Handbook of Research on Workforce Diversity in a Global Society:

Technologies and Concepts

Chaunda L. Scott
Oakland University, USA

Marilyn Y. Byrd
University Of Mary Hardin-Baylor, USA

Managing Director:	Lindsay Johnston
Senior Editorial Director:	Heather A. Probst
Book Production Manager:	Sean Woznicki
Development Manager:	Joel Gamon
Development Editor:	Hannah Abelbeck
Acquisitions Editor:	Erika Gallagher
Typesetter:	Christopher Shearer
Cover Design:	Nick Newcomer

Published in the United States of America by
Business Science Reference (an imprint of IGI Global)
701 E. Chocolate Avenue
Hershey PA 17033
Tel: 717-533-8845
Fax: 717-533-8661
E-mail: cust@igi-global.com
Web site: http://www.igi-global.com

Library of Congress Cataloging-in-Publication Data

Handbook of research on workforce diversity in a global society: technologies and concepts / Chaunda L. Scott and Marilyn Y. Byrd, editors.
p. cm.
Includes bibliographical references and index.
Summary: "This book highlights innovative research, theoretical frameworks, and perspectives that are currently being used to guide the practice of leveraging diversity in multiple organizational settings"--Provided by publisher.
ISBN 978-1-4666-1812-1 (hardcover) -- ISBN 978-1-4666-1813-8 (ebook) -- ISBN 978-1-4666-1814-5 (print & perpetual access)
1. Diversity in the workplace--Handbooks, manuals, etc. 2. Personnel management--Handbooks, manuals, etc. I. Scott, Chaunda L. II. Byrd, Marilyn Y.

HF5549.5.M5.H358 2012
658.3008--dc23

2012000295

British Cataloguing in Publication Data
A Cataloguing in Publication record for this book is available from the British Library.

All work contributed to this book is new, previously-unpublished material. The views expressed in this book are those of the authors, but not necessarily of the publisher.

Editorial Advisory Board

Table of Contents

Section 2
Leveraging Workforce Diversity and Leadership

Section 3
Strategies for Leveraging Workforce Diversity

Section 4
Initiatives for Leveraging Workforce Diversity

Detailed Table of Contents

Section 1
Leveraging Workforce Diversity in Higher Education

Chapter 1

Since its establishment in 1975, the Economic Community of West African States (ECOWAS) has faced the task of regional integration and cooperation in West Africa mainly through economic policies and treaties, and has substantially failed to achieve the desired goals. The sub-region is probably one of the most outstanding regional enclaves of human diversity in the world. However, ethnicity and other differences remain critical phenomena of politics and life in the sub-region. More often than not, these differences are exploited for negative purposes rather than leveraging them for the objectives of cooperation, integration, and development. The university system and its academic membership offer an opportunity for harnessing some of the diversity in the region for more fruitful integration and development. This chapter examines this expected role of academia and the university system towards leveraging human resource diversity for improved cooperation, integration, and development in West Africa.

Chapter 2

Properly managed diversity practices enable organizations to maximize human capital, create a sustainable competitive advantage, attract more customers, and become more profitable. Many organizations conduct diversity training to address workplace diversity issues. Top management communicates the value of and commitment to diversity, whereas managers facilitate an environment that embraces diversity. Diversity management has emerged as a prominent strategy to handle diversity issues. This chapter examines diversity curriculum of leading Executive MBA (EMBA) programs in the United States and highlights the current state of the educational environment in addition to explaining how curriculum supports diversity and inclusion reforms at the organizational level. Through content analysis, the authors summarized the diversity topics featured in 20 leading EMBA programs in the United States. None of the reviewed programs explicitly utilized the word "diversity" in any of their core or elective course titles, and only three (3) explicitly mentioned the words "diverse" or "diversity" within course descriptions. Nevertheless, the data suggest that programs do seek to offer some form of experiences which have the potential and intent to enhance cultural awareness. The majority of programs under study require students to travel to a foreign country to participate in global travel exploration. The authors provide recommendations for future research related to effectively implementing diversity practices and curriculum so that leaders become better equipped to address the challenges of diversity for their organizations.

Chapter 3

     Marilyn Y. Byrd, University of Mary Hardin-Baylor, USA
     Dominique T. Chlup, Texas A & M University, USA

This study is a qualitative, interpretative examination of nine African American women's encounters with race, gender, and social class (intersectionality) in predominantly white organizations and the learning experiences that emerged from these encounters. Rather than continuing to operate from a Eurocentric view of learning, this study contributes to the scholarly discussion the learning perspectives of African American Women (AAW). Black feminist theory is used as a socio-cultural framework to explain how AAW learn from issues emerging from intersectionality. A narrative approach to inquiry was the research strategy employed. Three major learning orientations emerged from the women's narratives: learning from influential sources, learning through divine guidance, and learning through affirmation of self. The authors contend that expanding the conversation of adult learning theories to include socio-cultural theories derived from black women's scholarship may be necessary to move the field of adult education toward more inclusive ways of theorizing adult learning. Implications for the field of adult education and the emerging workforce diversity paradigm are provided.

Chapter 4

     Julie Gedro, SUNY Empire State College, USA

Using a multi-disciplinary survey of educational studies, sociology, adult education, and human resources literature, this chapter explores the ways that racial minorities and sexual minorities (lesbian, gay, bisexual, and transgender) face oppression in organizational contexts. It examines and critiques organizational responses to diversity, and it uncovers the ways that these populations differ. Implications for diversity training programs are articulated, suggestions for training practice are offered, and recommendations for further research are provided.

Chapter 5

     Kemi Ogunyemi, Pan-African University, Nigeria

Diversity is an indisputable element of human life. In their bid to create value, employers have to face the challenges posed by putting together people coming from different backgrounds and with different paradigms. The Lagos Business School has also experienced this phenomenon. The School has a fair distribution of people from different ethnic groups. It also has a mission that identifies expressly with the Christian view of human nature and yet is open to people of all religious inclinations. As an academic environment, there is also the inevitable risk of distance between academic staff and administrative staff and between lecturers and students. The purpose of this chapter is to highlight the positive practices at the LBS that help them leverage workforce diversity and to make a few suggestions for improvement. This chapter will also highlight how the school reflects the importance of leveraging diversity in its academic curriculum.

Chapter 6

This chapter describes a Collaborative Inquiry (CI) process as experienced by six diverse female participants in a doctoral program. The focus of the inquiry was to deepen individual and group cross-cultural understanding, and to show how holistic learning can be promoted through integrating multiple ways of knowing and spirituality within a multicultural context. The purpose of this chapter is to provide the readers with sufficient information to apply CI in their practice and build on the research presented here. To meet this goal, the authors describe how CI has the potential to foster transformational learning and discuss the relationship between transformational learning, informational learning, global competencies, developmental capacity, and the paradoxical nature of diversity work. Lastly, the chapter ends with recommendations for creating a CI process that supports deep learning and change, and potential topics for future research.

Section 2
Leveraging Workforce Diversity and Leadership

Chapter 7

The purpose of this chapter is to examine some key trends in the workplace and marketplace that require successful corporate leaders to leverage workforce diversity. Such diversity poses certain challenges, which leaders can tackle and turn into lucrative opportunities to enhance not only productivity, sales, revenues, profits, brand, and reputation, but also the innovation so necessary for corporate survival. At the national level, the ability to compete in a global marketplace depends on successful innovation and has been a key driver of American eminence in the world. At the global level, innovation can empower people to move beyond fear of the future to actually shape their future; for example, we are currently seeing how technological innovations, such as cell phones and the Internet, are empowering people in the Middle East. The ability to understand and connect with people from diverse cultures also generates major opportunities to create peaceful relations as well as material abundance.

Chapter 8

The field of diversity and inclusion has experienced exponential growth over last 30 years. Yet, while these progressions have occurred, many of the core diversity and inclusion concepts have remained fairly stagnant. One critical example is around the concept of privilege. All of us find ourselves privileged in some way, but leaders in particular need to recognize and manage privilege to ensure inclusion in the workplace. Through personal examples and real stories, this chapter highlights the many positive outcomes leaders will experience by effectively managing privilege. These powerful outcomes include areas such as personal growth and effectiveness, more authentic relationships, increased levels of respect, expanded circle of influence, and maximized employee performance. To conclude, the authors look at the stages leaders go through before they are able to effectively manage this expanded view of privilege. These stages can be described as *bliss, awareness, overprotection, enlightened,* and ultimately *managing privilege.*

Chapter 9

Although the need to develop global leaders with adequate intercultural competencies has become obvious, global leadership, as an emerging field, has not received a great deal of attention. This chapter attempts to propose an integrative Intercultural Effectiveness (ICE) model for Human Resource Development (HRD) professionals. The model evolves a theoretical conceptualization to link ICE and global leadership with the theory of transformative learning and the process of cross-cultural learning. It provides a series of process guidelines for HRD professionals in designing, developing, and conducting HRD programs for the development of global leadership.

Chapter 10

With demographic change, organizations today are seeing changes in societal make-up translated to the composition of their workforce. In the future, younger and older employees will have to work together synergistically to achieve good performance. The authors argue that it will be largely up to leaders to prevent the negative effects of age diversity, i.e. social categorization and intergroup bias, and to facilitate the positive effects of age diversity, i.e. the sharing of unique knowledge resources held by young and old. The authors argue that certain leadership behaviors and especially their combinations have great promise in leading diverse teams, and highlight why they should be used in conjunction with positive beliefs about diversity.

Chapter 11

This chapter discusses the theoretical framework covering the relationship between top management team diversity determinants and certain organization-level variables in order to capture the essence of possible strategic outcomes. Accordingly, it attempts to summarize and clarify the theoretical and empirical literature regarding the effects of diversity on the functioning of top management teams. In this sense, the main aim of this study is to contribute to and improve the current literature on diversity through the viewpoint of strategic international business literature by directly focusing on the organizational unit—top management teams—which is responsible for formulating and implementing strategies that will leverage organizational performance in the long run.

Section 3
Strategies for Leveraging Workforce Diversity

This chapter describes the need for and development of a taxonomy of workplace diversity. It also examines the taxonomy's implications for understanding and predicting diversity outcomes at work. The context of diversity research is described, along with a problem the field is facing concerning consensus for a practical, operational definition. A seven-dimension taxonomy grounded in Social Identity Theory was developed by reviewing contemporary literature on diversity in the workplace. Preliminary research found that each of the seven dimensions of the taxonomy were present in 78 critical incidents describing work-relevant diversity scenarios. An instrument, the Workplace Diversity Inventory, has been developed and administered in order to empirically examine the seven-factor model of the taxonomy. Implications and directions for future research are discussed.

Workplace learning events can be categorized into a spectrum containing three major clusters: (a) the Navigation Cluster, containing those tasks that require planning, organizing, and structuring of content; (b) the Problem-Solving Cluster, containing those tasks that require innovative creativity or critical thinking skills; and (c) the Engagement Cluster, containing those tasks that require inter- and intra-personal skills required when working in situations that involve others. The purpose of this chapter is to propose an emerging 4-step framework that can be used to guide individuals, educators, and workplace trainers through a process to assist learners in identifying their learning strategies preferences and in leveraging these individual metacognitive processes in order to achieve specific workplace learning objectives.

As the world becomes smaller through globalization and the definition of diversity expands to accommodate new dimensions, it becomes increasingly important to identify and measure these changes and interpret how they influence strategic decision-making within organizations. To achieve an organization's stated goals, it is not only important to recognize this diversity, but also build programs to incorporate the benefits of diversity while minimizing any negative aspects associated with this construct. Sharing case studies of best practices will highlight successes that can be used as models for those organizations that are addressing their training needs in the area of organizational diversity. This chapter will share tools designed to help organizations evaluate their needs in terms of diversity training and development. These resources can help training and development professionals identify needs, design curriculum, create evaluation tools for assessment, and evaluate costs to deploy strategic training and development programs.

Chapter 15

The objectives of this chapter are to 1) introduce the idea of leveraging diversity through a career development paradigm shift and 2) to offer researchers ways to further explore this shift in thinking and enhance organizational and individual career development strategies. The suggestion is not for organizational leaders to choose diverse employees over others, but that they acknowledge and understand all employees and use that knowledge to enhance and improve organizational performance. To accomplish organizational success through career development, they must acknowledge the value of all employees.

Chapter 16

Diversity training is an area of growing interest within organizations. As organizations and society become more culturally diverse, there is a need to provide training across all hierarchical levels to make individuals more aware of and sensitized to elements of difference. Managing and valuing diversity is becoming increasingly important to delivering higher levels of performance and creativity, enhancing problem solving and decision-making, and gaining cultural insights into domestic and overseas markets. As facilitators of diversity training, line managers are increasingly tasked with the important role of equipping employees with the skills and competencies to work effectively in diverse multicultural teams. Consequently, this chapter looks at the mechanics of how diversity is discussed and delivered in organizations. It explores the necessity of diversity training in safeguarding and respecting individual identity and in fostering more welcoming inclusive workplaces.

Chapter 17

This chapter reviews the relationship between a selection of United States federal laws and Human Resource Development (HRD). The chapter specifically reviews United States federal Equal Employment Opportunity (EEO) laws related to race, gender, age, and national origin, discusses how the passage of these laws led to an increased diversity of the labor force, and demonstrates how utilizing this legislation can improve the research and practice of HRD. A comprehensive group of employment laws were passed between 1960 and 2000, and data from the U.S. Departments of Labor and Census indicate that these laws have served to substantially increase the percentage of minorities and women in the labor force. This increasing diversity requires practitioners to rethink the methods they use to deliver training and development programs to employees. In addition, researchers should examine how the increase in diversity impacts all areas of HRD, such as training, mentoring, and work-life balance.

Hale Öner, Dogus University, Turkey
Esra Kaya, CEVA Logistics, Turkey
Olca Surgevil, Dokuz Eylul University, Turkey
Mustafa Ozbilgin, Brunel University, UK

The purpose of this chapter is to review the global diversity management program at CEVA Logistics. CEVA is one of the world's leading supply chain companies with operating regions of Asia Pacific, Americas, Northern Europe and Southern Europe, Middle East, and Africa with its head office in The Netherlands. CEVA was formed in August, 2007, as a result of the merger of TNT Logistics and EGL Eagle Global Logistics. CEVA employs more than 49,000 people and runs a global network with operational facilities in more than 170 countries all over the world. The main Diversity and Inclusion activities of CEVA aim at increasing the participation of women at higher echelons of the management cadre, retaining diverse talent, and increasing the number of employees with disabilities. The diversity and integration understanding is the commitment to continuous improvement in every sub-region retaining the talented human capital with a focus on work and life balance initiatives and development by mentoring programs, network groups on the intranet, e-teams, and communities on gender and disability. Although diversity is integrated at CEVA at both the regional and global levels, the main motto in implementing the Diversity and Inclusion activities is "Think global, act local."

Section 4
Initiatives for Leveraging Workforce Diversity

Bertie M. Greer, Northern Kentucky University, USA
James A. Hill, The Ohio State University, USA

Important supply bases for buyers are those that emphasize minority-owned businesses. The increased focus on globalization, corporate social responsibility, supplier diversity, and additional benefits has established a need for buyers to develop sustainable relationships with minority-owned firms. Based on a review of the literature, and interviews with a minority supplier director, minority suppliers, and a purchasing manager, this chapter examines the relationship constructs that are important to buyer-minority-owned supplier relationships. Trust, perception of buyer's commitment, and minority-owned supplier commitment is explored. Research propositions, implications, and directions for further research are offered.

Aileen G. Zaballero, Pennsylvania State University, USA
Hsin-Ling Tsai, Pennsylvania State University, USA
Philip Acheampong, Pennsylvania State University, USA

This chapter will emphasize the importance of collaborative team-based work groups among diverse settings. First, the authors will discuss the factors of diverse teams and identify the stages of group development focusing on Tuckman's Model. In addition, Gert Hofstede's cultural dimension will be addressed. Finally, organizational contexts that impact the performance of diverse teams such will be explored.

Chapter 21

This chapter discusses the subject of workforce diversity as it directly relates to volunteerism, using the Peace Corps as an example. The aim of the chapter is to illustrate how nonprofit institutions can draw upon the value of workforce diversity in order to obtain competitive advantages. The Peace Corps' three-fold mission includes helping the people of interested countries in meeting their need for trained men and women, helping promote a better understanding of Americans on the part of the people served, and helping promote a better understanding of other peoples on the part of Americans. This chapter specifically discusses how the Peace Corps incorporate diversity in their volunteer program.

Chapter 22

Workforce diversity and the benefits resulting from its appropriate management is a topic that must be addressed from a strategic and not an emotional perspective; and more specifically, from the Human Resources Strategic Management perspective. This chapter intends to explore the Human Resources initiatives and practices in use, analyze which of them can be employed, and which are more appropriate for an optimal management of workforce diversity, creating a competitive advantage for companies.

Chapter 23

In recent years, the concept of generational diversity has gained increasing recognition in the United States. Each generation is shaped by historical, social, and cultural events that are unique to that particular age cohort. The purpose of this chapter is to help scholars, researchers, organizational leaders, practitioners, and graduate students understand diversity among generational cohorts and employ practices to utilize the wealth of knowledge that exists within today's multigenerational workforce. This chapter will describe the four generations in today's workplace and discuss gaps that can cause conflict. This chapter also provides tips and best practices for leveraging intergenerational diversity as well as scenarios and examples that demonstrate best practices. The result is a cohesive and productive workplace that respects multigenerational perspectives.

Chapter 24

Disclosure decisions for lesbian and gay employees have been researched in organizational contexts. While the dilemmas associated, factors affecting, and situations encouraging or discouraging disclosure have been studied, the relatively unexplored area is how alternate sexual orientation can be strategically deployed at workplace to contest the associated stigma and bring positive social and political changes in the organizational climate. While scholars believe that remaining closeted may be the best strategy in a heterosexist and homophobic environment, studies report psychological strain, lack of authenticity, behavioral dilemmas, etc. experienced by closeted individuals, which, at minimum, lead to conflicts in daily situations of identity management and, at the peak, suicidal attempts due to perceived burdensomeness and failed belongingness. To address this dilemma in leveraging sexual orientation diversity in workplaces, this chapter deals with the framework of identity deployment to explore how alternate sexual identity can be deployed in the workplace.

Section 5
Leveraging Workforce Diversity through Theoretical Frameworks and Technology

Chapter 25
Marilyn Y. Byrd, University of Mary Hardin-Baylor, USA

This chapter is a qualitative, narrative case study that seeks to unveil the social identity diversity of leadership from the perspective a Black woman leader. Social identity diversity is a form of difference that marginalized groups, such as Black women, experience in predominantly White organizational and institutional settings as a result of intersectionality. Social identity diversity creates multiple dynamics for groups such as Black women who hold leadership positions in the aforementioned settings. This study highlights the need for more inclusive and cultural perspectives of leadership, which calls for more inclusive theoretical frameworks that consider the social identity diversity of the leader. Critical race theory is presented as a theoretical framework that is useful for explaining how systems of power sustain domination and oppression in organizational and institutional settings. Implications for an emerging social justice paradigm are given.

Chapter 26
Rossella Riccò, University of Milan, Italy

In a global society, leveraging people's diversities is one of the major challenges faced by organizations of any size in developed countries. Factors such as demographic changes, international and national anti-discrimination measures, globalization, service-economy shifts, stakeholder pressures on organizational commitment to corporate social responsibility, and technological advances are heightening the international attention paid to the increase in people's diversities, thereby fostering discussion on their management in organizations. Since the end of the 1980s, professionals and academics have been debating how to devise efficient, effective, and equitable ways to manage workforce diversity in organizations; however, they have produced neither a shared definition of diversity management nor a general accepted assessment on the outcomes that diversity management can deliver for organizations and persons. The aim of this chapter is to expand the understanding of diversity management by systematizing it on the basis of McGregor's new human relations framework.

This chapter will include a brief description of the history of diversity; advantages of being culturally competent; paradigms/perspectives of diversity management; and a summary of the business case for diversity. In addition, theories and models of organization development and change management are further explained as a way to understand the organizational context surrounding diversity interventions.

Although Global Virtual Teams (GVTs) provide organizations with increased competitive advantages and greater flexibility due to their unique ability to transcend the traditional boundaries of time, location, and organizational constraints, managing globally dispersed and culturally diverse GVTs also poses unique challenges. This chapter explores some of the challenges affecting GVTs by examining extant literature on team diversity, team conflict, and collaboration technology, and further argues that organizations can greatly benefit from integrating the tenets of adaptable Collaboration Engineering technology and thinkLets into their GVT processes to develop sustainable team collaboration and a sense of structure in the virtual team context.

Chapter 29

In this chapter, the authors present a model for understanding the context and determinants of aggression within an on-line environment, known as cyber-aggression. They propose that the heterogeneity of global virtual teams along with other key individual characteristics such as Social Dominance Orientation, Identification Threat, and past experience with aggression/harassment will lead to greater likelihood of cyber-aggression occurring or being perceived by group members. Additionally, the use of lean communication media, as well as the distance between team members and the social and professional isolation that goes along with global virtual team work also contributes to greater likelihood of cyber-aggression occurring. Lastly, without any way to build meaningful trust in a virtual setting and a lack of cross-cultural competence, members of global virtual teams are more likely to engage in behaviors that do not demonstrate cultural sensitivity or cohesion on the team, resulting in poor communication which can lead to more aggressive behaviors. The authors conclude their chapter with recommendations on how to best combat these pitfalls of working in a virtual environment.

Chapter 30

Aileen G. Zaballero, Pennsylvania State University, USA

Tutaleni I. Asino, Pennsylvania State University, USA

Jessica Briskin, Pennsylvania State University, USA

This chapter connects technology and diversity and argues that technology can be leveraged to contribute to the diversification of a workforce. The authors discuss the changing global economy as it pertains to the diminution of labor market boundaries and diversified consumers, as well as current trends in technology usage and innovation as a means to accomplishing organizational goals. In addition, the authors analyze organizational learning and organizational performance, regarding the use of technology as a tool to overcome the challenges of a diverse workforce.

Preface

At present, a plethora of research exists emphasizing the importance of workforce diversity as it relates to valuing the similarities, differences, and talents of employees at all ranks. For example, these categories include, but are not limited to race, gender, disability, sexual orientation, age, language, religious beliefs, ethnicity, world view, height, weight, life experiences, cultural customs, economic status, educational level, job title, and years of work experience. Yet, there remains a need for more research that shows how corporate, nonprofit, government, educational, and health care institutions are actually drawing upon the value of workforce diversity in order to obtain competitive advantages.

One emerging paradigm being utilized in the 21st century to demonstrate the value of workforce diversity in its many forms is called leveraging diversity. The concept of leveraging diversity can be best understood as a set of transformational strategies that have been utilized to assist organizations in: 1) adapting to and managing cultural change due to demographic shifts in the workplace and society; 2) enhancing an organizational cultural and climate that is now more diverse culturally, ethnically, linguistically, intellectually, creatively, physically, and spiritually than ever before; 3) advocating for and developing policies and practices that support the total inclusion of all employees at all work levels; and 4) increasing organizational efficiency and profits to obtain a global and competitive edge (Scott, 2010).

The objectives of this handbook are threefold. First, it serves as a cutting edge resource for scholars, researchers, organizational leaders, practitioners, and graduate students who want to enhance their understanding of leveraging diversity in the workforce. Second, it serves to highlight innovative research in the areas of higher education, leadership, and technology along with theoretical frameworks, strategies, and initiatives that are currently being used to guide the practice of leveraging diversity in multiple organizational settings. Last, the aim of this handbook serves to provide insights on future workforce diversity trends.

In soliciting authors for this volume, the call for chapters was sent to several professional organizations, universities, consultants, academicians, and graduate programs that attracted vast interest in addressing and responding to leveraging workforce diversity issues and trends. After a rigorous blind review process, 30 chapters were selected for this first IGI handbook focused on the topic of workforce diversity.

The five sections highlighted in this handbook are as follows: leveraging workforce diversity in higher education, leveraging workforce diversity and leadership, strategies for leveraging workforce diversity, initiatives for leveraging workforce diversity, and leveraging workforce diversity through theoretical frameworks and technology. Below, the focus of each section is highlighted.

Section 1: Leveraging Workforce Diversity in Higher Education. Section 1 will explore numerous current teaching and program practices in higher education (as well as emerging ones) that seek to prepare students with the knowledge and skills needed to leverage workforce diversity in a global society.

Section 2: Leveraging Workforce Diversity and Leadership. Section 2 will explore leadership's responsibility, commitment, mission, vision, and action strategies used to leverage workforce diversity in a global society today and beyond.

Section 3: Strategies for Leveraging Workforce Diversity. Section 3 will explore a myriad of current strategies (as well as emerging ones) that are being put into practice to leverage workforce diversity in a global society.

Section 4: Initiatives for Leveraging Workforce Diversity. Section 4 will explore a number of current initiatives (as well as emerging ones) that are being put into practice to leverage workforce diversity in a global society.

Section 5: Leveraging Workforce Diversity through Theoretical Frameworks and Technology. Section 5 will explore varieties of current theoretical frameworks (as well as emerging ones) that are being used to leverage workforce diversity in a global society. This section will also highlight current and emerging workforce diversity technological trends

The target audience of this handbook is composed of scholars, researchers, organizational leaders, practitioners, and graduate students working in a variety of global settings and professional fields that include but are not limited to the following: human resource development, management, organizational psychology, organizational leadership, business administration, communication, counseling, criminal justice, social work, military education/training, workforce education and development, higher education, adult education, public administration, government relations, and health care.

Chaunda L. Scott
Oakland University, USA

Marilyn Y. Byrd
University of Mary Hardin-Baylor, USA

REFERENCE

Scott, C. L. (2010). Preface . In Scott, C. L. (Ed.), *Leveraging Diversity: Multiple Settings, Professions, Strategies and Theoretical Frameworks* (pp. 205–207). Geneva, Switzerland: Inderscience Enterprises Ltd.

Section 1
Leveraging Workforce Diversity in Higher Education

Chapter 1
Regional Integration in West Africa:
Exploring the Option of Leveraging Workforce Diversity in the Academia and University System

Ikeanyibe Okechukwu Marcellus
University of Nigeria, Nigeria

Ezeibe Chukwuebuka Christian
University of Nigeria, Nigeria

ABSTRACT

Since its establishment in 1975, the Economic Community of West African States (ECOWAS) has faced the task of regional integration and cooperation in West Africa mainly through economic policies and treaties, and has substantially failed to achieve the desired goals. The sub-region is probably one of the most outstanding regional enclaves of human diversity in the world. However, ethnicity and other differences remain critical phenomena of politics and life in the sub-region. More often than not, these differences are exploited for negative purposes rather than leveraging them for the objectives of cooperation, integration, and development. The university system and its academic membership offer an opportunity for harnessing some of the diversity in the region for more fruitful integration and development. This chapter examines this expected role of academia and the university system towards leveraging human resource diversity for improved cooperation, integration, and development in West Africa.

DOI: 10.4018/978-1-4666-1812-1.ch001

INTRODUCTION

The challenge of regional integration remains the primary objective of the Economic Community of West African States (ECOWAS) since its formation in 1975. The academia is one group that has the propensity to participate in policy making in most countries especially in Africa where a distinctive political class cannot be distinguished from other power centers. A good number of members of the academia find their way to appointments in governments; they act as resource persons at various levels and they produce a large chunk of personnel for both the government and the private sector. In terms of diversity, they possess the various differences that can be found among the rest of the population in the sub-region (ethnicity, language, sex, age, educational qualifications, temperaments, etc.). Above all, the nature of their engagement as researchers makes them most available to work together in various exchange programs. The academia and by extension the university system, therefore, present a unique opportunity that can easily be used to leverage diversity, build peace, and champion programs of regional cooperation and integration in West Africa. Despite the existing diversity in the region, the academia, and the university system has the high potency of bringing diverse human resources to work together in the West African Universities.

The general objective of this research work is to examine how the academia and the university system can be maximized as an option for leveraging human resource diversity for improved cooperation, integration and development of the sub-region. The specific objectives pursued in the chapter include, but were not limited to the following:

- discussing strategies for enhancing organizational culture and climate that is more diverse ethnically, culturally, linguistically, intellectually, creatively, etc. within the university system in the West Africa universities;

- exploring avenues of harnessing the diversity evident among the academia in the sub-region and leveraging this through various university exchange programs towards better integration of the sub-region, and

- advocating for and suggesting policies and practices that support inter-university exchanges and research cooperation among the academia of West Africa, the rest of Africa, and the world.

This research was conducted using documentary analysis as well as discourse analysis approaches. Relevant portions of documents like ECOWAS treaty and protocols were analyzed in relation to promoting cooperation in the area of study. The invaluable gains of university exchanges and research cooperation in other parts of the world and the emerging trend of leveraging workforce diversity were highlighted.

BACKGROUND OF THE STUDY

Diversity in West African Sub-Region

The West African sub-region is today made up of 15 countries in the central northwest bulge of the African Continent spanning from below the Sahara desert to the coast of the Atlantic Ocean. These countries include: Benin, Burkina Faso, Cote d'Ivoire, Cape Verde, Gambia, Ghana, Guinea, Guinea-Bissau, Liberia, Mali, Niger, Nigeria, Senegal, Sierra Leone, and Togo. These countries are populated by highly diverse ethnic folks that were forced together during colonialism by European Countries in the 19th and 20th centuries. Nigeria, with over 300 hundred ethnic groups, is considered to be the most important country of the sub-region in terms of size and ethnic composition. Ghana has an estimated 80 ethnic groups.

Before colonial rule, the numerous ethnic groups in the West African sub-region varied according to their politics, language, religion, trade, art, and culture. A general perception is that these types of differences are created by ethnicity. Prior to colonialism, these groups had separate developmental destinies with contacts with other groups like the Arabs and European groups from Portugal, Spain, the United Kingdom, Germany, and France. Colonialism brought the unification of these diverse groups under a few political sovereignties or states (sixteen). France and the United Kingdom are the two European linguistic cultures that had the dominant influence in the region, which also seems to dualize relations in the region into Franco-phone and Anglophone countries.

Efforts have been on serious the 1960s to increase cooperation and integration of countries in the sub-region. Today globalization has increased the propensity for intra regional relations that ought to increase opportunities for leveraging the diversity of the people in the sub-region. However, ethnicity and other forms of difference continue to negatively impact on political, economic, and social activities in the sub-region. This invariably affects developmental issues not only within country-specific regions, but also the integrative project of the sub-region that has been pursued by the ECOWAS.

Contextual Meaning of Leveraging Diversity

MacGrillivray and Golden (2007) explain diversity simply as any difference that makes a difference. In other words, diversity refers to all attributes of differences including race, gender, nationality, religion, age, class, physical disability, and sexual orientation as well as difference of experience,

thought, education, geography, and language. These and many more necessarily underline the differences that exist between individuals and such differences have been found to be strengths to be exploited rather than weaknesses to be feared or removed for effective and efficient organisations. The importance of recognizing and ensuring some level of diversity in contemporary organizations has become a significant human resource management strategy in recent years. Indeed:

Many companies appear to recognize this truism and the fact that diversity fosters ideas and learning. Some have established comprehensive strategies to recruit and retain employees from different cultures and backgrounds. Others promote diversity and its benefits in their corporate vision statements (Stevenson, 2004, p. 1).

This is essentially to reduce the effect of inbreeding and 'monolithic backgrounds' that will likely 'foster monolithic thinking,' to borrow the expression of William Donaldson as quoted by Stevenson (2004, p. 1). The system of education in South Africa during the apartheid regime could serve as a popular illustration here. It is observed that education in South Africa was previously organized along segregated racial lines, and the apartheid system of social engineering ensured that non-whites were denied equal access to white institutions and education of quality. This created a kind of social imbalance that continued to be the cause of student demonstrations, protests, and campus unrest experienced by many institutions of higher education (Norris, 2000). Since the end of apartheid in South Africa, social imbalances are being addressed in various ways including the use of affirmative action to infuse and manage diversity rather than segregate it. In higher education system, many institutions have changed their admission and recruitment policies in terms of staff appointments and student access (Norris, 2000). This definitely has contributed not only to peace in South Africa than what was obtained during the apartheid but has enhanced the status and development of the country generally. Diversity can therefore be a source of retrogression when perceived negatively and also a resource value that can be positively harnessed to advantage if properly managed and leveraged.

Managing diversity can be achieved through various means. Within the educational system for which we are concerned, it is explained as implying, among other things, "changing the organizational culture, re-conceptualizing appropriate leadership styles, restructuring organizations, reformulating what constitutes good teaching, and developing staff and students to work and learn in an organization that is very different from what it used to be" (Havenga, 1993, p. 11). It is a rather long process of social change and requires consistent and targeted transformational stages of the university education system and manpower breeding and utilization in the system.

An organization or a society that seeks to transform from a mono-cultural to a multicultural (diverse) one will expectedly pass through the following stages:

- mono-cultural stage, which is characterized by either implicit or explicit exclusion of some groups e.g. racial minorities or women;
- Non-discriminatory stage, which is characterized by a sincere desire to eliminate the majority group's unfair advantage. However, this is done without the organization or society significantly changing its dominant culture, but by ensuring that the climate is not hostile for new members; and
- multicultural which describes the organization or society that is either in the process of becoming or has become diverse in the most visionary sense that reflects the contributions and interests of the diverse cultural and social groups in the organization's or society's mission, operations,

products, or services. The entity commits to eradicate all forms of social discrimination and shares power and influence so that no one group is put at an exploitive advantage (Norris, 2000).

Unfortunately, most states and the university system in particular in West African sub region do not seem to have acknowledged the need of building a multi-cultural society and organisations by prioritizing programs of leveraging human resource diversity. In many state ethnicity and other divisive features are negatively exploited for political and economic reasons. In the university system particularly, policies of inter-university and interstate exchanges of staff and students are grossly advocated despite the regional declarations of cooperation and integration in the sub region. Even where diversity is accorded some importance in conventions and protocols of the regional body, ECOWAS and country specific policies and rules, these are hardly given any adequate attention in practice.

The Missing Link in the ECOWAS Cooperative, Integrative, and Development Efforts

ECOWAS has continued to pursue integration of the sub-region strongly on economic terms. But this has witnessed more of destabilizing effects. It has be revealed that the encouragement of free movement of goods and regional economic integration rather than yield the desired objectives facilitate the emergence of region-wide organized criminal syndicates and other problems rather than the anticipated integration and development of the sub-region (Alemika, 2009). Indeed, integrative efforts remain strongly hindered by the clear dichotomy of French-English speaking countries as well as fear of domination of small and poor countries by the more populous and advantaged states in the sub-region. The need to harness the obvious diversity in the sub-region towards better integration of the region is not doubted. The existing differences and diversity which create conflicts and acrimony can be exploited towards the objectives of cooperation, integration and development.

On another dimension, the university system from its very origin has been a scholastic guild very significant in knowledge production for the society. However, it usually operates under conditions removed from the society itself, it is very critical in generating ideas that propel the society (Benkler, 2011). Being an institution that appeals to the convergence of people from diverse background, it is bound to be an opportunity to exploit such diversity for the maximum benefit of the society. Universities abound in West African countries. The extent they have been the breeding grounds of knowledge, cooperation, and integration in the sub- region remains to be investigated.

Defining the Research Problem

This chapter investigates the contributions of pooling the academia and students in the West African sub-region through university exchanges as a viable strategy towards knowledge production, peace building, managing and harnessing the human resource diversity in the region and using it as an option for genuine regional cooperation, integration and development.

THE UNIVERSITY SYSTEM AND LEVERAGING HUMAN RESOURCE DIVERSITY

The University System in Historical Perspective

The university system began as an enclave of research and knowledge propagation. It also became an institution for the propagation of views and human cooperation. The origin of formal institutions of learning can be traced to the Greek philosophical institutions established by Plato (The Academy) and another by his student Aristotle (The Lyceum). The university system in particular had earliest beginning in Italy about the 9th Century. Earliest institutions were at Salerno in the course of the ninth century and Bologna in the eleventh century. At this time, they were known as *studia generalia*, or places to which scholars resorted from all parts of Europe. According to Cox (2000), the Latin word *universitas* often meant simply the student body, usually called the nation, organised for the communal protection of the foreign student body, men who otherwise, being aliens, were at the mercy of local innkeepers and tradesmen. It was rather a community or cooperation made up of scholars from various parts of Europe at that time. The idea of being a community that harbours and protects foreign student body implies the congregation of people from diverse culture and background. It also underscores the aloof character, which the university system tends to have in relation to other sectors of the society until date. This aloofness is described as the town-gown tension which has long typified the relationship of the university to the market and society as one of partial remove, that is, removed from the pressures and enticements of the market and a dedication to internal system values, usually embodied in the ideas of academic freedom, intellectual discipline, and peer review (Benkler, 2011). In other words, the university system, especially at the earlier period of its history and in the period that Benkler describes as the period of the industrial information economy, had maintained a stance apart from much of the rest of the society.

In spite of its aloofness from society, the university system has been instrumental to the tremendous knowledge production that has pushed the threshold of human and scientific development. Furthermore, the diversity that it has helped to congregate has been a factor in the intensity of knowledge production and scientific development in Europe since the mediaeval time. This opinion is even more appealing in today's networked society that is propelled by information and technological advancement of the contemporary society. Benkler (2011) emphasizes that:

As we move to a networked information economy, the distinct values of the university—its relative freedom from the pressures of the market, polity, and popular fashion—are a major source of strength. Universities can become an even more significant force in the knowledge production system, one that distinctly pulls in the direction of professional values.... University networks and technical platforms will have to focus on managing the increasingly permeable boundaries among universities, and between universities and the world outside them. University platform design should be focused on ensuring that faculty and students have the greatest degree possible of authority and capacity to act freely, innovate internally, and participate externally. And university systems should be attuned to the need to build platforms for cooperation, as the new practices of cooperation and sharing become more prevalent and more based in a broader shift from an image of hierarchical or market-oriented systems to systems based on individuals collaborating with each other in loose networks (p. 61).

The University System and West African Integration and Cooperation

It is significant to observe that universities in Africa have been less visible in world university web rankings. In the 2011 ranking for instance, no university in Africa was among the first 200 universities ranked in the world. In Africa itself, the West African universities lag behind those of North and Southern Africa. Only 12 universities in the sub-region featured among the top 100 universities in Africa in 2011 (4icu.org University Web Ranking, 2011). It is therefore necessary

to improve the status of these sub-regional universities as citadels of learning and knowledge production.

One of the most practicable ways of achieving this is to exploit the given heterogeneous nature of the countries in West Africa in terms of human resources and material endowment. This heterogeneity has been more of a minus than a plus for not only the countries of West Africa, but Africa as a whole. Indeed, some scholars regard conflict and violence as the most identifiable image of the African society. Idowu (2004) for instance, states that the most accurate image of Africa in the 70s, 80s, and 90s has been that of a continent of conflict and violence perennially on the edge of survival. Conflict and violence in Africa has not ended with the aforementioned decades. In the new millennium, serious conflicts and violence have been associated with countries particularly in the West African sub-region such as Nigeria, Sierra Leone, Liberia, and Cote D'Ivoire to mention a few.

Conflicts and violence are significant factors that affect the cooperative and integrative efforts made within the sub-region. A pragmatic attempt to initiate genuine integration and cooperation must lie in managing the critical sources of conflicts and violence that are largely rooted in the heterogeneity, which could be converted to a plus for development in the sub-region through effective management. Most countries in the sub-region have adopted some type of policies to recognize diversity in sharing resources, especially in government positions and employment. Nigeria for instance, has what is described as a federal character principle, which guides not only government employment and sharing of political positions, but even admission of students into government owned schools. As provided in the in the country's constitution since 1979, Section 14(3), the expression "federal character" is defined as:

The distinctive desire of the people of Nigeria to promote national unity, foster national/loyalty and give every citizen of Nigeria a sense of belonging to the nation, notwithstanding the diversities of ethnic origin, culture, language or religion which may exist and which is their desire to nourish and harness to the enrichment of the federal Republic of Nigeria (Federal Character Commission, 2011, p. iii).

The principle is a quota system, which aims at recognizing all kinds of diversity in the country to give every group a sense of belonging and fostering national loyalty as well as being a policy of leveraging the obvious diversities for the nourishment and enrichment of the nation. An Independent Commission formally enacted through Decree No. 34 of 1996 oversees the application of this principle in all stipulated instances.

Managing heterogeneity or diversity does not mean controlling or containing or stifling diversity. It means recognizing the utility of every feature of diversity and tapping the potential (Roosevelt, 1990). In a way, it is what is conceptually regarded as leveraging diversity. Realizing the efficacy of human resources as the most potent and central productive factor, contributing significantly to corporate or national bottom line and competitiveness, its importance in engendering cooperation, integration and development in West Africa becomes apt. Human beings are naturally equipped with different talents and aptitudes, and the university system is a relevant institution for further development of human resources, and pulling them together from far and wide. As a citadel of learning, it offers opportunity for developing the competences of individuals in relation to specific tasks, and changing or enhancing their attitudes, dispositions and behaviour (Alemika, 2008).

The ability of any nation or region to achieve its goals largely depends on the calibre, organization and motivation of its human resources (Ezeani, 2002). Harbinson (1973) once said that human resources, not capital or income or mate-

rial resources, constitute the ultimate basis for the wealth of nations. Capital and natural resources are passive factors of production. Human beings are the active agents who accumulate capital, exploit natural resources; build social, economic, and political organization and carry forward national development. Notably, human resource development is indispensable for the modern nation state and organizations to attain their objectives. For instance, the massive assembly of natural resources in West Africa requires practical indigenous knowledge available to the members of the sub-region for their better harness and utilization, and the university system and the academia remains central in exploiting and pooling the indigenous knowledge.

ECOWAS Protocols on Educational and Human Resource Development

ECOWAS has long realized the need of bringing together the efforts of various nations in the sub-region for greater development of the sub-region. In various articles of its revised treaty, the regional body has adopted protocols that aim at encouraging leveraging of human resources in the sub-region for educational and scientific development. Article 3 No 1 of the Revised Treaty of ECOWAS provides the aim and objectives of ECOWAS as follows:

The aims of the Community are to promote cooperation and integration, leading to the establishment of an economic union in West Africa in order to raise the living standards of its peoples, and to maintain and enhance economic stability, foster relations among Member States and contribute to the progress and development of the African Continent.

In order to achieve the goals established in the paragraph above, and in accordance with the relevant provisions of the Treaty, ECOWAS has tried to ensure the harmonization and coordination of various nations' policies and promotion of integration programs, projects and activities, particularly in food, agriculture and natural resources, industry, transport and communications, energy, trade, money and finance, taxation, economic reform policies, human resources, education, information, culture, science, technology, services, health, tourism, and legal matters. The Revised ECOWAS Treaty for instance, provides in Article 22 (g) that there shall be a Technical Commission to be known as Human Resources, Information, Social and Cultural Affairs. It is expected that the work of this Technical Commission will include designing various ways to encourage human resource development within the sub-region and contribute to the desired goals of integration and cooperation through information sharing and socio-cultural activities.

Below are the provisions of Articles 27 and 60 of the revised ECOWAS Treaty.

Member States shall:

a. strengthen their national scientific and technological capabilities in order to bring about the socio economic transformation required to improve the quality of life of their population;
b. ensure the proper application of science and technology to the development of agriculture, transport and communications, industry, health and hygiene, energy, education, and manpower and the conservation of the environment;
c. reduce their dependence on foreign technology and promote their individual and collective technological self-reliance;
d. cooperate in the development, acquisition and dissemination of appropriate technologies; and
e. strengthen existing scientific research institutions and take all necessary measures to prepare and implement joint scientific research and technological development programs.

In their cooperation in this field, member States shall:

a. harmonize, at the Community level, their national policies on scientific and technological research with a view to facilitating their integration into the national economic and social development plans;
b. coordinate their programs in applied research, research for development, scientific, and technological services;
c. harmonize their national technological development plans by placing special emphasis on indigenous and adapted technologies as well as their regulations on industrial property and transfer of technology;
d. coordinate their positions on all scientific and technical questions forming the subject of international negotiations;
e. carry out a permanent exchange of information and documentation and establish community data networks and data banks;
f. develop joint programs for training scientific and technological cadres, including the training and further training of skilled manpower;
g. promote exchanges of researchers and specialists among Member States in order to make full use of the technical skills available within the community; and
h. harmonize the educational systems in order to adapt better educational, scientific, and technical training to the specific development needs of the West African environment.

Member States shall undertake to cooperate in the full development of their human resources. To this end, they shall take measures to:

a. strengthen cooperation among themselves in the fields of education, training and employment; and to harmonize and coordinate their policies and programs in these areas;
b. consolidate their existing training institutions, improve the efficacy of their

educational systems, encourage exchanges between schools and universities, establish equivalences of academic, professional and technical qualifications, encourage literacy, promote the teaching and practice of the official languages of the community, and establish regional centers of excellence in various disciplines; and

c. encourage the exchange of skilled manpower between Member States (Afrimap, 2011).

There is no doubt that these are important provisions that can leverage human resources development at the regional level and encourage the much needed cooperation and integration through networks, fellowships and exchanges of researchers and students, but the extent of pursuing them, especially those that relate to promoting exchanges of researchers and specialists among member states within the community, is doubtful. However, a number of efforts are acknowledged.

Academic Cooperation and Collaboration in Africa and the West African Sub-Region

At the continental level of Africa, the African Union (AU) adopts policies to encourage cooperation in education and research. It has adopted the Second Decade of Education Action Plan, which includes the following as education plans:

*   knowledge generation through networks of centres of excellence, science technology and innovation,
*   quality assurance,
*   harmonization and regional integration, and
*   resource mobilization (Oyewole & Lamptey, 2008).

The Association of African Universities (AAU), a continental non-governmental organization has been very useful in the pursuit of policies of cooperation through networking and exchange of information and co-operation among institutions of higher education in Africa. The AAU was founded in Rabat, Morocco on November 12, 1967 following the recommendations made by the United Nations Educational Scientific and Cultural Organization (UNESCO). Initially, the AAU was to be the apex organization and forum that encouraged consultation, exchange of information, and co-operation among institutions of higher education in Africa. The AAU represents the voice of higher education in Africa on regional and international bodies and supports networking by institutions of higher education in teaching, research, information exchange, and dissemination.

The AAU had an initial membership of 34 higher institutions at inception. By June 2007, membership had reached 208 universities from 45 countries on the continent. However, this is not significant membership strength when compared to the number of universities on the continent. While statistics are not readily available, it important to note that Nigeria alone has 95 universities excluding other higher institutions like polytechnics, monotechnics, and colleges of education. Ghana has about 54 and most countries have not less than 30. The implication is that membership of the AAU is quite insignificant compared to the number of universities on the continent. In a situation where a large number of higher institutions do not participate in AAU programs, the overall impact will also be negligible.

AAU is organized in regions. The West African Regional association has its secretariat located in Ghana. The AAU has been very crucial in propagating the importance of cooperative and integrative activities among the academia in Africa and their counterparts in the rest of the World. Its core programs include:

*   serving as consultation and information exchange medium on key issues affecting education in Africa, such as building Data on African Thesis and Dissertation (DATAD),

- promoting cooperation and collaboration among member institutions,
- coordinating program activities especially promoting networks of African institutions,
- mobilizing regional capacity initiative, and
- designing an Academic Staff Exchange Program (ASEP) to foster inter-university cooperation through the exchange of staff between African universities.

The AAU seeks to accomplish these objectives by organizing conferences and attracting collaboration in establishing networks and fellowship programs, and developing infrastructure especially in ICT Development. AAU programs are directed at ensuring that faculty members are brought together through academic mobility in the form of exchange of staff for teaching assignments; serving as external examiners; participating at seminars, workshops and conferences; undertaking collaborative research assignments; facilitating the utilization of sabbatical leave appointments and enhancing the quality of teaching and research in African universities (Oyewole & Lamptey, 2008).

The AAU is greatly supported by a variety of international organizations. Some of these organizations are UNESCO, Ford Foundation International Fellowship Program, and USAID. For example, in its Networks for Regional Cooperation for Graduate Training and Research Project, the USAID provided $1,000,000 grants to AAU to establish multi-country networks for graduate training and research in the year 2000. The program ended in 2005, but some of networks secured other source of funding to continue with the program (Oyewole & Lamptey, 2008). Table 1 shows some fellowships and network programs in a number of Universities in Africa facilitated by AAU.

Three of the networks were implemented in West Africa Universities' Masters Program in Humanitarian and Refugee Studies, Degree Training Programs and Collaborative Research on Semi-Arid Agriculture and Graduate Program in

Microbiology Training and Research. A total of twenty-one Universities in the sub-region participated.

The AAU coordinates others programs provided by international donors. It coordinated IFP activities in Ghana, Nigeria and Senegal, the participating countries in collaboration with its partners Pathfinder International, Nigeria and the West African Research Center (WARC) in Senegal.

Within the ECOWAS region, the regional body and many other organizations have also made significant efforts to encourage the development of higher education through fellowship and research programs. ECOWAS has mainly developed and worked on adopting protocols for the countries in the region. These protocols as we have seen in the provisions of ECOWAS treaty seek to strengthen existing scientific research institutions and take all necessary measures to prepare and implement joint scientific research and technological development programs. It has also attempted a number of concerted actions through its various organs to embark on programs geared towards promoting learning and research through collaboration. Some of these efforts are in the way of infrastructural development.

In 2010, through its Department of Education, Culture, Science, and Technology, ECOWAS received a grant from the African Development Fund to finance Support of Network Institutions of Science and Technology Project. Nigeria's African University for Science and Technology, Abuja and Burkina Faso's International Institute for Water and Environmental Engineering, Ouagadougou benefitted. It has established an ECOWAS Education Fund through proceeds of the newly agreed Community Levy as well as other funding sources to promote education development in the sub-region. It is not obvious if any sponsorship of networks among the academia has been financed through the Fund. Despite these efforts, there seems to be poor or non-committal attitude by various countries in observing ECOWAS protocols and supporting inter-university exchanges,

Table 1. AAU facilitated networks, lead institutions, and participating institutions

Network	Lead Institution	Participating Institutions University
University Science, Humanities and Engineering Partnerships in Africa (USHEPiA) Program	University of Cape Town, Cape Town, South Africa	University of Cape Town; University of Dar Es Salaam; University of Botswana; Makerere University; Jomo Kenyatta University; University of Nairobi; University of Zimbabwe; University of Zambia
Masters Program in Humanitarian and Refugee Studies	University of Ibadan, Ibadan, Nigeria	University of Ibadan, Ibadan, Nigeria Rwanda; University of Burundi; University of Conakry, Guinea; University of Ghana; University of Liberia; University of Khartoum; University of Sierra Leone; Eduardo Mondlane University
Degree Training Programs and Collaborative Research on Semi-Arid Agriculture	Centre d'Etude Regional pour l'Amelioration de l'Adaptation a la Secheresse (CERAAS), Thies, Senegal	CERAAS, Senegal; ENSA, Senegal; Fourah Bay College, Sierra Leone; Universite Anta Diop, Senegal; Abia State University, Nigeria; Universite Ouagadougou, Burkina Faso.
Graduate Program in Microbiology Training & Research	University of Ouagadougou, Burkina Faso	University of Ouagadougou, Burkina Faso; Universite du Benin, Benin; Universite du Mali, Mali; University of Niamey, Niger; University of Conakry, Guinea; University of Cocody; Cote d'Ivoire
Masters Program on Humanitarian on Human Rights Law in Africa	University of Pretoria, South Africa	University of Pretoria; University of Mauritius; University of Zambia; University of Zimbabwe; University of Botswana; University of Namibia; University of Dar Es Salaam, Tanzania
Quality Assurance in the Field of Accountancy	University of South Africa, Pretoria	University of South Africa; University of Swaziland; University of Lesotho; University of Malawi, University of Zimbabwe; University of Namibia; University of Botswana

Source: Oyewole and Lamptey (2008)

efforts are still country specifics and the focus of ECOWAS in education development is vast to make impact in the specific area of interest of this chapter.

However, other groups have taken interest too in developing university network programs among the academia of West African universities. The impact of AAU programs is minimally felt in the sub-region. Some universities in the sub-region benefitted from the sample networks we showcased in Table 1. Many universities in the sub-region attract individual network, research, and fellowship sponsorships from many organizations both within and outside the sub-region. Many universities in America, Europe, Asia (China, Japan, for instance) have many linkage programs with universities in West Africa, but there are numerous challenges to effective inter-universities academic networks and linkage programs among the universities in West Africa that have affected optimisation of networks for regional integration and cooperation.

Most universities in the region lack academic autonomy and the finances that can help them to establish inter-university linkages in the sub-region without strong governmental funding. The governments in most of the states pay considerably low attention to education through their budgetary allocation to the sector. The private sector and non-governmental organizations are generally weak financially. In the case of private sector organizations, those that are relatively strong financially are the few multinationals that are unwilling to plough back a reasonable part of their profits as social responsibility. Thus, the greatest challenge of the university system and the academia in the West African universities seems to border on funding for research and collaboration that can facilitate inter-university exchanges and networks.

The issue of lack of comparability of academic degrees between the Anglophone countries and francophone, and the narrowness in scope of some academic programs run in some of the universities are also considerable challenges. It has been an important concern of AAU to develop effective frameworks that will facilitate mutual recognition of degrees and therefore help to promote academic mobility. Most programs run in some universities in the sub-region especially in the critical areas of physical sciences and technological studies are poorly equipped. The alternative is usually for students and researchers in those critical areas to travel overseas for such programs. Language barrier is another major constraint in the region. Apart from the two lingua Franca—English and French—spoken in the sub-region, numerous ethnic languages and dialects exist. Little effort is made within countries or sub-regional level to integrate these languages. Indeed, the two languages French and English have become sources of fundamental division among the countries in the sub-region rather than being a reason for more cooperative efforts and programs. It is impossible that such great number of languages existing in West Africa can all be recognized as means of regional or even country-wide communication as the case may be, but due diligence should be taken to preserve them and exploit their peculiar wisdom and thought patterns through research.

It is observable that in most of the existing linkage and network programs, the West African Universities are not considered as centers to run the programs. Many of these internationally supported exchange and network programs take places in universities outside the sub-region and even Africa. While Africans and West Africans in particular benefit from these programs, the expected utilities that will accrue in relation to regional cooperation and possible development of indigenous knowledge if the programs take place within the sub- region are lost. An increasing number of students are sent to universities in other regions of the world such as Europe and the United States, but few, if any are being sent

to Africa. Regrettably, the return rate of these scholars after their education has remained low as they tend to remain in those external countries for greener pastures. For instance, to date over 300 fellows have been selected from the West African sub-region and are studying in countries such as Britain, Canada, France, Switzerland, South Africa and the United States under the Ford Foundation's Fellowship International Program (FIP). Of these fellows, 200 have technically completed their studies and only about 150 have returned to the sub-region as of September 2008 (http://www. aau.org/?q=ffifp/backgrnd).

Furthermore, even where the programs take place within the continent or the West African sub-region, universities, which benefit from these collaborated programs and networks often limit the graduate training and research to universities located within specific countries. As a result, they lose the benefit of sub-regional interaction with people from other countries. Special projects like staff exchange for teaching or graduate supervision, exchange of external examiners, and research collaboration available in the developed economies rarely select from the African universities and the West African regional universities in particular.

It is also noticeable that most of the sponsorship of fellowships and other collaborated research programs come primarily from Europe and the United States. While acknowledging the high incidence of poverty among the sub-regional countries, it cannot be said to be the critical factor why investment is not made in this important aspect of human resource development and knowledge education in general. Nwoke (2005), remarks that discussions about cooperation and integration in West Africa seem to amount to 'defensive radicalism.' This is a concept coined by Ake (1981) to describe a situation where African leaders engage in political rhetoric and announce populist-sounding and grandiose plans and programs, which they were never committed to fulfill. Nwoke buttresses this assertion by arguing that:

An integration culture is also not yet conspicuous in the sub-region nor has it been accorded the high priority it really deserves. Ordinary people are not being encouraged to think in West African terms. And since 1975, when ECOWAS was formed, not many member-states have drawn up national development programs with regional considerations or the regional market as their point of reference (Nwoke, 2005, p. 132).

In our area of concern, little effort seems to be made by member states of ECOWAS to encourage inter-university academic and research exchanges. Apart from the West African Universities Sports Competition, there are minimal interaction in other areas of cooperation such as external examinations, networking, professorial assessments, and research cooperation generally. Regional cooperative and integrative policies are non-existent except as we have observed in some provisions of the ECOWAS treaty. Even in this, key challenges to the regional body are: 1) the political will to implement protocols, 2) weak institutional and administrative structures and capacity to support proposed projects, and 3) lack of resources to carry out programs. Above all, the divisive tendencies that arise from fear of domination and the fundamental political, economic, language, and educational differences between the Anglophone and Francophone major groups in the sub-region remain a major constraint (Nwoke, 2005).

The ineffectiveness of the ECOWAS states has some relationship with lack of functional education in the region. It is obvious from the foregoing that adequate attention has not been paid to the development of human resource development infrastructure needed for academic cooperation and integration in West Africa. There are still poor linkage programs for the members of the academia in the universities in the sub-region to share ideas, cooperate in common research projects, and network in official exchanges such as sabbatical leave, external examination appointments, and across the border employment opportunities. Indeed, there

seems to be more linkage and network projects between the West African universities and others in Europe, the United States, and Asia rather than among themselves.

The project of integration and cooperation in the sub-region that neglects creating opportunities for intra-regional interaction in one of the most critical sector of human resource development—the universities—will likely remain poorly articulated. If there is to be real progress in issues of integration and cooperation, both the regional body and country specific governments must take appropriate steps to encourage the development of a sub-regional manpower base that the university system can guarantee. No doubt, inter-universities cooperation through network in the sub-region could afford universities in West Africa the opportunity to share facilities, laboratories, equipments, library books, and journals. Hence, this will reduce the pace of "brain drain" from the region to other parts of the world and further integrate the region for political and economic collaborations. This cooperation will also help to raise the level of internal efficiency as universities strive to attract the best teachers and procure the most effective resources.

CONCLUSION AND RECOMMENDATIONS

Acknowledging the gallant efforts by past regional leaders to promote further cooperation among the West African countries and acknowledging the feasibility of this cooperation, we want to stress that a very fundamental aspect of integration and cooperation efforts have not been accorded the attention it deserves. Articulating collaborative economic and trade programs, peace and security operations, adopting mechanism for common market, establishing common parliament and court of justice without first addressing the basic differences that tear the people apart cannot yield much of the expected results. The people of West

Africa must first be made to realize that their differences are a source of strength if these can be properly harmonized and leveraged. The basic sources of difference, which has continued to be exploited for the underdevelopment, and violence that seems to be imminent in the region must be recognized and managed for development. The university system, through various exchange programs and networks, can be a real opportunity to bring students and the academia together in series of interactions that can gradually diffuse in both policies and human relationships within the sub-region. Finding ways of improving this all-important source of interaction in the sub-region becomes a *sine qua non*. In this measure, we want to highlight some pragmatic actions that can help to improve collaborative activities within the sub-regional universities.

In the first instance, ECOWAS must reassess the grounds on which it is hinging its integrative and cooperative efforts. Integration and cooperation cannot be possible when ethnic and religious differences are tearing nations apart in the sub-region. There is a need to first work on creating what Adolph Muschg calls "a synergy effect of inseparable national memories" (as cited in Guerot, 2003, p. 41).

A sense of oneness must be created by adopting policies and implementing programs that show that everybody whether from a large or small ethnic group, Muslim or Christian or indigenous religious worsher is important and has equal stake in both the national and sub-regional project. According to Ninsin (2009), integrative efforts must be based on the construction of an African cultural identity that is grounded in the history and culture of the people. Using West Africa as an example, Ninsin posits that:

West Africa's ancient history is replete with a succession of kingdoms that built extensive commercial and political networks of varying density with their immediate neighbors and penetrated distant lands. This was reinforced by constant

migration of people within the region, producing an ethno-linguistic map that binds most of the nation-states of the sub-region from Senegal in the West to Nigeria in the east, and from the coastal/ forest regions in the southern part of the region to the desert lands of the northeast (pp. 87-88).

The university system through research and interaction among different peoples of the sub- region can contribute significantly to this reconstruction of the grounds of identity that can ameliorate the antagonisms among groups in West Africa, apart from offering an opportunity for interaction and pooling of various talents.

ECOWAS may consider adopting protocols of 'regional character' in certain positions and programs run within the universities. By regional character is meant a recruitment policy for ensuring that all members are represented in the employees working in the identified positions and programs. Some of the countries in the sub-region have already enacted policies that the objectives include accommodating all sectional groups in employment. Nigeria for instance has a policy of federal character, which seeks to integrate all diverse groups in distribution of government largesse, employment inclusive. This policy option can help to raise the level of internal efficiency as universities strive to attract the best teachers from a larger employment market. While each country is contending with the problem of unemployment, a rationalization of such inter-country employment can ensure that the overall employees received are equivalent to that given out to other countries.

Each country in the sub-region should consider giving considerable priority in its fiscal budget to issues of education. The private sector should be encouraged to be more conscious of their social role to contribute to the development of human resources they use through reasonable commitment to sponsorship of fellowships and collaborative research within the sub-region where such opportunities or programs exist rather than overseas.

Finally, the universities in the sub-region should take the initiative to encourage collaboration. Such areas like appointment of external examiners, opportunities for sabbatical leave, international conferences, etc., can be embarked upon at minimal extra costs. If university officials consider the option of exploring the diversity within the sub-region in their teaching and research engagements, they can apply opportunity costs consideration by liberating funds from other important projects. In addition, generating and advancing knowledge through this unique avenue has the potential to provide a platform for leveraging diversity among the people of West Africa, which can tremendously enhance the regional concerns for cooperation and integration.

REFERENCES

Afrimap. (2011). *Treaty of ECOWAS*. Retrieved on 23/05/2011 from http://www.afrimap.org/english/images/treaty/ECOWAS%20Treaty.pdf.

Ake, C. (1981). *Revolutionary pressures in Africa*. London, UK: Zed Books.

Alemika, E. E. O. (2008). *Human resource management in the Nigeria police force: Challenges and imperatives*. Paper presented at the Police Service Commission Retreat on Understanding the Mandate and Operations of the Police Service Commission. Ada, Nigeria.

Alemika, E. E. O. (2009). Nature and pattern of transitional organized crime in West Africa. In A. O. Oluseyi & D. O. Ogaba (Eds.), *Transnational Crime and Security in West Africa,* (pp. 1-11). Lagos: Foreign Service Academy, Ministry of Foreign Affairs.

Benkler, Y. (2011). *The university in the networked economy and society: Challenges and opportunities*. Retrieved on 22/05/2011 from http://www.educause.edu/thetowerandthecloud/PUB7202f.

Cox, N. (2000). *Academical dress in New Zealand*. Retrieved on 20/05/2011 from http://www.academicapparel.com/caps/College-University-History.html.

ECOWAS. (2010). *General procurement notice*. Retrieved from http://www.afdb.org/fileadmin/uploads/afdb/Documents/Project-related Procurement/GPNNigeriaECOWAS%20%207-10.pdf.

Ezeani, E. O. (2002). Basic elements for effective human resource management in local government system. In Ezeani, E. O., & Nwankwo, B. C. (Eds.), *Human Resource Management in the Local Government System in Nigeria. Nsukka: Great Ap*. Express Publishers.

Federal Character Commission. (2011). *Federal character commission handbook*. Abuja: Federal Character Commission.

Guerot, U. (2003). *On the future of Europe* (p. 5). Deutschland.

Harbison, F. H. (1973). *Human Resources as the wealth of nations*. Oxford, UK: Oxford University Press.

Havenga, A. J. (1993). Beyond affirmative action there is diversity. *PRO Technida, 1*(10), 9–17.

4icu.org University Web Ranking. (2011). *Top 100 universities and colleges in Africa*. Retrieved 6/6/2011, from http://www.4icu.org/topAfrica/.

Idowu, W. (2004). Theorising conflict and violence: Contemporary Africa and the imperative of peaceful co-existence. *African Conflict Profile: Journal of the Centre for Ethnic and Conflict Studies, 1*(1), 1–17.

4International Universities and Colleges. (2011). *2011 world university ranking: Top 200 colleges and universities in the world by university web ranking*. Retrieved on 6/6/2011 from http://www.4icu.org/top200/.

MacGillivray, E. D., & Golden, D. (2007). Global diversity: Managing and leveraging diversity in a global workforce. *International Human Resource Journal*. Retrieved from http://www.orcnetworks.com/system/files/global%20diversity%20int%20HR%20summer07.pdf.

Ninsin, K. A. (2009). West Africa's integration: The logic of history and culture. In Adejumobi, S., & Adebayo, O. (Eds.), *The African Union and New Strategies for Development in Africa*. Nairobi, Kenya: Codesria and DPMF Publications.

Norris, B. (2000). Managing cultural diversity within higher education: A South African perspective. *Intercultural Communication, 3*. Retrieved 4/06/2011 from http://www.immi.se/intercultural/.

Nwoke, C. N. (2005). Nigeria and ECOWAS. In Ogwu, J. U. (Ed.), *New Horizons for Nigeria in World Affairs. Lagos*. Nigerian Institute of International Affairs.

Olusola-Oyewole, O., & Lamptey, A. S. (2008). *Developing links: EU-Africa cooperation in higher education through academic mobility*. Retrieved on 4/06/2011 from http://ec.europa.eu/education/external-relation-programmes/doc/confafrica/master3.pdf.

Roosevelt, T. R. (1990). From affirmative action to affirming diversity. *Harvard Business Review*, *2*(90), 107–117.

Stephenson, C. (2004). Leveraging diversity to maximum advantage: The business case for appointing more women to boards. *Ivey Business Journal*. Retrieved from http://c0524352.cdn.cloudfiles.rackspacecloud.com/101220-leveraging_diversity.pdf.

ADDITIONAL READING

Adejumobi, S., & Olukoshi, A. (2009). *The african union and new strategies for development in Africa*. Nairobi, Kenya: DPMF and CODESRIA.

Akiyemi, A. B., Falegan, S. B., & Aluko, I. A. (1983). *Readings and documents on ECOWAS. Lagos*. National Institute of International Affairs.

Bloom, D., Canning, D., & Chan, K. (2006). *Higher education and economic development in Africa*. Retrieved from http://www.arp.harvard.edu/AfricaHigherEducation/Reports/BloomAndCanning.pdf.

Devarajan, S., Monga, C., & Zongo, T. (2011). Making higher education finance work for Africa. *Journal of African Economies*, *20*(3), 133–154. doi:10.1093/jae/ejr020

Ezenwa, U. (1984). *ECOWAS and the economic integration of West Africa*. Ibadan: West Book.

Hazlewood, A. (1967). Problems of integration among African states. In Hazlewood, A. (Ed.), *African Integration and Disintegration: Case Studies in Economic and Political Union*. London, UK: Oxford University Press.

Lavergue, R. (1997). *Regional integration and cooperation in West Africa: A multi-dimensional perspective*. Trenton, NJ: Africa World Press.

United Nations University. (2009). *Revitalizing higher education in Sub-Saharan Africa: A United Nations University project report*. Retrieved from http://archive.unu.edu/africa/files/UNU_RevitalizingHigherEducation.pdf.

Utne, B. (2011). *Formulating higher education policies in Africa – The pressures from external forces and the neoliberal agenda*. Retrieved from http://www.netreed.uio.no/articles/high.ed_BBU.pdf.

KEY TERMS AND DEFINITIONS

Academia: Faculty members of a university system that engage in teaching and research.

Collaboration: Working together or joining efforts in pursuing a goal. It includes all opportunities for pursuing common education programs and projects among the universities, such as embarking on common research project, exchanging external examiners, providing opportunities for sabbatical leave for academics from other universities etc.

Cooperation: Ad hoc or temporary programs embarked on by various countries in the West African sub-region for the mutual benefit of all; separateness of countries is recognized.

Diversity Leverage: Recognizing and appreciating the worth of differences that exist among people. In this chapter, differences include ethnicity, nationality, talents, indigenous knowledge etc; essence is that such differences may constitute significant uniqueness and excellence in attributes, skills and talents which human beings possess.

Ethnicity: Differences in human groups rooted on such factors like, race, tribe, language, culture, and religion.

Integration: Attempt to associate or relate; establishing joint institutional mechanisms; implies a degree of shared sovereignty, which may be exercised by those joint institutional mechanisms distinguishable from those of individual countries in the region; aims to establish common markets, army, education system, employment etc.

Networking: Working together among the academia from various universities and countries. It encourages the pooling of individual efforts, talents, and aptitudes and also offers environmental opportunities for interaction and experience.

Chapter 2
Examining the Diversity Curriculum of Leading Executive MBA Programs in the United States

Mariya Gavrilova Aguilar
University of North Texas, USA

Pamela Bracey
University of North Texas, USA

Jeff Allen
University of North Texas, USA

ABSTRACT

Properly managed diversity practices enable organizations to maximize human capital, create a sustainable competitive advantage, attract more customers, and become more profitable. Many organizations conduct diversity training to address workplace diversity issues. Top management communicates the value of and commitment to diversity, whereas managers facilitate an environment that embraces diversity. Diversity management has emerged as a prominent strategy to handle diversity issues. This chapter examines diversity curriculum of leading Executive MBA (EMBA) programs in the United States and highlights the current state of the educational environment in addition to explaining how curriculum supports diversity and inclusion reforms at the organizational level. Through content analysis, the authors summarized the diversity topics featured in 20 leading EMBA programs in the United States. None of the reviewed programs explicitly utilized the word "diversity" in any of their core or elective course titles, and only three (3) explicitly mentioned the words "diverse" or "diversity" within course descriptions. Nevertheless, the data suggest that programs do seek to offer some form of experiences which have the potential and intent to enhance cultural awareness. The majority of programs under study require students to travel to a foreign country to participate in global travel exploration. The authors provide recommendations for future research related to effectively implementing diversity practices and curriculum so that leaders become better equipped to address the challenges of diversity for their organizations.

DOI: 10.4018/978-1-4666-1812-1.ch002

INTRODUCTION

The change in workforce demographics, increase of jobs in the service economy, continuing growth of globalization, and requirements for effective teamwork have emerged as significant forces in the business environment that drive the importance of diversity (Hitt, Miller, & Colella, 2006). Vecchio and Bullis (2001) stipulated that "as workplace diversity increases and supervisory ranks are staffed by a broader range of individuals, it becomes increasingly more common to be supervised by someone who is, in historical terms, an atypical supervisor" (p. 884). Having a multicultural workforce allows organizations to enhance marketing efforts, team building, problem solving, organizational flexibility, creativity, and innovation (Cox, 1993). Nevertheless, employees work in a workplace environment where diversity issues surface daily. Despite the US Census predictions of a more diverse US population, Buttner, Lowe, and Billings-Harris (2009) claimed that minority groups will still be underrepresented in professional occupations because of leader racial insensitivity, discrimination, (un)equal opportunity theory, and low organizational diversity strategic priorities. To some, this may be surprising provided that the first anti-discrimination legislation in the United States was introduced over 50 years ago. Currently, not only are US organizations witnessing inefficient diversity efforts but they are also facing a more significant challenge: lack of inclusion. "Diversity without inclusion does not work" (Miller & Katz, 2002, p. 17). Roberson (2004) explained diversity as emphasizing organizational demography and inclusion as being concerned with eliminating barriers to the integration of employees within the organization. How can we strive for inclusion if we are still struggling for diversity? Ultimately, the goal is to move away from compliance in the form of diversity quotas and mandatory training, and embrace integration within the organizational culture in the form of inclusion, which results in

a more committed workforce. McMahon (2006) discussed various diversity aspects depending on the desired goals of the organization: regulatory compliance; social justice; departmental responsibility (i.e., HR department), strategic planning outcome; or a community-focused activity. For the purposes of this chapter, the authors explored diversity from a strategic planning outcome perspective focusing on the roles of managers and leaders in leveraging diversity. Pursuing systemic and planned organizational change is one of the multi-faceted outcomes of diversity (Kreitz, 2008). This chapter examines the course curriculum and content areas emphasizing and promoting the importance of workforce diversity incorporated into 20 leading Executive MBA (EMBA) programs in the United States. The chapter also highlights the current state of the educational environment and how it supports diversity and inclusion reforms at the organizational level.

BACKGROUND

Business Case for Diversity

Effective diversity practices help organizations attract and retain human talent, enhance marketing efforts, increase creativity and innovation, improve problem solving, and develop flexibility (Cox, 1993). Loden and Rosener (1991) claimed that the primary dimensions of diversity such as race, ethnicity, gender, age, physical ability, and sexual orientation can create more tension at the workplace than secondary dimensions such as educational background, geographic location, income, marital status, parental status, and religion. Negative racial attitudes unfavorably affect human capital and can create a stressful environment for minorities (Brief, Dietz, Cohen, Pugh, & Vaslow, 2000; Clark, Anderson, Clark, & Williams, 1999). Properly managed diversity develops a better reputation as a minority employer and ability to respond to a more diverse market with a more diverse workforce (Cox & Blake, 1991). Because of the highly diverse population and the orientation toward a service economy, it is crucial that organizations have a workforce that understands the customer mindset and resolves customer concerns. Plummer (2003) discussed a diversity management approach that involves accepting and promoting diversity as inclusion. With this approach, organizations use diversity as a tool for growth while enhancing creativity, productivity, and morale. According to Yeo (2006), organizational policies promoting the recruitment, hiring, and retention of diverse employees and an organizational climate allowing employees to reach their full potential, encourage creativity and innovation, and champion inclusion of all employees. How can such outcomes be achieved?

Kirby and Richard (2000) determined that effectively managed diversity increased overall satisfaction and employee commitment. A degree of similarity between supervisors and their supervisees affected supervisees' organizational attachment (Mueller, Finley, Iverson, & Price, 1999). Organizational commitment of employees relates to a strong belief and acceptance of organizational goals and values, willingness to exert effort on behalf of the organization, and desire to maintain membership in it (Mowday, Porter, & Steers, 1982). Organizations are concerned about retaining and engaging their employees. Employee's organizational commitment has been correlated with the company's diversity initiatives (Wilborn, 1999). US chain retail stores with less supportive diversity climates had the largest racial-ethnic disparities disfavoring Black and Hispanic employees (McKay, Avery, & Morris, 2008). Buttner et al. (2009) concluded that inability to fulfill diversity promises resulted in lower levels of organizational commitment for professional employees of color. "The greater the difference in race between an individual and all other individuals in a work unit is, the lower the individual's attachment to the organization is" (Tsui, Egan, & O'Reilly, 1992, p. 568). Hicks-Clarke and Iles

(2000) concluded that women, racial and ethnic minorities, and people with disabilities harbored less positive attitudes towards their organization, jobs, and careers if the organization's diversity climate was poor. Regardless of whether an entry-level or a higher position is at stake, minority employees can recognize organizational lack of diversity commitment or ineffective diversity practices. This can ultimately lead to lower job and career satisfaction as well as low organizational commitment and engagement. The attitudes of men towards workplace hostility, turnover intentions, perceived promotion opportunity, job and supervisor satisfaction and supervisor-subordinate relationship are impacted by the organization's promotion of non-discrimination policies (Tejeda, 2006). Therefore, creating an organizational culture that promotes diversity, values all employees, and provides them opportunities to achieve their goals is paramount to both organizational and individual well-being.

Still, why do organizations face diversity management challenges? Poor training processes, outdated equipment, misguided incentive programs, discriminatory promotion and assignment practices, bylaws, exclusion from the golf tournament or being ignored at the board meeting represent some of the subtle barriers to inclusion (Miller & Katz, 2002). These instances of mistreatment or discrimination stem from the organizational culture and stifle the personal and professional development of employees, which may lead to indifference or lack of commitment toward the job, work team, and the company. Cox (1993) claimed that prejudice and discrimination negatively affected interpersonal trust, employee motivation, and performance, and multiplied the instances of sexual harassment. Collectively, these instances directly affected first-level organizational outcomes such as lost productivity, turnover, and absenteeism.

Choi (2008) found that demographic diversity (racial/ethnic) was negatively related to increased job satisfaction but was positively associated with turnover intentions in the public sector. Furthermore, it appeared that public agencies with effective diversity management practices perpetuated a positive relationship between racial/ethnic diversity and job satisfaction. Agencies that did not manage diversity effectively tended to have a negative relationship between racial/ethnic diversity and job satisfaction. Findings also revealed that minorities at diversified agencies demonstrated a higher level of job satisfaction and a lower intention to leave the organization in comparison with white employees. Women also demonstrated lower turnover intentions than men. This suggests that diverse employees of all levels who feel respected and appreciated develop a commitment toward the organization. Thus, the company gains positive exposure and builds a stronger reputation as a diverse employer.

Overall, diverse organizations promoted better performance and perpetuated effective decision-making (Nemeth, 1992). However, Mor Barak (2005) advocated a balanced focus on social justice as opposed to pure emphasis on the business case for diversity. There is much more to the business case for diversity than profitability. Norton and Fox (1997) explored the social and organizational responses to diversity. Social responses included legislative acts (i.e., 1964 Civil Rights Act, Age Discrimination Act), humanitarianism (i.e., raising awareness about the injustice minority groups suffered), and social responsibility (i.e., organizations which demonstrate corporate social responsibility by supporting disadvantaged individuals). Organizational responses included individuals facing exclusion, segregation, denial, and assimilation. Currently, organizations are oriented toward building relationships among individuals and workforce groups. Such an overall positive approach strengthened relationships between individuals from the same minority group, which defeats the purpose of diversity management. Diversity efforts have to be carefully managed and integrated into the overall organizational strategy in order to be effective. Therefore, industry leaders and administrators must be accountable for managing diversity initiatives.

Industry Needs for Leaders and Managers

Commitment of top management and alignment of diversity and strategic organizational goals represent another important aspect of diversity. Kreitz (2008) listed managerial influence as one of the best practices for successful implementation of diversity initiatives. An organization needs diversity-oriented executives; but how do we cultivate such individuals if they do not personally understand the benefits of diversity? Tudor (2011) encouraged managers to consider the diversity of their employees and create a suitable work environment. Organizational commitment to diversity perpetuates itself through CEO commitment, human capital, corporate internal and external communications, and supplier diversity (Slater, Weigand, & Zwirlein, 2008). For diversity to be effective, "the diversity mindset of senior management needs to change so that they can embrace a strategic view of diversity and develop policies that support the accumulation of diversity characteristics within the organization" (David, 2010, p. 41).

Organizations can develop a sustainable competitive advantage if they have "experienced, knowledgeable, highly skilled, and trained managers and workers" (Slater, et al., 2008, p. 202). How can organizations achieve this? Mor Barak (2005) overviewed the diversity evolution from equal rights laws, through affirmative action, to diversity management. Today, we are focusing on diversity management, which is "a voluntary organizational program designed to create greater inclusion of all individuals into informal social networks and formal company programs" (Gilbert, Stead, & Ivancevich, 1999, p. 1). What should organizations learn and managers emphasize? Diversity practices bring turmoil and require a substantial investment. Kreitz (2008) cautioned that leaders should embrace a multi-faceted strategy to manage diversity because recruitment and diversity training represent rather short-term approaches. Legislation and policies may prevent managers from embedding equality and diversity into their organizations (Preece, 2010). For example, risk-averse and stability-oriented organizations do not promote diversity (Tudor, 2011). Chrobot-Mason and Ruderman (2004) emphasized the role of leaders when recruiting and selecting team members, developing employees, and enhancing teamwork. In order to eliminate discrimination, promote diversity, and champion inclusion, managers should first understand the biases, stereotypes, and negative prejudice that affect their decisions. With respect to people development, leaders challenge, assess, recognize, and support employees as well as facilitate the communication between group members and enhance the overall productivity of the unit (Ruderman & Hughes-James, 1998).

Mor Barak (2005) discussed the Human Resource (HR) and Multicultural Organization (MO) paradigms as two of the most common diversity management strategies. These strategies provide a blueprint for diversity management that organizations can employ and the results they can expect. The HR approach manifests itself through diversity enlargement, diversity sensitivity, cultural audit, and organizational outcomes. As part of diversity enlargement, organizations recruit diverse employees. Diversity sensitivity involves training to increase awareness and improve communication and productivity in diverse work teams. The cultural audit is aimed at identifying and addressing problems while reviewing current practices in order to improve the overall workplace environment. Organizational outcomes are the result of the integration of diversity management with HR policy and strategic organizational as well as individual goals. The multicultural paradigm presented by Cox (1993) includes a monolithic

organization, a plural organization, and a multicultural organization. The monolithic organization is homogeneous and forces assimilation into the dominant culture. The plural organization is heterogeneous and committed to preventing discrimination; top management is still quite homogeneous although the rest of the organization is diverse. The multicultural organization should be used as a model of effective diversity management because it demonstrates a culture committed to equality and diversity. For the purposes of this chapter, the authors presented the HR and MO approaches because they encompass the multifaceted responses to diversity, which align with respective leader and organizational behaviors.

Another important contribution to diversity management reflected Thomas and Woodruff's (2001) characteristics of the diversity-mature individual. Such an individual accepts diversity management responsibility; possesses contextual clarity (knows himself or herself, knows his or her organization, understands key diversity concepts and definitions); is requirements-driven (differentiates among preferences, traditions, conveniences, and requirements; places differences in context when making include/exclude decisions); is comfortable with diversity tension; and engages in continual learning. As evident from these characteristics, diversity-mature individuals can represent any level of the organization. However, the key aspect is that these diversity-mature individuals are self-initiated and driven to accept the responsibility for developing and sustaining diversity change. Such individuals are aware of their role in the organization as well as their organization's strengths and weaknesses. This is a crucial aspect before any long-term change effort can be implemented. As we have already discussed, leaders must be able to effectively deal with or eliminate diversity tension consistently in order to focus on the overall benefits of diversity efforts. Being committed to constantly expanding his or her knowledge on the subject or gathering best practices represents the view that diversity management is a long-term and continuous effort.

Senior management is responsible for communicating the value of diversity and diversity management to the entire organization, whereas line management is responsible for implementing specific diversity strategies (Slater, et al., 2008). Nevertheless, a recent study noted that 50% of executives, middle managers, and supervisors named diversity as the least important leadership principle (AchieveGlobal, 2010). AchieveGlobal conducted a study of 971 business and government leaders and employees in Europe, Asia, and North America to identify the challenges they faced in the 21st century as well as the effective leadership practices that help them resolve these challenges. The study combined 42 behavioral and cognitive practices into 6 zones: Business, Reflection, Society, Diversity, Ingenuity, and People. Successful leadership in the diversity zone was characterized by the following:

In this zone, leaders value and leverage human differences, including gender, ethnicity, age, nationality, beliefs, and work styles. Here, leaders prove their ability to work with diverse people and appreciate cultural perspectives. To succeed in this zone, leaders:

- Strive to meet the needs of customers representing other cultures.
- Encourage collaboration among people from different groups.
- Display sensitivity in managing across cultural boundaries.
- Collaborate well with people very different from themselves.
- Effectively lead groups made up of very diverse people.
- Learn about the business practices of other cultures.
- Manage virtual teams with explicit customer-centric goals and practices.

It is imperative that leaders understand and respond to the needs of their diverse customers. This will result in higher customer satisfaction and loyalty. Leaders should focus on bridging the gaps between their diverse workforce by encouraging collaboration and effective teamwork. In order to demonstrate effective and dynamic leadership, leaders have to be culturally sensitive and able to manage diverse people. When conducting business internationally, leaders have to understand how the specific customs affect the business dynamics. Managing virtual teams represents the newest challenge from both a logistics and diversity perspective. Although the diversity leadership zone received the lowest rating of all six leadership zones, it was rated high among representatives from global organizations. This suggests that organizations already conducting business across nations have recognized the importance of managing a diverse workforce. For organizations still struggling with diversity management, we pose the following question: Who should be responsible for educating leaders and managers about the importance of diversity to the organization's bottom line, culture, and society?

Diversity Education

Diversity education is delivered through curriculum at institutions of higher learning or professional training courses to encourage managers and leaders to consider the impact of diversity on their organization. US universities have offered diversity awareness classes to prepare graduates for successful careers in a diverse workforce (Day & Glick, 2000). Adams and Zhou-McGovern (1993) advocated that the multicultural university environment spread diversity awareness and understanding. Gurin, Dey, Hurtado, and Gurin (2002) found that diverse experiences in higher education enhanced perspective-thinking, racial-cultural engagement, citizenship engagement, thus preparing individuals to participate and lead in a diverse democracy (p. 353). Diversity education programs emphasize self-reflection, awareness, and knowledge as opposed to skill development (King, Gulick, & Avery, 2009). Best practices in diversity education that can be incorporated into diversity training include providing frequent and structured feedback, using performance metrics, and exploring cognitive and affective processes (King, et al., 2009).

Pfeffer and Fong (2004) proposed several roles for business schools. Through knowledge development and management inquiry, business schools enhance the reputation of management. Business schools should be responsible for setting and enforcing the standards of management as a profession. More importantly, business schools develop critical thinking and analytical abilities. Business schools should also be charged with advancing management practice and enhancing economic development. Doria, Rozanski, and Cohen (2003) cautioned that business programs did not prepare students to handle the challenges of managing the workforce.

Examining the impact of diversity course requirements on student's racial prejudice, Chang (2002) found that students who took a mandatory diversity class had more favorable attitudes toward African-Americans than students who had just started the course. Bell, Connerley, and Cocchiara (2009) strongly advocated the introduction of mandatory diversity courses in management curriculum. The researchers stressed that diversity training offered at organizations was inadequate and too short to help managers face the diversity challenges. Diversity topics are usually addressed in human resources management and organizational behavior courses. Nevertheless, research also supports mandatory diversity education for the sake of not only promoting the "business case for diversity" but also to enhance the overall well-being of humans by improving the workplace environment.

Diversity training represents one of the most common methods to increase diversity awareness at the workplace. According to a study of

81 HR managers, organizations offered diversity training topics such as participation in teams, communication and listening, managing and supervising diversity, legal context, and cultural and international diversity (Day & Glick, 2000). According to Rynes and Rosen (1995), the most common workplace diversity training classes emphasized diversity awareness, working effectively and productively, balancing the needs of diverse groups, equal employment and affirmative action requirements, conflict management, special needs accommodations, and corporate cultural change. Backlash to diversity initiatives includes diversity training that is usually reactive, too brief, and perceived as remedial, as well as curriculum that is not adapted to the skills, needs, and experience of participants (Norton & Fox, 1997).

DIVERSITY CURRICULUM IN LEADING EMBA PROGRAMS

Research Design

To gain perspective into what graduate education currently offers experienced students regarding diversity training or instruction, the authors investigated the curriculum content of Executive MBA programs (EMBA) through content analysis. Typically, EMBA programs admit professionals with several years of managerial experience from a wide variety of institutions: Fortune 500 companies, non-profits, and small businesses. For example, the Kellogg Executive MBA program is "suitable for mid-career professionals who want to obtain senior leadership roles in their organizations or change industries." On average, students have between 12 and 15 years of work experience with a minimum requirement of eight years (Northwestern University, 2011).

The research population initially included all of the top ranked EMBA programs in American universities according to three separate 2010 reports from US News, Business Week, and The Wall

Street Journal. The rankings of these reports were collectively selected due to their public rapport of credibility and varying ranking methodologies. US News based EMBA rankings solely on feedback from business school deans and directors; BusinessWeek based their rankings on feedback from surveys of EMBA graduates and program directors; and The Wall Street Journal determined their rankings by surveying recent graduates and executives of companies that hire EMBA graduates (Porter, 2010). The research sample of this study only encompassed the 20 EMBA programs of US institutions holding rank on at least two of the three aforementioned published lists. Using rankings from all three reports enabled the authors to encompass reviews from a variety of perspectives. Because neither list of reported rankings was identical, the authors reviewed the top 25 EMBA programs on each list, and applied purposive sampling to create a more cohesive, unranked list of leading EMBA programs. Any institution located in another country was removed, in addition to US institutions that were only ranked on one list.

Following sample designation, a document review, and conceptual content analysis (Bauer, 2000) of program and course information available on university websites was conducted. Using an approach similar to Kuchinke's (2002) method of analyzing core curriculum, content was coded to identify both explicit and implicit references of diversity in the workplace within course titles and descriptions or academic experiences. Content Analysis is a research methodology used to determine the presence of certain words or concepts within texts or sets of texts, that allows quantification and analysis of the presence, meanings, and relationships of words and concepts, and then make inferences about the messages within the texts (Berelson, 1952). When conducting a content analysis, explicit terms are those that are obviously easy to identify, while implicit terms are those for which the researcher must base judgments on a slightly subjective system (Krippendorf, 1980).

Results

The sample of graduate institutions and business schools, listed in Table 1 (and reviewed in Tables 2 and 3), comprise the 20 leading Executive MBA programs reviewed in this study. None of the reviewed programs explicitly utilized the word "diversity" in any of their core or elective course titles, and only three (3) of them explicitly mentioned the words "diverse" or "diversity" within a course description. For example, the course description of an 'Organizational Behavior' course in one program read "…emphasizes skills needed to effectively manage diverse individuals through a variety of situations in organizations," and the course description of a 'Managing and Leading in Organizations' course read, "…topics include diversity, culture, and change…" Both of the aforementioned courses were core courses within their respective programs. The elective that mentioned 'diversity' was titled 'Communication for Developing Leaders,' which stated that students would learn to "negotiate diversity issues."

All but one (1) EMBA program had at least one (1) *implicit* reference of diversity in course titles, with 74% percent of these being part of the core curriculum of the programs. Course titles used to infer "diversity" are listed in Table 4.

Eighteen (18) of the 20 programs had at least one *implicit* reference of diversity within course descriptions, with 92% percent being part of the core curriculum. Examples of implicit references are listed in Table 5.

Although none of the 20 leading EMBA programs of our sample specifically denoted "diversity" training of any sort, the data suggest that programs do seek to offer some form of experiences for students, which have the potential and intent to enhance cultural awareness. The authors also determined that the majority of the programs under study require their students to travel to a foreign country to participate in some form of global travel exploration or seminar and enhance their cultural awareness, with the exception of

Table 1. A non-ranked compilation of 20 leading executive MBA programs

Top 2010 EMBA Rankings Based upon *US News*, *Business Week*, and *Wall Street Journal*
Boston University
Columbia University
Cornell University – Ithaca (Johnson)
Duke University (Fuqua)
Emory University – Atlanta (Goizueta)
Georgetown University – Washington (McDonough)
New York University (Stern)
Northwestern University (Kellogg)
Ohio State University (Fisher)
Southern Methodist University – Dallas
University of California – Los Angeles (Anderson)
University of California – Berkeley (Haas)
University of Chicago (Booth)
University of Michigan – Ann Arbor (Ross)
University of Notre Dame (Mendoza)
University of North Carolina – Chapel Hill (Kenan-Flagler)
University of Pennsylvania (Wharton)
University of Southern California – Los Angeles (Marshall)
University of Texas at Austin – Austin (McCombs)
University of Texas at Dallas

five (5). Related to the desired goals of the organization identified by McMahon (2006) and mentioned in the beginning of the chapter, the authors concluded that more is desired from EMBA programs in terms of preparing future executives to address diversity challenges. For example, regulatory compliance and social justice have dominated the field for a number of decades through Affirmative Action and Equal Employment Opportunity fighting to achieve equity and fairness in treatment. The authors are hopeful that the role of the HR department in educating the workforce and facilitating the understanding and implementation of diversity initiatives has been discussed throughout the overall curriculum since evidence of such was not found during our preliminary analysis. Involvement in community-based activities designed to enrich our understanding and appreciation for diversity has barely been addressed in the curriculum. With respect to strategic planning outcomes, organizations who truly strive to achieve a sustainable competitive advantage must regard diversity and inclusion as critical steps. It is expected that leading EMBA programs should prepare future executives to address the issues of diversity management. But if such programs do not embody diversity topics in their curriculum, who is responsible for helping middle managers become aware of, understand, accept and implement diversity and inclusion practices?

Implications and Recommendations

Diversity management is self-initiated, provides a broad definition, and aims at tangible benefits (Mor Barak, 2005). During the initial stages of any diversity initiative, supervisors and managers need to diffuse disagreements as soon as possible to avoid the build-up of tension between

Table 2. Executive MBA summary of results

	Program Total Yes	Course Type	Program Total No
Explicit Diversity Reference in Course Title	0	Core: 0 Electives: 0	20
Explicit Diversity Reference in Course Description	3	Core: 2 Electives: 1	17
Implicit Reference of Diversity in Course Title	19	Core: 39 Electives: 14	1
Implicit Reference of Diversity in Course Description	18	Core: 35 Electives: 2	2
Over Seas Trips	15		5

Table 3. Detailed breakdown of EMBA results

	Explicit Diversity Reference in Course Title	Explicit Diversity Reference in Course Description	Implicit Reference of Diversity in Course Title	Implicit Reference of Diversity in Course Description	Over Seas Trips
Institution 1	0	0	3	3	YES
Institution 2	0	0	0	1	NO
Institution 3	0	0	2	2	YES
Institution 4	0	0	2	0	YES
Institution 5	0	0	1	1	YES
Institution 6	0	0	2	3	YES
Institution 7	0	0	2	1	YES
Institution 8	0	0	2	3	NO
Institution 9	0	0	4	0	YES
Institution 10	0	0	2	3	YES
Institution 11	0	0	1	1	NO
Institution 12	0	1	1	2	YES
Institution 13	0	0	1	1	NO
Institution 14	0	1	2	3	NO
Institution 15	0	0	4	6	YES
Institution 16	0	0	1	1	YES
Institution 17	0	0	3	2	YES
Institution 18	0	0	3	2	YES
Institution 19	0	1	12	0	YES
Institution 20	0	0	5	2	YES
TOTALS	0	3	53	37	Yes: 15 No: 5

highly diverse individuals. Thereafter, managers can implement coaching and mentoring to help employees become more receptive toward diversity. Properly managed diversity develops a better reputation for the organization as a minority employer and enhanced the ability to respond to a more diverse market with a more diverse workforce (known as the marketing argument; Cox & Blake, 1991). In recent years, the trend to cater to a more diverse market has been considered a source of sustainable competitive advantage so managers must recognize the need to manage diversity effectively. Senior executives have to connect with all people at all levels in the organization, leverage diversity, integrate a culture of inclusion into their strategic and daily plans, as well as provide direction, focus, connections, and meaning to the inclusion strategies.

As evident from the curriculum examination, few EMBA programs offer a comprehensive focus on diversity through program content. The majority of curricula seems to focus on global cultural issues and ignores US cultural disparities and concerns. The scope of this study was to examine the current state of formal diversity education provided to executives. If research suggests that leaders should be educated in the area of diversity in order for them to understand the value of and incorporate diversity throughout their organizations, then how do leading EMBA pro-

Table 4. Examples of core course titles with implicit references of diversity

Titles
Competing Globally
Foreign Market Development
Global Business Environments
Global Financial Management
Global Logistics
Intercultural Management
International Business Strategy
International Managerial Policies and Strategies
Macroeconomics: Global External Environment
Multinational Business Administrations
Examples of Elective Course Titles with Implicit References of Diversity
Global Business Leadership
Global Immersion
Global Initiatives in Management
Globalization and Markets in the Changing Economic Landscape
International Finance
Leveraging Human Capital for Global Competitiveness
Thinking Globally
Working Mandarin
Working Portuguese
Working Spanish

grams respond to this need? The word "diversity" was explicitly mentioned in course curricula only three times. Perhaps there is a degree of stigma associated with the term that precludes leading programs from including it in their course titles and descriptions. Does that suggest that global topics of diversity have priority over issues encountered in the domestic workplace?

Summarizing results from Diversity Inc. rankings, Tudor (2011) concluded that successful diversity-oriented companies have supportive CEOs, incorporate diversity into every function, measure diversity effectiveness, and hold managers accountable for diversity initiatives. Diversity goals must be aligned with strategic organizational goals (Kreitz, 2008). Everyone from the CEO to the front line employee has to demonstrate diversity management skills (Harrington, 2009). When organizations struggle to establish an open communication process that allows them to keep every employee informed and build trust, the task is significantly complicated.

Thomas (1990) considered mandatory diversity training as ineffective when it failed to create long-term change. Therefore, top management should embrace a strategic vision for the organization with respect to diversity and promote it in its policies in order for these interventions to succeed (Buttner, et al., 2009). Managing diversity represents a lengthy process that requires top management commitment and understanding (Kreitz, 2008). As aforementioned, top management has to value diversity and promote its "well-being" in order for diversity to spread to all levels of the organization. However, a diversity revolution cannot occur overnight and key stakeholders must demonstrate patience and continue to focus on creating long-term cultural change. Managers utilizing reactive diversity training to address problems that have already occurred in the organization should also conduct a cultural audit in order to determine the reasons for the company's poor diversity climate. Mandatory diversity training is ineffective and fails to advance the organization when it only creates awareness and memorable discussions. Organizations need devoted leaders with a clear vision and practical strategies on how to incorporate and sustain diversity within the organizational culture.

The results of the study with respect to the explicit and implicit references to multicultural and global focus on diversity prompted further research into diversity in both the global and US specific contexts, which are beyond the scope of this chapter and are briefly mentioned here for clarification. Mor Barak (2005) offered various definitions of diversity: narrow category-based definitions focusing on gender, racial, or ethnic differences; broad category-based definitions focusing on education, marital status, among others; and definitions based on a conceptual rule encompassing variety of perspectives, actions, etc. When definitions of diversity are ethno-centric and

Table 5. Core course descriptions with implicit reference of diversity

Course Title	Example of Inference
Management of People at Work	*(... international models for managing employees)*
Governmental and Legal Business Environment	*(... emphasis on differences among countries)*
Financial Strategy	*(... case discussions of international firms...)*
Macroeconomics	*(... studies national and global economic activity)*
Negotiation Strategies	*(... debriefings that address multicultural issues...)*
The Manager and Business Relationships	*(... emerging trends of international trade)*
Corporate Governance	*(... consideration to international comparisons)*
Business Ethics	*(... focuses on intense global competition)*
Leadership Styles and Best Practices	*(... explore leadership in a global environment)*
Marketing Strategy and Analysis	*(... domestic vs. global competitive positioning)*
Environmental Analysis	*(... a global perspective of business environment)*
Financial Accounting	*(... US practice impacts the global corporation)*
Negotiations	*(... cultural, and gender differences on negotiations)*
Managerial Economics	*(... context of a changing international economy)*
Business and Government	*(... effects on government in US and abroad)*
Business as a System	*(... components of a complex global organization)*
Emerging Trends in Business and Society	*(... learn to view in broader global context)*
Strategy Formulation	*(.. companies in different industries & countries...)*
Operations Management & Strategy	*(.. emphasis on international operations...)*
Strategy	*(... gain advantage against competitors in the dynamic global market-place")*
Examples of Elective Course Descriptions with Implicit References of Diversity	
Negotiation and Dispute Resolution	*(... multi-party negotiations and cross-cultural issues)*
Modern Political Economy	*(... changes in American and international political economy)*

narrowly defined, the interpretation of *diversity* in other regions of the world becomes complicated. The Achieve Global report recommended that large-scale efforts were needed to leverage diversity in all its forms (2010).

The complex topic of diversity management cannot be successfully covered in one class. Therefore, the authors believe it is beneficial to incorporate diversity into the majority of courses taught in EMBA programs in addition to introducing a core diversity awareness course. Discussing diversity issues within specific courses will provide further reinforcement, as well as practical strategies for students to address the diversity challenges in those fields. Just as diversity is promoted at all levels of the organization, several courses in EMBA programs should explore how issues of diversity affect individuals, teams, and the organization as a whole.

FUTURE RESEARCH DIRECTIONS

Researchers interested in exploring the topic further have numerous perspectives to consider. More action research should focus on examining the different contexts of diversity and inclusion (Zanoni, Jansseses, Benschop, & Nkomo, 2010). In addition, executive board diversity has spurred significant discussion in recent years; the more diverse the board, the more effective decision-making is (Dalton & Dalton, 2005). Since many organizations still remain with a non-diverse board, researchers can empirically test the validity of this claim. Using this study as a blueprint, researchers should employ triangulation to incorporate data gathered from different sources: interviews with deans and program chairs, interviews with alumni, assessment of organizational culture, overview of institutional characteristics, and analysis of organizational systems and processes. Moreover, diversity education offered both through higher educational institutions as well as in-house or out-sourced diversity training seem to be insufficient in preparing leaders to encounter diversity challenges within their organization. Future diversity research should explore additional methods of not only increasing awareness but providing strategies to successfully implement diversity initiatives. Triandis (1995) recommended that researchers consider cultural distance, level of adaptation, history of intergroup relations, and acculturation when examining diversity. Linnehan and Konrad (1999) recommended more diversity research on the manifestation of prejudice, stereotyping, and discrimination at the workplace. Because of the fairly new emergence of the inclusion concept, research in this direction has had limited scope and tends to focus on the organizational practices from the perspective of executives/managers. Researchers should also consider conducting a longitudinal analysis of the diversity practices of organizations. Lastly, the levels of organizational diversity and commitment of international companies should be measured and compared to those of US headquartered companies; insight on these topics can help expatriates adjust to their foreign assignments more easily.

CONCLUSION

Leader racial insensitivity, discrimination, unequal opportunity theory, and low organizational diversity strategic priorities tumble effective diversity initiatives and minority group representation (Buttner, et al., 2009). Managers at all levels of the organization need to be aware of the ways diversity affects the commitment of their employees. Currently, as part of risk management and training and development initiatives, many organizations subject employees to mandatory diversity training to raise awareness of cultural issues. However, an organization cannot rely only on mandatory diversity training programs to address issues of discrimination, diversity, and inclusion; it has to also encourage diversity at all levels of its operations. A more diverse workforce that is not properly managed and supported through an organizational culture will not be more productive (Tudor, 2011). Supervisors and managers must defuse disagreements as soon as possible to avoid the build-up of tension between highly diverse individuals. Diversity should be a part of the organizational culture and not just a short-term initiative (Slater, et al., 2008). In order to be successful, large-scale diversity initiatives must have top management commitment but also have to be sustained through the interactions of all levels within the organization. Therefore, if organizations aspire to perform successfully in a global context, they must ensure that they accept and utilize the diversity of its workforce on a domestic level. Top management must be involved in diversity efforts and leadership must promote diversity as a core value of the organization (Norton & Fox, 1997). Diversity is not a human resource strategy or an approach to manage the workforce; stakeholders need to understand that diversity and inclusion perpetuate themselves through the full integration of members within the organization. Managers should lead teams that are inclusive, develop and retrain people, coach and mentor, and serve as role models promoting the culture of inclusion. Senior executives have to connect with all people at all levels in the organization, integrate leveraging diversity and a culture of inclusion into their strategic and daily plans, while providing direction, focus, connections, and meaning to the inclusion strategies. An inclusive organizational culture requires behavioral changes from all levels of the organization, and is the ultimate path to a profitable, responsible, and sustainable organization. Mandatory diversity education not only promotes the "business case for diversity" but it also enhances the overall well-being of humans by improving the workplace environment.

REFERENCES

AchieveGlobal Inc. (2010). *Developing the 21st century leader: A multi-level analysis of global trends in leadership challenges and practices.* Retrieved from http://www.achieveglobal.com.

Adams, M., & Zhou-McGovern, Y. (1993). *Connecting research to college teaching practice: Developmental findings applied to social diversity classes.* Paper presented at the 8th Annual Adult Development Society for Research in Adult Development. Amherst, MA.

Anderson Executive, M. B. A. Program. (2011). *University of California – LA's online course catalog.* Retrieved from http://www.anderson.ucla.edu/emba.xml.

Bauer, M. (2000). Classical content analysis: A review. In Bauer, M. W., & Gaskell, G. (Eds.), *Qualitative Researching with Text, Image, and Sound: A Practical Handbook* (pp. 131–151). London, UK: Sage.

Bell, M. P., Connerley, M. L., & Cocchiara, F. K. (2009). The case for mandatory diversity education. *Academy of Management Learning & Education, 8*(4), 597–609. doi:10.5465/AMLE.2009.47785478

Berelson, B. (1952). *Content analysis in communication research.* New York, NY: Free Press.

Berkeley-Columbia Executive, M. B. A. (2011). *University of California-Berkley's online course catalog.* Retrieved from http://berkeley.columbia.edu/.

Best Executive, M. B. A. Programs. (2010). *Wall Street Journal's online rankings.* Retrieved from http://online.wsj.com/public/resources/documents/EMBA-Top-25-Ranking.html.

Booth Executive, M. B. A. Program. (2011). *University of Chicago's online course catalog.* Retrieved from http://www.chicagobooth.edu/execmba/index.aspx.

Boston Executive, M. B. A. Program. (2011). *Boston University's online course catalog.* Retrieved from http://www.bu.edu/emba/?utm_source=adwords&utm_medium=cpc&utm_campaign=emba-adwords.

Brief, A. P., Dietz, J., Cohen, R. R., Pugh, S. D., & Vaslow, J. B. (2000). Just doing business: Modern racism and obedience to authority as explanations for employment discrimination. *Organizational Behavior and Human Decision Processes, 81,* 72–97. doi:10.1006/obhd.1999.2867

Buttner, H., Lowe, K., & Billings-Harris, L. (2009). The challenge of increasing minority-group professional representation in the United States: Intriguing findings. *International Journal of Human Resource Management, 20,* 771–789. doi:10.1080/09585190902770604

Chang, M. J. (2002). The impact of an undergraduate diversity course requirement on students' racial views and attitudes. *The Journal of General Education, 51,* 21–42. doi:10.1353/jge.2002.0002

Choi, S. (2008). Diversity in the US federal government: Diversity management and employee turnover in federal agencies. *Journal of Public Administration: Research and Theory, 19,* 603–630. doi:10.1093/jopart/mun010

Chrobot-Mason, & Ruderman, N. (2004). Leadership in a diverse workplace. In M. S. Stockdale & F. J. Crosby (Eds.), *The Psychology and Management of Workplace Diversity,* (pp. 100-121). Malden, MA: Blackwell.

Clark, R., Anderson, N. B., Clark, V. R., & Williams, D. R. (1999). Racism as a stressor for African Americans. *The American Psychologist, 54,* 805–816. doi:10.1037/0003-066X.54.10.805

Columbia Executive, M. B. A. (2011). *University of Columbia's online course catalog.* Retrieved from http://www4.gsb.columbia.edu/emba/overview.

Cornell Executive, M. B. A. (2011). *Cornell University's online course catalog.* Retrieved from http://www.johnson.cornell.edu/Academic-Programs/Executive-MBA.aspx.

Cox, T. Jr. (1993). *From cultural diversity in organizations: Theory, research and practice.* San Francisco, CA: Berrett-Koehler.

Cox, T. Jr. (2001). *Creating the multicultural organization: A strategy for capturing the power of diversity.* San Francisco, CA: Jossey-Bass.

Cox, T. H., & Blake, S. (1991). Managing cultural diversity: Implications for organizational competitiveness. *Academy of Management, 5,* 45–56.

Cox Executive, M. B. A. (2011). *Southern Methodist University's online course catalog.* Retrieved from http://www.cox.smu.edu/web/executive-mba.

Dalton, C., & Dalton, D. (2005). In defense of the individual: The CEO as board chairperson. *The Journal of Business Strategy, 26*(6), 8–9. doi:10.1108/02756660510632966

David, A. (2010). Diversity, innovation, and corporate strategy. In Moss, G. (Ed.), *Profiting from Diversity: The Business Advantages and the Obstacles to Achieving Diversity* (pp. 19–44). New York, NY: Palgrave Macmillan.

Day, N. E., & Glick, B. J. (2000). Teaching diversity: A study of organizational needs and diversity curriculum in higher education. *Journal of Management Education, 24*(3), 338–352. doi:10.1177/105256290002400305

Doria, J., Rozanski, H., & Cohen, E. (2003). What business needs from business schools. *Strategy +. Business, 32,* 39–45.

EMBA in Transition. (2011). *Bloomberg Businessweek's online business school rankings.* Retrieved from http://www.businessweek.com/bschools/rankings/.

Executive, M. B. A. Programs, Best Business Schools. (2011). *In US News' online rankings.* Retrieved from http://grad-schools.usnews.rankingsandreviews.com/best-graduate-schools/top-business-schools/executive-rankings.

Fisher Executive, M. B. A. (2011). *Ohio State University's online course catalog.* Retrieved from http://www.cob.ohio-state.edu/emba/.

Fuqua Weekend Executive, M. B. A. (2011). *Duke University's online course catalog.* Retrieved from http://www.fuqua.duke.edu/programs/duke_mba/weekend_executive/.

Georgetown Executive, M. B. A. (2011). *Georgetown University's online course catalog.* Retrieved from http://msb.georgetown.edu/gemba/.

Gilbert, J. A., Stead, B. A., & Ivancevich, J. A. (1999). Diversity management: A new organizational paradigm. *Journal of Business Ethics, 21,* 61–76. doi:10.1023/A:1005907602028

Glick, B. J., & Day, N. E. (2000). Teaching diversity: A study of organizational needs and diversity curriculum in higher education. *Journal of Management Education, 24*(3), 338–352. doi:10.1177/105256290002400305

Goizueta Executive, M. B. A. (2011). *Emory University's online course catalog.* Retrieved from http://www.goizueta.emory.edu/cgi-bin/generate/microsite_info_req.pl?display=form&section=emba&tactic=140.

Gurin, P., Dey, E. L., Hurtado, S., & Gurin, G. (2002). Diversity and higher education: Theory and impact on educational outcomes. *Harvard Educational Review, 72*(3), 330–336.

Harrington, M. (2009). What is your diversity management recession strategy? *Profiles of Diversity Journal.* Retrieved from http://www.aimd.org/.

Hicks-Clarke, D., & Illes, P. (2000). Climate for diversity and its effects on career and organizational perceptions. *Personnel Review, 29*, 324–347. doi:10.1108/00483480010324689

Hitt, M. A., Miller, C. C., & Collela, A. (2006). *Organizational behavior: A strategic approach.* New York, NY: John Wiley & Sons.

Kellogg Executive, M. B. A. Program. (2011). *Northwestern University's online course catalog.* Retrieved from http://www.kellogg.northwestern.edu/Programs/EMBA.aspx.

Kenan-Flagler MBA for Executives. (2011). *University of North Carolina's online course catalog.* Retrieved from http://www.kenan-flagler.unc.edu/programs/emba/index.cfm.

King, E. B., Gulick, L. M. V., & Avery, D. R. (2010). The divide between diversity training and diversity education: Integrating best practices. *Journal of Management Education, 34*(6), 891–906. doi:10.1177/1052562909348767

Kirby, S. L., & Richard, O. C. (2000). Impact of marketing work-place diversity on employee job involvement and organizational commitment. *The Journal of Social Psychology, 140*, 367–377. doi:10.1080/00224540009600477

Kreitz, P. A. (2008). Best practices for managing organizational diversity. *Journal of Academic Librarianship, 34*(2), 101–120. doi:10.1016/j.acalib.2007.12.001

Krippendorf, K. (1980). *Content analysis: An introduction to its methodology.* Beverly Hills, CA: Sage.

Kuchinke, K. P. (2002). Institutional and curricular characteristics of leading graduate HRD programs in the United States. *Human Resource Development Quarterly, 13*(2), 127–143. doi:10.1002/hrdq.1019

Linnehan, F., & Konrad, A. M. (1999). Diluting diversity: Implications for intergroup inequality in organizations. *Journal of Management Inquiry, 8*, 399–414. doi:10.1177/105649269984009

Loden, M., & Rosener, J. B. (1991). *Workforce America.* Homewood, IL: Business One Irwin.

Marshall Executive, M. B. A. (2011). *University of Southern California's online course catalog.* Retrieved from http://www.marshall.usc.edu/emba.

McKay, P. F., Avery, D. R., & Morris, M. A. (2008). Mean-racial ethnic differences in employee sales performance: The moderating role of diversity climate. *Personnel Psychology, 61*, 349–374. doi:10.1111/j.1744-6570.2008.00116.x

McMahon, M. A. (2006). *Responses to diversity: Approaches and initiatives.* Retrieved from http://www.shrm.org/.

Miller, F. A., & Katz, J. H. (2002). *The inclusion breakthrough: Unleashing the real power of diversity.* San Francisco, CA: Berrett-Koehler.

Mor Barak, M. E. (2005). *Managing diversity: Toward a globally inclusive workplace.* Thousand Oaks, CA: Sage.

Mowday, R., Porter, L., & Steers, R. (1982). Employee-organization linkages. In Warr, P. (Ed.), *Organizational and Occupational Psychology* (pp. 219–229). New York, NY: Academic Press.

Mueller, C., Finley, A., Iverson, R., & Price, J. (1999). The effects of group racial composition on job satisfaction, organizational commitment, and career commitment: The case of teachers. *Work and Occupations*, *26*(2), 187–219. doi:10.1177/0730888499026002003

Nemeth, C. J. (1992). Minority dissent as a stimulus to group performance. In Worchel, S., Wood, S. W., & Simpson, J. A. (Eds.), *Group Process and Productivity* (pp. 95–111). Newbury Park, CA: Sage.

Northwestern University. (2011). Kellogg school of management. *Kellogg Executive MBA*. Retrieved from http://www.kellogg.northwestern.edu.

Norton, J. R., & Fox, R. E. (1997). *The change equation: Capitalizing on diversity for effective change*. Washington, DC: American Psychological Association. doi:10.1037/10224-000

Pfeffer, J., & Fong, C. T. (2004). The business school 'business': Some lessons from the U.S. experience. *Journal of Management Studies*, *41*, 1501–1520. doi:10.1111/j.1467-6486.2004.00484.x

Plummer, D. L. (2003). Diagnosing diversity in organizations. In Plummer, D. L. (Ed.), *Handbook of Diversity Management: Beyond Awareness to Competency Based Learning* (pp. 1–49). Lanham, MD: University Press of America.

Porter, J. (2010). The best executive M.B.A. programs. *The Wall Street Journal*. Retrieved from http://online.wsj.com.

Preece, A. (2010). Embedding diversity: The obstacles faced by equality and diversity specialists. In Moss, G. (Ed.), *Profiting from Diversity: The Business Advantages and the Obstacles to Achieving Diversity* (pp. 137–148). New York, NY: Palgrave Macmillan.

Roberson, Q. M. (2004). *Disentangling the meanings of diversity and inclusion*. Center for Advanced Human Resource Studies (CAHRS) Working Paper. Ithaca, NY: Cornell University.

Ross Executive, M. B. A. (2011). *University of Michigan's online course catalog*. Retrieved from http://www.bus.umich.edu/Admissions/EMBA/Whyross.htm.

Ruderman, M. N., & Hughes-James, M. W. (1998). Leadership development across race and gender. In McCauley, C. D., Moxley, R. S., & Van Velsor, E. (Eds.), *The Center for Creative Leadership Handbook of Leadership Development* (pp. 291–335). San Francisco, CA: Jossey-Bass.

Rynes, S., & Rosen, B. (1995). A field survey of factors affecting the adoption and perceived success of diversity training. *Personnel Psychology*, *48*, 247–270. doi:10.1111/j.1744-6570.1995.tb01756.x

Slater, S., Weigland, R. A., & Zwirlein, T. J. (2008). The business case for commitment to diversity. *Business Horizons*, *51*, 201–209. doi:10.1016/j.bushor.2008.01.003

Stern Executive, M. B. A. (2011). *New York University's online course catalog*. Retrieved from http://www.stern.nyu.edu/AcademicPrograms/EMBA/Curriculum/index.htm.

Tejeda, M. J. (2006). Nondiscrimination policies and sexual identity disclosure: Do they make a difference in employee outcomes? *Employee Responsibilities and Rights Journal*, *18*(1), 45–59. doi:10.1007/s10672-005-9004-5

Texas Executive, M. B. A. (2011). *University of Texas at Austin's online course catalog.* Retrieved from http://new.mccombs.utexas.edu/MBA/EMBA.

The Executive MBA Program. (2011). *University of Texas at Dallas' online course catalog.* Retrieved from http://som.utdallas.edu/graduate/execed/execMba/.

The Nortre Dame Executive MBA. (2011). *University of Notre Dame's online course catalog.* Retrieved from http://business.nd.edu/executive_mba/.

Thomas, R. R. Jr. (1990). From affirmative action to affirming diversity. *Harvard Business Review*, *90*, 107–117.

Thomas, R. R. Jr, & Woodruff, M. (1999). *Building a house for diversity: How a fable about a giraffe & an elephant offers new strategies for today's workforce.* New York, NY: AMACOM.

Triandis, H. C. (1995). The importance of contexts in studies of diversity. In Jackson, S. E., & Ruderman, M. N. (Eds.), *Diversity in Work Teams: Researching Paradigms for a Changing Workplace* (pp. 225–233). Washington, DC: American Psychological Association. doi:10.1037/10189-009

Tsui, A. S., Egan, T. D., & O'Reilly, C. A. (1992). Being different: Relational demography and organizational attachment. *Administrative Science Quarterly*, *37*, 547–579. doi:10.2307/2393472

Tudor, P. (2011). *Adding value with diversity: What leaders need to know.* Retrieved from http://www.tudorconsulting.net.

Vecchio, R., & Bullis, R. (2001). Moderators of the influence of supervisor-subordinate similarity on subordinate outcomes. *The Journal of Applied Psychology*, *86*, 884–896. doi:10.1037/0021-9010.86.5.884

Wharton MBA for Executives. (2011). *University of Pennsylvania's online course catalog.* Retrieved from http://www.wharton.upenn.edu/mbaexecutive/academics/curriculum.cfm.

Wilborn, L. R. (1999). *An investigation of the relationships between diversity management training involvement with the personal inputs and outputs of managers in the lodging industry.* Unpublished Doctoral Dissertation. Memphis, TN: The University of Memphis.

Yeo, S. (2006). *Measuring organizational climate for diversity: A construct validation approach.* Unpublished Doctoral Dissertation. Columbus, OH: Ohio State University.

Zanoni, P., Janssens, M., Benschop, Y., & Nkomo, S. (2010). Guest editorial: Unpacking diversity, grasping inequality: Rethinking difference through critical perspectives. *Organization*, *17*, 9–29. doi:10.1177/1350508409350344

ADDITIONAL READING

Allen, W. R., Bonous-Hammarth, M., Teranishi, R. T., & Dano, O. C. (Eds.). (2006). *Higher education in a global society: Achieving diversity, equity, and excellence: Advances in education in diverse communities: Research, policy, and praxis,* (vol 5). Amsterdam, The Netherldands: Elsevier.

Battaglia, B. (1992). Skills for managing multicultural teams. *Cultural Diversity at Work*, *4*, 4–12.

Budd, R. W., Thorp, R. K., & Donohew, L. (1967). *Content analysis of communications.* New York, NY: Macmillan Company.

Chin, J. L. (2010). Introduction to the special issue on diversity and Leadership. *The American Psychologist*, *65*(3), 150–156. doi:10.1037/a0018716

Cox, T. Jr, & Beale, R. L. (1997). *Developing competency for managing diversity: Readings, cases, and activities*. San Francisco, CA: Berrett-Koehler.

Davenport, T. H., Prusak, L., & Wilson, H. J. (2003). *What's the big idea?* Boston, MA: Harvard Business School Press.

Gardenswartz, L., & Rowe, A. (1994). *The managing diversity survival guide*. Burr Ridge, IL: Irwin.

Golembiewski, R. T. (1995). *Managing diversity in organizations*. Tuscaloosa, AL: The University of Alabama.

Gottfredson, L. S. (1992). Dilemmas in developing diversity programs. In Jackson, S. E. (Ed.), *Diversity in the Workplace* (pp. 279–305). New York, NY: Guildford Press.

Judy, R. W., & D'Amico, C. (1999). *Work force 2020 – Work and workers in the 21st century* (5th ed.). Hudson Institute.

Kandola, B. (2009). *The value of difference: Eliminating bias in organizations*. Oxford, UK: Pearn Kandola.

Kandola, R., & Fullerton, J. (1998). *Managing the mosaic: Diversity in action* (2nd ed.). London, UK: Chartered Institute of Personnel and Development.

Kravitz, D. A. (2008). The diversity-validity dilemma: Beyond selection – The role of affirmative action. *Personnel Psychology, 61*, 173–193. doi:10.1111/j.1744-6570.2008.00110.x

Lieberman, S., Simons, G., & Berardo, K. (2009). *Putting diversity to work*. Mississauga, Canada: Crisp.

Lindsay, B., & Blanchett, W. (2011). *Universities and global diversity: Preparing educators for tomorrow*. New York, NY: Routledge.

Litvin, D. (1997). The discourse of diversity: From biology to management. *Organizations, 4*(2), 187–209. doi:10.1177/135050849742003

Moss, G. (Ed.). (2010). *Profiting from diversity: The business advantages and the obstacles to achieving diversity*. New York, NY: Palgrave Macmillan.

Pendry, L. F., Driscoll, D. M., & Field, S. (2007). Diversity training: Putting theory into practice. *Journal of Occupational and Organizational Psychology, 80*(1), 27–50. doi:10.1348/096317906X118397

Pfeffer, J., & Fong, C. T. (2002). The end of business schools? Less success than meets the eye. *Academy of Management Learning & Education, 1*, 78–95. doi:10.5465/AMLE.2002.7373679

Richard, O. C. (2000). Racial diversity, business strategy, and firm performance: A resource-based view. *Academy of Management Journal, 43*, 164–177. doi:10.2307/1556374

Shen, J., Chanda, A., D'Netto, B., & Monga, M. (2009). Managing diversity through human resource management: An international perspective and conceptual framework. *International Journal of Human Resource Management, 20*(2), 235–251. doi:10.1080/09585190802670516

Sonnenschein, W. (1997). *The diversity toolkit: How you can build and benefit from a diverse workforce*. Lincolnwood, IL: NTC Business Books.

Stockdale, M. S., & Crosby, F. J. (Eds.). (2004). *The psychology and management of workplace diversity*. Malden, MA: Blackwell.

Thomas, D. A., & Gabarro, J. J. (1999). *Breaking through: The making of minority executives in corporate America*. Boston, MA: Harvard Business School Press.

Thomas, R. R. Jr. (1992). Managing diversity: A conceptual framework. In Jackson, S., & Ruderman, M. (Eds.), *Diversity in Work Teams: Research Paradigms for a Changing Workplace* (pp. 306–318). Washington, DC: American Psychological Association.

Thomas, R. R. Jr. (1996). *Redefining diversity*. New York, NY: AMACOM.

Tyler, C. L., & Tyler, J. M. (2006). Applying the transtheoretical model of change to the sequencing of ethics instruction in business education. *Journal of Management Education, 30*(1), 45–64. doi:10.1177/1052562905280845

Webber, S. S., & Donahue, L. M. (2001). Impact of highly and less job-related diversity on work group cohesion and performance: A meta-analyses. *Journal of Management, 27*, 141–162.

Wright, P., Ferris, S. P., Hiller, J. S., & Kroll, M. (1995). Competitiveness through management of diversity: Effects of stock price valuation. *Academy of Management Journal, 38*, 272–287. doi:10.2307/256736

KEY TERMS AND DEFINITIONS

Diversity: Cultural or demographic differences among individuals.

Diversity Management: Maximizing diversity through voluntary organizational actions and implementation of specific policies and procedures.

EMBA: Executive Master of Business Administration; programs designed for managers seeking career and organizational advancement.

Explicit Terms: Terms used in content analysis that are obvious to identify; specific.

HR (Human Resources) Paradigm: A diversity management approach focused on aligning recruitment, selection, promotion, etc. policies and procedures with diversity goals.

Implicit Terms: Terms used in content analysis that are inferred; implicit.

Inclusion: Accepting all differences and involving individuals at all levels of the organization; the ultimate goal of diversity management.

MO (Multicultural Organization) Paradigm: This term, coined by Taylor Cox, refers to a diversity management approach that creates and sustains an organizational culture that provides opportunities for individuals of diverse backgrounds.

Monolithic Organization: A homogeneous organization that forces assimilation into the dominant culture.

Multicultural Organization: Demonstrates a culture committed to equality and diversity.

Plural Organization: A heterogeneous organization committed to preventing discrimination.

Chapter 3
Theorizing African American Women's Learning and Development:
Leveraging Workforce Diversity through Socio–Cultural Adult Learning Theories

Marilyn Y. Byrd
University of Mary Hardin-Baylor, USA

Dominique T. Chlup
Texas A & M University, USA

ABSTRACT

This study is a qualitative, interpretative examination of nine African American women's encounters with race, gender, and social class (intersectionality) in predominantly white organizations and the learning experiences that emerged from these encounters. Rather than continuing to operate from a Eurocentric view of learning, this study contributes to the scholarly discussion the learning perspectives of African American Women (AAW). Black feminist theory is used as a socio-cultural framework to explain how AAW learn from issues emerging from intersectionality. A narrative approach to inquiry was the research strategy employed. Three major learning orientations emerged from the women's narratives: learning from influential sources, learning through divine guidance, and learning through affirmation of self. The authors contend that expanding the conversation of adult learning theories to include socio-cultural theories derived from black women's scholarship may be necessary to move the field of adult education toward more inclusive ways of theorizing adult learning. Implications for the field of adult education and the emerging workforce diversity paradigm are provided.

DOI: 10.4018/978-1-4666-1812-1.ch003

INTRODUCTION

The intersection of race, gender, and social class are interlocking systems forming mutually constructing forms of social dominance (Collins, 1998). In North American society, constructions of race, gender, and social class reproduce hierarchical systems that privilege some while denying others. The workplace, like other areas of society, can play an important role in reproducing and maintaining the status quo. Together, perspectives and constructions of race, gender, and social class may work to the disadvantage of African American Women (AAW) in predominantly White organizations. For the purpose of this study, a predominantly White organization refers to an environment where an AAW enters and assumes a position of leadership.

In this study, we pursue the notion that adult learning theories should consider socio-cultural theoretical perspectives that address intersectionality in the learning and development process of AAW. Socio-cultural refers to theoretical perspectives that consider race, gender, and social class in analyzing power dynamics within bureaucratic and other systems where power can be used to oppress (Merriam & Caffarella, 1999). While scholars and educators in the field of adult education have addressed women's learning and development in terms of gender (Barr, 1999; Bierema, 2001, 1999; Belenky, Clinchy, Goldberger, & Tarule, 1986, 1998; Hayes & Flannery, 2000; McLaren, 1985; Thompson, 1983, 1995) there is a lack of studies which have addressed the intersection of race, gender, and social class and AAW's learning and development in predominantly White organizations. For this reason, there is a lack of research in the field that has used socio-cultural theoretical frameworks, such as black feminist theory, to examine the nexus between socio-cultural theories and traditional learning theories. The narratives of the AAW in this study shifts the discussion of learning and development from independent, separate categories of disadvantage to one that

focuses on the constructions of race, gender, and social class as an interactive, dynamic, and interlocking system of oppression.

For the purposes of this study, an African American woman is one who self-identifies as black and whose national origin of birth is the United States of America. Race is a socially constructed category that denotes differences among people and is politically sustained to assign people to categories (Banton, 2000). Gender is not only a social construct, it is a "set of assumptions and beliefs on both individual and societal levels that affect the thoughts, feelings, behaviors, resources, and treatment of women and men" (Bell & Nkomo, 2001, p. 16). Social class distinguishes the powerful from the powerless and can be one way of maintaining exclusion and sustaining oppression. In predominantly white settings, social class generally determines one's access to formal and informal social networks that grants social privilege and career success (Bell & Nkomo, 2001). Race, gender, and social class converge to form an interdependent, interactive, dynamic, and interlocking system referred to as intersectionality. While varying perspectives of intersectionality are emerging (Alcoff, 2006; Zack, 2005), the term "intersectionality" initially referred to the experiences of Black women whose experiences and struggles were not adequately captured in the feminist and anti-racist discourse. According to Crenshaw (1989), intersectionality denotes the various ways in which race, gender, and social class interact to shape the multiple dimensions in which AAW experience the world.

Statement of the Problem and Research Questions

According to Parker (2005), silencing the experiences of certain groups from the study of a phenomenon grants privilege to others and consequently produces the dominant, theoretical perspective that frames our understanding of what is accepted as the norm. By bringing the interlocking systems of race, gender, and social class to the conversation on adult learning, this study seeks to add a perspective of learning that challenges the traditional assumptions about the phenomenon of adult learning. To this end, the following research questions are posed:

1. How have AAW learned to develop in their professional roles in predominantly white organizations given their positionality within an interlocking social system of race, gender, and social class (intersectionality)?
2. How do traditional learning theories explain the learning experiences of African American women emerging from intersectionality?

Theoretical Framework

Black feminist theory will be used as a socio-cultural theoretical perspective that is emerging as a useful framework for explaining the intersection of race, gender, and social class in the experiences of AAW. The prevailing notion of black feminist theory is that AAW cannot be empowered unless intersecting systems of oppression are eliminated (Collins, 1990). Black feminist theory is a critical social theory that highlights power relationships that have maintained the marginalized status of AAW. Central to the goal of black feminist theory is the notion of collectivity and the commitment for social justice for those who are similarly positioned (Collins, 1998).

Black feminist theory brings to light the ways that AAW, individually and collectively, seek to understand injustices emerging from intersectionality. The shared knowledge that is gained in the process can be a stimulus for collective empowerment for social change. As a theoretical framework, black feminist theory emphasizes the empowerment of AAW and the quest for social justice. Hence, black feminist theory is useful for explaining intersectionality in the learning and development of AAW in predominantly white organizations.

SIGNIFICANCE OF CULTURALLY INFORMED LEARNING TO THE FIELD OF ADULT LEARNING AND EDUCATION

This study is significant to the field of adult learning and education because AAW's position within interlocking social systems may result in learning experiences that are different from their White counterparts. Since AAW are part of a larger body that has experienced historical oppression, their experiences cannot be and should not be generalized with the experiences of others. Collins (1986) uses the term *outsider-within* to describe Black women's social class position in society. Outsider-within identities are situational and attached to specific histories of social injustice, and it is the "unequal power relations of race, class, and gender that produce social locations characterized by injustice" (Collins, 1999, p. 86).

Schiele (1996) explains oppression as a "systematic and deliberate strategy to suppress the power and potentiality of people" (p. 288). Oppression "threatens to disempower men and women who have the capacity to be empowered, reflective actors" (Welton, 1993, p. 88). Similar to the broader society, the ways that AAW encounter oppression may influence the outcomes of professional learning and development. Hence, oppression is a strategy that is counter intuitive to learning and development.

Brookfield (2003) refers to adult education theorizing as racialized. A field of practice can be racialized when the dominant discourse that takes place is from the perspective of one particular group's perspective. In the case of adult education, the dominant discourse has been from the conceptualization of white, European American males. Alfred (2000) observes how the field of adult education should continue to challenge the universality of learning theories emanating from a Eurocentric epistemological orientation and embrace learning theories that consider social constructions such as race, gender, and social class. To accomplish this, more socio-cultural ways of learning and knowing are needed to explain experiences emerging from intersectionality and to enhance the learning theories traditionally associated with the field of adult learning and education.

The Absence of Socio-Cultural Perspectives in Traditional Adult Learning Theories

Adult learning is comprised of a collection of theories, ideas, models, and frameworks borrowed from other fields and disciplines, allowing us to view learning from different perspectives and angles. Merriam (2001) suggested that a universal theory of adult learning would simplify the task of explaining the field and informing the practice of adult education. A universal perspective for viewing adult learning would be ideal if learning could be applied to a group of learners that were common and whose worldviews were identical. According to Burns (2002), a general, universalized theory or adult learning is unrealistic given the multiple meanings and contexts of learning. More recently, Merriam (2007) offers new insight and suggests the need to embrace a knowledge base that captures more cultural and contextualized ways of learning and knowing.

Adult learning theories have generally assumed learning to be a generic phenomenon or process engaged in by middle class, white Americans (Brookfield, 1995). However, the learning experiences of AAW may be influenced by factors not perceived or comprehended by white Americans (or black men for that matter), rendering traditional

adult learning theories universally inapplicable. In this respect, the field of adult education has ignored the socio-cultural aspects that define learners' experiences in environments, such as workplace environments, that replicate societal beliefs and assumptions (Alfred, 2002). These learning experiences include ways that people make sense of their lives, transforming not only that which is learned but also the way learning occurs (Merriam, 2001). Moreover, learning cannot be separated from the context in which it is used. The context in which individuals make personal meaning of their learning experiences is the "larger systems in society, the culture, and the institutions that shape learning, the structural and historical conditions framing, indeed defining, the learning event" (Merriam & Caffarella, 1999, p. 360).

Theorizing AAW's learning and development in predominantly white organizations calls attention to race-neutral theorizing in the field of adult education. Race-neutral theorizing refers to theories that fail to recognize that organizations are not neutral settings where individuals are the same and are subjected to the same type of historical and cultural experiences (Parker, 2005). Furthermore, race-neutral theories establish a single and dominant perspective that becomes fixed in the literature and over a period of time becomes the informing and universally accepted perspective.

Rather than continuing to operate from a Eurocentric view of learning, this study introduces to the scholarly discussion the learning perspectives of AAW using black feminist theory as a socio-cultural framework that is appropriate for explaining how AAW learn from their experiences with intersectionality in predominantly white environments. Therefore, expanding the conversation of adult learning theories to include socio-cultural theories derived from black women's scholarship may be necessary to move the field of adult education toward more inclusive ways of theorizing adult learning.

AFRICAN AMERICAN WOMEN'S WAYS OF KNOWING: CULTURALLY INFORMED LEARNING

Similar to Ladson-Billings' (1995) culturally relevant teaching methodology which maintains that students' cultural backgrounds and experiences informs teaching methods, AAW's history and culture informs their way of knowing how to successfully overcome power dynamics stemming from intersectionality in predominantly White organizations. History and culture creates an ideology or tie that binds AAW (Bell & Nkomo, 2001). The tie that binds works as a unifying force that resists the oppressive forces created by simultaneous encounters with race, gender, and social class. Therefore, AAW have inherited culturally informed learning strategies from a historical and cultural background that has been rooted in oppression. Although traditional feminist perspectives have contributed to an awareness of gender bias in a male-dominated society, these feminist perspectives are generally advanced by white scholars and do not advance the issue of race. Johnson-Bailey and Cervero (2000) suggest that race is missing from feminist discourse because white perspectives are considered the accepted norm.

In addition, studies based on the experiences of white women do not effectively capture the positionality of AAW. For example, Bierema's (1999) study of how executive women learn and develop in corporate cultures that are maintained by patriarchal power structures consisted of thirteen women, 2 of whom were black. While this study sheds light on the challenges that women encounter in environments that are controlled and maintained by men, studies that attempt to universalize the experiences of educated and privileged white women with those of black women is problematic because the power dynamics emerging from racism are rendered invisible.

Adult educators and scholars studying the social constructions of learning have typically focused on ways that gender influences learning and development. When we refer to gender in terms of learning and development in the workplace or organizational settings, we might be referring to several things: learning to enhance knowledge and skills, learning as a continued lifelong process, learning the culture of the organization, or even learning to balance work and home. While these issues can be universally applied to all women, conversations on socio-cultural aspects of learning are needed to address the learning and development of women that are positioned at the intersection of race, gender, and social class. Bierema (2001) contends that:

...women's learning at work is challenging because it happens in a context that has been largely created, maintained, and controlled by white men. Success for many women often means accepting and even emulating male-dominated organizational culture. Yet this type of acculturation does not help eliminate systemic discrimination or asymmetrical power distribution, nor does it balance gender representation among the ranks of executives (p. 53).

While Bierema's (2001) explanation emphasizes gender discrimination in learning, for women positioned within the confines of race, gender, and social class, it is necessary to look deeper into ways that race and social class, in conjunction with gender, influences learning and development.

African American women view the world from discrete perspectives based on positionality within the confines of the larger structures of race and gender (Collins, 1990). In predominantly White organizations, AAW must learn to navigate hierarchies of power, barriers of exclusion, and structures of oppression that emerge from the interlocking system of race, gender, and social class. Because AAW are often perceived in terms of their race, gender, and social class, viewing their learning experiences through a culturally informed lens is essential to understanding their learning and professional development needs within predominantly white environments.

METHODOLOGY

This study is a qualitative, interpretative examination of nine African American women's encounters with race, gender, and social class (intersectionality) in predominantly white organizations and the learning experiences that emerged from these encounters. According to Seidman (1991), a qualitative methodology is useful in learning how people make meaning of their experiences and how their interpretations influence their reactions. Selected traditional learning theories will be examined to identify parallels or contradictions with black feminist theory, a socio-cultural theoretical framework. The ensuing discussion will examine how these selected theories are useful for explaining and gaining a better understanding of AAW's learning and development in predominantly White organizations.

Data Sources

Purposeful sampling (Creswell, 1999) was used to select the nine participants in this study. This sampling technique aims to discover, understand, and gain insight into individual experience. For this reason, it is necessary to select a sample from which the most can be learned.

The participants in this study ranged from age 40 to mid-60s with at least 5 years experience as an executive or senior-level manager in a predominantly white organization. They represented a variety of occupations and sectors of society. In this study, the term "executive" refers to chief operating officers, vice presidents, and the heads of business units with responsibilities such as change

initiatives, innovation, and business performance (Noe, 2002). A senior-level manager manages or has administrative authority over several groups or departments.

The participants were selected based on their affiliation with professional organizations such as the National Black MBA Association. Organizations with a large African American membership were targeted based on the likelihood that membership would include AAW executive and/or senior-level managers. The participants represented a variety of occupations and professions.

Data Collection

The data were collected from conducting face-to-face interviews in a neutral, mutually agreeable site. The interviews consisted of asking semi-structured, open-ended questions that were informed by the research questions. For example, participants were asked questions such as:

1. Tell me about a time that you found to be a disempowering experience or a challenge to your position of leadership. What was your way of responding, reacting, or resolving the difficulty?
2. Looking back over your professional life, can you talk about people that have influenced your leadership development?
3. Can you talk about mentors in your work environment that were valuable to your leadership development?

The goal of the interview process was to engage the participants in a conversation about disempowering situations where race, gender, and social class might have been a factor and the learning experiences that resulted from these encounters.

Narrative Analysis

A narrative approach to inquiry was employed since collecting the professional experiences of

AAW can produce a form of narrative that tells a story. From narratives, we learn one's philosophy of life. Philosophy expresses one's interpretations of the reality of life. Sharing realities grants us knowledge and perhaps greater wisdom that can be passed on. Using this premise, individual narrative should be a powerful tool for studying AAW because it "allows the person to withdraw from an experience in order to reflect upon it, then reenter active life with a new or deeper understanding of that experience" (Clark, 2001, p. 89).

Narratives offer an intimate perspective of a woman's life and provide deeper insight into interpreting and understanding her life unabridged (Etter-Lewis, 1993). The narratives produced in this study are grounded in encounters with race, gender, and social class biases and as such offers a deeper and more comprehensive understanding of the learning experiences and the socio-cultural realities of AAW.

LEARNING TO LEAD: REFLECTIONS OF AFRICAN AMERICAN WOMEN LEADERS

The following are selected passages from the narratives of nine AAW who are former or current leaders in predominantly White organizations. Three major learning orientations emerged from these women's experiences: learning from influential sources, learning through divine guidance, and learning through affirmation of self. These learning orientations represented life orientations (family, community, or spiritual values) that contributed to the participants' learning in predominantly White organizations. Life orientations are guiding forces that direct and determine how a woman arranges her life and represent the values and interests that direct her toward certain goals and opportunities (Bell, 1990).

Learning from Influential Sources

Social learning describes how people learn by interacting with and observing others (Bandura, 1986). In the workplace, learning can occur through the process of socialization or interactions between individuals.

Terhune (2008) found that African American women in predominantly white environments often experience feelings of social and cultural isolation, creating a need for connections to social support networks that can provide psychosocial buffers against disempowering situations. Furthermore, socialization provides access to formal and informal social networks that could increase opportunities for learning and skill development (Combs, 2003). However, informal social networks are more likely to represent access to power and authority and the development of social relationships that can positively influence and enhance career development. African American women's *outsider-within* social class status may inhibit participation in informal networks, which results in a lack of knowledge and the information exchange that can occur in these networks. Kezia (all names are pseudonyms), corporate executive, says AAW are locked out of social networking opportunities. She offers this perspective.

The thing that happens with a lot of AAW is that we're on the peripheral of the social circles and we can be locked out in many instances. I don't play golf or play squash. So I don't get those invitations. The informal nature of the social context is being pulled into that circle. I [emphasis added] have to build other relationships or look for opportunities to get together with other AAW who might be experiencing the same types of issues. Although my title is CIO, I am not a part of the executive management team—which is kind of funny in and of itself. And I know that from a socialization perspective I'm not on the dinner invitation list—have never been. In my current position, it's more of social cliques and I'm not in the social cliques. So I'm not invited to the table. There are other social contexts in which I can cross over. I guess maybe if I joined XX country club. But then I'm still not going to get invited into their group. But I should not have to go through that extent in order to get the information that I need. So that can be an inhibitor.

Central to social learning is the idea that people learn from role models. Thus, a key area is mentoring, a primary means of development in workplace interactions. Mentors are guides who "lead us along the journey of our lives… they cast light on the way ahead, interpret arcane signs, warn us of lurking dangers, and point out unexpected delights along the way" (Daloz, 1986, p. 17). Mentoring plays a crucial role in the psychosocial development of individuals, providing the interconnectedness and support needed to negotiate the challenges that are associated with new roles in the workplace (Mott, 2002). Because AAW entering predominantly White environments often experience isolation, they often find themselves assimilating with the dominant culture in order to find support systems (Hughes & Howard-Hamilton, 2002). Diana, retired executive manager, state government, confirms this perspective of mentoring:

I never had a mentor that I could identify with… but I had support of the (white) executive director at that time and two other top (white) administrators. And somebody that really pushed me hard was the former (white) executive director who was working as a professor at the local university. He encouraged, guided, directed, and coached me in many ways.

Judith, public school administrator, adds the following:

There were three (white) males and one (white) female that mentored me and that was wonderful! And the principals who gave me opportunities to use my skills, to shape and help mold me and just to learn by observing them—were white males!

Although Diana and Judith had positive experiences with cross-racial mentorships, their reflections describe more formal type relationships that are linked to superior/subordinate mentoring relationships that focus on task-related processes. The challenge, however for many AAW, is the lack of mentors and role models with whom they can form a support group and share counterstories of their lived experiences. The role models and facilitators of these groups should be other AAW (Hughes & Howard-Hamilton, 2003). For instance, Esther, retired manager of a public utility company, had this insight:

I trained under another African American woman and that was a wonderful experience because we could share the black experience. I could understand and relate to what she was sharing with me as opposed to a white person giving me this information. And I knew everything she said she was doing to get past certain situations, I was going to have to do it that same way.

Furthermore, in the absence of mentors to which they can identify from a socio-cultural perspective, AAW may be subjected to the worldviews of the dominant culture and therefore expected to act in accordance to worldviews that are contradictory to their cultural beliefs and background (Collins, 1986). In this respect, the traditional perspectives that support mentoring may be counter to the learning and development of AAW in predominantly White organizations. African American women's experiences with social issues that emerge from intersectionality require specialized insights and perspectives that are not shared with the dominant culture (Collins, 1990). For this reason, mentors must be aware of the subtleties and hidden injuries caused by racial differences so that protégés have a greater opportunity to learn and develop within organizations dominated by the status quo (Stanley & Lincoln, 2005). Furthermore, understanding the impact of experiences resulting from multiple layers of oppression may be invisible to members of the dominant group (Hughes & Howard-Hamilton, 2002). Johnson-Bailey and Cervero (2002) acknowledge that cross-cultural mentoring relationships are sites of struggle for learning and power because individuals are located in different social hierarchies of race and gender. Lydia, manager with a state agency, says:

It's sad to say but I did not have a mentor that I could identify with and that made it difficult. So I had to draw from, actually, common sense. Another thing that was really difficult for me as a female in a male dominated profession: my superior, a white male, made it known to me that he preferred all male managers because that's how he grew up. And there were others times when I felt—even knew—that he had a problem with the other...with me being black. So any problems I had, I had to work out on my own.

Research and discussions on mentoring that appear in major adult education and human resource development journals are typically presented from the perspective of white scholars and as a result issues emerging from intersectionality are not disclosed. For example Gibson's (2005) study of nine women faculty members supported the value of mentoring in personal and career learning. However, there needs to be more insight on

the unique mentoring needs of AAW in predominantly white organizations. The opportunity for an African American woman to engage in dialogue with a mentor in relation to issues emerging from intersectionality, and as a result, reflect and apply learning strategies is a challenge.

Learning from Divine Guidance

Success at work fulfills an individual's innate drive for what has been called self-actualization, or the need for achievement. Self-actualization is considered the primary goal of learning and is a central idea in Maslow's (1970) theory of motivation, a humanistic learning theory. Therefore, it is a natural tendency for individuals to be motivated towards goals in their work experiences. On the other hand, adverse experiences encountered from the intersection of race, gender, and social class can inhibit motivation to reach self-actualization.

Humanistic theories focus on development of the whole person. Beyond the basic levels of need, individuals possess needs that can be linked to moral or spiritual values. According to Mattis (2002), AAW draw upon faith and divine guidance when facing challenges by transforming those challenges into meaningful experiences that will move them towards a higher purpose. Hannah, school district administrator, shared how she learned to cope with these types of challenges in predominantly White organizations.

To successfully lead in these types of environments you have to trust God. Otherwise you'll spend a lot of energy trying to make things right that really you don't have the ability to make right. You cannot control how people feel about you or how they react towards you. But you can know that God will level the playing field. When we are in the middle of adversities, trying to work out our frustration and stress, we simply need to walk it out through faith.

Julia, a community and civic leader, shares another perspective of divine guidance:

It is difficult for an African American woman to be successful without being a Christian or a godly woman. Without strong spiritual faith and guidance, you'll become weakened or overstressed or you're just going to quit. God rewards those that diligently seek Him through their struggles.

Kezia, corporate executive, stated that she learned early in life the importance of keeping God in her life and that aspect of her life granted her the courage to endure issues she perceived were due to her race and gender.

My parents instilled in me the value of faith in God and how it would guide me later in life. I have experienced both race and gender issues—it just depends on the day of the week. Knowing that I can endure all things through Christ has sustained me.

Connection to a divine or spiritual source is one way that people construct knowledge and make meaning of lived experiences (Tisdell, 2003). Fundamental to divine guidance is the belief that in the "midst of fear and confusion, amid turmoil and uncertainty, appropriate actions and responses will somehow be revealed" (Dym & Hutson, 2005, p. 77). Walker (2009) says that because an African American woman is often the only person of color in her work setting, faith in God has provided a source of inspiration and strength to endure challenges that stem from intersecting levels of oppression.

Learning through Affirmation of Self

The intersection of race, gender, and social class in predominantly white organizations can produce dynamic, complex, and challenging problems and situations that are often difficult for AAW to resolve. Culturally informed learning strategies

that provide affirmation of self often provide the only solution to these difficult problems and situations (Collins, 1990).

Culturally informed learning strategies and the liberating empowerment that can be produced is linked to Freire's (1970) emancipatory philosophy, a major contributor to the transformational learning theory. The goal of emancipatory learning is to liberate individuals from oppressive forces that may control opportunities to reach a desired goal or that control individual autonomy to perform at the level to which that individual is capable. Being personally empowered even when conditions limit and restrict an individual's ability to act is necessary for a changed consciousness. Although traditionally applied to classroom experiences that emerge from critical pedagogy, emancipatory learning can be applied to work experiences and the concept of changed consciousness. Changed consciousness refers to AAW's ability to reach another level in their way of thinking about a situation because change has occurred from within (Collins, 1990). Rather than internalizing actions that are perceived as oppressive, AAW have developed strategies that reject the assumed power of others.

Paula, a bank vice-president, talked about a disempowering experience with a manager that was a source of frustration for her and a strategy she learned as a way to channel her frustration. Paula's boss (Pat) would refuse to recognize her ideas or suggestions, although she believed she could offer useful ideas from the experiential knowledge she had learned. She shared her strategy for coping with her frustration.

I had a manager once—a younger white male— who just did not want blacks in certain positions. When we needed to discuss certain ideas, he never asked for my thoughts. Well, I have sort of an experiential way of solving problems, but my Daddy had taught me to always know my role. So I made a sign and placed it on my computer. It said: PAT IS RIGHT in bold capital letters. The sign was a reminder that he is my superior and even if I knew there was a better way, it didn't matter what I thought. The bottom line is if Pat said it's blue he wants it blue! But the sign was really for me because it helped me through my frustration—it was my way of coping.

Experience and critical reflection is central to Freire's (1970) philosophy of emancipatory learning. According to Freire, the cycle of reflecting, acting on one's new understanding and then critically reflecting is praxis. Through praxis one may become empowered to develop capacities to act successfully and challenge systems of power. The system can be conceptualized as hierarchies of power such as corporations and organizations. Systems such as these can threaten to dis-empower marginalized groups who have the capacity and agency to be otherwise empowered and reflective (Welton, 1993). Esther talked about how she learned to evolve as a leader and how negative experiences strengthened her ability to speak up in meetings.

I evolved into leadership, because growing up I was actually shy. The management job I held made me stronger because I faced so many challenges alone. So I evolved out of my shyness and learned to speak up. I discovered a strength I didn't know I had. I never considered myself a spokesperson for black women, but in speaking up, I was speaking up for others who were still trying to find their strength.

However, critical reflection goes beyond reviewing one's experiences. The process of critical reflection involves examining underlying beliefs and assumptions and trying to make sense of what one discovers. The discovery of meaning and arriving at new understandings is tested through discourse with others. Claudia had a similar story about how she internalized difficult situations and how she learned to become assertive through a changed consciousness.

Being the only African American woman in my workplace has been difficult because I haven't had anyone to share those challenging times. It is hard to try to explain things that happen. You try to tell someone and it doesn't even seem real or sound like it makes sense. I don't expect to change people, so I had to learn how to change me. I had to learn how to assert myself, first quietly. And now, I just seem to know when, as my mother used to tell me...to choose my battles.

Emancipatory learning involves deconstructing power structures and developing ways of knowing to resist and challenge these structures. Emancipatory learning can lead to transformative learning experiences that empower and motivate individuals to act as change agents towards a more just society. While empowerment is liberating, emancipation involves resisting and challenging structures of power (Inglis, 1997). Hannah talked about a reaction strategy she learned that not only empowered her, but granted her peace of mind when dealing with a problematic boss. She called the strategy stop, drop, and roll.

I had a boss who operated in a crisis mode all the time. She was also racist and tried to turn everybody against me. Every time she came into my office it was a problem. Then the Lord gave me a strategy...it was stop, drop, and roll. Stop and know that God is in control. Drop my personal investment in the outcome because God has promised to take care of me. Roll and cast my cares on God. Once I learned that strategy, it was good for me and I carried it over into other areas of my life.

As AAW become empowered as individuals, a changed consciousness can promote collective empowerment. Individually, AAW are empowered to self-affirmation. Through group persistence, empowerment occurs to transform institutions (Collins, 1990). Identity with a cause larger than self is the point of departure in the process of self-definition. When linked to group action to change oppressive systems, individuals have the power to "change the world from one in which we merely exist to one over which we have some control" (p. 121). This philosophy speaks to AAW's goal of group uplift and the theme of lifting as we climb, a motto adopted by early AAW social activists. In the present study, Julia spoke of how she has been influenced and empowered by the strength and courage of her ancestors. In the same manner, she feels compelled to pass on this legacy of empowerment to other AAW.

You have to stay encouraged because things are going to discourage you daily. Pull from the strength of our ancestors and those that paved the road. You have to believe and know that all you go through is to strengthen you.

African American women's culturally ways of learning can produce an affirmation of self that is liberating and which has the potential to empower the larger group to advocate against social injustice.

When linked to group action, our individual struggles gain new meaning. Because our actions as individuals change the world from one in which we merely exist to one over which we have some control, they enable us to see everyday life as being in process and therefore amenable to change (Collins, 1990, p. 121).

As individual AAW experience personal, transformative learning, other AAW can become empowered to transform organizations into more democratic and socially just environments.

DISCUSSION OF THE ADULT LEARNING ORIENTATIONS EMERGING FROM THE NARRATIVES

The field of adult education is informed by a number of philosophical and theoretical learning orientations. In this study, observational learning (Bandura, 1986), self actualizing learning (Maslow, 1970), and emancipatory learning (Freire, 1970), can be identified in the learning themes that emerged from the participants' narratives.

Traditional adult learning theories support a Eurocentric ideology based on the universality of cultural perspectives (Schiele, 1996). The failure to consider the cultural values of people of color in developing models or theoretical frameworks can be viewed as an "implicit expression of Western ethnocentrism, or the belief that Eurocentric values are the only values that can explain behavior and should be the basis for solving people's problems" (p. 284). According to Lynham (2002), the application of a theory to a problem, issue, or phenomenon links the theory to the world of practice. Therefore, theories are used to give different perspectives, or frames that help us understand situations, problems, and daily activities in the workplace. A drawback may be that when theories refer to people they are not necessarily universal nor can they be generalized to all situations and circumstances. For this reason, theory should be inclusive of gender, social class, ethnicity, and age (Brookfield, 1992). Furthermore, consideration should be given to the ways that theory changes over time in response to the emergent nature of research and the changing dynamics in society.

For example, in this study, Bandura's (1986) observational theory, a social learning theory, applies to ways that the participants learned or received support from influential sources or mentors. The major drawback to this social learning orientation in respect to ways that AAW learn is that as AAW progress to higher levels in the organization's structure, the opportunities to form mentoring relationships with other AAW is limited. Male mentors may not provide the type of guidance needed from their own experiences as men. Furthermore, mentoring relationships with White men or White women do not offer the opportunity for AAW to share, reflect upon, and learn from their experiences with issues emerging from intersectionality.

While Maslow's (1970) theory of motivation is exemplified through the participants' persistence to confront their experiences, this theory does not adequately address the higher order of need that these women called upon to find relief from social issues emerging from intersectionality. Socio-cultural theories such as black feminist theory links spirituality to the history and culture of African American people and highlights the role spirituality has played in enduring oppression.

Freire's (1970) emancipatory philosophy explains adult learning as a transformative process with social change as an outcome. A common theme between emancipatory learning theory and Black feminist theory is empowerment and social change. These two theoretical perspectives speak to emancipation, empowerment, and social change and support common goals in the learning and development of African American women in predominantly white organizations.

Socio-Cultural Theories for Culturally Informed Learning

A socio-cultural theory that is useful for understanding culturally informed learning is Black feminist theory. According to Collins (1990), black feminist theory signifies the theoretical perspectives of those who live it. A basic assumption of black feminist theory is that AAW's experiences produces specialized knowledge. While this framework is recognized in areas such as sociology, it remains an untapped source for informing scholars across multiple disciplines of the realities of AAW within the larger confines of race, gender, and social class. Black feminist theory shares common and salient themes with adult learning theories that might be beneficial to educators and researchers interested in advancing the learning and development of African American women. On the other hand, it might be useful to educators and researchers to consider black feminist theory as an informing source for challenging some of the traditional and universally accepted theories of adult learning that do not adequately address the socio-cultural aspects of learning and development.

Black feminist theory explains the collective, lived experiences of AAW, the commonalities of these experiences, and the multiple contexts from which these experiences can be understood. Although the voices of AAW in contributing to knowledge construction is still largely unrecognized, Black feminist theory provides insight on how the realities and perspectives of AAW can be used to inform the traditional theories of adult learning. African American women's collaboration and group talk on issues that arise from common experiences produces specialized knowledge that requires strategies for coping that are common to the experiences of the larger society. Knowledge is fundamental to resisting, challenging, and being liberated from oppression, which can in turn produce learning. Black feminist theory places learning derived from experiences with intersectionality at the center of analysis and offers fresh insights to the study of adult learning. Therefore, identifying basic assumptions and goals between traditional adult learning theories and black feminist theory that promote or inhibit the learning of AAW may be a pivotal point for theorizing the intersections of race, gender, and social class in adult education.

Implications for the Field of Adult Education

The field of adult education has not adequately recognized or integrated socio-cultural theories such as Black feminist perspectives into research or theories. As shown in this study, AAW use culturally informed strategies for addressing issues that emerge from race, gender, and social class oppression. Therefore, socio-cultural theories are needed to explain the positionality of AAW, particularly in settings that are predominantly white.

The community of educators and scholars that represent the field of adult education are responsible for recognizing the perspectives of learning from the viewpoints of AAW rather than viewing them as insignificant to mainstream learning theory (Delany & Rogers, 2004). Theories that exclude the construct of race may influence who is studied and the type of questions that are addressed in research (Parker, 2005). By recognizing Black feminist theory as a contributor to mainstream scholarship, more inclusive perspectives of learning are made possible and offer a broader space for theorizing AAW's learning. If women are to advance in organizations and promote systemic change, their learning must address issues of power and oppression (Bierema, 2001). Building on this thought, we should be more explicit about ways that oppression might occur in settings, such as predominantly White organizations, where AAW experience isolation. To be truly representative of all women as learners, the field of adult education must offer more culturally informed ways for understanding how individuals learn and develop in settings where power and privilege are the norm.

Race, gender, and social class are constructions that order and influence the rights, privileges, and tribulations that AAW face every day. The effects of these social constructions cannot be separated out from the daily experiences of these women. It is hoped that this discussion is a beginning point toward addressing racial as well as gendered perspectives of adult learning in the workplace. The community of adult educators—all races—should be respectful of not only the learning experiences produced from AAW's experiences, but also how AAW, in general, experience the world and the wealth of knowledge they create during their journeys to reach self-definition.

Adult educators and scholars may not benefit from the valuable contribution that Black feminist theory makes to adult learning because this body of literature is not within the paradigm of epistemology generally associated with learning. The underlying assumption being that learners share a commonality of learning experiences and needs and do not differ in their subjection to the inequities of race, gender, and social class. In this respect, black feminist theory provides a socio-cultural perspective of learning and is a rich source for explaining and better understanding not only how AAW learn but also the uncommon areas in their learning in respect to women in general. Adult educators and scholars that support an Africentric philosophy (Asante, 1987; Collins, 1990; Schiele, 1996) would agree that although AAW have unique characteristics, core values, and philosophical assumptions originating from a shared history and culture (Alfred, 2000).

Understanding how to provide learning for the increasing number of women entering professional positions in organizations is an important task for the field of adult education (Brookfield, 1989). However, placing AAW at the center of analysis may require the field of adult education to consider theoretical perspectives that take into account the changing nature of work and issues confronting organizations in the 21st century. Furthermore, understanding the complexities of AAW's learning in predominantly white environments calls for synthesizing theories from multiple disciplines and fields with the traditional theories of adult learning. If the field of adult education is to be representative of all adults, more culturally informed ways of learning should be incorporated into research and theories. Using black feminist theory as a framework of analysis in addition to traditional learning theories may offer a more inclusive framework for understanding interactions of race, gender, and social class.

Implications for the Workforce Diversity Paradigm

Organizations and institutions hold leadership responsible for carrying out the strategic vision, mission, and goals of the organization. Leadership learning and development is necessary for leaders to carry out these strategic responsibilities. Yet, little consideration has been given in research and theory to the potential for an interlocking system of race, gender, and social class to interfere with leadership development—in this case, the leader being an African American woman. Therefore, more theoretical frameworks are needed to explain ways that counterproductive behaviors emerging from the positionality of the leader affects the leader's ability to perform and lead the organization towards its strategic goals.

REFERENCES

Alcoff, L. M. (2005). *Visible identities: Race, gender, and the self.* Oxford, UK: Oxford University Press.

Alfred, M. (2002). Linking the personal and the social for a more critical democratic adult education. In Alfred, M. V. (Ed.), *Learning in Sociocultural Context: Implications for Adults, Community, and Workplace Education* (*Vol. 4*, pp. 89–95). San Francisco, CA: Jossey-Bass. doi:10.1002/ace.82

Alfred, M. V. (2000). The politics of knowledge and theory construction in adult education: A critical analysis from an Africentric feminist perspective. In *Proceedings of the 41st Annual Adult Education Research Conference,* (pp. 6-10). Vancouver, Canada: University of British Columbia.

Asante, M. K. (1987). *The Afrocentric idea.* Philadelphia, PA: Temple University Press.

Bandura, A. (1986). *Social foundations of thought and action.* Englewood Cliffs, NJ: Prentice-Hall.

Banton, M. (2000). The idiom of race: A critique of presentation. In Back, L., & Solomos, J. (Eds.), *Racialization* (pp. 51–58). Oxford, UK: Oxford University Press.

Barr, J. (1999). *Liberating knowledge, research, feminism and adult education.* Leicester, UK: NIACE.

Belenky, M., Clinchy, B., Goldberger, N., & Tarule, J. (1986). *Women's ways of knowing.* New York, NY: Basic Books.

Belenky, M., Goldberger, N., Tarule, J., & Mcvicker, B. (1998). *Knowledge, difference, and power: Essays inspired by women's ways of knowing.* New York, NY: Basic Books.

Bell, E. L. (1990). The bicultural life experience of career-oriented black women. *Journal of Organizational Behavior, 11,* 459–477. doi:10.1002/job.4030110607

Bell, E. L., & Nkomo, S. (2001). *Our separate ways: Black and white women and the struggle for professional identity.* Boston, MA: Harvard Business School Press.

Bierema, L. L. (1999). A model of executive women's learning and development. *Adult Education Quarterly, 49*(2), 107–122. doi:10.1177/074171369904900203

Bierema, L. L. (2001). Women, work, and, learning. In Fenwick, T. J. (Ed.), *Sociocultural Perspectives on Learning through Work* (*Vol. 92*, pp. 53–62). San Francisco, CA: Jossey Bass.

Brookfield, S. (1992). Developing criteria for formal theory-building in adult education. *Adult Education Quarterly, 42*(2), 79–93. doi:10.1177/0001848192042002002

Brookfield, S. (1995). Adult learning: An overview. In Tuinjman, A. (Ed.), *International Encyclopedia of Education*. Oxford, UK: Pergamon Press.

Brookfield, S. (2003). Racializing criticality in adult education. *Adult Education Quarterly, 53*(3), 154–169. doi:10.1177/0741713603053003002

Brookfield, S. D. (1989). Facilitating adult learning. In Merriam, S. B., & Cunningham, P. (Eds.), *Handbook of Adult Education in the United States*. San Francisco, CA: Jossey-Bass.

Burns, R. (2002). *The adult learner at work: The challenges of lifelong education in the new millennium* (2nd ed.). Crows Nest, UK: Allen & Unwin.

Clark, M. C. (2001). Off the beaten path: Some creative approaches to adult learning. In Merriam, S. B. (Ed.), *The New Update on Adult Learning Theory* (*Vol. 89*, pp. 83–93). San Francisco, CA: Jossey Bass. doi:10.1002/ace.11

Collins, P. H. (1986). Learning from the outsider within: The sociological significance of black feminist thought. *Social Problems, 33*(6), 14–32. doi:10.1525/sp.1986.33.6.03a00020

Collins, P. H. (1990). *Black feminist thought: Knowledge, consciousness, and the politics of empowerment*. New York, NY: Routledge.

Collins, P. H. (1998). *Fighting words: Black women and the search for justice*. Minneapolis, MN: University of Minnesota Press.

Collins, P. H. (1999). Reflections on the outsider within. *Journal of Career Development, 26*(1), 85–88. doi:10.1177/089484539902600107

Combs, G. P. (2003). The duality of race and gender for managerial African American women: Implications of informal social networks on career advancement. *Human Resource Development Review, 2*(4), 385–405. doi:10.1177/1534484303257949

Crenshaw, K. (1989). Demarginalizing the intersection of race and sex: A black feminist critique of antidiscrimination doctrine, feminist theory and antiracist politics. *University of Chicago Legal Forum*. Retrieved from http://www.scribd.com/doc/28524679/Crenshaw-Demarginalizing-the-Intersection.

Creswell, J. W. (1998). *Qualitative inquiry and research design: The five traditions*. Thousand Oaks, CA. Sage.

Daloz, L. A. (1986). *Effective mentoring and teaching: Realizing the transformational power of adult learning experience*. San Francisco, CA: Jossey-Bass.

DeLany, J., & Rogers, E. (2004). Black women's leadership: Learning the politics of Afritics. *Convergence, 37*(2), 91–106.

Dym, B., & Hutson, H. (2005). *Leadership in nonprofit organizations*. Thousand Oaks, CA: Sage.

Etter-Lewis, G. (1993). *My soul is my own: Oral narratives of African American women in the professions*. New York, NY: Routledge.

Freire, P. (1970). *Pedagogy of the oppressed*. New York, NY: Seabury Press.

Hayes, E., & Flannery, D. D. (2000). *Women as learners: The significance of gender in adult learning*. San Francisco, CA: Jossey-Bass Publishers.

Hughes, R. L., & Howard-Hamilton, M. F. (2003). Insights: emphasizing issues that affect African American women. In M. F. Howard-Hamilton (Ed.), *Meeting the Needs of African American Women* (Vol. 104), (pp. 95-104). San Francisco, CA: Jossey-Bass.

Inglis, T. (1997). Empowerment and emancipation. *Adult Education Quarterly, 48*(1), 3–17. doi:10.1177/074171369704800102

Johnson-Bailey, J., & Cervero, R. M. (2000). The invisible politics of race in adult education. In Wilson, A., & Hayes, E. (Eds.), *Handbook of Adult and Continuing Education*. San Francisco, CA: Jossey-Bass.

Ladson-Billings, G. (1995). Toward a theory of culturally relevant pedagogy. *American Educational Research Journal, 32*(3), 465–491.

Lynham, S. A. (2002). The general method of theory-building research in applied disciplines. *Advances in Developing Resources, 4*(3), 221–241.

Maslow, A. (1970). *Motivation and personality*. New York, NY: Harper & Row.

McLaren, A. (1985). *Ambitions and realizations: Women in adult education*. London, UK: Peter Own.

Merriam, S. B. (2001). Andragogy and self-directed learning: Pillars of adult learning theory. In Merriam, S. B. (Ed.), *The New Update on Adult Learning Theory* (*Vol. 89*, pp. 3–13). San Francisco, CA: Jossey Bass. doi:10.1002/ace.3

Merriam, S. B. (2007). An introduction to non-western perspectives on learning and knowing. In Merriam, S. (Eds.), *Non-Western Perspectives on Learning and Knowing* (pp. 2–20). Malabar, FL: Krieger.

Merriam, S. B., & Caffarella, R. S. (1999). *Learning in adulthood*. San Francisco, CA: Jossey-Bass.

Noe, R. A. (2002). *Employee training and development*. New York, NY: McGraw-Hill.

Parker, P. S. (2005). *Race, gender, and leadership: Re-envisioning organizational leadership from the perspectives of African American women executives*. Mahwah, NJ: Lawrence Erlbaum Associates.

Schein, E. H. (1989). *Organizational culture and leadership*. San Francisco, CA: Jossey-Bass.

Schiele, J. H. (1996). Afrocentricity: An emerging paradigm in social work practice. *Social Work, 41*(3), 284–294.

Seidman, I. E. (1991). *Interviewing as qualitative research*. New York, NY: Columbia University.

Stanley, C. A., & Lincoln, Y. S. (2005). Cross race faculty mentoring. *Change*. Retrieved December 3, 2009 from http://www.findarticles.com/p/articles/mi_m1254/is_2_37/ai_n13794993.

Terhune, C. P. (2008). Coping in isolation: The experiences of black women in white communities. *Journal of Black Studies, 38*(4), 547–564. doi:10.1177/0021934706288144

Thompson, J. L. (1983). Women and adult education. In Tight, M. (Ed.), *Opportunities for Adult Education*. London, UK: Croom-Helm.

Thompson, J. L. (1995). Feminism and women's education. In Mayo, M., & Thompson, J. (Eds.), *Adult Learning Critical Intelligence and Social Change*. Leicester, UK: NIACE.

Tisdell, E. J. (2003). *Exploring spirituality and culture in adult and higher education*. San Francisco, CA: Jossey Bass.

Walker, S. A. (2009). Reflections on leadership from the perspective of an African American woman of faith. *Advances in Developing Human Resources, 11*(5), 646–656. doi:10.1177/1523422309352439

Welton, M. R. (1993). The contribution of critical theory to our understanding of adult learning. In Merriam, S. B. (Ed.), *An Update on Adult Learning Theory* (*Vol. 57*, pp. 81–90). San Francisco, CA: Jossey Bass. doi:10.1002/ace.36719935710

Zack, N. (2005). *Inclusive feminism: A third wave theory of women's commonality*. Lanham, MD: Rowman and Littlefield Publishers, Inc.

KEY TERMS AND DEFINITIONS

Emancipatory Learning: deconstructing power structures and developing ways of knowing to resist and challenge these structures.

Intersectionality: Term coined by Crenshaw (1989) that describes experiences and struggles of Black women not adequately captured in the feminist and anti-racist discourse.

Outsider-Within: Term coined by Collins (1986) that describes Black women's social identities that are situational and attached to specific histories of social injustice.

Self-Actualization: Based on Maslow's (1970) theory that describes an individual's natural tendency to be motivated towards goals in their work experiences.

Social Justice Paradigm: Research and theory-building that promotes socially-just work environments as places that are inclusive and uphold a culture of dignity and respect.

Social Learning: Foundational to Bandura's (1986) theory that describes how individuals learn by interacting with and observing others.

Socio-Cultural: Theoretical perspectives that explain how privilege can be used as a source of power for some and social identities can be used to oppress others.

Transformative Learning: Learning that empowers and motivates individuals to act as change agents towards a more just society.

Chapter 4

Leveraging Workforce Diversity through a Critical Examination of Intersectionalities and Divergences between Racial Minorities and Sexual Minorities

Julie Gedro
SUNY Empire State College, USA

ABSTRACT

Using a multi-disciplinary survey of educational studies, sociology, adult education, and human resources literature, this chapter explores the ways that racial minorities and sexual minorities (lesbian, gay, bisexual, and transgender) face oppression in organizational contexts. It examines and critiques organizational responses to diversity, and it uncovers the ways that these populations differ. Implications for diversity training programs are articulated, suggestions for training practice are offered, and recommendations for further research are provided.

INTRODUCTION

So we are working in a context of opposition and threat, the cause of which is certainly not the angers which lie between us, but rather that virulent hatred leveled against all women, people of Color, lesbians and gay men, poor people—against all of us who are seeking to examine the particulars of our lives as we resist our oppressions, moving toward coalition and effective action (Lorde, 1984, p. 128).

The phrase *workforce diversity* encompasses a broad spectrum of constructs, categories, and dimensions and it has become ubiquitous in the discourse and the practice of Human Resource and Organizational Development. Diversity represents "visible and non-visible aspects of identities by which individuals categorize themselves and others" (Ely & Thomas, 2001; Rocco, Landorf, & Delgado, 2009, p. 9). Harvey and Allard (2009) "define diversity as the ways in which people differ that may affect their organizational experience in terms of performance, motivation, communication, and inclusion" (p. 1). Issues of race,

DOI: 10.4018/978-1-4666-1812-1.ch004

class, gender, able-bodiedness, sexual orientation, religion, educational attainment, marital status, culture, ethnicity, and age comprise the fundamental aspects of ways that employees differ. Some of these aspects are visible while some are more nuanced or even invisible. Understanding the social, political, legal, environmental and organizational milieu is crucial for HRD practitioners and scholars to understand when designing and conducting diversity training programs. The field of Human Resource Development has begun to explore diversity, as evidenced by single issue journals on African American women's leadership experiences (Byrd & Stanley, 2009), diversity in the HRD curriculum (McDonald & Hite, 2010), disability awareness (Roessler & Nafukho, 2010), and sexual minority issues (Rocco, Gedro, & Kormanik, 2009). In the field of HRD, the current status of both of these diversity dimensions is that they are siloed. Each has been explored, but not in relation to each other. Each of these dimensions is situated within particular historical and social contexts that run counter to the dominant narrative of equal opportunity based upon merit. There are areas where these populations converge, and there are areas where they diverge. A critical examination of both areas—of convergence and divergence—is warranted so that such teasing out and unpacking provides Human Resource Development scholars and practitioners with deeper levels of understanding of "difference" and intersectionality. Such deeper level understanding provides a framework by which more effective diversity training and education can be imagined.

PURPOSE

Minorities in the United States continue to face oppression in the United States. This oppression persists in social, legal, political, and organizational systems and it occurs because of systematic discrimination against them. McNamee (2009) defines discrimination as "a set of exclusionary

practices by which individuals and groups use their power, privilege, and prestige to define criteria of eligibility for opportunity in terms of a set of characteristics...then to exclude those who lack those characteristics" (p. 190). Three decades of affirmative action efforts and anti-discrimination activities have not closed the gap between blacks and whites, and racial inequality persists in the United States (Massey, 2007, p. 38; McNamee, 2009). Organizational America is a sub-set of wider society, and its limitations for minorities mirror the larger systems of social, legal, and political oppressions. Despite the fact that "over $8 billion is spent annually on interventions" (Bierema, 2010, p. 566), the Equal Opportunity Commission has reported a record high 95,402 private sector discrimination charges filed in 2008 (Bierema, 2010). Sexual minority oppression exists concurrently with racial minority oppression. This chapter will use the term *sexual minority* to represent Lesbian, Gay, Bisexual, and Transgender (LGBT) people. Additionally, sexual minorities are those whose gender expression do not match traditionally ascribed gender roles (Gedro, 2010) and who instead dress, speak, act, and groom in ways that stray from those that are considered appropriate for men or for women.

This chapter will address the siloed nature of the dimensions of racial and sexual minorities by uncovering and exploring their intersections as well as their divergences. Each of these minority populations lacks significant representation and role models in the most senior roles of organizational America, each faces stigmatization and marginalization, and each faces of overt and covert workplace discrimination. However, there are distinctions between the two populations that merit a thoughtful exploration. Diversity training has become a ubiquitous feature of organizational training efforts in the United States, yet its affects remain questionable. Bierema (2010) highlights the example of Texaco as a striking example of failed diversity efforts. Texaco hired a renown diversity expert to conduct executive level diversity training, "yet white executives at the company were caught on tape mocking the diversity training and making racial slurs" (p. 565). These difference include federal legislation protections, visibility and invisibility (racial minorities have less choice in whether or not to "come out" as a racial minority), and most significantly, there are differences in the research and practice of allies. An *ally* is member of the dominant group who actively works to end discrimination of the oppressed population (Brooks & Edwards, in Rocco, Gedro, & Kormanik, 2009).

METHODOLOGY

Drawing upon a multi-disciplinary literature review, including an examination of the literature of HRD as well as the HRD practitioner background of the author, this chapter is mostly a conceptual piece. It is designed to problematize the mostly monolithic notion of workplace diversity. It will use some critical race theory, queer theory, educational studies, and sociology to develop a framework of difference within difference, to identify common ground, and to offer suggestions for practice and research. Emergent in the field of HRD is a conversation and critique about the opportunities for a deeper, richer, more critical exploration of diversity that challenges tacit assumptions about privilege and positionality. McDonald and Hite (2010) edited a special issue of the Advances journal entitled "Exploring Diversity in the Curriculum." In that journal, there were explorations of teaching diversity (Thomas, Tran, & Dawson, 2010), diversity education and strategies for educators (Bierema, 2010), race as an underexplored facet of diversity education (Alfred & Chlup, 2010), LGBT issues (Gedro, 2010), and workforce diversity and management training (Kormanik & Rajan, 2010).

This issue represents the emerging awareness of the importance of HRD scholarship that informs the field, challenges and field, and

presents a conceptual map for the field, rich with possibilities. Byrd and Stanley (2009) edited a special issue of Advances entitled "Giving Voice: The Socio-Cultural Realities of African-American Women's Leadership Experiences." In that journal, there were explorations of black women's leadership experiences (Jean-Marie, Williams, & Sherman, 2009), telling stories about leadership (Byrd, 2009), implications for race and gender in higher education administration (Lloyd-Jones, 2009), fostering an ethic of care in leadership (Bass, 2009), borrowed power (Petit, 2009), and reflections on leadership from a woman of faith (Walker, 2009).

Because the LGBT workplace equality movement has a mostly well developed, well articulated working notion of what an ally is and what an ally does, the movement has gained significant traction in the United States. However, there is no analogous visibility—through research or through practice—of what it means to be an ally of racial minorities. Racial minorities are particularly marginalized because they have to advocate for themselves. Through an examination Critical Race Theory, the chapter will illuminate marginalization and oppression of racial minorities as a result of the persistence and invisibility of racism. Racism, which as a result of federal legislation efforts aimed at discouraging overt discrimination, has not been effective in relieving United States society of the historical burden of race, racism and attendant discrimination against those who are of non-European descent. Race and racism have gone "underground" in the 21st century, yet racial minorities continue to lag behind whites in all markers of opportunity and privilege in United States society. Kormanik (2009) framed sexuality as a diversity dimension characterized by sexual orientation, gender identity, and sexual attraction. One's affectional or romantic attraction to the member of the same sex or the opposite sex is sexual orientation, which may be heterosexual (opposite sex attraction) or homosexual (same sex attraction). Gender identity represents one's internal sense of being male or female (Kormanik). A heteronormative society assumes that those born male have an internalized sense of themselves as male, and those born as female have an internalized sense of themselves as female (Kormanik). Corporate America, which remains a bastion of heterosexism (Gedro, 2004) as well as a bastion of heteronormativity (Gedro, 2010), expects those who are male to dress and act in masculine ways, and those who are female to dress and act in feminine ways.

THEORETICAL FRAMEWORKS

Because its focus is on two fundamental aspects of diversity: racial minorities and sexual minorities, this chapter is grounded in two theoretical frames. The first is Critical Race Theory (CRT). Race encompasses a myriad of identities, including African American, Latino, Native American and others, for purposes of this chapter, the chapter explores race as the social construction of otherness which is based upon dominant standards of European identity. Therefore, the use of the phrase "racial minority" means those who are of African or Latino descent, who are likely identifiable as members of these populations, and who do not share in the privileges, however tacit, of "whiteness." Whiteness is mostly an invisible characteristic, and that invisibility contributes to whites repeated misrecognition of their own "racially privileged location" (Ringrose, 2007, p. 325). McIntosh (1998; in Harvey & Allard, 2009) says that she has "come to see white privilege as an invisible package of unearned assets which I can count on cashing in each day, but about which I was meant to remain oblivious" (p. 35). The unspoken, tacit and mostly invisible assumptions of white privilege help to perpetuate a status quo in which racial minorities continue to lag behind whites in the attainment of education, housing, and for purposes of this chapter, career advancement opportunities.

Critical Race Theory

Critical Race Theory (CRT) serves as the guiding framework for understanding issues of race, racial minorities and the persistence of institutional racism in the United States today (Closson, 2010; Gilborn, 2006; Ringrose, 2007; Rozas & Miller, 2009). Trevino, Harris, and Wallace (2008) observe that the "explicit and sustained analysis of racial injustice…is deeply entrenched in the very foundations—the everyday thought processes, practices, and institutions—of US society" (p. 7). Critical Race Theory is an "iterative methodology for helping investigators remain attentive to equity while carrying out research, scholarship, and practice" (Ford & Airhihenbuwa, 2008, p. 31). This is the aspiration of this chapter, which seeks to unpack the clustering of different minorities within the discourse, research, and practice of diversity training and workforce inclusion interventions. In particular, the chapter presents two particular dimensions and populations of diversity: racial and sexual minorities, as mutually informing yet distinct sub-sets. Each of these populations experiences the deleterious effects of systematic and covert oppression. Diversity training efforts that are richly informed by theoretical foundations that contextualize the experiences and challenges of each population have the potential to create positive change.

Diversity training that fails to take into account the subtleties, the invisible veil of heteronormative, white privilege that creates a web of oppression, may perhaps build skills around vocabulary. It may even raise some awareness around privilege. However, it misses the opportunity to educate, create empathy, and inspire activism. Minorities have historically had to advocate for themselves. In *Changing Corporate America from the Inside Out,* Raeburn explains the progression of LGBT activism from within Fortune 500 corporations, as employees create the conditions by which senior leaders feel it appropriate and even necessary to provide benefits and resources for sexual minority employees. Ultimately, Raeburn presents, corporations begin to mimic each other in those provisions, because they realize the benefits of inclusion that accrue to all stakeholders. Building on the momentum gathered by sexual minorities advocating for themselves, which has resulted in a significant majority of Fortune corporations adopting anti-discrimination policies (prohibiting discrimination against LGBT employees), a movement of "straight allies" has become firmly established in the U.S. There exists a constellation of popular resources available to help educate and provide skills for virtually anyone interested in becoming an ally of the LGBT movement.

Critical Race Theory "challenges widely held beliefs that 'race consciousness' is synonymous with 'racism' and that 'colorblindness' is synonymous with the absence of racism" (Ford & Airhihenbuwa, 2010, p. 30). Critical Race Theory represents a multi-disciplinary methodology for "helping investigators remain attentive to equity while carrying out research, scholarship and practice and it also provides a way for scholars to conceive and pursue methods of transforming hierarchical social, political, legal, educational and occupational arrangements (Ford & Airhihenbuwa, 2010). Critical Race Theory rejects the idea that there is one master narrative that describes all phenomena (Ortiz & Jani, 2010) and rather, it argues that "race is a social construction, race permeates all aspects of social life, and race-based ideology is threaded throughout society" (p. 176). Rather than a fixed and objective definition, race is a category that exists for the purpose of "social stratification" (Ortiz & Jani, 2010, p. 177) and is established by the dominant group who purport that racial categories are determined by empirical methods as well as legal rules (Ortiz & Jani, 2010). As a category, race was first used to categorize human bodies by a French physician names Francois Bernier, and the notion of racial groupings was introduced by Carolus Linneaus

(Ford & Airhihenbuwa, 2008). Linneaus's concept of race devalued and degraded those who were not Europeans (Ford & Airhihenbuwa, 2008).

At its core, CRT is committed to advocating for justice for people who find themselves occupying positions on the margins—for those hold "minority" status. It directs attention to the ways in which structural arrangements inhibit and disadvantage some more than others in our society. It spotlights the form and function of dispossession, disenfranchisement, and discrimination across a range of social institutions, and then seeks to give voice to those who are victimized and displaced. CRT, therefore, seeks not only to name, but to be a tool for rooting out inequality and injustice (Trevino, Harris, & Wallace, 2008, p. 8).

Whiteness is a critical construct in Critical Race Theory. Whiteness, CRT scholars argue, is invisible yet it is a pervasive and organizing structure of United States society and culture:

Whiteness is (largely) invisible only to Whites, yet it tends to be less transparent to non-Whites, as is suggested by the long history of African-American analyses of whiteness that includes W.E.B. DuBois, Langston Hughes, James Baldwin, Richard Wright, and Toni Morrison. These differential visibility for different racialized groups is significant and reflects its social and cultural dominance and hegemony...although whiteness must be distinguished from mere skin color it nevertheless is embodied...whiteness is grounded in the interests, needs, and values of those racialized as White (Petitt, 2009, p. 637).

Recognizing that racism persists and is an organizing framework in the United States is a first step in imagining and then creating the conditions by which it can be dismantled. The invisible, pervasive, systematic ways that racism operates are the very qualities that ensure its persistence. Racism is "deeply entrenched" (Trevino, Harris, & Wallace, 2008, p. 7) and Critical Race Theory exposes the established order's claims of color-blindness and racial neutrality (Rabaka). Race continues to be an organizing framework that can be used as a predictor of educational quality, health, well being, job opportunity, and social mobility.

Queer Theory

Queer Theory complements Critical Race Theory because it is a method of inquiry that is intended to disrupt and question white, patriarchal, heterosexual hegemony, which is an organizing fact of United States life and all of its attendant microcosms, which include the workplace. Queer Theory creates a pause in the momentum gathered by heteronormative assumptions about the binaried essentialism of sexual orientation, gender identity, and gender expression. The term *queer* denotes "all variations in sexual desire, activity, and identity that are not straight" (Rocco & Gallagher, 2006, p. 30). The term "straight" represents those who have never engaged in any other sexual activity than that which has occurred with a member of the opposite sex, and has never engaged in outlawed sexual behavior (Rocco & Gallagher, 2006). Queer Theory, problematizes the taken for granted notion that gender is either male or female, and that romantic attraction is heterosexual. Queer Theory is an epistemological perspective that was developed in the 1990s, shaped by the critiques of gender and heterosexism by Judith Butler (1990) and Eve Sedgewick (1990; in Minton, 1997). Queer Theory also has its intellectual and activist roots in the work of Michel Foucault, who "conceives of power as a relation since power is everywhere, freedom cannot operate outside of power, one can never achieve freedom from power" (Foucault, 1978; Minton, 1997). The use of the term "queer," sometimes summarily resisted by heterosexuals for its perjoratively-laden tone, is actually a term

used in a strength-based way by many sexual minorities as an intentional linguistic distinction. While "some use the term queer as a catch-all for the LGBT conglomerate…many others prefer queer as a political term" (Meem, Gibson, & Alexander, 2010, p. 184). "The reclamation of the word queer, then, serves to defy normative, conventional society and its bigoted exclusions" (Meem, Gibson, & Alexander, 2010, p. 18).

SIMILARITIES

Discrimination

Prejudice refers to people's attitudes toward minority groups, and it takes various forms "ranging from hostile rejection to very subtle tokenism" (Brislin, 2000, p. 195). Both racial and sexual minority populations have to negotiate systems of oppression in which majoritarian assumptions about identify frame the workplace. Despite the legal inroads that signal an intention toward equality in the United States, as evidenced by the passages of Title VII of the Civil Rights Act of 1964, equality remains in an aspirational rather than an achieved status. There is a subtle and sometimes not so subject "othering" of those in sexual and racial minorities in society. Corporate and organizational America represent microcosms of the larger society, framed by racism and homogenativity.

Throughout the history of the United States, the definition of race, and the construction of racial groups, has gone through different evolutions depending on who is considered the in-group, or dominant group, or the out-group, or the minority group (Ortiz & Jani, 2010). Race is relational construct and its purpose is to separate and stratify (Ortiz & Jani, 2010). W.E.B. Du Bois developed the concept of "double consciousness" in which two selves reside in conflict and learn to negotiate a bi-cultural life (Trevino, Harris, & Wallace, 2008). Social theory in the 20th century lacked a critical analysis of race, and as a result, it lacked an analysis of racial injustice, "a pernicious problem that, then as now, is deeply entrenched in the very foundations—the everyday thought processes, practices and institutions—of U.S. society" (Trevino, Harris, & Wallace, 2008, p. 7). Even though whites may feel that their personal prejudices toward African have decreased, it is the persistence of racism and its effects in policies, systems and procedures continues to create inequities (McNickels & Baldino, 2009; in Harvey & Allard, 2009).

In a similar vein to the unpacking of the white knapsack (McIntosh) of privileges, those in the sexual majority have privileges as well. Carbado and Gulati (2003) note several of these privileges, or tacit assumptions. First, children of heterosexual parents do not have to explain why their parents have different genders. Second, heterosexuals do not have to worry about people trying to "cure" their sexual orientation (p. 1779). Third, heterosexuals can join the military without having to closet their sexual orientation. Fourth, heterosexuals do not have to worry about being "outed" (that is, being revealed by another, often times for malicious purposes) by another.

Those in positions of dominance and majority status did not have choice about their identity, any more so that those in positions of subordination had choice about theirs. Race and sexual orientation are immutable characteristics. However, because systems, structures, and institutions are arranged according to an implicit ordering, a hierarchy of privilege, those who are in positions of dominance are in many ways responsible for perpetuating the status quo. The rewards of society, using career mobility as proxy, are generally denied to those in racial and sexual minority populations.

There is, as a minimum, a legal mandate under Title VII to prohibit discrimination against minorities and historically marginalized groups. Title VII was enacted nearly 50 years ago. This is certainly time enough to presume that it is a commonly understood law in all but the small-est and most neophyte types of organizations or organizations who lack a formal Human Resource department. However, African Americans and Latinos continue to lag behind whites in virtually any measure of status. Overt discrimination has been "driven underground" (McNamee & Miller, 2009, p. 192) and "scratching just below the surface, however, reveals a continued pattern of political, occupational, education, housing and consumer distribution" (McNamee & Miller, 2009, p. 192).

Overwhelming evidence demonstrates that income and employment discrimination based on race in America lingers (McNamee & Miller, 2009, p. 193). In 2005, the average family income for blacks was only 60 percent that of whites, and the corresponding figure for Hispanics was only 64 percent (Mishel, Berstein, & Allegretto, 2007, p. 51; in McNamee & Miller, 2009, p. 195).

It would be possible to untangle sub-groups of both racial minorities and systematically define and analyze the experiences of African Americans, Latinos, Asian-Americans, Pacific Islanders, and others who are not of European heritage, for purposes of carefully deconstructing the impact of race and opportunity. It would also be possible to conduct the same type of analysis of sexual minorities, and explore the particular and unique challenges and experiences of lesbian, gay, bisexuals and transgender people. For purposes, however, of conceptual manageability, this chapter mostly considers race and sexual minority as two categories. Certainly, implications for further analysis of sub-groups within both of these populations warrant careful thought. However, the thrust of this work is to examine the nuanced nature of racism and heterosexism and identify what is similar about the experience of being a racial minority, and that of being a sexual minority. Admittedly, too, there are implications for exploration and analysis of intersectionalities within these two broad categories. In other words, it would be helpful and appropriate to the field of HRD to examine the experiences of those who belong to both racial and sexual minorities.

The Williams Institute (2009, Executive Summary) observed that:

Studies conducted from the mid-1980s to mid-1990s revealed that 16% to 68% of LGB respondents reported experiencing employment discrimination at some point in their lives. Since the mid-1990s, an additional fifteen studies found that 15% to 43% of LGB respondents experienced discrimination in the workplace. When asked more specific questions about the type of discrimination experienced, LGB respondents reported the following experiences that were related to their sexual orientation: 8%-17% were fired or denied employment, 10%-28% were denied a promotion or given negative performance evaluations, 7%-41% were verbally/physically abused or had their workplace vandalized, and 10%-19% reported receiving unequal pay or benefits.

Discrimination shows up in overt ways, as illustrated by data that confirms material inequalities between majority and minority populations. It also shows up in covert ways, as unconscious bias, that limit opportunities for minorities.

Internationalization of Oppression

Racial minorities and sexual minorities both experience internalized oppression, and both populations experience deleterious effects of that internalization. Internalized homophobia refers to pejorative social attitudes about homosexuals which result in a sense of inferiority, oppression, and negative distortions of self image (Russell & Bohan, 2006). Both populations have, as a matter of survival, acquired an instinctive habit of assessing a situation for its likelihood of hostility or friendliness. Just as Gedro, Cervero, and Johnson-Bailey (2004) learned that lesbians pre-screen a situation to determine the receptivity of an individual, group or situation toward lesbianism, racial minorities use "mental math:"

Mental math is the process many people of color go through as a result of racism, discrimination and prejudice. The process includes asking yourself questions such as: Was the person just rude, or is it because of my skin color being dark? That my surname has Latino roots? That my articulation of certain words does not fit in the dominant group? That my facial features relegate me to "other" status? Could one of these target determinants be responsible for what occurred between me and a person from a dominant group? (Rozas & Miller, 2009, p 35).

A negative sense of self leads to self-destructive behaviors ranging from the abandonment of career goals to substance abuse to self-loathing to suicide (Gedro, 2009; Russell & Bohan, 2006). Both racial and sexual minorities have learned how to negotiate their identities as members of the out-group and although racial minorities have less opportunity to closet, or hide their identities, both populations experience the psychic effects of operating as minorities within a dominant majority. LGBT identity development theories "hold that these identities are formed in a cultural context of extreme stigma toward same-sex romantic, emotional, and sexual behavior" (Szymanski & Kashubeck-West, 2008, p. 510) and that this stigmatization takes a toll in the form of self-doubt to overt self-hatred (Szymanski & Kashubeck-West, 2008).

DIVERGENCES

The Role of Family

There is a divergence between racial minorities and sexual minorities with respect to the role that the family of origin plays in helping one cope with the outside world. The homogeneity and the familiarity of family for racial minorities provide comfort, emotional protection, and connection against a word that is often hostile. For sexual minorities, the role of the family varies. Those who are sexual minorities often find themselves ostracized by the family of origin, and they are faced with the necessity of negotiating both a hostile outer world, as well as an alienated personal and family life. Parental reaction to disclosure by sexual minority child is "invariably negative, with the disclosure being perceived as a crisis by the family" (Strommen, 1993, p. 250), and this disclosure often results in parents suddenly sensing that their child is a stranger to them (Strommen, 1993; LaSala, 2004). This alienation stems from the lack of family roles for sexual minorities (Strommen, 1993). "In the developmental histories of gay men and women, periods of difficulty in acknowledging their homosexuality, either to themselves or to others, are often reported" (Drescher, 2004, p. 11). Gays and lesbians often grow up in environments where they receive little family support as they begin to acknowledge their homosexual orientation, and instead, gay people are often subjected to homophobia and moral condemnation from their own families (Drescher, 2004). This distinguishes the experiences of sexual minorities from racial minorities, with respect to the role of the family.

The Role of Religion

Religiousness is a predictor of prejudice against sexual minorities (Mak & Sang, 2008). Fundamentalist religion is adept at developing and distributing theological rationales for discrimination and marginalization of lesbian, gay, bisexual, and transgender people. Collins and Zimmerman (1983; in Strommen, 1993) posit that religious teaching tends to negatively sanction homosexual behavior. There are many examples of the role of religion in United States culture, society, and even politics, that range from a mild disgust for homosexuals and sexual minorities, to the offering of "cures" for homosexual feelings, to outright condemnation. Whitehead (2010) determined that religiosity is a predictor of a person's support of

same-sex unions (there is an inverse relationship, and he also observed that "Christians, conservative denominations, frequent attendees, biblical literalists, and those with active or angry images of God tend to be the most condemning of homosexual behavior" (p. 65). Macgillivray (2008) observed Christian Right opposes the inclusion of sexual orientation in school policies, arguing that such inclusion promotes homosexuality.

The centrality of religion to civil rights discourse is amplified when the civil rights struggle questions a status quo largely supported by religion. We may no longer remember the musty religious arguments today, but the Bible was once used to enforce segregation as much as to oppose it. God placed the races on different continents, segregationists said. God sanctioned slavery. Africans were heirs to the curse of Ham. And so on. Dr. King and his movement have so succeeded in their refraining of civil rights that these arguments may strike us today as bizarre. But just fifty years ago, they were preached from pulpits around the country. Yet unlike the debate over African American civil rights, our current national debate regarding equal rights for sexual minorities (I will speak primarily here of gays and lesbians, though most of the arguments apply to gender minorities such as transgender persons as well—and I use the broad term "gay rights" to encompass all of these), has so far included religion on only the negative side of the argument. The Bible forbids homosexuality, we are told. Heterosexual marriage is at the core of God's design for the universe. Traditional (read: "religious") values have been clear on this question for thousands of years.

The tension between religion and sexual minorities is not strictly an issue of culture, religion, society or politics. It has become a workplace issue, and it presents tensions for Human Resource Management and Development practitioners. Russell and Bohan (2006) distinguish the experiences of sexual minorities and their responses to the overarching heterosexist structures, institutions and attitudes framed by geography and history, social and family systems, religion, economic class, and other matters that shape one's life. For heterosexual people the messages about heterosexism and its attendant privileges are less disruptive to the psyche and one's internal sense of self and well being, because of the invisibility of the heterosexist assumption. For sexual minorities, however, the messages conveyed about sexuality through these different mechanisms can have negative impacts that range from mildly discouraging to significantly traumatic. The author, for example, is a practicing Episcopalian, currently a senior leader within the diocese of central New York. There is debate and contention, readily discernible, within the state of New York over the issue of same sex weddings within the Episcopal Church. Concurrent with the passing of same sex marriage in New York State, the diocese of Central New York has determined that it will begin to create specific liturgical rites that will be used for same sex weddings:

The Episcopal Church, which has been strained by gay-rights issues since the election of an openly gay bishop in New Hampshire eight years ago, is now divided over how to respond to the legalization of same-sex marriage in New York. As a result, gay and lesbian Episcopalians will be allowed on Sunday to get married by priests in Brooklyn and Queens, but not in the Bronx or Manhattan or on Staten Island; in Syracuse but not in Albany. That is because the church has not taken a firm position nationally on same-sex marriage, leaving local bishops with wide latitude to decide what priests may do when the law takes effect in New York State. In the state, with six Episcopal dioceses, the bishops are split: two have given the green light for priests to officiate at same-sex marriages, one has said absolutely not, two are undecided and one has staked out a middle ground, allowing priests to bless, but not officiate at, weddings of gay men and lesbians (Dewan, 2011).

In the workplace, there can be tensions between religion and sexual orientation, and companies are having to negotiate those tensions. "Employers who seek to balance religion and sexual orientation concerns in the workplace need to be aware of the fact that federal law does not afford these two characteristics equal protection" (Clark, 2004, p. 56). Title VII prohibits religious discrimination and harassment, and the Equal Opportunity Commission has indicated that employers must permit employees to engage in religious expression and it must accommodate employees' religious beliefs (Clark, 2004). As companies increasingly decide to not only create anti-discrimination policies for their employees, but also, to provide resources for LGBT employee resource groups, there can be backlash from employees who resist these efforts based on their religious beliefs. Thus, the tension between religion and sexual minority state is a very real, very present, and often times litigious matter.

The Role of Law

Clark (2004) indicates that federal law does not afford equal protection to those of sexual minority status. Although 85% of Fortune 500 corporations have policies that prohibit discrimination based upon sexual orientation, there remains no federal legislation that prohibits discrimination based upon sexual orientation. According to the Human Rights Campaign (2011):

The Employment Non-Discrimination Act (ENDA) would provide basic protections against workplace discrimination on the basis of sexual orientation or gender identity. ENDA simply affords to all Americans basic employment protection from discrimination based on irrational prejudice. The bill is closely modeled on existing civil rights laws, including Title VII of the Civil Rights Act of 1964 and the Americans with Disabilities Act. The bill explicitly prohibits preferential treatment and quotas and does not permit disparate impact suits. In addition, it exempts small businesses, religious organizations and the military, and does not require that domestic partner benefits be provided to the same-sex partners of employees.

While there are currently no federal laws that prohibit employment discrimination against sexual minorities, there have been attempts to do so. The Employment Non-Discrimination Act (ENDA) is proposed federal legislation that is modeled after Title VII of the Civil Rights Act of 1964 and the Americans with Disabilities Act. ENDA prohibits preferential treatment and quotas, and does not permit disparate impact suits (HRC, 2011). ENDA was first introduced to the 103rd Congress, and the Senate Labor and Human Resources Committee held its first hearings. Since that first introduction, the bill has been presented nine times, and has yet to be passed and signed into law. Despite what may sound like a simple landscape, then, of law related to sexual minorities, the legal landscape is astonishingly complex. 22 states have laws that prohibit discrimination based upon sexual orientation, of which 17 states include protections for transgender people. Rather, then, than having one law—federal law—that protects sexual minorities from employment discrimination, there are laws that differ from state to state. The experiences of sexual minorities, and their equal rights, can vary depending on the state where they live and work. This complicates what is already a complex issue, and the persistent failure of ENDA certainly represents the continued reluctance of representatives in government to establish federal protections for sexual minorities. This mirrors the ambivalence in society about the rights of sexual minorities.

Visibility and Invisibility

Visibility and invisibility present a complex set of considerations with respect to racial and sexual minorities. It is the construct, the oppressive and under-acknowledged hegemony of "whiteness" that creates the limiting conditions for all those who are not white. Racial minorities do not have the luxury to "pass" or to "hide" their other-ness, and yet whiteness is whiteness is invisible to all but those who are white (Petitt, 2009). Those in racial minorities, particularly African Americans, have little choice about whether or not to "come out" as racial minorities. There exists a long and persistent antipathy in the United States toward people who are darker skinned than the normative European fair skinned presentation. The famous golfer, Tiger Woods, is one quarter Chinese, one quarter Thai, one quarter Black, one eighth Native American, and one eighth Dutch (Sanchez-Huchles & Davis, 2010); however, "his black facial features influence others to perceive and treat him only as black" (p. 171). Moreover, he was once banned from playing a Georgia golf course because of this perception (that he was black).

Coming out is a complex and iterative process for sexual minorities. There are multiple strategies for negotiating one's identity; these strategies include passing as straight, lying about one's sexual orientation, distancing from others as a way to avoid discussions that could expose one's orientation, distracting the issue of sexual orientation by deliberately changing the subject from anything involving discussions of personal/familial/relational matters, or coming out. Coming out means identifying as a member of a sexual minority. Coming out of the closet can be particularly distressing not only because another person is disgusted by the person's sexual minority status, but also could result from the revelation inherent in coming out, that the person has heretofore been withholding important personal information (Adams, 2010). Because sexual minority status lacks permanent, visible, identifiable traits, coming out is a "canonical expression of being gay" (p. 236) and a necessary action (Adams). For the last 200 years, "the mere acknowledgement of gay and lesbian people in society was virtually nonexistent" (Lukenbill, 1999, p. 25). In many part of the United States over the last 100 years, same sex affection was looked upon as forbidden, illegal, and immoral. However, things are changing as the emancipation movement for lesbian and gay rights has begun to actively fight for protection, public visibility, and general public acceptance as a politically viable, morally legitimate group (Lukenbill, 1999).

The Role of Allies

According to the Gay and Lesbian Alliance Against Defamation (GLAAD, 2011), allies provide effective and powerful voices for the LGBT movement, and they are instrumental in helping help people in the coming-out process. They are also instrumental in helping others to understand principles of equality, fairness, acceptance and mutual respect (GLAAD). Allies are those members of the dominant group, who actively support members of the subordinate group and who take deliberate actions to eradicate oppressive conditions. With racial to minorities, then an ally would be a member of the dominant race (white) who seeks to end oppression of blacks. With respect to sexual orientation, an ally is a heterosexual person who seeks to end oppression of lesbians, gays, bisexuals and transgender people.

There is no handy, accessible, analogous phrase that describes whites who are affirming of the equal status and the equal rights of African American people. A general internet search using the terms "African American ally" or "African American allies" yielded no results that were related in any way to those who are in the majority, or dominant race, who are affirming, supportive, and encouraging of African Americans. The scholarly literature is not complete void of research and publications that conceptualize and write about whites who are African American affirming, but the scarcity is significant enough to responsibly claim that when compared with the information—both in general terms as well as in the scholarly literature—of information, writing, and resources that demonstrate the presence and visibility of heterosexuals who advocate for sexual

minorities, there is no analog for racial minorities, A search using EbscoHost using the same terms yielded one article that discussed cross cultural allies, but was not focused in particular on the issue of African American allies. A search using the same terms in JSTOR, ProQuest, PsychInfo, SocIndex, yielded no results. There was one result using Ebsco Host (Suyemoto & Fox Tree, 2006) that explored the relationships and alliances between people of color.

RECOMMENDATIONS AND CONCLUSION

Since more than 95% of leaders in the 500 largest companies in this country are white males (Livingston, 2009), and Title VII legislation is nearly 50 years old, there is clearly something that is not working entirely effectively with respect to diversity efforts in organizational American today. Diversity training has the potential to create workplaces that are characterized by equitable opportunities and inclusion (McGuire & Bagher, 2009). Effective diversity training must critically explore the conditions that create inequalities in the first place. Rather than operating from an operating assumption that focusing on "how to get along with those who are different," effective diversity training must explore what "different" is, how "different" became "different," who is "different" and why, and also, who is not "different." Diversity training can create conditions of backlash by those who are majoritarian and who feel that diversity training and its related efforts to ameliorate oppression are somehow efforts to privilege minority populations. Rather than focus on diversity as a skill building exercise, designed to help people develop social skills around negotiating a multi-cultural work context, diversity training efforts should provide education and context around nuanced contexts of privilege, taken for granted rights of those who are majoritarian, and unconscious biases. The exploration presented in this chapter that uncovers categories of convergence and divergence is designed to provide some foundation for imaging and developing diversity training interventions that create deep change and that dismantle structural and institutional oppression of all minorities. In particular, this chapter treated two intersectional minorities and provided insights about the ways that they intersect. To be specific, diversity training should begin with a model of awareness raising and leadership development, such as that presented by Santas (2000). This model suggests that effective diversity training should define and undo racism and homophobia, teach about the history of race and the history of the LGBT movement, and develop leaders to become change agents and executive sponsors of diversity initiatives and anti-oppressive structures and practices. Effective diversity training and change efforts should develop leaders at all levels of the organization, and it should hold them accountable for creating and sustaining cultures that support limitless opportunity for all organizational members and prospective members.

LIMITATIONS AND IMPLICATIONS FOR FUTURE RESEARCH

This chapter treated two populations—racial minorities and sexual minorities—for purposes of identifying intersections and divergences, to highlight the myriad of considerations and explanations for the persistence of marginalization of both. There remains an entire *constellation* of combinations, too, within and among these populations and the primary limitation of this chapter is that it simplified a very complex idea. That is, it would be possible to create a piece of work that treated each sub-set of sexual minorities: lesbians, gays, bisexuals and transgender people, as separate groups with unique considerations to which diversity training can respond. Similarly, there are

sub-sets within the category of racial minorities that deserve separate and thoughtful consideration. This chapter made an initial attempt to claim a way to conceptualize two conglomerated populations in order to provide HRD diversity scholars and educators with a set of considerations, and a way to think about how to develop, deliver, and evaluate organizational diversity training efforts so that they create positive change. As has been presented in this chapter, diversity-training efforts to date do not have sufficient evidence or justification for creating the types of changes that create truly equitable organizations in the U.S. today. The persistent presence and impact of racism bears out this claim. The persistent marginalization of sexual minorities, and the concomitant resistance to provide them with federal protections (at a minimum) and equitable career, employment and organizational opportunities (as an ideal) provide justification for the continued examination and suggestions for ways to make diversity training more effective. To be clear, the term "intersectionality" is used in this chapter to represent the shared challenges of racial and sexual minorities. It does not signify intersectionality in the way that third wave feminist writers suggest, that "gender, religion, ethnicity, social class, educational achievements, resident status, ethic regionalism, and other subordinating variables… shape identity, behavior, opportunities and access" (Ortiz & Jani, 2010, p. 187).

REFERENCES

Adams, T. (2010). Paradoxes of sexuality, gay identity, and the closet. *Symbolic Interaction, 33*(2), 234–256. doi:10.1525/si.2010.33.2.234

Bass, L. (2009). Fostering an ethic of care in leadership: A conversation with five African American women. *Advances in Developing Human Resources, 11*(5). doi:10.1177/1523422309352075

Bierema, L. (2010). Resisting HRD's resistance to diversity. *Journal of European Industrial Training, 34*(6), 565–576. doi:10.1108/03090591011061239

Brislin, R. (2000). *Understanding culture's influence on behavior.* Florence, KY: Wadsworth Publishing.

Byrd, M. (2009). Telling our stories of leadership: If we don't tell them they won't be told. *Advances in Developing Human Resources, 11*(5). doi:10.1177/1523422309351514

Byrd, M., & Stanley, C. (Eds.). (2009). Giving voice: The socio-cultural realities of African American women's leadership experiences. *Advances in Developing Human Resources, 11*(5).

Byrd, M., & Stanley, C. (2009). Bringing the voices together. *Advances in Developing Human Resources, 11*(5). doi:10.1177/1523422309351817

Clark, M. (2004, August). Religion vs sexual orientation. *HRMagazine*, 54–59.

Dewan, S. (2011, July 11). True to Episcopal Church's past, Bishops split on gay weddings. *New York Times*. Retrieved on August 31, 2011 from http://www.nytimes.com/2011/07/19/nyregion/new-episcopal-split-priests-role-in-ny-gay-weddings.html.

Drescher, J. (2004). The closet: Psychological issues of being in and coming out. *Psychiatric Times, 21*(12), 11–15.

Ford, C., & Airhihenbuwa, C. (2010). Critical race theory, race equity, and public health: Toward anti-racism praxis. *American Journal of Public Health, 100*, 30–35. doi:10.2105/AJPH.2009.171058

Garnets, L., & Kimmel, D. (1993). *Perspectives on lesbian and gay male experiences*. New York, NY: Columbia University Press.

Gedro, J. (2010). Lesbian presentations and representations of leadership, and the implications for HRD. *Journal of European Industrial Training, 34*(6), 552–564. doi:10.1108/03090591011061220

Gedro, J., Cervero, R., & Johnson-Bailey, J. (2004). How lesbians learn to negotiate the heterosexism of corporate America. *Human Resource Development International, 7*(2), 181–195. doi:10.1080/1367886042000243790

Harvey, C., & Allard, J. (2009). *Understanding and managing diversity* (4th ed.). Upper Saddle River, NJ: Prentice Hall.

Human Rights Campaign. (2009). *State of the workplace*. Retrieved August 25, 2011 from http://www.hrc.org/documents/HRC_Foundation_State_of_the_Workplace_2007-2008.pdf.

Human Rights Campaign. (2011). *Timeline: The employment non-discrimination act*. Retrieved on 9/1/11 from http://www.hrc.org/issues/workplace/5636.htm.

Jean-Marie, G., Williams, V., & Sherman, S. (2009). Black women's leadership experiences: Examining the intersectionality of race and gender. *Advances in Developing Human Resources, 11*(5). doi:10.1177/1523422309351836

Kormanik, M. (2009). Sexuality as a diversity factor. *Advances in Developing Human Resources, 11*(1), 24–36. doi:10.1177/1523422308329369

LaSala, M. (2004). Lesbians, gay men and their parents: Family therapy for the coming-out crisis. *Family Process, 39*(1), 67–81. doi:10.1111/j.1545-5300.2000.39108.x

Livingston, R. (2009, July 7). The baby-faced Black CEO phenomenon. *Forbes*.

Lloyd-Jones, B. (2009). Implications of race and gender in higher education administration: An African American woman's perspective. *Advances in Developing Human Resources, 11*(5). doi:10.1177/1523422309351820

Lorde, A. (1984). *Sister outsider*. Freedom, CA: The Crossing Press.

Lukenbill, G. (1999). *Untold millions: Secret truths about marketing to gay and lesbian consumers*. Binghamton, NY: Haworth Press.

Macgillivray, I. (2008). Religion, sexual orientation, and school policy: How the Christian right frames its arguments. *Educational Studies, 43*, 29–44.

Mak, H., & Sang, J. (2008). Separating the "sinner" from the "sin": Religious orientation and prejudiced behavior toward sexual orientation and promiscuous sex. *Journal for the Scientific Study of Religion, 47*(3), 379–392. doi:10.1111/j.1468-5906.2008.00416.x

McDonald, K., & Hite, L. (Eds.). (2010). Exploring diversity in the HRD curriculum. *Advances in Developing Human Resources, 12*(3). doi:10.1177/1523422310375032

McIntosh, P. (1998). White privilege and male privilege: A personal account of coming to see correspondences through work in women's studies. In Harvey, C., & Allard, J. (Eds.), *Understanding and Managing Diversity* (4th ed., pp. 35–47). Upper Saddle River, NJ: Prentice Hall.

McNamee, S., & Miller, R. (2009). *The meritocracy myth*. Lanham, MD: Rowman & Littlefield.

McNickels, J., & Baldino, C. (2009). Are African Americans still experiencing racism? In Harvey, C., & Allard, J. (Eds.), *Understanding and Managing Diversity*. Upper Saddle River, NJ: Prentice Hall.

Meem, D., Gibson, M., & Alexander, J. (2010). *Finding out: An introduction to LGBT studies*. Thousand Oaks, CA: Sage.

Michaelson, J. (2010). Ten reasons why gay rights is a religious issue. *Tikkun, 25*(4), 34–70.

Minton, H. (1997). Queer theory: Historical roots and implications for psychology. *Theory & Psychology, 7*(3), 337–353. doi:10.1177/0959354397073003

Ortiz, L., & Jani, J. (2010). Critical race theory: A transformational model for teaching diversity. *Journal of Social Work Education, 46*(2), 175–193. doi:10.5175/JSWE.2010.200900070

Petitt, B. (2009). Borrowed power. *Advances in Developing Human Resources, 11*(5). doi:10.1177/1523422309352310

Raeburn, N. (2004). *Changing corporate America from the inside out*. Minneapolis, MN: University of Minnesota Press.

Rocco, T., Landorf, H., & Delgado, A. (2009). Framing the issue/framing the question: A proposed framework for organizational perspectives on sexual minorities. *Advances in Developing Human Resources, 11*(1). doi:10.1177/1523422308328528

Rocco, T. S., Gedro, J., & Kormanik, M. B. (Eds.). (2009). Sexual minority issues in HRD: Raising awareness. *Advances in Developing Human Resources, 11*(1).

Roessler, R., & Nafukho, F. (Eds.). (2010). Disability, diversity, and discharge issues at the workplace: Implications for human resource development. *Advances in Developing Human Resources, 12*(4).

Russel, R., & Bohan, J. (2006). The case of internalized homophobia: Theory and/as practice. *Theory & Psychology, 16*(3), 343–366. doi:10.1177/0959354306064283

Sanchez-Huches, S., & Davis, D. (2010). Women and women of color in leadership. *The American Psychologist, 65*(3), 171–181. doi:10.1037/a0017459

Santas, A. (2000). Teaching anti-racism. *Studies in Philosophy and Education, 19*, 349–361. doi:10.1023/A:1005298916161

Stanley, C. (2009). Giving voice from the perspectives of African-American women leaders. *Advances in Developing Human Resources, 11*(5). doi:10.1177/1523422309351520

Strommen, E. (1993). You're a what? Family member reactions to the disclosure of homosexuality. In Garnets, L., & Kimmel, G. (Eds.), *Perspectives on Lesbian and Gay Male Experiences*. New York, NY: Columbia University Press.

Suyemoto, K., & Fox Tree, C. (2006). Building bridges across differences to meet social action goals: Being and creating allies among people of color. *American Journal of Community Psychology, 37*, 237–246. doi:10.1007/s10464-006-9048-1

Szymanski, D., Kashubeck-West, & Meyer, J. (2008). Internalized heterosexism: A historical and theoretical overview. *The Counseling Psychologist, 36*(4), 510–524. doi:10.1177/0011000007309488

Walker, S. (2009). Reflections on leadership from the perspective of an African American woman of faith. *Advances in Developing Human Resources, 11*(5). doi:10.1177/1523422309352439

Whitehead, A. (2010). Sacred rites and civil rights: Religion's effect on attitudes toward same-sex unions and the perceived cause of homosexuality. *Social Science Quarterly, 91*(1), 63–79. doi:10.1111/j.1540-6237.2010.00681.x

Williams Institute. (2009). *Bias in the workplace: Consistent evidence of sexual orientation and gender identity discrimination*. Retrieved on August 25, 2011 from http://services.law.ucla.edu/williamsinstitute/publications/Bias%20in%20the%20Workplace.pdf

ADDITIONAL READING

Butler, J. (1999). *Gender trouble*. New York, NY: Routledge.

Catalyst. (2011). *Website*. Retrieved from http://www.catalyst.org.

Duggan, L. (2004). *The twilight of equality: Neoliberalism, cultural politics, and the attack on democracy*. Boston, MA: Beacon Press.

Foucault, M. (1990). *The history of sexuality*. New York, NY: Vintage Books.

KEY TERMS AND DEFINITIONS

Ally: A member of the dominant group who has knowledge of the challenges faced by the minority group, who actively and intentionally seeks to champion the equal rights of the minority group.

Bisexual: A man or woman who is romantically and sexually attracted to men and to women.

Employee Resource Group: A collection of employees, typically having a particular common characteristic such as race, gender or sexual orientation, who are organized in an effort to mobilize for strategic and/or activist purposes within the organization, and also, across other networks of similarly characterized groups in other organizations or sectors.

Family: A set of people who are related, usually consisting of a nuclear system of husband, wife and children. Family can extend to grandparents, aunts, uncles, cousins.

Gay: A man who is romantically and sexually attracted to men.

Gender: The state of being masculine (male) or feminine (female).

Gender Expression: The manner in which a person exhibits masculine or feminine characteristics in dress, speech, hairstyle, grooming, mannerisms and behavior. It may or may not correspond to one's sex.

Gender Identity: A person's internal sense of gender, which may or may not correspond to one's physical gender.

Intersectionality: A place that two or more populations meet. A place, circumstance, or result that is common.

Lesbian: A woman who is romantically and sexually attracted to women.

Race: A social construction that groups people based upon physical characteristics.

Racial Minority: People who are not White.

Religion: An organized set of doctrine, accompanied by an established system of beliefs, rituals, and practices that are intended to honor the sacred.

Sex: The biological classification, assigned at birth as male or female.

Sexual Minority: People who are not heterosexual.

Transgender: A man or woman whose internal sense of self does not match the biology of one's sex.

Chapter 5
Workforce Diversity at the Lagos Business School, Pan-African University, Nigeria

Kemi Ogunyemi
Pan-African University, Nigeria

ABSTRACT

Diversity is an indisputable element of human life. In their bid to create value, employers have to face the challenges posed by putting together people coming from different backgrounds and with different paradigms. The Lagos Business School has also experienced this phenomenon.

The School has a fair distribution of people from different ethnic groups. It also has a mission that identifies expressly with the Christian view of human nature and yet is open to people of all religious inclinations. As an academic environment, there is also the inevitable risk of distance between academic staff and administrative staff and between lecturers and students. The purpose of this chapter is to highlight the positive practices at the LBS that help them leverage workforce diversity and to make a few suggestions for improvement. This chapter will also highlight how the school reflects the importance of leveraging diversity in its academic curriculum.

INTRODUCTION

Diversity is a given phenomenon of human existence. It can be viewed as an enabler or as an inhibitor in the workplace. Individuals in groups, because of their diversity, bring different experiences, knowledge, and information to the table when they come together, and also provide different validation sources and mechanisms for the information they bring (Phillips, Northcraft, & Neale, 2006). In this way, they enrich the organization and are potentially able to create great synergies. Numerous studies have shown, however, that diversity can lead to innovation and enrichment if it is understood, embraced and properly managed. This chapter discusses how the leveraging of workforce diversity is practiced and promoted in the Lagos Business School, a tertiary

DOI: 10.4018/978-1-4666-1812-1.ch005

institution in Nigeria. In this chapter, the Lagos Business School will be interchangeably referred to as the School.

The chapter will: 1) define diversity and explain the importance of and the ways of leveraging diversity in the workplace; 2) present a case-study of the efforts to leverage diversity in a business school in Nigeria; and 3) draw conclusions and offer suggestions to management practitioners that are interested in leveraging the diversity of their workforce.

Varying Definitions of Diversity

Moran, Harris, and Moran (2001) describe human diversity as comprising "differences of colour, ethnic origin, gender, sexual or religious preferences, age and disabilities" (p. 181). On the same page, quoting the American Express Financial Advisors, they include among diversity characteristics in organizations the following:

"race, gender, age, physical ability, physical appearance, nationality, cultural heritage, personal background, functional experience, position in the organization, mental, and physical challenges, family responsibilities, sexual orientation, military experience, educational background, style differences, economic status, thinking patterns, political backgrounds, city/state/region of residence, IQ level, smoking preference, weight, marital status, non-traditional job, religion, white collar, language, blue collar, and height" (p. 181).

These descriptions of diversity and its defining characteristics tend to show that all forms of human differences are elements of diversity. Each human being is unique and therefore may be motivated differently than others who seem to be in the same situation but may be of a different religion, age, functional expertise, family history and responsibilities, etc. it would be extremely difficult to find two human beings that are exactly alike, without any diversifying element. Even a set of identical twins could easily diverge in the experiences they live through, in the religion they embrace, or in their level of IQ or EQ. These differences mean that managers cannot take a one-size-fits-all in their approach to the people who work for or with them in their organizations, the people who make up their workforce. What motivates one person may not motivate another at all, and what makes one person less productive may actually raise the level of effectiveness of another person. If a manager were to be blind to the differences between the people who work with him, at best he might treat them all as he would expect himself to be treated. Since not everyone is like him, some people could feel offended or discriminated or insulted by his approach. He could easily end up allowing some friction to build up which might inhibit them from giving their best to their work, and thus some of the organization's goals may be frustrated or at least approached in a sub-optimal way. In today's globalized and competitive environment, it is doubtful that an organization can afford to maintain a workforce that is not performing optimally and constantly innovating to ensure product or service excellence and keep up with the competition.

According to DiTomaso, Post, and Parks-Yancy (2007), "workforce diversity refers to the composition of work units in terms of the cultural or demographic characteristics that are salient and symbolically meaningful in the relationships among group members" (p. 474). Such characteristics could include race (Dovidio, Kawakami & Gaertner, 2002; Moran, Harris & Moran, 2001), ethnicity (Moran, Harris & Moran, 2001; Portes & Rumbaut, 1996), gender (Chatman & O'Reilly, 2004; Moran, Harris & Moran, 2001), religion (Islam & Hewstone, 1993), education (Halaby, 2003), age (Moran, Harris & Moran, 2001; Zenger & Lawrence, 1989), type of academic and/or work experience (Cunningham & Chelladurai, 2005), and tenure or length of service (Reagans & Zuckerman, 2001). All these differences among the people can lead to internal divisions and affect interpersonal and management communication, turnover, job satisfaction, performance appraisals, and resource allocation (DiTomaso, Post, & Parks-Yancy, 2007). They can influence "who talks to whom, who notices whom, and who favours whom" (DiTomaso, Post & Parks-Yancy, 2007, p. 475). Small cliques may therefore be formed which consciously or unconsciously work against the efficiency of the organization and its best interests.

Surface and Deep Level Diversity

When studying or discussing diversity, attention should be paid to both surface level and deep level diversity and the positive and negative effects of each of them (Phillips, Northcraft, & Neale, 2006). Surface level diversity attracts more attention from scholars and most of the characteristics already mentioned fit into that category. Deep level diversity is premised on less visible characteristics such as attitudes, temperaments, personality, preferences, beliefs and values, and they sometimes manifest in external modes within which the subject acts, such as sense of urgency and extraversion (Harrison, Price, Gavin, & Florey, 2002; Mohammed & Angell, 2004).

When only surface level diversity is recognized, organizations may not work to smooth out the kinks created by deep level diversity, and with time, these could also cause problems for the organization. For example, a team may not have any conflicts or tensions arising from differences in ethnicity or gender, but may have problems resulting from resistance to another's view of what the instruction of a supervisor means; obstinacy in one's own construction of a customer request; or a resentment built up from a perception that others have a lower level of commitment than oneself. All of these are results of deep level diversity and thus their roots are less visible and could be overlooked. To prevent and/or resolve this kind of challenges, programs that: 1) increase the ability of workers to listen to one another respectfully

and argue purposefully rather than blindly; 2) increase self-knowledge and enhance interpersonal skills; or 3) broaden perspectives of individuals so that they recognize and value what in others is different from them, are invaluable. Training in emotional intelligence would also be helpful.

Leveraging Diversity in the Workplace

Effects of cultural diversity in teams have been the subject of much research (Colella & Varma, 2001; DiTomaso, Post, & Parks-Yancy, 2007; Heilman, Block, & Martell, 1995; Reskin, McBrier, & Kmec, 1999; Rosenbaum, Kariya, Settersen, & Maier, 1990; Sorensen, 2000). In the course of these studies, both positive and negative effects have been highlighted. On the positive side, diversity seems to drive creativity and innovation because of the pool of ideas it generates and integrates (Reagans & McEvily, 2003). Diversity of thought, background, experience, and perception can lead to greater synergy in groups where the members value the contribution of each individual. On the other hand, clashes of cultural values, etc. can inhibit effectiveness and productivity, by distorting communication within work teams (DiTomaso, Post, & Parks-Yancy, 2007) and inhibiting coordination and trust (Reagans & McEvily, 2003). Against this background, it is clear that leaders need to be aware of the possible negative inhibitors of true integration of a diverse team and motivate and manage them well in order to achieve efficiency and organisational goals (Moran, Harris, & Moran, 2001). The goals would be to find ways to drive the same levels of coordination, trust, which give rise to liking and cooperation in a homogenous environment to exist in a heterogeneous environment. In this endeavour two concepts that could help are that of 'swift trust' (DiTomaso, Post, & Parks-Yancy, 2007; Meyerson, Weick, & Kramer, 1996) and 'psychologically safe communication environment or climate' (Gibson & Gibbs, 2003). An organization that succeeds in quickly generating and sustaining trust among its members and in creating a climate in which they communicate effectively is more likely to overcome any negative consequences resulting from increasing diversity and further enhance the positive ones.

Furthermore, if diversity is to be an advantage for the organization, it must not only be accepted as a positive element but also directed and incorporated into strategy in order to ensure that the benefits to the organization are maximized and possible problems minimized. Strategic and purposeful pursuit of this desirable goal would in time yield better results than a chance or haphazard approach to take advantage of the fact of diversity. Thus, as a starting point, the organization would need to consciously embrace diversity and then follow up this by consciously leveraging diversity.

Consciously Embracing Diversity

Consciously embracing diversity involves an effort to treat people first as individuals before treating them as collectives, for example, celebrating birthdays of employees by sending electronic good wishes. It means acknowledging and resolving the circumstances or contexts that may lead to exclusion for some groups of people, for example, when determining the pricing for food in cafeterias, care could be taken to have options that are do not excessively tax the earning power of some of the staff or students. Forums could be set up within which people are valued for the contribution they make to the organization, for example, town-hall meetings to listen to everyone and ending with awards for extraordinary contribution that cut across the different departments or groups of people.

When setting up teams for projects, emphasis could be placed on the importance of the diversity of team members (ethnic, gender, functional expertise, age, etc.) to achieving success in the group's goals. In this way, the organization or unit shows that it values and promotes full utilization of work force diversity. The organization needs

to demonstrate cultural sensitivity and show that it is comfortable building diverse teams, for example, providing praying rooms for the different religious beliefs among the staff. In all its activities, demonstrating global awareness and readiness to take up opportunities to work with global teams will also send a message to both existing and prospective staff and students that the organization sees diversity as a plus.

Consciously Searching for Leverage

An organization that consciously wishes to leverage diversity would go on to ensure that its policies and activities avoid diminishing any person's sense of identity. It would indicate a dynamic approach to development and show openness to new ideas and innovation, for example by appreciating staff and students who bring up new ideas for positive change in the organization's systems and processes and implementing those ideas insofar as is possible in order to encourage more contributions.

In addition, such an organization would foster cross-pollination of ideas by tending to set up cross-functional teams to work together on projects and to organize activities within the organization. For example, the composition of staff and student teams would be carefully constructed to always include a diversity of people. The organization would need to encourage respectful attention to opposing views and an attitude of learn-ability in all staff and students, in appreciation of the variety of insights into the same issue that can be generated by seeing the same picture with different eyes. A customer-focused approach, both to the internal and external customer, also strengthens the leveragability of diversity and helps to leverage it to maximize the productivity of employees and the life value of customers. Employees are more inspired to give their best if they sense that the organization allows them a strong sense of self and exhibits appreciation for who they are and what value they bring to the organization.

Hiring policies and practices (interviews) are good indicators of the interest of the organization in leveraging diversity. From the beginning, there should be an interest in minimizing in-breeding, and in bringing in people whose experiences and opinions may be able to contrast with what is already obtainable in the organization and thus may add new value to what already is there.

CASE STUDY: LEVERAGING SURFACE AND DEEP-LEVEL DIVERSITY AT THE LAGOS BUSINESS SCHOOL

Nigeria is a country rich in ethnic diversity as well as other types of diversity. In a bid to create value, every employer in the country has to face the challenges posed by putting together people coming together from different backgrounds and with different paradigms. The Lagos Business School (LBS) is not left out of this endeavour. The mission statement on the School's website reads as follows:

"LBS is a community of people committed to creating and transmitting management and business knowledge based on a Christian conception of the human person and of economic activity and relevant to Nigeria and Africa at large. We strive to be a world-class business school which will have a significant impact on the practice of management.

In order to achieve this mission the School seeks to:

- *Provide high potential professionals with a general management education, which stresses professional ethics and service to the community through the practice of management.*

- *Have a positive impact on the professional and ethical standards of business management in Nigeria*
- *Make intellectual contributions which: a) support the practice of management; b) contribute to the advancement of the management disciplines; and c) create high quality teaching materials"[1] (*http://www. lbs.edu.ng/about-lbs/*).*

In order to achieve its mission, LBS has to work with over two hundred staff who must be committed to the same goal.

The School has an interesting distribution, shown in Tables 1 and 2, of people from both genders and from different ethnic groups as could be expected given the rich ethnic diversity (Moran, Harris, & Moran, 2001; Portes & Rumbaut, 1996) of the Nigerian people. It also has a mission that identifies expressly with the Christian view of human nature and yet is open to people of all religious inclinations, thus embracing religious diversity (Islam & Hewstone, 1993). As an academic environment, there is also the inevitable risk of distance between academic staff and administrative staff due to functional diversity (Cunningham & Chelladurai, 2005) and between lecturers and students, reflecting both functional diversity (Cunningham & Chelladurai, 2005) and age in the case of the full-time MBA students (Zenger & Lawrence, 1989). At the same time, LBS is trying to attain and maintain international standards while retaining local relevance (see mission statement quoted above). This chapter highlights the positive practices at the LBS that help them leverage on workforce diversity, and mentions some practices that could inhibit effectiveness as a diverse team. The chapter also includes some insight into how far the School goes in reflecting the importance of leveraging diversity in its curriculum for the MBA and PhD programs and the executive programs.

Leadership and Organizational Climate

Gibson and Gibbs (2003) mention the following as the problems usually associated with diversity in organizations seeking to foster innovation: differences in expectations; reduced identification, conflict, differences in worldviews, "misunderstanding, stereotyping, inability to reach agreement, make decisions, and take action" (p. 460). The same authors recommend that these potholes can be eliminated or minimized by building a psychologically safe communication climate, described as "a climate characterised by support, openness, trust, mutual respect, and risk taking" (p. 462) and which:

"*involves speaking up, raising differences for discussion, engaging in spontaneous and informal communication, providing unsolicited information, and bridging differences by suspending judgement, remaining open to other ideas and perspectives, and engaging in active listening*" (p. 462).

This is what the Lagos Business School had done deliberately and consciously, while maintaining an atmosphere of informality and spontaneity. The fact that the Dean is a woman, even though there are less women than men in the School, may has also contributed to passing across a clear message of non-discrimination and fair treatment.

Table 1. Demography of Lagos Business School workforce as of June 26, 2009

Gender	Ethnic Group[2]	Professional Training (1st degree)	Position
Male 97 Female 60	South-West 36 South-East 91 South-South 17 North 10	Legal & Arts 9 Technology 3 Health & Hospitality 11 Financial Services 7 Biological Sciences 1 Administration 10 Marketing 3 Others (still pre-degree) 84	Faculty 22 Senior Admin. Staff 32 Senior Technical Staff 8 Junior Staff 95

Total Workforce =157

Table 2. Demography of Lagos Business School student body as at Dec 26, 2010

Gender	Ethnic Group	Professional Training (1st degree)[3]	Functional Roles[4]	Religion
Male 195 Female 105	South-West 182 South-East 89 South-South 23 North 6	Law, Social Sciences & Arts 11 Technology & Engineering 27 Tourism & Hospitality 2 Financial Sciences 21 Biological Sciences 23 Administration & Education 12 Marketing & Sales 0 Others 4	Legal & Administration 27 Technology 24 Health & Consulting 19 Financial Control 64 Manufacturing 16 Logistics 11 Marketing & Sales 29 Others 10	Catholic 63 Other Christian 216 Moslem 20 Others 1

Total Students = 100 MBAs; 200 EMBAs

The composition of the staff and students reflect the openness to diversity that characterises the School. When a new employee arrives to the School, he or she is taken round to all the different departments and introduced to every staff. The Dean speaks personally as much as possible with individual staff members, encouraging them to share their views on how the School can do better.

Lagos Business School is indeed trying to innovate. No one else is doing what this organization is doing in the Nigerian environment, and so all hands are needed on deck. The management is ever open and welcomes all contributions. The leadership style is one that makes some effort to be attentive to the differences between individuals and to relate to each one accordingly (Yammarino, Dionne, Chun, & Dansereau, 2005). The management team tries to avoid conformism and inflexibility by remaining open to internal and external criticism, so that people can express their differences, and out of this open attitude, many improvements to the programs come—the more recent ones include the change in the time-schedule for the executive programs; the change in the mode of the family days; a staff choir at the Christmas party; etc.

The School organizes anthropology seminars for staff, similar to the course on the Nature of human beings, which is taught as a preparatory course to the full-time MBA. These seminars highlight the need to be aware of others' paradigms and differences, especially personality types, temperaments, etc.

Team Orientation and Team Processes

According to Mohammed and Angell (2004), to overcome challenges associated with diversity, especially deep level diversity, team orientation and team processes are needed. Team orientation means that people are ready to learn from others and are comfortable working with others, that they share a vision and hopeful of achieving it

as a team (Mohammed & Angell, 2004). At the Lagos Business School, this is part of the climate of the organization. The policies emphasize the importance of everyone working together to achieve the School's objective and doing this in an atmosphere of mutual respect and trust. They emphasize, in a document titled the Beliefs of the Lagos Business School, that the School expects staff to respect their subordinates as much as their superiors and to treat everyone with due dignity.

The different units are also encouraged not to work in silos but to all see their contribution to one another's job. Thus, for example, in order to plan the School calendar for each year, representatives from the MBA department meet with representatives of the Programs department, the Documents Room, the Marketing Department, the Facilities Unit, and all other stakeholders in the calendar, and together they work out the best sequence of events thinking of the customers and thinking of the effective use of the School's capacity. In much the same way, a multi-departmental team appointed on a project basis meets to plan special events such as graduation and convocation ceremonies, and every person on the team plays their part with a sense of responsibility and with gusto.

In the past years, the Lagos Business School has done a lot of work to achieve standardization of processes and procedures such that the role of natural liking and dislike or empathy in cooperation among people and units is minimal. To this end, there are procedures and processes for course schedules and course outlines, grading deadlines, admission process timelines, purchasing of supplies, etc. Fair appraisal systems, which express meritocracy (Castilla, 2008), are also part of these processes, and are conducted quarterly in the School with an emphasis on learning and development needs rather than on reward and sanctions. All the processes and procedures are updated constantly and audited on a quarterly basis. They help to deal with issues of deep level diversity, for example, by ensuring that disparities in sense of time urgency and in moods or preferences are normalized for everyone when a process, such as MBA projects supervision, has been officially given a standardized timeline. Two or three supervisors and administrators who may feel differently about whether two weeks from when the students submit project proposals is a far-off deadline or is too close for comfort can organize themselves as they please so long as they do meet the deadline eventually.

Policies, Inclusive Practices, and Observed Experiences Embracing and Leveraging Diversity

At the Lagos Business School, there is some effort to treat people as individuals as well as part of a collective. Birthdays are announced each month in the staff newsletter, and each person's photograph is displayed next to his or her date of birth. At the end of the month, all the birthdays of the month are celebrated at an end-of-month party, which all staff, academic and non-academic, try to attend. All the celebrants' names are written on one large cake, celebrating each person and at the same time all of them.

There are three cafeterias, one at the drivers' bay, one in the main building, and one at the gazebo, and each one operates as a separate unit and prices differently. This is an example of a context that could easily lead to the formation of cliques. However, since most of the staff have their meals in the main cafeteria, it is doubtful that there is any problem of exclusion.

Every three months, a town hall meeting is held and awards may be given on this occasion to staff that have been outstanding in their dedication to the organization's goals during that quarter. Two of the past awards were for customer service—one was given to a faculty assistant who went out of his way to attend to an external customer and the other was to an IT staff that showed a strong commit-

ment to her support function to other employees, internal customers. Through this medium, both were made to feel happy about their contribution towards the success of the organization.

Also, every quarter, an audit team is set-up to review the administrative processes and procedures of the whole school. This team is formed by people from different departments/units, in order to have a functional diversity that enhances their work. It also helps different people to understand and appreciate the work of people who work in other departments from theirs, so that staff do not work in silos but are aware of their links to those around them.

Every month, departments and units hold meetings at which people express their ideas freely. At each of these meetings, the staff will take turns to make presentations to the rest of the team about the School's values and goals. In this way, everyone's viewpoint is taken into account and those who may not be skilled at making presentations have an opportunity to practice.

The School shows its sensitivity to religious differences by setting apart a room for a Christian chapel and another for a Muslim prayer room. This also sends a message to Muslim staff and students that they are welcome and accepted as part of the team in a mission-driven organization, which mentions Christian ideals in its mission statement.

The Lagos Business School has worked in the past and continues partnering with other schools and entities from all over the world—Instituto de Estudios Superiores de la Empresa (IESE), Spain; Institut Européen d'Administration des Affaires (INSEAD), France; Strathmore Business School, Kenya; the Global Business School Network, just to mention a few. Awareness of these also ensures that the staff are not close-minded but rather open to embrace diversity and work happily with others who may hold different views from them or come from different backgrounds.

Workforce Education and Development

Through the programs of the Lagos Business School, there is also evidence of teaching respect for diversity and the value derived from leveraging it. Both the curricula and classroom sessions revealed these traits.

Openness to different viewpoints and appreciation for opposition is fostered through the case-study method. Emphasis is placed on respect for others' views and opinions, and everyone is encouraged to learn from whatever the other person contributes, even if it is only to learn that that other point of view exists. Gradually they are helped to realize that diversity is an asset that can substantially increase the competitiveness of a business enterprise.

In some of the longer programs such as the MBA and the Chief Executive Programme (CEP), participants are helped to grow in self-knowledge and in understanding of personality types, which lead to differences in worldviews and reasoning styles. The Myer-Briggs Type Indicator (MBTI) instrument is used for a psychometric assessment and thus people get to know their types and are taught how to relate better with teammates, colleagues, bosses, and subordinates that are different from them.

Both the full-time and executive MBA programs include a module referred to as the Life Project. This module provides an opportunity for each individual to receive feedback from others in the same class because they work closely with each other in the same small team during the program. The Life Project is often an eye-opener for the participants who see themselves through the eyes of others perhaps for the first time, and also gain new insights into what drives other people's thoughts, words, emotions, decisions and actions. Another module called Social Skills for Executives is also taught close to the beginning of the program, and the content includes rules of

etiquette and social relations that will ease the interaction among the students during their stay in the School.

Programs Curricula and Respect for Diversity

In the MBA program, diversity themes are included in certain course outlines, as shown in Table 3. One example is the course on Negotiation during which conflict resolution styles are taught. In addition, students are encouraged to learn about other cultures in order to be better equipped for cross-cultural negotiation in a global world.

Thus, out of the 32 courses examined, 17 (53%) contained strong elements of sensitization of the students to diversity. In the team building modules in both the Human Behaviour in Organizations (HBO) I and Project Management courses, an appreciation for the contribution of differences is emphasized, and teams are built in such a way that complementarities can be assured and leveraged for greater productivity.

For the full time program, a three-month internship program, through predominantly blind placements, emphasises openness to various fields and persons. In 2010, one of the interns went through a challenging period of having to adapt to a boss who was a difficult character. He initially found it very difficult, but advised and guided by his peers, he was able to overcome the issues and work well with a person with whom ordinarily he did not have anything in common on which to base a relationship.

Harnessing Diversity through Classroom Dynamics

The learning style in every program organized at the School is highly participatory, based on the premise that each person has something to offer, from which the others can be enriched. The lecturer (or the facilitator as he or she is called in

Table 3. Diversity themes in the MBA courses at the Lagos Business School

Course Title	Diversity theme
Analysis of Business Problems	Using objective and subjective criteria in decision-making
Corporate Financial Accounting	International and Local Standards
Business Ethics	Responsibilities of the firm towards its employees
Management Communication	Fundamental intra and interpersonal skills
	Emotional intelligence
	Handling interpersonal conflict
	Employee communication systems
Quantitative Analysis	Preference theory and risk aversion
Introduction to Marketing	Segmentation, targeting and positioning
Human Behaviour in Organizations I	Introduction to human problems in organization
Social and Political Environment of Business	Country competitiveness
Marketing Management	Personal selling
Human Behaviour in Organizations II	Organizational forms
	Leadership: theories of leadership
	Leadership values
	Change management
Negotiation	Conflict resolution styles
Strategic Management II	Creating new markets
Service Management	Understanding customer needs
Managing Corporate Power and Politics	Emotional intelligence
Human Resource Management	Employee relations
Project Management	Human resource planning and team building
Economic Environment of Business II	Business in the international environment

the Lagos Business School) is in the classroom as a guide who facilitates the synergy generated by the multiplicity of people. At the beginning of a program, sometimes participants may be shy to say what they think, but in a very short while, everyone catches the attitude and then the facilitator's role includes getting each one to listen to and respect others' views. By the time the program is over, participants usually have practiced embracing and celebrating diversity and can go on to continue doing so in their various workplaces.

Class participation is required for the MBA and Executive MBA programs in order to score up to thirty percent of the overall grade for each course. Therefore, every participant is motivated to contribute their viewpoints and reflections regarding the business decisions being discussed in class. In all the programs, both the academic and the executive, the case study teaching method is explained as a way to leverage diversity by sharing the learning generated from all the program participants' knowledge and experience. As such, the participants are encouraged to exchange ideas in permanently constituted groups, these groups having been constituted to achieve the maximum diversity of members, and then to take the same readiness to learn from their differences to the classroom.

The distribution of the students into the groups in which they will work during the two years of their program in the School is greatly predicated on diversity. It is done by the MBA Director, and the parameters for ensuring diversity are gender, professional background, type of work experience, length of work experience, industry, and ethnicity. As an example, the MBA Director would try to ensure that insofar as is possible there is in each group a lawyer, a doctor, an accountant or two, an engineer, etc., and that there is a mix of gender and ethnic origins in each group. The idea is to foster multi-cultural collaboration as much as possible while acknowledging each person's identity.

The MBA Director carries out this exercise of dividing the admitted candidates into teams before they arrive at the School the first day. This is done by using spreadsheets from the admissions office data to achieve maximum diversity. First of all, the academic background of the participants is considered. For example, if it is possible, each group should have an accountant, a lawyer, an engineer, someone from the biosciences and another from the arts. Following this pattern, a mixed gender distribution is ensured. Then the years of experience are considered, with the same idea of ensuring a mix. In turn, the industry in which the people have worked—or continue working in the case of the Executive MBA—comes up for consideration.

Ethnicity is the least considered basis for group distribution. It is taken for granted that the group will not lack ethnic diversity since there are so many varied tribes in Nigeria and so it is impossible for a whole group to belong to the same ethnic group. Even when people come from the same region of the country, they are often from different ethnic groups even within that region. Only on one occasion had this ever given rise to a complaint, from a student who felt that one or two groups reflected ethnic concentrations and that the minorities would not feel comfortable in their groups.

The MBA Internship

Companies that have hosted MBA interns reported that they found them a source of fresh and innovative ideas for the organization. They find the interns different from their permanent staff and full of new ideas, and so they often take advantage of having them there to review, restructure, redirect, reorient, re-strategize, etc. During the three-month internship, full-time MBA students are assessed, amongst other things, on how well they "articulate another's viewpoint through verbal and non-verbal interpretation" and "resolve interpersonal and team conflicts"—these are two of the assessment criteria included in the evaluation form sent to the intern's host company to be filled and returned to the School's career office.

Faculty and students interact very well despite the disparity in age and other diversity elements. The School encourages this by having a policy of everyone being addressed by their first name and by encouraging faculty to be accessible to students at all times to attend to their challenges with their academic work. Hence, faculty routinely give students their phone numbers during the first class they teach of each module. Even for those who may not use the phone numbers, this helps to create a climate of safe communication and high regard. Furthermore, each student on the MBA and Executive MBA is assigned a faculty advisor who is available for consultation for both academic and non-academic problems throughout the two years that the student spends in the School.

Student-led activities also help students to feel that their contribution is valued and appreciated by the School. Some of these activities—projects, events, clubs, etc.—are partly funded by the School. Very often, faculty are involved as advisers and patrons of the activities.

Gaps Yet to Be Filled

One instance in which there is a glaring lack of diversity in the Lagos Business School is the national homogeneity of the staff and students. There are two non-Nigerian out of 157 staff members, and two non-Nigerian out of 300 students. Perhaps going out to get more diversity in this aspect, starting by recruiting staff and students from other West-African countries could be a good way to enrich the School further and generate innovative ideas for its development. In the same vein, attracting students from the North of Nigeria could be an additional step towards greater diversity.

Greater interaction between the MBA classes and the Executive MBA classes or the Executive Education classes would also seem to be a desirable way to leverage the already existing diversity in age and work experience between these two sets of people in the School.

The School is yet to embark on student exchange programs. This is another area that could be profitably explored. To function well in a globalized business environment, business leaders need to be better prepared to work in tune with people from all over the world. This may require a level of exposure that the School's MBA program does not presently make adequate provision for.

CONCLUSION

The policies and practice of the Lagos Business School are generally directed towards leveraging diversity in order to achieve the goals of the School. Through leadership, enabling policies, team orientation and team processes, the staff are shown that their individuality is appreciated and at the same time that their contribution as individuals is needed for the team to be successful. The psychologically safe communication climate (Gibson & Gibbs, 2003) makes it easy for everyone to express themselves in their own way and yet feel an important part of the whole system.

Students at the Lagos Business School are treated as unique individuals. The approaches used for teaching them to foster an acceptance of diversity are aimed at empowering them to leverage diversity in the organizations where they may work. Their "perceptions of competence in their own abilities" (Ringer, Volkov, & Bridson, 2010, p. 6) is fostered in a way that teaches them how to treat others the same way and contribute to creating "an environment of cooperation and collaboration" (Ringer, Volkov, & Bridson, 2010, p. 6) around them.

However, there are still a few gaps in areas that the School could work on if it truly would like to harness synergies created by diversity in the accomplishment of its mission. One of these areas could be the marketing of the programs and recruiting strategically to attract a more diverse staff and student body. With every increase in diversity and inclusivity in a workplace, the company becomes more able to attract and motivate talented staff since each person is encouraged to contribute his or her best.

While not expecting that the Lagos Business School approach could automatically be workable for other organizations and or institutions in Nigeria or in any other developing country, it will at least serve as a guide to help optimize performance in an organization that has this degree of diversity and is interested in optimizing its existence. A diverse workforce not only increases the knowledge capital of the organization towards innovation, but also provides the organization with a massive toolkit with which to quickly spot new opportunities in the market, new value-propositions to customers, and new ways to partner with other stakeholders in the business environment in order to increase profitability and generally further the company's objectives.

REFERENCES

Becher, T., & Trowler, P. R. (2001). *Academic tribes and territories: Intellectual enquiry and the culture of disciplines* (2nd ed.). Buckingham, UK: Society for Research into Higher Education and Open University Press.

Castilla, E. J. (2008). Gender, race and meritocracy in organizational careers. *American Journal of Sociology, 113*(6), 1479–1526. doi:10.1086/588738

Chatman, J. A., & O'Reilly, C. A. (2004). Asymmetric reactions to work group sex diversity among men and women. *Academy of Management Journal, 47*, 193–208. doi:10.2307/20159572

Colella, A., & Varma, A. (2001). The impact of subordinate disability on leader-member exchange relationships. *Academy of Management Journal, 44*, 304–315. doi:10.2307/3069457

Cunningham, G. B., & Chelladurai, P. (2005). Affective reactions to cross-functional teams: The impact of size, relative performance, and common in-group identity. *Group Dynamic Theory Resource Practitioners, 8*, 83–97. doi:10.1037/1089-2699.8.2.83

DiMaggio, P. J. (1997). Culture and cognition. *Annual Review of Sociology, 23*, 264–287. doi:10.1146/annurev.soc.23.1.263

DiTomaso, N., Post, C., & Parks-Yancy, R. (2007). Workforce diversity and inequality: Power, status and numbers. *Annual Review of Sociology, 33*, 473–501. doi:10.1146/annurev.soc.33.040406.131805

Dovidio, J. F., Kawakami, K., & Gaertner, S. L. (2002). Implicit and explicit prejudice and interracial interaction. *Journal of Personality and Social Psychology, 82*, 62–68. doi:10.1037/0022-3514.82.1.62

Gibson, C. B., & Gibbs, J. L. (2006). Unpacking the concept of virtuality: The effects of geographic dispersion, electronic dependence, dynamic structure, and national diversity on team innovation. *Administrative Science Quarterly, 51*, 451–495.

Halaby, C. N. (2003). Where job values come from: Family and schooling background, cognitive ability, and gender. *American Sociological Review, 68*, 251–278. doi:10.2307/1519768

Harrison, D., Price, K. H., Gavin, J. H., & Florey, A. T. (2002). *Time, teams, and task performance: Changing effects of surface- and deep-level diversity on group functioning.* Retrieved May 29, 2011 from http://www.aom.pace.edu/amj/October2002/harrison.pdf.

Heilman, M. E., Block, C. J., & Martell, R. F. (1995). Sex stereotypes: Do they influence perceptions of managers? *Journal of Social Behavior and Personality, 10*, 237–252.

Islam, M. R., & Hewstone, M. (1993). Intergroup attitudes and affective consequences in majority and minority groups. *Journal of Personality and Social Psychology, 64*, 936–950. doi:10.1037/0022-3514.64.6.936

Kossek, E. E., & Lobel, S. A. (1996). *Managing diversity: Human resource strategies for transforming the workplace.* Retrieved May 29, 2011 from http://www.lavoisier.fr/livre/notice.asp?id=RAAWLSAXA6LOWB.

Kossek, E. E., Lobel, S. A., & Brown, J. (2005). *Human resource strategies to manage workforce diversity – Examining 'the business case'.* Retrieved May 29, 2011 from http://www.corwin.com/upm-data/7425_03_Konrad>02.pdf.

LBS. (2011). *About.* Retrieved from http://www.lbs.edu.ng/about-lbs/.

Meyerson, D., Weick, K. E., & Kramer, R. M. (1996). Swift trust and temporary groups. In Kramer, R. M., & Tyler, T. R. (Eds.), *Trust in Organizations: Frontiers of Theory and Research* (pp. 166–195). Thousand Oaks, CA: Sage Publications.

Mohammed, S., & Angell, L. C. (2004). Surface- and deep-level diversity in workgroups: Examining the moderating effects of team orientation and team process on relationship conflict. *Journal of Organizational Behavior*, *25*, 1015–1039. doi:10.1002/job.293

Moran, R. T., Harris, P. R., & Moran, S. V. (2007). *Managing cultural differences: Global leadership strategies for the 21st century*. London, UK: Butterworth-Heinemann.

Phillips, K. W., Northcraft, G. B., & Neale, M. A. (2006). Surface-level diversity and decision-making in groups: When does deep-level similarity help? *Group Processes & Intergroup Relations*, *9*(4), 467–482. Retrieved May 29, 2011 from http://peer.ccsd.cnrs.fr/docs/00/57/16/29/PDF/PEER_stage2_10.1177%252F1368430206067557.pdf.

Portes, A., & Rumbaut, R. G. (1996). *Immigrant America: A portrait*. Berkeley, CA: University of California Press.

Reagans, R., & McEvily, B. (2003). Network structure and knowledge transfer: The effects of cohesion and range. *Administrative Science Quarterly*, *48*, 240–267. doi:10.2307/3556658

Reagans, R., & Zuckerman, E. W. (2001). Networks, diversity, and productivity: The social capital of corporate R & D teams. *Organization Science*, *12*, 502–517. doi:10.1287/orsc.12.4.502.10637

Reskin, B. F., McBrier, D. B., & Kmec, J. A. (1999). The determinants and consequences of workplace sex and race composition. *Annual Review of Sociology*, *25*, 335–361. doi:10.1146/annurev.soc.25.1.335

Ringer, A., Volkov, M., & Bridson, K. (2010). Cultural diversity in the modern tertiary environment: The role of assessment and learning approaches. In *Proceedings of the 2010 Australian and New Zealand Marketing Academy Conference, ANZMAC*. Christchurch, New Zealand: ANZMAC.

Rosenbaum, J. E., Kariya, T., Settersen, R., & Maier, T. (1990). Market and network theories of the transition from high school to work: Their application to industrialized societies. *Annual Review of Sociology*, *16*, 263–299. doi:10.1146/annurev.so.16.080190.001403

Sorensen, J. B. (2000). The longitudinal effects of group tenure composition on turnover. *American Sociological Review*, *65*, 298–310. doi:10.2307/2657442

Yammarino, F. J., Dionne, S. D., Chun, J. U., & Dansereau, F. (2005). Leadership and levels of analysis: A state-of-the-science review. *The Leadership Quarterly*, *16*, 879–919. doi:10.1016/j.leaqua.2005.09.002

Zenger, T. R., & Lawrence, B. S. (1989). Organizational demography: The differential effects of age and tenure distributions on technical communication. *Academy of Management Journal*, *32*, 353–376. doi:10.2307/256366

ADDITIONAL READING

Devoe, D. (1999). *Managing a diverse workforce*. San Mateo, CA: InfoWorld Media Group.

Esty, K., Griffin, R., & Schorr-Hirsh, M. (1995). *Workplace diversity: A manager's guide to solving problems and turning diversity into a competitive advantage*. Avon, MA: Adams Media Corporation.

Jackson, S. E. (1990). *Diversity in the workplace: Human resources initiatives*. New York, NY: The Guilford Press.

KEY TERMS AND DEFINITIONS

Demography: The composition of the human population of a particular social entity, e.g. a country, a state, an organization.

Diversity: The level of variety and inclusiveness that characterizes a group of people.

Ethnicity: A set of cultural characteristics that distinguishes a group of people from others proceeding from another geographical origin.

Functional Diversity: Variety along the lines of the professional roles assigned to different people and in which they may have gained work experience.

Leverage: Gain some advantage from a possessed characteristic that might ordinarily be taken for granted.

Workforce: All the people employed by an organization.

ENDNOTES

[1]   LBS (2011).

[2]   Each geographical category includes a variety of ethnic groups; three foreigners are excluded.

[3]   Full-time MBA students only.

[4]   Executive MBA students only.

Chapter 6
A Collaborative Inquiry:
Raising Cross-Cultural Consciousness

Diversity Divas[1]
Teachers College, Columbia University, USA

ABSTRACT

This chapter describes a Collaborative Inquiry (CI) process as experienced by six diverse female participants in a doctoral program. The focus of the inquiry was to deepen individual and group cross-cultural understanding, and to show how holistic learning can be promoted through integrating multiple ways of knowing and spirituality within a multicultural context. The purpose of this chapter is to provide the readers with sufficient information to apply CI in their practice and build on the research presented here. To meet this goal, the authors describe how CI has the potential to foster transformational learning and discuss the relationship between transformational learning, informational learning, global competencies, developmental capacity, and the paradoxical nature of diversity work. Lastly, the chapter ends with recommendations for creating a CI process that supports deep learning and change, and potential topics for future research.

INTRODUCTION

Rapid changes in the global labor force call for the need to leverage workplace diversity (Ernst & Yip, 2008; Maltbia, 2001; McCuiston, Wooldridge, & Pierce, 2004). Organizations today have started to acknowledge the importance of increasing diversity within their structures, and recognize that cultural diversity can enhance their competitive advantage (Cox & Blake, 1991; Herriot

& Pemberton, 1995). For instance, key research that emerged out of the University of Michigan during the 1960's examined the quality of solutions to assigned problems (Cox & Blake, 1991). In this study, when the production of high quality solutions was compared between homogeneous and heterogeneous groups, researchers found that only twenty-one percent of the former produced high quality solutions, as compared to sixty-five percent of the latter (1991). Later findings also confirm the benefits of prioritizing diversity in the workplace (Amla, 2008).

DOI: 10.4018/978-1-4666-1812-1.ch006

As the workplace becomes more diversified, however, the construct of "diversity" has become even more challenging to define (Wentling & Palma-Rivas, 1998). While early attempts to create a succinct definition often resulted in only race and gender being identified, it was soon recognized that a more inclusive definition was needed (Ashkanasy, Hartel, & Daus, 2002; Oyler & Pryor, 2009). Maltbia and Power (2009) acknowledge the multiple layers and interpretations that exist when examining diversity, and identified some key components of diversity found in the literature. They include inborn human characteristics, personal experiences, organizational dimensions, personal style or tendencies, and external factors (2009).

R. Roosevelt Thomas, Jr. (1991) provides a comprehensive definition: "Diversity includes everyone. It is not something that is defined by race or gender. It extends to age, personal and corporate background, education, function, and personality. It includes lifestyle, sexual preference, geographic origin, and management or non-management" (p. 10). Scott (2010) concurs that organizations are now "more diverse culturally, ethnically, linguistically, intellectually, creatively, physically, and spiritually than ever before" (p. x). These views are all encompassing and take into account a more inclusive definition of "diversity" that allows for the support of all employees. Likewise, this handbook calls for an expanded view of "diversity" as well as "transformational strategies" that can be utilized to enhance the workplace. We define "transformational strategies" as those that support transformational learning that "…relates to the development of the cognitive, emotional, interpersonal, and intrapersonal capacities that enable a person to manage the complexities of work (e.g., leadership, teaching, learning, adaptive challenges) and life" (Drago-Severson, 2009, p. 11).

The current expanded view of "diversity" necessitates a theoretical framework as well as an adult learning structure that is more holistic in nature. We suggest that Collaborative Inquiry (CI),

a form of action research, integrated with Heron's (1992) holistic learning framework can serve as a "strategy for learning from experience" and leveraging workplace diversity (Alcantara, Hayes & Yorks, 2009, p. 251). CI is a "systematic process of action and reflection among co-inquirers who are tackling a common question of burning interest" (Ospina, El Hadidy, & Hofmann-Pinilla, 2008, p. 131). The main purpose is for "members of the inquiry group to change themselves. In response to a sense of personal disquiet or disorienting dilemma, an individual invites others with similar interests to join an inquiry. Together, inquirers formulate a compelling question that they can answer by examining "data" from their personal experience. Their goal is to develop their own capacities, either personal or professional" (Yorks & Kasl, 2002a, p. 5). We refer to "capacity" here as developmental in nature. "Developmental capacity concerns the cognitive, affective, interpersonal, and intrapersonal capacities that enable us to manage better the demands of leadership, teaching, learning, and life" (Drago-Severson, 2009. p. 8). Furthermore, for developmental capacity to increase, or become more complex, adaptive, and creative, individuals and groups need the right mix of supports and challenges, which has been referred to as a holding environment (Drago-Severson, 2009; Kegan, 1982).

CI thus involves creating a holding environment for a process of reflection and dialogue, and other Ways of Knowing, to occur. This can generate new knowledge for learning and working together. While learning that takes place during CI may take many forms, there is a potential for transformational learning and change (Alcantara, et al., 2009). Our research suggests that CI can serve as a tool to help individuals and groups engage with diversity issues. We found that to fully interact on cognitive, affective, and relational levels, it was necessary to utilize holistic and spiritual learning activities within the CI process. While cross-cultural relationships encourage exposure to varied ways of thinking and being in the world, incorporation of spirituality in contextualized, culturally-relevant settings allowed for exploration on various levels including the symbolic, relational, affective and cognitive (Chin, 2010; Merriam & Ntseane, 2008; Rosenwasser, 2002; Tisdell, 2003). Attending to our spirituality was essential for fostering a holistic transformational learning experience, and added a richer dimension to our inquiry. "Spirituality" is understood here as having "to do with a personal belief and experience of a higher power or higher purpose… to explore its potency for affective learning and change" (Chin, 2010, p. 28).

HOW WE USED CI TO INCREASE CROSS-CULTURAL AWARENESS

To address challenges in leveraging workplace diversity, we propose the use of CI as a creative process that can help build deeper cross-cultural understanding and develop a group "habit of being." We define "habit of being" based on Yorks and Kasl's (2002a) research which builds on Mezirow's (2000) notion of "habit of mind," defined as "a set of assumptions- broad, generalized, orienting predispositions that act as a filter for interpreting the meaning of experience" (p. 16). Attending to a "habit of being" is a more holistic approach (cognitive, affective, relational) to making meaning about and relating to the world around us. However, there exists the paradox of diversity, within any diverse context in that the more different people are in their "habits of minds" and "habits of being," the more likely for there to be a "disconnect" among group members (Yorks & Kasl, 2002a). At the same time, there is greater potential for deep and rich learning. Therefore, just creating cross-cultural groups is not sufficient for meaningful and deep growth to occur.

In this section, we describe how we used CI for our inquiry purposes. First, we introduce ourselves and then outline the steps used to initiate our CI process. These include creating the CI group,

shaping the inquiry framework—developing activities and protocols for action and reflection, and documenting what we learned about ourselves, and each other. Finally, we illustrate how through collaborative inquiry we developed a new understanding of others and ourselves.

Who We Are

We are doctoral candidates in a cohort-based adult learning and leadership program at Teachers College, Columbia University. We come from different ethnicities, cultures, spiritual traditions, academic disciplines, socioeconomic statuses, and professional backgrounds. Our ages range from 30-50 years old, and we represent six countries including Kenya, Singapore, the Philippines, England, Canada, and the United States. Our diverse backgrounds and common passion for learning about others and ourselves brought us together to undertake this journey of discovery.

We came together as co-inquirers and became sisters in the process. Like any family, this sisterhood has not always been easy. Conflicts and intense emotions have arisen but the CI process has given us a way of being with each other that helps to transcend these moments and enable us to reach our common goals. Through poetry, dance, music, art, dialogue, food, and writing, we learned to question our own beliefs, challenge each other's assumptions, listen to differing perspectives, and open our hearts and minds to new realities. Our experiences and identities are distinct, yet we share many similar histories, triumphs, and tribulations as women, doctoral candidates, professionals, daughters, wives, mothers, sisters, and friends. We are the *Diversity Divas*.

How We Initiated Our CI

Prior to undertaking this project, we studied the process of collaborative inquiry and dialogued about the questions that we hoped to explore. Since this was an academic requirement for our doctoral program, faculty members gave us guidance. We learned that "the inquiry group is an autonomous entity with its own rules and parameters, functioning as an independent association of peers. The goal of [which] is to create knowledge within the group and to observe the process" (Zelman, 1995, p. 353). Moreover, shaping the collaborative inquiry framework was driven by two dimensions- creation of space, and development of a context within this space, both of which must be grounded in a spirit of participation, dialogue and collaboration with all stakeholders (Trelevean, 1994).

Initially, our research questions were:

1. How does the way we make meaning of our multiple identities, and the intersections of these identities, influence development of our cross-cultural consciousness?
2. How is this expressed as Women's Ways of Knowing?
3. In what ways do the use of Heron's multiple Ways of Knowing and attentiveness to our spirituality enhance our whole-person understanding of ourselves and of others?

The discussion in this chapter will be based on the findings from questions one and three. However, all three questions give an example of the type of inquiry one may focus on during a CI process.

Shaping the Inquiry Framework and Development of the CI Process

Guided by Yorks and Kasl's (2002a) notion of "learning-within-relationship," or engaging in whole person knowing of self and other, we applied Heron's (1992) four interdependent Ways of Knowing (experiential, presentational, propositional, and practical) within the context of a CI to bridge the gap between felt encounter and whole person understanding in a diverse setting (Yorks & Kasl, 2002a). Figure 1 illustrates Heron's four epistemologies or multiple ways of sharing experiences in a meaningful way.

With our common theoretical interests in collaborative inquiry and Heron's Ways of Knowing, we set out to design our CI by creating three questions relating to fostering cross-cultural con-

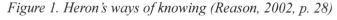

Figure 1. Heron's ways of knowing (Reason, 2002, p. 28)

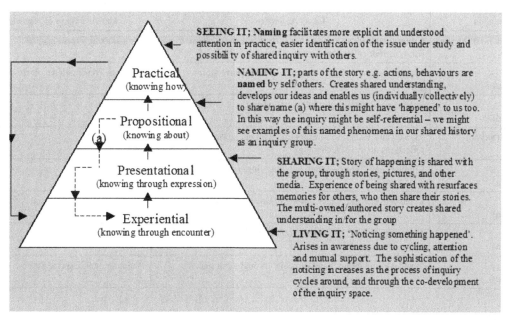

sciousness and agreed on the timeframe needed to complete the project. As co-inquirers, we committed ourselves to the space and time to engage in this collaborative inquiry from October 2010 through March 2011. This commitment included eight action-reflection cycles (six in person and two online via Skype).

Based on our CI experience, we witnessed how the process emerged organically. While we agreed to an overall timetable, we worked with the ambiguity of our busy schedules by meeting after class or on holiday weekends. We met in hotel rooms, in the library, and in the comfort of our homes. Each space fostered different emotions and set the tone for the specific session. We intentionally took turns leading each action/reflection session. While some explicit structures such as group norms were set up at the onset, the co-inquirers and the assigned facilitator(s) agreed to be flexible with regard to the focus or direction of the inquiry based on felt needs. The sessions were recorded using digital recorders and Garageband™ software. Each inquirer kept an on-going journal, and posted excerpts on a Google site for analysis. Table 1 illustrates the focus of each session using Heron's (1992) four Ways of Knowing.

What We Learned

In analyzing our data, based on our journal reflections, we individually and collectively used inductive and literature-based coding and presented our analysis and findings at an international conference. Our analysis revealed the following three themes:

The Volcano as a metaphor for life. Through this CI, we saw our life experiences in the forms of smoke, ash, and emerging lava, with shifting perspectives and new learning embroiling deep down in the core. We also recognized the paradox of diversity through the shifting tectonic plates resulting in an eruption of magma and gas. What lay beneath the surface of our physical diversity was a more complex and potentially volatile group dynamic. This volatile or conflictual part of our group dynamic would sometimes stay dormant and other times manifest in tears or arguments.

Table 1. CI sessions and Heron's ways of knowing (Heron, 1992, 1999)

Session	Topic/ Activities	Heron's Ways of Knowing
Session 1A + 1B (Skype)	Exploring our identity through poetry (*Phenomenal Women + Girl*) (include reflections on use of technology)	Propositional, Presentational
Session 2 (In-person)	Metaphor of the butterfly – change and transformation	Practical, Presentational, Experiential
Session 3 (In-person)	Sunrise awakening – spirituality and identity	Experiential
Session 4 (Skype)	Journey and Visual Art – resonating with our stories (include reflections on use of technology)	Presentational
Session 5 (In-person)	Conflicts and culture – inner and outer rings (include questions & answers)	Practical
Session 6 (In-person)	Exploring Self and 'Other' through Dance and Movement	Presentational, Experiential
Session 7 (In-person)	Notes and Post-its: Writing as a collaborative act (coding analysis)	Propositional
Session 8 (In-person)	"I and we" – a group 'habit of being' through quilt making	Presentational, Experiential

However, with each encounter and departure, there was a sense that the process in place was a safe but persistent container for surprise, play, unexpected interaction, and deeper authenticity. Because of alternative ways of expression and creativity, we were able to share aspects of ourselves, our identities, our relationships with others, the natural world, and spirituality, in a manner that led to greater openness and authenticity. We ultimately found ourselves experiencing personal transformation, which occurred organically, albeit in a spiral and complex manner. As we moved through cycles of action and reflection, engagement and relaxation, the experience of relational knowing evolved into an organic rhythm of increasing depth and unveiling, individually and collectively, like the "unpeeling of onion layers" and group metaphor of a volcano.

Integrating Heron's Ways of Knowing: A Holistic Learning Journey. As co-inquirers, we experienced "critical subjectivity" marked by an awareness and interplay of experiential, presentational, propositional and practical knowing (Heron, 1992). It is notable that predominantly presentational sessions (expressing our selves through art, play, stories, etc.) surfaced greater openness to creativity, to different Ways of Knowing, and to expressions of joy that ultimately lead to authenticity and most evidently powerful, impactful experiences. While all of the Ways of Knowing were incorporated into the various sessions, Yorks and Kasl's (2002a) assertion that presentational knowing is pivotal in creating congruence in the four interdependent Ways of Knowing, was corroborated by our experience. In particular, non-discursive modes of activity such as using art materials invoked potent sensations of imagination and play. At times, we were overcome with emotions, feelings and memories that surfaced when engaged in the simple art activity of a tactile nature. For instance, the use of colored markers, fluid paints and bare hands to fold origami papers brought out feelings of familiar, forgotten childish pleasures, instinctive delight for learning that have been put aside in our busy adult lives.

Weaving in Spirituality: Understanding Self, Other, the World and Beyond. A surprising theme that emerged from our data was a growing, more profound appreciation of the relationships of self, other, the natural world, and the unconscious and spiritual realms. In defining "spirituality," we did not limit ourselves to organized religion or a specific faith tradition but to a broader sense of connection to a larger purpose or being greater than ourselves. We underwent a process that encouraged us to examine our own perceptions and biases of our cultures, our womanhood, families and communities, and our work as adult educators. Through engagement in a number of different activities, our awareness of commonality and difference was accentuated. This was expressed and fostered through meditation, yoga, dance, song, food, prayer and poetry. Being purposefully open to each other's differing sensibilities of spirituality was a critical part of allowing for greater authenticity and openness. Based on these experiences, our data indicates: 1) spirituality is critical in mediating multiple and intersecting roles and identities, 2) spirituality promotes authenticity, and 3) spirituality is woven into our own personal experiences.

At the end of the process, every member of the group expressed pride and gratitude at the depth of their personal change as well as learning and insights into others' realities. We dialogued about "stepping out of (our) comfort zone," seeing "each other in different contexts," and helping us "find much comfort and assurance" in each other which led to "some surprising and powerful experiences." Personal metaphors shared in latter sessions led to common themes and the creation of a group metaphor that was both unified and diverse. The group metaphor of a volcano encapsulated the journey from 'me' to 'we.' However, as the group metaphor and our earlier comments indicate, the evolutionary dynamism, complexity and paradox of working together in a diverse setting was neither concretely linear nor without issue. The following section reviews how such concerns might be addressed in the broader context of the workplace.

THE COMPLEX AND PARADOXICAL NATURE OF DIVERSITY WORK: ISSUES, CONTROVERSIES, PROBLEMS

Javidan (2008a) argues that those working cross-culturally in a global environment have two major responsibilities. First, these individuals need to understand their own cultural lens. Second, and based upon the first, if individuals want to influence cross-culturally, they need to understand the other's cultural lens. While these reminders may be fairly basic, when missed, things can go very wrong (Irving, 2009, p. 3).

Globalization has intensified the need for cross-cultural and multicultural organizational strategies so that institutions can better leverage diversity for organizational success. As the above quote indicates, many organizations know to a certain level what to do to leverage diversity but what seems like a simple task is in actuality quite complex. This is because learning about our own cultural lens or worldview and then integrating other's perspectives into our own and/or co-creating a multicultural lens is a transformational process that takes considerable time and space (Drago-Severson, 2009; Kegan, 1982; Mezirow, 2000). Secondly, this process is complex and spiral in nature because inherent in cross-cultural and diversity work are a number of paradoxes (Fisher-Yoshida & Gellar, 2009), which are complex, ambiguous, and full of adaptive challenges—problems that are often systemic with no ready answers (Heifetz & Laurie, 1996).

Therefore, this section will discuss the need to incorporate transformational learning into diversity work, how a spiritual and holistic focus may be controversial but necessary for deep change to occur, the necessity for developing global competencies, and the issues inherent in managing the paradoxical nature of diversity work.

Collaborative Inquiry as a Transformational Learning Process

Based on our experience, we propose that a holistic CI aimed at increasing cross-cultural consciousness is a potentially transformational learning process, which assumes a "qualitative shift…in how a person actively interprets, organizes, understands, and makes sense of his or her experience" (Drago-Severson, 2009, p. 11). This process relates closely to transformative learning which has as its objective the creation of "a more dependable frame of reference….that is more inclusive, differentiating, permeable (open to other viewpoints), critically reflective of assumptions, emotionally capable of change, and integrative of experience" (Mezirow, 2000, p. 19). Both definitions are important for understanding transformation; however, we use Drago-Severson's definition in this chapter because she describes "transformational learning" as a holistic process of growth (cognitive, affective, and relational). This definition aligns well with Heron's multiple Ways of Knowing used in our research. Furthermore, the construct of transformational learning is especially helpful when describing its distinction from informational learning. Informational learning is about "increasing the amount of knowledge and skills a person possesses" (Drago-Severson, 2009, p. 11). Therefore, the challenge for the workplace is to offer both kinds of learning (informational and transformational) so that cross-cultural consciousness may be raised with the intent to create positive workplace change (Drago-Severson, 2009; Laiken, 2002; Torbert, 2004).

Building Global Competencies

One conceptual frame that integrates informational and transformational learning in relation to workplace diversity and cross-cultural awareness is the emergence of global competencies. Olson and Kroeger (2011) define a:

Globally competent person (as having) enough substantive knowledge, perceptual understanding, and intercultural communication skills to effectively interact in our globally interdependent world. Or in the case of a globally competent organization, there are both a sufficient number of people who have this knowledge, understanding, and skills and a culture that promotes such competency (p. 118).

Inherent in this definition is informational learning (substantive knowledge) and transformational learning (a qualitative shift in perception and meaning making). Hunter (2004) created a list of global competencies developed from experts in academia and practitioners in organizations. One can make a connection between Hunter's examples of knowledge and skills/experiences and informational learning, and his descriptions of attitudes with transformational learning as noted in Table 2.

In our own CI, we were primarily focused on transformational learning due to our key questions around building cross-cultural consciousness.

Therefore, our results are more consistent with Hunter's examples of attitudes. As our findings indicate, we grappled with the limitations of our own worldview by asking each other pointed and controversial questions about our cultures and multiple identities. We took risks within the holding environment we created by partaking in ethnic and spiritual activities different than our own such as engaging in yoga, dance, meditation, and song. When an experience (activity or discussion) was emotionally challenging, we expressed our feelings, gained support, and continued on with the exercise so that individual and group growth could be fostered. This sometimes involved tears and asking for additional time, follow-up through one-on-one discussion, and individually reflecting through journaling and then sharing our thoughts on our Google site for all to read. Many of our discussions were practical in nature and integrated cross-cultural strategies that we could implement in our lives and careers (e.g. discussions about "tiger mom" parenting to academic cross-cultural service learning and organizational diversity training).

However, based on our findings, it is also evident that many of Hunter's knowledge and skills/experiences were integrated into our CI. For example, we learned specific information about different cultures and practiced communicating and collaborating in a cross-cultural context. Heron's process is powerful because it intentionally fosters the development of informational

Table 2. Hunter's global competencies (Hunter, 2004)

Knowledge of...	Skills/Experience	Attitudes
...own culture	Intercultural project work and collaboration	Recognition of own worldview limits
...other cultures	Intercultural social competence in business	Willingness to experience life as "other" and take risks for growth
...globalization	Ability to live outside one's own culture	Openness to new experiences, even when emotionally challenging
...current world events	Ability to compete globally	Ability to cope with different cultures and attitudes
...world history	Effective global social and business participation	Celebrating diversity (non-judgmental)

and transformational learning which support the growth of competencies (the ability to perform tasks associated with a specific role) which in this case were global/multicultural in nature, and capacity (personal cognitive, affective development, and relational knowing) which helped us of foster a group "habit of being" which was transformational in nature (Drago-Severson, 2009; Kegan, 1982; Nicolaides, 2008; Yorks & Kasl, 2002a).

Spirituality as a Thematic Dimension

Organizations may also want to consider the spiritual aspects to creating a positive multicultural climate. What makes this approach controversial is the democratic notion in the United States of separation of church and state. However, by using a metaphysical and non-religious definition of spirituality, corporations can benefit from the strengths of such a theory and limit people's reluctance to engage in practices associated with it. One approach to spirituality that is especially useful for diversity work is described by Tisdell and Tolliver (2003), which comprises seven components:

1. a connection to a life force or higher self or purpose
2. a context that may or may not be related to a religious tradition
3. a sense of wholeness, healing, and the interconnectedness of all things
4. meaning making
5. knowledge construction through largely unconscious and symbolic processes (image, symbol, ritual, art, and music) that are deeply cultural
6. spiritual experiences that often happen by surprise
7. the ongoing development of identity (including one's cultural identity), of moving toward greater authenticity

Spiritual practices can help connect us with our unconscious process and make explicit our inner values and beliefs explicit to others and ourselves so that deep and meaningful conversations can be had. Oftentimes communication is purely cognitive and what is discussed is limited. Not only can we misunderstand another person but also we can be oblivious to or easily dismiss deeper inner feelings. Using spiritual practices (community celebration, music, metaphors, art, etc.) can help bring "habits of being" to the surface and create shared understandings, which is necessary and powerful in diversity work.

Furthermore, spirituality is often rooted in cultural traditions and holistic in nature. This makes it useful in exposing cultural influences on individuals and groups in a non-threatening way (Ottley, Rosser-Mims, & Palmer, 2011). Ottley et al. (2011) describe the "culturally competent educator" as one who incorporates an understanding of spirituality as well as other more traditional components of global or cultural competence into his/her practices. Though this example is focused on an educator, it is relevant to globally and multi-culturally competent leaders, employees, and community members alike.

Using CI in the Workplace

One way to incorporate informational and transformational learning to build competence and capacity aimed at leveraging diversity is by integrating Heron's four interdependent Ways of Knowing within a CI process. In our research, we specifically integrated a holistic focus that included spirituality. However, this approach might not be in line with organizational culture, particularly if the emphasis is on rational and cognitive discourse using primarily informational learning strategies. If this is the case, a holistic CI process may be seen as unconventional, unfamiliar and thus controversial. Raising awareness about this type of approach and gaining buy-in will be important. A way to do this is to pilot a CI process in your organization with people who are supporters of workplace diversity initiatives to gain their perspectives and feedback before integrating larger initiatives across the organization. We suggest that some of the sessions take place off-site so that a safe space is more easily created. It may also be important to hold an orientation session before starting on the CI action-reflection cycles. During this orientation session, literature relating to CI, adult education, and workplace diversity may be discussed. This would lay a foundation for using this type of approach (O'Neil & Marsick, 2007).

Ultimately, our findings and other key studies on the topic (Kasl & Yorks, 2002; Rosenwasser, 2002; Smith, 2002; Van Stralen, 2002; Zelman, 2002) support the idea that holistic and transformational processes are ways to increase effective cross-cultural relationships and in doing so, support creativity and innovation in the workplace. However, as our study indicates, this takes time and dedication. Our CI process took six months and we started the process after being graduate students together for over a year, which included individual research and group discussions on the core theoretical foundations of CI and diversity/multicultural issues. Therefore, this type of work takes long-term commitment but it can foster deep individual and group transformation that can ultimately impact the organizational culture. Therefore, time commitment is important to consider before implementation.

Paradoxes for Success

As discussed previously, the paradox of diversity (high potential for conflict and high potential for innovation, understanding and creativity) is a significant factor to consider when implementing diversity, multicultural, and cross-cultural initiatives in any setting. Furthermore, there are many paradoxes to consider in this line of work. The specific paradox of short term vs. long-term

focus, as described above, is only one example. We suggest that by also examining Fisher-Yoshida and Geller's (2009) description of the five paradoxes of Transnational Leadership, one can more intentionally plan CI processes that factor in the full paradoxical nature of this topic. The five paradoxes are defined as follows:

1. Paradox of knowing: Knowing self and honoring others
2. Paradox of focus: I centric, we centric
3. Paradox of communication: Communicating across differences
4. Paradox of action: Doing and reflecting
5. Paradox of response: Short term and long term responses

Furthermore, Fisher-Yoshida and Geller (2009) also take a holistic approach to diversity, cross-cultural and transnational work. These authors suggest that organizational culture (including the ability to leverage diversity) can be positively influenced because:

…transnational leaders need to lead in a relational way, taking the whole person into consideration; need to be culturally sensitive and appropriate to the context within which they are communicating; and need to be open to learning and change in the process by fostering and developing their own self-awareness and instilling these values throughout the organization (p. 7).

This notion has several connections with our holistic CI process including raising cross-cultural consciousness, a holistic or "whole person" focus, and a relational approach. This relational approach is especially useful in explaining how workplace paradoxes provide challenges to cross-cultural and multicultural work. Fisher-Yoshida and Geller's (2009) "transnational leadership" approach calls for leaders to engage with employees in managing and leveraging these paradoxes, and one way to do this is through using a holistic CI process.

Moreover, similar to our own CI experience, the authors describe the paradoxes as contradictory in nature and that a negative backlash may follow if one picks one side of the paradox over the other. The authors suggest that organizations should view each paradox as a continuum and work to balance the right mix of both in the workplace since individuals and groups have different reasons for supporting one side of a paradox over another.

To illustrate these paradoxes, we give examples from our CI process. The first paradox *knowing self and honoring others* "reflects the tension between awareness of our own needs and those of the other party with whom we are engaged" (Fisher-Yoshida & Geller, 2009, p. 13). This paradox was reflected in one of our co-inquirers who is white and North American as well as an extrovert. She learned to intentionally quiet her voice and moderate her input so that others, who had experienced less opportunity to share their voice in the past, had more time and space to do so in our CI. While doing this, she learned how to genuinely listen and through the process reflected that she not only learned more about others but gained a deeper sense of herself as well.

The second paradox *I centric, we centric* "introduces the contrasts in worldview that exist between those raised in cultures that focus primarily on the needs and interests of the individual (I-centric) and those raised in cultures that place primary emphasis on the collective needs (we-centric) of the group" (Fisher-Yoshida & Geller, 2009, p. 15). As discussed previously, this was a major theme throughout our work. As co-inquirers we spiraled between "I" and "we" depending on the activity and issues being discussed. This process was fluid and we did not necessarily discuss this paradox until we began coding and analyzing the data. We also often found ourselves operating as both "I" and "we" simultaneously. For example, during one of our presentations, we operated from a "we" orientation when giving our joint presentation on our CI process. At the same time we all had individualistic ("I") goals at the con-

ference in terms of attending specific presentations and networking. Although there was some tension and discussion around this paradox, by maintaining open and authentic communication and being flexible, our group was able to honor both perspectives.

The third paradox *communicating across differences* is about "identifying levels of directness and indirectness...recognizing how the understanding of certain words, expressions and phrases...impact subsequent actions and relationships (and) choosing to give information openly or waiting to share it..." (Fisher-Yoshida & Geller, 2009, p. 17). In our time together, we learned to negotiate the dynamics and interactions among each inquirer (direct vs. indirect), the meanings behind our words, expressions and actions (words vs. expressions), and how we showed up when we communicated with others (linear vs. circular). As co-inquirers from both Eastern and Western cultures, we learned that our communication styles varied greatly with some of us expressing ourselves more directly in words while others relying more on context to influence the conversation. This paradox had a significant impact on how we related and communicated with one another. Those times that we were not clear and intentional about our needs often triggered issues of dissonance and misunderstanding.

The fourth paradox *doing and reflecting* focuses on "creating a balance between doing and reflecting...(including) reflecting both in action and on action" (Fisher-Yoshida & Geller, 2009, p. 18). This paradox became evident later in our CI, particularly during the writing stages. For instance, some of us were more action-oriented, while others valued reflection, analysis and planning in relation to the larger picture. When this paradox was played out in a high stress context where a tight deadline for publication had to be met, it was not difficult to fall into the trap of assuming that someone might not be pulling her weight or that another might be too dominant in driving the project. It was therefore important to continuously engage in member checks and dialogue about these assumptions and emotions to foster a stronger and equitable working relationship and meet our goals.

The fifth and final paradox *short term and long term responses* considers our time focus including developing short and long-terms goals and the impact and consequences of those goals on the larger world (Fisher-Yoshida & Geller, 2009). As co-inquirers we continued to negotiate collective and individual goals for our CI in terms of publication and conference presentation opportunities. To do this, we have learned to communicate around short-term and long-term planning and thinking. For instance, we have developed an understanding of time and commitment to certain projects but also allowed for organic changes in structure, time and responsibility should any life issue occur or takes priority for the individual inquirer.

As co-inquirers working together to create knowledge and discover one another in the process, we concur with Fisher-Yoshida and Gellar (2009) that through dialogue and reflection people can decide together how to manage these paradoxes:

The five paradoxes of transnational leadership are about living and leading effectively in today's world- a global village. It's about letting go of our expectations or desire for sameness and accepting that our effectiveness with others can be enhanced by knowing, honoring, and welcoming difference. It is in our best interest to approach others who are not like us with an air of curiosity and openness to the potential of what could be. (2009, p. xv)

By attending to the transformational learning process, integrating a holistic and spiritual focus into diversity initiatives, and intentionally managing the many paradoxes inherent in multicultural work, there is great potential to prepare individuals and groups for the complexity of work and life in the 21st century. By learning to balance ambiguity and tackling adaptive challenges, employees at all

levels have a better chance of creating positive change in their organizations. This is difficult work that is dynamic in nature, much like our volcano metaphor describes. Therefore, learning to work organically and honoring oneself and others by focusing on relational knowing and creating a group "habit of being" is central to reaching group goals and making a positive impact on one's environment. However, much more applied research needs to be done to investigate the potential of using collaborative inquiry and holistic approaches to individual, group, and organizational transformation. The following section includes some solutions and recommendations for using CI in the workplace.

SOLUTIONS AND RECOMMENDATIONS

Although our CI was carried out in an academic setting, the results have relevancy for workplace settings where the goals are to raise cross-cultural awareness, support transformational learning, and/or foster more complex habits of mind/ being. Using the CI process in the workplace has the potential to build global competencies, incorporate transformational and informational learning, integrate a holistic and spiritual focus to foster deep change, and provide a framework to manage the many paradoxes inherent in diversity/ intercultural work. In this section, we propose how the CI process may be implemented in the workplace by describing: 1) the preparation process, 2) negotiating arrangements, 3) how to create the space, 4) the components of the process, and 5) documenting and analyzing the inquiry.

Initial Preparation

Support from senior management is pivotal in commencing the inquiry process (Bray, 2002). Initial preparation must examine stakeholder's interest and level of engagement. Co-inquirers must negotiate which workplace issues to address, goals of the CI, the questions to be tackled, the costs involved, the logistics or space needed, and the potential risks and benefits inherent in said process. Specific concerns may include:

- How much time and resources are needed?
- Who will be involved in the CI?
- Who can give appropriate guidance at the onset of the inquiry?
- Who will be involved in the design of the process?
- What are the benefits for the employees/ organization?
- Are there risks for the participants?
- How will involvement in the inquiry impact work-related responsibilities and obligations?
- How will learning be documented, analyzed and used?

Negotiating Arrangements

CI can be seen as "an intervention into a social system and culture" if implemented in the context of professional development in a workplace setting (Bray, 2002, p. 85). In the same vein, it is viewed as an opportunity to create a liberating structure for learning to take place (Fisher & Torbert, 1995) or a container for learning. Hence, negotiating arrangements at the onset is crucial.

Aside from the need to create a space appropriate for the inquiry process, other crucial arrangements include the role of the facilitator and membership of the inquiry group. Membership is an important issue due to the fact that the group should be intentionally diverse. However, assigning inquiry teams could foster a coercive element and this could become counterproductive. It is important to balance the need for diversity in the group through requesting participation with personal and group membership choice and ownership. Once the group is formed, the group may decide to be self-directed or use an outside facilitator. The facilitator and/or leaderless group should focus on laying the inquiry groundwork, including providing support in terms of organizing the members, taking care of logistics and leading the inquiry sessions.

Similar to our own process, we suggest having participants take turns in leading the sessions and assisting with logistics and record keeping. It is important to note that the more responsibility one person assumes during early stages of the process, the more difficult it is to distance him or herself from being looked upon as the "driver" of the CI (Bray, 2002). Furthermore, while voluntary participation is desired for "authentic participation," this may not be the case in organizations whose culture does not support these types of innovative practices (Bray, 2002, p. 85). It is also important to consider the positionality of the facilitator and personnel involved in the process as there can be tension in the group around democratic decision-making, especially if a supervisor is part of the group.

Creating the Space

Treleaven (1994) notes "establishing conditions that would generate a listening space in the workplace [is] a significant aspect of developing collaboration" (para. 67). Choosing a venue where sessions are held is important so that "re-entering that space over time became conducive to engagement in a different way of being" (Treleaven, 1994, para. 67). In our own CI process, we experienced each other differently in the library, hotel, or in our homes. Rich and often memorable discussions were held in places with comfortable chairs, soft lighting, and suitable ambiance. Moreover, sharing meals and rituals from different cultures evoked personal memories of our childhood and life journeys. Based on our experience, we suggest locating the CI sessions in a retreat center or more informal setting outside of the workplace, which might lead to a more relaxed and open opportunity for mutual growth and understanding.

Components of a Collaborative Inquiry

Mealman and Lawrence (1998) liken collaborative inquiry to cooking in an outdoor kettle wherein the various steps and ingredients involved in the process are results of complex and overlapping components that often make up CI such as: Developing Collaborative Knowledge, Relationship, Dialogue, Attentive Listening, Reflection, Openness to divergent views, Shared Passion and Commitment. One component that was especially significant to our CI process was fostering deep dialogue. For example, during our second session, which was guided by the metaphor of a butterfly, we engaged in dialogue, attentive, listening and reflection after participating in a creative, tactile activity (art and origami) and sharing artifacts from our personal histories. We broke into dyads to allow deeper dialogue about how we have experienced our own metamorphosis or growth in life, and then reconvened back into the large group to discuss how our personal growth is symbolized by the artifact we brought. Through this experience, relationships began to grow and we began to see each other differently. One woman reflected that:

as I listened to each woman share about their metaphors, peeling away layers of assumptions I may have had about each person, it was revealing to me how I had always thought of myself as sensitive and self-aware. Yet in my appreciation of each woman's sharing, I found myself recognizing a new beauty of their stories, and their journeys towards making sense of the world—in ways that were entirely different from mine.

Although our past individual experiences took place at different continuums and different spaces, we found a multitude of common experiences, learning and insights. A co-inquirer noted that: "I began to sense that our very different pasts had more in common then we realized." Particular sessions resonated very deeply for all inquirers and there were pivotal moments for the group when we began to take a deeper look into our similarities and differences. Although our presentational activities were crucial to creating openness and deepening our relationships, we also acknowledge the use of dialogue, attentive listening, and reflection to arrive at our learning.

Documenting and Analyzing the Inquiry Process and Emergent Themes

As a way of utilizing collaborative inquiry as both an adult learning strategy and research process, documentation played a critical role. Journaling and using critical incident questionnaires, as well as recording and transcribing sessions, contributed to a more meaningful understanding and analysis of the rich outcomes of the process. Additionally, creating a space or website for organizing correspondence and documentation related to the process was also necessary.

Engaging in this type of reflection and analyses is what gives CI powerful outcomes. It is through applied research or action science that individuals learn that they have significant thoughts and input to share. Participants come to understand that their voice matters and that through dialogue, reflection, inquiry, and application groups can create ideas and have a meaningful impact on their environment. Many organizational cultures are data driven and people in these contexts are used to giving reports and documenting processes. Using CI adds a qualitative component to quantitative data gathering and reporting. It incorporates a more in-depth look at a phenomenon so that a holistic view can be gained and ultimately better decisions made from having access to rich and contextualized information. It also emphasizes personal transformation, while not necessarily guaranteeing organizational change, can promote greater inclusivity and a healthier workplace environment.

FUTURE RESEARCH DIRECTIONS

From our collaborative inquiry process, which focused on raising cross-cultural consciousness and developing a group habit of being, we found that transformational change was possible as our worldviews were altered and more authentic relationships were created. However, further research is needed to investigate the relationship between collaborative inquiry processes that are holistic/spiritual and multicultural in nature to individual, group, and organizational outcomes. We feel that three potential research outcomes worthy of investigation include:

1. fostering the development of a learning organization;
2. increasing multicultural awareness and a positive cross-cultural organizational climate;
3. increasing individual and group developmental capacity and global/multicultural competencies

We believe that using a holistic/spiritual and cross-cultural CI process may assist an organization in expanding their own definition of diversity and help an institution engage in transformational learning. Furthermore, engaging in processes like CI may also support Watkins and Marsick's (1993, 1996) proposed learning organization model. Accordingly, this model of the learning organization includes seven dimensions: create continuous learning opportunities, promote inquiry and dialogue, encourage collaboration to its environment, establish systems to capture and share learning, empower people towards a collective vision, connect the organization to its environment, and leaders model and support learning. Therefore, future research may examine how CI can be used to foster the development of a learning organization or any of the components listed above. For example, CI could be used as a powerful tool to promote collaboration, inquiry, and dialogue. Based on Watkins and Marsick's model, these dimensions can assist an organization in creating a culture that encourages questioning, feedback, and experimentation.

Combining CI and the dimensions described above may result in knowledge creation for both organizational and individual learning. Yorks (2005) explores practitioner-based collaborative action inquiry, which strives to create social space in organizations and other social institutions for generative learning. The three-year project for the U.S. Department of Veterans Affairs (VA), which focused on stress and aggression as well as knowledge production, is an example of this type of initiative (Gibbons, et al., 1994). In this project, there was a focus on learning, reflection, and collaboration. The study results showed significant reductions in stress and all forms of aggression, as well as great improvements in employee satisfaction at all pilot sites. It is this holistic engagement in the learning process that supports our suggestion for the use of CI as a powerful tool in organizations.

CI may also be used to raise multicultural and cross-cultural consciousness. For instance, future studies could build on research conducted by Barlas et al. (2002) and Kasl and Yorks (2002a). Specifically, Barlas et al. (2002) investigated the impact of white consciousness on the participants' beliefs and behaviors. In this study, nineteen participants from four CI groups with varying levels of white consciousness took part in a cooperative/collaborative inquiry designed to understand how white privilege is lived and communicated across their daily lives. The findings indicated that a large majority claimed that the CI experience changed their beliefs and behaviors towards themselves and others. The researchers also noted significant shifts in perspective among co-inquirers particularly in an inquirer named Eleanor, who experienced a change in personal consciousness that impacted her ability to recognize her racist thoughts, her sense of responsibility to respond, and her behavior to take action.

Additional research is needed to investigate the relationship between CI and individual, group, and organizational outcomes, especially since these outcomes may not always be predictable. An organization could conduct a climate study that includes a focus on multicultural issues or cross-cultural communications and the dimensions of a learning organization before and after implementing a CI organizational-wide initiative. This suggestion would promote a holistic approach to learning, support the dimensions of a learning organization, and provide a way to accumulate both quantitative and qualitative data on the nurturing of a diverse workplace climate.

It may also be possible to collect qualitative and quantitative data on the growth of individual and group global competencies and developmental capacity (i.e. complexity/maturity). Again, using a pre and post-test research model, individuals who participate in a CI process could be assessed for particular competencies and developmental capacity. The Global Competence Aptitude Assessment (http://www.globalcompetence.org/GCAA-team.asp) based on Hunter's 2004 study could be used. Likewise, to gauge developmental capacity (cognitive, affective, and relational Ways of Knowing) the Subject-Object Interview based on Kegan's constructive-development theory (1982, 1994) or the SCTi-Map available from Cook-Greuter and Associates (http://www.cook-greuter.com/) could be applied. As noted earlier, global/multicultural competencies focus on knowledge, skills, and attitudes and these often overlap with developmental capacity but do not give an in-depth understanding of this construct (i.e. the way he/she makes meaning of the environment and his/her worldview). Therefore, we suggest that developmental capacity should be investigated as its own construct in future studies. Developmental capacity has been found to relate to a person's ability to deal with adaptive challenges, and developmental maturity/complexity is often associated with systems thinking and the ability to manage ambiguity (Drago-Severson, 2009; Kegan, 1994; Torbert, 2004) thus making developmental capacity an important construct to investigate in relation to CI and workplace diversity.

Furthermore, it may also be important to study the CI implementation process in relation to organizational outcomes because not all CI processes promote deep learning and change. Alcantara, Hayes, and Yorks (2009) argue that many types of learning may occur within a CI (not necessarily transformational learning) and because the inquiry should ideally be democratic, the role of the facilitator (external or internal to the group) is critical to guiding the inquiry. If the inquiry is guided mindfully the potential for transformational learning can be increased. Heron (1999) identifies six dimensions (planning, meaning, confronting, feeling, structuring, valuing, and three modes of facilitation (hierarchical, cooperative, autonomous) as well as critical reflexivity as important components that need to be managed when practicing CI. More research on how the role of the facilitator and Heron's modes of facilitation as well as the use of critical reflexivity could shed light on the relationship between CI processes and individual, group, and organizational outcomes.

Lastly, the focus of a CI (multicultural and holistic) and the individuals involved should be taken into account. As noted earlier, our CI included a holistic/spiritual and multicultural focus using participants who volunteered and were already committed to and passionate about the topic of diversity. Therefore, future research could take into account the process, focus, and/or participant competencies and capacities within CI initiatives and the impact these variables have on a variety of workplace outcomes such as increased innovation, creativity, and problem solving.

CONCLUSION

This collaboration of six women from diverse backgrounds across varying professional fields allowed for a unique space where personal histories were shared, voices were heard, and knowledge was co-constructed. In the course of our inquiry, we created a group "habit of being" by integrating spirituality and Heron's four Ways of Knowing into our collaborative inquiry. The inquiry enabled us to examine ourselves in light of our own spirituality, which is inherent in the learning process in any diverse setting (Heron, 1992). Furthermore, we found that spirituality was a powerful construct not dominated by one dogma or spiritual tradition, and learning occurred by sharing personal spiritual beliefs and being open to the practices of others.

Collaborative inquiry is a powerful tool that can be utilized to foster transformational learning. CI may assist groups with authentic sharing, intentionally examining cultural biases, and co-constructing knowledge. Used in the context of workplace settings, CI holds the potential for providing multiple benefits to various stakeholders. It could be an innovative tool that allows for holistic, transformational learning that is inclusive to diversity in the workplace. It could also be used to foster deeper individual learning via its process, which promotes cycles of reflection.

Since the nature of creating a multicultural and diverse positive organizational climate is difficult work and there are problems inherent in the paradoxical, developmentally complex, and spiritually oriented dimensions of cross-cultural initiatives, any intervention used to leverage workplace diversity should account for these issues when trying to foster transformational learning and leverage diversity. We believe that collaborative inquiry holds the potential for individual and organizational change toward an inclusive, multicultural, learning organization. Furthermore, deep learning can be supported and enhanced by incorporating Heron's Ways of Knowing and Tisdell's spirituality construct in the inquiry process.

REFERENCES

Alcantara, L., Hayes, S., & Yorks, L. (2009). Collaborative inquiry in action: Transformative learning through co-inquiry. In Mezirow, J., & Taylor, E. (Eds.), *Transformative Learning in Practice: Insights from Community, Workplace, and Higher Education* (pp. 251–261). San Francisco, CA: Jossey-Bass.

Amla, I. (2008). Managing and sustaining a world of workplace diversity: The Accenture experience. *Strategic HR Review*, 7(5), 11–16. doi:10.1108/14754390810893044

Ashkanasy, N. M., Hartel, C. E., & Daus, C. S. (2002). Diversity and emotion: The new frontiers in organizational behavior research. *Journal of Management*, 28(3), 307–338. doi:10.1177/014920630202800304

Barlas, C., Kasl, E., Kyle, R., MacLeod, A., Paxton, D., Rosenwasser, P., & Sartor, L. (2000). *Cooperative inquiry as a strategy for facilitating perspective transformation.* Retrieved on August 2, 2001, from http://www.iconoclastic.net/eccw/papers/barlasetal2000b.pdf.

Bray, J. (2002). Uniting teacher learning: Collaborative inquiry for professional development. *New Directions for Adult and Continuing Education*, 94, 83–92. doi:10.1002/ace.62

Chin, S. (2010). I am a human being, and I belong to the world: Narrating the intersection of spirituality and social identity. *Journal of Transformative Education*, 2(27), 27–42.

Cox, T. H., & Blake, S. (1991). Managing cultural diversity: Implications for organizational competitiveness. *The Academy of Management Executive, 5*(3).

Drago-Severson, E. (2009). *Leading adult learning: Supporting adult development in our schools.* Thousand Oaks, CA: Corwin Press.

Ernst, C., & Yip, J. (2008). Bridging boundaries: Meeting the challenge of workplace diversity. *Leadership in Action, 28*(1), 3–6. doi:10.1002/lia.1232

Fisher, D., & Torbert, W. R. (1995). *Personal and organizational transformations.* London, UK: McGraw-Hill.

Fisher-Yoshida, B., & Geller, K. (2009). *Transnational leadership development.* New York, NY: American Management Association.

Gibbons, M., Limoges, C., Nowotny, H., Schwartzman, S., Scott, P., & Trow, M. (1994). *The new production of knowledge: The dynamics of science and research in contemporary societies.* London, UK: Sage.

Heifetz, R., & Laurie, D. (1996). The work of leadership. *Harvard Business Review.* Retrieved on August 4, 2001, from http://mowgli.org.uk/wp-content/uploads/2011/02/laurie-jump-off-balcony-leadership.pdf.

Heron, J. (1992). *Feeling and personhood: Psychology in another key.* Newbury Park, CA: Sage.

Heron, J. (1999). *The complete facilitator's handbook.* London, UK: Kogan Page.

Herriot, P., & Pemberton, C. (1995). *Competitive advantage through diversity: Organizational learning from difference.* London, UK: Sage Publications.

Hunter, W. D. (2004). *Knowledge, skills, attitudes, and experience necessary to become globally competent.* Doctorial Dissertation. Bethlehem, PA: Lehigh University.

Irving, J. (2009). Educating global leaders: Exploring intercultural competence in leadership education. *Journal of International Business and Cultural Studies.* Retrieved on July 2, 2011, from http://aabri.com/manuscripts/09392.pdf.

Kasl, E., & Yorks, L. (2002). An extended epistemology for transformative learning theory and its application through collaborative inquiry. *TCRecordOnline.* Retrieved on January 30, 2011 from http://www.tcrecord.org/Content.asp?ContentID=10878.

Kegan, R. (1982). *The evolving self: Problems and process in human development.* Cambridge, MA: Harvard University Press.

Kegan, R. (1994). *In over our heads: The mental demands of modern life.* Cambridge, MA: Harvard University Press.

Laiken, M. (2002). *Managing the action/reflection polarity through dialogue: A path to transformative learning.* NALL Working Paper #53. Retrieved on August 4, 2011, from http://www.nall.ca/res/53MarilynLaiken.pdf.

Maltbia, T. E. (2001). *The journey of becoming a diversity practitioner: The connection between experience, learning, and competence.* Ed.D. Dissertation. New York, NY: Columbia.

Maltbia, T. E., & Power, A. (2009). *A leader's guide to leveraging diversity: Strategic learning capabilities for breakthrough performance.* Oxford, UK: Elsevier.

Marsick, V. J., & Watkins, K. E. (1999). *Facilitating learning organizations: Making learning count.* Aldershot, UK: Gower.

Merriam, S., & Ntseane, G. (2008). Transformational learning in Botswana: How culture shapes the process. *Adult Education Quarterly, 58*(183), 183–197. doi:10.1177/0741713608314087

Mezirow, J. (2000). *Learning as transformation.* San Francisco, CA: Jossey-Bass.

Nicolaides, A. (2008). *Learning their way through ambiguity: Explorations of how nine developmentally mature adults make sense of ambiguity.* Ed.D. Dissertation. New York, NY: Columbia.

O'Neil, J. A., & Marsick, V. J. (2007). *Understanding action learning.* New York, NY: AMACOM.

Olson, C. L., & Kroeger, K. R. (2001). Global competency and intercultural sensitivity. *Journal of Studies in International Education, 5*(2), 116–137. doi:10.1177/102831530152003

Ospina, S., El Hadidy, W., & Hofmann-Pinilla, A. (2008). Cooperative inquiry for learning and connectedness. *Action Learning Research and Practice, 5*(2), 131–147. doi:10.1080/14767330802185673

Ottley, A. H., Rosser-Mims, D., & Palmer, G. (2011). *The growing influence of spirituality in adult education: New opportunities to reach the adult learner.* PowerPoint Presentation. Retrieved on July 30, 2011, from http://www.indwes.edu/Search/?q=the%20growing%20influence%20of%20spirituality.

Oyler, J. D., & Pryor, M. G. (2009). Workplace diversity in the United States: The perspective of Peter Drucker. *Journal of Management History, 15*(4), 420–451. doi:10.1108/17511340910987338

Pritchard, C., & Sanders, P. (2002). Weaving our stories as they weave us. In Yorks, L., & Kasl, E. (Eds.), *Collaborative Inquiry as a Strategy for Adult Learning: Creating Space for Generative Learning.* San Francisco, CA: Jossey-Bass. doi:10.1002/ace.60

Reason, P. (2002). *Action research.* PowerPoint Presentation. Retrieved on May 19, 2011, from http://shsfaculty.swan.ac.uk/EmrysJenkins/Action%20Research/Power-point%20shows/Menu-web.htm.

Rosenwasser, P. (2002). Exploring internalized oppression and healing strategies. In L. Yorks & E. Kasl (Eds.), *Collaborative Inquiry as a Strategy for Adult Learning: Creating Space for Generative Learning.* San Francisco, CA: Jossey-Bass.

Scott, C. L. (2010). Preface. In Scott, C. L. (Ed.), *Leveraging Diversity: Multiple Settings, professions, Strategies and Theoretical Frameworks.* Geneva, Switzerland: Interscience Enterprises Ltd.

Smith, L. L. (2002). Using the power of collaborative inquiry: Community women learn and lead themselves. In L. Yorks & E. Kasl (Eds.), *Collaborative Inquiry as a Strategy for Adult Learning: Creating Space for Generative Learning.* San Francisco, CA: Jossey-Bass.

Thomas, R. R. Jr. (1991). *Beyond race and gender: Unleashing the power of your total work force by managing diversity.* New York, NY: American Management Association.

Tisdell, E. J. (2003). *Exploring spirituality and culture in adult and higher education.* San Francisco, CA: Jossey-Bass Publishers.

Tisdell, E. J., & Tolliver, D. E. (2003). Claiming a scared face: The role of spirituality and cultural identity in transformative adult higher education. *Journal of Transformative Education, 1*(4), 368–392. doi:10.1177/1541344603257678

Torbert, B. (2004). *Action inquiry: The secret of timely and transforming leadership.* San Francisco, CA: Berrett-Koehler.

Treleaven, L. (1994). Making a space: Collaborative inquiry as staff development. In P. Reason (Ed.), *Participation in Human Inquiry,* (pp. 138-162). London, UK: Sage. Retrieved from http://www.peterreason.eu/Participationinhumaninquiry/CHAP9.htm.

Van Stralen, S. (2002). Making sense of one's experience in the workplace. In Yorks, L., & Kasl, E. (Eds.), *Collaborative Inquiry as a Strategy for Adult Learning: Creating Space for Generative Learning*. San Francisco, CA: Jossey-Bass. doi:10.1002/ace.55

Watkins, K. E., & Marsick, V. J. (1993). *Sculpting the learning organization*. San Francisco, CA: Jossey-Bass.

Watkins, K. E., & Marsick, V. J. (Eds.). (1996). *In action: Creating the learning organization*. Alexandria, VA: ASTD Press.

Wentling, R. M., & Palma-Rivas, N. (1998). Current status and future trends of diversity initiatives in the workplace: Diversity experts' perspective. *Human Resource Development Quarterly*, *9*, 235–253. doi:10.1002/hrdq.3920090304

Yorks, L. (2005). Adult learning and the generation of new knowledge and meaning: Creating liberating spaces for fostering adult learning through practitioner based collaborative inquiry. *Teachers College Record*, *12*, 9–25.

Yorks, L., & Kasl, E. (2002a). Toward a theory and practice for whole-person learning: Reconceptualizing experience and the role of affect. *Adult Education Quarterly*, *52*(3), 176–192.

Yorks, L., & Kasl, E. (2002b). Collaborative inquiry as a strategy for adult learning. *New Directions for Adult and Continuing Education*, 94.

Zelman, A. W. (1995). Answering the question: How is learning experienced through collaborative inquiry? A phenomenological/hermeneutic approach. *Dissertation Abstracts International*, *7*(56), 2534.

KEY TERMS AND DEFINITIONS

Adaptive Challenges: Complex and ambiguous problems or opportunities that are often systemic with no readily understood answers (Heifetz & Laurie, 1996).

Collaborative Inquiry: A systematic process of action and reflection adopted by co-learners to investigate an agreed upon and meaningful topic or question (Ospina, El Hadidy, & Hofmann-Pinilla, 2008).

Developmental Capacity: The ability to use our internal resources (affective and cognitive) in complex ways so we can better manage the demands of life (Drago-Severson, 2009; Kegan, 1982).

Diversity: Includes inborn characteristics, personal experiences, education, organizational dimensions, and personal style. It is inclusive and incorporates lifestyle, sexual preference, geographic origin, and work experience (Maltbia & Powers, 2009; Scott, 2010; Thomas, 1991).

Global Competencies: Having knowledge and perceptual understanding as well as intercultural communications skills that assist one in interacting with the global and interdependent world (Olson & Kroeger, 2011).

Habit of Being: A holistic process for making meaning about and relating to the world (Yorks & Kasl, 2002a).

Informational Learning: Gaining knowledge and abilities (Drago-Severson, 2009).

Paradox of Diversity: The competing processes of diversity work including high potential for conflict and high potential for innovation, understanding, and creativity (Fisher-Yoshida & Geller, 2009; Yorks & Kasl, 2002a).

Spirituality: Personal beliefs, values, and experiences about a higher power or higher purpose. Connecting to something greater than ones self. Feeling interconnected to all things and fostering a more holistic identity (Chin, 2010; Tisdell & Tolliver, 2003).

Transformational Learning: Developing cognitive, emotional, interpersonal, and intrapersonal capacities that allow a person to manage the complexities of life. It has the potential to "shift" how a person actively interprets and understands his/her experiences and the world around him/her (Drago-Severson, 2009).

Ways of Knowing: One's individual perspective of a topic and/or the world including one's cognitive, affective, and relational capacity to make sense of phenomenon. It is about how a person makes meaning of his/her inner life and external experiences. It includes propositional, presentational, experiential, and practical Ways of Knowing (Drago-Severson, 2009; Heron, 1992; Kegan, 1982; Mezirow, 2000; Yorks & Kasl, 2002a).

ENDNOTE

[1] Diversity Divas is the name adopted by a collaborative inquiry group for purposes of group publication. Listed alphabetically the group consists of Maria Liu Wong, Naya Mondo, Ramona T. Sharpe, Aimee Tiu Wu, Connie Watson, Rosie Williams

Section 2
Leveraging Workforce Diversity and Leadership

Chapter 7
Leadership's Role in Leveraging Workforce Diversity

Norma Carr-Ruffino
San Francisco State University, USA

ABSTRACT

The purpose of this chapter is to examine some key trends in the workplace and marketplace that require successful corporate leaders to leverage workforce diversity. Such diversity poses certain challenges, which leaders can tackle and turn into lucrative opportunities to enhance not only productivity, sales, revenues, profits, brand, and reputation, but also the innovation so necessary for corporate survival. At the national level, the ability to compete in a global marketplace depends on successful innovation and has been a key driver of American eminence in the world. At the global level, innovation can empower people to move beyond fear of the future to actually shape their future; for example, we are currently seeing how technological innovations, such as cell phones and the Internet, are empowering people in the Middle East. The ability to understand and connect with people from diverse cultures also generates major opportunities to create peaceful relations as well as material abundance.

INTRODUCTION AND BACKGROUND

e pluribus unum—motto of the United States

The purpose of this chapter is to examine why leaders should leverage workforce diversity. We will explore many reasons, but perhaps the most powerful reason is that increased diversity, properly leveraged, can lead to greater innovation and wealth. At the corporate level, innovation has become essential to survival. At the national level, the ability to compete in a global marketplace depends on successful innovation and has been a key driver of American eminence in the world (Van der Vegt, 2003; Hong & Page, 2004). At the global level, innovation can empower people to move beyond fear of the future to actually shaping their future; for example, we are currently seeing how technological innovations, such as cell phones and the Internet, are empowering people in the Middle East. The ability to understand and connect with people from diverse cultures also generates major opportunities to create peaceful relations as well as material abundance.

DOI: 10.4018/978-1-4666-1812-1.ch007

Key trends in the workplace and marketplace make it essential that leaders learn how to leverage workforce diversity. Such diversity itself poses certain challenges, which leaders can tackle and even turn into advantages. More important, diversity offers lucrative opportunities for leaders to enhance not only corporate innovation, but also productivity, sales, revenues, profits, brand, and reputation (Hartenian & Gudmundson, 2000; Harvey, 1999; Richard, 2000).

KEY DIVERSITY TRENDS

The first step in leveraging the benefits to be reaped from a diverse workforce is to identify the key diversity trends that are affecting organizations and that are likely to impact their future (Fullerton & Tossi, 2001). The following trends highlight the areas that can shed light on this endeavor.

The first and most important trend is the dramatic increase in workplace diversity. More and more people from diverse groups are filling positions at all hierarchal levels of organizations. Diversity of ethnicity, gender, sexual orientation, age, and level of ability/disability, for example, is an increasingly substantial factor in the workplace. Traditionally Euro-American men constituted the large majority of workplace employees, especially in the better-paying, upwardly mobile positions. Now they represent about one-third of all employees, and perhaps only one-sixth of new entrants seeking jobs for the first time (McCuiston, et al., 2004; Pew, 2010; BLS, 2005; US Census Bureau, 2011).

The second trend is the higher expectations these diverse employees have for their jobs and careers. Expecting them to be grateful for anything they get from the organization is likely to alienate them. It is true that men of European ancestry have run virtually all the major American organizations, and they still dominate top management positions in the large corporations. They typically have set the rules of the game in the American culture and most corporate cultures. Employees from other groups were usually excluded from mainstream leadership roles. They worked on the periphery of our organizations as the workers who were told what to do and how to do it, as temporary employees and part-timers. Some were kept out completely—the unemployed and unemployable (US Glass Ceiling Commission, 1991, 1995).

Since the passage of civil rights laws and related legislation affecting workplace opportunities, members of previously excluded groups have gained higher levels of education and experience. Their higher career expectations are different from those of previous generations. Because diverse persons represent two-thirds of the population and five-sixths of new job applicants, leaders looking for qualified employees must be responsive to these heightened needs and aspirations. (BLS, 2009, 2011; Salomon & Schork, 2003).

Third, most companies now must sell to diverse market segments. The increasingly diverse U.S. workforce reflects the diversity of the U.S. population at large and the resulting growth in the market segments that these people represent. Businesses that want to survive and thrive learn how to market to diverse customers: women, Latino Americans, African Americans, Asian Americans, American Indians, and others. Companies with a workforce that "looks like America" have an advantage. They can project a multicultural image, deliver more on-target marketing insights, and relate better to a diverse customer base (Celent, 2003; MPA, 2008).

Fourth, most companies do business in the global marketplace these days. In the past most American businesses functioned primarily within U.S. borders. Now even very small businesses may do much of their business in global markets, which are intensely competitive (Hartenian, 2000). Success in those markets often depends on building positive, productive relationships with people from many cultures around the planet (McCuiston, 2007; Richard, 2000). Qualified employees from diverse cultural backgrounds are more crucial than ever for providing the diverse people skills that companies need in order to compete globally (Hong & Page, 2004; Harvey, 2003; Stevens, 2003).

Fifth, most companies must innovate in order to survive. The fast-paced global marketplace of the 21st century is networked, connected, changing moment by moment, and spewing out new products and services and processes by the thousands every day. In fact, most large American companies introduce more than one new product a day. Obviously, businesses must continually innovate in order to compete—and the pace keeps speeding up. If a company falls too far behind, it will die (Friedman, 2007).

The best CEOs and their consultants say that the United States must continue to lead the world in creativity and innovation—because they are the lifeblood of business success. "What's next?" is therefore the ongoing cry of the marketplace. Is it in cloud computing? nanotech? genomics?" These CEOs must have leaders, teams, and employees with the creative skills to contribute to the innovative process (Brown, 2009; Howkins, 2002; Sutton, 2002).

At IBM, innovation is the "outcome of a defined process of inclusion that is nurtured specifically for the purpose of enabling many" (Rao, et al., 2009, p. 1). This is a recognition that the most innovative teams tend to be widely diverse (Kelley, 2005). Diverse teams have a greater chance of coming up with unique ideas, according to many research studies (Hong & Page, 2004; Mayo, 1999). Firms that are most innovative try to hire for diversity in terms of culture, ethnicity, geography, age, gender, and fields or disciplines. Leaders have an economic interest in promoting diversity and reducing class divides. Successful leaders aim to tap the creativity of all diverse groups and to ensure that all are integrated into a multicultural workplace (Saloman & Schork, 2003; Van der Vegt, et al., 2005).

Finally, multicultural organizations are the ones attracting the best talent. Diverse employees expect more accommodation to their needs and identities than in the past. Fewer employees are willing to compromise their unique characteristics for the sake of "fitting in" with corporate cultures built exclusively on traditional Euro-American male values and norms still found in many corporations (Halter, 2000; Cox, 2001).

Multicultural organization have shaped their corporate cultures to be open, flexible, appreciative of diversity, and savvy about cultural and lifestyle differences. Having diverse employees at all levels in all functional areas enhances their competitive edge—and is becoming ever more crucial for success and profitability as reliance on innovation and global transactions increases (Council, 2001). Such organizations are overcoming the challenges that workforce diversity presents.

DIVERSITY CHALLENGES

The United States will find it far more difficult to maintain its competitive edge if it excludes those who are able and willing to help us compete. Bill Gates, Microsoft founder.

The major leadership challenge these days is how to meet the needs of the entire range of diverse employees in order to attract and retain the best and the brightest—and to bring out the best in them. For many employees, the primary career barriers are an incompatible corporate culture and the resulting systems and practices that exclude women and "minorities," thus blocking career progress. For leaders, the challenges include creating and implementing needed changes. In this section we will discuss the major types of diversity challenges that leaders must face and resolve in order to leverage diversity.

The first and most basic challenge stems from corporate cultures that alienate diverse persons. The corporate culture is the heart and soul of the organization. The basic beliefs and values of the culture determine all other aspects, such as policies, systems, procedures, programs, and practices. To many diverse employees, the corporate culture seems unfriendly and stressful (ELC, 2005; Lancaster, 1997).

At higher levels, diverse employees may be dramatically outnumbered by Euro-American men who treat them "differently," exclude them from social events and friendly camaraderie, and may view them as a curiosity (Kanter, 1991). Some of these newcomers sometimes report that the "insiders" watch them closely, over-scrutinize their work for mistakes, withhold information, and even sabotage their work. They say they must be better than the insiders just to keep up. Others say that when they cluster with employees from their own diversity group, they may be jokingly or seriously accused of plotting against the dominant group, being divisive, or excluding others. If they remain isolated, they may be seen as resentful or weird. If they try to join the insiders, they may be met with stereotyping or rejection (Carr-Ruffino, 1991; Graves, 1997).

The second challenge, therefore, is dealing with organizational systems and practices that ignore, neglect, and exclude diverse employees. Clearly, an organizational culture that supports or allows such practices calls for change. The most lasting and workable changes in the firm's systems and practices flow naturally from a commitment to corporate culture change. One reason affirmative action programs had such difficulty in the past is that leaders rarely built them upon a commitment to corporate culture change. Once this commitment is made by a critical mass of employees, changing the systems and practices becomes much easier (Bregman, 2009; Kravitz, 2007).

When the Korn Ferry Institute (2008) studied reasons why diverse professionals and managers leave organizations, it found that people of color were three times more likely to leave than Euro-Americans, and gay persons were twice as likely to leave. The types of unfairness they mentioned most often were:

- Being asked to attend extra recruiting or community-related events because of one's race, gender, religion, or sexual orientation
- Being passed over for a promotion due to one's personal characteristics
- Being publicly humiliated
- Being compared to a terrorist in a joking or serious manner

The third challenge is historical exclusion of diverse employees from "insider" status. Employees function most effectively when they perceive they are included in the organization's "inner circle." However, the inner circle of most large corporations was traditionally reserved for qualified Euro-American men because American culture harbored the belief that Euro-American men are the ones that should take the lead role in all arenas of power.

A fourth challenge is networking barriers that diverse employees find in some organizations. Many are unable to create and manage the networks of people who are essential to career success. Crucial information to be gleaned from such networks includes emerging industry trends, where the company is headed, and what is happening in company politics (Cox, 1993; Carr-Ruffino, 1991).

A fifth challenge is when conflict among subcultural groups creates another barrier to their success. When one underrepresented group competes with another for privileges, status, and power, infighting can occur and create a barrier for all. Managers have been known to use divide-and-conquer tactics to increase friction and infighting among diverse subgroups. Hate crime statistics indicate that backlash and infighting are problems in society at large, not just in organizations (FBI, 2009). The growing diversity in the population has increased inter-ethnic tension. In the workplace, leaders and managers have the greatest power to either inflame or to reduce such conflict (Lau, 2005; Cox, 2001).

A sixth and very important challenge occurs when Euro-American men in the organization resist the corporate culture changes so necessary to leveraging diversity. These traditional leaders in the business world usually hold the key to the changes needed to open the doors for people from other groups. Change leaders must therefore address Euro-American male concerns, which may relate to affirmative action backlash issues (Hebl, et al., 2008; Smither, et al., 1996). Such men may:

- fear that the firm might need to lower performance standards and quality
- fear that they will suffer from reverse discrimination
- fear the erosion of their income and job security
- feel a threat to existing social relationships or to old routines, rules, and habits
- worry that existing power relationships will change, leading to uncertainty
- dislike risk and be unwilling to experiment with the change that managing diversity requires
- stereotype people in outgroups and feel prejudiced toward them
- believe in the melting pot, that people should adapt to the current corporate culture
- suspect that any new diversity approach is an effort to sneak AA in through the back door
- believe they don't have the time or energy to deal with yet another initiative
- fail to see how managing diversity can help them achieve their goals, rather than being a distraction
- fail to see how a multicultural approach can be an effective tool for empowering employees

- fail to see how managing diversity can affect the success of their team or department

Open hostility and harassment are obvious forms of resistance. More subtle forms include different expectations of diverse persons, fewer informal ties to them, and facial expressions that signal exclusion. Such subtle discrimination can be even more insidious because it is more difficult to confront and resolve. Results for the targeted persons may include decreased emotional commitment, job satisfaction, and helping behaviors, as well as increased job stress and motivation to change jobs (Hebl, 2008; Davidson & Proudford, 2008).

A seventh challenge is the career development patterns typical of diverse employees. Euro-American men are often reluctant to assign nontraditional managers to those challenging, high-profile jobs that are needed to prepare people for senior management positions because they doubt diverse persons' potential abilities. Such assignments include leading a major start-up, troubleshooting (sometimes overseas), serving on important task forces, taking a headquarters staff job, and taking line jobs of increasing responsibility. They involve autonomy, visibility, access to senior management, and control over significant resources. They are considered the fast track in many organizations and may be used as tests and rewards for high-potential candidates. Such career-enhancing assignments are often not available to diverse employees, who tend to be found in staff rather than line positions (Catalyst, 2006; BLS, 2011).

The ultimate career barrier is the Glass Ceiling issue. The U.S. Glass Ceiling Commission reported in 1991, and again in 1995, that women and minority managers eventually hit a "glass ceiling" that is invisible until they realize that it is blocking them from top management positions in most large firms. The U.S. Bureau of Labor Statistics (BLS, 2011) reported that in 2010 about 30 percent of corporate middle management consisted of women, African Americans, and Latino Americans. However people from these groups made up less than 5 percent of senior management, even though they are about 65 percent of the workforce—meaning that 95 percent of top jobs in large corporations are still held by Euro-American men. Clearly, the glass ceiling still exists.

Finally, a challenge for change leaders, once a plan for leveraging diversity is underway, is how to avoid some typical change traps (Terry, 1990):

- Believing there is one best way. Solution: focus on the end result; the paths leading there may be many.
- Adopting a label, such as "diversity manager" or "change agent" but avoiding the real struggle. Solution: Get everyone involved in this effort.
- Assuming that everyone can comprehend and accept the new ideas. Solution: Deal with people according to where they are in their own development and take it one step at a time.
- Focusing only on the *reasons* change is needed or only on change *actions* themselves. Solution: Focus both on the actions needed *and* the reasons why.
- Holding Euro-American men responsible for solving exclusion problems. Solution: Get *all* stakeholders deeply involved in any solution.
- Becoming self-righteous about personal progress. Solution: Realize that even the most progressive among us can improve, and even the least progressive must start somewhere.
- Believing we have a choice about whether to change or not. Solution: Change is inevitable and constant, so people must change or be left behind.

These challenges to leveraging diversity center on organizational barriers to success for diverse employees, mostly stemming from traditional Euro-American male-centric corporate cultures. Change leaders therefore must understand the organizational culture and the barriers it may have erected. Such understanding can be a more important qualification for leadership than formal degrees, according to several surveys. In fact, courses and degrees may be less relevant to success in the executive suite than they once were because most programs omit the "soft skills" (Nancheria, 2009; i4CP, 2009). Other studies indicate that a key barrier has been Euro-American male reluctance to share power and privilege and their natural tendency to associate with people like themselves (Cox, 2001; Carr-Ruffino, 1991). Savvy leaders know it's time to break this cycle by giving everyone an equal chance. They are turning instead toward opportunities to leverage diversity.

OPPORTUNITIES TO LEVERAGE DIVERSITY

Leadership opportunities for successfully leveraging a diverse workplace are based on creating an inclusive organizational culture, where the "best and brightest" can thrive. The culture must be expanded to include important aspects of all the sub-cultures represented by employee groups. Once the organization's leaders adopt this multicultural approach, they can begin to modify corporate systems and practices so that all employees are included in the inner circle. Greater diversity offers great opportunities for the organization to leverage diversity in several ways.

First is the opportunity to create an inclusive corporate culture. Leadership opportunities for successfully managing a diverse workplace are all based on creating an inclusive organizational culture. The beliefs and values of an organization form its worldview and its mission in the world. These are the heart and soul of any organization. That is why change must start here. Organizations that ignore these basics—and start the change process with new programs or practices or even policies—cannot achieve optimal results. Surface-level, tacked-on programs soon fade away. Real, sustainable change must emanate from the heart, i.e. corporate culture (Bregman, 2009; McClenahen, 2005). Leaders can take on the role of corporate culture shape-shifter, working on key elements of the culture.

Beliefs and values, therefore, are the most basic aspect of changing the culture. Leaders can learn to adopt a worldview that sees "minority" persons as just as valuable and important as "majority" persons. For example, leaders can express their beliefs that diverse persons should be fairly valued, appreciated, recognized, and rewarded—and act on such beliefs.

Organizational heroes and heroines—the stars or champions of stories, legends, and myths that ripple through the networks and grapevines—should include diverse employees as well as Euro-American men. Leaders can begin to notice and reward these high achievers as role models of success. They can begin to tell stories about these new role models, and their ways of succeeding in an inclusive organization. Diverse stars can become the stuff of legend and myth, along with the traditional heroes. This is one way that the rituals and ceremonies—the ways of doing things and ways of interacting with each other—are expanded and become more flexible, so that they include customs that are typical of all the groups and that recognize people from all groups.

Then there are the organizational symbols—those shortcuts that signal significant meaning to everyone—which can be modified. Slogans, mottoes, and other symbols can be expanded so that they reflect people from all the groups and communicate an inclusive, multicultural worldview.

All these corporate culture changes can be thought of as expanding the culture, not as eliminating important aspects. When the corporate culture is broad and flexible enough for people from all the major groups to feel comfortable, members experience the freedom to be authentic, to express who they really are (Moss & Tilley, 2003).

A second opportunity is to adopt an inclusive multicultural approach that allows all employees to function with a sense of authenticity. They can be their best selves. A successful multicultural approach must be all-inclusive and must deal with employees as individuals, taking into account their cultural and experiential background against the backdrop of a diverse society. The inclusive approach is a diversity-within-unity approach (Cox, 2001). A key point: no one is a perfect reflection of his or her culture, so never use what you learn about cultural values and customs to assume that a person agrees with a particular cultural aspect. For example, a cultural belief may be that women belong in the home, not the workplace, but an individual woman may see this as nonsense (Chrobot, 2004).

Leaders can find ways to signal respect for the unique characteristics of another's culture. Small gestures can communicate respect, such as greeting persons in their native language, taking time to chat and learn more about a person, becoming aware of how the culture and the individual view sharing various types of personal information, and keeping a person's cultural and personal values in mind as you work together. Doing this effectively requires learning about diverse groups and building skills in relating to individual group members (Council, 2001; Bacharach, et al., 2005). Leaders can provide the types of diversity training needed for all employees at all levels to leverage this opportunity.

When people feel free to retain those distinctive and colorful ways that they treasure in their cultural heritage, the organization is enriched. Each individual decides those aspects of the culture's beliefs, stories, rituals, language, art, and cuisine that they want to hold dear and to express. This actually makes them more interesting and valuable to the whole organization and to society. They "prevent drab standardization in a culture dominated by advertising, brand names, malls, and sedative television" (Cox, 2001, p. 226). And, people feel free to contribute their unique viewpoints and ideas in pursuit of innovative endeavors.

A third opportunity is to build on equal opportunity principles. While a multicultural approach goes beyond Affirmative Action (AA) programs, it does not ignore equal opportunity principles or abandon AA programs. It does build on lessons business leaders have learned about how to make AA work most effectively for all groups (Harrison, et al., 2006; Carr-Ruffino, 1992).

For example, leaders can review the company's AA program to see if it needs revitalizing. Critical questions to ask include: Is it comprehensive enough? Does it have widespread support among the workforce, or does it cause conflict and resentment? Is it being energetically implemented? Are all its elements up to par? Leaders who have learned to manage AA effectively say that they 1) set high but realistic AA goals, 2) identify real job requirements and standards, not idealistic ones, 3) encourage an achiever self-concept and promote employee self-efficacy, 4) use leadership, not coercion, to get participation in all aspects of the program, and 5) focus on individuals, with awareness of "minority" backgrounds.

A fourth opportunity is to align corporate systems and practices with a multicultural approach to establishing an inclusive culture. If all the leaders are committed to creating unity-with-diversity, *e pluribus unum*, then people at all levels are likely to buy in. Leaders can include unity issues when they conduct a diversity audit to see what's needed. Then they have the basis for developing and implementing a plan that coordinates all major systems and practices (Eisenberger, et al., 1990).

A fifth opportunity is that of including all employees in innovative, bottom-line efforts. New multicultural systems and practices will naturally aim to include all employees in important projects that contribute to the firm's bottom-line success. Most people prefer feeling like a corporate insider rather than outsider, a winner rather than a loser, one whose ideas are valued.

People get excited about "Big I" innovations, those dramatic breakthroughs, decisive victories, and clear "wins" that are so impressive. But "little-i" innovations are easier to come by and can add up to big profits. They are the stuff of continuous improvement, which always leads to continuous learning for the diverse teams that are involved (Ely & Thomas, 2001; Mannix & Neal, 2005). An added bonus: diverse teams working together toward important common goals inevitably get to know each other at deeper levels, beyond stereotypes, and build powerful relationships (Dovidio, et al., 2003; Harrison, et al., 2006; Phillips, et al., 2009; Ponterotto & Pederson, 1993; Vescio, et al., 2003).

A sixth opportunity is to identify any resistance to these needed organizational changes and to develop the diversity training needed to resolve and prevent such problems. Resistance typically involves fear of losing the status quo, intergroup anxiety, and denial of the need for change. Change leaders can introduce effective training for all employees at all levels. Basic training should include the myths versus realities about the potential abilities of employees from the various diverse groups. Training should be required and ongoing in order to update and reinforce the basic training (Holladay, et al., 2003; Kidder, et al., 2004; Thomas, 2008).

Finally, a seventh opportunity is to build consensus for change across the spectrum of employees in order to successfully implement the multicultural approach. While the commitment of top management is the first step, lasting change requires the consensus of a critical mass of employees (Vescio, et al., 2003). Leaders can identify those factors that already motivate people toward change and build upon them. They can anticipate some typical types of resistance and change traps in order to defuse them. A good strategy is to designate certain people to serve as conscious change agents, who will influence others toward positive change. If change leaders want their organizations to change and are willing to devote the energy needed to do it, they can make remarkable progress in overcoming resistance and building consensus.

Organizations that meet diversity challenges head-on and leverage opportunities that diversity offers are reaping many benefits. They are developing corporate cultures that value relationships between teammates, customers, and suppliers, and the information that flows among them, as the lifeblood of the organization (Chatman & Flynn, 2001; Dahlin, et al., 2005). Such corporate cultures are increasingly built upon trust, collaboration, cooperation, and teamwork. In such organizations, it's more obvious than ever that people are the most valuable resource. How they work together creates either energy and innovation or lethargy and demoralization. Their interactions can spark the knowledge and information that fuel organizational growth and success. Leveraging workforce diversity actually begins with shaping the corporate culture to fit its diverse members. It culminates in reapring the many benefits of managing diversity well.

BENEFITS OF LEVERAGING DIVERSITY THROUGH ACTIVE LEADERSHIP

Business leaders who are achieving some success at leveraging diversity tend to use an active, change-oriented multicultural approach. Research studies point to benefits for the organization as well as its employees, suppliers, and customers. In this section we describe at least nine types of business advantage, ranging from attracting the best human talent to achieving organization objectives, including the profit objective.

The first benefit of leveraging diversity is that it helps the organization to attract and retain the best human talent. Talented people from across the whole range of diverse groups want to work with inclusive multicultural organizations. Perhaps the major benefit of effectively managing a diverse workforce is this ability to attract and retain the best talent available.

Attracting the best employees is challenging because most young employees want work that is meaningful to them, work that makes a contribution and brings a sense of fulfillment. Most of them, especially career women, expect to have a personal and family life and are less willing than were older generations to sacrifice a well-rounded life for career success. And most women and minority employees resist fitting into a Euro-American male corporate culture that requires them to squelch important parts of their persona. They need the comfort that comes with a sense of cultural fit (Deal, 2006).

The comfort factor is a feature of many research studies. When people are comfortable with others who are different and are able to build relationships across gender and cultural lines, the result is a more productive workplace (Harris & Kleiner, 1993; Council, 2001). Only when employees feel comfortable in their work environment are they motivated to work to their fullest potential (Freeman-Evans, 1994). In fact, employees who feel welcomed and valued become more passionate about their work (Salomon & Schork, 2003).

Retaining talented, high-potential employees is enhanced when leaders become truly committed to treating all employees fairly and to valuing diversity. Managers who appear to favor people from some demographic groups and to neglect people from minority groups, for example, risk paying the price of low productivity due to a restricted pool of applicants, employee dissatisfaction, lack of commitment, high turnover rates, and even sabotage. When diverse employees must consistently struggle to have their voices heard and their opinions valued, they eventually become exhausted—physically and emotionally. To them, the work environment seems hostile. These employees are more likely to quit their jobs because they see little hope for their future in the company (Salomon & Schork, 2003).

Employees who like the way they are treated are generally friendlier with their coworkers and managers. A key factor in holding onto talented employees is making sure they feel comfortable in the work environment, according to Patrick Council (2001), who says, "A diversified workforce allows people to socialize and relax with coworkers, which leads to higher job satisfaction and less employee turnover" (p. 22). Employees who feel comfortable and valued in the organization are likely to stay longer. One study of diverse persons who quit found that they probably would have stayed if their employer had offered better managers who recognized their abilities (Korn Ferry, 2008). Morris (2005) found that women are the largest group still being ignored in talent pools, despite research indicating they are just as hardworking and ambitious as men. Companies that gain a reputation for including, appreciating, and rewarding employees from all groups have the greatest success in attracting and retaining the best talent.

A second benefit of leveraging diversity is that the organization becomes more flexible, spontaneous, and nimble. When leaders of an organization develop multicultural skills and role model them to others, the company itself becomes better able to quickly adapt to shifting circumstances. Members can apply these diversity skills to working with coworkers as well as with people from other companies. For example, many companies form alliances with each other in order to pool their resources and to enhance their relationships with suppliers and customers. An alliance may require two teams or units from two different companies to blend together and serve as a link between the firms involved (Van den Steen, 2009). The most frequently cited source of problems with alliances is "different corporate cultures," according to a Harvard Business Review survey (Kanter, 1991).

The flexibility benefit has become more vital in recent years because companies must innovate and innovation requires flexibility. As a firm's products become commodities and competition to sell those products intensifies, the firm must create game-changing innovations. This cycle occurs over and over. Creative employees working in an innovative environment are essential for survival. Diversity breeds innovation; homogeneity does not. In a study conducted in 2003 at Northwestern University, 50 groups were asked to solve a murder mystery. Groups from varied social backgrounds did best. Homogeneous groups were more likely to get it wrong—and were more confident that their answers were right. The researchers concluded that if an organization wants creative ideas that contribute to good problem-solving and decision-making, a diversity of personality types works best (Phillips, et al., 2004; Gill, 2005). But how does an organization find the diversity it needs?

Flexibility is also necessary for finding the best talent. When managers are asked, "What is your greatest need?" most answer, "talented employees." In fact managers tend to constantly complain about how hard it is to find such applicants. Research indicates that when top managers say of a job candidate, "He'll be a great fit," they may mean, "He's someone who brings a needed talent." But they may also mean, "We like this person because he thinks like we do"; in other words, "He's likely to agree with us."

Hiring is one of most difficult tasks a manager faces, and the safest applicant often gets the job. This typically means someone with a background and personality similar to the Euro-American managers. This in turn can lead to a firm full of clones—at least in the main positions. Diversity of personality, sensibility, and work style are important too—and often reflect diverse cultural backgrounds (Gill, 2005). When making an important hire, managers must learn to focus on diversity of ethnicity, gender, and personality type—as well as on chemistry and fit. For example, in an organization of innovative achievers, a person with the ability and drive to change the game would normally fit well with the organization.

In fact, flexibility in hiring and promotion decisions can determine the level of investment capital an organization can attract. Research indicates that when leaders hire people who look and act like themselves, they risk losing venture capital funding. Savvy investors want to see that management will have people with a diversity of viewpoints and ideas, not a team of yes-persons (Gill, 2005). This diversity may mean that meetings are more boisterous and consensus is harder to come by. But arguments often spark new ideas. A certain amount of conflict is healthy, while too much can be detrimental, of course. In summary, a major benefit of managing diversity effectively is increased organization ability to be flexible, spontaneous, and nimble in responding to challenges and opportunities.

A third benefit is an improved reputation for social responsibility. The organization can become an agent for change, to make the world a better place by doing a great job at managing the diversity of all its stakeholders. And a good reputation can open many business doors. If one organization can thrive by creating an environment where diverse people can work effectively together, this can serve as a model for the entire world. A Los Angeles executive said, "In this area the situation is so desperate and so in need of role models, that if we in corporations can't advance minorities so they can turn around and do what needs to be done in their communities, I don't see any of us surviving. The bigger picture we have to deal with is the minority situation in this country" (Moss & Tilley, 2003, p. 238).

IBM's Chairman Samuel Palmisano said, "Businesses now operate in an environment in which long-standing concerns—in areas from diversity to equal opportunity, the environment and workforce policies—have been raised to the same level of public expectation as accounting practices and financial performance" (McClenahen, 2005, p. 2). Such indicators of corporate citizenship have become important to the general public.

A fourth benefit is the ability to increase market share. In fact, if a company wants to expand its share of local and global markets, it must learn how to manage diversity. For example, the combined purchasing power of the four major ethnic subcultural groups is huge and growing, as shown in Table 1. In 2002 it totaled about $1.45 trillion, in 2007 it was $2.25 trillion, and in 2010 it was $3.22 trillion, representing huge growth rates. By 2015, the purchasing power of these four groups is projected to be $4.68 trillion or about 25 percent of total U.S. expenditures of $18.72 trillion.

In 2006, the U.S. African American and Latino American consumer markets together were already larger than the entire economies of all but the 9 richest countries in the world. By 2010, the buying power of African Americans and Latino Americans exceeded the GDP of Canada, the ninth largest economy in the world.

Ethnic market niches are increasingly important; for example:

- **Ethnic personal care**—these areas were valued at $1.9 billion in 2007 (Millman, 2007).

Table 1. Purchasing power of US minorities

Ethnic Group	2002	2007	2010	Projected 2015
African Americans	$625 billion	$825 billion	$1.0 trillion	$1.5 trillion
American Indians	25	50	$ 68 billion	$90.4 billion
Asian Americans	225	450	$544 billion	$775 billion
Latino Americans	575	925	$1.0 trillion	$1.5 trillion
Total	**$1.45 trillion**	**$2.25 trillion**	**$3.22 trillion**	**$4.68 trillion**
Women all groups	*$5 trillion*	*n/a*	*$12 trillion*	*$15 trillion*

Source: Celent 2003; MPA 2008; Fahmy 2010

- **Telecommunications services**—33 percent of sales were to people of color, in 2007 (Insight, 2008).
- **Online retailing**—31 percent of Asian American consumers make at least five online purchases a year (MPA, 2008).
- **Business travel**—about half of business travelers are now women.

In fact, in 2002 women of all groups spent at least $5 trillion a year, over half the U.S. GDP. Several organizations estimate that women are actually responsible for about 80 percent of all consumer purchases—of everything from automobiles to healthcare, which would have been about $12 trillion in 2010 when total GDP was about $15 trillion. By 2015 women may be deciding on about $15 trillion worth of purchases in a total market of nearly $19 trillion (BCG, 2009; Silverstein, Sayre, & Butman, 2009).

The purchasing power of women and minorities has huge financial implications for virtually all businesses. If a company wants to understand these markets, it must depend on a diverse staff. It can reach untapped markets only if it has employees with the cultural experiences needed to sell effectively to those markets (Overell, 2004; Crockett, 1999; Segal, 1997). Diverse employees can help increase market share, boosting sales revenue and profits, when the company asks them to 1) identify diverse target markets, 2) contribute ideas for new products and services especially valuable to diverse groups, 3) advise on ways to represent and portray multicultural images that attract customers rather than offending them, 4) recommend approaches for selling to diverse targeted emergent markets, 5) show the company how to tap into the escalating purchasing power of diverse customers

Diverse employees tend to attract diverse customer segments. One reason is that diverse teams are more likely to produce products and services better tailored to diverse customers (Cox & Smolinski, 1994). For example, when experts assessed the problems that led to K-mart's bankruptcy, they concluded that K-mart had lost touch with its customer-base and failed to capitalize on multicultural markets that it once controlled. They suggested that K-mart place more emphasis on wooing consumers of color. Also, Avon discovered that when African American women are on the team, management is motivated to respond to growing market niches of African American women. In addition, customers tend to perceive that people of their own ethnicity or gender can best understand their needs, and this can influence them in choosing one service or product over another (Halter, 2000).

Tapping diverse employees to improve marketing skills within ethnically diverse domestic markets can help a company to market more effectively internationally, too. Learning how to be responsive to local markets and to project the right image there will help the company sharpen its skills for the international marketplace (Segal, 1997).

Diverse employees can help the organization to sidestep Public Relations (PR) problems. For example, diverse decision-making teams can help prevent PR problems that stem from not understanding the cultures of diverse customers, such as the following.

- A singing commercial that caused trouble: *Ay ay yay yay. I am the Frito bandito. I get Fritos corn chips. I steal them from you. I am the Frito Bandito.* Frito Lay was urged by the Mexican American community to halt this campaign because 1) the tune was based on the Mexican national anthem, and 2) the word "steal" implies that Mexicans are thieves.
- Some Manwich commercials showed a man eating a sandwich as he talked eagerly about something that typically excites women but not men, such as shopping, hairdo's, the theater. The man suddenly gets slapped around by a phantom hand, as a voiceover says, "It's called a Manwich."

A petition against the ad, on Change.org argued: "Violence against gender-non-conforming men and women is a serious problem in our country and should not be used for lazy jokes in advertising."

- A used car dealer's newspaper ad featured a woman posing rather provocatively along with this message to car buyers: "You know you're not the first. But do you really care?" Women's groups objected, saying the ad suggests that used vehicles are like "used women who've been around the block once or twice themselves."

- An American deodorant commercial showed an octopus putting antiperspirant under each of its eight arms. In Japan, octopus appendages are called "legs." When the commercial aired in Japan, people were puzzled to see an animal applying deodorant to its legs.

In summary, a diverse staff can prevent corporate actions that offend or confuse certain groups. They can promote actions that attract and keep diverse customers. Also, a diverse workforce provides a better image for an organization, making it a more attractive place to conduct business for a wide range of customers (Losey, 1993).

A fifth benefit of leveraging diversity is improved management effectiveness. For example, Euro-American male employees tend to perform better when ambitious minority newcomers join the competition, while the less competent performers are screened out. Also, managers who succeed in a diverse workplace learn fresh approaches to business problems; they learn how to see issues from new perspectives, and how to add diverse contacts to their business networks. Exposure to diverse colleagues can help managers develop breadth and openness. This in turn can actually boost their incomes. For example, even 15 or 20 years ago, Euro-American men who graduated from universities where African American students comprised 8 to 17 percent of the student body went on to earn roughly 15 percent higher wages than whose who graduated from "all-white" universities (Marshall, 1995).

In addition, much of what managers learn in training programs about how to treat diverse persons will also be broadly applied to all employees. For example, a major principle is to show appreciation for diverse employees' uniqueness and to respect their cultural values and customs. Such training establishes basic good human relations practices; all of us like to be appreciated for our uniqueness and to be treated with respect.

The multicultural approach to leveraging diversity enhances success in virtually every management area, including conflict resolution, negotiation, employee relationships, employee empowerment, leadership effectiveness, continuous improvement, continuous learning, innovation, productivity, total quality management, project teams, and trust building.

A sixth benefit is enrichment of team and corporate innovation efforts so essential to today's global, high-tech, networked economy. Post-industrial organizations, with their self-managing work teams, require creative thinking from the many rather than from the few in R&D departments. This is a huge shift from the corporate culture values of traditional assembly-line industrial organizations, which required creative thinking from only a few and typically resisted suggestions from most employees. Also, such Euro-American male corporate cultures expected women and minorities to change in order to adapt, thus failing to capitalize on the full creative potential of a diverse workforce. To leverage a diverse workforce toward innovative outcomes, leaders can learn how to create corporate cultures that promote innovation (Hong & Page, 2004).

The goal is to create environments where creativity and innovation can thrive. This effort is enhanced by diverse groups because they consist of people with different thoughts, attitudes, personalities, and experiences. Company cultures that are open to differences provide fertile ground for the growth of new ideas and innovations. When people feel comfortable communicating diverse viewpoints, the result is a larger pool of ideas that arise from members' various personalities and experiences. In a truly multicultural environment, people from diverse backgrounds feel respected, supported, and appreciated (Van der Vegt, et al., 2005). They are therefore willing to contribute their ideas to group sessions. This in turn provides the group with a broader range of diverse ideas to choose from, so group synergy is enhanced and groupthink is less likely (Chatman, 2001; Mayo, 1999). Diverse teams and organizations typically generate more options, especially more creative options and higher quality ideas—because opposing viewpoints are introduced and resolved (Nemeth, 1986; Cox, et al., 1991).

A diverse team is more likely to constantly hatch new ideas and to develop them in ways that think-alike teams never can. Research supports the belief that diverse teams enhance problem-solving, decision-making, and innovation. For example, one study concluded that higher-quality decisions are made when different solutions are evaluated and weighted (Mayo, 1999). Another showed that great decisions result from the merger of very different ideas (Salomon & Schork, 2003).

Chrysler VP James P. Holden said, "Teams become truly effective when they represent the full spectrum of diversity" (Mayo, 1999, p. 21). Raymond Gilmartin, CEO of Merck, states that "Competitive advantage in a business like ours rests on innovation. To succeed, we must bring together talented and committed people with diverse perspectives" (Salomon & Schork, 2003, p. 43).

A seventh benefit of leveraging diversity is saving on costs. A multicultural approach can save money in the long run and even in the short run. For example looking at short-term costs, women and minority employees quit their jobs more frequently than Euro-American male employees (Hom, 2007). In 2003, the median employee turnover rate was 12 percent for U.S. companies, according to the Bureau of National Affairs (2004), meaning that 12 of every 100 employees changed companies. Most companies aim to achieve much lower turnover rates in order to reduce costs.

The Korn Ferry Institute's (2008) study of reasons why diverse professionals and managers leave organizations revealed that U.S. companies lose more than $64 billion a year in turnover costs due solely to failed diversity management. In addition, the employees who walk away often discourage potential customers and job applicants from doing business with the company. Estimated costs of individual employee turnover vary from a few hundred dollars to four times the annual salary of the employee. On average, it costs a company one-third of a new hire's annual salary to replace an employee. Therefore, at minimum wage, the cost to replace an employee would be about $5,000; for an employee hired at $45,000, it would average $15,000 but could run as high as $180,000 (Mushrush, 2002).

Diversity efforts can reduce the high turnover rate of nontraditional employees and the costs that go with it. Jonathan Leonard and David Levine (2006) studied the effect of diversity in 800 workplaces and concluded that "Managers can benefit by helping employees thrive in a world of racial diversity—a prescription that is easier to state than to implement" (p. 569).

Long-range costs can result from endemic ongoing personnel problems, beginning with the implicit costs of job-related stress and low morale, racheting up to higher rates of absenteeism and turnover, leading to low productivity. Explicit costs add up when grievances and complaints are filed, and especially when lawsuits occur. For example, when companies such as Wal-Mart don't adequately manage diversity, they may end up paying dearly. The nation's largest employer, Wal-Mart has been fighting a class action suit by women employees for about 10 years; the case was appealed all the way to the Supreme Court. The women say they have consistently received lower wages and fewer promotions than men with comparable qualifications. Most settlements in such cases require companies to openly post job vacancies, to analyze all promotion and compensation decisions for potential bias, and to hold supervisors accountable for preventing discrimination (Olson, 2011). It makes sense for companies to take such actions *before* costly grievances and lawsuits are filed.

Lockheed Martin of Bethesda had to pay $2.5 million to an African American aviation electrician who said that Euro-American male coworkers harassed him with racial epithets and threatened him with bodily harm. They reportedly called him the N-word, and said, "We should do to blacks what Hitler did to the Jews," and "If the South had won, then this would be a better country." After he reported the harassment, the coworkers threatened to lynch him. Lockheed was criticized by the court for failing to discipline the harassers and allowing them to continue the discrimination during the African American's two-year tenure (Fears, 2008).

If management neglects such diversity issues, then once they set in, they are difficult to reverse. Savvy organization leaders take a proactive approach to appreciating diversity, managing it effectively, and nipping in the bud any disrespect or harassment.

A very important eighth benefit is ramping up employee productivity. All the benefits mentioned so far can work together to generally increase organizational productivity (Ely, 2000; Carpenter, 2002). Research indicates that groups that are diverse in terms of ethnicity, age, values, background, and training are more productive and innovative than homogeneous groups (Eisenberger, et al., 1990). A five-year research program, based on consultation with CEO's, revealed that diversity within a work team, if properly managed, will boost productivity and quality of output. Such diversity positively affects worker behavior, customer attitudes, productivity, and ultimately the bottom line (Harvey, 2003).

Diversity in senior management consistently correlates to superior corporate performance, ac-

cording to an American Management Association survey (AMA, 1999). The survey of more than 1,000 managers evaluated the impact of diversity on such performance measures as annual sales, gross revenues, market share, shareholder value, net operating profit, worker productivity, and total assets.

Smaller companies and service sector companies often have more women and minorities on senior management teams. They tend to report better organizational outcomes than larger companies and manufacturers. The communications industry—including telecommunications providers, broadcasters, and publishers—has senior management teams with more women and younger managers (33 percent compared to 21 percent for all industries). This industry is also far above average in increased sales, operating profits, and worker productivity (AMA, 1999).

Finally, all these benefits add up to the bottom line: increased profits, the reason business is in business, after all. Global competition is an established fact of life now, making it more challenging than ever for businesses to show a profit. The restructuring, re-engineering, and downsizing of the 1990s reflect the reality that United States business can no longer afford bureaucratic, hierarchical structures with a homogeneous group running the show (McCuiston, et al., 2004; Phillips, 2004). Businesses can no longer afford to pay layers of high-salaried managers to dole out company information and to set goals and make plans for workers and then try to motivate them and keep them productive. When employees can access needed information online, and when work teams can set their own goals and make their own plans, they are motivated to find ways to achieve them. Business can no longer afford to exclude people with the talents and skills so desperately needed for business success. All the benefits that talented diverse persons bring to the workplace can lead to increased company profits.

The need to leverage diversity is reflected in a study from Texas A & M University's Center of Retailing Studies. The conclusion: American retailers must understand the changing ethnic and cultural consumer market in order to survive (Stevens, 2003). Successfully engaging diversity in the marketplace is no longer an option for business. It's the key to economic survival. Studies show that firms with diverse top management teams get better financial returns by as much as 171 percent (Hartenian, 2000). Organizations today have little choice but to diversify in order to remain profitable and sustain a competitive advantage (Harvey, 1999; Richard, 2000).

CONCLUSION

Leaders who can read the key trends know that they must deal with ever-increasing workplace diversity. While leading in a diverse workplace and marketplace presents some challenges, it presents even greater opportunities to leverage diversity into innovative solutions, processes, products, and services. Given the potential benefits, leaders cannot afford to settle for outdated corporate cultures that exclude many potential contributors. They must create inclusive multicultural organizations. The benefits include greater productivity and profits for their organizations, which taken together can help to create a better life for all stakeholders at every level—locally, nationally, and globally.

REFERENCES

i4CP. (2009). *Study of leadership competencies*. New York, NY: Institute for Corporate Productivity.

AMA. (1999). *Diverse leadership teams are more productive: Findings from the American management association*. Retrieved from http://www.diversityweb.org.

Bacharach, S. B., Bamberger, P. A., & Vashdi, D. (2005). Diversity and homophily at work: Supportive relations among whites and African American peers. *Academy of Management Journal, 48*(4), 619–644. doi:10.5465/AMJ.2005.17843942

BCG. (2009, August 3). *Largest global survey of women finds that no matter where they live, women are over-worked, over-extended, over-stressed and under-served by businesses*. Retrieved April 2, 2011, from http://www.bcg.com.

BLS. (2009). *Employment projections 2008*. Retrieved from http://www.bls.gov.

BLS. (2011). *Women at work*. Retrieved April 2, 2011, from http://www.bls.gov/spotlight/2011/women/.

Bregman, P. (2009). A good way to change a corporate culture. *Harvard Business Review*. Retrieved November 2, 2010 from http://blogs.hbr.org.

Brown, T. (2009). *Change by design*. New York, NY: Harper Business.

Bureau of National Affairs. (2004). *Website*. Retrieved January 25, 2011, from http://www.bna.com.

Carpenter, M. S. (2002). The implications of strategy and social context for the relationship between top management team heterogeneity and firm performance. *Strategic Management Journal, 23*(3), 275–284. doi:10.1002/smj.226

Carr-Ruffino, N. (1991). U.S. women: Breaking through the glass ceiling. *Women in Management Review, 6*(5), 10–16. doi:10.1108/EUM0000000001801

Carr-Ruffino, N. (1992). Legal aspects of women's advancement. In Sekaran, U., & Leong, F. T. L. (Eds.), *Woman Power* (pp. 113–137). Thousand Oaks, CA: Sage.

Catalyst. (2006). *2005 catalyst census of women corporate officers and top earners of the fortune 500*. Retrieved October 3, 2010, from http://www.catalyst.org.

Catalyst. (2011). *Changing workplaces, changing lives: U.S. women in business*. Retrieved May 7, 2011 from http://www.catalyst.org.

Celent Communications. (2003). *Ethnic minorities, financial services, and the web*. Retrieved March 3, 2011, from http://www.celent.com.

Chatman, J. A., & Flynn, F. J. (2001). The influence of demographic heterogeneity on the emergence and consequences of cooperative norms in work teams. *Academy of Management Journal, 44*(5), 956–974. doi:10.2307/3069440

Chrobot, D., & Ruderman, M. N. (2004). Leadership in a diverse workplace. In Stockdale, M. S., & Crosby, F. J. (Eds.), *The Psychology and Management of Workplace Diversity* (pp. 100–121). Hoboken, NJ: Blackwell Publishing.

Council, P. (2001). Managing multiculturalism: Valuing diversity in the workplace. *Journal of Property Management, 66*(6), 22–25.

Cox, T. (2001). *Creating the multicultural organization: A strategy for capturing the power of diversity*. San Francisco, CA: Jossey-Bass.

Cox, T., Jr., & Smolinski, C. (1994). *Managing diversity and glass ceiling initiatives as national economic imperatives*. Working Paper #9410-01. Ann Arbor, MI: Michigan Business School.

Cox, T. H., Lobel, S. A., & McLeod, P. L. (1991). Effects of ethnic group, cultural differences, uncooperative and competitive behavior on a group task. *Academy of Management Journal, 34*, 827–847. doi:10.2307/256391

Crockett, J. (1999). Diversity: Winning competitive advantage through a diverse workforce. *HRFocus, 76*(5), 9–11.

Dahlin, K. B. (2005). Team diversity and information use. *Academy of Management Journal, 48*(8), 1107–1123. doi:10.5465/AMJ.2005.19573112

Davidson, M. N., & Proudford, K. L. (2008). Cycles of resistance. In Thomas, K. M. (Ed.), *Diversity Resistance in Organizations*. Mahwah, NJ: Lawrence Erlbaum Associates.

Deal, J. J. (2006). *Retiring the generation gap: How employees young and old can find common ground*. San Francisco, CA: Jossey-Bass/CCL.

Dovidio, J. F., Gaertner, S. L., & Kawakami, K. (2003). Intergroup contact: The past, present, and the future. *Group Processes & Intergroup Relations, 6*, 5–21. doi:10.1177/1368430203006001009

Eisenberger, R., Fasolo, P., & Davis-LaMastro, V. (1990). Perceived organizational support and employee diligence, commitment, and innovation. *The Journal of Applied Psychology, 75*(1), 51–59. doi:10.1037/0021-9010.75.1.51

ELC. (2005). News and publications. *Executive Leadership Council*. Retrieved November 5, 2005 from http://www.elcinfo.com.

Ely, R. J., & Thomas, D. A. (2001). Cultural diversity at work: The moderating effects of work group perspectives on diversity. *Administrative Science Quarterly, 46*, 229–273. doi:10.2307/2667087

Fahmy, S. (2010). *Despite recession, Hispanic and Asian buying power expected to surge in US. Annual Report of Selig Center*. Athens, GA: University of Georgia Terry College of Business.

FBI. (2009). *Federal bureau of investigation hate crimes report*. Retrieved from http://www.fbi.gov.

Fears, D. (2008, January 3). Lockheed to pay $2.5 million in racial discrimination case. *Washington Post*.

Freeman-Evans, T. (1994). The enriched association: Benefiting from multiculturalism. *Association Management, 46*(2), 52–57.

Friedman, T. L. (2007). *The world is flat 3.0: A brief history of the 21st century*. New York, NY: Macmillan Picador.

Fullerton, H. N., & Toossi, M. (2001). Employment outlook: 2000-10. *Monthly Labor Review*. Retrieved March 4, 2011, from http://www.bls.gov.

Gill, D. (2005, November). Dealing with diversity. *Inc Magazine*, 37-38.

Graves, E. G. (1997). *How to succeed in business without being white*. Scranton, PA: HarperBusiness.

Halter, M. (2000). *Shopping for identity: The marketing of ethnicity*. New York, NY: Schocken Books.

Harris, D., & Kleiner, B. (1993). Managing and valuing diversity in the workplace. *Equal Opportunities International, 12*(4), 6–10. doi:10.1108/eb010604

Harrison, D. A., Kravitz, D. M., Mayer, L. M., & Leslie, D. L.-A. (2006). Understanding attitudes toward affirmative action programs in employment. *The Journal of Applied Psychology, 91*(5), 1013–1036. doi:10.1037/0021-9010.91.5.1013

Hartenian, L., & Gudmundson, D. (2000). Cultural diversity in small business: Implications for firm performance. *Journal of Developmental Entrepreneurship, 5*(3), 209–220.

Harvey, B. H. (1999). Technology, diversity and work culture: Key trends in the next millennium. *HRMagazine, 44*(11), 58–60.

Harvey, G. (2003). *Program on redefining diversity*. Paper presented at 4th Annual Summit on Leading Diversity. Retrieved March 10 from http://www.linkageinc.com.

Hebl, M., Madera, J. M., & King, E. (2008). Exclusion, avoidance, and social distancing. In Thomas, D. M. (Ed.), *Diversity Resistance in Organizations* (pp. 127–150). New York, NY: Psychology Press.

Holladay, C. L. (2003). The influence of framing on attitudes toward diversity training. *Human Resource Development Quarterly, 14*(3), 245–263. doi:10.1002/hrdq.1065

Hom, P. (2007). *Women and minorities' high quit rates make corporate diversity difficult*. Retrieved March 10, 2011 from www.knowledge.wpcarey.asu.edu.

Hong, L., & Page, S. E. (2004). Groups of diverse problem solvers can outperform groups of high-ability problem solvers. *Proceedings of the National Academy of Sciences of the United States of America, 202*(46), 16385–16389. doi:10.1073/pnas.0403723101

Insight. (2008). *The 2007 telecommunications industry review: An anthology of market facts and forecasts*. Mountain Lakes, NJ: The Insight Research Corporation.

Kanter, R. M. (1991, May/June). Transcending business boundaries: 12,000 world managers view change. *Harvard Business Review*, 151–164.

Kelley, T. (2005). *The ten faces of innovation*. New York, NY: Random House Currency Books.

Kidder, D. L. (2004). Backlash toward diversity initiatives: Examining the impact of diversity program justification, personal, and group outcomes. *The International Journal of Conflict Management, 15*, 77–102. doi:10.1108/eb022908

Korn Ferry Institute. (2008). *The cost of employee turnover due to failed diversity initiatives in the workplace: The corporate leavers survey 2007.* Retrieved February 1, 2011, from http://www. kornferryinstitute.com.

Korn Ferry International. (2004). *Diversity in the executive suites: Good news and bad news.* Retrieved February 8, 2011 from http://www. kornferry.com.

Kravitz, D. A. (2007). Can we take the guesswork out of diversity practice selection? *The Academy of Management Perspectives, 21*(2). doi:10.5465/AMP.2007.25356517

Lancaster, H. (1997, February 4). Black managers often must emphasize building relationships. *Wall Street Journal,* p. A-1.

Lau, D. C., & Murnighan, J. K. (2005). Interactions within groups and subgroups: The effects of demographic faultlines. *Academy of Management Journal, 48*(4), 645–659. doi:10.5465/AMJ.2005.17843943

Leonard, J., & Levine, D. (2006, July). The effect of diversity on turnover: A large case study. *Industrial & Labor Relations Review,* 547–572.

Losey, M. R. (1993). Is sexual orientation an issue in the workplace? *HR News, 12,* 16–17.

Mannix, E., & Neale, M. (2005). What differences make a difference? The promise and reality of diverse teams in organizations. *Psychological Science in the Public Interest, 6*(2), 31–55. doi:10.1111/j.1529-1006.2005.00022.x

Mayo, M. (1999). Capitalizing on a diverse workforce. *Ivey Business Journal, 64*(1), 20–27.

McClenahen, J. S. (2005, January 1). Manufacturing & society: Creating values with values. *Industry Week.*

McCuiston, V., Wooldridge, B., & Pierce, C. (2004). Leading the diverse workforce: Profit, prospects and progress. *Leadership and Organization Development Journal, 25*(73), 1–2.

Millman, J. (2007). *Hot new data: Selig center tells you which multicultural markets are exploding.* Retrieved February 2, 2011 from http://www. diversityinc.com.

Morris, B. (2005). How corporate America is betraying women. *Fortune, 151*(1), 64–71.

Moss, P. I., & Tilly, C. (2003). *Stories employers tell: Race, skill, and hiring in America.* New York, NY: Russell Sage Foundation.

MPA. (2008). *Survey.* Retrieved March 1, 2011 from http://www.magazine.org.

Mushrush, W. (2004). Reducing employee turnover. *Creating Quality Newsletter.* Retrieved April 11, 2011 from http://www.MissouriBusiness.net.

Nancheria, A. (2009). Future leaders expected to wield soft power. *American Society of Training Directors.* Retrieved November 2, 2010 from http://www.astd.org.

Nemeth, C. J., & Wachtler, J. (1983). Creative problem solving as a result of majority vs. minority influence. *European Journal of Social Psychology, 13,* 45–55. doi:10.1002/ejsp.2420130103

Olson, E. G. (2011, April 4). Wal-Mart's gender bias case: What's at stake?. *Fortune.*

Overell, S. (2004). Painting over the cracks. *Personnel Today, 10.* Retrieved April 2, 2011 from http://www.personneltoday.com.

Pew Hispanic Center. (2005). *Hispanics: A people in motion.* Retrieved April 1, 2011 from http://www.pewhispanic.org.

Pew Hispanic Center. (2011). *Hispanics account for more than half of nation's growth in past decade*. Retrieved March 25, 2011, from http://www.pewhispanic.org.

Phillips, K. W. (2004). Diverse groups and information sharing: The effects of congruent ties. *Journal of Experimental Social Psychology, 40*(4), 497–510. doi:10.1016/j.jesp.2003.10.003

Phillips, K. W. (2009). To disclose or not to disclose? Status distance and self-disclosure in diverse environments. *Academy of Management Review, 34*(4), 710–732. doi:10.5465/AMR.2009.44886051

Ponterotto, J. G., & Pederson, P. B. (1993). *Preventing prejudice*. Thousand Oaks, CA: Sage.

Rao, J., Wilson, J., & Watkinson, J. (2009). What is innovation? Part 2: A web view of how IBM approaches innovation. *Innovation at Work*. Retrieved May 7, 2011, from http://innovation-atwork.wordpress.com.

Richard, O. C. (2000). Racial diversity, business strategy, and firm performance: A resource-based view. *Academy of Management Journal, 43*, 164–178. doi:10.2307/1556374

Salomon, M., & Schork, J. (2003). Turn diversity to your advantage. *Research Technology Management, 46*(4), 37–51.

Segal, J. A. (1997). Diversity for dollars. *HRMagazine, 42*(4), 134–140.

Silverstein, M. J., Sayre, K., & Butman, J. (2009). *Women want more: How to capture your share of the world's largest, fastest-growing market*. Scranton, PA: HarperBusiness.

Smither, R. D., Houston, J. M., & McIntire, S. D. (1996). *Organization development: Strategies for changing environments*. Scranton, PA: HarperCollins.

Stevens, J. (2003). *The power of diversity in corporate America*. Retrieved February 15, 2011 from http://www.Linkage-Inc.com.

Sutton, R. (2002). *Weird ideas that work*. New York, NY: Free Press.

Terry, R. W. (1990). *For whites only*. Grand Rapids, MI: William B. Eerdmans Publishing Company.

Thomas, K. M. (Ed.). (2008). *Diversity resistance in organizations*. Mahwah, NJ: Lawrence Erlbaum Associates.

US Census Bureau. (2001). *Website*. Retrieved from http://www.census.gov.

US Census Bureau. (2002). *Website*. Retrieved from http://www.census.gov.

US Census Bureau. (2010). *Website*. Retrieved from http://www.census.gov.

US Glass Ceiling Commission. (1991). *A report on the glass ceiling initiative*. Washington, DC: US Department of Labor.

US Glass Ceiling Commission. (1995). *Good for business*. Washington, DC: US Department of Labor.

Van den Steen, E. J. (2009, August). Culture clash: The costs and benefits of homogeneity. *Harvard Business Review*.

Van der Vegt, G. S. (2005). Location-level links between diversity and innovative climate depend on national power distance. *Academy of Management Journal, 48*(8), 1171–1182. doi:10.5465/AMJ.2005.19573116

Vescio, T. K., Sechrist, G. B., & Paolucci, M. P. (2003). Perspective taking and prejudice reduction: The mediational role of empathy arousal and situational attributions. *European Journal of Social Psychology, 33*, 455–472. doi:10.1002/ejsp.163

KEY TERMS AND DEFINITIONS

Corporate Culture: An organization's unique environment.

Innovation: Enhances the ability to compete at a local and global level.

Multicultural Approach: An organization's culture that is expanded to include all aspects of the sub-cultures as represented by employee groups.

Chapter 8
Managing Privilege as a Key to Inclusive Leadership

Doug Harris
Kaleidoscope Group, USA

Kasia Ganko-Rodriguez
Kaleidoscope Group, USA

ABSTRACT

The field of diversity and inclusion has experienced exponential growth over last 30 years. Yet, while these progressions have occurred, many of the core diversity and inclusion concepts have remained fairly stagnant. One critical example is around the concept of privilege. All of us find ourselves privileged in some way, but leaders in particular need to recognize and manage privilege to ensure inclusion in the workplace. Through personal examples and real stories, this chapter highlights the many positive outcomes leaders will experience by effectively managing privilege. These powerful outcomes include areas such as personal growth and effectiveness, more authentic relationships, increased levels of respect, expanded circle of influence, and maximized employee performance. To conclude, the authors look at the stages leaders go through before they are able to effectively manage this expanded view of privilege. These stages can be described as bliss, awareness, overprotection, enlightened, and ultimately managing privilege.

INTRODUCTION

While much has been written on the concept of privilege there is an opportunity to explore the concept specifically as it relates to leadership in today's organizations. In this chapter we look at privilege

across a wide and often subtle set of attributes that result in everyone, particularly leaders, being privileged in some form. As opposed to privilege being a passive factor that simply runs in the background for leaders, we conclude that leaders can in fact manage privilege actively. When leaders manage their privilege, it is argued that many individual, team and organization benefits can be achieved.

DOI: 10.4018/978-1-4666-1812-1.ch008

These positive outcomes include: personal growth and effectiveness, more authentic relationships, increased levels of respect, expanded circle of influence, and maximized employee performance. Understanding these outcomes is critical in helping leaders advance through the following stages that we label as bliss, awareness, overprotection, enlightened, and ultimately managing privilege. It is by sharing practical stories and tips that we hope that leaders can become better equipped to not only understand how they are privileged, but more importantly how they can manage that privilege to create an even more inclusive workplace, community and marketplace.

BACKGROUND: APPROACHES TO PRIVILEGE WITHIN THE LITERATURE

In order to discuss how managing privilege is a key to inclusive leadership, a definition of privilege is presented along with how the topic has been addressed to date in the literature. Privilege is a concept that surfaces in a variety of arenas. It is used in common language and every-day speech, for example, *I had the privilege to be included at last night's event.* It is a phenomenon that has been researched by scholars (e.g. Johnson, 2006; Kimmel & Ferber, 2010; Wildman, 1996). It is an area that has been studied in psychological experiments (e.g. Powell, Branscombe, & Schmitt, 2005). It is also a term frequently tossed around in the field of diversity of inclusion; for example, *that group of employees must be privileged, I wonder if they are even aware of it?* Through our work as Diversity and Inclusion (D&I) practitioners, consultants, and trainers, we have also experienced that the term frequently carries an emotional weight and evokes strong reactions. As Johnson (2006) noted, "privilege has become one of those loaded words we need to reclaim so that we can use it to name and illuminate the truth" (p. 21). Privilege has

been defined and addressed in the literature in a number of ways.

McIntosh's (1988) classic personal essay, *White Privilege and Male Privilege: A Personal Account of Coming to see Correspondence through Work in Women's Studies*, is a seminal work in the area of privilege. While McIntosh devoted the majority of the essay to the analysis of her own white privilege, she also recognized the need to expand the discussion beyond white and male privilege. Johnson (2006) credited McIntosh with identifying two types of privilege: "unearned entitlement" that should be granted to everyone but when restricted to some groups turns into "unearned advantage," as well as "conferred power," which "goes a step further by giving one group power over another" (pp. 22-23).

Historically, privilege has been frequently discussed in the context of oppression. Johnson (2006) believed oppression to be "the flip side of privilege" (p. 38) and Ferber (2010) stated: "privilege and oppression are two sides of the same coin" (p. 252). Hardiman, Jackson, and Griffin (2010) observed that "oppression is an interlocking, multileveled system that consolidates social power to the benefit of members of privileged groups and is maintained and operationalized on three dimensions: a) contextual dimension, b) conscious/unconscious dimension, and c) applied dimension" (pp. 26-27). These dimensions deal with whether oppression is intentional and unintentional, whether it happens on an individual, institutional, and social/cultural level and with how it is applied. Hardiman et al. added, however, that "it is not useful to argue about a hierarchy of oppressions" (p. 33).

Many authors on the topic have tended to focus only on one or two categories or dimensions of difference, where privilege appears. The most commonly discussed privilege dimensions are race and gender; privilege in the context of broader dimensions of difference, such as socio-economic status or education levels, has been less common. When reviewing literature on the topic, we obtained 1675 entries when searching for articles on White Privilege, 417 on Male Privilege, 61 on Heterosexual Privilege, 51 on Middle Class Privilege, and 46 on Christian Privilege, to list a few examples[1]. These statistics mirror our own experience working in the field of diversity and inclusion, where the most common dimensions associated with privilege we encounter are that of white and male privilege.

Some of the authors that described the existence of privilege across a number of social categories also discussed the notions of intersection and matrix. Collins (2000) argued that "Intersectionality refers to particular forms of intersecting oppressions, for example intersections of race and gender, or of sexuality and nation" (p. 18) and distinguished it from "matrix of domination" that "refers to how these intersecting oppressions are actually organized" (p. 18). Wildman and Davis (1996) observed "privilege can intersect with subordination or other systems of privilege as well. Seeing privilege at the intersection is complicated by the fact that there is no purely privileged or unprivileged person" (p. 21). Finally, Johnson (2006) stated "that the concept of a matrix reveals how the different dimensions of privilege and domination are connected to one another" (p. 52). Johnson also described how various dimensions of privilege can support each other and noted that being privileged on one dimension can impact being privileged on others or be used as a compensation for lack of others.

Leveraging some of the perspectives described above, Ferber (2010) proposed the "matrix framework" (p. 252) and urged readers to consider a number of privilege characteristics including the need to examine both privilege and oppression, the notion of intersection, social interpretations, acceptance that all are privileged, awareness that inequality harms everyone, the importance of self reflection, and a proactive focus on social change.

While the above literature highlights a range of definitions and approaches to privilege, our perspective offers another understanding.

AUTHORS' APPROACH TO PRIVILEGE

When we consult with our organizational clients at The Kaleidoscope Group, we define privilege as: *the absence of barriers and presence of unearned advantages*. Our philosophical approach to privilege in the context of the above literature review and our work as D&I practitioners is as follows. We are philosophically aligned with many of the privilege conceptualizations reviewed above, which can be summarized into three key areas. First, we support the notion that we are *all* privileged in some ways. We find this premise extremely impactful from the standpoint of encouraging both individual contributors and leaders to recognize and manage their own privilege, which assists in creating fairness for all. Second, we support that the privilege dialogue need not be held in the context of blame and guilt, but rather based in responsibility. Finally, we also agree that individuals do not choose to be privileged. Privilege exists in society and we are born into systems of privilege. However, as individuals, we have a choice to either manage privilege or *blissfully* benefit from its unearned advantages. Later in the chapter, we will share what we have observed to be the journey to managing privilege.

There are areas where our point of view diverges from the mainstream. For example, while one cannot deny the oppressive impact of unmanaged privilege, as D&I practitioners we have found that accentuating oppression and the victim/oppressor dichotomy often has had an alienating and counterproductive effect. Instead, we have seen individual contributors and leaders become motivated to increase fairness as a result of engaging in a privilege dialogue that is held in a non-threatening, non-blaming way. We also believe in the power of modeling our own challenges with recognizing and managing our own privilege and speaking from the vantage point of how we are privileged versus how we are not. We have witnessed people who become inspired to recognize and manage their privilege by hearing how, for example, our African American colleagues discuss their privilege associated with being male and physically able, how another colleague with physical disability shares a privilege of having access to health care and life-changing surgery, or by hearing a gay colleague highlight his privilege associated with class and education.

Along with others such as McIntosh (1988), Johnson (2006), and Ferber (2010), we are strong advocates that modeling cannot happen without self-reflection on how we are privileged. McIntosh (1988) shared how "[A]fter frustration with men who would not recognize male privilege, I decided to try to work on myself at least by identifying some of the daily effects of white privilege in my life" (pp. 4-5). It is this self-work that we believe is a key to managing privilege for creating inclusion, both on an individual and leadership levels. We also trust that change will happen when we all examine and focus on how we are privileged versus how we are not.

Our discussion of privilege also highlights the subtle nuances that occur specifically in organizational settings versus a general *societal* overview of all possible overt behaviors that may surface. Our experience shows that it is often the subtle and unconscious behaviors that create real barriers, especially in our workplaces. We are aligned with Jameson (2007) who observed that "privilege may mean subtle deference, respect and authority rather than explicit, tangible behaviors" (p. 221).

Lastly, our approach to privilege is designed to facilitate a dialogue, a real conversation. To that end we share our observations, our stories, and our insights on this topic in text that follows. Our sharing occurs, not in the framework of formal research, but as individuals committed to creating greater understanding and collaboration between people working to create a more fair and equitable world. We desire to continue the tradition inspired by McIntosh (1988) who said: "we need more down-to-earth writing by people about these taboo subjects" (p. 15).

BACKGROUND: INCLUSIVE LEADERSHIP WITHIN THE LITERATURE

Before we make connections between managing privilege and inclusive leadership, we need to define what inclusive leadership means. A lot has been written about leadership, different styles and keys to its effectiveness. Prewitt, Weil, and McClure (2011) observed that "it has been suggested by several authors that few terms inspire less agreement than the definition of leadership" (p. 13). The authors in addition point out:

With ever-increasing globalization and change, leaders will be challenged to manage relationships more than in the past. This will include the ability to interact effectively with diversity of partners and other business and with the larger context of differing cultures (Prewitt, Weil, & McClure, p. 19).

Prewitt, Weil, and McClure (2011) also noted that "by combining many of the concepts, including women as leaders into a new framework or model, insights can be offered into successful leadership (p. 18)." This model would address three areas of focus, such as "competence, character, and community" (p. 18).

Seemingly, less has been written about inclusive leadership per se, where the *per se* part is crucial. As Ryan (2007) argued in the context of inclusive leadership in academe:

There is no shortage of literature on inclusive leadership, that is, literature that explores or promotes participation of others besides administrators in governance processes, and/or advocates for leadership processes that promote the general principle of inclusion. Most of this literature, however, does not adopt the heading 'inclusive leadership.'

Ryan (2007) further showed how inclusive leadership connects with the notion of emancipatory leadership and is aligned with critical theories of leadership. "The emancipatory leadership literature contributes many things to our knowledge of inclusive leadership—especially its balanced account of inclusive leadership. It attends to both the process and the end-values of leadership."

Hollander (2009) underscored that "Inclusive Leadership (IL) is about relationships that can accomplish things for mutual benefit. Reaching leadership at this next level means 'doing things with people, rather than to people,' which is the essence of inclusion" (p. 3). He then identified: "Respect, Recognition, Responsiveness, and Responsibility" (p. 3) as four factors critical to inclusive leadership. Hollander and Park (cited in Hollander) have also developed the Inclusive Leadership Scale with items falling under three categories of "Support-Recognition, Communication-Action-Fairness, and Self-Interest-Disrespect" (p. 221). While managing privilege is not explicitly called out in this scale, we would argue that without managing their own privilege, leaders could not effectively exhibit any of the behaviors described in the scale.

Therefore, while there is much that can be intuited about how *effective leadership* ties to inclusion or even inherently contains inclusive behaviors, we find simply that it is not overt. Our premise is that these subtleties impact a leader's ability to make a connection as to how these behaviors may be both demonstrated with and perceived by broadly diverse employee, customer, and community populations.

Connecting the Dots between Inclusive Leadership and Privilege

In our view, leadership at one point was about power and control; the inclusive leadership of today is about empowering others. The reality is what is needed to empower people of diverse backgrounds and the barriers that get in the way of their empowerment are unique. Leaders who want to create inclusive workplaces and leverage today's global workforce need not only understand the privilege dynamics that can hinder or enable others' successes, but also manage their own privilege effectively.

Based on our work with organizations and having encountered leaders that were considered as either inclusive or exclusive, we have identified the following attributes of Inclusive Leadership: 1) integrating diversity and inclusion into the business strategy; 2) fostering an inclusive and fair work environment; 3) building effective relationships across lines of difference; 4) attracting, coaching, sponsoring, and developing diverse talent; 5) managing inclusively; and 6) managing privilege.

While many of the above attributes or competencies have been in some ways addressed (not necessarily under the heading of inclusive leadership per se) by scholars and other D&I practitioners (e.g. Adler, 2002; Miller & Katz, 2002, Ross, 2011[2], Tapia, 2009), one that we believe requires a more comprehensive discussion is that of managing privilege in the context of inclusive leadership. As argued by Rita E. Gardiner (2011):

[I]n Western society, certain kinds of leadership are privileged over others. The self-made man is often regarded as the epitome of the strong, successful leader. It is commonplace to read about an individual who was able to succeed through sheer willpower. Yet every person needs others to help them attain their goals, something that is missing in most discussions of authentic leadership (p. 100).

Like Gardiner, we would argue that a discussion of leadership must involve exploration of privilege. We have a fundamental belief that we live in a world of good people, but because we do not manage privilege effectively, we do not show up as *good* as we really are, whether as individual contributors or leaders. In the following section, we will seek to explore what managing privilege looks like for inclusive leaders, what outcomes it yields, and what stages are involved in the journey to managing privilege. Our perspective will be that of practitioners based on our collective, extensive experience in the field of diversity and inclusion. As such, our observations and conclusions are not grounded or validated by psychological or sociological studies, but are derived from years of practice.

THE BASIS FOR LEADERS' MANAGING PRIVILEGE

Managing privilege cannot take place without individuals first recognizing and then owning their privilege. However, because "privilege is not visible to the holder of the privilege, [appearing] as part of the normal fabric of daily life" (Wildman, 1996, p. 30), recognition of one's privilege may be a challenge[3].

In our work, we seek to explore what beliefs may get in the way of a leader's ability to recognize and own his or her privilege, the very prerequisites to managing it. For the sake of this chapter and given space limitations, we will only highlight a few of beliefs we have encountered that, in our view, serve as barriers to owning privilege: 1) *It's other people that are privileged*, 2) *I have earned all of my success*, and 3) *We all start at ground zero*.

Moving from *They are Privileged* to *I am Privileged*

In our D&I education with leader audiences, we often hear the following associations with privilege: *power, access, money, and being born with a silver spoon in one's mouth*. Participants call out multimillionaires, politicians, and famous celebrities—those powerful *others*. We have repeatedly observed that they think of other people as being privileged, hardly ever themselves. We also find that positioning privilege in the context of broader

cultural identity and highlighting it on various dimensions of diversity (beyond race, gender or sexual orientation, etc.), help leaders recognize that we are all privileged in some ways and therefore all have a responsibility to create fairness. The expanded approach also helps participants move from guilt and fear of being blamed to a sense of ownership and responsibility, which we think is a fundamental premise of managing privilege.

To highlight how we can be both privileged in some ways and not privileged in others, consider the selected dimensions of diversity through the lens of insiders and outsiders (see Table 1). We define *insiders* as those that are more of the norm, power base, and majority. To explore this concept we look at the United States society as a whole and look at organizations in the aggregate since the list in Table 1 might look differently for a specific individual organization, department or team, as well as for different global societies.

If we are an insider on any of the dimensions of diversity in Table 1, we are privileged on that dimension. Conversely, if we are an outsider, we are not privileged on that dimension. The list in Table 1 has only 10 dimensions. However, when we take workshop participants through a self-reflection activity in which they consider up to 20 dimensions of diversity, they find themselves to be privileged on more dimensions than they expected. As mentioned earlier, we often are not cognizant of our *insider-ness* and resulting privilege.

Similar frameworks have been also utilized by others. Kirko and Okazawa-Rey (2010) identified dominant and subordinate groups on a variety of social categories including gender, class, nation, ethnicity, age, etc., and Monaghan (2010) adapted Plummer's framework to capture how personal characteristics relate to societal norms around characteristics such as race/ethnicity, religion, and education, to name a few. Table 1 can also be adjusted to apply to global teams and organizations. As Hofstede & Hofstede (2005) noted, "inequality exists in any society" (p. 40) and according

Table 1. Diversity dimensions through the lens of insiders and outsiders

Insiders	Dimension	Outsiders
White	Race	People of Color
35-45	Age	Less than 35, more than 45
Male	Gender	Female, Transgender
Able-Bodied	Physical / Cognitive Abilities	Persons with a Disability
Heterosexual	Sexual Orientation	GLBTQ (Gay, Lesbian, Bisexual, Transgender, Questioning)
Native Speakers of English	Language/Accents	English as a 2nd Language/ Other languages
Middle Class and Above	Socio-Economics	Lower Middle Class and below
College Degree and Above	Education	No College Degree
Christian	Religion	Other Faiths/Religions, Non-believers
Married	Marital Status	Not Married

to Jameson (2007) "[in] intercultural business communication contexts, power and privilege are related to other components of cultural identity besides race, ethnicity, gender and age" (p. 221). Jameson shared further how person's professional field, the organization for which a person works, and his or her function within an organization can all confer power and privilege.

Recognizing Unearned Components of Our Success

Another belief barrier to managing privilege that we encounter in our D&I work is that associated with efforts invested in the success of individuals, and in this context, leaders. Many will often feel that *all of their* achievement was fully earned. Some have a hard time recognizing the subtle components that either facilitated or launched their success to another level. Yes, we worked hard to get our degree but who paid for it? Who encouraged us to go? Who set an example of the importance of a degree? Yes, we worked hard to get that promotion, but did we consider the extra points that go along with having attended a Big 10 school like all of the other leaders in our organization?

Privilege does not negate our efforts, but it does help catapult our efforts toward a greater likelihood of success. Getting our driver's license certainly involved efforts at learning and practicing, which comprise an earned portion of our success associated with getting a license. However, attending a high school which offered a driving school and having access to our parents' cars and their time for practice are examples of the unearned portion of our success.

Understanding that We did not all *Start at Ground Zero*

To illustrate this point, we will share a few personal examples of one of the authors of this chapter, Doug Harris. Doug attended Kingswood Oxford, a respected preparatory school in West Hartford, CT. While he did work hard to get into Kingswood Oxford, it was also his parents' 100% support that encouraged him to achieve at a high level. Doug was an athlete and his father was the only parent who showed up to every game. The other kids had fathers who were doing very well, often holding very senior level jobs as CEOs and COOs, but they were not able to be there for their children in the same way that Doug's dad was there for him. Doug recalls many of his teammates saying "Man I wish I had the relationship with my father that you have!"

Doug's privilege did not end there. His mother was a community organizer. Everybody who ran for mayor in Hartford would come by his house seeking her endorsement. When she finally made her decision, her decision would be in the local paper the next day. Doug recalls her going to the city council and just walking right into the mayor's office. This relates to Doug's privilege because when summer internship programs were announced or opportunities surfaced to involve local student leaders, Doug was always in the front of the line for those opportunities. The summer before he went to college he was in charge of managing a large summer program for the city, which was usually as staff member's job. In this position, he oversaw 12 individual sites, each having 15 to 20 students to manage. Normally, a 17-year-old would not have been given such huge responsibility.

That door was open to him because of his mother. She told people, "My son can do that." They responded, "He's only 17." She shot back, "I don't care how old he is. He can do that." And the next thing you know, he had the job. As he went to all of these sites, he remembers that his friends were doing very different summer work. They were sweeping the facilities he managed and helping at the park by playing with little children. Yet Doug was riding around in his parents' car, supervising their managers and making sure that everything was running smoothly...all at the age of 17. This all came about because the people who had the power to influence hiring and placement decisions had listened to his mother. Why? Because of her clout in the community, and he clearly benefited from that clout. He had not earned it. This is privilege at its most basic. What we have not shared with you is that Doug is also African American. However, it is his ability to manage his own privilege versus focus on lack thereof, that he attributes to his ability to become a leader.

OUTCOMES OF INCLUSIVE LEADERSHIP WHILE MANAGING PRIVILEGE

Leaders who effectively manage privilege gain in a number of ways. They can achieve more inclusive leadership, personally grow and become more effective, establish more authentic relationships, gain an increased level of respect, expand their circle of influence, enhance employee performance, and improve decision making. These outcomes culminate in enhancing leader's ability to create a truly diverse and inclusive environment.

Personal Growth and Effectiveness

When leaders manage privilege, it gives them insights into a broader viewpoint of how to see the world. The more perspectives they make their own, the more dynamic and versatile their leadership style becomes. To illustrate this point, we examine Doug's experience in growing as a leader.

Doug started his career in the consumer products industry. In his job 25 years ago, one would advance from an individual contributor to a manager by getting training, some of which included running team meetings. As part of the training, participants in the class were asked to pair up to run a meeting and Doug ended up working with a female colleague. After the meeting, their managers delivered feedback to Doug and his partner. Doug was told he had done a great job and she was told she had not taken enough control because they could not tell who was in charge. However, the feedback shared by the meeting participants surfaced a very different evaluation of Doug and his colleague. In fact, participants felt that she ran the best meeting that they had ever participated in.

How does privilege come into play here? They worked in an environment where a traditional, male style of leadership was considered to be the norm and best practice. In many ways Doug was conditioned for that style of leadership. He had moved through the company in several male dominated areas. He grew up with three brothers and one sister. He played college basketball. Doug also had been the president of his fraternity. In other words, his leadership behavior was aligned with the norm present in that work environment, which resulted in his getting an *unearned advantage* over his female colleague. At that time, one might say he was effective *enough* to progress and advance. The corporate world he was in told him that the best practice and desired behavior is what he had learned and displayed in that meeting. But was he as effective as he could be? No. And he definitely was not inclusive enough either.

Nonetheless, Doug chose to uncover what made his female counterpart's style more appealing to the meeting participants. He then expanded his own style by adding elements of what he observed from her into his leadership arsenal. These additions resulted in Doug feeling that his overall effectiveness had been enhanced significantly. Bottom line, back then he may have had two ways of running meetings; now he has twenty. Each time he has come across styles and ways that are effective yet out of the norm, he consciously works to incorporate aspects of them into his own style. Doug attributes the new variety of approaches he has gained from others along the way as helping him to not only be a better leader in the workplace, but also the approaches have helped him be a better husband and father to his seven children.

Our attempt here in sharing this personal example is to illustrate how managing privilege expands the possibilities of what is *best* leadership style. What is *best* has historically been associated with the majority, norm, and power. However, with the speed of change, technology advancements, and globalization ever increasing, it is the leaders who can experience new approaches, challenge their *go to* styles, and then quickly incorporate new adaptations that will be most successful. They not only expand their leadership repertoire and grow as leaders, but also become more effective. They particularly become more relevant and effective when leading employees of different backgrounds than their own, therefore gaining a higher chance to build a truly diverse and inclusive organization. Now as CEO of The Kaleidoscope Group, Doug attributes much of his success to his focus on expanding his leadership style and repertoire beyond what had been *the norm* to him or the work environments he has worked in. The result is that he has managed to create and sustain his diverse and inclusive organization as a result of his own personal growth.

More Authentic Relationships

We have found that particularly in relationships across lines of difference, employees expect their leaders to *really* understand them. We have also witnessed employees of diverse backgrounds *measure* their leaders' understanding of them based on two factors: will the leader take the time to understand their perspective and are they willing to admit that which they do not know. Based on this *assessment*, employees of diverse background would either choose to be or not to be authentic with that leader. Thus, we believe that leaders who manage privilege create a relationship in which employees feel that they are truly honored, heard, and included, which makes room for them to be authentic.

Unfortunately, the challenge we have seen leaders face is that they often thought they had authentic relationships, while in reality their reports felt otherwise. If a leader's direct reports did not *feel* valued, they consequently did not feel they could be authentic with their leaders; however, they might have still sent signals suggesting the opposite. After all, they were dealing with a position of authority. We believe that leaders need to manage their privilege associated with power and position of authority by actively soliciting, valuing and leveraging viewpoints from outside their usual circle and network, especially from those not in majority, norm and power, and from those having contrarian perspectives. This openness seems to create a strong foundation for building authentic relationships.

We have witnessed some powerful examples of how managing privilege creates authentic relationships. A few years ago, we were doing some work with a board of a not-for-profit located in an inner-city impoverished area. There was this kind, extremely caring, dedicated, and well-intended female on the board, who supported the community with both her time and substantial financial donations. She demonstrated a major commitment to the board and the relationships she had with people from her vantage point were very good. However, while others greatly appreciated her intent and recognized her financial contributions, the openness, trust, and honesty were lacking in their relationship with her.

Although she was a very well intended and generous person, she was also highly overprotective and unconsciously patronizing of others. One day we took her to the side and shared with her that when a person cares as much as she does, what was about to be said might be challenging for her to hear. We explained the unintended impact she was having on others and how she was being received as the *super angel on a mission to rescue the ill-equipped individuals*. She understood instantly and was visibly shaken by the feedback. She quickly apologized to the others, explained that it was not her intention to make them feel that way, and assured them that she appreciated the tough feedback. Her effectiveness improved tremendously and people became genuinely authentic with her. Her story exemplifies how effective management of privilege may result in authentic relationships.

Increased Levels of Respect

Wildman (1996) observed that "privilege often bestows a higher level of comfort in social interactions" (p. 30) and we would argue that managing privilege allows us to get out of *our shoes of comfort* and wear the shoes of others. We have

coached many leaders who thought that those they were leading were looking for agreement but, in reality, their employees were looking for respect. This was especially the case when leaders were managing a diverse workforce. What was the respect that their employees of different cultural backgrounds were looking for? The answer was quite simply that their leaders honestly took their vantage points into consideration. For leaders we have coached, the beginning of sincerely considering other viewpoints would start with a heartfelt conviction to consider their employees' viewpoints as valuable. Once employees felt truly respected, they in turn respected their leaders even more. The following concrete examples illustrate this point.

As open as Doug believes he is, he has no direct knowledge of what it is like for a person who was born elsewhere to enter the United States and balance their foundational heritage with existence in this country. He may have had his own challenges associated with living in the US but he still has the privilege of living in a country where many of his norms are considered the norms of most. Once he showed this understanding to those who do not experience this privilege, such as his immigrant employees, he immediately gained their respect, which empowered their relationship in so many ways.

A senior executive leader we worked with gave a speech that was broadcast to employees worldwide. During his presentation, he made a statement that while his wife was away, he was "playing mom." Immediately after his speech, he was flooded with several emails from offended employees, mostly women. They were bothered by the statement for two reasons. First, they felt he cannot "play mom"—he was simply fulfilling his role as a father. Secondly, that comment struck a chord with female employees who experienced challenges in the organization associated with gender. The leader's response was immediate and powerful. He sent a voice mail to 25,000 people in which he stated his intentions and that he truly heard the impact. He also apologized and shared that this was a major lesson for him, that he had a joking nature, and he now understood the inappropriateness of his joke. What is more, he created the message by himself, with no support of a communication expert, which was appreciated by his employees even more, as it was received as heart-felt.

The point of the above example is two-fold. First of all, the executive understood and managed his privilege associated with both gender and position, where the latter magnified the former. As a result, he gained more respect from his employees. Secondly, he took a negative situation—the mistake he had made—and turned it around it to gain better relationships. In our firm, we believe that diversity and inclusion is not so much about avoiding mistakes but about recovering from them.

Expanded Circle of Influence

One of the biggest objectives for leaders is to gain buy-in and acceptance of their direction, vision and goals (Prewitt, Weil, & McLure, 2011). We believe that leaders' circle of influence is instrumental to getting this buy-in and will be expanded by being in touch with those who they lead.

This is highlighted by our experience in a recent meeting with a group of employees who were early in their career. They were discussing their experience within their organization. In the midst of this discussion one of the individuals shared how a particular leader did not care about diversity and inclusion at all. Another person in the room, who had a very different experience, said vehemently: "She is one of the most open, caring and supportive leaders in this organization for all people." Other employees went on to share several personal stories about how this leader had supported and sponsored their efforts throughout their employment. They also stated how she took time to truly understand the challenge they were facing as a younger workforce. As a result, the leader gained a newfound respect and her influence to both support and gain support was enhanced

tremendously. It all began with the leader's sincerely managing privilege with one employee who then shared their positive experience with others.

This story illustrates the point that when leaders allow others to influence them, they in turn increase their ability to influence. The leader in the above scenario was taking in the issues of younger people, listening to difference perspectives that they had, how they communicated, how they structured work, and how they utilized technology. This leader displayed inclusion by valuing different approaches coming from another generation, while others responded to them with resistance or dismissal. As a result, this leader's circle of influence expanded.

Enhanced Employee Performance

One of the most important outcomes of managing privilege is maximizing employee performance. Sometimes leaders' abilities to manage privilege is the key factor in converting what is perceived as *low performance* into *high performance*. In one organization there was an employee, Frank, whose natural cultural style was laid back and reserved. Frank was an outstanding performer but was constantly told by his manager that if he wanted to get into management he had to adjust his style and become more forthright. Frank was well respected by peers and colleagues and was often called upon to help others perform their duties more effectively. Because Frank wanted to be promoted, he attempted to become more outspoken and forthright in his behaviors. Fellow colleagues began to share with his manager that working with Frank had become awkward and unproductive. Frank's manager concluded that he was not management material. The adjustment did not work.

Frank was then transferred to another area where his new manager managed his privilege well. The new manager was aware of the company norm but was also very interested in new approaches and styles to help enhance effectiveness. On Frank's first day of work in the new area, he was asked about his experience prior to being transferred. Frank shared the experience and was told immediately that different approaches were valued in this area. Frank had felt very valued and respected before starting his new assignment. In just a few weeks, he was back to being an outstanding performer. After several months of observing Frank, others in the area began to adapt Frank's style of effective questioning versus outright opinions. The manager was extremely pleased with Frank and suggested him for a promotion. His colleagues were appreciative of his style as well. Frank was promoted and often called upon as a mentor to others because of the effectiveness of his style.

The above story highlights how managing privilege leads to openness of possibilities. In order to be considered as inclusive leaders, we need to value and leverage abilities, talents, styles, and approaches of others. Managing privilege becomes a means to maximizing employee potential.

To summarize, in order to display inclusive leadership, one needs to manage the privilege associated with a historical notion of expertise by including outlier voices; those from outside of the majority, norm and power. In our consulting, we refer to that as *weighted input*, and coach leaders to ask the following questions at all stages of creating strategy: "Who are we not hearing from?; Who has a different way of seeing the issue?; Have we heard from those impacted by the solution/decision, etc.? Who disagrees with the recommendation at hand and why?" Consciously and consistently asking these questions ensures building D&I strategies relevant for all key stakeholders.

JOURNEY TO MANAGING PRIVILEGE

The reality is that becoming an inclusive leader who manages privilege may take time, motivation and effort. Based on the leadership behaviors we have observed and encountered in our D&I work, we have created a framework that describes *the journey to managing privilege* and lists various stages associated with it. This does not mean that an individual has to go through all stages in order to reach that of managing privilege. Some leaders move to the last stage relatively quickly. We have also seen many *get stuck* on what we call *over-protection* and a few others refuse to go beyond *awareness*. However, the journey always begins with the first step that we refer to as *coming out of bliss*. A close look at the stages follows below.

Bliss: "I Just Don't See It" – Bursting the Bubble

The foundation of the journey towards managing privilege is *coming out of bliss*. Bliss is essentially a state of unawareness; we may believe the world that we experience is the world that exists for everyone. As Johnson (2006) notes "the ease of not being aware of privilege is an aspect of privilege itself, what some call 'the luxury of obliviousness' (or, in philosophy, "epistemic privilege")" (p. 22). He then adds, "awareness requires effort and commitment" (p. 22). We would argue that to get out of unawareness we have to reach out to people who are aware and see the world differently. Unfortunately, we have observed both ourselves and others do the opposite—instinctively gravitate towards those that share the same perspective.

In our work, we sometimes witness, as an example, tenured employees talking with other tenured employees in order to get reassured that the organization is welcoming to new employees or mid-career hires. People without disabilities will seek confirmation from employees like them that employees with disabilities experience no issues. Men will approach other men to dismiss women's issues and Christians will gather to debate Muslim employee challenges without inviting their Muslim co-workers to the table, and the list goes on. As a result, we have seen many organizations not change.

One way that may help us get out of bliss is to find ourselves in situations where we are in some way not privileged. We once knew a leader extremely committed to the D&I process who did not approve of employee resource groups. He felt they were exclusive and caused dissension versus inclusion. He then was promoted to Japan and after six months of being abroad started a white male employee resource group. Our convictions and commitments can be misinformed when we are part of the norm and in a state of bliss. Table 2 summarizes characteristics of the bliss stage and provides suggestions for leaders to move forward.

Awareness: "Had No Idea It is *so* Hard for Them"

We have seen leaders *come out of bliss* and experience shock when realizing the lack of fairness and inequities in the organization. An organizational D&I culture assessment is used as an example. Leaders will often react with shock and anger at findings that contradict or challenge their perception of how diverse and inclusive their organization is. For well-intended leaders it will be hard to hear, for example, that a large percentage of their employees feel they are treated unfairly and inequitably, that they cannot advance and grow or that they do not see themselves represented amongst top ranks.

The key to moving from the Awareness stage lies, in our opinion, in overcoming initially adverse feelings that accompany the new, unprecedented insights into the experience of others. We were once called by a leader of diversity and inclusion who had just received feedback that their Hispanic/Latina population rated supervisor effectiveness at 32% favorability, while the overall organization rated supervisor effectiveness at 85% favorability. The shock associated with receiving this feedback overwhelmed her. This overwhelmed feeling led her to be stagnant and lose her effectiveness as a change agent.

On another occasion, a leader we once coached could not comprehend why his playing golf with a group of co-workers was perceived as an exclusionary practice and that others felt they could not get promoted unless they were privileged to play golf with him. Once he understood that the expectation of him was not to stop playing golf, but rather expand ways in which he engaged with other employees, he started moving to the next stage towards managing privilege. Table 3 summarizes characteristics of the aware stage and provides suggestions for leaders to move forward.

Overprotection: "Let Me Help…and Rescue You"

We have seen many empathetic leaders move from bliss straight to overprotection, and frankly, many feel very good about being in this stage. Overprotection can feel very rewarding to some of us, especially those with a strong desire to take care of others. While this desire is noble in itself, as leaders we need to understand that we cannot empower employees and set them up for success through overprotecting, rescuing, and removing barriers *for them* as opposed to *with* them. In fact, that is the last thing underprivileged employees

Table 2. Bliss stage: thoughts/beliefs and behaviors, and development steps

Stage / Focus	Thoughts/Beliefs	Behavior	Steps for Leaders to Develop
Bliss	• Differences do not impact opportunity • Sees most concerns from outsiders as illegitimate	Very minimal contact in circles of difference	1. Identify your own privilege 2. Understand how it has helped your own success 3. Engage in contact and conversations with outsiders and genuinely (without judgment) seek to understand their reality and obstacles faced due to being different

Table 3. Awareness stage: thoughts/beliefs and behaviors, and development steps

Stage/Focus	Thoughts/Beliefs	Behavior	Steps for Leaders to Develop
Awareness	• Differences can impact opportunities • Sees concerns from outsiders as legitimate but still often shocked	Contact in circles of difference is superficial	1. Manage your own discomfort when realizing the inequities impacting others' success 2. Engage in meaningful relationships across lines of difference to fully understand the perspective of outsiders, their lens and experience e.g. get on/create teams with outsiders, continuously seek their feedback 3. Seek to identify ways in which you can help create fairness

would expect from us. They want to feel heard, honored and supported in their *own* efforts to overcome their barriers.

We once worked with an organization that had received data that younger employees were leaving because their voice was not heard. Leaders felt very bad about this information and attempted to modify their behaviors to increase the retention of younger employees. As part of their attempts, they began to call on young people in meetings to answer every question. As a result, younger employees went from being *under-protected* to *over-protected*. The leaders' intentions were great, but the new behaviors created a spotlight factor with further isolated the younger population. The more inclusive way would have been to have regular check-ins with employees to find out the reasons why they were not feeling heard and what they needed to see and experience in order to feel included. Table 4 summarizes characteristics of the over protect stage and provides suggestions for leaders to move forward.

Enlightened: "I Want to Support You…Just Struggling How"

While an *overprotective* leader in the previous stage is extremely active in terms of engaging in behaviors aiming to remove barriers *for* outsiders, an *enlightened* leader is not only extremely aware of privilege, but also uncertain of what needs to be done to mitigate the impact. In the enlightened stage, leaders realize overprotection is not the right solution and at the same time, they do not seem to have a better one. We have encountered *enlightened* leaders who realized existing concerns around D&I, but due to internal discomfort, fear or lack of knowledge were unable to find a solution.

We like to say that inclusion is a *contact sport*, but many times the enlightened population attempts to find the appropriate responses on their own, without making contact with others who have dimensions of difference and therefore valuable insight. One leader we knew strongly believed that his organization was extremely conservative

Table 4. Overprotection stage: thoughts/beliefs and behaviors, and development steps

Stage/Focus	Thoughts/Beliefs	Behavior	Steps For Leaders To Develop
Over- Protection	• Outsiders are victims of oppression who need protection • Strongly empathize with outsiders	Seeking to understand and relating to outsiders versus supporting and challenging them to achieve.	1. Recognize your own need to overprotect and understand what is driving it (e.g. guilt, the need to be needed, a belief that outsiders are incapable of succeeding on their own, or they are not competent enough due to victimization) 2. Refrain from deciding for outsiders what they need 3. Ask outsiders what support they need

and that as a result, Gay, Lesbian, Bisexual, and Transgendered (GLBT) employees experienced fewer opportunities for advancement. He had a genuine desire to support the GLBT employees, but rather then reach out to them, he kept having conversations with his heterosexual colleagues attempting to find information that would help him empower GLBT colleagues for success. He was enlightened but his source of insight might not have been the best.

The difference between this leader and leaders in the other privilege stages was that he genuinely believed the validity of his GLBT co-workers' concerns and he wanted to address their challenges with inclusion; he just chose an incomplete path as the source of information. To offer a comparison, a *blissful* leader would overlook and dismiss the challenge, perhaps responding that *the world is not fair* or that *sexual orientation does not belong in the workplace anyway*. In contrast, the overprotective leader might rush to rescue his colleagues without getting their input.

Table 5 summarizes characteristics of the enlightened stage and provides suggestions for leaders to move forward.

Managing Privilege: "Tell Me What You Need from Me to Perform Your Best"

We believe that managing privilege refers to both leaders' mindset and behaviors. In order to become truly inclusive leaders, we must first see and believe that there is value in others and then have the courage and competence to bring that value to life. A CEO at one organization had lunch with employee resource group members once a month just to chat and understand what the organization's experience was like from their perspective. The power of this story is threefold. First, he realized his experience was not the norm. Second, he realized he probably could not gain this insight from his closest colleagues. Third, he was willing to *come down* to the level of employees to see the world from their perspective. This gave him personal knowledge to both understand and lead the entire population he was responsible for.

Managing privilege can also take place on a micro-level and yet have powerful impacts. In one of the organizations there was a younger female who started her work as an intern. Although she was eventually hired full time, the label *intern* followed her and she frequently complained of feeling not heard and valued. Unfortunately, many colleagues dismissed her concerns. She then approached a well-respected male with long tenure who truly heard her challenges. Then, one day, in a team meeting, he observed how the team was talking over her while she was giving a presentation and were somewhat dismissive of her input. He drew the team's attention to what was happening and all of a sudden they came *out of bliss* and realized that they had been unconsciously excluding that female. That employee managed his tenure

Table 5. Enlightened stage: thoughts/beliefs and behaviors, and development steps

Stage/Focus	Thoughts/Beliefs	Behavior	Steps for Leaders to Develop
Enlightened	• Aware of the unique talents and abilities of outsiders • Uncomfortable or doesn't know how to sponsor or challenge outsiders to achieve at a high level	Able to give insight to fellow insiders about the challenges of outsiders	1. Reach out to outsiders to find out what they expect in terms of opportunities, support, development and coaching, etc. 2. Uncover what stands in outsiders' way to fulfilling their potential and utilizing their talent and skills 3. Assist with equal opportunities and support outsiders' accountability to perform their own job

and male privilege to help include his younger co-worker. The key to managing privilege is not to do it in a way that creates overprotection. It is how you do it that makes a difference; you need to do it skillfully. Table 6 summarizes characteristics of the managing privilege stage and provides suggestions for leaders to move forward.

INCLUSIVE LEADERS EMPOWERING OTHER LEADERS

As inclusive leaders develop the ability to manage privilege, we believe that their next responsibility is to help other leaders manage privilege as well. There are three keys to leaders helping other leaders manage privilege: 1) be an open and sharing example of the benefits you personally have received through managing privilege; 2) question your fellow leaders by asking questions about how many different vantage points they have considered in their decisions; and 3) exhibit the skills of managing privilege when working alongside fellow leaders and colleagues.

There was a top leader that we worked with that proactively wanted to know what his direct reports' perspectives were regarding all key decisions. At the end of each meeting he had three questions he would always ask: 1) What are your reactions to the meeting? 2) What excited you most about the meeting? and 3) What concerns do you have about the meeting? After understanding and accepting the concept of managing privilege, he added a fourth question to his list: 4) Whose opinion have we not considered?

Once his fellow leaders responded to the above question, he would then probe to see how well they knew the thoughts of groups of people often not considered. If they were unaware of the varying perspectives, he would then task them to go find out more. He called about a year later after implementing this question and told us it was no longer needed. All of his leaders came to each meeting with intimate knowledge of the viewpoints of all of their people. At first, the input came from different levels and progressed to discussions about some of the often not-dealt-with dimensions. The quality and breadth of decisions was vastly enhanced. Even when decisions remained the same, they were communicated differently and approached differently to value the different viewpoints of all stakeholders.

We can therefore end where we began. A belief we shared early in this chapter was that the world is full of good people. Embracing the concept of managing privilege empowers those around us while at the same time puts a spotlight on the goodness that exists within all of us.

Table 6. Managing privilege stage: thoughts/beliefs and behaviors, and development steps

Focus / Stage	Thoughts/Beliefs	Behavior	Steps for Leaders to Develop
Managing Privilege	• To remain sustainable both today and in the future it is important to embrace differences and leverage all talent	Leveraging the unique talents and abilities of outsiders. Effectively challenging and supports outsiders to attain high level of achievement.	1. Continue to manage privilege and make sure to check in on how you are doing - seek feedback 2. Watch out for the risk of "resting in peace" and feeling like "you got it" and others don't – stay humble and continue to revisit your own privilege and its impact on your success 3. Be a champion and coach for others who are struggling with their journey to manage privilege

ACKNOWLEDGMENT

The authors would like to express their gratitude for editing contributions from Jay Colker and Scott Hoesman. Thank you!

REFERENCES

Adler, N. J. (2002). *International dimensions of organizational behavior* (4th ed.). Cincinnati, OH: South-Western/Thomson Learning.

Collins, P. H. (2000). *Black feminist thought: Knowledge, consciousness, and the politics of empowerment* (2nd ed.). New York, NY: Rutledge.

Ferber, A. L. (2010). Dismantling privilege and becoming an activist. In Kimmel, M. S., & Ferber, A. L. (Eds.), *Privilege: A Reader* (2nd ed.). Boulder, CO: Westview Press.

Gardiner, R. A. (2011). A critique of the discourse of authentic leadership. *International Journal of Business & Social Science, 2*(15), 99–104.

Hardiman, R., Jackson, B. W., & Griffin, P. (2010). Conceptual foundations. In Adams, M., Blumenfeld, W. J., Castaňeda, C., Hackman, H. W., Peters, M. L., & Zuňiga, X. (Eds.), *Readings for Diversity and Social Justice* (2nd ed.). New York, NY: Routledge/Taylor & Francis Group.

Hofstede, G., & Hofstede, G. J. (2005). *Cultures and organizations: Software of the mind.* New York, NY: McGraw-Hill.

Hollander, E. P. (2009). *Inclusive leadership: The essential leader-follower relationship.* New York, NY: Routledge/Taylor & Francis Group.

Jameson, D. A. (2007). Reconceptualizing cultural identity and its role in intercultural business communication. *Journal of Business Communication, 44*(3), 199–235. doi:10.1177/0021943607301346

Johnson, A. G. (2006). *Privilege, power and difference* (2nd ed.). New York, NY: McGraw-Hill.

Kimmel, M. S., & Ferber, A. L. (Eds.). (2010). *Privilege: A reader* (2nd ed.). Boulder, CO: Westview Press.

Kirk, G., & Okazawa-Rey, M. (2010). Identities and social locations: Who am I? Who are my people? In Adams, M., Blumenfeld, W. J., Castaňeda, C., Hackman, H. W., Peters, M. L., & Zuňiga, X. (Eds.), *Readings for Diversity and Social Justice* (2nd ed.). New York, NY: Routledge/Taylor & Francis Group.

McIntosh, P. (1988). *White privilege and male privilege: A personal account of coming to see correspondences through work in women's studies.* Working Paper 189. Boston, MA: Wellesley.

Miller, F. A., & Katz, J. H. (2002). *The inclusion breakthrough: Unleashing the real power of diversity.* San Francisco, CA: Berrett-Koehler Publishers, Inc.

Monaghan, C. H. (2010). Working against the grain: White privilege in human resource development. *New Directions for Adult and Continuing Education, 125,* 53–63. doi:10.1002/ace.362

Powell, A. A., Branscombe, N. R., & Schmitt, M. T. (2005). Inequality as ingroup privilege or outgroup disadvantage: The impact of group focus on collective guilt and interracial attitudes. *Personality and Social Psychology Bulletin, 31*(4), 508–521. doi:10.1177/0146167204271713

Prewitt, J., Weil, R., & McClure, A. (2011). Developing leadership in global and multi-cultural organizations. *International Journal of Business and Social Science, 2*(13), 14–20.

Rosette, A. S., & Plunkett Tost, L. (2007). Denying white privilege in organizations: The perceptions of race-based advantages as socially normative. In *Proceedings of the Academy of Management Annual Meeting,* (pp. 1-6). Academy of Management.

Ross, R. (2011, July). Creating an inclusive environment. *Training Journal,* 28-30.

Ryan, J. (2007). Inclusive leadership. *University of Toronto*. Retrieved from http://fcis.oise.utoronto.ca/~jryan/pub_files/incleadership.pdf.

Tapia, A. T. (2009). *The inclusion paradox: The Obama era and the transformation of global diversity*. Lincolnshire, IL: Hewitt Associates.

Wildman, S. M. (1996). Privilege in the workplace: The missing element in antidiscrimination law. In Wildman, S. M., Armstrong, M., Davis, A. D., & Grillo, T. (Eds.), *Privilege Revealed: How Invisible Preference Undermines AMERICA*. New York, NY: New York University Press.

Wildman, S. M., & Davis, A. D. (1996). Making systems of privilege work. In Wildman, S. M., Armstrong, M., Davis, A. D., & Grillo, T. (Eds.), *Privilege Revealed: How Invisible Preference Undermines America*. New York, NY: New York University Press.

KEY TERMS AND DEFINITIONS[4]

Diversity: Variety of abilities, skills, experiences, and cultural backgrounds, in all stakeholders.

Inclusion: Valuing and leveraging differences to achieve superior results.

Inclusive Leadership: Leadership characterized by: 1) integrating diversity and inclusion into the business strategy; 2) fostering an inclusive and fair work environment; 3) building effective relationships across lines of difference; 4) attracting, coaching, sponsoring, and developing diverse talent; 5) managing inclusively; and 6) managing privilege.

Insiders/Outsiders: Those who are/are not in the norm, majority, power.

Journey to Managing Privilege: The Kaleidoscope Group's model describing stages leaders go through before they are able to effectively manage privilege. These stages can be described as *bliss, awareness, overprotection, enlightened*, and ultimately *managing privilege*.

Managing Privilege: Effectively addressing the subtle, unearned advantages that enhance one's success and hinder the success of others.

Privilege: The absence of barriers and the presence of unearned positive advantages.

ENDNOTES

[1] We looked for the exact phrases such as White Privilege, etc. in the EBSCO host database.

[2] Schneider-Ross consultancy lists the following 6 competency clusters of inclusive leadership: "1. Listening and observation, 2. Open-minded and engaging, 3. Rapport-building, 4. Collaborative innovation, 5. Feedback exchange, 6. Flexible leadership style" (Ross, 2011, p. 29).

[3] Based on his interviews with HR managers, Allan (2006) lists additional reasons "why dominant groups don't see privilege as a problem" (pp. 69-71).

[4] The definitions are from The Kaleidoscope Group, L.L.C. All rights reserved.

Chapter 9
Developing Global Leaders:
Utilizing the Intercultural Effectiveness Competencies Model

Pi-Chi Han
University of Missouri – St. Louis, USA

ABSTRACT

Although the need to develop global leaders with adequate intercultural competencies has become obvious (Morrison, 2000; Suutari, 2002), global leadership, as an emerging field, has not received a great deal of attention (Morrison, 2000). Literature of developing global leadership has been focused on partial evidence to generate simple universality with an American bias (Dickson, Hartog, & Mitchelson, 2003). This chapter attempts to propose an integrative Intercultural Effectiveness (ICE) model for Human Resource Development (HRD) professionals. The model evolves a theoretical conceptualization to link ICE and global leadership with the theory of transformative learning and the process of cross-cultural learning. It provides a series of process guidelines for HRD professionals in designing, developing, and conducting HRD programs for the development of global leadership.

INTRODUCTION

Today's global economy has created an ever-changing environment in which most organizations must learn to cope with the change. Under the trend of globalization, the global environment has not only changed the way organization is conducted, it has also changed the criteria of effective leadership practices (Caligiuri & Tarique, 2009). Developing global leadership has become a critical issue discussed in much of international business literature (Brake, 1997; Bueno & Tubbs, 2004; Conner, 2000; Gregersen, et al., 1998; Kets de Vries & Mead, 1992; Moran & Riesenberger, 1994; Rhinesmith, 1996; Rosen & Digh, 2000; Speitzer, et al., 1997; Srinivas, 1995; Suutari, 2002).

DOI: 10.4018/978-1-4666-1812-1.ch009

Literature reveals that finding talented global leaders is getting harder due to the lack of global talent (Bhasin & Cheng, 2001). The most challenging task many global organizations are facing is developing a cadre of global leaders for helping them survive and move forward (Pucik, 1984). Conner (2000) asserted that accelerating globalization, new technology, and intense competition strengthens the need to develop future global leaders who are equiped with international skills and knowledge that help them to face the ever-changing world. The need to develop global leaders with adequate intercultural competencies has become obvious (Morrison, 2000; Suutari, 2002). The implication has made a significant impact on the field of Human Resource Development (HRD) (Osman-Gani, 2000; Yaw, McGovern, & Budhwar, 2000). The purpose of this chapter, therefore, is to propose an integrative model of Intercultural Effectiveness (ICE) competencies, to conceptualize intercultural competencies, to identify the processes and the outcomes of cross-cultural learning, and to highlight guidelines for HRD to develop global leaders.

GLOBAL LEADERSHIP

Global leadership is an emerging topic that has received far less attention than the more common topic of domestic leadership (Morrison, 2000). Jokinen (2005) defined global leaders as those who take on more global responsibilities and who have more global duties. The development and management of a global organization requires individuals who possess a global mindset, global competencies, and who think, lead, and act from a global perspective (Kim, 1997).

However, the primary problem in defining global leaders and identifying the competencies required for their development have not reached consensus. Without agreement on the intercultural competencies required for global leaders (Johnson, Lenartowicz, & Apud, 2006), planning for their

leadership development becomes problematic (Jokinen, 2005).

Gregersen et al.'s (1998) survey indicated that 85% of Fortune 500 firms reported limited numbers of global leaders. There are only eight percent of companies in Fortune 500 firms that report comprehensive systems for developing global leaders (Suutari, 2002). The shortage of global leaders has become a critical issue for many organizations to achieve success in the global arena (Shen, 2005). Therefore, it is necessary to explore the competencies that are required for developing global leaders in order to form a consensus for the area of global leadership.

Global Leadership Competencies

The competencies of global leaders empower them to perform jobs across cultures effectively. Caligiuri and Tarique (2009) pointed out that effectiveness of global leadership can be fostered by developing the intercultural competencies or facilitating the global mindset across the nations for leaders. Reviewing the literature, a summary of competencies for developing global leaders is presented in Table 1.

Similarly, Virjee (2004) asserted that the "single-most important skill to acquire in the 21st century is intercultural competence" (p. 35). Caligiuri and Tarique (2009) suggested by the practice of intercultural competencies, the effectiveness in global leadership activities can be facilitated.

Intercultural Effectiveness Competencies (ICE)

Intercultural competency is a concept that has been explored and researched under different terms, such as cross-cultural effectiveness (Kealey, 1989), cross-cultural adjustment (Benson, 1978), cross-cultural competence (Ruben 1989), cross-cultural communication effectiveness (Ruben, 1987), intercultural effectiveness (Cui& Van Den

Table 1. Global leader competency framework

Authors	Global Leader Competency Framework
Hofstede (1980)	The capacity to communicate respect, to be non-judgmental, to accept the relativity of one's own knowledge and perceptions, to display empathy, to be flexible, for turning-taking, tolerance for ambiguity
Ruben (1989)	Building an d maintaining relationship, transferring information, and gaining compliance
Kets de Vries and Mead (1992)	Envisioning; empowerment; networking; cognitive complexity; hardiness; and cultural adaptation
Moran and Riesenberger (1994)	Global mindset, quality with diversity, long-term orientation, facilitating organizational change, creating learning systems, motivating to excellence, negotiating conflicts, masterful the foreign deployment, leading multicultural teams, understanding self culture, profiling others' culture, demonstrating knowledge and respect to other countries.
Strinivas (1995)	A curiosity with context, acceptance of complexity and contradictions, diversity consciousness, seeking opportunity in uncertainties, trusting and delegating responsibility, focusing on continuous improvement, long-term view, stems thinking.
Rhinesmith (1996)	Global mindset, balancing contradictions, engaging process, flowing with change, valuing diversity, learning globally, personal characteristics (i.e. open, sensitive, flexible, strategic, analytical, and knowledgeable), managing competition, managing complexity, managing alignment, managing change, managing teams, and managing learning.
Brake (1997)	Business acumen (i.e. global perspective, entrepreneurial spirit, and professional expertise), relationship management (i.e. stakeholder orientation, organization astuteness, change agentry, community building, conflict management, cross-cultural communication, influencing), and personal effectiveness (competencies of accountability, curiosity and learning, maturity, thinking agility).
Speitzer et al. (1997)	Sensitiveness to cultural differences, business knowledge, courage to take action, interpersonal skills, acting with integrity, be insightful, Be committed to success, take risk, use feedback, be cultural adventurous, seek opportunities to learn, be open to criticism, seek feedback, be flexible.
Gregersen et al. (1998)	Inquisitiveness (i.e. having a desire to see and experience new things), exhibiting character (i.e. emotional connection and integrity), embracing duality (i.e. managing uncertainty and balancing tensions), demonstrating savvy.
Meldrum and Atkinson (1998)	Cognitive skills, emotional resilience, personal drive.
Goldsmith and Walt (1999)	Thinking globally, appreciating cultural diversity, demonstrating technology savvy, building partnerships, sharing leadership.
Conner (2000)	Business savvy, personal influence and communication skills, perspective, strong character, motivational and inspirational skills, entrepreneurial behavior.
Rosen and Digh (2000)	Personal literacy (i.e. competence of leading by example, being confident in the face of change and uncertainty, having strong principles and beliefs, having self-awareness, being committed to continuous learning), social literacy (i.e. being able to inspire others to action and excellence, being an effective listener and communicator, being able to encourage others to adopt common goals and values, being a teacher and coach, being able to transform conflict into creative action), business literacy (being able to build a culture of learning and innovation, helping people to adapt to change, focusing on leadership development, giving decision-making authority to others, educating people, promoting job security).
Lorange (2003)	A strategic capability, a partnership capability, a staffing capability, a learning capability, an organizational capability.
Bueno and Tubbs (2004)	Communication skills, motivation to learn, flexibility, open-mindedness, respect for others, and sensitivity.
Jokinen (2005)	The core of global leadership (i.e. self-awareness, engagement in personal transformation, inquisitiveness), desired mental characteristics (i.e. optimism, self-regulation, social judgment skills, empathy, motivation to work in international environment, cognitive skills, acceptance of complexity), desired behavioral competencies (i.e. social skills, networking skills, knowledge).

Berg, 1991; Hammer, Gudykunst, & Wiseman, 1978; Hanningan, 1990), intercultural competence (Dinges, 1983), and intercultural communication competence (Kim, 1991; Spitzberg, 1989; Wiseman, Hammer, & Nishida, 1989). One of most common definitions of intercultural competence is effectiveness (Han, 1997, 2008; Hawes & Kealey, 1979; Abe & Wiseman, 1983; Gudyskunst & Hammer, 1984).

The literature describes cultural competence as a learning process that results in the change of knowledge, attitude, and skill (Kim & Ruben, 1988; Shim & Paprock, 2002). Many researchers (Chang, 2007; Chin, Gu, & Tubbs, 2001; Taylor, 1994) asserted that acquiring intercultural competence is a personal transformational process or viewed it as an integrative and transformative process (Kim & Ruben, 1988; Mezirow, 1991). Taylor (1994) cited Mezirow's (1991) transformative learning theory and pointed out that "In effect, the literature seems to indicate that intercultural competence is a transformative process" (p. 155). He viewed intercultural competence as an adaptive capacity allowing individuals to become effective across cultures. Chang (2007) implied that personal transformation is the final stage for the cross-cultural learning process. Chin, Gu, and Tubbs' (2001) Global Leadership Competencies Model presents a three-level pyramidal hierarchy for developing global leadership. The final level of this model is a personal transformation in the behavioral level.

In addition to the personal transformation process, achieving success and effectiveness in a new culture can be the optimal outcome of cross-cultural learning (Han, 2011). Han (1997, 2008) proposed an ICE five-competence model to measure ICE competencies. In order to reach the optimal learning outcome of cross-cultural learning for acquiring ICE, the individual should develop the following ICE competencies: (a) the ability to handle psychological stress, (b) the ability to effectively communicate, (c) the ability

to establish interpersonal relationships, (d) the ability to have cross-cultural awareness, and (e) the ability to have cultural empathy.

Developing Global Leaders

Accordingly, scholars have asserted that acquiring intercultural competence is the result of cross-cultural learning and an on-going transformative learning (Bartel-Radic, 2006; Hannigan, 1990). Bartel-Radic (2006) has defined intercultural learning as "the acquisition or modification of the representations of intercultural situations" (p. 652). Mezirow (1991) elaborated that the change or modification from cross-cultural learning is an integrative and transformative learning process. During the period of interacting with others, the modification process takes place. In the assumption of intercultural learning, representations are the learning outcomes, while acquisition and modification are the learning processes (Han, 2011).

Kim and Ruben (1988) also confirmed that the process is transformational and it is a learning and growth process that allows individuals to function effectively across cultural and national boundaries. Mezirow (2000) concluded that "the process by which we transform our taken-for-granted frames of reference (meaning schemes, habits of mind, and mindsets) to make them more inclusive, discriminating, open, emotionally capable of change, and reflective so that they may generate beliefs and options that will prove more true or justified to guide action" (p. 8).

Although Taylor (1994) argued there is a significant relationship between intercultural competence and transformative learning, he has not provided theoretical conceptualizations of how individuals develop intercultural competencies. This chapter attempts to incorporate the theory of transformative learning and cross-cultural learning as the theoretical foundation to conceptualizing the process of how and what individuals acquire ICE competencies. An integrative ICE model (See

Figure 1) has been developed for helping Human Resource Development (HRD) professionals in designing, developing, and conducting HRD programs for individuals to obtain ICE competencies ICE (Han, 2011).

The following questions should be explored to examine the role of HRD in the personal transformation of individuals during the change process: (a) how can the individual transform the mindset from the resistance of the change to the willingness for change? (b) How does personal maturity levels of cognition and development impact cross-cultural learning acquisition and modification? (c) How can effective reflection serve as the means to obtain effective cross-cultural representation? (d) How can transformative learning be the process outcome of cross-cultural learning? and (e) How can the individual develop ICE competencies as the optimal outcomes of cross-cultural learning?

Brownell (2006) utilized a holistic approach and proposed a competency-based model for developing global leaders. There are two-fold ap-

proaches in his model: (a) common competencies such as the fundamental knowledge and skills, and (b) distinctive competencies including personal characteristics. Brownell (2006) suggested that it is not enough to focus on developing common competencies for global leadership and stated, "global leaders must be men and women of sound of character" (p. 309). Therefore, the quality of credibility, trustworthiness, fairness, honesty, respect for others, and humility, which belong to personal characters are imperative for the development of global leadership. Furthermore, Brownell (2006) argued that emotional intelligence competencies also become a crucial element in the development of global leaders. Interpersonal acumen (Aditya & House, 2002) and cultural acumen (Javidan & House, 2001) are presented as the necessities of global leaders. A global perspective, synergistic learning, and cross-cultural sensitivity (Townsend & Cairns, 2003) and cultural consciousness and global mindset (Cant, 2004) were described as the personal abilities and attributes of global leadership in those studies. The question is how and

Figure 1. Integrative model of ICE (Han, 2011)

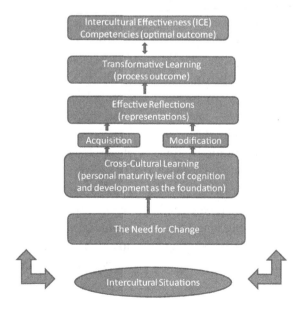

what HRD interventions of methods and strategies may help the organization develop global leaders. This inquiry directly requests HRD professionals' involvement.

HRD Interventions and Developing Global Leaders

Cross-cultural training has been related to the development of intercultural competencies of developing global leaders (Shen, 2005). Lee (1983) indicated that the importance of cross-cultural training in preparing an individual for an intercultural work assignment is crucial. Cross-cultural training is advocated as a means of facilitating effective cross-cultural interaction (Bochner, 1982; Han, 1997, 2008, 2011; Harris & Moran, 1987; Mendenhall & Oddou, 1986). Cardon (2006) asserted that cross-cultural training is vital to improve global leaders' job performance and satisfaction, and it is necessary to reduce global leaders' failure (Gudykunst, Guzley, & Hammer, 1996).

In addition to cross-cultural training, there are other interventions that help develop global leadership such as international assignments, short-term development assignments, international teams, action learning groups, international meetings and forums, and international travel (Suutari, 2002) and cultural mentorship (Shim & Paprock, 2002). Maznevski and DiStefano (2000) identified global leaders to be the global team players. Gregerson et al. (1998) proposed four strategies—international travel, the formation of diversified teams, international assignments, and training—for developing global leaders. Furthermore, Kramer (2005) suggested the three tactics for developing global leaders: (1) providing feedback for the performance and potential, (2) assigning long-term international assignments, and (3) developing international cross-functional team.

FUTURE RESEARCH DIRECTIONS

The topic of developing the intercultural competencies of global leaders makes several implications for future research in the field of HRD. First, leadership is rooted in the leaders' characteristics regarding personal qualities such as fairness, humility, and concern for the greater good. Educators and HRD professionals should embark on helping individuals identify key personal characteristics of global leadership (Brownell, 2006). Second, ICE acknowledges transfer and learning as based on experiential learning theory; and, we are able to understand the process of knowledge transfer (Kolb & Kolb, 2002). Learning is a continuous process rooted in experience. Different cultural contexts shape an individual's experience in diverse ways. Jokinen (2005) concluded that it is necessary to recognize and understand the importance of different types of previous experience in order to develop one's global leadership competencies.

Third, in terms of global assignments and global talent, Kramer (2005) has proposed a long-term international assignment as one of tactics to develop global talent. It is recommended to have more empirical studies to probe the relationship between duration of global assignments and development of global talent and leaders. In addition, it is recommended that empirical longitudinal studies investigating intercultural experiences of young households and personal lives or within the workplace and professional lives of individuals may provide the level of in-depth of understanding desired when striving to develop global talent.

Fourth, Dickson et al. (2003) revealed that many American biases exist in the current global leadership studies. Townsend and Cairns (2003) pointed out that the present theories for developing global leaders and managers have focused on western cultures that are not always relevant to the applications of Asian cultures. Much research (Caligiuri & Tarique, 2009; Dickson, et al., 2003) was based on the sample of Anglo leaders. To avoid the American bias, Merriam (2010) asserted that the blend of non-western perspectives in adult learning has been a trend under globalization and it is important for us to examine "the privileged position of Western assumptions about learning and knowing North American" (Merriam, 2010, p. 404).

Finally, higher education institutes, curriculum developers, and policy makers have faced the challenge of how to prepare their global-ready graduates with the intercultural competencies as the future global leaders. HR professionals and educators should work together in the development of high-performing global future leaders (Brownell, 2006). Finally, in terms of theory building for developing the ICE for global leaders, Lynham (2000) drew an attention to the role of theory building in advancing professionalism and maturity for the HRD professional. An integrative ICE model (Han, 2011) attempted to tackle this inquiry by incorporating theory of transformative learning and the process of cross-cultural learning to conceptualize ICE competencies for developing global leaders in the cross-cultural settings. Bueno and Tubbs (2004) believed personal transformation is the final developmental stage for developing global leadership. In the integrative ICE model (Han, 2011), the process outcome is personal transformative learning while the optimal outcomes are the ICE five competencies. The ICE integrative model enriches the literature for HRD to advance professionalism by the theory building process.

CONCLUSION

In the global arena, leaders have been requested to enhance their intercultural competence to work together, manage diversity, complexity, ambiguity, and even personal stress. "Developing tomorrow's global leaders is not an easy task, and the concept of leadership has never been simple or static" (Brownell, 2006, p. 329). Gregersen et al. (1998) asserted that global leaders are born and then made. They proposed three key elements, talent, opportunity, and training, to produce global leaders.

It may be hard to predict how individual's inherited talents can be identified for development while it may have a way to create and cultivate individual's learning. Opportunities may come from external physical world, while it actually starts from the internal thoughts and intention that individuals pursue and create on the way. In Bandura's (1977, 1986) social learning theory, he asserted that humans can regulate their own behaviors and have self-efficacy assisting to successfully perform and fulfill a behavior in a particular context or situation

Besides, literature (Bass & Steidlmeier, 1999; Black & Gregersen, 2000; Brownell, 2006; Johnson, Lenartowicz, & Apud, 2006) drew special attention to the relationship between personal characteristics and qualities and the development of global leaders. Personality traits such as self-efficacy and perseverance help global leadership in the direction of overcoming difficulties and challenges (Johnson, Lenartowicz, & Apud, 2004). Based on various levels of personal maturity in reacting to various difficulties and challenges in the cross-cultural interactions, individuals may either excuse themselves from the difficult scene or create the opportunity as it is triggered by the need of change.

Deriving from the theory of transformative learning, an integrative ICE model provides a theoretical conceptualization to transform the difficulties and challenges from the need of change. Based on the ICE model, the theory of transformative learning and the process of cross-cultural learning may navigate an optimal ICE learning journey of developing the five ICE competencies for the individual's cross-cultural learning. In addition, it provides HRD professional the direction to advance professionalism in developing global leadership with the integrative ICE model.

Training may be a crucial mechanism for HRD professionals to develop global leaders. It may be the only one element that HRD professional can have a real involvement. The model evolves a theoretical conceptualization to link ICE and global leadership with the theory of transformative learning, and provides a series of process guidelines for HRD professionals in designing, developing, and conducting HRD programs for the development of global leadership by acquiring ICE as the optimal learning outcome in cross-cultural interactions.

"Leadership doesn't simply happen. It can be taught, learned, and developed" (Giuliani, 2002, p. xii). The need of global leadership education becomes extremely important due to the increasing level of interactions between nations, cultures, and people from different cultural backgrounds creating possible conflicts and challenges (Funakawa, 1997). Therefore, HRD professionals need to take a proactive role in the process of developing global leaders. They must move from the reactive role to the proactive one in order to facilitate continuous learning, manage change, and develop intercultural competencies for the organization. A new mindset will evolve from the attempt of theory building of global leadership with an integrative ICE model. Once leaders begin to shift mindsets, they will be able to continue their cross-cultural learning journey to personal transformation and reach the optimal ICE competencies.

REFERENCES

Abe, H., & Wiseman, R. L. (1983). A cross-cultural confirmation of the dimensions of intercultural effectiveness. *International Journal of Intercultural Relations*, 7, 53–67. doi:10.1016/0147-1767(83)90005-6

Aditya, R., & House, R. J. (2002). Interpersonal acumen and leadership across cultures: Pointers from the GLOBE study. In Riggio, R. E., & Murphy, S. E. (Eds.), *Multiple Intelligences and Leadership* (pp. 215–240). Mahwah, NJ: Erlbaum.

Bandura, A. (1977). *Social learning theory*. Englewood Cliffs, NJ: Prentice-Hall.

Bandura, A. (1986). *Social foundations of thought and action: A social cognitive theory*. Englewood Cliffs, NJ: Prentice-Hall.

Bartel-Radic, A. (2006). Intercultural learning in global teams. *Management International Review*, 46(6), 647–677. doi:10.1007/s11575-006-0121-7

Bass, B., & Steidlmeier, P. (1999). Ethics, character, and authentic transformational leadership behavior. *The Leadership Quarterly*, 10(2), 181–217. doi:10.1016/S1048-9843(99)00016-8

Benson, P. G. (1978). Measuring cross-cultural adjustment: The problem of criteria. *International Journal of Intercultural Relations*, 2, 21–37. doi:10.1016/0147-1767(78)90027-5

Bhasin, B. B., & Cheng, P. L. K. (2001). *The fight for global talent: New directions, new competitors - A case study on Singapore*. Retrieved from http://www.emeraldinsight.com/Insight/ViewContentServlet:jsessionid=7CADD0491D61.

Black, J. S., & Gregersen, H. B. (2000). High impact training: Forging leaders for the global frontier. *Human Resource Management*, 39(2-3), 173–184. doi:10.1002/1099-050X(200022/23)39:2/3<173::AID-HRM7>3.0.CO;2-W

Bochner, S. (1982). The social psychology of cross-cultural relations. In Bochner, S. (Ed.), *Cultures in Contact: Studies in Cross-Cultural Interaction* (pp. 5–44). New York, NY: Pergamon.

Brake, T. (1997). *The global leader: Critical factors for creating the world class organization*. Chicagom, IL: Irwin Professional Publishing.

Brownell, J. (2006). Meeting the competency needs of global leaders: A partnership approach. *Human Resource Management, 45*(3), 309–336. doi:10.1002/hrm.20115

Bueno, C. M., & Tubbs, S. L. (2004). Identifying global leadership competencies: An exploratory study. *Journal of American Academy of Business, 5*(1/2), 80–87.

Caligiuri, P., & Tarique, I. (2009). Predicting effectiveness in global leadership activities. *Journal of World Business, 44*, 36–46. doi:10.1016/j.jwb.2008.11.005

Cant, A. (2004). Internationalizing the business curriculum: Developing intercultural competence. *Journal of American Academy of Business, 5*, 177–182.

Cardon, P. W. (2006). The changing nature of global assignments: Implications for cross-cultural training. *International Business*, 48-50.

Chang, W. (2007). Cultural competence of international humanitarian workers. *Adult Education Quarterly, 57*(3), 187–204. doi:10.1177/0741713606296755

Chin, C., Gu, J., & Tubbs, S. (2001). Developing global leadership competencies. *The Journal of Leadership Studies, 7*(3), 20–31. doi:10.1177/107179190100700402

Conner, J. (2000). Developing the global leaders of tomorrow. *Human Resource Management, 39*(2-3), 147–157. doi:10.1002/1099-050X(200022/23)39:2/3<147::AID-HRM5>3.0.CO;2-T

Cui, G. (1989). *Intercultural effectiveness: An integrative approach.* Paper presented at the 35th Annual Conference of the International Communication Association. San Francisco, CA.

Cui, G., & Van Den Berg, S. (1991). Testing the intercultural validity of intercultural effectiveness. *International Journal of Intercultural Relations, 15*, 227–241. doi:10.1016/0147-1767(91)90031-B

Dickson, M. W., Hartog, D. N. D., & Mitchelson, J. K. (2003). Research on leadership in a cross-cultural context: Making progress, and raising new questions. *The Leadership Quarterly, 14*, 729–768. doi:10.1016/j.leaqua.2003.09.002

Dinges, N. (1983). Intercultural competence. In Landis, D., & Brislin, R. W. (Eds.), *Handbook of Intercultural Training* (*Vol. 1*, pp. 176–202). New York, NY: Pergamon Press.

Funakawa, A. (1997). *Transcultural management: A new approach for global organizations.* San Francisco, CA: Jossey-Bass.

Giuliani, R. W. (2002). *Leadership.* New York, NY: Miramax Books.

Goldsmith, M., & Walt, K. (1999, December/January). New competencies for tomorrow's global leader. *CMA Management*, 20-24.

Gregerson, H. B., Morrison, A. J., & Black, G. S. (1998, Fall). Developing leaders in the global frontier. *Sloan Management Review*, 21–32.

Gudykunst, W. B., Guzley, R. M., & Hammer, M. R. (1996). Designing intercultural training. In Landis, D., & Bhagat, R. S. (Eds.), *Handbook of Intercultural Training.* Thousand Oaks, CA: Sage.

Gudykunst, W. B., & Hammer, M. R. (1984). Dimension of intercultural effectiveness: Culture specific or general. *International Journal of Intercultural Relations, 8*, 1–10. doi:10.1016/0147-1767(84)90003-8

Hammer, M. R., Gudykunst, W. B., & Wiseman, R. L. (1978). Dimensions of intercultural effectiveness: An exploratory study. *International Journal of Intercultural Relations, 2*, 383–393. doi:10.1016/0147-1767(78)90036-6

Han, P. C. (1997). *An investigation of intercultural effectiveness of international university students with implications for human resource development.* Unpublished Doctoral dissertation. Fayetteville, AR: University of Arkansas.

Han, P. C. (2008). An investigation of intercultural effectiveness for foreign-born faculty in Taiwan. *The International Journal of Learning, 15*(10), 165–174.

Han, P. C. (2011). Developing intercultural effectiveness competencies: The journey of transformative learning and cross-cultural learning for foreign-born faculty in American higher education. In Boden, C. J., & Kippers, S. M. (Eds.), *Pathway to Transformation: Learning in Relationship.* Charlotte, NC: Information Age Publishing.

Hannigan, T. P. (1990). Traits, attitudes, and skills that are related to intercultural effectiveness and their implications for cross-cultural training: A review of the literature. *International Journal of Intercultural Relations, 13*, 89–111. doi:10.1016/0147-1767(90)90049-3

Harris, P. R., & Moran, R. T. (1987). *Managing cultural differences* (2nd ed.). Houston, TX: Gulf Publishing Company.

Hawes, R., & Kealey, D. (1979). *Canadians in development: An empirical study of adaptations and effectiveness on overseas assignment.* Quebec, Canada: Canadian International Development Agency.

Hofstede, G. (1980). *Cultures consequences: International differences in working-related values.* Beverly Hills, CA: Sage.

Johnson, J. P., Lenartowicz, T., & Apud, S. (2006). Cross-cultural competence in international business: Toward a definition and a model. *Journal of International Business Studies, 37*, 525–543. doi:10.1057/palgrave.jibs.8400205

Jokinen, T. (2005). Global leadership competencies: A review and discussion. *Journal of European Industrial Training, 29*(3), 199–216. doi:10.1108/03090590510591085

Kealey, D. J. (1989). A study of cross-cultural effectiveness: Theoretical issues, practical applications. *International Journal of Intercultural Relations, 13*, 387–428. doi:10.1016/0147-1767(89)90019-9

Kelley, C., & Meyers, J. (1995). *CCAI (cross-cultural adaptability inventory) manual.* Minneapolis, MN: National Computer Systems, Inc.

Kets de Vries, M. F. R., & Mead, C. (1992). The development of the global leader within the multinational corporation. In Pucik, V., Tichy, N. M., & Barnett, C. K. (Eds.), *Globalizing Management: Creating and Leading the Competitive Organization* (pp. 187–205). New York, NY: John Wiley.

Kim, P. S. (1997). Globalization of human resource management in government: A cross-cultural perspective. In E. E. Holton, III (Ed.), *Academy of Human Resource Development Conference Proceedings,* (pp. 675-678). Atlanta, GA: Academy of Human Resource Development.

Kim, Y. Y. (1991). Intercultural communication competence. In Ting-Toomey, S., & Korzenny, F. (Eds.), *Cross-Cultural Interpersonal Communication* (pp. 259–275). Newberry Park, CA: Sage.

Kim, Y. Y., & Ruben, B. D. (1988). Intercultural transformation. In Kim, Y. Y., & Gudy Kunst, W. B. (Eds.), *Theories in Intercultural Communication* (pp. 299–321). London, UK: Sage.

Kolb, D. A., & Kolb, A. (2002). *Bibliography on experiential learning theory.* Retrieved from http://www.learningfromexperience.com/Research_Library.

Kramer, R. (2005). *Developing global leaders.* New York, NY: The Conference Board.

Lee, C. (1983). Cross-cultural training: Don't leave home without it. *Training (New York, N.Y.)*, *20*(7), 20–25.

Lorange, P. (2003, September/October). Developing global leaders. *BizEd*, 24-27.

Lynham, S. A. (2000). Theory building in the human resource development professional. *Human Resource Development Quarterly*, *11*(2), 159–178. doi:10.1002/1532-1096(200022)11:2<159::AID-HRDQ5>3.0.CO;2-E

Maznevski, M., & DiStefano, J. (2000). Global leaders are team players: Developing global leaders through membership on global teams. *Human Resource Management*, *9*(2-3), 195–208. doi:10.1002/1099-050X(200022/23)39:2/3<195::AID-HRM9>3.0.CO;2-I

McLean, G. N., Bartlett, K. R., & Chao, E. (2003). Human resource development as national policy: Republic of Korea and New Zealand. *Pacific-Asian Education*, *15*(1), 41–59.

Meldrum, M., & Atkinson, S. (1998). Meta-abilities and the implementation of strategy: Knowing what to do is simple not enough. *Journal of Management Development*, *17*(8), 564–575. doi:10.1108/02621719810228425

Mendenhall, M., & Oddou, G. (1986). Acculturation profiles of expatriate managers: Implications for cross-cultural training. *The Columbia Journal of World Business*, *21*(4), 73–79.

Merriam, S. B. (2010). Globalization and the role of adult and continuing education: Challenges and opportunities. In Kasworm, C., Rose, A., & Ross-Gordon, J. (Eds.), *Handbook of Adult and Continuing Education: 2010 Edition* (pp. 401–409). Thousand Oaks, CA: Sage.

Mezirow, J. (1991). *Transformative dimensions of adult learning*. San Francisco, CA: Jossey-Bass.

Mezirow, J. (2000). Learning to think like an adult: Core concepts of transformation theory. In Mezirow, J. (Eds.), *Learning as Transformation: Critical Perspectives on a Theory in Progress* (pp. 3–33). San Francisco, CA: Jossey-Bass.

Moran, R. T., & Riesenberger, J. R. (1994). *The global challenge: Building the new worldwide enterprise*. London, UK: McGraw-Hill Book Company.

Morrison, A. J. (2000). Developing a global leadership model. *Human Resource Management*, *39*(2-3), 117–131. doi:10.1002/1099-050X(200022/23)39:2/3<117::AID-HRM3>3.0.CO;2-1

Nadler, L., & Nadler, Z. (1989). *Developing human resources* (3rd ed.). San Francisco, CA: Jossey-Bass.

Osman-Gani, A. M (2000). Developing expatriates for the Asia Pacific region: A comparative analysis of multinational enterprise managers from five countries across three continents. *Human Resource Development Quarterly*, *11*(3), 213–236. doi:10.1002/1532-1096(200023)11:3<213::AID-HRDQ2>3.0.CO;2-#

Pucik, V. (1984). The international management of human resources. In Fombrun, C. J., Tichy, N. M., & Devanna, M. A. (Eds.), *Strategic Human Resource Management* (pp. 403–419). New York, NY: Wiley.

Rhinesmith, S. H. (1996). *A manager's guide to globalization: Six skills for success in a changing world*. New York, NY: McGraw-Hill.

Rosen, R., & Digh, P. (2000). *Global literacies: Lessons on business leadership and national cultures*. New York, NY: Simon & Schuster.

Ruben, B. D. (1989). The study of cross-cultural competence: Traditional and contemporary issues. *International Journal of Intercultural Relations*, *13*(3), 229–240. doi:10.1016/0147-1767(89)90011-4

Shen, J. (2005). International training and management development: Theory and reality. *Journal of Management Development, 24*(7/8), 656–666. doi:10.1108/02621710510608786

Shim, I. S., & Paprock, K. E. (2002). A study focusing on American expatriates' learning in host countries. *International Journal of Training and Development, 6*(1), 13–24. doi:10.1111/1468-2419.00146

Speitzer, G. M., McCall, M. W., & Mahoney, J. D. (1997). Early identification of international executive potential. *The Journal of Applied Psychology, 82*(1), 6–29. doi:10.1037/0021-9010.82.1.6

Spitzberg, B. H. (1989). Issues in the development of a theory of interpersonal competence in the intercultural context. *International Journal of Intercultural Relations, 13*, 241–268. doi:10.1016/0147-1767(89)90012-6

Srinivas, K. M. (1995). Globalization of business and the third world: Challenge of expanding the mindsets. *Journal of Management Development, 14*(3), 26–49. doi:10.1108/02621719510078957

Suutari, V. (2002). Global leader development: An emerging research agenda. *Career Development International, 7*(4), 218–233. doi:10.1108/13620430210431307

Taylor, E. W. (1994). Intercultural competency: A transformative learning process. *Adult Education Quarterly, 44*(3), 154–174. doi:10.1177/074171369404400303

Townsend, P., & Cairns, L. (2003). Developing the global manager using a capability framework. *Management Learning, 34*(3), 313–327. doi:10.1177/13505076030343002

Tung, R. L. (1981). Selection and training of personnel for overseas assignments. *The Columbia Journal of World Business, 16*(1), 68–78.

Virjee, Z. (2004). Cross-cultural learning in adult continuing education. *Education Canada, 44*(2), 35–37.

Wang, X., & McLean, G. N. (2007). The dilemma of defining international human resource development. *Human Resource Development Review, 6*(1), 96–108. doi:10.1177/1534484306296305

Wiseman, R. L., Hammer, M. R., & Nishida, H. (1989). Predictors of intercultural communication competence. *International Journal of Intercultural Relations, 13*, 349–369. doi:10.1016/0147-1767(89)90017-5

Yaw, A. D., McGovern, I., & Budhwar, P. (2000). Complementarities or competition: The development of human resources in a Southeast Asian growth triangle--Indonesia, Malaysia, and Singapore. *International Journal of Human Resource Management, 11*(2), 314–335. doi:10.1080/095851900339891

ADDITIONAL READING

Adler, N. J. (2001). Conclusion: Future issues in global development. In Mendenhall, M. E., Kuhlmann, T. M., & Stahl, G. K. (Eds.), *Developing Global Business Leaders* (pp. 257–271). Westport, CT: Quorum Books.

Aycan, Z. (2001). Expatriation: A critical step toward developing global leaders. In Mendenhall, M. E., Kuhlmann, T. M., & Stahl, G. K. (Eds.), *Developing Global Business Leaders* (pp. 119–135). Westport, CT: Quorum Books.

Bartlett, C. A., & Ghoshal, S. (1989). *Managing across borders: The transnational solution.* Boston, MA: Harvard Business School Press.

Bartlett, C. A., & Ghoshal, S. (1992). What is a global manager? *Harvard Business Review, 70*(5), 124–132.

Bird, A., & Osland, J. (2004). Global competencies: An introduction. In Lane, H., Mendenhall, M., Maznevski, M., & McNett, J. (Eds.), *Handbook of Global Management: A Guide to Managing Complexity* (pp. 57–80). Malden, MA: Blackwell Publishing.

Black, J. S. (2006). The mindset of global leaders: Inquisitiveness and duality. In Mobley, W. H., & Weldon, E. W. (Eds.), *Advances in Global Leadership* (Vol. 4, pp. 181–200). New York, NY: JAI Press. doi:10.1016/S1535-1203(06)04013-5

Black, J. S., Morrison, A. J., & Grgersen, H. B. (1999). *Global explorers: The next generation of leaders*. New York, NY: Routledge.

Caligiuri, P., & Di Santo, V. (2001). Global competence: What is it, and can it be developed through global assignments? *Human Resource Planning*, *24*(3), 27–35.

Earley, P. C., & Mosakowski, E. (2004). Cultural intelligence. *Harvard Business Review*, *82*(10), 1–9.

Engle, A. D., Mendenhall, M. E., Powers, R. L., & Stedham, Y. (2001). *Conceptualizing the global competency cube: A transnational model of human resource*. Paper presented at the Global Human Resource Management Conference. Barcelona, Spain.

Gelfand, M. J., Imai, L., & Fehr, R. (2008). Thinking intelligently about cultural intelligence: The road ahead. In Ang, S., & Van Dyne, L. (Eds.), *Handbook on Cultural Intelligence: Theory, Measurement and Applications* (pp. 375–387). New York, NY: M.E. Sharpe.

Goldsmith, M., & Walt, K. (1999, December/January). New competencies for tomorrow's global leader. *CMA Management*, 20-24.

Gupta, A. K., & Govindarajan, V. (2002). Cultivating global mindset. *The Academy of Management Executive*, *16*(1), 116–126. doi:10.5465/AME.2002.6640211

Hall, D. T., Zhu, G., & Yan, A. (2001). Developing global leaders: To hold on to them, let them go! *Advances in Global Leadership*, *2*, 327–349. doi:10.1016/S1535-1203(01)02126-8

Hanges, P. J., Dorfman, P. W., Shteynbert, G., & Bates, A. L. (2006). Culture and leadership: A connectionist information processing model. In Mobley, W. H., & Weldon, E. W. (Eds.), *Advances in Global Leadership* (Vol. 4, pp. 7–37). New York, NY: JAI Press. doi:10.1016/S1535-1203(06)04004-4

McCall, M. W. Jr, & Hollenbeck, G. P. (2002). *Developing global executives: The lessons of international experience*. Boston, MA: Harvard Business School Press.

Oddou, G., Mendenhall, M. E., & Richie, J. B. (2000). Leveraging travel as a tool for global leadership development. *Human Resource Management*, *39*(2/3), 159–172. doi:10.1002/1099-050X(200022/23)39:2/3<159::AID-HRM6>3.0.CO;2-J

Osland, J. S. (2001). The quest for transformation: The process of global leadership development. In Mendenhall, M. E., Kuhlmann, T. M., & Stahl, G. K. (Eds.), *Developing Global Business Leaders: Policies, Processes and Innovations* (pp. 137–156). Westport, CT: Quorum Books.

Pucik, V. (2006). Reframing global mindset: From thinking to acting. In Mobley, W. H., & Weldon, E. W. (Eds.), *Advances in Global Leadership* (Vol. 4, pp. 83–100). New York, NY: JAI Press. doi:10.1016/S1535-1203(06)04007-X

Roberts, K., Kossek, E. E., & Ozeki, C. (1998). Managing the global workforce: Challenges and strategies. *The Academy of Management Executive, 12*(4), 93–119. doi:10.5465/AME.1998.1333982

Rosen, R. H. (2000, April). What makes a globally literate leader?. *Chief Executive,* 46-48.

Thaler-Certer, R. E. (2000). Whither global leaders? *HRM Magazine, 45*(5), 82–86.

Tung, R. L., & Mille, E. L. (1990). Managing in the twenty-first century: The need for global orientation. *Management International Review, 30*(1), 5–18.

Van Velsor, E., Moxley, R. S., & Bunker, K. A. (2004). The leader development process. In McCauley, C. D., & Van Velsor, E. (Eds.), *Handbook of Leadership Development* (2nd ed., pp. 204–233). San Francisco, CA: Wiley.

Wills, S., & Barham, K. (1994). Being an international manager. *European Management Journal, 12*(1), 49–58. doi:10.1016/0263-2373(94)90046-9

Yamazaki, Y., & Kayes, D. C. (2004). An experiential approach to cross-cultural learning: A review and integration of competencies for successful expatriate adaptation. *Academy of Management Learning & Education, 3,* 362–379. doi:10.5465/AMLE.2004.15112543

Yukl, G. (1994). *Leadership in organizations* (3rd ed.). Englewood Cliffs, NJ: Prentice Hall.

KEY TERMS AND DEFINITIONS

Global Leaders: Jokinen (2005) defined global leaders as those who have international responsibilities and activities.

Human Resource Development: Nadler and Nadler (1989) defined HRD as "organizied learning experiences provided by employers within a specific period of time to bring about the possibility of performance improvement and/ or personal growth" (p. 6). HRD includes three context components-individual, work related issue, and organization (McLean, Barkett, & Cho, 2003).

Intercultural Competence: Taylor (1994) indicated that intercultural competence is "an adaptive capacity based on an inclusive and integrative world view which allows participants to effectively accommodate the demands of living in a host culture" (p. 154).

Intercultural Effectiveness (ICE) Competence: Kelley and Meyers (1995) defined ICE as cross-cultural competence and cross-cultural success. Cui (1989) defined ICE as the general assessment of a sojourner's ability to communicate effectively across culture. Han (1997) highlighted five measurable competencies for ICE.

Intercultural Learning: Bartel-Radic (2006) defined intercultural learning as "the acquisition or modification of the representations of intercultural situations" (p. 652).

International Human Resource Development: Wang and McLean (2007) defined "International HRD (also known, perhaps more appropriately, as cross-cultural HRD, transnational HRD, and global HRD is a field of study and practice that focuses on for-profit, not-for-profit, and /or governmental entities and individuals cooperating in some form across national borders" (p. 105).

International Training/Cross-Cultural Training: Tung (1981) defined cross-cultural training as any procedure or intervention used to increase the global manager's ability in coping with international assignments. Shen (2005) echoed Tung's idea and defined international training as the training for international assignments.

Chapter 10

Leveraging Age Diversity in Times of Demographic Change:
The Crucial Role of Leadership

Katharina Janz
Jacobs University Bremen, Germany

Claudia Buengeler
Jacobs University Bremen, Germany

Robert A. Eckhoff
Jacobs University Bremen, Germany

Astrid C. Homan
University of Amsterdam, The Netherlands

Sven C. Voelpel
Jacobs University Bremen, Germany & EBS Business School, Germany

ABSTRACT

With demographic change, organizations today are seeing changes in societal make-up translated to the composition of their workforce. In the future, younger and older employees will have to work together synergistically to achieve good performance. The authors argue that it will be largely up to leaders to prevent the negative effects of age diversity, i.e. social categorization and intergroup bias, and to facilitate the positive effects of age diversity, i.e. the sharing of unique knowledge resources held by young and old. The authors argue that certain leadership behaviors and especially their combinations have great promise in leading diverse teams, and highlight why they should be used in conjunction with positive beliefs about diversity.

DOI: 10.4018/978-1-4666-1812-1.ch010

INTRODUCTION

Globalization and demographic change are increasingly altering the composition of the workforce. Falling birthrates, extended life expectancies due to significant improvements in welfare systems and healthcare, as well as the aging of the baby boom generation contribute to shifts in societal and workforce composition (Fullerton & Toossi, 2001; Greller & Simpson, 1999). Therefore, one of the, arguably, most important diversity dimensions for business success in years to come will be age diversity, but organizations are not seeing the full impact of demographic change just yet (Leibold & Voelpel, 2006; Voelpel, Leibold, & Früchtenicht, 2007). Nonetheless, organizations have to face up to what sometimes appears daunting: to increasingly compete for the few well-educated young professionals with other companies, retaining their older employees and the knowledge they possess upon their retirement, and ultimately leveraging the potential that lies within their age-diverse workforce.

Inclusion of age diversity on any organizational agenda is vital because age has significant effects on team outcomes and individual behavior and cognition (e.g., Pelled, Eisenhardt, & Xin, 1999; Schaie, 1996; Wechsler, 1944; Zenger & Lawrence, 1989). As employees are increasingly likely to work in teams with significant age gaps between co-workers, employers seek to leverage the potentially positive effects of age diversity in the hope that a broadened perspective and knowledge base leads to superior performance. However, this does not come about automatically. In this chapter, we will highlight why and how leadership plays a crucial role in making age-diverse teams work.

First, we will give an overview of the current research on age diversity and its implications for organizations. We present empirical findings supporting both a positive and a negative view of age diversity for team functioning. Second, because understanding how individuals change with age

is important to understanding team functioning in age-diverse teams, we discuss changes in individuals over the lifespan, specifically intellectual functioning, goal orientations, and personality. Third, we highlight current research on leadership and diversity beliefs, a potential leverage of age diversity in teams. Finally, we conclude with a section on how to leverage age diversity in practice.

Background

Imagine an organization where innovation is key to business success. Existing products need to be improved; new products need to be invented. This organization is already feeling the impact of demographic change and has age-diverse teams in their research & development unit (R&D). Throughout this chapter, we will look at one particular R&D team from this organization to illustrate concepts and processes. There are 4 people working in this team: Sarah (23 years old), Peter (25), Rebecca (57), and Tom (62). That is, this R&D team consists of two relatively younger (Sarah and Peter) and two relatively older (Rebecca and Tom) members. How does this age diversity affect team processes and performance?

When it comes to diversity in work teams, it is difficult to predict whether performance will be hampered or improved as it can go either way. Two theoretical points of view help understand these contrasting findings (Williams & O'Reilly, 1999); taking the information-decision-making perspective (cf. De Dreu, Harinck, & van Vianen, 1999; van Knippenberg, De Dreu, & Homan, 2004), diverse teams will benefit from a wider range of knowledge, experiences, and perspectives than homogeneous teams. Making use of these differences is precisely what can make the performance of heterogeneous teams superior to homogeneous teams.

Looking at our age-diverse R&D team, Sarah and Peter (the younger members) have fairly recently graduated from university and do not have a lot of practical work experience. They have acquired new insights and are very experienced with new technologies. Rebecca and Tom (the older members), however, have spent their entire working lives in the organization. They are very experienced, know the history of the company really well, and know the organizational processes relevant to their work by heart. In theory, the unique knowledge and experience possessed by the younger and older members of our team are a perfect fit. If they bring these resources together, they can perform much better than other teams consisting of younger or older members alone. Yet powerful social processes may prevent young and old from coming together.

Theorizing and research from a social identity theory or the similarity/attraction paradigm has illustrated that dissimilarity between team members can lead to negative effects (Williams & O'Reilly, 1998). The similarity/attraction paradigm argues that people with similar backgrounds may share common life experiences and values, and should therefore find it easier to interact with one another (Berscheid & Walster, 1978; Byrne, 1971). Therefore, people may feel drawn to others who share the same age group, as similar birth cohorts will share similar values, perspectives on common topics, and experiences. Interacting with someone who is quite similar in age therefore provides positive reinforcement for one's own values, beliefs, and attitudes. Dissimilarity, i.e. working in an age heterogeneous team, however, constitutes a negative reinforcement.

Similarly, the social categorization theory would predict that age diversity can hamper effective team functioning as it can lead to the formation of subgroups (Hogg & Abrams, 1988; Tajfel, 1981; Tajfel & Turner, 1986; Turner, 1987; cf. van Knippenberg & Haslam, 2003). Subgroup formation can in turn lead to intergroup biases, due to which groups one belongs (in-groups) to are evaluated more favorably than groups one does not belong to (out-groups; Hewstone, Rubin, & Willis, 2002). These intergroup biases concern groups as well their individual members,

and can lead to discrimination, prejudice, and stereotyping. Ultimately intergroup biases may lead to people favoring their own age group, and derogating other age-groups and their members (Brewer, 1979; Mackie & Smith, 1998, Wilder & Simon, 2001), resulting in less trust, dishonesty, and low cooperation. This can be detrimental to organizational performance. Once the social categorization process has occurred and intergroup biases have been formed, it may be difficult to reverse, as positive behaviors of in-group members as well as negative behaviors of out-group members are then attributed to stable, internal causes (Stephan, 1985).

In terms of our example team, young and old may perceive that there is a visible age difference between them and split into subgroups on the basis of this observation. However, subgroup formation need not necessarily be based on visible characteristics alone, but can also be based on informational and experiential differences that co-vary with age. That is, members may therefore initially notice that there is a visible age difference between Sarah and Peter on the one hand and Rebecca and Tom on the other, but they may also realize that their knowledge and experiences differ systematically with their age differences. Because they find it much easier to interact with those members of the group who are similar to them, Sarah and Peter may form a younger subgroup, whereas Rebecca and Tom may form an older subgroup. If this social categorization process then leads to intergroup biases, whereby young and old favor their own subgroup and derogate the other, this means that our team will not pool their unique resources to work together synergistically.[1]

What is the empirical evidence regarding these two competing perspectives on diversity? Previous research shows more often than not negative rather than positive effects of diversity on individual-level (e.g., turnover, satisfaction, and commitment) and group-level (e.g., performance, cohesiveness) outcomes (van Knippenberg & Haslam, 2003; Guzzo & Dickson, 1996; Milliken & Martins,

1996; Williams & O'Reilly, 1998; van Knippenberg & Schippers, 2007). The most consistent finding appears to be that being different from fellow team members at the individual level and heterogeneity within a team at the group level tend to be associated with less positive evaluative and affective outcomes such as commitment as well as higher turnover (e.g., Riordan & Shore, 1997; Wagner, Pfeffer, & O'Reilly, 1984). Specifically regarding age diversity, research has consistently shown that there is a positive relationship between age diversity and turnover, i.e. that groups whose members are more dissimilar with respect to age tend to have higher turnover rates than age homogeneous groups (Jackson, Brett, Sessa, Cooper, Julin, & Peronnin, 1991; Wiersema & Bird, 1993). With respect to performance measures, results appear to be more varied, as diversity in general may be associated with both superior and inferior performance (e.g., Bantel & Jackson, 1989; Pelled, 1996). It has been suggested that diversity has more of a negative impact on performance when it relates to surface-level (demographic) dimensions than to deep-level dimensions such as informational diversity (cf. Jehn, Northcraft, & Neale, 1999; van Knippenberg & Haslam, 2003). As age is a demographic characteristic, one might argue that it will have a negative effect on team performance. However, although the distinction between demographic and informational diversity is intuitively appealing, it is not so insightful. For one, previous research has not been able to show consistent effects of the two categories on important team outcomes (van Knippenberg, et al., 2004; van Knippenberg & Schippers, 2007). Second, most demographic diversity dimensions go together with informational differences.

In this respect, age diversity is a perfect example of a demographic diversity dimension, which goes hand in hand with informational differences. Younger people acquire more and different knowledge than older people (e.g., technological, new scientific insights), and older people will have more experience, larger social networks

and a better memory for important organizational processes, norms, and guidelines.

Next to task-related informational and visible demographic differences, research from other perspectives illuminates that age diversity can also instigate motivational and personality differences, which can account for positive and negative effects of age diversity. We will discuss a number of variables changing over the lifespan that are of interest when studying age-diverse teams.

Age Diversity: Individual Changes Occurring over the Lifespan

As stated before, age diversity is especially interesting because it could instigate subgroup formation (i.e., young vs. old), but also introduces informational differences between team members. In this respect, it is vital to understand the underlying changes individuals experience over the lifespan. This section explains some of these relevant age-related changes occurring over the lifespan and illustrates why they may affect team functioning in age-diverse teams.

Fluid vs. Crystallized Intelligence

As our bodies and brains age, a number of changes occur with increasing age. We may see a decline in the acuity of our senses, as well as moving more slowly than in our youth. When it comes to the cognitive level, a decline in various functions such as the manipulation of information in working memory, reaction times, and information processing can be observed while other functions such as vocabulary see some improvement with age (Verhaegen, 2003; Woodruff-Pak, 1997).

Over the lifespan, individual intellectual abilities follow different change trajectories. In this context, research on life span psychology generally distinguishes between fluid mechanics and crystallized pragmatics of intelligence (Schaie, Willis, & Pennak, 2005). Fluid mechanics refer to the neurobiologically based mechanics of intelligence, such as processing speed, while crystallized intelligence refers to intellectual abilities that are primarily rooted in experience-based pragmatics of intelligence like professional knowledge. We use fluid intellectual abilities whenever we are required to think about something logically, e.g. when solving problems in novel situations, identifying relationships and patterns at the heart of these problems. Fluid intelligence, much like reaction times, peaks in young adulthood and then shows a steady decline over the lifespan (Horn & Cattell, 1967; Woodruff-Pak, 1997). Crystallized intelligence is the ability to use skills, knowledge, and experience built over the lifetime. Inherently to the definition, crystallized intelligence is more amenable and reflects—in an organizational context—our professional knowledge and experiences. Not surprisingly, crystallized intelligence therefore increases with age in line with our experiences (Horn & Cattell, 1967).

Thus, if organizations are to bring age-diverse teams to their full potential, younger individuals might be more apt for tasks demanding fluid intelligence whereas older individuals might contribute their large pool of crystallized knowledge and experience. For example, in R&D teams, younger team members may focus on solving complex technical problems and bringing in radical innovative ideas, whereas older team members will contribute through their experience and incremental innovative behavior, e.g. by being letting their team learn through what has or has not worked in the past. However, simply looking at cognitive gains and losses over the lifespan is not very revealing as individuals age differently and cognitive performance is very malleable depending on training.

Goal Orientations

From physical challenges, exams, and interviews to the performance expected of us at work: Our reaction to these challenges depends on our motivational approach called goal orientations. Like intelligence, motivations or goal orientations tend to change with age in accordance with changing demands and constraints across the lifespan as we try to adapt in order to maximize gains (promotion focus) and minimize losses (prevention focus; Staudinger, Marsiske, & Baltes, 1995).

The focus on possible gains leads to a more advantageous or risky processing style in which new possibilities are approached and explored. A focus on avoiding losses, in contrast, is accompanied by an aversion to risk, and the tendency to seek the tried and proven path. Indeed, while younger adults are predominantly oriented towards gain and growth, older adults are increasingly focused on maintenance and loss prevention (Ebner, Freund, & Baltes, 2006). This shift in motivational patterns has consequences on self-regulation and therefore on innovative capabilities as well as for the team functioning as a whole (cf. Kruglanski, et al., 2000). For instance, individuals in a promotion focus are more likely to generate creative ideas (Friedman & Foerster, 2001), while a prevention focus will improve performance in analytical tasks (Friedman & Foerster, 2005). In our age-diverse R&D team, these changes may mean that younger team members are the drivers behind radical innovations as they will be more likely to pursue goals more forcefully even if the pursuit is risky. Older team members, on the other hand, may not be as focused on pushing progress ahead quickly at all costs but on laying sound foundations before commencing to fulfill a task. While younger individuals may have initial advantages in the generation of creative ideas, they depend on their older counterparts for assessing those ideas and in order to analytically find and overcome problems. The innovation process inherently depends on both processes alike (George & Zhou, 2001). Thus, obtaining the right balance between fast and risky vs. slow and conservative is key to attaining team goals together. In age-diverse teams, young and old are likely to complement each other due to the differing nature of their self-regulatory focus.

Personality

People often assume that who we are, i.e. our characteristic way of thinking and behaving—our personality—is something that is rather stable. Adding to the relative stability of personality in adulthood, systematic changes in the Big Five personality factors (McCrae & Costa, 1985, 1987, 1990) tell a slightly different story. The five-factor model of personality proposes that there are five primary dimensions to personality: openness to experience, conscientiousness, extraversion, agreeableness, and emotional stability.

While conscientiousness, emotional stability, and agreeableness have been found to increase with age, extraversion and openness to experience tend to decrease (Helson & Kwan, 2000; Mroczek & Spiro, 2003). Specifically, research has shown that as people age they, (a) act more dutifully and be more self-disciplined (conscientiousness), (b) experience less negative emotions (emotional stability), (c) be more compassionate and cooperative to others (agreeableness), (d) seek out less stimulation and company of others (extraversion), and (e) be less imaginative and more conventional as they age (openness to experience).

Team personality composition, however, is an important lever for team performance (e.g. Neumann, Wagner, & Christiansen, 1999). Following the principle of maximizing person-team fit (Kristof, 1996), teams might profit from a high *supplementary* fit for some personality characteristics (e.g., conscientiousness; Humphrey, Hollenbeck, Meyer, & Ilgen, 2007), but a high *complementary* fit for others (i.e., extraversion and openness to experience; Humphrey, et al., 2007; Mohammed & Angell, 2003). As an example, it might be good if a team has members with similar levels of conscientiousness as this will help approaching a task with the same diligence. However, when all members are similar in terms of openness to experience, the team as a whole might not seize new opportunities (in case of low

openness) or might get lost in the abundance of possibilities that exist (in case of high openness). As a result, differing age-related personality constellations in age-diverse teams might both help and hinder team functioning and should be taken into account when trying to understand effects of age diversity.

These aspects that go hand in hand with age diversity could, similar to the demographic and informational aspects of age diversity, instigate both information elaboration as well as social categorization processes. In line with this theorizing, previous research on age diversity has shown minimal effects on performance (cf. Williams & O'Reilly, 1998). The reason for this lies in the fact that contextual moderators will determine whether the potential or harmful effects of age diversity will occur (cf. van Knippenberg, et al., 2004).

In sum, age-diverse groups should be able to benefit from their differences provided that they meet some requirements. The age differences should be related to a wider range of task-relevant information, skills, abilities, and expertise by virtue of having differing backgrounds. What each member of an age-diverse team adds to this broadened pool of information further needs to be distinct and non-redundant, so that all team members at best contribute knowledge and experience neither of the other possesses. These age-related differences should be conducive to different perspectives and opinions on the task that the group is to perform (van Knippenberg & Haslam, 2003). Also, the different opinions and perspectives thought to be prevalent in age-diverse groups need to be reconciled, which should enhance team performance by the task-relevant information being processed more elaborately (De Dreu, Hanrick, & van Vianen, 1999; van Knippenberg, et al., 2004). Whether the group will indeed elaborate will, among other things, depend on the style of the leader and the degree to which the team has a positive outlook on diversity.

LEVERAGING DIVERSITY THROUGH LEADERSHIP: HOW TO MAKE SURE THAT ORGANIZATIONS GET THE BEST FROM AGE DIVERSITY

Having established why and how age diversity can affect teams in the previous section of this chapter, we come to instruments organizations may use to utilize the potential inherent in age-diverse teams. Diversity has been argued and shown to be double-edged sword, but which measures are at an organizations' disposal to tip the balance in favor of increased instead of lowered team functioning? These measures need to be carefully considered, bearing in mind that is not only actual diversity that matters in this regard, but also the attitudes that exist towards functioning and performance of age-diverse team.

Merely knowing which age-related changes can be relevant to team functioning and performance is not sufficient in leveraging the potential of age-diverse teams. It takes a good leader to know the strengths younger and older team members possess, and to make use of these complementing capacities so that young and old work together synergistically. Leaders of age-diverse teams must be aware of the processes that can have an impact on good or poor performance (cf. background section of this chapter). Hence leaders must focus on creating a dual effect of preventing the negative effects of diversity and boosting the positive effects of diversity. It is their task to prevent their age-diverse team splitting into young and old, as—once categorization has occurred—it may be difficult to reverse. At the same time, they have to make sure that young and old share the different knowledge and perspectives they bring to the team adequately, so that the strengths of all involved are harvested.

We will argue here that adequate leadership is a powerful instrument and key determinant in making age-diverse teams work, and its success should depend on its adequacy for both actual diversity as well as respective beliefs regarding age diversity.

Leadership Behaviors and Age Diversity: Favorable and Unfavorable Effects

Team leaders have substantial influence on team processes and team outcomes (Zaccaro, Rittman, & Marks, 2001). Depending on the appropriateness for utilizing the potential of team diversity, leadership behaviors are assumed to be capable to either positively or negatively affect diverse teams (Kearney & Gebert, 2009). This will depend on whether leadership is able to induce a dual effect in diverse teams, i.e. to stimulate the potentially beneficial effects of age diversity, while at the same time counteracting the potentially harmful effects of age diversity. To date only few studies actually investigated the impact of leadership styles on diverse teams' functioning. In the following, we will discuss various behaviors from different leadership traditions and their potential effects on age-diverse teams. We will support this rationale with empirical findings related to leaders' impact on diverse teams.

Directive and Task-Focused Leadership

Directive leadership focuses on task fulfillment, role distribution, and establishing clear work procedures, and may thus maintain high team performance in diverse teams. However, without actively facilitating extra-role behavior and stimulating learning and development processes, followers might not use their diverging skills and knowledge bases (Druskat & Kayes, 2000). On the one hand, subgroup formation and arising conflicts might be superficially suppressed by tightly controlling subordinates and a decreasing necessity of interactions due to clearly structured briefings (Somech, 2006). On the other hand, this could also result in smoldering conflicts and lowered cooperation, bearing in mind that personal relations between team members are not fostered. Hence, the effectiveness of directive leadership in stimulating positive while hindering negative effects of team diversity is likely to be decreased. In line with this reasoning, Somech (2006) showed that directive leader behaviors were only able to stimulate team reflection when functional diversity was low rather than high.

Comparable to directive behaviors, task-focused leadership (e.g., Burke, Stagl, Klein, Goodwin, Salas, & Halpin, 2006; Fleishman, 1953; House, 1971) should yield similar outcomes in age-diverse teams: By focusing on the task instead of the employee, these behaviors are expected to suppress opinion differentials and smoldering conflicts despite diverging viewpoints, values and opinions (cf. Klein, Knight, Ziegert, Lim, & Saltz, 2011). Consequently, the option of avoiding being with age-dissimilar others is not left open to team members. In line with this, work ethics diversity was less positively related to conflict level, which in turn mediated team effectiveness (Klein, et al., 2011) under high levels of task-focused leadership.

Participative and Person-Focused Leadership

Participative leaders are all about getting their team members on board: They grant their followers a say in what is done by initially consulting their team before commencing with instructions and encouraging active discussion among team members. Participative leadership is assumed to enhance team performance via optimized cognitive processing as well as communication and planning processes within teams (Larson, Foster-Fishman, & Franz, 1998; Sagie & Koslowsky, 2000). Participative leaders may be able to reduce motivational, cognitive and emotional barriers by activating participation of all team members

(Durham, Knight, & Locke, 1997; Somech, 2006). By confronting team members with different perspectives and backgrounds, reflection of one's own as well as other perspectives is assumed to be enhanced (Drach-Zahavy & Somech, 2001)

However, increasingly complex interaction processes and the multitude of perspectives might also overwhelm team capacity and hinder efficient in-role performance in participative leadership (Somech, 2006). Without limiting communication possibilities, shared knowledge may not be integrated sufficiently so that problem-solving, decision-making and team performance are impaired. Moreover, knowing others' differing perspectives, values, and viewpoints also yields the potential for impaired interpersonal liking and increased conflicts (cf. Klein, et al., 2011). In sum, participative leadership is not very likely to suffice for tapping the potential of age diversity if leaders do not provide enough structure within which the team can thrive. Confirming these assumptions, Somech (2006) found that even though team reflection was increased, in-role performance of functionally diverse teams led by participative leaders suffered.

Although somewhat different, the tradition of relations- or person-oriented leadership (e.g., Burke, et al., 2006; Fleishman, 1953; House, 1971) is related to participative leadership and thus is expected to evoke similar effects on age-diverse teams: Fostering the specific perspective and contribution of each team member might increase conflicts within diverse teams as diverging, conflicting viewpoints and values might become obvious. These are likely to increase the potential for unfavorable social categorization processes and lowered cohesion among younger and older team members. Accordingly, Klein et al. (2011) found person-oriented leadership to strengthen the relationship between traditionalism diversity—a form of value diversity that may also be relevant for age-diverse teams—and conflicts, which in turn were negatively related to team effectiveness.

Transformational Leadership

Transformational leadership is able to strongly commit and intrinsically motivate followers towards performance beyond expectations (Bass & Riggio, 2006). This is rendered possible because transformational leaders simultaneously activate self-actualization and personal as well as collective growth in their subordinates. By completely engaging followers beyond their self-interest, identification with the leader as well as with the team is allowed.

There are four main sub-facets of transformational leadership (Bass, 1985): Idealized influence comprises the modeling of role behavior and reflects the charisma of the leader. Intellectual stimulation confronts followers with new perspectives and thus stimulates problem solving in previously unknown ways. Individualized consideration implies specific concern for and support of followers and their needs. Inspirational motivation comprises the communication of inspiring goals and vision as well as expectations toward followers.

By creating a common vision, team spirit, and value-in-diversity beliefs among team members, transformational leadership is expected to stimulate sharing and elaboration of task-relevant information present in age-diverse teams. Thus, the use of all available team resources is fostered to reach the common goal. At the same time, by personally considering the value of each team member as well as emphasizing the common team vision, unfavorable social categorization processes are hindered and team identification is facilitated. In line with this, Kearney and Gebert (2009) found that transformational leadership enhanced team identification as well as the elaboration of task-relevant information in teams that were diverse with regards to nationality and educational background diversity, which in turn led to increased performance. No such effects on performance were found under low diversity levels. Age diversity was unrelated to performance

under high levels of transformational leadership but yielded unfavorable effects in case of low transformational leadership. Additionally, Shin and Zhou (2007) found educationally diverse teams to be more creative when transformational leadership was high. These moderating effects were mediated by a team's creative efficacy.

Transactional Leadership

Transactional leadership operates via a mutual, mainly rational exchange relationship (Judge & Piccolo, 2004) and can be differentiated into the components "active management by exception" (i.e., searching for mistakes and punishing undesired follower behaviors), "passive management by exception" (i.e., punishing the followers' failures without actively looking for punishment), and "contingent reward" (Avolio & Bass, 2004). The latter implies both the clarification of necessary behavior and performance in order to obtain valued rewards and leader's contingency of rewards, recognition, and compliments on follower behavior (Dorfman, Howell, Hibino, Lee, Tate, & Bautista, 1997). Contingent reward has been consistently shown to have positive effects on performance and to sometimes even exceed transformational leadership's effectiveness (Judge & Piccolo, 2004). Due to the fact that performance outcomes of contingent reward are superior to those of the other transactional behaviors (Dumdum, Lowe, & Aviolo, 2002), we will only focus on contingent reward leadership for the purpose of this chapter when referring to transactional leadership.

Transactional leadership clearly links expected behaviors to material or psychological rewards and thus avoids misinterpretations of desired in-role performance, which might occur due to the multitude of different perspectives and opinions in age-diverse teams. Rewards contingent on the adequacy of followers' behaviors might help to motivate and commit older and younger team members to collaborate on a joint task. Nevertheless, the enlarged performance potential of age-diverse teams (e.g., effective mentoring relationships between older and younger team members, integrating fresh, innovative ideas with practical experiences) remains untapped: By directly reinforcing expected work behaviors, transactional leaders simultaneously decrease the probability of extra-role behaviors outside the leader's specific focus. Without capturing the full amount of age-diverse teams' assets, transactional leaders are in danger of losing sight of the importance of extra-role behaviors. If transactional leaders do manage to make their age-diverse team use its full range of task relevant knowledge and experience, this is likely done building an enabling structure (Burke et al., 2006). One important element of an enabling structure in teams are norms encouraging all team members to capitalize on the diverse perspectives and resources the team possesses (Hackman, 2002). Therefore, transactional leaders can create core norms that capture positive beliefs regarding members of age-diverse teams and their unique resources to enable young and old alike to contribute their resources for increased performance.

Getting the Best of Differing Worlds: Integrating Leadership Behaviors

As we have shown, directive or task-focused and participative or person-focused leadership behaviors have various shortcomings in either stimulating the exchange of and elaboration on different perspectives and backgrounds, and/or the fostering of team cohesion and interpersonal liking within diverse teams. Where participative/person-focused leadership stimulates the potential positive effects age-diverse teams can reap, it has shortcomings in securing team stability. The big advantage of directive/task-focused leadership is that it prevents teams splitting into subgroups and maintains in-role performance, but it neglects the important task leaders of diverse teams have in stimulating their subordinates to share and integrate information. However, it is not clear how

these shortcomings can be turned into an asset if leaders insist on a single leadership style alone. Preserving the positive effects of each leadership style, while eliminating their downsides, could be fulfilled by combining these leadership styles. Different leadership practices have often been viewed as separate entities that are used either alone or in addition to one another in the past. Yet, Blake and Mouton (1981, 1982) have advocated that task and team orientation are to be successfully integrated to achieve optimum results for team processes and performance.

If leaders combine two seemingly opposing but complementary leadership styles, e.g. by granting participation in discussions and decision-making and at the same time provide sufficient direction, this should positively affect team processes as well as performance. Using the combined power of directive and participative leadership, otherwise unshared information is highly likely to be shared and meaningfully integrated, while team functioning and in-role performance can be secured. The loose-tight leadership model (Sagie, 1997; Sagie, Zaidman, Amichai-Hamburgerm, Te'eni, & Schwartz, 2002) assumes that participative (loose) and directive (tight) behaviors are fully compatible rather than exclusive leadership practices. A related theoretical outline has been proposed by Gebert and Kearney (2011), who argue that ambidexterity, i.e. combining leadership practices that are seemingly opposing but in effect are complementary, is capable to boost the positive effects of each single leadership behavior while avoiding their negative effects.

Transformational leadership seems to evoke the required dual effect per se: It facilitates the positive effects of diversity while preventing its potential negative effects. In age-diverse teams, high levels of transformational leadership have been found to prevent performance deteriorations by means of two mediational mechanisms. Fostering team identification to build a strong team identity is assumed to hinder the potentially negative effects of subgroup formation into young and old, ingroupfavoritism, and outgroup-discriminations. Hence, older and younger team members alike share previously unshared task-relevant resources readily (i.e., networks, values, mindsets, and different knowledge bases), which allows for maintaining adequate team performance. Moreover, transformational leaders are assumed to actively support diversity by emphasizing the value of diversity (Bass & Riggio, 2006). By aligning team members toward collective goals, transformational leaders also create a super-ordinate identity which incorporates variety as unifying and – regarding other work units – distinguishing characteristic (Kark & Shamir, 2002; Kearney & Gebert, 2009).

However, research on the effects of transformational leadership in diverse teams is still sparse (Kearney & Gebert, 2009; Shin & Zhou, 2007). Even though previous findings point to predominantly positive effects, it has not yet been investigated when and under which circumstances transformational leadership is especially successful in leading age-diverse teams and whether its effectiveness can be further increased by using complementing leadership behaviors. Following the Full Range of Leadership Model (Bass, 1985; Bass & Riggio, 2006), transactional leadership builds the foundation on which transformational leadership might exert its transforming influence on followers. Under certain circumstances, transactional leadership (contingent reward) has even been found to be more successful than transformational leadership (Judge & Piccolo, 2004). However, the interactive effects of transformational leadership and transactional leadership are not yet known. Might their combined effects help ensure that transformational leadership does not only prevent negative effects of high age diversity (Kearney & Gebert, 2009) but instead is capable to make age-diverse teams' performance a success? We argue that this combination may be crucial for consistently obtaining favorable effects on functioning of age-diverse teams: By consistently rewarding successful and functional behaviors of teams members, each and every team member is required to bring in his/her share to teams' success. By reacting predictably to desirable behaviors, transactional leaders are able to build a reliable and trustful relationship with followers. Once a stable team functioning is established and secured, transformational leadership behaviors can exert their multifaceted influence on age-diverse teams: Based upon a stable transactional foundation, unifying team spirit can be built and an inspiring vision can be communicated. The leader of our age-diverse R&D team, for example, believes that his younger and older team members should share their different knowledge bases and that they should also learn from each other's experiences. He frequently makes this clear to his subordinates by encouraging to share their unique resources: he asks Sarah and Peter (the younger members) on their perspective from a technological stance, and Rebecca and Tom (the older members) to evaluate a problem from their experience. If young and old make use of their informational diversity, the leader of our R&D praises and reinforces his subordinates individually for their contributions, and as a team for their excellent teamwork. Through this, positive collective team identification is enabled, so that the leader of our R&D team now leads with an inspiring vision that is then shared and followed by the entire team.

Leaders' Beliefs Regarding Age Diversity: Why and How They Matter

Even if leaders are equipped with leadership strategies that show great promise for age-diverse teams, they may not succeed in facilitating the dual effect, e.g., transformational and transactional leadership or directive and participative leadership are assumed to have. Considering that the potentially negative effects of diversity are readily explained by the notion that most people prefer working with others similar to them in homogeneous groups—a notion that is mirrored by social identity theory and the similarity/attraction paradigm (van Knippenberg & Haslam, 2003)—organizations will also need to focus on what leaders think about diversity and its effects (cf. Greer, Homan, De Hoogh, & Den Hartog, 2011). After all, performance is likely to be influenced by what we believe about people around us.

Diversity beliefs comprise individuals' assumptions regarding the positive or negative consequences of diversity. When diversity beliefs held by individuals, teams, and organizations are positive, more favorable consequences of diversity are likely to result (van Knippenberg & Schippers, 2007). A number of studies have already examined attitudes towards diversity and the value attributed to it by individuals, as well as on the group or organizational level (e.g., Ely & Thomas, 2001; Homan, Hollenbeck, Humphrey, van Knippenberg, Ilgen, & van Kleef, 2008; Homan, Greer, Jehn, & Koning, 2010; Hostager & De Meuse, 2002; van Dick, van Knippenberg, Hägele, Guillaume, & Brodbeck, 2008; van Knippenberg & Haslam, 2003). Results show that positive beliefs regarding diversity and its value, have an impact on how well work teams and their respective members function. Hence, positive diversity beliefs lead to increased team identification, information elaboration, and desire to continue working within the team (e.g., Homan, van Knippenberg, van Kleef, & De Dreu, 2007; van Dick, et al., 2008). Therefore younger and older team members will be less likely to form subgroups and therefore obviate the potentially negative effects of demographic separation, while using their individual difference and informational variety (cf. Harrison & Klein, 2007).

Various 'images of aging' in the work place may be related to attitudes towards age-diverse teams. Employees' perceptions of how *other* people at their workplace perceive older workers are related to both younger and older employees' attitudes towards their work place, including their turnover intentions as well as older workers' self-rated work ability (Bowen, Noack, & Staudinger, 2010). Such images of aging likewise have particular relevance for attitudes and beliefs regarding age diversity and

can therefore potentially have a powerful impact on the success of age diversity in organizations as well as forming a positive overall age climate.

As much as leadership is about facilitating team members' functioning and performance, it is also about influencing people by shaping beliefs, desires, and priorities (Haslam, Reicher, & Platow, 2011; Yukl, 2010). Thus, it seems only natural that leaders of teams and organizations should foster positive diversity beliefs and thus help to create an enduring positive age climate in organizations. However, despite its presumed importance, to our knowledge the role of leaders' diversity beliefs has been neglected up to now. It is highly probable that the beliefs of leaders gain salience and power within teams through leader behaviors. Thus, leaders' attitudes come to life as they are perceived and internalized by subordinates. For example: what is said, jokes, expressions, how much time is spent with and on whom all reflects leaders' beliefs. If leaders of an age-diverse team choose to spend time with younger and older team members alike rather than favoring one subgroup, and are generally very inclusive in what they say and do, as well as conveying that age diversity is valuable and why, this is expected to have a two-fold effect: on the one hand, this focus on the whole team will make a split into subgroups highly unlikely. On the other hand, the team will emulate the leaders' pro-diversity beliefs so that positive team age climate and diversity beliefs will result. This, in turn, will have a positive impact on team functioning and performance (cf. Greer, et al., 2011). Leader inclusiveness also offers a good example to leaders who wish to facilitate the positive side of age-diverse teams while preventing its potential downsides. Leaders who include all members of their team irrespective of status and age invite and appreciate others' contribution through what they say and do (Nembhardt & Edmondson, 2006). Leading by example, they inspire their followers to also be inclusive, i.e. to value and seek out other team members' ideas and input and to likewise exchange information themselves.

Thus age-diverse teams, who can benefit from the informational variety they possess by virtue of young and old members being in their team, will make use of the full range of informational and experiential resources available to them.

Leaders therefore serve as role models and need to be aware of the power their own beliefs have in terms of shaping diverse team members' own beliefs. Especially team members of trans-formational leaders are likely to strongly identify and internalize leaders' values, goals, and attitudes (House, Spangler, & Woycke, 1991; Shamir, House, & Arthur, 1993), and thus also incorporate value-in-diversity beliefs. In sum, diversity beliefs of leaders should be intentionally used as a valuable instrument in organizations. However, for leaders to be able to successfully foster diverse teams' attitudes, functioning, and performance, positive organizational images of aging are required to support and facilitate leader's pro-diversity efforts (Bowen, et al., 2010). Hence, positive diversity beliefs at all hierarchical levels and in all kinds of teams (e.g., production teams, management teams, R&D teams) should be purposefully shaped and anchored in organizations to create a positive age climate in which age-diverse teams can thrive.

Leveraging Age Diversity in Practice

Having established that leaders must play a crucial role if organizations are to be successful with, in spite of and precisely because of their aging and increasingly age-diverse workforce, we will now focus on how organizations can reap the positive effects of age diversity on a practical level.

In promoting and planning for age diversity in organizations, the ultimate goal will have to be fostering and implementing a positive age climate and positive diversity beliefs. This has to take place via leaders at all hierarchical levels, as they act as role models and have the power to inspire beliefs in diversity and its value. They can enable a culture that values young and old, and knows that young and old work together synergistically to outperform age homogeneous teams. Best results will be achieved by organizations that embrace diversity at all organizational levels wholeheart-edly. Therefore, organizational culture needs to be shaped to include pro-diversity beliefs (Homan, et al., 2007). To provide guidance and direction to this goal at all organizational levels, pro-diversity beliefs may be included in the mission statement of an organization. Furthermore, leadership be-haviors that embrace value-in-diversity should be culturally anchored. This will help attain sustain-able effects of personnel development activities. Ultimately, pro-diversity beliefs should grow to be a part of teams' and leaders' social identity if organizations are to benefit from age diversity.

Since leaders will have to play a large part in shaping and anchoring diversity beliefs as well as letting their age-diverse teams perform at their best on a daily basis, personnel selection has to be focused on selecting leaders who (1) already have positive diversity beliefs, and (2) already show promising leadership and are able to com-bine various types of leadership behaviors at the same time (cf. ambidextrous leadership, Gebert & Kearney, 2011).

In personnel development leaders need to be trained to make use of leadership behaviors or combinations of leadership practices depending on the particular team composition and other situational circumstances. Leaders will also need to be made aware of the power they possess in not only facilitating the positive effects of age-diverse teams, and of how powerful their own beliefs are in inspiring and influencing followers (Greer, et al., 2011; Haslam, et al., 2011).

On the team level, age-diverse teams have to be supported in their efforts to actively utilize their broadened pool of task-relevant information and perspectives. To name but a few measures, this can be achieved by building strong teams, team-building activities, stressing the importance of sharing previously unshared knowledge, regular knowledge sharing meetings and circles, informal communication possibilities, job rotation and enrichment possibilities, as well as mentoring between young and old and vice versa. Furthermore, older workers should be actively retained and recruited to create age-diverse teams. New members, irrespective of their age, should be actively introduced into diverse teams, while stressing the benefits diversity can have. Finally, it is important to realize that all measures taken in recruitment as well as personnel and organizational development need time to work, i.e. the positive effects of age diversity may need time to emerge until performance improves measurably (van Knippenberg, et al., 2004).

FUTURE RESEARCH DIRECTIONS

Although age has been of interest in diversity research, this research has thus far not taken into account age-related changes in individuals that can affect team processes, team functioning, and performance of age-diverse teams. Yet the development of fluid vs. crystallized intelligence, goal orientations, as well as personality over the lifespan can lead to informational and social category differences, which should be explored in future research.

Even though research on diversity is thriving, there is still much to be learnt regarding the effects of leadership and diversity beliefs. Having identified specific combinations of leadership as promising in leading age-diverse teams, we find that there remains paucity in research on these leadership perspectives. Even though previous findings point to predominantly positive effects regarding transformational leadership alone, it has not yet been investigated whether transformational leadership combined with transactional leadership is more successful in leading age-diverse teams than its sole effect. Regarding the combination of directive or task-focused and participative or person-focused leadership behaviors it has been established that they are compatible (Gebert & Kearney, 2011; Sagie, et al., 2002), but interac-

tive effects of these and other leadership practices remain to be investigated.

A handful of studies investigated diversity beliefs at the individual and the team/organizational level (e.g., Ely & Thomas, 2001; Homan, et al., 2007, 2008, 2010; Hostager & De Meuse, 2002; van Dick, et al., 2008; van Knippenberg & Haslam, 2003). Here, research into the role of mental models concerning diversity beliefs that are shared by the team and with the leader might be a valuable path for further research. Given the crucial role leaders play in shaping beliefs, desires, and priorities (Haslam, et al., 2011), it is surprising that no attention has been paid to diversity beliefs of leaders yet. Therefore, future research should focus on leaders' diversity beliefs and how they can be utilized in leading diverse teams.

CONCLUSION

We started out by illustrating that due to demographic developments age diversity will be one of the most important diversity dimensions to influence business success in the future. We have then shown that there is great promise for performance in age-diverse teams, as they benefit from a broadened pool of task-relevant information: younger members possess fresh theoretical knowledge and ideas, while older members can contribute a wealth of experience. However, age-diverse teams do not function well automatically, as powerful social categorization processes and the resulting danger of sub-group formation into younger and older team members may occur. Even though organizations are not yet seeing the full impact of demographic change, it pays to be prepared to prevent those powerful effects while making full use of the smoldering potential.

Before examining which leadership styles show promise in leading diverse teams, we discussed the underlying changes individuals experience over the lifespan to illustrate how these may affect team functioning in age-diverse teams. This has highlighted the need to handle age-diverse teams well, as organizational reality frequently draws on resources possessed by both younger and older employees. In particular, the complementary use of specific leadership behaviors (transformational and transactional, directive and participative, person-focused and task-focused) exceeds the expectations in successfully leading diverse teams compared to solely confiding in only one part of the mentioned leadership style conjunctions. These combined leadership practices are expected to be valuable resources in avoiding possible negative effects, while boosting the positive effects of diversity.

Because what people think is just as important as adequate leadership of diverse teams, we emphasized leaders' diversity beliefs, and have discussed the power pro-diversity beliefs can have in successfully leading age diverse teams. Finally, we introduced measures that organizations can use to attain a pro-diversity climate and culture and to train leaders of age diverse teams for success—both with respect to adequate leadership practices and diversity beliefs. In sum, we have shown that age diverse teams are very promising due to the informational variety they possess. Yet, to leverage this potential, it takes a skillful leader who is able to combine specific leadership behaviors adequately, and who believes in the value of his age-diverse team.

ACKNOWLEDGMENT

Preparation of this chapter has been facilitated and financially supported by grants from the Volkswagen Foundation (II/82 811) and the Foundation of German Business (SDW).

REFERENCES

Avolio, B. J., & Bass, B. M. (2004). *MLQ - Multifactor leadership questionnaire*. Menlo Park, CA: Mind Garden.

Bantel, K., & Jackson, S. (1989). Top management and innovations in banking: Does the composition of the team make a difference? *Strategic Management Journal, 10*, 107–124. doi:10.1002/smj.4250100709

Bass, B. M. (1985). *Leadership and performance beyond expectations*. New York, NY: Free Press.

Bass, B. M., & Riggio, R. E. (2006). *Transformational leadership*. Mahwah, NJ: Erlbaum.

Berscheid, E., & Walster, H. (1978). *Interpersonal attraction*. Reading, MA: Addison-Wesley.

Blake, R. R., & Mouton, S. (1981). Management by grid principles or situationalism: Which? *Group & Organization Management, 6*, 439–455. doi:10.1177/105960118100600404

Blake, R. R., & Mouton, S. (1982, Spring). A comparative analysis of situationalism and 9, 9 management by principle. *Organizational Dynamics*, 20–43. doi:10.1016/0090-2616(82)90027-4

Bowen, C. E., Noack, C. M. G., & Staudinger, U. M. (2010). Aging in the work context. In Schaie, K. W., & Willis, S. (Eds.), *Handbook of the Psychology of Aging* (7th ed., pp. 263–278). San Diego, CA: Elsevier Academic Press.

Brewer, M. (1979). Ingroup bias in the minimal group situation: A cognitive-motivational analysis. *Psychological Bulletin, 86*, 307–324. doi:10.1037/0033-2909.86.2.307

Burke, C. S., Stagl, K. C., Klein, C., Goodwin, G. F., Salas, E., & Halpin, S. M. (2006). What type of leadership behaviors are functional in teams? A meta-analysis. *The Leadership Quarterly, 17,* 288–307. doi:10.1016/j.leaqua.2006.02.007

Byrne, D. (1971). *The attraction paradigm.* New York, NY: Academic Press.

De Dreu, C. K. W., Harinck, S., & van Vianen, A. E. M. (1999). Conflict and performance in groups and organisations. In Cooper, C. L., & Robertson, I. T. (Eds.), *International Review of Industrial and Organizational Psychology* (Vol. 14, pp. 369–414). Oxford, UK: Wiley. doi:10.1002/9780470696712. ch8

Dorfman, P. W., Howell, J. P., Hibino, S., Lee, J. K., Tate, U., & Bautista, A. (1997). Leadership in Western and Asian countries: Commonalities and differences in effective leadership processes across cultures. *The Leadership Quarterly, 8,* 233–274. doi:10.1016/S1048-9843(97)90003-5

Drach-Zahavy, A., & Somech, A. (2001). Understanding team innovation: The role of team processes and structures. *Group Dynamics, 5,* 111–123. doi:10.1037/1089-2699.5.2.111

Druskat, V. U., & Kayes, D. C. (2000). Learning versus performance in short-term project teams. *Small Group Research, 31,* 328–353. doi:10.1177/104649640003100304

Dumdum, U. R., Lowe, K. B., & Avolio, B. J. (2002). A meta-analysis of transformational and transactional leadership correlates of effectiveness and satisfaction: An update and extension. In Avolio, B. J., & Yammarino, F. J. (Eds.), *Transformational and Charismatic Leadership: The Road Ahead* (pp. 35–66). Amsterdam, The Netherlands: JAI.

Durham, C. C., Knight, D., & Locke, E. A. (1997). Effects of leader role, team-set goal difficulty, efficacy, and tactics on team effectiveness. *Organizational Behavior and Human Decision Processes, 72*(2), 203–231. doi:10.1006/obhd.1997.2739

Ebner, N. C., Freund, A. M., & Baltes, P. B. (2006). Developmental changes in personal goal orientation from young to late adulthood: From striving for gains to maintenance and prevention of losses. *Psychology and Aging, 21*(4), 664–678. doi:10.1037/0882-7974.21.4.664

Ely, R. J., & Thomas, D. A. (2001). Cultural diversity at work: The effects of diversity perspectives on work group processes and outcomes. *Administrative Science Quarterly, 46,* 229–273. doi:10.2307/2667087

Fleishman, E. A. (1953). The description of supervisory behavior. *Personnel Psychology, 37,* 1–6.

Friedman, R., & Förster, J. (2001). The effects of promotion and prevention cues on creativity. *Journal of Personality and Social Psychology, 81,* 1001–1013. doi:10.1037/0022-3514.81.6.1001

Friedman, R., & Förster, J. (2005). Effects of motivational cues on perceptual asymmetry: Implications for creativity and analytical problem solving. *Journal of Personality and Social Psychology, 88,* 263–275. doi:10.1037/0022-3514.88.2.263

Fullerton, F. N., & Toossi, M. (2001). Labor force projections to 2010: Steady growth and changing composition. *Monthly Labor Review, 124,* 21–38.

Gebert, D., & Kearney, E. (2011). Ambidextre führung: Eine andere sichtweise. *Zeitschrift für Arbeits- und Organisationspsychologie, 55,* 74–87. doi:10.1026/0932-4089/a000043

George, J. M., & Zhou, J. (2001). When openness to experience and conscientiousness are related to creative behavior: An interactional approach. *The Journal of Applied Psychology, 86,* 513–524. doi:10.1037/0021-9010.86.3.513

Greer, L. L., Homan, A. C., De Hoogh, A. H. B., & Den Hartog, D. N. (2012). Tainted visions: The effect of visionary leader behaviors and leader categorization tendencies on the financial performance of ethnically diverse teams. *The Journal of Applied Psychology, 97*(1), 203–213. doi:10.1037/a0025583

Greller, M. M., & Simpson, P. (1999). In search of late career: A review of contemporary social science research applicable to the understanding of late career. *Human Resource Management Review*, *9*, 309–347. doi:10.1016/S1053-4822(99)00023-6

Guzzo, R. A., & Dickson, M. W. (1996). Teams in organizations: Recent research on performance and effectiveness. *Annual Review of Psychology*, *47*, 307–338. doi:10.1146/annurev.psych.47.1.307

Hackman, J. R. (2002). *Leading teams: Setting the stage for great performances*. Boston, MA: HBS Press.

Harrison, D. A., & Klein, K. J. (2007). What's the difference? Diversity constructs as separation, variety, or disparity in organizations. *Academy of Management Review*, *32*, 1199–1228. doi:10.5465/AMR.2007.26586096

Haslam, A. S., Reicher, S. D., & Platow, M. J. (2011). *The new psychology of leadership: Identity, influence and power*. Hove, UK: Psychology Press.

Helson, R., & Kwan, V. S. Y. (2000). Personality development in adulthood: The broad picture and processes in one longitudinal sample. In Hampson, S. E. (Ed.), *Advances in Personality Psychology* (*Vol. 1*, pp. 77–106). London, UK: Routledge.

Hewstone, M., Rubin, M., & Willis, H. (2002). Intergroup bias. *Annual Review of Psychology*, *53*, 575–604. doi:10.1146/annurev.psych.53.100901.135109

Hogg, M., & Abrams, D. (1988). *Social identification*. London, UK: Routledge.

Homan, A. C., Greer, L. L., Jehn, K. A., & Koning, L. (2010). Believing shapes seeing: The impact of diversity beliefs on the construal of group composition. *Group Processes & Intergroup Relations*, *13*, 477–493. doi:10.1177/1368430209350747

Homan, A. C., Hollenbeck, J. R., Humphrey, S. E., van Knippenberg, D., Ilgen, D. R., & van Kleef, G. A. (2008). Facing differences with an open mind: Openness to experience, salience of intra-group differences, and performance of diverse groups. *Academy of Management Journal*, *58*, 1204–1222. doi:10.5465/AMJ.2008.35732995

Homan, A. C., van Knippenberg, D., van Kleef, G. A., & De Dreu, C. K. W. (2007). Bridging faultlines by valuing diversity: The effects of diversity beliefs on information processing and performance in diverse work groups. *The Journal of Applied Psychology*, *92*, 1189–1199. doi:10.1037/0021-9010.92.5.1189

Horn, J. L., & Cattell, R. B. (1967). Age differences in fluid and crystallized intelligence. *Acta Psychologica*, *26*, 107–129. doi:10.1016/0001-6918(67)90011-X

Hostager, T. J., & De Meuse, K. P. (2002). Assessing the complexity of diversity perceptions: Breadth, depth, and balance. *Journal of Business and Psychology*, *17*, 189–206. doi:10.1023/A:1019681314837

House, R. J. (1971). A path goal theory of leader effectiveness. *Administrative Science Quarterly*, *16*, 321–339. doi:10.2307/2391905

House, R. J., Spangler, W. D., & Woycke, J. (1991). Personality and charisma in the U. S. presidency: A psychological theory of leadership effectiveness. *Administrative Science Quarterly*, *36*, 364–396. doi:10.2307/2393201

Humphrey, S. E., Hollenbeck, J. R., Meyer, C. J., & Ilgen, D. R. (2007). Trait configurations in self-managed teams: A conceptual examination of the use of seeding for maximizing and minimizing trait variance in teams. *The Journal of Applied Psychology*, *92*, 595–615. doi:10.1037/0021-9010.92.3.885

Jackson, S. E., Brett, J. F., Sessa, V. I., Cooper, D. M., Julin, J. A., & Peyronnin, K. (1991). Some differences make a difference: Individual dissimilarity and group heterogeneity as correlates of recruitment, promotions, and turnover. *The Journal of Applied Psychology, 76*, 675–689. doi:10.1037/0021-9010.76.5.675

Jehn, K. A., Northcraft, G. B., & Neale, M. A. (1999). Why differences make a difference: A field study of diversity, conflict and performance in work groups. *Administrative Science Quarterly, 44*, 741–763. doi:10.2307/2667054

Judge, T. A., & Piccolo, R. (2004). Transformational and transactional leadership: A meta-analytic test of their relative validity. *The Journal of Applied Psychology, 89*, 755–768. doi:10.1037/0021-9010.89.5.755

Kark, R., & Shamir, B. (2002). The dual effect of transformational leadership: Priming relational and collective selves and further effects on followers. In Avolio, B. J., & Yammarino, F. J. (Eds.), *Transformational and Charismatic Leadership: The Road Ahead* (Vol. 2, pp. 67–91). Oxford, UK: Elsevier Science.

Kearney, E., & Gebert, D. (2009). Managing diversity and enhancing team outcomes: The promise of transformational leadership. *The Journal of Applied Psychology, 94*, 77–89. doi:10.1037/a0013077

Klein, K. J., Knight, A. P., Ziegert, J. C., Lim, B. C., & Saltz, J. L. (2011). When team members' values differ: The moderating role of team leadership. *Organizational Behavior and Human Decision Making Processes, 114*, 25–36. doi:10.1016/j.obhdp.2010.08.004

Kristof, A. L. (1996). Person-organization fit: An integrative review of its conceptualizations, measurement, and implications. *Personnel Psychology, 49*, 1–49. doi:10.1111/j.1744-6570.1996.tb01790.x

Kruglanski, A. W., Thompson, E. P., Higgins, E. T., Atash, M. N., Pierro, A., Shah, J. Y., & Spiegel, S. (2000). To "do the right thing" or to "just do it": Locomotion and assessment as distinct self-regulatory imperatives. *Journal of Personality and Social Psychology, 79*, 793–815. doi:10.1037/0022-3514.79.5.793

Larson, J. R. J., Foster-Fishman, P. G., & Franz, T. M. (1998). Leadership style and the discussion of shared and unshared information in decision-making groups. *Personality and Social Psychology Bulletin, 24*, 482–495. doi:10.1177/0146167298245004

Leibold, M., & Voelpel, S. (2006). *Managing the aging workforce: Challenges and solutions.* New York, NY: Wiley.

Mackie, D. M., & Smith, E. R. (1998). Intergroup relations: Insights from a theoretically integrative approach. *Psychological Review, 105*, 499–529. doi:10.1037/0033-295X.105.3.499

McCrae, R. R., & Costa, P. T. (1985). Updating Norman's 'adequate taxonomy': Intelligence and personality dimensions in natural language and in questionnaires. *Journal of Personality and Social Psychology, 49*, 81–90. doi:10.1037/0022-3514.49.3.710

McCrae, R. R., & Costa, P. T. (1987). Validation of the five-factor model of personality across instruments and observers. *Journal of Personality and Social Psychology, 52*(1), 81–90. doi:10.1037/0022-3514.52.1.81

McCrae, R. R., & Costa, P. T. (1990). *Personality in adulthood.* New York, NY: Guilford.

Milliken, F., & Martins, L. (1996). Searching for common threads: Understanding the multiple effects of diversity in organizational groups. *Academy of Management Review, 21*, 402–433.

Mohammed, S., & Angell, L. C. (2003). Personality heterogeneity in teams: Which differences make a difference for team performance? *Small Group Research, 34,* 651–677. doi:10.1177/1046496403257228

Mroczek, D. K., & Spiro, R. A. (2003). Modeling intraindividual change in personality traits: Findings from the normative aging study. *Journal of Gerontology, 58,* 153–165. doi:10.1093/geronb/58.3.P153

Nembhardt, I. M., & Edmondson, A. C. (2006). Making it safe: The effects of leader inclusiveness and professional status on psychological safety and improvement efforts in health care teams. *Journal of Organizational Behavior, 27,* 941–966. doi:10.1002/job.413

Neuman, G. A., Wagner, S. H., & Christiansen, N. D. (1999). The relationship between work- team personality composition and the job performance of teams. *Group & Organization Management, 24,* 28–45. doi:10.1177/1059601199241003

Pelled, L. H. (1996). Relational demography and perceptions of group conflict and performance: A field investigation. *The International Journal of Conflict Management, 7,* 230–246. doi:10.1108/eb022783

Pelled, L. H., Eisenhardt, K. M., & Xin, K. R. (1999). Exploring the black box: An analysis of work group diversity, conflict, and performance. *Administrative Science Quarterly, 44,* 1–28. doi:10.2307/2667029

Riordan, C., & Shore, L. (1997). Demographic diversity and employee attitudes: Examination of relational demography within work units. *The Journal of Applied Psychology, 82,* 342–358. doi:10.1037/0021-9010.82.3.342

Sagie, A. (1997). Leader direction and employee participation in decision making: Contradictory or compatible practices? *Applied Psychology: An International Review, 46,* 387–416.

Sagie, A., & Koslowsky, M. (2000). *Participation and empowerment in organizations.* Thousand Oaks, CA: Sage.

Sagie, A., Zaidman, N., Amichai-Hamburger, Y., Te'eni, D., & Schwartz, D. G. (2002). An empirical assessment of the loose-tight leadership model: Quantitative and qualitative analyses. *Journal of Organizational Behavior, 23,* 303–320. doi:10.1002/job.153

Schaie, K. W. (1996). *Intellectual development in adulthood: The Seattle longitudinal study.* Cambridge, UK: Cambridge University Press.

Schaie, K. W., Willis, S. L., & Pennak, S. (2005). A historical framework for cohort differences in intelligence. *Research in Human Development, 2,* 43–67.

Shamir, B., House, R. J., & Arthur, M. B. (1993). The motivational effects of charismatic leadership: A self-concept based theory. *Organization Science, 4,* 577–594. doi:10.1287/orsc.4.4.577

Shin, S. J., & Zhou, J. (2007). When is educational specialization heterogeneity related to creativity in research and development teams? Transformational leadership as a moderator. *The Journal of Applied Psychology, 92*(6), 1709–1721. doi:10.1037/0021-9010.92.6.1709

Somech, A. (2006). The effects of leadership style and team process on performance and innovation in functionally heterogeneous teams. *Journal of Management, 32*(1), 132–157. doi:10.1177/0149206305277799

Staudinger, U. M., Marsiske, M., & Baltes, P. B. (1995). Resilience and reserve capacity in later adulthood: Potentials and limits of development across the life span. In Cicchetti, D., & Cohen, D. (Eds.), *Developmental Psychopathology: Risk, Disorder, and Adaptation* (*Vol. 2,* pp. 801–847). New York, NY: Wiley.

Stephan, W. (1985). Intergroup relations. In Lindzey, G., & Aronson, E. (Eds.), *Handbook of Social Psychology* (pp. 599–658). New York, NY: Random House.

Tajfel, H. (1982). *Social identity and intergroup relations*. Cambridge, UK: Cambridge University Press.

Tajfel, H., & Turner, J. (1986). The social identity of intergroup behaviour. In S. Worchel &d W. Austin (Eds.), *Psychology and Intergroup Relations*, (pp. 7-24). Chicago, IL: Nelson-Hall.

Turner, J. (1987). *Rediscovering the social group: A social categorisation theory*. Oxford, UK: Blackwell.

van Dick, R., van Knippenberg, D., Hägele, S., Guillaume, Y. R. F., & Brodbeck, F. C. (2008). Group diversity and group identifications: The moderating role of diversity beliefs. *Human Relations, 61,* 1463–1492. doi:10.1177/0018726708095711

van Knippenberg, D., De Dreu, C. K. W., & Homan, A. C. (2004). Work group diversity and group performance: An integrative model and research agenda. *The Journal of Applied Psychology, 89*(6), 1008–1022. doi:10.1037/0021-9010.89.6.1008

van Knippenberg, D., & Haslam, S. A. (2003). Realizing the diversity dividend: Exploring the subtle interplay between identity, ideology, and reality. In Haslam, S. A., van Knippenberg, D., Platow, M. J., & Ellemers, N. (Eds.), *Social Identity at Work: Developing Theory for Organizational Practice* (pp. 61–77). Hove, UK: Psychology Press.

van Knippenberg, D., & Schippers, M. C. (2007). Work group diversity. *Annual Review of Psychology, 58,* 515–541. doi:10.1146/annurev.psych.58.110405.085546

Verhaegen, P. (2003). Aging and vocabulary score: A meta-analysis. *Psychology and Aging, 18,* 332–339. doi:10.1037/0882-7974.18.2.332

Voelpel, S., Leibold, M., & Früchtenicht, J.-D. (2007). *Herausforderung 50 plus: Warum sie erfahrene arbeitnehmer optimal managen müssen und wie es funktioniert*. Erlangen, Germany: Publicis-Wiley.

Wagner, W., Pfeffer, J., & O'Reilly, C. (1984). Organizational demography and turnover in top management groups. *Administrative Science Quarterly, 29,* 74–92. doi:10.2307/2393081

Wechsler, D. (1944). *The measurement of intelligence*. Baltimore, MD: Williams & Wilkins.

Wiersema, M. F., & Bird, A. (1993). Organizational demography in Japanese firms: Group heterogeneity, individual dissimilarity, and top management team turnover. *Academy of Management Journal, 36,* 996–1025. doi:10.2307/256643

Wilder, D., & Simon, A. F. (2001). Affect as a cause of intergroup bias. In Brown, R., & Gaertner, S. (Eds.), *Blackwell Handbook of Social Psychology: Intergroup Processes* (pp. 153–172). Malden, MA: Blackwell. doi:10.1002/9780470693421.ch8

Williams, K. Y., & O'Reilly, C. A. (1998). Demography and diversity in organizations: A review of 40 years of research. In Staw, B. M., & Cummings, L. L. (Eds.), *Research in Organizational Behavior* (*Vol. 20,* pp. 77–140). Greenwich, CT: JAI Press.

Woodruff-Pak, D. S. (1997). *The neuropsychology of aging*. Oxford, UK: Blackwell.

Yukl, G. A. (2010). *Leadership in organizations* (7th ed.). Upper Saddle River, NJ: Pearson.

Zaccaro, S. J., Rittman, A. L., & Marks, M. A. (2001). Team leadership. *The Leadership Quarterly, 12,* 451–483. doi:10.1016/S1048-9843(01)00093-5

Zenger, T. R., & Lawrence, B. S. (1989). Organizational demography: The differential effective of age and tenure distributions on technical communications. *Academy of Management Journal, 32*, 353–376. doi:10.2307/256366

ADDITIONAL READING

Bass, B. M., & Riggio, R. E. (2006). *Transformational leadership*. Mahwah, NJ: Erlbaum.

Harrison, D. A., & Klein, K. J. (2007). What's the difference? Diversity constructs as separation, variety, or disparity in organizations. *Academy of Management Review, 32*(4), 1199–1228. doi:10.5465/AMR.2007.26586096

Haslam, A. S., van Knippenberg, D., Platow, M. J., & Ellemers, N. (2003). *Social identity at work: Developing theory for organizational practice*. Hov, UK: Psychology Press.

Judge, T. A., & Piccolo, R. F. (2004). Transformational and transactional leadership: A meta-analytic test of their relative validity. *The Journal of Applied Psychology, 89*(5), 755–768. doi:10.1037/0021-9010.89.5.755

Lowe, K. B., Kroeck, K. G., & Sivasubramaniam, N. (1996). Effectiveness correlates of transformational and transactional leadership: A meta-analytic review of the MLQ literature. *The Leadership Quarterly, 7*(3), 385–425. doi:10.1016/S1048-9843(96)90027-2

van Knippenberg, D., De Dreu, C. K. W., & Homan, A. C. (2004). Work group diversity and group performance: An integrative model and research agenda. *The Journal of Applied Psychology, 89*(6), 1008–1022. doi:10.1037/0021-9010.89.6.1008

van Knippenberg, D., & Schippers, M. C. (2007). Work group diversity. *Annual Review of Psychology, 58*, 515–541. doi:10.1146/annurev.psych.58.110405.085546

Williams, K. Y., & O'Reilly, C. A. (1998). Demography and diversity in organizations: A review of 40 years of research. In Staw, B. M., & Cummings, L. L. (Eds.), *Research in Organizational Behavior* (*Vol. 20*, pp. 77–140). Greenwich, CT: JAI Press.

Zaccaro, S. J., Rittman, A. L., & Marks, M. A. (2001). Team leadership. *The Leadership Quarterly, 12*(4), 451. doi:10.1016/S1048-9843(01)00093-5

KEY TERMS AND DEFINITIONS

Age Diversity: Differences between within a team that pertain to age differences between team members (younger and older team members). Age differences do not only operate on the surface level but are also accompanied by informational diversity, i.e., younger team members possess recent theoretical and technological knowledge, while older team members will have a large experience base, knowledge of organizational processes, etc.

Demographic Change: Changes in the population affecting society at large as well as the workforce, e.g. due to a significant fall in birth rates, increased life expectancies.

Diversity Beliefs: Fundamental attitudes and values attributed to diversity in general or to specific diversity dimensions.

Information Elaboration: Sharing and expanding of knowledge through use of informational diversity within teams.

Leadership: Behaviors and practices used to influence others in order to attain their contribution towards team and organizational goals.

Life Span Development: Changes in physical, cognitive, social, and emotional development throughout the lifespan of individuals, which can have a bearing on age-diverse teams.

Social Categorization: Process in which others themselves as well as attitudes towards them are perceived as being similar or different from oneself and each other.

ENDNOTE

[1] Note that this team may also split into female and male subgroups if gender rather than age is a salient characteristic to the team. This could, for example, be the case in predominantly female professions such as nursing, where having few male members in a team is very likely to be noticeable and salient to a team. However, gender diversity does not necessarily go along with informational differences, as is the case in age diverse teams.

Chapter 11
Leveraging Multinational Firm Performance through the Use of Diversified Top Management Teams

Güven Alpay
Boğaziçi University, Turkey

Pınar Büyükbalcı
Yıldız Technical University, Turkey

ABSTRACT

This chapter discusses the theoretical framework covering the relationship between top management team diversity determinants and certain organization-level variables in order to capture the essence of possible strategic outcomes. Accordingly, it attempts to summarize and clarify the theoretical and empirical literature regarding the effects of diversity on the functioning of top management teams. In this sense, the main aim of this study is to contribute to and improve the current literature on diversity through the viewpoint of strategic international business literature by directly focusing on the organizational unit—top management teams—which is responsible for formulating and implementing strategies that will leverage organizational performance in the long run.

INTRODUCTION

The challenge for today's manager highly resides in managing the workforce diversity in organizations. In a way, diversity represents the unique talents, experiences, and intellectual assets introduced by the individual to the organiza-tion. In this sense, it provides a great potential that needs to be controlled wisely to improve competitiveness; otherwise, such power may be devastating for every organization. To state more specifically, when managed right, diversity becomes a source of creativity and innovation and act as a basis for competitive advantage. On the other hand, if managed wrong, it may become a cause of misunderstanding, and conflict in the

DOI: 10.4018/978-1-4666-1812-1.ch011

workplace, which result in absenteeism, poor quality, low morale and loss of competitiveness (Bassett-Jones, 2005). This "aggregated potential" brought by differences among organization members must be well-realized, respected and diverted in compliance with the individual's and the organization's best interest. In other words, workforce diversity makes sense only when it is turned into "workforce success" which depends on creating value through managing relationships in order to improve financial, operational and customer related firm performance (Huselid, Becker, & Beatty, 2005).

Accordingly, ignoring diversity is not an option for organizations any more. Rather, organizations seek out ways to understand the dynamics introduced by such diversity in order to develop necessary skills to cope with its possible impacts. These skills are especially important for multinational firms, which experience an extreme degree of workforce diversity at each organizational level. In these firms, the most strategic effects of diversity are observed at managerial levels. This is mainly due to the fact that operations of multinationals are carried out in many different regions all of which are managed by executives diversified mainly in terms of culture related dynamics. To provide coordination among these executives who are responsible for different operations in distant regions, teamwork becomes of crucial importance. While studying dynamics related to these Top Management Teams (TMTs), along with several mezzo level (organization level) and macro level (industry and operational region level) contextual factors, diversity related variables stemming from the individual level should also be considered to complement the whole theoretical framework.

Literature on workforce diversity presents both complementary and controversial views on the relation between Top Management Team (TMT) diversity and performance indicators. In this sense, the current study first attempts to briefly summarize these viewpoints and related findings. Following this, to extend current de-

bate on diversity, a new integrative perspective structured on the interaction of TMT diversity and certain organization-level variables (such as "nature of team task" and "the influence of board of directors") is presented. Regarding this framework, the chapter further states main issues and controversies along with certain solutions and recommendations. Finally, moving from this debate on, future research directions are put forth to open new venues in this field and thus contribute to the body of research on multinational TMT diversity.

BACKGROUND

Diversity is traced in terms of several different dimensions. According to Loden (1996), there are "primary" and "secondary" dimensions that cause diversity (p. 16). Among primary dimensions are age, gender, ethnic heritage, race, mental/physical abilities and characteristics, and sexual orientation, while secondary dimensions consist of variables such as education, work style, family status, religion, income, work experience, and geographical location. Similar to this, Erhardt, Werbe,l and Shrader (2003) puts forth two general distinctions described by the observable (demographic—gender, age, race, and ethnicity based) and non-observable (cognitive—knowledge, education, values, perception, affection, and personality based) dimensions. In terms of contextual variables affecting the degree of diversity, Triandis (1996) emphasize the importance of cultural distance, level of adaptation, history of intergroup relations, acculturation, and isomorphic attributions.

Despite of differences in terms of all these variables; future trends of internationalization, proclivity towards operating through virtual and decentralized organizations and acts against prejudice and discrimination foster extensive networking and collaboration (Allard, 2008). These high-coordination based mechanisms are especially important for the use of teamwork and its effects on strategic firm performance. This line of research has attracted attention in international business literature as well. According to Early and Gibson (2002) three theoretical domains provide the background for research on multinational work teams (p. 16-17). The first one relates to "multinational structures and technologies" which bases on a rather macro perspective with a focus on organizational context, technology, political systems, and economic systems. Second one relates to "top management team composition and functioning" and emphasizes the decision making power of the top managers constituting the dominant coalition of the firm. Finally, the third domain relates to "cognition, exchange, and conflict" and deals with problems pertaining to interpersonal and social aspects of multinational teams. Accordingly, this chapter adopts the second theoretical domain, "top management team composition and functioning," and focuses on diversity related dimensions in terms of top management team functioning.

Within the framework of studies on TMT dynamics, three related bodies of research; namely, TMT demography, group diversity, and multinational team research complement each other (Gong, 2006). Within this framework, proposing "upper echelon" perspective, Hambrick and Mason (1984) point out the importance of examining the relationship between Top Management Teams (TMTs) and organizational outcomes of strategic choices and performance levels. Specifically they suggest that demographic characteristics of top-level executives affect their cognitive styles and knowledge base, and thus divert their strategic actions. Apart from the individual demographic characteristics, certain team level variables are considered to be effective in this research stream as well. Among these; TMT tenure, TMT age and TMT international experience act as the most important and widely studies ones (Chen, 2011). In a supportive manner, Gupta (1988) argues that studying TMTs rather than the indi-

vidual manager, CEO, will much better clarify the impact of certain managerial level effects on organizational strategy. Similar to this, referring to related literature, Finkelstein (1992) supports that when the top management team is adopted as the unit of analysis rather than the individual CEO, studies yield superior results in terms of explained variance.

As presented in the seminal work of Carpenter, Geletkanycz and Sanders (2004), the scope of TMT varies in studies from being either consisted of top managers involved in strategic decision making by the CEO (e.g., Amason, 1996; West & Anderson, 1996; West & Schwenk, 1996; Papadikis & Barwise, 2002; Collins & Clark, 2003), or all executives above vice president level (e.g., Hambrick, Cho, & Chen, 1996; Carpenter & Fredrickson, 2001) to being limited with CEO and its direct reports (e.g., Tushman & Rosenkopf, 1996; Boeker, 1997). To generally state, three types of managers comprise TMTs in multinational firms; local nationals, home country expatriates and third country expatriates, all of which differ from each other in terms of their regional knowledge, sensitivity to local market and breadth of global perspective (Elron, 1997).

Regarding the variables related to diversity in teams, Jackson, Joshi and Erhardt (2003) differentiate between task-related (i.e., function, tenure, education) and relations-oriented (i.e., age, sex, and racio-ethnicity) attributes as well as readily detectable (i.e., age, sex, and racio-ethnicity) and underlying attributes (i.e., personality and attitudes). Similarly, basing on an extensive literature review, Early and Gibson (2002, p. 47), argue that sociocognitive characteristics, the team task, context, third parties, and the length of time members have interacted moderate the strategic impact of heterogeneity in multinational top management teams. In a more comprehensive manner, Jehn, Northcraft, and Neale (1999) introduce following classification to further clarify the types of diversity teams encounter (p. 743):

- *Informational Diversity*: This type of diversity refers to differences in knowledge bases and perspectives that members bring to the group.
- *Social Category Diversity*: This kind of diversity consists of explicit differences among group members in social category membership; such as race, gender, and ethnicity.
- *Value Diversity*: This type of diversity take place when members of a workgroup differ in terms of what they think the group's real task, goal, target, or mission should be.

Referring to a Fortune 100 executive research, Robinson and Dechant (1997) put forth that the stated reasons for engaging in diversity management generally focus on leverage opportunities rather than penalties of mismanagement. Among these reasons are better utilization of talent, increased marketplace understanding, enhanced breadth of understanding in leadership positions, enhanced creativity, and increased quality of team problem-solving (p. 22). Following this vein, recent studies have introduced "diversity" as an important variable in determining the functioning of TMTs and their performance leverage capacity, and studied the issue in terms of several diversity related dimensions (e.g. Wiersema & Bantel, 1992; Knight, et al., 1999; Tihanyi, et al., 2000; Carpenter & Fredrickson, 2001). An important portion of these studies put forth that diversity in terms of nationality and culture lead to conflict in multinational teams and thus affect their functioning (e.g. Gibson, 1996). Such conflict will render team effectiveness by causing miscommunication and low motivation and thus result in "process loss" which is defined as "less than optimal ways of combining members' resources" (Eigel & Kuhnert, 1996, p. 80).

Nevertheless, along with diversity related dimensions, two key factors should especially be emphasized in affecting a transnational team's composition, operations, and performance (Snow,

Snell, Davison, & Hambrick, 1996, pp. 52-53). One of them is the "task complexity and importance" as transnational teams work on highly complex projects; while the other one is the "multicultural dynamic" which refers to handling a variety of cross-cultural issues related to national culture, occupational culture, and company culture. However, it should also be kept in mind that, especially as they are at the top positions of the company, these teams are in close relation with certain external factors which shape their level of managerial discretion and thus, functioning. Accordingly, research in this field should also take possible impacts of these factors into account to provide a comprehensive perspective.

PUTTING IT INTO A FRAMEWORK: THE IMPACT OF DIVERSITY ON MULTINATIONAL FIRM TMT FUNCTIONING

Issues, Controversies, Problems

Top management teams are among the main tools to build and operate an ambidextrous organization, which is capable of simultaneously exploiting existing competencies and exploring new opportunities (Smith & Tushman, 2005; Tushman & O'Reilly, 1996; Raisch, Birkinshaw, Probst, & Tushman, 2009). According to Smith and Tushman (2005), top management teams are of crucial importance in that they "balance short-term performance and long-term adaptability through resource allocation trade-offs and organizational designs decisions" (Smith & Tushman, 2005, p. 524). Smith and Tushman (2005) moreover argue that the top management team serves as a point of integration in an organizational structure consisting of highly differentiated units, as in the "network structure" of multinational companies (e.g., Ghoshal & Bartlett, 1990; Parkhe, Wasserman, & Ralston, 2006; Contractor, Wasserman, & Faust, 2006). The role of top management teams in the integration of a differentiated structure has also been studied in relation with certain team specific variables like autonomy and knowledge management (e.g., Haas, 2010).

Without any doubt, the impact of diversity on the functioning of these teams becomes an even more crucial issue due to their strategic role. However, there are some controversial views regarding the way that diversity affects team functioning. For example, basing on related literature, Garcia-Prieto, Bellard, and Schneider (2003) emphasize that performance highly depends on the way in which diversity influences team processes. On the other hand, again basing on an extensive literature review, Jackson et al. (2003) state that "the general pattern across studies provides little support for the argument that the effects of diversity on performance are due to the effects of diversity on team processes" (p. 809). Taking its roots from this controversial framework, studies on the effects of diversity on team performance present mixed results as well. Despite of studies that reveal the positive impact of diversity on team functioning (e.g., Bantel & Jackson, 1989; Hambrick, et al., 1996), still there are many others empirically providing support for the negative impact of diversity on team performance (e.g., Ancona & Caldwell, 1992; Knight, Pearce, Smith, Olian, Sims, Smith, & Flood, 1999). Main premise of those supporting the positive impacts of diversity on team performance is that diversity improves the breadth of perspective and problem solving capacity, provides creativity and innovation along with greater tolerance for uncertainty and a propensity for strategic change (Hambrick, Davison, Snell, & Snow, 1998; Bantel & Jackson, 1989; Murray, 1989; Wiersema & Bantel, 1992). On the other hand, those who support the controversial viewpoint posits that homogeneity, instead of diversity promotes integration, trust, ease of communication, faster decision implementation and thus enhances group performance (O'Reilly & Flatt, 1989; Hambrick, Davison, Snell, & Snow, 1998).

Above stated controversial viewpoints lead to the need for considering the role of possible intervening variables within this research stream. These variables largely come from the context in which the team operates. As Jackson (1996) proposes, one should pay attention to the interaction between the specific nature of a team's diversity and the larger context that surrounds the team's activities. Following this vein, Priem (1990), for instance, proposes the level of dynamism in the external environment as a possible intervening variable and argues that TMT consensus will be associated with high performance in stable environments, rather than dynamic environments. Supportively, Keck and Tushman (1993) revealed that organizations, which survive dramatic environmental shifts, have executive teams that are heterogeneous in terms of functional diversity which provide both stability and the capacity for change, whereas periods of equilibrium are associated with low change and high homogeneity.

Additionally, there are several other variables affecting the role of diversity on team functioning. Among these variables, the type of work group is one of the most important ones. McGarth, Berdahl, and Arrow (1996) distinguish between "team," "task force," and "crew" as the major types of work groups. According to authors, teams consist of people with different array of knowledge, skills and abilities. Organizations train these people, equip and organize them into a team to be given the responsibility for carrying out a particular class of projects on a continuing basis. The other type, task forces, consists of people who are focused on completing a single, specific project. People are assigned to this work group and develop tools, rules, and procedures to complete the assigned project. After the project is completed, the group disbands. The final type, crew, is a rather technology - driven type of work group. Here, the organization establishes a focused technology for a specific class of projects and then assigns personnel to provide a crew for that project. The most relevant types of work groups, which reflect the characteristics of top manager work groups in multinational organizations, are teams and task forces. The other type, crews, is rather observed at a more technical level and thus reflects a more functional aspect of organizational structure. However, teams and task forces bear a lot of differences in their very nature and thus the impact of diversity will be highly differentiated among them. Supporting this notion, McGarth et al. (1996) argue that diversity should affect teams more than task forces and should affect crews least. Complementary to this, at the end of a thorough literature review, Early and Gibson (2002, p. 23) also identify nature of team tasks as an important variable related to diversity and team performance and note that "nonroutine task performance may be facilitated by multiculturalism, whereas performance on routine tasks should either be unaffected or possibly even negatively impacted." This is an important argument as it proposes diversity as a naturally positive contributor for one time-complex problem solving process, like that of task forces; while emphasizing its conflict causing role in more long term, continuity based processes, like that of teams.

Along with the nature of team tasks, Early and Gibson (2002) emphasize the impact of third parties as another important variable. Basing on Gibson and Saxton's (2001) and Jackson's (1992) findings, the authors note that; the type of third party input, timing of the input and heterogeneity of the team interact with each other to affect decision making process especially when the presence of a dominating third part is evident to help guide the team and keep the members on task.

Parallel with these, main premise of this chapter is that discussing possible effects of organization level variables that interact with the type of multinational work teams at top management level is necessary to reveal the impact of diversity on their functioning. In other words, this study proposes certain organizational-level variables such as the type of organizational task the team is involved

and the influence of third parties as major forces that interact with team diversity and affect team-level and organizational-level outcomes.

Solutions and Recommendations

Following Jackson's (1992) findings emphasizing that mixed results regarding the effects of diversity on team performance are due to the type of attributes studied (being either task-related or relations-related), this chapter adopts variables coming from organization-level and attempts to define them in terms of task and relations oriented indicators. Additional to this, the impact of third parties within the organization is also considered while building the discussion framework. Such an organization-level approach is believed to be much more clarifying in explaining the main points discussed in this chapter.

In this manner, two main groups of variables are thought to interact with different types of diversity dimensions in top management teams. The first group relates to the influence of task related attributes on the effects of diversity on TMT functioning. Regarding these task related attributes, Hambrick et al. (1998) provides a comprehensive but simple framework basing on three main types of tasks. One of them is the creative task which requires generating a broad array of better-refined ideas and coming up with rigorous solutions. The other type is computational task, which is based on obtaining and analyzing clear-cut information on objective standards for problem solving. The final type, coordinative task requires an elaborate and well-orchestrated interaction among group members to provide interpersonal reliability, prompt and timely interaction, and the potential for mutual adjustment among group members (p. 194). Basing on this classification, the authors further argue that, diversity of values positively impacts group functioning for creative tasks, while it has negative impacts on group functioning for coordinative tasks. For computational tasks, diversity of values is expected to be mostly irrelevant. Diversity of cognition, which is similar to informational diversity previously discussed, will enhance team functioning for creative tasks and for computational tasks as long as the information obtained is relevant to the issue on hand. However, its positive impact on coordinative tasks will be up to a certain level, since diversity in cognitions beyond that level will create conflict and thus be counter-productive. Finally, diversity in terms of variables like demeanors and language, similar to social category diversity, will have more harmful effects for groups dealing with coordinative tasks, rather than for those dealing with computational and creative tasks (for a more detailed discussion see Hambrick, et al., 1998, pp. 195-198).

This chapter builds on and extends this perspective proposed by Hambrick et al. (1998) by putting it into a framework based on the type of TMT. Specifically, there are two types of TMTs in multinational firms. One of them, "executive TMT," consists of permanent executives who are responsible for the worldwide operations of the firm. This group has a leader, CEO of the firm, and is directly responsible to board of directors. This long-term relations oriented team is in a continuous decision-making and problem-solving process on a daily basis and has a corporate-wide coordinative function. More specifically, this kind of team receives information from the internal and external environment on a daily basis, makes decisions and disseminates necessary knowledge and practical requirements to the whole corporate network, which makes it stand on an important liaison position and act as a "hub." Stemming from this position, main part of this team's activities consists of "coordinative" tasks. To successfully perform these tasks, a high degree of communication is required both internally and externally. Information obtained through this communication process should be interpreted from the viewpoint of a common mindset consisting of complementary (not conflicting) perspectives of the members. Accordingly, to act as a coordinative body in the

corporate network, the executive team has to be organic in nature and respond to external and internal needs with a shared behavioral pattern.

Apart from the permanent one consisting of executives, there is also another type of team in the multinational firm. This second type of team, which can be named as "project based TMT," also consists of top-level managers like regional executives and functional directors. However, rather than being relations oriented and having the responsibility of a corporate-wide coordinative function and continuous problem solving, this second type of team focuses on creating solutions for specific problems. In this sense, it can be described as a task-oriented, project-based, temporary team, which focuses on a sole problem that is rather complex in its nature and tries to come up with a decision on this problem. A large portion of this team's activities consists of "computational" and "creative" tasks.

These two teams also differ from each other in terms of their contextual network related dynamics. To put it in other words, the executive TMT heavily relies on the external network to manage knowledge flow needed to design the worldwide corporate strategies and make related decisions. On the other hand, project based top management team relies largely on knowledge coming from internal network dynamics for creating solution to a specific problem or designing a specific project. Thus, it can be argued that the executive TMT bases mainly on "feed-forward" mechanisms focusing "exploration" of new knowledge for the external network. However, the project based TMT mainly adopts internal oriented knowledge management systems and thus focuses more on "exploitation" of the knowledge on hand rather than exploring new knowledge from the wider external company network. In this sense, the ambidextrous nature of TMTs in multinational firms is emphasized once more as an anchor pointing out that different dynamics should prevail in the functioning of these teams. Accordingly, to understand and manage these teams in a way to leverage multinational firm performance, the impact of diversity should be discussed separately for each one.

As mentioned previously, the classification of Hambrick et al. (1998) is adopted in this chapter to illustrate a comprehensive framework, which describes diversity. As an underlying assumption, it should be noted that all members in TMTs are expected to have a certain level of international experience and as a result of this "experience based professionalism," members have skills and knowledge relevant to and fine-tuned with each other and the negative effects of informational diversity will be rasped in a large sense. Supportively, basing on previous research findings, Jackson (1996) takes attention to the fact that better decision making and problem solving occur when team members have "overlapping domains of expertise" (p. 61). Thus, it is assumed here that informational diversity among TMT members is rather complementary in its nature. However, the degree of informational diversity's impact on team functioning still differs in terms of team type and the task it deals with. For example, in project based TMTs, informational diversity is especially desired as it provides the necessary broad array of knowledge to be used to come up with appropriate solutions to complex problems. Thus, it can be defined even as a prerequisite for the proper functioning of these teams. Informational diversity is also important for executive TMTs. When informational diversity is high, each member presents the specific knowledge he or she acquires throughout the decision-making process, and due to the complementary nature of these relevant information, functioning of the team is fostered.

Basing on this discussion, it is proposed here that:

- *Proposition 1:* Informational diversity has positive impacts on TMT's performance leverage capacity; however this impact is much more critical for the proper functioning of "project based TMT" when compared to that of "executive TMT."

On the other hand, "social category diversity" and "value diversity" will both render the critical communication process, which is highly important in executive TMTs that carry out coordinative tasks. Social category diversity presents differences in language, age, race, etc. and in this sense damages the ability of team to act as a unified organ responsible for the worldwide coordination of multinational firm activities. Similarly, value diversity also raises conflict in the team as it emphasizes differences in terms of desired ends and priorities of members. Especially, as executive teams are more relations oriented and bear the responsibility of developing worldwide strategies in accordance with company-wide objectives, members should not differ from each other in terms of their perceptions of these objectives and priorities. However, the negative impact of diversity is seen in teams only after a while due to the "honeymoon effect" described by Kilduff, Angelmar, and Mehra (2000). Regarding this effect, the authors argue that people may initially strive to harmonize their thinking with other team members, but after a while, they become more comfortable in relying on thought patterns which are characteristic to their particular age-cohorts, national cultures, or functional specialties.

Nevertheless, contrary arguments regarding the above stated discussion should also be put forth to provide a comprehensive perspective. For instance, as revealed by Early and Mosakowski (2000), highly heterogeneous teams create a common identity after forming ways to interact and communicate, which takes a certain amount of time. This is also supported by Gong (2006) in a recent study conducted with subsidiary TMTs. He found that, the effect of TMT nationality diversity becomes more positive as the age variable increases. Gong (2006) justifies this finding by the extant international management literature proposing year of operation as a reasonable proxy for learning and institutionalism (e.g. Luo & Peng, 1999). Moving from these seemingly conflicting but actually complementary arguments, it can be claimed that the long-term focused nature of relationships in the executive TMT creates an advantageous situation as it creates the necessary conditions for institutionalism and learning which foster the positive effects of value and social category based diversity in a longer time frame. To put it altogether, the negative effects of value and social category diversity on executive team functioning show an inverse U-shaped pattern.

On the other hand, in project based TMTs, value diversity is expected to act as a positive moderator for the functioning of the team up to a specific point—which can be named as "beneficiary conflict edge"—in that it fosters presentation of new perspectives for the solution of complex problems the team deals with. These different perspectives provides new lenses to team members and the conflict emerging due to this diversity helps team members come up with alternative solutions and project designs. Different prioritization of objectives and different viewpoints to problems fosters this process of alternative solution design. On the other hand, social category diversity has a rather severe impact in more long-term oriented relationships, while it is mostly ignored in less relations-oriented and temporary teams. Contrary to the short-term, project oriented relations in project based teams, due to its relations oriented nature, the executive team inherits more intimate relationships which prepare a context for social category based differences to show up and be effective, at least in the midterm. However, in the long run, detrimental effects of these differences will diminish due to group socialization process which tunes members' values with each other.

Moving from this point on, it can be proposed that:

- *Proposition 2:* Negative impact of value diversity and social category diversity on the performance leverage capacity of executive TMT shows an inverse U-shaped pattern. Specifically, they will have no impact in the short term, while they have negative impacts in the midterm and positive impacts in the long term.

- *Proposition 3:* Value diversity has positive impact on the performance leverage capacity of project based TMTs in the short run; while social category diversity is not significantly influential on its functioning due to short term focus of relationships in these teams.

Additional to TMT type, there exists another important variable, which diverts TMT functioning and performance leverage capacity. This second organizational context related variable is the influence of third parties on the impact of diversity in TMTs. Supporting the important role of third parties, Kilduff et al. (2000) propose that the effects of demographic diversity (which is defined as a combination of age, nationality and functionality related heterogeneity) on cognitive diversity may be minimized under strong external effects.

The presence of a dominant third party as an external factor is discussed in this chapter in terms of the influence of board of directors in the corporate governance. As the board's influence is mostly traced in strategic decisions and other governance related issues, their impact on diversity's effects is especially observed in the functioning of executive TMT. In this vein, recent studies put forth the moderating impact of board of directors-related dynamics on the relationship between TMT diversity variables, certain organizational processes, and TMT strategic capabilities (e.g. Chen, 2011; Kim, Burns, & Prescott, 2009). Also related to this research stream, Alpay, Bodur, Ener, and Taluğ (2005) move from the importance of building and maintaining an effective monitoring process in multinational firms and study the role of several board related variables (like composition and size of the board, performance evaluation process variables, reporting process variables, etc.) on the functioning of this system by comparing the outcomes for both multinational firms and local firms.

Additional to these, related literature puts forth that the power of board of directors and autonomy of executive TMT highly bases on the type of knowledge obtained by the parties. In his pioneering studies, Pfeffer (1972, 1973) argues that companies use their boards as tools to deal with external environment through co-opting important actors with which they are interdependent. According to Pfeffer (1972, 1973) the percentage of members from financial organizations or law firms (and from other independent third party institutions) is contingent upon the interdependency of the organization to its environment, which is largely shaped by specific sectoral dynamics. When this dependency is high, knowledge coming from the network relations of these critical members turns out to be a great source of power, which increases their impact on executive TMT actions. Supporting this, Haas (2010) found that team effectiveness is contingent upon the characteristics of the knowledge, along with characteristics of the task, and increases when the content of knowledge is scarce. In a complementary way, Finkelstein and Hambrick (1990) revealed that top management teams operating in contexts in which managers have low levels of discretion have little effect on organizational outcomes, while in contexts that allowed managers to have high discretion, managers seem to matter greatly and thus team related variables gain importance. Accordingly, in firms with boards including significant number of outside shareholders, the managerial discretion will be significantly reduced (Hambrick & Finkelstein, 1987; Finkelstein, 1992). Under these circumstances, the directive impact of the board overrides the impact of diversity. In other words, the board deeply influences and limits the behaviors and decisions of the executive TMT, and thus limits any natural effects coming from sources

such as differences among members. Moving from this point on, it is argued here that the influence of third parties, in this case the "board of directors," depends highly on the strategic importance of the knowledge they obtain. Accordingly, the following proposition is suggested:

- *Proposition 4:* Impact of diversity on executive TMT's performance leverage capacity will be less when corporate board members acquire critical external network related knowledge which makes their influence on TMT functioning increase, and TMT members' managerial discretion level decrease.

At this point, it should be once more noted that the above stated proposition is especially valid for boards including independent members who hold strategic positions by virtue of their strong sectoral relationships. These relationships provide power to board members and make it possible for them to intervene decision-making process of executive TMT.

FUTURE RESEARCH DIRECTIONS

Additional to the framework and related perspectives provided here, future research should also take certain issues into consideration to further expand this research stream. Firstly, future research vein should focus on comparative studies regarding different effects of diversity attributes on the functioning of teams at all organizational levels. After all, no unit in the organization can be thought to be isolated from the other ones; thus, diversity variables affecting TMT functioning will also have certain interactions with other organizational level variables. Among these variables, structure and culture related ones especially bear importance in that these are the major integrative devices in every organization.

Secondly, apart from the organizational level variables, further studies also need to explain the effects of certain individual level variables on the effects of diversity. For example, introducing a new aspect for Hambrick and Mason's (1984) argument stating that managers' demographics influence their decisions, Giddens (1984) claims that manager's awareness of how their demographics affect their decisions has also severe impact on their decision making process. Presenting a complementary view, Garcia-Prieto et al. (2003) argue that individual level processes are also in great relevance with the effects of diversity on team functioning. Specifically they discuss that team members' subjective experiences of diversity affect their cognitive appraisals of events and issues. Moving from this discussion on, it is recommended that future research should be expanded in a way that care more about these individual level variables' possible effects on team level processes.

Thirdly, as pointed out by Jackson (1996), the issues of power and status stand as important variables on teams' agendas. Additional to diversity's direct effects, indirect ones that are incurred through the changes in power balances and related status differences within the TMTs should also be excavated in future research vein.

Finally, following Alpay et al.'s (2005) study, a promising future research vein will be presented by comparative studies incurred at the local and international levels. Without any doubt, the dynamics related to the impact of diversity will change in terms of different operating contexts. This makes it an imperative to conduct studies focusing on the effects of certain context related variables coming from the organization's local and wider international environment while designing future research. Among these variables, the most prominent ones are the effects of local and international regulations and local cultural norms.

CONCLUSION

Management, in a large sense, consists of making decisions among alternatives. As implied in this simplified expression, it is a rather complex process basing on evaluating all dynamics related to each alternative choice. In this sense, diversity comes into scene as a crucial factor, which affects the functioning of teams consisting of managers, like those of TMTs in multinational firms. Diversity has several different sub-dimensions, which affect the perspectives, mental models and preferences of the managers in TMTs, and thus makes it mandatory to reveal possible related mechanisms to understand certain effects on TMT functioning, which is directly related to its performance leverage capacity. Only in this way will it be possible to use the advantages of diversity for the purposes of growth and expansion in the global marketplace.

Moving from this point on and drawing upon the related literature on diversity's impact on team functioning, this chapter attempts to put the issue into a framework relevant to multinational firm TMT's performance leverage capacity. Within this debate, special attention is paid to variables such as the "nature of task" and "impact of corporate board of directors." In this sense, "nature of task" is used to describe the type of TMT—being either "executive TMT" and "project based TMT." The other dimension, "the impact of corporate board of directors" is also discussed throughout the chapter to reflect upon the role of external factors on diversity's team related outcomes. Such a viewpoint proposes team task related characteristics and the impact of board of directors as organizational level variables that interact with diversity's effects on TMT functioning and performance leverage capacity.

When the focus of this chapter and future research venues discussed in the previous sections are taken into account, it should be noted as a final word that, to further study the impact of diversity on multinational firm performance through TMT functioning, an integrative framework which takes all relevant aspects from individual, organizational, and macro-environmental levels should be adopted. Studies which take different aspects of such a framework will complement each other and thus altogether contribute to the flourishing of diversity related research stream in international business literature.

REFERENCES

Allard, J. M. (2002). Theoretical underpinnings of diversity. In Harvey, C., & Allard, M. J. (Eds.), *Understanding and Managing Diversity*. Upper Saddle River, NJ: Prentice Hall.

Alpay, G., Bodur, M., Ener, H., & Taluğ, C. (2005). Comparing board-level governance at MNEs and local firms: Lessons from Turkey. *Journal of International Management, 11*, 67–86. doi:10.1016/j.intman.2004.11.005

Amason, A. C. (1996). Distinguishing the effects of functional and dysfunctional conflict on strategic decision making: Resolving a paradox for top management teams. *Academy of Management Journal, 39*(1), 123–148. doi:10.2307/256633

Ancona, D., & Caldwell, D. (1992). Demography and design: predictors of new product team performance. *Organization Science, 3*, 342–355. doi:10.1287/orsc.3.3.321

Bantel, K., & Jackson, S. (1989). Top management and innovations in banking: does the composition of the top team make a difference? *Strategic Management Journal, 10*, 107–124. doi:10.1002/smj.4250100709

Bassett-Jones, N. (2005). The paradox of diversity management, creativity and innovation. *Creativity and Innovation Management, 14*(2), 169–175. doi:10.1111/j.1467-8691.00337.x

Boeker, W. (1997). Executive migration and strategic change: The effect of top manager movement on product market entry. *Administrative Science Quarterly, 42*(2), 213–236. doi:10.2307/2393919

Carpenter, M. A., & Fredrickson, J. W. (2001). Top management teams, global strategic posture, and the moderating role of uncertainty. *Academy of Management Journal, 44*(3), 533–546. doi:10.2307/3069368

Carpenter, M. A., Geletkanycz, M. A., & Sanders, W. G. (2004). Upper echelons research revisited: Antecedents, elements and consequences of top management team composition. *Journal of Management, 30*(6), 749–778. doi:10.1016/j.jm.2004.06.001

Chen, H. (2011). Does board independence influence the top management team? Evidence from strategic decisions toward internationalization. *Corporate Governance: An International Review, 19*(4).

Collins, C. J., & Clark, K. D. (2003). Strategic human resource practice, top management team social networks, and firm performance: The role of human resource practices in creative organizational competitive advantage. *Academy of Management Journal, 46*(6), 720–731. doi:10.2307/30040665

Contractor, N. S., Wasserman, S., & Faust, K. (2006). Testing multitheoretical, multilevel hypotheses about organizational networks: an analytic framework and empirical example. *Academy of Management Review, 31*(3), 681–703. doi:10.5465/AMR.2006.21318925

Early, P. C., & Gibson, C. B. (2002). *Multinational work teams: A new perspective*. Mahwah, NJ: Lawrence Erlbaum Associates, Inc.

Early, P. C., & Mosakowski, E. (2000). Creating hybrid team cultures: An empirical test of transnational team functioning. *Academy of Management Journal, 43*(1), 26–49. doi:10.2307/1556384

Eigel, K. M., & Kuhnert, K. W. (1996). Personality diversity and its relationship to managerial team productivity. In Ruderman, M. N., Hughes-James, M. W., & Jackson, S. E. (Eds.), *Selected Research on Work Team Diversity*. Washington, DC: APA-CCL Press. doi:10.1037/10507-004

Elron, E. (1997). Top management teams within multinational corporations: effects of cultural heterogeneity. *The Leadership Quarterly, 8*(4), 393–412. doi:10.1016/S1048-9843(97)90021-7

Erhardt, N. L., Werbel, J. D., & Shrader, C. B. (2003). Board of director diversity and firm financial performance. *Corporate Governance, 11*(2), 102–111. doi:10.1111/1467-8683.00011

Finkelstein, S. (1992). Power in top management teams: Dimensions, measurement, and validation. *Academy of Management Journal, 35*(3), 505–538. doi:10.2307/256485

Finkelstein, S., & Hambrick, D. C. (1990). Top management-team tenure and organizational outcomes: The moderating role for managerial discretion. *Administrative Science Quarterly, 35*, 484–503. doi:10.2307/2393314

Garcia-Prieto, P., Bellard, E., & Schneider, S. C. (2003). Experiencing diversity, conflict and emotions in teams. *Applied Psychology: An International Review, 52*(3), 413–440. doi:10.1111/1464-0597.00142

Gibson, C. (1996). Do you hear what I hear? A framework for reconciling intercultural communication difficulties arising from cognitive styles and cultural values. In Erez, M., & Early, P. C. (Eds.), *New Perspectives on International Industrial/Organizational Psychology*. San Francisco, CA: Jossey-Bass.

Gibson, C. B., & Saxton, T. (2001). *Consultants in the cupboard: How third party involvement affects team strategic decision outcomes*. Working Paper. Los Angeles, CA: University of Southern California.

Giddens, A. (1984). *The constitution of society: Outline of the theory of structuration*. Berkeley, CA: University of California Press.

Gong, Y. (2006). The impact of subsidiary top management team national diversity on subsidiary performance: Knowledge and legitimacy perspectives. *Management International Review, 46*(6), 771–789. doi:10.1007/s11575-006-0126-2

Gupta, A. K. (1988). Contingency perspectives on strategic leadership: Current knowledge and future research direction. In Hambrick, D. C. (Ed.), *The Executive Effect: Concepts and Methods for Studying Top Managers*. Greenwich, CT: JAI Press.

Haas, M. (2010). The double-edged swords of autonomy and external knowledge: Analyzing team effectiveness in a multinational organization. *Academy of Management Journal, 53*(5), 989–1008. doi:10.5465/AMJ.2010.54533180

Hambrick, D. C., Cho, T. S., & Chen, M. (1996). The influence of top management team heterogeneity on firms' competitive moves. *Administrative Science Quarterly, 41*(4), 659–684. doi:10.2307/2393871

Hambrick, D. C., Davison, S. C., Snell, S. A., & Snow, C. (1998). When groups consist of multiple nationalities: Towards a new understanding of the implications. *Organization Studies, 19*(2), 181–205. doi:10.1177/017084069801900202

Hambrick, D. C., & Finkelstein, S. (1987). Managerial discretion: A bridge between polar views on organizations. In Staw, B. M., & Gummings, L. L. (Eds.), *Research in Organizational Behavior*. Greenwich, CT: JAI Press.

Hambrick, D. E., & Mason, P. A. (1984). Upper echelons: The organization as a reflection of its top managers. *Academy of Management Review, 9*, 193–206.

Huselid, M. A., Becker, B. E., & Beatty, R. W. (2005). *The workforce scorecard: Managing human capital to execute strategy*. Boston, MA: Harvard Business School Press.

Jackson, S. (1992). Consequences of group composition for the interpersonal dynamics of strategic issue processing. *Advances in Strategic Management*, *8*, 345–382.

Jackson, S. (1996). The consequences of diversity in multidisciplinary work teams. In West, M. A. (Ed.), *Handbook of Work Group Psychology*. New York, NY: John Wiley&Sons.

Jackson, S. E., Joshi, A., & Erhardt, N. L. (2003). Recent research on team and organizational diversity: SWOT analysis and implications. *Journal of Management*, *29*(6), 801–830.

Keck, S. L., & Tushman, M. L. (1993). Environmental and organizational context and executive team structure. *Academy of Management Journal*, *36*(6), 1314–1344. doi:10.2307/256813

Kilduff, M., Angelmar, R., & Mehra, A. (2000). Top management-team diversity and firm performance: Examining the role of cognitions. *Organization Science*, *11*(1), 21–34. doi:10.1287/orsc.11.1.21.12569

Kim, B., Burns, M. L., & Prescott, J. E. (2009). The strategic role of the board: The impact of board structure on top management team strategic action capability. *Corporate Governance: An International Review*, *17*(6), 728–743. doi:10.1111/j.1467-8683.2009.00775.x

Knight, D., Pearce, C. L., Smith, K. G., Olian, J. D., Sims, H. P., Smith, K. A., & Flood, P. (1999). Top management team diversity, group process and strategic consensus. *Strategic Management Journal*, *20*, 445–465. doi:10.1002/(SICI)1097-0266(199905)20:5<445::AID-SMJ27>3.0.CO;2-V

Loden, M. (1996). *Implementing diversity*. Homewood, CA: Business One Irwin.

Luo, Y., & Peng, M. W. (1999). Learning to compete in a transition economy: Experience, environment, and performance. *Journal of International Business Studies*, *30*(2), 269–296. doi:10.1057/palgrave.jibs.8490070

McGrath, J. E., Berdahl, J. L., & Arrow, H. (1996). Traits, expectations, culture, and clout: The dynamics of diversity in work groups. In Jackson, S. E., & Ruderman, M. N. (Eds.), *Diversity in Work Teams*. Washington, DC: APA Publishing. doi:10.1037/10189-001

Murray, A. I. (1989). Top management group heterogeneity and firm performance. *Strategic Management Journal*, *10*, 125–142. doi:10.1002/smj.4250100710

O'Reilly, C. A., & Flatt, S. (1989). *Executive team demography, organizational innovation, and firm performance*. Working Paper. Berkeley, CA: University of California.

Papadakis, V. M., & Barwise, P. (2002). How much do CEOs and top managers matter in strategic decision-making? *British Journal of Management*, *13*(1), 83–95. doi:10.1111/1467-8551.00224

Parkhe, A., Wasserman, S., & Ralston, D. A. (2006). New frontiers in network theory development. *Academy of Management Review*, *31*(3), 560–568. doi:10.5465/AMR.2006.21318917

Pfeffer, J. (1972). Size and composition of corporate boards of directors: The organization and its environment. *Administrative Science Quarterly*, *17*(2), 218–228. doi:10.2307/2393956

Pfeffer, J. (1973). Size, composition, and function of hospital boards of directors: A study of organization-environment linkage. *Administrative Science Quarterly*, *18*(3), 349–364. doi:10.2307/2391668

Priem, R. L. (1990). Top management team group factors, consensus, and firm performance. *Strategic Management Journal*, *11*, 469–478. doi:10.1002/smj.4250110605

Raisch, S., Birkinshaw, J., Probst, G., & Tushman, M. L. (2009). Organizational ambidexterity: Balancing exploitation and exploration for sustained performance. *Organization Science*, *20*(4), 685–695. doi:10.1287/orsc.1090.0428

Robinson, G., & Dechant, K. (1997). Building a business case for diversity. *The Academy of Management Executive*, *11*(3), 21–31. doi:10.5465/AME.1997.9709231661

Smith, W. K., & Tushman, M. L. (2005). Managing strategic contradictions: A top management model for managing innovation streams. *Organization Science*, *16*(5), 522–536. doi:10.1287/orsc.1050.0134

Snow, C. C., Snell, S. A., Davison, S. C., & Hambrick, D. C. (1996). Use of transnational teams to globalize your company. *Organizational Dynamics*, *24*(4), 50–67. doi:10.1016/S0090-2616(96)90013-3

Tihanyi, L., Ellstrand, A. E., Daily, C. M., & Dalton, D. R. (2000). Composition of the top management team and firm international diversification. *Journal of Management*, *26*(6), 1157–1177. doi:10.1177/014920630002600605

Triandis, H. C. (1996). The importance of contexts in studies of diversity. In Jackson, S. E., & Ruderman, M. N. (Eds.), *Diversity in Work Teams* (pp. 225–233). Washington, DC: APA Publishing. doi:10.1037/10189-009

Tushman, M. L., & O'Reilly, C. A. (1996). Ambidextrous organizations: Managing evolutionary and revolutionary change. *California Management Review*, *38*, 8–30.

Tushman, M. L., & Rosenkopf, L. (1996). Executive succession, strategic reorientation and performance growth: A longitudinal study in the U.S. cement industry. *Management Science*, *42*(7), 939–953. doi:10.1287/mnsc.42.7.939

West, M. A., & Anderson, N. R. (1996). Innovation in top management teams. *The Journal of Applied Psychology*, *81*(6), 680–693. doi:10.1037/0021-9010.81.6.680

Wiersema, M. F., & Bantel, K. A. (1992). Top management team demography and corporate strategic change. *Academy of Management Journal*, *35*(1), 91–121. doi:10.2307/256474

ADDITIONAL READING

Bartlett, C. A., & Ghoshal, S. (2002). *Managing across borders: The transnational solution.* Boston, MA: HBS Press.

Bunderson, J. S., & Sutcliffe, K. M. (2002). Comparing alternative conceptualizations of functional diversity in management teams: Process and performance effects. *Academy of Management Journal*, *45*(5), 875–893. doi:10.2307/3069319

Carpenter, M. (2002). The implication of strategy and social context for the relationship between top management team heterogeneity and firm performance. *Strategic Management Journal*, *23*(3), 275–284. doi:10.1002/smj.226

Cox, T. (1993). *Cultural diversity in organizations: Theory, research and practice.* San Francisco, CA: Berret-Koehler Publishers.

Cox, T., & Blake, S. (1991). Managing cultural diversity: implications for organizational competitiveness. *The Academy of Management Executive*, *5*(3), 45–56.

Ely, R. J., & Thomas, D. A. (2001). Cultural diversity at work: The effects of diversity perspectives on work group processes and outcomes. *Administrative Science Quarterly, 43*(2), 229–273. doi:10.2307/2667087

Finkelstein, S., & Hambrick, D. C. (1996). *Strategic leadership: Top executives and their effects on organizations*. St. Paul, MN: West.

Haas, M. R. (2006). Acquiring and applying knowledge in transnational teams: The roles of cosmopolitans and locals. *Organization Science, 17*, 313–322. doi:10.1287/orsc.1060.0187

Hackman, J. R. (2002). *Leading teams: Setting the stage for great performance*. Boston, MA: HBS Press.

Harrison, D. A., Price, K. H., & Bell, M. P. (1998). Beyond relational demography: Time and the effects of surface- and deep-level diversity on work group cohesion. *Academy of Management Journal, 41*(1), 96–107. doi:10.2307/256901

Jackson, S. E., May, K. E., & Whitney, K. (1995). Under the dynamics of diversity in decision making teams. In Guzzo, R. A., & Salas, E. (Eds.), *Team Effectiveness and Decision Making in Organizations* (pp. 204–261). San Francisco, CA: Jossey-Bass.

Laurent, A. (1983). The cultural diversity of Western conceptions of management. *International Studies of Management and Organization, 13*(1/2), 75–96.

Maznevski, M. L. (1994). Understanding our differences: Performance in decision-making groups with diverse members. *Human Relations, 47*(5), 531–552. doi:10.1177/001872679404700504

Michel, J., & Hambrick, D. (1992). Diversification posture and top management team characteristics. *Academy of Management Journal, 35*(1), 9–37. doi:10.2307/256471

Nadler, D., Behan, B., & Nadler, M. (2006). *Building better boards: A blueprint for effective governance*. San Francisco, CA: Jossey-Bass.

Pelled, C. H. (1996). Demographic diversity, conflict, and work group outcomes: an intervening process theory. *Organization Science, 7*(6), 615–631. doi:10.1287/orsc.7.6.615

Pfeffer, J. (1983). Organizational demography. *Research in Organizational Behavior, 5*, 299–357.

Priem, R. L., Lyon, S. W., & Dess, G. G. (1999). Inherent limitations of demographic proxies in top management team heterogeneity research. *Journal of Management, 25*(6), 935–954. doi:10.1177/014920639902500607

Randel, A. E. (2002). Identity salience: A moderator of the relationship between group gender composition and work group conflict. *Journal of Organizational Behavior, 23*(6), 749–766. doi:10.1002/job.163

Ruigrok, W., Peck, S., & Keller, H. (2006). Board characteristics and involvement in strategic decision making: Evidence from Swiss companies. *Journal of Management Studies, 43*(5), 1201–1226. doi:10.1111/j.1467-6486.2006.00634.x

Sanders, W. M. G., & Carpenter, M. A. (1998). Internationalization and firm governance: The roles of CEO compensation, top team composition, and board structure. *Academy of Management Journal, 41*(2), 158–178. doi:10.2307/257100

Shaw, J. B., & Barrett-Power, E. (1998). The effects of diversity on small work group processes and performance. *Human Relations, 51*(10), 1307–1325. doi:10.1177/001872679805101005

Siciliano, J. (1996). The relationship of board member diversity to organizational performance. *Journal of Business Ethics, 15*(12), 1313–1321. doi:10.1007/BF00411816

Tsui, A. S., Egan, T. D., & O'Reilly, C. A. (1992). Being different: relational demography and organizational attachment. *Administrative Science Quarterly, 37*(4), 549–580. doi:10.2307/2393472

Tsui, A. S., & Gutek, B. A. (1999). *Demographic differences in organizations: Current research and future directions*. New York, NY: Lexington Books.

West, C. T. Jr, & Schwenk, C. R. (1996). Top management team strategic consensus, demographic homogeneity, and firm performance. *Strategic Management Journal, 17*, 571–576. doi:10.1002/(SICI)1097-0266(199607)17:7<571::AID-SMJ817>3.0.CO;2-C

KEY TERMS AND DEFINITIONS

Board of Directors: Corporate board members who are responsible to the shareholders for the successful governance of the firm.

Executive Top Management Team: Type of permanent tmt including top-level executives whose main responsibility is the design and execution of worldwide strategies in a continuous sense.

Informational Diversity: Diversity stemming from differences in individuals' knowledge and experience related background.

Project Based Top Management Team: Type of temporary tmt, which consists of top level executives chosen to design a specific project or solve a specific complex problem.

Social Category Diversity: Diversity stemming from differences in the social class related attributes (age, race, gender, cultural heritage, etc.) Of individuals.

Top Management Team: The group of top-level executives performing tasks that are relevant to worldwide operational context of the multinational company.

Value Diversity: Diversity stemming from differences in basic values, preferences, and priorities of individuals.

Section 3
Strategies for Leveraging Workforce Diversity

Chapter 12
Leveraging Workforce Diversity using a Multidimensional Approach

Aisha S. Taylor
Portland State University, USA

Keith James
Portland State University, USA

Adam Murry
Portland State University, USA

ABSTRACT

This chapter describes the need for and development of a taxonomy of workplace diversity. It also examines the taxonomy's implications for understanding and predicting diversity outcomes at work. The context of diversity research is described, along with a problem the field is facing concerning consensus for a practical, operational definition. A seven-dimension taxonomy grounded in Social Identity Theory was developed by reviewing contemporary literature on diversity in the workplace. Preliminary research found that each of the seven dimensions of the taxonomy were present in 78 critical incidents describing work-relevant diversity scenarios. An instrument, the Workplace Diversity Inventory, has been developed and administered in order to empirically examine the seven-factor model of the taxonomy. Implications and directions for future research are discussed.

INTRODUCTION

Workplace diversity is increasing, in the U.S. and internationally, and is increasingly important to organizational success (Cox, 2001; Mor Barak, 2005; Triandis, 2003). In contrast with that of

DOI: 10.4018/978-1-4666-1812-1.ch012

previous generations, today's workforce is more heterogeneous in terms of many social categories (e.g., age, gender, ethnicity, national origin), and research suggests that this trend will continue into the future (Judy & D'Amico, 1997). Due to globalization, international workforces are much more common and workplaces have become more diverse than ever before (Haq, 2004). The reality of today's increasingly diverse workforce creates a vital need to appreciate and value differences in order to work more effectively with people from diverse groups and varied backgrounds.

The urgency of addressing workplace diversity is evidenced by the fact that explicit, as well as covert, forms of racial prejudice have been shown to influence hiring decisions (Dovidio & Gaertner, 2000), and workplace discrimination has continued to increase (EEOC, 2010), in spite of greater awareness, increased training, and more social condemnation of the issue. There is a social and moral imperative to build diverse and inclusive working environments.

While workplace diversity has been shown to have both positive and negative effects (e.g., Guzzo & Dickson, 1996; Milliken & Martins, 1996), scholars agree that effective leadership and management are vital to leveraging the benefits of workplace diversity (Cox, 1991; Stockdale & Cao, 2004; Dahm, Willems, Ivancevich, & Graves, 2009). Effectively managing diversity leads to a number of organizational advantages, including greater inclusiveness, increased creativity and innovation, better decision-making capabilities, and, ultimately, performance gains (van Knippenberg & Schippers, 2007).

As a complex and elusive concept, diversity needs to be defined in terms that make it possible for organizations to measure, predict, and manage it effectively. It is not possible to accurately measure organizational diversity processes and outcomes or to specify the attributes of successful workplace diversity management unless we have a conceptually strong measurement tool with which to work. However, scholars have not yet come to consensus on one consistent, operational definition of workplace diversity. In the past 20 years, scholars have developed at least thirty definitions of workplace diversity (Mor Barak, 2011), yet none of them provide a clear way to assess the psychological constructs present in diverse organizations. To date, no published research has systematically defined the entire domain of

workplace diversity, nor has any comprehensive measure of all major dimensions of workplace diversity been developed. Therefore, there is a need to develop a detailed operational definition of diversity in the workplace, and a measure that examines all of its components. Defining diversity is important in order to make subsequent advances in implementing organizational diversity initiatives, in training that provides the skills necessary to navigate and manage increasingly diverse workforces, and in selecting workers that will contribute to bringing about the positive outcomes of diversity. To do so it is essential to develop a solid understanding of the underlying dynamics in diverse organizations. Accordingly, the purpose of this chapter is to describe the development of a cutting edge definition of workplace diversity and an instrument based on that definition, one which enables precise measurement of the patterns and experiences of employees in diverse U.S.-based and international work settings.

Two constructs that are commonly used to describe and measure diversity at work is diversity climate and inclusion. Research has demonstrated that a positive diversity climate is vital to the success of diversity initiatives (Rynes & Rosen, 1995; Kossek & Zonia, 1993). Scholars agree that a major problem in today's diverse workforce is that many employees perceive that they are not fully included—that they are not valued as integral parts of their organizations (Mor Barak, 2011). The definition offered in this chapter includes but also goes beyond diversity climate and the concept of inclusion-exclusion to incorporate all relevant factors that contribute to employees' perception of workplace diversity.

BACKGROUND

The term *diversity* is used often and in many different ways (Dass & Parker, 1999). Mor Barak (2011) provides a typology that includes thirty definitions of diversity developed by scholars from 1991 to 2010. Numerous authors have discussed diversity in relation to phenomena at the individual, team, and organizational levels, often using many different names and definitions for this concept (Stockdale & Cao, 2004; Hays-Thomas, 2004). Thomas (2005) asserts that diversity refers to "those individual differences that are socially and historically significant and which have resulted in differences in power and privilege inside as well as outside of organizations (p. 9)." Crosby and Stockdale (2004) describe diverse work organizations as, "those in which the people who work together differ along the dimensions that society has deemed important" (2004, p. xiii). Cox (1994, p. 6) has written, "Cultural diversity means the representation, in one social system, of people with distinctly different group affiliations of cultural significance." He focuses on race, ethnicity, gender, and nationality because he believes these dimensions to be particularly important in social interaction. To support this claim, he states that these bases of identity, unlike religion or age, do not change and that there is substantial social research on these dimensions. Differences based on these social categories have been sensitive to discuss and extremely difficult to alter (Hays-Thomas, 2004). In contrast to the above definitions, a broader approach was developed and promulgated by Roosevelt Thomas (1996), which downplays power differentials and treats all bases of difference, such as personality and professional background, as more or less equivalent in terms of systematic analyses (Hays-Thomas, 2004). Linnehan and Konrad (1999) argue against this approach, stating that it is vital to focus on the ways in which privilege, power, and inequality affect intergroup relations. While R. Thomas' approach has an important place in the research literature, it is of secondary interest in this chapter. We focus on diversity among consequential social categories, not only within the U.S., but also in the global workforce. In an attempt to address the limitations of both approaches, Mor Barak (2011) developed the following definition of

global workforce diversity: "Workforce diversity refers to the division of the workforce into distinct categories that (a) have a perceived commonality within a given cultural or national context and that (b) impact potentially harmful or beneficial employment outcomes such as job opportunities, treatment in the workplace, and promotion prospects—irrespective of job-related skills and qualifications" (p. 148). This definition provides a way to include any and all relevant categories in specific cultural or national environments, thus allowing the inclusion of categories that may be relevant in some cultural contexts and not in others (e.g., regional differences, HIV status). It also emphasizes the importance of the *consequences* of social categorization in terms of its potential to affect important workplace outcomes, which addresses the limitation of broad definitions of diversity that include inconsequential characteristics.

Currently, a strong majority of available measures explicitly state specific demographic categories within the items of the scale, which makes it difficult for these scales to be effective in cross cultural or global settings. In terms of the definition of workplace diversity in a global context, the need to have flexibility in the referent identity constructs that are salient in a particular organizational context is vital. The references to certain categories, most commonly race and gender, make those scales less relevant in organizations outside the U.S. and in multinational organizations, where specific categories may not be relevant in different cultural or national contexts.

In addition to needing options for multiple social categories, these measures do not encompass the multidimensionality of workplace diversity. With the multitude of academic definitions of diversity at work, there has been confusion regarding the construct itself and which dimensions comprise it, not the mention a consistent way to measure it that encompasses all of its psychological constructs.

Social Identity and Self-Categorization Theories

Social identity (Tajfel & Turner, 1986) and self-categorization (Turner, 1987) theories posit that individuals classify themselves and others into personally meaningful groups. These groups may include demographic categories. These classifications are important because individuals use them to draw distinctions between in-group and out-group members (Avery, McKay, & Wilson, 2007). Because individuals have a strong desire to maintain and enhance their own self esteem, they tend to "(a) respond unfavorably to social identity threats, such as discrimination, (b) exhibit bias in favor of in-group members; and (c) seek information affirming identification with in-group membership" (Avery, McKay, & Wilson, 2007, p. 1543). The motivation to preserve a positive identity drives individuals' cognitions, emotions, and behaviors (James, Lovato, & Cropanzano, 1994).

Maintaining positive in-group characteristics are important for an individual to maintain a positive sense of self-worth; however, these theories predict that evaluations of in-group characteristics are made possible through comparisons of the in-group and out-group. The distinctions made between in-group and out-group membership has the potential to bring about negative consequences at work, especially for those who are perceived to be in the minority of the relevant social category (James, et al., 1994). This often happens "when the characteristic(s) on which that grouping is based are normatively associated with low status and negative stereotypes" (James, et al., 1994, p. 1575).

Social identity-based diversity dynamics manifest in a variety of both positive and negative ways in the workplace. When managed effectively, diversity can result in increased creativity, better problem solving, and higher effectiveness; however, diversity also has the potential to create miscommunication, lower cohesion, and stress, especially when management has not placed enough importance on eliminating discrimination and building a culture of inclusion and appreciation for differences. To ensure that organizations are able to leverage the potential benefits of diversity, a tool that assesses employee perceptions of how diversity is fairing within their organization and which social categories are relevant is a necessity.

DEVELOPING THE WORKPLACE DIVERSITY TAXONOMY

Summary of Workplace Diversity Measurement Literature

Several instruments have been published that measure workplace diversity, inclusion-exclusion, discrimination, and prejudice: the Mor Barak Inclusion-Exclusion Scale (Mor Barak, 2005), the Diversity Perceptions Scale (Mor Barak, Cherin, & Berkman, 1998), the Workplace Prejudice/Discrimination Inventory (WPDI; James, Lovato, & Cropanzano, 1994), the Attitudes Toward Diversity Scale (ATDS; Montei, Adams, & Eggers, 1996), the Organizational Diversity Inventory (ODI; Hegarty & Dalton, 1995), the Workforce Diversity Questionnaire (WDQ; Larkey, 1996), and the Perceived Occupational Opportunity Scale–Form B (POOS), and Perceived Occupational Discrimination Scale–Form B (PODS; Chung & Harmon, 1999). However, with the exception of the first three measures, the conceptualization, development, and validation of these measures are in the preliminary stages of research (Burkard, et al., 2002). More importantly, although these instruments cover various aspects of the domain of workplace diversity, such as inclusion-exclusion, discrimination, workplace diversity attitudes, and certain dimensions of organizational diversity, not one of them encompasses the entire range of psychological constructs, patterns, and experiences that manifest in diverse workforces. Researchers have recognized a void in these models and have called for expansion of workplace diversity assessments to include: (a) prevalence rates of subtle forms of racism in the United States (e.g., modern racism [McConahay, 1986] and aversive racism [Gaertner & Dovidio, 1986]), (b) theories of prejudice and discrimination that acknowledge explicit and implicit cognitive processes that are independent of one another (e.g., Devine, 1989; Greenwald & Banaji, 1995), and (c) conceptualizations and accompanying measures that examine the appreciation of cultural diversity or the motivation to control prejudice reactions (e.g., Dunton & Fazio, 1997; Miville, et al., 1999).

The vital issues of diversity's multidimensionality and recent theoretical developments yet to be incorporated in diversity measurement are liabilities in an organization's ability to leverage diversity. Burkard (2002) states that future research should assess subtle forms of racism and oppression and use the above conceptualizations to develop workplace diversity measures that are reflective of the multidimensional nature of workplace discrimination and prejudice. As of yet, there is no instrument that measures the broad domain of workplace diversity described in the literature. To make progress in our understanding and management of the issues, our team developed a measurement tool that attempted to respond to the need to address aversive racism by examining how diversity plays out among co-workers, supervisors, and higher management across multiple dimensions.

Taxonomy of Workplace Diversity

The process of building a taxonomy to encompass the multi-faceted experience of workplace diversity began with a review of the literature to identify the major constructs that define the operations of diverse workforces. This review was used to develop a preliminary nomological network of the constructs that characterize diverse organizations. The following seven dimensions were identified: Identity, Values, Schemas, Communication, Organizational Justice, Diversity Climate, and Leadership. The definitions of each dimension in the taxonomy are provided in Table 1. In each section below, examples are provided of positive and negative manifestations of workplace diversity.

Identity. Perceived identity shapes peoples' in-group and out-group perceptions, emotions, and behaviors (Hogg & Terry, 2000; Turner, 1981), and in the context of the workplace, both intra-group and inter-group feelings and relations are affected (Hogg & Terry, 2000; Messick & Mack-

Table 1. Taxonomy of workplace diversity

Taxonomy Dimension	Definition
Identity	The extent to which one perceives, feels, and behaves as if they are included or excluded in a diverse work setting.
Values	The extent to which one's central guides influence his/her perceptions of appropriate identity, preferences, beliefs and behaviors in a diverse workplace.
Schemas	The extent to which cognitive guides lead to the organization of information and the perceived patterns of behaviors, including stereotypes and behavioral scripts, in diverse work settings.
Communication	The extent to which language barriers and differences in communication styles, nonverbal communication, language fluency, and cultural fluency manifest in diverse work settings.
Organizational Justice	The extent to which employees perceive fairness of the distribution of resources, procedures, and interactions within a diverse organization.
Diversity Climate	The extent to which employees share the perception that a diverse organization's policies, practices, and procedures communicate a strong priority given to fostering & maintaining diversity and inclusion.
Leadership	The extent to which the leaders, or managers, in a diverse organization support diversity as a priority in the workplace.

ie, 1989). While in-group perceptions are important for positive self-worth (James, et al., 1994), distinctions made between in-groups and out-groups at work can bring about exclusion, discrimination and prejudice based on one's perceived social identity. Additionally, individuals' experiences in the workplace and their perceptions of organizational actions and policies will be affected by their identity group memberships (Mor Barak, 2011). In the workplace diversity taxonomy, Identity is defined as the extent to which one perceives, feels, and behaves as if they are included or excluded in a diverse work setting.

Perceptions of inclusion/exclusion have been found to correlate with job satisfaction, employee well-being, organizational commitment, organizational justice, and job performance (Mor Barak & Levin, 2002; Acquavita, Pittman, Gibbons, & Castellanos-Brown, 2009; Mor Barak, Findler, & Wind, 2003; Findler, Wind, & Mor Barak, 2007; Cho & Mor Barak, 2008). In this context, Identity encompasses the social or informal aspects of an employee's perception that he or she is an integral part of the organization, department, or work group.

For example, the Identity dimension could manifest in a workplace composed of mostly younger people. The older employees may perceive they are highly dissimilar to their co-workers due to age. The perception of being a member of the out-group (due to younger workers being the majority) will likely result in feeling that their social identity is threatened, which is likely to lead to disengagement (Avery, McCay, & Wilson, 2007).

Values. In the taxonomy, values are defined as the extent to which one's *central guides* influence his/her perceptions of appropriate identity, preferences, beliefs and behaviors in a diverse workplace. Employees' values may influence their attitudes toward people from different backgrounds and social identity groups (Mor Barak, 2011). Because of these influences, differences in values impact organizational diversity outcomes (Harvey & Allard, 2005; House, Hanges,

Javidan, Dorfman, & Gupta, 2004; Markus & Kitayama, 1991). Strong associations have been found between value items, organizational justice, and organizational inclusion (Caldwell, Mack, Johnson, & Biderman, 2002).

Value dynamics can manifest negatively in a religiously diverse workplace when members of the in-group demonstrate intolerance for the cultural values and behavior-norm differences of people who are of lesser represented religions, the out-group members in this case. In such a workplace, conformity pressures can be strong (Cox & Nkomo, 1986) and the benefits of diversity may not be achieved (Adler & Gunderson, 2008).

Schemas. Schemas are defined as the extent to which cognitive guides lead to the organization of information and the perceived patterns of behaviors in diverse work settings. Schemas include stereotypes, mental maps, and behavioral scripts that guide thinking and actions toward in-group and out-group members in particular situations (Cox, 2001; Dunning & Sherman, 1997; James, Lovato, & Cropanzano, 1994; Schaller, 1991). They provide a mental framework that often provides a sense of confidence when one encounters a person from another group. This framework is commonly developed through a combination of social, cultural, and political influences that include other encounters with people of the group, popular media images, cultural norms of tolerance, partial truths from various sources, as well as contextual variables that are influenced by current events (Bar-Tal, 1997; Bar-Tal & Labin, 2001). These perceptions are often inaccurate and offensive when applied to an individual member of a group, as well as to the group as a whole, and they are commonly used to steer expectations and serve to justify actions that may turn out to be harmful or immoral (Tavris & Aronson, 2007).

Schemas often manifest as stereotypes, which are "standardized, oversimplified mental picture[s] that [are] held in common by members of a group" (Taylor & Moghaddam, 1994, p.159). Enteman (1996) states, "a stereotype imposes a rigid mold on the subject and encourages repeated mechanical usage… The person who substitutes a stereotype for careful analysis simply does not want to work harder than necessary to achieve a superficially acceptable result." (p. 9) For example, negative attitudes toward people who are Lesbian, Gay, Bisexual, or Transgender (LGBT) "can be based on stereotypes, which help people make sense of the world by categorizing their past experiences" (Lubensky, et al., 2004, p. 209). Between 25-66 percent of gay and lesbian employees report discrimination (see reviews by Ragins, 2004; King & Cortina, 2011). On the other hand, Schemas can manifest positively, or at least in a neutral manner, and more recent studies have put less emphasis on the negative aspects of stereotyping–viewing it as a basic cognitive process that is not necessarily bad (Blair, 2002; Taylor & Moghaddam, 1994). One way this may occur in organizations is when managers and co-workers use the schema that an expatriate has different experiences and perspectives to bring to the table because they are from a different country. If organizational members use this schema to their advantage by encouraging and supporting expatriates to share their ideas (rather than trying to force them to assimilate to the host country's way of thinking), this is likely to inspire creativity and innovation within the organization, which can lead to a competitive edge in the global economy.

Communication. In its most basic form, communication is the use of symbols to express meaning. Symbols can include words, tone of voice, gestures, or use of objects (Mor Barak, 2011). In today's diverse work settings, communication is becoming increasingly cross-cultural. Communication in work settings between people from different cultures and backgrounds involves surmounting language barriers, including cultural differences in communication styles, nonverbal communication differences, language fluency and cultural fluency (Mor Barak, 2011; Harvey & Allard, 2005). Nonverbal communication includes body language (e.g., movement, gestures,

and postures) and the use of objects, such as personal adornments and the physical setting. For example, clothing is often used to signify rank, mood, occasion, and seasons. Trust and respect are often conveyed through nonverbal rather than verbal communication (Mor Barak, 2011). While language fluency and cultural fluency are related, they are not the same. The former is the mastery of linguistic skills that enables one to function much like a native speaker of the language. Cultural fluency, however, refers to the ability to "identify, understand, and apply the communicative behaviors of members of the other group… the ability to go back and forth between two cultures, to send and receive messages in a way that assures that the meanings of both the sender and the received regularly match" (Glazier, 2003; Molinsky, 2005; Scott, 1999; quoted in Mor Barak, 2011, p. 206).

When team members have effective cross-cultural communication skills, the capacity to understand each other across differences and conflicting opinions increases (Alder & Gunderson, 2008) and they are better able to navigate many types of interactions and organizational functions. On the other hand, miscommunication occurs when the original intent and message of the person transmitting the message is different from the meaning that is received by the other person, and this is more likely to occur between co-workers who are different from each other. Pekerti and Thomas (2003) examined intercultural and intra-cultural communication styles between two culturally different groups in New Zealand and found that interacting with members of a different culture increased the tendency to use the cultural communication style of their own culture. That is, the dominant tendency in cross-cultural communication is exaggeration of one's own cultural behaviors rather than adaptation. The authors attributed this behavior to the uncertainty and anxiety often provoked by cross-cultural interactions. In light of this finding, it is relevant for organizations to know the extent to which employees feel comfortable in communicating with co-workers from different cultures, backgrounds, and life experiences. In the workplace diversity taxonomy, Communication is defined as the extent to which language barriers and differences in communication styles, nonverbal communication, language fluency, and cultural fluency manifest in diverse work settings.

Organizational Justice. Previous researchers have suggested that organizational fairness and workers' justice perceptions are central to diversity management (Ely & Thomas, 2001; Roberson & Colquitt, 2005). For instance, when procedures are fair, it conveys the message that employees have a common organizational identity (e.g. Brewer, 1991; Koper, et al., 1993). Similarly, distributive, procedural, interpersonal and informational justice all help shape intra-, inter-, and organizational climates for diversity (Rupp, Bashur, & Liao, 2007; Cropanzano, Li, & James, 2007). Within this taxonomy, Organizational Justice is defined as the extent to which employees perceive fairness of the distribution of resources, procedures, and interactions within a diverse organization.

Organizational Justice is also tied to the concept of inclusion/exclusion, and as such, it is likely to be highly correlated with the Identity dimension of the taxonomy. While Identity as defined above encompasses the affective experiences of perceiving inclusion/exclusion in the workplace, Organizational (in)Justice in this context is most often reported in the form of limited access to, or exclusion from, informal social networks that provide critical information for job effectiveness and career advancement (Gray, Kurihara, Hommen, & Feldman, 2007; McDonald, Lin, & Ao, 2009). The Federal Glass Ceiling Commission identified "information isolation," or the exclusion from information networks, as one of the main barriers that blocks the career advancement of women and ethnic minorities, particularly in the private sector (Federal Glass Ceiling Commission, 1995). This effect is compounded in people who have multiple identities with minority groups and/or who are women (e.g., women who are

African-American, Hispanic gay men; Combs, 2003). Informational Justice is one of the four factors Colquitt (2001) found in the factor structure of the overall Organizational Justice construct.

In industries that are dominated by men, such as engineering and technology, men are members of the in-group because they are in the majority, oftentimes paid more, and have enjoyed positions of power within these industries for a long time. Women are members of the out-group because they are the significant minority, often paid less, and find it difficult to break into the highest levels of leadership. Women can feel excluded and that this "good old boys club" is not fair. This power imbalance can be, and is often, perceived as organizational injustice.

Diversity Climate. Many organizations have implemented diversity initiatives in order to more effectively manage diversity. The success of these efforts depends on the broader context of the organization (Rynes & Rosen, 1995; Kossek & Zonia, 1993), which has been termed diversity climate. Diversity climate has been defined in the literature as shared perceptions (at the organizational or team levels) of relationships among members of diverse groups and organizational (or team) norms and aspirations for such relationships (Cropanzano, Li, & James, 2007; Rotundo, Nguyen, & Sackett, 2001). Gelfand et al. (2005) defined diversity climate as "employees' shared perceptions of the policies, practices, and procedures that implicitly and explicitly communicate the extent to which fostering and maintaining diversity and eliminating discrimination is a priority in the organization." In other words, diversity climate is employees' common understanding about "the way things are around here" regarding diversity (Reichers & Schneider, 1990). Diversity climates are essentially internalized beliefs about past organizational (or team) diversity practices, and current organizational (or team) diversity attitudes, norms and policies. In the context of this study, Diversity Climate is defined as the extent to which employees share the perception that a diverse organization's policies, practices, and procedures communicate a strong priority given to fostering and maintaining diversity and inclusion.

The main characteristics of a positive diversity climate include public support from top management, supportive policies, and a high organizational priority on diversity (Rynes & Rosen, 1995). The limited existing research indicates that diversity climate in organizations plays a critical role in many important organizational outcomes, such as training transfer (Rynes & Rosen, 1995) and intention to accept a position (McKay & Avery, 2006). Kossek, Markel, and McHugh (2003) found some evidence that greater workgroup heterogeneity in terms of gender and race was associated with several indicators of a positive diversity climate. Other research has shown that specific human resource policies and practices, such as hiring practices that specifically consider an individual's race or ethnicity, lead to perceptions of the organization being supportive of diversity (Highhouse, Stierwalt, Bachiochi, Elder, & Fisher, 1999; Kim & Gelfand, 2003). McKay and Avery (2006) developed a theoretical model for how, when job seekers are on site visits, organizational and community attributes contribute to perceptions of the organization's diversity climate, which impacts subsequent job acceptance decisions. McKay et al. (2007) found that individual-level diversity climate perceptions were negatively associated with turnover intentions, and these effects were stronger for Black employees.

Social Identity Theory predicts that in a work setting in which heterosexuals are the majority, people who are Lesbian, Gay, Bisexual, or Transgender (LGBT) may feel like members of an out-group and they may perceive that heterosexuals are members of the in-group, regarding sexual orientation. One way a positive Diversity Climate can alleviate this naturally occurring phenomenon is for managers and co-workers to provide supervisor and peer support, as well as social integration, for LGBT employees (Beck,

Horan, & Tolbert, 1980). This can result from LGBT friendly policies, as well as from the use of inclusive language (such as "partner" instead of "husband" or "girlfriend").

Leadership. Research has consistently shown that leader vision for, support of, and approach to diversity at work has a significant impact on employees' identities and motivation; on organizational justice systems and practices; on diversity climates and communications and, therefore; on individual and organizational diversity outcomes (D'Almeida, 2007; Wieland, 2004). Leadership is defined here as the extent to which the leader, or manager, in a diverse organization supports diversity as a priority. For example, leadership can manifest negatively in a predominantly Caucasian/White workplace, when leaders display harsh scrutiny and criticism of members of ethnic minority groups, the out-group individuals in this case, which often leads to prejudice and discrimination (Dworkin, Dworkin, & Chafetz, 1986; Pettigrew & Martin, 1987).

Workplace Diversity Taxonomy Construct Model

In Figure 1, a model is presented that provides a depiction of how the taxonomy can be tested for validity. On the left side of the graph are the influences on workplace diversity, including the individual, organizational, and contextual factors that impact one's experiences within diverse work settings. In the middle of the graph, the dimensions of the workplace diversity taxonomy are listed as the ways in which employees experience and perceive diversity at work. Finally, on the right side, are the outcomes that we expect will be predicted by the dimensions of the taxonomy.

Preliminary Research on a Model of Workplace Diversity

Preliminary research explored the extent to which empirical support based on qualitative data could

Figure 1. Workplace diversity taxonomy construct model

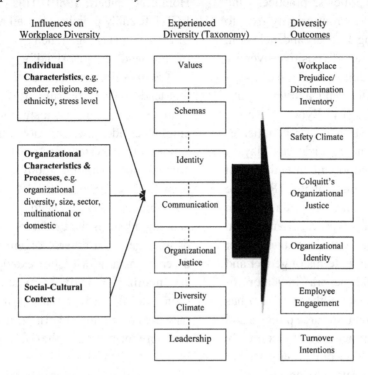

be found to verify the existence of the seven workplace diversity dimensions suggested by the literature and discussed above. This was accomplished by using the Critical Incident Technique (Flanagan, 1954), in which approximately 100 critical incidents that described real-world examples of the dynamics that arose in diverse work environments were reviewed and content analyzed. This effort supported the seven-dimension taxonomy of workplace diversity (Taylor & James, 2010), providing evidence that each of the seven dimensions are part of the patterns that people in diverse organizations experience.

The important implications of this research for designing the WDI to evaluate workplace diversity were that diversity is multidimensional and the seven dimensions appear to be present in diverse workplaces. With these findings in support of the seven-dimension taxonomy, the

Workplace Diversity Inventory was designed to further examine the taxonomy.

Empirical Test of the Workplace Diversity Taxonomy

With the supportive preliminary evidence from the qualitative study, the Workplace Diversity Inventory (WDI) was developed based on the definitions of the seven dimensions of the taxonomy. A sample of 209 employees who worked at least 20 hours per week was collected via an online survey. A demographic questionnaire was included that asked about participants' ethnicity, language, gender, age, sexual orientation, faith/religion, socioeconomic status, disability, education, job level, and about the participants' organization size, sector, industry, country of origin, and whether or not it was a multinational firm.

The WDI examines employees' perceptions about diversity in their organization. The measure focuses on perceptions because research has found that employees' behavior is often driven by perceptions of reality, even if their beliefs are incorrect (e.g., Eisenberger, Fasolo, & Davis-LaMastro, 1990). The WDI included 47 items with the seven dimensions of the taxonomy: Identity, Values, Schemas, Communication, Diversity Climate, Organizational Justice and Leadership. The items evaluate a person's perceptions in relation to five different system levels: individual, work group, supervisor, higher management, and organization. Participants indicated their level of agreement with each item using a 7-point Likert-type response scale with anchors of 1 = *strongly disagree* and 7 = *strongly agree*. Higher scores on the WDI reflect more positive perceptions of workplace diversity (negatively phrased questions were reverse-scored), so higher ratings reflect more positive diversity dynamics. In addition, the instructions provided for the instrument were developed intentionally to encourage participants to think about diversity on a wide range of demographic categories, and those that are given as examples are offered for clarity only.

The online survey included questions asking participants to rank the importance of different social groups or demographic categories to which they belong. The main purpose of these questions is for researchers and/or practitioners to be able to tease out the specific aspects of diversity that are important to employees. The ranking question asks, "Based on your responses, please rank the most important aspect of your identity that impacts your interactions with co-workers." The next question asks participants to rank the second most important aspect as well. The survey also included two questions regarding the organization's level of diversity: 1) How diverse is your organization across all major areas of diversity? 2) Name the top three (3) areas in which it is diverse. An overall qualitative question about current workplace diversity experience is also included: "What do you think about the way your organization handles diversity?"

To initially evaluate the WDI, reliability estimates for each of the expected seven dimensions were computed. To test the validity of the WDI, I used an eleven-step process, which included both principle components and confirmatory factor analyses on the full seven-dimension model, individual dimensions, and simpler models to examine the underlying factor structure of the data. Results of these analyses provided promising evidence for the validity of the WDI and the multidimensional nature of diversity.

Summary of Findings

Due to the increasing influence of globalization and the stubborn persistence of discrimination based on social identity in the workplace, it is vital to gain a more complete understanding of workplace diversity. Scholars have not yet come to consensus on a definition of diversity that systematically defines the entire domain of diversity at work. In the past 20 years, 30 academic definitions of diversity have been put forward, and this does not include the plethora of definitions developed within applied settings. Nor have scholars decided which scale is best to use to accurately measure diversity at work. It is not possible to accurately research any construct without strong conceptual and measurement tools. This review and subsequent research is an important step in articulating the specific psychological constructs that employees experience in diverse work settings, and it contributes to the academic study of workplace diversity in three important ways. Although it seems reasonable that diversity is multidimensional given the wide range of constructs that have been associated with workplace diversity in the literature, this research is the first effort that has been undertaken to systematically identify the potential dimensions of diversity and to empirically examine its multidimensionality. In doing so, it offers a conceptual framework and an operational definition, the Workplace Diversity Taxonomy, that helps expand our understanding and ability to measure the constructs present in increasingly diverse work settings. This taxonomy has been created in an attempt to classify the entire domain of workplace diversity in order to clarify and detail the essential patterns of experience found in diverse work settings. In applying the taxonomy, an instrument, the WDI, has been developed and promising evidence of validity has been found. The WDI includes but goes beyond two common measures of diversity: diversity climate and inclusion. While diversity climate and inclusion are important, they do not encompass the entire range of psychological patterns and experiences that manifest in diverse workforces.

It is also important to note that the dimensions of the WDI are correlated, and each item has an intentionally built-in frame-of-reference for diversity at work. These two features of the scale demonstrate the additional utility that the taxonomy provides. Researchers cannot simply use separate, currently validated scales for each dimension of the WDI to measure workplace diversity. The dimensions are part of an interlocking pattern of experiences, the taxonomy classifies them as such, and the WDI measures them that way.

A further contribution of the scale is that it has the potential to be used in global work settings. Unlike most commonly used measures of workplace diversity (with the exception of Mor Barak's [2005] Perception of Inclusion-Exclusion Scale), the WDI items do not include specific reference to one or more demographic categories. The instrument can be used to reference the categories that are specific to different cultural or national contexts. It is not limited to using the common types of diversity in the U.S., e.g., race, gender, age. The instructions can be modified to include the most salient referent-identity examples for the culture or context in question.

FUTURE RESEARCH DIRECTIONS

Future research should be conducted to examine the validity of the instrument further, since construct validity cannot be demonstrated conclusively in just one study (Hogan & Nicholson, 1998; Landy 1986). A more parsimonious model of workplace diversity may emerge from future research using other measures of the dimensions proposed here. In addition, new dimensions may surface if the data are collected during periods of organizational transition.

One limitation of the WDI itself is that it is a self-report measure, the limits of which have long been recognized in psychology in the measurement of prejudice, discrimination, and workplace diversity (Crosby, et al., 1980; Dunton & Fazio, 1997; Ponterotto & Casas, 1991). It would be beneficial for future research to measure workplace diversity with multiple, alternate assessment methods to help control for the limitations of self-report measures. In previous research, qualitative methods have been used to focus on aspects of diversity involving individual, group, or institutional dynamics that operate in work settings. Perhaps administering the WDI at multiple organizational levels could mimic the strengths of this approach. Observational methods can be used to target specific variables of interest, such as conflict, creativity, and decision-making ability. Longitudinal studies would provide evidence regarding whether WDI assessments predict later individual and organizational outcomes (e.g., health and well-being, turnover rates, profitability), directly and indirectly, related to diversity. Archival data may be able to provide objective outcomes to measure the effect of positive or negative diversity climate changes as well. Ultimately, future research should utilize multiple methods of assessment to provide a more complete picture and to cross validate findings (Burkard, et al., 2002).

Although this chapter focused on developing an operational definition of workplace diversity, future research could specify the knowledge, skills, abilities, and other characteristics that underlie successful diversity management and predict more positive scores in the WDI dimensions. Future research should also include measures of important workplace outcomes to build a body of literature that indicates that the WDI predicts such constructs as employee engagement, organizational identity, creativity and innovation, job satisfaction, performance, turnover intentions and conflict. In addition to focusing on general organizational outcomes, another extension of this research could be to focus on diversity training and its outcomes, which could be measured, at least in part, by the WDI. Diversity training is a common method organizations use to improve workplace diversity. Goldstein and Ford (2002) describe the three main types of this training. The first focuses on raising awareness about diversity, including knowledge of the legal aspects, examination of the concept itself and how it relates to organizational effectiveness, and identification of factors that influence attitudes and behaviors toward others. The second type of diversity training focuses more directly on attitude change and increased understanding of how actions impact others. It uses role playing, videos, and interactive exercises to go beyond simple awareness to greater understanding of the negative emotional and performance effects of stereotypes, values, and behaviors on members of minority groups. The third type directly addresses the enhancement of leadership skills, such as coaching and mentoring skills, conflict management techniques, and effectively providing performance feedback. However, there are few systematic research studies that have examined the impact of diversity training or the different types of training programs on the subsequent behaviors of leaders (Goldstein & Ford, 2002). Future research is needed to document whether the WDI has predictive validity for diagnosing training needs and assessing training outcomes.

The themes of this chapter have important implications for both theory and practice. As stated above, one theoretical implication is that it provides evidence that workplace diversity is multidimensional and a taxonomy that delineates these dimensions. Practically speaking, the taxonomy and resultant WDI is a promising tool for organizations to use in diagnosing and solving issues related to diversity. The present research has the potential to aid organizational leaders in determining the particular types of selection measures, training strategies, and/or organizational development initiatives needed for an organization to maximize diversity's prospective positive outcomes.

The WDI in particular provides an empirical measure of the areas in which an organization must develop in order to increase its potential to obtain the competitive edge that diversity can create. Specifically, the WDI provides a score on each of the dimensions as well as an overall composite score, so organizational leaders can use empirical information in deciding how to best invest in and focus on diversity interventions. Using the instrument in this way would enable organizational leaders to see exactly which dimensions they are excelling in, and which dimensions they need to work on. For example, an organization may receive a high score on Communication across diverse groups, but if there is a poor Diversity Climate, the organization's overall score on the WDI would not be as high as expected if one was only focusing on the fact that people in the organization communicate well across differences. This way, organizational leaders can celebrate the areas in which the organization demonstrates competency, which is important because managing diversity can often seem overwhelming, while at the same time, be more efficient in their use of resources toward their diversity and inclusion goals.

Because the WDI provides empirical assessment of the psychological constructs that manifest in diverse work settings, it also has the potential to provide a convenient way to evaluate diversity initiatives. Organizations could use the WDI scores as baseline measures prior to the implementation of a diversity initiative, and then use it again at different intervals as the initiatives are rolled out as a way to track and evaluate organizational progress. The WDI may also be useful as a first step in conducting a thorough needs assessment. In terms of diversity training, the WDI could provide a way for organizations to set a baseline for their training program and to focus the training on the dimensions with lower baseline scores in order to determine which type of diversity training that would be most effective. For example, Communication may be linked to specific competencies, so the third type of diversity training may be best suited for this purpose, whereas Values may be improved more successfully with the second type.

As a supplement to the WDI, the qualitative question used in the online survey would provide information for leaders to delve deeper into the specific issues that may be leading to positive or negative outcomes. In addition, if an organization used the demographic questionnaire used in the online survey in combination with the WDI items, it could prove to be a useful tool for determining anonymous information on an organization's overall demographic statistics on categories that are not collected by human resources, such as sexual orientation and religion.

Providing a concrete description of the ways in which an organization is benefiting and growing from its diversity initiatives may prove effective in helping managers and employees take "bitable chunks" by knowing the specific areas to apply often limited resources. Prior to the development of this taxonomy and instrument, there was no theory-driven and psychometrically tested way to empirically measure the dynamics that arise in diverse workforces, and thus no means of making this vital information available to capitalize on the critical competitive edge of effectively-managed diversity.

CONCLUSION

The attention on workplace diversity grown tremendously in the past 20 years, and this trend will only continue. Due to rapid globalization, diversity in the workplace is increasing and becoming more complex. Thus, it is becoming more difficult to manage. There is a shortage of leaders who are able to effectively manage diversity in the U.S. and beyond. This is in part due to the lack of clarity regarding the definition of diversity or having a precise way to measure it. The confusion has impacted research on this topic in that diversity researchers have not been able to consistently and reliably measure, predict and provide advice on how to manage diversity in such a way as to maximize its benefits. As with most newly developed definitions and measures, further research is needed to more fully develop evidence of validity. However, the Workplace Diversity Taxonomy, and the Workplace Diversity Inventory that measures it, represents a promising step toward building diverse workplaces that are inclusive and fair and that contribute to the well-being of all employees equally.

REFERENCES

Acquavita, S. P., Pittman, J., Gibbons, M., & Castellanos-Brown, K. (2009). Personal and organizational diversity factors' impact on social workers' job satisfaction: Results from a national internet-based survey. *Administration in Social Work*, *33*(2), 151–166. doi:10.1080/03643100902768824

Adler, N. J., & Gunderson, A. (2008). *International dimensions of organizational behavior* (5th ed.). Mason, OH: South-Western Cengage Learning.

Avery, D. R., McKay, P. F., & Wilson, D. C. (2007). Engaging the aging workforce: The relationship between perceived age similarity, satisfaction with coworkers, and employee engagement. *The Journal of Applied Psychology, 92*(6), 1542–1556. doi:10.1037/0021-9010.92.6.1542

Bar-Tal, D. (1997). Formation and change of ethnic and national stereotypes: An integrative model. *International Journal of Intercultural Relations, 21*(4), 491–523. doi:10.1016/S0147-1767(97)00022-9

Bar-Tal, D., & Labin, D. (2001). The effect of a major event on stereotyping: Terrorist attacks in Israel and Israeli adolescents' perceptions of Palestinians, Jordanians, and Arabs. *European Journal of Social Psychology, 31,* 1–17. doi:10.1002/ejsp.43

Blair, I. V. (2002). The malleability of automatic stereotypes and prejudice. *Personality and Social Psychology Review, 6*(3), 242–261. doi:10.1207/S15327957PSPR0603_8

Brewer, M. (1991). The social self: On being the same and different at the same time. *Personality and Social Psychology Bulletin, 17,* 475–482. doi:10.1177/0146167291175001

Burkard, A. W., Boticki, M. A., & Madson, M. B. (2002). Workplace discrimination, prejudice, and diversity measurement: A review of instrumentation. *Journal of Career Assessment, 10,* 343. doi:10.1177/10672702010003005

Caldwell, Q. S., Mack, D., Johnson, C. D., & Biderman, M. D. (2002). *Value for diversity as a moderator of organizational relationships.* Paper presented at the 17th Annual Meeting of the Society for Industrial and Organizational Psychology. Toronto, Canada.

Cho, S., & Mor Barak, M. E. (2008). Understanding diversity and inclusion in a perceived homogenous culture: A study of organizational commitment and job performance among Korean employees. *Administration in Social Work, 32*(4), 100–126. doi:10.1080/03643100802293865

Chung, Y. B., & Harmon, L. W. (1999). Assessment of perceived occupational opportunity for Black Americans. *Journal of Career Assessment, 7,* 45–62. doi:10.1177/106907279900700104

Colquitt, J. A. (2001). On the dimensionality of organizational justice: A construct validation of a measure. *The Journal of Applied Psychology, 86*(3), 386–400. doi:10.1037/0021-9010.86.3.386

Combs, G. M. (2003). The duality of race and gender for managerial African American women: Implications of informal social networks on career advancement. *Human Resource Development Review, 2*(4), 385–405. doi:10.1177/1534484303257949

Cox, T. (1991). The multicultural organization. *The Academy of Management Executive, 5,* 34–47.

Cox, T. (1994). *Cultural diversity in organizations: Theory, research and practice.* San Francisco, CA: Berrett-Koehler.

Cox, T. (2001). *Creating the multicultural organization: A strategy for capturing the power of diversity.* San Francisco, CA: Jossey-Bass.

Cox, T. (2004). Problems with research by organizational scholars on issues of race and ethnicity. *The Journal of Applied Behavioral Science, 40,* 124–145. doi:10.1177/0021886304263851

Cox, T., & Blake, H. (1991). Managing cultural diversity: Implications for organizational competitiveness. *The Academy of Management Executive, 5*(3), 45–57.

Cropanzano, R., Li, A., & James, K. (2007). Intraunit justice and interunit justice and the people who experience them. In Dansereau, F., & Yammarino, F. J. (Eds.), *Research in Multilevel Issues* (*Vol. 6*, pp. 415–438). Englewood Cliffs, NJ: Erlbaum. doi:10.1016/S1475-9144(07)06019-5

Crosby, F., Bromley, S., & Saxe, L. (1980). Recent unobtrusive studies of Black-and-White discrimination and prejudice: A literature review. *Psychological Bulletin, 87,* 546–563. doi:10.1037/0033-2909.87.3.546

D'Almeida, C. M. (2007). *The effects of cultural diversity in the workplace.* Unpublished Dissertation. Ann Arbor, MI: Capella University.

Dahm, M. J., Willems, E. P., Ivancevich, J. M., & Graves, D. E. (2009). Development of an organizational diversity needs analysis instrument. *Journal of Applied Social Psychology, 39*(2), 283–318. doi:10.1111/j.1559-1816.2008.00439.x

Dass, P., & Parker, B. (1999). Strategies for managing human resource diversity: From resistance to learning. *The Academy of Management Executive, 13,* 68–80. doi:10.5465/AME.1999.1899550

Devine, P. G. (1989). Stereotypes and prejudice: Their automatic and controlled components. *Journal of Personality and Social Psychology, 56,* 5–18. doi:10.1037/0022-3514.56.1.5

Dunning, D., & Sherman, D. A. (1997). Stereotypes and tacit inference. *Journal of Personality and Social Psychology, 73,* 459–471. doi:10.1037/0022-3514.73.3.459

Dunton, B. C., & Fazio, R. H. (1997). An individual difference measure of motivation to control prejudiced reactions. *Personality and Social Psychology Bulletin, 23,* 316–326. doi:10.1177/0146167297233009

Dworkin, F., Dworkin, D., & Chafetz, I. (1986). The effects of tokenism on work alienation among urban public school teachers. *Work and Occupations, 13,* 399–420. doi:10.1177/0730888486013003006

EEOC. (2010). *Job bias charges approach record high in fiscal year 2009, EEOC reports.* Retrieved November 16, 2010, from http://www.eeoc.gov/eeoc/newsroom/release/1-6-10.cfm.

Eisenberger, R., Fasolo, P., & Davis-LaMastro, V. (1990). Perceived organizational support and employee diligence, commitment, and innovation. *The Journal of Applied Psychology, 75*(1), 51–59. doi:10.1037/0021-9010.75.1.51

Ely, R. J., & Thomas, D. A. (2001). Cultural diversity at work: The effects of diversity perspectives on work group processes and outcomes. *Administrative Science Quarterly, 46,* 229–273. doi:10.2307/2667087

Enteman, W. (1996). Stereotyping, prejudice, and discrimination. In Lester, P. M. (Ed.), *Images that Injure: Pictorial Stereotypes in the Media* (pp. 9–14). Westport, CT: Praeger.

Federal Glass Ceiling Commission. (1995). *Good for business: Making full use of the nation's human capital: The environmental scan, a fact-finding report of the federal glass ceiling commission.* Washington, DC: Government Printing Office.

Findler, L., Wind, L., & Mor Barak, M. E. (2007). The challenge of workforce management in a global society: Modeling the relationship between diversity, organizational culture, and employee well-being, job satisfaction and organizational commitment. *Administration in Social Work, 31*(3), 63–94. doi:10.1300/J147v31n03_05

Flanagan, J. C. (1954). The critical incident technique. *Psychological Bulletin, 51*(4), 327–358. doi:10.1037/h0061470

Gaertner, S. L., & Dovidio, J. F. (1986). The aversive form of racism. In Gaertner, S. L., & Dovidio, J. F. (Eds.), *Prejudice, Discrimination, and Racism* (pp. 61–89). New York, NY: Academic Press.

Gelfand, M. J., Nishii, L. H., Raver, J., & Schneider, B. (2005). Discrimination in organizations: An organizational level systems perspective. In Dipboye, R., & Colella, A. (Eds.), *Discrimination at Work: The Psychological and Organizational Bases* (pp. 89–116). Mahwah, NJ: Erlbaum.

Glazier, J. A. (2003). Developing cultural fluency: Arab and Jewish students engaging in one another's company. *Harvard Educational Review*, *73*(2), 141–163.

Goldstein, I. L., & Ford, J. K. (2002). *Training in organizations* (4th ed.). Belmont, CA: Wadsworth Group.

Gray, M., Kurihara, T., Hommen, L., & Feldman, J. (2007). Networks of exclusion: Job segmentation and social networks in the knowledge economy. *Equal Opportunities International*, *26*(2), 144–161. doi:10.1108/02610150710732212

Greenwald, A. G., & Banaji, M. R. (1995). Implicit social cognition: Attitudes, self-esteem, and stereotypes. *Psychological Review*, *102*, 4–27. doi:10.1037/0033-295X.102.1.4

Guzzo, R., & Dickson, M. (1996). Teams in organizations: Recent research on performance and effectiveness. *Annual Review of Psychology*, *47*, 307–338. doi:10.1146/annurev.psych.47.1.307

Haq, R. (2004). International perspectives on workplace diversity. In Stockdale, M. S., & Crosby, F. J. (Eds.), *The Psychology and Management of Workplace Diversity* (pp. 277–298). Malden, MA: Blackwell.

Harvey, C. P., & Allard, M. J. (2005). *Understanding and managing diversity: Readings, cases and exercises*. Upper Saddle River, NJ: Pearson Education.

Hays-Thomas, R. (2004). Why now? The contemporary focus on managing diversity. In Stockdale, M. S., & Crosby, F. J. (Eds.), *The Psychology and Management of Workplace Diversity* (pp. 3–30). Malden, MA: Blackwell.

Hegarty, W. H., & Dalton, D. R. (1995). Development and psychometric properties of the organizational diversity inventory (ODI). *Educational and Psychological Measurement*, *55*, 1047–1052. doi:10.1177/0013164495055006014

Highhouse, S., Stierwalt, S. L., Bachiochi, P., Elder, A. E., & Fisher, G. (1999). Effects of advertised human resource management practices on attraction of African American applicants. *Personnel Psychology*, *52*, 424–442. doi:10.1111/j.1744-6570.1999.tb00167.x

Hogan, R., & Nicholson, R. A. (1988). The meaning of personality test scores. *The American Psychologist*, *43*, 621–626. doi:10.1037/0003-066X.43.8.621

Hogg, M. A., & Terry, D. J. (2000). Social identity and self-categorization processes in organizational contexts. *Academy of Management Review*, *25*, 121–140.

House, R. J., Hanges, P. J., Javidan, M., Dorfman, P. W., & Gupta, V. (Eds.). (2004). *Culture, leadership and organizations: The GLOBE study of 62 societies*. Thousand Oaks, CA: Sage.

James, K., Lovato, C., & Cropanzano, R. (1994). Correlational and known-group comparison validation of a workplace prejudice/discrimination inventory. *Journal of Applied Social Psychology*, *24*, 1573–1592. doi:10.1111/j.1559-1816.1994.tb01563.x

Judy, R. W., & D'Amico, C. (1997). *Workforce 2020: Work and workers in the 21st century*. Indianapolis, IN: Hudson Institute.

Kim, S. S., & Gelfand, M. J. (2003). The influence of ethnic identity on perceptions of organizational recruitment. *Journal of Vocational Behavior, 63*, 396–416. doi:10.1016/S0001-8791(02)00043-X

King, E. B., & Cortina, J. M. (2011). Stated and unstated barriers and opportunities to creating LGBT-supportive organizations. *Industrial-Organizational Psychology: Perspectives of Science and Practice, 3*, 103–108. doi:10.1111/j.1754-9434.2009.01209.x

Koper, G., Knippenberg, D., Bouhuijs, F., Vermunt, R., & Wilke, H. (1993). Procedural fairness and self esteem. *European Journal of Social Psychology, 23*, 313–325. doi:10.1002/ejsp.2420230307

Kossek, E. E., Markel, K. S., & McHugh, P. P. (2003). Increasing diversity as an HRM change strategy. *Journal of Organizational Change Management, 16*, 328–352. doi:10.1108/09534810310475550

Kossek, E. E., & Zonia, S. C. (1993). Assessing diversity climate: A field study of reactions to employer efforts to promote diversity. *Journal of Organizational Behavior, 14*(1), 61–81. doi:10.1002/job.4030140107

Landy, F. J. (1986). Stamp collecting versus science: Validation as hypothesis testing. *The American Psychologist, 41*, 1183–1192. doi:10.1037/0003-066X.41.11.1183

Larkey, L. K. (1996). The development and validation of the workforce diversity questionnaire: An instrument to assess interactions in diverse workgroups. *Management Communication Quarterly, 9*, 296–337. doi:10.1177/0893318996009003002

Lubensky, M. E., Holland, S. L., Wiethoff, C., & Crosby, F. J. (2004). Diversity and sexual orientation: Including and valuing sexual minorities in the workplace. In Stockdale, M. S., & Crosby, F. J. (Eds.), *The Psychology and Management of Workplace Diversity* (pp. 206–223). Malden, MA: Blackwell.

Markus, H. R., & Kitayama, S. (1991). Culture and the self: Implications for cognition, emotion, and motivation. *Psychological Review, 98*, 224–253. doi:10.1037/0033-295X.98.2.224

McConahay, J. B. (1986). Modern racism, ambivalence, and the modern racism scale. In Dovidio, J. F., & Gaertner, S. L. (Eds.), *Prejudice, Discrimination, and Racism* (pp. 91–125). Orlando, FL: Academic Press.

McDonald, S., Lin, N., & Ao, D. (2009). Networks of opportunity: Gender, race and job leads. *Social Problems, 56*(3), 385–402. doi:10.1525/sp.2009.56.3.385

McKay, P. F., & Avery, D. R. (2006). What has race got to do with it? Unraveling the role of racioethnicity in job seekers' reactions to site visits. *Personnel Psychology, 59*, 395–429.

McKay, P. F., Avery, D. R., Tonidandel, S., Morris, M. A., Hernandez, M., & Hebl, M. R. (2007). Racial differences in employee retention: Are diversity climate perceptions the key? *Personnel Psychology, 60*, 35–62. doi:10.1111/j.1744-6570.2007.00064.x

Messick, D. M., & Mackie, D. M. (1989). Intergroup relations. *Annual Review of Psychology, 40*, 51–81. doi:10.1146/annurev.ps.40.020189.000401

Milliken, F., & Martins, L. (1996). Searching for common threads: Understanding the multiple effects of diversity in organizational groups. *Academy of Management Review, 21*, 402–433.

Miville, M. L., Gelso, C. J., Pannu, R., Liu, W., Touradji, P., Holloway, P., & Fuertes, J. (1999). Appreciating similarities and valuing differences: The Miville-Guzman Universality-diversity scale. *Journal of Counseling Psychology, 46*, 291–307. doi:10.1037/0022-0167.46.3.291

Molinsky, A. L. (2005). Language fluency and the evaluation of cultural faux pa: Russians interviewing for jobs in the United States. *Social Psychology Quarterly, 68*(2), 103–120. doi:10.1177/019027250506800201

Montei, M. S., Adams, G. A., & Eggers, L. M. (1996). Validity of scores on the attitudes toward diversity scale (ATDS). *Educational and Psychological Measurement, 56*, 293–303. doi:10.1177/0013164496056002010

Mor Barak, M. E. (2011). *Managing diversity: Toward a globally inclusive workplace* (2nd ed.). Thousand Oaks, CA: Sage Publishing.

Mor Barak, M. E., Cherin, D. A., & Berkman, S. (1998). Organizational and personal dimensions in diversity climate. *The Journal of Applied Behavioral Science, 34*, 82–104. doi:10.1177/0021886398341006

Mor Barak, M. E., Findler, L., & Wind, L. (2003). Cross-cultural aspects of diversity and well-being in the workplace: An international perspective. *Journal of Social Work Research and Evaluation, 4*(2), 49–73.

Mor Barak, M. E., & Levin, A. (2002). Outside the corporate mainstream and excluded from the work community: A study of diversity, job satisfaction and well-being. *Community Work & Family, 5*(2), 133–157. doi:10.1080/13668800220146346

Neal, A., & Griffin, M. A. (2006). A Study of the lagged relationships among safety climate, safety motivation, safety behavior, and accidents at the individual and group levels. *The Journal of Applied Psychology, 91*(4), 946–953. doi:10.1037/0021-9010.91.4.946

Neal, R. A., Griffin, M. A., & Hart, P. M. (2000). The impact of organizational climate on safety climate and individual behavior. *Safety Science, 34*, 99–109. doi:10.1016/S0925-7535(00)00008-4

Pekerti, A. A., & Thomas, D. C. (2003). Communication in intercultural interaction: An empirical investigation of indicentric and sociocentric communication styles. *Journal of Cross-Cultural Psychology, 34*(2), 139–154. doi:10.1177/0022022102250724

Pettigrew, T. F., & Martin, J. (1987). Shaping the organizational context for black American inclusion. *The Journal of Social Issues, 43*, 41–78. doi:10.1111/j.1540-4560.1987.tb02330.x

Ponterotto, J. G., & Casas, J. M. (1991). *Handbook of racial/ethnic minority counseling research.* Springfield, IL: Charles C Thomas.

Pugh, S. D., Dietz, J., Brief, A. P., & Wiley, J. W. (2008). Looking inside and out: The impact of employee and community demographic composition on organizational diversity climate. *The Journal of Applied Psychology, 93*(6), 1422–1428. doi:10.1037/a0012696

Ragins, B. R. (2004). Sexual orientation in the workplace: The unique work and career experiences of gay, lesbian and bisexual workers. *Research in Personnel and Human Resources Management, 23*, 37–122. doi:10.1016/S0742-7301(04)23002-X

Roberson, Q. R., & Colquitt, J. A. (2005). Shared and configural justice: A social network model of justice in teams. *Academy of Management Review, 30*(3), 595–607. doi:10.5465/AMR.2005.17293715

Rotundo, M., Nguyen, D. H., & Sackett, P. R. (2001). A Meta-analytic review of gender differences in perceptions of sexual harassment. *The Journal of Applied Psychology, 86*, 914–922. doi:10.1037/0021-9010.86.5.914

Rupp, D. E., Bashshur, M., & Liao, H. (2007). Justice climate past, present, and future: Models of structure and emergence. In Dansereau, F., & Yammarino, F. J. (Eds.), *Research in Multilevel Issues* (*Vol. 6*). Englewood Cliffs, NJ: Erlbaum. doi:10.1016/S1475-9144(07)06017-1

Rynes, S., & Rosen, B. (1995). A field survey of factors affecting the adoption and perceived success of diversity training. *Personnel Psychology, 48*, 247–270. doi:10.1111/j.1744-6570.1995. tb01756.x

Schaller, M. (1991). Social categorization and the formation of social stereotypes: Further evidence for biased information processing in the perception of group-behavior correlations. *European Journal of Social Psychology, 21*, 25–35. doi:10.1002/ejsp.2420210103

Scott, J. C. (1999, January/February). Developing cultural fluency: The goal of international business communication instruction in the 21st century. *Journal of Education for Business*, 140–143. doi:10.1080/08832329909601676

Stockdale, M. S., & Cao, C. (2004). Looking back and heading forward: Major themes of the psychology and management of workplace diversity. In Stockdale, M. S., & Crosby, F. J. (Eds.), *The Psychology and Management of Workplace Diversity* (pp. 300–316). Malden, MA: Blackwell.

Tajfel, H., & Turner, J. C. (1979). An integrative theory of intergroup conflict. In Austin, W. G., & Worchel, S. (Eds.), *The Social Psychology of Intergroup Relations* (pp. 33–47). Pacific Grove, CA: Brooks/Cole.

Tavris, C., & Aronson, E. (2007). *Mistakes were made (but not by me): Why we justify foolish beliefs, bad decisions, and hurtful acts*. Orlando, FL: Harcourt.

Taylor, A. S., & James, K. (2010). *Toward the well-being of all: Integrating diversity dynamics and organizational justice dimensions*. Paper presentation at the Academy of Management Meeting. Montreal, Canada.

Taylor, D. M., & Moghaddam, F. M. (1994). *Theories of intergroup relations: International social psychological perspectives* (2nd ed.). New York, NY: Praeger.

Thomas, K. (2005). *Diversity dynamics in the workplace*. Belmont, CA: Thomson Wadsworth.

Triandis, H. C. (2003). The future of workforce diversity in international organisations: A commentary. *Applied Psychology: An International Review, 52*, 486–495. doi:10.1111/1464-0597.00146

Turner, J. C. (1981). The experimental social psychology of inter-group behavior. In Turner, J. C., & Giles, H. (Eds.), *Intergroup Behavior* (pp. 66–101). Chicago, IL: University of Chicago Press.

van Knippenberg, D., & Schippers, M. C. (2007). Work group diversity. *Annual Review of Psychology, 58*, 515–541. doi:10.1146/annurev. psych.58.110405.085546

ADDITIONAL READING

Bassett-Jones, N. (2005). The paradox of diversity management, creativity and innovation. *Creativity and Innovation Management, 14*(2), 169. doi:10.1111/j.1467-8691.00337.x

Black, J. S. (1990). Locus of control, social support, stress, and adjustment in international transfers. *Asia Pacific Journal of Management, 7*, 1–29. doi:10.1007/BF01731881

Chrobot-Mason, D., & Ruderman, M. N. (2004). Leadership in a diverse workplace. In Stockdale, M. S., & Crosby, F. J. (Eds.), *The Psychology and Management of Workplace Diversity* (pp. 100–121). Malden, MA: Blackwell.

Foldes, H. J., Duehr, E. E., & Ones, D. S. (2008). Group differences in personality: Meta-analyses comparing five U.S. racial groups. *Personnel Psychology*, *61*, 579–616. doi:10.1111/j.1744-6570.2008.00123.x

Ibarra, H. (1995). Race, opportunity, and diversity of social circles in managerial networks. *Academy of Management Journal*, *38*, 673–703. doi:10.2307/256742

King, E. B., & Cortina, J. M. (2010). The social and economic imperative of LGBT-supportive organizations. *Industrial-Organizational Psychology: Perspectives of Science and Practice*, *3*(1), 69–78. doi:10.1111/j.1754-9434.2009.01201.x

Lau, D. C., & Murnighan, J. K. (1998). Demographic diversity and faultlines: The compositional dynamics of organizational groups. *Academy of Management Review*, *23*, 325–340.

Mannix, E., & Neale, M. A. (2005). What differences make a difference? The promise and reality of diverse teams in organizations. *Psychological Science in the Public Interest*, *6*, 31–55. doi:10.1111/j.1529-1006.2005.00022.x

Nelson, E. S., & Krieger, S. L. (1997). Changes in attitude toward homosexuality in college students: Implementation of a gay men and lesbian peer panel. *Journal of Homosexuality*, *33*, 63–81. doi:10.1300/J082v33n02_04

Offermann, L. R., & Phan, L. U. (2002). Culturally intelligent leadership for a diverse world. In Riggio, R. E., Murphy, S. E., & Pirozzolo, F. J. (Eds.), *Multiple Intelligences and Leadership* (pp. 187–214). Mahwah, NJ: Lawrence Erlbaum Associates.

Rynes, S., & Rosen, B. (1995). A field survey of factors affecting the adoption and perceived success of diversity training. *Personnel Psychology*, *48*, 247–270. doi:10.1111/j.1744-6570.1995.tb01756.x

Slaughter, M. (2010). How U.S. multinational companies strengthen the U.S. economy: Data update. *Business Roundtable*. Retrieved May 3, 2011 from http://www.uscib.org/docs/foundation_multinationals_update.pdf.

Sniderman, P., & Tetlock, P. (1986). Symbolic racism: Problems of motive attribution in political analysis. *The Journal of Social Issues*, *42*, 423–447. doi:10.1111/j.1540-4560.1986.tb00229.x

Tomaskovic-Devey, D., Zimmer, C., Stainback, K., Robinson, C., Taylor, T., & McTague, T. (2006). Documenting desegregation: Segregation in American workplaces by race, ethnicity, and sex, 1966–2003. *American Sociological Review*, *71*, 565–588. doi:10.1177/000312240607100403

US Department of Health and Human Services. (2011). *Prevalence and impact, fact sheet*. Retrieved May 3, 2011 from http://www.hhs.gov/od/about/fact_sheets/prevalenceandimpact.html.

Weiland, A. J. (2004). *Business leadership and diversity: The relationships between team diversity climate, leaders' diversity attitudes, and leadership styles*. Unpublished Dissertation. Iowa City, IA: University of Iowa.

KEY TERMS AND DEFINITIONS

Communication: The extent to which language barriers and differences in communication styles, nonverbal communication, language fluency, and cultural fluency manifest in diverse work settings.

Diversity Climate: The extent to which employees share the perception that a diverse organization's policies, practices, and procedures communicate a strong priority given to fostering and maintaining diversity and inclusion.

Identity: The extent to which one perceives, feels, and behaves as if they are included or excluded in a diverse work setting.

Leadership: The extent to which the leaders, or managers, in a diverse organization support diversity as a priority in the workplace.

Organizational Justice: The extent to which employees perceive fairness of the distribution of resources, procedures, and interactions within a diverse organization.

Schemas: The extent to which cognitive guides lead to the organization of information and the perceived patterns of behaviors, including stereotypes and behavioral scripts, in diverse work settings.

Values: The extent to which one's central guides influence his/her perceptions of appropriate identity, preferences, beliefs and behaviors in a diverse workplace.

Workforce Diversity: The division of the workforce into distinct categories that (a) have a perceived commonality within a given cultural or national context and that (b) impact potentially harmful or beneficial employment outcomes such as job opportunities, treatment in the workplace, and promotion prospects—irrespective of job-related skills and qualifications

Chapter 13
Leveraging the Power of Diversity in Workplace Learning Strategies

Rita C. McNeil
Idaho State University, USA

ABSTRACT

Just as adult learning strategies can be categorized into three major learning strategy preference groups (Conti & Kolody, 1998), workplace learning events can also be similarly categorized into a spectrum containing three major clusters: (a) the Navigation Cluster, containing those tasks that require planning, organizing, and structuring of content; (b) the Problem-Solving Cluster, containing those tasks that require innovative creativity or critical thinking skills; and (c) the Engagement Cluster, containing those tasks that require inter- and intra-personal skills required when working in situations that involve others. The purpose of this chapter is to propose an emerging 4-step framework that can be used to guide individuals, educators, and workplace trainers through a process to assist learners in identifying their learning strategies preferences and in leveraging these individual metacognitive processes in order to achieve specific workplace learning objectives.

INTRODUCTION

"As educators, we teach students the skills to become competent entry-level employees, but unfortunately, we often fail to teach them the one skill that will span their entire careers—that of learning how to learn."

DOI: 10.4018/978-1-4666-1812-1.ch013

Although the rate of career advancement is often dependent upon one's ability to learn and apply new concepts quickly and efficiently in the workplace, scant effort is spent within post-secondary programs or in the workplace to prepare individuals to manage the steep learning curve often experienced by employees in new roles. Awareness of one's personal learning processes, and specifically learning strategy preferences, improves one's learning performance and ultimately, workplace performance (Conti, Kolody, & Schneider, 1997).

Workplace learning traditionally occurs through activities such as lecture, observation, experience, or practice; however, learning tasks can be accomplished with greater efficiency when approached in a purposeful, analytical, and systematic fashion. This systematic approach requires metacognitive awareness – that of knowing one's strengths and shortcomings in learning processes. Metacognition is associated with reflective practice. The reflective practice serves to assist in people being able to draw from experiences to minimize a problematic situation by detracting the complexity, uncertainty, uniqueness, and value conflict found within this circumstance (Schön, 1983). As such, learners make use of this reflective practice, which is presented with new events from real-life experiences to develop a source of reference that can create a repertoire of responses, and theories that can be used in future dilemmas (Smith, 1983). Metacognition is a conscious reflective action implemented while analyzing, assessing, and managing the thought processes" (Conti & Kolody, 1999, p. 3). Moreover, "it has become evident that the learner who is conscious of his or her learning processes exercises more control over those processes and becomes a more effective learner" (Fellenz & Conti, 1993, p. 9). When learners are aware of their cognitive strengths, they can then more appropriately match these natural, innate, and comfortable learning processes to specific learning events that require strategies best suited to the learners' preferences.

Learning processes are less efficient, however, when one experiences shortcomings required for specific learning objectives. Learners often attempt to compensate for the shortcomings with less efficient processes or they avoid the learning task altogether. When this occurs, workplace performance efficiency is compromised.

It is encouraging to note that shortcomings in learning processes, and specifically learning strategies, can be overcome. Metacognitive awareness can be increased by identifying and applying a variety of learning strategies (not only those that fall within their preferences)—in essence, by learning how to learn. Not only is individual performance increased through enhanced metacognitive awareness, the diversity that comes with learning strategy preference can be embraced for optimum organizational leveraged results.

Consequently, employees can master a spectrum of workplace learning strategies that they can select and apply appropriately, as required. The 4-step framework proposed in this chapter can be used to guide individuals, educators, and workplace trainers through processes to acquire the skills for learning how to learn in the workplace.

BACKGROUND

Diversity

Diversity too often is considered in workplace training only when the diversity is visible in dimensions such as race, gender, age, and lifestyle choice. Because individuals approach learning in a variety of cognitive styles that are not readily visible and are often difficult to identify, this dimension of diversity is often overlooked in the workplace. According to Thomas and Ely, (as cited by Stalinski, 2004, p. 14), diversity has most commonly become a compliance issue. Stalinski further suggests that the basic belief in a diverse workforce is simply not enough; diversity must become a source of organizational benefit (2004).

One way of addressing diversity in the workplace is to leverage individual differences in individual learner's cognitive styles. Sternberg and Grigorenko (1997) define cognitive styles as "people's characteristic and typically preferred modes of processing information," and often refer to concepts such as learning styles, learning modalities, thinking styles, personality styles, and learning strategy preference. While most cognitive styles are innate, diverse learning strategies, if not developed naturally, can be learned, applied, and leveraged effectively to enhance learning efficiency in workplace settings, in academic environments, and in real-life learning situations.

Adult Learning Strategies

Learning strategies are those techniques or specialized skills that the learner has developed and elects to use in both formal and informal learning situations (McKeachie, 1988; Fellenz & Conti, 1993). Learning strategies identify ways in which adults perceive factors in their learning environment and in their metacognitive processes "that advance the understanding of the individuality of learning experiences and that promote learner self-knowledge and control of personal perceptions and judgments...for potential empowerment of the individual" (Fellenz & Conti, 1993, p. 23).

In the Self-Knowledge Inventory of Lifelong Learning Strategies (SKILLS) instrument, Fellenz and Conti (1993) have focused on the role of learning strategies used in real-life learning situations by adults. As such, they have identified five areas of learning strategies upon which to center their investigation; metacognition, metamotivation, memory, critical thinking, and resource management. Each of these five constructs consists of three learning strategies (Conti & Fellenz, 1991; Fellenz & Conti, 1993).

Metacognition Strategies. Metacognition is defined as the knowledge and control over one's thinking and learning (Brown, 1985). It is a conscious, reflective endeavour; it is one that requires the learner to analyze, assess, and manage learning activities. The three learning strategies involved in the area of metacognition identified in the SKILLS instrument are Planning (creating a step-by-step learning plan), Monitoring (self-checking to compare planned progress to actual progress), and Adjusting (revising the plan to meet objectives if off-track).

Metamotivation Strategies. Metamotivation is the "awareness of and control over factors that energize and direct one's learning" (Fellenz & Conti, 1993, p. 12). The prefix "meta" is used to differentiate the concept from external motivation prevalent in traditional education institutions (Fellenz & Conti, 1993). The three learning strategies involved in the area of metamotivation identified in the SKILLS instrument are Attention (deciding to pay attention), Reward/Enjoyment (having fun, or experiencing satisfaction with the learning activity), and Confidence ("the learner's perceptions of self-efficacy and self-control in learning situations") (McCombs, 1988, p. 142). All metamotivational strategies are associated with the affective domain (Fellenz & Conti, 1993).

Memory Strategies. Memory is "the capacity of humans to retain information, to recall it when needed and recognize its familiarity when they later see it or hear it again" (Wingfield & Byrnes, 1981, p. 4). "Metamemory is practical knowledge acquired about our own memory capacities and what we must do to remember; or simply, what people know about how they remember" (Fellenz & Conti, 1993, p. 22). Learners can improve their memory performance and the efficiency of their learning by developing metamemory skills; thus, difficulties encountered in learning may not be due to the inabilities of the learner but rather may be the result of not using the appropriate memory strategy for the learning task (Wingfield & Byrnes, 1981). The memory strategies used in the SKILLS model include Organization (the manner in which the memory reorders or restructures information from that in which it was originally presented), External Aids (tools and list to enhance recall), and Memory Application (the use of those internal strategies involved in Memory Organization for the purpose of planning, completing, and evaluating learning.

Critical Thinking Strategies. Critical Thinking is a reflective thinking process utilizing higher order thinking skills in order to improve learning

(Brookfield, 1987). The three learning strategies involved in the area of Critical Thinking identified in the SKILLS instrument include Testing Assumptions (identifying and examining assumptions), Generating Alternatives (identifying alternate solutions), and Conditional Acceptance (questioning simplistic answers and predicting consequences).

Resource Management Strategies. Resource Management involves the ability to identify, evaluate, and use resources relevant to the learning task (Fellenz & Conti, 1993). The three learning strategies involved in the area of Resource Management identified in the SKILLS instrument include Identification (locating a variety of physical, electronic, and/or human resources), Critical Use (selection of the most appropriate resource rather than simply those that are readily available), and Human Resources (integrating others into the social and political processes of learning).

Learning Strategy Preference

According to research based on a self-scoring instrument used to identify learning strategy preference, Assessing The Learning Strategies of AdultS (ATLAS – Appendix B, Conti & Kolody, 1998), learners can be categorized into three major groups, each with a set of commonalities and general characteristics. ATLAS has been translated into several languages and has been used globally to assess learning strategy preferences within diverse populations in fields such as business, tribal communities, nursing, the military, public school administration, and leadership. The distribution of the three groups has consistently been relatively equal among a variety of populations: Navigators—36.5%, Problem Solvers—31.7%, and Engagers—31.8% (Conti & Kolody, 1998, 1999, 2004). Descriptions of these learning strategy preference groups are detailed later in this chapter.

The ATLAS instrument arose out of a need for a self-scoring tool that was easy to administer, that could be completed rapidly, and that could

be used immediately by both facilitators and learners. Depending upon reading level, ATLAS can be completed in approximately one to three minutes. Although it appears to be a very simple instrument, the contents of this valid and reliable instrument are based on powerful multivariate statistical procedures (Conti & Kolody, 1998). Instrumented learning is the process by which learners use instruments to learn about themselves (Blake & Mouton, 1972). Instruments used to describe how people choose to undertake a task can serve to enlighten them of both their strengths and ineffective strategies. They can replace discovered weaknesses with more effective strengths when managing best-case practices (Sanders, 2008).

It is important to note that, as with any concepts that have the potential of labeling individuals, care must be taken not to stereotype or to make assumptions regarding learners in any one specific learning group. Certainly, individual differences will appear within the groups. The commonalities found, however, can provide useful insights to help learners better understand how they go about the learning process (Conti & Kolody, 2004).

WORKPLACE LEARNING STRATEGIES

Issues, Controversies, Problems

Defining Learning Strategies

The term "learning strategies" is ill-defined in the education community; the concepts of learning strategies are misunderstood, and the benefits of learning strategies are underutilized. Educators loosely use the term to refer to concepts such as study strategies, reading strategies, test-taking strategies, and anxiety-reduction strategies. Perpetuating this confusion not only does injustice to the learners but also impedes the progress required to come to a universal definition and understanding that will lead to learners developing the learning strategies to accomplish learning tasks and to organizations benefitting from efficient workplace learning. Educators, researchers, practitioners, training professionals, and learners would benefit greatly by adopting the precise language associated with learning strategies and by promoting the use of proper terminology. Efficiencies in the workplace and in educational settings rely on the acceptance of a common definition. Leveraging the diversity of learning strategy preference within an organization can only occur once a common "playing field" has been established. One of the objectives of this chapter is to present a well-researched definition of learning strategies and to then guide the readers through a process by which they can identify and use learning strategies to optimize performance in the workplace.

Learning How to Learn

Robert Smith (1983) played a pivotal role in adult education in regards to understanding the concept of learning how to learn. "Learning how to learn involves possessing, or acquiring, the knowledge and skill to learn effectively in whatever learning situation one encounters" (p. 19). Smith emphasized the fundamental importance of learners knowing their own "characteristic ways of processing information, feeling, and behaving in learning situations" (p. 24) and of having "the ability to recognize one's own learning style, interests, aptitudes and aspirations, including the ability to identify affective considerations" (p. 65). As educators, we teach students the skills to become competent entry-level employees, but unfortunately, we fail to teach them the one skill that will span their entire careers—that of *learning how to learn* (McNeil, 2011).

Incorporating metacognitive awareness and self-directed learning principles into academic programs would benefit students greatly in preparing them for the workplace.

Knowles (1975) contributed to the development of the concept of self-directed learning. "In its broadest meaning, 'self-directed learning' describes a process in which individuals take the initiative, with or without the help of others, in diagnosing their learning needs, formulating learning goals, identifying human and material resources for learning, choosing and implementing appropriate learning strategies, and evaluating learning outcomes" (p. 18). Other theorists such as Tough (1971) expanded and developed the concept. Self-directed learning

not only takes learners into account but also considers the context of the learning and the nature of the learning. In Danis's (1992) model (as cited by Sanders, 2008), learning strategies, phases of the learning process, the content, the learner, and the environmental factors in the context must all be taken into account in mapping the process of self-directed learning.

SOLUTIONS AND RECOMMENDATIONS

Workplace Learning Strategy Spectrum

Workplace learning events can be categorized into a spectrum containing three major clusters: (a) the Navigation Cluster (those tasks that require planning, organizing, and structuring of content); (b) the Problem-Solving Cluster (those tasks that require innovative creativity or critical thinking skills); and (c) the Engagement Cluster (those tasks that require inter- and intra- personal skills required when working in situations that involve others (Figure 1).

In order to fulfil performance expectations in most positions in the workplace, employees must master skills in each of the three learning strategy clusters. However, most individuals have a pref-

Figure 1. Workplace learning strategies spectrum

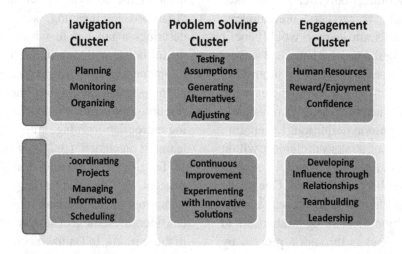

erence for one of these three sets and, as such, tend to use one of these three sets more predominantly that the others, even when the learning event clearly requires skills outside of their preferred set.

Often, complex workplace functions require the application of learning strategies from all three clusters. For example, implementation of an innovation or process within an organization might include Problem-Solving Strategies to *identify* and *critically assess* and *select* creative solutions; the Navigation Strategies of *planning* and *organizing* to purchase and install equipment and to schedule training for maintenance and operations; and Engagement Strategies might then be used to garner *influence* and *manage employee morale* during the change management phase. An employee involved in this type of project may perform some of the functions better than others, but all functions can be performed equally well if the employee has mastered the identification and application of the appropriate learning strategies for each task.

4-Step Workplace Learning Strategy Framework

The 4-Step Workplace Learning Strategy Framework (Figure 2) can be used by:

- **Individuals** in a self-study format that desire a means of learning how to learn
- **Educators** who would like to teach their students the art of learning how to learn both for learning purposes and to prepare them for the world of work
- **Workplace Trainers** who would like to promote individual employee learning within their organization in order to enhance performance and productivity.

Step One: Establish a Shared Definition of Workplace Learning Strategies

Promoting a learning culture within an organization requires discourse. Attention to the concepts and importance of intentional learning must be sur-

Figure 2. 4-step workplace learning strategy framework

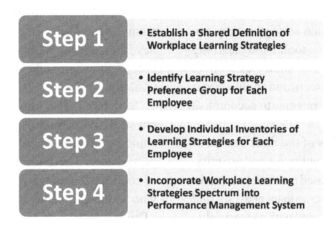

faced and promoted throughout the organization. If the metacognitive processes of "learning how to learn" are not currently a part of the organization's practices, then to successfully facilitate a cultural change, an initial announcement and rollout program should be embarked upon to introduce the "learning how to learn" culture.

As with any change management efforts within an organization, the entire organization must be aware of the new language and terms associated with the proposed concepts. A shared definition throughout the organization is critical to the success of the cultural change. Written materials could be distributed; training and conversations could occur to ensure alignment and to categorize workplace learning events into their appropriate clusters. Employees can then expand upon the concepts provided in the learning strategies spectrum and customize definitions with details specific to the organization.

The recommended starting point is to begin with the five constructs of learning strategies and the three learning strategies within each construct identified in the Quick Reference Guide adapted by the Self-Knowledge Inventory of Lifelong Learning Strategies (SKILLS) instrument (see Appendix A). The constructs and corresponding learning strategies found in the Quick Reference

Guide provide a solid foundation for further considerations with the Workplace Learning Strategies Spectrum discussed previously in this chapter.

Step Two: Identify Individual Learning Strategy Preference Group for Each Employee

The second step within the 4-Step Workplace Learning Strategies Framework is to identify each employee's learning strategy preference group. When learners are aware of their cognitive strengths, they can then more appropriately match these seemingly natural processes to specific learning events. The metacognitive awareness that results from understanding one's natural preferences likewise provides a deeper understanding of one's learning developmental needs.

Using the self-scoring Assessing the Learning Strategies of AdultS (ATLAS) instrument found in Appendix B of this chapter, employees will be able to identify their own individual learning strategy preference group and then compare the generalities described in the group descriptions to their own preferred learning practices. Employees will most often identify some similarities within each group to their own preferences to some degree, but they will most likely also detect a marked affinity with one particular preference group. Once learners are able to define and identify their individual learning strategy preferences and strengths, they can then enhance their "learning toolkits" by learning to master additional learning strategies with an increased ability to best discern and apply a larger spectrum of appropriate strategies to accomplish specific learning tasks.

The following profiles of the three groups of learners are the results of qualitative and quantitative research projects that used the statistical methods of cluster analysis, discriminant analysis, and analysis of variance conducted with each variable when the participants were grouped by clusters. Qualitative comments from learners within each cluster collected during focus groups and personal interviews are also included to enrich descriptions (Armstrong, 2001; Bighorn, 1997; Courtnage, 1998; GhostBear, 2001; Hinds, 2001; Kolody, 1997; Korinek, 1997; Lively, 2001; Lockwood, 1997; Ungricht, 1997; Willyard, 2000).

Navigators

Navigators predominantly use the learning strategies of Attention, Planning, and Organizing. As such, they are the learners to first make a conscious decision to create a learning plan. They readily identify the "Big Picture," in other words the goals, objectives, and anticipated outcomes, and then map out a set of activities by which to "navigate" their way through the learning event. Navigators are conscientious, results-oriented high achievers who favor making logical connections (Conti & Kolody, 1998, 1999).

Planning involves knowing "how to elicit purpose from both themselves and the situations and how to organize and identify the steps essential to the learning process" (Yussen, 1985, p. 280). Because of the great importance of planning to Navigators, schedules are important to them, and they reportedly become stressed if their schedules or plans are disrupted. For this reason, group work is not often appealing to Navigators as the risk

of schedule disruption is higher with multiple people within a group, especially if teamed with members less focused than themselves. Navigators have "a tendency to take over and dominate the group" to ensure adherence to scheduled plans (Kolody, 1997).

Structure is also important to the Navigator's physical environment. A Navigator's slogan in life could be "a place for everything and everything in its place." These learners like to be in control of their surroundings and to work with others who value the same clean, organized setting. "Things are to be done a certain way and in a certain order to keep things running smoothly" (Kolody, 1997). Metacognitive structure involves linear thinking and making logical connections (chunking, step-by-step processes, beginning at the beginning). Navigators are most likely to use planning aids such as to-do lists, schedulers, and electronic organizers.

Navigators also rely heavily on the learning strategy of attention, which involves the arousal of interest in learners, the stimulation of an attitude of inquiry, and the maintenance of attention. This group of learners systematically and purposefully creates an environment that facilitates learning. This often will include a specific location for studying which is free from distractions "with all my pencils, erasers, and materials neatly in place"(Kolody, 1997). Navigators all agreed that studying at a particular and consistent time of day also helped them to stay focused on their learning.

Navigators also rely heavily on the learning strategies of Identification of Resources and Use of Resources, which is knowing how to locate and use the best information (Fellenz & Conti, 1993). "When I want to find out about something, I want the facts; not other people's opinions. So I go to the library or ask a professional." Although the group participants were divided when asked whether they preferred human or physical resources in their learning, all displayed an ability to know how to locate and use the best information for them (Kolody, 1997).

Problem Solvers

Problems Solvers predominantly use the Critical Thinking learning strategies of Testing Assumptions, Generating Alternatives, and Conditional Acceptance. Problem Solvers test assumptions to evaluate the specifics and generalizability within a learning situation; they generate alternatives to create additional learning options; and they are open to conditional acceptance of learning outcomes while keeping an open mind to other learning possibilities (Conti & Kolody, 1998, 1999).

Although curious, inventive, and intuitive, the Problem Solver's ability to generate alternatives and consider various solutions can also tend to result in increased difficulty in making decisions. Thus, Problem Solvers do not generally do well on multiple-choice exams and are better assessed with open-ended questions and problem-solving activities.

Critical thinkers rely on a reflective thinking process, which utilizes higher order thinking skills (Brookfield, 1987). Problem Solvers' critical thinking skills are sustained by their use of the Adjusting learning strategy, which is the ongoing modification and revision of their learning plans in relationship to their evaluation of their own learning process. Problem Solvers have a significant sense of self-efficacy, which provides them a sense of confidence to have the ability to "figure it out as they go along." Unlike Navigators, it is not a source of stress to not have a plan, and it many cases, they find working to a plan to be oppressive and restricting. They much prefer the freedom to experiment and adjust as needed (Conti & Kolody, 1998, 1999).

Engagers

The most distinguishing characteristic of Engagers is their heightened ability to manage human resources, defined as "integrating others into the social and political process of learning through dialogues, discussions, and networking" (Fellenz & Conti, 1993). As such, they most often listen to and consider others' opposing views during their decision-making processes. Proficient at maximizing human resources, they possess enhanced interpersonal skills that allow them to excel in activities such as teamwork, leadership, relationship building, having difficult conversations, and conflict management. In the workplace, Engagers seem to best understand the connection between employee engagement and performance and are often placed in roles of mediation, morale building, and performance improvement.

Engagers predominantly use the Metamotivational learning strategies of Reward/Enjoyment and Confidence. Engagers seek out learning activities that provide the greatest opportunity for engagement, which Kidd (1973) defines as "a relationship between the learner, the task or subject matter, the environment, and the teacher" (p. 266). Interaction and collaboration are major motivators for entering into the learning task.

For this learning strategy preference group, the affective domain is the dominant factor in learning. Engagers monitor the value of the learning experience and the personal level of motivation on an economy of scale to determine if the expected reward is worth the effort. If the learning activity is not perceived or expected to be a worthwhile or enjoyable experience, the Engager will seek out another activity that they will find more meaningful (Kolody, 1997).

Although the Engagers were not aware of the term "transformational learning" coined by Mezirow (1990), they described this concept as part of their learning in their constant pursuit of learning activities that enhanced understanding of themselves and their world around them (Conti & Kolody, 1998, 1999). While competent in completing short-term learning activities, these hold no emotional value to the Engager who finds superficiality and details to be painfully tedious. Rather, the Engager pursues long-term learning activities that will result in self-development and will aid in a permanent personal change and growth.

Confidence is another metamotivational learning strategy in which Engagers scored high. However, the group participants pointed out that their confidence is not dependent so much on the learners believing that they can complete the learning task successfully as it is on whether they are confident that the learning task will keep them interested enough to complete the learning task. In evaluating their learning, the Engager's focus is on meeting their internal needs rather than meeting external standards. Because of the great emotional investment in their learning, Engagers take great pride in their work and often their self-worth is determined or validated by their accomplishments.

Engagers make heavy use of the Memory strategies of Memory Application, using mental images or other memories to facilitate problem solving. Group members agreed that they do not memorize material. Rather, visualization was a more common memory technique used by most participants of this group, and many identified themselves as either visual or kinesthetic learners (Conti & Kolody, 1998, 1999).

Step Three: Develop Individual Inventories of Learning Strategies for Each Employee

The third step in the 4-Step Workplace Learning Strategies Framework is to increase the tools in one's learning toolbox by learning to use those strategies that do not come naturally or that are not one's preference. The more sophisticated we become as learners, the more diverse our learning strategy toolkits become. We learn to identify and apply the appropriate "tools" or learning strategies to the learning event.

When optimum learning strategies do not match an individual's learning strategy preference, then learning is compromised. It would behoove educators and workplace training professionals to teach students and employees how to increase their use of learning strategies beyond their natural preferences, so that they may develop the learning sophistication to identify, select, and employ the most efficient learning strategy for the specific learning objective.

A learner's effective choice of learning strategies "usually results in greater learning" (McKeachie, 1988, p. 3). "The skills or techniques selected to accomplish the task often have a great influence on the success of that learning activity. Adeptness and insight in the use of learning strategies appears to be a significant part of one's ability to learn how to learn (Fellenz & Conti, 1993, p. 3).

The lesson for individuals and organizations alike is to concentrate on development activities to increase the toolkit. If an individual is not naturally organized, then develop strategies to master organizational requirements; if an individual is not naturally creative, then develop skills to promote creative and critical thought processes; if an individual is not naturally charismatic and engaging, then develop teamwork, leadership, and interpersonal skills to master the art of relationship building.

Developing Navigation Cluster Skills. The workplace competencies within this cluster are those requiring planning, organizing, scheduling, and coordinating. Sometimes, events need to be organized; at other times, thoughts need to be sorted out and organized; and in certain instances, people need to be organized, either in determining who is going to fulfill certain functions within specific roles, or in the scheduling of those functions. Navigators, because of their natural tendencies for linear and step-by-step thought processes, tend to perform these organizational tasks well and with little direction. Often, Navigators will undertake these organizational tasks, even when these tasks are not assigned within their roles. It is reported that they often assume the function out of frustration with their perceived lack of organization (Kolody, 1997).

However, many employees who function within the abstract realm (instead of the Navigation linear realm) often grapple with organizational skills, manifested by their constant struggle to meet deadlines. Extreme cases even find it a challenge to arrive at work on time every day. Organization simply is not their forte and they often need assistance in learning how to become focused and organized when work tasks require these skills. Although organization does not come naturally to most abstract thinkers, these navigation skills can be learned, developed, and applied as required. Individuals who are in the process of developing navigation skills report that learning is most effective when graphic organizers (also termed concept maps or mind maps) are modeled. They report that, before they can use the tools efficiently on their own, it is helpful to see examples of organizational tools in use (Kolody, 1997).

Examples of graphic organizers that can be used to identify objectives and expectations may include:

- Spider Maps (to identify and organize anticipated outcomes)
- Continuum Charts

Examples of graphic organizers that can be used to create schedules, deadlines, and logically sequenced project plans may include:

- Herringbone Maps to identify Who, Does What, When, Where, How, and Why
- Cycle Flow Charts
- Linear Flow Charts
- Series of Events Chains

Examples of graphic organizers that can be used to organize thoughts and information may include:

- Venn Compare-Contrast Organizers
- Matrix Compare-Contrast Organizers
- Hierarchical Organizers

Teaching the use of electronic organizers is also helpful to promote navigation skills to those who struggle with organization. To-do lists, day timers, and electronic calendars are samples of effective tools to develop and appreciate methods to help organize thoughts and events.

Developing Problem-Solving Cluster Skills. Unless an organization promotes a culture of continuous improvement, creative and critical thinking processes in the workplace are not always appreciated, much less rewarded. Oftentimes, it is considered much "safer" for employees to simply follow established policies and procedures than to explore creative innovations. However, unless processes are mandated legislatively or unless there are safety issues, valuable returns on investment can be realized by exploring creative approaches to organizational issues. Much can be gained by challenging the status quo, brainstorming, and experimenting with innovative practices to solve problems in the workplace. Promoting the use of a risk assessment model to identify anticipated outcomes of proposed workplace solutions hones awareness and increases the capacity for possibility thinking.

Another common and effective method of developing critical thinking skills is to foster a multi-solutioned mindset in which there is not always a right and a wrong answer. Rather than searching for "*the*" solution, Problem-Solving processes involve generating alternatives for multiple solutions and then assessing the viability of each alternative. This critical thinking activity can be accomplished individually or in groups.

Critical thought processes are often manifested by the art of asking good questions. Modeling the following questions and promoting their use in reflective conversations within an organization encourage evaluation of assumptions. Paul and Elder, 2009 recommend the following questions in developing critical thinking skills:

- How did I reach this conclusion?
- Is there another way to interpret the information?
- What am I taking for granted?

- What assumption has led me to that conclusion?
- Is there another point of view that I should consider?
- Does this really make sense?
- Are we considering all relevant viewpoints in good faith?
- Are we more concerned about our vested interests than the common goal?

It is interesting to note that some individuals (most often Navigators) report that they did not know it was sometimes acceptable not to have a plan before beginning a project. In fact, they considered beginning a project without a plan to be irresponsible. Because they gravitate towards being "rules people," they did not know that it was okay to challenge the norm. They thought good employees fell into step with established policies and procedures and that it was not acceptable to "make waves." Not surprisingly, when Navigators become supervisors, they expect their direct reports not to make waves, not to challenge the status quo, and not to violate policies and procedures, resulting in potential interpersonal conflicts within the team (Conti & Kolody, 2004).

Developing Engagement Cluster Skills. Engagement is synonymous with connectivity and most successful employees are highly connected with their metacognitive and intrapersonal strengths as much as with their digital technology that allows them to stay connected with others. Engagers understand the power of self-awareness, communication, and relationship building and demonstrate skills associated with the Affective Domain (Bloom, et al., 1964). Fortunately, for those who do not find these skills to be innate, these Engagement skills can be learned. Arguably the most difficult lessons to be taught, employees can learn Engagement concepts such as empathy, appreciation, teamwork, leadership, congeniality, ethics, and charisma. Valuable development activities of these critical interpersonal skills can be offered in the workplace through workshops that provide opportunity for case studies and role-play, one-on-one coaching and mentoring for real-life incidents, or through a variety of online, self-study, and discussion formats. Critical to the success of Engagement skills training is ongoing reinforcement and, most importantly, modeling of engagement strategies by administration and supervisors. Employees who feel engaged and respected will imitate behaviors and will strive to perpetuate a culture of Engagement within their sphere of workplace contacts. Employees who have mastered Engagement learning strategies demonstrate skills in areas such as conflict management, having difficult conversations, morale boosting, celebrating success, and improving performance in one's self and in co-workers.

With the ever-increasing electronic communication and physical geographic distance often experienced in the workplace, employee engagement is becoming more challenging to achieve. When used effectively, digital communication modes can help to overcome the challenge by increasing contact opportunities and by decreasing response time in social learning opportunities. Providing the technology, training, support, and assessment for real-time communication and training-on-demand formats can greatly enhance the development rate and skill application of online engagement learning strategies.

Step Four: Incorporate Workplace Learning Strategies Spectrum into Performance Management System

There is an adage in business, often attributed to Peter Drucker (as cited by Gill, 2010), which suggests that what gets measured, gets done. The fourth and final step in the 4-Step Workplace Learning Framework is to incorporate intentioned and purposeful learning activities into ongoing evaluations within a systemic performance management practice. Including learning as an assessment metric in each individual employee's evaluations requires a paradigm shift from a training-centered to a learner centered practice in which the responsibility shifts from teaching and training housed within and delivered by training departments to individuals accepting accountability for their own learning throughout their careers. As employee performance goals for the upcoming period are identified, appropriate learning strategies required to accomplish the specific goals can then be incorporated into the employee's learning plan.

When individual learning is promoted as a performance expectation, and metacognitive practices are supported and rewarded by management, then intentioned learning becomes a part of performance conversations and employees are better equipped to utilize further learning strategy practices to best manage their professional development opportunities and career promotion. In competing within the war for talent, Michaels, et. al suggest that organizations that offer exceptional learning opportunities and accelerated career advancement attract and retain top performers (2001). Incorporating the 4-Step Workplace Learning Strategies Framework into daily organizational practice demonstrates to these career-oriented employees the organizational attention to employee learning and career advancement. As a result, workplace learning strategy diversity is leveraged at both the individual employee and the organizational levels – employees gain learning skills to manage their performance and subsequent advancements; organizations enjoy engaged employees with heightened awareness and capacity to enhance learning, performance, and productivity.

FUTURE RESEARCH DIRECTIONS

The technology explosion trend has changed the ways we conduct business and shows no indications of slowing down any time soon. One might erroneously assume that technology would be the solution to managing the ever-increasing demand of our fast-paced business world, but technological advances seem, at times, to be working counter to that notion. Since technology has increased the speed with which we now function and communicate, increased productivity and quickly paced responses are now also an expected norm. As a result of this digital information explosion experienced over the past decade, more time is being spent managing the information overload and "sifting through" the available information for that which is appropriate and valuable. Individuals and corporations alike are searching for innovative resource management strategies to maximize digital learning opportunities. McNulty (2010) suggests that the basis for successfully navigating the knowledge economy is to populate it with "workers creating and relying upon quick access to, and acquisition of, information that they need – organizations can range from construction to IT…as long as they depend on the acquisition of relevant info/knowledge in order to perform and improve…" (Orbitalrpm, 2009).

Another emerging trend is business is that of social learning. Training departments are no longer considered to hold the primary accountability for the learning function within organizations. Additionally, the requirement for instant information has often out-paced the rate of a training department's ability to identify and respond to training needs. Organizational learning efficiency is increased when individual employees identify and satisfy their specific learning needs. Bingham, ASTD CEO (as cited in Ketter, 2010) states:

Historically, the learning community has stayed away from informal learning and social learning, and that is where most of the learning is taking place. We now have the tools, and the catalysts, to engage [employees] with that kind of learning. I think that is going to help the learning community take it to the next level.

Lave and Wagner (1991) encourage social learning through Communities of Practice (CoPs), which they define as a process of sharing information and experiences with the group in which the members learn from each other, and have an opportunity to develop themselves personally and professionally. The authors suggests that CoPs can exist online with activities such as discussion boards and newsgroups, or in face-to-face environments such as the lunch room at work, in a field setting, or on a factory floor.

Leveraging diversity within an organization is a major component of maintaining a competitive advantage when each individual's exceptionalities are recognized, addressed, and oftentimes celebrated.

Organizational success results from individual performance and productivity, and as such, efficiency has become a key expectation. To function efficiently in our current world of work, mastering the workplace learning strategies spectrum is becoming critical. Successful and upwardly mobile employees will demonstrate competencies in all three clusters of the spectrum: the capacity to plan and organize proficiently, to create viable and effective solutions to workplace challenges, and to engage others in the social and political processes to improve individual and organizational productivity.

CONCLUSION

Recognizing, celebrating, and leveraging the diversity among individual employees regarding their strengths and ongoing training needs in workplace learning strategy development provides a profitable return on investment for both individual employee career advancement and for collaborative organizational results. Healthy organizations that communicate an appreciation of diversity enjoy employees who are engaged, self-directed, high performers with a willingness to learn and a desire to make valuable contributions to the overarching sustainability and success of the company.

Organizations that promote the concept of learning how to learn in the workplace demonstrate an appreciation of individual capacity. Employees most often respond well to being treated with this level of respect and dignity and this validation frequently translates into increased job satisfaction, employee retention, productivity, customer satisfaction, and profitability.

Employees, especially those in succession for leadership roles, have the metacognitive roadmap to learn the varied functions within their roles once they master the three clusters of learning strategies contained within the workplace learning strategy spectrum. The foundation of workplace learning is metacognitive awareness and the spectrum enhances awareness to develop skills to plan and organize, to creatively solve problems, and to maintain healthy professional relationships. Acquiring these skills sets has value added benefits in that employees might also transfer these workplace learning skills to their personal lives, facilitating development both personally and in the workplace.

REFERENCES

Armstrong, N. (2001). *Learning strategy preferences of international graduate students at Oklahoma State University*. Unpublished Doctoral Dissertation. Norman, OK: Oklahoma State University.

Bighorn, R. (1997). *Learning strategies in the Fort Peck reservation community*. Unpublished Doctoral Dissertation. Bozeman, MT: Montana State University.

Blake, R., & Mouton, J. (1972a). What is instrumented learning? Part I--Learning instruments. *Industrial Training International, 7*(4), 113–116.

Bloom, B., Mesia, B., & Krathwohl, D. (1964). *Taxonomy of educational objectives*. New York, NY: David McKay Co Inc.

Brookfield, S. (1987). *Developing critical thinkers*. San Francisco, CA: Jossey-Bass.

Conti, G., & Fellenz, R. (1991). Assessing adult learning strategies. In *Proceedings of the 32nd Annual Adult Education Research Conference*. Norman, OK: University of Oklahoma.

Conti, G., & Kolody, R. (1998). Development of an instrument for identifying groups of learners. In *Proceedings of the 39th Annual Adult Education Research Conference*, (pp. 109-114). San Antonio, TX: Sacred Heart University.

Conti, G., & Kolody, R. (1999). *Guide for using ATLAS*. Stillwater, OK: Oklahoma State University.

Conti, G., & Kolody, R. (2004). Guidelines for selecting methods and techniques. In Galbraith, M. W. (Ed.), *Adult Learning Method* (3rd ed., pp. 181–192). Malabar, FL: Krieger.

Conti, G., Kolody, R., & Schneider, B. (1997). Learning strategies in the corporate setting. In *Proceedings of the 38th Annual Adult Education Research Conference*, (pp. 67-72). Stillwater, OK: Oklahoma State University.

Courtnage, L. (1998). *Advertising industry survey: Learning strategies of advertising sales people*. Unpublished Doctoral Dissertation. Bozeman, MT: Montana State University.

Fellenz, R., & Conti, G. (1993). *Self-knowledge inventory of lifelong learning strategies (SKILLS): Manual*. Bozeman, MT: Center for Adult Learning Research.

Ghost Bear, A. (2001). *Adult learning on the Internet: Engaging the eBay auction process*. Unpublished Doctoral Dissertation. Stillwater, OK: Oklahoma State University.

Gill, S. (2010, February 8). What gets measured gets done...or not. *The Performance Improvement Blog*. Retrieved from http://stephenjgill.typepad.com/performance_improvement_b/2010/02/what-gets-measured-gets-doneor-not.html.

Hinds, B. (2001). *Learning strategies in the African-American community of Enid, Oklahoma*. Unpublished Doctoral Dissertation. Stillwater, OK: Oklahoma State University.

Ketter, P. (2010). *Six trends that will change workplace learning forever*. Retrieved from http://www.astd.org/LC/2010/1210_ketter.htm.

Kolody, R. (1997). *Learning strategies of Alberta college students*. Unpublished Doctoral Dissertation. Bozeman, MT: Montana State University.

Korinek, D. (1997). *An investigation of learning strategies utilized by Air Force officers*. Unpublished Doctoral Dissertation. Bozeman, MT: Montana State University.

Lave, J., & Wenger, E. (1991). *Situated learning: Legitimate peripheral participation*. Cambridge, UK: Cambridge University Press.

Lively, S. (2001). *Learning, growing, and aging: Lifelong learners in the Academy of Senior Professionals in Bethany, Oklahoma*. Unpublished Doctoral Dissertation. Stillwater, OK: Oklahoma State University.

Lockwood, S. (1997). *An investigation of learning strategies utilized by nursing students in Montana*. Unpublished Doctoral Dissertation. Bozeman, MT: Montana State University.

McKeachie, W. (1988). The need for study strategy training. In Weinstein, C., Goetz, E., & Alexander, P. (Eds.), *Learning and Study Strategies*. San Diego, CA: Academic Press.

McNeil, R. (2011). The use of learning strategies in a learner-centered classroom. In *Proceedings of the 9th Hawaii International Conference on Education*, (pp. 4383-4393). Honolulu, HI: Hawaii International.

McNulty, J. (2009). *Workplace learning in 10 years – My thoughts*. Retrieved from http://www.orbitalrpm.com/2009/workplace-learning-in-10-years-my-thoughts.

Mezirow, J. (1990). How critical reflection triggers transformative learning. In Mezirow, (Eds.), *Fostering Critical Reflection in Adulthood*. San Francisco, CA: Jossey-Bass.

Michaels, E., Handfield-Jones, H., & Axelrod, B. (2001). *The war for talent*. Boston, MA: Harvard Business Press.

Orbitalrpm. (2009). *Website*. Retrieved from http://www.orbitalrpm.com/2009/workplace-learning-in-10-years-my-thoughts/.

Paul, R., & Elder, L. (2009). *The miniature guide to critical thinking concepts and tools* (5th ed.). Dillon Beach, CA: Foundation for Critical Thinking Press.

Sanders, P. (2008). *The decision-making styles, ways of knowing, and learning strategy preferences of clients at a one-stop career center*. Unpublished Doctoral Dissertation. Stillwater, OK: Oklahoma State University.

Schön, D. (1983). *The reflective practitioner: How professionals think in action*. New York, NY: Basic Books.

Smith, R. (1983). *Learning how to learn*. Milton Keynes, UK: Open University Press.

Stalinski, S. (2004). Leveraging diversity: Moving from compliance to performance. *Journal for Quality and Participation, 27*(4), 14.

Sternberg, R., & Grigorenko, E. (1997). Are cognitive styles still in style? *The American Psychologist, 52*, 700–712. doi:10.1037/0003-066X.52.7.700

Tough, A. (1971). *The adult's learning project*. Toronto, Canada: The Ontario Institute for Studies in Education.

Ungricht, T. (1997). *Learning strategies of concurrent enrollment students at Utah Valley State College*. Unpublished Doctoral Dissertation. Bozeman, MT: Montana State University.

Willyard, P. (2000). *Learning strategies of first-generation community college students*. Unpublished Doctoral Dissertation. Stillwater, OK: Oklahoma State University.

Wingfield, A., & Byrnes, D. (1981). *The psychology of human memory*. New York, NY: Academic Press.

Yussen, S. (1985). The role of metacognition in contemporary theories of cognitive development. In Forrext-Pressley, D. L., MacKinnon, G., & Waller, T. (Eds.), *Metacognition, Cognition, and Human Performance* (*Vol. 1*). Orlando, FL: Academic Press.

ADDITIONAL READING

Bingham, T., & Conner, M. (2010). *The new social learning*. Alexandria, VA: ASTD Press.

Govaerts, N., Kyndt, E., Dochy, F., & Baert, H. (2011). Influence of learning and working climate on the retention of talented employees. *Journal of Workplace Learning, 23*(1), 35–55.

Illeris, K. (2011). *The fundamentals of workplace learning: Understanding how people learn in working life*. New York, NY: Routledge.

Kearsley, G., & Shneiderman, B. (1999). *Engagement theory: A framework for technology-based teaching and learning*. Retrieved from http://home.sprynet.com/~gkearsley/engage.htm.

Kidd, J. R. (1973). *How adults learn* (2nd ed.). Chicago, IL: Follett.

Knowles, M. (1975). *Self-directed learners: A guide for learners and teachers*. Chicago, IL: Follett.

Knowles, M. (1980). *The modern practice of adult education: From pedagogy to andragogy.* Chicago, IL: Follet.

Kolb, D. (1984). *Experiential learning: Experience as the source of learning and development.* Englewood Cliffs, NJ: Prentice Hall.

Merriam, S. (2001). Andragogy and self-directed learning: Pillars of adult learning theory. In Merriam, S. B. (Ed.), *The New Update on Adult Learning Theory.* San Francisco, CA: Jossey-Bass. doi:10.1002/ace.3

Nuriddin, H. (2010). Learning theories have practical uses in the workplace. *Adult Education Examiner.* Retrieved from http://www.examiner.com/adult-education-in-national/learning-theories-have-practical-uses-the-workplace#ixzz1PhQlW1DS.

Raelin, J. (2008). *Work-based learning: Bridging knowledge and action in the workplace* (Revised Ed.). San Francisco, CA: Jossey-Bass.

Robinson, D., & Robinson, J. (1995). *Performance consulting: Moving beyond training.* San Francisco, CA: Berrett-Koehler.

Rowden, R. (2006). *Workplace learning: Principles and practice.* Malabar, FL: Krieger.

Sommerlad, E., & Stern, E. (1999). *Workplace learning, culture and performance.* London, UK: Institute of Personnel and Development.

Steensma, H., & Groeneveld, K. (2010). Evaluating a training using the four levels model. *Journal of Workplace Learning, 22*(5), 319–331. doi:10.1108/13665621011053226

Stolovitch, H., & Keeps, E. (2010). *Telling ain't training* (2nd ed.). Alexandria, VA: ASTD Press.

KEY TERMS AND DEFINITIONS

Adult Learning: Also referred to as Andragogy, the processes and learning principles specific to adults.

ATLAS: Assessing The Learning Strategies of Adults instrument. Developed in 1998 by Conti and Kolody, a self-scoring instrument to measure learning strategy preference.

Learning Strategies: The techniques and processes selected by the learner by which to achieve a specific learning objective.

Learning Strategy Preference Groups: Three differentiated groups of learners whose placement in a group is based upon the results of the ATLAS instrument to determine patterns and preferences of the learner.

Metacognition: Self-awareness of one's learning styles, preferences, patterns, and strategies.

SKILLS: Self Knowledge Inventory of Lifelong Learning Strategies, an instrument to measure learning strategy preference.

Workplace Learning: Learning strategies specific to a work environment such as performance management, leadership, and competency and capacity development.

Workplace Learning Strategies Spectrum: A collection of learning strategies that include examples of strategies from the Navigation, Problem-Solving, and Engagement clusters.

APPENDIX A: ATLAS Learning Strategy Quick Reference Guide

Table 1. ATLAS quick reference guide

5 Constructs	15 Learning Strategies
Metacognition – knowledge and control over one's thinking and learning	Planning – accepting responsibility and taking control over one's learning experience. *Learning Activities: overviewing, focusing on purpose, and acknowledging one's learning style*
	Monitoring – being cognizant of one's learning progress and closely monitor one's learning. *Learning Activities: self-testing, comparing progress from previous learning situations, asking for feedback, checking new resources for information, and keeping track of diverse steps in learning*
	Adjusting – modifying and revising learning plans in relationship to the evaluation of the learning progress. *Learning Activities: revising one's learning plan, changing learning strategies, restructuring learning to satisfy one's knowledge level*
Metamotivation – knowing and understanding how or why one is motivated to participate or remain in a learning activity	Attention – focused engagement. *Learning Activities: arousal of interest in learners, the stimulation of an attitude or inquiry, and the maintenance of attention*
	Reward/Enjoyment – anticipating or recognizing the value to one's self. *Learning Activities: identifying the benefits of the activity; reminding one's self of the meaningfulness of the activity to self or to others*
	Confidence – learner's perceptions of self-efficacy and self-control. *Learning Activities: using self talk to remind one's self of strengths and past successes that predict future success; approach new activities with a positive mindset*
Memory – the capacity of humans to retain and recall information, and recognize its familiarity when they later see it or hear it again	Organization – arranging the material to be learned in patterns that direct the retrieval process. *Learning Activities: patterns that direct the retrieval process such as mnemonics and chunking.*
	External Aids – reviewing materials. *Learning Activities: using appointment books, to-do lists, placing visual items on display, and asking others to provide reminders at relevant times.*
	Memory Application – using those internal strategies involved in Memory Organization for the purpose of planning, completing, and evaluating learning. *Learning Activities: repeating material to be learned; practicing applying content under a variety of circumstances*
Critical Thinking – a reflective thinking process utilizing higher order thinking skills in order to improve learning	Testing Assumptions – ability and willingness to challenge assumptions. *Learning Activities: identify relationships, spot inconsistencies, or question value sets.*
	Generating Alternatives – hypothesizing while grounding options. *Learning Activities: brainstorming or envisioning the future, ranking the order of alternatives, and identifying alternate solutions.*
	Conditional Acceptance – Advocating reflective skepticism to avoid absolutes or over simplifications. *Learning Activities: questioning simplistic answers and predicting consequences.*
Resource Management – management of resources to find solutions to real-life, everyday problems	Identification – judging whether obtaining the resource is equal in value to the time, energy, and expense in gathering it. *Learning Activities: compare options (electronic, paper, or people) for efficiency in information gathering methods*
	Critical Use – selection of the most appropriate resource. *Learning Activities: contacting an expert or an outsider, checking the information with a second source, and observing or asking questions to check for bias*
	Human Resources – integrating others into the social and political processes of learning. *Learning Activities: dialogue that involves listening to people with different opinions or insights, developing networks.*

Adapted from SKILLS (Fellenz & Conti, 1993)

APPENDIX B: Assessing the Learning Strategies of AdultS

Directions: Read the sentence stem in the box, and choose the option that best applies to you. Follow the arrow to the next box (Figure 3).

Figure 3. ATLAS

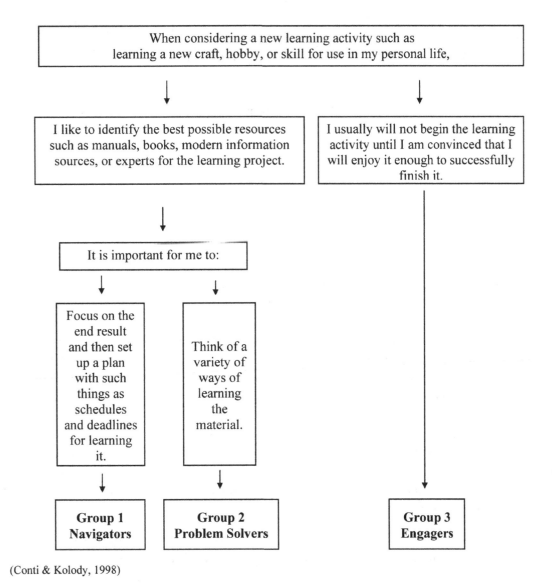

(Conti & Kolody, 1998)

Chapter 14
Training and Development:
Leveraging Diversity to Gain Strategic Advantage in Corporate Settings

Denise R. Philpot
University of North Texas, USA

Laura A. Pasquini
University of North Texas, USA

ABSTRACT

Organizations, in their strategic plans to gain competitive advantage, must utilize training and development initiatives that recognize and exploit the current diversity of the entity as well as developing trends that will impact future operations (Wentling & Palma-Rivas, 1997). Unfortunately, in many organizations, these initiatives are frequently the victim of cost cutting measures in a tough economy. It is critical that organizations design and implement programs that recognize the diversity of the organization and the customers they serve. It is important to consider how training and development models can support any desired organizational outcomes and diversity objectives. As our definition of diversity changes, this evolution and its impact on training and development curriculum will challenge organizations to review learning curriculum trends, program goals, expenditures, organizational commitment, and achievement. Because of these changes, training professionals should continuously assess learning outcomes, analyze the results, and implement improvements as indicated.

As the world becomes smaller through globalization and the definition of diversity expands to accommodate new dimensions, it becomes increasingly important to identify and measure these changes and interpret how they influence strategic decision-making within organizations. To achieve an organization's stated goals, it is not only important to recognize this diversity, but also build programs to incorporate the benefits of diversity while minimizing any negative aspects associated with this construct. Sharing case studies of best practices will highlight successes that can be used as models for those organizations

DOI: 10.4018/978-1-4666-1812-1.ch014

that are addressing their training needs in the area of organizational diversity. This chapter will share tools designed to help organizations evaluate their needs in terms of diversity training and development. These resources can help training and development professionals identify needs, design curriculum, create evaluation tools for assessment, and evaluate costs to deploy strategic training and development programs.

INTRODUCTION

In today's corporate world, organizations need to create value and develop innovative practices that will lead to a competitive advantage in the marketplace. To manage effectively, organizations must value diversity and make it an integral part of the organization (Gilbert, Stead, & Ivancevich, 1999). By using diversity management strategies in training and development programs, corporations have the ability to enhance their organizational effectiveness and maximize profits. Cox and Blake (1991) indicated that diversity management can lead to the following competitive advantages for organizations: cost savings, resource acquisition, marketing success, enhanced creativity, and problem-solving and system flexibility.

As a result of this paradigm shift, many corporate settings are creating a culture which values and appreciates diversity in the workplace. Organizational benefits for managing cultural diversity to achieve competitive advantage include cost reduction, effective use of recruitment resources, and cultural insight among all employee groups, increased problem-solving capability, and promotion of system flexibility (Gilbert, Stead, & Ivancevich, 1999). The presence of a diverse organization allows a corporation to reach a broader consumer base and market share. When implemented appropriately, training and development initiatives that support diversity management strategies have the potential to dramatically enhance an organizational structure and achieve the objectives of all stakeholders.

Another way to interpret how an organization uses human resources to support the organizational objectives is to determine if an HR system is utilized. According to Lepak, Liao, Yunhyang, and Harden (2006), an HR system is comprised of the organization's HR practices and policies. An example of an HR practice that supports diversity training is making diversity training part of the onboarding process for all new employees as well as refresher courses during the course of employment. The corresponding HR policy that supports that practice would be a policy that requires all new hires to attend training sessions designed to introduce the new employee to the organizational culture, code of conduct, business practices, and commitment to diversity in the workplace. The HR system, comprised of the HR policies and practices that support the strategic goals of the organization, should influence an employee's knowledge, skills, abilities, motivation and effort, and create opportunities for employees to contribute in a meaningful way to the overall success of the organization (Lepak, et al., 2006).

This chapter will address the subject of diversity management strategies as it directly relates to training and development initiatives within the corporate setting. Further, the authors seek to widen the definition of diversity to support the growth of an effective training and development program that utilizes theory, systems, processes, and tools to advance organizational learning and support effective human resource practices.

MODEL DEVELOPMENT

Definitions for Understanding

To best discuss the area of training and development, with respect to leveraging diversity, it is necessary to define a few terms that the authors will be utilizing throughout this chapter. Although there may be other specific definitions for commonality and referencing we will define these terms used in this chapter. Training and development is the process of systematically teaching employees to acquire and improve job-related skills and knowledge set by specific learning and performance outcomes (Greenberg, 2011). Today the term diversity represents much more than age, gender, ethnicity, or religious beliefs. Diversity now encompasses various levels of education, experience, technical skills, and learning preferences. These are just a few of the considerations that must be incorporated into effective training and development programs (Kormanik & Rajan, 2010).

Diversity management is a voluntary organizational program designed to create greater inclusion of all individuals into informal social networks and formal company programs, and is an intentional design to foster appreciation of demographic, ethnic, and individual differences (Gilbert, Stead, & Ivancevich, 1999). Many organizations create diversity management programs that promote recognition and appreciation of the differences between people and encourage the creation of a supportive work environment (Greenberg, 2011). The term organization refers to a structured social system consisting of groups and individuals working together to meet objectives (Greenberg, 2011).

Diversity Management

Corporations interested in diversity management strategies need to consider this a complete organizational culture change, rather than an isolated component. To accomplish cultural change it is important to consider current procedures, practices, and human resources with regards to the organizational model (Gilbert, Stead, & Ivancevich, 1999). The integrated model (Figure 1) provides an example for incorporating diversity management practices into an organization.

Figure 1 is an example of the common human resource systems targeted at diversity management programs. Benefits of effectively managed diversity can also impact other areas, including orga-

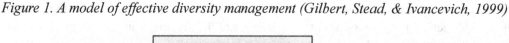

Figure 1. A model of effective diversity management (Gilbert, Stead, & Ivancevich, 1999)

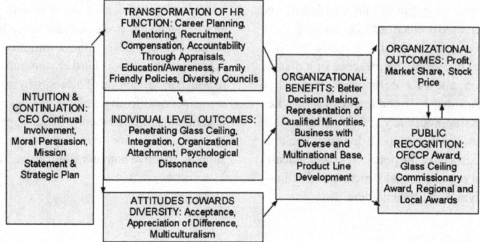

nizational outcomes. The purpose for diversity strategies in training and development programs is to foster employee integration and support development across the work environment. By considering how diversity fits into your training and development program, human resource departments can support other objectives within the organization's culture.

Corporate training and development programs need to consider diversity needs and how employees identify with the organizational group. Social capital, which is a derivative of social identity theory and related theories on the self, plays a vital role in the development of more cooperative relationships within groups and organizations (Kramer, 2006). Organizational processes that allow accommodations for individuals will create value in its workforce. Employers that recognize the impacts of social capital and an individual's psychological identification with a work environment, enhance their willingness to engage in behaviors and increase performance within that particular organization (Kramer, 2006). As employees feel individually appreciated and valued, their contributions to the organization accumulate.

Training and Development: Organizational Strategic Plan

It is important that human resource departments and organizational leaders consider innovative and sustainable practices to best support the organizational goals. Increasingly, a large number of corporations now encourage creative thinking and different application strategies to help enhance the workplace. Innovative thinking strategies can translate into solutions of change and support corporate values, policies, programs, and initiatives, such as diversity management.

Diversity training can be developed as part of diversity awareness training or diversity skills-based training. Diversity awareness training is intended to raise the awareness level of employees regarding the various diversity issues being ad-

dressed such as gender, age, ethnicity, orientation, or religion. This type of training often begins with a self-assessment that is used to help participants recognize their biases and assumptions regarding stereotypes. Diversity skills-based training is used to improve the skills employees need to be successful in the workplace and can include communication skills, negotiation skills, and problem solving or conflict resolution skills. As a training and development professional, knowing which type of training is needed and promoting it appropriately to management and employees is key to the success of the training events (Williams, 2011).

When designing a strategic plan for training and development, it is important to consider the innovative diagnostics constructs outlined in Figure 2 for effecting organization growth.

The fundamental organizational practice for successful innovation is visible commitment from senior management to establish and promote innovative culture (SHRM, 2009). As the work environment population is expanding, it is important to consider the various employee populations corporations are now required to manage. In considering sustainable practices such as diversity management, it is critical to include strategies, processes, resources and organizational culture into your plan. It will be necessary for human resource departments to guide the evolution of strategic planning, specifically to support organizational learning, rewards and evaluation metrics (SHRM, 2009).

Organizational Commitment to Diversity

It is not enough to verbalize an organization's commitment diversity. Diversity within an organization, broadly defined, encompasses race/ethnicity, gender, age, religion, knowledge/skill level, intellectual/physical ability, job function, and tenure. Organizations have evolved from mandated compliance in the 1960s to voluntary inclu-

Figure 2. Assessing strategic plan and innovation diagnostics tool (adopted from the SHRM model for assessing organizational innovation policies and strategies, 2009)

What is the Strategy?	☐ Yes	☐ No	• Are innovation initiatives clearly aligned with the strategic plans of the organization? • Is management support for the innovative strategy visible and understood by employees? • Do employees understand customer needs and how those needs drive the innovation strategy? • Is there a tangible relationship between customer needs, innovation strategy and organizational goals?
Do the Processes support the strategy?	☐ Yes	☐ No	• Are there processes that promote idea generation? • Do the established processes support fast innovation, quality control and process improvement, and idea screening based upon a defined standard? • Are project management tools used to support processes and effective implementation? • Does the work team review processes for gaps and compliance?
Effective use of Resources	☐ Yes	☐ No	• To ensure the most effective use of resources, are business and technology departments aligned and engaged in collaborative efforts supporting innovation? • Is there diversity in staffing to ensure nontraditional perspectives are represented in design and implementation teams? • Does training and development support core competencies and increase in knowledge and skills? • Are partnerships developed to support innovation growth and goal achievement?
Have the Organizational needs been met?	☐ Yes	☐ No	• Does the current leadership support and embrace innovation? • Is the appropriate reward system in place that includes incentives for innovation? • Are senior managers held accountable for collaboration and success of innovation projects? • Are successes publicized with benefits documented and continued innovation success promoted throughout the organization?

sion and recognition of the benefits gained from embracing and promoting diversity (Lockwood, 2005). The challenge is to strike the right balance between seeing everyone as the same while recognizing, appreciating, and utilizing what makes everyone unique. Organizations that successfully embrace diversity may enjoy the many benefits, measured in a variety of ways, including improved employee retention, increased employee motivation/satisfaction, effective succession planning, positive community engagement/recognition, and a strategic advantage in the marketplace (Dass & Parker, 1999).

Human capital is an organization's most valuable asset. The labor pool in the United States has changed dramatically in the last 50 years. The U.S. labor market has shifted to include more women and minorities, with 34% of the U.S. workforce predicted to be non-Caucasian by 2010 (Hewitt, 2004). Our workforce is also aging with the largest growth in the 45-64 age group and a very slight decline in the 18-44 age group. Many organizations have four generations represented in their labor force including Baby Boomers, Generation X, Generation Y, and Millenials. Each of these groups have distinct characteristics that present both management and training challenges as well as many opportunities to embrace the strengths each group brings to the workplace. As with any type of change, an organization that can simultaneously recognize the changes in their workforce and adapt their processes, procedures, and training to meet these evolving needs, will position the organization to do more than simply sustain (see Table 1).

Corporate America is not the only sector addressing diversity among their employee groups. The Federal Government is also aware of their employee demographics and has created initiatives to promote diversity and inclusion in the workplace. These goals include diversity training for all employees and recruitment and selection activities designed to attract applicants from all demographic profiles. Table 2 contains the demographics, as collected by the Office of Personnel Management (OPM) for the federal government. These numbers reflect an increase of 9.4% of minorities at the senior pay levels including 31.2% of senior-level positions held by women. Like their corporate counterparts, OPM is developing student recruitment programs, sharing best practices within federal agencies, and focusing on diversity management and leadership development (Pace, 2011).

A complicated challenge for any training and development professional is both recognizing and sharing how diversity issues can impact an organization. The forward-thinking professional will champion the importance of the well-trained workforce enabled by the strategic implementation of learning at all levels of the organization. In support of diversity initiatives, successful orga-

nizations link diversity to business goals (HRFocus, 2010). Finding the appropriate measures to demonstrate the value of diversity to the organization presents some of the same challenges that are experienced when looking for the best way to show the value of training and development.

In the recent Global Diversity and Inclusion survey conducted by SHRM (2009), 53% of the respondents believe it is important to tap into the broad range of employee backgrounds and skill sets to improve internal efficiency. Of these same respondents, 47% saw diversity as a matter of fairness and doing the right thing. This same group indicated that they needed to be mindful of diversity with their customers/vendors. When asked to identify categories of diversity, 79% of the respondents identified women as the most important minority group. Additional groups identified in the survey as a focus for diversity management included individuals of 50 years of age or more (46% considered this group a target group) and ethnic minorities which were considered important by 39% of the respondents. Filho, Lockwood, and Williams (2009) developed an assessment matrix that includes 4 levels of diversity development and 4 stages of corporate diversity development. Use of this tool can help an organization determine the types of initiatives necessary to reach diversity goals. It is important to note that global organizations will need to make

Table 1. US demographic projections as reported by the National Center for Public Policy and Higher Education (2005)

Demographic group	Actual population in 1980	Projected population in 2020
Whites	82%	63%
All Minorities	18%	37%
African-Americans	10%	13%
Hispanics/Latinos	6%	17%
Asian-Americans	2%	6%
Native Americans	0.6%	0.8%

Table 2. Federal workforce demographics, fiscal year 2010 (Source: Office of Personnel Management)

White	66.2%
Black	17.7%
Hispanic	8%
Asian/Pacific Islander	5.6%
Native American	1.8%
Non-Hispanic/Multiracial	0.7%
Men	56.1%
Women	43.9%

assessments and design interventions locally as each country of operation will have different needs and solutions (see Figure 3).

As organizations embrace diversity, resources are committed to ensure initiatives are successful and goals are met. It is estimated that diversity training expenditures have exceeded $8 billion annually (Hansen, 2003). Many organizations have created programs and/or have dedicated staff such as a Director of Equity and Diversity, whose primary function is to ensure that the organization not only is legally compliant but also achieves diversity goals, provides training and support to HR, and tracks both successes and opportunities for improvement as the organization grows and changes. Konrad (2003) believed that three primary arguments could be made for implementing diversity initiatives. These include the competitive nature of the job market and the need to reach out to a diverse labor pool, employing a labor pool that reflects the diversity of your customer base, and unleashing the creative talents of your em-

ployees through their diverse demographics. One could also argue that embracing diversity, at the organizational level, is simply the right thing to do, regardless of the legal requirements to do so (Jayne & Dipboye, 2004).

Strategic Management Responses

Three different strategic responses for implementing diversity initiatives have been proposed by Dass and Parker (1999). Each approach is based upon the organization's perception of their need to implement diversity initiatives based upon internal and external pressures. At the lowest level, The Episodic Approach is generally used when there are few pressures and diversity is viewed by management as a marginal issue. Programs and actions tend to be isolated, disjointed, and do not necessarily support or reflect the organizational mission or vision. When moderate pressures are present, management may adopt The Freestanding Approach. This approach can result in a

Figure 3. Global diversity assessment matrix (Filho, Lockwood, & Williams, 2009)

		Ethnocentric ⟵————————————————————⟶ Geocentric				
Stages of Diversity Development	Empower and leverage					Strategic ⟰ ⟱ Tactical
	Learn from diversity					
	Accept and value					
	Comply					
		Domestic	Import/Export	International/ Multinational	Global	
		• Differences in work style and language • Difference domestic ethnic markets • Scan globally for competitors	• Cross-cultural business practices • Differences in language • Local practices alignment with headquarters • Public relations / image management	• Cross-cultural values, norms and business practices • Differences in language and HR laws • Cross-border employee exchange • Workforce development	• Cross-border systems integration • Global leadership development and worldwide staffing • Communication • Balancing corporate culture with national /regional perspectives	
		Stages of Corporate Development and Diversity Issues				

multitude of programs that are not effectively linked to organizational goals. It is critical to link the freestanding programs to diversity objectives and ensure that benefits outweigh sanctions. The third response, The Systemic Approach, is usually adopted by executives that respond to the high pressures for diversity and view diversity as a strategic issue. The key to this approach is linking diversity initiatives with existing programs and processes. This comprehensive approach should be flexible, fully integrated, and include rewards as well as consequences for non-compliance. As with any model, organizations can exhibit different responses based upon a particular set of circumstances. The right solution for an organization will evolve as the internal and external pressures change and are satisfied by management responses and organizational culture embracing diversity as a strategic advantage.

On the surface, it is not only logical to develop and implement a diversity strategy but would seem to be essential in today's global business environment. A diversity strategy of inclusion that embraces and leverages employee uniqueness is different than policies and practices that address legal requirements such as equal employment opportunities and affirmative action (Jayne & Dipboye, 2004). As organizations work to evaluate their strategies and programs, what is lacking is strong empirical evidence that successful implementation of these strategies leads to the desired outcomes. In addition, the level of assessment and evaluation needs to be considered, as some assessments can be done quickly while others require both time and newly developed measurement tools. For example, it is easy to track where recruiting efforts are focused as well as the demographics of both new and current employees. Organizations can also compare their demographics with that of their communities and customer base. What becomes more difficult is to measure how diversity policies and practices impact organizational

outcomes. Can the increase in market share be traced directly to diversity practices or is it a function of other economic factors, market maturity, or product enhancements?

Suggested Practices

Research provides us with some insights into best practices that have been shown to lead to desired outcomes of diversity strategies. Diversity strategies, like other organizational initiatives, are most likely to be successfully implemented when they receive senior management support and include accountability measures at the highest level of the organization (Jayne & Dipboye, 2004). Line managers must be active supporters of the initiatives and be accountable for leveraging diversity to achieve organizational goals. They must support training initiatives as well as building teams that effectively utilize the contributions made by members representing diverse demographics. As you would with any initiative, a thorough needs assessment should be conducted to understand the current state of the organization with respect to diversity. All aspects about the workforce would be included in addition to demographics, so that the analysis captures knowledge, skills, attributes, tenure, job scope/description, and employee attitudes/perceptions. This assessment is a critical component in developing the organization's diversity strategy. In addition, when developing the organization's diversity strategy, success must be tied to business results. Business results should include more measures than just revenue and profit. Key measures of success might include improved retention rates, increased employee satisfaction, reduced absenteeism, reduced discrimination and harassment litigation, and high levels of employee engagement. Richard (2000) found a positive link between racial diversity and firm performance for those organizations that implemented a growth strategy. The important finding documented in his study was the positive relationship between racial diversity and growth strategies. Organizations that were downsizing did not have the same positive experiences with racial diversity.

Key to the success of any new or updated strategy/initiative, employee training and team building must be developed. With the desired goal of a diverse employee population, special care must be taken to capitalize on the unique benefits that these employees bring to the workplace. Team-building activities can promote understanding and appreciation of the contributions each member can make with the understanding that the sum is greater than the parts. Developing "interpersonal congruence" will ensure team members perceive that both their skills and the unique skills of their team members are in sync with one another, which can lead to improved creative task performance (Polzer, Milton, & Swann, 2002).

Managers must also be trained to facilitate team conflicts, engage in effective communications, and anticipate potential challenges diverse teams may experience (Jayne & Dipboye, 2004). Realistic expectations should be included in this training as results will not be achieved overnight and sometimes it may take months before the diverse group is able to take advantage of the strengths of each team member in creating solutions to complex problems. Finally, to evaluate the success of the strategy, meaningful metrics must be developed. This is perhaps the most difficult part of developing the diversity strategy.

Many organizations often fail to collect sufficient data to analyze the effects of the strategy on organizational outcomes. Whether it is because they fear the results will not justify the investment or they are worried an undesirable situation will be uncovered, it is important to examine the results and make modifications as necessary. Employees want to see that the organization is truly committed to diversity and that program failures will

be addressed and resolved. Successes should be celebrated and rewards should be commensurate with the significance of milestones achieved. As with any strategy, time is a necessary component for sustained results and benefits integration into work processes.

Diversity Advantage

Yang (2005) has defined the diversity advantage based upon the human resource advantage concept. Diversity advantage is defined as the rare value from a relatively immobile and appropriable diverse work force. To be fully realized, this specific type of human resource advantage is derived from successful diversity management. Included in the diversity advantage is diversity capital and process advantages. Of importance here is the concept of diversity capital, the organization's superior composition of different demographic groups that can ensure the organization outperforms its competitors in terms of the availability of a variety of knowledge, skills and perspectives. Closely tied to the diversity capital advantage is the diversity process advantage. This represents the superior problem solving and social integration and communication processes derived from different demographic groups that can help an organization to execute operations more quickly, efficiently, and effectively, ultimately outperforming the competition (Yang, 2005).

In support of this concept, Yang examines several diversity management structures and presents theories explaining the relationship between these structures and diversity advantage. The most advantageous structure, configurationally diversity structures, benefit the most from an organization's diversity capital advantage yielding a very strong positive outcome that is greater than the sum of the strategic and institutional diversity structures.

IMPLEMENTATION MODEL

Case Study: IBM

There is abundant evidence that many companies embraced diversity before it was recognized as a way to gain a strategic advantage in the labor market and guard against competitors. IBM, a corporate giant, led the way in 1953 with a letter from Tom Watson, Jr. to his management team regarding a conversation he had with two southern governors involving the negotiation of tax incentives to build manufacturing plants. In his letter he emphasized that there would not be "equal but separate" treatment of minorities at IBM. This was not the first time IBM took a stand in favor of diversity.

In 1899, IBM hired their first female and black employees (Childs, 2005). This commitment to diversity has not wavered and continues to be a cornerstone of IBM's business strategy. All employees must complete a diversity training program annually. A $50 million Global Work/Life Fund Strategy was implemented in 2000 to address basic child and dependent care needs of employees. Over $1.3 billion has been spent on developing their supplier diversity programs of which about 20% was spent outside of the United States. In May, 2010, DiversityInc named IBM the number one company for global diversity. Diversity 3.0 is IBM's current version of the policies and practices that support diversity at all levels and in all countries where they do business.

Case Study: Texas Instruments

The technology innovator, Texas Instruments, has a well-known practice of inclusion as the foundation of its diversity strategy. With annual results published in their corporate citizen report, TI shares their commitment to diversity and inclusion both internally and externally. Rich Templeton, Chairman and CEO, promotes the importance of diversity through a globally inclusive environment

that is based upon trust. He is the sponsor of the TI Diversity Network and actively participates in recruiting efforts based upon diversity initiatives. TI firmly believes that their competitive edge comes from recognizing and developing the talents of people from different backgrounds, experiences, and perspectives (2011). At TI, every employee is expected to promote an environment of inclusiveness, respecting the individual and valuing the contributions of all team members. Because of the global nature of their business, they acknowledge that workforce diversity is unique to each location and country but that all business entities must have appropriate strategies in place to create an inclusive work environment. In addition to traditional diversity workshops, TI educates employees about a variety of diversity topics through newsletters, conferences, emails, brochures, and their internal diversity website.

As proof of their commitment to diversity, TI has significantly increased the number of women and minorities in management positions in the last 20 years. At the end of 2010, the TI board included four women, one of which is a woman of color. At the officer level, 20 percent are women and 15 percent are minority. At the heart of innovation and research at TI, more than 5 percent of the TI Fellows are women or people of color. TI has received many forms of recognition for their commitment to diversity including being named as a "Most Admired Employer" by US Black Engineer, Hispanic Engineer, and Women of Color magazines (Texas Instruments, 2011).

Research Initiative

While companies like IBM lead the way in their commitment to diversity, companies that are still developing their diversity strategies look to empirical research to help guide them in their efforts. In 1996, a group of executives and human resource professionals formed a non-profit organization called Building Opportunities for Leadership Development (BOLD) Initiative to learn more about leveraging diversity to gain competitive advantage in the marketplace. They began a large-scale, longitudinal field research study in 1997 to address the lack of empirical data to support commonly held beliefs about the impact of diversity strategies (Kochan, et al., 2002). Not surprising, during the course of their review of existing research, BOLD found conflicting results in terms of diversity initiatives and positive impact on the organization. Also frustrating was the lack of empirical data to support either case as many organizations either did not collect the data necessary to support their assumptions or were reluctant to release it due to fears of legal repercussions. The research team developed a model, shown in Figure 4, to explain the complex relationship between diversity and business outcomes.

Human resource policies and practices, which include training and development activities, is a key moderator in this relationship. According to the BOLD team, HR practices that support a diverse workforce by recruiting and hiring the skills necessary to embrace diversity and then providing the necessary training to enable these groups to be successful, have the potential to lead to positive performance outcomes. Conversely, human resource practices that are only focused on organizational diversity, without providing diversity management training, are likely to experience

negative performance outcomes. To test their model, BOLD set out to study a variety of Fortune 500 companies. Knowing that the data they hoped to capture was sensitive in nature, they were able to engage four major organizations in the study. Two companies were in the information processing industry, the third company was a major financial services firm and the fourth a large retail operation.

The participating organizations were all different and participated in different ways. One provided data they collected on their own activities including demographics, training, performance numbers, and employee satisfaction. Others allowed the researchers to distribute surveys and access employees for interviews. Each organization was large enough to provide large enough samples so that data could be analyzed and validated for each organization. All of the organizations embraced diversity with commitment evidenced by executive behaviors and company policies. All organizations focused primarily on two aspects of diversity: gender and race[1].

The first organization, an information processing firm with over 26,000 employees, has embraced diversity for over 70 years. In the late 1980s, the organization became aware of advancement issues for women and minorities. In addition to the resource groups what were formed to advance

Figure 4. The effects of diversity of group processes and outcomes model (Kochan, et al., 2002)

the interests of women and minorities, a Diversity Task Force was created in 1992. Diversity plans, created by an employee council, are created every year with end of year results reported for each business unit. Diversity is a topic in each unit's internal newsletter. Managers create Development Plans for work groups and address diversity and training needs. These same unit/group leaders evaluate their leadership competencies in areas that include diversity, organizational cultures, and human resource practices. This organization has embraced and valued diversity for a very long time. Surprisingly, the data analysis yielded results that showed no significant direct effects of either racial or gender diversity on performance. One very important finding had to do with the impact of training and development activities relating to diversity issues. While these activities, including training, coaching, open communications, and providing challenging assignments did not increase positive results, they were shown to reduce negative effects of racial diversity on constructive group processes. Also, in support of training activities that focused on career development and diversity management, the negative relationship between racial diversity and group processes was largely absent in groups that received appropriate training.

The next organization that participated was a large financial services firm with dozens of retail branches. Not only does this company have a wonderful record for embracing diversity, the CEO chairs the Diversity Council and all senior managers are held accountable for managing their region's formal diversity plan which includes components addressing education, recruiting, succession planning, career development and business growth. The organization is committed to diversity and focuses recruiting efforts designed to target populations represented in the communities in which they do business. They have established relationships with Historically Black Colleges and their internship program provides opportunities for both high school and college students.

An important detail about this organization is that 480 retail branch locations are staffed primarily by women. These operations ranged in size from 4 to 70 employees, with an average of 15, of which 83% were women and the racial composition included 49% Caucasian. The data used to analyze the organization was archival, collected by the company in 1999, 2000, and 2001. Included in this data were demographics, the results from their employee attitude-satisfaction survey, and branch performance data used to allocate bonuses. Based upon prior theories, the BOLD researchers expected to see higher levels of performance in branches that adopted the integration-and-learning perspective as this perspective provides the rationale and guidance needed to achieve sustained benefits from diversity (Kochan, et al., 2002). Focusing on the results that can be linked to training and development, there was a positive relationship between racial diversity and higher overall performance in branches that implemented and promoted the integration-and-learning perspective on diversity. Branches that leveraged racial diversity as a resource for innovation and learning had a positive relationship between diversity and overall performance. This supports that concept that an organization that promotes racial diversity learning programs can benefit even when commitment to diversity is deeply embedded within the organization.

The third organization that participated in this research study, also an information processing firm, provided data from their U.S. sales and service employees (sales n=3970 employees; service n=8636 employees). As with the first two studies, this organization was known for its commitment to diversity. Their U.S. workforce is comprised of 33% females, 17% African Americans, and fewer than 10% Hispanics. Annual targets are set for achieving diversity goals with representation expectations at every level of the organization. There were a very low percentage of female employees in service (6%) while the sales force was over one third female. Because of the differences in the nature of the work and the overall differences in the demographics of the groups, sales and service were analyzed separately. Performance measures for the sales teams were goal achievement and sales-based bonuses. The service performance measures were tied to machine performance and service response times. This organization was evaluated at both the team level and larger organizational units. At the team level, there was no statistically significant relationship between diversity and team processes or team performance. However, at the larger organizational level, greater levels of racial and gender diversity were associated with greater levels of cooperation. It was also found that diverse teams performed better if they were a part of a larger organizational unit that was also diverse. The results of the studies of this third organization support the idea that organizational context matters. In other words, diversity must be embraced and supported enterprise-wide, not just at the team level, for there to be a positive impact on performance.

The last organization that participated in this study was a large retail organization with locations all over the United States. Each retail location was examined to see if the employee make-up of the stores matched that of the communities in which they are located. The BOLD research study did not examine any training/development relationships with diversity management. The focus of this study was the relationship between diversity and workplace performance. Stores generally employed 15 to 40 part-time employees with a couple of managers and assistant managers. Employee demographics were collected from employee records from 1996 to 1998 and compared with census data from 1990. The results of this analysis found no evidence that consumer purchases were related to the diversity of the retail store.

From a sales volume performance perspective, diversity appeared to have a mixed relationship with outcomes. On one hand, the index of racial diversity predicted higher sales. Conversely, stores with more white employees sold more than racially diverse stores. Although these results are frustrating when trying to explain the relationship between diversity and performance, another way to view the results is they present an opportunity for additional research to see if these results are repeated in other retail operations. There are many factors that make retail a unique environment to study including the part-time workforce, turnover rate, consumer loyalty (or lack thereof), tenure, and autonomy of each retail location.

The initiative, while it is rather limited in scope, provides important insights into the relationship between diversity management and performance. Although this study was not singularly focused on training, an important validation is the value of diversity training and development initiatives and their impact on reducing negative effects that result from racial diversity. The authors also recommend an updated business case for diversity based upon their findings. They have proposed the following business case:

"Diversity is a reality in labor markets and customer markets today. To be successful in working with and gaining value from this diversity requires a sustained, systematic approach and long-term commitment. Success is facilitated by a perspective that considers diversity to be an opportunity for everyone in an organization to learn from each other how better accomplish their work and an occasion that requires supportive and cooperative organizational culture as well as group leadership and process skills that can facilitate effective group functioning. Organizations that invest their resources in taking advantage of the opportunities that diversity offers should outperform those that fail to make such investments" (Kochan, et al., 2002, p. 31).

Justification of Diversity Training

Diversity in the labor market and customer markets, and how to leverage that diversity to gain a competitive advantage, will continue to be the subject of research studies well into the future. The conflicting results by researchers provides motivation to those training and development professionals that need to present empirical evidence to senior management to support initiatives designed to increase the exploitation of diversity in achieving desired results. There is agreement that the commitment to diversity must be institutionalized and embraced from the top down to the entry level employees. Some data that would be reported back to senior management is generally easy to collect. Capturing basic demographic data is critical for tracking the results of recruiting efforts. Acquiring current demographic information about the community in which an organization does business is as easy as the click of a mouse in today's information rich environment. Performance numbers will be organization specific and can include data such as sales, billable hours, productivity, waste/scrap/errors, bonus earned, tenure, absence rates, injuries reported, or some other metric based upon the industry and market segment supported.

Part of an organization's overall diversity management strategy usually involves new hire training modules that address diversity and focus on cultural awareness, communication skills, and identification of personal biases that could become barriers to productive work-based relationships. While it might not make sense to administer a pre- and post-test to newly hired employees that are receiving diversity training, it is recommended that a follow-up assessment be completed. As with any training, it is important to verify that the desired behaviors are being exhibited after the employee is working in their assigned position. Organizations recognize the importance of an effective on-boarding or new hire training/orientation program. Capturing the costs associated with this event, as it tends to be regular and repeated, is not complicated if the training and development or human resource professional keeps accurate records and is able to incorporate the salary of the employees being trained.

Return On Investment (ROI) is always the most difficult figure to calculate for training and development professionals and attempting to derive that figure for specific training programs that support diversity initiatives is problematic at best. As evidenced in the research results included in this text, results of studies that examine the relationship between diversity and business outcomes or performance are mixed. However, this should not dissuade the human resource or training professional from calculating ROI based upon the data they are able to collect. Regular evaluation of training programs is essential and should be done in the spirit of continuous improvement as well as providing input to senior management on the effectiveness of diversity strategies and human resource initiatives. Gaining access to the data necessary to complete this analysis might require that the human resource or training professional establish relationships with all functional areas within the organization. This might include developing a relationship with the production supervisor, sales manager, service director, operations manager, and director of marketing. This trust-based relationship should benefit both parties—support of the organizations training needs and acquisition of the data that enables assessment of the effectiveness of training programs and identifies current and future training needs.

CONCLUSION

Despite the difficulty in finding empirical research that supports a positive relationship between diversity management and business results, this business strategy is worth supporting and should not be abandoned due to lack of statistical significance. Many organizations, while committed to diversity, lack the measurement metrics necessary to truly assess the value of these policies and practices to the organization. Other organizations can report the obvious statistics such as changes in recruiting, training hours completed, reduction in harassment complaints, and bonuses paid, but they guard much of their data due to privacy concerns and fear of legal actions should the data reveal inconsistencies. It is commonly accepted that participating in the global marketplace requires a global perspective in human resource practices. It seems only logical that effective implementation of diversity strategies can help any organization achieve their goals while embracing the unique skills, knowledge, experiences, and perspectives that a heterogeneous workforce brings to the organization.

One theme that was consistently supported is that effective diversity training programs can reduce the negative effects of racial diversity in an organization. While the research did not find a positive relationship between diversity and business results, reducing negative effects could result in the reduction of organizational costs. For instance, negative effects would include things like lawsuits claiming racial discrimination, excessive turnover due to perceived racially hostile environments, and reduced productivity due to racial conflict. Human resource departments must become better at collecting the data necessary to evaluate diversity strategies to support executive level commitment of these programs and to ensure that the programs evolve and change as the demographics of the organization's employees and customers change.

Creating a culture, which values and appreciates differences requires major, systematic, planned change efforts, which are typically not part of affirmative action plans; however, diversity management has been considered a new organizational paradigm in that it moves beyond a human resource model based solely on a legal compliance to one that suggests there is inherent value in diversity. (Gilbert, Stead, & Ivancevich,

1999). Corporations must continue to embrace strategies that support the evolution of organizational culture. Change is constant, the growth of globalization in the marketplace adds new issues to business processes, and cultivation of talented and diverse employment populations adds a new level of recruiting complexities for today's forward thinking organizations.

Having a highly trained workforce is a business imperative. Jayne and Dipboye (2004), in their research on leveraging diversity, found that training programs to support diversity initiatives generally include awareness training, issue-based/prevention training, team building, and group process training. Effective assessment of employee knowledge, skills, and attitudes is the basis of creating an effective training and development program. The organizational benefits of successful implementation of an effective diversity awareness training program can be transformational for both the employees and the organization.

Future Research

Deming and others have promoted manage by fact as part of a continuous improvement practice. This is the theme for decision-making processes by organizations that use quality control process such as Six Sigma to address areas for improvements in their organizations, for any issue that can benefit from quality control procedures. To understand the complete impact of diversity strategies in organizations, it is necessary to develop the appropriate measurement metrics. Conducting the research over a period of time will be necessary to establish long-term and short-term impact of the training and development programs. Organizational context is also important to take into consideration. The research done by the BOLD Initiative showed different relationships between diversity and organizational results with respect to the type of organization. It might be necessary to propose different models based upon the type industry developing and deploying strategic diversity initiatives. Comprehensive research involving a variety of industries is recommended before any results can be generalized across organizations.

REFERENCES

Childs, J. T. Jr. (2005). Managing workforce diversity at IBM: A global HR topic that has arrived. *Human Resource Management, 44*(1), 73–77. doi:10.1002/hrm.20042

Cox, T. H., & Blake, S. (1991). Managing cultural diversity: Implications for organizational competitiveness. *The Academy of Management Executive, 5,* 45–56.

Dass, P., & Parker, B. (1999). Strategies for managing human resource diversity: From resistance to learning. *The Academy of Management Executive, 13*(2), 68–80. doi:10.5465/AME.1999.1899550

Filho, R. P., Lockwood, N. R., & Williams, S. (2009). Global diversity advantage: The next competitive edge. *SHRM*. Retrieved from http://www.shrm.org/Research/Articles/Articles/Pages/GlobalDiversityAdvantage.aspx.

Focus, H. R. (2010, January). Link diversity to business goals for best results. *HRFocus*, 5–10.

Gilbert, J. A., Stead, B. A., & Ivancevich, J. M. (1999). Diversity management: A new organizational paradigm. *Journal of Business Ethics, 21*(1), 61–76. doi:10.1023/A:1005907602028

Greenberg, J. (2011). *Behavior in organizations* (10th ed.). Upper Saddle River, NJ: Prentice Hall.

Hansen, F. (2003). Diversity's business case doesn't add up. *Workforce*. Retrieved from http://findarticles.com/p/articles/mi_m0FXS/is_4_82/ai_99986376/?tag=content;col1.

Hewitt Associates. (2004). *Preparing the workforce of tomorrow*. Retrieved from http://www.hewitt.com.

Jayne, M. E. A., & Dipboye, R. L. (2004). Leveraging diversity to improve business performance: Research findings and recommendations for organizations. *Human Resource Management, 43*(4), 409–424. doi:10.1002/hrm.20033

Kochan, T., Bezrukova, K., Ely, R., Jackson, S., Joshi, A., & Jehn, K. … Thomas, D. (2002). *The effects of diversity on business performance: Report of the diversity research network*. Cambridge, MA: MIT Sloan School of Management.

Konrad, A. (2003). Defining the domain of workplace diversity scholarship. *Group & Organization Management, 28*(1), 4–17. doi:10.1177/1059601102250013

Kramer, R. M. (2006). Social capital and cooperative behavior in the workplace: A social identity perspective. *Advances in Group Processes, 23,* 1–30. doi:10.1016/S0882-6145(06)23001-7

Lepak, D. P., Liao, H., Yunhyun, C., & Harden, E. E. (2006). A conceptual review of human resource management systems in strategic human resource management research. *Research in Personnel and Human Resource Management, 25,* 217–271. doi:10.1016/S0742-7301(06)25006-0

Lockwood, N. R. (2005). *Workplace diversity: Leveraging the power of difference for competitive advantage*. Retrieved from http://www.shrm.org/Research/Articles/Articles/Documents/0605RQ.pdf.

Lockwood, N. R., Anderson, L., Gundling, E. O., Moore, K., Jr., Olivas-Lujan, M. R., Williams, S., & Wilson, J. R. (2009). *Creativity and innovation in human resource management: A sign of the times*. Retrieved from http://www.shrm.org.

National Center for Public Policy and Higher Education. (2005). *FACT #1: The U.S. workforce is becoming more diverse*. Retrieved from http://www.highereducatin.org/reports/pa_decline/decline-f1.shtml.

Pace, A. (2011). OPM makes diversity a top priority. *T&D, 65*(6), 16-17.

Polzer, J. T., Milton, L. T., & Swann, W. B. Jr. (2002). Capitalizing on diversity: Interpersonal congruence in small work groups. *Administrative Science Quarterly, 47,* 296–324. doi:10.2307/3094807

Richard, O. C. (2000). Racial diversity, business strategy, and firm performance: A resource-based view. *Academy of Management Journal, 43,* 164–177. doi:10.2307/1556374

Society for Human Resource Management. (2009). *Creativity and innovation in human resource management: A sign of the times.* Retrieved from http://www.shrm.org/Research/Articles/Documents/09-0525_RQ_3_2009.pdf.

Texas Instruments. (2011). *2010 corporate citizen report.* Retrieved from http://www.ti.com/corp/docs/csr/index2.shtml.

Williams, C. (2011). Managing individuals and a diverse work force. In *Management* (pp. 452–487). Mason, OH: South-Western Cengage Learning.

Yang, Y. (2005). Developing cultural diversity advantage: The impact of diversity management structures. In *Academy of Management Best Conference Paper 2005,* (pp. H1-H6). Academy of Management.

ADDITIONAL READING

Addison, R., Haig, C., & Kearny, L. (2009). *Performance architecture: The art and science of improving organizations.* San Francisco, CA: Pfeiffer.

Citkin, F., & Spielman, L. (2011). *Transformational diversity: Why and how intercultural competencies can help organizations to survive and thrive.* Alexandria, VA: Society for Human Resource Management.

Halsey, V. (2011). *Brilliance by design: Creating learning experiences that connect, inspire, and engage.* San Francisco, CA: Berrett-Koehler.

Johnson, M., & Johnson, L. (2010). *Generations, inc.: From boomers to linksters—Managing the friction between generations at work.* New York, NY: AMACOM.

Kirkpatrick, J. D., & Kirkpatrick, W. K. (2010). *Training on trial: How workplace learning must reinvent itself to remain relevant.* New York, NY: AMACOM.

KEY TERMS AND DEFINITIONS

Diversity: Represents much more than age, gender, ethnicity or religious beliefs. Diversity now encompasses various levels of education, experience, technical skills, and learning preferences. These are just a few of the considerations that must be incorporated into effective training and development programs (Kormanik & Rajan, 2010).

Diversity Advantage: The rare value from a relatively immobile and appropriable diverse work force (Yang, 2005).

Diversity Capital Advantage: The organization's superior composition of different demographics groups that can ensure the organization outperforms its competitors in terms of the availability of a variety of knowledge (Yang, 2005).

Diversity Management: Is a voluntary organizational program designed to create greater inclusion of all individuals into informal social networks and formal company programs, and is an intentional design to foster appreciation of demographic, ethnic and individual differences (Gilbert, Stead & Ivancevich, 1999).

Diversity Management Program: A specific program that promotes recognition and appreciation of the differences between people and encourages the creation of a supportive work environment (Greenberg, 2011).

Diversity Management Strategies: As it directly relates to training and development initiatives within the corporate setting. Further, the authors seek to widen the definition of diversity to support the growth of an effective training and development program that utilizes theory, systems, processes and tools to advance organizational learning and support effective human resource practices.

Diversity Process Advantage: The superior problem solving and social integration and communication processes derived from different demographic groups that can help an organization execute operations more quickly, efficiently, and effectively, ultimately outperforming the competition (Yang, 2005).

Organization: Refers to a structured social system consisting of groups and individuals working together to meet objectives (Greenberg, 2011).

Training and Development: Is the process of systematically teaching employees to acquire and improve job-related skills and knowledge set by specific learning and performance outcomes (Greenberg, 2011).

ENDNOTE

[1] It should be noted that since this study was done, the concept of diversity has expanded dramatically to include other constructs including skill/knowledge level, tenure, job variety and many other attributes that make each individual contributor unique. The results of this study that link to training and development will be discussed with suggestions for future research.

Chapter 15
Leveraging Workforce Diversity through a Career Development Paradigm Shift

Claretha Hughes
University of Arkansas, USA

DeVaughn Stephens
University of Arkansas, USA

ABSTRACT

Many diverse individuals may not have previously been considered mainstream within organizational career development strategies (Avery, 2011). The objectives of this chapter are to 1) introduce the idea of leveraging diversity through a career development paradigm shift and 2) to offer researchers ways to further explore this shift in thinking and enhance organizational and individual career development strategies. The suggestion is not for organizational leaders to choose diverse employees over others, but that they acknowledge and understand all employees and use that knowledge to enhance and improve organizational performance. To accomplish organizational success through career development, they must acknowledge the value of all employees.

INTRODUCTION

For the heart to thrive it must be nourished (Lawler, 2003) and if organizations believe that people are the heart of the organization's existence, the process and practice of career development is one way for organizations to provide proper nourishment to employees in the workplace. The bottom-line performance of organizations is affected by having the right people in the right jobs, doing the right things at the right time. Choosing the most suitable career development strategy that is appropriate for both the organization and the individuals impacting the bottom-line performance is vital. Organizations and individuals must understand career development strategies because expectations, goals, and/or aspirations are essential to the successful execution of the strategy.

DOI: 10.4018/978-1-4666-1812-1.ch015

Some organizations make the mistake of establishing career development strategies built on the lofty premise of "if we build it, they will come" as there is no guarantee that "they" will come. Instead, this effort requires active analysis and involvement by all stakeholders helping to ensure the appropriateness and allocation of resources. There is no absolute right choice, but there should be an attempt to achieve a return on investment from a human capital and financial perspective. Generally, younger employees are sometimes more eager than senior staff members for career development. However, in this fast-paced economic environment, all employees need to be current in all areas of their development. This condition mandates and establishes a mind-set of system-wide application, flexibility, and the selection of relevant organizational talent management and career development strategies.

A pattern of work-related experiences that encompass the course of a person's work life is one description of a career and obtaining the most suitable and applicable career development is crucial if the individual seeks a successful, long-term career. Individuals are expected to own and held responsible for their personal career development. In today's global economy, this expectation of career ownership and responsibility represents a tremendous adjustment for some workers especially when the previous situation only required them to show up for work as scheduled, exhibit appropriate workplace conduct, and follow the documented script of instructions to meet performance goals. Yet, with the advancement of technology and the explosion of the information-powered workplaces, the speed of change has forced individuals and organizations to change and adapt rather quickly.

Understanding the career progression process and the potential benefits for both the individual and the organization is a key to success for all involved. No one individual worker is the same. This acknowledgement of the differences necessitates finding a "fit" between organizational and individual goals if one adheres to Boudreaux's

(2001) description of career development as focusing "on the alignment of individual subjective career aspects and the more objective career aspects of the organizations in order to achieve the best fit between individual and organizational needs as well as personal characteristics and career roles" (p. 806). In the end, the individual benefits through understanding what it takes to carve out a career that aligns with their diverse Knowledge, Skills, and Abilities (KSAs). Career development is considered to be one of the three pillars of Human Resource Development (HRD) (Chalofsky, 1992; Swanson, 2001) and "organizational career development theories should focus the interaction between individual and organization, and can also be regarded as change theories on an individual level, which make them central to HRD" (Swanson & Holton, 2001; van Dijk, 2004, p. 772). The organization also benefits from dedicated employees who want to stay and build a career with the organization.

These employees include many diverse individuals who have not been previously considered mainstream within organizational career development strategies (Avery, 2011). One means of building a solid interaction between the individual and the organization's career development is leveraging and promoting workplace diversity. Career development has not been examined to the extent possible with regards to developing and leveraging workforce diversity across all levels of the organization. The objectives of this chapter are to 1) introduce the idea of leveraging diversity through a career development paradigm shift and 2) to offer researcher ways to can further explore this shift in thinking and enhance organizational and individual career development strategies.

BACKGROUND

In many instances, the impact of workplace diversity comes from the power and structure inside organizations, which may be derived from the central position of individuals (Burkhardt & Brass, 1990; Brass & Burkhardt, 1993). This central position translates to the value of an employee's location in the organization. The impact of employees' actual and perceived power within organizations is based upon their strategic placement or location within the organization (Brass & Burkhardt, 1993; Pfeffer, 1994). The valuation of workplace diversity instigates an organization "understanding the impact of diversity on performance and formulating a strategy to manage diversity that is connected to the career development plan (Pitts, 2006). Incorporating policies that encourage diversity and career development make it desirable for all people, especially women and minorities, to remain in the organization (Pitts, 2006) and become fully optimized in the workplace environment.

Avery (2011) suggests that "prioritizing diversity throughout organizational human-resource management practices" (p. 251) is a key to unlocking diversity's potential inside the organization. He also notes that:

Through their human-resource management policies and procedures, organizations have a considerable impact on the diversity climates they facilitate and the employees they attract and retain. If they wish to encourage employee diversity activism, it is imperative that they take steps to ensure that the climates, supervisors, and coworkers employees routinely encounter convey that diversity is valued and supported (p. 252).

These suggestions apply to career development leaders within organizations. Career development requires that the organization provide a supportive climate, supervisors, and coworkers for diverse employees to feel comfortable interacting with mentors (Bingham, Gewin, Hu, Thomas, & Yanchus, 2005). Organizations and employees must adapt to changes to survive in the global economy. One method for adapting is through career development. As individuals compete,

they are competing against low wage, high skilled workers throughout the world (Friedman & Mandelbaum, 2011). Skill enhancement must become a constant, if workers and organizations are to remain nimble at adjusting to changes.

MAIN FOCUS OF THE CHAPTER

As organizations continue to expand their capabilities, they seek to invest their resources in ways that will enhance their business. Investments have been made in people and career development strategies have been developed; yet, there are still opportunities for improvement. The Global Recession of 2008 clearly shed light on the limitations of the career development plans and strategies of organizations and the people they employed. With rampant layoffs around the world and millions of people unemployed, society has been negative impacted by the sudden and drastic changes (Friedman & Mandelbaum, 2011). Many organizations and employees had no career strategy or career plan for successful transitioning or adaptation to the changes.

Issues, Controversies, Problems

The location value (Hughes, 2010) that an organization may gain from employees can be established through their placement within the career development structure of the organization (Banks, 2006; Banks & Nafukho, 2008, Holland, 1973; Kaye, 1997, Schein, 1975, Super, 2002; Vardi, 1980; Vroom & MacCrimmon, 1968). The employee provides both the internal and external location value to the organization as well and "organizations develop rules or policies that impose some control over personnel movements, such as retirement at 65, promotion from within, giving new college graduates a variety of training assignments before assigning them to positions of responsibility and so on" (Vroom & MacCrimmon, 1968, p. 28). These factors remain relevant in today's global economy with internal and external location value of the employee has the potential to significantly impacting the employee's performance and value to the organization.

An individual's location value (Hughes, 2010) within the organization structure means that the access to the diversity of talent happens at all levels of the enterprise regardless of position, job title, or physical placement. This recognition enables individuals to be fully optimized in the workplace, which represents the paradigm shift in career development. In essence, the focus does not only rely on an individual's capability but also on the total organization's capability. Concentrating on the organization's capability allows access across multiple levels. It is a contemporary, pragmatic approach to career development that encourages the elimination of the cultural and environmental barriers that prevent the promotion of diversity in the overall career development scheme.

The organizational culture has to be accepting of diversity and career development (Avery, 2011; Deal & Kennedy, 1984). The unique traits of the individual, the variation of group dynamics, and the distinctive application of policies and procedures are all found within the organization system and of course fluctuate based upon the idiosyncratic nature of the organization. Yet, individuals entering the workplace must recognize and understand these elements and prepare to develop their careers within the opportunities presented, despite the constraints that they may encounter. Robbins (2005) suggests that in the:

boundaryless career, the organization's responsibility is to build employees' self-reliance and help them maintain marketability through continuous learning. This "boundaryless career" paradigm shifts the attention from an isolated location perspective to an enterprise-wide conception accessible by all. Specific ways that this can be accomplished are to clearly communicate the

organization's goals and future strategies, create growth opportunities, offer financial assistance, and provide time for employees to learn (p. 594).

If employees are entering, re-entering, and transitioning within the workplace they must remain cognizant of the continuous shifting nature of career planning and adapt accordingly (Hayes, 2000; Karsten & Igou, 2005).

Solutions and Recommendations

Career Paths and Location Value

Career paths represent the chronological order of career progression in an organization (Isaacson & Brown, 1997; Leibowitz, Farren, & Kaye, 1986) and are used to assist with development of career plans for individuals providing sources of self-fulfillment, welcomed challenges, and source of income (Baruch, 2004). Usually career paths are developed for each job based upon organizational promotional practices (Isaacson & Brown, 1997). Yet, few organizations provide career counseling or planning assistance to employees as they seek to progress along the paths and since this institutional, procedural barrier to career development support exists, a realistic expectation is that there should be many opportunities for employees to obtain career development formation both inside and outside of the organization. Gathering new information about all possible career options (Hayes, 2000) is vital when changing units within or moving to a different organization. It may be in the organization's best interest to establish transparent career paths for its employees so that they can have some control over and better management of employee location value (Hughes, 2010) throughout the organization.

Employees' location value (Hughes, 2010) is intuitively known when they make an error on the job they are reprimanded or in some cases fired because of the loss value caused by the error to the organization. Employee location value is also evident when they receive compensation for work produced when present at work. There are times when assumptions regarding causality are made and people are moved from one location to another to the detriment of the employee and the organization. These actions beg the question of whether organizations are providing career development opportunities that include adequate, clear, and consistent feedback regarding an individual's actions and how those actions translate into performance (Kerno & Kuznia, 2007). This proposition also seeks to enhance employee location value by ensuring that all employees are on the job contributing and delivering value. The value of diverse employees within organizations is essential to productivity, competitive advantage, and long-term performance strategy. These elements should be measurable and directly expressed on the balance sheet. Effective career development, deliberate management of workplace diversity, and consideration of an employee's location value are linked to the investment organization's make in human capital and career capital (Human Capital, 2011; Hughes, 2010). Integrating this paradigm shift with human capital and career capital theories provides an opportunity for two complimentary points of integrated HRD to be leveraged by organizations (Baruch, 2006; Baruch, 2004; Dickman & Harris, 2006).

Many employees have not had to think about anything other than doing their assigned job at their place of work. They have not been asked to map their career or if they even have an individual career strategy, which further suggests that they may not be able to distinguish between having a career and having a job. Career change occurs for many workers after they have been laid off from a job and are tasked with obtaining another one. The next step on their journey tends to be the unemployment office, temporary agencies, and/ or "one-stop" centers for re-training. Some lucky

individuals may have a copy of their resume or employee development plan to help them map out a career strategy. They may know the job they were on and understand the value of their having been on that job to the organization; however, they may not be aware or know how to transfer the skills, nor how to fit that knowledge or the totality of their experiences into a future career or career development strategy.

Since the introduction of the Workforce Investment Act in 1999 and the introduction of the American Jobs Act bill under the Obama administration (American Job Act, 2011), the field of career development continues to expand. As workforce development efforts are streamlined and agencies are combined within regions of the states, organizations must be flexible and open to change and understand that employees and potential employees are in need of career development assistance. The many stakeholders who interact with these "one-stop" centers such as businesses and educational institutions must remember that the employee is the essential ingredient to workplace success. Assisting them with establishing a career track and obtaining needed education and/or training will be a benefit for all involved. If the employee is not developed, businesses will not succeed to the fullest extent possible, educational institutions will not meet student enrollment goals, and private practitioners will be seeing fewer clients. All of these potential consequences challenge the critical objective of career development and limits the transformative power of workplace diversity.

Because of historical discriminatory practices in the United States, there are many laws that organizations must adhere to that they cannot make decisions perceived to be stereotypical and judgmental. The ability to forecast workplace selection strategies have been hampered by these laws. In the past organizations tended to plan ahead only when required by laws as opposed to integrating based upon business demands. Organizations must develop ways to manage the location value of employees from positions that are not mandated, preventatively influenced to avoid punishment, and fear of legal action.

Legal and Ethical Consideration of Diversity Management

If asked the question is diversity a legal or ethical issue, what would the response be? There are many debates regarding diversity, but there are no clear, definitive definitions and interpretations to which all organizations and individuals adhere. The management of diversity is not a legal issue. To date, there are no known state laws, federal legislation, or municipal statues leveling the requirement of diversity on any situation. Further, there are no court cases at any level that make diversity a mandate in the workplace or any other institution. Consequently, sometimes diversity is often mistaken for Equal Employment Opportunity (EEO) and Affirmative Action (AA); however, diversity goes beyond the legal requirements that EEO and AA provide. Actually, "for many organizations, the definition of diversity has evolved from a focus on legally protected attributes such as race, gender, and age to a much broader definition that includes the entire spectrum of human differences" (Jayne & Dipboye, 2004, p. 410).

The concept of diversity does not stand alone. It was born out of the burdens of the 1960's civil rights legislation and employment laws (Holvino & Kamp, 2009). Specifically, AA and EEO laws emerged at the height of the United States (U.S.) civil rights movement to rectify past discrimination and preclude future discrimination in employment and several presidential Executive Orders (e.g. 10925, 11246, and 11375); these legally required mandates are leveled upon federal contractors and subcontractors (Kelly & Dobbin, 1998). Principally,

equal employment opportunity ensures that employment decisions (e.g. hiring, promotion, pay) are made without regard to legally protected attributes... [and] affirmative action programs, in turn, seek to remedy past discrimination by taking proactive steps based on race and gender to prevent current or future discrimination (Jayne & Dipboye, 2004, p. 410).

Essentially, diversity has materialized to strengthen and further add qualitative, good faith reinforcement to EEO and AA requirements. Diversity is an inclusive force that like EEO and AA, also involves protecting the classifications of age, race, gender, and several other legally identified demographics under the civil rights laws, but it is not officially enforced by any authorized/legal entities. Jayne and Dipboye (2004) contend that "inclusion as a diversity strategy differs from policies and programs such as equal employment opportunity and affirmative action" (p. 410). Over time, the recasting of EEO/AA measures as part of the diversity management and touting the competitive advantages offered by these practices (Kelly & Dobbin, 1998) has become the acceptable means of ensuring that non-discriminatory decisions are made and comprehensive programs are embedded across an organization.

Perhaps the key to managing diversity is practical education and learning. Based on this suggestion, achieving a diverse, pluralistic, and democratic society that meets its ideal of equity and social justice is inextricably linked to the pedagogical practices of its educational institutions (Ginsberg & Wlodowski, 2009). This position suggests that instead of attempting to legislate diversity through laws like EEO and AA, the awareness of diversity should be perpetuated by building learning organizations that promote its value and meaning (Avery, 2011; Thomas, 2008). Konrad (2006) argues that:

a truly multicultural organization that values variety and shows flexibility can only be achieved through programmatic change over the long term [and] managers should expect the diversity frontier to continue to move forward, and to take the actions needed to keep pace with these changes in society (p. 182).

Undeniably, managing diversity effectively is difficult and complex; considerable barriers significantly challenge the implementation of the business case for diversity (Konrad, 2006). These barriers come in the form of human, psychological, organization, and institutional resistance (Avery, 2011). For these reasons, "building support for a diversity initiative requires a clearly defined strategy for communicating the business case and clear roles and responsibilities for the senior leadership team, managers, and employees" (Jayne & Dipboye, 2004, p. 418). Marques (2007) explains "if conscientiously applied and facilitated at all levels, diversity can elevate an organization's long term performance to levels that are beyond all expectations"(p. 24). The goodness of diversity is reflected in the fact that despite huge challenges American society is transforming away from its historical assimilationist melting philosophy towards cultural pluralism. This transformation supports societal members who are diverse in many ways such as cultural, social, racial, or religious groups. These members can now maintain their own identity yet concurrently share common political organization, economic system, and social structure (Banks, 2006; Ginsberg & Wlodkowski, 2009). The compounding effect of all these dynamic elements provides evidence to support that diversity is not a legal issue but rather a constructive mindset, strongly influencing individuals and organizations toward strategic thinking, interactive and collective discourse, and ethical behavior.

It almost seems natural to hear labor unions being blamed for diminishing relationships between organizations and their employees, but legal action through class action lawsuits has had more impact on reducing the effectiveness of unions than anything else other than government agencies that are lacking in their enforcement of their guidelines. After legal actions are complete, organizations are forced through court order to make adjustments and many of these adjustments force modifications in job training, skills development, human resources and talent management procedures, and location/placement of employees. The combination of these workplace actions evokes the strategic execution of career development and diversity management (Avery, 2011; Den Hond & DeBakker, 2007; Thomas, 2008). Keep in mind, that neither workplace diversity nor career development is necessarily a matter of legal obligation but rather a pressing organizational imperative.

FUTURE RESEARCH DIRECTIONS

With attention placed on the future of a sustainable workforce and skills capabilities to perform the type of work (Friedman & Mandelbaum, 2011; Reich, 2010), organizations must make rapid adjustments and many of these adjustments force modifications in job training, skills development, human resources and talent management procedures, and location/placement of employees (Hughes, 2010). This attentiveness to human resource development programs design changes compels organizations to continue working towards defining and clarifying the term workforce diversity (Carrell, Mann, & Honeycutt-Sigler, 2006).

Along with career development, talent management, succession planning, diversity programs, and organizational leadership practices are all areas that require more empirical studies to inform practice. Some research questions to consider include:

1. Does the employee position in the organization limit them from career development opportunities?
2. Is your location value significant enough to the organization to warrant career development?
3. To what extent can organizational leaders leverage their understanding of diversity to enhance career development opportunities for all employees?
4. To what extent can enhanced career development strategies increase productivity within the organizations?

CONCLUSION

Organization leaders and practitioners within the field of career development have a difficult job, but must be committed to helping employees succeed. Global workplace expansion requires leaders to understand different cultures and the needs of employees who are of different nationalities (Friedman & Mandelbaum, 2011). Organizations must restructure and reinvent themselves as they adapt to continuously changing economic conditions. Technological means allow for quick adaptations but leaders must begin to view people changes in ways that are similar (Hughes, 2010). The needs of dedicated employees must be acknowledged regardless of differences, but consideration of location value within the structure, the physical placement, and the effect on career progression is also important for those who want the organization to invest in their potential. The development of individual's careers and the priority of managing workplace diversity moves from the mundane tasks of getting people to work to a forward-thinking approach of establishing unity within individuals' assigned environment, adaptation to the organizational culture, and confirmation that career development and growth is attainable and sustainable.

Organization leaders should understand the extent to which the cultural environment affects diverse employees in the workplace (Avery, 2011). They may also want to understand the way(s) location value of employees essential to productivity and/or competitive advantage of an organization (Hughes, 2010). This chapter is not suggesting that organizational leaders choose diverse employees over others, but that they acknowledge and understand all employees and use that knowledge to enhance and improve organizational performance.

REFERENCES

Avery, D. R. (2011). Support for diversity in organizations: A theoretical exploration of its origins and offshoots. *Organizational Psychology Review*, *1*, 239–256. doi:10.1177/2041386611402115

Banks, C. H. (2006). Career planning: Toward an inclusive model. In Karsten, M. (Ed.), *Gender, Race and Ethnicity in the Workplace* (*Vol. 3*, pp. 99–116). Westport, CT: Greenwood. Publishing Group, Inc.

Banks, C. H., & Nafukho, F. M. (2008). Career transitions across and within organizations: Implications for human resource development. In T. M. Chermack & J. Storberg-Walker (Eds.), *2008 Academy of Human Resource Development Annual Research Conference Proceedings*, (pp. 1096- 1102). Bowling Green, OH: Academy of Human Resource Development.

Banks, J. A. (2006). *Race, culture, and education: The selected works of James A. Banks*. New York, NY: Routledge.

Baruch, Y. (2004). Transforming careers from linear to multidirectional career paths: Organizational and individual perspectives. *Career Development International*, *9*(1), 58–73. doi:10.1108/13620430410518147

Baruch, Y. (2006). Career development in organizations and beyond: Balancing traditional and contemporary viewpoints. *Human Resource Management Review, 16*(2), 125–138. doi:10.1016/j.hrmr.2006.03.002

Bingham, K., Gewin, A., Hu, C., Thomas, K., & Yanchus, N. (2005). The roles of protégé race, gender, and proactive socialization attempts on peer monitoring. *Advances in Developing Human Resources, 7*(4), 540–555. doi:10.1177/1523422305279681

Boudreaux, M. A. (2001). Career development: What is its role in human resource development? In O. A. Aliaga (Ed.), *Academy of HRD 2001 Conference Proceedings,* (pp. 805-812). Bowling Green, OH: Academy of Human Resource Development.

Brass, D. J., & Burkhardt, M. E. (1993). Potential power and power use: An investigation of structure and behavior. *Academy of Management Journal, 36*(3), 441–470. doi:10.2307/256588

Burkhardt, M. E., & Brass, D. J. (1990). Changing patterns or patterns of change: The effects of a change in technology on social network structure and power. *Administrative Science Quarterly, 35,* 104–127. doi:10.2307/2393552

Carrell, M., Mann, E., & Honeycutt-Sigler, T. (2006). Defining workforce diversity programs and practices in organizations: A longitudinal study. *Labor Law Journal, 57*(1), 5–12.

Chalofsky, N. (1992). A unifying definition for the human resource development profession. *Human Resource Development Quarterly, 3*(2), 175–182. doi:10.1002/hrdq.3920030208

Deal, T., & Kennedy, A. (1984). *Corporate cultures.* Reading, MA: Addison-Wesley.

Den Hond, F., & De Bakker, F. G. A. (2007). Ideologically motivated activism: How activist groups influence corporate social change activities. *Academy of Management Review, 32,* 901–924. doi:10.5465/AMR.2007.25275682

Dickman, M., & Harris, H. (2006). Developing career capital for global careers: The role of international assignments. *Journal of World Business, 40*(4), 399–408. doi:10.1016/j.jwb.2005.08.007

Friedman, T. L., & Mandelbaum, M. (2011). *That used to be us: How America fell behind in the world it invented and how we can come back.* New York, NY: Farrar, Strauss, and Giroux.

Ginsberg, M., & Wlodowski, R. (2009). *Diversity & motivation: Culturally responsive teaching in college.* San Francisco, CA: Jossey-Bass.

Hayes, K. H. (2000). *Managing career transitions: Your career as a work in progress* (2nd ed.). Upper Saddle River, NJ: Prentice Hall.

Holland, J. L. (1973). *Making vocational choices: A theory of careers.* Upper Saddle River, NJ: Prentice-Hall.

Holvino, E., & Kamp, A. (2009). Diversity management: Are we moving in the right direction? Reflections from both sides of the North Atlantic. *Scandinavian Journal of Management, 25*(4), 395–403. doi:10.1016/j.scaman.2009.09.005

Hughes, C. (2010). "People as technology" conceptual model: Towards a new value creation paradigm for strategic human resource development. *Human Resource Development Review, 9*(1), 48–71. doi:10.1177/1534484309353561

Human Capital. (2011). *Dictionary.* Retrieved on October 31, 2011 from http://dictionary.reference.com/browse/human+capital.

Isaacson, L. E., & Brown, D. (1997). *Career information, career counseling, and career development* (6th ed.). Boston, MA: Allyn & Bacon.

Jayne, M., & Dipboye, R. (2004). Leveraging diversity to improve business performance: Research findings and recommendations for organizations. *Human Resource Management, 43,* 409–424. doi:10.1002/hrm.20033

Karsten, M. F., & Igou, F. (2005). Career planning: A model for a diverse workforce. In *Proceedings of the North American Management Society track at the 2005 Midwest Business Administration Association Conference.* Chicago, IL: MBAA.

Kaye, B. (1997). *Up is not the only way.* Englewood Cliffs, NJ: Davies-Black.

Kelly, E., & Dobbin, F. (1998). How affirmative action became diversity management: Employer response to antidiscrimination laws, 1961 to 1996. *The American Behavioral Scientist, 41,* 960–984. doi:10.1177/0002764298041007008

Kerno, S., & Kuznia, K. (2007). Modern career navigation: Preparing for success despite uncertainties. *Industrial Engineer, 39*(10), 31–33.

Konrad, A. (2006). Leveraging workplace diversity in organizations. *Organization Management Journal, 3*(3), 194–189. doi:10.1057/omj.2006.18

Lawler, E. E. III. (2003). *Treat people right! How organizations and individuals can propel each other into a virtuous spiral of success.* San Francisco, CA: Jossey-Bass.

Leibowitz, Z. B., Farren, C., & Kaye, B. L. (1986). *Designing career development systems.* San Francisco, CA: Jossey-Bass.

Marques, J. (2007). Diversity as a win-win strategy. *Management Services, 51*(1), 22–24.

Pfeffer, J. (1994). *Competitive advantage through people: Unleashing the power of the workforce.* Boston, MA: Harvard Business School Press.

Pitts, D. (2006). Modeling the impact of diversity management. *Review of Public Personnel Administration, 26*(3), 245–268. doi:10.1177/0734371X05278491

Reich, R. B. (2010). *Aftershock: The next economy and America's future.* New York, NY: Alfred A. Knopf.

Robbins, S. P. (2005). *Organizational behavior* (11th ed.). Upper Saddle River, NJ: Pearson Prentice Hall.

Schein, E. H. (1975). How career anchors hold executives to their career paths. *Personnel, 52,* 11–24.

Super, D. (2002). A life-span, life-space approach to career development. In Brown, D., & Brooks, L. (Eds.), *Career Choice and Development* (2nd ed.). San Francisco, CA: Jossey-Bass. doi:10.1016/0001-8791(80)90056-1

Swanson, R. A. (2001). The discipline of human resource development. In Swanson, R. A., & Holton, E. F. (Eds.), *Foundations of Human Resource Development* (pp. 88–100). San Francisco, CA: Berrett-Koehler Publishers.

Swanson, R. A., & Holton, E. F. (2001). *Foundation of human resource development.* San Francisco, CA: Berrett-Koehler Publishers.

Thomas, K. M. (2008). *Diversity resistance in organizations.* New York, NY: Lawrence Erlbaum.

van Dijk, M. (2004). Career development within HRD: Foundations or fad? In T. M. Egan & M. L. Morris (Eds.), *2004 Academy of Human Resource Development Annual Research Conference Proceedings,* (pp. 771-778). Bowling Green, OH: Academy of Human Resource Development.

Vardi, Y. (1980). Organizational career mobility: An integrative model. *Academy of Management Review, 5*(3), 341–355.

Vroom, V. H., & MacCrimmon, K. R. (1968). Toward a stochastic model of managerial careers. *Administrative Science Quarterly*, *13*(1), 26–46. doi:10.2307/2391260

White House. (2011). *American jobs act*. Retrieved on October 31, 2011 from http://www.whitehouse. gov/economy/jobsact/read-the-bill.

KEY TERMS AND DEFINITIONS

Career Capital: A resource based view of "knowing how" to acquire career relevant skills and work-related knowledge, "knowing why" or what energizes, provides a sense of purpose, motivates, and allows an individual to identify with work, and "knowing whom" to build interpersonal relationships, organizational partnerships, and social alliance with to access information and forge channels for self-promotion in the workplace.

Career Development: A pillar of HRD, focuses on the alignment of individual subjective career aspects and the more objective career aspects of the organization in order to achieve the best fit between individual and organizational needs as well as personal characteristics and career roles. Essentially, it is the process of assessing current career reality and determining the appropriate means of changing or progressing along a career path through the acquisition, retention, and transference of relevant Knowledge, Skills, and Abilities (KSAs).

Career Path: The process of guiding and developing employees' work experiences and positions within jobs that build career knowledge.

It is a major life accomplishment that revolves around work, provides a sense of purpose, challenge, self-fulfillment, and a source of income.

Employee Location Value: The value an organization may gain from employees, established by their placement within the career development and organizational hierarchy or structure. A concept that takes into account both the internal and external location value of the employee to the organization in the consideration of career development experiences and opportunities to leverage workplace diversity across multiple organization levels.

Human Capital: An economic concept emphasizing the abilities and skills of any individual, especially those acquired through investment in education and training, and that fundamentally enhance potential earning of income.

Human Resource Development (HRD): The study and practice of increasing the learning capacity of individuals, groups, collectives, and organizations through the development and application of learning-based interventions for the purpose of optimizing human and organizational growth and effectiveness.

Workplace Diversity: A focus on the ways that individuals differ that can affect a task or relationship within an organization. An understanding of the varied approaches that members of different identity groups bring to the workplace to include perspectives on discrimination and fairness, access and legitimacy, and learning and effectiveness.

Chapter 16
Diversity Training in Organizations

David McGuire
Queen Margaret University, UK

Nicola Patterson
Northumbria University, UK

ABSTRACT

Diversity training is an area of growing interest within organizations. As organizations and society become more culturally diverse, there is a need to provide training across all hierarchical levels to make individuals more aware of and sensitized to elements of difference. Managing and valuing diversity is becoming increasingly important to delivering higher levels of performance and creativity, enhancing problem solving and decision-making, and gaining cultural insights into domestic and overseas markets. As facilitators of diversity training, line managers are increasingly tasked with the important role of equipping employees with the skills and competencies to work effectively in diverse multicultural teams. Consequently, this chapter looks at the mechanics of how diversity is discussed and delivered in organizations. It explores the necessity of diversity training in safeguarding and respecting individual identity and in fostering more welcoming inclusive workplaces.

INTRODUCTION

Diversity is an increasingly important issue within organizations, with diversity management in particular positioned as an effective managerial response to the challenges posed by globalization and an increasingly heterogeneous workforce (Groschl, 2011). Recent special issues of the *Journal of European Industrial Training*, *International Journal of Human Resources Development and Management*, and *Advances in Developing Human Resources* have focused on diversity and equal opportunities, signaling that the Human Resource Development (HRD) field is finally beginning to address diversity training in earnest.

DOI: 10.4018/978-1-4666-1812-1.ch016

For too long, diversity has been missing from university curricula, programmes, textbooks and research, despite the field of HRD claiming diversity as a vital responsibility and key competency (Bierema, 2010). For his part, Gibb (2008) highlights the changing nature of the workforce as a key factor underpinning HRD's newfound commitment to diversity. He identifies six factors for the greater visibility and attention to diversity:

- Higher levels of employment participation by women
- A significant percentage of the workforce with dependent children or "carer" responsibilities
- Increased number of dual income families
- Changes in the family structures of employees—sole parents, fewer men and women in traditional family roles
- An ageing workforce
- Higher levels of cultural diversity with substantial labour migration

Multiculturalism has become an important facet of modern society and global organizations. As Scullion and Collings (2011) point out, organizations are increasingly sourcing, developing, and retaining key employees on a global scale. In such contexts, they argue that the effectiveness of global talent systems is increasingly being recognized as a major source of success or failure in international business. Cultural competencies have become critical to successful operations at a national, regional, and global level, and Mc-Donnell and Collings (2011) report that many organizations are looking for leaders who possess a global mindset and who can communicate and work with different cultures, manage uncertainty and global complexity.

With widening diversity, organizations are increasingly becoming aware of the need to develop and run diversity training programmes to prepare and equip employees with the skills to meet the needs of other employees and customers from linguistic, cultural and social backgrounds (Vielba & Edelshain, 1997). Moreover, organizations are also realising that the benefits of running diversity programmes go beyond legal compliance towards the attainment of sustainable competitive advantages, whereby diversity insights can lead to enhanced creativity, innovation and products and services more directly aligned to customer needs (Page, 2007; Finkelstein & Hambrick, 1996). As Keogh (2005, p. 261) points out: "Customers are increasingly looking through the front door of companies they buy from. If they do not like what they see in terms of social response, they will not go in." Subsequently, diversity management can be utilised as a mechanism to help organizations model themselves as attractive, progressive employers who embrace difference (Guerrier & Wilson, 2011).

However, diversity management programmes are not without their critics. Within organizations, there are many opponents of diversity training programmes who see diversity training as a form of "political correctness" leading to a nervousness and guilt being placed at the door of the majority group. Such individuals see diversity training as an attempt to blame the majority group for historical segregation and an attempt to force minority values and beliefs onto those of the majority (Stewart, et al., 2008; Holladay & Quinones, 2008). A second criticism leveled is that diversity advocates often engage in "distant cheerleading," heralding new diversity initiatives, without involving themselves in practical day-to-day workplace issues (Dick & Cassell, 2002). Furthermore, Dickens and Hall (2006) posit that organizations are only interested in diversity issues to the degree to which they coincide with business needs and are easy and straightforward to tackle. Such views suggest that many organizations adopt a contingent, cost-based approach to diversity, rather than a deeper commitment to underlying diversity values and principles. A final criticism comes from Rees *et al.* (2007) who argue that emphasizing differences between employees rather than unity can exacerbate problems and stereotypes that already exist, rather than resolve them.

This chapter examines the importance of diversity training in organizations. First, the business rationale for diversity is explored from a resource-based view, looking at why organizations engage with diversity issues. A resource-based view of the firm is adopted looking at how organizations can gain competitive advantage from managing diversity effectively. The second section in the chapter looks at the role of line managers who are increasingly asked to deliver diversity training to front-line employees. It considers the impact of structural changes within the HR function and the knowledge and skills required from line managers to effectively work with employees on diversity issues. The chapter goes on to look at identity and privilege in diversity training drawing upon gender to illustrate how diversity training can affect individual attitudes and behaviour. The final concluding section pull together the key issues discussed in the chapter and looks at the future of diversity training in organizations.

THE BUSINESS RATIONALE FOR ENGAGING WITH DIVERSITY ISSUES

A key proposition for addressing diversity issues in organizations is the belief that managing diversity will lead to improved performance outcomes. For many years, organizations have viewed a diverse workforce as a resource that needs to be valued and managed. A resource-based view of the firm sees employees as instruments conferring competitive advantages on the firm to the degree to which employee skills remain scarce or hard to duplicate, have no direct substitute, and enable organizations to pursue opportunities (Richard, 2000). Such perspectives can position employees in an exploitative relationship with management where the uniqueness of an employee is valued, not for its intrinsic importance, but for the net worth

and cash value that it brings to the organization. However, as valuable commodities that are rare and hard to imitate, employees, under the resource-based view are worthy of investment to the degree to which they continue to yield a beneficial return on investment. Watkins and Cseh (2009) argue that the skills and talents of key managers represent critical core competencies that allow an organization to excel and create customer value relative to competitors. They argue that the development of cultural and diversity competencies, built up over time, allow organizations to be transformed from pedestrian to successful ventures in the global market.

Underpinning the resource-based view of the firm is the notion that core competencies can be identified and used as the basis of diversity training initiatives. Prahalad and Hamel (1990) define core competencies as the collective learning in the organization, which can be leveraged to achieve competitive advantages. In so doing, competencies become a repository for organizational knowledge and learning. Gillert and Chuzischvili (2004) challenge the view that there is a specific set of cultural or diversity competencies and question whether dealing with diversity is just using social and communicative skills under more difficult circumstances. For their part, Iles and Hayers (1997) see diversity competencies as comprising of cultural awareness and communicative, affective, and cognitive competencies. Consequently, core diversity competencies incorporate an ability for employees and managers to recognize difference and communicate, behave and interact appropriately and positively.

Empowering the resource-based view of the firm has been the language that organizations have adopted to discuss diversity issues. The language of diversity has become more acceptable and palatable than the legal precepts and number-focused strategies associated with equal opportunities and affirmative action in the US. In research examining the language of diversity, Kirby and Harter (2003) argue that the discourse on diversity management is primarily framed to align with the interests of management. They argue that much of the material written about diversity is targeted at higher-level management, often white males: the underlying assumption being that those that are managed are white women and people of color. They also argue that the discourse within much of the management literature is that diversity is something that can and should be "managed" with individuals grouped into categories, where individuality may be lost at the expense of effort-saving objectifying generalizations.

The resource-based view of the firm is only helpful to organizations if there is a clear linkage between diversity management competencies and performance outcomes. There exists an ever-accumulating body of research detailing the organizational benefits that accrue from diversity training programmes. Both Ely and Thomas (2001) and McLeod *et al.* (1996) suggest that workforce diversity leads to a broadening of perspectives resulting in greater levels of creativity and innovation. Furthermore, Cox and Blake (1991) argue that firms that manage diversity well will benefit in terms of integration costs, greater cultural sensitivity, and insights into foreign markets, enhanced organizational reputation, better problem-solving capabilities, and a more fluid organizational system. Other research points to the beneficial impact of diversity on profitability and managerial effectiveness (Dallas, 2002; Sarra, 2002) as well as increasing organizational competitive advantage (Barney & Wright, 1998) and expanding access to diverse markets (Cook & Glass, 2009).

Perhaps surprisingly, the resource-based view of the firm has been brought to the fore in the public sector as much as the private sector. Within the public sector, Greene and Kirton (2011) argue that the ascendancy of the business case has often been to the exclusion or diminution of the social justice case. The authors suggest the greater inclusion of private sector bodies in public service delivery has weakened diversity outcomes at a societal level,

as private sector involvement typically lessens the power of trade unions and social groups to affect positive change. Such modernisation programmes may have resulted in greater efficiencies in the public sector, but at the cost of lower levels of social equality and participation. A contrary view is advanced by Harris and Foster (2010) who argue that a culture of equality, public accountability and a stronger union presence makes the public sector more predisposed to fairness in equality and diversity management. However, importantly they do indicate that tensions exist in relation to new management practices such as talent management approaches, which favour individualistic and selective approaches, which may run contrary to the sameness of treatment or equal opportunities culture prevalent in much of the public sector.

DELIVERING DIVERSITY TRAINING

In recent years, a transformation has occurred in relation to how human resources services are structured and delivered in organizations. The impetus for this change resulted from a re-visioning of the core role and functions of HR and a realization that HR needed to become more strategically focused to meet the needs of the 21st century workforce. The work of Ulrich and Brockbank (2005) assigned five new HR roles: employee advocate; strategic partner, functional expert, human capital developer and HR leader and created and four new HR delivery mechanisms: corporate HR, embedded HR, centres of expertise and line managers. These changes have driven HR out of centralised functions and placed HR at the business coalface, making HR accountable for enacting and enabling business development. Within such structures, line managers are now playing an increasingly significant role, being empowered to step up and accept many aspects of HR operational delivery (Truss & Gratton, 1994; Mello, 2007). In the context of diversity, line managers are often front-line facilitators in delivering diversity training to employees. As Hales (2005) points out, organizations are adopting more participative management styles leading to line managers taking on the role of "coach," "conductor" or "leader" of motivated work teams. He argues that this has been accompanied with line managers acquiring more middle-management functions and becoming more "mini general managers" in charge of more HR delivery with less emphasis on supervision.

Increased involvement of line managers in HR delivery—and in this case, diversity training poses many organisational challenges, not least whether line managers have the necessary skills to deliver such training effectively. Hailey *et al.* (2005) are skeptical that line managers will have the skills, knowledge and expertise necessary to engage with front-line HR delivery and maintain that line managers will require extensive training to ensure their overall effectiveness. Engagement with diversity training and HR issues will inevitably come on top of an already burgeoning workload leading to feelings amongst some line managers that they are being "dumped upon" (Renwick, 2003, p. 265) or "pushed upon to take new HR responsibilities" (Harris, et al., 2002, p. 219). Indeed, research by both Foster and Harris (2005) and Greene and Kirton (2011) indicates that line managers may be at a genuine loss to know what they are required to do to demonstrate their commitment to diversity issues and that they may have a very limited understanding of the business case.

While the new HR structures allocates overall responsibility for diversity with diversity advocates (so-called "functional experts" under Ulrich's framework), Kirton *et al.* (2007) maintain that diversity advocates are often driven by moral convictions as much as the business case. They suggest that diversity advocates often occupy a difficult position balancing organizational change roles with social justice and policy-making functions, whilst building and developing relationships with line managers and other stakeholder groups. For her part, Jones (2004) sees a conflict between the social change agenda pursued equal opportunities officers (now increasingly replaced by diversity advocates) and the private sector individualistic language of HR professionals and departments who see managing diversity as a less threatening sanitizing discourse enabling the pursuit of an organizationally-driven agenda—thereby fostering a potentially exploitative relationship between employers and workers.

In delivering diversity training, one of the challenges faced by line managers is to define the parameters under which diversity will be discussed. As Khan *et al.* (2010) point out, diversity may be examined across various spectrums including: "readily detectable versus less observable" diversity; "surface level versus deep level" diversity and "highly job related" versus "less job related" diversity. To date, much reliance has been placed on interventions such as lectures, videos, role-plays, discussions and case studies to get employees to engage with their feelings about diversity and outline the consequences and impact of discrimination experiences (McGuire, 2011; Hite & McDonald, 2006). Such interventions focus on making diversity more personal to individuals—rather than a cold legalistic framework. In this regard, they are aimed at winning hearts and minds, but such interventions can equally under-play the potency of organizational barriers facing employees from minority groups. As such, Foster and Harris (2005) caution that relying on case studies and role-play scenarios can lead to an unrealistic view of how diversity issues are approached in practice. They posit that diversity training needs to provide line managers with relevant, durable work-based solutions than sets of policies handed out for implementation.

To deliver diversity training, it is arguable that line managers need to be equipped with both emotional intelligence skills (Goleman, 2004) and cultural intelligence skills (Earley & Mosakowski, 2004). Emotional intelligence is critical in delivering diversity training, as line managers need empathy and social skills in developing relationships with others and increasing employee awareness of diversity issues and support adaptation to new behaviors that may be required. Line managers will need to have both tact and diplomacy skills in confronting unacceptable behaviors and attitudes and helping employees embrace more inclusive approaches. In relation to cultural intelligence, Earley and Mosakowski (2004) argue that it is a development of emotional intelligence, related to an individual's ability to interpret gestures and behavior and position them within a cultural context. Successful managers need to be able to cope and adapt to different national, corporate and divisional/unit cultures. Cultural intelligence requires managers to understand that cultures exert powerful forces upon individuals and groups and that understanding such cultures is essential to bring about sustainable lasting change.

IDENTITY AND PRIVILEGE

Identity is a critical issue in employee interactions in the workplace. Employees need to feel that they can express themselves freely and appropriately in a safe working environment. A core tenet of managing diversity is the development of an organizational environment, which respects and protects individuals' identities from discrimination and fosters a culture of acceptance and tolerance. Ely and Thomas (2001) identify diversity as being forged in an individual's identity, encompassing membership of different social groups and including both visible and invisible components through which individuals categorise themselves. Giovannini (2004) goes further to assert that diversity is a differentiator, which enables individuals to distinguish themselves as unique and distinctive. Similarly, Cohn and Mullennix (2007) see diversity as an inescapable and intrinsic part of the human experience, requiring individuals to develop skills to learn and adapt to difference.

Dealing with difference and adjusting to worldviews dissimilar from your own can often be a daunting prospect. This may be particularly demanding as diversity discussions often necessitate an exploration of power dynamics and associated privilege. As such, diversity training can often involve discussions of sensitive issues of identity and worldview, with Cavaleros *et al.* (2002, p. 51) arguing that diversity training is often met with "with confusion, disorder, approval, reverence, bewilderment and even hostility." Such a range of emotional reaction often results from a realisation of how hierarchies within organizations are constructed based upon social group membership (McKay & Avery, 2006; Aquino, et al., 2005) and the hidden privileges and advantages that members of the dominant group possess, often without their own awareness of them (McGuire & Bagher, 2010). Two core characteristics underpinning the concept of privilege is that privilege is unearned and invisible—in other words, the individual is likely to be unaware of the benefits being gained by virtue through its possession and the individual has not been accrued the entitlement on his/her own merits (McIntosh, 1993). The existence of privilege means that the experience of organizations will not be uniform across all demographic groups—and that individuals who belong to majority groups will find greater acceptance, recognition and reward than individuals belonging to minority groups.

As social constructs, organizations are hotbeds of unacknowledged inequalities, discrimination, and subjugation. To recognise organizations as such requires individuals to leave their privileged positions (privilege positions being those occupied on the basis of being in the dominant group for the characteristic of gender, age, sexual orientation, race, disability, class, or religion) to one side and look at the range of vested interests across the organization as a whole. In the remainder of this section, we examine how identity is constructed in the areas of gender, race, and sexual orientation.

Gender is drawn upon now to illustrate; inequalities within organizations, how the privilege of masculinity and men go unnoticed and highlight the importance for the need to raise awareness of the gendered nature of organizations through diversity training and how this can affect individuals' attitudes and behavior.

Gender is understood to be socially constructed characteristics of masculinities and femininities (Fonow & Cook, 2005), "forms of subjectivities... that are present in all persons, men as well as women" (Alvesson & Due Billing, 1997, p. 85) accomplished through action and interaction with others (Messerschmidt, 2009). However, gender is often used as "variable-orientated fixation on 'men' and 'women' using the bodies as a firm criterion for classification" (Alvesson & Due Billing, 1997, p. 82). Consequently, masculinities are understood to be the "values, experiences, and meanings that are culturally interpreted as masculine and typically feel 'natural' to or are ascribed to men more than women" (Alvesson & Due Billing, 1997, p. 83). Descriptive characteristic of masculinities are "hard, dry, impersonal, objective, explicit, outer focused, action-orientated, analytical, dualistic, quantitative, linear, rationalist, reductionist, and materialist" (Hines, 1992, p. 328). Femininity is described in contrast, with the prioritization of feelings, creativity, and imagination (Hines, 1992), cooperation, interdependence, acceptance, emotion (Marshall, 1993), nurturing, empathy, and compassion (Grant, 1988).

Gender is infused in all action and interactions (Fletcher, 1999) and cannot be removed or detached from the organizational context (Martin, 2006). Organizational practices have embodied attributes of masculinities (sex role stereotyped to men) and such practices are referred to as gendered as they "reflect and reinforce prevailing conceptions of masculinity" (Maier, 1999, p. 71). Masculine practices have become so deeply rooted within organisational culture (Martin, 2006) they have become "silent actions" (Czarniawska, 2006,

p. 234), and accepted as mainstream and legitimate practices. The dominance of masculinity within organisations over time has normalized masculine practice, stripping gender from the context and enabling masculinity to become invisible (Lewis, 2006; Simpson & Lewis, 2005). Consequently, we are unable to identify organisational experiences in relation to gender (Acker, 1992), which enables the gendered nature of organizational practices to continue unchallenged.

Women are marginalised and disadvantaged (Martin, 2006) as attributes most commonly associated with women are not valued or embedded within organisational processes and practices. Therefore, to suggest that organisations are gender neutral masks understandings of everyday organisational realities (Acker, 1998) of the symbolic order of gender (Gherardi, 1994). Assumptions based on essentialist notions of women's skills set, based upon their perceived domestic skills and experience perpetuates women's role as caregivers and their second place within the social order (Due Billing & Alvesson, 2000; Elliott & Stead, 2008). Consequently, women's skills are often devalued in terms of their significance and potential contribution within organizations (Due Billing & Alvesson, 2000). Biological determinism of gender results in individuals' sex at birth shaping organizational perceptions and expectations of women (and men) in relation to their assigned gender category (women are perceived to be naturally suited to domestic labour and men better to waged labour (Pilcher & Whelehan, 2004), subsequently affecting their identities and future opportunities. The category 'woman' has come to symbolise a common identity (Butler, 1990) for all women, as does the category of 'man,' resulting in women and men becoming prisoners of gendered identities (Gherardi, 1996), as attributes bestowed to one gender are implicitly denied to the other (Gherardi, 1994; Maier, 1999), denying diversity within and between the sexes (Stanley & Wise, 1993).

Providing an understanding of gender as something we all do (West & Zimmerman, 1987) through gender practice (dress, behaviour, language, interests) provides an understanding of how people conform or rebel against institutionalised gender status (Martin, 2006; Nencel, 2010). Most importantly for trainers it highlights the subtle nature of gender practice which results in gender "often [being] instantaneous, often barely noticed or made a theme in conversation" (Connell, 2003, p. 370). Highlighting the subtle nature of gender practices draws attention to the invisibility of masculine hegemony within organizations and consequential male privilege and emphasizes the need to increase awareness of the 'gender we think' (Gherardi, 1994), in order to understand experiences of gender, become more aware of the gender in our own action and to begin to challenge the gendered nature of organizations.

In conceptualising the 'gender we think,' Gherardi (1994) highlights that gender goes beyond interactional behaviour to a deeper, trans-psychic level, informed by tacit knowledge below the level of consciousness. Therefore, although we are aware of our decisions and actions, we may not be aware of how gender is implicated (Martin, 2006) within them. Nencel (2010, p. 73) assert "that much of how we construct gender...is done non-reflexively, unless we have a gender consciousness. Czarniawska's (2006, p. 234) study highlights that subtle forms of gender are invisible and, consequently, perceived as legitimate enabling individuals to "do gender unto the other... ascribing gender to people through discriminatory action." Furthermore, she argues that such discriminatory action may be accepted by both the individuals to whom the discriminatory action is aimed and society more broadly, for example men and women using different toilets. She maintains that discrimination cannot continue to hide behind other criteria for example "she lacks leadership qualities." At this 'deeper' level of the 'gender we think' (Gherardi, 1994), our gendered assumptions must be surfaced, to articulate, highlight

and challenge the more subtle forms of the gender we do (Martin, 2003, 2006) to understand how we continue to perpetuate gendered assumptions.

For example, Martin (2006, p. 257) illustrates gender practice as the "practice of referring to women who are in no sense 'girls' relative to age, as 'girls'." She contends that:

a man who refers to women at work as 'girls' enacts a practice made available to him by the institutionalized system of gender relations. He knows about the practice; he uses it correctly, relative to (some) norms of the gender order. Yet in using it he may communicate a message he does not intend. (On the other hand, he may intend it.) The social and cultural context in which the term is used will affect the way women interpret and react to it. For instance, they may accept it when a male friend calls them 'girls' at a dinner party but resent it if he does so at work. They may especially dislike it if their boss, man or woman, uses the term. The meanings people attach to gender are contextually dependent. Contexts influence workers' intellectual and emotional responses to gendering practice; thus context as well as content must be addressed if gender's resilience and influence at work is to be unmasked (Ferre, 2003; Ridgeway & Correll, 2004, p. 257).

Katila and Merilainen's (1999) research draws upon the same example, referring to women as 'girls.' Whilst this may be accepted in one social context as free spirited and playful, in an organisational setting it may be rejected as derogatory, with a perceived intent of undermining women's credibility (Katila & Merilainen, 1999). Responses to such comments are often made unreflexively (Martin, 2006; Nencel, 2010). HRD practitioners therefore have a responsibility to highlight "the shape, fluidity and dynamism of gender in practice" (Martin, 2006, p. 254) in order to understand the 'gender we do' and the 'gender we think' (Gherardi, 1994) within organizational contexts that perpetuate privileging specific groups.

In relation to race, Bernal *et al.* (1990) define ethnic or racial identity as the set of ideals, values, attitudes and behaviours that distinguishes an individual as a member of a particular race or social group. Understanding the traditions and cultural backgrounds of minority employees is crucial to ensuring that an individual's identity is safeguarded and respected within organisations. In many cases, race/ethnicity forms part of a multiple social identity whereby the individual may be a member of more than one minority grouping (Frable, 1997). In some cases, this can lead to double-marginalisation or concealment of a component/element of one's identity. However, research does point to the importance of race/ethnicity as a factor in how individuals relate and interact with organizations. For their part, Buttner *et al.* (2010) argue that individuals from a minority racial/ethnic background exhibit greater racial awareness in organisations and will monitor the organisational climate to evaluate levels of fairness and trust.

The phenomenon of racism casts a long shadow on society and is an important factor when dealing with racial diversity in organisations. As Oikelome (2011, p. 195) states: "There are forms of social influence—racism and its effects—that are experienced almost exclusively by members of minority ethnic groups—racism cannot be taken to be a given feature of society; its historical roots and current social origins need to be explored." The implications from this quote are that racism exists at a structural level across organisations and society. For their part, Barrett *et al.* (2004) identify institutional barriers and personal barriers affecting the progression of minority racial groups in organizations and society. In relation to institutional barriers, they identify limited access to vocational guidance, tracking in appropriate jobs and discrimination in selection and promotion processes, whilst in terms of personal barriers they cite lack of self-confidence, less career exploration and an inability or unwillingness to play the political game as factors affecting advancement.

Consequently, Thomas (2001) identifies the need for minority ethnic employees to develop competence, confidence, and credibility in the early stages of their career as tools to help counter institutional and personal barriers.

Sexual orientation is an important component of an individual's identity. Wright (2011, p. 238) argues that sexual orientation and sexuality may be distinct from other diversity categories and require specific attention due to the process of "invisibilization." Gedro *et al.* (2004) argue that hetrosexism is prevalent in organizational environment and poses a persistent threat to Lesbian, Gay, Bisexual, and Transgendered (LGBT) employees in terms of employment status and income, constricted job mobility, constrained relationships with supervisors and peers and a hostile working environment. They argue that the homosexual presence in the workplace can often refer to the hidden "erotic" in organizations—a transgression from the organizational heterosexual norm leading to rejection and marginalization. Crocker *et al.* (1998) argue that for an LGBT person to disclose their sexuality in the workplace is to announce an association with a group that has been historically devalued and persecuted; thus, it is a decision taken with great care and after much reflection. However, King *et al.* (1998) argue that disclosure in a safe organizational environment allows LGBT people to form an authentic and stable sense of self, foster a positive homosexual image, and reduce the burden of cognitive dissonance and identity management.

Closeting or passing is a common strategy employed by LGBT people to avoid persecution, rejection, and alienation in the workplace. Goffman (1963, p. 53) defines passing as "the management of undisclosed discrediting information" and it is used by LGBT employees to conceal their sexual orientation in work environments judged to be hostile towards sexual minorities. Clair *et al.* (2005) identify the three tactics of fabrication, concealment, and discretion as strategies used to pass off ones sexual identity in the workplace. DeJordy

(2008) argues that the projection of conformity to the heterosexual norm can be very damaging as it creates a conflict between expressed and personal values leading to considerable discomfort and internal dissonance. Whilst he argues that closeting and passing may be done to increase levels of opportunity, he indicates that such strategies are invariably accompanied by increased stress, fear, and emotional exhaustion.

CONCLUSION

Diversity training in organizations represents a growing and important area of research and practice. Globalisation, employee mobility, and an emphasis on finding skilled employees means that organizations can no longer afford to neglect diversity issues. Working across different linguistic, cultural, and social contexts requires organizations to embed diversity at the heart of internationalization strategies. It challenges organizations to confront insular, discriminatory attitudes and values and adopt a more open inclusive organizational environment that respects and safeguards difference.

A solid business case is emerging for engaging with diversity in organizations. Companies which develop competence in managing diversity have been proven to be more innovative and creative, achieve higher levels of performance and productive, engage in more effective problem solving and decision-making and are more connected to local communities and customers. That said, attention needs to be paid to how diversity is delivered in organizational settings. Recent changes to HR structures now mean that line managers are increasingly tasked with diversity training. In many instances, line managers are overworked and neither have the time or skill set to deliver diversity training effectively. Organizations and HR departments in particular need to pay attention that the value of diversity training is not diluted or diminished due to poor trained line managers.

Issues of identity lie at the heart of strategies to manage and value diversity. Organizations need to understand that identity is a social construct comprised of an individual's membership of various social groups and there is a strong need to have such memberships validated and respected through fair, non-discriminatory organizational practices. Through diversity training all organisational stakeholders should be encouraged to be cognizant and critical of the own actions and how they may perpetuate discriminatory understandings and relationships within organizations (Bierema & Cseh, 2003) enabling the continuation of power and privilege to specific groups. As Metcalfe (2008, p. 449) contends, practitioners play a central role in fostering a renewed vision of diversity through the development programmes they facilitate to enable 'gender (and other diversity categories) to be placed firmly on the agenda.' Through seeking to address workplace inequalities, diversity training programmes provide a vehicle for examining issue of power and privilege and bringing a positive difference to the lives of organizational employees.

REFERENCES

Acker, J. (1992). From sex roles to gendered institutions. *Contemporary Sociology*, *21*(5), 565–569. doi:10.2307/2075528

Acker, J. (1998). The future of 'gender and organizations': Connections and boundaries. *Gender, Work and Organization*, *5*(4), 195–206. doi:10.1111/1468-0432.00057

Alvesson, M., & Due Billing, Y. (1997). *Understanding gender and organizations*. London, UK: Sage Publications.

Aquino, K., Stewart, M. M., & Reed, A. (2005). How social dominance orientation and job status influence perceptions of African-American affirmative action beneficiaries. *Personnel Psychology*, *58*, 703–744. doi:10.1111/j.1744-6570.2005.681.x

Barney, J. B., & Wright, P. M. (1998). On becoming a strategic partner: The role of human resources in gaining competitive advantage. *Human Resource Management, 37*, 31–46. doi:10.1002/(SICI)1099-050X(199821)37:1<31::AID-HRM4>3.0.CO;2-W

Barratt, I. C., Cervero, R. M., & Johnson-Bailey, J. (2004). The career development of black human resource developers in the United States. *Human Resource Development International, 7*(1), 85–100. doi:10.1080/1367886022000032354

Bernal, M. E., Knight, G. P., Ocampo, K. A., Garza, C. A., & Cota, M. K. (1990). The development of ethnic identity in Mexican-American children. *Hispanic Journal of Behavioral Sciences, 12*(1), 3–24. doi:10.1177/07399863900121001

Bierema, L. (2010). Resisting HRD's resistance to diversity. *Journal of European Industrial Training, 34*(6), 565–576. doi:10.1108/03090591011061239

Bierema, L. L., & Cseh, M. (2003). Evaluating AHRD research using a feminist research framework. *Human Resource Development Quarterly, 14*(1), 5–26. doi:10.1002/hrdq.1047

Butler, J. (1990). *Gender trouble: Feminism and the subversion of identity.* London, UK: Routledge.

Cavaleros, C., Van Vuuren, L. V., & Visser, D. (2002). The effectiveness of a diversity awareness training programme. *South African Journal of Industrial Psychology, 28*(3), 50–61.

Clair, J. A., Beatty, J. E., & MacLean, T. (2005). Out of sight but not out of mind: Managing invisible social identities in the workplace. *Academy of Management Review, 30*, 78. doi:10.5465/AMR.2005.15281431

Cohn, E., & Mullennix, J. (2007). Diversity as an integral component of college curricula. In Branche, J., Mullennix, J., & Cohn, E. (Eds.), *Diversity across the Curriculum: A Guide for Faculty in Higher Education* (pp. 213–218). Boston, MA: Anker.

Connell, R. W. (2003). Developing a theory of gender as practice: Notes on Yancey Martin's feminist lecture. *Gender & Society, 17*(3), 370–372. doi:10.1177/0891243203017003004

Cook, A., & Glass, C. (2009). Between a rock and a hard place: Managing diversity in a shareholder society. *Human Resource Management Journal, 19*(4), 393–412. doi:10.1111/j.1748-8583.2009.00100.x

Cox, T. H., & Blake, S. (1991). Managing cultural diversity: Implications for organisational competitiveness. *The Academy of Management Executive, 5*(3), 45–57.

Crocker, J., Major, B., & Steele, C. (1998). Social stigma. In Gilbert, D. T., & Fiske, S. T. (Eds.), *The Handbook of Social Psychology* (4th ed., Vol. 2, pp. 504–553). New York, NY: McGraw-Hill.

Czarniawska, B. (2006). Doing gender unto the other: Fiction as a mode of studying gender discrimination in organizations. *Gender, Work and Organization, 13*(3), 234–253. doi:10.1111/j.1468-0432.2006.00306.x

Dallas, L. L. (2002). The new managerialism and diversity on corporate boards of directors. *Tulane Law Review, 76*, 1363.

DeJordy, R. (2008). Just passing through: Stigma, passing and identity decoupling in the workplace. *Group & Organization Management, 33*(5), 504–531. doi:10.1177/1059601108324879

Dick, P., & Cassell, C. (2002). Barriers to managing diversity in the UK constabulary: The role of discourse. *Journal of Management Studies, 39*(7), 953–976. doi:10.1111/1467-6486.00319

Dickens, L., & Hall, M. (2006). Fairness up to a point: Assessing the impact of new labours employment legislation. *Human Resource Management Journal, 16*(4), 338–356. doi:10.1111/j.1748-8583.2006.00024.x

Due Billing, Y., & Alvesson, M. (2000). Questioning the notion of feminine leadership: A critical perspective on the gender labelling of leadership. *Gender, Work and Organization, 7*(3), 144–157. doi:10.1111/1468-0432.00103

Earley, P., & Mosakowski, E. (2004). Cultural intelligence. *Harvard Business Review, 82*(9), 139–146.

Elliott, C., & Stead, V. (2008). Learning for leading women's experience: Towards a sociological understanding. *Leadership, 4*(2), 159–180. doi:10.1177/1742715008089636

Ely, R. J., & Thomas, D. A. (2001). Cultural diversity at work: The effects of diversity perspectives on work group processes and outcomes. *Administrative Science Quarterly, 46*(2), 229–273. doi:10.2307/2667087

Finkelstein, S., & Hambrick, D. C. (1996). *Strategic leadership: Top executives and their effects on organizations*. Minneapolis, MN: West Educational Publishing.

Fletcher, J. K. (1999). *Disappearing acts: Gender, power and relational practice*. Cambridge, MA: The Massachusetts Institute of Technology.

Fonow, M. M., & Cook, J. A. (2005). Feminist methodology: New application in the academy and public policy. *Signs: Journal of Women in Culture and Society, 30*(4), 2211–2239. doi:10.1086/428417

Foster, C., & Harris, L. (2005). Easy to say, difficult to do: Diversity management in retail. *Human Resource Management Journal, 15*(3), 4–17. doi:10.1111/j.1748-8583.2005.tb00150.x

Frable, D. E. S. (1997). Gender, racial, ethnic, sexual, and class identities. *Annual Review of Psychology, 48*(1), 139–163. doi:10.1146/annurev.psych.48.1.139

Gedro, J., Cervero, R. M., & Johnson-Bailey, J. (2004). How lesbians learn to negotiate the heterosexism of corporate America. *Human Resource Development International, 7*(2), 181–195. doi:10.1080/1367886042000243790

Gherardi, S. (1994). The gender we think the gender we do in our everyday organisational lives. *Human Relations, 47*(6), 591–610. doi:10.1177/001872679404700602

Gherardi, S. (1996). Gendered organisational cultures: Narratives of women travellers in a male world. *Gender, Work and Organization, 3*(4), 187–201. doi:10.1111/j.1468-0432.1996.tb00059.x

Gibb, S. (2008). *Human resource development: Process, practices and perspectives* (2nd ed.). Hampshire, CT: Palgrave Macmillan.

Giovannini, M. (2004). What gets measured gets done: Achieving results through diversity and inclusion. *Journal for Quality and Participation, 27*, 21–27.

Goffman, E. (1963). *Stigma: Notes on the management of spoiled identity*. New York, NY: Simon & Schuster.

Goleman, D. (2004, January). What makes a Leader? *Harvard Business Review*, 22–34.

Grant, J. (1988). Women as managers: What they can offer to organizations? *Organizational Dynamics, 16*(1), 56–63. doi:10.1016/0090-2616(88)90036-8

Greene, A. M., & Kirton, G. (2011). Diversity management meets downsizing: The case of a government department. *Employee Relations, 33*(1), 22–40. doi:10.1108/01425451111091636

Groschl, S. (2011). Diversity management strategies of global hotel groups: A corporate web site based exploration. *International Journal of Contemporary Hospitality Management, 23*(2), 224–241. doi:10.1108/09596111111119347

Guerrier, Y., & Wilson, C. (2011). Representing diversity on UK company websites. *Equality, Diversity and Inclusion. International Journal (Toronto, Ont.), 30*(3), 183–195.

Hailey, V. H., Farndale, E., & Truss, C. (2005). The HR department's role in organisational performance. *Human Resource Management Journal, 15*(3), 49–66. doi:10.1111/j.1748-8583.2005. tb00153.x

Hales, C. (2005). Rooted in supervision, branching into management: Continuity and change in the role of first-line manager. *Journal of Management Studies, 42*(3), 471–506. doi:10.1111/j.1467-6486.2005.00506.x

Harris, L., Doughty, D., & Kirk, S. (2002). The devolution of HR responsibilities – Perspectives from the UK's public sector. *Journal of European Industrial Training, 26*(5), 218–229. doi:10.1108/03090590210424894

Harris, L., & Foster, C. (2010). Aligning talent management with approaches to equality and diversity. *Equality, Diversity and Inclusion. International Journal (Toronto, Ont.), 29*(5), 422–435.

Hines, R. D. (1992). Accounting: Filling the negative space. *Accounting, Organizations and Society, 17*(3/4), 313–341. doi:10.1016/0361-3682(92)90027-P

Hite, L. M., & McDonald, K. S. (2006). Diversity training pitfalls and possibilities: An exploration of small and mid-size US organizations. *Human Resource Development International, 9*(3), 365–377. doi:10.1080/13678860600893565

Holladay, C. L., & Quinones, M. A. (2008). The influence of training focus and trainer characteristics on diversity training effectiveness. *Academy of Management Learning & Education, 7*(3), 343–354. doi:10.5465/AMLE.2008.34251672

Iles, P., & Hayers, P. K. (1997). Managing diversity in transnational project teams: A tentative model and case study. *Journal of Managerial Psychology, 12*(2), 95–117. doi:10.1108/02683949710164190

Jones, D. (2004). Screwing diversity out of workers? Reading diversity. *Journal of Organizational Change Management, 17*(3), 281–291. doi:10.1108/09534810410538333

Katila, S., & Merilainen, S. (1999). A serious researcher or just another nice girl? Doing gender in a male-dominated scientific community. *Gender, Work and Organization, 6*(3), 163–173. doi:10.1111/1468-0432.00079

Keogh, K. E. (2008). Workplace diversity and training – More than fine words. In Wilson, J. P. (Ed.), *Human Resource Development* (2nd ed.). London, UK: Kogan Page.

King, E. B., Reilly, C., & Hebl, M. (2008). The best of times, the worst of times: Exploring dual perspectives of "coming out" in the workplace. *Group & Organization Management, 33*(5), 566–601. doi:10.1177/1059601108321834

Kirby, E. L., & Harter, L. M. (2003). Speaking the language of the bottom-line: The metaphor of "managing diversity". *Journal of Business Communication, 40*(1), 28–49. doi:10.1177/002194360304000103

Kirton, G., Greene, A. M., & Dean, D. (2007). British diversity professionals as change agents – Radicals, tempered radicals or liberal reformers? *International Journal of Human Resource Management, 18*(11), 1979–1994. doi:10.1080/09585190701638226

Lewis, P. (2006). The quest for invisibility: Female entrepreneurs and the masculine norm of entrepreneurship. *Gender, Work and Organization, 13*(5), 453–469. doi:10.1111/j.1468-0432.2006.00317.x

Maier, M. (1999). On the gendered substructure of organization: Dimensions and dilemmas of corporate masculinity. In Powell, G. N. (Ed.), *Handbook of Gender and Work*. London, UK: Sage.

Marshall, J. (1993). Organizational communication from a feminist perspective. In Deetz, S. (Ed.), *Communication Yearbook* (*Vol. 16*). Newbury Park, CA: Sage.

Martin, P. Y. (2001). Mobilizing masculinities: Women's experiences of men at work. *Organization, 8*, 587–618. doi:10.1177/135050840184003

Martin, P. Y. (2003). Said and done versus saying and doing: Gendering practices, practicing gender at work. *Gender & Society, 17*(3), 342–366. doi:10.1177/0891243203017003002

Martin, P. Y. (2006). Practising gender at work: Further thoughts on reflexivity. *Gender, Work and Organization, 13*(3), 254–276. doi:10.1111/j.1468-0432.2006.00307.x

McDonnell, A., & Collings, D. (2011). The identification and evaluation of talent in MNEs. In Scullion, H., & Collings, D. G. (Eds.), *Global Talent Management*. Oxford, UK: Routledge.

McGuire, D. (2011). Diversity training and HRD. In McGuire, D., & Jorgensen, K. M. (Eds.), *Human Resource Development: Theory and Practice*. London, UK: Sage.

McGuire, D., & Bagher, M. (2010). Diversity training in organizations: An introduction. *Journal of European Industrial Training, 34*(6), 493–505. doi:10.1108/03090591011061185

McIntosh, P. (1993). White privilege and male privilege: A personal account of coming to see correspondences through work in women's studies. In Minas, A. (Ed.), *Gender Basics: Feminist Perspectives on Women and Men* (pp. 30–38). Belmont, CA: Wadsworth.

McKay, P. F., & Avery, D. R. (2006). What has race got to do with it? Unravelling the role of racioethnicity in job seekers reactions to site visits. *Personnel Psychology, 59*, 395–429.

McLeod, P. L., Lobel, S. A., & Cox, T. H. (1996). Ethnic diversity and creativity in small groups. *Small Group Research, 27*, 248–264. doi:10.1177/1046496496272003

Mello, J. A. (2007). *Strategic human resource management*. Delhi, India: Thomson.

Messerschmidt, J. W. (2009). Doing gender: The impact of a salient sociological concept. *Gender & Society, 23*(1), 85–88. doi:10.1177/0891243208326253

Metcalfe, B. D. (2008). A feminist poststructuralists analysis of HRD: Why bodies, power and reflexivity matter. *Human Resource Development International, 11*(5), 447–463. doi:10.1080/13678860802417569

Nencel, L. (2010). Que viva la minifalda! Secretaries, miniskirts and daily practices of sexuality in the public sector in Lima. *Gender, Work and Organization, 17*(1), 69–90.

Oikelome, F. (2011). Relevance of US and UK national histories in the understanding of racism and inequality in work and career. In Healy, G., Kirton, G., & Noon, M. (Eds.), *Equality, Inequalities and Diversity: Contemporary Challenges and Strategies*. London, UK: Palgrave Macmillan.

Page, S. E. (2007). Making the difference: Applying the logic of diversity. *The Academy of Management Perspectives, 21*(4), 6–20. doi:10.5465/AMP.2007.27895335

Pilcher, J., & Whelehan, I. (2004). *50 key concepts in gender studies*. London, UK: Sage.

Prahalad, C. K., & Hamel, G. (1990). The core competence of the corporation. *Harvard Business Review, 3*, 79–91.

Rees, C., Mamman, A., & Bin Braik, A. (2007). Emiratization as a strategic HRM change initiative: Case study evidence from a UAE petroleum company. *International Journal of Human Resource Management, 18*(1), 33–53. doi:10.1080/09585190601068268

Renwick, D. (2003). Line manager involvement in HRM: An inside view. *Employee Relations, 25*(3), 262–280. doi:10.1108/01425450310475856

Richard, O. C. (2000). Racial diversity, business strategy and firm performance: A resource-based view. *Academy of Management Journal, 43*(2), 164–177. doi:10.2307/1556374

Sarra, J. (2002). Rose-colored glasses, opaque financial reporting and investor blues: Enron as con and the vulnerability of Canadian corporate law. *St. John's Law Review, 76*, 715–766.

Scullion, H., & Collings, D. G. (2011). *Global talent management*. London, UK: Routledge.

Simpson, R., & Lewis, P. (2007). *Voice, visibility and the gendering of organization*. Basingstoke, UK: Palgrave Macmillan.

Stanley, L., & Wise, S. (1993). *Breaking out again: Feminist ontology and epistemology*. London, UK: Routledge.

Stewart, M. M., Crary, M., & Humberd, B. K. (2008). Teaching value in diversity: On the folly of espousing inclusion, while practicing exclusion. *Academy of Management Learning & Education, 7*(3), 374–386. doi:10.5465/AMLE.2008.34251674

Thomas, D. A. (2001, April). The truth about mentoring minorities: Race matters. *Harvard Business Review*, 98–109.

Truss, C., & Gratton, L. (1994). Strategic human resource management: A conceptual approach. *International Journal of Human Resource Management, 5*(3), 663–686. doi:10.1080/09585199400000053

Ulrich, D., & Brockbank, W. (2005). *The HR value proposition*. Boston, MA: Harvard Business School Press.

Vielba, C., & Edelshain, D. (1997). Are business schools meeting the challenge of International communication? *Journal of Management Development, 16*(2), 80–92. doi:10.1108/02621719710164265

Watkins, K., & Cseh, M. (2009). Competence development in the USA: Limiting expectations or unleashing global capacities. In Illeris, K. (Ed.), *International Perspectives on Competence Development*. Oxford, UK: Routledge.

West, C., & Zimmerman, D. H. (1987). Doing gender. *Gender & Society, 1*, 125–151. doi:10.1177/0891243287001002002

Wright, T. (2011). Exploring the intersections of gender, sexuality and class in the transport and construction industries. In Healy, G., Kirton, G., & Noon, M. (Eds.), *Equality, Inequality and Diversity: Contemporary Challenges and Strategies*. London, UK: Palgrave Macmillan.

Chapter 17

Demographic Changes and Equal Employment Opportunity Legislation:
Implications for Leveraging Workforce Diversity in the Field of Human Resource Development

Shani D. Carter
Rhode Island College, USA

ABSTRACT

This chapter reviews the relationship between a selection of United States federal laws and Human Resource Development (HRD). The chapter specifically reviews United States federal Equal Employment Opportunity (EEO) laws related to race, gender, age, and national origin, discusses how the passage of these laws led to an increased diversity of the labor force, and demonstrates how utilizing this legislation can improve the research and practice of HRD. A comprehensive group of employment laws were passed between 1960 and 2000, and data from the U.S. Departments of Labor and Census indicate that these laws have served to substantially increase the percentage of minorities and women in the labor force. This increasing diversity requires practitioners to rethink the methods they use to deliver training and development programs to employees. In addition, researchers should examine how the increase in diversity impacts all areas of HRD, such as training, mentoring, and work-life balance.

INTRODUCTION

The United States Presidential Primary season of 2008 made the issue of diversity more salient than ever. During the season, for the first time, we witnessed the participation of a viable of group multicultural candidates, including members of several races, religions, and both genders. This diversity was accompanied by an unprecedented level of citizen participation in the Primary election process in donations and voting. We have seen, then, that diversity has an energizing effect on many people. Given this effect, Human Resource Development (HRD) scholars and practitioners

DOI: 10.4018/978-1-4666-1812-1.ch017

should take a fresh look at diversity in the labor force and how this diversity can be harnessed to energize organizations. To this end, this chapter reviews the major federal laws covering diversity and Equal Employment Opportunity (EEO) in the workplace, and examines how these laws relate to the research and practice of HRD.

The chapter begins with a review of federal EEO laws related to race, gender, age, and national origin, in view of fleshing out their richness and comprehensiveness. This is followed by a discussion of how the federal laws have led to increased diversity of the labor force and how this diversity impacts the practice of HRD. Next, the chapter gives an overview of the current knowledge of the benefits of diversity for organizations in regard to HRD. The section discusses the potential impact of diversity on organizations as a whole and the impact of diversity on HRD programs, such as mentoring programs.

The chapter then reviews how diversity relates to research in HRD, with a discussion of the Kirkpatrick (2005) model of training evaluation under the assumption that HRD practices should adapt to the changing workforce. The chapter concludes with implications for research and practice and a discussion of issues organizations should consider for the future.

HRD, DEMOGRAPHIC CHANGES, AND EEO LEGISLATION

Overview and Relationship of EEO to HRD

There have been significant changes in the composition of the workforce in the last 30 years. Specifically, there has been increased growth in the percentage of employees who are Black, Hispanic, and Asian. In addition, there has been an increase in the labor force participation rate of women, and a continued shift in the age composition of the labor force. The labor force will continue to change significantly in the coming decades.

Due to these demographic changes in the composition of the labor force, organizations should plan to tailor their HRD strategies to the needs of the diverse employees who will enter employment. It is critical that organizations manage diversity in a way that is deliberate and planned, and that the programs have CEO support to be successful (Ng, 2008).

Historic Foundations of Current Legislation

Following the end of Civil War in 1865, the United States federal government wanted to ensure that all people would be treated equally. To this end, the federal government enacted two pieces of legislation that are the basis of modern EEO laws. First, the states ratified the 14th amendment to the U.S. Constitution in 1868. This amendment guaranteed equal benefits under the law for all citizens, such that all people could own property and make contracts. Employment is considered a contract, so the amendment makes fair employment possible.

Second, the federal government passed the Civil Rights Act of 1871. This act gave everyone the right to sue in federal court. This right enabled people to sue for enforcement of the 14th Amendment, which includes the right to sue for fair employment practices. The following sections review some of the major EEO laws that grew out of the 14th amendment and their relationship to HRD.

Gender

Overview of the Laws and Relationship to HRD

There are three major laws that ensure that women and men will be treated equally in the workplace. These laws offer important safeguards for women, which are especially important given that women were laid off in higher numbers during the most economic recent recession than during prior recessions (US Congress, 2008). Organizations can benefit from following these laws because employees will have equal access to development opportunities regardless of gender. Further, employees have higher job satisfaction and productivity when they believe their compensation, development, and work assignments are based upon merit rather than on gender.

Equal Pay Act of 1963

This law requires equal pay, benefits, and pensions across genders for jobs with primarily equivalent skill, effort, responsibility, and working conditions within the same organization. Organizations are, however, permitted to offer compensating wage differentials for seniority, merit, and incentives (EEOC, 1963).

Pregnancy Discrimination Act of 1978

This law categorizes pregnancy as a disability or generic medical condition. Therefore, employees who are pregnant must be treated equally to employees with other medical conditions, and they cannot be refused a job or a promotion because of the pregnancy if employees with other medical conditions are not denied these opportunities (EEOC, 1978).

Sexual Harassment

Sexual harassment is covered under a broader law, Title VII of the Civil Rights Act of 1964, which prohibits all forms of gender-based workplace discrimination. The first type of sexual harassment is labeled Quid Pro Quo (i.e., this for that). This harassment occurs when conditions of employment are contingent upon submission to sexual advances. The second type of sexual harassment is labeled hostile environment. This harassment occurs when the work environment or culture make

it difficult for someone to comfortably perform tasks of a job. This form of harassment is in the eye of the beholder, therefore, what is offensive to one person may be inoffensive to another. Employees must, therefore, make each other aware of their own level of comfort (see Figure 1).

Changes in the Labor Force

The passage of the Equal Pay Act in 1963, Title VII in 1964, and the Pregnancy Discrimination Act in 1978 led to greater employment opportunities for women. As a result, the Labor Force Participation Rate (i.e., percentage of all people who are working or looking for work) of women has risen steadily during the last forty years, from 44.7% in 1973 to 59.3% in 2007 (US Bureau of Labor Statistics, 2008). This compares with a slight decline for men, from 78.8% in 1973 to 73.2% in 2007. The result is that, while in 1973 only 38.9% of workers were women, today 46.4% (nearly half) of the total labor force is comprised of women (U.S. Bureau of Labor Statistics, 2008).

Impact on HRD of Gender-Based Changes

It is known that women's career paths often differ from those of men, frequently due to work-life balance (Sullivan & Mainiero, 2008). Organizations can therefore design career paths to accommodate the needs of employees with young children, perhaps including flextime, job-sharing, and telecommuting arrangements. These arrangements should be available to all employees (not just to women or to those with children) so that all employees are encouraged to view the programs as a means to balance their work and personal lives (American Federation of Teachers, 2011). An appropriate balance in the work-life area can positively impact an employee's career development (Kahnweiler, 2008; MacDermid & Wittenborn, 2007).

Figure 1. Increase of women in the labor force (Source: US Bureau of Labor Statistics)

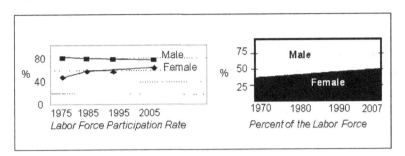

Other reasons for different career paths of men and women is women's high desire for meaning and challenge in their work (Sullivan & Mainiero, 2008). To meet the need for meaning at work, organizations should increase organizational social responsibility and offer programs related to total wellness, and community service. To meet the need of challenge at work, organizations should provide job rotation and succession planning (Sullivan & Mainiero, 2008).

Organizations also should provide company-wide programs to promote gender equality and neutrality. For example, organizations should offer mentoring and training on gender-related issues. Topics can include gender-based differences in management styles and negotiation. For example, frequently, women are expected to be kind and sweet, and when they behave in an assertive manner, they are labeled as being inappropriately aggressive (Jaschik, 2011). Conversely, when women do not behave assertively, they are said to need mentoring and coaching in assertiveness (Lublin, 2011). This creates a no-win situation for women, therefore organizations should provide training company-wide to lessen this bias.

In addition, organizations should offer training on sexual harassment and misogyny prevention. It is known that as women rise to higher positions in their organizations, they often face increasing amounts of harassment (McLaughlin & Blacktone, 2009). It is hypothesized that this increased harassment may be due to some male coworkers feeling social identity threat from the increased

number of women moving into higher level positions (Carter, 2010). This increased harassment can demotivate women from obtaining developmental opportunities and from advancing in their careers. The harassment also can demotivate male and female witnesses to the harassment because it leads them to believe work environment is unprofessional (McLaughlin & Blacktone 2009). Therefore, in order for organizations to ensure that women pursue and benefit from development opportunities, all employees should be trained in regard to these issues.

In regard to performance appraisal, it is widely known that women with the same productivity as men are frequently rated lower than men are rated, both by men and by women (Fisher, 2008; Jaschik, 2011; Sander & Hall, 1986; Wennerds & Wold, 1997). Therefore, organizations should construct performance appraisal documents that lessen bias (e.g., Behaviorally Anchored Rating Scale). Organizations also should provide training to all managers in conducting appraisals in order to ensure high validity and reliability in the appraisal process, and to create fair opportunities for development and advancement for women.

Ethnic Background

Overview of the Law and Relationship to HRD

Federal law requires that all employees will be treated fairly in the workplace, without regard to race and national origin. Organizations can benefit from adherence to these laws because employees have higher job satisfaction and productivity when they believe their compensation, development, and work assignments are based upon merit rather than on their personal characteristics. The laws also specifically state that access to training and apprentice programs must be based on merit. The laws, therefore, enable organizations to gain the benefits of having a diverse workforce by opening training programs to all workers.

Civil Rights Act (CRA) of 1964, Title VII, amended 1991

This law requires equal treatment across race, color, religion, creed, gender, and national origin in regard to all human resources activities (EEOC, 1964). The law applies to nearly all employers, including: private employers with more than 15 employees; state and local government; employment agencies; apprenticeship programs; training programs; unions with more than 15 members; and educational institutions. In addition, several Presidential Executive Orders (i.e., 11246 of 1965; 11375 of 1967; and 11478 of 1969) apply the requirements of Title VII to the Federal Government.

Amendment to Title VII

In 1990, Congress passed CRA 1991 to amend Title VII of CRA 1964 in response to several 1980's Supreme Court decisions. There are six major areas of the amendment, including: burden of proof; HR practices covered; mixed motives; consent decrees; international employment; and seniority systems. Most of the details of the 1991 amendment will not be discussed in this chapter because they are not directly related to HRD, but tend more toward finer points of definitions in the law.

The one area of the amendment that relates directly to HRD is mixed motives. Mixed motives occur when a decision regarding an employee is based upon valid work-related reasons and upon demographic reasons. For example, if a female manager with acceptable-level performance were not promoted to vice president because she wore pants instead of skirts, this would be a mixed motive. In this case, the decision to deny the promotion would be illegal because it was partially based on gender (i.e., skirts).

Changes in the Labor Force

The percentage of the labor force that is Black, Latino, and Asian has doubled since the early 1970's. From 1973 to 2007, this percentage has increased from 13.6% to 27%. This percentage is projected to grow at a faster rate, and will increase to 32% of the labor force by 2020. In addition, the U.S. Census Bureau projects that minorities will make up 54% of the total U.S. population by 2050 (Navarrette, 2008) (see Figure 2).

Impact on HRD of Changes in Ethnicity

This continued increase in the number of Black, Latino, and Asian employees will have numerous effects on organizations. Specifically, employees of different cultural backgrounds may need to be trained to interact effectively with each other, thus increasing organizations' cultural sensitivity development needs (Combs & Griffith, 2007). Employee development in regard to having productive cross-cultural interactions can be accomplished via formal workshops. If workshops are held, it is imperative that the workshop leaders represent a cross-section of ethnicities in order for the workshop to be seen as valid by employees (Cross, 2010).

Employee development also can be accomplished by having employees regularly meet with their peers who are from different cultural backgrounds, because there is some evidence that frequent contact with others lessens stereotype biases (Combs & Griffith, 2007). In other words, ensuring that teams and committees have

Figure 2. Percentage of the U.S. labor force by race

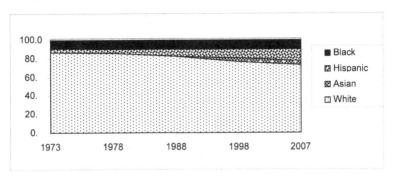

a mixture of races and national origins represented in membership, can, over time, lead to greater cross-cultural understandings.

In addition, increased immigration might affect the skill mix available to organizations. Organizations may find that school systems outside the United States have emphasized different skill sets than those that are emphasized in the United States, leading to skill gaps between what an organization needs and what employees offer. For example, U.S. based organizations may have a high need of communication skills, but employees whose first language is not English, but who have high technical skills, may find themselves at a disadvantage. For a second example, it has been found that cooperation is a cultural norm (Keller & Loewenstein, 2011). Given that U.S. based schools and colleges frequently emphasize competition between peers, but other countries (e.g., China, Japan) emphasize cooperation between peers (Keller & Loewenstein, 2011) organizations will need to provide developmental opportunities to all employees to enable them to work together effectively. For example, within Toyota, teamwork is a critical part of the corporate culture. Toyota must provide extensive training in teamwork at its facilities in the United States because U.S. employees tend to place their own interests ahead of those of the company (Editor, 2006).

Further, employees from different cultural backgrounds may have different learning styles, thus requiring organizations to use multiple train-ing methods. For example, employees from the United States may prefer participative learning methods while employees from other countries may prefer lecture-based training. Organizations may, therefore, need to tailor their HRD programs to the needs of employees of different cultural backgrounds.

Age and Generations

Overview of the Laws and Relationship to HRD

Over the last 30 years, life expectancy and mean retirement ages have risen. Given that there are more older workers in the labor force, it is beneficial for organizations to ensure that older workers are treated equally to younger workers in regard to developmental activities such as training, mentoring, and succession planning. In addition, there are cultural differences between older workers and younger workers, and organizations should provide developmental opportunities to ensure that all employees can work together effectively.

The Age Discrimination in Employment Act (ADEA) of 1967 and 1990

This law protects employees age 40 and older, and mandates that employers cannot discriminate on the basis of age if an employee is older than another employee. The law covers all human resources activities for employers with more than 20 employees (EEOC, 1967). There are several exceptions in the law in regard to public safety, the most notable being that airline pilots are required to retire from flying jumbo jets at age 65.

Three Generations

There are currently three large generations in the workforce, each having come of age amidst very different social eras, and having highly divergent value sets and attitudes towards the workplace. The Baby Boom generation, consisting of people born between 1945 and 1964, is the largest of the three generations, consisting of 47.2% of the labor force. Due to the large size of the generation, they have faced high competition for advancement, and because there are relatively few promotions available, organizations have difficulty finding substitutable incentives and rewards to motivate these employees (Hall & Richter, 1990). Also, due to the high competition for advancement, these employees have, of necessity, sacrificed their personal lives for the sake of their careers. They have very high company loyalty and tend to remain at the same organization for a large part of their careers. Research shows that workers around age 50 face a high level of age-based discrimination, such as termination and harassment (Santora & Seaton, 2008), and most of the members of the Baby Boom generation have passed this age milestone.

The next youngest generation is labeled Generation X, consisting of those born between 1965 and 1980, which make up 31.2% of the labor force. These workers came of age during an era of social, political, and economic turmoil, including Watergate, the 1970's OPEC oil crisis and stagflation, mass layoffs without notice during the early 1980's, and the rise of two-income households without access to daycare. They, therefore, witnessed an era when organizations routinely cast aside loyal workers, and when they themselves became "latchkey children," needing to care for

themselves after school at an early age so that both parents could work. The result is that they are self-sufficient, rarely trust organizations, have low company loyalty, and engage in job hopping. Generation X members are primarily concerned with quality-of-life issues, rather than career issues. Baby Boomers sometimes view Generation X members as being lazy and disloyal. Further, each generation harbors stereotypes about the others, which are often untrue (Rossi, 2007).

The youngest generation is labeled Generation Y, whose members were born between 1980 and 2000, and who represent 8.1% of the labor force. They are primarily the children of Baby Boomers, and learned to have high organization loyalty from their parents. They tend to remain at the same organization for many years. They also have strong social ties, and are highly skilled with computer-based technology (see Figure 3).

Impact on HRD of Age Differences

Organizations should offer training regarding workplace behavioral norms and expectations. Members of the three generations sometimes clash regarding work-related issues such as schedules, workload, autonomy, and time off and also regarding social issues such as acceptable jokes, gender roles, and other social norms. These

Figure 3. Population and labor force by age and generation 2009 (Source: US Bureau of Labor Statistics)

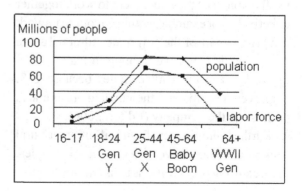

disagreements can lead to less effective group decision making, lower productivity, and higher turnover. Organizations should help employees balance work-life issues as part of their development plans to better integrate Generation X and Generation Y employees into the organization (Morris & Madsen, 2007).

There also may be generational-based differences in HRD needs regarding skill sets and training methods. Organizations should ensure that older employees have access to development opportunities rather than assuming that only new or younger employees are in need of development (Callanan & Greenhaus, 2008). The older generations tended to be educated in lecture-based formats, and also are adept at self-study. Generation Y was educated in a more interactive educational system, and its members tend to perform less well in lecture-based and reading-list based methods. They prefer multi-media teaching methods, therefore, organizations may need to change the form of training.

Relationship of EEO Laws to Measurement in HRD

Enforcement mechanisms for Title VII were created by the EEO Act of 1972. This law gave the Equal Employment Opportunity Commission (EEOC) enforcement powers. In 1978, the U.S. Department of Labor wrote guidelines defining discrimination, which were derived from the law and from standard statistical reliability and validity procedures. These are known as the Uniform Guidelines on Employee Selection Procedures, which require organizations to demonstrate job relatedness of measurement tools using several criteria, including: content validity; concurrent validity; and predictive validity (US DOL, 1978). Therefore, the federal EEO guidelines use the same measurement guidelines that had been used by the field of HRD for decades.

The Uniform Guidelines also define several types of discrimination, including methods that focus on types of discrimination and comparisons across groups. The types of discrimination are disparate treatment (i.e., intentionally treating an individual differently because of demographics) and disparate impact (i.e., facially neutral [unintentional] device negatively impacts a group). Disparate impact occurs when a measurement device causes rejection of a significantly higher percentage of one group compared to another group. For example, a training admissions test for firefighters might fail nearly all women while passing nearly all men.

Organizations can use what is called the "4/5 rule" as a as rule-of-thumb, but are not required to do so. This rule states that the pass rate for each group should be at least 80% (4/5) as high as the pass rate for all other groups. For example, if 20% of men pass the test, then at least 16% of women should pass the test, also (16%=80% times 20%). If a test does not meet the 4/5 rule, then an organization should double-check the validity and reliability of the test. If the test is reliable and valid, and if no viable non-discriminatory test exists, then the organization can continue to use the test. Organizations also should use the 4/5 rule to compare the availability, (i.e., percentage of people by Title VII categories in company who are qualified and interested in training) with its utilization (i.e., percentage trained by Title VII categories). In summary, by using the Uniform Guidelines, organizations can monitor whether they are adhering to the laws in regard to access to training and development opportunities.

BENEFITS OF DIVERSITY FOR ORGANIZATIONS AND IMPACT ON DEVELOPMENT PROGRAMS

Diversity of demographic characteristics of an organization's workforce can bring a multitude of backgrounds, work styles, and skills to an organization. This diversity of knowledge, skills, and abilities can advance organizational change and development and can improve an organization's competitive advantage. This section gives a brief overview of some of the types of impact diversity can have on HRD.

Current Issues of Organizations and Diversity

Organizational Change

When an organization's members hail from different backgrounds, they often hold a diversity of views, and these divergent views can lead to increased organizational flexibility because employees consider a greater number of options and scenarios when planning than they would consider if all the employees had the same background (Page, 2007). This increased flexibility might help increase the organization's ability to respond to changes in its environment, but some researchers believe this area needs further study (Curtis & Dreachslin, 2008).

A second issue to consider in regard to organizational change and diversity relates to the different types of employment relationships that are frequently held by different groups. Specifically, often, women, very young workers, and older workers hold part-time or temporary positions in organizations (Gumbrell-McCormick, 2011). Given that women, very young workers, and older workers are a growing part of the labor force, organizations will need to change their operational methods and management styles in order to integrate these part time and temporary workers effectively into the organizations if the organizations are to remain competitive (Gumbrell-McCormick, 2011).

Recruitment, Staffing, and Retention

Applicants' beliefs about whether an organization has a favorable climate in regard to diversity impacts recruiting. Organizations that have a favorable reputation in regard to diversity can more easily recruit and hire diverse applicants, which can have a positive impact on the organization (Cross, 2010). Organizations should form partnerships with Historically Black Colleges and Universities (HBCUs), Hispanic-Serving Institutions (HSIs), tribal colleges to improve their recruitment and retention of diverse applicants (American Federation of Teachers, 2010).

Further, organizations that successfully integrate diverse employees into the organization face lower turnover of these employees, and thereby obtain a higher return on their training and development expenses. These organizations also have better communication between employees, higher productivity, and lower amounts of internal complaints and lawsuits (Cross, 2010).

Organizational change to increase acceptance of diversity in organizations should be fully supported by top management (Gonzalez, 2010). These top managers should initiate, monitor, and support the organizational change. Throughout the change process, they should make their vision known, grant authority and influence to employees from diverse backgrounds, and ensure that all employees have the opportunity to participate in diversity-related activities (Gonzalez, 2010).

Current Issues of Employee Development and Diversity

Currently, one of the areas of focus in regard to diversity is mentoring for women and minorities, because mentoring is seen as a way to give long-term, individualized development to employees who may not have other means of access to organizational social networks. Mentoring for women and minorities should differ from standard mentoring programs because these employees' expectations sometimes differ from expectations of White males. For example, women and minorities depend more upon objective human capital items such as education, prior experience, and performance appraisals for career development compared to White males (Daley, 1996). Mentoring of women and minorities tends to focus on job-specific issues, and does not include social capital such as networking. Further, their supervisors tend to lack information on individual-to-organizational fit.

Mentoring and Gender

Mentors believe there are significant personal and organizational benefits from mentoring (de Vries, Webb, & Eveline, 2006). For example, long-term, cross-gender mentoring for women can foster organizational change because men involved in cross-gender mentoring gain an increased understanding of gender issues at work. Thus, cross-gender mentoring should be seen as a developmental opportunity for the mentor and for the employee being mentored.

Unfortunately, women are often denied access to traditional organizational networks which are male dominated, which makes women-to-women mentoring critical for female career success (Cross & Armstrong, 2008). Women-to-women mentoring may at first feel unnatural to women, but women-to-women mentoring can reduce workplace stress (American Federation of Teachers, 2011). Women who feel professionally disconnected from each other can connect by mentoring each other (Keating, 2002). Again, mentoring should be seen as a developmental opportunity for the mentor and for the employee being mentored.

Mentoring and Ethnicity

Minorities also have different mentoring needs than White males. Minority professionals, especially minority women, tend to participate heavily in community service outside work and in recruiting, mentoring, and committee work in the workplace (Hewlett, Luce, & West, 2005). This involvement can increase organizations' competitive advantage; therefore, mentors should respect and value these tasks, as opposed to viewing these activities as unimportant, which is common. Mentors should help the employees being mentored utilize their community service and organizational service as opportunities to develop professional networks and as opportunities to develop leadership and managerial skills. In addition, mentors should recognize how remaining connected to the outside community can increase the employees' work-life balance, job satisfaction, and knowledge of customer preferences.

Mentoring and Age

In regard to the aging of the Baby Boom generation, many of these employees are beginning to retire, so organizations will need to find development opportunities to encourage them to remain in the organization. In addition, these employees should be encouraged to mentor younger workers in order to pass their knowledge on to younger generations prior to their retirement (Kaye & Cohen, 2008). Generation X and Generation Y members prefer participative forms of management, so mentoring programs will need to be more participative and less directive than programs offered for Baby Boomers.

Some of the older workers who plan to continue working often face stereotypes and discrimination. They are seen as being warmer but less competent than younger workers, and face age-related bias in employment (Krings, Sczesny, & Kluge, 2011). Organizations should train younger workers to avoid stereotyping older workers.

Summary

This section gave a brief overview of several relationships between HRD and diversity. It gave a brief view of how the experiences of women, minorities, and older workers in the workplace differ from those of White men. The fact that these experiences differ indicates that the field of HRD should be attentive to the demographic characteristics of employees.

THE FUTURE OF THE PRACTICE OF HRD AND DIVERSITY

Self Reflection of Practitioners

HRD practitioners should examine how diversity issues affect their relationships with their colleagues and trainees. They also should examine how the laws impact their activities. Practitioners should ask themselves several questions in regard to diversity. For example, how do the laws impact organizations and the way practitioners should conduct activities such as orientation, training, and mentoring? HRD practitioners should take a fresh look at their training and development activities in light the Equal Pay Act, Title VII CRA 1964, and the Age Discrimination in Employment Act.

Access to Training

In regard to the Equal Pay Act, which mandates equal pay for equal compensable factors across gender, HRD practitioners should examine whether access to and participation rates in their programs are equal for men and women. If access and participation differ by gender, practitioners should determine whether it is due to employee motivation, supervisor practices, or to the practices of the practitioners themselves. Practitioners also should examine whether learning outcomes differ by gender. If gender-related learning differences exist, practitioners should determine whether these differences are due to employees or due to pedagogy. Last, practitioners should examine whether employment outcomes, such as pay raises and promotions differ by gender. Practitioners should work closely with supervisors to ensure that all employees are given the opportunity to utilize their new skills in the workplace and that they are rewarded fairly for doing so.

Pedagogy and Diversity

HRD practitioners should determine what changes in regard to diversity in employee characteristics have occurred in their organizations. HRD practitioners should gather data on the age, gender, race, and national origin of employees with the goal of creating developmental programs that will benefit all employees and the organization. These programs should be tailored to the demographic characteristics of the employees to ensure that they obtain job-related skills.

Cultural Sensitivity Training

In addition, if an organization's diversity has increased markedly, or if the organization is experiencing difficulties due to diversity, then the HRD practitioners should develop programs to increase cultural diversity acceptance throughout the organization. Organizations should focus on evaluating the effectiveness of diversity training and development programs because, currently, about 25% of these programs are not evaluated on their effectiveness (Nancherla, 2008). Using the Kirkpatrick (2005) model, organizations should first conduct a needs assessment to determine which types of programs are needed, and then determine whether the programs met their objectives. The programs should be evaluated for their impact on the trainees, trainee coworkers, departments, and organizational results, which can include a wide array of variables such as employee turnover, profit, productivity, volume, and product launches.

Relationships with Researchers

HRD practitioners should continue to maintain relationships with HRD researchers, and they also should reach out into other areas of research. For example, HRD practitioners should read articles and journals related to diversity in addition to reading articles related to HRD. Broadening their reading list beyond HRD publications is particularly important because diversity issues are often not mentioned in HRD publications. For example, the classic textbook of HRD, Foundations of Human Resource Development, by Swanson and Holton (2001) does not have the words race, gender, women, or diversity in either the table of contents or the index. It devotes only two pages (of 385) to globalization.

FUTURE OF RESEARCH IN HRD AND DIVERSITY

Self Reflection of Researchers

Professors of both genders and all ethnicities should examine how diversity issues relate to their roles as professors, such as, their relationships with their colleagues, students, and universities. For example, it has been found that for Blacks and Latinos, parental encouragement and financial concerns have the strongest impact on the decision to become business professors (Stewart, 2008). Colleges should examine how these variables influence the ongoing careers of their minority professors.

Professors should consider how their own demographic characteristics impact their relationships with each other. For example, Baby Boom professors and Generation X professors may have very different beliefs regarding work-life balance and organizational loyalty. It may be the case that Generation X professors have lower company loyalty, making them less likely to spend their entire careers at a single college, or to sacrifice their social lives for the sake of their careers, preferring instead to maintain social relationships with people outside of the workplace rather than exclusively with coworkers.

Last, all professors also should consider how diversity issues shape their teaching and research. While some professors teach and research directly in diversity issues, other professors do not touch upon these topics, while other professors briefly mention diversity in the context of other issues. All professors should examine current research in diversity issues to determine how diversity impacts their area of expertise, and also to determine how best to approach their students who are from diverse backgrounds.

Training Methods and Diversity

There are many areas which HRD researchers can examine in regard to training methods and diversity. The literature indicates that employers are increasing their use of multiple training methods (e.g., lecture, case studies, simulation, and discussion) in training programs. One question to address is whether demographic characteristics (e.g., race, gender, religion, national origin) of trainers and trainees influence the choice of pedagogy / andragogy. For example, are male trainers more likely to use lecture while female trainers are more likely to use discussion groups? For a second example, are trainers more likely to use lecture when offering training to women than to men?

Researchers also should determine the relationship between diversity and the Kirkpatrick (2005) model of training evaluation (i.e., reaction, knowledge, behavior, results) For example, does reaction to training methods vary across demographics? That is, researchers should address the question of whether demographic characteristics of trainees has an influence on reaction to training and motivation to learn across training methods. For example, Baby Boom trainees may feel insulted at being asked to listen to a lecture without participating in discussion, which might lead them to believe the training is worthless.

Second in the Kirkpatrick (2005) model, does learning (i.e., knowledge) vary across demographics and training methods? Researchers should address the question of whether demographic characteristics of trainees influences performance in different training methods. For example, do Generation Y trainees learn more in multi-media training methods than they learn in lectures? Do trainees from Japan learn more in discussion groups than they learn in lectures?

Training Transfer and Diversity

Third in the Kirkpatrick (2005) model, does training transfer (i.e., behavior) vary across demographics? Researchers should address the question of whether demographic characteristics of trainees influences their ability to use their new skills on the job. Trainers should ensure that all trainees learn how to transfer their skills to the job. Trainers may need to include diversity-specific elements in the program, if the trainer is aware that the work environment is not entirely accepting of diversity (e.g., female carpenters). Here, elements of the work environment will be involved. Specifically, researchers should determine the extent to which supervisors foster or hinder transfer, and whether trainees are granted equal access to resources and equipment to use their new skills effectively.

Fourth in the Kirkpatrick (2005) model, does training effectiveness (i.e., results) vary across demographics? Researchers should address the question of whether demographic characteristics of trainees influences their impact on organizational results such as productivity and profit. In some cases, trainees may successfully transfer their new skills to the job, but elements outside the trainees' sphere of influence may prevent the trainees' work from impacting the larger organization. For example, a supervisor or higher-level manager may refuse to publish an employee's report, or may take credit for the employee's work.

CONCLUSION

This chapter has reviewed EEO laws, subsequent changes in demographics in the workplace, and areas researchers and practitioners can examine to improve the practice of HRD. A number of laws governing diversity were passed between 1960 and 1991, several of which were reviewed in this chapter, including the Equal Pay Act, Title VII CRA 1964, and the Age Discrimination in Employment Act. These laws aim to ensure that employees are treated fairly in regard to race, color, religion, creed, gender, national origin, and age in all employment activities. Passage of the laws increased the percentage of women, minorities, and older workers in the labor force. These demographic changes require organizations to change in order to recruit and retain talented workers.

In regard to HRD practitioners, gaining knowledge of the relationship of the laws to research and practice of HRD will enable them to operate their training and development activities in ways that maximize the benefits of having a diverse workforce. HRD practitioners should create programs that meet the needs of diverse workers. They also should create programs that lead organizations to accept diverse workers and to treat them fairly.

In regard to HRD researchers, gaining knowledge of the relationship of the laws to research and practice of HRD will add to the richness of their teaching and research. Researchers and professors should become aware of the characteristics of different demographic groups, and how these characteristics impact learning. Researchers also should examine how diversity impacts fundamental assumptions of the field of HRD, given that there is a relative dearth of research in this area.

Last, for researchers and practitioners, gaining knowledge of the laws and the impact of diversity on HRD will empower them to be treated fairly in their own careers. Researchers and practitioners can develop methods to enable them to take advantage of opportunities and to avoid pitfalls related to diversity.

REFERENCES

American Federation of Teachers. (2010). *Promoting racial and ethnic diversity in the faculty: What higher education unions can do*. Washington, DC: AFT Higher Education.

American Federation of Teachers. (2011). *Promoting gender diversity in the faculty: What higher education unions can do*. Washington, DC: AFT Higher Education.

Anonymous. (2004). Blended is better. *T + D, 58*(11), 52-55.

Callanan, G. A., & Greenhaus, J. H. (2008). The baby boom generation and career management: A call to action. *Advances in Developing Human Resources, 10*(1), 70–85. doi:10.1177/1523422307310113

Carter, S. D. (2010). Pushback: The negative HRD experiences afforded to post-tenure female faculty in the United States 1988-2004. In *Proceedings of the Academy of Human Resource Development Annual International Conference*. Knoxville, TN: HRD.

Combs, G. M., & Griffith, J. (2007). An examination of interracial contact: The influence of cross-race interpersonal efficacy and affect regulation. *Human Resource Development Review, 6*(3), 222–244. doi:10.1177/1534484307303990

Cross, C., & Armstrong, C. (2008). Understanding the role of networks in collective learning processes: The experiences of women. *Advances in Developing Human Resources, 10*(4), 600–613. doi:10.1177/1523422308320495

Cross, E. Y. (2010). Managing diversity: A continuous process of change. *Diversity Factor, 18*(2), 1–4.

Curtis, E. F., & Dreachslin, J. L. (2008). Diversity management interventions and organizational performance: A synthesis of current literature. *Human Resource Development Review, 7*(1), 107–134. doi:10.1177/1534484307311700

Daley, D. M. (1996). Paths of glory and the glass ceiling: Differing patterns of career advancement among women and minority federal employees. *Public Administration Quarterly, 20*(2), 143–162.

de Vries, J., Webb, C., & Eveline, J. (2006). Mentoring for gender equality and organisational change. *Employee Relations, 28*(6), 573. doi:10.1108/01425450610704506

(Ed.). (2006). Survey: Inculcating culture. *The Economist, 378*(8461), 13.

EEOC. (1963). *Equal pay act*. Retrieved from http://www.eeoc.gov/policy/epa.html.

EEOC. (1964). *Title VII civil rights act*. Retrieved from http://www.eeoc.gov/policy/vii.html.

EEOC. (1967). *Age discrimination in employment act*. Retrieved from http://www.eeoc.gov/policy/adea.html.

EEOC. (1978). *Pregnancy discrimination act*. Retrieved from http://www.eeoc.gov/abouteeoc/35th/thelaw/pregnancy_discrimination-1978.html.

Fisher, M. J. (2008). Study: Women professors at UCI face discrimination. *The Orange County Register*. Retrieved from http://www.ocregister.com.

Gardner, H. (1983). *Frames of mind: The theory of multiple intelligences*. New York, NY: Basic Books.

Gardner, H. (2006). *Multiple intelligences: New horizons*. New York, NY: Basic Books.

Gonzalez, J. A. (2010). Diversity change in organizations: A systemic, multilevel, and nonlinear process. *The Journal of Applied Behavioral Science*, *46*(2), 197–219. doi:10.1177/0021886310367943

Gumbrell-McCormick, R. (2011). European trade unions and 'atypical' workers. *Industrial Relations Journal*, *42*(3), 293. doi:10.1111/j.1468-2338.2011.00628.x

Hall, D. T., & Richter, J. (1990). Career gridlock: Baby boomers hit the wall. *The Academy of Management Executive*, *4*(3), 7–22.

Hewlett, S. A., Luce, C. B., & West, C. (2005). Leadership in your midst. *Harvard Business Review*, *83*(11), 74.

Jaschik, S. (2011). The enduring gender gap in pay. *Inside Higher Education*. Retrieved from http://www.insidehighered.com/news/2011/04/052/the_enduring_gender_gap_in_faculty_pay.

Jaschik, S. (2011). The MIT again reviews status of women. *Inside Higher Education*. Retrieved from http://www.insidehighered.com/news/2011/03/21/mit_issues_new_report_on_status_of_women.

Kahnweiler, W. M. (2008). The work-life conundrum: Will HRD become more involved? *Human Resource Development Quarterly*, *19*(1), 75–83. doi:10.1002/hrdq.1226

Kaye, B., & Cohen, J. (2008, April). Safeguarding the intellectual capital of baby boomers. *T&D*, 30-33. S

Keating, L. (2002). Women mentoring women: The rewards of giving. *Women in Business*, *54*(1), 28.

Keller, J., & Loewenstein, J. (2011). The cultural category of cooperation: A cultural consensus model analysis for China and the United States. *Organization Science*, *22*(2), 299–320. doi:10.1287/orsc.1100.0530

Kirkpatrick, D. L., & Kirkpatrick, J. D. (2005). *Evaluating training programs: The four levels* (3rd ed.). Alexandria, VA: American Society for Training and Development.

Krings, F., Sczesny, S., & Kluge, A. (2011). Stereotypical inferences as mediators of age discrimination: The role of competence and warmth. *British Journal of Management*, *22*(2), 187. doi:10.1111/j.1467-8551.2010.00721.x

Lublin, J. S. (2011, April 4). Coaching urged for women. *The Wall Street Journal*. Retrieved from http://online.wsj.com/article_email/SB10001424052748704530204-576237203974840800-lMyQjAxMTA-xMDAwNDEwNDQyWj.html.

MacDermid, S. M., & Wittenborn, A. K. (2007). Lessons from work-life research for developing human resources. *Advances in Developing Human Resources*, *9*(4), 556–568. doi:10.1177/1523422307305493

McLaughlin, H., Uggen, C., & Blacktone, A. (2009). *A longitudinal analysis of gender, power, and sexual harassment in young adulthood*. Paper presented at the American Sociological Association 104th Annual Meeting.

Morris, M. L., & Madsen, S. R. (2007). Advancing work-life integration in individuals, organizations, and communities. *Advances in Developing Human Resources*, *9*(4), 439–454. doi:10.1177/1523422307305486

Nancherla, A. (2006). The art of great training delivery: Strategies, tools, and tactics. *T + D*, *60*(12), 87.

Nancherla, A. (2008, May). Nobody's perfect: Diversity training study finds common flaws. *T&D*, 20.

Navarrette, R. (2008). Commentary: What Olympic gold says about diversity in America. *CNN*. Retrieved from http://www.cnn.com/2008/politics/08/21/navarrette.demograhics/index.html.

Ng, E. S. W. (2008). Why organizations choose to manage diversity? Toward a leadership-based theoretical framework. *Human Resource Development Review*, *7*(1), 58–78. doi:10.1177/1534484307311592

Page, S. E. (2007). Making the difference: Applying a logic of diversity. *The Academy of Management Perspectives*, *21*(4), 6–20. doi:10.5465/AMP.2007.27895335

Rampak, S. Z. (2001, July 26). Matching workplace skills with technology renewal. *Business Times*, 7.

Sandler, B. R., & Hall, R. (1986). The campus climate revisited: Chilly for women faculty, administrators, and graduate students. *Association of American Colleges and Universities*. Retrieved from http://dynamic.uoregon.edu/~jjf/chillyclimate.html.

Santora, J. C., & Seaton, W. J. (2008). Age discrimination: Alive and well in the workplace? *The Academy of Management Perspectives*, *22*(2), 103–104. doi:10.5465/AMP.2008.32739764

Stewart, M. M., Williamson, I. O., & King, J. E. (2008). Who wants to be a business PhD? Exploring minority entry into the faculty "pipeline". *Academy of Management Learning & Education*, *7*(1), 42–55. doi:10.5465/AMLE.2008.31413861

Sullivan, S. E., & Mainiero, L. (2008). Using the kaleidoscope career model to understand the changing patterns of women's careers: Designing HRD programs that attract and retain women. *Advances in Developing Human Resources*, *10*(1), 32–49. doi:10.1177/1523422307310110

Swanson, R. A., & Holton, E. F. (2001). *Foundations of human resource development*. San Francisco, CA: Berrett Koehler. Rossi, J. (2007, November). What generation gap? *T&D*, 10-11.

US Bureau of Labor Statistics. (2008). *Employed persons in agriculture and related and in non-agricultural industries by age, sex, and class of worker*. Retrieved from ftp://ftp.bls.gov/pub/special.requests/lf/aat15.txt.

US Bureau of Labor Statistics. (2008). *Customized tables of data on gender of workers*. Retrieved from ftp://ftp.bls.gov/pub/special.requests/lf/aat2.txt.

US Bureau of Labor Statistics. (2008). *Customized tables of data on race of workers*. Retrieved from http://www.bls.gov/cps/cpsatabs.htm.

US Congress. (2008). *Equality in job loss: Women are increasingly vulnerable to layoffs during recessions*. Washington, DC: Majority Staff of the Joint Economic Committee.

US DOL. (1978). *Uniform guidelines on employee selection procedures*. Retrieved from http://www.dol.gov/esa/regs/cfr/41cfr/toc_Chapt60/60_3_toc.htm.

Wennerds, C., & Wold, A. (1997). Nepotism and sexism in peer review. *Nature*, *307*, 341. doi:10.1038/387341a0

KEY TERMS AND DEFINITIONS

4/5 Rule: Guideline that shows whether disparate impact exists. Demonstrates whether a less preferred group was selected at least 80% as often as the most preferred group was selected.

Age Discrimination in Employment Act: Law that bans discrimination in employment against people who are over the age of 40, on the basis that they are older than other workers.

Andragogy: Training methods or teaching methods. Often used to define teaching methods that are used with adults.

Availability: Number or percentage of people in a demographic group who are qualified & interested in a position.

Baby Boom Generation: People born between 1945 and 1964.

Behaviorally Anchored Rating Scale: Type of performance appraisal that lists specific work behaviors (e.g., smile at customers) and which can require a supervisor to indicate how frequently an employee performed the behavior during a year.

Career Path: The workplace experiences and occupations a person holds from the first job until retirement.

Demographics: The innate characteristics of a person, such as race, color, religion, creed, gender, national origin, or age.

Disability: Within the Americans with Disabilities Act, it is defined as a physical or mental impairment that substantially limits one or more of life's major activities (e.g., walking, seeing).

Disparate Treatment: Intentionally treating an individual differently because of demographics.

Disparate Impact: Unintentionally discriminating against a group because of use of a facially neutral device (e.g., a math test, on its face, looks like it is fair to all demographic groups).

Diversity: State of being that exists when a group contains people from more than one demographic group.

Equal Employment Opportunity: Fair treatment without regard to demographic characteristics. EEO does not require quotas (i.e., that specific numbers of people per demographic group be hired).

Equal Employment Opportunity Commission (EEOC): Branch of the federal government that enforces most diversity-related laws.

Equal Pay Act: Law that bans discrimination in compensation and benefits by gender.

Flex-Time: Allowing employees to set their own work schedules, within limits, such as working from 6:00 a.m. until 2:00 p.m. or from 12:00 p.m. until 8:00 p.m.

Generation X: People born between 1965 and 1980.

Generation Y: People born between 1980 and 2000.

Hostile Environment: Type of workplace harassment, such as bullying, that makes it difficult to perform the duties of a job.

Human Resource Development (HRD): Training and development activities in an organization conducted to increase the knowledge, skills, and abilities of employees.

Job-Sharing: Allowing two highly-skilled employees to share one full-time job, with each employee working part time.

Labor Force Participation Rate: Percentage of all people who are working or looking for work.

Latchkey Child: Young child who has a house key who lets herself into her family's home after school and who stays at home alone for several hours after school until her parents return home from work.

Mentoring: One-on-one, long term training and development with the goal of preparing an employee for higher-level positions.

Pedagogy: Training methods or teaching methods. Often used to define teaching methods that are used with children.

Practitioner: A person whose primary tasks are to deliver HRD to corporate employees.

Presidential Executive Orders: Decree written by the U.S. President ordering the branches of the Federal Government to do something. Does not require permission or approval of Congress or the Supreme Court. Can be withdrawn by any time by any U.S. President.

Quid Pro Quo: Literally, this for that. A type of sexual harassment that requires submission to sexual advances as a condition of employment.

Reliability: A state of being that exists when an instrument (e.g., test) score is stable (e.g., each time a person takes a test, the score is the same; or if two supervisors rate an employee, they agree on the quality of the employee's work).

Researcher: A person whose primary tasks are to teach and conduct research at the university level.

Telecommuting: Allowing employees to work at home via the use of technology such as cell phones and the internet.

Title VII CRA 1964: Law that bans discrimination in employment on the basis of race, color, religion, creed, gender, and national origin.

Uniform Guidelines on Employee Selection Procedures: Documents produced by the U.S. Department of Labor which define discrimination, validity, and reliability.

U.S. Departments of Census: Branch of the federal government that gathers population statistics, and which shares some data with the Bureau of Labor Statistics.

U.S. Departments of Labor: Branch of the federal government that oversees workforce issues, and which includes the Bureau of Labor Statistics.

Utilization: Number or percentage of people in a demographic group who were selected for a position.

Validity: A state of being that exists when an instrument (e.g., test) represents or predicts something. For example, a math test contains math questions; or a math test predicts job performance.

Work-Life Balance: A state of being wherein an employee successfully balances time and emotional demands between personal life and professional life.

Chapter 18
Global Diversity Management Programs and Strategies at CEVA Logistics

Hale Öner
Dogus University, Turkey

Esra Kaya
CEVA Logistics, Turkey

Olca Surgevil
Dokuz Eylul University, Turkey

Mustafa Ozbilgin
Brunel University, UK

ABSTRACT

The purpose of this chapter is to review the global diversity management program at CEVA Logistics. CEVA is one of the world's leading supply chain companies with operating regions of Asia Pacific, Americas, Northern Europe and Southern Europe, Middle East, and Africa with its head office in The Netherlands. CEVA was formed in August, 2007, as a result of the merger of TNT Logistics and EGL Eagle Global Logistics. CEVA employs more than 49,000 people and runs a global network with operational facilities in more than 170 countries all over the world.

The main Diversity and Inclusion activities of CEVA aim at increasing the participation of women at higher echelons of the management cadre, retaining diverse talent, and increasing the number of employees with disabilities. The diversity and integration understanding is the commitment to continuous improvement in every sub-region retaining the talented human capital with a focus on work and life balance initiatives and development by mentoring programs, network groups on the intranet, e-teams, and communities on gender and disability. Although diversity is integrated at CEVA at both the regional and global levels, the main motto in implementing the Diversity and Inclusion activities is "Think global, act local."

DOI: 10.4018/978-1-4666-1812-1.ch018

INTRODUCTION

Diversity management from domestic and international perspectives is often defined as recognizing and leveraging differences at work. Local approaches to diversity management originate from the North American context and date back to the late 1980s (Tatli & Özbilgin, 2009). Global Diversity Management (GDM) is a management philosophy, which underpins a set of strategies, policies, initiatives, and training and development activities that seek to transcend national differences in diversity management policies and practices by recognizing and leveraging diverse sets of social and individual backgrounds, interests, beliefs, values, and ways of work across branch networks of organizations with international, multinational, global, and transnational workforces (Özbilgin & Tatli, 2008). Diversity management as a management philosophy aims to create awareness about heterogeneity in organizations, campaigning for global coordination of activities and following a set of actions and processes in accordance with strategies and policies so as to recognize and value this heterogeneity within a legal framework. However, there is a vested interest of multiple stakeholder groups over the aims and processes as expected outcomes of diversity management coupled with the legitimacy issues with respect to legal issues (Özbilgin & Tatli, 2011). Much work on diversity has been carried out either in domestic settings with little attention to its global counterpart or drawn on a single-level analysis with a focus on managerial or trade union dimensions of diversity.

This case study focuses on a global supply chain management company, CEVA, as a company that has considerable input in promoting diversity to reflect with its diverse customer and community base. This case study is based on extensive documentary evidence shared by CEVA Turkey and shows how CEVA displays commitment to diversity in its strategy.

CEVA's 2010 – 2012 Diversity and Inclusion (D&I) strategy focuses on the following five areas embedded in D&I plans for employees, customers, partners and communities. The first three items below are the D&I global Key Performance Indicators (KPIs) that are regularly monitored:

- Engaging employees: Gender and disability networks are in place to cover all workforce
- Recruiting diverse talent: Ensure recruitment process is not limiting diverse talents
- Retaining diverse talent: Improve career and development plan to ensure long term attainment
- Building CEVA's reputation: Explain how CEVA demonstrates D&I program internally and externally
- Building an evidence base: Setting up a reporting process and regular follow up

The focus of this case study is to analyze the key drivers of diversity initiatives at regional, national, organizational, and individual levels. Diversity encourages and capitalizes on diverse views, thoughts, and team contributions to continuously improve the business.

BACKGROUND

Global Diversity Management (GDM) is a management philosophy that underpins a set of strategies, policies, initiatives, training, and development activities that seek to transcend national differences in diversity management policies and practices by recognizing and leveraging diverse sets of social and individual backgrounds, interests, beliefs, values, and ways of work across branch networks of organizations with international, multinational, global, and transnational workforces (Özbilgin & Tatli, 2008). Seeking to explain the difference between domestic diversity management and GDM concepts, Stumpf, Watson, and Rustogi (1994) noted that while domestic diversity management is about leveraging individual differences in order to generate positive organizational outcomes, GDM is about transcending national differences in order to arrive at workable solutions for international coordination of domestic diversity management initiatives. According to Nishii and Özbilgin (2007), GDM is about, first, gaining an understanding of contexts, and meanings of domestic approaches to diversity management from a cross-national perspective, and second, management of diversity in multinational and global organizations from public, private, and voluntary sectors. In the former case, a comparative approach is taken with the aim of unpacking cross-national similarities and differences in terms of recognition and treatment of workforce diversity. The latter, on the other hand, corresponds to multinational, international, or global approaches that focus on devising strategies for the coordination of diversity management in ways that can overcome national boundaries. GDM has emerged as a response to a lack of translation of diversity management practices to suit the new international settings (Boxembaum, 2006) and the observed failure of ill-planned transposition of domestic diversity management approaches from one country to another (Cooke & Saini, 2010; Nishii & Özbilgin, 2007; Özbilgin, 2008; Sippola & Smale, 2007).

In terms of organizational diversity management practices and approaches, the increasing diffusion of GDM, particularly amongst US Multi-National Corporations (MNCs) can be understood as an answer to the growing impact of globalization on the workforce of organizations, making an international perspective of diversity management crucial (Shen, Chanda & D'Netto, 2009; Wentling & Palma-Rivas, 2000). Numerous MNCs have workforces located outside the company's home country. At its core, GDM is a tool relating the management of workforces across different countries (Mor Barak, 2005). Moreover,

top management and Human Resources Management (HRM) strategies are increasingly focused on capability and knowledge as drivers of competitive advantage (Evans, Pucik, & Björkman, 2011), which puts diversity and the global management hereof in a central role. However, little is known about how multinationals are responding to the increasing globalization of their workforces (Sippola & Smale, 2007).

There were multiple drivers for the development of the GDM theory and practice, ranging from business and economic justifications to social and legal changes in the international context. Harvey and Buckley (1997) explain that global organizations pursue strategies to leverage differences among their employees in order to accrue competitive advantages in the international context. Besides the ambitions of global firms to gain strategic advantages, there are also contextual changes such as the expansion of international law to cover issues of equality in recent decades. International diversification of highly skilled workers (Al Ariss & Özbilgin, 2010) and increased competition for talent not only in industrialized countries but also in emerging economies (Özbilgin & Vassilopoulou, 2010) have been another driver for GDM theorization and practice. Another reason for the emergence of GDM as distinct from domestic variants has been the failures in transposing North American approaches to diversity management to other national contexts. Agocs and Burr (1996) explain transposing diversity management approaches across national borders bodes ill for business success as the usefulness and appropriateness of a specific approach to diversity management should be considered in the light of key national priorities, assessed in terms of its contribution to core business objectives and overall fit with the systems and structures in the workplace.

Within this setting, a global supply chain management company, CEVA, is studied in this extended case study, as an organization which has considerable input in promoting Diversity and

Inclusion to keep up with its diverse customer base. This case study shows how CEVA has set its commitment to Diversity and Inclusion.

CEVA LOGISTICS: A GLOBAL SUPPLY CHAIN MANAGEMENT COMPANY

CEVA was formed in August 2007 as a result of the merger of TNT Logistics and EGL Eagle Global Logistics. CEVA is one of the world's leading non-asset based supply chain management companies, providing end-to-end design, implementation, and operational capabilities in freight forwarding, contract logistics, transportation management, and distribution management. CEVA offers every customer a service tailored to their specific needs, built on our formidable experience across a broad range of market sectors. They have particular expertise in automotive and tires; technology; consumer and retail; industrial; publishing; energy; aerospace; and healthcare. CEVA is a non-listed company, owned by affiliates of Apollo Management LP, one of the leading private equity investors in the world. CEVA employ more than 49,000 people and run a global network with facilities in more than 170 countries. CEVA operates worldwide, and its regions are Asia Pacific, the Americas, Northern Europe and Southern Europe, Middle East and Africa. Reported combined revenues in fiscal year 2010 were €6.8 billion.

CEVA has been providing logistics, warehousing and transport services for its customers in Turkey since 2000. CEVA in Turkey obtained ISO10002 (Customer Satisfaction Standard) in 2008 building on the ISO9001, ISO14001, and OHSAS18001 standards received in 2005, and exemplifying its Operational Excellence philosophy. It received the Investor in People award in 2007. CEVA in Turkey has gained great success by winning the "Respect for Candidates Award" in the logistics sector for the eighth year in row

given by Kariyer.net (internet job search Website). CEVA's Turkish business has been selected as Turkey's and Central Eastern Europe's best employer according to the "Best Employers" study by Hewitt Associates too. It has also been granted with double awards by PERYON (The Association of Human Resource Managers of Turkey) in 2009. It has been elected first place in the Performance Management and Training and Development Management categories—the first time a company has ever received both awards.

Mission and Vision

CEVA's mission is 'making business flow' that ensures CEVA supports its customers' business through effective supply chains, CEVA has the vision to become the 'most admired company' in the supply chain industry exemplifying Unity (One company—one team), Growth (Outperform market growth) and Excellence (Perfection is our goal), and a magnet for diverse talent. Supporting this aim and very clear brand imperatives, is its goal to be an employer of choice. CEVA is committed to considering how CEVA embraces this diversity—of its employees and of customers—to capitalize on the opportunities to bring benefits to its communities, customers, and employees. In line with CEVA's vision, CEVA Management says '*At CEVA, we believe that to succeed in today's multi-cultural and Global environment, embracing Diversity and Inclusion will allow us to be better equipped to understand the demographics and thus to thrive in a global market. Our employees are our key asset and our goal is to attract, motivate, and retain the highest performing workforce in our industry. We will never realize our full potential unless we allow our best talent—from any background—to rise to the top.*' CEVA values were also determined by its people within the business and shown through real employees. The company values are listed as follows:

- We are passionate about customers: we go the extra mile to understand and delight them, placing them at the center of all we do.
- We are energetic and eager: a young company and proud of it – we are open to new ideas and enthusiastic about innovation. We promote a positive, energizing, and fun environment.
- We are performance driven: we judge ourselves and others on results, and how they are achieved. We set a high bar for achievement and are driven by a spirit of constructive dissatisfaction.
- We are successful: we deliver on our promises and celebrate our successes. We have a 'can do' attitude.
- We are agile and responsive: we value speed and flexibility. We minimize reporting layers and bureaucracy to enable fast, effective communication.
- We promote and value diversity: we are proud to be a company that is a rich mix of cultures and backgrounds that stimulates diversity of thought and action. This enables superior performance.
- We value people: we provide great opportunities for all to make a real difference to our business and to help them achieve their full potential.
- We are supply chain masters: our business is running supply chains. We cultivate and value operations excellence and continually develop industry-leading operations.
- Integrity and respect are our way of life: our code of conduct provides the foundation for the way we do business and protect the environment.

CEVA has established an organizational structure to support the Diversity and Inclusion strategy to drive progress and monitor organizational performance. CEVA has a Global Diversity Council, which includes members of the Executive Board, to ensure top-level commitment. The Council meets bi-quarterly to review progress and set direction. It is chaired by the Executive Diversity Champion. The Global Diversity Council proactively monitors company performance in meeting these standards and policies, and sets targets for the achievement and maintenance of this policy. The Champions manage Regional Diversity Councils that helps CEVA to 'think global, act local' in planning and implementation of actions that are relevant to the circumstances, cultures and legislation of each region. These councils are chaired by Regional Presidents who lead and drive progress across their regions, and D&I project managers' champion of the Region follow and implement D&I applications in every sub-region. CEVA's management and Diversity Champions are committed to Diversity and have a plan to achieve their objectives. They are committed to creating a culture of Diversity and Inclusion, which means they provide the necessary resources to assure a truly diverse and inclusive environment. It is their responsibility to establish an executable plan and be accountable for progress at CEVA. Employee Working Groups and Employee Networks to ensure CEVA is connected to its employees in all fields including office and operational sites. Diversity & Inclusion Global Council develops Global Employee Network charter and guidelines, supports the global network, and provides reward/recognition. Their activities can be listed as monthly virtual meetings coordinated by the group sponsor, creation of group network community (e-team) on CEVA intranet (CEVA net), participation of a group member in the D&I Global Council, regular information about open positions at CEVA, management events, trainings, news, conferences, etc., participation in one of the proposed activities for each session such as events, trainings, conferences given by senior executive members or other CEVA employees or external speakers about topics of interests to the group. Moreover, employees have a chance to be a gender and disability strand champion, executive champion and regional D&I project managers' champion.

On its journey to becoming the most admired company in the industry, one of CEVA's global strategic priorities is Organizational Capability, which is designed to equip people with the skills, training and development opportunities to support CEVA in attracting the right candidates and retaining the best Employees into the business in the future. The Organizational Capability program has five building blocks, and its objectives are to:

- Train: provide skill and competency based training, create training processes and content
- Motivate: improve employee communication, motivation and culture in general e.g. through the implementation of two way communication vehicles
- Develop: improve the processes and content of its management development approach
- Organize: address areas where the organization's processes and structure hamper effectiveness
- Attract: improve its ability to recruit a constant flow of high caliber individuals

Consequently, by embracing Diversity and Inclusion, CEVA's concentration is to create an inclusive workplace and release the full potential of all the employees regardless of their background. CEVA's vision is underpinned by a belief that CEVA's reputation as a leader in Diversity and Inclusion will enable CEVA to access new talent pools, develop, and inspire all of their employees, and moreover, deliver better solutions to its customers.

CEVA's Global Diversity and Inclusion Policy

The Diversity and Inclusion program was first mentioned in 2005, CEVA launched the D&I program in 2008 and kept its commitment to success. Since January 2009, the program started speeding up globally.

As CEVA thinks globally, but acts local, disability and gender are priorities for all regions but each country and region's D&I KPI's are linked with the local priorities and realities. To support this practice, CEVA in Turkey always is aiming of creating a difference in hiring, retaining disabled candidates with Diversity and Inclusion program, while in the UK there is also the LGBT working group, and Ethnicity in the USA within the D&I program. Activities are determined by calendar dates and quarterly activities supporting 'think global/act local' philosophy. The impact of these activities is monitored by various questionnaires such as gender and disability, entrance/exit results, through monthly monitors, quarterly KPI targets, and regional analysis worldwide. All activities and regional priorities are shared and discussed in each Regional and Global D&I meetings to share best practices. The philosophy of CEVA's Diversity & Inclusion policy is as follows:

CEVA is committed to promoting and valuing diversity in all areas of recruitment, employment, training, and promotion based on merit and inclusiveness without regard to race, gender, marital/civil status, sexual orientation, disability, age, religion or belief, ethnic or national origin. They strive to provide a positive environment where everyone feels valued and respected, benefiting employee productivity and engagement.

Diversity is about understanding and maximizing differences—the variety of perspectives, opinions, and contributions that we each bring to the business. Inclusion is about leveraging diversity to create an environment and culture that is welcoming, collaborative and productive. To build a sustainable and high performance organization, CEVA seeks to create a workplace that reflects on differences and be open to the fresh perspectives that are generated in a diverse work environment. Diversity brings innovation and improvements that benefit staff, customers, and shareholders and reflects the global nature of the company and its customers. All of these mentioned characteristics of D&I are important to CEVA, however gender and disability have been chosen as key strands of diversity.

CEVA recognizes that people from different backgrounds with different experiences and abilities can bring fresh knowledge and ideas to improve the working practices and business by enhancing decision making and increasing innovation. CEVA can better understand its customers and better identify the needs of its customers when they have a diverse workforce that mirrors CEVA's worldwide customer base. Thus, CEVA embraces and celebrates the differences in a positive environment, and is committed to engage with the needs of its diverse employees, customers and communities to enable them to achieve company goals both at individual and corporate level.

Managing diversity is in line with CEVA's values, foundation competencies and consistent with the CEVA Code of Conducts. It emphasizes the business need for valuing the differences between people, rather than just complying with the law. Businesses that grasp the opportunities generated by managing diversity effectively have a competitive advantage over those which do not, because they can attract new markets, a wider customer base and have the ability to provide more tailored service or range of solutions from a wider range of suppliers. Thus, D&I is one of the four foundation competencies of all employees. As a competency, it is evaluated at understanding, behavior, and outcome/application stages with

respect to a set of levels i.e. master, expert, professional, practitioner, novice, and problem levels.

The scope of the D&I policy is designed as to attract, engage and retain the best employees through supporting CEVA's aspiration to be the most admired company. The policy helps ensure that Diversity & Inclusion is embedded in the corporate culture, reflected in employees, and recognized by customers and suppliers. CEVA will endeavor to:

- Attract applications from candidates without regard of race, gender, marital/civil status, sexual orientation, disability, age, religion or belief, ethnic or national origin.
- Improve performance and development opportunities in order to prepare all individuals for other roles and responsibilities in accordance with the company strategy.
- Ensure that employment conditions support employees' needs and the individual's ability to do a job.
- Enhance decision-making, innovation, and involvement.
- Increase the ability to relate to and serve customer/clients wherever they exist.
- Identify the various behaviors that discrimination can take, and understand the negative effect these have for the company and its employees and customer/clients.
- Monitor the application of this policy eliminating any practices, which may hinder or prevent CEVA from achieving its objectives.

Within the framework of D&I policy, CEVA aims to make diversity a priority, ensure everyone is committed to diversity, provide uniform expectations, promote an open-door policy, protect people rights, promote compliance and prevention, and create a respectful and dignified work environment, CEVA seeks to create an environment where attitudes and biases that hinder the progress of individuals and groups are dismantled so that people can work together in mutual respect and tolerance for all. At this point, it is worthwhile mentioning about CEVA's diversity needs statement, which emphasizes the following:

Improving Customer Satisfaction

Global markets require diversity of thoughts, approaches, and cultures. With customers and revenues linked to countries around the world, a globally diverse workforce is a competitive advantage. Growth through increased customer satisfaction will be achieved by having employees whose backgrounds mirror the communities they live and work in, and the diverse markets CEVA operates in. Understanding local customers' needs improves customer satisfaction and retention rates while also generating new businesses.

Improving Employee Satisfaction

Wherever CEVA operates, employees are the most important asset for the corporation. Unity (One company—one team) through increased employee satisfaction will be achieved by creating an environment where everyone's contribution is valued, everyone's talents are fully utilized, and shared organizational goals are aligned together. Inclusion of people of all backgrounds will improve employee satisfaction, productivity, and retention rates as well as facilitate the recruiting of external talent.

Improving Financial Performance

Research shows that in today's globalized economy, all industrial companies with a diverse workforce and an inclusive culture outperform their peer group. This is especially true of organizations operating in environments with a low level of legal protection of employees' rights, i.e., these companies go above and beyond mere compliance. Here, diversity, coupled with inclusion, becomes a competitive advantage and bottom-line contributor.

Improving Recruitment

A diverse workforce is a pre-requisite to leadership with the company stakeholders and in the markets served. To accomplish CEVA's ambitious growth objectives, they encourage each employee to help identify, recruit, and retain the most talented individuals, who can bring diverse perspectives and capabilities. Within an environment of trust and openness employees of different lifestyles and backgrounds can reach their full potential and contribute to the collective success.

Improving Leadership Quality

Diversity and Inclusion coupled with Integrity and Respect are CEVA Foundation Competencies reflected in KPI's (Key Performance Indicators) against which progress is measured and assessed. Thus, all employees should both understand and be responsible for how these competencies should be applied in their own workplace. Through mentoring and career planning across geographies the full creativity and innovation potential within the organization will be tapped, allowing the most capable to develop international experience and grow into decision-making positions, and significantly increasing the depth of the company's leadership. In line with these foundation competencies and reward policy, managers are responsible for developing and encouraging a positive environment, where all employees are treated with integrity and respect.

Within this framework, CEVA aims to tackle barriers to participation and create a culture in which equal opportunities and equal treatment are priorities for all employees. The company is committed to supporting employees and managers in the achievement of a diverse workplace.

Infrastructure and Implementation of D&I Strategy

The reason CEVA is working on Diversity and Inclusion is quite simply to achieve better business results. Based on extensive research in many countries, there is strong evidence that companies with inclusive/diverse cultures perform better as they are able to utilize the broadest range of talents and perspectives to enable better, more creative decisions; moreover, they can stay 'in touch' with markets and trends through having a holistic view on events, they have access to a wider talent pool; typically inclusive companies become "magnets" for talent.

If CEVA is to become the most admired company in the sector, they need to take the lead in D&I. Inclusion is still a new and underdeveloped area in the logistics industry but, in many other industry sectors, leading companies are driving ahead with powerful programs. CEVA must learn from these companies and develop itself into a role model for it exits in.

For CEVA Diversity means creating a workforce who is demographically in line with the societies where it operates. In practice, this typically means increasing the numbers of employees from 'minority' groups to create a more diverse mix. Within CEVA, the management intends to focus on 'gender diversity' as the initial priority. Inclusion means creating a meritocratic culture where the voices and ideas of all these demographic groups are heard within the company. It is only by inviting and valuing the contributions of all staff that they will start to unlock the true potential within CEVA.

Some people think of inclusion as a positive discrimination program for minorities based on 'looking good' to the outside world. This is not how CEVA operates, CEVA, as a performance driven company, will only hire and promote the best available candidates regardless of gender, race, ethnicity, background, age, etc. However, CEVA hopes its commitment to inclusion will create a stronger pipeline of talent within CEVA and create a more level playing field for employees from minority groups.

CEVA creates a policy framework, provides diversity training, establishes support groups, and tracks D&I progress. This is the basic role of CEVA's Diversity and Inclusion program. A detailed implementation plan will follow its communication. The company will ensure the compliance with current local legislations in order to implement the D&I strategy. CEVA's CEO is personally committed to leading this transformation and convinced that inclusion will make them a stronger company, relying on leadership and support for this breakthrough project.

Within this policy framework mentioned above CEVA wants to promote the development, advancement, and effectiveness of women in support of CEVA's business goals, values, and objectives by supporting the formation and operation of a 'Women Leaders Network' that provides professional growth for participants, education, and awareness for other employees and promotes the Company's mission, values, and corporate goals. The participants are senior management women within CEVA and are nominated by the HR Regional Director, representing the top management women within the region. Emerging talent women are also invited to participate for a period of 18 months. They are empowered as ambassadors internally/externally to provide input to Diversity and Inclusion plans and priorities, provide employee referrals and customer insights. Their roles and responsibilities are briefly summarized below.

- Support and further business objectives
- Support recruitment of women within CEVA
- Support the professional development of women within CEVA
- Contribute to the community
- Increase awareness of Diversity and Inclusion

- Self-organized group of women that support each other
- Completely voluntary
- Support to develop leadership skills
- Opportunity to network with other leaders at CEVA

The network sponsor has to display visible leadership support, set agenda, oversee the program and host meaningful dialogues and engage participants, via town hall and virtual meetings, Webinars/forums, and leadership access.

As for the D&I communication tools, CEVA issued a newsletter called 'Diverse Times' as of May, 2011. The newsletter aims to inform employees about CEVA's Gender and Disability program, networks, activities and achievements, as well as LGBT programs. At CEVA, there are also local Newsletters aiming to share general company information with local employees, Newsletter in Turkey called Üçgen (Triangle) is published quarterly to increase awareness among the Turkish employees about the local projects; it refers to D&I practices, news, and progress, since January 2009.

Training Programs on D&I Program

The objective of the D&I program is to establish training programs to upgrade the knowledge of CEVA's employees on why D&I matters to them and facilitate specific training to managers to help and guide them build a confident and inclusive organization, starting with their teams.

The training courses at CEVA have the following modules:

1. D&I Awareness: Aim is to present the Global D&I policy that includes statement on equal opportunities and dignity at work.
2. Gender:
   a. Gender Matters (awareness training)
   b. Inclusive recruitment
   c. Senior women leadership training
   d. How to set up a local gender network/mentoring

The leadership training proposal to develop women leaders aims to teach women how to become comfortable in the spotlight; unlock the power of their voice; create strong scripts, and achieve a dynamic presence.

3. Disability: Disability tool kit for managers including the following subjects.
   a. Disability Awareness and Adjustment
   b. Reasonable accommodations/adjustments
   c. How to interview people with disabilities
   d. How to communicate with people with disabilities

'Beyond the Limits' Awareness training shows successful stories about people effected with disabilities, breaking the false assumptions and concerns about their real capabilities. It explains how important for CEVA's success is to create a truly diverse and inclusive culture and the goals of the Disability Program. For training purposes, there is a 'Beyond the Limits—Managers Tool Kit,' which introduces the disability business case and showcase success stories of people with disabilities that have been able to run their jobs successfully despite their disability. It also provides tips on how to make reasonable adjustments in order to remove barriers and make CEVA accessible to everyone.

GLOBAL WiN (Women's international Network)

One of the Gender Working Group's goals and targets is to ensure the engagement and satisfaction of employees by increasing the number of employees joining network groups and CEVA local networks. This goal coupled with Diversity and Inclusion strategy, the Gender Program which aims to capitalize on all market opportunities in relation to gender is designed to promote fair recruitment practices, development opportunities and other support activities that help CEVA to become a leading employer, who equitably attracts and retains female and male talent.

CEVA's WiN (Women international Network) is a self-organized group of employees that support each other based on completely voluntary participation. It supports group to develop leadership skills, creates opportunity to network with other colleagues at CEVA and serves as a benefit for CEVA as it engages employees in the organization.

CEVA's WiN is an internal platform that connects employees who are interested in supporting CEVA's Gender Program, sharing knowledge and opinions, participating in events and discussions that help them to develop within the company and its mission is to promote the development, advancement and effectiveness of women in support of CEVA's business goals, values and objectives by creating a mutually supportive network and safe environment for shared experiences. CEVA's WiN plans to provide professional growth for participants, provide awareness for other employees, and promote the Company's mission, values, and corporate goals.

The key roles and responsibilities of CEVA's WiN is to support gender program with recommendations for improvement of current local policies and practices, set agenda of activities for WiN members and oversees the program. Also host meaningful dialogues and engage participants, via town hall and virtual meetings, Webinars/forums and leadership access, support recruitment and professional development of women, and increase awareness of Diversity and Inclusion among women within CEVA.

This gender working program supports the gender E-community with WiN chapters in each sub-region or country with the following some key roles and responsibilities such as visible leadership support and obtain internal senior support, define direction for the gender agenda, lead the Gender Working Group, raise profile of the Gender agenda internally and externally, and regularly report on performance to the Global D&I Council.

The Gender Working Group (GWG) is composed of volunteer employees representing all regions and functions that are invited to join the GWG after a selection process for a period of six months. GWG has the following key roles and responsibilities such as shape the purpose and objectives of the gender strategy, take ownership for defining and achieving mutually agreed outcomes, promote the strategy by agreeing on gender initiatives, provide leadership and direction to the network.

The Gender e-community formed of any of the CEVA employees interested in gender issues has two key roles and responsibilities such as to connect people who are interested in the skills and talents of all employees are fully leveraged for the benefit of the business, and the fulfillment of the employees, and to connect employees with the colleagues globally to share knowledge and opinions and take part in discussions.

Current CEVA's WiN groups and contacts are in the US, UK, Brazil, Mexico, Singapore, Melbourne and Bangkok. These groups and contacts set the stage for mentoring programs as CEVA aims to use these mentoring activities as a catalyst for career advancement. It is a crucial initiative initiated by UK and Ireland.

Disability Program

CEVA is willing to become a leading disability confident employer, who equitably attracts and retains disabled and non-disabled talent and who is recognized by communities and stakeholders as an accessible and disability aware industry leader. CEVA aims to build disability confidence, creating an inclusive and accessible organization for colleagues with disabilities, those caring for others with disabilities and for all interested stakeholders internally and externally and increase the number of people with disabilities employed by CEVA across a range of grades and roles.

CEVA's Disability Working Group (DWG) wants to engage with diversity leaders specialized in 'People with Disabilities,' in a learning relationship that can increase the awareness and education about disability in the countries that are due to meet the legal requirement on quotas by 2012, as well as other countries. CEVA's Disability Working Group is a global network of employees who have volunteered to support the disability agenda by giving their expert opinion while working on some tangible actions that move CEVA forward as a disability confident employer. This initiative creates an inclusive culture at CEVA as it is the 'ability in disability that matters' celebrating empowerment through independence, inclusiveness and choice'

The DWG is working on some tangible actions that move CEVA forward as a disability confident employer. Some of these deliverables of the disability program for 2011 are created according to the list of set actions. Action1: Sustainable deployment provides tangible and clear suggestions to the organization to show how to improve the number of disabled employees within the company. Disability data tracking system and survey launched in Europe helped to identify internal best practices within CEVA. The survey aimed to ask managers what they think to work with an employee with disability in their team. Disability elements are also included to the Site Classification Assessment program, an ongoing initiative to bring substantial benefits to our customers in terms of the highest levels of performance, which uses 35 standardized metrics globally to assess each location. CEVA also provides recruitment tools i.e. tool kit distributed to HR country leads. Action2: CEVA aims to create awareness of the disability program and engagement among the employees by utilizing global disability awareness campaign. Action3: Company aims to develop

tools and processes i.e. develop global processes and line manager's toolkit such as a disability tool kit for managers.

CEVA's disability target for 2012 is that all countries meet the legal requirement on quotas. This is the minimum requirement to CEVA's ambition to further the increase in the number of employees with disabilities across the organization. In order to provide the necessary tools to achieve this goal, the objective is to increase the awareness and education on disability within the organisation by learning from other best in class companies.

Each D&I Regional project manager is responsible for monitoring that the project plan is implemented by the countries included in their region. The country contacts will engage with their D&I country leader in order to get information about three specific areas: Local regulations, Civil, and/or governmental associations they partner with, and main activities they develop in those countries aiming to increase the number of employees with disabilities.

In order to have an inventory of the existing situation at CEVA, the disability survey has been carried out in Southern Europe and Northern Europe countries to explore current employees with disabilities employed, their positions, the kind of disabilities they have, the reasons for the choice of these employees, the duration they have been in the company, their performance evaluation, level of absenteeism, turnover, adjustments/accommodations made for the employees and their cost, additional investments necessary to employ more employees with disabilities, contribution of employees with disabilities to create a more positive environment, awareness of the existence of the disability program at CEVA, the effectiveness of the program and intention to join the CEVA disability network. The results of these surveys are in use for increasing confidence to self declare a disability, developing opportunities to the existing talent pool and increasing diverse talent via recruitment and/or promotion to higher grades.

The implementation of the disability program is different in each country in terms of the nature of disabled people and different quota regulations.

Disability Working Group (DWG) collaborates with regional and local teams for the strategy implementation. The aim is the ultimate support to employees across the organisation that is effected by disability and search new opportunities to employ more disabled people thereby tapping new talent opportunities.

The disability data and survey in Southern Europe and Northern Europe countries aims to serve action 1: sustainable development giving tangible and clear suggestion, guidance to the organisation as how sustainability can improve the conditions of disabled employees. The results show that employing disabled employees help to improve the work environment. However, the awareness should be increased about their disability program. Action 2 is the disability awareness campaign and engagement. The disability awareness campaign 'Beyond the Limits—Awareness' shows successful stories about people with disabilities, breaking false assumptions and concerns about their real capabilities. Moreover, it explains the importance of a truly diverse and inclusive culture at CEVA. The awareness sessions are intended to be presented to all the employees at CEVA coupled with train the trainer sessions. Finally action 3 is the training part i.e. processes and tools called 'Beyond the Limits—Adjustments' that was created for all CEVA managers to show them how critic their role in daily business life when they meet a disabled person.

The disability recruitment tool kit aims to develop global processes and tools for line managers so that they are better equipped to welcome disabled employees at CEVA. Even a recruitment statement, reviewed by the Employers Forum on Disability, has been agreed to be included in the Careers section on CEVA's Website. The statement reads as follows, *'All qualified applicants will re-ceive consideration for employment without regard to race, color, national origin, genetics, disability, age, veteran status or any other characteristic.'*

Solutions and Recommendations

The challenges for CEVA during the target setting and implementation stages of the D&I program is to find a balance between the requirements of the local setting and CEVA's goals i.e. the accordance with the local understanding as well as the legal requirements of the countries where operated. The difficulty of getting members on network groups in the intranet such as e-teams, e-training, and e-communities for diversity, gender, and disability to share opinions and discussions is another hurdle.

Although CEVA has a set of competencies and skills for 'Diversity Champions' that are applicable to anyone, these competencies are not easy to establish in a short period of time and may need active reinforcement all through the year strengthened by continuous mentoring programs. These competencies have been recommended: to listen everyone effectively, be open to learning and be able to create a safe environment for everyone, to be trusted, and to be able to engage with a wide range of people. It is also important to have empathy, in other words to be able to 'put oneself in someone else's shoes.' The major competencies for CEVA are: having influencing skills, acting as a change agent, good communicator and credible role model for other employees, willing to learn, having ability to handle the conflicts and create solutions, achieving results through one's own actions and actions of others, recognizing the challenges of global workplace and working across cultures, coupled with recognizing the behaviors and language that may be seen as inappropriate or intimidating by others. CEVA has a number of pointers for recruitment and retention of women. These competencies are formulated in a set of questions that are posed to managers such as what CEVA can do to attract and retain women, how CEVA can increase the brand reputation as an employer of choice for women, what women need to feel supported and be successful, how CEVA can increase gender understanding of male colleagues and etc. In addition, there are some questions related to flexible working conditions (For example: Flexible working solutions, part time, etc.) and family commitments are often quoted as potential barriers to women's career progression. Is this true at CEVA? If so, what does CEVA need to do to change it? such as training interventions, and culture. Lastly, how can CEVA be the most admired company in the supply chain industry, is the critical question. Thus, these above questions search answers for benefits, work-life balance and flexible working conditions to make all employees' work life balance much better.

To promote diversity and inclusion, supplier diversity is included in the current global procurement policy, government relations, community and social responsibility projects are being planned. In order to form alliances, CEVA also has established partnerships with many organizations in different parts of the world.

FUTURE RESEARCH DIRECTIONS

There is need for research to explore dominant discourses of diversity at work in light of the evidence of practice, processes, and outcomes. Such research may come in the form of case studies or surveys, which provide evidence for the oft-stated aims, processes, and outcomes of diversity in organizational settings. Furthermore, most of the research on diversity management is limited to studies, which are not intrusive. Participant observations, visual ethnography, action research, and longitudinal case studies may bring depth to CEVA's understanding of diversity management.

CONCLUSION

CEVA aims to be an inclusive organisation where everyone is treated with respect and dignity, and where there is equal opportunity for all. As such CEVA seeks to integrate D&I throughout its organizational processes. In order to achieve integration of diversity in organizational processes, CEVA has created institutional structures, such as networks and committees, offices that tackle different aspects of D&I. It is important to note that although a wide range of diversity categories are supported at CEVA, two categories, i.e. gender and disability, are prioritized since 2010, however all differences are respected and valued by CEVA's management and employees. In order to ensure Gender and Disability Network Group's success, the implication of this is that specific activities and interventions are planned for both working groups.

CEVA's Diversity and Inclusion understanding is not limited only with gender and disability CEVA also committed to respects differences, encourages new ideas and perspectives, promotes fairness and allows everyone to contribute to goals and share in success and as well as helps to create a stronger, more successful organization.

Overall, GDM activities appear to be sensitive to local demands as well as global need to standardize efforts. In recognition of these polarized demands, company invests considerable amount of resources in facilitating communication across national branches.

Most benefits that CEVA expects to accrue from GDM are yet to materialize. The coming years can reveal the true contribution that GDM interventions make to CEVA. Furthermore, GDM activities are primarily centered on single strands. What remain to explore are the intersections among multiple strands of diversity. Moving from single strands of diversity to multiple and intersecting strands of diversity remains as key challenges for the future.

REFERENCES

Agocs, C., & Burr, C. (1996). Employment equity affirmative action d managing diversity: Assessing the differences. *International Journal of Manpower*, *17*, 30–45. doi:10.1108/01437729610127668

Al Ariss, A., & Ozbilgin, M. (2010). Understanding self-initiated expatriates: Career experiences of Lebanese self-initiated expatriates in France. *Thunderbird International Business Review*, *52*(4), 275–285. doi:10.1002/tie.20355

Boxenbaum, E. (2006). Lost in translation? The making of Danish diversity management. *The American Behavioral Scientist*, *49*(7), 939–948. doi:10.1177/0002764205285173

Cooke, F. L., & Saini, D. S. (2010). Diversity management in India: A study of organizations in different ownership forms and industrial sectors. *Human Resource Management*, *49*(3), 477–500. doi:10.1002/hrm.20360

Evans, P., Pucik, V., & Björkman, I. (2011). *The global challenge: International human resource management* (2nd ed.). New York, NY: McGraw-Hill.

Harvey, M. G., & Buckley, M. R. (1997). Managing inpatriates: Building a global core competency. *Journal of World Business*, *32*, 35–53. doi:10.1016/S1090-9516(97)90024-9

Mor Barak, M. E. (2005). *Managing diversity: Toward a globally inclusive workplace*. Thousand Oaks, CA: Sage.

Nishii, L. H., & Özbilgin, M. F. (2007). Global diversity management: Towards a conceptual framework. *International Journal of Human Resource Management*, *18*(11), 1883–1894. doi:10.1080/09585190701638077

Ogbonna, E., & Harris, L. C. (2002). Organizational culture. *Journal of Management Studies*, *39*(5), 673–706. doi:10.1111/1467-6486.00004

Özbilgin, M. F. (2008). Global diversity management. In Smith, P., Peterson, M. F., & Thomas, D. C. (Eds.), *The Handbook of Cross-Cultural Management Research* (pp. 379–396). London, UK: Sage Press.

Özbilgin, M. F., & Tatli, A. (2008). *Global diversity management: An evidence based approach*. Basingstoke, UK: Palgrave.

Özbilgin, M. F., & Vassilopoulou, J. (2010). *Global talent management: The case of emerging economies*. London, UK: Chartered Institute of Personnel and Development.

Shen, J., Chanda, A., & D'Netto, B. (2009). Managing diversity through human resource management: An international perspective and conceptual framework. *International Journal of Human Resource Management*, *20*, 235–252. doi:10.1080/09585190802670516

Sippola, A., & Smale, A. (2007). The global integration of diversity management: A longitudinal case study. *International Journal of Human Resource Management*, *18*(11), 1895–1916. doi:10.1080/09585190701638101

Stumpf, S. A., Watson, M. A., & Rustogi, H. (1994). Leadership in a global village: Creating practice fields to develop learning organizations. *Journal of Management Development*, *13*, 16–25. doi:10.1108/02621719410071946

Tatli, A., & Özbilgin, M. (2009). Understanding diversity managers' role in organizational change: Towards a conceptual framework. *Canadian Journal of Administrative Sciences*, *26*(3), 244–258. doi:10.1002/cjas.107

Wentling, R. M., & Palma-Rivas, N. (2000). Current status of diversity initiatives in selected multinational corporations. *Human Resource Development Quarterly*, *11*(1), 35–60. doi:10.1002/1532-1096(200021)11:1<35::AID-HRDQ4>3.0.CO;2-#

KEY TERMS AND DEFINITIONS

CEVA's WiN: An internal platform that connects employees who are interested in supporting CEVA's Gender Program, sharing knowledge and opinions, participating in events and discussions that help them to develop within the company, and its mission is to promote the development, advancement and effectiveness of women in support of CEVA's business goals, values and objectives by creating a mutually supportive network and safe environment for shared experiences. CEVA's WiN plan to provide professional growth for participants, provide awareness for other employees, and promote the Company's mission, values and corporate goals.

Gender Working Group (GWG) and the Disability Working Group (DWG): These are group of volunteer employees representing all regions and functions that are invited to join the GWG and/or DWG after a selection process for a period of six months has some key roles and responsibilities such as to shape the purpose and objectives of the gender / disability strategy, take ownership for defining and achieving mutually agreed outcomes, promote the strategy by agreeing on gender / disability initiatives, provide leadership and direction to the network.

Global Diversity Management (GDM): A management philosophy which underpins a set of strategies, policies, initiatives, and training and development activities that seek to transcend national differences in diversity management policies and practices by recognizing and leveraging diverse sets of social and individual backgrounds, interests, beliefs, values and ways of work across branch networks of organizations with international, multinational, global and transnational workforces.

KPI (Key Performance Indicators): Indicators against which progress is measured and assessed.

Section 4
Initiatives for Leveraging Workforce Diversity

Chapter 19
Leveraging Workforce Diversity in Practice:
Building Successful Global Relationships with Minority-Owned Suppliers

Bertie M. Greer
Northern Kentucky University, USA

James A. Hill
The Ohio State University, USA

ABSTRACT

Important supply bases for buyers are those that emphasize minority-owned businesses. The increased focus on globalization, corporate social responsibility, supplier diversity, and additional benefits has established a need for buyers to develop sustainable relationships with minority-owned firms. Based on a review of the literature, and interviews with a minority supplier director, minority suppliers, and a purchasing manager, this chapter examines the relationship constructs that are important to buyer-minority-owned supplier relationships. Trust, perception of buyer's commitment, and minority-owned supplier commitment is explored. Research propositions, implications, and directions for further research are offered.

INTRODUCTION

Research across many different fields has begun to explore the disparities that exist because of racial, cultural, and gender differences. Often times, studies assume a "one size fits all" conclusion. For example, Hayes et al. (2010) in their study on coronary heart disease, heart failure, and stroke discuss the underrepresentation of women and minorities in clinical trials and how this lack of race-specific and sex-specific reporting compounds problems such as patient care. When research fails to be inclusive, the resulting studies contribute to a gap in knowledge in that field. This resulting gap in knowledge ultimately translates to a gap in problem recognition, attention, and solutions. This type of research oversight occurs not only in the field of medicine, but in other fields too.

DOI: 10.4018/978-1-4666-1812-1.ch019

General research in the field of operations management in the area of buyer supplier relationships, not only offers minimum insight and input from the suppliers' perspective, but there is also minimum insight and input from the minority-owned business perspective. This oversight limits the ability of businesses or buyers to build and maintain successful relationships with minority businesses. Research that highlights and confronts challenges based on racial, cultural, and gender differences can close the gap of misunderstanding and lead to healthy functional business relationships. In this chapter, we attempt to minimize this gap by discussing differences between minority owned businesses who supply non-minority owned businesses (hereafter referred to as buyers) with necessary resources, products and services and non minority-owned businesses who supply buyers with the same. We use this knowledge to suggest ways that non-minority buyers can build successful relationships with minority owned businesses (minority owned businesses and minority suppliers will be used interchangeably).

Two critical relationship variables that contribute to business relationship success are trust and commitment. It has been well established in the social sciences that trust has a critical role in facilitating successful relationships (Blau, 1964; Zucker, 1986; Coleman, 1988). In a business relationship, each business must be able to have confidence that they can rely on the other to successfully carry out said responsibilities. Moreover, a successful relationship between two businesses involves commitment. Each business must be assured that the other will be obliged to carry out those said responsibilities.

In this chapter, we define trust based on research in social psychology (Larzelere & Huston, 1980) and relationship marketing (Ganesan, 1994; Doney & Cannon, 1997) trust is defined along two dimensions. The first dimension focuses on the objective *credibility of a supply chain's partner, expectancy that the partner's word or written statement can be relied on*. The second dimension focuses on *benevolence, which is based on the extent to which one partner is genuinely interested in the other partner's welfare and motivated to seek joint gain.*

We define commitment from research on social exchange (Cook & Emerson, 1978), organizations (Meyer & Allen, 1984) and relationship marketing (Anderson & Weitz, 1992). We define commitment as *a buyer/supplier's belief that the relationship is important enough to warrant maximum efforts at maintaining it; that is, the committed party values the relationship to an extent that it is worth continuing indefinitely.* Our definition corresponds almost exactly with that developed by Morgan and Hunt (1994).

Existing literature is abounding with research pertaining to the role of trust and commitment between buyers and suppliers. The majority of these studies explaining the importance of trust and commitment, however, discuss trust and commitment from the buyers' point of view. Conversely, less attention has been paid in existing literature to the suppliers' point of view. Moreover, extant literature also has failed to offer much insights on minority owned businesses and their perspective on trust and commitment in buyer supplier relationships.

Obtaining and maintaining relationships with minority owned businesses is considered a strategic and competitive advantage for most companies. Yet, the ability for organizations to realize this advantage has been challenging.

RESEARCH MOTIVATION

Many companies are seeking innovative and sustainable methods to develop and improve their relationships with their suppliers. One important segment of the supply base that has caught the attention of corporate America and gained increased attention is minority- owned suppliers. Many companies place the responsibility of building relationships with minority owned business in their supplier diversity programs. In a recent survey, it was reported that 65% of the respondents indicated that supplier diversity was either a mid-level or high-level priority (Teague & Hannon, 2005). One of the reasons supplier diversity has increased in importance and evolved into a market-driven strategy is that it makes the kind of bottom-line sense that corporations understand. In a recent article on partnering for profit, John Barth, chairman and CEO of Johnson Controls and chairman of the National Minority Supplier Development Council (NMSDC) stated that "Corporate America's strategic relationship with its minority suppliers is also part of the effort to become more like the customer base it serves. The bottom line is that by helping our customers sell more products or gain more business, we help ourselves" (http:// www.time.com/, p. 4). Atsushi Niimi, president and CEO, Toyota Motor Manufacturing North America, Inc. states that "we believe the continuous growth of our supplier diversity program is a must, and we are striving to be the best in our industry, and our commitment to supplier diversity is an integral part of our success, and we know that this commitment must continue to grow" (http:// www.time.com/, p. 45). Other companies are also realizing benefits. AT&T documented that supplier diversity was a factor in generating $1.1 billion dollars in revenue for 2006 (Varmazis, 2007). Time Warner Cable stated that supplier diversity has fostered new levels of innovation, creativity and customer focus (Britt, 2007). Others have stated that supplier diversity has brought about a fresh approach to the look of cars, fresh designs for the use and look of technology and a broader base for its products (Witherspoon, 2006). Consequently, organizations are realizing that they do not want to be restricted when looking for the best partners that will impact their business success and competitiveness. Michael Porter (1995) highlights the value of minority businesses by explaining why we should grow the businesses in the inner city. He suggests that these businesses

are advantageous because they meet the cultural and ethnic needs of the US. For example, he points to the many businesses that supply food products (Parks Sausage and Brooks Sausage), and hair products (Soft Sheen, Proline, Dudley, and Luster products). These companies meet the needs of many minorities and have gained success over larger and established businesses such as Procter and Gamble.

Moreover, as US businesses seek to have a greater global presence, they must understand that other countries operate differently. How are minority business defined in Europe or South Africa? Are these countries proactive with minority programs? What are the expectations for European business and the business relationships they have with minority owned businesses? Ethnic entrepreneurship has been identified as a solution to reducing immigrant unemployment in the Netherlands (Masurel, et al., 2002). In Sweden, they have high expectations that self-employment will foster the integration of immigrants into the larger society (Alund, 2003). In Great Britain, the creation and operation of successful ethnic businesses are seen as catalyst to urban regeneration (Ethnic Business, 2003).

It is with these facts in mind, that we explore relationship building with minority owned businesses as a critical supply base that is worthy of sustaining and important enough that organizations should allocate resources and extra effort to enhancing. We first, define minority-owned businesses and discuss reasons for an increased focus on the minority owned business supply base through supplier diversity and basic program success. Next, we discuss the challenges that organizations face when building relationships with minority owned businesses. Finally, we propose a theoretical framework for building successful relationships with minority owned businesses, highlight the associated propositions for future research, and offer practical implications.

DEFINING "MINORITY" IN MINORITY-OWNED BUSINESSES

Defining the term minority has many definitions, depending on the company. For example, the National Supplier Diversity Council (2009) defines minority as a for profit business physically located in the US in which 51 percent ownership and operation is by a U.S. citizens and/or 51 percent of the stock is owned by individuals who are at least 25% minimum of the following ethnic backgrounds: African American, Hispanic Americans (Mexican, Cuban, South American, Puerto Rican, or other Hispanic or Latino Americans), Native American, Asian-Pacific American, and Asian Indian American.

Other organizations such as MWBE (Minority and Women owned Business Enterprises), established in 1998 to address the needs of upscale minority and women-owned small businesses seeking opportunities in private-sector supplier diversity programs define a minority-owned business as "being owned, capitalized, operated and controlled by a member of an identified minority group. The business must be a for-profit enterprise, which physically resides in the United States or one of its territories. Identified "Minority groups" are generally defined as having an ethnic background consisting of Asian, Black, Hispanic, East Asian Indian and/or Native American. Some applications require that the applicant have 75% ethnic heritage others accept as little as one fourth" (http://www.mwbe-enterprises.com/).

While women are not a minority group identified by census population numbers, they are still classified as a "minority" in business. Minority group means "singled out for unequal treatment." Thereby, the more dominant group, white men, would be the majority group because white men have "greater power, privileges, and social status" (Henslin, 2008). The MWBE Enterprises defines women-owned businesses as "being owned, capitalized, operated and controlled by a woman or group of women. The business must be a "for-profit" business which is physically in the United States or one of its territories" (http://www.mwbe-enterprises.com/). As stated previously, ownership means that the business is at least 51% owned by a women or group of women.

Other qualifications are based on a minority of influence or power in the company, thereby it is possible to see "minority" defined as veteran-owned businesses, disabled-owned business and businesses located in Historically Under-Utilized Business zones (HUB) (Greer, Maltbia, & Scott, 2008). The MWBE Enterprises defines a Small Disadvantaged Business (SDB) or Disadvantaged Business Enterprises (DBE) as a small or disadvantaged business that is at least 51% owned, operated, controlled by women, a minority or minority group, a disabled person or a veteran who owns a business. "The business must be a for-profit enterprise which physically resides in the United States or one of its territories" (http://www.mwbe-enterprises.com/). This makes the term minority very broad and gives organizations the flexibility to define "minority" according its mission or history of past discrimination in the company or region.

It is important to note that the previously mentioned definitions are used in the United States. In other countries, the definitions vary. For example, in the UK, labels such as "ethnic business" or "Black and Minority Ethnic business (BME)" or "Ethnic Minority Business (EMB)" are commonly used. The groups identified as ethnic minority tend to be African-Caribbean, Indian, Pakistani, Bangladeshi, and Chinese (Centre for Enterprise and Economic Development Research, 2001). In Europe, most minority groups are immigrants. Consequently, EMB's are usually considered as a part of the larger issue of immigration.

Other countries are grappling with the use of the word minority when the group may be a numerical majority. For example, in South Africa, blacks are a numerical majority, but since black-owned businesses are weak in comparison to white-owned businesses, the government has issued policies to give priority and support to black-owned businesses.

It is also important to note that in Europe, the EMB's are owned solely by minorities. Thus, their definitions for minority do not include percentages (Sonfield, 2005).

INCREASED GROWTH IN SUPPLIER DIVERSITY

Combat Economic Disparity

When buyers improve their relationships with minority owned business, there exist a means to combat economic disparity in disadvantaged communities. The underlying logic is that as relationships with buyers and minority owned suppliers improve, benefits will accrue not only to minority owned businesses, but also to corporations and society as a whole since there will be more disposable income to spend on products and services; particularly, the products/services of companies who invest in minority communities (Varmazis, 2007). Indeed, a recent study by the Women's Business Enterprise National Council (WBENC) revealed that 80% of female consumers polled between the age of 35 and 55 indicated that they would try a product or service from a company who sourced with a women-owned business (Varmazis, 2007).

Moreover, demographic trends suggest that the move to embrace minority-owned businesses will only increase. Minority groups are increasing their business ownership at a much higher rate than the national average, according to the U.S. Census Bureau's 2002 survey of Business Owners. While the number of U.S. businesses increased by 10 percent between 1997 and 2002, the rate of growth for minority owned businesses was far higher, ranging from 20 percent to 67 percent depending on the ethnic or racial group.

Global pressures are also being used to combat economic disparity. Countries such as Europe are requiring all those doing business in their country to operate by their rules on minority business inclusion (Sonfield, 2005). Such facts only increase the need for businesses to learn how to develop successful relationships with minority owned businesses.

Corporate Social Responsibility

Organizations are increasingly becoming more concerned with being socially responsible. Examples of Corporate Socially Responsible (CSR) acts are corporate philanthropy, socially responsible hiring, cause-related marketing and minority support programs (Varadarajan & Menon, 1988). Regardless of the act, organizations have found that there is a positive relationship between their CSR and its customers' attitude about them, their products, and/or services (Sen & Bhattacharya, 2001).

Many companies include supplier diversity as part of their overall corporate responsibility and community engagement initiative. Apple Inc. states that their strong and longstanding commitment to a diverse supply base is a good example of how they take their social responsibilities seriously (http://www.Apple.com/). PepsiCo believes that a diverse supplier base creates mutually beneficial relationships that expand PepsiCo's sphere of activity. It helps build community infrastructure by providing employment, training, role models, products from other minority and women-owned businesses and support from community organizations (http://www.PepsiCo.com/). Businesses have come to realize that there is something socially irresponsible about taking billions of dollars from minority communities and neglecting to hire or partner with people who look like them, and to invest in their communities. As stated by the President of a supplier to UPS, "A meaningful supplier diversity program extends beyond just including small businesses that present the best numbers. The most effective supplier diversity program is one that includes businesses that share our commitment to making positive changes to the communities we serve" (Townes, 2007, p. 7).

Initiatives headed by corporate America are having some success. Corporate spending with minority-owned businesses has increased from $360 million in 1974 to $87.4 billion in 2004 (National Minority Supplier Development Council, 2005). Typical spending goals range from 5-8% (National Minority Supplier Development Council, 2008). For example, Toyota set a 7.5% spending goal for purchases from minority suppliers (Witherspoon, 2006). These spending goals are generally distributed throughout the supply chain with expectations for all suppliers. In fact, diversity as a criterion for procurement is rising (Bhayani, 2007). Some contracts now require bidders to ensure diversity of not only employees, but also in their supply chain. Such forms can be called pre-bid diversity forms and require companies to state their action plans on how they will increase diversity in their organization and in the supply chain. (Bhayani, 2007). Over the past 20 years, with support from both private and public companies, minority firms have seen their revenue rise approximately 10 percent annually, have created 23 percent more jobs, and have an overall growth rate three times higher than that of non-minority owned businesses (Boston Consulting Group, 2005). However, even though minority businesses are growing at a rate faster than non-minority businesses, their proportion does not fully reflect the growing size of minority communities in the United States. Such results indicate that CSR efforts may not always lead to business results as expected. Hence, if organizations wish to improve their relationship with minority owned suppliers other avenues must be sought.

It should be noted that countries other than the US offer little assistance for their ethnic businesses (DG Enterprise for the European Commission, 2000). The situation is slowing changing, however. In England and Scotland, governments are recognizing that ethnic minority firms are growing and in need of external financing. These countries have established programs to assist their needs (Deakins, et al., 2003). They have also begun to recognize that existing European policies and legislation are working against ethnic minority business development. Thus, programs to "set-aside" work are growing (Cormack & Niessen, 2002).

CHALLENGES OF MAINTAINING RELATIONSHIPS WITH MINORITY SUPPLIERS

Building relationships with minority suppliers can be very challenging. One problem is the constant struggle that purchasing has in reaching minority-purchasing goals under extreme pressure to reduce costs. Supply chain management initiatives continually advocate the consolidation and reduction of suppliers (Teague & Hannon, 2005). Such goals can work counterproductive to supplier diversity programs as many minority-owned suppliers are likely to be smaller in terms of capacity and depth of capabilities. In addition, without a proven record indicating past success and potential for future growth, a minority-owned supplier's chance of competing are minimized. Purchasing agents and minority-owned suppliers also have to deal with affirmative action backlash (Morgan, 2002). Supplier diversity programs and their champions constantly have to defend their initiatives and explain their importance to the organization. Moreover, it complicates the selection of minority owned suppliers, because some suppliers refuse to be labeled as such.

Other problems hindering buyer minority owned supplier relationship success are issues of cash flow, understanding business processes and corporate politics (Shah & Ram, 2006; Pullins, et al., 2004). For example, the director of minority suppliers at Dana Corporation stated that, "Non-minority owned suppliers have an advantage because they have been in business a lot longer. In many cases, they have the infrastructure, money, and sales and marketing staff. They have the ability to navigate through the political arena. They have been at the table longer. They know the questions to ask and more importantly, they know which people to ask." Such issues are critical to achieving successful business relationships.

Buyers must be prepared to sustain and maintain the relationships they have. We propose a theoretical model that depicts important relationship variables that we believe impact minority owned supplier's relationship satisfaction with a buyer. These variables include trust, commitment, and relationship satisfaction. It is important to note that these variables are common to buyer supplier relationships, in general. However, based on our review of the literature, to date, we have found no research exploring key determinants of sustaining relationships with minority owned suppliers and how buying firms can increase the minority owned supplier's satisfaction. Current research places much of the responsibility of relationship building on the supplier. Moreover, our proposed model is developed from the minority supplier's perspective at the individual level giving them a voice in the relationship process, which is also negligent in extant research.

The relationship variables important for non-minority owned business such as, trust and commitment, will be similarly important for minority owned businesses, but for different reasons. In Figure 1, an organizing framework summarizes our view of buyer-minority owned supplier relationship satisfaction and maps the territory that is covered in this article. Our framework identifies the importance of understanding the role of trust (benevolence and credibility), minority owned supplier's perception of buyer's commitment and the minority owned supplier's commitment. The proposed framework could aid buyers with building and maintaining their relationships with their minority owned suppliers. Understanding such a framework could eliminate the perception that buyers need to treat minority owned suppliers differently than non-minority owned suppliers when building and establishing relationships. Thereby, if the process and key determinants of building relationships with minority owned suppliers are similar to non-minority suppliers, buyers can modify existing strategies and begin to develop more innovative and successful programs and practices that will actually enhance and sustain this unique minority owned supply base.

As we describe the framework, we will highlight the unique issues that make minority owned suppliers different from non-minority suppliers. This understanding can be used as information that can increase the success of supplier diver-

Figure 1. Building relationships with minority suppliers

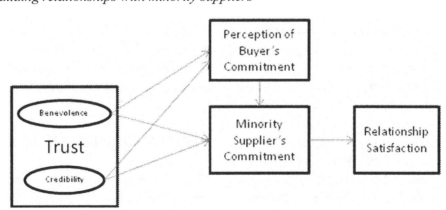

sity goals, the success of social responsibility agendas and increase retention and performance of minority owned suppliers with their buying firms.

The remainder of the chapter is as follows. We review the past research on supplier diversity. We then discuss our model and introduce specific research propositions. We conclude with insights for practicing managers, contributions to theory, and directions for future research.

PREVIOUS RESEARCH ON MINORITY-OWNED SUPPLIERS

Research dating back as early as the 1970's indicate differences and difficulties that minority owned businesses face. Recent research also discusses the challenges to implementing supplier diversity programs. Gumpert (1970) describes the difficulties in changing long-standing purchasing practices and the problems that minority-owned companies are having in sustaining long term relationships. Enz, Dollinger, and Daily (1990) discussed how Minority Business Enterprises (MBEs) appear to align their organizational based values to those of their customers as a means of building trust. Based on a survey of both buyers and suppliers, Pearson, Fawcett, and Cooper (1993) found that purchasing managers and MBEs view the impediments to successful relationships quite differently. MBEs perceive a higher level of difficulty in developing strong buyer/supplier relationships than their purchasing counterparts. Krause, Ragatz, and Hughley (1999) focused on assessing the effectiveness of a large industrial manufacturing firm's minority supplier development program, in terms of the outcomes of the program for minority owned suppliers, and examining potential barriers to success.

Other research has focused on supplier diversity implementation. Giunipero (1981) identifies the stages of supplier diversity program implementation and discusses the key elements needed in developing these programs. Shah and Ram (2006) conducted interviews with three US companies to understand the rationale, drivers and challenges to implementing supplier diversity programs. Whitfield and Landeros (2006) empirically examined the influence of organizational culture on supplier diversity. Adobor and McMullen (2007) offered guidelines for large corporations and MBEs to sustain and develop supplier diversity initiatives.

While these studies are noteworthy and further our knowledge on minority owned businesses, we have not found any research to date that has explored the key determinants of sustaining relationships with minority owned suppliers. One argument for this oversight could be that minority classification is not an issue because objective performance outcomes are all that matter. Thereby, there is no need to highlight and/or address this difference. However, research on diversity continues to indicate that culture, ethnicity, and gender difference are complications to business relationships and are worthy of strategies to minimize their negative effects (Cox & Blake, 1991; Hofstede, 1984; Lewicki, McAllister, & Bies, 1998; Doney, Cannon, & Mullen, 1998). A second argument could also be made that research in supply chain management is generally done from the buyer perspective because that is who has the control and economic power; consequently, supplier relationship satisfaction in not an issue. However, research continues to mount that demonstrates the value of building relationships with suppliers and including their perspective in decision-making (Liker & Choi, 2004). Indeed, a recent survey of the operations management literature uncovered an imbalance to the detriment of the supplier (van der Vaart & van Donk, 2008).

CONCEPTUAL FRAMEWORK

The following constructs are a part of our conceptual framework that leads to minority owned supplier's satisfaction with their buying firms (see

Figure 1). These variables are common to buyer supplier relationships and research has proven their importance. We first define the variables and in a later section discuss their relationship to the other variables and our propositions.

Trust

It has been well established in the social sciences literature that trust is an important social resource that can facilitate cooperation and enable coordinated social interactions (Blau, 1964; Zucker, 1986; Coleman, 1988). We also established trust's importance through structured interviews, in 2003, with practicing managers of the Minority Supplier Development Council of Middle Tennessee. During these interviews with minority owned suppliers, it became apparent that it is often difficult to develop trust and cooperation across group boundaries because people often perceive individuals from other groups as potential adversaries with conflicting goals.

Fiske and Neuberg (1990) propose that when individuals are viewed as representatives of a social group, interpersonal and intergroup interactions fuse such that the affect and beliefs associated with that social group influence interpersonal interactions. Williams (2001) argues that it is this fusion that is likely to influence trust development, because beliefs about trustworthiness are often associated with social group membership. Williams (2001) also discusses how people's perceptions of their own interdependence with other groups influence both their beliefs about group members' trustworthiness and their affect for group members. Moreover, there is evidence that suggests that individuals from dissimilar groups, such as different demographic categories view members of contrasting groups with distrust (Kanter, 1977; Cox, 1993).

Trust is invaluable to organizations that depend on inter-organizational partnerships and other cooperative structures because it facilitates informal cooperation and reduces negotiation costs by reducing the need to monitor others' behaviors, formalize procedures and to completely specify contracts (Williams, 2001). Trust in business relationships is important because when it is present, complex problems can be diminished more quickly and economically than by using formal authority or policies. This means that operational expenses and overall cost structures can be reduced.

Handfield et al. (2000) discussed how cultivating mutual trust is one of the biggest challenges in supplier development. Johnston et al. (2004) in their research on the effect of supplier trust on performance found that higher levels of inter-organizational cooperative behaviors such as shared planning and flexibility in coordinating activities were strongly linked to the supplier's trust in the buyer firm.

Because trust has been examined in different streams of research, it is important that we clearly define trust in the context of our research. Drawing on literature in social psychology (Larzelere & Huston, 1980) and relationship marketing (Ganesan, 1994; Doney & Cannon, 1997) trust is defined along two dimensions. The first dimension focuses on the objective *credibility of a supply chain's partner, expectancy that the partner's word or written statement can be relied on.* The second dimension focuses on *benevolence, which is based on the extent to which one partner is genuinely interested in the other partner's welfare and motivated to seek joint gain.*

Commitment

Building a successful relationship between two businesses involves a long-term commitment from both the buying firm and the supplying firm. Commitment is viewed as critical in the literature of social exchange (Cook & Emerson, 1978), organizations (Meyer & Allen, 1984) and relationship marketing (Anderson & Weitz, 1992). Drawing on the conceptualization of commitment in social exchange theory, we define commitment as *a buyer/supplier's belief that the relationship is important enough to warrant maximum efforts at maintaining it; that is, the committed party values the relationship to an extent that it is worth continuing indefinitely.* Our definition corresponds almost exactly with that developed by Morgan and Hunt (1994).

Commitment is also viewed as critical in the area of supplier development and supplier evaluations. Krause (1999) in his study of supplier development programs concluded that the buying firm's perception of supplier commitment is an important antecedent to further commitment on the part of the buying firm. Prahinski and Benton (2004) found similar results in that buying firms can influence the supplier's commitment through increased efforts of cooperation and commitment. Anderson and Weitz (1992) in their study on channel relationships found that manufacturers and distributors appear to factor the other side's commitment into its perceptions. Distributors attribute greater commitment to manufacturers that are more committed, and manufacturers do likewise. These facts intensify our interest in what role commitment can play in buyers trying to sustain successful relationships with minority owned suppliers.

Based on these studies, we include both the minority owned supplier's level of commitment and the minority owned supplier's perception of the buyer's commitment in our conceptual framework along with trust.

PROPOSITION DEVELOPMENT

Trust and Commitment

An important component of business-to-business relationships is that of reciprocity. The principle of reciprocity in exchange theory suggests that members of a dyad must perceive the other to be trustworthy in order to ensure a successful and continuing relationship (Blau, 1964; Anderson & Weitz, 1989). Berry and Parasuraman (1991)

maintain that "relationships are built on the foundation of mutual commitment." Moreover, previous literature on successful marketing relationships maintains that those networks characterized by relationship commitment and trust engender cooperation (Morgan and Hunt, 1994). Trust will be crucial to the buyer-minority owned supplier relationship because supply chain success is dependent upon cooperation (Moberg & Speh, 2003). However, research has established that cooperation across group boundaries can be difficult because individuals often perceive those who belong to other groups as potential adversaries with conflicting goals, beliefs, and styles (e.g. Fiske & Ruscher, 1993; Kramer & Messick, 1998). This makes trust a vital element in buyer minority owned supplier relationships because research has established that it is natural for individuals to group themselves according to their demographic characteristics (ie. age, gender, race, etc.). The concern, however, is that self-categorization generally results with in-group members perceiving out-group members as being untrustworthy (Brewer, 1979). Indeed, research indicates that in three types of trust (overall trust, trust of superiors, and trust of colleagues) that managers of similar nationality held significantly higher levels of trust for their superiors of similar nationality than for superiors of different nationality (Banai & Reisel, 1999).

Research suggests that trust and commitment have a close relationship in buyer supplier relationships. Trust and commitment have been shown to be necessary for successful buyer supplier relationships, with trust being an antecedent to commitment (Geyskens, Steenkamp, & Kumar, 1998). Moreover, Adobor and McMullen (2006) found in their research on supplier diversity in the supply chain that commitment was an important factor. Commitment in supplier diversity programs establishes legitimacy (Aldrich & Fiol, 1994) and helps to gain support from internal stakeholders (Shah and Ram, 2006). Indeed, in a survey of minority owned businesses, Pearson et al. (1993), found that MBEs believed that large firms lacked commitment to supplier diversity programs and only used such programs merely as a means to meet government regulations and/or for creating a positive public image. Commitment is also important because businesses apart of a supply chain must conduct business with direct competitors and may have to share sensitive operational and strategic information with other members. Thereby, the supplier must be committed to the strategy and be trusted to keep sensitive information private.

Such research indicates the importance of trust as an antecedent to commitment and the importance of both the minority owned supplier's commitment and the minority owned supplier's perception of the buyer's commitment to the relationship. Thus, trust and commitment will have a direct relationship to cooperative behaviors that are conducive to building strong relationships with minority owned suppliers and increasing supplier diversity program success.

Thereby we propose that:

- *Proposition 1a: A minority supplier's perception that the buying firm is credible will have a positive effect on the minority supplier's commitment to the buying firm.*
- *Proposition 1b: A minority supplier's perception that the buying firm is benevolent will have a positive effect on the minority supplier's commitment to the buying firm.*
- *Proposition 1c: A minority supplier's perception that the buying firm is credible will have a positive effect on the minority supplier's perception of the buying firm's commitment*
- *Proposition 1d: A minority supplier's perception that the buying firm is benevolent will have a positive effect on the minority supplier's perception of the buying firm's commitment*

Perception of Buyer's and Minority-Owned Supplier's Commitment

The minority owned supplier is aware of and will develop a perception of the buyer's commitment. As indicated earlier, Pearson et al. (1993), revealed in their survey of minority owned businesses that MBEs believed that large firms lacked commitment to supplier diversity programs and only used such programs merely as a means to meet government regulations and/or for creating a positive public image. Other reports reveal that firms have used minorities as "fronts" to gain business, or simply falsifying their classification (Boston Consulting Group, 2005). Companies simply appoint minorities to be a partner or assign them to other ownership positions without giving them real responsibility. Awareness of these types of actions will affect the minority owned suppliers' commitment because they will view the buyer's motives as opportunistic. According to Bagozzi's (1992) attitude theory, employees generally react positively to an idea when they believe that top management is committed. We can apply such logic to the buyer minority owned supplier relationship. If the minority owned supplier views the buyer to be committed, they will be too. Thereby we propose that:

- *Proposition 2: A minority's supplier's perception that the buying firm is committed will have a positive effect on the minority supplier's commitment to the buying firm.*

Commitment and Relationship Satisfaction

Organizational commitment and job satisfaction are popular topics in the study of work-related attitudes. The majority of theoretical and empirical evidence suggests that job satisfaction is an antecedent to organizational commitment (Bagozzi, 1980; Bartol, 1979; Brown & Peterson, 1994; Mathieu & Hamel, 1989; Reichers, 1985). However, some support exists for the role of job satisfaction as an outcome of organizational commitment (Baseman & Strasser, 1984). Koslowsky et al. (1991) found no evidence to support a causal relationship, but determined that a high correlation exists. This finding was consistent with a number of studies that include both variables (Knoop, 1995; Mathieu & Zajac, 1990; Shore & Martin, 1989). Research has identified commitment as one of the key characteristics of successful relationships (Dwyer, et al., 1987; Morgan & Hunt, 1994). Jap and Ganesan (2000) found that retailers are more likely to be satisfied with suppliers whom they perceive to be committed. In the supplier development literature, Krause (1999) concluded that the buying firm will proceed with its supplier development investment, if it perceives that the supplier is committed to the relationship. Thereby we propose that:

- *Proposition 3a: The minority supplier's commitment to the buying firm will have a positive effect on relationship satisfaction.*
- *Proposition 3b: The minority supplier's positive perception of the buyer's commitment will have a positive effect on relationship satisfaction.*

PRACTICAL IMPLICATIONS AND FUTURE RESEARCH

The preceding conceptual framework and related research propositions represent relationship variables that we see as essential to buyers and their need to sustain minority owned suppliers, a crucial component of their supply base. An increase in corporate initiated supplier diversity spending goals, corporate social responsibility and need for innovation will force buyers to, not only, spend

more with minority owned suppliers, but also to sustain ongoing relationships. Research is needed to assist business owners, purchasing and supply chain managers with the knowledge needed to achieve desired goals.

Our model proposes that buyers will have a responsibility to manage their image and the manner in which they interact with minority owned suppliers. The information gathered during formal and informal interactions and from the media may have a direct effect on the minority owned supplier's perception of the buyer's commitment, which could determine overall relationship satisfaction. Moreover, we propose that buyers will need to understand that relationships are built on mutual commitment with trustworthiness being the core foundation. Strategies based on this understanding will not have to be an isolated or separate agenda for minority owned firms as non-minority suppliers will benefit from the same policy.

Research indicates that minority owned suppliers may be more sensitive to trust issues than non minority owned suppliers (Boston Consulting Group, 2005). Consequently, buyers will need to be conscious of policies, procedures, and practices that may be hindering their ability to sustain successful supplier diversity programs. Moreover, buyers will likely need to continue grass root and community programs that invest in communities and communicate a level of commitment beyond financial gain. We propose that such actions will aid in assisting buyers find and build successful relationships with minority owned suppliers.

Given the importance of relationship building with minority owned suppliers, buyers will need to commit to efforts geared toward creating an environment that enables trust and commitment. Such environments are necessary for both non-minority owned and minority owned suppliers. Building trust and displaying commitment will need to be established over-time with consistent efforts that focus on common goals, honesty and integrity, courtesy and respect, open communication, and cultural empathy. Such efforts can create a relationship that is functional and successful.

We have proposed a conceptual framework grounded in practical realities and research theory. We hope that our study generates additional research in this area. We intend to further investigate this topic by testing our proposed model and determining statistical significance and the implications of those results. Additional research could investigate to determine other factors that either enhance or deter the minority owned supplier's buyer relationship. Future research could also seek to investigate the specific obstacles that minority owned supplier's in specific industries endure when dealing with buyers and supply chain issues. Other studies could seek to highlight critical success factors based on case studies with specific minority owned suppliers who have ongoing successful relationships with buyers.

CONCLUSION

As we continue moving toward a global society, building relationships with minority owned businesses is a diversity goal that is becoming an important competitive initiative for organizations. Our study introduces research propositions from the minority business owners' (supplier's) voice that we see as critical in building successful buyer-minority supplier relationships. Savvy buyers who wish to build successful relationships with minority owned businesses and increase their overall supply diversity will need to understand the role that trust and commitment plays in relationship building. Buyers will need to continue to invest in proactive mentoring and other programs such as supplier diversity to increase the opportunity to build relationships.

REFERENCES

Adobor, H., & McMullen, R. (2007). Supplier diversity and supply chain management: A strategic approach. *Business Horizons, 50,* 279–329. doi:10.1016/j.bushor.2006.10.003

Aldrich, H. E., & Fiol, C. M. (1994). Fools rush in? The institutional context of industry creation. *Academy of Management Review, 19*(4), 645–670.

Alund, A. (2003). Self-employment of non-privileged groups as integration strategy. *International Review of Sociology, 13*(1), 77–87.

Anderson, E., & Weitz, B. (1989). Determinants of continuity in conventional industrial channel dyads. *Marketing Science, 8,* 310–323. doi:10.1287/mksc.8.4.310

Anderson, E., & Weitz, B. (1992). The use of pledges to build and sustain commitment in distribution channels. *JMR, Journal of Marketing Research, 29,* 18–34. doi:10.2307/3172490

Apple. (2009). *Apple and procurement.* Retrieved May 1, 2009 from http://www.apple.com/procurement/.

Bagozzi, R. P. (1980). Performance and satisfaction in an industrial sales force: An examination of their antecedents simultaneity. *Journal of Marketing, 44*(2), 65–77. doi:10.2307/1249978

Banai, M., & William, R. D. (1999). Would you trust your foreign manager? An empirical investigation. *International Journal of Human Resource Management, 10*(3), 477–487. doi:10.1080/095851999340431

Baseman, T. S., & Strasser, S. (1984). A longitudinal analysis of the antecedents of organizational commitment. *Academy of Management Journal, 27*(1), 95–112. doi:10.2307/255959

Berry, L. L., & Parasuraman, A. (1991). *Marketing services.* New York, NY: The Free Press.

Bhayani, H. (2007, May 15). Efforts to prove workforce diversity fail to help win contracts. *Personnel Today, 3.*

Blau, P. M. (1964). *Exchange and power in social life.* New York, NY: Wiley.

Boston Consulting Group. (2005). *The new agenda for minority business development.* Boston, MA: Boston Consulting Group.

Brewer, M. B. (1979). In group bias in the minimal intergroup situation: A cognitive-motivational analysis. *Psychological Bulletin, 86,* 307–324. doi:10.1037/0033-2909.86.2.307

Britt, G. (2007, September 17). Diversifying the supply chain. *Multichannel News.* Retrieved from http://www.highbeam.com/doc/1G1-168740825.html.

Brown, S. P., & Peterson, R. A. (1994). The effect of effort on sales performance and job satisfaction. *Journal of Marketing, 58*(2), 70–81. doi:10.2307/1252270

Business, E. (2003). Ethnic business support vital for urban regeneration. *Engineering Management, 13*(2), 5.

Centre for Enterprise and Economic Development Research. (2001). *Website.* Retrieved on May 20, 2009 from http://sbs.gov.uk/content/pdf/embf/BBA_Access_to_Finance_Research.pdf.

Coleman, J. S. (1988). Social capital in the creation of human capital. *American Journal of Sociology, 94,* 95–120. doi:10.1086/228943

Cook, K. S., & Emerson, R. M. (1978). Power, equity, and commitment in exchange networks. *American Sociological Review, 43,* 721–739. doi:10.2307/2094546

Cormack, J., & Niessen, J. (2002). Immigrant and minority businesses: Making the policy case. *European Journal of Migration and Law, 4*(3), 329–337. doi:10.1163/157181602322768939

Cox, T. H. (1993). *Cultural diversity in organizations: Theory, research and practice.* San Francisco, CA: Berrett-Koehler Publishers.

Cox, T. H., & Blake, S. (1991). Managing cultural diversity: Implications for organizational competitiveness. *The Executive, 5*(3), 45–56. doi:10.5465/AME.1991.4274465

Davis, K., & Blomstrom, R. L. (1966). *Business and its environment.* New York, NY: McGraw-Hill.

Doney, P. M., & Cannon, J. P. (1997). An examination of the nature of trust in buyer-seller relationships. *Journal of Marketing, 61,* 35–51. doi:10.2307/1251829

Doney, P. M., Cannon, J. P., & Mullen, M. R. (1998). Understanding the influence of national culture on the development of trust. *Academy of Management Review, 23*(3), 601–620.

Dwyer, F. R., Schurr, P. H., & Oh, S. (1987). Developing buyer-seller relationships. *Journal of Marketing, 51,* 11–27. doi:10.2307/1251126

Enterprises, M. W. B. E. (2010). *Website.* Retrieved on May 2010 from http://www.mwbe-enterprises.com/.

Enterprises, M. W. B. E. (2011). *Website.* Retrieved from http://www.mwbe-enterprises.com.

Enz, C. A., Dollinger, M., & Daily, C. (1990). Value orientations of minority and non-minority small business owners. *Entrepreneurship Theory and Practice, 15*(1), 23–36.

Fiske, S. T., & Neuberg, S. L. (1990). A continuum of impression formation: From category-based to individuating processes: Influences of information and motivation on attention and interpretation. In Zanna, M. (Ed.), *Advances in Experimental Social Psychology* (pp. 1–74). San Diego, CA: Academic Press. doi:10.1016/S0065-2601(08)60317-2

Fiske, S. T., & Ruscher, J. B. (1993). Negative interdependence and prejudice: Whence the affect? In Mackie, D. M., & Hamilton, D. L. (Eds.), *Affect, Cognition, and Stereotyping: Interactive Processes in Group Perceptions* (pp. 239–269). New York, NY: Academic Press.

Ganesan, S. (1994). Determinants of long-term orientation in buyer-seller relationships. *Journal of Marketing*, *58*, 1–19. doi:10.2307/1252265

Geyskens, I., Steenkamp, J. E. B. M., & Kumar, N. (1998). Generalizations about trust in marketing channel relationships using meta-analysis. *International Journal of Research in Marketing*, *15*(3), 223–248. doi:10.1016/S0167-8116(98)00002-0

Giunipero, L. (1981). Developing effective minority purchasing programs. *Sloan Management Review*, *22*(2), 33–42.

Greer, B., Matlbia, T., & Scott, C. (2006). Supplier diversity: A missing link in HRD. *Human Resource Development Quarterly*, *17*(3), 325–341. doi:10.1002/hrdq.1177

Gumpert, D. E. (1979). Seeking minority-owned businesses as suppliers. *Harvard Business Review*, *57*(1), 110–116.

Handfield, R. B., Krause, D. R., Scannell, T. V., & Monczka, R. M. (2000). Avoid the pitfalls in supplier development. *Sloan Management Review*, *41*(2), 37–49.

Hayes, S. N., Ofili, E. O., & Mitchell, J. E. (2010). *Racial/ethnic disparities: CVD in African American women*. Retrieved on February 26, 2010 from http://www.medscape.org/viewprogram/30681.

Henslin, J. M. (2008). *Essentials of sociology: A down to earth approach* (8th ed.). Boston, MA: Allyn & Bacon.

Hofstede, G. (1984). *Culture's consequences: International differences on work related values*. Beverly Hills, CA: Sage.

Jap, S. D., & Ganesan, S. (2000). Control mechanisms and the relationship life cycle: Implications of safeguarding specific investments and developing commitment. *JMR, Journal of Marketing Research*, *37*(2), 227–245. doi:10.1509/jmkr.37.2.227.18735

Johnston, D. A., McCutcheon, D. M., Stuart, F. I., & Kerwood, H. (2004). Effects of supplier trust on performance of cooperative supplier relationships. *Journal of Operations Management*, *22*, 23–38. doi:10.1016/j.jom.2003.12.001

Kanter, R. M. (1977). *Men and women of the corporation*. New York, NY: Basic Books.

Knoop, R. (1995). Relationship among job involvement, job satisfaction, and organizational commitment for nurses. *The Journal of Psychology*, *129*, 643–649. doi:10.1080/00223980.1995.9914935

Koslowsky, M., Caspy, T., & Lazar, M. (1991). Cause and effect explanations of job satisfaction and commitment: The case of exchange commitment. *The Journal of Psychology*, *125*(2), 153–162.

Kramer, R. M., & Messick, D. M. (1998). Getting by with a little help from our enemies: Collective paranoia and its role in intergroup relations. In Sedikides, C. (Ed.), *Intergroup Cognition and Intergroup Behavior* (pp. 233–255). Mahwah, NJ: Lawrence Erlbaum Associates.

Krause, D. R. (1999). The antecedents of buying firms' efforts to improve suppliers. *Journal of Operations Management*, *17*, 205–224. doi:10.1016/S0272-6963(98)00038-2

Krause, D. R., Ragatz, G. L., & Hughley, S. (1999). Supplier development from the minority supplier's perspective. *The Journal of Supply Chain Management*, *35*(4), 33–41. doi:10.1111/j.1745-493X.1999.tb00242.x

Larzelere, R. E., & Huston, T. L. (1980). The dyadic trust scale: Toward understanding interpersonal trust in close relationships. *Journal of Marriage and the Family, 42,* 595–604. doi:10.2307/351903

Lewicki, R. J., McAllister, D. J., & Bies, R. J. (1998). Trust and distrust: New relationships and realities. *Academy of Management Journal, 23*(3), 438–458.

Liker, J. K., & Choi, T. (2004). Building deep supplier relationships. *Harvard Business Review, 82*(12), 104–113.

Masurel, E., Nijkamp, P., Tastan, M., & Vindigni, G. (2002). Motivations and performance conditions for ethnic entrepreneurship. *Growth and Change, 33*(2), 238–260. doi:10.1111/0017-4815.00189

Mathieu, J. E., & Hamel, K. (1989). A causal model of the antecedents of organizational commitment among professionals and nonprofessionals. *Journal of Vocational Behavior, 34,* 299–317. doi:10.1016/0001-8791(89)90022-5

Mathieu, J. E., & Zajac, D. (1990). A review and meta-analysis of the antecedents, correlates, and consequences of organizational commitment. *Psychological Bulletin, 108,* 171–194. doi:10.1037/0033-2909.108.2.171

McGee, J. (1998). Commentary on corporate strategies and environmental regulations: An organizing framework by A. M. Rugman and A. Verbeke. *Strategic Management Journal, 19*(4), 377–387. doi:10.1002/(SICI)1097-0266(199804)19:4<377::AID-SMJ988>3.0.CO;2-S

Meyer, J. P., & Allen, N. J. (1984). Testing the side-bet theory of organizational commitment: Some methodological considerations. *The Journal of Applied Psychology, 69*(3), 372–378. doi:10.1037/0021-9010.69.3.372

Moberg, C. R., & Speh, T. W. (2003). Evaluating the relationships between questionable business practices and strength of supply chain relationships. *Journal of Business Logistics, 24*(2), 1–19. doi:10.1002/j.2158-1592.2003.tb00043.x

Morgan, J. (2002). How well are supplier diversity programs doing? *Purchasing, 131*(13), 29–33.

Morgan, R. M., & Hunt, S. D. (1994). The commitment-trust theory of relationship marketing. *Journal of Marketing, 58,* 20–38. doi:10.2307/1252308

NMSDC. (2008). *The new realities for minority business.* New York, NY: National Minority Supplier Development Council.

Pearson, J. N., Fawcett, S., & Cooper, A. (1993). Challenges and approaches to purchasing from minority-owned firms: A longitudinal examination. *Entrepreneurship Theory and Practice, 18*(2), 71–88.

Pepsi. (2009). *Supplier diversity.* Retrieved on May 5, 2009 from http://www.pepsico.com/Purpose/Diversity-and-Inclusion/Supplier-Diversity.aspx.

Porter, M. (1995, May-June). The competitive advantage of the inner city. *Harvard Business Review,* 55–71.

Prahinski, C., & Benton, W. C. (2004). Supplier evaluations: Communication strategies to improve supplier performance. *Journal of Operations Management, 22,* 39–62. doi:10.1016/j.jom.2003.12.005

Pullins, E. B., Reid, D. A., & Plank, R. E. (2004). Gender issues in buyer-seller relationships: Does gender matter in purchasing? *Journal of Supply Chain Management, 40*(3), 40–48. doi:10.1111/j.1745-493X.2004.tb00173.x

Ram, M., & Smallbone, D. (2003). Ethnic minority enterprise: Policy in practice. *Entrepreneurship & Regional Development, 15,* 99–102. doi:10.1080/0898562032000075186

Reichers, A. E. (1985). A review and reconceptualization of organizational commitment. *Academy of Management Review, 10*(3), 465–476.

Rogerson, C., & Rogerson, J. (1997). The changing post-apartheid city: Emergent black-owned enterprises in Johannesburg. *Urban Studies (Edinburgh, Scotland), 34*(1), 85–103. doi:10.1080/0042098976285

Sen, S., & Bhattacharya, C. B. (2001). Does doing good always lead to doing better? Consumer reactions to corporate social responsibility. *JMR, Journal of Marketing Research, 38*(2), 225–243. doi:10.1509/jmkr.38.2.225.18838

Shah, M., & Ram, M. (2006). Supplier diversity and minority business enterprise: Case study experience of three US multinationals. *Supply Chain Management: An International Journal, 11*(1), 75–81. doi:10.1108/13598540610642493

Shore, L. M., & Martin, H. J. (1989). Job satisfaction and organizational commitment in relation to work performance and turnover intentions. *Human Relations, 42*, 625–638. doi:10.1177/001872678904200705

Sonfield, M. (2005, May 17). A new US definition of minority business: Lessons from the first four years. *Entrepreneurship & Regional Development*, 223-235.

Teague, P., & Hannon, D. (2005). The changing face of supplier diversity. *Purchasing, 134*(13), 52–55.

Time Inc. (2005). *Partnering for profit*. Retrieved on January 7, 2009 from http://www.timeinc.net/fortune/services/sections/fortune/corp/2005_04MinorityBiz.html.

Townes, G. (2007). M/WBE suppliers find business opportunities with UPS. *New York Amsterdam News, 98*(44), 6–34.

US Census Bureau Economic Census. (2002). *Survey of business owners*. Washington, DC: US Census Bureau.

Van der Vaart, T., & Van Donk, D. P. (2008). A critical review of survey-based research in supply chain integration. *International Journal of Production Economics, 111*(1), 42–55. doi:10.1016/j.ijpe.2006.10.011

Varadarajan, P. R., & Menon. (1988). Cause related marketing: A coalignment of marketing strategy and corporate philanthropy. *Journal of Marketing, 52*(3), 58–74. doi:10.2307/1251450

Varmazis, M. (2007). Supplier diversity yields growth. *Purchasing*, 57-58.

Whitfield, G., & Landeros, R. (2006). Supplier diversity effectiveness: Does organizational culture really matter? *The Journal of Supply Chain Management, 42*(4), 16–28. doi:10.1111/j.1745-493X.2006.00019.x

Williams, M. (2001). In whom we trust: Group membership as an affective context for trust development. *Academy of Management Review, 26*(3), 377–396.

Witherspoon, R. (2006). Who's who in supplier diversity? *USBE & Information Technology, 19*(54), 28–31.

Zenisek, T. J. (1979). Corporate social responsibility: A conceptualization based on organizational literature. *Academy of Management Review, 4*(3), 359–368.

Zucker, L. G. (1986). Production of trust: Institutional sources of economic structure, 1840-1920. In B. M. Staw & L. L. Cummings (Eds.), *Research in Organizational Behavior, 8*, 53-111.

KEY TERMS AND DEFINITIONS

Benevolence: The extent to which one partner is genuinely interested in the other partner's welfare and motivated to seek joint gain.

BME: Black and Minority Ethnic Business.

Buyers: A business that purchases products/services from another business.

Commitment: Belief that the relationship is important enough to warrant maximum efforts at maintaining it; that is, the committed party values the relationship to an extent that it is worth continuing indefinitely.

Corporate Social Responsibility: Corporate initiative to assess and take responsibility for the company's effects on the environment and impact on social welfare.

Credibility: Expectancy that the partner's word or written statement can be relied on.

DBE: Disadvantaged Business Enterprise.

EMB: Ethnic Minority Business.

MBE: Minority Business Enterprises.

Minority: A group having little power or representation relative to other groups within a society.

MWBE: Minority and Women owned Business Enterprises.

NMSDC: National Minority Supplier Development Council.

SBA: Small Business Administration.

SDVOB: Service Disabled Veteran-Owned Businesses.

Suppliers: A business that supplies a product and/or service to another business or customer.

Supplier Diversity: Is a proactive business program that encourages the sourcing of products and services from MWBE, VOB, SDVOB, historically underutilized business, and SBA defined small business vendors as suppliers.

Trust: Firm belief in the reliability, truth, ability, or strength of someone or something.

WBENC: Women's Business Enterprise National Council.

VOB: Veteran Owned Businesses.

Chapter 20
Leveraging Workforce Diversity and Team Development

Aileen G. Zaballero
Pennsylvania State University, USA

Hsin-Ling Tsai
Pennsylvania State University, USA

Philip Acheampong
Pennsylvania State University, USA

ABSTRACT

In this broadening landscape of business, corporations are encouraged to develop global leaders. "Changes in workforce demographics resulting from globalization, combined with the rising popularity of team-based management techniques, have resulted in a practical concern with the management of multicultural groups" (Thomas, 1999, p. 242). Organizations are challenged to implement a comprehensive approach to global development that encompasses different cultural perspectives. This chapter proposes to utilize team-based learning within a cross-cultural work-group. The use of a collaborative approach supports the social dimensions of learning and can exhibit greater productivity for individuals. According to Jonassen, Strobel, and Lee (2006) as cited by Schaffer, Lei, and Paulino (2008), "Knowledge exists not only in the heads of learners, but also in the conversations and social relations among collaborators" (p. 144).

This chapter will emphasize the importance of collaborative team-based work groups among diverse settings. First, the authors will discuss the factors of diverse teams and identify the stages of group development focusing on Tuckman's Model. In addition, Gert Hofstede's cultural dimension will be addressed. Finally, organizational contexts that impact the performance of diverse teams such will be explored.

DOI: 10.4018/978-1-4666-1812-1.ch020

INTRODUCTION

Due to globalization, emerging markets, boundary-less labor pool, the workforce of most organizations have become much more diverse. Many corporations must also address workplace inequalities while harnessing the power associated with the concept of diversity (Gopal, et al., 1997). In many industrialized nations, it is not uncommon to visit institutions or organizations that employ individuals from a multitude of cultural backgrounds. In 2003, it was estimated that international foreign workers globally consisted of approximately 25 million people, of which an estimated 14 million live in United States; 5 million in Northwestern Europe; half a million in Japan and about 5 million in Saudi Arabia (Knox, Agnew, & McCarthy, 2003). These groups of professional experts are drawn to fill positions as blue-collar workers; language teachers and entertainers. In 2008, the United States granted permanent resident status to over one million people (US Department of Homeland Security, 2009). The labor pool is no longer limited by national boundaries and cross-cultural work groups have become the norm.

Concerns of workers among cross-cultural groups not only pose challenges to employers, but barriers such as communication skills, cultural difference, lack of training, and culturally inept programs have impede efforts and productivity. Working collaboratively among diverse workgroups and cultures requires education where employees with good working skills can enhance organization's output and create opportunities for others to improve.

Collaboration can be a key step to learning that fosters innovation and growth. The use of collaborative approach supports the social dimensions of learning and can exhibit greater productivity for individuals. Following with the rapid technological change, globalization and aging labor-force, the workforce landscape now requires diversity of skills and education (Judy & D'Amico, 1997). As organizations become more diverse, it is important

to have strong communication skills, problem solving abilities, interpersonal relations, and the capacity to work effectively within diverse team.

Understanding the role of diversity in the underpinnings of a global workforce is one of the most important issues in the field of international business (Jain & Tucker, 1995). As cross-cultural teams continue to be part of the everyday business, the need to understand teams beyond western concepts continues to grow. The following section will define team both from functional and diverse perspective

TEAM WITHIN DIVERSE SETTINGS

Value of Team

Globalization has caused a network of relationships and organizational links within the business world. To stay competitive in today's market, organizations seek ways to create an equitable workplace environment that will make use of the knowledge, skill, and attitude of a diverse workforce. Throughout this chapter, the authors use the term *team* to refer to organizational work group that work interdependently towards a common goal and produces an output that is the result of the team's collective efforts (Oertig & Buergi, 2000).

Teams are made of individuals, often with different backgrounds. As diversity contributes to the creative innovation of a group, it is also diversity that poses challenges. Understanding individual work styles, group dynamics, and cultural variations is important to avoid potential conflicts.

Diverse Teams

The business case for diversity has emerged as a key strategy in a globally competitive market and has become an important business function for American businesses. With the labor pool and the customer base becoming more diverse many organizations are attempting to capitalize on these demographic changes (Dansky, Weech-Maldonado, De Souza, & Dreachslin, 2003). Several studies show that "culturally diverse organizations outperform their more homogeneous counterparts" (2003, p. 243) and research has identified potential positive outcomes (Dreachslin, 2007; Egan & Bendick, 2007). To enhance innovation and productivity, organizations continue to emphasize collaborative efforts; however, diversity must be managed appropriately. Companies must develop a culture that empowers everyone to be respectful, inclusive, and utilize their individual knowledge skills to expand the company knowledge (Egan & Bendick, 2007).

To capitalize on the unique contributions of each member it is imperative to identify the strengths of diverse teams and understand the individual strengths and cultural variations. Loden and Rosener (1991) defined individual dimensions as "those immutable human differences that are inborn and/or that exert an important impact on our early socialization and ongoing impact throughout our lives" (p. 18) such as age, ethnicity, gender, physical abilities/qualities, race and sexual orientation. Other contributors to diversity are: educational background, geographic location, income, marital status, military experience, parental status, religious belief and work experience.

It is important to develop teams and the relationship that exist among its members, furthermore to understand various communication and working styles various cultural orientation must be considered. The following section will discuss the stages of team development and explore the cultural dimensions as identified by Gert Hofstede.

TEAM DEVELOPMENT

In many sectors Team Building (TB) and Team Development (TD) are aware especial for multicultural group. If we want to understand team development well the first we need to indentify the difference between team building and team development. There are many methods for the process of team development. In third section of this Chapter, we review Action Learning Model, Tuckman's five-stage model of team development, Jones' Group Development Assessment and Process Consultation. Each of them has important role in process of team development as we introduced in the fourth section of this chapter.

Team Building and Team Development

Both team building and team development involve some similar characters such as common tasks, communication between individual and group and a facilitator. The difference between two is external and internal facilitator. Pfeiffer (1991) mentioned in *The Encyclopedia of Team-Building Activities*, the role of facilitator in team development "is not a professional, but the team's own formal leader or a designated member of the team" and facilitator is also a participant. Compare to team building intervention usually facilitated by outside professional consultant or outside of work unit professional (Dyer, 1987). Either team building or team development is aim to build group of people for working together and have more effective operation.

Tuckman's Model

Second model that we like to illustrate in this chapter is five-stage model: Tuckman's model of group development. This model describes stages of team development as Forming, Storming, Norming, Performing, and Adjourning (Tuckman, 1965; Tuckman & Jensen, 1977). Tuckman's model of group development is one of the mostly commonly cited models for the maturation process of groups and teams (Kreitner & Kinicki, 2007) (see Table 1).

Group Development Assessment

Groups will develop at different rates and levels of cooperation will fluctuate among members. The GDA model is presented by Jones (1973) and focuses on group development in both dimensions and is parallel with Tuckman's model. "Orientation and dependency are equivalent to Tuckman's forming stage, organization and conflict to storming, open data flow and cohesion to norming, and problem solving and interdependence to performing" (Ito & Brotheridge, 2008, p. 217). The GDA evaluates how the group is functioning such that improvement is available to support the group's action plan.

The GDA examines eight clusters of behaviors and four stages for task and process behaviors. Figure 1 demonstrates the comparison of stages in GDA and Tuckman's model. Unlike the Tuckman's model, GDA separates task behaviors from process behaviors where each contains four stages of group development. The model suggests that groups tend to go through predictable stages of growth as a result of the interaction of the two behavioral dimensions. As a diagnostic tool, GDA is designed to help managers, leaders, consultants, and group facilitators determine how to improve group functioning. To develop an effective team, individuals must be able to engage simultaneously in both task and process behaviors.

Overall, Tuckman's model assists team-based work groups as a maturation indicator. This model helps identify the current situation of teams as they develop. The GDA is a tool that teams can utilize to evaluate their current functioning in both task and interpersonal dimensions. It provides a comprehensive picture of what is necessary to become a successful team.

Process Consultation

Another tool we like to introduce in this chapter is process consultation which Process Consultation is used to enhance team effectiveness and address conflict. This tool helps teams develop strategies to work together successfully and efficiently. Cummings and Worley (2001) mentioned " process consultation is used not only as a way of helping groups become effective but also as a means whereby group learn to diagnose and

Table 1. Five stages

Stages	Climate	Key Tasks
Forming	Individual members are uncertain of their roles and the goals of the group. As various types of leadership emerge, trust and involvement tends to be low.	groups tend to require leadership for guidance (role) and direction (goals). individual members are getting to know each other as they get to know each other
Storming	The group will attempt to identify the purpose and goals of the team, as well as how they will function independently. Subgroups often develop and differences usually surface possibly causing a contentious environment.	Individuals and leadership is confronted during this phase. Individuals begin to open up to each other and challenge ideas and perspectives.
Norming	Individual roles are identified and behaviors will adjust to develop a feeling of team spirit creating group cohesiveness. Rules, values, and group norms are collectively developed.	Uncertainty about leadership and authority are mostly resolved. Team members begin to trust each other and the motivation of the group increases
Performing	The team develops a climate of open communication, strong cooperation, and commitment. Boundaries are established and conflict is resolved in a constructive and effective manner.	Accomplishing the collective goals and solving problems are the key focus of the group.
Adjourning	Wrap up	involves accomplishing the goals and disperse the team so that everyone can move on to new things

Figure 1. Comparison of stages in the GDA and Tuckman model (adapted from Ito & Brotheridge, 2008)

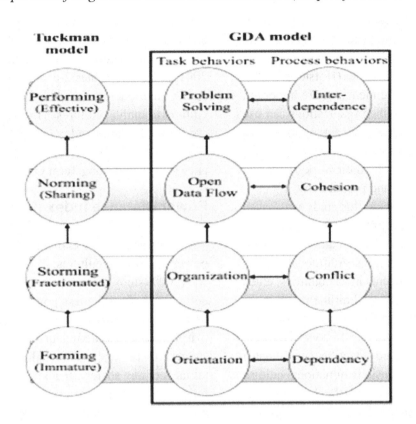

solve their own problem and continue to develop their competence and maturity." Therefore, process consultation can be utilized collaboratively with Tuckman's model and GDA along team development. Process consultation utilizes a set of activities to increase group awareness and understanding. Teams or organizations can take steps to improve the way that its members work together. According to Edgar Schein, "Any form of consultation implies that one person is helping another person, hence the central focus of analysis will be on deciphering that is helpful and what is not helpful in any given human situation" (Schein, 1999, p. 3). Process consultation can be any key initiative that takes place within an Organization Development (OD) and/or learning effort. In general, the intention is to help group members develop a more effective way of working together.

GEERT HOFSTEDE CULTURAL DIMENSIONS

Cultures have been defined in many ways, according to the Hofsted (2009) study, "Dimentionalizing Cultures." Geert Hofstede defines culture as, "the collective programming of the mind that distinguishes the members of one group or category of the group from others." Culture is always a collective phenomenon but can be connected to different collectives (Hofstede, 2009). Hofstede asserts individual characteristics using the concept of bell curve, as variation between cultures is the shift of the bell curve when one migrates from one culture to another (Hofstede). Generally the term "culture" is used for tribes, or ethnic groups (in anthropology), for nations (in political science, sociology, and management), and for organizations (sociology and management), Hofstede asserts. The term is applied to culture of occupations such as engineers, accountants, and academics of diverse disciplines and also gender to generations to social classes (Hofstede, 2009). Why Hofsted cultural dimensions are important is the extent to which the organizations can use determines cultural variations among the workgroups. Organizations can certain that identifying the differences among their workgroups can enhance performance and productivity.

According to Hofstede this study was based on a large research project into national cultural differences across units of multinational corporations (IBM) in 64 countries. Additional studies by others covered students in 23 countries, elites in 19 countries, commercial airline pilots in 23 countries, up-market consumers in 15 countries and civil service managers in 14 countries.

This section of the study identifies and validates five independent dimensions of national culture differences. Hofstede notes that the changing level of what he calls aggregation alters the nature and concept of culture. Comparing cultures, Hofstede explains culture as societal, national and gender that is acquired by birth are much deeper that rooted in human mind than occupational culture acquired through academic or organization. The academic

and organizational cultures are exchangeable when people take new jobs however societal cultures reside in values in the sense of broad tendencies to prefer certain states of affairs to others (Hofstede, 2001, p. 5). The Tables 2-6 use Hofstede (2003) study; the model of five dimensions of national cultures to analyze cultures of the world. Included are Power Distance Index (PDI), Individualism (IDV), Masculinity (MAS), Uncertainty Avoidance (UAI), and Long Term Orientation (LTO)

Power Distance Index (PDI)

Power distance index explains the hierarchy of power and role in cultures. According to Hofstede (2009) study, power distance index has been defined to reflect the less powerful members of organizations and institutions to accept and expect that power is distributed unequally. Hofstead study suggests that Power and inequality are fundamental facts of any society. It acknowledges that the followers endorse a society's level of inequality as much as the leaders. The study claims all societies are unequal but some are more equal than others. In comparing differences of cultures, Table 2 lists some cultural dimensions that can be used to compare cultures.

Table 2. Ten differences between small and large power distance societies

Small Power Distance	Large Power Distance
Parents treat children as equals	Parents teach children obedience
Use of power should be legitimate and is subject to criteria of good and evil	Power is a basic fact of a society antedating good or evil: its legitimacy is irrelevant.
Older people are neither respected nor feared	Older are respected and feared
Student-centered education	Teacher-centered education
Hierarchy means inequality of roles, established for convenience	Hierarchy means existential inequality
Subordinates expect to be consulted	Subordinates expect to be told what to do
Pluralist governments based on majority vote and change peacefully	Autocratic governments based on co-optation and change by revolution
Corruption rare; scandals end political careers	Corruption frequent, scandals are covered up
Income distribution in society rather even	Income distribution in society very uneven
Religions stressing equality of believers	Religions of hierarchy of priests

Source: (Hofstede, 2009)

Statistical data of summary shows content of each dimension opposing cultures with low and high scores. These oppositions are base on correlation with studies by others. The relationship is statistical and not every line applies equally strong to every country (Hofstede, 2009). Power index scores were higher in Eastern Europe, Latin America, Asia, and African countries and lower for Germanic and English-speaking Western countries (Hofstede, 2009).

Uncertainty Avoidance Index

According to Hofstede (2009) dimensions of national cultures, uncertainty avoidance is not the same as risk avoidance, it deals with a society's tolerance for ambiguity. Societies are occupied with issues of uncertainties. Hofstede uses a term unstructured to indicate he degree to which a culture programs its members to feel either uncomfortable or comfortable in situations, which are not defined or guided by the rule of law. Unstructured situations are novel, unknown, surprising, and different from usual (Hofstede, 2009). In comparing differences of cultures,

Table 3 lists some cultural dimensions that can be used to compare cultures. Hofstede describes the disapproval of deviant opinions and a belief in absolute Truth. Studies have shown that people in uncertainty avoiding countries are more emotional and motivated by inner nervous energy (Hofstede 2009). Uncertainty accepting cultures are more tolerant of opinions different from what they are used to, Hofsted asserts. They prefer fewer rules and on philosophical and religious level they tend to be close but not easily influenced and more contemplative.

Uncertainty avoidance scores are higher in East and Central European countries, in Latin American countries, in Japan, and in German speaking countries, lower in English speaking, Nordic and Chinese culture countries (Hofstede, 2009). In comparing differences of cultures, Table 3 lists difference between weak and strong uncertainty avoidance societies.

Individualism (IDV)

Hofstede's (2009) definition of individualism draws comparisons of the opposite; collectivism

Table 3. Ten differences between weak-and strong-uncertainty avoidance societies

Weak Uncertainty Avoidance	Strong Uncertainty Avoidance
The uncertainty inherent in life is accepted and each day is taken as it comes	The uncertainty inherent in life is felt as a continuous threat that must be fought
Ease, lower stress, self control, low anxiety	High stress, emotionality, anxiety, neuroticism
Higher scores on subjective health and well-being	Lower scores on subjective health and well-being
Tolerance of deviant persons and ideas: what is different is curious	Intolerance of deviant persons and ideas: what is different is dangerous
Comfortable with ambiguity and chaos	Need for clarity and structure
Teachers may say I don't know	Teachers supposed to have all the answers
Changing jobs no problem	Staying in jobs even disliked
Dislike of rules-written or unwritten	Emotional need for rules-even if not obeyed
In politics, citizens feel and are seen as competent towards authorities	In politics, citizens feel and are seen as incompetent towards authorities
In religion, philosophy and science: relativism and empiricism	In religion, philosophy and science: belief in ultimate truth and grand theories

Source: (Hofstede, 2009)

as a societal, not an individual characteristic, is the extent to which people in society are integrated into groups. Cultures that tend to be individualism focus more on themselves and their immediate families. On the other hand cultures that are base on collectivism in which people are integrated from birth tend to have strong, cohesive in-groups often termed extended families (uncles, aunts, and grandparents). This group of families enjoys continuous protection and loyalty from family members.

Individualism scores are higher in the western counties while collectivism is less in the emerging economies and Eastern countries; Japan takes a middle position on this dimension (Hofstede, 2009). Table 4 lists differences between collectivist and individualist societies.

Masculinity (MAS)

Hofstede (2009) defines masculinity versus its opposite; femininity as a national and not as an individual characteristics, refers to distribution of values between genders. According to Hofsteade (2009), IBM studies women's values differ less among societies than men's. The men's values

from one country to another contain a dimension from very assertive and competitive and maximally different from women's. While the study identifies women to be modest and caring, men tend to be the assertive with reflective characteristics; masculinity and femininity. The women in the feminine countries are perceived to have the same modest and caring values as the men, although they are perceived to be assertive and competitive, they fall below the men in the masculine countries which indicate a gap between women's and men's values (Hofstede, 2009). The perception of taboos in masculine cultures is raised in this study where the author explains its bases from a deeply rooted values around this dimension (Hofstede, et al., 1998). According to Hofstede (2009), this taboo shows that masculine and feminine dimensions in some societies touches basic and often unconscious values too sensitive to discuss. In comparing differences, Table 5 lists some cultural dimensions between feminine and masculine societies.

According to Hofstede's (2009) study, masculinity is high in Japan, German-speaking countries, and in some Latin countries like Mexico. It is moderately high in English speaking Western

Table 4. Ten differences between collectivist and individualist societies

Individualism	Collectivism
Everyone is suppose to take care of him or herself and his or her immediate family	People are born into extended families or clans which protect them to exchange for loyalty
I "consciousness"	We "consciousness"
Right of property	Stress on belonging
Speaking one's mind is healthy	Harmony should always be maintained
Others classified as individuals	Others classified as in-group or out-group
Personal opinion expected: one person one vote	Opinions and votes predetermine by in-group
Transgression of norms leads to guilt feelings	Transgression of norms leads to shame
Languages in which the word "I" is indispensable	Languages in which the word "I" is avoided
Purpose of education is learning how to learn	Purpose of education is learning how to do
Task prevails over leadership	Relationship prevails over task

Source: (Hofstede, 2009)

Table 5. Ten differences between feminine and masculine societies

Femininity	Masculinity
Minimum emotional and social role differentiation between genders	Maximum emotional and social role differentiation between genders
Men and women should be modest and caring	Men should be and women may be assertive and ambitious
Sympathy for the weak	Admiration for the strong
Both fathers and mothers deal with facts and feelings	Fathers deal with facts, mothers deal with feelings
Both boys and girls may cry but neither should fight	Girls cry, boys don't, boys should fight back, girls shouldn't fight
Mothers decide on number of children	Fathers decide on family size
Many women in elected political positions	Few women in elected in political positions
Religion focuses on fellow human beings	Religion focuses on God or gods
Matter-of-fact attitudes about sexuality; sex is a way of relating	Moralistic attitudes about sexuality; sex is a way of performing

Source: (Hofstede, 2009)

countries; it is low in Nordic countries and in The Netherlands and moderately low in some Latin and Asian countries like France, Spain, Portugal, Chile, Korea, and Thailand.

Long Term Orientation (LTO)

According to Hoftede's (2009) study, the fifth dimension concluded with students from 23 countries with questionnaire designed by Chinese scholars (Hofstede, 1988). The author describes values associated with long-term orientation are thrift and perseverance; values associated with short term are respect for tradition; fulfilling social obligations; and protecting one's face. The author makes reference to both positive and negatively related rated values of this dimension found in the teachings of Confucius around 500 B.C. The rationale of comparing the long-term orientation with the teachings of Confucianism is perceived to represents a focus on the future-oriented maxims of Confucianism, at the expense of the past-oriented ones. The study applies equally well to countries without a Confucian heritage. Table 6 lists differences between short an long term orientated societies.

Countries that reflect Long-term orientation are East Asian countries, particularly in China, Hong Kong, Taiwan, Japan, and South Korea. Countries with lesser extent of reflection are India, and Brazil. In most European countries, a medium term orientation is found; however, United States and Britain are found to be short-term orientation.

Statistical data of summary shows content of each dimension opposing cultures with low and high scores. These oppositions are base on correlation with studies by others. The relationship is statistical and not every line applies equally strong to every country (Hofstede, 2009). Power index scores were higher in Eastern Europe, Latin America, Asia, and African countries and lower for Germanic and English-speaking Western countries (Hofstede, 2009). Uncertainty avoidance scores are higher in East and Central European countries, in Latin American countries, in Japan, and in German speaking countries, lower in English speaking, Nordic, and Chinese culture countries (Hofstede, 2009). Individualism scores are higher in the western counties while collectivism is less in the emerging economies and Eastern countries; Japan takes a middle position on this dimension (Hofstede, 2009). According

Table 6. Ten differences between short and long term orientated societies

Short-Term Orientation	Long Term Orientation
Most important events in life occurred in the past or take place now	Most important events in life occur in the future
Immediate need of gratification is expected	Need gratification deferred until later
There are universal guidelines about what is good and what is evil	What is good and evil depends upon the circumstances
Traditions are sacrosanct	Traditions are adaptable to changed circumstances
Family life guided by imperatives	Family life guided by shared tasks
What one thinks and says should be true	What one does should be virtuous
Children should learn tolerance and respect	Children should learn to be thrifty
Social spending and consumption	Saving investing
Unstructured problem solving	Structure, mathematical problem solving
In business, stress on short term profits	In business, stress on future market position

Source: (Hofstede, 2009)

to Hofstede's (2009) study, masculinity is high in Japan, German-speaking countries, and in some Latin countries like Mexico. It is moderately high in English speaking Western countries; it is low in Nordic countries and in The Netherlands, and moderately low in France, Spain, Portugal, Chile, Korea, and Thailand.

Countries that reflect long-term orientation are East Asian countries, particularly in China, Hong Kong, Taiwan, Japan, and South Korea. Countries with lesser extent of reflection are India and Brazil. In most European countries, a medium term orientation is found; however, United States and Britain are found to be short-term orientation.

Workforce demographics resulting from globalization, combined with the rising popularity of team-based management techniques have resulted a practical need of multicultural workgroups (Hoerr, 1989). Because of globalization, organizations of workforce have become broader and much more diverse than ever before. This is evidently witnessed by most industrialized nations. Today multicultural workforce is seen as the reality of growing number of organizations impacting cultural diversity and work group effectiveness (Thomas, 1999). Business professionals and researchers have recognized the importance

of work group functioning for more than 40 years (Thomas, 1999). However, until recently extensive reviews of literature had consistently show little empirical research on culturally diverse groups (Goodman, Ravlin, & Argote, 1986; McGrath & Kravitz, 1982). Using Hofstsde national cultural dimensions can identify issues confronting many organizations. Effective use of the model can certainly impact team-based work groups performances.

ORGANIZATIONAL CONTEXT

The value of a team will depend on the organization's ability to empower each individual to utilize their unique individual talents to improve the group performance and contribute to the organization's success. However, environmental factors such as organizational culture is important to consider.

Individuals from diverse backgrounds bring a plethora of knowledge that include perspectives about how to design processes, innovate solutions, reach goals, communicate effectively and lead teams (Thomas & Ely, 1996). However, various organizations perceive diversity from different lenses. Some view diversity from a discrimination and fairness perspective. Instead of accepting and embracing the differences between people in the workplace, they ignore all of those differences in the name of fairness. The underlying logic is to consider fairness and to comply with federal mandates, and work toward restructuring the makeup the organization to let it more closely reflect that of society. Although demographic diversity in the workplace has increased and promoted fair treatment, everyone is the same and assimilates. Therefore, minimizing the opportunity to optimize the unique qualities each person has to offer (Thomas & Ely, 1996). The employees may be diversified, but not the work.

Companies that follow this idea implement a color blind or gender blind idea to promote fair treatment, but lose the prospect to explore how people's differences generate potential innovation to generate effective business practices. Success is often measured by recruitment and retention of underrepresented groups (Thomas & Ely, 1996).

Other organizations view diversity as a means to get access to markets that otherwise might be a challenge to conquer (Thomas & Ely, 1996). The legitimacy portion refers to the trust that is intrinsic when dealing with people that look similar to you. The underlying motivation of the access-and-legitimacy perspective is the recognition of an increasingly multicultural country, and new ethnic groups are quickly gaining consumer power. Therefore, to stay competitive companies needs a demographically more diverse workforce to gain access to these differentiated segments. Diversity is not just fair; it makes business sense (1996, p. 5). Although this perspective has increased competitive advantage in culturally dominant communities, employees are often pigeonholed in certain markets where they may feel exploited and closed to other opportunities in the organization. Cultural differences are emphasized within certain conditions but the skills, beliefs and practices that are unique are not identified or integrated to create a learning opportunities into the larger organization (Thomas & Ely, 1996).

The most optimal organizational perspective of diversity incorporates aspects of the fairness and business where employee's perspectives are integrated into rethinking primary tasks and redefining business practices (Thomas & Ely, 1996). This context of diversity creates an environment where people's differences and perspective can be valued and allowed to influence positively their experience and contribution to the work of the organization. Because work environments are dynamic and constantly changing, the ability to adapt relies on the ability to leverage diversity.

Organizations that have taken full advantage of the cultural differences of diverse employees are more productive and efficient. This may lead to new and transformational ways of doing business and placing these companies on the cutting edge of their industry. The process requires a high level of commitment from the whole organization (Thomas & Ely, 1996). The desire to create an organizational culture where everyone could work in requires cultural competence and an environment that advocates for "inclusion" (Anand & Winters, 2008, p. 362).

SUMMARY

Workforce demographic changes occurring in corporate America have a profound impact on the way organizations think, feel, and see the world, as well as how they hire and govern their organizations and businesses. Collaboration within and among organizations has become increasingly important in this competitive market. Managers encourage employees to collaborate to create an environment of innovation and to improve quality and knowledge sharing. However, many companies are still unable to successfully manage team-based work group, particularly diverse teams.

Collaboration among diverse employees can facilitate the learning process as well as develop skills to work in team based learning groups. Effective working structures across departmental functional lines are difficult to introduce in multicultural organizations. Management must provide the companies with an effective team model and a rationale for teamwork and providing skill-building opportunities.

REFERENCES

Adler, S. (2000). Project management competence: Building key skills for individuals, teams, and organizations. *Personnel Psychology, 53*(3), 778–780.

Banutu-Gomez, M., & Rohrer, W. G. (2011). Teams in organization. *The Cambridge Business Review, 18*(1), 54–60.

Carnoy, M., & Rhoten, D. (2002). What does globalization mean for educational change? A comparative approach. *Comparative Education Review, 46*(1), 1–9. doi:10.1086/324053

Chaudhuri, S., & Ravallion, M. (2007). Partially awakened giants uncover growth in China and India. In Winters, L. A., & Yusuf, S. (Eds.), *Dancing with Giants: China, India, and the Global Economy*. Washington, DC: World Bank.

Cummings, T. G., & Worley, C. G. (2001). *Organization development and change* (7th ed.). Cincinnati, OH: South-Western.

Dansky, K. H., Weech-Maldonado, R., De Souza, G., & Dreachslin, J. L. (2003). Organizational strategy and diversity management: Diversity-sensitive orientation as a moderating influence. *Health Care Management Review, 28*(3), 243–253.

Dass, P., & Parker, B. (1999). Strategies for managing human resource diversity: From resistance to learning. *The Academy of Management Executive, 13*(2), 68–80. doi:10.5465/AME.1999.1899550

Dirani, K. (2006). Exploring socio-cultural factors that influence HRD practices in Lebanon. *Human Resource Development International, 9*(1), 85–98. doi:10.1080/13678860500523270

Dreachslin, J. L. (1996). *Diversity leadership*. Chicago, IL: Health Administration Press.

Dreachslin, J. L. (2007). Diversity management and cultural competence: Research, practice, and the business case. *Journal of Healthcare Management, 52*(2), 79–86.

Dyer, W. G. (1987). *Team building: Issues and alternatives* (2nd ed.). Reading, MA: Addison-Wesley.

Egan, M., & Bendick, M. (2007). *Teaching cultural competence: What multicultural management courses can learn from diversity*. Retrieved October 19, 2008, from http://www.bendickegan.com/pdf/10012007/EganBendickMulticultural 2007.pdf.

Egan, M., & Bendick, M. (2008). Combining multicultural management and diversity into one course on cultural competence. *Academy of Management Learning & Education, 7*(3), 387–393. doi:10.5465/AMLE.2008.34251675

Gibson, C. B., Zellmer-Bruhn, M., & Schwab, D. P. (2003). Team effectiveness in multinational organizations: Evaluation across contexts. *Group & Organization Management, 28*(4), 444–474. doi:10.1177/1059601103251685

Gill, R. H., & Creighton-Zollar, A. (1998). Diverse self-directed work teams: Developing strategic initiatives for 21st century organizations. *Public Personnel Management, 27*(2), 187–200.

Golembiewski, R. T. (1979). *Approaches to planned change: Part 2*. New York, NY: Marcel Dekker.

Goodman, P. S. Ravlin, E. C., & Argote, L.(1986). Current thinking about groups: Setting the stage for new ideas. In P. S. Goodman (Ed.), *Designing Effective Work Groups*. San Francisco, CA: Jossey-Bass.

Gray, K., & Paryono, P. (2004). A conceptual model of workforce education and development systems. In Rojewski, J. W. (Ed.), *International Perspectives on Workforce Education and Development* (pp. 17–42). Greenwich, CT: Information Age.

Gregory-Mina, H. (2010). The importance of teams and how to lead teams through change initiatives in 21st century organizations. *The Business Review, Cambridge, 16*(1), 60–66.

Hatch, E. K. (1995). Cross cultural team building and training. *Journal for Quality and Participation, 18*(2), 44–48.

Hoerr, J. (1989, July 10). The payoff from teamwork. *Business Week*, 55-62.

Ilgen, D. R., Hollenbeck, J. R., Johnson, M., & Jundt, D. (2005). Teams in organizations: From input-process-output models to IMOI models. *Annual Review of Psychology, 56*, 517–543. doi:10.1146/annurev.psych.56.091103.070250

Jain, S. C., & Tucker, L. R. (1995). The influence of culture on strategic constructs in the process of globalization: An empirical study of North American and Japanese MNCs. *International Business Review, 4*(1), 19–37. doi:10.1016/0969-5931(94)00029-L

Judy, R. W., & D'Amico, C. (1997). *Workforce 2020: Work and workers in the 21st century*. Indianapolis, IN: Hudson Institute.

Leibold, M., & Voelpel, S. C. (2009). *Managing the aging workforce: Challenges and solutions*. Hoboken, NJ: Wiley.

Leinonen, P., & Bluemink, J. (2008). The distributed team members' explanations of knowledge they assume to be shared. *Journal of Workplace Learning, 20*(1), 38–53. doi:10.1108/13665620810843638

Liang, P. J., Rajan, M. V., & Ray, K. (2008). Optimal team size and monitoring in organizations. *Accounting Review, 83*(3), 789–822. doi:10.2308/accr.2008.83.3.789

Loden, M. (1996). *Implementing diversity*. Chicago, IL: Irwin Professional Publishing.

Loden, M., & Rosener, J. B. (1991). *Workforce America! Managing employee diversity as a vital resource*. Homewood, IL: Business One Irwin.

McLean, G. (2001). Human resource development as a factor in the inevitable move to globalization. In *Proceedings of the Academy of Human Resource Development 2001 Conference*, (pp. 731-738). Tulsa, OK: Academy of Human Resource Development.

Montebello, A. R. (1995). Inside teams: How 20 world-class organizations are winning through teamwork. *Personnel Psychology, 48*(3), 686.

Montebello, A. R. (2003). Beyond teams: Building the collaborative organization. *Personnel Psychology, 56*(4), 1070–1073.

Oertig, M., & Buergi, T. (2006). The challenges of managing cross-cultural virtual project teams. *Team Performance Management, 12*(1), 23–30. doi:10.1108/13527590610652774

Santos-Paulino, A. U., & Wan, G. (2010). Introduction: Southern engines of global growth. In Santos-Paulino, A. U., & Wan, G. (Eds.), *Southern Engines of Global Growth* (pp. 1–7). New York, NY: Oxford University Press. doi:10.1093/acprof:oso/9780199580606.003.0001

Chapter 21
Leveraging Workforce Diversity through Volunteerism

Ashwini Joshua-Gojer
University of North Texas, USA

Jeff M. Allen
University of North Texas, USA

ABSTRACT

This chapter discusses the subject of workforce diversity as it directly relates to volunteerism, using the Peace Corps as an example. The aim of the chapter is to illustrate how nonprofit institutions can draw upon the value of workforce diversity in order to obtain competitive advantages. The Peace Corps' three-fold mission includes helping the people of interested countries in meeting their need for trained men and women, helping promote a better understanding of Americans on the part of the people served, and helping promote a better understanding of other peoples on the part of Americans (Peace Corps, 2011a). This chapter specifically discusses how the Peace Corps incorporate diversity in their volunteer program. "The agency has always reflected the diversity of America and is actively recruiting the next generation of Peace Corps Volunteers" (Peace Corps, 2011b).

INTRODUCTION

The concept of workforce diversity is no longer an alien concept. According to the National Center for Public Policy and Higher Education (2005) the United States (U.S.) workforce is becoming more diverse. A globalized workforce has given rise to the understanding that diversity is all encompassing and has proved to be beneficial (Kossek, Lobel, & Brown, 2006). There are many arguments that

support diversity, suggesting that society is better when we work together. Workplace diversity is increasingly viewed as an essential success factor to be competitive in today's marketplace. In an opinion poll, 81% of respondents said that it is somewhat or very important "to have employees of different races, cultures and backgrounds in the workplace or businesses" (Barrington & Troske, 2001). Diversity is touted as being 'good business' by corporate leaders (Crockett, 2003). Even though research supports the value that workforce diversity adds to organizations, nonprofits seems

DOI: 10.4018/978-1-4666-1812-1.ch021

to lack diversity (Tempel & Smith, 2007; Allison, 2001). In the nonprofit sector, many organizations are involved in working and serving traditionally under-represented and marginalized groups. In these circumstances, the need for responsive and diverse workers takes on greater significance. Diversity not only assumes that all individuals are unique, but that difference is indeed value-added (Rodriguez, 1997).

DEFINING WORKFORCE DIVERSITY

One of the major stumbling blocks in discussions surrounding diversity is its very definition. There are different diversity definitions available in management literature (Weisinger, 2005). According to a survey by the Society for Human Resource Management (SHRM), only 30 percent of human resources professionals say that their company even has an official definition of diversity (SHRM, 2008). A study done by the U.S. Department of Commerce and Vice President Al Gore's National Partnership for Reinventing Government (NPR) Diversity Task Force determined that diversity needed to be defined broadly and that it should encompass a wide range of initiatives that meet the changing needs of customers and workers (US Department of Commerce, 1999). In the context of nonprofits that includes the individuals served by the nonprofit as well as the volunteers and employees who work there. The study suggested that leaders and employees should take active roles in implementing diversity processes and in order for them to succeed they needed to be fully aligned with core organizational goals and objectives. The findings in the report illustrated that the benefits of diversity are for everyone. It also emphasized that diversity, more than a moral imperative, is a global necessity. For the purpose of this chapter, we use the following definition of diversity: Diversity includes all characteristics and experiences that define each of us as individuals (US Department of Commerce, 1999).

THE HISTORY OF WORKFORCE DIVERSITY IN THE USA

Prior to World War I and up until the late 1970s, the human resources field found its roots in scientific management practices, bureaucratization, employment protective legislation, and unionization (Langbert & Friedman, 2002). Frederick W. Taylor (1911), who is regarded as the father of scientific management, promoted the practice of setting performance standards based on individual piece-rate incentives and cooperation of employees and employer through the economically motivated mutuality of interest. Additionally, Taylor emphasized the need to match employee abilities with the specific demands of the jobs through his 'first-class' man standard which required for his system's success (Wren & Bedeian, 2009).

In the 1960s and 1970s, the U.S. took its first steps toward promoting diversity in the workplace. During this period, several important pieces of federal legislation were passed in the U.S. in order to promote equity among workers. In 1961, President John F. Kennedy established the President's Committee on Equal Employment Opportunity. The goal of this committee was to end discrimination in employment by the government and its contractors. Workplaces were faced with a new business mandate of complying with the increasing legislations and regulations that required organizations to focus on achieving demographic variation in order to comply with federal Equal Employment Opportunity requirements. The first of its kind in the early 1960s, the Civil Rights Act of 1964 prohibited discrimination in any federal program or activity. In 1965, President Johnson went one step further, with Executive Order 11246 to promote equal employment opportunity through a positive, continuing program in each department and agency (US Department of Labor, 1965). The Order prohibits federal contractors and federally assisted construction contractors and subcontractors that do more than $10,000 in government business in one year from discriminating in employment decisions on the basis of race, color, religion, sex or national origin. Contractors are also required to 'take affirmative action to ensure that applicants are employed, and that employees are treated during employment, without regard to their race, color, religion, sex, or national origin' (US Department of Labor, 2002). This was a critical juncture, because it went beyond prohibiting the consideration of race, creed, color, or national origin to acting on the principle that fairness required more than a commitment to impartial treatment.

Title VII of the Civil Rights Act of 1964 was a landmark legislation that made it illegal for employers with more than 15 employees to discriminate in hiring, termination, promotion, compensation, job training, or any other term, condition, or privilege of employment based on race, color, religion, sex, or national origin. Since then, Title VII has been supplemented with legislation prohibiting pregnancy, age, and disability discrimination. Sexual harassment is also prohibited by Title VII. The Equal Employment Opportunity Commission (EEOC) is charged with enforcing Title VII. Affirmative action programs require employers to set goals to increase the utilization of underrepresented groups to achieve equality based on their labor force availability. The Department of Labor's Office of Federal Contract Compliance Programs (OFCCP) is charged with enforcement of the Executive Order. Because the legislation focused on 'protected class' employees (i.e., discrimination was illegal based on race, ethnicity, sex, or religion, initially; protection for other groups, such as people with disabilities followed later), individuals who did not belong to the 'protected class' often resented their exclusion and believed that affirmative action led to the hiring of unqualified candidates and to preferential treatment for the targeted groups. As an outcome of these early efforts and the resulting effects experienced by those who felt excluded, today the term "diversity," which was introduced in the late 1970s, is sometimes used interchangeably with

affirmative action and EEO and still carries some negative connotations (SHRM, 2008).

In 1967 the Age Discrimination in Employment Act (ADEA) was passed. It protects individuals who are 40 years of age or older from employment discrimination based on age (EEOC, 2008). While it seemed that the American industry was booming, the American executive was aging due to complications from the Great Depression and previous wars. Specifically, many highly talented workers were removed from the working ranks due to these proceedings. During this same period in the U.S., the percentage of total employment in the goods-producing sector began to decline while shares of employment in the services sector experienced steady growth (Bhide´, 2008; Urquhart, 1984). A historical analysis of the employment shift to services revealed that this growth was not due to an exodus of workers as assumed earlier, but was ascribed to an expansion of the workforce through the addition of people from backgrounds other than white and English speaking (Urquhart, 1984).

During the 1960s, the U.S. experienced an exceptional boom that was occasionally interrupted by a short-term recession. As the early generation of Baby Boomers began to reach adulthood, their aspirations and values were markedly different from their parents' generation (Oyler & Pryor, 2009). Many Baby Boomers valued education, and the number of granted undergraduate and graduate degrees doubled from 1957 to 1967 (Gitlin, 1987). Moreover, the Baby Boomer generation experienced many new directions in civil rights with the United States Supreme Court Decision in a court case in 1954 to end racial segregation in schools, the racial integration crisis at Little Rock Central High School in Arkansas in the Fall of 1957, the United States Civil Rights Act of 1964 that banned segregation in public places and discrimination in employment, and the rise of Dr Martin Luther King, Jr., who was a civil rights activist (Oyler & Pryor, 2009).

The technological revolution and the increase in the number of increases in the service industry required American companies and labor unions to re-think and modify traditional business practices that were already in place. Simultaneously, these changes brought about changes in the workplace that were rare earlier, ranging from different generations working together, dual-income households, and individuals from different ethnicities working together. All these changes played a role in the impact they had on the effective functioning of the organization. Organizations had to take these workforce changes into consideration when they re-engineered their HR practices. Some of these organizational changes included developing recruiting and selection practices that targeted minorities and formulating organizational benefits that were tailored to diverse populations (Drucker, 1960).

Before World War I and up until the late 1970s, in the period referred to as the Bureaucratic period, Peter Drucker, along with other organizational researchers, discovered that industrialization and corresponding advances in technology required a new managerial mindset. The workforce had expanded to include not just unskilled labor, but also knowledge workers. Human resources progressed from being seen as an overhead expenditure to a valuable and strategic asset of the organization. Furthermore, the drastic changes in demographics, including age, gender, and ethnic/racial diversity pushed forth the perspective that all employees should have access to equal opportunities. Oyler and Pryor (2009) maintain that Drucker's early prescriptive advice remains intriguing because he touted specific HR practices for employees from diverse backgrounds. In terms of research, there was a dearth of ethnic/racial and gender diversity research until the passage of Title VII of the Civil Rights Act in 1964 in the U.S. However, the passage of the federal Civil Rights Act led to significant changes in the composition of the workforce and provided the foundation for future management research in gender and ethnic issues (Cox & Nkomo, 1990).

In the late 1970s, the Supreme Court in Regents of the University of California v. Bakke held in a closely divided decision that race could be one of the factors considered in choosing a diverse student body in university admissions decisions (Anderson, 2005; SHRM, 2008). The Court also ruled that the use of quotas in affirmative action programs was not permissible; thus the University of California, by maintaining a 16% minority quota, discriminated against Allan Bakke. This was a landmark judgment in terms of affirmative action. Firstly, it led to a visible association of diversity with affirmative action and secondly, to viewing diversity as equivalent with efforts to have a numerically representative workforce with respect to race, gender, ethnicity, and other demographic dimensions. These perceptions resulted in the Civil Rights milestones being seen as the origin of diversity and efforts to achieve representation being referred to as managing diversity (SHRM, 2008).

Peter Drucker's emphasis on valuing diversity in organizations is related to the living values challenge (Oyler & Pryor, 2009). Living values look at the extent to which the organization values economic, ethical, legal, and strategic dimensions (Wright & Snell, 2005). Oyler and Pryor (2009) mention that even though this challenge has not been typically discussed under the rubric of HRM and usually falls under social issues management, it is a viable component of the HR profession. In two of his later books, Managing in Turbulent Times and Managing in the Next Society, he extensively explored major demographic themes and predicted that the relatively homogenous American workforce would evolve to include more women, ethnic minorities, and older workers (Drucker, 1980, 2002). What was unique about Drucker's conjecture was not his arguments about the consequences of population structure and growth, but his ideas about their potential impact. Drucker encouraged businesses to take advantage of the opportunities of future demographic patterns. He addressed the importance of understanding and valuing age, ethnic/racial, and gender diversity (Drucker, 1980, 2002).

Drucker emphasized three changes and their ultimate impacts. Firstly, he stated that increased life expectancies coupled with low birth rates in the U.S. would continue to increase the proportion of older people in the workplace (Drucker, 1980, 2002). He maintained that "because the supply of young people will shrink, creating new employment patterns, to attract and hold the growing number of older people (especially older educated people) will become increasingly important" (Drucker, 2002, p. 237). Secondly, he illustrated that the American population structure is constantly changing to include more ethnic diversity (Drucker, 1980, 2002). "There is no way to prevent mass migration from Mexico over an open 2,000-mile border into the United States . . . . Whether they are officially 'legal,' 'illegal,' or 'quasi-legal' is immaterial. Socially and culturally, a mass migration of Mexicans to the United States will exacerbate racial and ethnic tensions . . . . Economically, the mass migration from Mexico . . . should be beneficial and should in fact endow American manufacturing with competitive strength such as it has not known for some time." (Drucker, 1980, p. 92-93). Thirdly, he espoused that the U.S. working population is regularly evolving to include more women (Drucker, 1980). Drucker wrote: "The labor force has become heterogeneous; and its fragmentation will continue. Such splintering will continue in respect to age and sex distribution . . . . Perhaps the majority of both older and younger women will expect different benefits. What appears as a 'benefit' or as an 'opportunity' to the traditional male employee often has little appeal to the working woman" (Drucker, 1980, p. 81). Thus, Peter Drucker showed a lot of foresight in his predic-

tions of the future of the U.S. workforce and the impact it would have. However, he was not the only one predicting the change that was to come.

In 1987, the Hudson Institute released the landmark study Workforce 2000, which predicted that rapid technological change, globalization, the demand for skills and education, an aging workforce and greater ethnic diversification in the labor market would forever change the employment landscape (SHRM, 2008). This new data introduced a model that focused more on how to assimilate large numbers of women and minorities into existing, homogenous corporate cultures rather than how to comply with legal mandates. The assimilation approach sought to increase conformity to the dominant (homogeneous) culture's ways of thinking and behaving. Minority employees resented and even challenged the notion that they were not recognized nor appreciated for their individual differences (SHRM, 2008). The slogan 'We are a melting pot' that emerged in the early 1980s was touted to reject individual differences rather than appreciating them.

The approach to strategically conform minorities into the majority's mold was backfiring. The corporate world had already begun to experience difficulty in achieving its affirmative action goals. While recruiting underrepresented groups posed a significant challenge, retaining women and minorities was an even greater problem (SHRM, 2008). Turnover data was revealing that as many underrepresented groups as were being recruited were also exiting. This was dubbed the 'revolving door syndrome' (SHRM, 2008). Steps had to be taken to understand the reasons behind the high attrition rate. This led to more research being done on the problem and ways in which to correct the situation. While legal procedures had set the ball rolling with regards to workforce diversity, actual behaviors at work were what needed to be changed.

The Civil Rights Act of 1964 and other legal proceedings did not change attitudes, behaviors and subtle discrimination. While organizational human resource efforts improved, the behavior of individual employees within organizations often did not. In addition, employers found that only hiring a diverse workforce did not bring some of the expected benefits. Evidence suggested that management would have to take a more sustained and committed approach in order to realize the benefits of diversity. This remedial approach gave way, during the 1980s, with the recognition that diversity should not only be legislated or mandated, but also valued as a business attribute. Diversity training came be to be implemented in many organizations. Training at the time focused on employee attitudes, as businesses and government agencies tried to raise awareness of and increase employee sensitivity to diversity issues.

The concept of workplace diversity continues to evolve. In the present century, the workforce has evolved rapidly to reflect multiple dimensions of diversity that include age, ethnicity, gender, disability, national origin, and sexual orientation (Thomas, 2005; Bell, 2007; Carr-Ruffino, 2007; Harvey & Allard, 2008; Shore, et al., 2009). While a significant number of organizations continue to focus their diversity efforts on compliance and representation, an increasing number of leading organizations are focusing on the business case for diversity and on building inclusive cultures in the workplace (SHRM, 2008). Human resources together with a diversity orientation that brings about the appropriate individual and organizational outcomes have the potential to create a sustained competitive advantage for the organization. As global demographics change, understanding and valuing diversity has become a reality for modifying workplace policies and procedures (Bell, 2007; Carr-Ruffino, 2007; Harvey & Allard, 2008). The case for workplace diversity as a business necessity is gaining recognition by organizational leaders. At a symposium sponsored by The Conference Board regarding diversity in the workplace, for example, 400 executives agreed that "diversity programs help to ensure the creation, management, valuing and leveraging of a diverse workforce that will lead to organizational effectiveness and

sustained competitiveness" (SHRM, 2008, p. 9). Diversity management in the United States is misconstrued many times to mean a lot of different things. A few years ago, only some companies recognized diversity as a priority, and even among those pioneers in the field, it had little impact beyond increasing representation among women and minorities (SHRM, 2008). It is important to remember that diversity is more than just another word for affirmative action, or quotas, or a win-lose proposition, a means of blaming or changing work ethic. Managing diversity is considered a necessity by forward-thinking companies that want to empower employees, expand market share, and sustain the enterprise.

The future of workforce diversity lies not just in 'managing' diversity, but also in understanding the complexity and multidimensionality of the issue (Tatli, 2006). It requires both organizations and employees to be proactive; building on and sustaining the momentum of best practices and proven theory. Not all organizations approach the issue of diversity in the same manner, as we discussed earlier. Research has shown that private, public, and non-profit organizations face similar challenges when faced with the issue of diversity (Gajewski, 2005; Grunin, 2011). There needs to be a system in place to support best practices so that private, public, and nonprofit organizations can reap the benefits of having a diverse workforce.

WORKFORCE DIVERSITY IN NONPROFITS

While major American nonprofit organizations have greatly assisted minority communities in the U.S., and have increased their racial and ethnic composition, their boards, executives, staff and roughly 90 percent of foundation leadership remain largely white (O'Neill, 2002; Tempel & Smith, 2007). One study found that only 14.3% of nonprofit managers were minorities, and of the managers with some graduate education, 12.5%

were people of color (Rogers & Smith, 1994). Weisinger (2005) states that although race and ethnicity are not the only dimensions of representational diversity, "[i]n diverse societies, race, and race-like ethnicity create the most stark divides" (McPherson, Smith-Lovin, & Cook, 2001, p. 429).

There exists a wealth of research and resources related to cultural diversity in philanthropy (Kasper, Ramos, & Walker, 2004; Weisinger, 2005). The development of diversity literature in nonprofit organizations is fairly recent. Much of the research has focused on board composition and governance issues (Weisinger, 2005). Very few studies have focused on diversity among staff and volunteers, nor on issues of diversity that move beyond representational demographics and composition. Because the systematic study of diversity in the nonprofit domain is at a nascent stage (Weisinger & Salipante, 2005), it is useful to analyze how diversity is dealt with in one nonprofit, viz., the Peace Corps.

HISTORY OF THE PEACE CORPS

The Peace Corps are celebrating their 50th anniversary in 2011. The agency commemorates 50 years of promoting peace and friendship around the world. To understand diversity in the Peace Corps, it is important to know a little bit about the history of the Peace Corps. Peace Corps is an independent U.S. government agency that provides volunteers for countries requesting assistance around the world. The Peace Corps traces its roots and mission to 1960, when then-Sen. John F. Kennedy challenged 10,000 students at the University of Michigan in Ann Arbor to serve their country in the cause of peace by living and working in developing countries (Peace Corps, 2011c). That inspirational challenge gave birth to a federal government agency devoted to world peace and friendship. It was a bold new experiment in public service. The reaction to the call was both swift and enthusiastic, and since 1961,

more than 45 years, more than 200,000 Americans have responded to this enduring challenge. Ever since that early morning day on 14th October, 1960, the Peace Corps has demonstrated how the power of an idea can capture the imagination of an entire nation.

Throughout its history, the Peace Corps has adapted and responded to the issues of the times. At present the Peace Corps has approximately 8,655 volunteers in 71 posts serving in 77 countries (Peace Corps, 2011d). In an ever-changing world, Peace Corps Volunteers are involved in a variety of services ranging from fighting HIV/AIDS in Africa and the Caribbean to providing technical training and support to groups and organizations that want to make better use of information and communications technology. The kinds of service Peace Corps volunteers provide are very varied. The volunteers work with local governments, communities, schools and entrepreneurs to address changing and complex needs in education, health, HIV/AIDS, business and Information Communication Technology (ICT), environment, agriculture, and youth development (Peace Corps, 2011e). Peace Corps volunteers are constantly meeting new challenges with innovation, creativity, determination, and compassion (Peace Corps, 2011d). Peace Corps Volunteers have helped people build better lives for themselves. Their work in villages, towns, and cities around the globe represents a legacy of service that has become a significant part of America's history and positive image abroad.

DIVERSITY IN THE PEACE CORPS

The Peace Corps' statement on diversity is "An organization that represents America should be representative of America" (MPCA, 2011a). The Peace Corps Fact sheet states that the agency reflects the diversity of America with volunteers ranging in age from 18 to 86 (seven percent of the volunteers are over 50 years of age), and representing all 50 states of America. The demographic differences do not end there—60 percent of the volunteers are women, 93 percent are single, 19 percent are minorities, and 90 percent have at least an undergraduate degree (Peace Corps, 2011e).

A casual glance through the Peace Corps website will strengthen one's belief that the organization is truly diverse. Under the recruiting tab, there is an announcement listed about an information session with a diversity panel in Chicago. The text reads, "Come and participate in an active discussion with a group of diverse Returned Peace Corps Volunteers at Hosteling International. Hear their stories and learn why they chose Peace Corps, what kind of work they accomplished and the relationships they formed through this life changing experience" (Peace Corps, 2011f). Another article under the 'Press and Multimedia' tab, lists a diversity write up published in Texas in 2005. The article itself references Gaddi H. Vasquez, the first Hispanic Director of the Peace Corps (Peace Corps, 2011g). The Peace Corps' attempt at touting the diversity within the Corps is also reflected in their stories from the field listed on the website. The stories documented are varied, ranging from those of married couples serving together, to older Americans, to Empty Nesters as well as Asian and Pacific Islander Americans (Peace Corps, 2011h). The tab on 'Who volunteers' contains photographs and stories of volunteers past and present who reflect the diversity of America (Peace Corps, 2011b). Last, but not least, the Peace Corps is making an effort to propose a wider view of diversity by sharing on their website the stories of their volunteers with disabilities (Peace Corps, 2011i). Besides the Peace Corps itself encouraging diversity, Returned Peace Corps Volunteers (RPCVs) have formed nonprofit groups to help encourage diversity, share stories from the field, and recruit future Peace Corps volunteers.

In 1993, the Peace Corps Gay, Lesbian, or Bisexual Employees (GLOBE) group was formed at Peace Corps headquarters (Peace Corps GLOBE, 2009). It is part of a network of GLOBE chapters in many different government agencies under the umbrella of Federal GLOBE: Gay, Lesbian, or Bisexual Employees of the Federal government. The purpose of Peace Corps GLOBE has been to work toward improving the volunteer and employee work environment by fostering a better understanding on the part of the general Peace Corps community about issues of importance to Gay, Lesbian, Bisexual, Transgender (G/L/B/T) employees and volunteers. The Peace Corps GLOBE website lists the following goals of the group:

- Work to improve Agency operations, personnel management practices, employee effectiveness, and service to the Volunteers by facilitating the exchange of information about G/L/B/T diversity issues.
- Encourage the celebration of diversity through inclusive, appreciative programming, projects, and purpose.
- Work toward establishment and maintenance of equal civil rights for G/L/B/T employees within the federal workforce.

In order to achieve these goals, Peace Corps GLOBE has sought to raise awareness of Peace Corps' nondiscrimination policy that is inclusive of sexual orientation diversity issues through resource development and distribution, forums, public speakers, and other educational activities (Peace Corps GLOBE, 2009). The Peace Corps, due to the cross-cultural nature of its goals, has gained a reputation as an agency that celebrates diversity. However, Peace Corps GLOBE claims that deficiencies currently exist, especially in relation to G/L/B/T issues. Peace Corps GLOBE intends to work closely with Peace Corps staff to ensure that these issues are appropriately addressed. They intend to work with the Office of Communications to insure that G/L/B/T inclusive language is incorporated into all forms of outreach and communication with the public, including documents such as the Peace Corps catalog and application form, as well as on the Peace Corps web site. They also intend to reach potential G/L/B/T Peace Corps Volunteers during the application process, so that they can make an informed decision when considering volunteer service with the Peace Corps.

Another group formed by RPCVs is the Minority Peace Corps Association (MPCA). The MPCA was birthed when RPCVs of color met informally to discuss their Peace Corps experiences. What sprang from discussions about the life-changing Peace Corps experience is now a national nonprofit organization (MPCA, 2004). The MPCA aims to (MPCA, 2011b):

- Promote community service,
- Provide support and assistance to returned and serving Peace Corps volunteers and applicants of color,
- Enhance the awareness and participation of Americans of color in international experience, international careers, and international affairs.

Through partnership, special events and outreach activities MPCA strives to strengthen Americans' understanding about the world and its peoples.

As we have seen, the Peace Corps exemplifies diversity both in the field and in their leadership. Other nonprofits can take inspiration from the example that the agency has laid, especially since it is one of the world's most successful and respected development organizations (Peace Corps, 2011j).

WORKFORCE DIVERSITY AND HRD IN NONPROFITS

The changing economic and organizational environments are pressuring organizations to address issues of diversity in new ways. The past few decades have seen a shift that nonprofits have needed to address and adapt to in order to merely survive. The following section highlights trends that point to diversity as a strategic HR resource for nonprofit organizations and long-term diversity plans organizations can undertake.

The Case for Diversity

The nonprofit sector, like the rest of the nation, has been affected by the first great economic crisis of the new century (Nonprofit Finance Fund, 2011). The national and global trends have already changed and continue to change the environment for nonprofits. A study by Guidestar (2010), an agency analyzing nonprofit financial trends, reveals that there is an increased demand for services in the face of limited supply of services. It is important for nonprofits in this environment to be attuned to rapid and continual shifts in the environment; continually evaluating and interpreting how organizations can best adapt; and experimenting with new responses and approaches (Gowdy, Hildebrand, La Piana, & Mendes Campos, 2009). Even before the recession, Halpern (2006) had suggested that working across generations is but one of the challenges presented by changing demographics. Research indicates that the workforce is one of the nonprofit sector's most valuable resources. Light (2002) found nonprofit employees to be highly motivated, hard working, and deeply committed, but he also discovered that nonprofit employees experience high levels of stress and burn out, and report that their organizations do not provide enough training and staff to succeed. In cases such as these, where the workforce is comprised mainly of volunteers, it becomes imperative that these issues are addressed. Younger generations comprise an increasing percentage of the workforce, and they bring with them new values and expectations around work, activism and the use of technology. This dynamic may challenge the ability of nonprofit organizations to attract and provide a place for this new generation to find meaningful participation (Gowdy, Hildebrand, La Piana, & Mendes Campos, 2009).

Census figures show that by 2042, the United States will be a minority-majority society, and ongoing and shifting immigration patterns are changing the face of countless communities around the country, with profound implications for nonprofits (Frey, 2011). Additionally, the millennial generation, or Generation Y (comprising those born between 1981 and 1999) is proving more diverse than any preceding generation, with many more young people of color, first- and second-generation immigrants and mixed-race individuals. This diversity highlights how the intersection of generational and other demographic shifts will continue to impact the nonprofit workforce (Gowdy, Hildebrand, La Piana, & Mendes Campos, 2009). To succeed, nonprofits must rethink how they serve as well as how they manage. The business case for diversity in nonprofits is important.

Research on organizations working toward inclusiveness reveals several important factors regarding the process. The single and most important factor affecting the success and endurance of diversity initiatives is leadership (Sidberry, 2002). The commitment towards diversity initiatives must be long-term and should integrate inclusiveness holistically into the organization. A comprehensive approach aimed at changing organizational culture and practices should examine external elements, such as how an organization relates to underserved populations, and internal elements, including the recruitment, retention, and treatment of diverse members. While most nonprofits that involve volunteers excel at the external elements, it is the internal elements that need a boost. Halpern (2006) also insists that special attention must be given to recruitment and retention of diverse staff. Those organizations that are most inclusive tend to have very high leadership commitment to hiring diverse staff and reach out to diverse individuals in the hiring process. This is noticed in

the Peace Corps recruitment effort, as they reach out to a diverse population to recruit volunteers. The most critical retention factor is making sure that volunteers know that the leadership is committed to inclusiveness. Research indicates that barriers to creating an inclusive workplace include insufficient time or financial resources, conflicting priorities, failed integration with organizational mission, and a flawed understanding of oppression and diversity (Halpern, 2006).

BUILDING DIVERSITY IN YOUR ORGANIZATION

A national study produced in partnership by Commongood Careers and Level Playing Field Institute (Schwartz, Weinberg, Hagenbuch, & Scott, 2011) reports that there are five strategies for organizations to shift from just valuing diversity to building and sustaining diversity. They include:

- Open conversations about race that include executive leadership,
- Effective communications about diversity commitments that include measured results,
- Building partnerships and networks that facilitate effective recruiting,
- A hiring process free from subtle bias, and
- Taking the time to develop, mentor and promote a diverse staff.

Successful nonprofits will:

- Acknowledge and discuss generational differences, diversity, inclusion and cultural competency—and clarify their relevance to organizational effectiveness and the ability to effect social change
- Develop new structures and ways of managing both staff and volunteers to meet generational needs; and adapt to changing workplace values and expectations

- Go beyond generational and representational diversity and focus on developing organizational strategy and leveraging diverse ideas, approaches and talents in support of the mission
- Will institutionalize a mentoring system that will help in overcoming stereotypes and invisibility.

The barriers and challenges to more diverse nonprofit organizations are many and varied. But by understanding and addressing them, and learning from the likes of the Peace Corps, organizations can begin to change, and in doing so can strengthen leadership in this sector. Nonprofits are at risk of losing touch with the populations they are organized to serve if diversity initiatives are not leveraged. Embracing a diverse and talented workforce is an objective nonprofits owe their stakeholders, customers, and employees.

REFERENCES

Allison, M. T. (2001). *Diversity issues and challenges facing youth-related nonprofit agencies: A report prepared for the center for nonprofit leadership and management.* Tempe, AZ: Arizona State University. Retrieved September 8, 2005, from http://www.asu.edu/copp/nonprofit/res/div_issue_fr.pdf.

Anderson, T. H. (2005). *The pursuit of fairness: A history of affirmative action.* New York, NY: Oxford University Press.

Barrington, L., & Troske, K. (2001). *Workforce diversity and productivity: An analysis of employer-employee matched data.* Working Paper Series EPWP#01–02. New York, NY: Conference Board Economics Program.

Bell, M. P. (2007). *Diversity in organizations.* Mason, OH: Cengage.

Bhide´, A. (2008). *The venturesome economy.* Princeton, NJ: Princeton University Press.

Carr-Ruffino, N. (2007). *Managing diversity: People skills for a multicultural workplace* (7th ed.). Boston, MA: Pearson Custom Publishing.

Cox, T. Jr, & Nkomo, S. M. (1990). Invisible men and women: A status report on race as a variable in organizational behavior research. *Journal of Organizational Behavior*, *11*(6), 419–431. doi:10.1002/job.4030110604

Crockett, R. O. (2003). *Why diversity is good business.* Retrieved June 17, 2011, from http://www.businessweek.com/bwdaily/dnflash/jan2003/nf20030117_6373.htm.

Drucker, P. F. (1960). Build tomorrow's workforce today. *Nation's Business, 48*(8), 76–79.

Drucker, P. F. (1980). *Managing in turbulent times.* New York, NY: Harper & Row.

Drucker, P. F. (2002). *Managing in the next society.* New York, NY: Truman Talley.

EEOC. (2008). *Facts about age discrimination.* Retrieved June 17, 2011, from http://www.eeoc.gov/facts/age.html.

Frey, W. H. (2011). *America's diverse future: initial glimpses at the U.S. child population from the 2010 census.* Retrieved June 17, 2011, from http://www.brookings.edu/~/media/Files/rc/papers/2011/0406_census_diversity_frey/0406_census_diversity_frey.pdf.

Gajewski, M. (2005). Strategic diversity to increase human capital in public and nonprofit organizations. *Nonprofit Management Good Practice Guide.* Retrieved from http://www.np-goodpractice.org/Management/GVSU/.

Gitlin, T. (1987). *The sixties: Years of hope, days of rage.* New York, NY: Bantam Books.

Gowdy, H., Hildebrand, A., La Piana, D., & Mendes Campos, M. (2009). *How five trends will reshape the social sector*. Irvine, CA: The James Irvine Foundation.

Grunin, S. (2011). *Becoming more competitive: How diversity and inclusion can transform your organization*. Paper presented at the Presentation on the Diversity & Inclusion White Paper Activity at the May 12, 2011 ACT-IAC Human Capital SIG Meeting. Retrieved June 17, 2011, from http://www.actgov.org/knowledgebank/documentsandpresentations/Documents/Shared%20Interest%20Groups/Human%20Capital%20SIG/How%20Diversity%20and%20Inclusion%20Can%20Transform%20Your%20Organization%20-%20Susan%20Grunin-HC%20SIG%2005-11-11.pdf.

Guidestar. (2010). *The nonprofit research collaborative: November 2010 fundraising survey*. Retrieved June 17, 2010 from http://www2.guidestar.org/ViewCmsFile.aspx?ContentID=3117.

Halpern, P. (2006). *Workforce issues in the nonprofit sector: Generational leadership change and diversity*. Kansas, MO: American Humanics.

Harvey, C. P., & Allard, M. J. (2008). *Understanding and managing diversity: Readings, cases, and exercises* (4th ed.). Upper Saddle River, NJ: Prentice-Hall.

Kasper, G., Ramos, H. A. J., & Walker, C. J. (2004). Making the case for diversity in philanthropy. *Foundation News & Commentary, 45*(6). Retrieved June 17, 2011, from http://www.foundationnews.org/CME/article.cfm?ID=3054.

Kossek, E., Lobel, S., & Brown, J. (2006). Human resource strategies to manage work force diversity: Examining "the business case". In Konrad, A. M., Prasad, P., & Pringle, J. K. (Eds.), *Handbook of Workplace Diversity* (pp. 53–74). Thousand Oaks, CA: Sage.

Langbert, M., & Friedman, H. (2002). Continuous improvement in the history of human resource management. *Management Decision, 40*(7/8), 782–787. doi:10.1108/00251740210437734

Light, P. (2002). The content of their character: The state of the nonprofit workforce. *The Nonprofit Quarterly, 9*(3), 6–16.

McPherson, J., Smith-Lovin, L., & Cook, J. (2001). Birds of a feather: Homophily in social networks. *Annual Review of Sociology, 27*, 415–444. doi:10.1146/annurev.soc.27.1.415

MPCA. (2004). *Peace corps hotline*. Retrieved June 17, 2011, from http://multimedia.peacecorps.gov/multimedia/pdf/returned/hotline/hotline030104.pdf.

MPCA. (2011a). *Peace Corps' statement on diversity*. Retrieved June 17, 2011, from http://www.minoritypca.org/Peace.Corps.Diversity.pdf.

MPCA. (2011b). *MPCA*. Retrieved June 17, 2011, from http://www.minoritypca.org/index1001a.html.

National Center for Public Policy and Higher Education. (2005). *Policy alert*. Retrieved June 17, 2011 from http://www.highereducation.org/reports/pa_decline/pa_decline.pdf.

Nonprofit Finance Fund. (2011). *2011 state of the sector survey*. Retrieved June 17, 2011 from http://nonprofitfinancefund.org/files/docs/2011/2011survey_brochure.pdf.

O'Neill, M. (2002). *Nonprofit nation: A new look at the third America*. San Francisco, CA: Jossey-Bass.

Oyler, J. D., & Pryor, M. G. (2009). Workplace diversity in the United States: The perspective of Peter Drucker. *Journal of Management History, 15*(4), 420–451. doi:10.1108/17511340910987338

Peace Corps. (2011a). *Mission*. Retrieved June 17, 2011, from http://www.peacecorps.gov/index.cfm?shell=about.mission.

Peace Corps. (2011b). *Who volunteers?* Retrieved June 17, 2011, from http://www.peacecorps.gov/index.cfm?shell=learn.whovol.

Peace Corps. (2011c). *History.* Retrieved June 17, 2011, from http://www.peacecorps.gov/index.cfm?shell=about.history.

Peace Corps. (2011d). *Peace Corps today*. Retrieved June 17, 2011, from http://www.peacecorps.gov/index.cfm?shell=about.pctoday.

Peace Corps. (2011e). *Peace Corps fact sheet*. Retrieved June 17, 2011, from http://multimedia.peacecorps.gov/multimedia/pdf/about/pc_facts.pdf.

Peace Corps. (2011f). *Information session with diversity panel*. Retrieved June 17, 2011, from http://www.peacecorps.gov/index.cfm?shell=meet.regrec.event&eventid=97507.

Peace Corps. (2011g). *Press and multimedia: Press Corps director touts diversity*. Retrieved June 17, 2011, from http://www.peacecorps.gov/index.cfm?shell=resources.media.medstories.view&news_id=1104.

Peace Corps. (2011h). *Stories from the field*. Retrieved June 17, 2011, from http://www.peacecorps.gov/index.cfm?shell=resources.media.stories.

Peace Corps. (2011i). *Press and media: Diversity in the Peace Corps*. Retrieved June 17, 2011, from http://www.peacecorps.gov/index.cfm?shell=resources.media.medstories.view&news_id=1503.

Peace Corps. (2011j). *Agency jobs*. Retrieved June 17, 2011, from http://www.peacecorps.gov/index.cfm?shell=jobs.

Peace Corps, G. L. O. B. E. (2009). *Lesbian, gay, bisexual & transgender US Peace Corps alumni*. Retrieved June 17, 2011, from http://www.lgbrpcv.org/articles/11_00globe.htm.

Rodriguez, S. (1997). Diversity and volunteerism: Deriving advantage from difference. *The Journal of Volunteer Administration, 15*(3), 18–20.

Rogers, P., & Smith, J. P. (1994). *Nonprofit management and leadership: The status of people of color*. New York, NY: Nonprofit Academic Centers Council.

Schwartz, R., Weinberg, J., Hagenbuch, D., & Scott, A. (2011). *The voice of nonprofit talent: Perceptions of diversity in the workplace*. Retrieved June 17, 2011, from http://www.cgcareers.org/diversityreport.pdf.

Shore, L. M., Chung-Herrera, B. G., Dean, M. A., Ehrhart, K. H., Jung, D. I., Randel, A. E., & Singh, R. (2009). Diversity in organizations: Where are we now and where are we going? *Human Resource Management Review, 19*(2), 117–133. doi:10.1016/j.hrmr.2008.10.004

SHRM. (2008). *2007 state of workplace diversity management: A survey report by the society for human resource management*. Alexandria, VA: SHRM.

Sidberry, T. B. (2002). Building diversity in organizations. *The Nonprofit Quarterly, 8*(2), 28–33.

Tatli, A. (2006). Handbook of workplace diversity. *Equal Opportunities International, 25*(2), 160–162.

Taylor, F. W. (1911). *The principles of scientific management*. New York, NY: Harper & Brothers.

Tempel, E. R., & Smith, L. (2007). *Nonprofits have a spotty record on diversity: Nonprofit times*. Retrieved June 17, 2011, from http://www.humanics.org/atf/cf/%7BE02C99B2-B9B8-4887-9A15-C9E973FD5616%7D/Smith-Tempel%20Article.pdf.

Thomas, K. M. (2005). *Diversity dynamics in the workplace*. Belmont, CA: Thomson Wadsworth.

Urquhart, M. (1984). The employment shift from services: Where did it come from? *Monthly Labor Review, 107*(4), 15–22.

US Department of Commerce. (1999). *Best practices in achieving workforce diversity benchmarking study / U.S. Department of Commerce and Vice President Al Gore's national partnership for reinventing government*. Online doc. PRVP 42.2:R 27/2003012037. Retrieved June 17, 2011, from http://purl.access.gpo.gov/GPO/LPS30263.

US Department of Labor. (1965). *Executive order 11264, as amended*. Retrieved June 17, 2011, from http://www.dol.gov/ofccp/regs/statutes/eo11246.htm.

US Department of Labor (2002). *Facts on executive order 11264 – Affirmative action*. Retrieved June 17, 2011, from http://www.dol.gov/ofccp/regs/compliance/aa.htm.

Weisinger, J. (2005). *Understanding the meaning of diversity in a nonprofit organization*. White Paper. Retrieved June 17, 2011 from http://www.naccouncil.org/pdf/ARNOVA%202005%20Paper%20Judy%20Weisinger.pdf.

Weisinger, J., & Salipante, P. (2005). A grounded theory for building ethnically bridging social capital in voluntary organizations. *Nonprofit and Voluntary Sector Quarterly, 34*(1), 29–55. doi:10.1177/0899764004270069

Wren, D. A., & Bedeian, A. G. (2009). *The evolution of management thought*. Hoboken, NJ: John Wiley & Sons.

Wright, P. M., & Snell, S. A. (2005). Partner or guardian? HR's challenge in balancing value and values. *Human Resource Management, 44*(2), 177–182. doi:10.1002/hrm.20061

KEY TERMS AND DEFINITIONS

Baby Boomers: People born at the end of World War II and the late 1960s.

Melting Pot: A place where immigrants of different cultures or races form an integrated society.

Nonprofit: An organization, corporation or association that conducts business for the benefit of the general public without shareholders and without a profit motive.

Peace Corps: A federal government organization that trains and sends American volunteers abroad to work with people of developing countries on projects for technological, agricultural, and educational improvement.

Revolving Door Syndrome: Turnovers in organizations, specifically amongst underrepresented groups, where as many groups as were being recruited were also exiting.

Volunteer: A person who voluntarily offers himself or herself for a service or undertaking.

Workforce Diversity: Similarities and differences including all characteristics and experiences of employees including age, cultural background, physical abilities and disabilities, race, religion, sex, and sexual orientation.

Chapter 22
Leveraging Workforce Diversity through Human Resource Management Initiatives

Mercedes Sánchez-Apellániz
University of Seville, Spain

Rafael Triguero-Sánchez
University of Seville, Spain

ABSTRACT

Workforce diversity and the benefits resulting from its appropriate management is a topic that must be addressed from a strategic and not an emotional perspective; and more specifically, from the Human Resources Strategic Management perspective. This chapter intends to explore the Human Resources initiatives and practices in use, analyze which of them can be employed, and which are more appropriate for an optimal management of workforce diversity, creating a competitive advantage for companies.

INTRODUCTION

A diverse workforce includes multiple beliefs, values, forms of understanding the world and specific information. Internationalization and globalization have favored an increase and reinforcement of the significance of workforce diversity. A multicultural workforce is a common element not only to organizations of western societies but also to corporations at global scale. As a result, diversity is increasingly becoming a hot button at political, legal, corporate, and educational levels (Shen, Chanda, & Monga, 2009).

Diversity must be understood as a competition issue. It must be approached from a strategic perspective and not from an emotional one. However, diversity by itself does must not necessarily have an impact, either negative or positive, on business results. The key lies in management, and more specifically in Human Resources Management.

DOI: 10.4018/978-1-4666-1812-1.ch022

Researchers widely recognize that effective diversity management can only be achieved by means of the use of appropriate human resources strategies (Richard & Johnson, 2001; Litvin, 1997). This chapter intends to explore such practices, analyze which of them can be employed and which are more appropriate for an optimal management of workforce diversity and to obtain a competitive advantage for companies.

The chapter is structured into the following main sections: Diversity as a Strategic Value will focus on the analysis of the benefits resulting from workforce diversity and on how diversity is a strategic rather than emotional issue; Approaches to Diversity will include a review of the main diversity perspectives, attitudes, and paradigms focusing on the most appropriate models to achieve benefits from it; The role of Human Resources Management in Diversity Management will focus on the widely shared position that diversity by itself does not mean any valued-added for the company if it does not go together with management processes of such diversity, processes related to the management of diverse Human Resources; and Human Resources Policies that Leverage Diversity Management will analyze the different existing human resources management practices leading to an appropriate management of diversity, which are the possible options available to companies, and how to improve existing practices.

DIVERSITY AS A STRATEGIC VALUE

There is a widespread recognition of the value provided by a diverse workforce. It is related, among others, to an improved quality in management decision making (Beeth, 1997), more innovative problem solving thanks to the contribution of new ideas (Cox, 1994; Elsass & Graves, 1997), the possibility of gaining access to new markets since it reflects the diversity of clients and suppliers (Ford, 1996; Cox, 1994; Cox & Blake, 1991), an improved corporate image (Kandola,

1995), and, as suggested by the resource-based view, the development of a sustainable competitive advantage due to the use of valuable, rare, inimitable and irreplaceable (human) resources (Barney, 1991).

Valuable because firms must have jobs requiring employees with different skills and employees that differ in the skills they have. Organizations that exclude certain people as potential employees based on irrelevant factors limit their ability to hire employees who may master some skills others in the company do not have (McMahan, Bell, & Virick, 1998). Moreover, the availability of different skills is something valuable inasmuch as it has been proven that diverse groups are more effective in identifying problems and finding solutions than homogeneous groups (Watson, Kuman, & Michaelsen, 1993).

Rare because candidates with a high potential are rare, and organizations that exclude potential employees based on irrelevant factors limit their ability to attract and hire candidates with a high potential; and also rare because it is relatively common that in organizations of all sizes the workforce is quite homogeneous, which determines that employees tend to be segregated within organizations (on grounds of gender, hierarchical levels, occupations,...). Having a workforce in which diverse individuals are present at different levels and occupations is something rare.

Inimitable because the policies supporting diversity in an organization may have been the outcome of changes in certain policies and measurement practices developed as a response to litigation on discrimination, or result from a type of leadership associated to the recruitment of diverse employees, or be the result of interconnecting different human resources functions to each other, or of interconnecting to other functional areas; all of which makes them inimitable.

Irreplaceable because a workforce is made up by individuals who are inherently different and who contribute different experiences, knowledge, skills, and capacities to the organization. An organization employing such a workforce must necessarily have employees who have learned from each other and their assets may be used as required.

Therefore, diversity must be understood as a competition issue. It must be approached from a strategic perspective and not as an emotional one. Diversity initiatives must be part of the business' strategic objectives and be connected to the other business strategies and objectives. Successful diversity management should be a key element in corporate mission statements, business objectives and other corporate strategies.

APPROACHES TO DIVERSITY

The literature agrees in that organizations may adopt different attitudes, models or paradigms towards diversity. Thus, Joplin and Dauss (1997) write about the attitudes of tolerance, intolerance and appreciation; Cox (1991) describes monolithic, plural and multicultural organizations; and Thomas and Ely (1996) state the presence of 3 paradigms in terms of diversity management (discrimination and justice, access and legitimacy, and learning and effectiveness).

According to Cox (1991), based upon how organizations implement diversity initiatives, there is a continuum made up by three types of organizations: monolithic, plural, and multicultural.

Monolithic organizations are homogeneous in demographic and cultural terms. This homogeneity minimizes intergroup conflict. The extent of their commitment to diversity is limited to the presence of an affirmative action plan.

Plural organizations develop an imbalanced representation of their workforce. Whereas the organization may be culturally diverse, its leadership stays homogeneous. The trend in plural organizations is to bring in new members and encourage them to adopt the central leadership culture (assimilation of minorities). These organizations may recruit and promote minorities more actively, but such minorities are expected to assimilate the dominant culture.

Multicultural organizations are culturally diverse along their entire hierarchy. They do not just tolerate diversity, they value it. They use pluralism in an acculturation process that makes emphasis on two-way learning, adaptation, interdependence, and mutual appreciation among the different cultures. They represent the ideal model, a place in which differences are appreciated and are used to obtain a competitive advantage. They promote the integration of minorities both attitudinally and structurally and manage corporate diversity in an effective manner.

These 3 organizational models coincide with the main individual attitudes towards diversity defined by Joplin and Daus (1997): intolerance, tolerance, and appreciation.

In the state of intolerance organizations meet the legal requirements on workforce make-up. Diversity is managed at a superficial level, but the organization is not committed to the idea that diversity has its own advantages. Organizational routines and practices go on "as they have always been."

This state coincides with the first of the paradigms described by Thomas and Ely (1996), called the *discrimination and justice paradigm*, which is probably the most widespread form of understanding diversity. Companies operating according to this philosophy measure their progress in diversity in terms of to what extent they achieve their minority group recruitment and retention targets, rather than the extent to which they allow their employees to contribute their personal perspectives on how to work more effectively. Workforce is diversified, but work is not.

These organizations usually have bureaucratic structures and cultures that are easy to identify in which it is assumed that "we are all equal" or that "we all aspire to be equal." Although this allows for an increase of the demographic diversity of organizations, it is unlikely that they will explore how differences among individuals can generate a diverse potential of effective ways of working, motivating, analyzing markets, managing staff and learning. This paradigm undermines the organization's ability to learn and to improve its own strategies, processes and practices.

The second of the states described by Joplin and Daus (1997) is the state of tolerance, in which culturally diverse groups are incorporated into the daily practices and routines of the organization.

This state coincides with the *access and legitimacy paradigm* (Thomas & Ely, 1996) according to which differences are accepted and celebrated. When this paradigm is in place many organizations usually focus on reaching out to a diverse client base, which in some cases leads to a substantial increase in organizational diversity. Their market-based motivation and their potential to obtain a competitive advantage are their main qualities.

However, in their pursuit of market niches they place their staff with specific skills for each niche in separated pigeonholes, without trying to understand what those skills are and how they could be integrated into the company's master lines. Work teams differentiated according to this principle operate independently applying their "exotic and slightly mysterious" cultural diversity within their market niche.

This may sometimes cause individuals to feel underestimated and perceive that the organization does not give them any opportunity. Furthermore, whenever organizations undertake staff reductions they tend to be the first ones affected.

In the state of appreciation (Joplin & Daus, 1997), organizations go beyond acceptation and become actively involved in diversity. They are fully committed to the incorporation of diverse members into routines, practices, and participation levels.

This coincides with the *learning and efficiency paradigm* (Thomas & Ely, 1996), in which the different perspectives of employees are incorporated into the main work lines. Tasks are reconsidered;

and markets, products, strategies, missions and even cultures are redefined. This paradigm is characterized by a full integration.

This form of managing diversity allows organizations to internalize the differences among employees, learning from and growing with them. If the model is firmly established the organization's members can declare that they are members of the same team, with their differences and not despite them. These are the organizations that truly benefit from cultural diversity.

It seems that it is only with an appreciation attitude, in multicultural organizations and under the learning and effectiveness paradigm, when workforce diversity is valued as a true asset, where there is an active engagement of the organization with diversity and where the above-mentioned benefits from cultural diversity may be achieved (Awbrey, 2007; Sánchez Apellániz & Román, 2008)

ROLE OF HUMAN RESOURCES MANAGEMENT IN DIVERSITY MANAGEMENT

However, the different versions agree in that the potential benefits of diversity do not occur just as a result of having a more diverse workforce. Diversity by itself does not need to have an impact, either negative or positive, on business results. The key lies in management, and more specifically in Human Resources Management.

As Cox (1994) mentioned, for diversity to become an asset for the company, it must be properly managed; otherwise, if it is poorly managed or neglected, it can become an obstacle to business results. Richard and Johnson (2001) proposed that diversity will affect the effectiveness of the firm depending upon the Human Resources Policy, the characteristics of the environment and the strategy adopted. Focus on diversity shall become then a Human Resources model in which policies reinforce each other with a culture that values diversity as something desirable.

From a review of the recent literature (i.e. Martin-Alcazar, Romero-Fernandez, & Sánchez-Gardey, 2011) it can be deduced that the Human Resources system is an interesting tool to model the effects of diversity in work groups. According to Wright and McMahan (1992), such system is made up by a set of interrelated elements by means of which the organization manages its human capital consistently with the business strategy. In this perspective, in addition to its orientation to the achievement of business objectives, there are also benefits in terms of employee satisfaction (Richard & Johnson, 2001). Such arguments allow companies to get access to increasingly heterogeneous resources and achieve greater levels of international competitiveness, and additionally provide valid and socially accepted responses to certain minority or women groups (Shen, et al., 2009).

Therefore, the issue for organizations (Shen, et al., 2009) is not about just accepting that individuals are different, but rather about creating an inclusion atmosphere and achieving a compromise to value diversity. The key to managing diversity lies in strategic thinking and in policies focusing on people.

Diversity Management and Human Resources Management (HRM) overlap each other. The former is an approach that focuses on employees; the latter is the custodian of the management processes of individuals. Both issues are related mainly to the contribution of the human resources function to the business strategy, and both are related to the individual differences, the development, and wellbeing of each and every one of the individuals.

Researchers widely recognize that an effective diversity management can only be achieved by means of the use of appropriate human resources strategies (Richard & Johnson, 2001; Litvin, 1997). Effective human resources strategies focus on promoting organizational learning, flexibility,

knowledge production and developing a working environment that facilitates diversity management.

HR diversity management has gained momentum due to the pressures experienced by companies to be competitive at international level, to the changing composition of their workforce, to the increasing awareness of the importance of human resources management and to the backlash generated by the perceptions of special treatment for women and minorities (Shen, et al., 2009).

HUMAN RESOURCES POLICIES THAT LEVERAGE DIVERSITY MANAGEMENT

HRM is a set of activities, functions, and processes aimed at attracting, managing, and retaining an organization's human resources. This function has expanded over the decades to cover a wide spectrum of management processes of individuals.

The literature suggests that there is some level of agreement on what practices constitute, or may constitute, an organization's human resources system. They are practices limited to more specific functional areas, whereas policies are in an intermediate level between them and the human resources strategy, since they require the coordination of two or more practices in order to achieve specific objectives. Among them, we can find job design, staff management, recruiting and selection, socialization, performance assessment, etc.; in conclusion, a series of areas that must be managed taking into account the diversity existing among its members and the goals set by the organization.

The literature has addressed diversity in multiple areas of human resources, as well as at all organization levels (Brooks & Clunis, 2007; Wentling & Palma-Rivas, 2000). There are important contributions in the field of recruitment and selection (i.e. Ng. & Burke, 2005; Taber & Hendricks, 2003), in compensation policies (Chiang & Birtch, 2007; Jackson, Colquitt, Wesson, &

Zapata-Phelan, 2006), in performance assessment processes (Barkema & Shvyrkov, 2007; Tyran & Gibson, 2008), in employee training and development (i.e. Schaubroeck & Lam, 2002), as well as its impacts on the working atmosphere (i.e. Gonzalez & Denisi, 2009; Kamenou & Fearfull, 2006).

To summarize, from a strategic perspective human resources practices can be a valuable instrument for diversity management. They can be used by organizations to improve not only their outputs and the effectiveness of their workforce, but also the satisfaction and wellbeing of the people making part of them.

One of the main limitations researchers have found in studying Diversity Management is the lack of typologies that can help us to better understand the potential alternatives in managing Human Resources (Lopez & Sánchez-Gardey, 2010). Therefore, in this chapter we will try to clarify which are the initiatives that provide for diversity management in the field of Human Resources.

Cultural Auditing

Effective management of cultural diversity is becoming increasingly important for all the organizations operating both in domestic and international markets. Understanding and valuing differences among employees and clients translates directly into economic prosperity and survival in a global economy. Hence, it is important for internal auditors to understand the fundamental aspects of culture, the impact of culture on the short term and long-term feasibility of the organization, and how to introduce cultural audits as a routine practice (Ricaud, 2006).

Culture may come up in different ways, by means of language, religion, the way we dress, business practices, work patterns… However, the drivers of all cultures are their values. This is why the first initiative we should take should be an internal cultural audit examining our motivations before starting to think about Diversity Manage-

ment and its meaning for us: Is it a problem to be solved? Is it an opportunity? Is it a threat? How far are we going to get?

The answers to the above questions will depict an image of the organizational mentality towards diversity, but a cultural audit not only requires answers about the explicit mental attitude of each and everyone towards diversity, but also intends to find the implicit values, assumptions and rules to deal with individuals and get the work done within the organization, what is what hinders or supports an inclusive environment.

At first glance, many of these values, assumptions, and rules seem to have little, if anything, to do with diversity. Cox (1993) describes this phenomenon with the term "institutional prejudice" referring to the fact that the preference models underpinning the way we manage organizations frequently and unpremeditatedly set up barriers to the comprehensive participation of the members of the organization that stem from cultural experiences that are different from the typical cultural experience of the majority group.

Some of the practices that help to create these institutional prejudices are: too long working hours emphasizing employees "being present," separating personal life from professional life, tending to overall standardization, using just one language, favoring individualism in reward systems, using informal recommendations and personal references as the primary recruitment and promotion tool, recruitment and/or promotion interviews held mainly by members of the majority group, trend towards defining effective leadership in terms reflecting mainly the typical features of the dominant group. Cultural audits make these rules and assumptions visible and unveil the potential impact they have in limiting the contribution of some employees.

Ideally, audits are a powerful tool for organizational self-reflection and to generate an internal view, setting the foundations for designing effective initiatives. They help to assess how both organizational insiders and outsiders perceive the success of the organization in its quest to embrace diversity (Hoobler, Basadur, & Lemmon, 2007). In the worst-case scenario, their outcomes can encourage internal conflicts or just be shelved.

Recruitment and Selection

Despite of the several decades of legislation on equality and an explicit commitment to equal opportunities, there is still systematic discrimination in recruitment and selection processes. Most organizations apply just an approximation to equality rather than a full deployment of measures aimed at building a more supportive organizational climate (Shen, et al., 2009)

Recruitment and selection should prevent the "ASA cycle" (Attraction-Selection-Attrition) (Schneider, 1987) in order to develop multiple cultures in the organization. Some of the initiatives that can be applied to achieve this objective are the following (Gentile, 1998):

- Expanding recruitment grounds: For example, in order to find female candidates with some business experience it would be appropriate to consider recruitment within the different businesswomen association existing in the country rather than recruiting in traditional grounds.
- Reviewing employment pre-requirements. It is about determining which employment requirements are truly related to the competences, knowledge, abilities, and skills required for the job and which ones are just a matter of tradition. For example, Subeliani and Tsogas (2005) identified in the Dutch bank Rabobank that having a workforce that reflects its clients' interests and needs provided it with a substantial increase in commercial operations.
- Expanding the pipeline. Some organizations may have traditionally focused on homogeneous labor market sections in their recruitment processes, but in many

cases they had to develop new programs to be able to recruit highly-skilled candidates. Indeed, some research studies suggest that individuals with high skill levels usually prefer to work in organizations that are interested in having a diverse workforce (Ng & Burke, 2005).

- Training the organization's recruitment team. The idea is to avoid prejudices, stereotypes, etc. so that they do not introduce a bias in candidate assessments. Human Resources managers and line managers recruiting and interviewing job seekers in a multicultural workforce must know how the beliefs, attitudes and stereotypes of interviewers affect their behavior.
- Developing, controlling, and assessing outcomes in recruitment objectives. It is important to explain the overall approach and discuss aspects or objections to this process. In particular, it is important to make clear the commitment to rigorous scores and the difference between agreed and imposed "quotas" with regards to other objectives. According to Tipper (2004), in order to develop an effective diversity recruitment strategy it is crucial to develop a business case1, which will be helpful in getting managers to support diversity management.
- Recruiting and promoting individuals from certain groups to the upper levels of the organization. Efforts to find top managers will take less time and be more effective if we consider all the talent available, a practice that will have an impact on future recruitments and promotions. According to a report of Diversity Best Practices (2006, p. 109) *"the recruitment of top performing staff and managers is one of the primary responsibilities of leading companies"* and it has been considered to be an excellent business practice.

Recruitment and selection are among the Human Resources practices that have most frequently been related to diversity management. Hodes (2008) and the European Institute for Diversity Management (2011) assure that it is the best-valued activity in the companies committed to diversity.

Hodes' study (2008) on the best diversity practices reveals that the sources most frequently used by companies to find diverse candidates are the recommendations of their own employees, followed by diversity events and associations representing a diverse population. In general terms, smaller organizations tend to make a greater use of informal channels, with a predominance of internal recruitment in individualistic and risk-aversion cultural contexts, rejecting what is new and therefore unknown (Aycan, 2005).

In some cases it is the behavior of minority groups, which must be redirected in order to achieve the desired recruitment levels. For example, Shantz, Wright, and Latham (2011) detected that women seldom used *"contact networks"* for engineering jobs. However, this underuse rather than being a self-limitation may be due to their smaller presence in a sector or industry, which is self-supplied through its own social networks. Therefore, firms must be aware of the fact that the use of references provided by their current employees has limitations resulting from the make-up of their workforce (Taber & Hendricks, 2003). Chrysler Group (2011) seems to have learned from this shortfall and shows its pride in being one of the employers that finds more technical talent among women and minorities.

Training

There is anecdotal evidence showing that training in diversity issues receives substantial attention by the organization's management (Shen, et al., 2009). Furthermore, most of the training programs seem to reinforce the rules, values and perspectives of the dominant organizational culture (Tung, 1993).

Companies must clarify their training objectives and carry out systematic assessments of their training needs. Participants should know whether the training program aims at raising awareness on diversity or at developing multicultural skills. In any case, education and training must suit the specific needs of the organization, division, level, team, or individual. Moreover, the critical element for any training program to be successful is to link training to the organization's strategic objectives.

In recent times diversity training has been gaining importance within organizations and this is due to its contribution to understanding the value and relevance of diversity for their business objectives (Byrd, 2007). Yap, Holmes, Hannan, and Cukier (2010) have concluded in a large longitudinal study including more than 11,000 managers, professional, and executives of Canadian firms that if employees, when they receive diversity training, perceive it to be effective, their levels of professional satisfaction and commitment to the organization are higher than when they consider it to be of little use or when they do not receive such training.

These actions must target the whole workforce, with a special care devoted to that aimed at supervisors and line managers, since they will play a key role in the implementation of any plan or program (Diversity Best Practices, 2006). Likewise, the training of top managers shall not be neglected because in addition to their privileged and influential situation, they tend to be one of the most biased groups in the organization (Capowsky, 1996).

Some of the training action initiatives than can be implemented are the following (Gentile, 1998):

- Introduction to diversity and its impacts on business. The purpose of this type of program is to start developing a shared definition and vocabulary around diversity, to share the fundamentals and objectives of the organization and to raise interest for ulterior individualized training.

- In depth-programs focusing on raising awareness. The purpose of these programs is to expand the individual understanding of what it actually means to change behavior towards other employees. A high quality training developing awareness towards diversity is a Human resources initiative that improves the effective integration of members from diverse groups. Training aimed at raising such awareness creates a common understanding of the value of diversity, helping to reinforce the social cohesion, which results in improved individual and organizational outcomes.

- Skill-development seminars. These programs teach specific skills on how to listen despite the differences, solve conflicts, interview, and mentor, making emphasis on race and gender issues and other differences.

- Seminars for specific groups. These programs are usually addressed at members of minority groups to give them specific training. For example, training programs for women holding intermediate manager positions in order to inhibit the perceived effects of the "glass ceiling."

- Seminars on mobbing. These programs focus on teaching the legal definition of mobbing and disseminating the organizational policies and practices designed to prevent it. Frequently these efforts generate debates in which conflicting feelings are aired and discussed.

- Integrated diversity training. In these programs, diversity is a complementary objective to other ones that intend to develop specific functional skills for business activities. For example, a client service program may include the particular opportunities and challenges of serving a diverse client base. These integrated efforts have the benefit of combining diversity with other regular activities in the company, making them more feasible.

According to Hodes (2008) the diversity training method can be implemented through the orientation programs of firms. It should be supported by hiring external consultants that can provide customized training at the workplace. To a lesser extent, employees themselves can give the training or design seminars. In any case, this practice has become a business imperative that is increasingly attracting more attention and recognition. At a symposium sponsored by The Conference Board regarding diversity in the workplace, for example, 400 executives agreed that diversity programs help to ensure the creation, management, valuing and leveraging of a diverse workforce that will ultimately lead to greater organizational effectiveness and sustained competitiveness (Hart, 1997). Likewise, training and education prior to the implementation of diversity programs will greatly contribute to their success (Combs & Luthans, 2007).

Communication

Communication processes are important both for companies and for the groups and individuals that form them. If the mentality of the organization or its objectives in terms of diversity are not properly transmitted to managers and employees, it is very unlikely that they will feel committed to the project. Notwithstanding, there are many companies that do not have an effective communication system for all its employees in place.

For example, in the well-known "Fortune 500" list of firms, Fegley (2006) found that more than 26% of the companies studied did not have a communications plan for their whole workforce; this hinders the adoption of a (global) strategy allowing the top management and all its employees to get involved in the diversity process. Moreover, and in the words of the general manager of "MCR Activos Humanos," communication must also project a good corporate image, of coherence with all its different audiences, showing its inclusion policy to all its stakeholders, and this because diversity is its differential capital (Rink & Ellemers, 2007). Indeed, there has been a recent proliferation of prestigious companies that actively disseminate this type of information, for example, the widely disseminated meeting of the main Wall Street banks (Bank of America, Merrill Lynch, Barclays, Citi …) to discuss issues related to diversity: culture change, recruitment, career development (Diversity Best Practices, 2011).

Some of the actions recommended to facilitate these communication practices include presentations made by top managers, videoconferences, statements of the corporate vision and mission regarding diversity, CEO memorandums, diversity brochures, employee newsletters, or communication in a second language (Wheeler, 1996). Conklin (2006) has grouped the best diversity communication practices into seven action lines:

1. Develop a strategic communications plan aligned with the company's business plan.
2. Build consensus and buy-in to the plan.
3. Define the audience(s) and outcome(s).
4. Identify and craft key message(s).
5. Determine the best methods and media for reaching your audience(s).
6. Test your plan before rolling it out.
7. Measure, follow up, and refine.

Networks, Discussion Groups, and Work Teams

The establishment of employee groups is an increasingly common diversity initiative. Although their objectives may differ, they all tend to focus on the problems of a particular community. In terms of their composition, they may range from 25 to more than one thousand members (Bye, 2003).

A wide range of group initiatives can be deployed to develop diversity in organizations. Some of them are:

- Support networks and groups. They may be created by the groups or directly by the organization and they have a social, educational and self-development purpose. As social networks, they offset the lack of power and the isolation of some employee groups that for geographic circumstances or social exclusion reasons have poor access to information networks (Cox, 1993). Support groups provide a comfortable environment to those that otherwise might feel excluded from the corporate master lines or lost in a bureaucracy managed by people that are different from them (Gómez-Mejía & Balkin, 2002).

Merely for information purposes, we can mention some companies that have developed such support groups, as it has been the case in IBM, Allstate, Avon, Digital Equipment, and Xerox. DuPont has declared that it has got more than 100 of those networks. In the general headquarters of Apple in Cupertino, California, there is a Jewish cultural group, a gay/lesbian group and women groups.

- Consultative work groups. Networks may also have a consultative and/or defense role, since those represented in them try to inform on and recommend changes in the policies and behaviors of organizational leaders. Its members are usually selected on purpose to be representative, being such groups one of the few places in which members abide to "equality rules" rather than "proportional and representation rules" (Cox, 1993), and so they can be used to study and discuss different topics and perspectives. An example is the case of PricewaterhouseCoopers (PwC) that set up in 2006 a Gender Consultative Board made up by 14 international leaders, men and women, that has been working actively to improve the employment conditions of women; this has led them to receive the prize for being the best world company for diversity in 2009 awarded by Diversityinc printers in the United States.

- Discussion groups. They are small groups made up by employees of different races, gender, or hierarchical level that give their members a chance to interact with others different from them and on topics related to their differences.

- Diversity learning labs (Gomez-Mejía & Balkin, 2002). These initiatives improve the knowledge and perception of the market niches of different client populations. Their purpose is to learn key aspects for the management of projects in different market segments. American Express has set up 15 diversity learning labs that receive funding and practical support from the regional and corporate offices. They focus on market segments such as African Americans, gays and lesbians, and women. A further recent example is PwC in the United States with the launching of a video on diversity in which more than 10,000 people and organizations have been involved (Diversity Best Practices, 2011).

- International teams. The increasingly global economy seems to have encouraged the development of teams made up by employees coming from different geographic areas, a circumstance that has been associated to competitive advantages. Indeed, firms such as Intel (Intel Business Practices Network) have developed multicultural teams that seem to produce a large number of innovative ideas. According to Aycan (2005), the proliferation of these teams may be slowed down by an organizational culture with focus strong on performance, a trend that has been associated to the use of highly formal and standardized processes.

In addition to the groups mentioned above, other ones can be established to encourage the participation and involvement of employees and managers. They may include (Wheeler, 1996) thematic study groups or groups focusing on specific issues, corporate advisory committees, business unit steering committees, etc.

In order to achieve the best practices in this type of diversity initiatives we can mention the following recommendations: (Bye, 2003)

1. Recognize employee participation.
2. Establish executive forums.
3. Use these internal resources to the benefit of all.
4. Enhance external community presence.

Career Management

Many leading companies have not succeeded in retaining and promoting women and minorities. The managers of organizations in which there is a deficit of effective Human Resources policies are likely to will promote or grade better subordinates with experiences and backgrounds similar to theirs (Shen, et al., 2009).

Professional development and career planning are areas in which discrimination is visible and it requires a careful attention while designing diversity management policies. If Human Resources practices for career development do not reflect diversity issues properly, diverse employees may have a negative perception of the process as a whole.

Providing equal opportunities in promotion and personal development to all employees, including minorities in the panels evaluating, selecting and promoting managers, including non-traditional managers in decision-making processes and in the evaluation of candidates for promotion, establishing mentoring programs… They are all strategies that must be followed if we want candidates not only to be recruited but also to be properly prepared as to opt for a management position.

Organizations use a wide range of methods to manage these issues (Gentile, 1998; Gómez-Mejía & Balkin, 2002; Wheeler, 1996), among them the following:

- Improving performance assessment systems: Informal performance assessment systems frequently carry unfair career opportunities. Effective performance assessment practices in the field of Diversity Management should be objective and not subjective, relevant for the position and the company and fair to all employees without offering a special treatment (Schuler, Dowling, & DeCieri, 1993). There are certain consistent evidences suggesting that a greater demographic similarity between supervisors and their subordinates in age, race, or gender is correlated to certain results such as better performance levels (Shen, et al., 2009). Establishing guidelines on performance feedback, ensuring that all employees receive them at least a certain number of times every year, considering different feedback sources (360 degree feedback) or including non-traditional managers in assessment panels are some initiatives that can be implemented to stop the trend towards informal or subjective appraisals. The objective should be to make assessments as culturally neutral as possible.
- Including employee performance as an objective in manager performance. Employee development outcomes can be included in the managers' performance assessment. This would reflect the organization's commitment to Diversity Management. However, it is important to design mea-

surement systems carefully, with demonstrable qualification criteria and realistic time horizons.

- Career plan appraisal and control. Understanding what are the typical steps in the promotion to managerial positions allows for the determination of the knowledge areas, critical skills, and visibility level required to grow in professional terms. Once these factors are known we can assess whether those implicit requirements are necessary or just a matter of tradition. We can also determine whether there are common obstacles some employees must face unnecessarily.
- Job redesign. Job design is a further practice that plays an important role in the potential success of organizations, especially if they have a loose hierarchy, since it enhances the commitment of its employees. In this area, multifunctional, self-managing, or project-based teams, in which an adequate job design and proper employee qualification are important, have gained relevance. Likewise, employee-training plays also an important role in the management of a heterogeneous workforce, particularly for "key positions," and the same applies to multidisciplinary training for the different tasks usually assigned to self-managing and similar teams (Hoerr, 1989).
- Mentoring programs. Women and other minority employees may face greater difficulties in finding mentors. The purpose of the mentor is to help underrepresented minority groups to overcome the invisible barriers and progress in their careers. Due to the importance of their role, some organizations have developed formal assignments of mentors to all new employees, others only to minorities; however, it seems that the relation works better when it is entirely voluntary on both sides. In any

case, it is recommendable to train mentors and mentored ones in giving and receiving feedback, communication skills, and other areas.

- Reward systems. Wage inequality is one of the main reasons of labor dissatisfaction and demotivation, and therefore a main issue on diversity management. Although the implementation of the equal pay principle has significantly reduced wage differences between men and women, wage inequality is still a global problem (Brainerd, 2000). It is fundamental to review the types and levels of rewards, more specifically compensations, promotions and bonuses to assess whether there are disparities between different groups.

Working Conditions

An important aspect in diversity management arises when individuals try to reach a balance between their personal and their professional lives. In this regard, flexible working arrangements have great advantages over the traditional employment system. Flexible working arrangements allow individuals to choose a working scheme based on their personal abilities. Flexibility provides a reasonable balance and allows employees to manage significant issues (Shen, et al., 2009). Moreover, if there is not a certain balance between personal and professional life, individual issues might spill over and end up affecting organizational productivity (Cox, 1993). Organizations should therefore provide support services to help mitigate certain aspects that are connected to the personal life-professional life balance.

The initiatives that may be applied in this field can be grouped into different blocks (Chinchilla, Poelmans, & León, 2003; Lavara, 2004; Hoobler, et al., 2007):

- Working flexibility in terms of time. In many sectors and jobs, time and physical presence are not relevant criteria for assessment and compensation any more. The key elements are objectives and performance. Hence, strict timetables are replaced by flexible timetables, self-control, and assessment based on objectives. Flexible working hours, part-time work, shared jobs, shortened working week, reduced workdays, and yearly count of work hours are some of the available alternatives.

- Working flexibility in terms of space: working at home or in the office. In the era of information technologies flexibility in terms of time and distance is not science fiction any more. The responsibility for using those technological developments for the benefit of both the employee and the company rests on the latter. What is most important is that employees have more control of their working hours and their working space. The ethical issue is whether those measures are used as the prelude for the separation of the worker, not only in spatial terms but also in terms of employment contract. Initiatives in the field may include satellite offices close to home, working at home, videoconferences, and teleoffices.

- Professional support policies: in order to adapt the job as a result of changes in personal situations, the company must have a system in place to detect, address and follow those changes. There are several types of counseling for these problems: professional trajectory counseling, psychological/family counseling, legal counseling, and counseling for expatriates.

- Counseling policies: some say that training is an indication of the fact that the company is taking preventive measures against stress because it enables individual employees to manage their stress, conflicts, time constraints, and the new responsibilities they have acquired in the family.

Others say that it is not enough because it does not tackle the root of the problem; there are even some who think that it is a hypocritical attitude if the company increases working hours at the same time. In any case, preventing occupational stress is becoming more and more necessary. If companies do not do it for the health of their employees, they should do it for their own interest: hundreds of studies have proven that social support is an essential protection against stress, and so, if companies allow occupational stress brim over, they are endangering the productivity of their employees. The potential courses to be covered are: time management, stress management, and conflict management, among others.

- Family services. Services that reduce the burden placed on the employee outside of the company. This is in line with a service policy attitude in parallel to a wage policy, because people not only require money to live, they also need quality of life, time, and therefore, services. Information on childcare services, nursery in the company, financial support by employers for the payment of childcare expenses during work trips or overtime work, information on elderly care centers and other household services (dry cleaner's, shopping, transport, parking, restaurant, sports/fitness facilities) can be included in this section.

- Additional social benefits: This last category includes different types of non-compulsory benefits, labeled also as "social" which can make less worried about other issues such as medical care of their families. Some examples are medical insurance for spouses, medical insurance for children, disability insurance, global medical insurance, retirement plans, life insurance, etc. Some companies are acknowledging the different priorities of their employees

in terms of life conditions and they are starting to offer non-salary benefits to the registered partners both heterosexual and homosexual. Other companies are starting to develop resources and contact networks for employees in charge of dependents.

FINAL REMARKS

The growing attention devoted to Diversity Management both in practice and in Human Resources Management is not just a temporary fashion, but rather reflects the unavoidable consequences of a global economy and of demographic changes (Jayne & Dipboye, 2004). Diversity alone does not guarantee immediate and tangible improvements in organizational, group and individual performance. Nevertheless, having a diverse workforce and managing it in an effective manner may lead to great benefits.

There is a continuous need for effective diversity management and Human Resources Management plays an essential role in this. Operating under monolithic (Cox, 1991), intolerant (Joplin & Daus, 1997) mechanisms, or under the discrimination and justice paradigm (Thomas & Ely, 1996) leads to understanding diversity as something connected to merely fulfilling legal requirements and not to Human Resources Management. Ineffective management of diversity along these schemes is very likely going to lead to conflicts, demotivation, and a poorer organizational performance. For this reason Diversity Management must become a priority issue in Human Resources Management practices in all organizations (Shen, et al., 2009) if we want to achieve the benefits resulting from a diverse workforce.

However, such benefits will only become tangible if diversity is adopted at all levels in the company and if the commitment to diversity is a value deeply rooted in the corporate culture, capable of producing the appropriate rules for all employees to develop constructive and productive behaviors (Slater, Weigand, & Zwirlein, 2008).

REFERENCES

Awbrey, S. M. (2007). The dynamics of vertical and horizontal diversity in organization and society. *Human Resource Development Review*, *6*(1), 7–32. doi:10.1177/1534484306295638

Aycan, Z. (2005). The interplay between cultural and institutional/structural contingencies in human resource management practices. *International Journal of Human Resource Management*, *16*(7), 1083–1119. doi:10.1080/09585190500143956

Barkema, H. G., & Shvyrkov, O. (2007). Does TMT promote or hamper foreign expansion? *Strategic Management Journal*, *28*, 663–680. doi:10.1002/smj.604

Barney, J. (1991). Firm resources and sustained competitive advantage. *Journal of Management*, *17*, 99–120. doi:10.1177/014920639101700108

Beeth, G. (1997, May). Multicultural managers wanted. *Management Review*, 17–21.

Brainerd, E. (2000). Women in transition: Changes in gender wage differentials in Eastern Europe and former Soviet Union. *Industrial & Labor Relations Review*, *54*(1), 138–162. doi:10.2307/2696036

Brooks, A. K., & Clunis, T. (2007). Where to now? Race and ethnicity in workplace learning and development research: 1980-2005. *Human Resource Development Quarterly*, *18*(2), 229–251. doi:10.1002/hrdq.1201

Bye, L. B. (2003). Best practices for employee resource groups. *Diversity in Practice*, *11*(2), 7–10.

Byrd, M. (2007). Educating and developing leaders of racially diverse organizations. *Human Resource Development Quarterly*, *18*(2), 275–279. doi:10.1002/hrdq.1203

Capowsky, G. (1996). Managing diversity. *Management Review*, *85*(6), 12–20.

Chiang, F., & Birtch, T. (2007). The transferability of management practices: Examining cross-national differences in reward preferences. *Human Relations*, *60*(9), 1293–1330. doi:10.1177/0018726707082849

Chinchilla, M. N., Poelmans, S., & León, C. (2003). *Políticas de conciliación trabajo-familia en 150 empresas españolas. Documento de investigación número 498*. Pamplona, Spain: IESE Business School, Universidad de Navarra.

Combs, G. M., & Luthans, F. (2007). Diversity training: Analysis of the impact of self-efficacy. *Human Resource Development Quarterly*, *18*(1), 91–120. doi:10.1002/hrdq.1193

Conklin, W. (2006). Seven best practices in diversity communications. *Managing Diversity Communications*, *14*(2), 11–16.

Cox, T. (1991). The multicultural organization. *The Academy of Management Executive*, *5*, 34–47.

Cox, T. (1993). *Cultural diversity in organizations: Theory, research & practices*. San Francisco, CA: Berret-Koehler.

Cox, T. (1994). *Review of research on diversity and organizational performance, in cultural diversity in organizations: theory, research & practice*. San Francisco, CA: Berrett-Koehler Publisher Inc.

Cox, T., & Blake, S. (1991). Managing cultural diversity: Implications for organizational competitiveness. *The Academy of Management Executive*, *5*(3), 45–56.

Diversity Best Practices. (2006). *Winning the race for diverse talent: A major report*. Washington, DC: Diversity Best Practices.

Diversity Best Practices. (2011). *PwC says "it gets better" in support of LGBT youth.* Retrieved from http://www.diversitybestpractices.com/news-articles/pwc-says-it-gets.

Elsass, P. M., & Graves, L. M. (1997). Demographic diversity in decision-making groups: The experience of women and people of colour. *Academy of Management Review, 22*(4), 946–973.

European Institute for Diversity Management. (2011). *Diversity for talent and competitiveness: The SME business case for diversity, 2011.* Retrieved from http://iegd.org/spanish800/charter.html.

Fegley, S. (2006). Workplace diversity and changes to the EEO-1 process survey report. *Society for Human Resource Management.* Retrieved from http://www.shrm.org/surveys.

Ford, V. (1996, February). Partnership is the secret of progress. *People Management,* 34-36.

Gentile. (1998). *Managerial excellence through diversity.* Long Grove, IL: Waveland Press, Inc.

Gómez-Mejía, L. R., & Balkin, D. B. (2002). *Administración.* Spain: McGraw-Hill.

Gonzalez, J., & Denisi, A. (2009). Cross-level effects of demography and diversity climate on organizational attachment and firm effectiveness. *Journal of Organizational Behavior, 30,* 21–40. doi:10.1002/job.498

Hart, M. (1997). *Managing diversity for sustained competitiveness.* New York, NY: The Conference Board.

Hodes, B. (2008). *Diversity best practices research for HCI summit: Full Report.* Bernard Hodes Group. Retrieved from http://emarketing.hodes.com/hci_may08/pdfs/HCI_ExecutiveSum_050208_FINAL.pdf.

Hoerr, J. (1989). The payoff from teamwork. *Business Week,* 56-62.

Hoobler, J., Basadur, T., & Lemmon, G. (2007). Management of a diverse workforce: Meanings and practices. *The Journal of Equipment Lease Financing, 25*(1), 1–8.

Jackson, C., Colquitt, J. A., Wesson, M. J., & Zapata-Phelan, C. P. (2006). Psychological collectivism: A measurement validation and linkage to group member performance. *The Journal of Applied Psychology, 91*(4), 884–899. doi:10.1037/0021-9010.91.4.884

Jayne, M. E. A., & Dipboye, R. L. (2004). Leveraging diversity to improve business performance: Research findings and recommendations for organizations. *Human Resource Management, 43*(4), 409–424. doi:10.1002/hrm.20033

Joplin, J. R. W., & Dauss, C. S. (1997). Challenges of leading a diverse workforce. *The Academy of Management Executive, 11*(3), 32–47. doi:10.5465/AME.1997.9709231662

Kamenou, N., & Fearfull, A. (2006). Ethnic minority women: A lost voice in HRM. *Human Resource Management, 16*(2), 154–172. doi:10.1111/j.1748-8583.2006.00010.x

Kandola, R. (1995). Managing diversity: New broom or old hat? In Cooper, C. L., & Robertson, I. T. (Eds.), *International Review of Industrial and Organizational Psychology.* Chichester, UK: Wiley.

Lavara, N. (2004). Los empresarios se implican en la conciliación de la vida familiar y laboral. *Entorno Social.* Retrieved from http://www.entornosocial.es.

Litvin, D. (1997). The discourse of diversity: From biology to management. *Organizations, 4*(2), 187–209. doi:10.1177/135050849742003

Lopez, M., & Sánchez-Gardey, G. (2010). Managing the effects of diversity on social capital. *Equal Diversity and Inclusion: An International Journal, 29*(5), 491–516. doi:10.1108/02610151011052780

Martin-Alcazar, F., Romero-Fernandez, P. M., & Sánchez-Gardey, G. (2011). Effects of diversity on group decision-making processes: The moderating role of human resource management. *Group Decis Negot.* Retrieved from http://wenku.baidu.com/view/5b7fb1f1f90f76c661371aa9.html.

McMahan, G. C., Bell, M. P., & Virick, M. (1998). Strategic human resource management: Employee involvement, diversity and international issues. *Human Resource Management Review, 8*(3), 193–214. doi:10.1016/S1053-4822(98)90002-X

Ng, E. S., & Burke, R. J. (2005). Person-organization fit and the war for talent: Does diversity management make a difference? *International Journal of Human Resource Management, 16*(7), 1195–1210. doi:10.1080/09585190500144038

PR Newswire Association. (2011). *Chrysler group named among nation's top supporters of engineering programs of historically black colleges and universities, 2011.* Retrieved from http://search.proquest.com/docview/863149112?accountid=14744.

Ricaud, J. S. (2006). Auditing cultural diversity. *The Internal Auditor, 63*(6), 57–61.

Richard, O. C., & Johnson, N. B. (2001). Understanding the impact of human resource diversity practices on firm performance. *Journal of Managerial Issues, 13*(2), 177–195.

Rink, F., & Ellemers, N. (2007). Diversity as a basis for shared organizational identity: The norm congruity principle. *British Journal of Management, 18*, 17–27. doi:10.1111/j.1467-8551.2007.00523.x

Sánchez-Apellániz, M., & Román, M. L. (2008). *Gestionar la diversidad: Políticas de recursos humanos para afrontar el entorno global.* Seville, Spain: Edición Digital@tres.

Schaubroeck, J., & Lam, S. K. (2002). How similarity to peers and supervisor influences organizational advancement in different cultures. *Academy of Management Journal, 45*(6), 1120–1136. doi:10.2307/3069428

Schneider, B. (1987). The people make the place. *Personnel Psychology, 40*(3), 437–456. doi:10.1111/j.1744-6570.1987.tb00609.x

Schuler, R. S., Dowling, P. J., & DeCieri, H. (1993). An integrative framework of strategic international human resource management. *International Journal of Human Resource Management, 5*(3), 717–764. doi:10.1080/09585199300000056

Shantz, A., Wright, K., & Latham, G. (2011). *Networking with boundary spanners: A quasi-case study on why women are less likely to be offered an engineering role.* Bradford, UK: Emerald Group Publishing.

Shen, J., Chanda, A., D'Netto, B., & Monga, M. (2009). Managing diversity through human resource management: An international perspective and conceptual framework. *International Journal of Human Resource Management, 20*(2), 235–251. doi:10.1080/09585190802670516

Slater, S. F., Weigand, R. A., & Zwirlein, T. J. (2008). The business case for commitment to diversity. *Business Horizons, 51*(3), 201–209. doi:10.1016/j.bushor.2008.01.003

Subeliani, D., & Tsogas, G. (2005). Managing diversity in the Netherlands: A case study of Rabobank. *International Journal of Human Resource Management, 16*(5), 831–851. doi:10.1080/09585190500083392

Taber, M. E., & Hendricks, W. (2003). The effects of workplace gender and race demographic composition on hiring through employee referrals. *Human Resource Development Quarterly, 14*(3), 303–319. doi:10.1002/hrdq.1068

Thomas, D. A., & Ely, R. J. (1996, September/October). Making differences matter: A new paradigm for managing diversity. *Harvard Business Review*.

Tipper, J. (2004). How to increase diversity through your recruitment practices. *Industrial and Commercial Training, 36*(4), 158–161. doi:10.1108/00197850410542392

Tung, R. (1993). Managing cross-national and intra-national diversity. *Human Resource Management, 32*, 461–477. doi:10.1002/hrm.3930320404

Tyran, K. L., & Gibson, C. (2008). Is what you see, what you get? The relationship among surface –and deep- level heterogeneity characteristics, group efficacy, and team reputation. *Group & Organization Management, 33*(1), 46–76. doi:10.1177/1059601106287111

Watson, W. E., Kumar, K., & Michaelsen, L. K. (1993). Cultural diversity's impact on interaction process and performance: Comparing homogeneous and diverse task groups. *Academy of Management Journal, 36*, 590–602. doi:10.2307/256593

Wentling, R. M., & Palma-Rivas, N. (2000). Current status of diversity, initiatives in selected multinational corporations. *Human Resource Development Quarterly, 11*(1), 35–60. doi:10.1002/1532-1096(200021)11:1<35::AID-HRDQ4>3.0.CO;2-#

Wheeler, M. L. (1996, December 9). Diversity: Making the business case. *Business Week*.

Wright, P. M., & McMahan, G. C. (1992). Theoretical perspectives for strategic human resource management. *Journal of Management, 18*(2), 295–320. doi:10.1177/014920639201800205

Yap, M., Holmes, M. R., Hannan, C., & Cukier, W. (2010). The relationship between diversity training, organizational commitment, and career satisfaction. *Journal of European Industrial Training, 34*(6), 519–538. doi:10.1108/03090591011061202

ENDNOTE

[1] The Business Case is a document used to assess or analyze the financial and/or economic impact of a proposal made within a company, as well as to document the most relevant aspects considered in making the analysis. It serves as a support to the planning and decision-making process. It provides us with a framework and methodology to carry out a sound assessment of one or more alternatives and their impacts on the further evolution of our area, division, business, and/or company. This methodology allows for the financial or operational analysis of a proposal or alternative, measuring the impact it may have on the company. It intends to answer the question: *What would happen both from a financial perspective and a business (operations, administration, etc.) perspective if we make one decision or the other?* The Business Case focuses on measuring the specific impact of the proposal on the company, demonstrating with figures that what we are proposing is feasible and real, and that it will have an economic impact (positive or negative). It documents each of the assumptions, methodologies, risks, contingencies, and impacts, among others, resulting from putting our Case into practice.

Chapter 23

Leveraging Intergenerational Diversity to Meet Business Goals

Sherita L. Jackson
Thomson Reuters IP Management Services, USA

ABSTRACT

In recent years, the concept of generational diversity has gained increasing recognition in the United States. Each generation is shaped by historical, social, and cultural events that are unique to that particular age cohort. The purpose of this chapter is to help scholars, researchers, organizational leaders, practitioners, and graduate students understand diversity among generational cohorts and employ practices to utilize the wealth of knowledge that exists within today's multigenerational workforce. This chapter will describe the four generations in today's workplace and discuss gaps that can cause conflict. This chapter also provides tips and best practices for leveraging intergenerational diversity as well as scenarios and examples that demonstrate best practices. The result is a cohesive and productive workplace that respects multigenerational perspectives.

INTRODUCTION

Each generation imagines itself to be more intelligent than the one that went before it, and wiser than the one that comes after it—George Orwell

I sat with my colleagues and had lunch one afternoon after a team meeting. It was one of the rare opportunities that we had to talk about issues that affect our training department. Most of us are Baby Boomers or Generation Xers. One of my colleagues talked about how difficult it was to get her trainees to understand technology. I asked, "Do you think it is a generational issue?" Her response was yes. She believes that the older generation is afraid to try new technology. Another colleague told us that when computers were introduced into the workplace some 30 years ago, there were mass retirements because some people did not want to deal with the new technology. Another colleague lamented about the poor spelling skills of many Millennials. She attributed some of this to the way they were taught (or not taught) how to spell in school. We laughed at the style of writing that many young people use as they text their friends, and agreed it was inappropriate for

DOI: 10.4018/978-1-4666-1812-1.ch023

business communications. Comments like these are not uncommon in today's workplace. People from one generation may display characteristics that are confusing and sometimes even annoying to another generation.

Generational diversity is a dimension of diversity that we need to better understand in today's workforce. Unlike other dimensions of diversity, generational diversity transcends race, ethnicity, gender, religion, disability, sexual identity, and economic class. Regardless of these dimensions, age cohorts tend to be influenced by the time in which they were born, and the events that shaped their formative years can have lasting impressions on their beliefs, values, and perceptions. Understanding differences between the generations is essential in establishing a successful intergenerational workplace. For each generation there, are particular experiences that mold preferences, expectations, beliefs, work style, and professional goals. For the purposes of this chapter, we define a generation as a "group of individuals born contemporaneously who have common knowledge and experiences that affect their thoughts, attitudes, values, beliefs, and behaviors" (Johnson & Johnson, 2010, p. 6). In other words, the era in which you were born has an effect on your worldview including your views on workplace issues. Each generation has signposts that are "events or cultural phenomenon that is specific to one generation" (Johnson & Johnson, 2010, p. 4). The signpost tends to influence a generation's ideas about life including issues related to loyalty and work ethics. For example, a member of the Traditionalists generation may be loyal to a company because he has had a 40-year career there; a Generation Xer may be seen as less loyal because she was laid off in her late 20s and has changed jobs every few years since.

Life laws are "events that have social, political, or economic influence on our lives but occurred before we were old enough to remember any difference" (Johnson & Johnson, 2010, p. 5). We

automatically take life laws for granted because we do not know any different. The use of the internet is a life law for Millennials because they came of age with the internet. Older generations had to adapt to the changes the Internet brought to the workplace.

It is common today to observe four generations in the Unites States' workplace: Traditionalists (born between 1922 and 1945), Baby Boomers (born between 1946 and 1964), Generation Xers (born between 1965 and 1980), and Millennial (born between 1981 and 2000). Because each generation tends to hold values and viewpoints that are closely tied to the culture and environment in which they were raised, there are differences in the approach to work and the meaning of employment that can be attributed to generational differences. These differences can create conflicts that hinder progress, creativity, and positive results in the workplace. Success in the workplace depends on engaging and communicating effectively with a demographically diverse worker population and mitigating intergenerational conflict to create a cooperative and respectful workforce.

This chapter will provide a perspective on topics related to multigenerational diversity including:

- Describe the four generations in today's workplace
- Provide scenarios of intergenerational workers that highlight conflict among different generations
- Discuss seven major intergenerational gaps that cause conflict in the workplace
- Present perspectives on how to build a team-centric culture in an intergenerational workplace
- Dispel stereotypes related to the generations
- Provide examples of companies that are leveraging intergenerational diversity
- Present best practices for leveraging generational diversity

Note: Any discussion of generations tends to describe generational cohorts as being homogenous, and this is untrue. However, "generalities about generations can provide insight on values and expectations in the workplace" (HR Magazine, 2009, p. 1). It is helpful to understand that people born within a certain time span have shared life experiences that influence their viewpoint. There may also be overlap between the generations, especially when individuals are born near the beginning or end of a generation. These so-called cuspers can usually relate to both generations. The information presented in this chapter should not be used to stereotype members of a particular generation but to help better understand how subtle differences can cause considerable conflict that can lead to dissatisfaction and affect profitability.

IDENTIFYING GENERATIONAL COHORTS

Scenario: Generational Conflict

Harvey is a Traditionalist in charge of a training department at Blue Bank, a small local bank that has been in business for over 50 years. Harvey's boss has asked him to create a training and development team consisting of two instructional designers, a Web developer, and a graphic artist to design and develop a training module for a brand new computer system the bank will use. Harvey is reluctant, but he knows he has to do what his boss asks, and he feels as though he should not question the boss at all. Harvey likes to share stories about what Blue Bank was like in the past. "We had six men all dressed up in suits and ties in the good old days," he says. "No casual Fridays back then."

After careful consideration, Harvey chooses Maxine, Gabrielle, Dora, and Brandon. Maxine is a Baby Boomer who has worked for Blue Bank for over 30 years. She remembers when female tellers first began working at the bank and when the first computer system was installed. Maxine

started out as a clerk at the bank after graduating from high school and worked her way up to a position in the training department as an instructional designer. She is team-oriented, hardworking, and is usually the first one in and the last one out of the office. Gabrielle is a Gen Xer with a Masters degree in training and development. Gabrielle has been an instructional designer for over a decade and has worked for many companies. Although she is an expert in training design and development, she is relatively new to the banking industry. Gabrielle is technically inclined and uses many tools to design training, and she is not afraid to learn new technology. She has worked for Blue Bank for about a year. Dora is a Gen Xer and the lead Web developer at Blue Bank. Dora is fast and efficient; she gets her work done and moves on to the next project. Dora holds a Bachelors degree in computer science and manages a small team of developers. Brandon is a Millennial who holds an Associate degree in graphic design, but Brandon is brand new to Blue Bank.

Harvey notices that there is tension among the individuals and his first instinct is to lay down the law and forbid the team from debating. It is evident that these team members need an intervention if they are to work together successfully. After two weeks, Harvey decides to meet with the team to gain some insight on the source of conflict. Maxine is the first to speak and states that Gabrielle, Dora, and Brandon are not taking their job seriously. "Gabrielle is not willing to put in the hours to collaborate on the project and Brandon wants constant praise," says Maxine. Gabrielle complains that Maxine does not understand the technology. "Maxine wants to sit here all night instead of finishing the job and moving on. She needs to get a life," says Gabrielle. Brandon complains that he is not receiving enough feedback on the graphics he creates. "I can't seem to get either one of them to tell me if they like my graphics," says Brandon. Dora says, "I don't have time for the bickering. I have to finish here and go do my consulting in the evenings." Harvey tells the team, "back in his day, you came to work, did what your boss said, and went home." All four remind him that things have changed since he started at the bank many years ago. Harvey is clueless as to what to do. By the end of this chapter, you will gain insight to help Harvey's team and teams like them in your organization.

Each generation has a distinct set of values, perceptions, and perspectives that influence attitudes about work. Values, perceptions, and performance are related to success in the workplace and when they collide, they can cause tension and create challenges in the workplace. Let's take a closer look at each of the four generations to gain some perspectives about their values, attitudes, and work styles.

Traditionalists

The oldest generation in today's workplace is Traditionalists, and they were born before 1946. Traditionalists grew up in a world that valued the nuclear family and saw work as a privilege due in part to the lack of work during the Great Depression, one of the signposts of this generation. Another signpost in their lives was World War II, and they can remember the celebrations that took place to honor the veterans who fought for freedom. Influential messages from their formative years included "make do or do without, stay in line, sacrifice, be heroic, [and] consider the common good" (AARP, 2007, p. 9).

Members of this generation make up the smallest percentage of today's workforce; however, their influence is quite prevalent in corporations. The idea of the corporate ladder and management chain of command is due in large part to Traditionalists. According to Quinn (2010), "traditionalists endeavor to build a lasting legacy—one of stability, order, and structure" (p. 34). The traditionalist's legacy includes a hierarchical approach to problem solving, classroom training, top-down communication style, and a military-like leadership style where no news is good news. Traditionalists

entered the workforce at a time when it was almost exclusively run by white males. Remember Harvey's comment about the male tellers at the bank in the opening scenario. It is hard for some people to believe that tellers used to be considered a prestigious job. Most people now consider it an entry-level position.

Baby Boomers

The largest and most influential population in today's workforce is the Baby Boomers generation. Baby Boomers were born between 1946 and 1964 and constitute the largest population in U.S. history. Baby Boomers grew up in a time of revolution and change; from the prosperous postwar era to the turbulent 1960s when the nation began to acknowledge diversity in race and gender, the baby boomers challenged the rules. Signposts for Baby Boomers include the Civil Rights movement, assassinations of President John F. Kennedy, Dr. Martin Luther King, Jr., and other leaders, the Vietnam War, and the Women's Liberation movement. Their parents raised them to believe that they could transform society. Influential messages from their formative years include "be anything you want to be, change the world, work well with others, [and] live up to expectations" (AARP, 2007, p. 11).

Baby Boomers entered the workforce with a positive attitude and the belief that they could make a difference. They introduced collaboration and consensus building into the workplace. They also introduced long hours and working weekends into the equation as they tried to go the extra mile and prove themselves. Ironically, many of these former flower children embraced the corporate structure and worked hard to succeed within the structure. Although they questioned the Traditionalist's autocratic style of managing, "Baby Boomers tend to be workaholics who measure their self-worth by how far they have climbed up the corporate ladder" (Quinn, 2010, p. 34). Baby Boomers were the first generation who had to learn to embrace technology to keep up. While some Traditionalists refused to embrace technology or left the workforce through retirement, Baby Boomers who wanted to succeed had to learn the latest software programs and use the latest equipment in order to progress in their jobs.

Baby Boomers tend to value teamwork as a work style and learning style. We can thank Baby Boomers for corporate meetings used to inform members of a work group or cross-functional business team. However, their leadership style tends to be unilateral. The annual review is a major means of communicating feedback for Baby Boomers. Baby Boomers also expected the 60-hour work week to bring recognition and rewards. Baby Boomers were the first generation to struggle with diversity in the workplace as a result of the Civil Rights Act of 1964. Women and people of color entered a variety of levels in corporate America during the early work lives of Baby Boomers, and Baby Boomers dealt with the struggles that resulted from the new laws and changing attitudes in the workplace.

Generation X

Generation X was born between 1965 and 1980 and is the smallest population in the U.S., representing a significant decrease in the birthrate from the previous generation. Gen Xers, as they are also known, grew up with signposts such as the global energy crisis, the Challenger disaster, and a stagnant job market. Generation X was affected by divorce and both parents working outside the home, and therefore became the first generation to be self-reliant while parents were away. This generation is known as latch-key generation. Influential messages from their formative years are "don't count on it, heroes don't exist, get real, take care of yourself, [and] always ask why" (AARP, 2007. p. 12).

Gen Xers tend to be pragmatic about work and strive for a balance between their work life and the rest of their life. Gen Xers tend to avoid defining themselves strictly by their careers and more by their broader responsibilities in life. While the Baby Boomers tended to challenge the rules of the Traditionalist, Gen Xers sought to change the rules altogether. They were the first generation to enter the workforce using computers and they are technologically savvy. Gen Xers grew up at a time of distrust for institutions, and uncertainty in the job market. Gen Xers tend to be more independent and autonomous in learning and problem solving as well as motivated and driven by the task. Gen Xers work to live, and this generation does not like to waste time because they want to get on with the rest of their lives. Gen Xers also accept diversity in the workplace, and most members of the generation expect to see women and people of color throughout an organization.

Millennials

Millennials were born between 1981 and 2000 and represent the fastest growing cohort in the workplace. This generation grew up with technology and tends to use it constantly in every aspect of life including the workplace. Signposts for Millennials include the Columbine shootings, Enron and other corporate scandals, and the September 11 attacks. Despite these tragedies, members of this generation tend to be ambitious and optimistic because they were nurtured. Unlike Gen Xers who were often left to care for themselves, the parents of Millennials tended to be highly engaged and acted as advocates for their children. Influential messages from their formative years include "you are special, leave no one behind, connect 24/7, achieve now, [and] serve your community" (AARP, 2007, p. 13).

Unlike previous generations, Millennials seek out companies that satisfy their technology and social networking needs. If a Millennial is dissatisfied at work, he or she is more likely to seek employment elsewhere by using technology to reach out to other companies that meet their wants and needs. More than any other generation,

Millennials embrace diversity and inclusion in the workplace and tend to have friends who represent all dimensions of diversity. Table 1 provides a snapshot of the four generations.

AREAS OF THE INTERGENERATIONAL GAPS

People naturally view the world based on their own values and perceptions, which are influenced by the time in which they were born; therefore, employees and managers of different generations might fail to unite in preferred tone and style as a result of differing values and perspectives. When this occurs, the work product is adversely impacted. Gallagher (2004) cautions that misunderstandings between managers and employees of different generations can lead to hurt feelings, impede production, interfere with delegating, and decrease communication effectiveness" (p. 2). According to Bernstein, Alexander & Alexander, there are seven key areas of gaps among generations in the workplace that can cause tension and stress: work style, authority and leadership, communication, technology, recognition and reward, work and family, and loyalty.

Work Style

Work style is the method by which people approach work, and they tend to vary among the four generations. Traditionalists tend to see work as an obligation from the hours of 9 to 5, and they show great dedication to their jobs. Traditionalists tend to like to learn the hard way but will attend formal classroom training when it is required. To motivate a Traditionalist, connect their actions to the overall good of the organization.

Baby Boomers believe in working hard and paying their dues. For them, work is an adventure, and Baby Boomers value dedication, quality, and teamwork. Baby Boomers favor a facilitated learning style, but they prefer training in moderation. To motivate a Baby Boomer, demonstrate that they are valued and needed by the organization.

Generation X sees work as a challenge that involves eliminating the task. Gen Xers value autonomy, flexibility, and informality. Gen Xers have changed the rules involving work; hours do not matter as long as the job is done. Gen Xers prefer solving problems independently but also include the team in the decision. Their learning style is independent, and they expect an organization to provide training in order to retain them. Gen Xers are motivated by freedom and removal of rules.

Millennials view work as fulfillment. They value feedback, advanced technology, and fun. Millennials use technology to challenge traditional work schedules and create new rules. Millennials believe in networking and feedback. Millennials prefer a collaborative approach to problem solving where decisions are made by the team. For Millennials, training is continuous and expected

Table 1. Generations at a glance

Generation	Born	Characteristics	Stereotyped As
Traditionalist	Before 1946	Hardworking; dedicated; respectful of authority; conservative	Rigid; Risk averse; Old-fashioned
Baby Boomers	1946-1964	Youthful self-identity, Optimistic; Team player, Competitive	Unrealistic; Workaholic; Self absorbed
Generation X	1965-1980	Work/life balance; Self-reliant; Pragmatic	Slackers; Selfish; Impatient; Cynical
Millennials	1980-2000	Fast-paced, Fun-seeking, Technology savvy	Short attention span; Technology dependent; Spoiled

as part of the job. They are motivated by working collaboratively with other bright people.

Authority and Leadership

When it comes to their view of authority and leadership, the generations are quite different. Traditionalists lean towards a command and control view of leadership and authority in the workplace. Traditionalists follow the rules and believe in a hierarchical problem solving strategy. They rarely question the rules and seek approval from managers who they view as authority figures.

Baby Boomers respect power and accomplishment. Unlike Traditionalists, Baby Boomers use a horizontal method of problem solving that involves a team centric approach in decision-making.

By contrast, Generation X tends to question authority. For Gen Xers, rules are flexible, and collaboration is more important than a hierarchical organizational structure. Competence is the most important characteristics in a leader to Gen Xers.

Millennials value autonomy and are less likely to seek formal leadership positions in an organization. Millennials believe in leadership by achievement not hierarchy.

Communication

Communication is the method and means by which people correspond with each other. Communication is important in any relationship including intergenerational relationships in the workplace. Therefore, it is appropriate to examine communication patterns across the generations.

Traditionalists have a formal, detail-oriented style of communication. They appreciate information to be delivered by an authority figure in print, by telephone, or face-to-face within a reasonable timeframe. They prefer communication to be delivered in appropriate amounts as needed. When communicating with a Traditionalist, use a polite and professional tone, proper grammar, and limit slang.

Baby Boomers have a semi-formal communication style, and they accept rules as created by Traditionalists. They prefer information to be delivered in digestible chunks via print, face-to-face, or by online resource as needed and whenever it is relevant to the bottom line or their reward. When communicating with a Baby Boomer, affiliation and business results may be interrelated so be more relational and make the conversation participative by asking about shared interests.

Generation Xers have an informal and sometimes irreverent communication style. They prefer to receive relevant messages, and the sender of the message should get to the point. Gen Xers prefer communication via online resources and on demand. Face-to-face meetings should occur only when absolutely necessary. They openly question the messenger and are sometimes referred to as skeptical because they do not necessarily accept the message at face value. When communicating with Gen Xers, be straightforward and get to the point. Use e-mail and voicemail to state what is required.

Millennials tend to have a fun communication style and use technology to stay linked in all the time. The message should be relevant, and it should come from a respected authority figure who communicates constantly. When communicating with Millennials, be positive and relate the message to the person's goals.

Technology

Attitudes toward technology may differ among the four generations. When Traditionalists entered the workforce, computer, the Internet, and other forms of technology we take for granted today were unimaginable. Some Traditionalists have been slower than others to adapt to technology in the workplace. As my colleague mentioned during our informal discussion, some even retired rather than learn how to use computers.

Baby Boomers were the first generation forced to learn new technologies in order to survive in the workplace. This was the generation that transitioned from the typewriter to the computer. They have had to accept technology to keep up in the workplace.

Generation X views technology as a practical way to get the job done. Most Gen Xers began using technology as young adults so they appreciate the fact that it is a useful way to save time and accomplish the task at hand. Gen Xers expect employers to stay up to date with the latest technology to make their jobs easier.

Millennials take technology a step further by embodying it. Millennials learned how to use computers and the Internet as children and expect the modern workplace to embrace their technical savvy and keep up with their need to use technology to integrate work and personal life.

Recognition and Reward

Everyone wants to be recognized and rewarded for a job well done; however, the definition of recognition and reward varies by generations. However, according to McDonald (2008), "workers from different generations respond to different sets of motivators and rewards and seek to derive varying experiences and benefits from work" (p. 62). Traditionalists prefer personal acknowledgement and compensation. Baby Boomers prefer public acknowledgement and promotions. Gen Xers seek a balance between fair and equitable compensation with ample time off as a reward. Millennials seek individual and public praise as well as opportunities to learn more.

Work and Family

When it comes to the balance and compromises the generations are willing to make for work, there are significant differences. For Traditionalists, work and family should remain separate. For Baby Boomers, work comes first. Generation X

by contrast values and seeks a balance between work and life. Millennials tend to blend the two.

Loyalty

Loyalty is an interesting concept in the workplace. Loyalty perhaps more than any other gap discussed is based on perception of cost over benefit. Traditionalists are loyal to the organization because they perceive that the organization is loyal to them. Baby Boomers are loyal to the importance and meaning of work because work is so much a part of them. Gen Xers are loyal to people and their individual career goals because they have experienced a job market that requires them to sustain themselves through corporate downsizing and reorganizations. Millennials are loyal to people involved with the project. Table 2 highlights the differences among the generations.

CLOSING GENERATIONAL GAPS

There are methodologies available that can help leaders close the generation gap. These include reflecting on commonalities that exist between the generations and appreciated the uniqueness that different generations bring to the workplace.

Reflect on Commonalities

It is important to consider the commonalities among the generations and people when attempting to leverage the potential in the workplace. Work is important in the lives of all people regardless of their generation. According to Gallagher (2004), the generations have more commonalities than differences.

Everyone needs to feel valued and believe that he or she is making a positive contribution to the workplace. People want to feel respected by everyone in the organization and feel that their job provides a valuable skill or service to the organi-

Table 2. Seven gaps in the workplace

	Traditionalists	Baby Boomers	Generation X	Millennials
1. Work style	Dedicated Individual	Driven Teams	Balanced Entrepreneurial	Ambitious Participative
2. View of Authority and Leadership	Respectful	Love/Hate	Unimpressed	Relaxed Polite
3. Communication	Formal through proper channels	Semi-formal through structured network	Casual and direct; sometimes skeptical	Casual and direct; eager to please
4. Technology	"If it ain't broke, don't fix it"	Necessary for progress	Practical tools for getting things done	What else is there?
5. Rewarded by...	A job well done	A title	Freedom	Meaningful work
6. Work/Family	Work and family are separate	Sacrifice personal life for work	Value work/life balance	Values blending personal life and family
7. Loyal to...	The company	The company and self	People	Self and professional advocate

zation. Managers should provide an environment that respects the contributions of all generations.

All people need to feel a healthy balance between their work life and outside life. Whether it is raising a family, leisure time, or both, it is unhealthy for individuals to define themselves exclusively by a job. Flexible schedules help to resolve this issue.

Individuals need to feel as though they receive fair compensation for the work performed regardless of their generation. Everyone also likes to be recognized for extra efforts or for an exceptional job. Compensation and reward programs should be structured in a way that values contributions made by everyone regardless of life stage.

It is appropriate to provide learning opportunities to all employees at all levels of the organization because career development is highly valued among people of all generations. Different generations may prefer different types of training, but training should be relevant for the employee regardless of his or her generation. Provide different training formats such as classroom, online, and interactive training to cover the variety of preferences among the generations.

All people need to be well informed to perform at optimal standards. Organizations should make an effort to provide various modes of communication that will attract members of all generations.

Appreciate the Differences

Most managers would agree that the ideal employee would embody enthusiasm and energy, share innovative ideas, display wisdom that usually comes from years of experience, demonstrate unwavering loyalty to the organization, and refuse to take no for an answer when trying to sell an idea. Leaders can create this nirvana by leveraging the strengths of all four generations in the workplace. By title, a manager can force an employee to complete a task and the employee cannot refuse a delegated task because he was not approached in his 'preferred' manner. What is likely to occur, however, is that the employee loses morale, performs at a lower standard, and spreads negative rumors about the organization. This can leave managers clueless as to why employees are not performing well.

When leaders understand the forces that have influenced each generation, they can adapt their style to more effectively structure workflow, engage employees, and foster communication. Incorporating a range of strategies that promote collaborative relationships among the generations is a business imperative. Leveraging generational strengths requires strategic commitment but the outcome is a stronger, more innovative, adaptable, and profitable organization (Ballone, 2007).

According to Salopek (2006), however, many organizations do not understand generational awareness and "wait for failure to occur before taking action" (p. 22). Leaders can harness the strengths that come from an intergenerational workforce by understanding the unique characteristics of each generation and adopting competencies that utilize the strengths and minimize the weaknesses in each generation and individual. This goes a long way in attracting and retaining workers of all generations. According to Bernstein, Alexander and Alexander, "the personality profile of an ideal employee is found not in the individual but in the multigenerational workforce on whom organizations now and in the future will be increasingly dependent on" (p. 6). This suggests that leaders need to be able to recognize the differences among the generations, embrace the differences, and find ways to help employees work in a cohesive environment. To gain a better understanding of intergenerational diversity, an organization's leaders should take the initiative to learn about intergenerational differences and help employees understand the subtle issues that can cause conflict because "the existence of four generations is a major factor in talent management" (HR Magazine, 2009).

Case Study: Recruitment and Retention

For decades Thomas Engineering recruited high achieving graduates from local university engineering programs to work for the company. The firm's rigorous processes tended to weed out employees who could not handle the job and retain employees who could keep up with the high performance expectations. Recently, the firm experienced a generation shift from Traditional-

ists and Baby Boomers to Generation Xers. The tried and true hiring practices suddenly seemed to fail. The Generation Xers were discontent regarding the rigid work schedule that would not allow flextime or options to work from home. Employees who traveled regularly complained about the requirement to travel on the weekends, which took time away from their families. Many of the engineers left the company and accepted positions in companies that provided more flexibility and autonomy.

The firm realized that they would have to make changes to attract and retain the best and brightest engineers. The company implemented a policy that allowed engineers the option to work at home as long as their projects were completed, and they were available via e-mail or cell phone. The company also provided cell phones and laptops to make the flexible scheduling more viable. No longer were employees required to travel on weekends; they were able to fly out on Monday mornings and return Thursday evening. The attrition rate has fallen 25%.

BEST PRACTICES FOR LEVERAGING INTERGENERATIONAL DIVERSITY

Intergenerational diversity is an attribute of diversity that is often overlooked. AARP (2007) offers a list of best practices that fall into six important categories: workplace culture, employee retention, benefits options, compensation, training and development, and mentoring.

Culture

Workplace culture is an important indicator of employee satisfaction. If an employee rates the company's culture positively, he or she is more likely to be satisfied with the job. Organizations should study their generational composition and facilitate conversation about generational differences. It is the subtle nuisances that when ignored can create problems in the workplace. Organizations should also create an environment where everyone is valued and employees feel free to express their opinions without reprimand. Another tip is to make sure the workforce mirrors the customer base or desired customer base. Boards, committees, and councils should also represent all generations.

Retention

Another best practice is employee retention. Managers should be rewarded for retaining their direct reports because it is more efficient to retain than to train new employees. To keep employees engaged, organizations should offer special assignments and other horizontal movements within the organization. Organizations should also develop methods to transfer and retain knowledge so there is not a knowledge deficit when employees separate from the company. Organizations should also consider phased retirements to serve two benefits: (1) help employees transition slowly into retirement and (2) help organizations to retain some of the employee's expertise for a longer period of time. Another best practice is to stay in contact with former employees by creating an alumni program to share knowledge. This also increases the potential that a former employee will rejoin the organization at some point in the future.

Benefits

Benefit options are an important part of total compensation so organizations should offer benefits that are flexible rather than a standard, one-size-fits-all benefits package. For example, a Millennial who has no dependents may have very different benefit needs than a Baby Boomer who has college-aged children and elderly parents, and the benefits plan should reflect differences.

Organization should also offer health and wellness plans to support employee well being. Examples include on-site exercise classes, massages, and nutrition classes.

Compensation

Although money is not a sole motivator for all individuals or all generations, everyone wants to receive fair pay for work performed. Compensation plans should reward performance and accomplishments not merely how many years on the job. Employees should also offer organization-matched contributions such as 401(K) and profit sharing.

Training

Training and development is important because it helps employees perform at their optimal level. Organizations should provide training in generational diversity so that employees can better understand and mitigate issues that can lead to intergenerational conflict. Both leadership and employees should be taught how to work together in a respectful and productive manner. Employees should also be given opportunities to strengthen skills and develop new ones. This is especially important to Generation X and Millennials who expect performance improvement opportunities as part of the job.

According to Ware, Craft, and Kerschenbaum (2007), "training and technology will need to fit both the learning styles and lifestyles of a multigenerational workforce" (p. 56). Baby Boomers tend to respond well to traditional classroom training and Gen Xers tend to like e-learning. Millennials expect training to be offered via wikis, blogs, or in a way, which allows it to be downloaded to a MP3 player. A blended approach to training that provides various modes helps address generational differences. Trainers and instructional designers will need both organizational support and training to help them design, develop, and deliver training that is flexible and serves these needs.

Mentoring

It is not uncommon for companies to have mentoring programs, and these programs can be used to leverage intergenerational differences in the workplace. One of the ways that Traditionalists and Baby Boomers can feel engaged and help with knowledge transfer is through mentoring younger generations. Mentoring can improve intergenerational relationships and provide a means of transferring institutional knowledge to the next generation. Some mentoring tips for Generation X include providing a casual and open environment, actively involving the protégé, providing flexibility and freedom, and providing a learning environment. Tips for mentoring Millennials include providing a structured environment that gives support and personal interactions. Technology should also be incorporated whenever possible. There is also a reverse effect to mentoring according to McDonald (2008) because, "experienced professionals are likely to find that younger workers can help them gain a new perspective on their work, and may have valuable skills to share with their mentors" (p. 67).

The Department for the Aging's *Intergenerational Work Study Program* (IWSP) in New York City, NY integrates academic study, community service, and work experience for public high school students. IWSP connects students with members of older generations by allowing students to students deliver needed services to elders in senior centers, nursing homes and in-home settings. During these supervised encounters, the seniors serve as mentors. The benefit is mutual; students gain valuable work experience and respect for elders while seniors share their life experience with younger generation.

Survey

The following statements can help your organization identify its success at creating a culture where all generations can thrive. The more statements that match your organization the more generation-friendly your organization is likely to be.

1. There is diversity among people who are successful in the organization.
2. The organization's project teams include a variety of viewpoints.
3. Employees are treated like customers.
4. The organization discusses diverse opinions.
5. Employees talk candidly about what they want from the job.
6. The organization's policies are based on what customers and employees want.
7. The organization is known for its honesty with others.
8. Employees understand the big picture as well as specific objectives and measures and feel empowered to find the best way of accomplishing them.
9. The organization expects top performance from all employees and treats them as if they can make a considerable contribution so they are motivated to do their best.
10. The organization focuses on retention every day.

COMPANIES THAT ARE HAVING SUCCESS

There are many organizations that are using methods and practices to maximize generational diversity in the workplace. This section highlights actual companies that are successfully leveraging intergenerational differences and seeing positive results.

A Lesson in Understanding Generational Diversity

In 2001, Scripps Health of San Diego, CA was experiencing high attrition from its nursing staff. The company began to take a look at how it could leverage intergenerational differences to create a stronger company and a happier staff. Managers began to receive training on how generational differences can affect the workplace. The company completed a survey to analyze the generational statistics within the workplace. One of the outcomes of the analysis was a life cycle benefits program, which replaced the one-size-fits-all benefit package. The new program provides a monetary allowance for participants to use toward a benefit that they prefer such as childcare, elder care, or to pay for a health and wellness class. The company also began a work/life balance program that includes flexible scheduling. The company implemented a generational diversity-training program that was implemented across the company.

Scripps Health Instituted a mentoring program that paired experienced nurses with less experienced nurses to share ideas, and the company also revised its new hire orientation to reflect the intergenerational workplace. In addition, the company created meaningful work opportunities and enhanced its communication strategy, and career topic planning. Scripps Health also focused on improving the physical work environment by performing an ergonomic needs analysis to ensure that work areas were properly designed to minimize physical exertion.

Training and Intergenerational Awareness

Inova Health Systems of Falls Church, VA has a diversified workforce of approximately 12,500 employees. With over $2,000,000 in tuition reimbursement, Inova recognizes the life-long learning needs of their multigenerational workers and helps create career opportunities. In addition,

Inova sponsors annual multigenerational fairs to give employees a chance to explore work/life issues ranging from eldercare to adoption resources.

Work and Job Design and Flexible Benefits

Life Works Online, the intranet service of Pitney Bowes' Life Balance Resources Program, was established to meet the varied needs of employees at different points in the "life cycle." Examples of how individuals use this intranet service include Boomers downloading college applications for their kids or Medicare forms for their parents. Generation Xers can locate childcare or summer programs for school-age children. Millennials might surf the site to find an apartment or purchase a vehicle. The online tool also allows employees to provide input on what benefits are useful to them and what additional offerings are of interest to employees. Company executives monitor the online suggestions and use these recommendations when renewing company benefits each year.

Generation-Specific Recruitment and Retention

Chevy's Fresh Mex restaurant chain includes more than 100 stores with sales beyond two million dollars per year. To recruit & retain Generation Xers managers, Chevy's hired more staff to reduce the number of hours managers are expected to work. To limit employee separation, they redesigned their training program to include career development and readily shared corporate information that clearly expresses the expectations and performance objectives that need to be attained in order to stay and advance within the company.

Scenario: Generational Conflict Revisited

Harvey (Traditionalist) and his team used the best practices and suggestions discussed in this chapter to make their workgroup more cohesive. First, the team was trained on generational differences, to get a better understanding of how different generations may have different values and perceptions. The team members now appreciate what each member brings to the table: Harvey's historical perspective, Maxine's teamwork, Gabrielle's business acumen, Dora's tenacity, and Brandon's fresh ideas. Nowadays when Harvey shares stories about Blue Bank he is mindful of colleagues of all generations and refrains from making comments about the good old days that could alienate other generations. Maxine (Baby Boomer) and Gabrielle (Gen Xer) have come to an understanding about the differences in their work styles. Maxine is even working less overtime now because Gabrielle has shown her tips and tricks to make her work more efficient. They make a great team with Maxine's knowledge of banking and Gabrielle's knowledge of training. Dora is also getting along better with the team and understands that it is necessary to relate to her Traditionalist, Baby Boomer, and Millennial team members in a more personable manner. Brandon has learned to work with his colleagues to get the feedback he needs without interrupting the workflow. Harvey notices the increase in morale and productivity as a result of taking a generation-centric approach to team work.

DISPELLING STEREOTYPES ABOUT THE GENERATIONS

- **Stereotype**: Millennials are self-centered.
  - **Fact**: Millennials care about society as a whole. According to a 2008 study by the Higher Education Research Institute at UCLA, helping others was the third highest common value held by incoming students in 2006, the highest it has been in 20 years.

- **Stereotype**: Gen Xers are not willing to work hard.
  - **Fact**: Generation X is willing to work hard. Gen Xers are task oriented and practical. They do, however, think it is unfair to work 60 hour work weeks for 40 hours pay. Speaking for my own generation, we want a life beyond work. Generation Xers are good at multitasking and using the latest technology to get the job done. Remember to give them constructive feedback to assist then in performing more efficiently. Do not micro-manage these employees and give them time to pursue other interests.

- **Stereotype**: Baby Boomers have quit learning.
  - **Fact**: According to Generation Target.com, Baby Boomers are returning to college at a record-breaking rate. They are also working longer and gaining new skills on the job. Baby Boomers like a personal approach from their bosses. They appreciate public recognition and awards for their hard work and the long hours they work. If you are working with Baby Boomers, remember to get consensus because they may be insulted if you do not include them in the decision making process.

- **Stereotype**: Older workers are not as productive as younger employees.
  - **Fact**: According to The Business Case for Workers age 50+, "employers can expect that a 50+ worker will be more productive than someone younger and with less experience" (p. 19). Remember that Traditionalists bring value to the workplace with their experience and knowledge and are diligent and reliable.

FUTURE RESEARCH DIRECTION

Generational diversity remains one of the areas that is largely overlooked, even by progressive companies. According to Jamison (2007), "the distrust and sense of competition between generations can make constructive communication and effective work partnerships difficult" (p. 15). The key to addressing this lies in a paradigm shift:

"We need to shift FROM thinking of age as a relatively innocuous dimension of diversity—one where we accept limiting and stereotypical notions as fact—TO seeing the value inherent in an organization that is truly multigenerational—that utilizes the best thinking and wisdom of all ages and leverages opportunities that can only come from cross-generational innovation and creativity" (Jamison, 2007, p. 14).

Areas for future research include but are not limited to incorporating social media in the workplace, strategies for engaging multiple generations, cross-generational partnerships in management, multi-way mentoring, and eliminating ageism.

CONCLUSION

"The challenges facing today's organizations are too complex for members of a single generation to solve alone. They need collaboration from all age groups" (Jamison, 2007, p. 16). This chapter provided perspectives on topics related to leveraging intergenerational diversity in organizations. Intergenerational conflict is often the result of different values and perspectives. Organizations that have not yet started intergenerational diversity awareness programs should assume that intergenerational obstacles exist, even if this has not been specifically stated by employees. Employees, managers, and HR Department staff must recognize potential intergenerational conflicts and move to quickly remove barriers.

Values, perceptions, and performance are inextricably linked to generational differences. An Arab proverb explains that *People resemble their times more than they resemble their parents.* Therefore, we need to better understand this dimension of diversity. The only constant in today's workplace is change. As our world continues to become more diverse, organizations that choose to leverage all facets of diversity and inclusion will maintain and gain an overwhelming advantage over organizations that do not.

REFERENCES

AARP. (2005). *The business case for workers age 50+: Planning for tomorrow's talent needs in today's competitive environment.* Washington, DC: AARP. Retrieved May 21, 2011 from http://assets.aarp.org/rgcenter/econ/workers_fifty_plus_1.pdf.

AARP. (2007). *Leading a multigenerational workforce.* Washington, DC: AARP. Retrieved May 14, 2011 from http://assets.aarp.org/www.aarp.org_/articles/money/employers/leading_multigenerational_workforce.pdf.

Ballone, C. (2007). Consulting your clients to leverage the multigenerational workforce. *Journal of Practical Consulting, 2*(1), 9-15. Retrieved May 27, 2011 from http://www.regent.edu/acad/global/publications/jpc/vol2iss1/ballone/JPCVol2Iss1_Ballone.pdf.

Bernstein, L., Alexander, D., & Alexander, B. (2011). *Generations: Harnessing the potential of the multigenerational workforce.* Retrieved May 18, 2011 from http://www.trainingsolutions.com/pdf/Generations_Perspective.pdf.

Fogg, P. (2009). When generations collide. *Education Digest, 74*(6), 25–30.

Gallagher, A. (2004). *Multigenerational diversity in U.S. workplaces: Eliminating intergenerational conflict on route to organizational success.* Retrieved May 13, 2011 from http://www.pittsburghhra.org/UserFiles/File/carrer_bank/GenerationalDiversityPHRAProject.pdf.

Higher Education Research Institute of University of Southern California. Los Angeles. (2008). *The American freshman forty-year trends: 1966 – 2006.* Retrieved May 22, 2011, from http://www.heri.ucla.edu/PDFs/pubs/briefs/40yrTrendsResearchBrief.pdf.

Jamison, C. (2007). Tapping the wisdom of the ages: Ageism and the need for multigenerational organizations. *OD Practitioner, 39*(2), 14-17. Retrieved May 27, 2011 from http://www.kjcg.com/resources/articles/documents/KJ_TappingTheWisdom_AR_051507 .pdf.

Johnson, M., & Johnson, L. (2010). *Generations, inc: From boomers to linksters – Managing the frictions between generations at work.* New York, NY: American Management Association.

Magazine, H. R. (2009). The multigenerational workforce: Opportunity for competitive success. *HRMagazine, 54*(3), 1–9.

McDonald, P. (2008). The multigenerational workforce. *Internal Auditor, 65*(5), 61–67.

Quinn, P. (2010). A multigenerational perspective on employee communications. *Risk Management, 57*(1), 32–34.

Reynolds, L., Bush, E., & Geist, R. (2008). The gen y imperative. *Communication World.* Retrieved May 11, 2011 from http://www.emerginghealthleaders.ca/resources/Reynolds-GenY.pdf.

Salopek, J. J. (2006). Leadership for a new age. *T+D, 60*(6), 22-23.

Simons, N. (2010). Leveraging generational work styles to meet business objectives. *Information & Management, 44*(1), 28–33.

University of Iowa School of Social Work – National Resource Center for Family Centered Practice. (2009). *Supervision of intergenerational dynamics.* Retrieved February 13, 2011 from http://www.uiowa.edu/~nrcfcp/training/documents/Participant%20Packet%20Intergen%20 Dynamics.pdf.

Ware, J., Craft, R., & Kerschenbaum, S. (2007). Training tomorrow's workforce. *T+D, 64*(4), 58-60.

ADDITIONAL READING

Adams, A. (2008). Redefining the rules of the generation game. *People Manage, 14*(16), 12–13.

Aker, J. M. (2009). Managing a multigenerational workforce. *Buildings, 103*(1), 46–48.

Altes, K. (2009). Social media: Young professionals effect change in the workplace. *Journal of Property Management, 74*(5), 44–47.

Atkinson, W. (2003). Managing the generation gap poses many challenges. *Hotel & Motel Management, 218*(19), 72–74.

Clark, C. (2009). Generational differences: Turning challenges into opportunities. *Journal of Property Management, 74*(5), 41–43.

Elmore, L. (2010). The workplace generation gap. *Women in Business, 62*(2), 8–11.

Giancola, F. (2006). The generation gap: more myth than reality. *Human Resource Planning, 29*(4), 32–37.

Hannam, S., & Yordi, B. (2011). *Engaging a multi-generational workforce: Practical advice for government managers.* Retrieved May 27, 2011 from http://www.businessofgovernment.org/sites/default/files/Engaging%20a%20Multi-Generational%20Workforce.pdf.

Harvey, P. (2003). Entitlement or creativity. *Industrial Engineer, 42*(7), 14.

Houlihan, A. (2008). When gen-x is in charge: How to harness the young leaderships style. *Super Vision, 69*(4), 11–13.

Lancaster, L. C., & Stillman, D. (2002). *When generations collide: Who they are, why they clash, how to solve the generational puzzle at work.* New York, NY: HarperCollins.

Le Beau, E. (2010). From conflict to 'cohorts'--When young, older workers mix. *Workforce Management, 89*(10), 12.

Leopold, R. (2007). The hows and whys of gen x benefits. *Best's Review, 108*(2), 38.

Marston, C. (2007). *Motivating the what's in it for me workforce: Manage across the generational divide and increase profits.* Hoboken, NJ: John Wiley & Sons, Inc.

McDonald, P. (2008). The multigenerational workforce. *The Internal Auditor, 65*(5), 60-63, 65, 67.

Messmer, M. (2006). Managing a multigenerational workforce. *National Public Accountant, 5*(5), 32D.

Murphy, E. F., Gibson, J. W., & Greenwood, R. A. (2010). Analyzing generational values among managers and non-managers for sustainable organizational effectiveness. *Advanced Management Journal, 75*(1), 33-43, 55.

Podmolik, M. E. (2001). Talkin' 'bout my generation. *Crain's Chicago Business, 24*(23), E18–E19.

Rossi, J. (2007). What generation gap?. *T+D, 61*(11), 10-11.

Smith-Trudeau, P. (2008). How an intergenerational workforce will affect nursing. *ARN Network, 25*(4), 8-10. Retrieved February 13, 2011 from http://www.rehabnurse.org/uploads/files/pubs/network/AprilMay08.pdf.

Thau, R. (2001). Are we heading for intergenerational war? *Across the Board, 38*(4), 70–78.

Wagner, C. G. (2009). When mentors and mentees switch roles. *The Futurist, 43*(1), 6–7.

Ware, J., Craft, R., & Kerschenbaum, S. (2007). Training tomorrow's workforce. *T+D, 61*(4), 58-60.

Wieck, L. (2007). Motivating an intergenerational workforce: Scenarios for success. *Orthopedic Nursing, 26*(6), 366–371. doi:10.1097/01. NOR.0000300948.88494.9b

Zemke, R., Raines, C., & Filipczak, B. (2000). *Generations at work: Managing the clash of veterans, boomers, xers, and nexters in your workplace.* New York, NY: American Management Association.

KEY TERMS AND DEFINITIONS

Cohort: A group of individuals in the same age range or generation.

Diversity: Differences that exist among individuals.

Generation: Cohorts who shared similar cultural experiences during their formative years.

Intergenerational/Multigenerational: Across generations.

Signposts: Major life events that influence a generation.

Stereotype: Misconceptions about a particular group based on flawed generalizations.

Values: A set of beliefs that a person or group of people hold based on perceptions and experiences.

Chapter 24
Leveraging Sexual Orientation Workforce Diversity through Identity Deployment

Apoorva Ghosh
XLRI School of Business and Human Resources, India

ABSTRACT

Disclosure decisions for lesbian and gay employees have been researched in organizational contexts. While the dilemmas associated, factors affecting, and situations encouraging or discouraging disclosure have been studied, the relatively unexplored area is how homosexuality can be strategically deployed at workplace to contest the associated stigma and bring positive social and political changes in the organizational climate. While scholars believe that remaining closeted may be the best strategy in a heterosexist and homophobic environment, studies report psychological strain, lack of authenticity, behavioral dilemmas, etc. experienced by closeted individuals, which, at minimum, lead to conflicts in daily situations of identity management and, at the peak, suicidal attempts due to perceived burdensomeness and failed belongingness. To address this dilemma in leveraging sexual orientation diversity in workplaces, this chapter deals with the framework of identity deployment offered by Bernstein (1997) to explore how homosexuality can be deployed in the workplace.

INTRODUCTION

"Since the late 1980s, FinCo, one of the oldest corporations in the Twin Cities, has had what many insiders and outsiders alike described as a strong diversity initiative as part of its corporate strategy. Yet, there was no organized GLBT group until January 1993, when a series of unrelated

events catalyzed two unacquainted employees to start the Gay, Lesbian, and Friends Network. For Dean, a gay man, it was an exercise in a team-training session, in which participants were asked to write the name of a celebrity dream date on a card; as a team-building exercise, they would make a game of matching cards to participants. Faced with the choice of coming out on the spot or hiding, he left the card blank and was later chastised for not being a team player (In later

DOI: 10.4018/978-1-4666-1812-1.ch024

educative encounters, he used this story to answer the frequent question, "What does sexual orientation have to do with work?")" (Creed & Scully, 2000, p. 399).

With the demedicalizing of homosexuality by American Psychological Association and American Psychiatric Association in 1973 (Conger, 1975; Berkley & Watt, 2006) and the shift of conservative mindsets, making one's homosexuality visible is being increasingly seen as normal and accepted. Contrary to the previous phase when homosexuality was considered psycho-pathological and social deviance and concealing was considered more appropriate (Cain, 1991) and discourses on homosexuality were limited to criminology and psychiatry (Gruszczynska, 2009), now it is finding place in the mainstream sociological, economic, and psychological discourses (Badgett, 2001). As a result, organizational scholars are also equally eager to study this diversity after realizing that much focus was on visible social identities such as age, race, and gender (Williams & O'Reilly, 1998).

Woods (1993) captures the pervasiveness of sexual orientation identity in organizations as he observes that peer group functions and gatherings demand the presence of a spouse or partner as social obligation, especially for people holding senior positions. Managing information about their sexual identity, hence, becomes important for lesbian and gay employees (Herek, 1996; Woods, 1993; Woods & Harbeck, 1991) in such situations. The interdependence of relationship and career (Browning, et al., 1991; O'Ryan & McFarland, 2010), referring to spouse or partner during regular chats and meetings in workplaces (Creed & Scully, 2000), and congruence of sexual identity between work and non-work settings (Ragins, 2004, 2008) bring sexual identity to the workplace which may be very normal, usual and obvious for heterosexual employees, but not for gay and lesbian employees (Creed & Scully, 2000). This brings sexual identity in the same league of other invisible identities like religion, occupation,

national origin, club or social group memberships, illness (Clair, et al., 2005) etc., where disclosures may not be always easy.

The belief that lesbian and gay employees constitute microscopic minority at workplace holds no good. Up to 17% of population in workplaces of USA can consist of non heterosexual workers (Powers, 1996; Gonsiorek & Weinrich, 1991). This figure is reported to be 2 to 10 percent depending on small town or metropolitan environment in another study (Michael, et al., 1994). Nonetheless, these figures still cannot reflect the true picture in organizations where closeted gay identity is reality due to fears of social exclusion, or norm due to policies in organizations like military and defense services, conservative religious institutions, and organizations that serve children (Friskopp & Silverstein, 1995; Herek, et al., 1996). Though the neglect of studying homosexuality in organizations is felt (Gonsiorek & Weinrich, 1991; Croteau, 1996; Ragins & Wiethoff, 2005), organizational scholars have still made sexual orientation an area ripe for research especially in the last two decades by dealing with issues like strategies of identity management in workplaces (Clair, et al., 2005; Creed & Scully, 2000; Button, 2004; Chrobot-Mason, et al., 2001, etc.), workplace benefits for lesbian and gay employees (Raeburn, 2004; Day & Greene, 2008), interdependence of work and same-sex relationship (O'Ryan & McFarland, 2010), LGB[1] leadership and organizational citizenship behavior (Fasinger, et al., 2010; Brenner, et al., 2010), role of legal environment (Beatty & Kirby, 2006; Berkley & Watt, 2006; Herek, 1990), workplace disclosures (Ragins, et al., 2007; Griffith & Hebl, 2002; Day & Schoenrade, 1997), etc.

However, at the same time, homosexuality does not escape from the stigma associated with invisible identities (Goffman, 1963) and disclosure decisions still remain risky, calculative and planned (Ragins, 2004). Thus, management of homosexuality has received considerable scholarly attention in recent times. A review of these identity management strategies reveal that they run on a continuum from being closeted across work and life settings to openly explicit, depending on the work environment and peer attitudes (Woods & Harbeck, 1991; Griffin, 1992; Woods, 1993; Herek, 1996; Ragins, 2004, 2008; Button, 2004; Clair, et al., 2005). However, these identity management strategies do not account for the possibility of deploying identity to create inclusive mindsets towards homosexuality and making workplace equal for lesbian and gay employees. Hence, this chapter explores the framework for deploying homosexuality (Bernstein, 1997) by lesbian and gay employees to leverage sexual orientation diversity at workplaces.

IDENTITY DEPLOYMENT: THEORETICAL BACKGROUND

Bernstein's (1997) framework of identity deployment is focused on contesting the stigma associated with a collective identity, with particular emphasis on homosexuality. Identity deployment receives intellectual inputs from the explanation of social movements by *Resource Mobilization theory* and *Political Opportunity theory*. Social movement refers to "collective challenges [to elites, authorities, other groups, or cultural codes] by people with common purposes and solidarity in sustained interactions with elites, opponents, and authorities" (Tarrow, 1994). Bernstein (1997) adds insights from the *New Social Movement theory* to arrive at her conceptual framework.

Resource Mobilization Theory explains the interaction of "the variety of resources that must be mobilized, the linkages of social movements to other groups, the dependence of movements upon external support for success and the tactics used by authorities to control or incorporate movements" (McCarthy & Zald, 1977, p. 133). It argues that the activists of social movement make rational strategic decisions to mobilize a constituency to achieve pre-determined goals of a movement. For

this, they mobilize resources using the pre-existing organizational structures (McCarthy & Zald, 1977, Zald & McCarthy, 1988). While deprivation and the resulting grievance are key reasons to mobilize, they are not sufficient in doing so when the movement lacks sufficient resources (Wilkening, 2005; Jenkins, 1983).

Though Resource Mobilization theory offers initial insight on the ways and means to mobilize, it largely ignores the political contexts in which the social movements operate (Mayer, 1991). McAdam et al. (1996) believe that social movements are "shaped by the broader set of political constraints and opportunities unique to the national context in which they are embedded" (p. 3). Political Opportunity theorists believe that the political structures and events have major bearing upon the course of social movement. Activists do not decide upon the strategies and goal without assessing the constraints and opportunities imposed by the political environment. In other words, politically achievable goals are adopted. Efforts for mobilizing are hurt when the activists are denied access or when the immediate demands of the social movement are met by the ruling elite. However, when the polity is fragmented and makes itself open to the movement demands, mobilization is strongest. This fragmentation leads to political opportunities and activists make rational and strategic decisions on the modus of collective mobilization to achieve the success of movement (reviews by Cortese, 2004; Gruszczynska, 2009). The "changing political opportunity, meaningful access to power and influential allies and significant splits in the ruling alignment or cleavages among the elite" boost the efforts of collective mobilization for a movement (Tarrow, 1994, p. 18).

Though these two frameworks explain the formulation of goals and strategy for political mobilization, they are criticized for ignoring the cultural mobilization in a social movement (Mayer, 1991; Bevington & Dixon, 2005). Bernstein (1997) observes that these theories overemphasize strategy as instrument for change in policy structure and 'access to the structure of political bargaining' (p. 534) as the main goals of collective mobilization. This leaves the theorists unable to explain the movements that aim to challenge the mainstream culture, contest the dominant values, beliefs and norms about social identities, and at times 'working at cross purposes to achieving policy change' (p. 534). Pichardo (1997) emphasizes that the New Social Movement (NSM) theory fills this gap by explaining the aspects like culture, identity, and role of civic sphere in social movements. At macro level, NSM explains the role of culture in social movements, whereas at micro level, it is concerned with how identity and personal behavior shape up the movements. The NSM paradigm offers credence to the civic sphere as an equally important arena of social movements as the economic and political spheres. Buechler (1995) observes that unlike the social movements of industrial period which attracted the working class as major activists, the agendas of NSMs are carried by the middle class. The NSM paradigm accommodates in its theoretical framework new forms of collective action that arise from the shift of industrial to post-industrial society, are centered round culture, identity (women and minority groups), environment, peace and youth groups, and have, inter alia, apolitical goals (Boggs, 1986; Olofsson, 1988).

Social identity refers to 'the portion of an individual's self concept which derives from his/her knowledge of membership in a social group or groups' (Tajfel, 1978; quoted by Schneider, 1993, p. 121). Viewing from NSM perspective, Bernstein (1997) observes that "identity movements seek to transform dominant cultural patterns, or gain recognition for new social identities, by employing expressive strategies" (p. 533) that create new organizational forms aiming towards participation and empowerment of stigmatized minority identities like gays and lesbians. Bernstein's framework of identity deployment centers round the mobilization of collective identity as means of empowering a constituency to achieve

the identity goals using strategic actions. Collective identity refers to "an individual's cognitive, moral, and emotional connection with a broader community, category, practice, or institution" (Polletta & Jasper, 2001, p. 285). Bernstein's identity deployment framework is based on three analytic dimensions of identity: identity for empowerment, identity as goal, and identity as strategy (Table 1). These are explained in the next section.

The Three Analytic Dimensions of Identity

Identity for empowerment. Bernstein (1997) defines *identity for empowerment* "to mean the creation of collective identity and the feeling that political action is feasible" (p. 536). It is the first step towards initiating activism and paving way towards future action by creating and mobilizing a constituency. This dimension also empowers the activists to assume legitimate political standing in the movement by reinforcing their identity. Leitz (2011) explains how the oppositional identities of peace movement against the pro-Iraq war frames in USA legitimized their standing as the advocates of peace. The activists, being military veterans, ex-soldiers, and military families, asserted their insider position on the war that allowed them to be heard by people who may choose to otherwise ignore the stereotyped traditional peace activists.

Identity as goal. Bernstein explains that *Identity as goal* seeks to attain the broad outcomes of the movement, such as to contest the stigmatization of an identity by challenging the dominant cultural norms and values. The aim is to bring the individuals holding this identity from the fringes of social milieu to the mainstream and achieve belongingness and respect for what they are. The goal could also be to deconstruct restrictive social categories of identities like "man," "woman," "gay," "straight," "black," or "white." that create barriers of 'us' versus 'them' and restrict access to social structures and resources. The goal could also be the recognition for emerging identities, such as

Table 1. The three analytic dimensions of 'identity'

Dimension	Description
Identity for empowerment	Activists must draw on an existing identity or construct a new collective identity in order to create and mobilize a constituency. The particular identity chosen will have implications for future activism.
Identity as goal	Activists may challenge stigmatized identities, seek recognition for new identities, or deconstruct restrictive social categories as goals of collective action.
Identity as strategy	Identities may be deployed strategically as a form of collective action. *Identity deployment* is defined as expressing identity such that the terrain of conflict becomes the individual person so that the values, categories, and practices of individuals become subject to debate. *Identity for critique* confronts the values, categories, and practice of the dominant culture. *Identity for education* challenges the dominant culture's perception of the minority or is used strategically to gain legitimacy by playing on uncontroversial themes.

(Source: Bernstein, 1997, p. 537)

mixed races (Bernstein & Cruz, 2009), alternate cultural forms like the New Left organizations of the 1960s (Bernstein, 1997), and new categories such as specialist versus generalist identities (Swaminathan, 2001).

Identity as strategy. Bernstein (1997) believes that "cultural resources also have an external, strategic dimension" (Williams, 1995, p. 125). She defines identity deployment as "expressing identity such that the terrain of conflict becomes the individual person so that the values, categories, and practices of individuals become subject to debate" (Bernstein, 1997, pp. 537-538). By deploying identity, activists make their identity visible in a way that seeks to contest its attributed stigma for the purposes of institutional change (Taylor & Raeburn, 1995) or "transform mainstream culture, its categories and values (and perhaps by extension its policies and structures), by providing alternative organizational forms" (Bernstein, 1997, p. 538).

The strategic action adopted to realize the broad cultural goals of collective identity depends on how the activists wish to deploy their identity. Bernstein explains that the strategy for identity deployment could be to either celebrate or suppress the differences from mainstream culture. She expresses the possibility of deploying identity both collectively as well as individually along a continuum from critique to education by 'identity for critique' and 'identity for education.' *Identity*

for critique 'confronts the values, categories, and practices of the dominant culture' (p. 538). The efforts concentrate on contesting the existing structural forms, norms, and values created by dominant culture by making visible the differences of the alternate culture from the dominant culture. *Identity for education* "challenges the dominant culture's perception of the minority or is used strategically to gain legitimacy by playing on uncontroversial themes" (p. 538). In other words, without challenging the morality, values and beliefs of the dominant culture, 'identity for education' attempts to change the popular notions about the stigmatized identity by emphasizing oneness and similarity with the dominant culture.

ORGANIZATIONAL VIEW OF IDENTITY DEPLOYMENT: NORMALIZING AND DIFFERENTIATING STRATEGIES

Creed and Scully (2000) argue that identity deployment by lesbian and gay employees is a form of 'micromobilization' and is capable of bringing organizational change. Identity deployment in workplace is manifested through strategic actions aimed towards changing the organizational mindsets towards homosexuality. Equal Treatment for lesbian and gay employees in matters of hiring, compensation, benefits, career progression, and termination could be one goal of deploying homosexuality. Equality is also sought in matters of corporate recognition of same-sex partnership and adopting gay-inclusive policies and practices, including non-discrimination policies like domestic partner and healthcare benefits (Raeburn, 2004, Köllen, 2007; HRC, 2008). At the same time, making workplaces inclusive for lesbian and gay employees by preventing any disparate treatment due to heterosexism and homophobic behaviors could be another goal (Ragins, 2004; Collela & Dipboye, 2005).

Identity deployment is understood as strategic action of suppressing or celebrating differences with the dominant culture to achieve broad cultural and political goals for stigmatized identity group. The identity deployment strategies-identity for education and identity for critique are explored in the workplace context of lesbian and gay employees. Clair et al. (2005) explain these two mechanisms through normalizing and differentiating tactics at workplace to make the identity visible. Using differentiating tactics, lesbian and gay employees emphasize differences from the heterosexual workforce in matters like gender of their partners, associated stigma with their sexual identity and adverse impact due to institutional discrimination, which heterosexual employees do not have to face. Thus, they "reveal differences in ways that challenge perceptions, values, practices, and perspectives of the dominant group or organizational culture vis-a-vis stigmatized others' (Clair, et al., 2005, p. 84) and demand equitable benefits such as domestic partner benefits including their dependent partner's health insurance and corporate recognition of same-sex partnership, which are denied so far because of these 'differences.'

Normalizing is the attempt to establish, pretend, and maintain to be living as "normal" as others, and denying any fundamental difference from others due to the alternate identity. This could be done by assimilating into the local organizational culture and making homosexuality visible as nor-

mally as done by the heterosexual counterparts in day-to-day conversations and information sharing (Clair, et al., 2005). The employees contest the stigma associated with their homosexuality by emphasizing *homonormativity,* a term coined by Duggan (2003) to emphasize that heterosexual ideals and constructs could be assimilated in the gay identity as well. Normalizing tactics can thus help in making workplaces more inclusive.

Because these two forms of tactics practically mean strategic action by employees (Clair, et al., 2005), I use the terms normalizing and differentiating strategies henceforth. In the following section, I discuss four strategies that are seen as largely normalizing-claiming encounters, educative encounters, discretion strategy and teaming up, and three differentiating strategies-advocacy encounters, legal encounters, and immersion-emersion attitudes. Then, I discuss 'mixed model of identity deployment' (Bernstein, 1997; Bernstein & Olsen, 2009), wherein employees deploy normalizing and differentiating strategies alternately or simultaneously.

Claiming Encounters

Woods (1993) observes that in high profile and senior positions, the presence of spouse or partner is expected in the social gatherings and peer group functions. Similarly, a casual mention of one's partner or spouse during routine conversations or displaying family pictures on computer desktop at workplace is common. Even in organizations that do not encourage bringing family obligations in casual encounters, employees may not really fear using a gendered name for their partners (Creed & Scully, 2000). These are some of the numerous occasions when employees accept their heterosexuality. Accepting heterosexuality may not be seen a very big event, given that the normalcy associated with it downplays the significance associated with it. However, for lesbian and gay employees, this could be an event, or more precisely an 'encounter.' Creed and Scully (2000, p.

392) define encounter as *"pivotal moments in a larger process whereby beliefs about and attitudes toward an identity are mediated and altered and discriminatory workplace policies and practices are challenged and, in some cases, changed."* When tacit or direct disclosures of their sexual identity is done by lesbian and gay employees without thought on daily basis, similar to their heterosexual counterparts, Creed and Scully (2000) term these as claiming encounters. These encounters are the 'first step in staking a claim to the legitimate social standing' (p. 397) because they associate normalcy with homosexuality and assert its social recognition equally important as the heterosexual ways of life.

Creed and Scully (2000) observe the dynamics associated with claiming encounters. Lesbian and gay employees may take cautious steps by claiming initially to their trusted peers to receive their feedback on the suitability of doing so with rest of the peers. Organizational climate and the perceived heterosexist and homophobic reactions play major moderating role in this process. Pfeffer (1981) observes that in organizations where diversity is promoted, employees may feel safer to claim their identity to the senior diversity managers or officers since they are more sensitized to such issues. Such managers are likely to be more appreciative to such honesty and may take symbolic actions to include them with the mainstream on the issue of sexual orientation.

Though claiming encounters involve the process of 'coming out' of the closet, the two are not exactly the same. While 'coming out' is an individual process of revealing, claiming encounters makes the person "consciously or accidentally… political in order to initiate a challenge to the social status quo" (Creed & Scully, 2000, p. 399). This is the reason why claiming encounter is seen as identity deployment and not simply disclosure at workplace.

Educative Encounters

Lesbian and gay employees often encounter heterosexism in organizations that result from the comparison of a) their virtual stigmatized social identity existing as mental representation or cognitive schemata in the minds of heterosexual peers and b) the actual social identity for which equal treatment policies are fostered (Stone, et al., 1992, p. 391). Bernstein (1997) finds that activists try to change the mainstream perceptions about the stigmatized identity and educate the legislators and public to dispel the associated myths and stereotypes. To adopt a similar inclusive approach in organizations, Creed and Scully (2000) explain the deployment of homosexuality through education by educative encounters. Educative encounters are the face-to-face meetings for addressing the various contentions of the peers and employer. Educative encounters invite questions, which offer the lesbian and gay employees to explain realities about their lives, which are largely unknown to their heterosexual peers and employers.

In their qualitative study, Creed and Scully (2000) offer examples of how educative encounters are deployed in organizations. In their study of FinCo, they find that the first official act of the lesbian and gay employee group after its formation was placing a request for extending partner benefits to them. This was turned down by Tom, a heterosexual white man and the Senior Vice President, HR, at the very first instance. However, Maria, the lead representative of the group was successful in scheduling a luncheon meeting to have an initial discussion. During this meeting, Tom was replied to all his questions. After this encounter, explaining the transformation and the shift of mindset, Tom says:

"It was apparent that this is an issue that I needed to pay attention to. I didn't understand it. . . . I think the breakthrough was, "How is it that I can see the needs of all these other groups?" On the gay and lesbian side of the equation, [it was],

"This is a personal issue." That was part of the learning. From there [Maria, a lesbian employee activist] was very instrumental and very helpful in walking me through that. I asked a lot of questions, and she was very blunt and candid in explaining things" (p. 399).

This example shows that when the senior management is ready to hear issues with an open mind, the heterosexist views can be contested. Educative encounter from outsiders can sometimes be more effective than efforts from the insider lesbian and gay employees. Addressing the issue with authentic accounts from one's own life can transform the views of senior management. Creed and Scully (2000) recount another example of such an encounter. The case of Karen Thompson, who fought an eight-year legal battle with her in-laws to take care of her partner who was seriously injured in a car accident (Thompson & Andrzejewski, 1988), was invited by a newly form lesbian and gay employee group to deliver a talk on her experiences. Though many senior executives declined to attend, the Executive Vice President, HR, Cathy accepted the invitation. After listening to the talk, explaining her transformation, Cathy said that she made an attempt to view herself in Karen's place. The pain, anxiety, and frustration experienced in such situations are quite the same as in a heterosexual relationship. Hence, the issue is to recognize the equal rights of lesbian and gay individuals and not to evaluate the moral, religious, and cultural sanctity of same-sex relationships. Cathy, thus, championed the cause of domestic partner benefits for lesbian and gay employees, both inside and outside her organization, and actively advocated in the senior management meeting, since she felt so strongly about it.

Educative encounters can also be deployed collectively through tactical repertoires that contest the stigma associated with the identity by challenging the mainstream cultural values, beliefs and sanctions (Taylor, et al., 2009). Gay employee groups organize educative events that invite employees across the organization and sensitize them about the need to be inclusive towards diversity (Raeburn, 2004). Of course, these events are likely to succeed when a favorable environment is created to conduct them. The "GLUE" (Gay and Lesbian United Employees) association of a telecommunication company in Raeburn's study developed such an initiative of establishing personal connection with heterosexual peers so that gay and lesbian issues were "brought home" rather than marginalizing or alienating them. To operationalize this philosophy, they compiled a "GLUE Family Album" that contained, in the words of the national co-president, "stories of our gay and lesbian lives." It contained "a collection of short autobiographical sketches of members, primarily those in long-term committed relationships, to help overcome society's stereotypes" (p. 194). The album was circulated to everyone, including the top executives of the organization. This initiative won their as well as coworkers' support towards inclusion of lesbian and gay employees.

Discretion Strategy

Though keeping homosexuality in the closet may be harmful for such employees psychologically (Griffith & Hebl, 2002) as well for their workplace productivity (Brenner, et al., 2010; Day & Schoenrade, 1997), remaining so and opting for counterfeiting their identity or simply avoiding such matters may still be preferred by them given the possibilities of heterosexist and homophobic reactions (Chrobot-Mason, et al., 2001). However, even in such situations, homosexuality can be deployed through *discretion strategy*. Discretion here does not mean being selective in disclosing personal information (Herek, 1996), nor does it mean choosing conversations, activities, or contexts that selectively hide personal information (Clair, et al., 2005). Discretion strategy can be understood as to postpone the decision of making the identity visible and remaining alert in choosing the right time to do so which impacts positively on the coworkers and makes the workplace inclusive for lesbian and gay employees. Discretion, thus, means to *choose the right time to make the identity visible*, and not choosing the information, conversation, activities, and contexts to disclose.

Contrary to earlier times when homosexuality was seen as socio-pathological deviance and a subject matter of psychiatry and criminology (Gruszczynska, 2009), disclosure or coming out of closet is now being increasingly seen as normal and accepted mainly because of the demedicalization of homosexuality by APA in 1973 (Conger, 1975). Thus after this period more number of people came out of closet (Cain, 1991). It can be argued that lesbian and gay individuals sensed it to be the right time to make their identity visible when medical science contested the stigmatized view of their sexual identity.

In her study of homosexuality in American Corporate, Raeburn (2004) finds that a closeted lesbian employee, who was also an assistant to the CEO of a firm established in scientific and photographic industry, joined the gay employee network after three years of its formation. The group was overwhelmed with the inclusion of this high profile member, but was more surprised when she came out of her closet in a high profile educative event organized by this group, which had among other senior executives, her own boss too. The time chosen by her to narrate the pain, frustration, anxiety and anger in her journey of being queer was, indeed, politically and strategically correct. This push in the presence of senior management gave serious impetus to lesbian and gay inclusive policies in the organization.

Making identity visible at the right time not only saves oneself from political repercussions, but can also impact profoundly on the lesbian and gay movement. In their study of Sociologist's lesbian and gay caucus in American academia, Taylor and

Raeburn (1995) came across a gay sociologist who kept his homosexuality at a very low profile until he was tenured. After getting the tenure, he went back to television events and gay meetings to participate in the lesbian and gay movement. While making identity visible at such times not only saves a person in terms of career prospects, the movement also benefits from high socio-educational status achieved by such individuals.

Teaming Up

The influence of partner could be significant in deploying identity at workplace. This area, though less researched, has significant implications. Partner's influence in disclosure decisions is observed by Rostosky and Riggle (2002), who, in a study of 118 lesbian and gay couples, found that individuals were more likely to disclose at work when their partner worked at an organization that had gay-friendly environment. However, in wake of perceived low peer support, how dual career gay couples combat the initial hesitation and apprehension towards the identity deployment process? In such scenarios, O'Ryan and McFarland (2010), from their qualitative study of dual career gay couples, suggest the strategy of *"shifting from marginalization to consolidation and integration."* I term this strategy, in short, as *teaming up*. Starting from marginalization and usually avoiding such situations that make the disclosure likely, the same-sex partners initially kept their relationship separate from work in the process of securing their roles in the workplace. The next phase of *teaming up* was a stage when they maintained their work identities while solidifying their relationship. This involved bringing personal and work world together, overcoming anxiety, frustration, and discomfort during microencounters and at the same time, being strong and protective towards each other. The last phase, *"consolidation and integration"* involved overcoming barriers in the workplace and presenting their relationship more authentically and gaining social acceptability in official gatherings and informal encounters. Identity deployment could thus be a team activity in the workplace garnering social support through integration with the coworkers in a phased process.

Advocacy Encounters

Goffman (1961) argues that encounters a) are gatherings having single focus, b) involve "heightened awareness of the mutual relevance of each others' acts," and c) have a clear beginning and end, often marked by ritual or ceremonial expressions (quoted in Creed & Scully, 2000, p. 393; and Gamson, et al., 1982, p. 10). Gamson et al. (1982), offering input to the resource mobilization theory, observe that encounters are face-to-face interactions by which activists 'micromobilize' themselves and alter the course of long-term mobilization. In organizational contexts, Creed and Scully (2000) refer to the face-to-face encounter with policy makers as advocacy targets to claim equal treatment in the organization as advocacy encounter. They argue that an advocacy encounter is a process of micromobilization that contests organizational injustice to the employees based on their sexual orientation and claims remedy. It seeks to mitigate the discriminatory organizational policies and practices, like keeping the benefits enjoyed by the heterosexual coworkers inaccessible to the lesbian and gay employees, and social discrimination.

Advocacy encounters can emanate from the voice of gay employee groups which advocate for official corporate recognition of same sex partnerships, and making the policies and practices gay inclusive, such as extending domestic-partner benefits to lesbian and gay employees and equal treatment in hiring and career progression (Raeburn, 2004). Creed and Scully (2000) believe that successful advocacies are those in which employees take advantage of their insider status and don't make the issue radical and contentious.

Raeburn's discussion on shareholder activism in her study (2004) offers an illustration to this. In AT&T, when a resolution to remove the protection to lesbian and gay employees from diversity policy was moved by the conservative group in May 2001, the lesbian and gay employee group made the board of director as their advocacy target. Employing their persuasive tactics, it convinced the board to urge the shareholders to vote against the resolution. This advocacy encounter was successful and the board influenced the majority shareholders to vote against the resolution.

However, all said, advocacy encounters require imaginative leadership and collective efficacy to succeed. The extent of openness of the organization and gay friendliness of the industry in which the firm is operating (Raeburn, 2004) plays crucial role in the success of advocacy encounters. Creed and Scully (2000) observe that advocacy encounters may also not succeed when the employee activists are not assertive enough to put their contentions or when the senior executives are not willing to take the responsibility of change. Also, advocacy encounters may not work where organizations clearly express their unwillingness to take steps beyond an extent, such as including sexual orientation in diversity policy, but unwilling to consider the demand of domestic partner benefits (Creed & Scully (2000).

Legal Encounters

The legal premises addressing sexual orientation discrimination are different across countries and states. A mixed instance occurs in USA where sexual orientation is not a federally protected identity in employment under Title VII of Civil Rights Act (CRA), 1963 (Berkley & Watt, 2006). However under state laws, it is protected in 21 states and district counties of USA[2] (HRC, 2011).

Employees have deployed their homosexuality by making legal claims against injustice meted in their workplaces. Fitzpatrik (2007) offers a review of cases in UK where sexual orientation identity is protected in employment relations since 2003 (Aransheibani, et al., 2007). In *Mr David John Hubble v Mr Brian Brooks* (Case No 1600381/05 (4902/90) July 2005) case, the tribunal upheld that the gay couple could not be refused employment only on the grounds of their sexual orientation. In another case (*Mr P Lewis v HSBC Bank Plc* (EAT/0364/06/RN) (Clark J) 19 December 2006), the tribunal sensitized the employer that the staff must receive diversity training to avoid any kind of homophobic or heterosexist treatment in disciplinary proceedings. Further, any discriminatory treatment based on sexual orientation should not be tolerated. In *Mr E Ho v University of Manchester* (Case No. 2401255/05 (4901/103) July 2005) case, the court upheld that sexual orientation regulations also cover students at institutes of higher education. And finally, sexual orientation protection is not only confined to the plaintiff's own sexual orientation, but also includes his/ her professional endeavors related to homosexuality, such as research on gays and lesbian sexualities (*Brian Lacey v The University of Ulster and Paul Davidson* (Case Ref: 970/05, February 2007).

Deploying identity through legal encounters could be an uphill task where explicit legal protection is absent. In the states and district counties of USA where sexual identity is not protected, plaintiffs have claimed justice by seeking remedy towards discrimination against their gender identity and not sexual orientation, taking benefit from 'sex' as a protected identity under Title VII of CRA. (e.g. *MGM Grand Hotel v. Rene*, No. 02-970 (March, 2003), cited in Berkley & Watt, 2006). In these cases, courts have upheld decisions in favor of lesbian and gay employees considering that discrimination was due to not behaving according to the socially accepted gender norms, and thus the cases were within the ambit of Title VII. However, such cases may create bad precedents for deployment of homosexuality in two ways: one, the stereotyping approach adopted by the courts is inconsistent with identity deployment

strategies like advocacy and educative encounters. Second, plaintiffs who rely on such claims create bad precedents for lesbian and gay employees who face discrimination only because of their sexual orientation and not for disobeying gender stereotypes (Bible, 2001, 2002). Hence, the continual efforts are ongoing since over three and a half decades to include sexual orientation in Title VII protection, and the amendment has faced numerous legislative and political hurdles so far (Sung, 2011), but given the return of Democrats, who are perceived to be more liberal than Republicans in matters of lesbian and gay issues (Cortese, 2004), the chances of success are now brighter.

Immersion-Emersion Attitudes

Cross's (1971, 1978) model of nigrescence is widely used and referred model of racial identity development in people of African origin. Because non-white race and homosexuality both attract societal stigmas (e.g. Ragins, 2004), Walters and Simoni (1991) borrowed this model in study of sexual identity development in lesbian and gay individuals and found empirically that its four stages pre-encounter, encounter, immersion-emersion attitudes and internalization represent homosexuality development process as well.

In case of lesbian and gay individuals, immersion-emersion attitudes make them fascinated and involved towards the gay culture and they celebrate their differences from the larger heterosexual majority. At the same time, these are also found to help in integrating the lesbian and gay employees with their heterosexual counterparts (Walters & Simoni, 1991; Button, 2001). Immersion-emersion attitudes are manifested by participation in gay pride march, celebrating gay pride month at workplace and involvement in "National Coming-out day" during the month of October every year. Such participations are likely to impact on the organizational mindsets towards gay issues. It is reported that organizations where gay employee groups actively participate in the celebration of their identity in these events, there is far more equitable working environment in terms of domestic partner benefits and corporate recognition of same-sex partnerships compared to those where such participations are minimal (Raeburn, 2004).

MIXED MODEL OF IDENTITY DEPLOYMENT

Bernstein (1997; Olsen, 2009) argues that activists may follow a mixed model of identity deployment or mixed identity presentation (Dugan, 2008) wherein they emphasize both sameness and differences. Activists may deploy identity for critique and identity for education simultaneously or alternately to achieve the identity goals. This means that activists may shift their course of strategy over a period of time or they can use both strategies at the same time.

Alternate Mixed Model of Identity Deployment

In cases where activists shift their strategies with course of time, Bernstein and Olsen (2009) argue that such moves depend on the level of political access of the activists and changing political environment. When activists' political access is delegitimized, identity for critique is the strategy mostly resorted to, and when otherwise, identity for education is used to suppress the glorification of contentious differences with the broader culture. Bernstein (2011) observes that with the coming of Republican President Ronald Reagan in 1980 with support from Religious Rights Wing, and the reduced access to federal agencies compared to that at the time of Democratic President Jimmy Carter, the lesbian and gay movement's strategies and goals saw drastic shift. With the proliferation of attempts to repeal the sexual orientation clauses from antidiscrimination ordinances, the mobilization now shifted its focus from identity

for education to gaining political legitimacy by identity for critique. Drawing parallel to the workplace situations, it can be expected that normalizing strategies are most likely to be resorted by gay employee groups when they have access to the senior management positions or have ally relationships with people manning such positions. On the other hand, when political equations change resulting in hostile workplaces, differentiating strategies are most likely to be used.

Bernstein and Olsen (2009) argue that the shift in identity deployment strategy may also result from internal efforts by the organizational members. Gilmore and Kaminsky's (2007) study of National Organization for Women (NOW) explains the hostility of its members towards lesbian feminists in the organization. When the demand for their inclusivity gained momentum, moving from differentiating approach, NOW focused on mitigating the differences between the two groups (lesbian and non-lesbian feminists). It built a new organizational identity that stressed more on the oneness of these groups by merging these two identities to join these erstwhile separate groups.

Bernstein's discussion of mixed model of identity deployment explains the shift of strategy with course of time. Cortese (2004), based on his field research in USA, argues that shift of strategy may vary, instead with time, depending on the "distinct political environments contingent upon its geographical location" (p. 30). He finds that SAGA (Straight and Gay Alliance), a gay organization founded on ally relationships with heterosexuals, deployed identity for education in geographical areas that have gay friendly legislations, conducive political environment to foster gay inclusive policies (mostly where democrats are ruling or have occupied political offices) and have liberal mindsets towards same-sex unions. He observes that in these areas, SAGA's main focus is towards broadening the fundraising base from the heterosexual allies. However, in conservative areas, SAGA has to expend most of its energy for the visibility of heterosexual allies to gain political legitimacy for gay inclusive policies and legislation. Thus, in such areas, identity for critique is the widely used strategy.

Simultaneous Mixed Model of Identity Deployment

Though normalizing and differentiating strategies may be significantly different means to make identity visible, their contributions may be complimentary. Dugan (2008) observes that mixed identity presentation strategies based on simultaneous deployment of sameness and differences may work depending on the audience and venue of deployment. She explains how Christian Rights Movement achieved its identity goals against the gay rights movement in Cincinnati during 1992-93 by mixed identity deployment. When the mayor of Cincinnati included homosexuality as protected identity in the Human Rights ordinance in 1992, the right wing Christian Rights group initiated a protest campaign "Issue 3" in which they brought visibility to the gay identity in two ways. First, they emphasized their difference from the larger heterosexual population. They argued that the amendment was a reality because the gay wing is far more influential and politically well resourced and connected than the rest. Second, emphasizing their similarity with the rest, they advocated that the lesbian and gay individuals are really not a minority group that needs protection. By seeking to be a protected group, they are being treated 'specially' and not 'equally.' This active campaign of both celebrating and suppressing the differences reached to a large population, including the African Americans who expressed their oneness with Issue 3. On the other end, the gay rights wing, responding to this campaign, resorted to the more traditional way of reacting by condemning the proponents of Issue 3 as villains advocating discrimination in legislation. This static approach was cited the main reason for not being able to stop the anti-gay ballot initiative of 1993.

Just the way Christian rights group deployed mixed identity to achieve its goals, an active campaign by lesbian and gay employees at the workplace which ascends above the rhetoric of discrimination against their sexual identity by celebrating and suppressing differences simultaneously can achieve diversity management goals like equality and inclusion at the same time. Lesbian and gay employees have partners, family, and way of living similar to their heterosexual peers. They too like to enjoy holidays and being invited to the corporate social gatherings and peer group functions with their partners. The need for belongingness with their partnered status is same as for any heterosexual couple. Most of them are visibly indistinguishable from their heterosexual peers and the gender stereotypes about lesbians and gays really do not fit many of them (Creed & Scully, 2000). Hence, they are very much like others and deserve inclusion in the social network of peers. At the same time, they are different because their partners are of the same sex. Hence, local and state laws which do not approve same-sex relationships hurdle the normal way of living as compared to their heterosexual counterparts. When the workplace also does not recognize the same, they cannot take care of their partners when they are ill or injured since there is no ground to seek a leave of absence. Similarly, they also do not have access to health insurance for their dependent partners, nor can they enjoy tax benefits that married or partnered heterosexual employees are entitled to. Thus, because of these differences, lesbian and gay employees often advocate for the corporate recognition of their same-sex union (Köllen, 2007) which the heterosexual employees do not have to. Hence, by making these differences visible, gay employee networks often advocate for equal treatment policies. Owing to these differences, they also argue for non-discrimination in hiring, career progression, compensation, termination of employment, and redressal of such grievances. Otherwise, gay employees may face prejudiced treatment from superiors who have heterosexist and homophobic mindsets (cf. Ragins, 2004).

CONCLUSION AND FURTHER SCOPE

This chapter extends the identity deployment framework to organizations from the realm of sociological discourses on identity movement. I do this by acknowledging previous writings, which have wholly or partially done so (e.g. Taylor & Raeburn, 1995; Creed & Scully, 2000; Raeburn, 2004; Clair, et al., 2005; Bernstein & Olsen, 2009)

This chapter explains the importance of acknowledging homosexuality at workplace and its importance in leveraging the workforce diversity. Focusing on the lesbian and gay employees, identity deployment process for contesting the stigmatized view of identity and fostering inclusive mindsets at workplace is dealt at length. This narration begins with the conceptual inputs from resource mobilization theory, political opportunity theory and new social movement theory that shape the framework of identity deployment. Then, explaining the three analytic dimensions of identity and the identity deployment strategies-identity for critique and identity for education, this chapter takes a micro view into the workplace contexts and explores the normalizing and differentiating strategies adopted by employees at workplace to deploy their homosexuality. Hence, augmenting Bernstein's framework of three analytic dimensions of identity further, this chapter adds another level of normalizing and differentiating strategies at workplace, which clarifies further how identity for critique and identity for education are operationalized in organizational contexts to achieve the identity goals.

Figure 1 illustrates the three levels of identity deployment framework. The *first level* at the top consists of the three analytic dimensions of identity from Bernstein's framework. I view 'identity as goal' and 'identity for empowerment' as foundational concepts for identity deployment since they express the purpose and prerequisite for the process. The goal of de-stigmatizing the identity and deconstructing restrictive social categories (Bernstein, 1997) explains the purpose. *Identity for empowerment*, i.e., realizing the collective identity and mobilizing a constituency (here, the lesbian and gay employees) to gain a legitimate political standing to take strategic actions, explains the prerequisite. To achieve the goal, Bernstein suggests the third dimension-identity as strategy. She argues that the strategy could be to suppress or celebrate the differences with the dominant culture (here, the heterosexual workforce) through identity for education and identity for critique. This is the *second level* in the model. The *third level* explains the normalizing and differentiating strategies at workplace. I discuss these strategies at length and how these can help the lesbian and gay employees achieve their identity goals. Considerable attention is given to the mixed model of identity deployment as well, wherein the differentiating and normalizing strategies are used alternately or simultaneously.

An important focus of identity deployment could be whether the strategies are deployed individually, collectively or both. A few strategies, by their definition, nature and the way of deployment, are most likely to be seen as individual strategies. For example, claiming encounter is about making an explicit or tacit disclosure by the employee in a way that creates inclusive mindsets in their coworkers. Discretion strategy is about remaining alert for the right time to make the identity visible in an appropriate way. Similarly, a legal encounter depicts the litigation filed by a lesbian or gay employee to redress the discrimination and injustice meted at the workplace, with an aim towards claiming equal treatment from the employer. Hence, these three strategies can be seen as individual strategies. On the other hand, there are some strategies, which utilize the strength provided by collective force of employees. In my discussion, advocacy encounters and

Figure 1. Identity deployment framework for workplace context

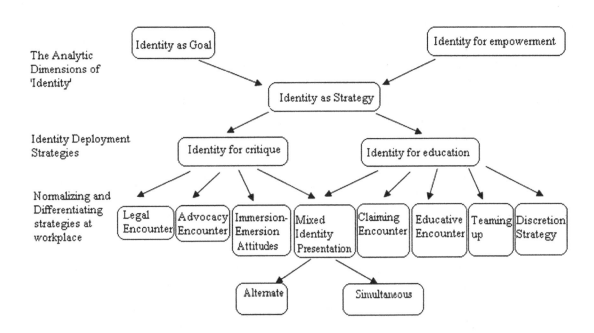

immersion-emersion attitudes are the strategies that are mostly deployed by gay employee groups through their collective voices. The 'teaming up' strategy explains a unique case of collective strategy, wherein identity deployment is by two people-the employee and their partner, and not a group.

Finally, there are strategies, which could be deployed both individually and collectively. As we saw, for an educative encounter, the source could be either an individual or an employee group. Similarly, besides demonstrating collectively, immersion-emersion attitudes can also be deployed individually. In a first of its kind precedent, Ralph J Hexter, the President of Hampshire College, celebrated his gay identity by letting himself out as an openly gay executive in the print media through an article, "Being an out president." Following this, subsequent reports swelled this

number up to eleven, demonstrating, probably, the contagious effect of immersion-emersion attitude (Fassinger, et al., 2010). Mixed model of identity can also be deployed individually, besides collectively. Claiming encounters, though largely seen as normalizing, may be deployed as special case of mixed identity deployment. Creed and Scully (2000) observe that during claiming encounters, individuals may claim both the oneness as well as the differences of their homosexuality from the heterosexual identity.

The categorization of identity deployment strategies into individual and collective can be contrasted with their normalizing versus differentiating nature. This model can be presented in a 2 X 2 matrix, as shown in Figure 2. Mixed identity presentation takes center-stage in this matrix as it can occupy all the four quadrants.

The framework of identity deployment to leverage workforce diversity offers at least three compelling reasons to research further in this area. *First*, organizational scholars may be interested in exploring what could be the identity goals of this deployment process. Equality and inclusion could be two prominent goals in the workplace context (Bell, 2009; Özbilgin, 2009). By creating inclusive mindsets in the heterosexual coworkers, employees contest the stigma associated with homosexuality. Simultaneously, they deconstruct restrictive social categories by claiming equal treatment through organizational policies. Scholars may be interested in exploring other identity goals as well. Next, having categorized the normalizing and differentiating strategies into individual and collective, one may like to explore the identity deployment process in these two streams. Thus, the *second* area of research could be to explore what individual and organizational characteristics (Chrobot-Mason, et al., 2001) affect identity deployment, when done individually. And the *third* stream could be to explore the role of collective efficacy beliefs (Bandura, 1982) in deploying identity collectively. "Though forceful collective action is prompted by detrimental conditions, it is initiated by those "not... who have lost hope, but (by) the more able members whose efforts at social and economic betterment have met with at least some success" (p. 143). Hence, this course could explore the relationship of collective efficacy beliefs of the employee groups with their identity deployment strategies and how contextual factors affect these relationships.

As seen in the chapter, many sociologists of contemporary times have expressed interest in taking identity deployment framework further (e.g. Dugan, 2008; Taylor, et al., 2008, Bernstein, et al., 2008). Organizational scholars (e.g. Creed & Scully, 2000; Swaminathan, 2001; Raeburn, 2004; Clair, et al., 2005) have also offered significant inputs in this area. However, the field is still very ripe with a lot of possibility of conceptual and empirical contributions, which can enhance our knowledge in the area of workforce diversity.

Figure 2. A 2 X 2 matrix explaining the types and levels of identity deployment strategies

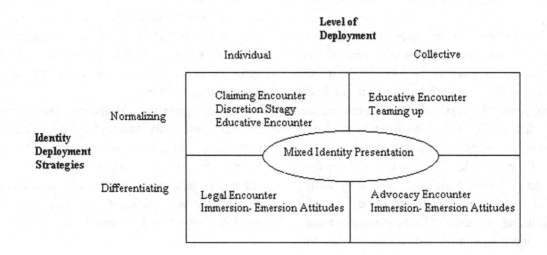

REFERENCES

Arabsheibani, R., Marin, A., & Wadsworth, J. (2007). Variations in gay pay in the USA and in the UK. In Badgett, M. V. L., & Frank, J. (Eds.), *Sexual Orientation Discrimination: An International Perspective* (pp. 44–61). London, UK: Taylor & Francis/Routledge.

Badgett, L. (2001). *Money, myths, and change: The economic lives of lesbians and gay men*. Chicago, IL: University of Chicago Press.

Bandura, A. (1982). Self efficacy mechanism in human agency. *The American Psychologist*, *37*(3), 122–147. doi:10.1037/0003-066X.37.2.122

Beatty, J. E., & Kirby, S. L. (2006). Beyond the legal environment: How stigma influences invisible identity groups in the workplace. *Employee Responsibilities and Rights Journal*, *18*(1), 29–44. doi:10.1007/s10672-005-9003-6

Bell, M. P. (2009). Effects of the experience of inequality, exclusion and discrimination on scholarship. In Özbilgin, M. F. (Ed.), *Equality, Diversity and Inclusion at Work: A Research Companion* (pp. 17–26). Cheltenham, UK: Edward Elgar.

Berkley, R. A., & Watt, A. H. (2006). Impact of same-sex harassment and gender-role stereotypes on title VII protection for gay, lesbian, and bisexual employees. *Employee Responsibilities and Rights Journal*, *18*(1), 3–19. doi:10.1007/s10672-005-9001-8

Bernstein, M. (1997). Celebration and suppression: The strategic use of identity by the lesbian and gay movement. *American Journal of Sociology*, *103*(3), 531–565. doi:10.1086/231250

Bernstein, M. (2011). Multi-institutional politics, social movements and the state: Lesbian and gay activism in the U.S. In Johnson, C., Paternotte, D., & Tremblay, M. (Eds.), *The Lesbian and Gay Movement and the State: Comparative Insights into a Transformed Relationship*. London, UK: Ashgate.

Bernstein, M., & Cruz, M. (2009). "What are you?" Explaining identity as a goal of the multiracial hapa movement. *Social Problems*, *56*(4), 722–745. doi:10.1525/sp.2009.56.4.722

Bernstein, M., & Olsen, K. A. (2009). Identity deployment and social change: Understanding identity as a social movement and organizational strategy. *Social Compass*, *3*(6), 871–883. doi:10.1111/j.1751-9020.2009.00255.x

Bevington, D., & Dixon, C. (2005). Movement-relevant theory: Rethinking social movement scholarship and activism. *Social Movement Studies*, *4*(3), 185–208. doi:10.1080/14742830500329838

Bible, J. (2001). Gender stereotyping: Courts open the door to title VII claims by homosexuals. *Journal of Employment Discrimination Law*, *3*(1), 27–33.

Bible, J. D. (2002). Same-sex sexual harassment: When does a harasser act 'because of sex'. *Labor Law Journal*, *53*(1), 3–10.

Boggs, C. (1986). *Social movements and political power: Emerging forms of radicalism in the west*. Philadelphia, PA: Temple University Press.

Brenner, B. R., Lyons, H. Z., & Fassinger, R. E. (2010). Can heterosexism harm organizations? Predicting the perceived organizational citizenship behaviors of gay and lesbian employees. *The Career Development Quarterly*, *58*, 321–335. doi:10.1002/j.2161-0045.2010.tb00181.x

Browning, C., Reynolds, A., & Dworkin, S. (1991). Affirmative psychotherapy for lesbian women. *The Counseling Psychologist*, *19*, 177–196. doi:10.1177/0011000091192004

Buechler, S. M. (1995). New social movement theories. *The Sociological Quarterly*, *36*(3), 441–464. doi:10.1111/j.1533-8525.1995.tb00447.x

Button, S. B. (2004). Identity management strategies utilized by lesbian and gay employees. *Group & Organization Management, 29*(4), 470–494. doi:10.1177/1059601103257417

Cain, R. (1991). Disclosure and secrecy among gay men in the United States and Canada: A shift in views. *Journal of the History of Sexuality, 2*(1), 25–45.

Chrobot-Mason, D., Button, S. B., & DiClementi, J. D. (2001). Sexual identity management strategies: An exploration of antecedents and consequences. *Sex Roles, 45*, 321–336. doi:10.1023/A:1014357514405

Clair, J. A., Beatty, J., & MacLean, T. (2005). Out of sight but not out of mind: Managing invisible social identities in the workplace. *Academy of Management Review, 30*(1), 78–95. doi:10.5465/AMR.2005.15281431

Collella, A., & Dipboye, B. (Eds.). (2005). *Discrimination at work: Psychological and organizational bases.* Mahwah, NJ: Lawrence Erlbaum.

Conger, J. J. (1975). Proceedings of the American psychological association, incorporated, for the year 1974: Minutes of the annual meeting of the council of representatives. *The American Psychologist, 30*, 620–651. doi:10.1037/h0078455

Cortese, D. K. H. (2004). *Are we thinking straight? Negotiating political environments and identities in a lesbian, gay, bisexual, and transgender social movement organization.* Doctoral Dissertation. Austin, TX: The University of Texas at Austin.

Creed, W. E. D., & Scully, M. (2000). Songs of ourselves: Employees' deployment of social identity in workplace encounters. *Journal of Management Inquiry, 9*, 391–412. doi:10.1177/105649260000900410

Cross, W. E. (1971). The negro-to-black conversion experience. *Black World, 20*, 3–27.

Cross, W. E. (1978). The Thomas and Cross model of psychological nigrescence: A literature review. *The Journal of Black Psychology, 4*, 13–31. doi:10.1177/009579847800500102

Croteau, I. M. (1996). Research on the work experiences of lesbian, gay and bisexual people: An integrative review of methodology and findings. *Journal of Vocational Behavior, 48*, 195–209. doi:10.1006/jvbe.1996.0018

Day, N. E., & Greene, P. G. (2008). A case for sexual orientation diversity management in small and large organizations. *Human Resource Management, 47*(3), 637–654. doi:10.1002/hrm.20235

Day, N. E., & Schoenrade, P. (1997). Staying in the closet vs. corning out: Relationships between communication about sexual orientation and work attitudes. *Personnel Psychology, 50*, 147–163. doi:10.1111/j.1744-6570.1997.tb00904.x

Dugan, K. B. (2008). Just Like You: The Dimensions of Identity Presentations in an Antigay Contested Context. (pp. 21–46). In J. Reger, D. J. Meyers & R. L. Einwohner (Eds.). *Identity Work in Social Movements.* Minneapolis: University of Minnesota

Duggan, L. (2003). *The twilight of equality: Neoliberalism, cultural politics, and the attack on democracy.* New York, NY: Beacon Press.

Fassinger, R. E. (2008). Workplace diversity and public policy. *The American Psychologist, 63*, 252–268. doi:10.1037/0003-066X.63.4.252

Fassinger, R. E., Shullman, S. L., & Stevenson, M. R. (2010). Toward an affirmative lesbian, gay, bisexual and transgender leadership paradigm. *The American Psychologist, 65*(3), 201–215. doi:10.1037/a0018597

Fitzpatrick, B. (2007). *Sexual orientation and religion or belief cases.* Retrieved March 06, 2011, from http://www.tuc.org.ukextrasSOR-Breport.pdf.

Friskopp, A., & Silverstein, S. (1996). *Straight jobs, gay lives: Gay and lesbian professionals, the Harvard business school, and the American workplace*. New York, NY: Touchstone/Simon & Schuster.

Gamson, W. A., Fireman, B., & Rytina, S. (1982). *Encounters with unjust authorities*. Homewood, IL: Dorsey.

Goffman, E. (1961). *Encounters*. Indianapolis, IN: Bobbs-Merrill.

Goffman, E. (1963). *Stigma: Notes on the management of spoiled identity*. New York, NY: Jason Aronson.

Gonsiorek, J. C., & Weinrich, J. D. (1991). The definition and scope of sexual orientation. In Gonsiorek, J. C., & Weinrich, J. D. (Eds.), *Homosexuality: Research Implications for Public Policy* (pp. 1–12). Newbury Park, CA: Sage.

Griffith, K. H., & Hebl, M. R. (2002). The disclosure dilemma for gay men and lesbians: "Coming out" at work. *The Journal of Applied Psychology*, *87*(6), 1191–1199. doi:10.1037/0021-9010.87.6.1191

Gruszczynska, A. (2009). *Queer enough? Contested terrains of identity deployment in the context of gay and lesbian public activism in Poland*. Doctoral Dissertation. Birmingham, UK: Aston University.

Herek, G. M. (1990). The context of anti-gay violence. *Journal of Interpersonal Violence*, *5*, 316–333. doi:10.1177/088626090005003006

Herek, G. M. (1996). Why tell if you're not asked? Self-disclosure, intergroup contact and heterosexuals' attitudes towards lesbians and gay men. In Herek, G. M., Jobe, J. B., & Carney, R. M. (Eds.), *Coming Out in Force: Sexual Orientation and the Military* (pp. 197–225). Chicago, IL: University of Chicago Press.

Herek, G. M., Jobe, I. B., & Carney, R. M. (Eds.). (1996). *Coming out in force: Sexual orientation and the military*. Chicago, IL: University of Chicago Press.

HRC. (2008). *State of the workplace for gay, lesbian, bisexual and transgender Americans: 2006-07*. Retrieved January 27, 2011 from http://www.hrc.org/documents/State_of_the_Workplace.pdf.

HRC. (2011). *Statewide employment laws and policies*. Retrieved April 06, 2011 from http://www.hrc.org/documents/Employment_Laws_and_Policies.pdf.

Jenkins, C. J. (1983). Resource mobilization theory and the study of social movements. *Annual Review of Sociology*, *9*(1), 527–553. doi:10.1146/annurev.so.09.080183.002523

Köllen, T. (2007). Part of the whole? Homosexuality in companies' diversity policies and in business research: Focus on Germany. *The International Journal of Diversity in Organisations. Communities and Nations*, *7*(5), 315–322.

Mayer, M. (1991). Social movement research and social movement practice: The U.S. pattern. In Rucht, D. (Ed.), *Research on Social Movements: The State of the Art in Western Europe and the USA* (pp. 47–120). Boulder, CO: Westview Press.

McAdam, D., McCarthy, J. D., & Zald, M. N. (1996). *Comparative perspectives on social movements: Political opportunities, mobilizing structures, and cultural framings*. Cambridge, UK: Cambridge University Press.

McCarthy, J., & Zald, M. N. (1977). Resource mobilization and social movements. *American Journal of Sociology*, *82*(6), 133–167. doi:10.1086/226464

Michael, R. T., Gagnon, J. H., Laumann, E. O., & Kolata, G. (1994). *Sex in America*. New York, NY: Little, Brown.

O'Ryan, L. W., & McFarland, W. P. (2010). A phenomenological exploration of the experiences of dual-career lesbian and gay couples. *Journal of Counseling and Development, 88,* 71–79. doi:10.1002/j.1556-6678.2010.tb00153.x

Olofsson, G. (1988). After the working-class movement? An essay on what's 'new' and what's 'social' in the new social movements. *Acta Sociologica, 31*(1), 15–34. doi:10.1177/000169938803100103

Osigweh, C. A. B. (1989). Concept fallibility in organizational science. *Academy of Management Review, 14*(4), 579–594. doi:10.2307/258560

Özbilgin, M. F. (Ed.). (2009). *Equality, diversity and inclusion at work: A research companion.* Cheltenham, UK: Edward Elgar.

Pfeffer, J. (1981). Management as symbolic action. In Staw, B., & Cummings, L. L. (Eds.), *Research in Organizational Behavior* (pp. 1–52). Greenwich, CT: JAI.

Pichardo, N. A. (1997). New social movements: A critical review. *Annual Review of Sociology, 23*(1), 411. doi:10.1146/annurev.soc.23.1.411

Polleta, F., & Jasper, J. M. (2001). Collective identity and social movements. *Annual Review of Sociology, 27,* 283–305. doi:10.1146/annurev.soc.27.1.283

Powers, B. (1996). The impact of gay, lesbian, and bisexual workplace issues on productivity. In Ellis, A. L., & Riggle, E. D. B. (Eds.), *Sexual Identity on the Job: Issues and Services* (pp. 79–90). New York, NY: Haworth Press. doi:10.1300/J041v04n04_05

Raeburn, N. (2004). *Changing corporate America from inside out: Lesbian and Gay workplace rights.* Minneapolis, MN: University of Minnesota Press.

Ragins, B. R. (2004). Sexual orientation in the workplace: The unique work and career experiences of gay, lesbian and bisexual workers. *Research in Personnel and Human Resource Management, 23,* 37–122.

Ragins, B. R. (2008). Disclosure disconnects: Antecedents and consequences of disclosing invisible stigma across life domains. *Academy of Management Review, 33*(1), 194–215. doi:10.5465/AMR.2008.27752724

Ragins, B. R., Singh, R., & Cornwell, J. M. (2007). Making the invisible visible: Fear and disclosure of sexual orientation at work. *The Journal of Applied Psychology, 92,* 1103–1118. doi:10.1037/0021-9010.92.4.1103

Ragins, B. R., & Wiethoff, C. (2005). Understanding heterosexism at work: The straight problem. In Dipboye, B., & Colella, A. (Eds.), *Discrimination at Work: Psychological and Organizational Base* (pp. 177–201). Mahwah, NJ: Lawrence Erlbaum Association.

Rostosky, S. S., & Riggle, E. D. B. (2002). Out at work: The relation of actor and partner workplace policy and internalized homophobia to disclosure status. *Journal of Counseling Psychology, 49,* 411–419. doi:10.1037/0022-0167.49.4.411

Schneider, B. H. (1993). *Children's social competence in context: The contributions of family, school and culture.* London, UK: Routledge.

Stone, E. F., Stone, D. L., & Dipboye, R. L. (1992). Stigmas in organizations: Race, handicaps and physical unattractiveness. In Kelly, K. (Ed.), *Issues, theory, and research in industrial/organizational psychology* (pp. 385–457). Amsterdam, The Netherlands: Elsvier. doi:10.1016/S0166-4115(08)62608-4

Sung, W. C. (2011). Taking the fight back to title VII: A case for redefining "because of sex" to include gender stereotypes, sexual orientation and gender identity. *Southern California Law Review, 84*, 487–539.

Swaminathan, A. (2001). Resource partitioning and the evolution of specialist organizations: The role of location and identity in the U.S. wine industry. *Academy of Management Journal, 44*(6), 1169–1185. doi:10.2307/3069395

Tajfel, H. (1978). *Differentiation between social groups: Studies in the social psychology of intergroup relations*. London, UK: Academic Press.

Tarrow, S. (1994). *Power in movement: Social movements, collective action, and politics*. Cambridge, UK: Cambridge University Press.

Taylor, V., & Raeburn, N. C. (1995). Identity politics as high-risk activism: Career consequences for lesbian, gay, and bisexual sociologists. *Social Problems, 42*(2), 252–273. doi:10.1525/sp.1995.42.2.03x0113i

Taylor, V., Van Dyke, N., Kimport, K., & Andersen, E. A. (2009). Culture and mobilization: Tactical repertoires, same-sex weddings, and the impact on gay activism. *American Sociological Review, 74*(6), 865–890. doi:10.1177/000312240907400602

Thompson, K., & Andrzejewski, J. (1988). *Why can't Sharon Kowalski come home?* San Francisco, CA: Spinsters/Aunt Lute.

Williams, R. H. (1995). Constructing the public good: Social movements and cultural resources. *Social Problems, 42*(1), 124–144. doi:10.1525/sp.1995.42.1.03x0458p

Wilkening, B. (2005). *Political opportunities in the post-Soviet realm: A comparative case study of anti-regime mobilization and success in Azerbaijan and Georgia*. Paper presented at the Illinois State University Conference for Students of Political Science. Normal, IL.

Williams, K. Y., & O'Reilly, C. A. III. (1998). Demography and diversity in organizations: A review of 40 years of research. *Research in Organizational Behavior, 20*, 77–140.

Woods, J. D. (1993). *The corporate closet: The professional lives of gay men in America*. New York, NY: Free Press.

Woods, S. E., & Harbeck, K. M. (1991). Living in two worlds: The identity management strategies used by lesbian physical educators. *Journal of Homosexuality, 22*, 141–166. doi:10.1300/J082v22n03_06

Zald, M. N., & McCarthy, J. (1988). *Social movements in an organizational society*. New Brunswick, NJ: Transaction.

Zuckerman, A. J., & Simons, G. F. (1996). *Sexual orientation in the workplace*. Thousand Oaks, CA: Sage.

KEY TERMS AND DEFINITIONS

Advocacy Encounter: Face-to-face encounter with policy makers as advocacy targets to claim equal treatment in the organization.

Claiming Encounter: Tacit or direct disclosure of sexual identity done by lesbian and gay employees without thought on daily basis, similar to their heterosexual counterparts.

Collective Identity: An individual's cognitive, moral, and emotional connection with a broader community, category, practice, or institution.

Differentiating Strategy: A term used for 'identity for critique' at workplace.

Discretion Strategy: To postpone the decision of making the identity visible and remaining alert in choosing the right time to do so, which impacts positively on the coworkers and makes the workplace inclusive for lesbian and gay employees.

Educative Encounter: Face-to-face meetings for addressing the various contentions of the peers and employer. Educative encounters invite questions, which offer the lesbian and gay employees to explain realities about their lives, which are largely unknown to their heterosexual peers and employer.

Identity as Goal: The goal of mobilizing collective identity to contest the associated stigma, deconstruct restrictive social categories that limit access to resources or seek recognition for an emerging identity.

Identity as Strategy: The strategic actions taken to deploy collective identity.

Identity Deployment: A way of expressive collective identity that brings positive cultural and political shifts in the organizational mindsets.

Identity for Critique: The strategy to confront the values, categories, and practices of the dominant culture. The emphasis here is on highlighting differences from the dominant culture

Identity for Education: The strategy to challenge the dominant culture's perception of the minority to gain legitimacy by playing on uncontroversial themes. The emphasis here is on highlighting sameness with the dominant culture.

Identity for Empowerment: To mean the creation of collective identity and the feeling that political action is feasible.

Immersion-Emersion Attitudes: Fascination and involvement towards the gay culture and celebrating their differences from the larger heterosexual majority.

Legal Encounter: Litigation filed by lesbian or gay employee to fight discrimination based on sexual orientation at workplace.

Lesbian and Gay: Women and men who are attracted to the members of same sex. The commonly used term for this, homosexual, was coined by psychiatrists around 1890 to connote homosexuality as an illness. Hence, it is more appropriate to use lesbian and gay, instead of homosexuals (Zuckerman & Simons, 1996). In many contexts, however, 'gay' incorporates both lesbian and gay, which too is fine.

Mixed Identity Presentation/ Mixed Model of Identity Deployment (Alternate): Shift from normalizing to differentiating strategies or vice versa in the course of identity deployment.

Mixed Identity Presentation/ Mixed Model of Identity Deployment (Simultaneous): Deployment of normalizing and differentiating strategies simultaneously with the same target.

Normalizing Strategy: A term used for 'identity for education' at workplace.

Teaming Up: Collective efforts of a dual career lesbian or gay couple to deploy their homosexuality at workplace.

ENDNOTES

[1]   LGB stands for Lesbian, Gay, and Bisexual. The literature on sexual minorities deals with broad class of identities, like lesbian, gay, bisexual, transgender, trans-sexual, and intersexual. Hence, acronyms like LGB, LGBT, and LGBTI are used in various writings. Though the author realizes the importance and responsibility of being inclusive, academic scholarship demands focus on specific social identities to make the framework and conceptualization more generalizable than if an all-inclusive approach were adopted (Osigweh, 1989). Hence, the social identity considered in this chapter is 'homosexuality,' and thus the group under the discussion ambit is lesbian and gay employees.

[2]   As of March 08, 2011.

Section 5
Leveraging Workforce Diversity through Theoretical Frameworks and Technology

Chapter 25

Critical Race Theory:
A Framework for Examining Social Identity Diversity of Black Women in Positions of Leadership

Marilyn Y. Byrd
University of Mary Hardin-Baylor, USA

ABSTRACT

This chapter is a qualitative, narrative case study that seeks to unveil the social identity diversity of leadership from the perspective a Black woman leader. Social identity diversity is a form of difference that marginalized groups, such as Black women, experience in predominantly White organizational and institutional settings as a result of intersectionality. Social identity diversity creates multiple dynamics for groups such as Black women who hold leadership positions in the aforementioned settings. This study highlights the need for more inclusive and cultural perspectives of leadership, which calls for more inclusive theoretical frameworks that consider the social identity diversity of the leader. Critical race theory is presented as a theoretical framework that is useful for explaining how systems of power sustain domination and oppression in organizational and institutional settings. Implications for an emerging social justice paradigm are given.

INTRODUCTION

For the most part, the leadership experiences of Black women leaders has been subsumed within the larger discussion of women leaders, as well as the more traditional discussion that has been articulated from and towards the leadership of White, middle-class men. Although feminist literature speaks to the issue of gender equality,

feminist perspectives do not make an issue for equality in terms of racial oppression or social class designation. As a result, gender equality has not adequately captured the convergence of gender with race and social class. The convergence or intersection of race, gender, and social class has been commonly referred to as intersectionality, a term that denotes the various ways these social constructs interact and shape multiple dimensions of Black women's experiences (Crenshaw, 1989). This intersection is an interlocking system

DOI: 10.4018/978-1-4666-1812-1.ch025

of oppression containing a multiplier effect; that is racism multiplied by sexism multiplied by classism (King, 1988). Intersectionality can create social identity diversity, a form of difference that marginalized groups (such as Black women) experience in predominantly White organizational and institutional settings. Social identity diversity creates multiple dynamics for marginalized groups such as Black women who hold leadership positions in the aforementioned settings.

This study highlights the need to re-emphasize social constructs (race, gender, social class) as foundations for diversity in organizational and institutional settings. Discussions on diversity now include lifestyles, ideas, education, personality, and an emerging array of schools of thought that have minimized the historical and legally mandated need to ensure equality. As new topics are added to the diversity list, the "isms" of diversity (racism, sexism, and classism) have become minimized and relegated to the sidelines. In order to frame the term diversity within a historical background, it is necessary to recognize social identity diversity as the diversity upon which bias, prejudice, and discrimination in this country is rooted.

Statement of the Problem

While some discussion has been given to the obstacles Black women encounter in reaching positions of leadership in predominantly White organizations, less conversation has taken place concerning how Black women are disempowered to lead in settings where their social identity is associated with socially disadvantaged groups (Byrd, 2009a). Socially disadvantaged refers to individuals who have been subjected to ethnic prejudice or cultural bias because of their identity as a member of a group without regard to their individual qualities (SBA, 2004). One reason for the disempowerment of Black women is that the idealized and fixed image in Western culture of who leads in organizations has generally fit the

stereotype of middle-class, White men and more recently White women (Byrd, 2008; Parker, 2005). Black women entering predominantly White organizations in positions of leadership are confronted with disrupting this fixed image of 'leader.' To address the aforementioned, research and theory is needed that explains how Black women struggle in their everyday, lived leadership experiences to disrupt an image associated with their social identity and create a new image of 'who leads.'

In order to better understand the social identity diversity of Black women as leaders, the discourse on leadership should reflect the lived experiences of the leader (Gostnell, 1996). Lived experience is not secondhand; rather, it is how an individual perceives, describes, feels, judges, remembers, makes sense of, and talks about the experience (Patton, 2002). "A person cannot reflect on experience while living through the experience… reflection on lived experience is always recollective; it is reflection on experience that is already passed or lived through" (Van Manen, 1997, p. 9). Consequently, lived experiences are ways that people experience life based on their social location within society (Byrd, 2009a).

This study will therefore explore the following research question: *How does social identity diversity influence the everyday, lived leadership experiences of Black women in predominantly White organizations?* A goal of this study is to bring the perspectives of Black women to the discourse on leadership and shift conversations of leadership to the social identity of the leader. The ultimate goal is to begin conceptualizing new and more inclusive theories of leadership.

SOCIO-HISTORICAL PERSPECTIVES OF BLACK WOMEN AS LEADERS

Black women have developed an innate sense of survival that is grounded in the historical struggle against oppression that has been experienced by the Black community (Byrd, 2009b). Being forced to assume an existence of "dissemblance and self-reliance in order to survive…and having embarked upon the heroic task of re-imaging themselves" (Hine, 1992, p. 14), Black women have emerged as the new image of 'who leads' (Byrd, 2009b). For this reason, it is insightful to examine the leadership of Black women from a historical perspective to discover the interrelatedness of the part to the whole (Dilthey, 1976).

Historically, Black women have been portrayed in subordinate or subservient roles. As a result, the anomalous presence of Black women in leadership roles challenges society's perceptions of who leads (Gostnell, 1996) in organizational settings. Therefore, the image of Black women as leaders in organizations may be distorted by the historical images and stereotypes that continue to oppress their leadership experiences. The socio-historical leadership experiences of Black women, grounded in a culture of oppression and dominance, is in sharp contrast to traditional and dominant leadership styles based on control and competitive behavior and written from the perspectives of White men (Parker, 2005). Today's Black woman challenges the traditional perspectives and speaks from a social epistemology based on the quest for liberation and social change.

Organizational Perspectives of Black Women's Leadership

Parker (2001) describes organizational leadership as the practice of leadership within a context where individuals are held to norms, values, expectations, and beliefs that are defined by the organization's culture. Schein (1992) popularized the concept of organizational culture as the norms and values that are perceived by the members of the organization. In predominantly White organizations, the culture is most reflective of the norms and values of the dominant group to which organizational members are expected to adapt. A basic characteristic of organizational culture is that the leader plays a crucial role in defining the organization's culture

(Byrd, 2009b; Parker, 2001). In predominantly White organizations, Black women leaders are faced with the following dilemma--adapt to the norm or seek to create new norms and values based on the multiple perspectives they bring to the leadership experience (Byrd, 2009b).

The belief that the survival of an organization rests largely on effective leadership is not likely to be challenged, but neither is it likely that the image conjured from that statement is that of a Black woman as the leader. Historically, research on the phenomenon of leadership has used White men as the model. Consequently, there appears to be little research on how social identity constructs touches the lived experiences of the Black woman leader.

Parker (2005) argues against the notion of the feminist advantage model in organizational leadership because it represents a universal, race-neutral model of leadership based on the experiences of middle-class White women. Race neutral models fail to recognize that organizations are not neutral settings where all leaders are the same and are subjected to the same type of historical and cultural experience (Byrd, 2009b). Instead, Parker (2005) advances an inclusive framework of leadership, which supports social identity diversity as a means of interpreting and analyzing leadership. Social identity diversity suggests that the everyday lived leadership experiences of Black women in predominantly White organizations are not located within separate spheres of race, gender, or social class. Given the fact that Black women are simultaneously situated within at least two groups that are subjected to broad subordinations, the convergence of these social constructs challenges the notion that diversity issues can be viewed as mono-causal (Crenshaw, 1989).

Consistent with Parker's (2005) argument Hooks (1984) asserts that, "White women who dominate feminist discourse, who for the most part make and articulate feminist theory, have little or no understanding of White supremacy as a racial politic, of the psychological impact of class, of their political status within a racist, sexist, capitalist state" (p. 3). As a result, the distinct leadership experiences of Black women in predominantly White organizations are not effectively captured from the perspective of leadership discussions led by White women. According to hooks (1984), traditional feminist perspectives offer a universal, collective representation of women's experiences and do not effectively capture the lived experiences of Black women.

Consequently, in settings like predominantly White organizations, Black women are caught in another dilemma of trying to operate within an organizational system without adequate authority or support and only symbolic power (Dumas, 1980). The strategy of distancing Black women from the base of power and authority is one way of maintaining the status quo.

METHODOLOGY

This study is a qualitative, narrative, case study that examined the leadership experiences of a Black woman senior manager in a predominantly White organization. A narrative method is used because it allows the participant to describe her everyday, lived leadership experiences in a predominantly White organization by telling her story. Through storytelling, the participant is enabled to withdraw and reflect upon those experiences, then re-emerge with a new insight and deeper understanding of what she experienced (Clark, 2001). According to Yin (2003), the single case study method is best when there is a need to study a critical or unique situation. This study is unique in that it brings to the discourse of leadership the concept of social identity diversity.

Theoretical Framework

Critical Race Theory (CRT) is the framework used to discuss the findings from this study. As-

sociated with the critical theory paradigm, CRT is an appropriate framework for studying Black women in predominantly White organizations because this framework considers the multiple social identities and roles of a Black woman's life. Creswell (1998) describes the critical theory paradigm as a research paradigm that generally seeks to explore the oppression, exploitation, and struggle of individuals within institutions and organizations where power can be used to dominate and control. Researchers from the social sciences use critical theories for understanding, describing, and explaining how people experience the world.

Critical Race Theory (CRT) is based on the notion of social construction and reality of race (Bell, 1993; Delgado, 1995; Ladson-Billings & Tate, 1995). CRT provides a means for people of color to communicate experiences and realities through narratives and storytelling and consequently, critically examine racial issues within the context of the workplace (Byrd, 2009b). According to Taylor (2004), CRT posits, "issues of race, class, and gender are inextricably bound by economic, social, and political hegemonic power structures" (p. 35). Therefore, using counter stories based on experiences are useful for challenging the discourse and beliefs of the dominant group that have been reinforced through traditional research and theories.

The goal of CRT is emancipation of the individual. Emancipation occurs through the conscious experiences of self, which can be realized through discourse or the telling of one's story. CRT provides the means to dismantle the social structures and power dynamics that are exposed during discourse. Emancipation can lead to transformation, which could result in self-definition. Self-definition is the point in a woman's life where she overcomes societal stereotypes, dispels myths, becomes empowered, and begins a journey towards self-expression, defining her life in her own terms (Collins, 1990).

Study Participant

The participant in this study is a Black woman, former manager in the public utility industry in central United States, and current senior level administrator for a state agency. The participant's true name has been changed to maintain anonymity. Selection criteria were: 1) self-identifying as a Black woman, 2) holding a senior level or executive manager's position at a predominantly White organization, and 3) agreeing to an audio-taped interview. The participant was identified based on membership affiliation with a Black professional organization.

Data Collection

The data was collected by conducting an in-depth face-to-face interview that lasted approximately two hours. In a qualitative study, an in-depth interview is an appropriate technique for "locating the meanings people place on the events, processes, and structures of their lives: their perceptions, assumptions, prejudgments, presuppositions, and for connecting these meaning to the social world around them" (Miles & Huberman, 1994, p. 10). Semi-structured, open-ended questions were used as these type questions generally lend themselves to further and deeper probing. The interview took place at neutral, mutually agreeable site.

Data Analysis

This study was analyzed using a narrative, case-study method. First, the interview with the participant was transcribed and organized according to the perceptions of the experiences she encountered. Collecting the professional experiences of Black women produces a form of narrative analysis—the telling of one's own story (Byrd, 2009a). Telling one's story is an analysis of Black women's ways of knowing and interpreting structured patterns of racism, sexism, and social classism. In this study, the analysis lies significantly within the story

itself as the participant exposes the bureaucracy and social hierarchy that restricted her leadership within predominantly White organizations.

Second, a case study analysis bounds the study within a specific problem, context, and related issues. According to Lincoln and Guba (1985) a case study analysis is useful when a specific problem is being explored, in a specific context, with identifiable issues, that leads to new insight on the problem being explored. In the present study, the participant is presented with a number of dilemmas in her experiences as a leader in predominantly White organizations. A case study analysis thereby provides a holistic and realistic account of the problems she encountered (Lloyd-Jones, 2009; Merriam & Caffarella, 1999; Patton, 1990).

JEAN'S STORY: TO ENTER AND LEAD

It didn't take long for me to realize that I was constantly being watched. But after a while I began to recognize this as an opportunity to prove to those that were curious about me that I could "pass the test"—because there is much more to me than what they are willing to see.

While feminist perspectives offer a universal, collective representation of women's experiences, these perspectives do not effectively capture the lived experiences of Black women in predominantly White organizations (Byrd, 2009a). Instead experiences such as feeling alone, being excluded, needing support, being stigmatized, and being disempowered are the types of lived experiences Black women encounter in predominantly White organizations. The burden of having to perform while hiding the pain of oppression (Terhune, 2008) stemming from social identity is the untold story of leadership.

The following case study is the story of Jean, a Black woman, mid-forties, who worked for a number of years as a senior manager in the public service industry. Jean's story continues after she eventually transitioned to another management position with a state agency. In her story, Jean describes her everyday, lived experiences as a leader in predominantly White settings. Her story not only unveils multiple dynamics of oppression such as exclusion and disempowerment, her story highlights a social advocacy response to confront these problems in order to become a more effective leader; rather than react to the issues which she perceived were caused from her social identity.

Feeling Alone

Terhune (2008) questions how a Black woman can subsist when she finds herself to be one of a few or the only one in predominantly White organizations or settings. The answer most likely lies in coping mechanisms and strategies for overcoming the feeling of being alone. Jean begins her story by talking about her experiences of feeling alone.

I began my career with [name of company] in an entry-level customer service position. Within a year, I qualified for a management position. After I had gone through a management-training program, I was offered a position as a chief assigner in [name of city] which meant I was in charge of the company's records in the district I was assigned. I was the first woman to hold that position in that city. In the departmental area that I managed I was the only Black person, period. There were also 2 females [White] reporting to me that held skill level positions. But my department—the plant area—was really where men were dominant. When I assumed the position, there was not much accountability among the staff. So all of a sudden, I show up, not only a woman, but a Black woman at that. So I had to go through a period of "passing the test." I believe my survival during that initial phasing in period was due to

the support I received from the Black workers that were employed as janitors and general maintenance workers.

In the office area I managed, I faced an all White staff of 12 men and women, all over 40. The first thing I discovered was that the enforcement of policies in the department had been somewhat lax. Many of them had a practice of leaving late just to earn overtime--which I had no problem with as long as work was actually being done. So when I began to set policies that addressed this concern, I posed a threat to their paychecks. And they exuded negativity in every way! One of my first challenges was trying to sort out job responsibilities, balance the duties, and make people more accountable. The way I approached this was by spending the day with each of my staff and trying to establish some system of accountability. I did not necessarily meet with visible resistance, but they would want to control how these meetings played out, like they needed to be the one to teach me something. They played the game of you are dumb and we have to show you. Here I am the one with the degree and most of them were barely out of high school! And so you go along with the game, but you know all the time you still have the upper hand. It did not take long for me to become aware of people snitching and talking about me to upper management.

Then there were the rough looking and racist acting guys from other departments that I had to deal with on a daily basis because they depended on my department to do their jobs. On Monday morning department meetings, I came to anticipate them blaming my department for some delay in their operation. On top of that I was the only female (and Black) in those meetings. Several times my "knowledge" of what goes on the field was questioned. So I had to learn the "field" which meant I literally spent a day riding with one of my field workers who I suspected was conducting personal business while he was on duty. One particular day, I confronted him with information I had that confirmed my suspicion that he was riding around all day, drawing overtime, but not doing the work. He fussed and jumped and ranted, threatening to quit and he's going to have me fired, that sort of thing. But in the end, he knew I had the power--not him.

The manager who I reported to always sat behind closed doors, but he was aware of the battles I was fighting. He would not necessarily walk down the hall and come to the fight, but he would hear about the fight; because I would usually go to him and complain. I can say that if it came to my needing help because [others] were really jumping me, he would stand up and say, hey we are going to have to work it the way she says. But I am sure that if it came down to being something that he might have gotten in trouble about, he would have probably blamed me.

Being Excluded

According to the U. S. Small Business Association's designation, social class denotes a Black woman's socially disadvantaged status. Historically, social class has represented a socioeconomic stratification that is measured in terms of education, occupation, wealth, and income. In recent years, social class represents a system that distinguishes the powerful from the powerless. In light of this representation, social class can play a significant role in determining one's access to social networks that influence success and social privilege in the workplace (Byrd, 2009a). Therefore, social class can be one way of asserting power, maintaining exclusion, and sustaining oppression (Stanley, 2009).

According to Gostnell (1996), access and the freedom to exercise one's authority often lies in informal social networking systems. One such social networking system is the good ole boy network. The good ole boy network is an informal social

networking "system that allows racial prejudice to linger and endure and as a result create a social stratification usually across racial lines" (Byrd, 2009a, p. 591). As a result this system creates a barrier that excludes Black women from social networks where opportunities to advance may exist. Bell and Nkomo (2001) refers to this barrier as a concrete ceiling--a barrier that is denser and more difficult to break through than the glass ceiling. Jean continued her story with this recollection:

Numerous times, I was the only Black person period in formal meetings or other gatherings. On one occasion, I was among a group of managers that attended a two-day out-of-town meeting. At the end of the first day's meeting, we went out to eat at sports bar type restaurant where drinking was permitted. Some people get in those environments and try to act cool just to fit in. So that particular night, there was a lot of drinking and loud talk about something I wasn't interested in. After a while, I excused myself by pretending not to feel well. The following morning, I go into the meeting ready to attend to business. As I am going over the day's agenda, I am surprised to discover that the items on the agenda had already been discussed and decided upon the previous night!

So I soon learned that was where the decisions were made. Like people who golf. One of the top managers took up golfing. And guess what? Because he was into the sport other managers began golfing. And so you learn to do those sorts of things to get access to information. But I never played games when it came down to my job because I never wanted to do anything that was compromising.

Needing Support

In predominantly White settings, Black women have limited opportunities to form mentoring relationships (Byrd, 2009a). Mentoring is a supportive relationship whereby individuals learn to reflect on and examine their personal sense of self, integrating self-confidence and personal fulfillment with professional development (Merriam & Caffarella, 1999). For Black women, access to mentors to which they can identify, share, and reflect on lived experiences emerging from their social identity is crucial because these lived experiences require specialized insights and perspectives that are not shared with the dominant culture (Collins, 1990). Jean shared the following experience of needing support:

When you are a new manager, you are often a little reluctant to ask direct questions because it sounds like you have a lesser understanding of something. So what you do is, you try to find someone you are comfortable with. When I first got the position of chief assigner there were no other Black women managers for me to relate to. But eventually I was sent to a training workshop where I met another Black woman from another region. She managed a larger department compared to me. But it was a wonderful experience to connect with her—because she was Black and we could share the Black experience. It also enabled me to form an alliance with her although we were not in the same geographic area. She shared a lot with me and I really appreciated that because I knew coming from another Black woman, she knew what she was talking about as opposed to a White person giving me this information. And I knew everything she said she was doing to get past certain situations, I was going to have to do it that same way. I was fortunate to get another Black woman's perspective because she was sharing how to make that social thing work in that environment. Eventually a Black male transferred to my region and being more seasoned about company operations, he was a valuable source of information and support for me.

Being Stigmatized

Black women entering organizations to lead are challenged to de-myth (disrupt) the stigmas and images that has been assigned by society merely by nature of group membership (Byrd, 2009a). According to Jean, overcoming the stereotypes associated with Black people in general, and Black women in particular was ultimately a source of strength for her.

I was constantly in the mode of proving that I could do something. I wanted to prove that I wasn't some exceptional Black woman that didn't fit the stereotype they had in their heads. Most Black people, who work in these type environments, have good work ethics and we want to prove ourselves in terms of what people think about all Black people. Because everybody is assessing you more than the White male, who is not fair, but they expect the Black woman to be fair and we tend to become very fair minded. This is another way I evolved because right now I'm extremely fair-minded and I can't tolerate people who are not, I don't care who it is.

So I evolved because I had to build up a strength I didn't know I had. I can remember a time sitting quietly. But over the years I slowly came out of that shell. I never considered myself a spokesperson for Black women, but in speaking up for myself, I was speaking up for someone who was still trying to find their strength. I have a really good work ethic. I have often found myself trying to set the standard for all the Black people; because many of the times the whole is judged by a single part. Throughout my career, I gained more courage to speak out and stand alone.

Being Disempowered

The convergence of social identity constructs are fundamentally structured by the existence of a power hierarchy at the macro and micro levels in this society. Therefore in challenging the dynamics produced, the politics of "power to disempower" as well as to "dominate and control" should be central to the analysis.

Whites often use their privilege to undermine and control the actions of Blacks in organizational or other settings (Deitch, et al., 2003). Privilege and control can create an outsider within experience for Black women--a term coined by Collins (1998) to describe feelings of disempowerment within interactive systems of power, race, gender, and social class. Disempowerment may occur in the form of challenging, resisting, resenting, circumventing or even ignoring a person's authority (Byrd, 2009a). A Black woman that experiences disempowerment is often the only person of color in a group setting. Quite often, Whites appear unaware or insensitive to how this experience can create feelings of being alone, alienated, or undervalued (Byrd, 2009a). Jean recalled the following:

Most of the resistance I got came from the other department managers [White men] who were always trying to make my department look inefficient. But on Monday mornings when we would have department meetings, I had documentation that showed their crews, not my employees, were responsible for customers' complaints. It didn't take me long to realize I had that power. So I implemented a procedure that if customers did not receive service as requested, those managers needed to be accountable for why their crews didn't make it happen. It really annoyed them when I did this. But that was just one of the many times I found myself having to prove to them that I could manage my department, despite my inexperience as a manager. But what I did, I had to neutralize my inexperience by learning more

about the company's procedure. So I memorized the procedures manual! I found out real quick they didn't read anything. They would just go into a meeting and talk off the top of their heads. So whenever I spoke during these Monday meetings, I would have procedural information from the manual and that's how I would talk and that would always frustrate the men. But rather than acknowledging my efficiency, they challenged me by saying things like, you think you know this, but it doesn't work that way...what's in that book is not what we're out there doing.

Another thing they did was to try and block me out. I would try to call them [department managers] all day on the phone, but they wouldn't call me back. Or they would go around me and treat me like I was not really the manager of my department. When they would contact my department they would talk to my employees and have them relay a message to me. By then I had gained some knowledge about the department to basically understand how things worked. And I was more confident. So even though they called in and talked to my employees, I would still have to say yes or no to whatever they were calling about. When I refused to accept any more messages, that problem took care of itself, because I made it clear they were not going to ignore me.

After I left [the utility company] I accepted a position as administrator for a state agency. I report to a White woman who has tried in every way to control me. In fact, initially I was not even able to use the official title I was hired into because this woman was using this title as well. One thing she recognized though is my writing skill. Numerous times, she has claimed ownership of documents I have written by replacing my name with her own. Finally, I told her secretary she would need to speak directly to me before she used any information with my signature on it. It was not so much having the recognition, but at least being acknowledged for my contribution.

Another way she has tried to control my authority was by blocking everything I tried to implement by withholding funding for projects or programs. When I successfully pulled off projects, this woman would be so outdone because things turned out so well. One particular project earned us national recognition at a major conference; it is even on the web. After the conference, we were at a staff meeting, and the Executive Director [of the organization] was present. When my manager got up to make remarks, she recognized everything but my involvement and success with that national project. But when the Executive Director got up, he went on and on about my work on the project. I think she realized how this made her look.

For the first six months after I got the position, I didn't even have a computer. A guy from another department felt so bad for me that he gave me a laptop. In fact, the project that gained us national attention--I typed that up myself on that laptop.

On top of that, initially I was not provided with support staff. Other administrators had staff they didn't know what to do with and all I had asked for was one clerk. During staff meetings when I gave a report, I would say, "me, myself, and I" did this or that. After one particular staff meeting her secretary called for me to come and sign paperwork for a clerk. My manager had never discussed this with me, but it finally hit her that maybe she needed to give me the clerk. Because it looked sort of obvious—I was the only Black administrator without staff to assist me.

She rarely includes me in information sharing meetings that I will eventually have some role. Then when she eventually has a conversation with me, she approaches me like I had been in on every moment of the discussion on whatever it was. One occasion I asked her to explain my role, and she responded in an exasperated tone like I'm the one wrong just for asking! Now all the other administrators had gone out to lunch

and dinner with her. But I'm the one that hadn't, so being outside the loop, I need her to explain things to me. And something else, she always wants me to do the behind the scenes jobs, but she wants to carry the ball into the room. I understand her role as my superior, but I do not accept her dominance and control.

Stories like Jean's suggest that leadership is not confined to a singular reality. For Black women leaders, leadership is based on facing multiple social identities that emerge from a system of race, gender, and social class. Based on the findings from this study, the lived experience of being a Black woman leader in a predominantly White organization brings a sociocultural theoretical perspective to leadership. Sociocultural theoretical perspectives refer to theories that consider social constructs in analyzing power dynamics within bureaucratic and other systems where power can be used to oppress (Merriam & Caffarella, 1999).

Critical Race Theory (CRT) is an appropriate framework for explaining the leadership experiences of Black women in predominantly White organizations (Byrd, 2009a; Howard-Hamilton, 2003). As a socio-cultural framework, CRT considers the multiple identities and roles of Black women that are associated with their social identity and are not captured in traditional leadership theories and frameworks.

CRITICAL RACE THEORY: TOWARD A SOCIO-CULTURAL FRAMEWORK

Critical race theory originated in the area of legal scholarship and evolved during a period of social unrest in the United States (Crenshaw, 2002). CRT is based on the premise that systems of oppression such as racism, have become so embedded as a norm in our society that its practice is assumed to be natural (Ladson-Billings, 1998).

CRT is associated with a critical theory paradigm that uses stories and narratives to counter the status quo and in the process unveil the unique experiences of disadvantaged groups (Bernal, 2002; Byrd, 2009a). Moreover, CRT uses a social justice framework to address the inequalities that are pervasive in society. As a critical theory, CRT raises an awareness of the everyday experiences of oppressed groups that have been hidden or distorted by the status quo. The ultimate goal for using CRT as a socio-cultural framework is activism and social change.

The stories, beliefs, and experiences of oppressed groups (women, people of color, etc.) are often lost in the stories, beliefs, and perspective of the dominant group (Delgado, 1995). Although members of the dominant group engage in storytelling, they are unable to see the subjectivity of their narratives and therefore take advantage of their position of privilege in advancing their perspective as the norm. On the other hand, CRT uses narratives and storytelling, usually from the perspective of an oppressed group, to deconstruct the norm and reconstruct perspectives that are more inclusive and reflective of social identity diversity. In this study, CRT helps to explain Jean's lived leadership experiences in several ways.

First, Jean challenged the status quo by telling her story. Stories are a form of giving voice which can counter the dominant discourse, challenge the traditional way of knowing, and stimulate our thinking on what constitutes knowledge (Bernal, 2002; Byrd, 2009a). Relinquishing one's right to be heard relinquishes one's power. Through storytelling, Jean was given voice, which granted her a source of power. Because dilemmas and problems that stem from the social identity of the leader are not common to the discourse of leadership, the experiences of Black women leaders have been silent. Therefore, the critical examination of Black women's experiences infers that the discourse of a phenomenon is not complete until all voices have been heard (Andersen & Collins, 2001; Stanley, 2009).

Second, Jean described encounters with issues that she perceived were related to her social

identity. Encountering issues that are oppressive in relation to one's social location is consistent with how CRT gives centrality to racism and other forms of social identity diversity (Byrd, 2009b). "Race-gendered epistemologies emerge from ways of knowing that are in direct contrast with the dominant Eurocentric epistemology partially as a result of histories that are based on the intersection of racism, sexism, classism and other forms of subordination" (Bernal, 2002, p. 110).

Finally, Jean was willing to take a risk by speaking out against disempowering situations that challenged her authority and effectiveness to lead. In some situations, Black women find themselves accepting circumstances rather than challenging the bureaucracy of a social hierarchy. In the present study, Jean's willingness to use initiative, to speak out, and stand-alone defines a commitment to social justice and social change. These qualities are consistent with the aspired outcome of CRT, which is to promote social justice and create social change in society. Therefore, CRT offers a useful framework for exploring social justice issues and gaining a deeper insight on ways of knowing from the experiences of socially disadvantaged groups.

CONCLUSION AND RECOMMENDATION

This qualitative study investigated the everyday, lived leadership experiences of a Black woman in a predominantly White organization. The findings revealed that the participant experienced feeling alone, being excluded, needing support, being stigmatized, and being disempowered. By presenting leadership from the perspective of social identity diversity, this study contributes new insights for developing leadership theories.

Moreover, bringing discussions of social identity diversity into the conversation of leadership is enlightening because it challenges the taken for granted notion that White, middle class men are the defining group for studying leadership

(Byrd, 2009a). While the findings from this study are not intended to generalize the experiences to all Black women leaders in predominantly White organizations, the experiences of the participant gave voice to a social identity perspective that is not generally articulated through traditional, mainstream leadership literature. Therefore, sociocultural frameworks such as critical race theory are needed to give voice to the socially disadvantaged, challenge the status quo, and bring to light the significance of a social justice approach for explaining social identity diversity in organizations and institutions.

It is often difficult to separate the influence of race from that of sex; there is no doubt, however that the combination levies a heavy toll on the black woman who tries to exercise her authority and responsibility in groups. Herein lies the most significant challenge to black women [leaders]... and to all who are concerned with the development of social and psychological theories of organizational leadership (Dumas, 1975, p. 49).

REFERENCES

Andersen, M. L., & Collins, P. H. (Eds.). (2001). *Race class and gender: An anthology* (4th ed.). Belmont, CA: Wadsworth Thomson Learning.

Bell, D. A. (1993). Remembrance of racism past: The civil rights decline. In Hill, H., & Jones, J. E. (Eds.), *Race in America: The Struggle for Equality* (pp. 73–82). Madison, WI: University of Wisconsin Press.

Bell, E. L., & Nkomo, S. (2001). *Our separate ways: Black and White women and the struggle for professional identity*. Boston, MA: Harvard Business School Press.

Bernal, D. (2002). Critical race theory, Latino critical theory, and critical raced-gendered epistemologies: Recognizing students of color as holders and creators of knowledge. *Qualitative Inquiry, 8*(1), 105–126.

Byrd, M. (2008). Negotiating new meanings of "leader" and envisioning culturally informed theories for developing African American women in leadership roles: An interview with Patricia Parker. *Human Resource Development International, 11*(1), 101–107. doi:10.1080/13678860701782477

Byrd, M. (2009a). Telling our stories of leadership: If we don't tell them they won't be told. *Advances in Developing Human Resources, 11*(5), 582–606. doi:10.1177/1523422309351514

Byrd, M. (2009b). Theorizing African American women's leadership experiences: Socio-cultural theoretical alternatives. *Advancing Women in Leadership Journal, 27*(2).

Clark, M. C. (2001). Off the beaten path: Some creative approaches to adult learning. In Merriam, S. B. (Ed.), *The New Update on Adult Learning Theory* (pp. 83–93). San Francisco, CA: Jossey Bass. doi:10.1002/ace.11

Collins, P. H. (1990). *Black feminist thought: Knowledge, consciousness, and the politics of empowerment*. New York, NY: Routledge.

Collins, P. H. (1998). *Fighting words: Black women and the search for justice*. Minneapolis, MN: University of Minnesota Press.

Crenshaw, K. (1989). Demarginalizing the intersection of race and sex: A black feminist critique of antidiscrimination doctrine, feminist theory and antiracist politics. *The University of Chicago Legal Forum*, 139–167.

Crenshaw, K. W. (2002). The first decade: Critical reflections or a foot in the closing door. *UCLA Law Review. University of California, Los Angeles. School of Law, 49*(5), 1343–1373.

Creswell, J. W. (1998). *Qualitative inquiry and research design: The five traditions*. Thousand Oaks, CA: Sage.

Deitch, E. A., Barsky, A., Butz, R. M., Chan, S., Brief, A. P., & Bradley, J. C. (2003). Subtle yet significant: The existence and impact of everyday racial discrimination in the workplace. *Human Relations*, *56*(11), 1299–1324. doi:10.1177/00187267035611002

Delgado, R. (1995). Storytelling for oppositionists and others: A plea for narrative. In Delgado, R. (Ed.), *Critical Race Theory: The Cutting Edge* (pp. 267–277). Philadelphia, PA: Temple University Press. doi:10.2307/1289308

Dilthey, W. (1976). *Wilhelm Dilthey: Selected writings*. Cambridge, UK: CambridgeUniversity Press.

Dumas, R. G. (1975). *The seed of the coming free: An essay on black female leadership*. Barbourville, KY: The Union Graduate School.

Dumas, R. G. (1980). Dilemmas of black females in leadership. In Rodgers-Rose, L. (Ed.), *The Black Woman*. Thousand Oaks, CA: Sage.

Gostnell, G. M. (1996). *The leadership of African American women: Constructing realities, shifting paradigms*. Portland, OR: Portland State University.

Hine, D. C. (1992). The black studies movement: Afrocentric-traditionalist-feminist paradigms for the next stage. *The Black Scholar*, *22*, 11–18.

hooks, b. (1984). *Feminist theory: From the margin to center*. Boston, MA: South End Press.

Howard-Hamilton, M. F. (2003). Theoretical frameworks for African American women. *New Directions for Student Services*, *104*, 19–27. doi:10.1002/ss.104

King, D. K. (1988). Multiple jeopardy, multiple consciousness: The context of a black feminist ideology. *Signs*, *14*(1), 42–72. doi:10.1086/494491

Ladson-Billings, G. (1998). Just what is critical race theory and what's it doing in a nice field like education. *Qualitative Studies in Education*, *11*(1), 7–24. doi:10.1080/095183998236863

Ladson-Billings, G., & Tate, W. (1995). Toward a critical race theory of education. *Teachers College Record*, *97*(1), 47–68.

Lincoln, Y. S., & Guba, E. G. (1985). *Naturalistic inquiry*. Beverly Hills, CA: Sage.

Lloyd-Jones, B. (2009). Implications of race and gender in higher education administration: An African American woman's perspective. *Advances in Developing Human Resources*, *11*(5), 606–618. doi:10.1177/1523422309351820

Merriam, S. B., & Caffarella, R. S. (1999). *Learning in adulthood*. San Francisco, CA: Jossey-Bass.

Miles, M. B., & Huberman, A. M. (1994). *Qualitative data analysis: An expanded sourcebook* (2nd ed.). Newbury Park, CA: Sage.

Parker, P. S. (2001). African American women executives within dominant culture organizations: (Re)conceptualizing notions of instrumentality and collaboration. *Management Communication Quarterly*, *15*(1), 42–82. doi:10.1177/0893318901151002

Parker, P. S. (2005). *Race, gender, and leadership: Re-envisioning organizational leadership from the perspectives of African American women executives*. Mahwah, NJ: Lawrence Erlbaum Associates, Publishers.

Patton, M. Q. (2002). *Qualitative research and evaluation*. Thousand Oaks, CA: Sage Publications.

Schein, E. H. (1992). *Organizational culture and leadership*. San Francisco, CA: Jossey-Bass.

Stanley, C. (2009). Giving voice from the perspectives of African American women leaders. *Advances in Developing Human Resources, 11*(5), 551–561. doi:10.1177/1523422309351520

Taylor, C. R. (2004). *An inquiry into the experiences of the African American women principal: Critical race theory and black feminist perspectives*. Augusta, GA: Georgia Southern University.

Terhune, C. P. (2008). Coping in isolation: The experiences of Black women in White communities. *Journal of Black Studies, 38*(4), 547–564. doi:10.1177/0021934706288144

United States Small Business Administration. (2004). *Small business act (15 USC 637)*. Retrieved from http://www.sba.gov/regulations/sbaact/sbaact.html.

Van Manen, M. (1997). *Researching lived experiences: Human science for an action sensitive pedagogy* (2nd ed.). London, UK: The Althouse Press.

Yin, R. K. (1999). Enhancing the quality of case studies in health services research. *Health Services Research, 34*(5), 1209–1224.

KEY TERMS AND DEFINITIONS

Critical Race Theory: Is a framework based on the premise that systems of oppression such as racism, have become so embedded as a norm in our society that is practice is assume to be natural (Ladson-Billings, 1998).

Intersectionality: Refers to the convergence or intersection of race, gender, and social class; denotes the various ways these social constructs interact and shape multiple dimensions of Black women's experiences (Crenshaw, 1989).

Lived Experience: Is experience that is not secondhand. It is experienced in how an individual perceives, describes, feels, judges, remembers, makes sense of, and talks about the experience (Patton, 2002).

Organizational Leadership: Refers to the practice of leadership within a context where individuals are held to norms, values, and beliefs of the organization's culture (Parker, 2001).

Social Identity Diversity: Is a form of difference that marginalized groups experience in predominantly White organizational and institutional settings as a result of intersectionality.

Socially Disadvantaged: Refers to individuals who have been subjected to ethnic prejudice or cultural bias because of their identity as a member of a group without regard to their individual qualities (SBA, 2004).

Sociocultural Theories: Refer to theories that consider social constructs in analyzing power dynamics within bureaucratic and other systems where power can be used to oppress (Merriam & Caffarella, 1999).

Chapter 26
Utilizing a New Human Relations Framework to Leverage Workforce Diversity

Rossella Riccò
University of Milan, Italy

ABSTRACT

In a global society, leveraging people's diversities is one of the major challenges faced by organizations of any size in developed countries. Factors such as demographic changes, international and national anti-discrimination measures, globalization, service-economy shifts, stakeholder pressures on organizational commitment to corporate social responsibility, and technological advances are heightening the international attention paid to the increase in people's diversities, thereby fostering discussion on their management in organizations. Since the end of the 1980s, professionals and academics have been debating how to devise efficient, effective, and equitable ways to manage workforce diversity in organizations; however, they have produced neither a shared definition of diversity management nor a general accepted assessment on the outcomes that diversity management can deliver for organizations and persons. The aim of this chapter is to expand the understanding of diversity management by systematizing it on the basis of McGregor's new human relations framework.

INTRODUCTION

We live in a global society, "a diverse social universe in which the unifying forces of modern production, markets, communications, and cultural and political modernization interact with many global, regional, national, and local segmentations and differentiations" (Shaw, 2000, p. 11). As

underlined by McGrew (1992), this global society is a "shrinking world where relations, networks, activities and interconnections of all kinds" (p. 64), especially socio-economic, environmental and political, extend beyond national boundaries. In this global society, leveraging people's diversities (Jayne & Dupboye, 2004; Scott, 2010) is one of the major challenges facing organizations of any size in developed countries.

DOI: 10.4018/978-1-4666-1812-1.ch026

But what is "diversity"? Academics have defined "diversity" in rather different ways (Carnevale & Stone, 1994; Cox, 1994; Kandola & Fullerton, 1998; Kossek & Lobel, 1996; Milliken & Martins, 1996; Thomas, 1991; Zanoni & Jassens, 2004). Here, by "diversity" is meant the multiplicity of differences and similarities that exist among people (Kreitner & Kinicki, 2004) and which, combined together, create each person's multiple and intersecting identities. These identities define a person's uniqueness, which is expressed in how s/he lives with, sees, and relates to other people and to the world in general. Kossek and Lobel (1996) emphasize that "each of these potentially overlapping identity group memberships can affect an employee's attitudes and behaviors in the workplace, as well as influence his or her ability to work well with other organizational members" (p. 2). According to Thomas's idea that "diversity is inherently neither good nor bad, but rather a reality" (2004, p. 10), companies have to gain a sense of how to plan and implement "organizational systems and practices to manage people so that the potential advantages of diversity are maximized while its potential disadvantages are minimized" (Cox, 1993, p. 11). This induces organizations to shift from a management undifferentiated in terms of strategy, policy, solutions, and tools to a "conscious" diversity management. However, there is no generally accepted definition of "diversity management," and academics and professionals too often use this concept without stating the meaning that they give to it, thus leaving one unsure as to what they are really talking about. Indeed, even though since the end of the 1980s professionals and academics have been engaged in animated debate on how to devise efficient, effective, and equitable ways to manage people's diversities in organizations, they have produced neither a shared definition of diversity management nor a generally accepted assessment, be it positive or negative, of the outcomes that diversity management can deliver to organizations and persons (Curtis & Dreachslin, 2008; Kirton &

Greene, 2005; Shen, Chanda, D'Netto, & Monga, 2009; Zanoni & Jassens, 2004). Academics are divided into two main groups: those who support diversity management on the basis of the business case, and those who adopt a more critical approach to the issue. Despite this division, it is possible to identify general agreement on certain features regarded as distinctive of the diversity management approach, namely:

- People are considered key assets for organizational success, moreover they are diverse, and their diversities should be managed by the organization
- Diversity management is a contextual issue, that is to say, there is no "best" diversity strategy or a "one-size-fits-all" solution
- Diversity management is a long-term approach that requires the commitment of the organization's board and managers
- Diversity management requires organizations to carry out changes in both cultural and organizational terms.

In order to systematize the concept of diversity management starting from these elements and using a new human relations framework revolving around McGregor's thought (2006), this chapter proposes a definition of diversity management and explains it in depth.

BACKGROUND

The increasing diversity of markets, customers, and workforces is one of the main characteristics of global society. It is possible to identify a plurality of factors, external to the organizations, that have direct the attention of academics and professionals to people's diversities, most notably: demographic changes (feminization of the labor force; the increase in working age with the interconnected growing presence of different age cohorts in organizations; the increase of people of different nationalities at work) (Johnston & Packer, 1987; Kirton & Greene, 2005; Kossek & Lobel, 1996); international and national anti-discrimination laws (Cox, 1993; Kelly & Dobbin, 1998); socio-political concerns with people's life and work quality (Dickens, 1999; O'Leary & Weathington, 2006); trade expansion in time and space (globalization) (Nishii & Özbilgin, 2007); service-economy shifts (customers' heterogeneity; the personalization of services and products) (Kossek & Lobel, 1996); stakeholder pressures for the organization's commitment to corporate social responsibility (Kossek & Lobel, 1996; Wright, Ferris, Hiller, & Kroll, 1995); and technological advances (Kossek & Lobel, 1996). Over time, these factors have influenced the attention paid by academics and professionals to people's diversities, and on their management in organizations, in different ways.

Academics and professionals started to focus their attention on people's diversities in the US in the second half of the 1960s. As well described by Kelly and Dobbin (1998), the interest in diversity was initially driven by legal factors. Following Kennedy's 1961 executive order 10925, which required federal contractors to commit themselves to ending discrimination by means of affirmative action, in 1964 the Civil Rights Act (Title VII) declared the unlawfulness of employment discrimination (on grounds of race, ethnicity, nationality, and thereafter gender and religion). Consequently, at the beginning of the 1970s, concern for diversity in organizations was mandated by laws (Affirmative Action Law, 1971; Equal Employment Opportunity Act, 1972) and was regarded as an onerous compliance to legal requirements. During the 1980s, organizational attention to diversity shifted from legal to political factors. Regan's political actions, in fact, were contrary to affirmative action (especially quotas) and had the effect of reducing the effectiveness of these laws. Regan's administration (January 1981 – January 1989) sought to identify a managerial model that would be perceived as politically cor-

rect and accepted by American boards and managers. However, this managerial model did not yet exist. At the end of the 1980s, as Ivancevich and Gilbert (2000) show, organizational attention to people's diversities turned to demographic factors as a consequence of Johnston and Parker's (1987) study on changes in the composition of the US workforce, which forecasted a considerable further enlargement in workforce diversity in the twenty-first century. Johnston and Parker urge organizations to consider how to face this new challenge. Following this recommendation, at the beginning of the 1990s academics and professionals shifted their attention from the issue of workforce diversity to that of the management of people's diversity in organizations. In 1990 Thomas Roosevelt Jr. stated that organizations should commit themselves to creating "an environment where no one is advantaged or disadvantaged, an environment where 'we' is everyone…where everyone will do their best work" (p. 109). One year later, the same author introduced the expression *managing diversity*[1] defining it as organizational commitment to attract, recruit, retain, reward and develop an heterogeneous mix of productive, motivated and committed employees, including people of different colors, genders and physical or mental abilities. Since then, diversity management has become an *organizational approach* aimed at creating a work environment (workplace, job, and relationships) that enables organizations to enhance and to integrate people's diversities in order to achieve better results (to increase the organization's effectiveness). This still undefined organizational approach captured the political attention of George H. W. Bush's administration because it was identified as the ideal solution to boost in organizations as a replacement for affirmative action. In fact, diversity management was deemed politically correct (it required that the potential of each person be respected, enhanced and integrated within the organization) without imposing any specific organizational solution. It thus became more easily acceptable by organizations.

In the 1990s the grounds for organizational attention to diversity management moved from legal and political reasons to economic ones. In those years academics focused on the so-called diversity management *"business case,"* that is, the number of economic, competitive, and reputational reasons ascribable to a more differentiated, efficient, effective, and equitable way of managing people's diversities. The diversity management business case concerns three different areas (economic, competitive and reputational) and it can bring five main advantages to the organization: reduction of organizational costs, increase in stock values, increase in individual, group and organizational productivity and performance, better customers relations, improvement of organizational image and reputation. Table 1 summarizes the main areas, elements, and organizational results that compose the diversity management business case.

It was especially because of the diversity business case that diversity management spread from North America to Canada, the English-speaking countries and North European countries as an organizational approach able to assure organizational competitiveness or survival in the medium-long run (Cox & Blake, 1991; Curtis & Dreachslin, 2011; Ivancevich & Gilbert, 2000; Kandola & Fullerton, 1998). However, it should be stressed

Table 1. The diversity management business case (adapted from Riccò, 2008, pp. 217-219; Riccò, 2011, pp. 6-7)

Area	Elements that Compose the Diversity Management Business Case	Organizational Results
ECONOMIC	Working environment improvements and workforce motivation enhancements reduce the organization's costs relative to: o health and stress o demotivation o absenteeism o strikes o mobbing-discrimination Cuts in selection and training costs through: o reduced turnover rates, which reduce the costs due to selection and training o hiring better employees (those right for the vacant positions and for the organization) selecting them among a wider pool of potential candidates Elimination of costs connected to: o legal cases (legal sanctions) o internal conflicts (exclusions, discriminations or mobbing) o market sanctions in terms of negative endorsements that have • internal effects on actual employees (reduction in employees' effort, strikes or quits); • external effects on potential candidates (who do not consider the organization because it is perceived to be a bad place to work) • external effects on customers because they do not approve of how the organization manages its employees • external effects due to reduction of public funds or access to public notifications	COST REDUCTION (Cox & Blake, 1991; Milliken & Martins, 1996; Kandola & Fullerton, 1998; Worman, Bland & Chase, 2005)
	Increase in stock value for organizations committed to adopting diversity management (Wright, Ferris, Hiller & Kroll, 1995; Wang & Schwarz, 2010)	INCREASE IN STOCK VALUE
REPUTA-TIONAL	Organization's image and reputation improvements o worth recognized by institutions and costumers in relation to diversity management effort o enhancement of Corporate Social Responsibility (Anderson & Metcalf, 2003; Cox & Blake, 1991; Worman, Bland & Chase, 2005) Better organizational capacity to attract qualified candidates and to retain high-potential employees (Cox & Blake, 1991; Kandola & Fullerton, 1998; Worman, Bland & Chase, 2005)	IMAGE AND REPUTATION IMPROVEMENT

continued on following page

Table 1. Continued

Area	Elements that Compose the Diversity Management Business Case	Organizational Results

COMPETITI-VENESS	Employees more committed to the organization
	  o more willingness to take on extra-role actions/activities
	  o more effort
	  o more loyalty
	  (Ivanchevich & Gilbert, 2000; Worman, Bland & Chase, 2005)
	Increase in internal flexibility
	  o working hours solutions
	  o work organizations
	  o rewarding solutions (total rewards idea)
	  (Golembiewski, 1995; Kandola & Fullerton, 1998)
	Improvement of employees' behaviors
	  o promotion of personal and professional development
	  o promotion of interaction among employees with different backgrounds and characteristics
	Better organizational climate
	  o strengthening of the organization's cultural values
	  o improvement of internal respect and cooperation
	  o better internal relations
	  o better quality of work and working environment and consequent increase in workforce motivation, participation, satisfaction and productivity
	  o unexpressed potentials come to light
	  (Gordon, DiTomaso & Farris, 1991; Mulholland, Özbilgin & Worman, 2005)
	Increase in creativity and innovation
	  o diversity promotes the sharing of ideas and a variety of perspectives that lead to better decisional processes
	  (Anderson & Metcalf, 2003; Armstrong et al., 2010; Milliken & Martins, 1996)
	Better group problem-solving capabilities
	  (Cox & Blake, 1991; Worman, Bland & Chase, 2005)
	Increase in productivity
	  (Armstrong et al., 2010; Cox & Blake, 1991; Mulholland, Özbilgin & Worman, 2005)
		INCREASE IN PRODUCTIVITY

	Better customer relations
	  o workforce diversity reflects customer diversity
	  o increase in the organization's ability to understand customers' needs
	  o improvement in service levels and, consequently, in customer satisfaction
	  (Cox & Blake, 1991; Mulholland, Özbilgin & Worman, 2005)
	Increase in organizational sales, market shares and profit margins
	  o invention and introduction of new more targeted goods and services
	  o expansion of reference market
	  (Anderson & Metcalf, 2003)
		IMPROVEMENT OF CUSTOMER RELATIONS

that the diversity management business case is more declared than proven (Foster & Harris, 2005; Kandola & Fullerton, 1998; Kirton & Greene, 2005; Curtis & Dreachslin, 2008). Indeed, as widely recognized in organizational studies, it is extremely difficult to measure the direct effect of human resource management solutions on organizational results (Becker & Huselid, 1998), and it is even more difficult to demonstrate that improvements in organizational results are due to diversity management solutions (Benschop,

2001). At the end of the 1990s, these difficulties in measuring the effects of diversity management on organizational results induced academics, especially in the UK, to adopt a more critical approach to diversity management. These authors focused on the lack of effective demonstration of the business case (Kirton & Greene, 2005; Zanoni & Jassens, 2006); the theoretical vagueness of the concept of diversity management (Foster & Harris, 2005; Lorbiecki & Jack, 2000); the "rhetoric" connected to the diversity management approach (Ivancevich & Gilbert, 2000; Kirton & Greene, 2005; Zanoni & Jassens, 2006); the reduced anti-discrimination force of diversity management compared with equal opportunity and affirmative action (Liff & Dickens, 2000; Kelly & Dobbin, 1998; Kirton & Greene, 2005); as well as problems related to the integration of people's diversities (Foster & Harris, 2005), intra- and inter-group conflicts related to diversities (Gordon, 1995; Wrench, 2001) and diversity management costs in economic, organizational, legal and change terms (UE, 2003). Today, academics and professionals are still divided between those who support diversity management and those who are critical of it. Figure 1 illustrates the evolution of American academics' and professionals' attention to workforce diversity and diversity management. It shows how, over time, there has been a shift in the debate from the issue of workforce anti-discrimination (which arose outside organizations; non-business reasons) to that of workforce diversity management (which arose within the organizations as a way to achieve a competitive advantage; business reasons).

Although academics and professionals, especially in the US and the UK, have engaged in lively debate on people's diversities and their management in organizations for more that thirty years, they still have not agreed on a definition of diversity management, and one currently witnesses a division in the international community between those who support diversity management and those who are instead more critical of it. The academics and professionals who support diversity management focus on the diversity management business case (Armstrong, et al., 2010; Dass & Parker, 1999; Jayne & Dipboye, 2004; Kandola & Fullerton, 1998; Kossek & Lobel, 1996; Thomas, 1990; Worman, Bland, & Chase, 2005). They consider diversity management to be an approach that aims at achieving better organizational results through the diversified, efficient, effective, and equitable management of people's diversities. On the other hand, academics who adopt a more critical approach to diversity management (Foster & Harris, 2005; Gordon, 1995; Ivancevich & Gilbert, 2000; Liff & Dickens, 2000; Kelly & Dobbin, 1998; Kirton & Greene, 2005; Zanoni & Jassens, 2006; Wrench, 2001) tend to concentrate on anti-discrimination and equal opportunity issues, assessing the capacity of diversity management to overcome workplace discrimination and to grant equal opportunities to all employees.

Figure 1. Evolution of the US academics' and professionals' attention to workforce diversity and diversity management

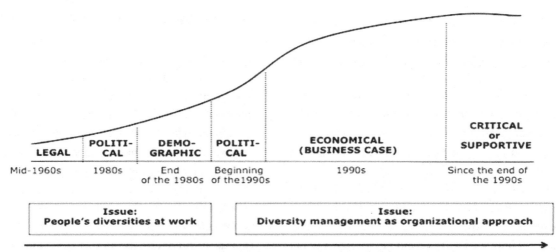

Despite this division, it is possible to identify general agreement on some elements regarded as distinctive of the diversity management approach.

Firstly, diversity management is grounded on the idea that people are key assets for organizational success. By recognizing that people are characterized by many intersected diversities that need to be managed, a diversity management approach maintains that only the "conscious" management of these diversities can establish a real, outstanding, and lasting competitive advantage for the organization (Thomas, 1990; Worman, Bland, & Chase, 2005). Indeed, this conscious management should be made in a diversified, effective, efficient and equitable way.

Secondly, diversity management is claimed to be a highly "contextual" matter. There is no single way for organizations to manage people's diversities, nor is there a *one best diversity strategy*. On the contrary, the management of diversities requires a *fit* with the specific organizational context (Cox, 1993; Dass & Parker, 1999; Kandola & Fullerton, 1998; Nishii & Özbilgin, 2007; Shore, et al., 2009; Syed & Özbilgin, 2009; Thomas, 1995). This means that organizations will make their decisions about diversity management on the basis of their different national characteristics in terms of history, culture (Nishii & Özbilgin, 2007; Trompenars & Hampden-Turner, 1998), laws, and economic, social, and political background; as well as on the basis of their business characteristics and specificities (organizational culture, goals, values, available economic, financial, human, technological and temporal resources). Moreover, they will consider diversity management costs and benefits in the short and long run and also the aspirations, identities and beliefs of the people involved in the choice.

Thirdly, in order to be effective, the adoption of this progressive, incremental, and long-term approach requires the commitment of both the organization's board and managers (Eddy, 2008; Kandola & Fullerton, 1998; Kirton & Greene, 2005; Thomas, 1990). Eventually, these people will be responsible for extending the awareness of, and the attention and commitment to people's diversities to all employees, inducing them to respect, enhance, include and integrate these diversities in the workplace.

Finally, it should be borne in mind that diversity brings complexity into organizations (Kandola & Fullerton, 1998; Thomas, 1990, 1995). On undertaking a "conscious" diversity management, organizations should be willing to promote and carry out an internal cultural and organizational change (Dass & Parker, 1999; Pless & Maak, 2004; Shen, Chanda, D'Netto, & Monga, 2009; Thomas, 1990).

Keeping the above-described evolution of the diversity management discourse and the key diversity management elements clearly in mind, the purpose of the present chapter is to systematize the concept of diversity management, thereby eliminating two causes of criticism: the lack of a theoretical foundation for diversity management, and the vagueness of the concept. To this end, the chapter first grounds the organization's commitment to leveraging workforce diversity on McGregor's new human relations theory, and then, in the light of this theoretical framework, it provides a definition of diversity management and explains it in depth.

DIVERSITY MANAGEMENT: TOWARDS A DEFINITION

Too often in organizational studies on diversity management, the theoretical frame—that is the *lens* adopted by the writer to interpret an organization's/person's choices and actions—is not clearly expressed. Recognizing that "theory and practice are inseparable" (McGregor, 2006, p. 8) and consequently that "our thinking, our belief system, our mindset determines our priorities, our procedures, our processes, what we expect from people and the way we deal with them" (Heil, Bennis, & Stephens, 2000, p. 47), it is important to start systematizing the diversity management concept by explaining the basic theoretical assumptions on which the approach is grounded.

This chapter considers McGregor's new human relation theory to be the most appropriate framework in which to leverage workforce diversity in organizations.

McGregor's New Human Relations Framework

In the introduction to the twenty-fifth anniversary printing of *The Human Side of Enterprise* Warren Bennis explained that Douglas McGregor introduced an outstanding novelty in the field of management by replacing the concept of organizational man "with a new paradigm that stressed human potentials, emphasized human growth, and elevated the human role in industrial society" (McGregor, 2006, p. xv). McGregor argues that the most appropriate organizational model to adopt in order to face the increasing complexity of society and the work environment is to unleash human potential at every level of the organization (Heil, Bennis, & Stephens, 2000). His basic assumption is that employees are key elements in an organization's success. He maintains that each person is unique, worthy of trust and respect, and that s/he has knowledge, attitudes, capabilities, and competences that the organization should be able to recognize and develop because "if we don't stretch our goals, offer a valuable cause, and give people an opportunity to realize their potential, chances are that they won't give us the best they have to give" (Heil, Bennis, & Stephens, 2000, p. 120). Another key component of McGregor's thought concerns the relevance of managers' assumptions, beliefs and behaviors in regard to the management of the organization. He underlines that the theoretical assumptions that a manager, implicitly or explicitly, holds about human nature, human behavior, and the most efficient way to manage human resources "determine the whole

character of the enterprise" (McGregor, 2006, p. xxii).

McGregor recognizes the tendency of managers to believe that "the average human being has an inherent dislike of work and will avoid it if s/he can" (McGregor, 2006, p. 45): this is why most people "must be coerced, controlled, directed, threatened with punishment to get them to put forth adequate effort toward the achievement of organizational objective" (McGregor, 2006, pp. 45-46). Moreover, such managers are convinced that "the average human being prefers to be directed, wishes to avoid responsibility, has relatively little ambition, wants security above all" (McGregor, 2006, p. 46). This set of assumptions by managers about human nature and human beings gives rise to the so-called Theory X. Managers who adhere to Theory X organize the resources available (economic and technological, as well as materials, equipments and people) in pursuit of the organization's economic ends. As Heil, Bennis, and Stephens (2000) emphasize, in order to direct people's efforts towards organizational ends, managers become committed to motivating people, to controlling their actions, and to modifying their behaviors "to fit the needs of the organization" (p. 132). Managers who adopt Theory X believe that if the organizational performance is ineffective "it is due to the nature of the human resources with which we must work" (McGregor, 2006, p. 66).

However, Theory X is not the only possible way to look at people in organizations. Indeed, McGregor puts forward another group of assumptions about human nature and human beings that managers can adopt, Theory Y:

1. *The expenditure of physical and mental effort in work is natural as play or rest.* The average human being does not inherently dislike work. Depending upon controllable conditions work may be a source of satisfaction (and will be voluntarily performed) or a source of punishment (and will be avoided if possible).

2. External control and the threat of punishment are not the only means for bringing about effort toward organizational objectives. Man will exercise self-direction and self-control in the service of objectives to which he is committed.
3. *Commitment to objectives is a function of the rewards associated with people's achievements...*
4. *The average human being learns, under proper conditions, not only to accept but also to seek responsibility...*
5. The capacity to exercise a relatively high degree of imagination, ingenuity, and creativity in the solution of organizational problems is widely, not narrowly, distributed in the population.
6. *Under the condition of modern industrial life, the intellectual potentialities of the average human being are only partially utilized* (McGregor, 2006, pp. 65-66).

In building his theory, Douglas McGregor embraces Maslow's (1982) motivation theory, which organizes human needs into five main hierarchical levels: physiological needs (i.e. air, food, drink, rest, exercise, shelter, clothes), safety needs (i.e. protection against danger, threat, deprivation), social needs (i.e. sense of belonging, acceptance, friendship, love), ego needs (self esteem and reputation), and self-fulfillment needs (becoming able to realize one's own potentialities and achieve a continued self-development). McGregor then merges these levels of needs into three main categories: physical needs (physiological and safety needs), social needs and egoistic needs (ego and self-fulfillment needs). According to Maslow's theory, human behaviors and actions are driven by the desire to fulfill one's needs, starting from the lowest level and moving to the next level when the previous one has been reasonably satisfied. That means that when a need is satisfied, or reasonably satisfied, it ceases to be a motivator factor. On these assumptions, McGregor claims

that money (rewards, benefits) and control (authority, punishments) are not effective means to satisfy higher-level needs; rather, intrinsic motivation enablers are needed. To foster employees' long-term loyalty, trust and performance, an organization should build and continually modify a work environment in which motivated people can fulfill their needs and uptake their potentialities "while pursuing the goals of the organization" (Heil, Bennis, & Stephens, 2000, p. 87). That is to say, the challenge for organizations is not to find ways to adapt people to the organization's ends, motivating them through coercion (*hard management approach*: "Making them do what they are told" – p. 162) or other extrinsic motivator factors (*soft management approach*: being good and giving them something, so we can manipulate them and lead them to do what we want they do). Instead, the challenge is continually to promote a process of work environment rearrangement founded on the integration of the organization's and the individual's needs, so that each person in the organization is voluntarily willing to cooperate, developing and utilizing his/her capabilities, knowledge, skills and creativity in ways which contribute to the success of the organization. In McGregor's opinion, integration is "the creation of conditions such that the members of the organization can achieve their own goals best by directing their efforts toward the success of the enterprise" (McGregor, 2006, pp. 67-68). Integration between the individual's and the organization's needs requires a shift in the mindset of the organization from a *top-down* one (Theory X) to a *bottom-up* approach. This implies the direct participation of employees in development of their work and career, giving them voice through self-direction, promoting mutual involvement in the definition of personal targets, self-control, and self-appraisal. McGregor maintains that if integration between the individual's and the organization's needs is not achieved, "the organization will suffer" (McGregor, 2006, p. 71). To clarify this statement, it is necessary to explain McGregor's concept of an organization. McGregor considers an organization to be an organic, open, and social system. It is a "system" because it is composed of interrelated elements (people, values, strategies, policies, and economic, financial, technical, and technological resources). This system is "social" because it is made up of persons bound to each other and to the organization by functional relationships (satisfaction of different needs). This social system is "organic": over time, it learns, develops, grows, and changes. Finally, this organic social system is "open" because it is influenced by a political, social, and economic milieu that affects its managerial practices; at the same time, it may be partially influenced by organizational actions. This conception of an organization reflects the belief that organizational ends can be achieved only through the attainment of employees' well-being (connected to physical needs), on-the-job satisfaction (connected to social end egoistic needs), and commitment. In Theory Y, it is assumed that if employees adopt negative behaviors and are not committed to the organization's ends, thus attaining ineffective organizational performance, "the causes lie in management's method of organization and control" (McGregor, 2006, p. 66).

Through Theory Y, McGregor promotes a new managerial approach, which focuses organizational attention on persons with their specificities and needs. He maintains that the achievement of organizational goals can be attained only through the availability of committed employees and through the integration of the organization's and the individual's needs. There are no organizational tools or easy solutions that enable an organization to obtain committed employees and integration; on the contrary, it is necessary to create and continually to readjust a work environment which is "based upon values of respect and integrity" (McGregor, 2006, p. xxxi) and enables each person to participate actively in the definition of his/her work and career. Theory Y challenges organizations "to innovate, to discover new ways of organizing and directing human effort" (McGregor, 2006, p. 74) and it is well suited to approaching the diversity management issue.

Utilizing McGregor's New Human Relations Framework to Define Diversity Management

On the basis of McGregor's new human relations framework (Theory Y), diversity management is defined here as:

a strategic, micro-founded and diversified organizational approach that considers people as core resources for the success of the organization. Thus, in order to achieve better organizational results, it focuses the organization's attention on the person and her/his specificities and needs by promoting and fulfilling a cultural and an organizational process of change so as to create a non-discriminatory and equitable work environment where people's diversities are recognized, respected, enhanced and integrated, and the individual's potential expression is fostered.

Because the purpose of this chapter is to systematize the concept of diversity management and to remove its vagueness, it cannot merely give a definition of diversity management. It must also itemize the various components of this definition and explain each of them in depth.

Firstly, diversity management is an *approach*. It identifies a way in which the organization and the relationships within and outside it are perceived, analyzed, assessed and managed.

Diversity management is then defined as an *organizational* approach because it affects the management of the organization in its entirety (culture, time organization, power division, employees' autonomy and participation in decision-making processes, human resource management, leadership, content, and way of communicating, internal relationships, as well as the organization's internal and external image). It operates on three levels: strategic, tactical, and operational (Shen, Chanda, D'Netto, & Monga, 2009). At the strategic level, diversity management influences the organization's mission, vision, and business strategies in the direction of recognizing, respecting, enhancing and integrating people's diversities by creating a work environment characterized by mutual respect, individual commitment, and cooperation. At the tactical level, diversity management acts on organizational policies, especially on those related to the management of human resources, to attract, motivate, retain, and develop people in the organization (Kossek & Lobel, 1996; Dass & Parker, 1999; Shen, Chanda, D'Netto, & Monga, 2009). At the operational level, diversity management concerns the actual implementation of organizational solutions aimed at building an inclusive work environment that secures employees' commitment to the organization.

Furthermore, diversity management is said to be *strategic* because, besides adopting a holistic view of both organization and people, it falls within a plan of action that identifies clear strategic goals that may contribute to producing structural long-term and permanent effects on employees' commitment and work conditions. Hence, it must be integrated into the general management system, and a long-term perspective must be adopted. In particular, to draw on Pless and Maak (2004) and expand their ideas, diversity management pursues five main strategic goals:

1. To achieve better organizational results in economic, competitive and reputational terms by leveraging people's diversities through their diversified, effective, efficient, and equitable management
2. To raise employees' awareness of diversity in order to fight existing mental schemes (stereotypes, prejudices, ethnocentrism, intolerance and hostility towards certain categories of people, resistance to change), thereby

helping them to understand people's diverse viewpoints and encouraging reflection
3. To develop and disseminate a vision of inclusion and integration at individual, group and organizational level
4. To rethink core concepts and principles of management relative to business values, principles, leadership, decision-making, information and communication processes by considering people's work-life balance needs
5. To induce organizations to create and integrate a system which translates founding principles into observable and measurable behaviors, and which fosters the development, reinforcement, and recognition of inclusive behaviors. For the organization, this will require operating on the processes of recruitment, performance evaluation, development, reward and compensation, as well as creating a non-discriminatory, equitable, and inclusive work environment where "different voices are respected and heard, diverse viewpoints, perspectives and approaches are valued and everyone is encouraged to make a unique and meaningful contribution" (pp. 130-131).

As just set out, the main aim of the diversity management approach is to improve individual, group, and organizational results through the enhancement, inclusion, and integration of people's diversity in the organization. In other words, the diversity management approach is first of all strategically driven by business ends. Nevertheless, the other above-mentioned strategic goals show that it seeks to eliminate stereotypes and prejudices, and to build a work environment where everyone can be themselves, fully expressing their knowledge, capabilities, skills, needs and potentialities. This implies that organizations cannot undertake diversity management without first guaranteeing equal opportunities. Thomas (1990), too, underlines this concept by explaining that diversity management requires equitable management of the organization "without unnatural advantage or disadvantage for any member of your diverse workforce" (p. 117). However, this entails that the organization "must first have a work force that is diverse at every level, and if you don't, you're going to need affirmative action to get from here to there" (p. 117). Diversity management, equal opportunity, and affirmative action are interrelated because they all concern workforce diversity in organizations. But, at the same time, they are very different concepts. Numerous authors have discussed these three different perspectives on workforce diversity and made comparisons among them (Kelly & Dobbin, 1998; Kreitner & Kinicki, 2004; Maxwell, Balir, & McDougall, 2001; Riccò, 2008; Yakura, 1996). In regard to these studies, Table 2 summarizes the main features of diversity management, equal opportunity, and affirmative action.

As shown by Table 2, only diversity management is an organizational approach (driven by business ends), while equal employment opportunity is a socio-political approach (driven by the struggle against work discrimination in organizations driven by laws) and affirmative actions are practical interventions voluntary implemented to amend and to eliminate work discrimination within organizations thereby achieving equal opportunity. The interrelationship among them resides in the inclusiveness of the work environment that diversity management requires to be built. This inclusiveness cannot be achieved without guaranteeing equal employment opportunities to all.

Moreover, diversity management is termed *micro-founded* because it analyzes the relation between the organization and the person underpinning people's diversities, thereby focusing managerial attention on the specific contributions and subjective needs of each employee. The person/organization relation is a highly complex matter inasmuch as it is "specific" (each person is unique because of his/her characteristics and history, hence each person/organization relation is

exclusive), it is "contextualized" (it is built through the organization which contains and gives form to it), and it "takes place in a precise historical context" (Solari, 2004). The person/organization relation is therefore so complex, dynamic and full of hidden implications that large part of its facets remain indefinite at a legal level, and it is instead managed through informal and unwritten agreements constructed by actors and incorporated into the so-called *psychological contract*. The psychological contract is a mental scheme, moderately stable and enduring, consisting of employee's perceptions and beliefs concerning the terms of the reciprocal exchange agreement between the person and her/his organization. This mental scheme is built, developed, and changed through interaction among both employee and organization representatives (i.e. boards, managers, department heads, line-managers) and through the employee's perception of organizational procedures, policies, communications and culture (Rousseau, 1989, 1995). The psychological contract affects people's motivations, choices and behaviors, and it assigns a leading role to trust, loyalty, coherence, communication, and direct participation in the person/organization relation. Rousseau (1995) identifies a continuum of psychological contract types ranging between two ideal-typical extremes: the transitional psychological contract and the relational psychological contract. Table 3 summarizes the main characteristics of the transitional and relational psychological contracts described by Rousseau (1989, 1995) and Solari (2004).

Organizations that choose to adopt a diversity management approach will tend to build and cultivate person/organization relations grounded on psychological contracts that are relational in their nature.

Thereafter, this micro-founded, strategic, organizational approach is *diversified* because—on recognizing people's diversities in terms of physical, psychological, and temperamental characteristics as well as knowledge, capabilities, skills, motivational systems, needs, and life-cycle—it

Table 2. Comparison among diversity management, equal employment opportunity, and affirmative action: three different ways to look at workforce diversity in organizations

	Diversity Management	Equal Employment Opportunity	Affirmative Action
SOURCE	Human resources specialists (academics and professionals)	Laws	Executive order and regulations
PROBLEM	Underutilization of people's knowledge, capabilities, skills and potentialities	Exclusion from, or limited access to, work for some *groups* of people	Exclusion, limited access and development for some *groups* of people in the workplace
AIM	To achieve better organizational results by managing people's diversities (business case and social justice)	To eliminate discrimination in the workplace (social justice and ethical and human rights)	To put right work discrimination effects (social justice and ethical and human rights)
SAFEGUARDED INTERESTS	Both the organization's and people's ends	People's interests	People's interests
IDENTIFIED SOLUTIONS	To realize a cultural and organizational change by creating an inclusive work environment where people's specificities, potentialities and needs are taken into account, respected, enhanced	To allow a minority group to enter the workplace by formalizing organizational commitment to non-discrimination	To allow minority groups not only to enter the workplace but also to advance in it by realizing targeted programs for recruitment, selection and promotion
RATIONALE FOR ADOPTION	Strategic choice driven by economic ends and, perhaps, ethical ends (internal)	Compliance with laws (external) Ethical/Moral choice (internal)	Compliance with laws (external) Ethical/Moral choice (internal)
VALUES PROMOTED	Respect, inclusiveness and integration of people's diversity by means of equity	Equality	Equality and equity
RECIPIENTS	All people	Specific social groups identified as *minorities*	Specific social groups identified as *minorities*
ORGANIZATION ATTITUDE	Proactive The commitment to respecting, enhancing, including and integrating people's diversities affects all the organization's solutions. It starts as a top-down approach but then becomes a circular approach (a combination of both bottom-up and top-down)	Reactive Interventions reflect legal requirements Top-down approach	Active Interventions reflect the organization's determination to do pragmatically something which eliminates discrimination effects Top-down approach
DIVERSITY IS IDENTIFIED AS	All the visible and non-visible characteristics of people that, combined together, create the uniqueness of the multiple and intersecting identities of each person	Multiple and intersecting identities expressed through categories (the main ones are: race, gender, age, disability, religion, sexual orientation)	Multiple and intersecting identities expressed through categories (the main ones are: race, gender, age, disability, religion, sexual orientation)
DIVERSITY IS SEEN	Positively: as a resource in which to invest	Negatively: as a source of discrimination, a limit	Positively: as an opportunity
IN THE ORGANIZATION DIVERSITY IS	Integrated by means of a new culture, new management, and a new work environment	Assimilated	Assimilated

Table 3. Main characteristics of transitional and relational psychological contract

Characteristic	Transitional Contract	Relational Contract
CONTRACT ELEMENTS	Economic	Social and economic
FORMALIZATION	Written	Written and unwritten
AGREEMENT TERMS	Well-defined, not ambiguous	Loosely-defined, subject to personal interpretation
TIME FRAME	Closed-ended	Open-ended
RELATION DURATION	Short-term	Long-term
FORMAT RELATION	Static	Dynamic (subject to change)
ORGANIZATION UPTAKE	Existing employee's competence	Employee's social capital
EXPECTED OUTPUT	Good performance	High level of identification, commitment and loyalty, which will bring good performance
EMPLOYEE'S IDENTIFICATION	Organizational role	Organizational mission and values
PERSONAL WORK INVOLVEMENT	Limited	Whole
EMPLOYEE'S EMOTIONAL AFFECTION	Little	Quite substantial
EMPLOYEE'S MOTIVATION	Self-regarding (individual well-being)	Other-regarding (equity, reciprocity, other's well-being) Process-regarding (procedural justice, involvement)
EMPLOYEE'S MAIN INCENTIVE	Economic conditions (External motivator factors)	Emotional involvement (Internal motivator factors)
EMPLOYEE'S EXPECTATIONS	Salary, professional training, career, status, accessory benefits	Uncertainty and stress reduction, work security, work environment, interesting and stimulating job, autonomy, flexibility, responsibility

treats undifferentiated human resources management solutions as unsuitable. Rather, it requires to establish *for what reasons* (values and motives that induce the organization to realize diversified solutions), *in which cases* (diversity dimensions or specific situations that require the organization to adopt diversified solutions), and *on what basis* (availability of economic, financial, technological, temporal, and human resources that enable the organization to realize diversified solutions) diversified management solutions, pointedly respectful of organizational justice[2] (Kirton & Greene, 2005; O'Leary & Weathington, 2006) can be provided. This implies that not all diversity dimensions will be managed by dedicated organizational solutions (Dass & Parker, 1996; Thomas, 1991, 1995; Thomas & Robin, 1996). Nevertheless, even when a certain workforce diversity is not managed by means of diversified solutions, diversity management gives the organization the awareness necessary to internally and externally motivate its choices, because it builds a conscious approach to the management of people's diversities.

The above definition states that diversity management considers people as *core resources for the success of the organization*. Indeed, every activity within an organization is realized through the work of people (technologies and machinery, too, need the action of employees to be invented, installed, used, updated, monitored, repaired, or replaced). Understanding how to take advantage of people's existing and potential specificities through their management becomes a central objective of the organization. It entails finding the way to put the right person in the right place with the right remuneration; above all, it requires building a work environment that enables each person to give of his/her best thereby "making a difference at work."

The aim of diversity management is to obtain *better organizational results* by improving individual and group performances. This goal can be achieved through exploitation of the diversity management business case connected with a management of people's diversity which is conscious (the organization is aware of its choices relative to the management of people's diversities), diversified, effective (it achieves the goals set), efficient (it prevents the wasteful use of resources), and equitable (people perceive the outcomes and the processes followed to define those outcomes as fair) (Cox & Blake, 1991; Golembiewski, 1995; Wright, Ferris, Hiller, & Kroll, 1995; Kandola & Fullerton, 1998; Kossek & Lobel, 1996; Thomas, 1995).

To this end, diversity management requires organizations to have intention and capability to promote and shape a *cultural change* establishing a *"culture of inclusion."* Here by "organizational culture" is meant the cluster of principles, values and behavioral rules that a group has discovered, invented and adapted to solve issues concerning both external environment adaptation (how to achieve goals and how the organization relates with external actors) and inter-group integration (i.e. tacit assumptions, organizational identity, languages, symbols, ceremonies, accepted behaviors, procedures followed to attribute status and power). The organizational culture is a set of basic assumptions that have worked sufficiently well to be considered valid and to be taught to new employees as the right way to perceive, think, and feel in similar situations (Daft, 2004). Diversity management influences individuals, groups, and the organization in its entirety in the direction of recognizing, respecting, enhancing and integrating people's diversities through the creation of a work environment characterized by mutual respect, individual commitment, and cooperation.

"If such commitment is inconsistent with the current organizational culture, then a significant culture change may be necessary" (Shen, Chanda, D'Netto, & Monga, 2009, p. 245). The aim of this change in culture is to reshape the organization's fundamental principles, values, and strategic programs by introducing awareness of, and the respect for, people's diversities, as well as the organization's commitment to managing people's specificities recognizing that people's diversities are influential in achieving better organizational results. Accomplishment of this cultural change should enable each person to feel that her/his dignity, identities, characteristics and needs are respected and taken into account by those with whom s/he must work within the organization, so increasing the employees' commitment to both their work and the organization. This particular process of change entails redefinition of the relation between the person and the organization, opening it up to mutual adaptation. It can be said that diversity management promotes the fulfillment of an organizational culture of inclusion, a culture where diversities:

are recognized, valued and engaged. Different voices are understood as being legitimate and as opening up new vistas; they are heard and integrated in decision making and problem solving processes; they have an active role in shaping culture and fostering creativity and innovation; and eventually in adding value to the company's performance (Pless & Maak, 2004, p. 130).

The requisite cultural change in its turn requires the development of a contextual *organizational change* by increasing the ways in which a competitive advantage can be achieved, namely, managing people's diversities in a diversified, efficient, effective and equitable way and creating an inclusive work environment. Dass and Parker (1999), Lawler and Finegold (2000), and Riccò (2009, 2011) point out that the organizational change connected to diversity management consists of:

- Identification of the dimensions of diversity that the organization wants to manage through targeted solutions
- The diversity management strategic logic that the organization chooses to adopt in managing each dimension of diversity that it wants to handle through targeted solutions[3]
- The characteristics of these solutions (single vs. several; ad hoc vs. planned; directed towards individual or specific groups of people or the totality of people that exhibit a given problem; integrated or not integrated among themselves and/or within the general organizational strategy)
- The organizational areas affected by these solutions.

Finally, the proposed definition of diversity management recognizes that the organization can achieve better organizational results if it builds a *non-discriminatory and equitable work environment*. That is to say, an organization cannot have diversity management if it does not guarantee people's equal opportunities. Such a work environment is inclusive if *people's diversities are:*

- *Recognized* (there is awareness of the existence of people's diversities)
- *Respected* (there is a strong regard for others' feelings and rights)
- *Enhanced* (people's diversities are welcomed in the organization and everyone can express him/herself)
- *Integrated* (people's diversities are combined in order to create new ways to communicate and collaborate by analyzing and affording situations enriched by the integration of the complementarities that arise from diversity).

In such work environment, *the individual's potential expression is fostered*. This means that each person feels able to be him/herself and that s/he works in an organization that gives him/her voice, space, responsibility and resources with which to make an active contribution to improving the organization's results by means of his/her uniqueness as a human being.

When diversity management is well established in the organizational culture, and when its guiding principles have become organizational values in themselves, it turns into an organizational philosophy: a group of ideas, values, beliefs, and behaviors that are taken as points of reference to drive the organization's choices and actions which define how to leverage and integrate people's diversities to promote the organization's sustainability.

FUTURE RESEARCH DIRECTIONS

This chapter has systematized the concept of diversity management by grounding its definition on McGregor's new human relations theory, and thus countering the criticisms of the concept's lack of clarity. In the future, it is important that researchers on this topic should clearly define their assumptions about human beings, what they regard as the most appropriate ways to manage them and their diversities in the organization, and the meaning that they attribute to the concept of diversity management.

Systematization of the concept has made it possible to describe the interrelation among diversity management, equal employment opportunity, and affirmative action, and to highlight that non-discrimination is not a direct aim of diversity management although it is embodied in it. This counters the criticism that *diversity management has less anti-discrimination force than equal opportunities and affirmative action* because diversity management, equal employment opportunities, and affirmative action are not comparable on these terms. In fact, they are grounded on different issues: the first is an organizational business-driven approach; the second is a socio-political-ethical anti-discrimination approach; and the third is a group of solutions aimed at realizing equal opportunities in organizations.

Another very important criticism remains to be dealt with: the *lack of effective demonstration of the business case* that still today characterizes diversity management studies (Curtins & Dreachslin, 2011) and which fuels the connected criticism of *diversity management's "rhetoric."* Further diversity management studies should more consistently track and objectively measure the impact of diversity management on the productivity of individuals and groups and then on the organization's results. For this purpose, it is important to create a collaborative bridge between diversity management researchers and human resource and organizational development professionals. The necessary collaboration between these two worlds (academic and organizational) raises an important challenge: finding effective ways to translate diversity management theory into practice. This means creating operational guidelines, which are sufficiently detailed to accompany human resource and organizational development professionals step by step in applying diversity management principles, but, at the same time, which are explained in a flexible and personalized manner so that they can be adapted to the specific organization (O'Flynn, et al., 2001; Riccò, 2011).

CONCLUSION

The increasing presence of diversity that characterizes global society has direct the attention of academics and professionals to the conscious, effective, efficient, and equitable management of people's diversities in organizations, introducing the issue of diversity management. Since the beginning of the 1990s, diversity management has been a lively topic of discussion among academics and professionals. Too often, however, this concept is used without explanation of the assumptions on which it is grounded and the meaning attributed to it. Assuming McGregor's new human relations framework, this chapter has defined diversity

management as a strategic, micro-founded, and diversified organizational approach that considers people to be core resources for the organization's success. Thus, in order to achieve better organizational results, it focuses the organization's attention on the person and her/his specificities and needs by promoting and fulfilling a cultural and an organizational process of change so as to create a non-discriminatory and equitable work environment where people's diversities are recognized, respected, enhanced and integrated, and the individual's potential expression is fostered.

This definition does not suggest that diversity management requires organizations to implement specific organizational solutions or solutions directed at managing all categories of diversities. On the contrary, it emphasizes that a change in the organizational culture and in people's culture within the organization is necessary in order to create an inclusive work environment fostering synergies among people's diversities so as to achieve better organizational results. This evolving process, which requires commitment by individuals, groups and the organization, time and effort, can be realized in infinite ways.

Presented thus, diversity management is an approach that can be adopted not only by multinationals or large companies but also by small and medium-sized companies in any area provided that they:

- Recognize the existence of people's diversities and their importance for achievement of the organization's ends
- Choose to strategically handle the management of human resources aiming at fully involving and utilizing human resources
- Are willing to undertake a cultural and organizational process of change.

The next challenge facing academics and professionals is to determine how to move from theory to practice, demonstrating both the advantages and costs of the diversity management approach.

REFERENCES

Anderson, T., & Metcalf, H. (2003). *Diversity: Stacking up the evidence*. London, UK: CIPD.

Armstrong, C., Flood, P. C., Guthrie, J. P., Liu, W., Maccurtain, S., & Mkamwa, T. (2010). The impact of diversity and equality management on firm performance: beyond high performance work systems. *Human Resource Management, 49*(6), 977–998. doi:10.1002/hrm.20391

Becker, B. E., & Huselid, M. A. (1998). High performance work systems and firm performance: A synthesis of research and managerial implications. *Research in Personnel and Human Resources Journal, 16*(1), 53–101.

Benschop, Y. (2001). Pride, prejudice and performance: Relations between HRM, diversity and performance. *International Journal of Human Resource Management, 12*(7), 1166–1181. doi:10.1080/09585190110068377

Carnevale, A., & Stone, S. (1994). Diversity beyond the golden rule. *Training & Development, 48*(10), 22–40.

Cox, J. T. (1993). *Cultural diversity in organizations: Theory, research and practice*. San Francisco, CA: Berrett-Koehler Publishers.

Cox, J. T. (1994). A comment on the language of diversity. *Organization, 1*(1), 51–58. doi:10.1177/135050849400100109

Cox, J. T., & Blake, S. (1991). Managing cultural diversity for organizational competitiveness. *The Academy of Management Executive, 5*(3), 45–56.

Curtis, E. F., & Dreachslin, J. L. (2008). Diversity management interventions and organizational performance: A synthesis of current literature. *Human Resource Development Review, 7*(1), 107–134. doi:10.1177/1534484307311700

Daft, R. L. (2004). *Organizzazione aziendale*. Milano, Italy: Apogeo.

Dass, P., & Parker, B. (1999). Strategies for managing human resource diversity: From resistance to learning. *The Academy of Management Executive, 13*(2), 68–80. doi:10.5465/AME.1999.1899550

Dickens, L. (1999). Beyond the business case: A three-pronged approach to equality action. *Human Resource Management Journal, 9*(1), 9–19. doi:10.1111/j.1748-8583.1999.tb00185.x

Eddy, S. W. N. (2008). Why organizations choose to manage diversity? Toward a leadership-based theoretical framework. *Human Resource Development Review, 7*(1), 58–78. doi:10.1177/1534484307311592

Folger, R., & Cropanzano, R. (1998). *Organizational justice and human resource management*. Thousand Oaks, CA: Sage Publications.

Foster, C., & Harris, L. (2005). Easy to say, difficult to do: Diversity management in retail. *Human Resource Management Journal, 15*(3), 4–17. doi:10.1111/j.1748-8583.2005.tb00150.x

Golembiewski, R. T. (1995). *Managing diversity in organizations*. Birmingham, AL: University of Alabama Press.

Gordon, G. G., DiTomaso, N., & Farris, G. F. (1991). Managing diversity in R&D groups. *Research Technology Management, 34*(1), 18–23.

Gordon, J. (1995, May). Different from what? Diversity as a performance issue. *Training (New York, N.Y.)*, 25–33.

Heil, G., Bennis, W., & Stephens, D. C. (2000). *Douglas McGregor, revisited: Managing the human side of enterprise*. New York, NY: John Wiley & Sons, Inc.

Ivancevich, J. M., & Gilbert, J. A. (2000). Diversity management: Time for a new approach. *Public Personnel Management, 9*(1), 75–92.

Jayne, M. E. A., & Dupboye, R. L. (2004). Leveraging diversity to improve business performance: Research findings and recommendations for organizations. *Human Resource Management, 43*(4), 409–424. doi:10.1002/hrm.20033

Johnston, W. B., & Packer, A. E. (1987). *Workforce 2000: Work and workers for the twenty-first century*. Indianapolis, IN: Hudson Institute.

Kandola, R., & Fullerton, J. (1998). *Diversity in action: Managing the mosaic* (2nd ed.). London, UK: CIPD.

Kelly, E., & Dobbin, F. (1998). How affirmative actions became diversity management. *The American Behavioral Scientist, 4*(7), 960–984. doi:10.1177/0002764298041007008

Kirton, G., & Greene, A. M. (2005). *The dynamics of managing diversity: A critical approach* (2nd ed.). Oxford, UK: Elsevier Butterworth-Heinemann.

Kossek, E. E., & Lobel, S. A. (1996). *Managing diversity: Human resource strategies for transforming the workplace*. Oxford, UK: Blackwell Publishers.

Kreitner, R., & Kinicki, A. (2004). La gestione delle diversità: Liberare il potenziale di ogni persona. In Kreitner, R., & Kinicki, A. (Eds.), *Comportamento Organizzativo* (pp. 39–68). Milano, Italy: Apogeo.

Lawler, E. E. III, & Finegold, D. (2000). Individualizing the organization: Past, present and future. *Organizational Dynamics, 29*(1), 1–15. doi:10.1016/S0090-2616(00)00009-7

Liff, S., & Dickens, L. (2000). Ethics and equality: Reconciling false dilemmas. In Winstanley, D., & Woodall, J. (Eds.), *Ethical Issues in Contemporary Human Resource Management* (pp. 85–101). New York, NY: Palgrave Macmillan.

Lorbiecki, A., & Jack, G. (2000). Critical turns in the evolution of diversity management. *British Journal of Management, 11*, 17–31. doi:10.1111/1467-8551.11.s1.3

Maslow, A. H. (1992). *Motivazione e personalità*. Roma, Italy: Armando Editore.

Maxwell, G. A., Balir, S., & McDougall, M. (2001). Edging towards managing diversity in practice. *Employee Relations, 23*(5), 468–482. doi:10.1108/01425450110405161

McGregor, D. (2006). *The human side of enterprise*. New York, NY: McGraw-Hill.

McGrew, T. (1992). A global society? In McGrew, T., Hall, S., & Hel, D. (Eds.), *Modernity and Its Futures: Understanding Modern Society* (pp. 61–116). Cambridge, UK: Polity Press.

Milliken, F. J., & Martins, L. L. (1996). Searching for common threads: Understanding the multiple effects of diversity in organizational groups. *Academy of Management Review, 21*(2), 402–433.

Mulholland, G., Özbilgin, M. F., & Worman, D. (2005). *Managing diversity linking the theory and practice to business performance. Change Agenda*. London, UK: CIPD.

Nishii, L. H., & Özbilgin, M. F. (2007). Global diversity management: Towards a conceptual framework. *International Journal of Human Resource Management, 18*(11), 1883–1894. doi:10.1080/09585190701638077

O'Flynn, J., Sammartino, A., Lau, K., Riciotti, A., & Nicholas, S. (2001). *Attract, retain and motivate: A toolkit for diversity management*. Retrieved May 25, 2011, from http://www.mibru.unimelb.edu.au/template-assets/07/includes/diversity/Attract_retain_motivate_toolkit_diversity.pdf.

O'Leary, B. J., & Weathington, B. L. (2006). Beyond the business case for diversity in organizations. *Employee Responsibilities and Rights Journal, 18*(4), 283–292. doi:10.1007/s10672-006-9024-9

Pless, N. M., & Maak, T. (2004). Building an inclusive diversity culture: Principles, processes and practice. *Journal of Business Ethics, 54*, 129–147. doi:10.1007/s10551-004-9465-8

Riccò, R. (2008). Teoria e pratica della gestione delle diversità. In Neri, M. (Ed.), *Studi e Ricerche sul Tema Delle Relazioni di Lavoro* (pp. 188–225). Bologna, Italy: Pitagora Editrice.

Riccò, R. (2009). *Shedding light on the Italian way to diversity management.* Paper presented at the 25th EGOS Colloquium Conference. Barcelona, Spain.

Riccò, R. (2011). *Guida operativa al diversity management.* Milano, Italy: OD&M Consulting. Retrieved May 25, 2011, from http://www.odmconsulting.com/survey/diversity-management/.

Rousseau, D. M. (1989). Psychological and implied contracts in organizations. *Employee Responsibilities and Rights Journal, 2*, 121–139. doi:10.1007/BF01384942

Rousseau, D. M. (1995). *Psychological contracts in organizations: Understanding written and unwritten agreements.* London, UK: Sage Publications.

Scott, C. L. (2010). Preface. *International Journal of Human Resources Development and Management, 10*(3), 205–207.

Shaw, M. (2000). *Global society and international relations: Sociological concepts and political perspectives.* Cambridge, UK: Polity Press. Retrieved May 9, 2011, from http://www.sussex.ac.uk/Users/hafa3/global.htm.

Shen, J., Chanda, A., D'Netto, B., & Monga, M. (2009). Managing diversity through human resource management: An international perspective and conceptual framework. *International Journal of Human Resource Management, 29*(2), 235–251. doi:10.1080/09585190802670516

Shore, L. M., Chung-Herrera, B. G., Dean, M. A., Ehrhart, K. H., Jung, D. I., Randel, A. E., & Singh, G. (2009). Diversity in organizations: Where are we and where are we going? *Human Resource Management Review, 19*, 117–133. doi:10.1016/j.hrmr.2008.10.004

Solari, L. (2004). *La gestione delle risorse umane: Dalle teorie alle persone.* Roma, Italy: Carocci.

Syed, J., & Özbilgin, M. (2009). A relational framework for international transfer of diversity management practices. *International Journal of Human Resource Management, 20*(12), 2435–2453. doi:10.1080/09585190903363755

Thomas, D. A., & Robin, E. J. (1996). Making differences matter. *Harvard Business Review, 74*(5), 79–90.

Thomas, R. Jr. (1990). From affirmative action to affirming diversity. *Harvard Business Review, 68*(2), 107–117.

Thomas, R. Jr. (1991). *Beyond race and gender: Unleashing the power of your total workforce by managing diversity.* New York, NY: AMACOM.

Thomas, R. Jr. (1995). A diversity framework. In Chemers, M. M., Oskamp, S., & Costanzo, M. A. (Eds.), *Diversity in Organizations: New Perspectives for Changing Workforce* (pp. 245–263). Newbury Park, CA: Sage Publications.

Thomas, R., Jr. (2004). *Diversity management and affirmative action: Past present and future.* Paper presented at the Diversity Symposium: Equity, Affirmative Action and Diversity. Lansdowne, VA.

Trompenaars, F., & Hampden-Turner, C. (1998). *Riding the waves of culture: Understanding diversity in global business* (2nd ed.). New York, NY: McGraw-Hill.

UE. (2003). *I costi e i benefici della diversità*. Retrieved May 25, 2011, from http://www.ec.europa.eu/social/BlobServlet?docId=1440&langId=it.

Wang, P., & Schwarz, J. L. (2010). Stock price reactions to GLBT non discrimination policies. *Human Resource Management, 49*(2), 195–216. doi:10.1002/hrm.20341

Worman, D., Bland, A., & Chase, P. (2005). Managing diversity: People make the difference at work: But everyone is different. In *Change Agenda*. London, UK: CIPD.

Wrench, J. (2001). *Diversity management in the European context: A critical examination of organisational strategies for combating ethnic discrimination and exclusion*. Paper presented at the International Perspectives on Cross-Cultural Workforce Diversity: The Inclusive Workplace. Bellagio, Italy.

Wright, P. M., Ferris, S. P., Hiller, J. S., & Kroll, M. (1995). Competitiveness through management of diversity: Effects on stock price valuation. *Academy of Management Journal, 38*(1), 272–287. doi:10.2307/256736

Yakura, E. K. (1996). EEO, law and managing diversity. In Kossek, E. E., & Lobel, S. A. (Eds.), *Managing Diversity: Human Resources Strategies for Transforming the Workplace* (pp. 25–50). Oxford, UK: Blackwell Publishers.

Zanoni, P., & Janssens, M. (2004). Deconstructing difference: The rhetoric of human resource managers' diversity discourses. *Organization Studies, 25*(1), 55–74. doi:10.1177/0170840604038180

ADDITIONAL READING

Cox, J. T. (2001). *Creating the multicultural organization: A strategy for capturing the power of diversity*. San Francisco, CA: Jossey-Bass.

CSES. (2003a). *Methods and indicators to measure the cost-effectiveness of diversity policies in enterprises. KE-55-03-899-EN-N*. New York, NY: CNES.

D'Netto, B., & Sohal, A. S. (1999). Human resource practices and workforce diversity: An empirical assessment. *International Journal of Manpower, 20*(8), 530–547. doi:10.1108/01437729910302723

Delery, J. E., & Shaw, J. D. (2001). The strategic management of people in work organizations: Review, synthesis, and extension. *Research in Personnel and Human Resource Management, 20*, 165–197. doi:10.1016/S0742-7301(01)20003-6

Duglas, D. (2004). Ethical challenges of an increasingly diverse workforce: The paradox of change. *Human Resource Development International, 7*(2), 197–210. doi:10.1080/1367886032000099053

European Commission. (2005). *The business case for diversity: Good practices in the workplace*. Retrieved October 25, 2011, from http://www.diversityatwork.net/EN/Docs/busicase_diversity.pdf.

Guest, D. E. (2002). Human resource management, corporate performance and employee well-being: Building the worker into HRM. *The Journal of Industrial Relations, 44*(3), 335–358. doi:10.1111/1472-9296.00053

Hall, D. T., & Parker, V. A. (1993). The role of workplace flexibility in managing diversity. *Organizational Dynamics, 22*(1), 4–18. doi:10.1016/0090-2616(93)90078-F

Kirby, E. L., & Harter, L. M. (2003). Speaking the language of the bottom-line: The metaphor of managing diversity. *Journal of Business Communication, 40*(1), 28–49. doi:10.1177/002194360304000103

Kirton, G., & Greene, A. M. (2009). The costs and opportunities of doing diversity work in mainstream organizations. *Human Resource Management Journal, 19*(2), 159–175. doi:10.1111/j.1748-8583.2009.00091.x

Liff, S. (1996). Two routes to managing diversity: Individual differences or social group characteristics? *Employee Relations, 19*(1), 11–26. doi:10.1108/01425459710163552

Orlando, C. R., & Kirby, S. L. (1999). Organizational justice and the justification of workforce diversity programs. *Journal of Business and Psychology, 14*(1), 109–118. doi:10.1023/A:1022962618674

SHRM. (2008). *2007 state of the workplace diversity management*. Alexandria, VA: SHRM. Retrieved June 27, 2008, from http://www.shrm.org/diversity.

Singh, V., & Point, S. (2004). Strategic responses by European companies to the diversity challenge: An on-line comparison. *Long Range Planning, 37*, 295–318. doi:10.1016/j.lrp.2004.05.009

Sonnenschein, W. (1999). *The diversity toolkit: How you can build and benefit from a diverse workforce*. New York, NY: McGraw-Hill.

Süß, S., & Kleiner, M. (2007). Diversity management in Germany: Dissemination and design of the concept. *International Journal of Human Resource Management, 18*(11), 1934–1953. doi:10.1080/09585190701638150

Wentling, R. (2004). Factors that assist and barriers that hinder the success of diversity initiatives in multinational corporations. *Human Resource Development International, 7*(2), 165–180. doi:10.1080/1367886042000243781

KEY TERMS AND DEFINITIONS

Business Case: Is the number of economic, competitive and reputational reasons ascribable to a more differentiated, efficient, effective and equitable way of managing people's diversities.

Diversity: Is the multiplicity of differences and similarities that exist among people and which, combined together, create the uniqueness of each person.

Diversity Management: Is an organizational approach aimed at achieving better organizational results by creating a non-discriminatory and equitable work environment where people's diversities are recognized, respected, enhanced, and integrated, person's needs are taken into account, and the individual's potential expression is fostered.

Inclusive Workplace: Is a workplace characterized by mutual respect, individual commitment, and cooperation, where people's diversities are recognized, respected, enhanced, and integrated, and individual needs are taken into account. In an inclusive workplace, people have the voice, space, responsibility, and resources with which they can actively contribute to improving organizational results by means of their uniqueness.

Integration: Is the process whereby people's diversities are combined in the organization to create new ways of communicating, collaborating, analyzing, and coping with situations.

Leveraging Workforce Diversity: Is the process whereby the organization recognizes the importance of people's diversities for the achievement of business ends, and chooses to manage them in a conscious, differentiated, effective, efficient, and equitable way to maximum advantage.

Theory Y: Is a managerial approach proposed in 1960 by McGregor. It focuses organizational attention on persons and their proactive participation in the organization. It maintains that organizational goals can only be achieved through the availability of committed employees and through the integration of the organization's and the individual's needs.

ENDNOTES

[1]   In this chapter, "managing diversity" and "diversity management" are used synonymously. Nevertheless, it should be pointed out that some academics use these terms in order to refer to two different approaches: one individualistic (managing diversity) and one collectivistic (diversity management). See Kirton and Greene (2005) for further explanation on this distinction.

[2]   The concept of "organizational justice" is used here as defined by Folger and Cropanzano (1998): "In organizations, justice is about the rules and social norms governing how outcomes (e.g., rewards and punishment) should be distributed, the procedures used for making such distribution decisions (as well as other types of decisions) and how people are treated interpersonally" (p. xiii).

[3]   Among the various diversity management strategic logics presented in the literature, we cite in particular: Dass and Parker (1999); Ivancevich and Gilbert (2000); Kossek and Lobel (1996); Riccò (2008); Thomas and Robin (1996); Thomas (1995).

Chapter 27
Theoretical Frameworks and Models Supporting the Practice of Leveraging Workforce Diversity

Aileen G. Zaballero
Pennsylvania State University, USA

Yeonsoo Kim
University of Nevada Las Vegas, USA

ABSTRACT

Generally defined, diversity is multidimensional, but the key to diversity is the "valuing and managing of differences in such a way that the results lead to inclusion"(Plummer, 2003, p. 10). The term diversity refers to the presence of a wide variety of cultures, ethnic groups, languages, physical features, socio-economic backgrounds, opinions, religious beliefs, gender identity, and neurology within one population. Diversity, in this chapter, will be defined as it is above, but within an organizational context.

When organizations became aware of the demographic changes in the workforce and customer base, organizational diversity became a key topic for success. As a result of legislation mandating Equal Employment Opportunity and Affirmative Action, leaders and managers began to examine the minority representation within their own companies' (Plummer, 2003) organizational framework. Diversity refers to "making use of and leveraging human differences toward organizational effectiveness and productive business goals that maintain a high performing workforce" (2003, p.13).

Thomas (1991) shifted anti-discrimination initiatives from compliance to one that promoted diversity as a business imperative. He also argued that managing diversity went beyond race and gender and includes the primary and secondary dimensions of the individual (1991). On the organizational level, diversity management addresses issues such as business rationale, diversity strategic planning, recruiting, and retaining a diverse workforce (Plummer, 2003). According to Cox (1993), "a potential benefit

DOI: 10.4018/978-1-4666-1812-1.ch027

of diversity will be to promote organizational effectiveness in creativity, marketing, problem-solving, and quality of decision making by being conscious of individual identities" (p.251).

This chapter will include a brief description of the history of diversity; advantages of being culturally competent; paradigms/perspectives of diversity management; and a summary of the business case for diversity. In addition, theories and models of organization development and change management are further explained as a way to understand the organizational context surrounding diversity interventions.

INTRODUCTION

Diversity Defined

Cox (2001) defines "diversity as the variation of social and cultural identities among people existing together in a defined employment or market setting" (p. 3). Cox and Smolinski (1994) define diversity as "the representation of people of different group identities in the same organization social system"(p. 12). Generally defined, "diversity is multidimensional, but the key to diversity is the valuing and managing of differences in such a way that the results lead to inclusion"(Plummer, 2003, p. 10).

The term diversity refers to the presence of a wide variety of cultures, ethnic groups, languages, physical features, socio-economic backgrounds, opinions, religious beliefs, gender identity, and neurology within a one population. Diversity, in this study, will be defined as it is above, but within an organizational context.

When organizational leaders became aware of the demographic changes in the workforce and consumer base, it became apparent that a focus on organizational diversity was critical. As a result of legislation mandating Equal Employment Opportunity and Affirmative Action, leaders and managers began to examine the employment demographics within their own companies (Plummer, 2003). Within an organizational framework, diversity refers to "making use of and leveraging human differences toward organizational effectiveness and productive business goals" that maintain a high performing workforce (p.

13). A potential benefit of diversity will be "to promote organizational effectiveness in creativity, marketing, problem-solving, and quality of decision-making by being conscious of individual identities" (Cox, 1993, p. 251).

When identifying individual diversity, it is suggested one distinguishes between the primary and secondary dimensions. Loden and Rosener (1991) defined "primary dimensions of diversity as those immutable human differences that are inborn and/or that exert an important impact on our early socialization and ongoing impact throughout our lives" (p. 18) such as age, ethnicity, gender, physical abilities/qualities, race, and sexual orientation. Secondary dimensions contain elements of control and are things that can be changed such as: educational background, geographic location, income, marital status, military experience, parental status, religious belief and work experience. Both are extremely important because they influence people's identity, how they define themselves in the world, and how others react to them (1991). Figure 1 shows both primary and secondary dimensions of diversity. The inner circle represents the primary dimensions and the outer circle represents the secondary dimensions.

Historical Background

Diversity can be one of the most controversial and least understood business topics because of the issues regarding quality, leadership, and ethics (Anand & Winters, 2008). Although its effectiveness has been questioned over the past 30 years, diversity training has become a common practice

Figure 1. Primary and secondary dimensions of diversity

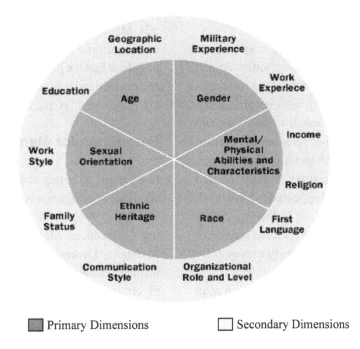

in the corporate arena. The emphasis of training has evolved from compliance-oriented content to one focusing on acceptance and leveraging of all dimensions of diversity based on the belief that it will enhance business performance (Anand & Winters, 2008).

The Civil Rights Act of 1964 launched government legislation such as Title VII that prohibits employment discrimination based on race, color, religion, sex and national origin (Thomas, 1991; Plummer, 2003; Anand & Winters, 2008). During this time, diversity training was implemented as a reaction to the Equal Employment Opportunity Commission (EEOC). Companies wanted to avoid negative publicity and costly lawsuits and as a result, organizations introduced training programs that mainly focused on delivering information on legal requirements to managers. The objective was to recite the law and company policy that dictated appropriate behavior in the workplace however,

the content of these trainings did not connect how the recommended changes would improve business results. Therefore, these trainings made minimal impact (Anand & Winters, 2008).

By the early 1980's President Ronald Regan deregulated polices and appointed Clarence Thomas as head of the EEOC who disapproved of a timetable to increase the underrepresented groups in the workforce. With less government regulations, companies scaled back on affirmative action and equal employment trainings (Anand & Winters, 2008).

Anand and Winters (2008), cite the Hudson Institute which published a report in 1987, entitled Workforce 2000. This report was prophetic in many ways, predicting the retirement of the baby boomers, increased immigration, and the influx of women and ethnic minorities in the workforce. It also indicated that women, minorities, and immigrants would account for over 80 percent of the new entrants in the workforce. As a result of this report, corporations shifted and included in their discussions ways of retraining women and minorities (Anand & Winters, 2008).

By the end of the 1990s, most corporations executed some form of diversity initiative and recognized the value of diversity as an ongoing business process. Many also embraced the philosophy that everyone needs to be aware and sensitive to the needs and differences of others to enhance working relationships (Anand & Winters, 2008). Most training programs generally focused on individual attitudes and appeared to have modest effects (Bendick, Egan, & Lofhjelm, 2001). Organizations with a diverse workforce zontinued to struggle with managing diversity successfully (Plummer, 2003).

Thomas (1991) shifted anti-discrimination initiatives from compliance to one which promoted diversity as a business imperative. He approached diversity from a management perspective and said: managing diversity means approaching diversity at three levels simultaneously: individual, interpersonal, and organizational. The traditional focus has been on individual and interpersonal aspects alone. What is new is seeing diversity as an issue for the entire organization, involving the very way organizations are structured (Thomas, 1991, p. 12). He also argued that managing diversity went beyond race and gender and includes the primary and secondary dimensions of the individual (Thomas, 1991). On the organizational level, diversity management addresses issues such as business rationale, diversity strategic planning, recruiting and retaining a diverse workforce (Plummer, 2003).

Diversity Management

Diversity management is a cross-disciplinary field that draws research and theory from various applied behavioral sciences including: anthropology, economics, education, human resource management, organization behavior, organization development, political science, psychology, social work and sociology (Plummer, 2003, p. 52). Managing diversity refers to "implementing organizational systems and practices to manage people so that the potential advantages of diversity are maximized while its potential disadvantages are minimized" (Cox, 1993, p. 11).

Paradigms for Managing Diversity

In an effort to better understand why companies should concern themselves with diversity, Thomas and Ely (1996) wrote an article entitled, "Making Differences Matter: A New Paradigm for Managing Diversity," a research focused on the influence a diverse group of individuals can make on organizational effectiveness. They postulated that diversity goes beyond social justice to minimize adversities on underrepresented groups the corporate world, but is more insider information on niche markets. Diversity should be understood as "the varied perspectives and approaches to work that members of different identity groups bring"(Thomas & Ely, 1996, p. 2). Individuals from diverse backgrounds bring a plethora of knowledge that include perspectives about how to design processes, innovate solutions, reach goals, communicate effectively, and lead teams (1996).

Thomas and Ely (1996) introduced three different paradigms: *discrimination-and fairness paradigm, access and legitimacy paradigm and learning and effectiveness paradigm*. The first two paradigms have directed most organizations on their approach to diversity. Table 1 illustrates Anand and Winter's (2008) outline of the three different paradigms.

The Discrimination and Fairness Paradigm is one of the main diversity theories in practice today and resembles affirmative-action efforts. Instead of accepting and embracing the differences between people in the workplace, the discrimination and fairness paradigm tends to ignore all of those

Table 1. Thomas and Ely's three paradigms of diversity

Discrimination and Fairness Paradigm	Access and Legitimacy Paradigm	Learning and Effectiveness Paradigm
• Equal Opportunity • Compliance with EEO regulations • Fair treatment • Focus on the numbers • Concern with creating mentoring and career development programs for women and people of color • Supports assimilation and color and gender-blind conformism	• Acceptance and celebration of difference • Market-based motivation for competitive advantage • Motivation is to attract multicultural talent to understand and serve customers and gain legitimacy with them	• Different perspectives and approaches to work are valuable • Acknowledgement that learning and re-learning are central to leveraging diversity • Organization fosters personal development that brings out people's full range of skills • Recognition that employees often make business choices that draws on their cultural backgrounds. • We are all on the same team with our differences-not despite them

Source: Anand and Winters (2008)

differences in the name of fairness (Thomas & Ely, 1996). The paradigm's underlying logic can be expressed as follows:

"Prejudice has kept members of certain demographic groups out of organizations such as ours. As a matter of fairness and to comply with federal mandates, we need to work toward restructuring the makeup of our organization to let it more closely reflect that of society. We need managerial processes that ensure that all our employees are treated equally and with respect and that some are not given unfair advantage over others" (1996, p. 2).

The Discrimination and Fairness Paradigm has increased demographic diversity and promoted fair treatment, but under this paradigm, everyone is the same and should assimilate, minimizing the opportunity to optimize the unique qualities each person has to offer (Thomas & Ely, 1996). The employees may be diversified, but not the work.

Companies that follow this paradigm are usually bureaucratic in structure where initiatives are enforced by top down directives. This color blind or gender blind idea can be beneficial in promoting fair treatment, but loses the prospect to explore how people's differences generate potential innovation to generate effective business practices. Success

is often measured by recruitment and retention of underrepresented groups (Thomas & Ely, 1996).

The idea that diversity should be implemented in order to gain market share advantage is sometimes called the Access and Legitimacy Paradigm. Hiring diverse workers can give you access to markets that otherwise might be a challenge to conquer (Thomas & Ely, 1996). The legitimacy portion refers to the trust that is intrinsic when dealing with people that look similar to you. The underlying motivation of the access-and-legitimacy paradigm can be expressed this way:

"We are living in an increasingly multicultural country, and new ethnic groups are quickly gaining consumer power. Our company needs a demographically more diverse workforce to help us gain access to these differentiated segments. We need employees with multilingual skills in order to understand and serve our customers better and to gain legitimacy with them. Diversity ins't just fair; it makes business sense" (1996, p. 5).

The Access and Legitimacy Paradigm has led to new specialized and managerial opportunities for underrepresented groups. It has also increased competitive advantage in culturally dominant communities, but under this paradigm employees are sometimes pigeonholed in certain markets where they may feel exploited and closed to other opportunities in the organization. Cultural differences are emphasized within certain conditions but the skills, beliefs, and practices that are unique are not identified or integrated to create a learning opportunities into the larger organization (Thomas & Ely, 1996).

The third paradigm, Learning-and-Effectiveness, incorporates aspects of the first two but goes beyond by connecting diversity to learning opportunities at work. Employee's perspectives are integrated into rethinking primary tasks and redefining business practices (Thomas & Ely, 1996). Three distinctions of this paradigm are:

a. it sees similarities and differences as dual aspects of workforce diversity;
b. it seeks multiple objectives from diversity including efficiency, innovation, customer satisfaction, employee development, and social responsibility;
c. it views diversity as having long-term as well as short term ramifications (Thomas and Ely as cited by Dass & Parker, 1999, p. 72).

In an interview with Saposnick, Thomas describes the underlying motivation of the Learningand-Effectiveness paradigm which can be expressed this way (2003):

"When we talk about managing diversity, we're referring to creating an environment where peopls'se differences in perspective can be valued and allowed to influence positively their experience in and contribution to the work of the organization. Because we work in dynamic environments whose constantly changing labor and customer pools require adaptation much of our ability to adapt lies in our ability to leverage diversity" (2003, p. 7)

Organizations that have taken full advantage of the cultural differences of diverse employees are more productive and efficient. This may lead to new and transformational ways of doing business and placing these companies on the cutting edge of their industry. The process requires a high level of commitment from the whole organization (Thomas & Ely, 1996). The desire to create an organizational culture where everyone could work in requires cultural competence and an environment that advocates for "inclusion"(Anand & Winters, 2008, p. 362).

Cultural Competence (CQ)

Culture can strongly influence business. The term "culture" is often used interchangeably with "ethnicity," "nationality," and "race"(Plummer, 2003, p. 22). Culture influences the way an individual thinks and behaves and is most often transferred through family settings, educational systems and social experiences (2003). Everyone is culturally programmed from a variety of sources therefore; no one has the exact cultural identity (Gardenswartz & Rowe, 1993). One of the challenges of managing cultural diversity within organizations is allowing the individual to fully express themselves, while maintaining a respectful and cohesive work environment. An alternative solution to managing diverse backgrounds is employing Cultural Intelligence (CQ), the key competencies that are essential for individuals to better understand the impact of culture. The competencies necessary for cultural intelligence are: constant awareness, cultural understanding, and cultural intelligence skills (Bucher, 2008).

It is natural as humans to make judgments about other cultures that are different from our own. However, cultural comparison is not the issue. The concern is the tendency for some to see other cultures as less adequate and unfavorable which may lead to biases and stereotypical assumptions (Gardenswartz & Rowe, 1993). To minimize such results, cultural competence is necessary when managing diverse teams.

According to Bucher, employees with CQ can impact the overall success and survival of an organization (2008). CQ is a skill that can be learned, developed and managed. Bucher identifies nine specific mega-skills to promote cross-cultural understanding: understanding cultural identity, checking cultural lenses, global consciousness, shifting perspectives, intercultural communication, managing cross-cultural conflict, multicultural teaming, managing bias, and understanding the dynamics of power. Cultural diversity of workers and customers affects everyone within an organization; therefore, CQ is viewed as an essential competency that impacts the bottom line (2008). Table 2 identifies the importance of cultural intelligence and distinguishes the rationale for developing CQ.

Cultural competence is defined as "set of behaviors, attitudes, and policies that help organizations and staff work effectively with people of different cultures. It explores the rich dynamics of cross cultural interactions and provides individuals with knowledge and skill to bridge the gaps"(Lynch & Hanson, 1992, p. 35). In a multicultural world and global economy, cultural misunderstandings can threaten effective operations. According to current management education, cultural competencies include (Egan & Bendick, 2007, pp. 3-4):

- cultural self awareness - an understanding of the cultural conditions that shape an individual's own values, assumptions and beliefs;
- cultural consciousness - sensitivity and adaptability to operate outside the comfort of one's own culture;
- multicultural leadership - the ability to collaborate with and lead individuals with diverse cultural perspectives;
- multicultural negotiations - an understanding of individual's varying negotiating approaches, styles and "rules of the game,"
- "global thinking" - an appreciation of the strategic implications of global commerce.

As today's global market becomes increasingly diverse, businesses must adapt in order to stay competitive. To improve the health and effectiveness of organizations, companies employ diversity management (Plummer, 2003). Cultural competence is just one of the components to assess and measure the current state and identify the organization's business case for diversity.

BUSINESS CASE FOR DIVERSITY

Interest in diversity and diversity management continue to grow in both the academic and business communities (O'Leary & Weathington, 2006); however getting people to understand and support

Table 2. Rationale of CQ

Bottom-Line Issue	Rationale for Developing CQ
• Avoiding lawsuits and other forms of intolerance that devalue diversity and threaten productivity • Being flexible and innovative • Maximizing utilization of human capital • Solving problems • Reaching out to a changing, global marketplace and new populations	• Bias, including discrimination, is expensive. Even if it does not result in a lawsuit, bias wastes human potential and alienates customers. • Being able to shift perspective makes it possible to continually reexamine basic, traditional assumptions. In turn, this can foster development of new and better products and services and recognition of new opportunities. • Respecting and valuing differences breaks down walls, increases trust, and improves performance. • Seeking, understanding, and evaluating multiple perspectives allows for better solutions. • Designing and developing products and services are much easier when we understand markets

Source: Bucher (2008)

diversity is a process that requires continuous reinforcement (Gardenswartz & Rowe, 1993). Kahn and Gomez (as cited by Gardenswartz & Rowe, 1993) identify diversity as an internal and external workforce issue. Properly managed, diversity could improve community relations in addition to improving the organizational functions (O'Leary & Weathington, 2006). In order to attract potential customers and deliver the appropriate services, it is important that businesses understand their community and the residents (2006). "the business case also argues that it is important that organizations adequately represent the communities they serve, again with an eye on improving profitability by increasing the attractiveness of their employees to their customer base"(2006, p. 6). Diversity related efforts should be aligned with key business goals (SHRM, 2008).

Cox (2001) states that, well-managed diversity can add value to an organization by (1) improving problem solving, (2) increasing creativity and innovation, (3) allowing for organizational flexibility, (4) improving the quality of personnel through better recruitment and retention, and (5) using effective marketing strategies, especially for organizations that sell products or services (Cox, 2001, pp. 19-22). Diversity impacts the ability to achieve organizational goals and influences the attitudes of employees (2001).

Recognizing that all employees bring a unique quality to the workplace, diverse perspectives can offer alternative solutions and innovative approaches to business problems (Cox, 2001; O'Leary & Weathington, 2006). Furthermore, it has been argued that diversity can potentially provide competitive advantage for organizations through increased creativity and problem solving capabilities (Richard, Kochan, & McMillan-Capehart, 2002).

Diverse teams can produce better results than their homogenous counterparts (Cox, 2001; SHRM, 2008). Recognizing that the subject of diversity in business has reached a critical state,

the Society of Human Resource Management (SHRM) in 2007 conducted the largest and most comprehensive study on the state of workplace diversity management in the U.S. (2008). SHRM identified ten global trends that are expected to have a major impact on the workplace of the future (2008, pp. 10-11):

1. Desire of companies to expand into the global market.
2. Economic growth of Asia.
3. Continued acceleration of global change.
4. Stricter cross-border policies for global business settings.
5. Cross-cultural understanding/savvy in business settings.
6. Growing economic interdependence among the world's countries.
7. Increased off-shoring.
8. Heightened awareness of cultural differences.
9. Pressure for development of global labor standards.
10. Increased security for expatriates aboard.

Furthermore, talent acquisition is going global. Emerging countries are producing university-educated young professionals four times the rate of the United States (2008). Considering the global realities and the organizational goals, business success will require strategic planning for diversity in order to capitalize on the "interaction between, and collaboration among, people of diverse cultures, religion, histories, and perspectives"(SHRM, 2008, p. 12). Diversity integration requires a strategic long-term commitment.

Strategies for Diversity Management

Dass and Parker in Strategies for Managing Human Resource Diversity: From Resistance to Learning (1999) have identified strategic responses for managing workforce diversity expanding on Thomas and Ely's diversity paradigm.

Implementation of diversity initiatives depends on pressures, perspectives and strategic responses. The episodic approach is viewed as a marginal issue and these initiatives tend to be isolated and separate from core organizational activities (Dass & Parker, 1999). Companies who implement the freestanding approach usually experience moderate pressure. These programmatic initiatives are formal but are not integrated fully with business core activities. When diversity is considered as a strategic issue, company executives usually adopt a systematic approach where diversity initiatives are comprehensive and integrated into the existing system (1999).

Organizational learning from a diversity perspective is a systematic approach which is incorporated through multiple applications: organization development, transition management, transformational leadership, action research, reengineering, total quality management and team learning. Although top executives usually select the strategy used to approach diversity, it is the middle and lower level managers who must implement the programs and the line level employees who must put them into operation (Dass & Parker, 1999).

In general, diversity initiatives are an amalgamation of ideas and approaches and will not be as isolated as those represented in Figure 2. Matching internal resources with external opportunities will determine the strategy. Often times conflicting pressures and approaches exist within a single organization. As executive leaders select the appropriate strategy for diversity, they must also identify their individual business goals. When selecting a strategy, "consistency between perspectives and action is certain to reduce employee confusion about roles they are expected to play in managing diversity" (1999, p. 78). Figure 2 illustrates a matrix that combines the four perspectives (reactive, defensive, accommodative, and proactive) the associated strategic response towards diversity, and the three general approaches to implementing diversity initiatives.

Considering global realities, business success will require long range strategic planning that is supported by top management with collaborative participation from all employees to implement diversity in order to capitalize on the "interaction between, and collaboration among, people of diverse cultures, religion, histories, and perspectives"(SHRM, 2008, p. 25).

Research reveals that corporations which have responded to issues of diversity by implementing a strategic plan have recruited and retained a diverse workforce. It also improved their marketability with diverse populations and improved their workers?attitudes on issues of diversity (Cox, 2001).

Cox (1993) presents a comprehensive conceptual model that ties together learning with dimensions of diversity to create a generic model of the impact on work behavior and outcomes. Figure 3 illustrates effects of cultural diversity on individual and organizational outcomes as a response to the identities of its members, thus defining the diversity climate of an organization. This climate may influence individual morale and satisfaction regarding work and their employer, as well as influence actual career achievement, ultimately impacting organizational performance (Cox, 1993).

The model presented in Figure3 proposes that the impact of diversity on organizational outcomes is a complex interaction with the individuals of the company and the environment. The model hypothesizes that "our individual-level factors, three intergroup factors, and four organizational factors collectively define the diversity climate of an organization"(Cox, 1993, p. 9). In addition, the level of diversity will impact factors such as: creativity/innovation, problem solving, and cohesiveness/communication.

The survival of an organization in a rapidly expanding global climate will depend on how they manage and value diversity. This requires understanding and addressing complex organizational systems. To empower a diverse group

Figure 2. Strategic responses for managing diversity and their implementation

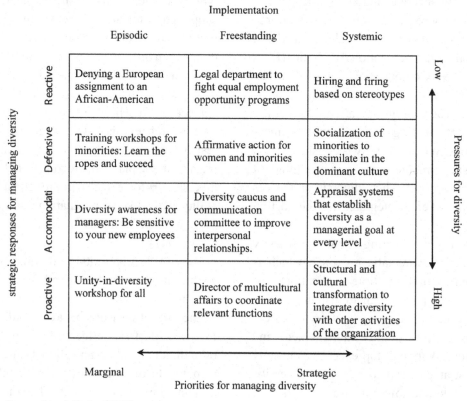

Source: Dass & Parker (1999)

of employees, the organizational system must be changed, and the core culture modified (Thomas, 1991). Organization development theories and practices may support the comprehension of the values that operate within the organization from the leadership all the way to the cultural climate within the company.

DRIVING CULTURAL AND ORGANIZATIONAL CHANGE

Utilizing diversity as a strategic asset keeps an organization's competitive edge sharp for a long period of time. This makes diversity a prime source of economical potential that can be sustainable. However, to realize this potential, diversity profes-

sionals must understand the organizational change process to implement diversity. A strategic plan for developing and sustaining diversity through-out the organization is best approached through systems thinking.

A systems approach to diversity is more than employees and employers working effectively together, but a process where these individuals work together to achieve the success of all stake-holders. This requires an alteration in corporate philosophy and practices (Gilbert & Ivanevich, 2000). Organization Development (OD) is an alternative to implement organization change and modify employee behavior. A system planned approach, can support management to implement a corporate wide impact to promote a culture of diversity (Allen & Montgomery, 2001). In order

Figure 3. An interactional model of the impact of diversity on individual career outcomes and organizational effectiveness

Source: Cox (1993)

for the change effort to be effective, the diversity program must be based on the "organization's own unique culture, internal strengths, weaknesses and needs"(Allen & Montgomery, 2001, p. 152). In addition, it is important to create an Organization Development (OD) strategy that has a long range plan; supported change by top managers; applied organization-wide learning; and collaborative participation of all employees (Rothwell & Sullivan, 2005, p. 21).

Bendick, Egan, and Lofhjelm (2001) identified nine benchmarks for organization development approach to diversity initiatives (pp. 17-19):

1. Support from top management: Without top management support, organizations will be challenged to implement diversity programs or diversity initiatives (Allen & Montgomery, 2001). Executives, Chief Executive Officers (CEOs), and top management control the resources (Rothwell & Sullivan, 2005).

2. Initiatives are tailored: Tailoring involves pre-training audits to identify the organization's current circumstances and priority issues (Bendick, Egan, & Lofhjelm, 2001).

3. Diversity initiatives are linked to central operating goals: Connecting to operational goals "through increased productivity, reduced cost, easier recruitment, enhanced creativity, improved client service, or expanded markets"builds a business case

and creates opportunity of lasting impact (Bendick, Egan, & Lofhjelm, 2001, p. 17).

4. Trainers are organization development professionals: Diversity impact is directly tied to organization's operational performance (Bendick, Egan, & Lofhjelm, 2001).

5. Diversity initiatives enroll all levels of employees: "Influencing an organization's corporate culture does not start to form until about twenty-five percent of all personnel at a work site have received training" (Bendick, Egan, & Lofhjelm, 2001, p. 18).

6. Diversity initiatives include discussions about discrimination as a general process. A broader approach can address all forms of discrimination without isolating any single group as the culprit (Bendick, Egan, & Lofhjelm, 2001).

7. Diversity initiatives explicitly address individual behavior: "Developing and practicing new ways of speaking and acting is more likely to affect post-training behavior" (Bendick, Egan, & Lofhjelm, 2001, p. 18).

8. Diversity initiatives are complemented by changes in human resource practices: Organization's procedures and policies pertaining to "recruitment, hiring, assignment, compensation, training, evaluation, promotion, and dismissal" must reflect changes to promote diversity (Bendick, Egan, & Lofhjelm, 2001, p. 18).

9. Diversity initiatives impact the corporate culture such as internal systems of beliefs and values and ways of behaving must reflect diversity goals (Bendick, Egan, Lofhjelm, 2001).

Marilyn Loden (1996), in her book Implementing Diversity also identified ten best practices for enhancing organizational diversity. She found that the best practices shared certain characteristics that included the following: "support the long-term goal of cultural change, position valuing diversity as a business strategy, emphasize inclusion, mutual respect, cooperation, and encourage innovation and empowerment?" (Loden, 1996, p. 166).

Cox's Change Model for Work on Diversity (2001) is a comprehensive conceptual method that identifies the main activities for effective organizational change. Figure 4 illustrates a flow chart identifying the change effort cycle. This model utilizes a system approach to managing diversity. Cox recommends that an effective organizational change effort should include all of the elements depicted in Figure 4. "As the flow of the arrows suggests, the change effort cycles through all of the elements and is continually assessed and refined over time in a process of continuous loop learning" (Cox, 2001, p. 18).

Cox's Change Model for Work on Diversity has five components. Within each component there are subcomponents. The following section will discuss the five components in the following order: (1) leadership, (2) research and measurement, (3) education, (4) alignment of management systems, and (5) follow-up.

Leadership

In the context of organizational change, leadership is a behavior that determines the directions or objectives for change; provides a sense of exigency and significance for the vision; facilitates the motivation of others; and, encourages the necessary conditions for achievement of the vision. "Leadership is the most essential element for change; without it, nothing happens" (Cox, 2001, p. 18).

Under leadership, Cox (2001) provides six subcomponents. The first is management philosophy. This is the sense of direction in which the leader wants to take the organization. Management philosophy differs from the vision. The vision of the organization is "the ability to decide what is to be done and how to get there" (Cox, 2001, p. 40). The leader recognizes that they will not get there unless they can light a fire under the people

Figure 4. Cox's change model for work on diversity

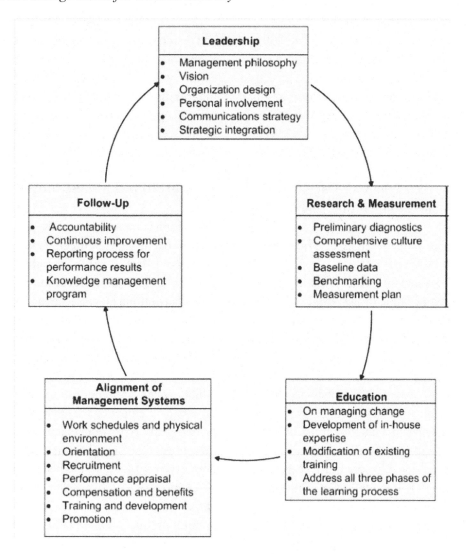

with whom they have influence to embrace this vision for change (Cox, 2001).

Vision is a portrayal of what needs to happen and provides a direction for those who lead. Moreover, it guides what should be measured to determine the success of the change effort. To implement diversity throughout the organization, leaders must create a shared vision. Cox (2001) identifies the following to facilitate a collective vision (p. 42):

- Demonstrate some personal passion for the needed change.
- Provide a compelling case for why it is the right vision.
- Communicate profusely.

Organizational Design is a formal guided process to align people's collective efforts to implement a change process. Through the formation of steering committees and advisory groups, leaders can monitor the transformational effort. These teams are "normally charged with creating a diversity business plan or strategy" (Cox, 2001, p. 48). A diversity plan corresponds with the vision and mission of the change initiatives. Through the design process, organizations perform to improve the possibility that the cooperative efforts of members will be successful. The following criteria should be considered (Cox, 2001, p. 48):

- Highly respected and knowledgeable;
- Personal interest in the work and a desire to serve;
- Knowledge about diversity or a high motivation to learn about it;
- Willingness and ability to invest a significant amount of time in the work;
- Diversity of members on gender and other dimensions of difference that are salient in the workforce.

Personal Involvement in diversity work shows personal commitment. If the change effort is to succeed, the norms of behavior must change, and the leaders must be the first to demonstrate this shift in behavior. Leaders must be able to walk the walk and talk the talk (Cox, 2001). An additional task of leadership is the development of an explicit strategy for communicating to the organization about the developmental work on diversity. Three key factors for an effective communication strategy are "(1) the nature of the work itself deals with sensitive and sometime emotional issues, (2) many organization have several other initiatives involving cultural change occurring at the same time and, (3) how, when, and to whom organizational data are collected as part of the development process should be communicated" (Cox, 1993, pp. 233-234). Communication is important to maintain momentum.

Finally, the last subcomponent of leadership is strategic integration. According to Cox (2001) four essential elements are involved. The first type of strategy integration that must occur is the diversity strategy for the overall mission of the organization. The second is establishing goals and action steps for managing diversity. The third is the placement of the strategy for managing people within the strategic framework. Finally, the fourth requirement is to ensure that the work on managing diversity becomes an integral part of the overall strategy for managing people in the organization (Cox, 2001).

Research and Measurement

The second component of the Cox's model is Research and Measurement. Research and Measurement is beneficial to education and schools because at the campus level individuals can see their contribution increased awareness, improved feelings, and increased satisfaction among groups. At the district level, it is a real missed opportunity if these small contributions are over looked. "research is the purposeful collection of data by which we can answer questions about some environmental element or phenomenon" (Cox, 2001, p. 20). Many types of data are needed, including measures of the organizational culture, equal opportunity profile data, analysis of attitudes and perceptions of employees, and data that highlight career experiences of members from different cultural groups (Cox, 1993).

Measurement means the use of research to keep score in the progress of a change initiative. This component is included in the model because successful organizational change work must be well-informed by relevant data, with results systematically measured at pertinent intervals during the process (Cox, 2001).

One aspect of the research program should be to obtain baseline data on key indicators of the diversity environment that can be updated periodically to assess programs (Cox, 1993). Gathering data is helpful only in term of good or bad data. Cox (2001) states because there are few absolute standards of excellence in the area of organizational climate for people, benchmarking or calibration often requires some sort of comparison. Thse areas are external benchmarking, internal benchmarking, and comparing data for the same work unit at different times and triangulation (Cox, 2001).

Education

Education is the third component of the cultural change model. The term "education" is used rather than "training" to signify that learning must be approached through a variety of methods (Cox, 2001, p. 21). Although there has been a great deal of activity in the area of diversity training, early returns on its effectiveness are questionable. On managing change one must be cautious to the resistance of change. One reason for this resistance is fear among the majority group members that change will produce a zero-sum game in which others gain and lose (Cox, 2001). This resistance is partly due to a misunderstanding of diversity. In the development of in-house expertise it is paramount for long-term success in organizational change for the creation of internal resources to carry out education on diversity. The internal resources, trainers or facilitators in diversity must be skilled at dealing with issues that are "(1) laden with emotion, such as experiences with prejudice and discrimination, (2) controversial, such as affirmative action, and (3) deeply personal, such as topics that touch on the spiritual life of participants"(Cox, 2001, p. 98). In addressing the three learning processes associated with diversity, trainers of diversity must be aware of the objective/s. According to Cox (2001) if the objective of the training is to raise awareness, this is facilitated by the participant being self-reflective and hearing about the experiences and interpretation of others. If the objective is deeper knowledge, the participant is given new information concerning research about the subject. If the objective to change behavior, then the training must require participants to think about action steps for translating new insights into doing something differently as they perform their job.

Alignment of Management Systems

Alignment of Management Systems is the fourth components of Cox's Change Model for Work on Diversity. Management systems include any organization policy, practice, rule or procedure. This covers the major human resources activities like recruitment, promotion, and development, as well as other conditions such as work schedules or the design of the physical work environment. All of these systems must be aligned with the goal of leveraging diversity. When this part of the change process gets little attention, or is omitted, the result is that the overall goals of the diversity effort are not realized (Cox, 2001). Organizations have traditionally focused on how to more successfully target qualified people from underrepresented identity groups through recruiting. Some organizations have encountered strong resistance from certain members of the workforce whose personal attitudes, beliefs, and personality traits lead them to oppose efforts to make the workplace more inclusive of people who are different from the traditional social-cultural mix (Cox, 2001).

Follow-Up

The last component of Cox's Change Model for Work on Diversity is the concept of follow-up. This involves "implementing action, establishing accountability for results, and capturing and recycling the learning so that the action steps become more and more precise"(Cox, 2001, p. 22). This component intersects with all the other four components but is connected especially to the research and measurement component. An effective organizational change effort should include all of the elements (Cox, 2001).

An effective leadership requires top leaders to proactively establish real accountability for results on diversity with their direct report. Many leaders leave the implementation of goals to others assuming that people will follow through. Leaders fail to understand that making these goals a part of the culture will require a deployment process and that it is up to them to make sure the process is being used. The result is that accountability will cascade down through the organization, leading to the kind of comprehensive follow-up effort that is needed to make change happen (Cox, 2001).

CONCLUSION

Diversity is an amorphous topic both in academia and business. Many researchers and professionals have developed guidelines, paradigms and models which show how to embrace diversity. Yet, many companies still have difficulty embedding the management of diversity into their daily practices and procedures (Gilbert & Ivanevich, 2000). It is recommended that a systematic planned approach be identified when attempting to design a diversity management initiative. Through effective leadership and strategic planning, diversity can enhance the culture of any organization (Loden, 1996; Plummer, 2003; Thomas, 1991).

The incorporation of diverse people, cultures, values, and norms remains one of the most significant challenges facing organizations. In order to successfully develop an organizational culture where diversity is a priority, organizational structure must reflect the changing workforce (Bendick, Egan, & Lofhjelm, 2001). Diversity is not just a "nice thing to do," it is a business imperative (Plummer, 2003, p. 236). When diversity is effectively utilized it can produce innovative solutions, higher efficiency in business practices, and better employee competencies (Plummer, 2003).

REFERENCES

Allen, R. S., & Montgomery, K. A. (2001). Applying an organizational development approach to creating diversity. *Organizational Dynamics, 30*(2), 149–161. doi:10.1016/S0090-2616(01)00049-3

Anand, R., & Winters, M. (2008). A retrospective view of corporate diversity training from 1964 to the present. *Academy of Management Learning & Education, 7*(3), 356–372. doi:10.5465/AMLE.2008.34251673

Bendick, M. Jr, Egan, M. L., & Lofhjelm, S. M. (2001). Workforce diversity training: From anti-discrimination compliance to organizational development. *Human Resource Planning, 24*(2), 10–25.

Bucher, R. D. (2008). *Building cultural intelligence (CQ)*. Upper Saddle River, NJ: Pearson Education, Inc.

Cox, T. (1993). *Cultural diversity in organizations: Theory, research, & practice*. San Francisco, CA: Berrett-Koehler.

Cox, T. (2001). *Creating the multicultural organization: A strategy for capturing the power of diversity*. San Francisco, CA: Jossey-Bass.

Cox, T., & Smolinski, C. (1994). *Managing diversity and glass ceiling initiatives as nation economic imperatives*. Washington, DC: Key Workplace Documents Federal Publications.

Dass, P., & Parker, B. (1999). Strategies for managing human resource diversity: From resistance to learning. *The Academy of Management Executive, 13*(2), 68–80. doi:10.5465/AME.1999.1899550

Dreachslin, J. L. (2007). Diversity management and cultural competence: Research, practice, and the business case. *Journal of Healthcare Management, 52*(2), 79–86.

Egan, M., & Bendick, M. (2007). *Teaching cultural competence: What multicultural management courses can learn from diversity*. Retrieved October 19, 2008, from http://www.bendickegan.com/pdf/10012007/EganBendickMulticultural2007.pdf.

Egan, M., & Bendick, M. (2008). Combining multicultural management and diversity into one course on cultural competence. *Academy of Management Learning & Education*, *7*(3), 387–393. doi:10.5465/AMLE.2008.34251675

Gardenswartz, L., & Rowe, A. (1993). *Managing diversity: A complete desk reference and planning guide*. Homewood, IL: Business One Irwin.

Gilbert, A. J., & Ivancevich, J. M. (2000). Valuing diversity: A tale of two organizations. *Academy of Management Executives, 14*(1), 93-105. Retrieved from http://web.ebscohost.com.ezproxy.library. unlv.edu/bsi/pdf?vid=19&hid=5&sid=1358b5cf-cbb2-4bcd-9062-b9e27e267f8a%40sessionmgr7.

Gladwin, T. N., Kenelly, J. J., & Krause, T. (1995). Shifting paradigms for sustainable development: Implications for management theory and research. *Academy of Management Review, 20*(4), 874–907.

Loden, M. (1996). *Implementing diversity*. Chicago, IL: Irwin Professional Publishing.

Loden, M., & Rosener, J. B. (1991). *Workforce America! Managing employee diversity as a vital resource*. Homewood, IL: Business One Irwin.

Lynch, E. W., & Hanson, M. J. (1992). *Developing cross-cultural competence*. Baltimore, MD: Paul H. Brookes Publishing Co.

O'Leary, B. J., & Weathington, B. L. (2006). Beyond the business case for diversity in organizations. *Employee Responsibilities and Rights Journal, 18*(4), 1–10.

Plummer, D. L. (2003). *Handbook of diversity management: Beyond awareness to competency based learning*. Lanham, MD: University Press of America, Inc.

Richard, O. C., Kochan, T. A., & McMillan-Capehart, A. (2002). The impact of visible diversity on organizational effectiveness: Disclosing the contents in Pandora's black box. *Journal of Business and Management, 8*(3), 265–291.

Rothwell, W. J., & Sullivan, R. L. (2005). *Practicing organization development: A guide for consultants*. San Francisco, CA: Pfeiffer.

Saposnick, K. (2003). *Managing diversity as a key organizational resource: An interview with David Thomas*. Retrieved from http://www.pegasuscom. com/levpoints/thomasint.html.

SHRM. (2008). *Leadership summit on diversity and inclusion*. Alexandria, VA: SHRM. Retrieved from http://moss07.shrm.org/hrdisciplines/Diversity/Pages/inclusion.aspx.

Thomas, D. A., & Ely, R. J. (1996). Making differences matter: A new paradigm for managing diversity. *Harvard Business Review*, *90*(2), 107–117.

Thomas, R. (1991). *Beyond race and gender: Unleashing the power of your total work force by managing diversity*. New York, NY: American Management Association.

KEY TERMS AND DEFINITIONS

Change: Implies movement toward a goal, an idealized state, or a vision of what should be and movement away from present conditions, beliefs, or attitudes.

Corporate Culture: Basic assumptions and beliefs that are shared by members of an organization, that operates unconsciously, and that is defined in a basic "taken-for-granted" fashion an organization's view of itself and its environment. These assumptions and beliefs are learned responses to a group's problems. They come to be taken for granted because they solve those problems repeatedly and reliably.

Cultural Competence: The capacity to function effectively with all cultures and to successfully navigate a multicultural society.

Cultural Diversity: The inclusion and acceptance of the unique worldviews, customs, norms, patterns of behavior, and traditions of many groups of people.

Diversity: Differences among people with respect to age, class, ethnicity, gender, health, physical and mental ability, race, sexual orientation, religion, stature, education level, job level and function, personality trait, and other human differences.

Diversity Management: Uses applied behavioral science methods, research and theory to manage organizational change and stability processes, that support diversity in organizations and eliminate oppression based on race, gender, sexual orientation, and other human differences, in order to improve the health and effectiveness of organizations while affirming the values of respect for human differences, social justice, participations, community, authenticity, compassion, protection and humility, effectiveness and health, and lifelong learning.

Leveraging Diversity: Enhancing organizational effectiveness and performances by making use of the different perspectives, experiences, and abilities that people bring to the workplace.

Organizational Cultural Competence: The capacity to function effectively with all cultures and to make creative use of a diverse workforce in a way that meets business goals and enhances performance.

Chapter 28
Using Global Virtual Teams to Leverage Workforce Diversity in Global Environments:
Applications of CE Technology and ThinkLets

Cecilia Santillan
University of St. Thomas, USA

Sujin K. Horwitz
University of St. Thomas, USA

ABSTRACT

Although Global Virtual Teams (GVTs) provide organizations with increased competitive advantages and greater flexibility due to their unique ability to transcend the traditional boundaries of time, location, and organizational constraints, managing globally dispersed and culturally diverse GVTs also poses unique challenges. This chapter explores some of the challenges affecting GVTs by examining extant literature on team diversity, team conflict, and collaboration technology. Additionally, it further argues that organizations can greatly benefit from integrating the tenets of adaptable Collaboration Engineering technology and thinkLets into their GVT processes to develop sustainable team collaboration and a sense of structure in the virtual team context.

INTRODUCTION

There has been growing interest for utilizing the collective knowledge among employee teams as organizations are increasingly integrating work teams into their permanent organizational structure

DOI: 10.4018/978-1-4666-1812-1.ch028

(Alavi & Leidner, 2001). Additionally, with the advent of technological innovation and globalization, virtual teams have emerged as another popular, contemporary format of teams (Boudreau, Loch, Robey, & Straub, 1998; Townsend, DeMarie, & Hendrickson, 1998). The information age has indeed provided organizations with technologies that can potentially lead to cost reductions, operational efficiency, and acquisition of highly skilled employees without geographical and time barriers (Duarte & Snyder, 2006; Martins, Gilson, & Maynard, 2004; Zaccaro & Bader, 2003). While virtual teams can overcome traditional constraints of time, location, and organizational boundaries for globally-operated organizations, they are not immune from potential disadvantages and their use poses unique challenges to organizations. One of the most significant challenges for organizations is the lack of direct member interactions due to geographical and temporal separation found in virtual teams and how virtual collaboration should thus be fostered for synergistic teamwork in the absence of such interactions (Hymowitz, 1999).

This chapter explores some of the challenges affecting global virtual teams by examining extant literature on team diversity, team conflict, and technology applied to the global virtual context. It is proposed that organizations can adopt the idea behind Collaboration Engineering (CE) to increase the efficacy of virtual teamwork. CE is a research-based approach to designing, deploying, and sustaining collaborative processes, which can be executed by practitioners in an organization (Briggs, de Vreede, & Nunamaker, 2003). Specifically, we explore the feasibility of using CE models for virtual teams to develop predictable patterns of member behavior and a sense of structure often lacking in the virtual team context.

Operationalizing Global Virtual Teams

A virtual team is generally defined as a group of geographically dispersed individuals cooperating to achieve a common goal with the aid of technology to link them across time, space, and other organizational barriers (Cascio & Shurygailo, 2003; Jarvenpaa & Leidner, 1998). However, virtual teams are a relatively new form of teaming in that the term "virtual" has been applied rather liberally in the literature to represent varying types of teams (Cascio & Shurygailo, 2003).

Virtual teams can take various formats and configurations contingent upon organizational needs and resource availability (Jarvenpaa & Leidner, 1998). For instance, virtual teams can be formed within the same organization but can connect departmental members operating in geographically dispersed locations. Virtual teams can also be configured for facilitating collaborative work among different departments within the same organization. Finally, in some virtual teams, culturally and geographically diverse individuals are specifically brought together to elicit a common understanding of a goal. While recognizing multiple forms and configurations inherent in virtual teams, this chapter specifically focuses on Global Virtual Team (GVT) and defines GVT as globally dispersed, culturally diverse, and technologically connected individuals who work interdependently with a limited life span of membership in order to accomplish a common goal.

TWO SALIENT FEATURES OF GVTs AND CONFLICT

Virtualness in GVTs

It is necessary to explain the dimensions of virtualness in order to fully elucidate the dynamic nature of GVTs. Neale and Griffith (2001) have provided a multidimensional framework to understand the range of virtualness by classifying it into three dimensions: 1) physical distance ranging from close to far; 2) the level of technology support ranging from low to high; and 3) the percentage of time that team members are apart on the task ranging from 0 to 100 percent (Figure 1). The framework by Neale and Griffith offers an insightful conceptualization of virtualness in analyzing GVTs, which is a relatively recent phenomenon of teaming in globally operating organizations. In traditional (face-to-face) teams, members need to be physically close, require low technology support, and spend little time apart, whereas in hybrid teams, collocated and geographically dispersed members work collaboratively and require a medium level of technology support with occasional face-to-face meetings. Finally, teams considered "purely" virtual are physically distant, spend the majority of their time apart when collaborating, and require a great deal of technology support (Neale & Griffith, 2001).

Note that virtualness is not a mutually exclusive category but rather a continuous construct, where varying forms of virtual teaming can take place depending on where a team lies on the three dimensions (Neale & Griffith, 2001; Kirkman & Mathieu, 2005). As Figure 1 depicts, virtualness lies on a three dimensional continuum with GVTs lying on the far right ("highly to purely virtual") due to a large physical distance, the majority of time on a task spent apart, and a high level of technology support although the degree of virtualness in GVTs can vary in terms of their technology support and physical/task distance actually separating members.

Figure 1. Traditional, hybrid, and virtual teams (Neale & Griffith, 2001)

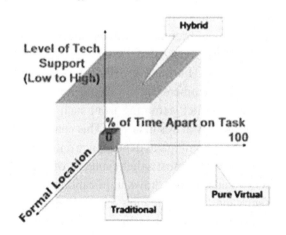

Diversity in GVTs

Another significant feature of GVTs is team member diversity as such global teams tend to be more diverse than traditional or hybrid teams (Kiesler & Cummings, 2002). There are various ways to recognize diverse attributes in teams and researchers have created several classifications for parsimoniously categorizing the multitude of team diversity attributes. For example, in their narrative review, Jackson et al. (1995) distinguished between readily detectable and less observable team diversity in which the former represented bio-demographic markers and the latter indicated ability and cognitive resources. Harrison, Price, and Bell (1998) examined the impact of surface-level (demographic) and deep-level (attitudinal) diversity on team integration. The researchers defined surface-level diversity as member differences in immediately observable biological characteristics such as age, gender, and race/ethnicity and deep-level diversity as differences in attitudes, beliefs, and values, which are learned through member interactions. Similarly, Milliken and Martins (1996) categorized diversity into two broad types, observable individual differences, and underlying attributes. Of the common diversity attributes in the team literature, deep-level diversity was examined in this chapter, particularly cultural diversity, and its effects on GVTs. It is acknowledged that a host of other diversity attributes as presented in these multiple frameworks can influence GVT processes other than cultural effects discussed here. However, as GVT members tend to be more nationally and culturally diverse than collocated teams, socio-cultural diversity is assumed to hold the most significant impact on the complex dynamics of virtual team performance (Kieler & Cummings, 2002; Mortensen & Hinds,

2001). The ensuing section examines the potential effects of GVTs' two salient characteristics, distance due to virtualness and diversity due to varying national and cultural backgrounds, on team processes with a particular focus on conflict. Team conflict is especially problematic as virtual teams operating in a geographically distant and culturally diverse environment have been found to experience more process loss and dysfunctional conflict than non-virtual teams (Crowston, Sieber, & Wynn, 2007; Gibson & Cohen, 2003).

Team Conflict in GVTs

Team conflict has been an area widely researched by organizational scholars (De Dreu & Weingart, 2003; Jehn, 1995). While the reduction of conflict is a paramount goal, not all conflict is destructive, and in some cases conflict can lead to operational improvements (Amason & Mooney, 1999, Jehn & Mannix, 2001). In part, whether conflict is constructive or destructive depends on whether it results from relational-based or task-driven origins (Jehn, 1995). Studies of work groups in organizations have suggested that while relationship conflict does hamper group performance, conflict regarding the group's task may actually facilitate performance to a certain extent (Jehn, 1995, 1997). In particular, when tasks are of a non-routine nature, open conflict can enhance the depth of problem evaluation and assessment of options. Consistent with the above notion, it has been empirically shown that too little dissent, or the extreme need to arrive at a consensus, can lead to overlooking potential options hence resulting in poor decisions (Payne, 1982). Although an excessive amount of any of these conflict types was deemed to be detrimental to team performance, a moderate level of task-based conflict was found to produce positive effects by generating ideas, evaluating alternatives, and encouraging constructive criticism, all of which improved evaluation and decision-making (Klien & Harrison, 2007). This finding was consistent with other studies, demonstrating that task-related conflict can enhance creativity through eliciting divergent viewpoints, and thus represents an advantage diverse teams have relative to homogenous teams, provided the diverse team is properly managed (Friedman & Berger, 2004; Jehn & Bendersky, 2003). In contrast, outcomes of bickering, low satisfaction, and decreased performance were reported when conflicts were relationship-based.

As in traditional teams, GVTs often suffer from conflict arising from member differences (Hinds & Bailey, 2003; Jarvenpaa & Leidner, 1998). However, the two most salient features of GVTs, distance and technological dependence due to virtualness and cultural diversity due to the global composition of GVTs, can hamper the coordination of team processes and further exacerbate conflict in GVTs as shown in Figure 2. Several studies of geographically dispersed teams posit that conflict among such distributed team members is not only pervasive but also difficult to identify and manage (Hind & Bailey, 2003; Mannix, Griffith, & Neale, 2002). Particularly, spatial distance significantly reduces member interactions and communications relative to face-to-face interactions (Allen, Tushman, & Lee, 1979; Te'eni, 2001). Furthermore, as GVTs typically consist of members from varying nations and cultures, conflict stemming from such diversity also frequently arises in GVTs. This chapter thus discusses technological dependence and cultural diversity as two most salient sources of conflict in GVTs and further draws implications for their effectiveness by reviewing extant literature on team diversity, team conflict, and technology in the global virtual context.

TWO ANTECEDENTS OF GVT CONFLICT: DIVERSITY AND TECHNOLOGY

Conflicts Arising from Cultural Diversity

Creating a virtual team for multinational organizations is an opportunity to embrace global talents without the constant outflows of travel coordination and relocation expenses—an optimal solution for highly integrated global businesses. Theoretically, diversity in GVTs capitalizing on global talents should benefit team performance (Townsend, et al., 1998) until diversity itself begins to introduce and highlight disparities amongst team members. Indeed, diversity in teams is a mixed blessing in that simply bringing people with diverse skills, knowledge, and experience together does not guarantee that they will be aligned in their understanding of team goals (Horwitz & Horwitz, 2007). Although a strong business case for diversity has been made in both academics and practice, barriers to capitalizing on diversity still

exist in organizations (Cox & Blake, 1991). One of the potential pitfalls of team diversity is that such diversity can increase intra-team conflict, both cognitive and affective types, as diversity prompts different perspectives on and approaches to tasks and further fuels different attitudes and expectations (Jehn, 1997; Pelled, 1996). Because GVT members are globally dispersed, there tends to be diverse regional, national, ethnic, linguistic, and other complex cultural dimensions, which can negatively affect member behaviors and interactions hence creating more serious conflicts in GVTs than traditional teams.

Cultural diversity is a multidimensional construct embracing an array of differences in individuals with unique socio-cultural backgrounds (Benhamou & Peltier, 2007). While reflecting on the multifaceted nature of cultural diversity, much attention is given to variations in national, linguistic, socio-cultural, and value differences in GVTs in this chapter (Hofstede, 1991). Particularly, norms for appropriate team behavior are heavily influenced by the value, belief, and even idiosyncratic emotional displays of the countries

Figure 2. The effects of virtualness and diversity on GVT process

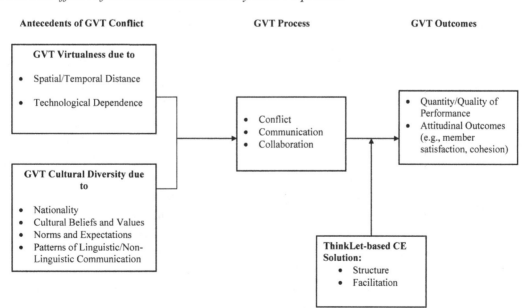

in which individual members reside (Janssens & Brett, 1997). Consequently, GVTs consisting of members with varying socio-cultural beliefs, values, norms, and linguistic differences (cultural diversity) tend to lack a unified view of appropriate team behaviors while having different interpretations of each other's actions and undermining the member relationships.

Research suggests that cultural diversity influences the frequency and intensity of conflict in culturally diverse teams (Blackburn, Furst, & Rosen, 2003; Gibson & Zellmer-Bruhn, 2001; Kirkman & Shapiro, 2001). Particularly, negative effects of affective conflict stemming from non-substantive issues such as personality clashes, dislike, confusion, and annoyance tend to be much more pronounced than cognitive, task-oriented conflict in culturally diverse teams. As Blackburn et al. (2003) reported in their qualitative study of virtual teams, culturally diverse members often encounter conflicts arising from different protocols and expectations of the communication process. Another example of relationship conflict originated from cultural diversity includes the difference in members' preferred mode of team dynamics between collaboration and competitiveness, which has been both theoretically and empirically linked to the efficacy of team collaboration (Gibson & Zellmer-Bruhn, 2001). For example, Kirkman and Shapiro (2001) discovered that team members from the highly individualistic U.S. culture were more resistant to team-aspects of self-managed teams and more receptive to the autonomy-aspects than members from the collectivistic Philippine culture. Similarly, many Western cultures expect direct communication in which messages are transparent, while the Eastern communication norm relies more on implications and inferences, particularly in conflict situations (Ting-Toomey, 1992). A team member may pose a situation, which needs to be addressed as a hypothetical situation instead of directly stating the facts in order to be less assertive and non-confrontational in email correspondence. While this indirect method may

construe as an evasive and ineffective way of communication from the Western perspective, it is expected and even encouraged in the Eastern standard of communication. Likewise, individuals with East Asian ethnicities (e.g., Korean, Chinese, and Japanese) are more concerned with preserving "face" and thus act to limit embarrassment by avoiding to ask sensitive questions directly (Oetzel & Ting-Toomey, 2003).

As shown in the aforementioned examples, a great deal of diversity-related conflict in GVTs occurs from cultural and linguistic misunderstandings and confusion, which is largely non-task oriented and relational in nature (or becomes relational-conflict if such conflict is not managed properly). Furthermore, misunderstandings between GVT members are often aggravated by the absence of non-verbal cues and contextual information due to the heavy reliance on computer-mediated communication and technology. Although this heavy reliance on technology is necessary for GVTs to collaborate, such technological dependence for member interactions can also reduce opportunities for monitoring crucial non-linguistic communication essential to accurately interpreting messages and increase the potential for escalating conflict.

Conflict Arising from Technological Dependence

Research suggests that capabilities for monitoring and managing member behavior are significantly reduced in virtual environments, thereby creating a difficulty for team leaders and managers to guide the team process for optimal performance (Zhao, Nunamaker, & Briggs, 2002). Armstrong and Cole (2002), for example, reported that conflicts in geographically dispersed teams connected with technology went unidentified and unaddressed longer than conflicts in collocated teams. Different time zones (temporal distance) due to a high level of virtualness in GVTs also trigger reductions in spontaneous communications and decrease the potential for synchronous interactions, hence affecting real-time problem solving and decision-making (O'Leary & Cummings, 2007). A recent study, which interviewed 56 GVTs (Cordery & Soo, 2008), demonstrated that the virtual teams struggled in effective directory updating, information allocation, and retrieval coordination mechanisms. In the study interviews, the team members expressed that technology-mediated communication was not ideal for discussion and decision-making. Another issue addressed in the study was the team's concern for sharing vital organizational information with others without direct, face-to-face interactions.

Several studies have reported that decision making via technology poses a unique temporally-oriented challenge to GVTs as the speed and scrutiny necessary to make a comfortable decision and arrive at a consensus can vary greatly on the quality and capacity of technology infrastructures available to members (Hertel, Geister, & Konradt, 2005; King & Majchrzak, 2003). Additionally, GVT members with varying cultures have different norms and protocols for sharing knowledge and exchanging feedback, which further aggravates potential conflict in computer mediated decision making processes (Hollingshead, 1996a, 1996b). Hall (1987) reported that there was less feedback exchange between members from different cultures. Some national cultures are, for example, "high context" and others are "low context," referring to the importance of non-verbal, contextual cues in interpreting messages (Hall, 1987). Overall, delays in technology combined with cultural variations in temporal-orientation can engender both process and affective conflict while affecting GVTs' real-time problem solving and time-sensitive decision-making.

In technology-mediated communication, individuals tend to interpret virtual communications such as synchronized video/audio conferences and electronic texts/messages based on their own conventions and contextual knowledge which are local to them. However, communication through electronic texts/messages is often time-consuming and laborious in that individuals tend not to fully express details they would otherwise communicate verbally (Graetz, Boyle, Kimble, Thompson, & Garloch, 1998). Consequently, omitted details and qualifications coupled with the absence of social cues lead to lower communication efficiency and higher instances of miscommunication in technology-mediated virtual teams as compared to collocated teams (DeSandtis & Monge, 1999). Furthermore, relationship-oriented, non-substantive, and dysfunctional conflict can be aggravated by inadequate or delayed technology such as a long time lapse or absence of rich auditory and visual cues, which distorts the subtle meaning of messages sent to GVT members in another country or culture (Staples & Zhao, 2006). Thus, complex information exchanged between GVT members through technology can be subject to multiple interpretations, particularly across cultures.

Interestingly, some researchers have found that an anonymous virtual setting can promote more uninhibited member behavior, even uncivil behavior at times, than face-to-face interactions (Siegel, Dubrovsky, Kiesler, & McGuire, 1986; Sproull & Kiesler, 1986). Siegel et al. (1986) reported that uninhibited behavior such as swearing, insults, and name-calling was significantly more likely to occur in computer-mediated distributed teams than in traditional teams with face-to-face interactions. Similarly, Sproull and Kiesler (1986) discovered that greater self-absorption (individuals focused more on themselves than on others) and uninhibited behavior in email messages. Team composition also played a role in virtual teams' proclivity for engaging in uninhibited behavior; particularly, all male virtual teams used more confrontational and crude language than members of all female teams (Savicki, Lingenfelter, & Kelley, 1996). As Kankanhalli et al. (2006) aptly pointed out, "Virtual teams that relied more heavily on technology were found to experience more conflict, and the conflict seemed to be more detrimental for such teams than traditional teams" (Kankanhalli, Tan, & Wei, 2006, p. 242).

TECHNOLOGY TO AID COLLABORATION AND REDUCE CONFLICT IN GVTs

Collaboration requires individuals to consciously work together towards a common goal in a coordinated fashion with organizational support. The transition to virtual collaboration in today's dynamic global environment is a complex, process-driven task necessitating the effective mediation of technology, team facilitation, and organizational support to help GVT members capitalize on their expertise and produce a synergistic team output. In the virtual context, the development of team cohesion has been found to be more difficult than in conventional teams, because there are reduced member interactions due to a high level of virtualness (Blackburn, et al., 2003). Additionally, GVTs characteristically have greater member heterogeneity than collocated or hybrid teams, with team boundaries spanning several geographical zones and exhibiting multiple cultures, thereby presenting unique challenges for creating a shared sense of team identity. Streamlining collaborative team activities has been thus found to be critical to virtual team effectiveness, because such a streamlined process can provide GVT members with a much-needed structure to guide members to operate toward the shared goal (Gibson & Cohen, 2003). Similarly, extant research in the fields of e-commerce and marketing posits that ensuring structure in virtual transactions, also known as "structural assurance" (McKnight, Choudhury, & Kacmar, 2002) helps build trust and improve member interactions (Huang, Wei, Watson, & Tan, 2002; Lurey & Raisinghani, 2001).

Although it may seem like a bureaucratic nuisance, GVT members need to have established deadlines, formats, documentation, and other procedural structures to overcome potential conflict and process loss stemming from distance and diversity (Zhao, et al., 2002). In doing so, optimizing technology to facilitate collaborative processes and channels of communication is of utmost importance to GVTs as technology is a key part of linking temporally, spatially, and culturally dispersed members. As Workman pointed out, "The virtual environment has less externally supplied structure, is more isolated, and creates greater degrees of ambiguity about tasks and interpersonal relationships than in proximal settings" (Workman, 2007, p. 795). The section below examines how Group Support Systems (GSS) can be used to structure and facilitate virtual team processes.

COLLABORATION ENGINEERING FOR STRUCTURE AND FACILITATION IN GVT

Group Support Systems: Added Values, Designs, and Problems

The availability of groupware technologies has been expanded exponentially since the proliferation of the internet and digital communications. These technologies include useful features such as video and audio capabilities that have shown to enhance group interactions in virtual teams, where members rarely meet face-to-face. However, practitioners continue to show preference for Group Support Systems (GSS) for their virtual team collaboration (Huang, et al., 2002; Townsend, et al., 1998). GSS provide teams with multi-feature software tools to communicate, exchange information, and manage data to accomplish team tasks (Briggs, de Vreede, & Nunamaker, 2003; Harder, Keeter, Woodcock, Ferguson, & Wills, 2005; Nunamaker, 1997). For instance, team members may be using a Smart Board to illustrate a task while simultaneously using an audio feature for explanation. In distributed environments, research consistently shows that synchronous communication and multi-feature capabilities found in GSS greatly increase the number of responses and the depth of analysis in virtual teams (Briggs, de Vreede, & Nunamaker, 2003; Davison & Briggs, 2000). Another benefit derived from GSS use in

GVTs is that these technologies foster the development of much needed structures for virtual collaboration. Specifically, GSS tools enable team members to interchange individualized work with collaborative work depending on the progression of the task, thereby facilitating the mode of interaction at dispersed locations (Rao, Luk, & Warren, 2005) and this capability to merge individual users into a group space is optimal for GVTs. Finally, by using the same software tools, team members are able to predict the functions or modules that their colleagues are likely to use and such predictability is important for GVTs to define and structure collaborative activities in order to reduce misunderstandings and confusions stemming from distance and diversity (Kolfschoten & de Vreede, 2009). Ultimately, without the aid of dependable groupware technology such as GSS, the manifestation of diversity- and distance-related conflicts is likely to worsen hence impeding effective GVT performance (Davison & Briggs, 2000).

Although a positive association between GSS use and virtual teamwork has generally been reported in the literature, there have been several instances of failure and slow diffusion of GSS into business operations (Briggs, et al., 2003; Harder, et al., 2005). One major drawback is the complexity of GSS technology for its users. As GSS tools are becoming increasingly sophisticated by incorporating more functions and modules for team facilitation, not all users are versed in such complex, automated tools for collaboration. Consequently, users must be trained to use various configurations of GSS to fully reap the benefits. There is, however, relatively a stiff learning curve for a novice user (particularly for an employee with limited time, resources, and technological expertise) to be skilled in using various features within GSS to produce intended outcomes as such technologies utilize full-featured platforms with hundreds of configurable features (Briggs, et al., 2003). For example, the GroupSystems Electronic Brainstorming Tool has more than 20 independently configurable features, hence creating a total of 1,048,576 possible combinations. Other dimensions pertinent to individual users must also be considered prior to adopting GSS for team facilitation. These dimensions include the perceived usefulness of technology, cognitive load, economic, political, and social utility derived from using GSS technology in their work. Additionally, team facilitation in GSS requires an extensive set of communication and moderation skills, which are often difficult to develop and transfer within the existing employee pool in an organization (Bragge, et al., 2004). Indeed, due to the high cognitive load and team facilitation skills needed for the optimal use of GSS, GSS interventions are generally prepared and guided by professional facilitators, either hired externally or trained internally, who possess the requisite skills for running the system and facilitating the team's collaborative process (Briggs, et al., 2003). Although organizations are increasingly investing in various groupware technologies for distributed teamwork, sustainable GSS use is often difficult to be accomplished for the aforementioned issues. In reality, the decision to adopt GSS for enhanced virtual team collaboration is not only driven by innovation or competitive advantage but also based on an organization's long-term commitment to investing in such technology, training personnel, and willingness to embrace an organic approach to augmenting business workflows in distributed global environments.

In this chapter, it is suggested Collaboration Engineering (CE) and thinkLets, a feature within CE, to complement the functions of GSS for a sustained use of collaboration technology that structures and facilitates GVT processes. CE is a research-based approach that designs, models, and deploys structured, collaboration processes and thinkLets within CE are the units of facilitation which can be encoded into GSS in order to develop a streamlined line of activities for a given team task (Bragge, et al., 2007). The preponderance of collaboration technology research demonstrates that the CE approach combined with thinkLets (thinkLet-based CE approach) can provide organizations with two crucial types of support necessary for effective GVT collaboration: structure and facilitation. Under this approach, a well-defined and streamlined structure can reduce ambiguity, uncertainty, and unpredictability in member interactions due to virtualness while well-executed team facilitation can mitigate conflict arising from confusions and misunderstandings due to cultural diversity. With a high level of structural support and facilitation provided by the CE approach, GVT members will be more likely to share the common goal, create a common identity, communicate openly, and develop appropriate protocols for their virtual collaboration (Cramton, 2001). The following sections further examine the CE approach and thinkLets as venues to manage team behaviors in GVTs.

Collaboration Engineering and ThinkLets

In the CE approach, a collaboration engineer designs an efficacious, predictable, and reusable pattern of team activities, which is then transferred to a GVT member who has most understanding of the task and team dynamics. After this transition, which requires a short training, the team member can facilitate the collaboration process, without an on-going support from a professional facilitator and without having to learn extensive facilitation skills. Consequently, the thinkLet-based CE approach is one of the few collaboration approaches that provide novice facilitators with codified and scripted, thus directly applicable, expert-level advice on how to conduct successful team collaboration (Bragge, et al., 2007; Nabukenya, Van Bommel, Proper, & de Vreede, 2011). Therefore, in adopting the tenet of CE, it is critical that an organization in conjunction with collaboration engineers designs a user-friendly, instrumental, and transferable collaboration process to offer its users a recurring added value (Kolfschoten, de Vreede, & Briggs, 2007). To design such

high-value, transferable CE, thinkLets are used. Briggs et al. (2006) defined thinkLets as "named, packaged facilitation interventions that create predictable, repeatable patterns of collaboration among people toward a goal" (p. 314). ThinkLets form a pattern of language, which generates sustainable team collaboration. Practitioners who understand the specification of a given thinkLet can produce the pattern of collaboration that the thinkLet is intended for and further replicate the collaboration pattern for similar tasks in the future.

ThinkLet-Based CE Approach

CE supports sustainable team collaboration in terms of structure, facilitation, and transferability by using thinkLets that encode a facilitator's best practices into the existing GSS to generate clear and scripted prompts for guiding collaborative activities (Briggs, et al., 2003). There are six primary patterns of collaborative behavior utilized by thinkLets: 1) diverge; 2) converge; 3) clarify; 4) organize; 5) evaluate and; 6) build consensus (Briggs, et al., 2003; Harder, et al., 2005). Approximately 60 to 70 thinkLet dimensions of these five patterns have been codified, capturing effective team facilitation practices and encoding such practices into repeatable processes for future use (Briggs, et al., 2003; Kolfschoten, et al., 2007). Table 1 provides an example of a divergent thinkLet named "LeafHopper." As shown in the table, thinkLets have three components which constitute a specific stimulus for creating the thinkLet-based CE approach: 1) tool, or the GSS used; 2) configuration, referring to the features employed by the GSS; and 3) script, or the instructions encoded into the GSS (Briggs, et al., 2003). Team members should know each of these components of thinkLets in order to recreate the intended patterns of behavior in their team collaboration. Once all team activities are specified and validated, a process manual for the team members should be created containing the configuration, a script for each activity, and activity cue cards. It should be noted that thinkLets are not to be used as the "cookie cutter" solution to team facilitation. Rather, thinkLets are designed to be copied and modified to fit the task as it progresses. Specifically, the script of a thinkLet can be "reworded" to include or exclude new aspects of the task; once the thinkLet is re-scripted, it is called a modifier (Kolfschoten & Santanen, 2007).

In one study, the "LeafHopper" thinkLet example in Table 1 was used within an existing GSS tool to facilitate a team decision-making task involving diverse stakeholders of a US software company. In this organizational application of the "LeafHopper" thinkLet, a commercial software development team had twelve high-stake, complex issues to be resolved relatively quickly while incorporating input from all stakeholders ranging from engineers to customers (Briggs, et al., 2001). The team soon realized that for any given stakeholders, they only had an interest in about 1/3 of the issues; however, the mix of issues and interest was such that the team could not ideally schedule

multiple sub-sessions around each topic. The team, therefore, employed a LeafHopper thinkLet to overcome the conflict. The development team posted the twelve issues to their GSS, the Group-Systems Topic Commenter, and asked the participants to work first on the topics in which they had the most stake, and on which they had the most expertise. The participants proposed options for resolving each issue by prioritizing the twelve issues based on their interest and expertise and then discussed the pros and cons of the proposals. The whole discussion of twelve topics took approximately an hour and a half. In the subsequent, follow-up discussion, the group reached the consensus on seven outstanding issues and assigned action items for collecting information on the five that remained unresolved. The entire group of the stakeholders was fully engaged in the discussions using the LeafHopper, with one participant commenting on the outcome, "We just did a week's work in three and a half hours" (Briggs, et al., 2001, p. 4). The underlying conceptualization of

Table 1. LeafHopper: a divergence thinkLet example

Select this thinkLet,	when you know in advance that the team must brainstorm on several topics at once. when different participants will have different levels of interest or expertise in the different topics. when it is not important to assure that every participant contributes to every topic.
Do not select this thinkLet,	when it is important to assure that each person addresses each topic.
Overview	Participants start with an electronic list of several discussion topics; Each item on the list links to an instance of a simultaneous comment window; Each participant hops among the topics to contribute as dictated by interest and expertise. *Inputs: A list of topics that must be addressed by the team.* *Outputs: A set of comments organized by discussion topic.*

How to use LeafHopper	*Tool:* GroupSystems Topic Commenter
	Configuration:
	    1. Participants may contribute comments under each topic.
	    2. Participants may not contribute new topics.
	    3. Contributions will be anonymous.
	    4. Create one topic card for each brainstorming question in Topic Commenter or one of the other list/ comments tools.
	Script:
	    5. Explain the topics to the team and verify that the participants understand them.
	    6. Explain the kinds of ideas to which the team must contribute.
	    7. Explain how to open the comment window under each discussion item.
	    8. Say this:
	        a. Start working on the topics in which you have the most interest or the most expertise. If you have time, move to each of the other topics to read and comment on the contribution of others.
	        b. You may not have time to work on every topic; so work first on the topics that are most important to you.

thinkLets is to design clear rules and thus team members can logically produce an optimal pattern of collaborative behavior (Knoll, Hörning, & Horton, 2009).

As discussed previously, cultural diversity in GVTs, combined with a heavy reliance on technology, can create depersonalized interactions and promote inappropriate behaviors among members hence increasing the potential for relationship conflict (Hinds & Bailey, 2003). Dysfunctional relationship conflict can be substantially reduced with the thinkLet-based CE approach by automatically limiting the parameters of member responses to the tasks at hand. For instance, a thinkLet called "StrawPoll" builds a consensus by directing team members to anonymously register their opinion on a single topic and then discuss the pros and cons of the topic for a certain time period. The team members can change their vote anonymously as the discussion progresses, which encourages more honest responses and criticism (more thinkLet examples are shown in Appendix A). The thinkLet-based CE approach is not limited to special projects but can also be exercised in managerial tasks as presented below.

ORGANIZATIONAL APPLICATION OF THINKLETS TO VIRTUAL COLLABORATION

Example 1: Policy-Making Using the ThinkLet-Based CE Approach

Organizational policy-making is a complex and recurring collaborative process involving a diverse group of stakeholders with different values, interests, and agendas. Nabukenya et al. (2011) have argued that the complex and political nature of the policy making process is often caused by bringing multiple parties with different backgrounds and conflicting objectives together to create an acceptable policy solution for all. Consequently, the process of organizational policy making needs to

be well-defined and structured to mitigate conflict and politics while integrating needs and interests of multiple stakeholders. Once proven successful, an organization should be able to reuse the same template with some modifications for improving future policy-making (Nabukenya, et al., 2011). In this real-life application, the thinkLet-based CE approach was found to be an appropriate mechanism to provide structural support and facilitate a mission-critical, recurring, collaborative policy-making process (Nabukenya, et al., 2011). The thinkLet-model used in this case created three primary patterns of collaborative behavior[1]: 1) identifying various policy solutions using the "Generate" thinkLet pattern; 2) filtering key policy solutions using the "Converge" thinkLet pattern; and 3) prioritizing key policy solutions using the "Evaluate" thinkLet pattern. Organizations can greatly benefit from automating specific patterns of behavior through thinkLets in policy-making processes as shown in this example.

Example 2: Developing Organizational Strategy with the Use of ThinkLets

ThinkLets encoded into GSS have proven beneficial not only for traditional, for-profit organizations but also for not-for-profit, public organizations such as educational institutions. Bragge et al. (2007), for example, conducted an e-collaboration using thinkLets with representatives from thirteen Finnish universities for multi-organizational strategy development. Strategy development is one of the most critical functions within an organization to establish and execute goals to remain competitive (Bragge et al., 2007; Eden & Ackerman, 2001). When strategy development involves multiple organizations, the strategy development process is even more difficult and complex than for a single organization because it involves diverse organizational goals, issues of power dominance, and politics thereby creating conflict between the organizations. Eden and Ackerman (2001) have further argued that a key to developing a successful multi-organizational strategy is grounded in the social processes between organizations and their ability to agree on the strategy direction and plans of implementation among the collaborating organizations.

Bragge et al. observed and intervened in the educational strategy development process by the Oodi Consortium, a Multi-Organizational Collaborative Team (MCT) Committee, composed of representatives from thirteen Finish universities. The main objective of the Oodi MCT Committee was to revise the current "Oodi" system to implement more up-to-date and cost-effective student information system which could be accessed by faculty, administrators, and students across multiple Finish member universities (Bragge, et al., 2007). For the Oodi MCT Committee facilitation technology, a centralized GSS called GroupSystemsTM MeetingRoom was used in conjunction with thinkLets (Bragge, et al., 2007). Several types of thinkLets were used to facilitate the strategy development process in the Oodi meeting, and the selection of the thinkLets was mainly based on the goals and the time frame given to the team members for each activity. The Oodi MCT's participation level was very active throughout the entire e-collaboration session; for instance, the FreeBrainstorm thinkLet registered 198 comments in 35 minutes for an internal environmental analysis question such as "What needs and challenges will your university, and especially your student administration, face in the coming years with respect to the Oodi System?" (Bragge, et al., 2007)[2]. The one-day Oodi strategy development e-collaboration session was concluded with an electronic feedback survey and a wrap-up review.

The results and feedback from the Oodi MCT Committee members were mostly positive. The team members seemed to be relaxed and more willing to comment due to the anonymity of the computer-mediated discussions. The e-collaboration accompanied by thinkLets also provided the Oodi MCT members with technological support and process structure hence encouraging democratic involvements by all participating stakeholders. Additionally, the team members expressed that the quantity and quality of the responses were far superior to those generated by conventional means of virtual team facilitation (Bragee, et al., 2007). However, some participants expressed concerns and limitations regarding the thinkLet-based e-collaboration in the study. One of the notable concerns was that deep face-to-face interaction was still needed to complement the e-collaboration, while another was related to the inherent problem of voting-based selection, which omitted potentially good but radical ideas during the voting process. Finally, there were divergent opinions on whether the process to train novice practitioners to replicate the thinkLet process was adequate (Bragee, et al., 2007). Overall, the e-collaboration session employing thinkLets provided the team with the process support (electronic, anonymous and parallel communication with group memory), the process structure (e.g. predefined agenda), and the task structure (e.g. predefined categories and automated questions) to improve the development of a multi-organizational strategy for the Oodi MCT Committee.

IMPLICATIONS FOR PRACTICE

Although there are various ways to manage virtual team interactions, research suggests that the use of the thinkLet-based CE approach can be particularly beneficial for managing GVT collaboration which puts a premium on standardized and structured technology for facilitating such teamwork (Deokar, Kolfscheoten, & de Vreede, 2008; Kolfscheoten & de Vreede, 2007). Furthermore, the majority of GVT facilitations and interventions are recurring activities due to their high levels of virtualness, thereby making the thinkLet approach as an optimal collaboration solution for GVTs. There are, however, costs incurred by the adoption of the thinkLet-based CE approach as in any technology adoptions in organizations. Dean, Deokar, and Bush (2006), for example, classified Collaborative Intervention (CI) into three types: 1) level one ad hoc interventions which happen at the exact moment of the collaborative process; 2) level two interventions which are planned but not designed to be replicated; and 3) level three interventions which are planned and intended to be replicated for future use. Reflecting on Dean et al.'s classifications of CI, it is likely that the thinkLet-based CE approach primarily affects CI levels two and three, hence incurring a moderate to high amount of initial investment due to the necessary selection, customization, and deployment of thinkLets.

In addition, there are several managerial considerations in adopting the thinkLet-based CE approach for GVTs such as team members' general knowledge and comfort level of technology, training, and resources involved for the effective use of thinkLets, and potential for an additional, experienced facilitator for GVT collaboration (Dean, et al., 2006). The thinkLet-based CE approach is more advantageous and cost-effective for organizations than other traditional means of collaboration technology, because practitioners learn and deploy their own set of collaborative activities without constant help of a professional facilitator. However, professional and skilled facilitators may not be completely eliminated from some GVT projects due to their highly complex and critical nature of tasks (Dean, et al., 2006). Indeed, organizations considering the thinkLet-based CE approach for GVT collaboration must be cognizant of various investment requirements prior to introducing the approach to their GVT processes. In doing so, they need to clearly define desired project outcomes while considering the scope and complexity of the task and evaluating whether the project is a right fit for the thinkLet-based CE approach. Key dimensions of the task such as the intensity and frequency of member interactions, the amount of information to be shared, and processing intensity of data collected

should all be carefully considered (Dean, et al., 2006). Other criteria for the optimal match include the number of participants, resource availability for on-going technology support, and most importantly, the availability of a process champion responsible for ensuring the thinkLet-based CE approach is sustained for recurring virtual tasks (Dean, et al., 2006). The process champion should be a key participant in the project and responsible for accessing the organization's resources and support for the sustainable use of thinkLets. It should be emphasized that the process champion in tandem with the cooperation from team members, not thinkLets or GSS tools, must drive the team process.

Along with technology, organizations should also create a team environment conducive to maximizing virtual collaboration. For example, organizations can create a positive team climate by providing specific training aimed at helping GVT members recognize their similarities and bridge differences (e.g., team building, conflict-resolution, cross-cultural communication training, and so forth). There is a long stream of research suggesting that such training benefits organizations employing diverse teams (Peters & Waterman, 1988). Specifically, by illuminating potential opportunities teams can attain through diversity, GVT members can significantly appreciate the benefits from member diversity while becoming more cognizant of potential problems arising from cultural differences.

IMPLICATIONS FOR RESEARCH

Although a great deal of research has been conducted on different factors impacting globally distributed teams (Carmel, 1999; Hertel, et al., 2005), there is still a paucity of studies examining cost-effective, process-driven, and user-friendly technology options enabling practitioners and organizations to facilitate GVT collaboration. This chapter aims to build a case for such an efficacious and practitioner-oriented technology by employing the thinkLet-based CE approach to complement GSS while considering the unique features of GVTs. Using thinkLets as identifiable collaboration tools is a relatively novel approach despite the concept of thinkLets has been understood and utilized as tacit knowledge among GSS facilitators for quite some time (Briggs, et al., 2001). Consequently, many existing thinkLets are still embedded in the implicit knowledge of expert GSS users, and as such are unavailable to others (Briggs, et al., 2001). Future research efforts should thus be made to document, publish, and disseminate these thinkLets to benefit a wider community of practitioners and organizations. Additionally, more empirical studies should be conducted to describe how thinkLets can be scripted and utilized in organizational settings. Despite growing interest in the benefits of thinkLets (Bragge, et al., 2006; Briggs, et al., 2001, 2003), there is a significant lack of studies reporting thinkLet procedures as well as the physical design of a thinkLet-based model in sufficient detail to allow users to apply the concepts to their practices (Knoll, et al., 2009). Therefore, it is crucial for the GSS research community to expand the use of thinkLets and CE technology by means of empirically validating such outcomes to better assist organizations with managing GVTs. Concurrently, future research endeavor should also focus on establishing theoretical foundations for different types of GVT processes and defining a set of thinkLets applicable to unique types of GVT processes.

ThinkLets are by no means a technological panacea to produce effective GVT collaboration. Rather, thinkLets are research-based practical tools, which can create and replicate desired patterns of team behavior, and thus provide users with a means to manage their own team collaboration. As Briggs and associates (2001) cautioned, individuals can still produce different team outcomes even with the identical scripts depending on individuals' facilitation abilities and team

building techniques. Much work remains to be done to validate how thinkLets can be combined to create predictable, repeatable, and sustainable success in collaborative team tasks in the virtual context. Consequently, researchers in the fields of GSS and CE need to work closely with organizational researchers to transfer the benefits of the thinkLet-based CE approach to organizations.

CONCLUDING REMARKS

This chapter started with a discussion on the two salient features of GVTs, virtualness marked by distance and technology and cultural diversity characterized by the global composition of GVTs. It then elaborated on GVT conflict mediated by technology and cultural diversity as these features have been found to intensify conflict among team members. The use of technology, in particular, is further complicated by distance and diversity inherent in GVTs. Initial structures and processes are thus more crucial in GVTs than in collocated teams because such structures help develop the common ground needed to bridge differences and facilitate team cohesion in virtual situations. Therefore, it is recommended that the thinkLet-based CE approach should be adopted as a potential solution to improve collaboration by creating sustainable patterns of team behavior. As GVTs provide organizations with increased competitive advantages and greater flexibility, adaptable and cost-efficient technology to enhance virtual collaboration will continue to be of significant importance to organizational practitioners and researchers alike. It is, however, important for organizations to recognize that GVTs are not simply a technologically mediated formation of teams. Rather, they are dynamic sociotechnological systems intricately comprised by individuals with diverse beliefs, values, and norms, which makes the management of GVTs especially challenging and important. We believe that GVTs can become one of the most critical tools for organizations to compete and cooperate in the global market when the right set of technology is implemented and diverse intelligence is well leveraged in the team.

REFERENCES

Alavi, M., & Leidner, D. E. (2001). Knowledge management and knowledge management systems: Conceptual foundations and research issues. *Management Information Systems Quarterly*, *25*(1), 107–136. doi:10.2307/3250961

Allen, T. J., Tushman, M. L., & Lee, D. M. (1979). Technology transfer as a function of position in the spectrum from research through development to technical services. *Academy of Management Journal*, *22*(4), 694–708. doi:10.2307/255809

Amason, A. C., & Mooney, A. C. (2000). The effects of past performance on top management team conflict in strategic decision making. *The International Journal of Conflict Management*, *10*, 340–359. doi:10.1108/eb022829

Armstrong, D., & Cole, P. (2002). Managing distances and differences in geographically distributed work groups. In Hinds, P., & Kiesler, S. (Eds.), *Distributed Work* (pp. 167–189). Cambridge, MA: MIT Press. doi:10.1037/10189-007

Benhamou, F., & Peltier, S. (2007). How should cultural diversity be measured? An application using the French publishing industry. *Journal of Cultural Economics*, *31*(2), 85–107. doi:10.1007/s10824-007-9037-8

Blackburn, R., Furst, S., & Rosen, B. (2003). Building a winning virtual team: KSAs, selection, training and evaluation. In Gibson, C., & Cohen, S. (Eds.), *Virtual Teams that Work: Creating Conditions for Virtual Team Effectiveness* (pp. 95–120). San Francisco, CA: Jossey-Bass.

Boudreau, M. C., Loch, K. D., Robey, D., & Straub, D. (1998). Going global: Using information technology to advance the competitiveness of the virtual transnational organization. *The Academy of Management Executive*, *12*(4), 120–128. doi:10.5465/AME.1998.1334008

Bragge, J., Merisalo-Rantanen, H., Nurmi, A., & Tanner, L. (2007). A repeatable e-collaboration process based on thinkLets for multi-organization strategy development. *Group Decision and Negotiation*, *16*(4), 363–379. doi:10.1007/s10726-006-9055-5

Briggs, R. O. (2006). The value frequency model: Towards a theoretical understanding of organizational change. In S. Seifert & C. Weinhardt (Eds.), *International Conference on Group Decision and Negotiation*. Karlsruhe, Germany: Karlsruhe University Press.

Briggs, R. O., de Vreede, G. J., & Nunamaker, J. F. (2003). Collaboration engineering with thinkLets to pursue sustained success with group support systems. *Journal of Management Information Systems*, *19*(4), 31–64.

Briggs, R. O., de Vreede, G. J., Nunamaker, J. F., & David, T. H. (2001). ThinkLets: Achieving predictable, repeatable patterns of group interaction with group support systems. In *Proceedings of the 34th International Conference on System Sciences*. Maui, HI: System Sciences.

Brown, S., & Eisenhardt, K. (1995). Product development: Past research, present findings, and future directions. *Academy of Management Review*, *20*(2), 343–378.

Carmel, E. (1999). *Global software teams: Collaborating across borders and time zones*. Upper Saddle River, NJ: Prentice Hall.

Cascio, W. F., & Shurygailo, S. (2003). E-leadership and virtual teams. *Organizational Dynamics*, *31*, 362–376. doi:10.1016/S0090-2616(02)00130-4

Cordery, J. L., & Soo, C. (2008). Overcoming impediments to virtual team effectiveness. *Human Factors and Ergonomics in Manufacturing, 18*(5), 487–500. doi:10.1002/hfm.20119

Cox, T., & Blake, S. (1991). Managing cultural diversity: Implications for organizational competitiveness. *The Academy of Management Executive, 5*(3), 45–56.

Cramton, C. D. (2001). The mutual knowledge problem and its consequences for dispersed collaboration. *Organization Science, 12*(3), 346–371. doi:10.1287/orsc.12.3.346.10098

Crowston, K., Sieber, S., & Wynn, E. (Eds.). (2007). Virtuality and virtualization. In *Proceedings of IFIP*. New York, NY: Springer.

Davison, R. M., & Briggs, R. O. (2000). GSS for presentation support: Supercharging the audience through simultaneous discussions during presentations. *Communications of the ACM, 43*(9), 91–97. doi:10.1145/348941.349006

De Dreu, C. K., & Weingart, L. R. (2003). Task versus relationship conflict and team effectiveness: A meta-analysis. *The Journal of Applied Psychology, 88*(4), 741–749. doi:10.1037/0021-9010.88.4.741

Dean, D. L., Deokar, A., & Bush, R. T. (2006). Making the collaboration engineering investment decision. In *Proceedings of the 39th International Conference on System Sciences*. Kauai, HI: System Sciences.

Deokar, A., Kolfscheoten, G. L., & de Vreede, G. J. (2008). Prescriptive workflow design for collaboration-intensive processes using the collaboration engineering approach. *Global Journal of Flexible Systems Management, 9*(4), 13–24.

DeSandtis, G., & Monge, P. (1999). Introduction to the special issue: Communication process for virtual organization. *Organization Science, 10*(6), 693–694. doi:10.1287/orsc.10.6.693

Duarte, D. L., & Snyder, N. T. (2006). *Mastering virtual teams: Strategies, tools, and techniques that succeed*. New York, NY: Wiley.

Eden, C. L., & Ackerman, F. (2001). SODA—The principles. In Rosenhead, J., & Mingers, J. (Eds.), *Rational Analysis for a Problematic World Revisited* (pp. 21–41). Chichester, UK: John Wiley & Sons.

Friedman, D. M., & Berger, D. L. (2004). Improving team structure and communication: A key to hospital efficiency. *Archives of Surgery, 139*(11), 1194–1198. doi:10.1001/archsurg.139.11.1194

Gibson, C. B., & Cohen, S. G. (2003). *Virtual teams that work: Creating conditions for virtual team effectiveness*. San Francisco, CA: Jossey-Bass.

Gibson, C. B., & Gibbs, J. L. (2006). Unpacking the concept of virtuality: The effects of geographic dispersion, electronic dependence, dynamic structure, and national diversity on team innovation. *Administrative Science Quarterly, 51*(3), 451–495.

Gibson, C. B., & Zellmer-Bruhn, M. E. (2001). Metaphors and meaning: An intercultural analysis of the concept of teamwork. *Administrative Science Quarterly, 46*(2), 274–303. doi:10.2307/2667088

Graetz, K. A., Boyle, E. B., Kimble, C. E., Thompson, P., & Garloch, J. L. (1998). Information sharing in face-to-face, teleconferencing, and electronic chat groups. *Small Group Research, 29*(6), 714–743. doi:10.1177/1046496498296003

Hall, E. T. (1987). *Hidden differences: Doing business with the Japanese*. Garden City, NY: Anchor Press/Doubleday.

Harder, R., Keeter, J. M., Woodcock, B. W., Ferguson, J. W., & Wills, F. W. (2005). Insights in implementing collaboration engineering. In *Proceedings of the 38th Hawaii International Conference on System Sciences*. Big Island, HI: System Sciences.

Harrison, D. A., Price, K. H., & Bell, M. P. (1998). Beyond relational demography: Time and the effects of surface- and deep-level diversity on work group cohesion. *Academy of Management Journal, 41*(1), 96–107. doi:10.2307/256901

Hertel, G., Geister, S., & Konradt, U. (2005). Managing virtual teams: A review of current empirical research. *Human Resource Management Review, 15*(1), 69–95. doi:10.1016/j.hrmr.2005.01.002

Hinds, P. J., & Bailey, D. E. (2003). Out of sight, out of sync: Understanding conflict in distributed teams. *Organization Science, 14*(6), 615–632. doi:10.1287/orsc.14.6.615.24872

Hofstede, G. (1991). *Cultures and organizations: Software of the mind.* London, UK: McGraw-Hill International.

Hollingshead, A. B. (1996). Information suppression and status persistence in group decision making: The effects of communication media. *Human Communication Research, 23*, 193–219. doi:10.1111/j.1468-2958.1996.tb00392.x

Hollingshead, A. B. (1996). The rank order effect in group decision making. *Organizational Behavior and Human Decision Processes, 68*, 181–193. doi:10.1006/obhd.1996.0098

Horwitz, S. K., & Horwitz, I. B. (2007). The effects of team diversity on team outcomes: A meta-analytic review of team demography. *Journal of Management, 33*(6), 987–1015. doi:10.1177/0149206307308587

Huang, W. W., Wei, K. K., Watson, R. T., & Tan, B. C. (2002). Supporting virtual team-building in GSS: An empirical investigation. *Decision Support Systems, 34*, 359–367. doi:10.1016/S0167-9236(02)00009-X

Hymowitz, C. (1999, April 6). Remote managers find ways to narrow the distance gap. *The Wall Street Journal*, p. B1.

Jackson, S. E., May, K. E., & Whitney, K. (1995). Understanding the dynamics of diversity in decision-making teams. In Guzzo, R. A., & Salas, E. (Eds.), *Team Effectiveness and Decision Making in Organizations* (pp. 204–261). San Francisco, CA: Jossey-Bass.

Janssens, M., & Brett, J. M. (1997). Meaningful participation in transnational teams. *European Journal of Work and Organizational Psychology, 6*(2), 153–168. doi:10.1080/135943297399141

Jarvenpaa, S. L., & Leidner, D. E. (1998). Communication and trust in global virtual teams. *Organization Science, 10*(6), 791–815. doi:10.1287/orsc.10.6.791

Jehn, K. A. (1995). A multimethod examination of the benefits and detriments of intragroup conflict. *Administrative Science Quarterly, 40*(2), 256–282. doi:10.2307/2393638

Jehn, K. A. (1997). A qualitative analysis of conflict types and dimensions in organizational groups. *Administrative Science Quarterly, 42*, 530–557. doi:10.2307/2393737

Jehn, K. A., & Bendersky, C. (2003). Intragroup conflict in organizations: A contingency perspective on the conflict-outcome relationship. *Research in Organizational Behavior, 25*, 189–244. doi:10.1016/S0191-3085(03)25005-X

Jehn, K. A., & Mannix, E. A. (2001). The dynamic nature of conflict: A longitudinal study of intragroup conflict and group performance. *Academy of Management Journal, 44*(2), 238–251. doi:10.2307/3069453

Kankanhalli, A., Tan, B. C. Y., & Wei, K. K. (2005). Contributing knowledge to electronic knowledge repositories: An empirical investigation. *Management Information Systems Quarterly, 29*(1), 113–143.

Kiesler, S., & Cummings, J. N. (2002). What do we know about proximity and distance in work groups? A legacy of research. In Hinds, P., & Kiesler, S. (Eds.), *Distributed Work* (pp. 83–112). Cambridge, MA: MIT Press.

King, N., & Majchrzak, A. (2003). Technology alignment and adaptation for virtual teams involved in unstructured knowledge work. In Gibson, C., & Cohen, S. (Eds.), *Virtual Teams that Work: Creating Conditions for Virtual Team Effectiveness* (pp. 265–291). San Francisco, CA: Jossey-Bass.

Kirkman, B., & Mathieu, J. E. (2005). The dimensions and antecedents of team virtuality. *Journal of Management, 31,* 700–718. doi:10.1177/0149206305279113

Kirkman, B. L., & Shapiro, D. L. (2001). The impact of cultural values on job satisfaction and organizational commitment in self-managing work teams: The mediating role of employee resistance. *Academy of Management Journal, 44,* 557–568. doi:10.2307/3069370

Klein, K. J., & Harrison, D. A. (2007). On the diversity of diversity: Tidy logic, messier realities. *The Academy of Management Perspectives, 21*(4), 26–33. doi:10.5465/AMP.2007.27895337

Knoll, S. W., Hörning, M., & Horton, G. (2009). Applying a thinkLet- and thinXel-based group process modeling language: A prototype of a universal group support system. In *Proceedings of the 42nd International Conference on System Sciences*. Waikoloa, HI: System Sciences.

Kolfschoten, G. L., Appelman, J. H., Briggs, R. O., & de Vreede, G. J. (2004). Recurring patterns of facilitation interventions in GSS sessions. In *Proceedings of the 37th International Conference on System Sciences*. Big Island, HI: System Sciences.

Kolfschoten, G. L., & de Vreede, G. J. (2009). A design approach for collaboration processes: A multimethod design science study in collaboration engineering. *Journal of Management Information Systems, 26*(1), 225–256. doi:10.2753/MIS0742-1222260109

Kolfschoten, G. L., & Santanen, E. L. (2007). Reconceptualizing generate thinkLets: The role of the modifier. In *Proceedings of the 40th International Conference on System Sciences*. Waikoloa, HI: System Sciences.

Lurey, J. S., & Raisinghani, M. S. (2001). An empirical study of best practices in virtual teams. *Information & Management, 38,* 523–544. doi:10.1016/S0378-7206(01)00074-X

Mannix, E. A., Griffith, T. L., & Neale, M. A. (2002). The phenomenology of conflict in distributed work teams. In Hinds, P., & Kiesler, S. (Eds.), *Distributed Work* (pp. 213–233). Cambrdige, MA: MIT Press.

Martins, L. L., Gilson, L. L., & Maynard, M. T. (2004). Virtual teams: What do we know and where do we go from here? *Journal of Management, 30*(6), 805–835. doi:10.1016/j.jm.2004.05.002

McKnight, D. H., Choudhury, V., & Kacmar, C. (2002). Developing and validating trust measures for e-commerce: An integrative typology. *Information Systems Research, 13*(3), 334–359. doi:10.1287/isre.13.3.334.81

Milliken, F. J., & Martins, L. L. (1996). Searching for common threads: Understanding the multiple effects of diversity in organizational groups. *Academy of Management Review, 21*(2), 402–433.

Mortensen, M., & Hinds, P. (2001). Conflict and shared identity in geographically distributed teams. *The International Journal of Conflict Management, 12*(3), 212–238. doi:10.1108/eb022856

Nabukenya, J., Van Bommel, P., Proper, H. A., & de Vreede, G. J. (2011). An evaluation instrument for collaborative processes: Application to organizational policy-making. *Group Decision and Negotiation, 20*(4), 465–488. doi:10.1007/s10726-009-9177-7

Neale, M. A., & Griffith, T. L. (2001). Information processing in traditional, hybrid, and virtual teams: From nascent knowledge to transactive memory. In Staw, B., & Sutton, R. (Eds.), *Research in Organizational Behavior* (pp. 379–421). Greenwich, CT: JAI Press.

Nunamaker, J. F. (1997). Future research in group support systems: Needs, some questions and possible directions. *International Journal of Computer Studies, 47,* 357–385. doi:10.1006/ijhc.1997.0142

O'Leary, M., & Cummings, J. N. (2007). The spatial, temporal, and configurational characteristics of geographic dispersion in work teams. *Management Information Systems Quarterly, 31*(3), 433–452.

Oetzel, J. G., & Ting-Toomey, S. (2003). Face concerns in interpersonal conflict: A cross-cultural empirical test of the face negotiation theory. *Communication Research, 6*(3), 599–624. doi:10.1177/0093650203257841

Payne, R. (1990). The effectiveness of research teams: A review. In West, M. A., & Farr, J. L. (Eds.), *Innovation and Creativity at Work* (pp. 101–122). Chichester, UK: Wiley.

Pelled, L. H. (1996). Demographic diversity, conflict, and work group outcomes: An intervening process theory. *Organization Science, 7,* 615–631. doi:10.1287/orsc.7.6.615

Peters, T., & Waterman, R. H. (1988). *In search of excellence.* New York, NY: Warner.

Rao, S. V., Luk, W., & Warren, J. (2005). Issues in building multiuser interfaces. *International Journal of Human-Computer Interaction, 19*(1), 55–74. doi:10.1207/s15327590ijhc1901_5

Savicki, V., Lingenfelter, D., & Kelley, M. (1996). Gender language style and group composition in internet discussion groups. *Journal of Computer Mediated Communication, 2*(3). Retrieved May 14, 2011, from http://jcmc.indiana.edu/vol2/issue3/.

Siegel, J., Dubrovsky, V., Kiesler, S., & McGuire, T. W. (1986). Group processes in computer-mediated communication. *Organizational Behavior and Human Decision Processes, 37*(2), 157–187. doi:10.1016/0749-5978(86)90050-6

Sproull, L., & Kiesler, S. (1986). Reducing social context cues: Electronic mail in organizational communication. *Management Science, 32,* 1492–1512. doi:10.1287/mnsc.32.11.1492

Staples, D. S., & Zhao, L. (2006). The effects of cultural diversity in virtual teams versus face-face teams. *Group Decision and Negotiation, 15*(4), 389–406. doi:10.1007/s10726-006-9042-x

Tan, B. C., Wei, K., Watson, R. T., Clapper, D. L., & McLean, E. R. (1998). Computer-mediated communication and majority influence: Assessing the impact in an individualistic and a collectivistic culture. *Management Science, 44*(9), 1263–1278. doi:10.1287/mnsc.44.9.1263

Te'eni, D. (2001). Review: A cognitive-affective model of organizational communication for designing IT. *Management Information Systems Quarterly, 25*(2), 251–312. doi:10.2307/3250931

Ting-Toomey, S. (1992). Intercultural communication. In Lederman, L. (Ed.), *Communication Pedagogy: Approaches to Teaching Undergraduate Courses in Communication* (pp. 157–171). Norwood, NJ: Ablex.

Townsend, A. M., DeMarie, S. M., & Hendrickson, A. R. (1998). Virtual teams: Technology and the workplace of the future. *The Academy of Management Executive*, *12*(3), 17–29. doi:10.5465/AME.1998.1109047

Workman, M. (2007). A proximal-virtual team continuum: A study of performance. *Journal of the American Society for Information Science and Technology*, *58*(6), 794–801. doi:10.1002/asi.20545

Zaccaro, S. J., & Bader, P. (2003). E-leadership and the challenges of leading e-teams: Minimizing the bad and maximizing the good. *Organizational Dynamics*, *31*(4), 377–387. doi:10.1016/S0090-2616(02)00129-8

Zhao, J. L., Nunamaker, J. F., & Briggs, R. O. (2002). Intelligent workflow techniques for distributed group facilitation. In *Proceedings of the 35th International Conference on System Sciences*. Big Island, HI: System Sciences.

KEY TERMS AND DEFINITIONS

Collaboration Engineering: Research-based approach to designing, deploying, and sustaining repeatable collaborative processes which can be executed by practitioners in an organization.

Global Virtual Teams: Globally dispersed, culturally diverse, and technologically connected individuals who work interdependently with a limited life span of membership in order to accomplish a common goal.

Group Support Systems: Multi-feature software tools used by a team facilitator and members to communicate, exchange information, and manage data to accomplish team tasks.

Team Conflict: A dynamic process occurring between interdependent parties as they experience disagreements and interference with the attainment of their goals.

Team Diversity: Different attributes and characteristics of individual members in a team.

ThinkLets: Named, packaged facilitation interventions that create predictable, repeatable patterns of collaboration among people toward a goal.

Virtualness: Feature of virtual teaming that describes a level of virtual work within the range of a continuum on three dimensions: 1) physical distance; 2) technology support; and 3) time that team members are apart on the task.

ENDNOTES

[1] For more information on the thinkLets used in Nabukenya et al.'s study, please refer to Nabukenya et al. (2011).

[2] For more information on the thinkLets used in the Oodi MCT case, please refer to Bragge et al. (2007).

APPENDIX A: THINKLET EXAMPLES

Organize: RichRelations (Contributed by Bill Becker, U.S. Dept. of Defense)

Choose this thinkLet...

   . . . to create a set of categories for organizing brainstorming comments.

   . . . after any divergence thinkLet and before a thinkLet where ideas will be sorted into categories

Overview

Participants browse their brainstorming comments and find two items that are related in some way. They articulate the relationship between the two items, and if the group agrees, that relationship becomes the name of a category.

Setup

Post the brainstorming comments as list items in one bucket (category) of the Categorizer tool.
Display the bucket (category) column
Prepare to add a new bucket (category).

Script

1.   Say this:
   a.   Please read through the comments on your screen. If you find two more comments that are related in some way, tell me how they are related.
   b.   Add a new bucket (category) with the relationship as a label.
   c.   Continue the process until participants can find no more relationships.

Build Consensus: MoodRing

Choose this thinkLet...

   . . . to track patterns of consensus on a single issue in real time.

   . . . to know when it is time to stop the talking and make a decision.

Overview

Participants register their opinion on a single topic, then begin an oral discussion. As they talk, if they hear something that changes their opinion either direction, they change their vote. Results update in real time.

Setup

1. Post a statement about an issue in the Opinion Meter tool.
2. Open the Opinion Meter on the participants' screens.
3. Make sure the group understands the issue.

Script

1. Say this:
   a. Please register your opinion in the Opinion Meter tool.
   b. Now let's talk about the issue. If you hear anything that changes your mind in either direction, shift your vote accordingly. We will keep talking until we've reached some sort of consensus on this issue.

Chapter 29
Leveraging Diversity in a Virtual Context:
Global Diversity and Cyber–Aggression

Robyn A. Berkley
Southern Illinois University – Edwardsville, USA

Roxanne Beard
Ohio Dominican University, USA

David M. Kaplan
Saint Louis University, USA

ABSTRACT

In this chapter, the authors present a model for understanding the context and determinants of aggression within an on-line environment, known as cyber-aggression. They propose that the heterogeneity of global virtual teams along with other key individual characteristics such as Social Dominance Orientation, Identification Threat, and past experience with aggression/harassment will lead to greater likelihood of cyber-aggression occurring or being perceived by group members. Additionally, the use of lean communication media, as well as the distance between team members and the social and professional isolation that goes along with global virtual team work also contributes to greater likelihood of cyber-aggression occurring. Lastly, without any way to build meaningful trust in a virtual setting and a lack of cross-cultural competence, members of global virtual teams are more likely to engage in behaviors that do not demonstrate cultural sensitivity or cohesion on the team, resulting in poor communication which can lead to more aggressive behaviors. The authors conclude their chapter with recommendations on how to best combat these pitfalls of working in a virtual environment.

DOI: 10.4018/978-1-4666-1812-1.ch029

INTRODUCTION

When members of a global team experience conflict, they often have difficulty communicating with one another (Korac-Kakabadse, Kouzmin, Korac-Kakabadse, & Savery, 2001; Von Glinow, Shapiro, & Brett, 2004), particularly if they are connected virtually. These global teams have to rely on emergent team culture because they do not have a pre-existing identity, as few commonalities exist among team members (Matveev & Nelson, 2004) due to their distance and differing cultures. This exacerbates the obvious barrier of language. When people do not communicate face-to-face, it is often not possible to detect tone or body language, which hinders the ability to correctly interpret what another person is saying. Further, individuals tend to use and interpret language culturally, so even what appears to be a straightforward comment can result in misunderstandings. Depending on the scope and pervasiveness of these misunderstandings, conflict can emerge.

These problems are exacerbated when the source of conflict has an emotional component (Von Glinow, et al., 2004). In situations such as these, when emotions are running high, the messages that team members need to communicate effectively with one another should be information rich. Unfortunately, Global Virtual Team (GVT) members are often limited to lean communication media (Daft & Lengel, 1984), which decreases the likelihood that messages will be properly conveyed between team members. As a result, conflict, both task related and emotional/relationship related seems inevitable. Understanding the sources of such conflict is essential to limiting it and thereby promoting global diversity and organizational effectiveness.

GVTs are by definition separated by vast distances and are limited in their ability to communicate face-to-face. While new forms of communication enable individuals to send information rich messages across large distances (e.g., video-conferencing); these communication modes assume that individuals are synchronous in time. GVT members are often asynchronous, separated not only by distance, but also by time (Lurey & Raisinghani, 2001). Additionally, Von Glinow et al. (2004) note that virtual actions, such as not responding promptly to an e-mail, will be interpreted differently by team members from different national cultures. Such differences can lead to friction and conflict, or if a conflict already exists, can escalate it. Similarly, one person may consider a particular statement innocent or even a complement, but another person may interpret the same statement as harassing (Berkley & Kaplan, 2009).

The purpose of this chapter is to present a model for understanding how structural factors (e.g., media richness) and interpersonal factors (e.g., trust) moderate the relationship between team heterogeneity (focusing on cross-cultural differences) and aggression, while also acknowledging the role of individual characteristics (e.g., past experience). Further, we will take the model a step beyond understanding the heterogeneity-aggression relationship by proposing how heterogeneous global teams can be rife for manifesting cyber-aggression, ranging from simple name-calling to threats of harm. Finally, the chapter will address how organizations can promote harmony and effectiveness. Implications for training and team member selection are also proposed.

TEAM HETEROGENEITY AND AGGRESSION

While team heterogeneity can be measured along multiple dimensions, given the emphasis here on global diversity, the proposed model and associated discussion will focus on cross-cultural differences. Specifically, the model uses the typology developed by Hofstede (2001) to define these differences. Included among these dimensions are individualism-collectivism, uncertainty avoidance, power distance, masculinity-femininity, and time orientation. Individualism-collectivism refers to the extent that members of a society focus on personal (individual) versus group (collectivist) goals and outcomes. As for uncertainty avoidance, those societies that are considered strong on this dimension disdain ambiguity and risk while those from weak uncertainty avoidance cultures have greater comfort and even preferences for these. Finally, power distance represents the extent to which members of the culture expect and accept that power will not be distributed equally within a society or organization. These dimensions have important implications for how someone may interact as a member of a GVT (Korac-Kakabadse, et al., 2001; Li, 2009; Matveev & Nelson, 2004).

Individualistic cultures tend to be low-context cultures while collectivist cultures tend to be high-context (Korac-Kakabadse, et al., 2001). Low-context cultures tend to be explicit in their messages (Matveev & Nelson, 2004); the words that are used are normally all that is needed to understand the message. High-context cultures, on the other hand, tend to convey messages through the individual's internalized values, beliefs, and norms (Matveev & Nelson, 2004). Without an awareness of one another's contextual situations, it can be extremely difficult to understand the actions or reactions of GVT members (Korac-Kakabadse, et al., 2001) and conflict can arise.

By definition, not understanding the context of a situation creates a degree of ambiguity. Therefore, at least initially, uncertainty represents an inherent characteristic of GVTs. This can be problematic for those from strong uncertainty avoidance cultures as they have a discomfort with such ambiguity. Not surprisingly, organizations based in countries categorized as strong in uncertainty avoidance have smaller percentages of employees working virtually from home (Peters & den Dulk, 2003). Interestingly though, members of these cultures can exacerbate the problem through a reluctance to share information as this, at times, can be considered risky (Li, 2009).

The conflict that emerges within GVTs can be split into two categories: task and emotional/relationship (Jehn, 1995; Pelled, Eisenhardt, & Xin, 1999). Task conflict arises when group members disagree about "task issues, including goals, key decision areas, procedures, and the appropriate choice for action" (Pelled, et al., 1999). Functional background differences (i.e., tenure, educational background) among group members often results in task conflict (Pelled, et al., 1999).

GVTs can experience a higher level of task conflict because of the differences in nationality among group members. As Pelled et al. (1999) state, divergent perspectives of goals and tasks can lead to higher levels of task conflict. For example, Oetzel (1998) discusses how people from different cultures will pursue different types of goals. Oetzel (1998) found that people in individualistic cultures often pursue personal goals over collective goals when the two types of goals come into conflict. By contrast, someone from a collectivist culture would be more likely to pursue the collective goal. Similarly, Cox, Lobel, and McLeod (1991) found that groups from collectivist cultures display more cooperative behaviors than those from individualistic cultures.

Frustration resulting from task conflict, due to the perception of interference with one's goal-directed behavior, can lead to aggression (Baron & Neuman, 1998). Gibson and Zellmer-Bruhn (2001) demonstrated that definitions of teamwork differ around the globe. They explored what types of metaphors for teams, (i.e., sports, family, military, or community) were used by individuals in different nations. They showed that teams within nations with greater power distance were less likely to use metaphors containing clear role content. Teams within individualistic nations were less likely to use team metaphors that were broad in scope and considered the individual to be tied to a long-lasting team. As a result, individuals from individualistic nations may be more task focused/instrumental and less focused on relationship building than a person from a collectivist culture. The discrepant views on the longevity of group membership could result in interpersonal clashes and emotional/relationship conflict. Additionally, differences in perceptions of how team members should interact and define roles and goals could possibly lead to both task-related and emotional-related conflict.

Pelled et al. (1999) found that differences on impermeable personal attributes (such as race and gender) can also result in emotional conflict for members of face-to-face teams. They explain that this is because individuals tend to categorize others based on demographic attributes. In order to maintain self-esteem, individuals will develop positive opinions of their own groups and negative opinions of others. As a result, resentment and conflict can occur when individuals realize that they themselves have also been categorized and stereotyped by others. They found that an increased diversity among group members on race and tenure led to a higher level of experienced emotional conflict. Increased diversity, if it results in negative effect, may result in decreased levels of interpersonal attraction and an increased potential for aggression (Baron & Neuman, 1998).

According to Kickul, Lester, and Finkl (2002) globalization of the workforce has created a new psychological contract. Employers now have the ability to access employment talent from many nations. This opportunity often makes the regional labor force expendable, leaving employees with an unprecedented sense of uncertainty in terms of employer loyalty, in-role job performance, and job security. This is exacerbated by stories where domestic workers have been asked to train their off-shored replacements. This reduction in the psychological trust between employer and employee leads to a short-term orientation in the employment relationship and a less than optimal set of organizational citizenship behaviors toward other employees. These findings align with that of Beck (1992) who wrote that due to globalization any course of action is likely to have "side-effects" on others, therefore workers engage in sub-politics to create meaning, negotiate change, and leverage new technologies in the process of individualization as their personal interests are now at the center of all work efforts.

Although the benefits of a GVT are tangible—broader employee skill sets and multiple perspectives resulting in higher quality problem solving—the increased workplace diversity creates more contact between individuals and groups with differing cultural backgrounds. Similar to diversity from other sources, the benefits of GVTs are not a given, as they require proper management and support which explains why prior research has found conflicting results (Kaplan, Wiley, & Maertz, 2011). For GVTs, challenges exist due to differences in perceptions, stereotyping, ethnocentrism, differences in motives, cognitive rigidity, bias, ineffective communication patterns, and frustration, all leading to decreased team cohesion and aggression. Aggression in the workplace occurs when employees, not connected to the workplace or teammates, rationalize their response to a situation or event. A study by Baron and Neuman (1996) found increased workplace diversity was significantly related to witnessed and experienced aggression and that verbal and passive forms of aggression are more common in the workplace than physical and direct acts. Lurey and Raisinghani (2001) published work demonstrating virtual team performance and member satisfaction was affected most by team identification and that the virtual team's social network is responsible for its members. Successful virtual teams "care for its members and provide the right opportunities for personal development and growth" (p. 526).

The global workplace, especially those with geographically dispersed locations, offer limited opportunities to develop loyalty, connectedness, and personal commitment. A lack of cultural understanding, decreased commitment to the organization and fellow employees, and a sense of social and professional isolation increase the risk employees will act individualistically. For example, Gunawardena, Nolla, Wilson, Lopez-Islas, Ramirez-Angel, and Megchun-Alpizar (2001) studied group processes across several different nationalities and found significant differences in perceptions in the Norming and Performing stages of group development. The study found group processes were influenced by the cultural dimensions of power distance, language, gender roles, collectivistic versus individualistic tendencies, social presence, time frame, conflict, and technical skills. Additionally, Earley (1993) found the tendency toward social loafing behavior to more likely in individualistic cultures.

Geographic boundaries can significantly impact the effectiveness of GVTs. For example, when teams are distributed geographically, members are very aware of location-specific sub-groups. This leads to an ethnocentric bias for one's own group, which weakens team cohesion, and reduces the likelihood of cooperation and team success (Cramton & Hinds, 2005; Lau & Murnighan, 1998). It is important to note that geographic boundaries do not necessarily refer to political/national boundaries but simply any spatial separation that regularly impedes face-to-face interactions that are the norm in traditional office settings. Shapiro, Furst, Spreitzer, and Von Glinow (2002) found that the inability to have face-to-face time locally caused a reliance on electronic communication. This reliance was linked to loss of self-identification, withholding effort, and negative influences on team performance. Specifically, the researchers found that time zone, language, and differences in understanding of what constitutes appropriate and desirable behavior led to differing interpretations of member actions and reduced socio-emotional understanding.

In order to be successful, virtual GVTs must manage a broad scope of influences. In addition to the social and cultural factors described earlier, teams must negotiate both technological and Internet influences. According to Beck (1992) computer information systems are changing the hierarchical structures of organizations, creating interdependence across the organization, changing communication processes and employee participation, and are the catalyst for the development of new organizational structures, moving accountability down the hierarchy. Beck also notes that computer information systems cause the line between management and employees to be blurred, thus influencing power distribution and authority. With this distribution of power comes the need for lower level employees to self-manage because the more central one is to the flow of information the more power one has. This can also create discomfort among those from high power distance cultures who expect power differentials and hence are less comfortable with more egalitarian systems. Layered onto the technological aspect, virtual teams must overcome the Internet culture with its own language, ambiguities, and netiquette. Normalized communication processes—metaphors, values, expectations for clear and concise language, time management, and preferred type of technology—must all be negotiated and optimized for a GVT to be successful. Members should be knowledgeable of differences in online and offline language and meaning. Awareness of cultural meaning requires members be competent in several levels and types of communication.

For GVTs that communicate electronically, there are two culture gaps that influence workplace interactions: the culture gap between individuals and the culture gap between individuals and the dominant cyber-culture. When dealing with teams comprised of members from various cultures, there is often an ethnocentric expectation about how the technology will be set up and utilized. For example, team members from the United States typically assume English will be the language of choice for all electronic communications. This expectation may complicate communication processes, as electronic translation media may not be able to convey nuanced messaging and concepts of other languages. This means team members must intuit meaning in the absence of visual, verbal and aural cues. This, of course, can lead to miscommunication of the message and marginalization of the sender. Even if the sender attempts to mitigate potential communication problems, users are challenged to determine which tools are most appropriate based on content of message and audience (Campion, et al., 1996; Papper & Medsker, 1996).

Although teams may select from either synchronous or asynchronous forms of technology, Campion et al. (1996), found that, in general, virtual teams rely on individual communication methods—email and phone—rather than team-based communication, and that team-based communication technologies were used infrequently despite the opportunity to mitigate the lack of face-to-face interaction. When selecting a communication medium, the most common synchronous technologies available to employees include electronic display, desktop conferencing, video-conferencing, audio-conferencing, electronic meeting systems, and instant messaging. If real-time interaction is not important, or practical, asynchronous technologies may be utilized. These include email, bulletin boards, PDAs, team or VPN websites, workflow applications, and group calendars. Despite the expectation that synchronous technologies would enhance workplace communication, trust, and interdependence, Campion et al. (1996) found some teams reported the use of video conferencing failed to have the same impact as face-to-face interaction. Ferris (1996) found that rather than mitigating the communication challenges experienced by gender bias, computer mediated communications often exacerbated the problems. And, despite efforts to use video-conferencing to help virtual teams develop trust, the "virtual blindness" limitations of the technology actually aggravated trust issues (Duarte & Snyder, 2006).

INDIVIDUAL CHARACTERISTICS AND AGGRESSION

Although Team Heterogeneity is the main focus of this chapter and the model presented, we acknowledge there are other important individual characteristics that may have an effect on aggressive actions within a GVT. We identify three individual characteristics: Past Experience with Aggression, Social Dominance Orientation, and Identification Threat. In each case, we explain how the characteristic can result in aggressive actions but given the focus of this volume reserve our discussion of moderating effects to Team Heterogeneity.

Past Experience

Individuals who have experienced aggression interpret potentially aggressive messages differently from those who have not been the target of aggression. Similarly, Glomb and Liao (2003) found that aggression can escalate within a work group. The authors found that aggressive behaviors exhibited by others within the work group significantly predict an individual's interpersonal aggressive behavior. Additionally, the authors noted that victims of aggressive behaviors tended to also engage in aggressive behaviors towards other group members. It would seem that similar to the idea that miscommunication begets miscommunication, aggressive behaviors lead to more aggression.

Social Dominance Orientation

Social Dominance Orientation (Pratto, Sidanius, Stallworth, & Malle, 1994) is a personality variable that measures the belief in individuals that some groups are superior relative to others and those individuals therefore approve of inequality/

social hierarchy within in-group relationships. Wilson and Liu (2003) found that gender group identification moderated the relationship between gender and Social Dominance Orientation. Male respondents tended to score similarly on the Social Dominance Orientation scale, regardless if they identified strongly or weakly with the male gender. Low-identifying females (females who had low levels of identification with the female gender), however, scored much higher on the Social Dominance Orientation scale than high-identifying females.

Aquino and Byron (2002) found that males reported being victims of aggression more frequently if they demonstrated high levels or low levels (as opposed to moderate levels) of dominating behaviors. For females, however, the report of being a victim of aggression was not a function of displayed dominating behaviors. The authors suggested that for males, demonstrating high levels of dominating behaviors may have violated social norms within the workgroup, or challenged others' social identities, while demonstrating low levels of dominating behaviors may have made the individual appear weak and easily exploited. The authors found that for females, there was not as much of a difference in the perception of being the victim of aggressive behaviors, regardless of the dominating behaviors exhibited.

Identification Threat

Maass, Cadinu, Guarnieri, and Grasselli (2003) conducted a study during which male participants were exposed to different types of threat (legitimacy threat, threat to group value, distinctiveness threat, prototypicality threat, or no threat) and were given the opportunity to sexually harass a female interaction partner by sending her pornographic material online. *Legitimacy threat* occurs when groups are recognized as distinct categories, but the legitimacy of status differences between groups is challenged (thereby challenging the social standing or privileges deriving from a particular

group membership). *Threat to group value* occurs when one encounters information suggesting that one's own group is valued less, performs less well, or is morally inferior to a relevant out-group. *Distinctiveness threat* occurs when someone encounters information that challenges the distinctiveness of the in-group compared with an out-group. *Prototypicality threat* occurs when one encounters information that challenges the individual's status as a good or as a prototypical group member. The authors found that legitimacy threat, prototypicality, and distinctiveness threats were factors in on-line harassment.

Aquino and Douglas (2003) defined identity threat as "any overt action by another party that challenges, calls into question, or diminishes a person's sense of competence, dignity, or self-worth" (196). Aquino and Douglas (2003) discuss that an individual who perceives an identity threat will react with aggressive behaviors which can be directed towards the perpetrator, but can also be displaced and directed towards any "convenient, available, or powerless target" (p. 196). The authors found that perceived identity threat was related to higher levels of antisocial behavior.

Simeon, Nicholson, and Wong (2001) found that people's views on gender roles and societal attitudes toward assertiveness and male dominance in business vary as a function of nationality. The authors discuss that across national cultures, individuals vary in what is considered typical tasks for men and women. In relation to the above research, if a woman is performing a job which male team members typically consider masculine, then that woman may pose a threat to the male members' identity.

CYBER-AGGRESSION

Aggression can be defined as an intentional effort to intimidate, emotionally harm, or exert power over another. It is a relationship-based phenomenon. Baron and Neuman (1998) posit there are three primary forms of workplace aggression, all of which can easily manifest within a cyber, or on-line, context. These include Verbal/Non-verbal aggression, Obstructionism and Violence. Verbal/Non-verbal aggression includes behaviors that are primarily verbal or symbolic in nature (e.g. dirty looks, belittling other's opinions, talking behind the target's back, giving someone the "silent" treatment). Obstructionism is behaviors that impede the target's ability to perform effectively his/her job (e.g. failure to return phone calls respond to memos, failure to transmit needed information, interfering with activities important to the target, showing up late for meetings). Behaviors included in this factor represent primarily passive forms of aggression. Violence includes behaviors such as physical attack, theft, or destruction of property, threats of physical violence, stealing or damaging company property needed by the target person. While employees who are not co-located might not be able to directly inflict violence on their team member in bodily form, they can threaten violence and/or hack into the victim's work files, destroy their work or perhaps spread a virus that could affect a team member's computer, and engage in sexual harassment.

Cross-cultural differences such as Power Distance or Collectivism with its in- versus out-group identities can result in marginalization of an individual or group. GVTs are subject to several unique aspects of aggression. Cyber-aggression, as it applies to GVTs, can represent both intentional and unintentional behavior. This is due to differences in cultural perceptions, values, beliefs, communication patterns, expected behaviors, geographic distance, and technological limitations. When a team member responds, or acts in a way that is discordant with the cultural expectations of another team member, the response may be perceived as aggressive in intent. Because GVTs often operate in different time zones, aggression may occur both on-line and off-line, synchronously or asynchronously, which differs significantly from teams that operate in the same geographic location and interact primarily through face-to-face, or real-time, interaction.

Few studies have been completed on workplace cyber-aggression. Fewer yet have been completed addressing cyber-aggression as it applies to a culturally diverse workforce. In a study with limited generalizabilty, Privitera and Campbell (2009) found that 11% of the respondents reported being cyberbullied. This number represents what the victims recognized as intentional, or overt, aggression. Baron and Neuman (1996) note passive forms of aggression occur when the actor attempts to harm the victim by withholding information or action. For example "withholding information from others, failing to notify them about important meetings, failing to deny false rumors about others, withholding needed support from target persons when they request" (p. 170). Shapiro et al. (2002) described other passive effort-withholding behaviors seen in multinational teams. These include social loafing, cognitive loafing, shirking, and free riding.

The negative consequences of workplace cyber-aggression are costly across all levels of the organization: individual, team, and organizational. At the individual level, the negative impact on a cyber-aggression victim's health and emotional well-being is well-documented (Hoel, Faragher, & Cooper, 2004; Kieseker & Marchant, 1999; Leymann & Gustafsson, 1996). Due to the stressors associated with victimization, employees often take extended, or more frequent sick leave (Thompson, 1997). This negative performance behavior jeopardizes opportunities for career advancement (Richards & Freeman, 2002). Although witnesses to cyber-aggression are usually unintended victims, they often experience negative mental health consequences (Bjorkqvist, Osterman, & Hjelt-Back, 1994; Hoel & Cooper, 2000; Kieseker & Marchant, 1999; Lewis & Orford, 2005). Both victims and witnesses may demonstrate a variety of negative work-related behaviors such as reduced employee commitment (Gandolfo, 1995; Richards & Freeman, 2002), low morale (Gandolfo, 1995; Richards & Freeman, 2002), and reduced job satisfaction (Richards & Freeman, 2002). Finally, both victims and witnesses may experience problems with workplace relationships and ineffective performance in teams (Lewis & Orford, 2005).

Cyber-aggression can have a significantly negative financial impact on the organization. For example, organizational effectiveness, profitability, and productivity (Gandolfo, 1995; Richards & Freeman, 2002) often fall off as a consequence of the increased rate of employee absenteeism (Kieseker & Marchant, 1999; Richards & Freeman, 2002). As described above, victims often suffer from poor job satisfaction and low morale (Gandolfo, 1995; Kieseker & Marchant, 1999; Richards & Freeman, 2002). These problems cause often lead to an increased rate of turnover. Human resources management costs associated with recruiting, retention, and training may increase. Finally, there may be long-term financial consequences linked to the organization's inability to successfully manage human resources due to a poor public image and reputation of being a challenging place to work (Kieseker & Marchant, 1999).

Employers across the globe have an obligation to maintain a safe workplace. Although national and international definitions of a "safe workplace" vary significantly, addressing the liability issues associated with cyber-aggression can be challenging. As previously described, cyber-aggression may take several forms—overt or covert—with the primary form being covert. The indirect, often behind-the-scenes, behaviors such as loafing, devaluing an individual or group, ignoring opinions, withholding necessary information, slow response, discounting an individual or group, and isolating individuals (Hoel & Cooper, 2000) make it difficult to identify cyber-aggression. This increases the liability risk associated with a hostile workplace. However, many nations have developed discrimination, harassment, and workplace aggression legislation to address the

problem. In some instances, specific legislation has been considered in an effort to address workplace aggression.

STRUCTURAL AND INTERPERSONAL MODERATING FACTORS

While the relationship between cultural heterogeneity and conflict and aggression is not in debate, understanding the moderating factors that may lead to a greater likelihood to engage in cyber-aggression is imperative. We classify these moderating factors into two categories: Structural and Interpersonal Factors. Structural factors are those that reflect the situation within which the team functions. These include: proximity of team members, media richness of the communication medium they use, and social/professional isolation depending on whether members are socially isolated not only from each other but from their local organization as well (e.g., an employee is a telecommuter). Interpersonal factors are those that reflect the characteristics of members of the group or are reflective of group dynamics. Trust and Cross-Cultural Competence are two of these factors included in the model that is presented in Figure 1.

STRUCTURAL FACTORS

Media Richness

Media richness theory (Daft & Lengel, 1984) suggests that communication channels differ in the extent to which they can convey content. When messages are equivocal, additional information does not increase understanding. In order to enact a solution to an equivocal problem, individuals must redefine or create the answer, rather than search for more information (Daft & Lengel, 1986). In this case, a richer communication medium is desired

Figure 1. Moderating factors

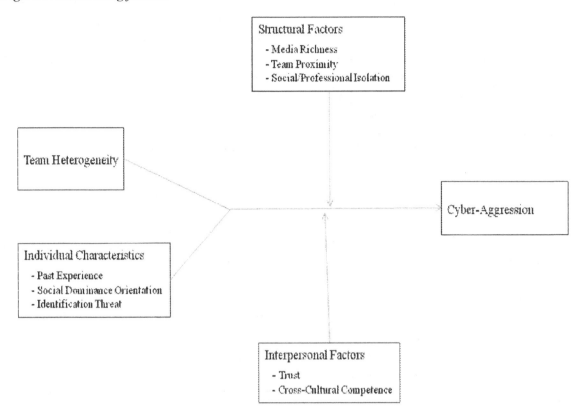

in order to convey multiple verbal and nonverbal cues, immediate feedback, and personal focus. Rich communication media include face-to-face conversations and video-conferencing. Rich media allow for better understanding of both verbal and non-verbal communication cues. When a message is unequivocal, this extra richness is not necessary in order to convey the message. In this case, lean communication media, such as letters or emails, can be used to effectively communicate the message.

Each communication medium has its costs and benefits. Rich media may be able to effectively communicate a message, but the costs rise when there are difficulties coordinating the sender and the recipient of the message. Lean media may not be able to communicate all messages effectively, but they can be used when individuals are distant from one another, or when multiple recipients are involved.

Because GVT members are generally limited to lean communication media, the messages that members try to convey may be more easily misinterpreted. Additionally, individuals are more likely to engage in "flaming" behaviors (where the individual communicates a negative and hostile attitude) when communicating online, rather than face-to-face. People also experience an increased willingness to deliver bad news when communicating through lean media (Sproull & Kiesler, 1986). Lean communication leads to a decrease in the satisfaction with the interaction and decreased effectiveness (Baltes, Dickson, Sherman, Bauer, & LaGanke, 2002). Lean communication media has also been associated with a decreased sense of team identity and an increase in the propensity to withhold effort (Shapiro, et al., 2002). Therefore, within GVTs, as they use more lean communication media than rich, cyber-aggression is more likely to occur over standard face-to-face forms of aggression.

While the leanness of communication is expected to have an overall impact, it has important implications for GVTs with cross-cultural differences. Those from collectivist cultures can become frustrated with a message's leanness. Such frustration can erupt into conflict and aggression. A similar outcome would be expected among those from strong uncertainty avoidance cultures because lean messages are inherently more ambiguous.

Team Proximity

Trevino, Webster, and Stein (2000) found that when message equivocality was high, individuals were more likely to choose rich media than lean media. However, when message recipients were physically removed from the sender, individuals were more likely to choose lean media. This enabled the sender to have a greater ease of use and fewer coordination problems than was possible with more rich media such as face-to-face meetings.

Due to their lack of proximity to one another, global virtual team members are often restricted to the use of lean media such as electronic mail. These communication media lack social context cues and are already extremely open to subjective interpretation (Weisband & Reinig, 1995). Additionally, when using media such as computer-mediated communications, people tend to "lose their fear of social sanctions and criticism due to limited reminders of conventional human interaction" (Weisband & Reinig, 1995, p. 45).

There are three ways in which team proximity is expected to moderate the relationship between Team Heterogeneity and Aggression. First, a consequence of not being co-located is a reliance on leaner communication channels that as previously discussed can increase frustration levels among individuals from collectivist that have a need for higher context communication. Second, another consequence of not being co-located and

leaner communication is increased ambiguity, which similarly is expected to make individuals from Strongly Uncertainty Avoidance cultures uncomfortable. Finally, ambiguity could also be a function of less clear lines of authority, which would be expected to have a negative impact on individuals from High Power Distance societies.

Social/Professional Isolation

Because the members of GVTs are not co-located, problems can develop because of individuals may be physically and psychologically isolated. The most extreme degree of physical isolation occurs when the member of a virtual team is also a telecommuter and as such does not meet face-to-face with anyone in the organization. However, someone could still be physically isolated if he or she was the only member of a team working at a particular worksite. Psychologically, anyone can feel isolated but for simplicity isolation will be discussed as a singular construct. As such, the discussion of this moderator is grounded in the research and example of the teleworker.

Researchers have also noted that teleworkers are prone to feeling both socially and professionally isolated (Golden, Veiga, & Dino, 2008; Mann, Varey, & Button, 2000; Mello, 2007; Tan-Solano & Kleiner, 2001). Individuals who are isolated may have a greater propensity for engaging in aggressive behaviors as well as being more susceptible to co-worker aggression. Isolation can represent an excuse or rationale for aggressive behavior or communication. There is some research that indicates that the colleagues of teleworkers experience negative work outcomes (Golden, 2007). Someone who is jealous or envious of colleagues who do not have to come into the office may retaliate through aggressive behavior. Conversely, someone who feels socially or professionally thwarted may engage in aggressive behavior or communication to retaliate or compensate for being marginalized within the organization.

As a further consequence of being professionally isolated, an individual is likely to have weaker developmental networks such as mentors (Golden, et al., 2008; Tan-Solano & Kleiner, 2001). Face-to-face contact with colleagues and/or interacting with mentors provide valuable social cues and role modeling for individuals to learn behavioral norms and how to interpret communication (Golden, et al., 2008; Mann, et al., 2000). The lack of this socialization increases the opportunity for misinterpreting behaviors or communications as aggressive. However, teleworkers are also more susceptible to genuinely aggressive behavior or communication. This is because they may lack another important benefit of mentoring relationships, an organizational champion to help avoid or deflect situations that foster aggression. Once targeted, the lack of a strong developmental network may prevent the teleworker from receiving vital psychosocial support.

There are two important implications of social/professional isolation that cause it to be included as a moderator in the proposed model. An association of being isolated would be membership in an out-group, whether real or perceived. Because out-group status is a more relevant factor in interpersonal relations for members of collectivist cultures, this would differentially impact those employees on a virtual team resulting in higher levels of aggression than those from individualistic cultures. Another implication of isolation is increased ambiguity. Depending on the strength of the culture's Uncertainty Avoidance, there would be increasing levels of aggression as the result of an interaction with social/professional isolation.

INTERPERSONAL FACTORS

Trust

According to Mancini (2010), trust is built upon frequent interaction, shared information, and the development of a joint organizational culture.

Global virtual teams are at a distinct disadvantage in developing trust because of the lack of proximity of members and the methods of communication upon which they depend. Layer in cultural differences between team members and it creates an even greater challenge to achieving trust. As Mancini (2010) argues, it is the shared experiences among team members that create the mortar necessary to build a wall of trust.

Bekmeier-Feuerhahn and Eichenlaub (2010) posit that communication style is a determinant of trust development. Through the maintenance of "facework commitments" (Gilbert, 2005, p. 407) trust is developed through personal communication among team members. The challenge that faces GVTs is that the methods for personal communication are very limited and can be removed from the rich communication media needed to communicate both verbal and non-verbal cues. Luhmann (2000) argues that trust is built upon familiarity. When groups are more homogeneous, trust develops much easier than it does with heterogeneous groups. Familiarity provides the group members with experiential knowledge of the integrity and competence of others. Past behaviors predict future behaviors, so if a person has behaved with integrity in the past, then the assumption is they will behave that same way in the future. This form of familiarity, predictability, and consistency will lead to greater trust. Bekmeier-Feuerhahn and Eichenlaub (2010) further argue that similarity, or the perception of similarity influences trust building.

In an interesting study by Bicchieri and Lev-On (2011) they found results that contrast, yet also reinforce those of Bekmeier-Feuerhahn and Eichenlaub (2010). Bicchieri and Lev-On discovered that communication medium does not have a big impact on trust building and maintenance, but pre-play communication and group size does impact trust. In their lab experiment, they found those groups that were given an opportunity to meet face to face before beginning work together developed more trust than those groups that either began working immediately, or were using lean communication media such as texting or on-line chats before they began working together. So it is not the method by which the group performs it tasks that is important to building trust, but the types of opportunities to build "familiarity" the team is allowed before they begin working together that appears to have the greater impact.

The importance of team trust with respect to team performance cannot be understated. Palanski, Kahai, and Yammarino (2011) found that team transparency, operationalized as openness, availability and disclosure of information, was positively related to team integrity and, in turn, team trust. They further found evidence that team trust had a positive relationship with team performance. Therefore, developing team trust is particularly salient for global virtual teams if we want them to perform at maximum effectiveness. Without trust, virtual teams would have lower performance and greater conflict, resulting in a greater likelihood of manifesting into cyber-aggression.

Trust is predicted to moderate Team Heterogeneity and Aggression through the degree of collectivism in a culture. Collectives exhibit a greater amount of trust among members WITHIN the group, however, may have little trust with out-group members. Individualistic cultures would also require a great deal of trust to function and may not be able to develop that trust when members are not co-located and sharing common experiences.

Cross Cultural Competence

In order to optimize the development of interpersonal relationships and trust in cross-cultural teams, members need to develop cross-cultural communication. Matveev and Nelson provide guidance in this area offering, "Cultural empathy is the most important psychological predisposi-

tion for effective cross cultural communication" (2004, p. 260). According to Neuliep, (2009), cross-cultural communication competence is comprised of four components:

a. Knowledge component – knowledge of the other's cultural values, beliefs, verbal and non-verbal communication styles, cultural dimensions, and ethnocentrism.

b. Affect component – the individual's willingness to communicate in an intercultural situation.

c. Psychomotor component – is the application of the knowledge and affect components as a means to become competent.

d. Situational component – the actual situation in which the intercultural communication takes place. Successfully navigating non-local communication requires management of information loads, developing trust over time, managing status differences, and the dynamic changes that can occur in the communication environment.

Unlike the other factors identified in the model, Cross-Cultural Competence is expected to moderate the overall level of team heterogeneity and aggression rather than specific dimensions (e.g., Power Distance). The more heterogeneous the team, the more important it will be for the individual members to be culturally competent. Individuals who are culturally competent will be able to promote the positive aspects of diversity will mitigating potential sources of conflict and aggression. Regardless of the cultural mix, someone who is culturally competent will be less likely to misinterpret messages and/or be understanding of differences that would cause frustration leading to conflict and aggression than individuals who have a low level of cross-cultural competence.

RECOMMENDATIONS AND CONCLUSION

Based on the model presented in this chapter, there are several things that an organization can do to decrease the potential occurrences and negative implications of aggressive communications and actions by individuals in GVTs. Among the several options that will be identified in this section, developing and rewarding Cross-Cultural Competences among employees will have some of the most far-reaching effects. When discussed as a moderator, Cross-Cultural Competence supports all forms of team heterogeneity. Therefore, developing and rewarding these competencies is useful regardless of the cross-cultural difference. Further, it is essential that employees be rewarded for being competent in addition to just being trained. Employees who are not rewarded for being competent may be less motivated to employ his or her competencies when needed and/or allow them to atrophy.

Another useful development tool is mentoring. Mentors serve many positive psychosocial functions that can help deter and minimize employee aggression. Not the least of these is the fact that mentors are role models and therefore if they model non-aggressive behavior then their protégés would also be expected to be less aggressive. Mentors can also serve as a sounding board for their protégés that provides an outlet for misunderstandings and frustrations that could otherwise erupt into aggression. Providing employees with mentors is also a direct intervention to prevent individuals from feeling socially/professionally isolated.

Related to mentoring is the need to create opportunities for GVT members to meet face-to-face. Face-to-face interactions should have an immediate impact on reducing a sense of social/professional isolation. Face-to-face interactions are also a valuable source of rich communication that can prevent misunderstandings from occurring. These interactions are also important for establishing trust and building relationships that will deter employee aggression even when communicating virtually.

It is also important that organizations do not take the easy way out and rely on standard-operating procedures. This applies to both communication channels and programmed decision-making. Although it is possible to reduce conflict through programmed decision-making, this is likely to undermine the creativity and potential that the GVT was created to realize. Similarly, it is all too easy for team members who are not co-located to communicate via email, especially when there are large time-differences. Unfortunately, an over reliance on lean communication methods such as email increases the potential for conflict. Even though it may be logistically difficult, GVT members should be encouraged to use richer and more synchronous communication methods as these will build relationships and trust while also reducing the potential for misunderstandings and aggression.

A final recommendation is to take even what you may consider low levels of conflict seriously. Even low levels of conflict can eventually erupt into aggression if it becomes pervasive enough. Similarly, as outlined in the model, past experience is an important personal characteristic that can result in aggression. Individuals who have been the target of even low-level conflict may be more likely to engage in future acts of aggression even if the situation is unrelated. If the normative reasons for wanting to reduce aggression are not sufficient, keep in mind that even low levels of aggression can create a hostile work environment that can result in legal liability. An organization is at increased liability for an employee's harassing behavior if it cannot show that they have taken steps to prevent it and/or created an environment that discourages such aggressive acts.

REFERENCES

Andolsek, D. M., & Stebe, J. (2004). Multinational perspectives on work values and commitment. *International Journal of Cross Cultural Management*, *4*(2), 181–209. doi:10.1177/1470595804044749

Aquino, K., & Byron, K. (2002). Dominating interpersonal behavior and perceived victimization in groups: Evidence for a curvilinear relationship. *Journal of Management*, *28*(1), 69–87. doi:10.1177/014920630202800105

Aquino, K., & Douglas, S. (2003). Identity threat and antisocial behavior in organizations: The moderating effects of individual differences, aggressive modeling, and hierarchical status. *Organizational Behavior and Human Decision Processes*, *90*, 195–208. doi:10.1016/S0749-5978(02)00517-4

Baltes, B. B., Dickson, M. W., Sherman, M. P., Bauer, C. C., & LaGanke, J. S. (2002). Computer-mediated communication and group decision making: A meta-analysis. *Organizational Behavior and Human Decision Processes*, *87*(1), 156–179. doi:10.1006/obhd.2001.2961

Baron, R. A., & Neuman, J. H. (1996). Workplace violence and workplace aggression: Evidence on their relative frequency and potential causes. *Aggressive Behavior*, *22*, 161–173. doi:10.1002/(SICI)1098-2337(1996)22:3<161::AID-AB1>3.0.CO;2-Q

Baron, R. A., & Neuman, J. H. (1998). Workplace aggression – The iceberg beneath the tip of workplace violence: Evidence on its forms, frequency, and targets. *Public Administration Quarterly*, *21*(4), 446–464.

Beck, U. (1992). *Risk society: Towards a new modernity*. Thousand Oaks, CA: Sage.

Bekmeier-Feuerhahn, S., & Eichenlaub, A. (2010). What makes for trust relationships in on-line communication. *Journal of Communication Management*, *14*(4), 337–355. doi:10.1108/13632541011090446

Berkley, R. A., & Kaplan, D. M. (2009). Assessing liability for sexual harassment: Reactions of potential jurors to email versus face-to-face incidents. *Employee Responsibilities and Rights Journal*, *21*, 195–211. doi:10.1007/s10672-009-9110-x

Bicchieri, C., & Lev-On, A. (2011). Studying the ethical implications of e-trust in the lab. *Ethics and Information Technology*, *13*, 5–15. doi:10.1007/s10676-010-9258-y

Bjorkqvist, K., Osterman, K., & Hjelt-Back, M. (1994). Aggression among university employees. *Aggressive Behavior*, *20*, 173–184. doi:10.1002/1098-2337(1994)20:3<173::AID-AB2480200304>3.0.CO;2-D

Campion, M. A., Papper, E. M., & Medsker, G. J. (1996). Relations between work team characteristics and effectiveness: A replication and extension. *The Personnel Journal*, *49*(2), 429–452.

Cox, T. H., Lobel, S. A., & McLeod, P. L. (1991). Effects of ethnic group cultural differences on cooperative and competitive behavior on a group task. *Academy of Management Journal*, *34*(4), 827–847. doi:10.2307/256391

Cramton, C. D., & Hinds, P. J. (2005). Subgroup dynamics in internationally distributed teams: Ethnocentricism or cross-national learning. In Staw, B. M., & Kramer, R. (Eds.), *Research in Organizational Behavior* (*Vol. 26*, pp. 231–263). San Diego, CA: Elsevier.

Daft, R. L., & Lengel, R. H. (1984). Information richness: A new approach to managerial behavior and organizational design. *Research in Organizational Behavior*, *6*, 191–233.

Duarte, D., & Snyder, N. T. (2006). *Mastering virtual teams: Strategies, tools, and techniques that succeed*. San Francisco, CA: Jossey-Bass.

Earley, P. C. (1993). East meets west meets mideast: Further explorations of collectivistic and individualistic work groups. *Academy of Management Journal, 36*, 319–348. doi:10.2307/256525

Ferris, S. P. (1996). Women on-line: Cultural and relational aspects of women's communication in on-line discussion groups. *Interpersonal Computing and Technology: An Electronic Journal for the 21st Century, 4*(3-4), 29-40. Retrieved from http://www.helsinki.fi/science/optek/1996/n3/ferris.txt.

Flaherty, S., & Moss, S. A. (2007). The impact of personality and team context on the relationship between workplace injustice and counterproductive work behavior. *Journal of Applied Social Psychology, 37*(11), 2549–2575. doi:10.1111/j.1559-1816.2007.00270.x

Gandolfo, R. (1995). MMPI-2 profiles of worker's compensation claimants who present with complaints of harassment. *Journal of Clinical Psychology, 51*, 711–715. doi:10.1002/1097-4679(199509)51:5<711::AID-JCLP2270510517>3.0.CO;2-R

Gibson, C. B., & Zellmer-Bruhn, M. E. (2001). Metaphors and meaning: An intercultural analysis of the concept of teamwork. *Administrative Science Quarterly, 46*, 274–303. doi:10.2307/2667088

Gilbert, D. U. (2005). Kontextsteuerung und systemvertrauen in strategischen unternehmensnetzwerken. *Die Unternehmung, 59*(5), 407–422.

Glomb, T. M., & Liao, H. (2003). Interpersonal aggression in work groups: Social influence, reciprocal, and individual effects. *Academy of Management Journal, 46*(4), 486–496. doi:10.2307/30040640

Golden, T. (2007). Co-workers who telework and the impact on those in the office: Understanding the implications of virtual work for co-worker satisfaction and turnover intentions. *Human Relations, 60*(11), 1641–1667. doi:10.1177/0018726707084303

Golden, T. D., Veiga, J. F., & Dino, R. N. (2008). The impact of professional isolation on teleworker job performance and turnover intentions: Does time spent teleworking, interacting face-to-face, or having access to communication-enhancing technology matter? *The Journal of Applied Psychology, 93*(6), 1412–1421. doi:10.1037/a0012722

Gunawardena, C. N., Nolla, A. C., Wilson, P. L., Lopez-Islas, J. R., Ramirez-Angel, N., & Megchun-Alpizar, R. M. (2001). A cross-cultural study of group process and development in online conferences. *Distance Education, 22*(1), 85–121. doi:10.1080/0158791010220106

Hoel, H., & Cooper, C. L. (2000). *Destructive conflict and bullying at work*. Retrieved from http://www.workplacebullying.org/res/umist.pdf.

Hoel, H., Faragher, B., & Cooper, C. L. (2004). Bullying is detrimental to health, but all bullying behaviors are not necessarily equally damaging. *British Journal of Guidance & Counselling, 32*(3), 367–387. doi:10.1080/03069880410001723594

Hofstede, G. H. (2001). *Culture's consequences: Comparing values, behaviors, institutions and organizations across nations* (2nd ed.). Thousand Oaks, CA: Sage.

Jehn, K. A. (1995). A multimethod examination of the benefits and detriments of intragroup conflict. *Administrative Science Quarterly, 40*, 256–282. doi:10.2307/2393638

Kaplan, D. M., Wiley, J. W., & Maertz, C. P. (2011). The role of calculative attachment in the relationship between diversity climate and retention. *Human Resource Management, 50*(2), 271–287. doi:10.1002/hrm.20413

Kickul, J., Lester, S. W., & Finkl, J. (2002). Promise breaking during radical organizational change: Do justice interventions make a difference? *Journal of Organizational Behavior, 23,* 469–488. doi:10.1002/job.151

Kieseker, R., & Marchant, T. (1999). Workpalce bullying in Australia: A review of current conceptualizations and existing research. *Australian Journal of Management and Organisational Behaviour, 2*(5), 61–75.

Korac-Kakabadse, N., Kouzmin, A., Korac-Kakabadse, A., & Savery, L. (2001). Low- and high-context communication patterns: Towards mapping cross-cultural encounters. *Cross Cultural Management, 8*(2), 3–24. doi:10.1108/13527600110797218

Lau, D. C., & Murnighan, J. K. (1998). Demographic diversity and faultlines: The compositional dynamics of organizational groups. *Academy of Management Review, 23,* 325–340.

Lewis, S. E., & Orford, J. (2005). Women's experiences of adult workplace bullying: A process model of changes in social relationships. *Journal of Community & Applied Social Psychology, 15,* 29–47. doi:10.1002/casp.807

Leymann, H., & Gustafsson, A. (1996). Mobbing at work and the development of post-traumatic stress disorders. *European Journal of Work and Organizational Psychology, 5*(2), 251–275. doi:10.1080/13594329608414858

Li, W. (2009). Online knowledge sharing among Chinese and American employees: Explore the influence of national cultural differences. *International Journal of Knowledge Management, 5*(3), 54–72. doi:10.4018/jkm.2009070104

Luhmann, N. (2000). *Vertrauen ein mechanismus der reduction sozialer komplexitat* (4th ed.). Stuttgart, Germany: Lucius & Lucius.

Lurey, J. S., & Raisinghani, M. S. (2001). An empirical study of best practices in virtual teams. *Information & Management, 38,* 523–544. doi:10.1016/S0378-7206(01)00074-X

Maass, A., Cadinu, M., Guarnieri, G., & Grasselli, A. (2003). Sexual harassment under social identity threat: The computer harassment paradigm. *Journal of Personality and Social Psychology, 85*(5), 853–870. doi:10.1037/0022-3514.85.5.853

Mancini, D. J. (2010). Building organizational trust in virtual teams. *Journal of Behavioral Studies in Business, 2,* 1–5.

Mann, S., Varey, R., & Button, W. (2000). An exploration of the emotional impact of tele-working via computer-mediated communication. *Journal of Managerial Psychology, 15*(7), 668–690. doi:10.1108/02683940010378054

Matveev, A. V., & Nelson, P. E. (2004). Cross cultural communication competence and multicultural team performance: Perceptions of American and Russian managers. *International Journal of Cross Cultural Management, 4*(2), 253–270. doi:10.1177/1470595804044752

Mello, J. A. (2007). Managing telework programs effectively. *Employee Responsibilities and Rights Journal, 19,* 247–261. doi:10.1007/s10672-007-9051-1

Neuliep, J. W. (2009). *Intercultural communication: A contextual approach.* Thousand Oaks, CA: Sage.

Neuman, J. H., & Baron, R. A. (1998). Workplace violence and workplace aggression: Evidence concerning specific forms, potential causes, and preferred targets. *Journal of Management, 24*(3), 391–419.

Oetzel, J. G. (1998). Culturally homogeneous and heterogeneous groups: Explaining communication processes through individualism-collectivism and self-construal. *International Journal of Intercultural Relations, 22*(2), 135–161. doi:10.1016/S0147-1767(98)00002-9

Palanski, M. E., Kahai, S. S., & Yammarino, F. J. (2011). Team virtues and performance: An examination of transparency, behavioral integrity, and trust. *Journal of Business Ethics, 99*, 201–216. doi:10.1007/s10551-010-0650-7

Pelled, L. H., Eisenhardt, K. M., & Xin, K. R. (1999). Exploring the black box: An analysis of work group diversity, conflict, and performance. *Administrative Science Quarterly, 44*, 1–28. doi:10.2307/2667029

Peters, P., & den Dulk, L. (2003). Cross-cultural differences in managers' support for home-based telework: A Theoretical elaboration. *International Journal of Cross Cultural Management, 3*(3), 329–346. doi:10.1177/1470595803003003005

Pratto, F., Sidanius, J., Stallworth, L. M., & Malle, B. F. (1994). Social dominance orientation: A personality variable predicting social and political attitudes. *Journal of Personality and Social Psychology, 67*(4), 741–763. doi:10.1037/0022-3514.67.4.741

Privitera, C., & Campbell, M. A. (2009). Cyberbulling: The new face of workplace bullying? *Cyberpsychology & Behavior, 12*(4), 395–400. doi:10.1089/cpb.2009.0025

Richards, H., & Freeman, S. (2002). *Bullying in the workplace: An occupational hazard*. Pymble, Australia: Harper Collins.

Shapiro, D. L., Furst, S. A., Spreitzer, G. M., & Von Glinow, M. A. (2002). Transnational teams in the electronic age: Are team identity and high performance at risk? *Journal of Organizational Behavior, 23*, 455–467. doi:10.1002/job.149

Simeon, R., Nicholson, J. D., & Wong, Y. Y. (2001). Comparisons of Asian and US workplace gender roles. *Cross Cultural Management, 8*(2), 47–59. doi:10.1108/13527600110797236

Sproull, L., & Kiesler, S. (1986). Reducing social context cues: Electronic mail in organizational communication. *Management Science, 32*(11), 1492–1512. doi:10.1287/mnsc.32.11.1492

Tan-Solano, M., & Kleiner, B. H. (2001). Effects of telecommuting on organizational behaviour. *Management Research News, 24*, 123–126. doi:10.1108/01409170110782720

Trevino, L. K., Webster, J., & Stein, E. W. (2000). Making connections: Complementary influences on communication media choices, attitudes, and use. *Organization Science, 11*(2), 163–182. doi:10.1287/orsc.11.2.163.12510

Volkema, R. J. (2004). Demographic, cultural, and economic predictors of perceived ethicality of negotiation behavior: A nine-country analysis. *Journal of Business Research, 57*, 69–78. doi:10.1016/S0148-2963(02)00286-2

Von Glinow, M. A., Shapiro, D. L., & Brett, J. M. (2004). Can we talk and should we? Managing emotional conflict in multicultural teams. *Academy of Management Review, 29*(4), 578–592.

Weisband, S. P., & Reinig, B. A. (1995). Managing user perceptions of email privacy. *Communications of the ACM, 38*(12), 40–47. doi:10.1145/219663.219678

Wiesenfeld, B. M., Raghuram, S., & Garud, R. (1999). Communication patterns as determinants of organizational identification in a virtual organization. *Organization Science, 10*(6), 777–790. doi:10.1287/orsc.10.6.777

Wilson, M. S., & Liu, J. H. (2003). Social dominance orientation and gender: The moderating role of gender identification. *The British Journal of Social Psychology, 42*, 187–198. doi:10.1348/014466603322127175

KEY TERMS AND DEFINITIONS

Asynchronous Communication: Any form of communication in which the sender and receiver are not concurrently communicating.

Cross-Cultural Competence: An individual's set of knowledge, skills, and dispositions that facilitate adaptation in cross-cultural environments.

Cyber-Aggression: A relationship-based phenomenon whereby an individual intentionally intimidates, emotionally harms, or exerts power over another in an on-line environment.

Global Virtual Team (GVT): Workplace teams separated by vast distances and limited ability to communicate face-to-face.

Global Workplace: The concept that organizations can exist in more than one country across the globe or can interact with organizations in different locations worldwide

Psychological Contract: The mutual beliefs, perceptions, and informal obligations between an employer and an employee

Social Dominance Orientation: A personality variable that measures the belief in individuals that some groups are superior relative to others and those individuals therefore approve of inequality/social hierarchy within in-group relationships.

Synchronous Communication: Any form of communication in which the sender and receiver are concurrently communicating.

Virtual Team: A team made up of individuals dispersed across time, geography, or organizational structures. These teams typically rely on a variety of communication technologies to complete work tasks.

Chapter 30

Leveraging Workforce Diversity:
Utilizing Technology

Aileen G. Zaballero
Pennsylvania State University, USA

Tutaleni I. Asino
Pennsylvania State University, USA

Jessica Briskin
Pennsylvania State University, USA

ABSTRACT

Technology is affecting and transforming nearly every aspect of society. It has not only facilitated increased access to information, but has also changed the functioning of the workforce. The manner in which a technology is used can offer organizations a competitive advantage or place them at a disadvantage; hence, it is the manner in which technological tools are utilized in the organization that determines their value.

This chapter connects technology and diversity and argues that technology can be leveraged to contribute to the diversification of a workforce. The authors discuss the changing global economy as it pertains to the diminution of labor market boundaries and diversified consumers, as well as current trends in technology usage and innovation as a means to accomplishing organizational goals. In addition, the authors analyze organizational learning and organizational performance, regarding the use of technology as a tool to overcome the challenges of a diverse workforce.

INTRODUCTION

Technology and diversity are alike in that both are continually evolving, making the task of nailing down a definition of either akin to hitting a moving target. Each year, many new technologies emerge, some eventually altering not only the ways in which work is done, but also altering society as a whole. Similarly, with each passing year, new conceptualizations of diversity emerge, leading to broader definitions and serving as a testament to the existence and persistence of globalization and a global workforce.

DOI: 10.4018/978-1-4666-1812-1.ch030

The interconnected nature of today's economy presents organizations with the potential for chaotic systems, characterized not by disorder but rather by unpredictability, as even small changes can lead to unexpected behaviors (Thietart & Forgues, 1995). Consequently, when this is combined with the age of information and globalization, managers must not only face, but also conquer, the challenges of increased competition and rapidly changing conditions (Yuksel & Turkey, 2011). The organization's ability to effectively deal with these challenges and maintain both sustainable and sizeable momentum is heavily dependent on having high performing and competent employees (Yuksel & Turkey, 2011).

One way to maintain this momentum and generate new ideas is through increased diversity. Originally defined based on visible attributes, globalization has forced organizations to shift their definition of workforce diversity. The term diversity has now expanded to encompass more inclusive ideas, comprised of values, goals, education, and experience. This new conceptualization is not only based on political correctness, but also on a necessity for recruitment. According to the Business-Higher Education Forum, it is projected that by 2028 there will be 19 million more jobs than there will be qualified workers, with many of these jobs in the Information Technology (IT) field (as cited by Moody, et al., 2003). Facing such a shortage, organizations will be (and some already have been) forced to push beyond their usual arenas and expand beyond traditional borders in order to find qualified candidates.

As organizations continue to concern themselves with diversification of their workforce, they are also addressing workplace inequalities while harnessing the power associated with the concept of diversity (Gopal, et al., 1997). There is ample evidence from various studies showing a direct positive correlation between technological success and communities that are socially, culturally and ethnically diverse (Moody, et al., 2003, p. 63). Recruiting, engaging and educating a diverse workforce, as well as identifying the emerging markets and creating capacity-building relationships, are therefore necessary practices in order to stay competitive in a changing global market. A global market expands not only a customer base, but also the labor supply market. As a result, the demographics of the marketplace and workforce are morphing from homogenous communities into ethnically diverse populations.

CHANGING GLOBAL ECONOMY

In the event that there is still a debate about the changing nature of the global economy, one needs only go to any supermarket, department store, or shopping centre. Simply surveying items in any aisle in almost any store, one will find evidence of manufacturing from different parts of the world. There is no longer just one main supplier. Even for the nations with large economies, their goods are often produced in or have components from emerging economies.

According to the International Monetary Fund (IMF), emerging market economies face turmoil with respect to rising food and fuel prices. Consequently, they "will need to play a growing leadership role, joining with advanced economies in learning to operate in unfamiliar terrain" (Collyns & Srinivasan, 2008). With volatile conditions and competition soaring, the need to employ high performing and competent employees is becoming increasingly imperative. Fewer people must work together to achieve ever-higher standards of quantity and quality through the utilization of virtual teams, networks, and flatter organizational structures. Leveraging knowledge and effectively distributing resources are necessary practices to maintain a competitive advantage in an information-driven economy. This is of significance because the internet is altering the global production of work. Unskilled workers are being displaced by information-intensive jobs. The diffusion of technology and the world-wide-connectivity has created pressures of continuous change (Yuksel, 2011). Therefore, the development and management of human resources must encompass strategic and innovative competencies simultaneously designed to optimize technology.

Emerging Economies

There has been a continuous discussion regarding the world economic situation and the redistribution of power since the 1990s. However, there is still no consensus about the definitions of the term emerging economies or markets (Hoskisson, et al., 2000). Arnold and Quelch (1998) note that emerging economies have two characteristics: relatively fast economic growth and restructuring of government policies to liberate national trade agreements and establishment of a market-oriented system. Hoskisson et al. (2000) identify emerging economies as low-income countries that through economic liberation have achieved fast growth.

This increased and relatively rapid economic growth occurring primarily in developing countries is being experienced as a result of market-oriented economic reform and expanding policies. Regardless of the definition, the fact remains that the expansion of world trade and economic globalization has brought new players to the business arena. According to The Development of Emerging Economies Annual Report 2009 (The Baoa Forum of Asia, 2009, p. 7) the top ten new players that form the emerging countries are:

- Argentina
- Brazil
- India
- Indonesia
- Mexico
- People's Republic of China
- Republic of Korea
- Russia
- Saudi Arabia
- South Africa

As a testament to the power of emerging markets and globalization, products and services are being consumed beyond their own country. Organizations must now cooperate with greater economic interdependence on issues of diversity in the workplace that impacts employment relations, competitive advantages, and market share.

Reflecting and recognizing changing global patterns, an increasing number of organizations are utilizing offshore outsourcing and shifting business functions to emerging countries such as India, Philippines, and Malaysia. As stated in the 2002-2003 Society for Human Resource Management (SHRM) Workplace Forecast, companies such as Ford, General Motors, and Nestle are outsourcing and employing workers in foreign countries because they provide highly educated workforces, but at a low labor cost. This trend is expected to continue and it is projected "that 3.3 million U.S. service-and knowledge-based jobs will be shipped overseas by the year 2015, 70 percent of which will move to India" (Tan, 2011). In multiple languages and in various cultures, the communication of information is being shared across the globe.

In the 1980s and 1990s, workers from India and China entered the international labor pool. Although these workers have always existed, the compounding difference is that these countries have become key players in the global system of production and consumption. In 2000, India and China supplied 1.47 billion workers to the global labor workforce. As a result, the world's interconnected workforce doubled (National Intelligence Council, 2008). Furthermore, China and India are developing millions of competent college graduates who are as productive as the college graduates of Europe, Japan, and the United States, but at a much lower pay (National Intelligence Council, 2008). In addition, China holds over a trillion dollars in hard currency reserves. Additionally, the high-tech sector of India is growing exponentially. These factors create intense pressures on labor markets throughout the world.

Although in 2008 the global financial created seismic stress, the world economy rebounded quicker than expected. China's economy expanded by 8.7% in 2009 as a result of the government's effective stimulus policies. They increased imports, expanded outbound investment, developed international cooperation, and provided trade financing and currency exchanges with other countries. India also maintained a relatively powerful economic growth momentum of 5.6% in 2009. India focused on domestic demands; set restrictions on investment in its financial sectors; and finally "adopted a series of stimulus measures such as tax cuts, interest rate cuts, increasing expenditures and providing export guarantee to stimulate the economy" (Boao Forum for Asia, 2010, p. 34).

Expansion of National Labor Markets

As the rise of emerging markets continues to impact global businesses, international employment opportunities continue to expand. Potential employees are no longer competing just within local and national borders, but must now also contend within the international labor market. However, the population growth in many countries has not kept up with the job growth since the 1950's. Furthermore, there has been an expansion of world trade, a shift from manual labor to knowledge intensive work, and the adoption of labor-reduction technologies.(Jacobs & Slaus, 2011, p. 60). As globalized labor markets continue to increase, the approach of recruitment, retaining, and developing must shift to a human-centered global perspective. To achieve efficient and effective employment strategies on a global basis, organizations must optimize every available resource, particularly technological innovations. According to Jacobs and Slaus (2011), technology has transformed the 20th century as the business world is revolutionized and the way work is done is altered. Technology becomes a mixed blessing as communication and information travel faster and faster. New products and services are cre-

ated; however, resistance to depend on machines permeates (2011).

More people compete for fewer jobs as the global population continues to increase and diversify. To survive in this global market, individuals, organizations, and nations must evolve to a new way of thinking regarding economic and social space and time (Carnoy, 1999). Various organizations are taking the lead and because of their ability to capitalize on the rapid global technological innovations and the ability to lead a knowledge-based learning process.

Emerging global economies are contributing to the diversification of the global labor pool. Therefore, the development and management of human resources must encompass strategic and innovative competencies simultaneously designed to optimize human capital within organizational levels and across borders. The advancement of various information and communication technologies has manifested the diversification of employees. The following section will discuss the uses and development of various innovations that are contributing to the knowledge-based workforce.

INNOVATION AND TECHNOLOGY

Technological innovations have existed for centuries, from the discovery and recreation of fire to the printing press to the computers and everything else in between. With each new innovation, new challenges and opportunities emerge. Organizations that manage to understand the emergent trends and technologies often have a keen advantage over their competitors. The current rate of innovation is rapid and new tools are offering various affordances to organizations.

Technological innovations have had significant impact on the economy and labor movement. This change has been documented by many and is eloquently told by Thomas Friedman in his 2005 book *The World is Flat*. In it, Friedman details the role that technology has played in globalization and how it has flattened the world, allowing now more than ever for the masses to have access to the knowledge that was once enjoyed only by a small minority and controlled by even fewer gatekeepers. The question is no longer about whether technology can or will change how business is conducted, but rather what should become the new technological questions and focus. How is technology changing the global market and how can organizations benefit from such innovations? In this section, six categories of technological innovation are examined with a special focus on how they have affected the labor market and the ways in which they can be harnessed to facilitate diversity in the workforce.

Internet and World Wide Web

The creation of the Internet ushered in a new period in human history that rivals any that came before and affects multiple aspects of human life. Perhaps the only other technological innovation that can rival the Internet is the invention of the printing press, which made the printed word more accessible to the masses.

The term Internet has been loosely used and has taken on various meanings for different people. The usage of it in this section is a reference to the series of a worldwide system of computers connected through the use of a standard known as the Transmission Control Protocol/Internet Protocol, commonly referred to as TCP/IP. The Internet is in essence a network of networks because it is a global telecommunications system that connects millions of other, smaller computer networks. This is significant because anything that is on the internet is potentially available to the billions of people all over the globe on any network, whether they are in academic, government, and business, private, and public networks. This connectivity makes it possible for people to communicate with each other from distant places. From its inception in the 1960s, when it was primarily used by the United States' Department of Defense

(DoD) researchers shared information across the country, the Internet proved to be a powerful tool. The internet not only served that purposes it was intended for, but also became the impetus for many other usages and inventions that may not have been envisioned by the DoD researchers.

The introduction of the World Wide Web in the 1990s made the Internet much more accessible to everyone through the use of Web browsers to obtain information. Web browsers allowed users to interact with the Internet in a point and click manner that they were already familiar with through software such as word processing programs like Microsoft Word. One of the earliest browsers that was introduced to the masses was Mosaic developed by the National Center for Supercomputing Applications (NCSA) at the University of Illinois Urbana Champaign, and introduced in 1993, and was followed up by popular browsers such as Netscape, Internet Explorer, AOL, Opera, Safari, and Firefox. The introduction of the Web browser took away the intimidation factor of the technology and made it popular by imposing order and making it user-friendly on the front end by allowing for the inclusion of various media (Cockburn & Wilson, 1995).

Early examinations of the Internet and its impact on organizations tended to focus on the benefit for businesses to extend there. The focus was more on marketing and reaching new customer bases through e-commerce. It was seen as a tool to offer organizations an easier way to sell directly to customers by shortening the supply chain; improving research & development; and making communication and collaboration more efficient (Cockburn & Wilson, 1995). As argued by Ng et al. (1998), the Internet was seen as a way for organizations to have a global reach, to be more competitive, efficient, and save money.

Early researches on the internet seem to advocate for a one-way model where businesses are both the beneficiary and the ones in control of its effect. In actuality, the more organizations extended their reach through the Internet, the more they let in different people. Each new person expanded the organization's diverse views, introducing a new and expansive culture to the company.

Social Networking/Marketing

The internet has brought into existence various forms of technologies that have effectively changed how many communicate and perhaps also changed one's understanding of community. Nowhere is this more apparent than with the emergence of social networks.

As a result of the Internet, the term social networks no longer refers to people one meets at events and exchanges business cards with; it is now a virtual networking experience that allows people to be able to network and benefit from such an experience from anywhere in the world. As explained by Boyd and Ellison (2008), social networking sites are internet-based services that allow users to create public or semi-public profiles that connect them to other users. Once users joins a network, they can then view profiles of others as well as have their profiles viewed by others on the same network, depending on the privacy and security permissions that each individual enacts.

Social networking sites allow members to share information and share in each other's experiences regardless of location. They allow people who may have not communicated in a long time to re-establish contact and also allow for people who do not know each other to connect and network for business or job-seeking purposes.

There are a multitude of social networking sites that exist today and seemingly new ones emerge regularly. In their research on social networks in the workplace, Skeels and Grudin (2009) listed LinkedIn, Facebook, Live Spaces, MySpace, Orkut, Friendster, and Twitter as the most popular social networks that exist today. Regardless of popularity and variance in what the social site offers, one key feature of all social networking sites is its ability to function both synchronously and asynchronously. For example, in a social network

like Facebook, the user can chat (synchronous) and can also send each other messages (asynchronous) to be read later. It is these features that can help facilitate diversity in the organization.

Social networking sites can allow for an organization to easily obtain feedback from all members of an organization and not simply those that are a more versed in expressing their opinions in public. It is now possible for an organization to easily post a document for discussion or a question to respond to on a social network and obtain feedback from their employees. This ensures that a wider diversity of voices is incorporated in the organization's conversation and avoids a groupthink mentality. Considerations can also be given to those who want to respond anonymously.

Regardless of whether or not an organization understands the true value of social networks, the fact remains that their employees are using the sites and software often as a mean by which they regularly communicate. Although it can be argued that these methods of communication tend to be adopted by a younger workforce, it is still important or perhaps even more so critical that organizations dedicate efforts to address these differences in adoption as a way of addressing this seemingly generational divide between the young and old (DiMicco, et al., 2008, p. 719). In concluding their research on the social network "Beehive" at IBM, DiMicco (2008) and her colleagues warn that if companies do not provide a way for employees to utilize social networking sites, particularly by providing them internally, employees will actively seek out these tools on their own and leave the organization devoid of an important communication channel.

It is however also worth pointing out that the use of social networking sites is not without challenges. The inclusion of social networking sites can also begin to blur the line between professional space and personal space. It may lead to the employees feeling that the organization is encroaching on their privacy and fatigue from feeling that they are always plugged in.

Adaptive and Assistive Technologies Computer Tools

The current economic crisis is making it difficult for many to find jobs. However, for a person with a disability, the problem is compounded and leads to the statistic of people with disabilities being 5% more likely to be unemployed (Gewin, 2011). In the United States, the 1990 signing of the Americans with Disabilities Act, which prevents discrimination on the basis of disability, has contributed to the improved situation of access by persons with disability in the workforce. Equally so are the changes in attitudes towards the disabled and advances in technologies to enable persons with disabilities to more easily, effectively and efficiently perform their duties. Technologies that enable persons with disabilities to work more efficiently are often referred to as adaptive or assistive technologies. Such technologies can, for example, take information on the computer screen, magnify it, read it or translate into Braille to enable those who are visually impaired to access it (Ray & Ray, 1998).

Adaptive and assistive technologies however are not the magic pill to a way of including people with disabilities in the workforce. Ray and Ray (1998) argue that although the technology is important, other factors must be considered. For example, what has regularly been considered an effective form of visual communication "using color to convey meaning, fonts to distinguish between different kinds of information, column and table formats to clarify information, and graphics to summarize information is often problematic because not all adaptive technologies can translate these cues and some that do it still require improvements. This leaves out many visually impaired individuals by excluding them from fully participating, contributing, and accessing information" (p. 573). It is therefore important that other steps are taken not only to introduce the technology, but also to fully integrate it so that organizations can include those with disabilities in the workforce and be able to benefit for the diversity of skills, views and ideas that they offer.

ORGANIZATIONAL LEARNING

Technology has played a dominant role in transforming the culture of the United States, particularly in regards to the way individuals communicate and collaborate with one another. These advancements have enabled the construction of computer environments, which offer varying degrees of user immersion, participation, and collaboration.

Digital Divide

Individuals are now inundated with different methods of technological communication, including text-messaging, email, and instant messaging (just to name a few). Due to the relatively recent growth in these technologies, a "digital divide" has been created between older and younger generations. While younger generations have grown up in a technology-saturated society, enabling them to become fluent in navigating, understanding and using these new methods, older generations tend to have a difficult time adapting to this new language, first struggling to decipher it before finally achieving a level of fluency (Prensky, 2001). This divide fuels conflict in the workplace, and the impact will become an increasingly important consideration as patterns continue to shift due to both networked communication technologies as well as the influx of digital natives entering the workforce.

Another generational shift will greatly impact the workforce as well. Many baby boomers, those born from 1943 to 1960 (Gelston, 2008), are beginning to retire and the influx of new workers is not large enough to fill these now vacant positions. A majority of the workforce is comprised of individuals aged 24 to 55 years old, with this group accounting for 71.1% of the total working group in 2000. 2000 is an important benchmark, as it signifies the year by which all members of the baby boomer generation had entered this majority range, and the beginning of when the older members would cross into the next category of 55+. In the ensuing period from 2000 to 2005 as baby boomers continued to age, the percentage of the workforce in this 24 to 55 year old range decreased to 68.8%, and in 2050 this percentage is projected to fall to 64% (Toosi, 2006). There are simply an inadequate number of Generation Y workers, those born after 1982 (Gelston, 2008), as well as Generation X workers to fill these vast leadership positions. Generation X workers are those born between 1961 and 1981 (Gelston, 2008). These numbers are significant, as the estimated 77 million baby boomers that will retire between 2010 and 2025 will take their skills and knowledge with them out of the workforce (Dodd, 2009). Organizations that fail to replace the baby boomers with new leaders who have learned from their predecessors will surely suffer as the great asset of knowledge leaks freely from the internal system.

How does one tackle the problem of the digital divide? How does the workforce capture the knowledge of its current leaders? and how does one use this knowledge to guide the new generation of leaders? An organization's success and competitive edge depends upon its ability to embrace diversity and realize its benefits. Multiple benefits are reported when organizations actively assess their internal handling of workplace diversity plans. A diverse workforce, in which one feels comfortable communicating varying points of view, provides a larger collection of ideas and experiences. The organization can draw from that collection in order to meet both business strategy needs, as well as those of customers, in a more effective manner.

Distance Learning

There is a multitude of technology already being utilized in the workplace as a means to foster employee development and collaboration, especially for those working at a distance (i.e. telecommuting). The available technology can be tailored to fit each individual's unique situation. Development needs may include the continual honing of skills and competencies in alignment with strategic business goals and performance objectives for succession planning. This occurs in both formal and informal settings, and includes: a Learning Management System (LMS), Knowledge Management System (KMS), and collective learning.

Learning Management System

Organizations are able to develop their diverse workforce by incorporating a LMS. This is a secure software application that enables administration to identify learning needs and quickly build development plans to prevent skill gaps and promote complete competency (Ellis, 2009). An LMS can provide reports and track a range of employee learning activities from attendance, to test scores as well as additional course requirements (Ellis, 2009). Organizations that integrate an LMS to track social networking content are able to see who utilizes this tool and link it those who are developing and building their expertise. An LMS also aids in performance management, helping individuals track their performances. It tracks how workers are doing in relation to objectives and accesses skill growth and competencies. An LMS is helpful for organizational success in developing both new and old employees alike.

Knowledge Management System

A Knowledge Management System (KMS) "refers to a class of information systems applied to managing organizational knowledge" (Alavi & Leidner, 2001, p. 114). That is, they are IT-based systems to capture and support the creation, organization, and distribution of knowledge. A KMS will help to store and retrieve information. Some reasons why an individual would use a KMS include, sharing of information throughout organizational hierarchy and with new employees, working together in virtual teams, or accessing information on past projects (Alavi & Leidner, 2001).

Collective Learning

The development of a diverse workforce can also be facilitated through the incorporation of collective learning with the use of eLearning 2.0. This increases employee collaboration, development, and performance. eLearning 2.0 refers to implementations of Web 2.0/social networking technologies to complement traditional learning processes (Downes, 2005). This includes blogs, wikis, and other social software useful to promote eLearning communities of practice. By incorporating eLearning 2.0 and Web 2.0 tools, knowledge sharing can grow in new directions and will serve the younger generation. Younger generations have grown up with these tools and have become accustomed to using them for networking and communication purposes. Not only is this beneficial for existing employees of the Gen Y cohort, but it will also be useful for on-boarding new employees (Downes, 2005).

Achieving Digital Equity

LMS, KMS, and eLearning 2.0 can each boost collaboration and communication among internal employees, external partners, and customer communities. An LMS is a tool that helps leaders coach and give feedback to their employees, while a KMS and eLearning 2.0 encourage knowledge sharing. These are three of the biggest challenges that diverse organizations face today (Jacobs, 2004). The continuing acceptance and adoption

of these applications/services is changing not only the ways in which individuals configure and use software and storage, but also the ways in which we conceptualize those functions. It does not matter where our work is stored; what matters is that our information is accessible from any location or device. Globally, in huge numbers, we are growing accustomed to a model of browser-based software that is device-independent. While challenges still remain, specifically with regard to the notions of privacy and control, the promise of significant cost savings is an important motivating force behind the search for solutions (Johnson, Levine, Smith, & Stone, 2010).

ORGANIZATIONAL PERFORMANCE

Considering global realities, more and more businesses implement long-range strategic plans to employ diversity to capitalize on the "interaction between, and collaboration among, people of diverse cultures, religion, histories, and perspectives" (SHRM, 2008, p. 25). As today's global market becomes increasingly diverse, businesses must adapt and innovate in order to stay competitive. Long-term, organization-wide strategies to improve internal operations such as processes and work- flow management continue to be a key challenge. An additional challenge is preparing for globalizations and the information revolution, particularly in regards to diverse internal and external customers. "Policy-makers, business executives, NGO activists, academics, and ordinary citizens are increasingly concerned with the need to make their societies competitive in the emergent information economy" (Pascual, 2003, p. 1). Technology is playing an increasingly vital role in transitioning markets from industrial-based economies to knowledge-based societies. As opportunities for global expansion and outsourcing increase, so does the trend for global diversity in the workplace. The following section will focus on the impact technology has had on organizational performance and how innovative strategies have supported a diverse workforce in maintaining a competitive advantage.

Knowledge Driven Competitive Advantages

Throughout the world, a knowledge-intensive economy is prevalent. Nations and organizations alike are seeking to capitalize on their available resources—specifically people, technology, and skills—to maintain core competencies in certain industry sectors (Rajshekhar, et al., 2011). Contributions from various major nations built the current global knowledge economy. In general, information and communication technologies are playing an important role. It is essential that organizations understand the issues of knowledge acquisition in various contexts, particularly in diverse settings (Rajshekhar, et al., 2011; Tong & Shaikh, 2010). The continuous advantage in business performance from utilizing technology is imperative for all organizations. Companies that embrace technology are able to gain more in sales and profit than firms that are late in optimizing technological resources. Environmental turbulence and competitive intensity moderate the necessity to optimize business performance.

Knowledge strategies impact both within and beyond an organization. Solutions to optimize technology must impinge upon roles and interactions all through the organization. Knowledge strategies use the right information in the right context at the right time to ensure the organization's performance. Knowledge by itself will not transform businesses. However, knowledge coupled with new technologies can provide countless opportunities if the organizations are willing to change business structures and adapt to new strategies. Continuous learning is necessary to optimize the appropriate use of technology as a means to provide a competitive advantage.

Learning Organization

As information and technology continues to be a key component of society and a catalyst for new economies, the need to change and evolve becomes necessary. Seeking new ways to work makes learning a condition of survival for individuals, companies, schools, and nations. In the new business model, knowledge is the principal value of reference. Learning to progress beyond the Industrial-Era education is crucial. Organizations' learning requires a higher level of awareness. It is suggested by Esposito (2010) "that 'how' questions really are the fundamental issues, which political leaders, researchers, business people and educators must strive to address fast" (p. 1). The strength and potential of an organization no longer lies in the tangible assets, but in the collective knowledge of the organization itself and the ability to promote continuous learning in every aspect of its business function.

Businesses need information and the powerful capability in processing and delivering results effectively. The key to survival and success lies in the ability to get work done accurately, efficiently and with limited resources (Kehoe, et al., 2005; Lawler & Mohrman, 2001). The use of technology can save time and optimize performance, "minimize cost and strengthen the organizational sustainability to progressively evolve the system to satisfy changing requirements and to capitalize on technology improvements" (Capelli, 2001). The ability to develop and change systems will depend on how learning and information acquisition is implemented. Technology then becomes both a commodity and a tool.

Kozlowski et al. (2001) as cited by Zin and Talat (2011) states that "estimated on-line distance learning can reduce the indirect costs of training (for example, costs associated with travel to training facilities, hotel accommodations for trainees, lost work time for employees attending training) that have estimated to account for 80 percent of overall organizational training expenditures" (p. 49). Research also shows that between 70 and 90 percent of large firms use e-recruiting systems, computerized performance-monitoring technology, and revolutionized human resource management appraisal systems (Capelli, 2001; Gale, 2005; Kozlowski, et al., 2001).

In a highly competitive global economy, the conceptualization of an organization and its success changes. Business entities must "evolve from a big machine to a creative thinking brain" (Esposito, 2010, p. 4). A learning organization identifies the employees as a long-term strategic investment and recognizes the vital importance to develop the unique individual competencies of their diverse workforce. Through the use of technology, organizations can streamline the development process and information technology competencies become more important.

Information Technology (IT) Competencies

The work environment has acquired many complex and novel challenges. Companies such as IBM and Kodak are now providing "trans-related medical care; while 125 Fortune 500 companies now protect transgender employees from job discrimination" (Rosenberg, 2007; as cited by Zin & Talat, 2011, p. 49). In addition, recruiting, retaining and developing a diverse workforce continue to be important to preventing a decline in productivity. With the use of IT, organizations are able to detect potential problems, allocate resources, update policies and strategies, and communicate more effectively with all members of the organization (Zin & Talat, 2011). Furthermore, organizational constructs vary considerably from administrative structures to multi-site communication. IT competency is fundamental in all business functions including: collecting, summarizing, generating, disseminating, converting, and synthesizing information. In addition, technology

literacy among all employees becomes crucial and a prerequisite since all aspects of business now become dependent on knowledge and the communication of information.

Utilizing Technology to Optimize Organizational Strategic Goals

In an information-driven economy, technology has become critical to leverage knowledge throughout the organization. Global business has been transformed by the mass use of the Internet. Management of human capital in a global context has been facilitated by the diffusion of technology. Many organizations are investing more time and money to develop technological infrastructures to manage their people effectively and are redesigning their organizational frameworks to stay competitive. According to Yuksel and Turkey (2011), "all employees need to continuously upgrade their skills to be able to understand business as a whole and its processes" (p. 104) in order to optimize the workplace effectiveness, employees need continuous development of business acumen to create partners in the comprehension of strategy and cost. Utilizing the individual knowledge of a diverse workforce becomes complex and requires strategic approaches to talent management.

Talent Management System (TMS)

The management of talent is now focusing on managing knowledge workers. Interestingly, "the most common approach to high-end knowledge work…can be summarized as 'hire smart people and leave them alone'" (Davenport, et al, 2002, p. 26-27). However, supervising information-intense work cannot be computerized, forecasted, or micromanaged (Thompson & Heron, 2005). To optimize knowledgeable workers, flexibility and creativity of new ideas must be promoted as a means to synthesize new information. Organizational structures must be established such that knowledge sharing happens naturally (Davenport, 2004; Thompson & Heron, 2005). As project-based work becomes the norm of business structures and organizations grow flatter, the need to network and process information effectively becomes vital. The use of technology can aid in communication and support knowledge processing among diverse employees while promoting collaborative opportunities.

Increasing Collaborative Opportunity

Collaboration enables employees of all skills and experience to combine their efforts, benefiting the whole organization rather than individual interest (Yuksel & Turkey, 2011). When an organization promotes team and collaborative work environment, shared learning experiences becomes a norm (Carleton, 2011). Technology supports information sharing and can bridge the geographic distances between individuals through the use of email, shareware, and virtual meetings. Using these mediums facilitate the sharing of information among knowledge workers, thus optimizing social capital (Thompson & Heron, 2005; as cited by Carleton, 2011). Organizational policies and structures must create an environment that encourages diverse employees with various knowledge, skills, and background to engage in communities of practice to facilitate knowledge sharing.

CONCLUSION

In times of rapid change, when knowledge and information are among the most vital of resources, organizational competitiveness is dependent on how well groups are able to address such issues as globalization, an emerging workforce, knowledge management, and innovation. Along the same lines, the demographics of the workforce continue to diversify. The workforce talent pool extends beyond national borders, making the ability to attract and retain the very best employee essential to securing a competitive advantage. However, the

diversity of the workforce is no longer restricted only to categories of race, gender, age, social class, etc., but comprises of individual attributes such as values, goals, education, experience, and the ability to learn. The workforce advantage is not only assessed by labor potential, but also by knowledge abilities.

Considering all these predominant factors, the appropriate use of technology and the advancements of communication tools have enhanced how individuals can work together. Networking technologies have made both asynchronous and real-time communications between different communities feasible, creating collaborative and knowledge sharing experiences within diverse settings. Individuals are no longer simply employed for physical labor, but instead for their ability to acquire and develop information. The diversity of knowledge of workers and the potential of each individual becomes the organizational advantage. Different contexts of technology that must be understood include policy, infrastructure, regulation, and cultures of different regions. Proper management and development of intangible assets is key to optimal performance and the use of technology and innovative strategies can contribute to organizational diversity The diffusion and adoption of interactive, adaptive, and assistive technologies continue to illustrate the power of technology as a contributing factor to workforce diversification.

REFERENCES

Alavi, M., & Leidner, D. E. (2001). Review: Knowledge management and knowledge management systems: Conceptual foundations and research issues. *Management Information Systems Quarterly, 25*(1), 107–236. doi:10.2307/3250961

Banutu-Gomez, M., & Rohrer, W. G. (2011). Teams in organization. *The Cambridge Business Review, 18*(1), 54–60.

Cappelli, P. (2001). Making the most of on-line recruiting. *Harvard Business Review, 79*, 139–146.

Carleton, K. (2011). How to motivate and retain knowledge workers in organizations: A review of the literature. *International Journal of Management, 28*(2), 459–468.

Cockburn, C., & Wilson, T. D. (1995). Business use of the world-wide web. *Information Research, 1*(1). Retrieved from http://informationr.net/ir/1-2/paper6.html.

Davenport, T. H., Thomas, R. I., & Cantrell, S. (2002). The mysterious art and science of knowledge-worker performance. *MIT Sloan Management Review.* Retrieved from http://sloan-review.mit.edu/the-magazine/2002-fall/4412/the-mysterious-art-and-science-of-knowledge-worker-performance/.

DiMicco, J., Millen, D., Geyer, W., Dugan, C., Brownholtz, B., & Muller, M. (2008). Motivations for social networking at work. In *Proceedings of the ACM Conference on Computer Supported Cooperative Work.* San Diego, CA: ACM Press.

Dodd, A. (2009). *The flexible workforce: A secret weapon in the war for talent.* Retrieved January 12, 2009, from http://www.talentmgt.com/recruitment_retention/2009/January/848/index.php.

Education and Training. (2001). Learning to bridge the digital divide. *Education & Training, 43*(2), 125-126.

Esposito, M. (2010). The role of learning organizations in the growing discussion on social responsibility. *International Journal of the Academy of Executives & Administrators, 1*(8), 1–18.

Gale, S. F. (2005). Making c-learning more than "pixie dust". *Workforce Management, 82*, 112–122.

Gelston, S. (2008). *Gen y, gen x, and the baby boomers: Workplace generation wars.* Retrieved January 12, 2009, from http://www.cio.com/article/178050/Gen_Y_Gen_X_and_the_Baby_Boomers_Workplace_Generation_Wars.

Gewin, V. (2011). Equality: The fight for access. *Nature, 469*, 255–257. doi:10.1038/nj7329-255a

Giulianelli, D., Cruzado, G., Rodriguez, R., Vera, P. M., Trigueros, A., & Moreno, E. (2011). Advances in new technologies, interactive interfaces, and communicability. *Lecture Notes in Computer Science, 6616*, 62–72. doi:10.1007/978-3-642-20810-2_7

Irons, L. (2008). E-learning 2.0 and learning management systems (LMS). Retrieved December 7, 2008, from http://skilfulminds.com/2008/05/19/elearning-20-and-learning-management-systems-lms/.

Jacobs, D. (2004, September). In search of future leaders. *Human Resource Management*, 22–27.

Johnson, L., Levine, A., Smith, R., & Stone, S. (2010). *The 2010 horizon report.* Austin, TX: The New Media Consortium. Retrieved June 20, 2011, from http://wp.nmc.org/horizon2010/.

Kehoe, J. F., Dickter, D. N., Russell, D. P., & Sacco, J. M. (2005). e-Selection. In Gueutal & Stone (Eds.), *The Brave New World of e-HR*, (pp. 54-103). San Francisco, CA: Jossey-Bass.

Kozlowski, S. W. J., Tone, U., Mullins, M. E., Weissbein, D. A., Brown, K. G., & Bell, B. S. (2001). Developing adaptability: A theory for the design of integrated-embedded training systems. In Salas, E. (Ed.), *Advances in Human Performance and Cognitive Engineering Research* (pp. 59–123). Amsterdam, The Netherlands: JAI/Elsevier Science. doi:10.1016/S1479-3601(01)01004-9

Ng, H., Pan, Y. J., & Wilson, T. D. (1998). Business use of the world wide web: A report on further investigations. *Information Research, 3*(4). Retrieved from http://informationr.net/ir/3-4/paper46.html.

Oreilly, T. (2007). What is web 2.0: Design patterns and business models for the next generation of software. *Communications & Strategies, 1*, 17. Retrieved from http://ssrn.com/abstract=1008839.

Pascual, P. J. (2003). *E-government, e-asean task force, UNDP-APDIP*. Retrieved from http://www.apdip.net/publications/iespprimers/eprimer-egov.pdf.

Prensky, M. (2001). Digital natives, digital immigrants. *Horizon, 9*(5), 1–6. doi:10.1108/10748120110424816

Rajshekhar, R. G., Javalgi, A. C., Gross, W., Benoy, J., & Granot, E. (2011). Assessing competitive advantage of emerging markets in knowledge intensive business services. *Journal of Business and Industrial Marketing, 26*(3), 171–180. doi:10.1108/08858621111115895

Ray, D. S., & Ray, E. J. (1998). Adaptive technologies for the visually impaired: The role of technical communicators. *Technical Communication, 45*(4), 573–579.

SHRM. (2003). *Workplace forecast: A strategic outlook 2000–2003*. Alexandria, VA: Society for Human Resource Management.

Skeels, M. M., & Grudin, J. (2009). When social networks cross boundaries: A case study of workplace use of Facebook and LinkedIn. In *Proceedings of the ACM 2009 International Conference on Supporting Group Work (GROUP 2009)*, (pp. 95-104). New York, NY: ACM Press.

Thompson, M., & Heron, P. (2005). The difference a manager can make: Organizational justice and knowledge worker commitment. *International Journal of Human Resource Management, 16*(3), 383–404. doi:10.1080/0958519042000339561

Tong, J., & Shaikh, S. A. (2010). Communications: Wireless in developing countries and networks of the future. *IFIP Advances in Information and Communication Technology, 327*, 60–71. doi:10.1007/978-3-642-15476-8_7

Toosi, M. (2006). A new look at long-term labor force projections to 2050. *Monthly Labor Review*. Retrieved from http://www.bls.gov/opub/mlr/2006/11/art3full.pdf.

Weaver, A. C., & Morrison, B. B. (2008). Social networking. *Compute, 41*(2), 97–100. doi:10.1109/MC.2008.61

Yuksel, M. (2011). Core competencies of managers in an emerging market. *Journal of American Academy of Business, 17*(1), 104–111.

Zin, R. M., & Talat, N. A. (2011). Can functional performances of HRM be improved with the adoption of IT? *The Cambridge Business Review, 18*(1), 48–53.

KEY TERMS AND DEFINITIONS

Adaptive/Assistive Technology: Technologies that enable persons with disabilities to work more efficiently by adapting the information on computer screen to make it easier to read, translate it to Braille or other forms.

Digital Divide: A gap between generations with regard to technology.

Emerging Economies/Markets: Low-income countries that through economic liberation, restructuring of government policies and the liberation of national trade agreements have achieved global shares of the international market.

Knowledge Management System (KMS): An information system used to capture, organize, and create knowledge to enhance organizational processes.

Learning Management System (LMS): A software application that automates the administration, tracking and reporting of training events. (Ellis, 2009)

Learning Organization: An organization that identifies the employees as a long-term strategic investment and recognizes the vital importance to develop the unique individual competencies of each member.

Social Networking/Marketing: Social networking sites are Internet-based services that allow users to create public or semi-public profiles that connect them to other users (Boyd and Ellison, 2008)

Talent Management System (TMS): A comprehensive Human Resource process that integrates recruitment, performance management; compensation management, training and development, and succession planning.

TCP/IP: Transmission Control Protocol/Internet Protocol - Commonly referred to as TCP/IP, it is a standard that connects computers around the world to create what we have now come to know as the Internet.

Compilation of References

4 icu.org University Web Ranking. (2011). *Top 100 universities and colleges in Africa*. Retrieved 6/6/2011, from http://www.4icu.org/topAfrica/.

4 International Universities and Colleges. (2011). *2011 world university ranking: Top 200 colleges and universities in the world by university web ranking*. Retrieved on 6/6/2011 from http://www.4icu.org/top200/.

AARP. (2005). *The business case for workers age 50+: Planning for tomorrow's talent needs in today's competitive environment*. Washington, DC: AARP. Retrieved May 21, 2011 from http://assets.aarp.org/rgcenter/econ/workers_fifty_plus_1.pdf.

AARP. (2007). *Leading a multigenerational workforce*. Washington, DC: AARP. Retrieved May 14, 2011 from http://assets.aarp.org/www.aarp.org_/articles/money/employers/leading_multigenerational_workforce.pdf.

Abe, H., & Wiseman, R. L. (1983). A cross-cultural confirmation of the dimensions of intercultural effectiveness. *International Journal of Intercultural Relations, 7*, 53–67. doi:10.1016/0147-1767(83)90005-6

AchieveGlobal Inc. (2010). *Developing the 21st century leader: A multi-level analysis of global trends in leadership challenges and practices*. Retrieved from http://www.achieveglobal.com.

Acker, J. (1992). From sex roles to gendered institutions. *Contemporary Sociology, 21*(5), 565–569. doi:10.2307/2075528

Acker, J. (1998). The future of 'gender and organizations': Connections and boundaries. *Gender, Work and Organization, 5*(4), 195–206. doi:10.1111/1468-0432.00057

Acquavita, S. P., Pittman, J., Gibbons, M., & Castellanos-Brown, K. (2009). Personal and organizational diversity factors' impact on social workers' job satisfaction: Results from a national internet-based survey. *Administration in Social Work, 33*(2), 151–166. doi:10.1080/03643100902768824

Adams, M., & Zhou-McGovern, Y. (1993). *Connecting research to college teaching practice: Developmental findings applied to social diversity classes*. Paper presented at the 8th Annual Adult Development Society for Research in Adult Development. Amherst, MA.

Adams, T. (2010). Paradoxes of sexuality, gay identity, and the closet. *Symbolic Interaction, 33*(2), 234–256. doi:10.1525/si.2010.33.2.234

Aditya, R., & House, R. J. (2002). Interpersonal acumen and leadership across cultures: Pointers from the GLOBE study. In Riggio, R. E., & Murphy, S. E. (Eds.), *Multiple Intelligences and Leadership* (pp. 215–240). Mahwah, NJ: Erlbaum.

Adler, N. J. (2002). *International dimensions of organizational behavior* (4th ed.). Cincinnati, OH: South-Western/Thomson Learning.

Adler, N. J., & Gunderson, A. (2008). *International dimensions of organizational behavior* (5th ed.). Mason, OH: South-Western Cengage Learning.

Adler, S. (2000). Project management competence: Building key skills for individuals, teams, and organizations. *Personnel Psychology, 53*(3), 778–780.

Adobor, H., & McMullen, R. (2007). Supplier diversity and supply chain management: A strategic approach. *Business Horizons, 50*, 279–329. doi:10.1016/j.bushor.2006.10.003

Afrimap. (2011). *Treaty of ECOWAS*. Retrieved on 23/05/2011 from http://www.afrimap.org/english/images/treaty/ECOWAS%20Treaty.pdf.

Agocs, C., & Burr, C. (1996). Employment equity affirmative action d managing diversity: Assessing the differences. *International Journal of Manpower, 17*, 30–45. doi:10.1108/01437729610127668

Ake, C. (1981). *Revolutionary pressures in Africa*. London, UK: Zed Books.

Al Ariss, A., & Ozbilgin, M. (2010). Understanding self-initiated expatriates: Career experiences of Lebanese self-initiated expatriates in France. *Thunderbird International Business Review, 52*(4), 275–285. doi:10.1002/tie.20355

Alavi, M., & Leidner, D. E. (2001). Knowledge management and knowledge management systems: Conceptual foundations and research issues. *Management Information Systems Quarterly, 25*(1), 107–136. doi:10.2307/3250961

Alavi, M., & Leidner, D. E. (2001). Review: Knowledge management and knowledge management systems: Conceptual foundations and research issues. *Management Information Systems Quarterly, 25*(1), 107–236. doi:10.2307/3250961

Alcantara, L., Hayes, S., & Yorks, L. (2009). Collaborative inquiry in action: Transformative learning through co-inquiry. In Mezirow, J., & Taylor, E. (Eds.), *Transformative Learning in Practice: Insights from Community, Workplace, and Higher Education* (pp. 251–261). San Francisco, CA: Jossey-Bass.

Alcoff, L. M. (2005). *Visible identities: Race, gender, and the self*. Oxford, UK: Oxford University Press.

Aldrich, H. E., & Fiol, C. M. (1994). Fools rush in? The institutional context of industry creation. *Academy of Management Review, 19*(4), 645–670.

Alemika, E. E. O. (2008). *Human resource management in the Nigeria police force: Challenges and imperatives*. Paper presented at the Police Service Commission Retreat on Understanding the Mandate and Operations of the Police Service Commission. Ada, Nigeria.

Alemika, E. E. O. (2009). Nature and pattern of transitional organized crime in West Africa. In A. O. Oluseyi & D. O. Ogaba (Eds.), *Transnational Crime and Security in West Africa*, (pp. 1-11). Lagos: Foreign Service Academy, Ministry of Foreign Affairs.

Alfred, M. V. (2000). The politics of knowledge and theory construction in adult education: A critical analysis from an Africentric feminist perspective. In *Proceedings of the 41st Annual Adult Education Research Conference*, (pp. 6-10). Vancouver, Canada: University of British Columbia.

Alfred, M. (2002). Linking the personal and the social for a more critical democratic adult education. In Alfred, M. V. (Ed.), *Learning in Sociocultural Context: Implications for Adults, Community, and Workplace Education* (*Vol. 4*, pp. 89–95). San Francisco, CA: Jossey-Bass. doi:10.1002/ace.82

Allard, J. M. (2002). Theoretical underpinnings of diversity. In Harvey, C., & Allard, M. J. (Eds.), *Understanding and Managing Diversity*. Upper Saddle River, NJ: Prentice Hall.

Allen, R. S., & Montgomery, K. A. (2001). Applying an organizational development approach to creating diversity. *Organizational Dynamics, 30*(2), 149–161. doi:10.1016/S0090-2616(01)00049-3

Allen, T. J., Tushman, M. L., & Lee, D. M. (1979). Technology transfer as a function of position in the spectrum from research through development to technical services. *Academy of Management Journal, 22*(4), 694–708. doi:10.2307/255809

Allison, M. T. (2001). *Diversity issues and challenges facing youth-related nonprofit agencies: A report prepared for the center for nonprofit leadership and management*. Tempe, AZ: Arizona State University. Retrieved September 8, 2005, from http://www.asu.edu/copp/nonprofit/res/div_issue_fr.pdf.

Alpay, G., Bodur, M., Ener, H., & Taluğ, C. (2005). Comparing board-level governance at MNEs and local firms: Lessons from Turkey. *Journal of International Management, 11*, 67–86. doi:10.1016/j.intman.2004.11.005

Alund, A. (2003). Self-employment of non-privileged groups as integration strategy. *International Review of Sociology, 13*(1), 77–87.

Alvesson, M., & Due Billing, Y. (1997). *Understanding gender and organizations*. London, UK: Sage Publications.

AMA. (1999). *Diverse leadership teams are more productive: Findings from the American management association*. Retrieved from http://www.diversityweb.org.

Amason, A. C. (1996). Distinguishing the effects of functional and dysfunctional conflict on strategic decision making: Resolving a paradox for top management teams. *Academy of Management Journal, 39*(1), 123–148. doi:10.2307/256633

Amason, A. C., & Mooney, A. C. (2000). The effects of past performance on top management team conflict in strategic decision making. *The International Journal of Conflict Management, 10*, 340–359. doi:10.1108/eb022829

American Federation of Teachers. (2010). *Promoting racial and ethnic diversity in the faculty: What higher education unions can do*. Washington, DC: AFT Higher Education.

American Federation of Teachers. (2011). *Promoting gender diversity in the faculty: What higher education unions can do*. Washington, DC: AFT Higher Education.

Amla, I. (2008). Managing and sustaining a world of workplace diversity: The Accenture experience. *Strategic HR Review, 7*(5), 11–16. doi:10.1108/14754390810893044

Anand, R., & Winters, M. (2008). A retrospective view of corporate diversity training from 1964 to the present. *Academy of Management Learning & Education, 7*(3), 356–372. doi:10.5465/AMLE.2008.34251673

Ancona, D., & Caldwell, D. (1992). Demography and design: predictors of new product team performance. *Organization Science, 3*, 342–355. doi:10.1287/orsc.3.3.321

Andersen, M. L., & Collins, P. H. (Eds.). (2001). *Race class and gender: An anthology* (4th ed.). Belmont, CA: Wadsworth Thomson Learning.

Anderson Executive, M. B. A. Program. (2011). *University of California – LA's online course catalog*. Retrieved from http://www.anderson.ucla.edu/emba.xml.

Anderson, E., & Weitz, B. (1989). Determinants of continuity in conventional industrial channel dyads. *Marketing Science, 8*, 310–323. doi:10.1287/mksc.8.4.310

Anderson, E., & Weitz, B. (1992). The use of pledges to build and sustain commitment in distribution channels. *JMR, Journal of Marketing Research, 29*, 18–34. doi:10.2307/3172490

Anderson, T. H. (2005). *The pursuit of fairness: A history of affirmative action*. New York, NY: Oxford University Press.

Anderson, T., & Metcalf, H. (2003). *Diversity: Stacking up the evidence*. London, UK: CIPD.

Andolsek, D. M., & Stebe, J. (2004). Multinational perspectives on work values and commitment. *International Journal of Cross Cultural Management, 4*(2), 181–209. doi:10.1177/1470595804044749

Anonymous. (2004). Blended is better. *T + D, 58*(11), 52-55.

Apple. (2009). *Apple and procurement*. Retrieved May 1, 2009 from http://www.apple.com/procurement/.

Aquino, K., & Byron, K. (2002). Dominating interpersonal behavior and perceived victimization in groups: Evidence for a curvilinear relationship. *Journal of Management, 28*(1), 69–87. doi:10.1177/014920630202800105

Aquino, K., & Douglas, S. (2003). Identity threat and antisocial behavior in organizations: The moderating effects of individual differences, aggressive modeling, and hierarchical status. *Organizational Behavior and Human Decision Processes, 90*, 195–208. doi:10.1016/S0749-5978(02)00517-4

Aquino, K., Stewart, M. M., & Reed, A. (2005). How social dominance orientation and job status influence perceptions of African-American affirmative action beneficiaries. *Personnel Psychology, 58*, 703–744. doi:10.1111/j.1744-6570.2005.681.x

Arabsheibani, R., Marin, A., & Wadsworth, J. (2007). Variations in gay pay in the USA and in the UK. In Badgett, M. V. L., & Frank, J. (Eds.), *Sexual Orientation Discrimination: An International Perspective* (pp. 44–61). London, UK: Taylor & Francis/Routledge.

Armstrong, N. (2001). *Learning strategy preferences of international graduate students at Oklahoma State University*. Unpublished Doctoral Dissertation. Norman, OK: Oklahoma State University.

Armstrong, C., Flood, P. C., Guthrie, J. P., Liu, W., Maccurtain, S., & Mkamwa, T. (2010). The impact of diversity and equality management on firm performance: beyond high performance work systems. *Human Resource Management, 49*(6), 977–998. doi:10.1002/hrm.20391

Armstrong, D., & Cole, P. (2002). Managing distances and differences in geographically distributed work groups. In Hinds, P., & Kiesler, S. (Eds.), *Distributed Work* (pp. 167–189). Cambridge, MA: MIT Press. doi:10.1037/10189-007

Asante, M. K. (1987). *The Afrocentric idea*. Philadelphia, PA: Temple University Press.

Ashkanasy, N. M., Hartel, C. E., & Daus, C. S. (2002). Diversity and emotion: The new frontiers in organizational behavior research. *Journal of Management, 28*(3), 307–338. doi:10.1177/014920630202800304

Avery, D. R. (2011). Support for diversity in organizations: A theoretical exploration of its origins and offshoots. *Organizational Psychology Review, 1*, 239–256. doi:10.1177/2041386611402115

Avery, D. R., McKay, P. F., & Wilson, D. C. (2007). Engaging the aging workforce: The relationship between perceived age similarity, satisfaction with coworkers, and employee engagement. *The Journal of Applied Psychology, 92*(6), 1542–1556. doi:10.1037/0021-9010.92.6.1542

Avolio, B. J., & Bass, B. M. (2004). *MLQ - Multifactor leadership questionnaire*. Menlo Park, CA: Mind Garden.

Awbrey, S. M. (2007). The dynamics of vertical and horizontal diversity in organization and society. *Human Resource Development Review, 6*(1), 7–32. doi:10.1177/1534484306295638

Aycan, Z. (2005). The interplay between cultural and institutional/structural contingencies in human resource management practices. *International Journal of Human Resource Management, 16*(7), 1083–1119. doi:10.1080/09585190500143956

Bacharach, S. B., Bamberger, P. A., & Vashdi, D. (2005). Diversity and homophily at work: Supportive relations among whites and African American peers. *Academy of Management Journal, 48*(4), 619–644. doi:10.5465/AMJ.2005.17843942

Badgett, L. (2001). *Money, myths, and change: The economic lives of lesbians and gay men*. Chicago, IL: University of Chicago Press.

Bagozzi, R. P. (1980). Performance and satisfaction in an industrial sales force: An examination of their antecedents simultaneity. *Journal of Marketing, 44*(2), 65–77. doi:10.2307/1249978

Ballone, C. (2007). Consulting your clients to leverage the multigenerational workforce. *Journal of Practical Consulting, 2*(1), 9-15. Retrieved May 27, 2011 from http://www.regent.edu/acad/global/publications/jpc/vol2iss1/ballone/JPCVol2Iss1_Ballone.pdf.

Baltes, B. B., Dickson, M. W., Sherman, M. P., Bauer, C. C., & LaGanke, J. S. (2002). Computer-mediated communication and group decision making: A meta-analysis. *Organizational Behavior and Human Decision Processes, 87*(1), 156–179. doi:10.1006/obhd.2001.2961

Banai, M., & William, R. D. (1999). Would you trust your foreign manager? An empirical investigation. *International Journal of Human Resource Management, 10*(3), 477–487. doi:10.1080/095851999340431

Bandura, A. (1977). *Social learning theory*. Englewood Cliffs, NJ: Prentice-Hall.

Bandura, A. (1982). Self efficacy mechanism in human agency. *The American Psychologist, 37*(3), 122–147. doi:10.1037/0003-066X.37.2.122

Bandura, A. (1986). *Social foundations of thought and action: A social cognitive theory*. Englewood Cliffs, NJ: Prentice-Hall.

Banks, C. H., & Nafukho, F. M. (2008). Career transitions across and within organizations: Implications for human resource development. In T. M. Chermack & J. Storberg-Walker (Eds.), *2008 Academy of Human Resource Development Annual Research Conference Proceedings,* (pp. 1096- 1102). Bowling Green, OH: Academy of Human Resource Development.

Banks, C. H. (2006). Career planning: Toward an inclusive model. In Karsten, M. (Ed.), *Gender, Race and Ethnicity in the Workplace* (*Vol. 3*, pp. 99–116). Westport, CT: Greenwood. Publishing Group, Inc.

Banks, J. A. (2006). *Race, culture, and education: The selected works of James A. Banks*. New York, NY: Routledge.

Bantel, K., & Jackson, S. (1989). Top management and innovations in banking: does the composition of the top team make a difference? *Strategic Management Journal, 10*, 107–124. doi:10.1002/smj.4250100709

Banton, M. (2000). The idiom of race: A critique of presentation. In Back, L., & Solomos, J. (Eds.), *Racialization* (pp. 51–58). Oxford, UK: Oxford University Press.

Banutu-Gomez, M., & Rohrer, W. G. (2011). Teams in organization. *The Cambridge Business Review, 18*(1), 54–60.

Barkema, H. G., & Shvyrkov, O. (2007). Does TMT promote or hamper foreign expansion? *Strategic Management Journal, 28*, 663–680. doi:10.1002/smj.604

Barlas, C., Kasl, E., Kyle, R., MacLeod, A., Paxton, D., Rosenwasser, P., & Sartor, L. (2000). *Cooperative inquiry as a strategy for facilitating perspective transformation.* Retrieved on August 2, 2001, from http://www.iconoclastic.net/eccw/papers/barlasetal2000b.pdf.

Barney, J. (1991). Firm resources and sustained competitive advantage. *Journal of Management, 17,* 99–120. doi:10.1177/014920639101700108

Barney, J. B., & Wright, P. M. (1998). On becoming a strategic partner: The role of human resources in gaining competitive advantage. *Human Resource Management, 37,* 31–46. doi:10.1002/(SICI)1099-050X(199821)37:1<31::AID-HRM4>3.0.CO;2-W

Baron, R. A., & Neuman, J. H. (1996). Workplace violence and workplace aggression: Evidence on their relative frequency and potential causes. *Aggressive Behavior, 22,* 161–173. doi:10.1002/(SICI)1098-2337(1996)22:3<161::AID-AB1>3.0.CO;2-Q

Baron, R. A., & Neuman, J. H. (1998). Workplace aggression – The iceberg beneath the tip of workplace violence: Evidence on its forms, frequency, and targets. *Public Administration Quarterly, 21*(4), 446–464.

Barratt, I. C., Cervero, R. M., & Johnson-Bailey, J. (2004). The career development of black human resource developers in the United States. *Human Resource Development International, 7*(1), 85–100. doi:10.1080/1367886022000032354

Barrington, L., & Troske, K. (2001). *Workforce diversity and productivity: An analysis of employer-employee matched data.* Working Paper Series EPWP #01 – 02. New York, NY: Conference Board Economics Program.

Barr, J. (1999). *Liberating knowledge, research, feminism and adult education.* Leicester, UK: NIACE.

Bar-Tal, D. (1997). Formation and change of ethnic and national stereotypes: An integrative model. *International Journal of Intercultural Relations, 21*(4), 491–523. doi:10.1016/S0147-1767(97)00022-9

Bar-Tal, D., & Labin, D. (2001). The effect of a major event on stereotyping: Terrorist attacks in Israel and Israeli adolescents' perceptions of Palestinians, Jordanians, and Arabs. *European Journal of Social Psychology, 31,* 1–17. doi:10.1002/ejsp.43

Bartel-Radic, A. (2006). Intercultural learning in global teams. *Management International Review, 46*(6), 647–677. doi:10.1007/s11575-006-0121-7

Baruch, Y. (2004). Transforming careers from linear to multidirectional career paths: Organizational and individual perspectives. *Career Development International, 9*(1), 58–73. doi:10.1108/13620430410518147

Baruch, Y. (2006). Career development in organizations and beyond: Balancing traditional and contemporary viewpoints. *Human Resource Management Review, 16*(2), 125–138. doi:10.1016/j.hrmr.2006.03.002

Baseman, T. S., & Strasser, S. (1984). A longitudinal analysis of the antecedents of organizational commitment. *Academy of Management Journal, 27*(1), 95–112. doi:10.2307/255959

Bass, B. M. (1985). *Leadership and performance beyond expectations.* New York, NY: Free Press.

Bass, B. M., & Riggio, R. E. (2006). *Transformational leadership.* Mahwah, NJ: Erlbaum.

Bass, B., & Steidlmeier, P. (1999). Ethics, character, and authentic transformational leadership behavior. *The Leadership Quarterly, 10*(2), 181–217. doi:10.1016/S1048-9843(99)00016-8

Bassett-Jones, N. (2005). The paradox of diversity management, creativity and innovation. *Creativity and Innovation Management, 14*(2), 169–175. doi:10.1111/j.1467-8691.00337.x

Bass, L. (2009). Fostering an ethic of care in leadership: A conversation with five African American women. *Advances in Developing Human Resources, 11*(5). doi:10.1177/1523422309352075

Bauer, M. (2000). Classical content analysis: A review. In Bauer, M. W., & Gaskell, G. (Eds.), *Qualitative Researching with Text, Image, and Sound: A Practical Handbook* (pp. 131–151). London, UK: Sage.

BCG. (2009, August 3). *Largest global survey of women finds that no matter where they live, women are overworked, over-extended, over-stressed and under-served by businesses.* Retrieved April 2, 2011, from http://www.bcg.com.

Beatty, J. E., & Kirby, S. L. (2006). Beyond the legal environment: How stigma influences invisible identity groups in the workplace. *Employee Responsibilities and Rights Journal, 18*(1), 29–44. doi:10.1007/s10672-005-9003-6

Becher, T., & Trowler, P. R. (2001). *Academic tribes and territories: Intellectual enquiry and the culture of disciplines* (2nd ed.). Buckingham, UK: Society for Research into Higher Education and Open University Press.

Becker, B. E., & Huselid, M. A. (1998). High performance work systems and firm performance: A synthesis of research and managerial implications. *Research in Personnel and Human Resources Journal, 16*(1), 53–101.

Beck, U. (1992). *Risk society: Towards a new modernity.* Thousand Oaks, CA: Sage.

Beeth, G. (1997, May). Multicultural managers wanted. *Management Review*, 17–21.

Bekmeier-Feuerhahn, S., & Eichenlaub, A. (2010). What makes for trust relationships in on-line communication. *Journal of Communication Management, 14*(4), 337–355. doi:10.1108/13632541011090446

Belenky, M., Clinchy, B., Goldberger, N., & Tarule, J. (1986). *Women's ways of knowing.* New York, NY: Basic Books.

Belenky, M., Goldberger, N., Tarule, J., & Mcvicker, B. (1998). *Knowledge, difference, and power: Essays inspired by women's ways of knowing.* New York, NY: Basic Books.

Bell, D. A. (1993). Remembrance of racism past: The civil rights decline. In Hill, H., & Jones, J. E. (Eds.), *Race in America: The Struggle for Equality* (pp. 73–82). Madison, WI: University of Wisconsin Press.

Bell, E. L. (1990). The bicultural life experience of career-oriented black women. *Journal of Organizational Behavior, 11*, 459–477. doi:10.1002/job.4030110607

Bell, E. L., & Nkomo, S. (2001). *Our separate ways: Black and White women and the struggle for professional identity.* Boston, MA: Harvard Business School Press.

Bell, M. P. (2007). *Diversity in organizations.* Mason, OH: Cengage.

Bell, M. P. (2009). Effects of the experience of inequality, exclusion and discrimination on scholarship. In Özbilgin, M. F. (Ed.), *Equality, Diversity and Inclusion at Work: A Research Companion* (pp. 17–26). Cheltenham, UK: Edward Elgar.

Bell, M. P., Connerley, M. L., & Cocchiara, F. K. (2009). The case for mandatory diversity education. *Academy of Management Learning & Education, 8*(4), 597–609. doi:10.5465/AMLE.2009.47785478

Bendick, M. Jr, Egan, M. L., & Lofhjelm, S. M. (2001). Workforce diversity training: From anti-discrimination compliance to organizational development. *Human Resource Planning, 24*(2), 10–25.

Benhamou, F., & Peltier, S. (2007). How should cultural diversity be measured? An application using the French publishing industry. *Journal of Cultural Economics, 31*(2), 85–107. doi:10.1007/s10824-007-9037-8

Benkler, Y. (2011). *The university in the networked economy and society: Challenges and opportunities.* Retrieved on 22/05/2011 from http://www.educause.edu/thetowerandthecloud/PUB7202f.

Benschop, Y. (2001). Pride, prejudice and performance: Relations between HRM, diversity and performance. *International Journal of Human Resource Management, 12*(7), 1166–1181. doi:10.1080/09585190110068377

Benson, P. G. (1978). Measuring cross-cultural adjustment: The problem of criteria. *International Journal of Intercultural Relations, 2*, 21–37. doi:10.1016/0147-1767(78)90027-5

Berelson, B. (1952). *Content analysis in communication research.* New York, NY: Free Press.

Berkeley-Columbia Executive, M.B.A. (2011). *University of California-Berkley's online course catalog.* Retrieved from http://berkeley.columbia.edu/.

Berkley, R. A., & Kaplan, D. M. (2009). Assessing liability for sexual harassment: Reactions of potential jurors to email versus face-to-face incidents. *Employee Responsibilities and Rights Journal, 21*, 195–211. doi:10.1007/s10672-009-9110-x

Berkley, R. A., & Watt, A. H. (2006). Impact of same-sex harassment and gender-role stereotypes on title VII protection for gay, lesbian, and bisexual employees. *Employee Responsibilities and Rights Journal, 18*(1), 3–19. doi:10.1007/s10672-005-9001-8

Bernal, D. (2002). Critical race theory, Latino critical theory, and critical raced-gendered epistemologies: Recognizing students of color as holders and creators of knowledge. *Qualitative Inquiry, 8*(1), 105–126.

Bernal, M. E., Knight, G. P., Ocampo, K. A., Garza, C. A., & Cota, M. K. (1990). The development of ethnic identity in Mexican-American children. *Hispanic Journal of Behavioral Sciences, 12*(1), 3–24. doi:10.1177/07399863900121001

Bernstein, L., Alexander, D., & Alexander, B. (2011). *Generations: Harnessing the potential of the multigenerational workforce*. Retrieved May 18, 2011 from http://www.trainingsolutions.com/pdf/Generations_Perspective.pdf.

Bernstein, M. (1997). Celebration and suppression: The strategic use of identity by the lesbian and gay movement. *American Journal of Sociology, 103*(3), 531–565. doi:10.1086/231250

Bernstein, M. (2011). Multi-institutional politics, social movements and the state: Lesbian and gay activism in the U.S. In Johnson, C., Paternotte, D., & Tremblay, M. (Eds.), *The Lesbian and Gay Movement and the State: Comparative Insights into a Transformed Relationship*. London, UK: Ashgate.

Bernstein, M., & Cruz, M. (2009). "What are you?" Explaining identity as a goal of the multiracial hapa movement. *Social Problems, 56*(4), 722–745. doi:10.1525/sp.2009.56.4.722

Bernstein, M., & Olsen, K. A. (2009). Identity deployment and social change: Understanding identity as a social movement and organizational strategy. *Social Compass, 3*(6), 871–883. doi:10.1111/j.1751-9020.2009.00255.x

Berry, L. L., & Parasuraman, A. (1991). *Marketing services*. New York, NY: The Free Press.

Berscheid, E., & Walster, H. (1978). *Interpersonal attraction*. Reading, MA: Addison-Wesley.

Best Executive, M. B. A. Programs. (2010). *Wall Street Journal's online rankings*. Retrieved from http://online.wsj.com/public/resources/documents/EMBA-Top-25-Ranking.html.

Bevington, D., & Dixon, C. (2005). Movement-relevant theory: Rethinking social movement scholarship and activism. *Social Movement Studies, 4*(3), 185–208. doi:10.1080/14742830500329838

Bhasin, B. B., & Cheng, P. L. K. (2001). *The fight for global talent: New directions, new competitors - A case study on Singapore*. Retrieved from http://www.emeraldinsight.com/Insight/ViewContentServlet:jsessionid=7CADD0491D61.

Bhayani, H. (2007, May 15). Efforts to prove workforce diversity fail to help win contracts. *Personnel Today*, 3.

Bhide´, A. (2008). *The venturesome economy*. Princeton, NJ: Princeton University Press.

Bible, J. (2001). Gender stereotyping: Courts open the door to title VII claims by homosexuals. *Journal of Employment Discrimination Law, 3*(1), 27–33.

Bible, J. D. (2002). Same-sex sexual harassment: When does a harasser act 'because of sex'. *Labor Law Journal, 53*(1), 3–10.

Bicchieri, C., & Lev-On, A. (2011). Studying the ethical implications of e-trust in the lab. *Ethics and Information Technology, 13*, 5–15. doi:10.1007/s10676-010-9258-y

Bierema, L. (2010). Resisting HRD's resistance to diversity. *Journal of European Industrial Training, 34*(6), 565–576. doi:10.1108/03090591011061239

Bierema, L. L. (1999). A model of executive women's learning and development. *Adult Education Quarterly, 49*(2), 107–122. doi:10.1177/074171369904900203

Bierema, L. L. (2001). Women, work, and, learning. In Fenwick, T. J. (Ed.), *Sociocultural Perspectives on Learning through Work* (Vol. 92, pp. 53–62). San Francisco, CA: Jossey Bass.

Bierema, L. L., & Cseh, M. (2003). Evaluating AHRD research using a feminist research framework. *Human Resource Development Quarterly, 14*(1), 5–26. doi:10.1002/hrdq.1047

Bighorn, R. (1997). *Learning strategies in the Fort Peck reservation community*. Unpublished Doctoral Dissertation. Bozeman, MT: Montana State University.

Bingham, K., Gewin, A., Hu, C., Thomas, K., & Yanchus, N. (2005). The roles of protégé race, gender, and proactive socialization attempts on peer monitoring. *Advances in Developing Human Resources*, *7*(4), 540–555. doi:10.1177/1523422305279681

Bjorkqvist, K., Osterman, K., & Hjelt-Back, M. (1994). Aggression among university employees. *Aggressive Behavior*, *20*, 173–184. doi:10.1002/1098-2337(1994)20:3<173::AID-AB2480200304>3.0.CO;2-D

Blackburn, R., Furst, S., & Rosen, B. (2003). Building a winning virtual team: KSAs, selection, training and evaluation. In Gibson, C., & Cohen, S. (Eds.), *Virtual Teams that Work: Creating Conditions for Virtual Team Effectiveness* (pp. 95–120). San Francisco, CA: Jossey-Bass.

Black, J. S., & Gregersen, H. B. (2000). High impact training: Forging leaders for the global frontier. *Human Resource Management*, *39*(2-3), 173–184. doi:10.1002/1099-050X(200022/23)39:2/3<173::AID-HRM7>3.0.CO;2-W

Blair, I. V. (2002). The malleability of automatic stereotypes and prejudice. *Personality and Social Psychology Review*, *6*(3), 242–261. doi:10.1207/S15327957PSPR0603_8

Blake, R. R., & Mouton, S. (1981). Management by grid principles or situationalism: Which? *Group & Organization Management*, *6*, 439–455. doi:10.1177/105960118100600404

Blake, R. R., & Mouton, S. (1982, Spring). A comparative analysis of situationalism and 9, 9 management by principle. *Organizational Dynamics*, 20–43. doi:10.1016/0090-2616(82)90027-4

Blake, R., & Mouton, J. (1972a). What is instrumented learning? Part I--Learning instruments. *Industrial Training International*, *7*(4), 113–116.

Blau, P. M. (1964). *Exchange and power in social life*. New York, NY: Wiley.

Bloom, B., Mesia, B., & Krathwohl, D. (1964). *Taxonomy of educational objectives*. New York, NY: David McKay Co Inc.

BLS. (2009). *Employment projections 2008*. Retrieved from http://www.bls.gov.

BLS. (2011). *Women at work*. Retrieved April 2, 2011, from http://www.bls.gov/spotlight/2011/women/.

Bochner, S. (1982). The social psychology of cross-cultural relations. In Bochner, S. (Ed.), *Cultures in Contact: Studies in Cross-Cultural Interaction* (pp. 5–44). New York, NY: Pergamon.

Boeker, W. (1997). Executive migration and strategic change: The effect of top manager movement on product market entry. *Administrative Science Quarterly*, *42*(2), 213–236. doi:10.2307/2393919

Boggs, C. (1986). *Social movements and political power: Emerging forms of radicalism in the west*. Philadelphia, PA: Temple University Press.

Booth Executive, M. B. A. Program. (2011). *University of Chicago's online course catalog*. Retrieved from http://www.chicagobooth.edu/execmba/index.aspx.

Boston Consulting Group. (2005). *The new agenda for minority business development*. Boston, MA: Boston Consulting Group.

Boston Executive, M. B. A. Program. (2011). *Boston University's online course catalog*. Retrieved from http://www.bu.edu/emba/?utm_source=adwords&utm_medium=cpc&utm_campaign=emba-adwords.

Boudreau, M. C., Loch, K. D., Robey, D., & Straub, D. (1998). Going global: Using information technology to advance the competitiveness of the virtual transnational organization. *The Academy of Management Executive*, *12*(4), 120–128. doi:10.5465/AME.1998.1334008

Boudreaux, M. A. (2001). Career development: What is its role in human resource development? In O. A. Aliaga (Ed.), *Academy of HRD 2001 Conference Proceedings*, (pp. 805-812). Bowling Green, OH: Academy of Human Resource Development.

Bowen, C. E., Noack, C. M. G., & Staudinger, U. M. (2010). Aging in the work context. In Schaie, K. W., & Willis, S. (Eds.), *Handbook of the Psychology of Aging* (7th ed., pp. 263–278). San Diego, CA: Elsevier Academic Press.

Boxenbaum, E. (2006). Lost in translation? The making of Danish diversity management. *The American Behavioral Scientist, 49*(7), 939–948. doi:10.1177/0002764205285173

Bragge, J., Merisalo-Rantanen, H., Nurmi, A., & Tanner, L. (2007). A repeatable e-collaboration process based on thinkLets for multi-organization strategy development. *Group Decision and Negotiation, 16*(4), 363–379. doi:10.1007/s10726-006-9055-5

Brainerd, E. (2000). Women in transition: Changes in gender wage differentials in Eastern Europe and former Soviet Union. *Industrial & Labor Relations Review, 54*(1), 138–162. doi:10.2307/2696036

Brake, T. (1997). *The global leader: Critical factors for creating the world class organization*. Chicagom, IL: Irwin Professional Publishing.

Brass, D. J., & Burkhardt, M. E. (1993). Potential power and power use: An investigation of structure and behavior. *Academy of Management Journal, 36*(3), 441–470. doi:10.2307/256588

Bray, J. (2002). Uniting teacher learning: Collaborative inquiry for professional development. *New Directions for Adult and Continuing Education, 94*, 83–92. doi:10.1002/ace.62

Bregman, P. (2009). A good way to change a corporate culture. *Harvard Business Review*. Retrieved November 2, 2010 from http://blogs.hbr.org.

Brenner, B. R., Lyons, H. Z., & Fassinger, R. E. (2010). Can heterosexism harm organizations? Predicting the perceived organizational citizenship behaviors of gay and lesbian employees. *The Career Development Quarterly, 58*, 321–335. doi:10.1002/j.2161-0045.2010.tb00181.x

Brewer, M. (1979). Ingroup bias in the minimal group situation: A cognitive-motivational analysis. *Psychological Bulletin, 86*, 307–324. doi:10.1037/0033-2909.86.2.307

Brewer, M. (1991). The social self: On being the same and different at the same time. *Personality and Social Psychology Bulletin, 17*, 475–482. doi:10.1177/0146167291175001

Brewer, M. B. (1979). In group bias in the minimal intergroup situation: A cognitive-motivational analysis. *Psychological Bulletin, 86*, 307–324. doi:10.1037/0033-2909.86.2.307

Brief, A. P., Dietz, J., Cohen, R. R., Pugh, S. D., & Vaslow, J. B. (2000). Just doing business: Modern racism and obedience to authority as explanations for employment discrimination. *Organizational Behavior and Human Decision Processes, 81*, 72–97. doi:10.1006/obhd.1999.2867

Briggs, R. O. (2006). The value frequency model: Towards a theoretical understanding of organizational change. In S. Seifert & C. Weinhardt (Eds.), *International Conference on Group Decision and Negotiation*. Karlsruhe, Germany: Karlsruhe University Press.

Briggs, R. O., de Vreede, G. J., Nunamaker, J. F., & David, T. H. (2001). ThinkLets: Achieving predictable, repeatable patterns of group interaction with group support systems. In *Proceedings of the 34th International Conference on System Sciences*. Maui, HI: System Sciences.

Briggs, R. O., de Vreede, G. J., & Nunamaker, J. F. (2003). Collaboration engineering with thinkLets to pursue sustained success with group support systems. *Journal of Management Information Systems, 19*(4), 31–64.

Brislin, R. (2000). *Understanding culture's influence on behavior*. Florence, KY: Wadsworth Publishing.

Britt, G. (2007, September 17). Diversifying the supply chain. *Multichannel News*. Retrieved from http://www.highbeam.com/doc/1G1-168740825.html.

Brookfield, S. (1987). *Developing critical thinkers*. San Francisco, CA: Jossey-Bass.

Brookfield, S. (1992). Developing criteria for formal theory-building in adult education. *Adult Education Quarterly, 42*(2), 79–93. doi:10.1177/0001848192042002002

Brookfield, S. (1995). Adult learning: An overview. In Tuinjman, A. (Ed.), *International Encyclopedia of Education*. Oxford, UK: Pergamon Press.

Brookfield, S. (2003). Racializing criticality in adult education. *Adult Education Quarterly, 53*(3), 154–169. doi:10.1177/0741713603053003002

Brookfield, S. D. (1989). Facilitating adult learning. In Merriam, S. B., & Cunningham, P. (Eds.), *Handbook of Adult Education in the United States*. San Francisco, CA: Jossey-Bass.

Brooks, A. K., & Clunis, T. (2007). Where to now? Race and ethnicity in workplace learning and development research: 1980-2005. *Human Resource Development Quarterly, 18*(2), 229–251. doi:10.1002/hrdq.1201

Brownell, J. (2006). Meeting the competency needs of global leaders: A partnership approach. *Human Resource Management, 45*(3), 309–336. doi:10.1002/hrm.20115

Browning, C., Reynolds, A., & Dworkin, S. (1991). Affirmative psychotherapy for lesbian women. *The Counseling Psychologist, 19*, 177–196. doi:10.1177/0011000091192004

Brown, S. P., & Peterson, R. A. (1994). The effect of effort on sales performance and job satisfaction. *Journal of Marketing, 58*(2), 70–81. doi:10.2307/1252270

Brown, S., & Eisenhardt, K. (1995). Product development: Past research, present findings, and future directions. *Academy of Management Review, 20*(2), 343–378.

Brown, T. (2009). *Change by design.* New York, NY: Harper Business.

Bucher, R. D. (2008). *Building cultural intelligence (CQ).* Upper Saddle River, NJ: Pearson Education, Inc.

Buechler, S. M. (1995). New social movement theories. *The Sociological Quarterly, 36*(3), 441–464. doi:10.1111/j.1533-8525.1995.tb00447.x

Bueno, C. M., & Tubbs, S. L. (2004). Identifying global leadership competencies: An exploratory study. *Journal of American Academy of Business, 5*(1/2), 80–87.

Bureau of National Affairs. (2004). *Website.* Retrieved January 25, 2011, from http://www.bna.com.

Burkard, A. W., Boticki, M. A., & Madson, M. B. (2002). Workplace discrimination, prejudice, and diversity measurement: A review of instrumentation. *Journal of Career Assessment, 10*, 343. doi:10.1177/10672702010003005

Burke, C. S., Stagl, K. C., Klein, C., Goodwin, G. F., Salas, E., & Halpin, S. M. (2006). What type of leadership behaviors are functional in teams? A meta-analysis. *The Leadership Quarterly, 17*, 288–307. doi:10.1016/j.leaqua.2006.02.007

Burkhardt, M. E., & Brass, D. J. (1990). Changing patterns or patterns of change: The effects of a change in technology on social network structure and power. *Administrative Science Quarterly, 35*, 104–127. doi:10.2307/2393552

Burns, R. (2002). *The adult learner at work: The challenges of lifelong education in the new millennium* (2nd ed.). Crows Nest, UK: Allen & Unwin.

Business, E. (2003). Ethnic business support vital for urban regeneration. *Engineering Management, 13*(2), 5.

Butler, J. (1990). *Gender trouble: Feminism and the subversion of identity.* London, UK: Routledge.

Buttner, H., Lowe, K., & Billings-Harris, L. (2009). The challenge of increasing minority-group professional representation in the United States: Intriguing findings. *International Journal of Human Resource Management, 20*, 771–789. doi:10.1080/09585190902770604

Button, S. B. (2004). Identity management strategies utilized by lesbian and gay employees. *Group & Organization Management, 29*(4), 470–494. doi:10.1177/1059601103257417

Bye, L. B. (2003). Best practices for employee resource groups. *Diversity in Practice, 11*(2), 7–10.

Byrd, M. (2009b). Theorizing African American women's leadership experiences: Socio-cultural theoretical alternatives. *Advancing Women in Leadership Journal, 27*(2).

Byrd, M. (2007). Educating and developing leaders of racially diverse organizations. *Human Resource Development Quarterly, 18*(2), 275–279. doi:10.1002/hrdq.1203

Byrd, M. (2008). Negotiating new meanings of "leader" and envisioning culturally informed theories for developing African American women in leadership roles: An interview with Patricia Parker. *Human Resource Development International, 11*(1), 101–107. doi:10.1080/13678860701782477

Byrd, M. (2009). Telling our stories of leadership: If we don't tell them they won't be told. *Advances in Developing Human Resources, 11*(5). doi:10.1177/1523422309351514

Byrd, M., & Stanley, C. (2009). Bringing the voices together. *Advances in Developing Human Resources, 11*(5). doi:10.1177/1523422309351817

Byrd, M., & Stanley, C. (Eds.). (2009). Giving voice: The socio-cultural realities of African American women's leadership experiences. *Advances in Developing Human Resources, 11*(5).

Byrne, D. (1971). *The attraction paradigm.* New York, NY: Academic Press.

Cain, R. (1991). Disclosure and secrecy among gay men in the United States and Canada: A shift in views. *Journal of the History of Sexuality, 2*(1), 25–45.

Caldwell, Q. S., Mack, D., Johnson, C. D., & Biderman, M. D. (2002). *Value for diversity as a moderator of organizational relationships.* Paper presented at the 17th Annual Meeting of the Society for Industrial and Organizational Psychology. Toronto, Canada.

Caligiuri, P., & Tarique, I. (2009). Predicting effectiveness in global leadership activities. *Journal of World Business, 44*, 36–46. doi:10.1016/j.jwb.2008.11.005

Callanan, G. A., & Greenhaus, J. H. (2008). The baby boom generation and career management: A call to action. *Advances in Developing Human Resources, 10*(1), 70–85. doi:10.1177/1523422307310113

Campion, M. A., Papper, E. M., & Medsker, G. J. (1996). Relations between work team characteristics and effectiveness: A replication and extension. *The Personnel Journal, 49*(2), 429–452.

Cant, A. (2004). Internationalizing the business curriculum: Developing intercultural competence. *Journal of American Academy of Business, 5*, 177–182.

Capowsky, G. (1996). Managing diversity. *Management Review, 85*(6), 12–20.

Cappelli, P. (2001). Making the most of on-line recruiting. *Harvard Business Review, 79*, 139–146.

Cardon, P. W. (2006). The changing nature of global assignments: Implications for cross-cultural training. *International Business*, 48-50.

Carleton, K. (2011). How to motivate and retain knowledge workers in organizations: A review of the literature. *International Journal of Management, 28*(2), 459–468.

Carmel, E. (1999). *Global software teams: Collaborating across borders and time zones.* Upper Saddle River, NJ: Prentice Hall.

Carnevale, A., & Stone, S. (1994). Diversity beyond the golden rule. *Training & Development, 48*(10), 22–40.

Carnoy, M., & Rhoten, D. (2002). What does globalization mean for educational change? A comparative approach. *Comparative Education Review, 46*(1), 1–9. doi:10.1086/324053

Carpenter, M. A., & Fredrickson, J. W. (2001). Top management teams, global strategic posture, and the moderating role of uncertainty. *Academy of Management Journal, 44*(3), 533–546. doi:10.2307/3069368

Carpenter, M. A., Geletkanycz, M. A., & Sanders, W. G. (2004). Upper echelons research revisited: Antecedents, elements and consequences of top management team composition. *Journal of Management, 30*(6), 749–778. doi:10.1016/j.jm.2004.06.001

Carpenter, M. S. (2002). The implications of strategy and social context for the relationship between top management team heterogeneity and firm performance. *Strategic Management Journal, 23*(3), 275–284. doi:10.1002/smj.226

Carrell, M., Mann, E., & Honeycutt-Sigler, T. (2006). Defining workforce diversity programs and practices in organizations: A longitudinal study. *Labor Law Journal, 57*(1), 5–12.

Carr-Ruffino, N. (1991). U.S. women: Breaking through the glass ceiling. *Women in Management Review, 6*(5), 10–16. doi:10.1108/EUM0000000001801

Carr-Ruffino, N. (1992). Legal aspects of women's advancement. In Sekaran, U., & Leong, F. T. L. (Eds.), *Woman Power* (pp. 113–137). Thousand Oaks, CA: Sage.

Carr-Ruffino, N. (2007). *Managing diversity: People skills for a multicultural workplace* (7th ed.). Boston, MA: Pearson Custom Publishing.

Carter, S. D. (2010). Pushback: The negative HRD experiences afforded to post-tenure female faculty in the United States 1988-2004. In *Proceedings of the Academy of Human Resource Development Annual International Conference.* Knoxville, TN: HRD.

Cascio, W. F., & Shurygailo, S. (2003). E-leadership and virtual teams. *Organizational Dynamics, 31*, 362–376. doi:10.1016/S0090-2616(02)00130-4

Castilla, E. J. (2008). Gender, race and meritocracy in organizational careers. *American Journal of Sociology, 113*(6), 1479–1526. doi:10.1086/588738

Catalyst. (2006). *2005 catalyst census of women corporate officers and top earners of the fortune 500.* Retrieved October 3, 2010, from http://www.catalyst.org.

Catalyst. (2011). *Changing workplaces, changing lives: U.S. women in business.* Retrieved May 7, 2011 from http://www.catalyst.org.

Cavaleros, C., Van Vuuren, L. V., & Visser, D. (2002). The effectiveness of a diversity awareness training programme. *South African Journal of Industrial Psychology, 28*(3), 50–61.

Celent Communications. (2003). *Ethnic minorities, financial services, and the web.* Retrieved March 3, 2011, from http://www.celent.com.

Centre for Enterprise and Economic Development Research. (2001). *Website.* Retrieved on May 20, 2009 from http://sbs.gov.uk/content/pdf/embf/BBA_Access_to_Finance_Research.pdf.

Chalofsky, N. (1992). A unifying definition for the human resource development profession. *Human Resource Development Quarterly, 3*(2), 175–182. doi:10.1002/hrdq.3920030208

Chang, M. J. (2002). The impact of an undergraduate diversity course requirement on students' racial views and attitudes. *The Journal of General Education, 51*, 21–42. doi:10.1353/jge.2002.0002

Chang, W. (2007). Cultural competence of international humanitarian workers. *Adult Education Quarterly, 57*(3), 187–204. doi:10.1177/0741713606296755

Chatman, J. A., & Flynn, F. J. (2001). The influence of demographic heterogeneity on the emergence and consequences of cooperative norms in work teams. *Academy of Management Journal, 44*(5), 956–974. doi:10.2307/3069440

Chatman, J. A., & O'Reilly, C. A. (2004). Asymmetric reactions to work group sex diversity among men and women. *Academy of Management Journal, 47*, 193–208. doi:10.2307/20159572

Chaudhuri, S., & Ravallion, M. (2007). Partially awakened giants uncover growth in China and India. In Winters, L. A., & Yusuf, S. (Eds.), *Dancing with Giants: China, India, and the Global Economy.* Washington, DC: World Bank.

Chen, H. (2011). Does board independence influence the top management team? Evidence from strategic decisions toward internationalization. *Corporate Governance: An International Review, 19*(4).

Chiang, F., & Birtch, T. (2007). The transferability of management practices: Examining cross-national differences in reward preferences. *Human Relations, 60*(9), 1293–1330. doi:10.1177/0018726707082849

Childs, J. T. Jr. (2005). Managing workforce diversity at IBM: A global HR topic that has arrived. *Human Resource Management, 44*(1), 73–77. doi:10.1002/hrm.20042

Chin, C., Gu, J., & Tubbs, S. (2001). Developing global leadership competencies. *The Journal of Leadership Studies, 7*(3), 20–31. doi:10.1177/107179190100700402

Chinchilla, M. N., Poelmans, S., & León, C. (2003). *Políticas de conciliación trabajo-familia en 150 empresas españolas. Documento de investigación número 498.* Pamplona, Spain: IESE Business School, Universidad de Navarra.

Chin, S. (2010). I am a human being, and I belong to the world: Narrating the intersection of spirituality and social identity. *Journal of Transformative Education, 2*(27), 27–42.

Choi, S. (2008). Diversity in the US federal government: Diversity management and employee turnover in federal agencies. *Journal of Public Administration: Research and Theory, 19*, 603–630. doi:10.1093/jopart/mun010

Cho, S., & Mor Barak, M. E. (2008). Understanding diversity and inclusion in a perceived homogenous culture: A study of organizational commitment and job performance among Korean employees. *Administration in Social Work, 32*(4), 100–126. doi:10.1080/03643100802293865

Chrobot, D., & Ruderman, M. N. (2004). Leadership in a diverse workplace. In Stockdale, M. S., & Crosby, F. J. (Eds.), *The Psychology and Management of Workplace Diversity* (pp. 100–121). Hoboken, NJ: Blackwell Publishing.

Chrobot-Mason, & Ruderman, N. (2004). Leadership in a diverse workplace. In M. S. Stockdale & F. J. Crosby (Eds.), *The Psychology and Management of Workplace Diversity,* (pp. 100-121). Malden, MA: Blackwell.

Chrobot-Mason, D., Button, S. B., & DiClementi, J. D. (2001). Sexual identity management strategies: An exploration of antecedents and consequences. *Sex Roles, 45*, 321–336. doi:10.1023/A:1014357514405

Chung, Y. B., & Harmon, L. W. (1999). Assessment of perceived occupational opportunity for Black Americans. *Journal of Career Assessment, 7,* 45–62. doi:10.1177/106907279900700104

Clair, J. A., Beatty, J., & MacLean, T. (2005). Out of sight but not out of mind: Managing invisible social identities in the workplace. *Academy of Management Review, 30*(1), 78–95. doi:10.5465/AMR.2005.15281431

Clark, M. (2004, August). Religion vs. sexual orientation. *HR Magazine,* 54–59.

Clark, M. C. (2001). Off the beaten path: Some creative approaches to adult learning. In Merriam, S. B. (Ed.), *The New Update on Adult Learning Theory* (Vol. 89, pp. 83–93). San Francisco, CA: Jossey Bass. doi:10.1002/ace.11

Clark, R., Anderson, N. B., Clark, V. R., & Williams, D. R. (1999). Racism as a stressor for African Americans. *The American Psychologist, 54,* 805–816. doi:10.1037/0003-066X.54.10.805

Cockburn, C., & Wilson, T. D. (1995). Business use of the world-wide web. *Information Research, 1*(1). Retrieved from http://informationr.net/ir/1-2/paper6.html.

Cohn, E., & Mullennix, J. (2007). Diversity as an integral component of college curricula. In Branche, J., Mullennix, J., & Cohn, E. (Eds.), *Diversity across the Curriculum: A Guide for Faculty in Higher Education* (pp. 213–218). Boston, MA: Anker.

Colella, A., & Varma, A. (2001). The impact of subordinate disability on leader-member exchange relationships. *Academy of Management Journal, 44,* 304–315. doi:10.2307/3069457

Coleman, J. S. (1988). Social capital in the creation of human capital. *American Journal of Sociology, 94,* 95–120. doi:10.1086/228943

Collella, A., & Dipboye, B. (Eds.). (2005). *Discrimination at work: Psychological and organizational bases.* Mahwah, NJ: Lawrence Erlbaum.

Collins, C. J., & Clark, K. D. (2003). Strategic human resource practice, top management team social networks, and firm performance: The role of human resource practices in creative organizational competitive advantage. *Academy of Management Journal, 46*(6), 720–731. doi:10.2307/30040665

Collins, P. H. (1986). Learning from the outsider within: The sociological significance of black feminist thought. *Social Problems, 33*(6), 14–32. doi:10.1525/sp.1986.33.6.03a00020

Collins, P. H. (1990). *Black feminist thought: Knowledge, consciousness, and the politics of empowerment.* New York, NY: Routledge.

Collins, P. H. (1998). *Fighting words: Black women and the search for justice.* Minneapolis, MN: University of Minnesota Press.

Collins, P. H. (1999). Reflections on the outsider within. *Journal of Career Development, 26*(1), 85–88. doi:10.1177/089484539902600107

Collins, P. H. (2000). *Black feminist thought: Knowledge, consciousness, and the politics of empowerment* (2nd ed.). New York, NY: Rutledge.

Colquitt, J. A. (2001). On the dimensionality of organizational justice: A construct validation of a measure. *The Journal of Applied Psychology, 86*(3), 386–400. doi:10.1037/0021-9010.86.3.386

Columbia Executive, M. B. A. (2011). *University of Columbia's online course catalog.* Retrieved from http://www4.gsb.columbia.edu/emba/overview.

Combs, G. M. (2003). The duality of race and gender for managerial African American women: Implications of informal social networks on career advancement. *Human Resource Development Review, 2*(4), 385–405. doi:10.1177/1534484303257949

Combs, G. M., & Griffith, J. (2007). An examination of interracial contact: The influence of cross-race interpersonal efficacy and affect regulation. *Human Resource Development Review, 6*(3), 222–244. doi:10.1177/1534484307303990

Combs, G. M., & Luthans, F. (2007). Diversity training: Analysis of the impact of self-efficacy. *Human Resource Development Quarterly, 18*(1), 91–120. doi:10.1002/hrdq.1193

Combs, G. P. (2003). The duality of race and gender for managerial African American women: Implications of informal social networks on career advancement. *Human Resource Development Review, 2*(4), 385–405. doi:10.1177/1534484303257949

Conger, J. J. (1975). Proceedings of the American psychological association, incorporated, for the year 1974: Minutes of the annual meeting of the council of representatives. *The American Psychologist*, *30*, 620–651. doi:10.1037/h0078455

Conklin, W. (2006). Seven best practices in diversity communications. *Managing Diversity Communications*, *14*(2), 11–16.

Connell, R. W. (2003). Developing a theory of gender as practice: Notes on Yancey Martin's feminist lecture. *Gender & Society*, *17*(3), 370–372. doi:10.1177/0891243203017003004

Conner, J. (2000). Developing the global leaders of tomorrow. *Human Resource Management*, *39*(2-3), 147–157. doi:10.1002/1099-050X(200022/23)39:2/3<147::AID-HRM5>3.0.CO;2-T

Conti, G., & Fellenz, R. (1991). Assessing adult learning strategies. In *Proceedings of the 32nd Annual Adult Education Research Conference*. Norman, OK: University of Oklahoma.

Conti, G., & Kolody, R. (1998). Development of an instrument for identifying groups of learners. In *Proceedings of the 39th Annual Adult Education Research Conference*, (pp. 109-114). San Antonio, TX: Sacred Heart University.

Conti, G., Kolody, R., & Schneider, B. (1997). Learning strategies in the corporate setting. In *Proceedings of the 38th Annual Adult Education Research Conference*, (pp. 67-72). Stillwater, OK: Oklahoma State University.

Conti, G., & Kolody, R. (1999). *Guide for using ATLAS*. Stillwater, OK: Oklahoma State University.

Conti, G., & Kolody, R. (2004). Guidelines for selecting methods and techniques. In Galbraith, M. W. (Ed.), *Adult Learning Method* (3rd ed., pp. 181–192). Malabar, FL: Krieger.

Contractor, N. S., Wasserman, S., & Faust, K. (2006). Testing multitheoretical, multilevel hypotheses about organizational networks: an analytic framework and empirical example. *Academy of Management Review*, *31*(3), 681–703. doi:10.5465/AMR.2006.21318925

Cook, A., & Glass, C. (2009). Between a rock and a hard place: Managing diversity in a shareholder society. *Human Resource Management Journal*, *19*(4), 393–412. doi:10.1111/j.1748-8583.2009.00100.x

Cooke, F. L., & Saini, D. S. (2010). Diversity management in India: A study of organizations in different ownership forms and industrial sectors. *Human Resource Management*, *49*(3), 477–500. doi:10.1002/hrm.20360

Cook, K. S., & Emerson, R. M. (1978). Power, equity, and commitment in exchange networks. *American Sociological Review*, *43*, 721–739. doi:10.2307/2094546

Cordery, J. L., & Soo, C. (2008). Overcoming impediments to virtual team effectiveness. *Human Factors and Ergonomics in Manufacturing*, *18*(5), 487–500. doi:10.1002/hfm.20119

Cormack, J., & Niessen, J. (2002). Immigrant and minority businesses: Making the policy case. *European Journal of Migration and Law*, *4*(3), 329–337. doi:10.1163/157181602322768939

Cornell Executive, M. B. A. (2011). *Cornell University's online course catalog*. Retrieved from http://www.johnson.cornell.edu/Academic-Programs/Executive-MBA.aspx.

Cortese, D. K. H. (2004). *Are we thinking straight? Negotiating political environments and identities in a lesbian, gay, bisexual, and transgender social movement organization*. Doctoral Dissertation. Austin, TX: The University of Texas at Austin.

Council, P. (2001). Managing multiculturalism: Valuing diversity in the workplace. *Journal of Property Management*, *66*(6), 22–25.

Courtnage, L. (1998). *Advertising industry survey: Learning strategies of advertising sales people*. Unpublished Doctoral Dissertation. Bozeman, MT: Montana State University.

Cox Executive, M. B. A. (2011). *Southern Methodist University's online course catalog*. Retrieved from http://www.cox.smu.edu/web/executive-mba.

Cox, N. (2000). *Academical dress in New Zealand*. Retrieved on 20/05/2011 from http://www.academicapparel.com/caps/College-University-History.html.

Cox, T., Jr., & Smolinski, C. (1994). *Managing diversity and glass ceiling initiatives as national economic imperatives.* Working Paper #9410-01. Ann Arbor, MI: Michigan Business School.

Cox, J. T. (1993). *Cultural diversity in organizations: Theory, research and practice.* San Francisco, CA: Berrett-Koehler Publishers.

Cox, J. T. (1994). A comment on the language of diversity. *Organization, 1*(1), 51–58. doi:10.1177/135050849400100109

Cox, J. T., & Blake, S. (1991). Managing cultural diversity for organizational competitiveness. *The Academy of Management Executive, 5*(3), 45–56.

Cox, T. (1991). The multicultural organization. *The Academy of Management Executive, 5*, 34–47.

Cox, T. (1993). *Cultural diversity in organizations: Theory, research, & practice.* San Francisco, CA: Berrett-Koehler.

Cox, T. (1994). *Cultural diversity in organizations: Theory, research and practice.* San Francisco, CA: Berrett-Koehler.

Cox, T. (1994). *Review of research on diversity and organizational performance, in cultural diversity in organizations: theory, research & practice.* San Francisco, CA: Berrett-Koehler Publisher Inc.

Cox, T. (2001). *Creating the multicultural organization: A strategy for capturing the power of diversity.* San Francisco, CA: Jossey-Bass.

Cox, T. (2004). Problems with research by organizational scholars on issues of race and ethnicity. *The Journal of Applied Behavioral Science, 40*, 124–145. doi:10.1177/0021886304263851

Cox, T. H. (1993). *Cultural diversity in organizations: Theory, research and practice.* San Francisco, CA: Berrett-Koehler Publishers.

Cox, T. H., & Blake, S. (1991). Managing cultural diversity: Implications for organisational competitiveness. *The Academy of Management Executive, 5*(3), 45–57.

Cox, T. H., & Blake, S. (1991). Managing cultural diversity: Implications for organizational competitiveness. *The Academy of Management Executive, 5*(3).

Cox, T. H., & Blake, S. (1991). Managing cultural diversity: Implications for organizational competitiveness. *The Executive, 5*(3), 45–56. doi:10.5465/AME.1991.4274465

Cox, T. H., Lobel, S. A., & McLeod, P. L. (1991). Effects of ethnic group cultural differences on cooperative and competitive behavior on a group task. *Academy of Management Journal, 34*(4), 827–847. doi:10.2307/256391

Cox, T., & Blake, S. (1991). Managing cultural diversity: Implications for organizational competitiveness. *The Academy of Management Executive, 5*(3), 45–56.

Cox, T. Jr. (1993). *From cultural diversity in organizations: Theory, research and practice.* San Francisco, CA: Berrett-Koehler.

Cox, T. Jr. (2001). *Creating the multicultural organization: A strategy for capturing the power of diversity.* San Francisco, CA: Jossey-Bass.

Cox, T. Jr, & Nkomo, S. M. (1990). Invisible men and women: A status report on race as a variable in organizational behavior research. *Journal of Organizational Behavior, 11*(6), 419–431. doi:10.1002/job.4030110604

Cox, T., & Smolinski, C. (1994). *Managing diversity and glass ceiling initiatives as nation economic imperatives.* Washington, DC: Key Workplace Documents Federal Publications.

Cramton, C. D. (2001). The mutual knowledge problem and its consequences for dispersed collaboration. *Organization Science, 12*(3), 346–371. doi:10.1287/orsc.12.3.346.10098

Cramton, C. D., & Hinds, P. J. (2005). Subgroup dynamics in internationally distributed teams: Ethnocentricism or cross- national learning. In Staw, B. M., & Kramer, R. (Eds.), *Research in Organizational Behavior* (Vol. 26, pp. 231–263). San Diego, CA: Elsevier.

Creed, W. E. D., & Scully, M. (2000). Songs of ourselves: Employees' deployment of social identity in workplace encounters. *Journal of Management Inquiry, 9*, 391–412. doi:10.1177/105649260000900410

Crenshaw, K. (1989). Demarginalizing the intersection of race and sex: A black feminist critique of antidiscrimination doctrine, feminist theory and antiracist politics. *University of Chicago Legal Forum.* Retrieved from http://www.scribd.com/doc/28524679/Crenshaw-Demarginalizing-the-Intersection.

Crenshaw, K. W. (2002). The first decade: Critical reflections or a foot in the closing door. *UCLA Law Review. University of California, Los Angeles. School of Law*, *49*(5), 1343–1373.

Creswell, J. W. (1998). *Qualitative inquiry and research design: The five traditions*. Thousand Oaks, CA: Sage.

Crocker, J., Major, B., & Steele, C. (1998). Social stigma. In Gilbert, D. T., & Fiske, S. T. (Eds.), *The Handbook of Social Psychology* (4th ed., *Vol. 2*, pp. 504–553). New York, NY: McGraw-Hill.

Crockett, R. O. (2003). *Why diversity is good business*. Retrieved June 17, 2011, from http://www.businessweek.com/bwdaily/dnflash/jan2003/nf20030117_6373.htm.

Crockett, J. (1999). Diversity: Winning competitive advantage through a diverse workforce. *HRFocus*, *76*(5), 9–11.

Cropanzano, R., Li, A., & James, K. (2007). Intraunit justice and interunit justice and the people who experience them. In Dansereau, F., & Yammarino, F. J. (Eds.), *Research in Multilevel Issues* (*Vol. 6*, pp. 415–438). Englewood Cliffs, NJ: Erlbaum. doi:10.1016/S1475-9144(07)06019-5

Crosby, F., Bromley, S., & Saxe, L. (1980). Recent unobtrusive studies of Black-and-White discrimination and prejudice: A literature review. *Psychological Bulletin*, *87*, 546–563. doi:10.1037/0033-2909.87.3.546

Cross, C., & Armstrong, C. (2008). Understanding the role of networks in collective learning processes: The experiences of women. *Advances in Developing Human Resources*, *10*(4), 600–613. doi:10.1177/1523422308320495

Cross, E. Y. (2010). Managing diversity: A continuous process of change. *Diversity Factor*, *18*(2), 1–4.

Cross, W. E. (1971). The negro-to-black conversion experience. *Black World*, *20*, 3–27.

Cross, W. E. (1978). The Thomas and Cross model of psychological nigrescence: A literature review. *The Journal of Black Psychology*, *4*, 13–31. doi:10.1177/009579847800500102

Croteau, I. M. (1996). Research on the work experiences of lesbian, gay and bisexual people: An integrative review of methodology and findings. *Journal of Vocational Behavior*, *48*, 195–209. doi:10.1006/jvbe.1996.0018

Crowston, K., Sieber, S., & Wynn, E. (Eds.). (2007). Virtuality and virtualization. In *Proceedings of IFIP*. New York, NY: Springer.

Cui, G. (1989). *Intercultural effectiveness: An integrative approach*. Paper presented at the 35th Annual Conference of the International Communication Association. San Francisco, CA.

Cui, G., & Van Den Berg, S. (1991). Testing the intercultural validity of intercultural effectiveness. *International Journal of Intercultural Relations*, *15*, 227–241. doi:10.1016/0147-1767(91)90031-B

Cummings, T. G., & Worley, C. G. (2001). *Organization development and change* (7th ed.). Cincinnati, OH: South-Western.

Cunningham, G. B., & Chelladurai, P. (2005). Affective reactions to cross-functional teams: The impact of size, relative performance, and common in-group identity. *Group Dynamic Theory Resource Practitioners*, *8*, 83–97. doi:10.1037/1089-2699.8.2.83

Curtis, E. F., & Dreachslin, J. L. (2008). Diversity management interventions and organizational performance: A synthesis of current literature. *Human Resource Development Review*, *7*(1), 107–134. doi:10.1177/1534484307311700

Czarniawska, B. (2006). Doing gender unto the other: Fiction as a mode of studying gender discrimination in organizations. *Gender, Work and Organization*, *13*(3), 234–253. doi:10.1111/j.1468-0432.2006.00306.x

D'Almeida, C. M. (2007). *The effects of cultural diversity in the workplace*. Unpublished Dissertation. Ann Arbor, MI: Capella University.

Daft, R. L. (2004). *Organizzazione aziendale*. Milano, Italy: Apogeo.

Daft, R. L., & Lengel, R. H. (1984). Information richness: A new approach to managerial behavior and organizational design. *Research in Organizational Behavior*, *6*, 191–233.

Dahlin, K. B. (2005). Team diversity and information use. *Academy of Management Journal*, *48*(8), 1107–1123. doi:10.5465/AMJ.2005.19573112

Dahm, M. J., Willems, E. P., Ivancevich, J. M., & Graves, D. E. (2009). Development of an organizational diversity needs analysis instrument. *Journal of Applied Social Psychology*, *39*(2), 283–318. doi:10.1111/j.1559-1816.2008.00439.x

Daley, D. M. (1996). Paths of glory and the glass ceiling: Differing patterns of career advancement among women and minority federal employees. *Public Administration Quarterly*, *20*(2), 143–162.

Dallas, L. L. (2002). The new managerialism and diversity on corporate boards of directors. *Tulane Law Review*, *76*, 1363.

Daloz, L. A. (1986). *Effective mentoring and teaching: Realizing the transformational power of adult learning experience*. San Francisco, CA: Jossey-Bass.

Dalton, C., & Dalton, D. (2005). In defense of the individual: The CEO as board chairperson. *The Journal of Business Strategy*, *26*(6), 8–9. doi:10.1108/02756660510632966

Dansky, K. H., Weech-Maldonado, R., De Souza, G., & Dreachslin, J. L. (2003). Organizational strategy and diversity management: Diversity-sensitive orientation as a moderating influence. *Health Care Management Review*, *28*(3), 243–253.

Dass, P., & Parker, B. (1999). Strategies for managing human resource diversity: From resistance to learning. *The Academy of Management Executive*, *13*(2), 68–80. doi:10.5465/AME.1999.1899550

Davenport, T. H., Thomas, R. I., & Cantrell, S. (2002). The mysterious art and science of knowledge-worker performance. *MIT Sloan Management Review*. Retrieved from http://sloanreview.mit.edu/the-magazine/2002-fall/4412/the-mysterious-art-and-science-of-knowledgeworker-performance/.

David, A. (2010). Diversity, innovation, and corporate strategy. In Moss, G. (Ed.), *Profiting from Diversity: The Business Advantages and the Obstacles to Achieving Diversity* (pp. 19–44). New York, NY: Palgrave Macmillan.

Davidson, M. N., & Proudford, K. L. (2008). Cycles of resistance. In Thomas, K. M. (Ed.), *Diversity Resistance in Organizations*. Mahwah, NJ: Lawrence Erlbaum Associates.

Davis, K., & Blomstrom, R. L. (1966). *Business and its environment*. New York, NY: McGraw-Hill.

Davison, R. M., & Briggs, R. O. (2000). GSS for presentation support: Supercharging the audience through simultaneous discussions during presentations. *Communications of the ACM*, *43*(9), 91–97. doi:10.1145/348941.349006

Day, N. E., & Glick, B. J. (2000). Teaching diversity: A study of organizational needs and diversity curriculum in higher education. *Journal of Management Education*, *24*(3), 338–352. doi:10.1177/105256290002400305

Day, N. E., & Greene, P. G. (2008). A case for sexual orientation diversity management in small and large organizations. *Human Resource Management*, *47*(3), 637–654. doi:10.1002/hrm.20235

Day, N. E., & Schoenrade, P. (1997). Staying in the closet vs. corning out: Relationships between communication about sexual orientation and work attitudes. *Personnel Psychology*, *50*, 147–163. doi:10.1111/j.1744-6570.1997.tb00904.x

De Dreu, C. K. W., Harinck, S., & van Vianen, A. E. M. (1999). Conflict and performance in groups and organisations. In Cooper, C. L., & Robertson, I. T. (Eds.), *International Review of Industrial and Organizational Psychology* (Vol. 14, pp. 369–414). Oxford, UK: Wiley. doi:10.1002/9780470696712.ch8

De Dreu, C. K., & Weingart, L. R. (2003). Task versus relationship conflict and team effectiveness: A meta-analysis. *The Journal of Applied Psychology*, *88*(4), 741–749. doi:10.1037/0021-9010.88.4.741

de Vries, J., Webb, C., & Eveline, J. (2006). Mentoring for gender equality and organisational change. *Employee Relations*, *28*(6), 573. doi:10.1108/01425450610704506

Deal, J. J. (2006). *Retiring the generation gap: How employees young and old can find common ground*. San Francisco, CA: Jossey-Bass/CCL.

Deal, T., & Kennedy, A. (1984). *Corporate cultures*. Reading, MA: Addison-Wesley.

Dean, D. L., Deokar, A., & Bush, R. T. (2006). Making the collaboration engineering investment decision. In *Proceedings of the 39th International Conference on System Sciences*. Kauai, HI: System Sciences.

Deitch, E. A., Barsky, A., Butz, R. M., Chan, S., Brief, A. P., & Bradley, J. C. (2003). Subtle yet significant: The existence and impact of everyday racial discrimination in the workplace. *Human Relations, 56*(11), 1299–1324. doi:10.1177/00187267035611002

DeJordy, R. (2008). Just passing through: Stigma, passing and identity decoupling in the workplace. *Group & Organization Management, 33*(5), 504–531. doi:10.1177/1059601108324879

DeLany, J., & Rogers, E. (2004). Black women's leadership: Learning the politics of Afritics. *Convergence, 37*(2), 91–106.

Delgado, R. (1995). Storytelling for oppositionists and others: A plea for narrative. In Delgado, R. (Ed.), *Critical Race Theory: The Cutting Edge* (pp. 267–277). Philadelphia, PA: Temple University Press. doi:10.2307/1289308

Den Hond, F., & De Bakker, F. G. A. (2007). Ideologically motivated activism: How activist groups influence corporate social change activities. *Academy of Management Review, 32*, 901–924. doi:10.5465/AMR.2007.25275682

Deokar, A., Kolfscheoten, G. L., & de Vreede, G. J. (2008). Prescriptive workflow design for collaboration-intensive processes using the collaboration engineering approach. *Global Journal of Flexible Systems Management, 9*(4), 13–24.

DeSandtis, G., & Monge, P. (1999). Introduction to the special issue: Communication process for virtual organization. *Organization Science, 10*(6), 693–694. doi:10.1287/orsc.10.6.693

Devine, P. G. (1989). Stereotypes and prejudice: Their automatic and controlled components. *Journal of Personality and Social Psychology, 56*, 5–18. doi:10.1037/0022-3514.56.1.5

Dewan, S. (2011, July 11). True to Episcopal Church's past, Bishops split on gay weddings. *New York Times*. Retrieved on August 31, 2011 from http://www.nytimes.com/2011/07/19/nyregion/new-episcopal-split-priests-role-in-ny-gay-weddings.html.

Dickens, L. (1999). Beyond the business case: A three-pronged approach to equality action. *Human Resource Management Journal, 9*(1), 9–19. doi:10.1111/j.1748-8583.1999.tb00185.x

Dickens, L., & Hall, M. (2006). Fairness up to a point: Assessing the impact of new labours employment legislation. *Human Resource Management Journal, 16*(4), 338–356. doi:10.1111/j.1748-8583.2006.00024.x

Dickman, M., & Harris, H. (2006). Developing career capital for global careers: The role of international assignments. *Journal of World Business, 40*(4), 399–408. doi:10.1016/j.jwb.2005.08.007

Dick, P., & Cassell, C. (2002). Barriers to managing diversity in the UK constabulary: The role of discourse. *Journal of Management Studies, 39*(7), 953–976. doi:10.1111/1467-6486.00319

Dickson, M. W., Hartog, D. N. D., & Mitchelson, J. K. (2003). Research on leadership in a cross-cultural context: Making progress, and raising new questions. *The Leadership Quarterly, 14*, 729–768. doi:10.1016/j.leaqua.2003.09.002

Dilthey, W. (1976). *Wilhelm Dilthey: Selected writings*. Cambridge, UK: CambridgeUniversity Press.

DiMaggio, P. J. (1997). Culture and cognition. *Annual Review of Sociology, 23*, 264–287. doi:10.1146/annurev.soc.23.1.263

DiMicco, J., Millen, D., Geyer, W., Dugan, C., Brownholtz, B., & Muller, M. (2008). Motivations for social networking at work. In *Proceedings of the ACM Conference on Computer Supported Cooperative Work*. San Diego, CA: ACM Press.

Dinges, N. (1983). Intercultural competence. In Landis, D., & Brislin, R. W. (Eds.), *Handbook of Intercultural Training* (*Vol. 1*, pp. 176–202). New York, NY: Pergamon Press.

Dirani, K. (2006). Exploring socio-cultural factors that influence HRD practices in Lebanon. *Human Resource Development International, 9*(1), 85–98. doi:10.1080/13678860500523270

DiTomaso, N., Post, C., & Parks-Yancy, R. (2007). Workforce diversity and inequality: Power, status and numbers. *Annual Review of Sociology, 33*, 473–501. doi:10.1146/annurev.soc.33.040406.131805

Diversity Best Practices. (2006). *Winning the race for diverse talent: A major report*. Washington, DC: Diversity Best Practices.

Diversity Best Practices. (2011). *PwC says "it gets better" in support of LGBT youth.* Retrieved from http://www.diversitybestpractices.com/news-articles/pwc-says-it-gets.

Dodd, A. (2009). *The flexible workforce: A secret weapon in the war for talent.* Retrieved January 12, 2009, from http://www.talentmgt.com/recruitment_retention/2009/January/848/index.php.

Doney, P. M., & Cannon, J. P. (1997). An examination of the nature of trust in buyer-seller relationships. *Journal of Marketing, 61*, 35–51. doi:10.2307/1251829

Doney, P. M., Cannon, J. P., & Mullen, M. R. (1998). Understanding the influence of national culture on the development of trust. *Academy of Management Review, 23*(3), 601–620.

Dorfman, P. W., Howell, J. P., Hibino, S., Lee, J. K., Tate, U., & Bautista, A. (1997). Leadership in Western and Asian countries: Commonalities and differences in effective leadership processes across cultures. *The Leadership Quarterly, 8*, 233–274. doi:10.1016/S1048-9843(97)90003-5

Doria, J., Rozanski, H., & Cohen, E. (2003). What business needs from business schools. *Strategy +. Business, 32*, 39–45.

Dovidio, J. F., Gaertner, S. L., & Kawakami, K. (2003). Intergroup contact: The past, present, and the future. *Group Processes & Intergroup Relations, 6*, 5–21. doi:10.1177/1368430203006001009

Dovidio, J. F., Kawakami, K., & Gaertner, S. L. (2002). Implicit and explicit prejudice and interracial interaction. *Journal of Personality and Social Psychology, 82*, 62–68. doi:10.1037/0022-3514.82.1.62

Drach-Zahavy, A., & Somech, A. (2001). Understanding team innovation: The role of team processes and structures. *Group Dynamics, 5*, 111–123. doi:10.1037/1089-2699.5.2.111

Drago-Severson, E. (2009). *Leading adult learning: Supporting adult development in our schools.* Thousand Oaks, CA: Corwin Press.

Dreachslin, J. L. (1996). *Diversity leadership.* Chicago, IL: Health Administration Press.

Dreachslin, J. L. (2007). Diversity management and cultural competence: Research, practice, and the business case. *Journal of Healthcare Management, 52*(2), 79–86.

Drescher, J. (2004). The closet: Psychological issues of being in and coming out. *Psychiatric Times, 21*(12), 11–15.

Drucker, P. F. (1960). Build tomorrow's workforce today. *Nation's Business, 48*(8), 76–79.

Drucker, P. F. (1980). *Managing in turbulent times.* New York, NY: Harper & Row.

Drucker, P. F. (2002). *Managing in the next society.* New York, NY: Truman Talley.

Druskat, V. U., & Kayes, D. C. (2000). Learning versus performance in short-term project teams. *Small Group Research, 31*, 328–353. doi:10.1177/104649640003100304

Duarte, D. L., & Snyder, N. T. (2006). *Mastering virtual teams: Strategies, tools, and techniques that succeed.* New York, NY: Wiley.

Duarte, D., & Snyder, N. T. (2006). *Mastering virtual teams: Strategies, tools, and techniques that succeed.* San Francisco, CA: Jossey-Bass.

Due Billing, Y., & Alvesson, M. (2000). Questioning the notion of feminine leadership: A critical perspective on the gender labelling of leadership. *Gender, Work and Organization, 7*(3), 144–157. doi:10.1111/1468-0432.00103

Duggan, L. (2003). *The twilight of equality: Neoliberalism, cultural politics, and the attack on democracy.* New York, NY: Beacon Press.

Dumas, R. G. (1975). *The seed of the coming free: An essay on black female leadership.* Barbourville, KY: The Union Graduate School.

Dumas, R. G. (1980). Dilemmas of black females in leadership. In Rodgers-Rose, L. (Ed.), *The Black Woman.* Thousand Oaks, CA: Sage.

Dumdum, U. R., Lowe, K. B., & Avolio, B. J. (2002). A meta-analysis of transformational and transactional leadership correlates of effectiveness and satisfaction: An update and extension. In Avolio, B. J., & Yammarino, F. J. (Eds.), *Transformational and Charismatic Leadership: The Road Ahead* (pp. 35–66). Amsterdam, The Netherlands: JAI.

Dunning, D., & Sherman, D. A. (1997). Stereotypes and tacit inference. *Journal of Personality and Social Psychology, 73*, 459–471. doi:10.1037/0022-3514.73.3.459

Dunton, B. C., & Fazio, R. H. (1997). An individual difference measure of motivation to control prejudiced reactions. *Personality and Social Psychology Bulletin, 23*, 316–326. doi:10.1177/0146167297233009

Durham, C. C., Knight, D., & Locke, E. A. (1997). Effects of leader role, team-set goal difficulty, efficacy, and tactics on team effectiveness. *Organizational Behavior and Human Decision Processes, 72*(2), 203–231. doi:10.1006/obhd.1997.2739

Dworkin, F., Dworkin, D., & Chafetz, I. (1986). The effects of tokenism on work alienation among urban public school teachers. *Work and Occupations, 13*, 399–420. doi:10.1177/0730888486013003006

Dwyer, F. R., Schurr, P. H., & Oh, S. (1987). Developing buyer-seller relationships. *Journal of Marketing, 51*, 11–27. doi:10.2307/1251126

Dyer, W. G. (1987). *Team building: Issues and alternatives* (2nd ed.). Reading, MA: Addison-Wesley.

Dym, B., & Hutson, H. (2005). *Leadership in nonprofit organizations*. Thousand Oaks, CA: Sage.

Earley, P. C. (1993). East meets west meets mideast: Further explorations of collectivistic and individualistic work groups. *Academy of Management Journal, 36*, 319–348. doi:10.2307/256525

Earley, P., & Mosakowski, E. (2004). Cultural intelligence. *Harvard Business Review, 82*(9), 139–146.

Early, P. C., & Gibson, C. B. (2002). *Multinational work teams: A new perspective*. Mahwah, NJ: Lawrence Erlbaum Associates, Inc.

Early, P. C., & Mosakowski, E. (2000). Creating hybrid team cultures: An empirical test of transnational team functioning. *Academy of Management Journal, 43*(1), 26–49. doi:10.2307/1556384

Ebner, N. C., Freund, A. M., & Baltes, P. B. (2006). Developmental changes in personal goal orientation from young to late adulthood: From striving for gains to maintenance and prevention of losses. *Psychology and Aging, 21*(4), 664–678. doi:10.1037/0882-7974.21.4.664

ECOWAS. (2010). *General procurement notice*. Retrieved from http://www.afdb.org/fileadmin/uploads/afdb/Documents/Project-related Procurement/GPNNigeriaECOWAS%20%207-10.pdf.

Eddy, S. W. N. (2008). Why organizations choose to manage diversity? Toward a leadership-based theoretical framework. *Human Resource Development Review, 7*(1), 58–78. doi:10.1177/1534484307311592

Eden, C. L., & Ackerman, F. (2001). SODA—The principles. In Rosenhead, J., & Mingers, J. (Eds.), *Rational Analysis for a Problematic World Revisited* (pp. 21–41). Chichester, UK: John Wiley & Sons.

Education and Training. (2001). Learning to bridge the digital divide. *Education & Training, 43*(2), 125-126.

EEOC. (1963). *Equal pay act*. Retrieved from http://www.eeoc.gov/policy/epa.html.

EEOC. (1964). *Title VII civil rights act*. Retrieved from http://www.eeoc.gov/policy/vii.html.

EEOC. (1967). *Age discrimination in employment act*. Retrieved from http://www.eeoc.gov/policy/adea.html.

EEOC. (1978). *Pregnancy discrimination act*. Retrieved from http://www.eeoc.gov/abouteeoc/35th/thelaw/pregnancy_discrimination-1978.html.

EEOC. (2008). *Facts about age discrimination*. Retrieved June 17, 2011, from http://www.eeoc.gov/facts/age.html.

EEOC. (2010). *Job bias charges approach record high in fiscal year 2009, EEOC reports*. Retrieved November 16, 2010, from http://www.eeoc.gov/eeoc/newsroom/release/1-6-10.cfm.

Egan, M., & Bendick, M. (2007). *Teaching cultural competence: What multicultural management courses can learn from diversity*. Retrieved October 19, 2008, from http://www.bendickegan.com/pdf/10012007/Egan-BendickMulticultural2007.pdf.

Egan, M., & Bendick, M. (2008). Combining multicultural management and diversity into one course on cultural competence. *Academy of Management Learning & Education, 7*(3), 387–393. doi:10.5465/AMLE.2008.34251675

Eigel, K. M., & Kuhnert, K. W. (1996). Personality diversity and its relationship to managerial team productivity. In Ruderman, M. N., Hughes-James, M. W., & Jackson, S. E. (Eds.), *Selected Research on Work Team Diversity*. Washington, DC: APA-CCL Press. doi:10.1037/10507-004

Eisenberger, R., Fasolo, P., & Davis-LaMastro, V. (1990). Perceived organizational support and employee diligence, commitment, and innovation. *The Journal of Applied Psychology*, *75*(1), 51–59. doi:10.1037/0021-9010.75.1.51

ELC. (2005). News and publications. *Executive Leadership Council*. Retrieved November 5, 2005 from http://www.elcinfo.com.

Elliott, C., & Stead, V. (2008). Learning for leading women's experience: Towards a sociological understanding. *Leadership*, *4*(2), 159–180. doi:10.1177/1742715008089636

Elron, E. (1997). Top management teams within multinational corporations: effects of cultural heterogeneity. *The Leadership Quarterly*, *8*(4), 393–412. doi:10.1016/S1048-9843(97)90021-7

Elsass, P. M., & Graves, L. M. (1997). Demographic diversity in decision-making groups: The experience of women and people of colour. *Academy of Management Review*, *22*(4), 946–973.

Ely, R. J., & Thomas, D. A. (2001). Cultural diversity at work: The effects of diversity perspectives on work group processes and outcomes. *Administrative Science Quarterly*, *46*(2), 229–273. doi:10.2307/2667087

Ely, R. J., & Thomas, D. A. (2001). Cultural diversity at work: The moderating effects of work group perspectives on diversity. *Administrative Science Quarterly*, *46*, 229–273. doi:10.2307/2667087

EMBA in Transition. (2011). *Bloomberg Businessweek's online business school rankings*. Retrieved from http://www.businessweek.com/bschools/rankings/.

Enteman, W. (1996). Stereotyping, prejudice, and discrimination. In Lester, P. M. (Ed.), *Images that Injure: Pictorial Stereotypes in the Media* (pp. 9–14). Westport, CT: Praeger.

Enterprises, M. W. B. E. (2010). *Website*. Retrieved on May 2010 from http://www.mwbe-enterprises.com/.

Enz, C. A., Dollinger, M., & Daily, C. (1990). Value orientations of minority and non-minority small business owners. *Entrepreneurship Theory and Practice*, *15*(1), 23–36.

Erhardt, N. L., Werbel, J. D., & Shrader, C. B. (2003). Board of director diversity and firm financial performance. *Corporate Governance*, *11*(2), 102–111. doi:10.1111/1467-8683.00011

Ernst, C., & Yip, J. (2008). Bridging boundaries: Meeting the challenge of workplace diversity. *Leadership in Action*, *28*(1), 3–6. doi:10.1002/lia.1232

Esposito, M. (2010). The role of learning organizations in the growing discussion on social responsibility. *International Journal of the Academy of Executives & Administrators*, *1*(8), 1–18.

Etter-Lewis, G. (1993). *My soul is my own: Oral narratives of African American women in the professions*. New York, NY: Routledge.

European Institute for Diversity Management. (2011). *Diversity for talent and competitiveness: The SME business case for diversity, 2011*. Retrieved from http://iegd.org/spanish800/charter.html.

Evans, P., Pucik, V., & Björkman, I. (2011). *The global challenge: International human resource management* (2nd ed.). New York, NY: McGraw-Hill.

Executive, M. B. A. Programs, Best Business Schools. (2011). *In US News' online rankings*. Retrieved from http://grad-schools.usnews.rankingsandreviews.com/best-graduate-schools/top-business-schools/executive-rankings.

Ezeani, E. O. (2002). Basic elements for effective human resource management in local government system. In Ezeani, E. O., & Nwankwo, B. C. (Eds.), *Human Resource Management in the Local Government System in Nigeria*. Nsukka: Great Ap. Express Publishers.

Fahmy, S. (2010). *Despite recession, Hispanic and Asian buying power expected to surge in US. Annual Report of Selig Center*. Athens, GA: University of Georgia Terry College of Business.

Fassinger, R. E. (2008). Workplace diversity and public policy. *The American Psychologist*, *63*, 252–268. doi:10.1037/0003-066X.63.4.252

Fassinger, R. E., Shullman, S. L., & Stevenson, M. R. (2010). Toward an affirmative lesbian, gay, bisexual and transgender leadership paradigm. *The American Psychologist, 65*(3), 201–215. doi:10.1037/a0018597

FBI. (2009). *Federal bureau of investigation hate crimes report*. Retrieved from http://www.fbi.gov.

Fears, D. (2008, January 3). Lockheed to pay $2.5 million in racial discrimination case. *Washington Post.*

Federal Character Commission. (2011). *Federal character commission handbook*. Abuja: Federal Character Commission.

Federal Glass Ceiling Commission. (1995). *Good for business: Making full use of the nation's human capital: The environmental scan, a fact-finding report of the federal glass ceiling commission*. Washington, DC: Government Printing Office.

Fegley, S. (2006). Workplace diversity and changes to the EEO-1 process survey report. *Society for Human Resource Management*. Retrieved from http://www.shrm.org/surveys.

Fellenz, R., & Conti, G. (1993). *Self-knowledge inventory of lifelong learning strategies (SKILLS): Manual*. Bozeman, MT: Center for Adult Learning Research.

Ferber, A. L. (2010). Dismantling privilege and becoming an activist. In Kimmel, M. S., & Ferber, A. L. (Eds.), *Privilege: A Reader* (2nd ed.). Boulder, CO: Westview Press.

Ferris, S. P. (1996). Women on-line: Cultural and relational aspects of women's communication in on-line discussion groups. *Interpersonal Computing and Technology: An Electronic Journal for the 21st Century, 4*(3-4), 29-40. Retrieved from http://www.helsinki.fi/science/optek/1996/n3/ferris.txt.

Filho, R. P., Lockwood, N. R., & Williams, S. (2009). Global diversity advantage: The next competitive edge. *SHRM*. Retrieved from http://www.shrm.org/Research/Articles/Articles/Pages/GlobalDiversityAdvantage.aspx.

Findler, L., Wind, L., & Mor Barak, M. E. (2007). The challenge of workforce management in a global society: Modeling the relationship between diversity, organizational culture, and employee well-being, job satisfaction and organizational commitment. *Administration in Social Work, 31*(3), 63–94. doi:10.1300/J147v31n03_05

Finkelstein, S. (1992). Power in top management teams: Dimensions, measurement, and validation. *Academy of Management Journal, 35*(3), 505–538. doi:10.2307/256485

Finkelstein, S., & Hambrick, D. C. (1990). Top management-team tenure and organizational outcomes: The moderating role for managerial discretion. *Administrative Science Quarterly, 35*, 484–503. doi:10.2307/2393314

Finkelstein, S., & Hambrick, D. C. (1996). *Strategic leadership: Top executives and their effects on organizations*. Minneapolis, MN: West Educational Publishing.

Fisher Executive, M. B. A. (2011). *Ohio State University's online course catalog*. Retrieved from http://www.cob.ohio-state.edu/emba/.

Fisher, M. J. (2008). Study: Women professors at UCI face discrimination. *The Orange County Register.* Retrieved from http://www.ocregister.com.

Fisher, D., & Torbert, W. R. (1995). *Personal and organizational transformations*. London, UK: McGraw-Hill.

Fisher-Yoshida, B., & Geller, K. (2009). *Transnational leadership development*. New York, NY: American Management Association.

Fiske, S. T., & Neuberg, S. L. (1990). A continuum of impression formation: From category-based to individuating processes: Influences of information and motivation on attention and interpretation. In Zanna, M. (Ed.), *Advances in Experimental Social Psychology* (pp. 1–74). San Diego, CA: Academic Press. doi:10.1016/S0065-2601(08)60317-2

Fiske, S. T., & Ruscher, J. B. (1993). Negative interdependence and prejudice: Whence the affect? In Mackie, D. M., & Hamilton, D. L. (Eds.), *Affect, Cognition, and Stereotyping: Interactive Processes in Group Perceptions* (pp. 239–269). New York, NY: Academic Press.

Fitzpatrick, B. (2007). *Sexual orientation and religion or belief cases*. Retrieved March 06, 2011, from http://www.tuc.org.ukextrasSORBreport.pdf.

Flaherty, S., & Moss, S. A. (2007). The impact of personality and team context on the relationship between workplace injustice and counterproductive work behavior. *Journal of Applied Social Psychology, 37*(11), 2549–2575. doi:10.1111/j.1559-1816.2007.00270.x

Flanagan, J. C. (1954). The critical incident technique. *Psychological Bulletin, 51*(4), 327–358. doi:10.1037/h0061470

Fleishman, E. A. (1953). The description of supervisory behavior. *Personnel Psychology, 37,* 1–6.

Fletcher, J. K. (1999). *Disappearing acts: Gender, power and relational practice.* Cambridge, MA: The Massachusetts Institute of Technology.

Focus, H. R. (2010, January). Link diversity to business goals for best results. *HRFocus,* 5–10.

Fogg, P. (2009). When generations collide. *Education Digest, 74*(6), 25–30.

Folger, R., & Cropanzano, R. (1998). *Organizational justice and human resource management.* Thousand Oaks, CA: Sage Publications.

Fonow, M. M., & Cook, J. A. (2005). Feminist methodology: New application in the academy and public policy. *Signs: Journal of Women in Culture and Society, 30*(4), 2211–2239. doi:10.1086/428417

Ford, V. (1996, February). Partnership is the secret of progress. *People Management,* 34-36.

Ford, C., & Airhihenbuwa, C. (2010). Critical race theory, race equity, and public health: Toward antiracism praxis. *American Journal of Public Health, 100,* 30–35. doi:10.2105/AJPH.2009.171058

Foster, C., & Harris, L. (2005). Easy to say, difficult to do: Diversity management in retail. *Human Resource Management Journal, 15*(3), 4–17. doi:10.1111/j.1748-8583.2005.tb00150.x

Frable, D. E. S. (1997). Gender, racial, ethnic, sexual, and class identities. *Annual Review of Psychology, 48*(1), 139–163. doi:10.1146/annurev.psych.48.1.139

Freeman-Evans, T. (1994). The enriched association: Benefiting from multiculturalism. *Association Management, 46*(2), 52–57.

Freire, P. (1970). *Pedagogy of the oppressed.* New York, NY: Seabury Press.

Frey, W. H. (2011). *America's diverse future: initial glimpses at the U.S. child population from the 2010 census.* Retrieved June 17, 2011, from http://www.brookings.edu/~/media/Files/rc/papers/2011/0406_census_diversity_frey/0406_census_diversity_frey.pdf.

Friedman, D. M., & Berger, D. L. (2004). Improving team structure and communication: A key to hospital efficiency. *Archives of Surgery, 139*(11), 1194–1198. doi:10.1001/archsurg.139.11.1194

Friedman, R., & Förster, J. (2001). The effects of promotion and prevention cues on creativity. *Journal of Personality and Social Psychology, 81,* 1001–1013. doi:10.1037/0022-3514.81.6.1001

Friedman, R., & Förster, J. (2005). Effects of motivational cues on perceptual asymmetry: Implications for creativity and analytical problem solving. *Journal of Personality and Social Psychology, 88,* 263–275. doi:10.1037/0022-3514.88.2.263

Friedman, T. L. (2007). *The world is flat 3.0: A brief history of the 21st century.* New York, NY: Macmillan Picador.

Friedman, T. L., & Mandelbaum, M. (2011). *That used to be us: How America fell behind in the world it invented and how we can come back.* New York, NY: Farrar, Strauss, and Giroux.

Friskopp, A., & Silverstein, S. (1996). *Straight jobs, gay lives: Gay and lesbian professionals, the Harvard business school, and the American workplace.* New York, NY: Touchstone/Simon & Schuster.

Fullerton, H. N., & Toossi, M. (2001). Employment outlook: 2000-10. *Monthly Labor Review.* Retrieved March 4, 2011, from http://www.bls.gov.

Fullerton, F. N., & Toossi, M. (2001). Labor force projections to 2010: Steady growth and changing composition. *Monthly Labor Review, 124,* 21–38.

Funakawa, A. (1997). *Transcultural management: A new approach for global organizations.* San Francisco, CA: Jossey-Bass.

Fuqua Weekend Executive, M. B. A. (2011). *Duke University's online course catalog.* Retrieved from http://www.fuqua.duke.edu/programs/duke_mba/weekend_executive/.

Gaertner, S. L., & Dovidio, J. F. (1986). The aversive form of racism. In Gaertner, S. L., & Dovidio, J. F. (Eds.), *Prejudice, Discrimination, and Racism* (pp. 61–89). New York, NY: Academic Press.

Gajewski, M. (2005). Strategic diversity to increase human capital in public and nonprofit organizations. *Nonprofit Management Good Practice Guide*. Retrieved from http://www.npgoodpractice.org/Management/GVSU/.

Gale, S. F. (2005). Making c-learning more than "pixie dust". *Workforce Management, 82*, 112–122.

Gallagher, A. (2004). *Multigenerational diversity in U.S. workplaces: Eliminating intergenerational conflict on route to organizational success*. Retrieved May 13, 2011 from http://www.pittsburghhra.org/UserFiles/File/carrer_bank/GenerationalDiversityPHRAProject.pdf.

Gamson, W. A., Fireman, B., & Rytina, S. (1982). *Encounters with unjust authorities*. Homewood, IL: Dorsey.

Gandolfo, R. (1995). MMPI-2 profiles of worker's compensation claimants who present with complaints of harassment. *Journal of Clinical Psychology, 51*, 711–715. doi:10.1002/1097-4679(199509)51:5<711::AID-JCLP2270510517>3.0.CO;2-R

Ganesan, S. (1994). Determinants of long-term orientation in buyer-seller relationships. *Journal of Marketing, 58*, 1–19. doi:10.2307/1252265

Garcia-Prieto, P., Bellard, E., & Schneider, S. C. (2003). Experiencing diversity, conflict and emotions in teams. *Applied Psychology: An International Review, 52*(3), 413–440. doi:10.1111/1464-0597.00142

Gardenswartz, L., & Rowe, A. (1993). *Managing diversity: A complete desk reference and planning guide*. Homewood, IL: Business One Irwin.

Gardiner, R. A. (2011). A critique of the discourse of authentic leadership. *International Journal of Business & Social Science, 2*(15), 99–104.

Gardner, H. (1983). *Frames of mind: The theory of multiple intelligences*. New York, NY: Basic Books.

Gardner, H. (2006). *Multiple intelligences: New horizons*. New York, NY: Basic Books.

Garnets, L., & Kimmel, D. (1993). *Perspectives on lesbian and gay male experiences*. New York, NY: Columbia University Press.

Gebert, D., & Kearney, E. (2011). Ambidextre führung: Eine andere sichtweise. *Zeitschrift für Arbeits- und Organisationspsychologie, 55*, 74–87. doi:10.1026/0932-4089/a000043

Gedro, J. (2010). Lesbian presentations and representations of leadership, and the implications for HRD. *Journal of European Industrial Training, 34*(6), 552–564. doi:10.1108/03090591011061220

Gedro, J., Cervero, R. M., & Johnson-Bailey, J. (2004). How lesbians learn to negotiate the heterosexism of corporate America. *Human Resource Development International, 7*(2), 181–195. doi:10.1080/1367886042000243790

Gelfand, M. J., Nishii, L. H., Raver, J., & Schneider, B. (2005). Discrimination in organizations: An organizational level systems perspective. In Dipboye, R., & Colella, A. (Eds.), *Discrimination at Work: The Psychological and Organizational Bases* (pp. 89–116). Mahwah, NJ: Erlbaum.

Gelston, S. (2008). *Gen y, gen x, and the baby boomers: Workplace generation wars*. Retrieved January 12, 2009, from http://www.cio.com/article/178050/Gen_Y_Gen_X_and_the_Baby_Boomers_Workplace_Generation_Wars.

Gentile. (1998). *Managerial excellence through diversity*. Long Grove, IL: Waveland Press, Inc.

George, J. M., & Zhou, J. (2001). When openness to experience and conscientiousness are related to creative behavior: An interactional approach. *The Journal of Applied Psychology, 86*, 513–524. doi:10.1037/0021-9010.86.3.513

Georgetown Executive, M. B. A. (2011). *Georgetown University's online course catalog*. Retrieved from http://msb.georgetown.edu/gemba/.

Gewin, V. (2011). Equality: The fight for access. *Nature, 469*, 255–257. doi:10.1038/nj7329-255a

Geyskens, I., Steenkamp, J. E. B. M., & Kumar, N. (1998). Generalizations about trust in marketing channel relationships using meta-analysis. *International Journal of Research in Marketing, 15*(3), 223–248. doi:10.1016/S0167-8116(98)00002-0

Gherardi, S. (1994). The gender we think the gender we do in our everyday organisational lives. *Human Relations, 47*(6), 591–610. doi:10.1177/001872679404700602

Gherardi, S. (1996). Gendered organisational cultures: Narratives of women travellers in a male world. *Gender, Work and Organization, 3*(4), 187–201. doi:10.1111/j.1468-0432.1996.tb00059.x

Ghost Bear, A. (2001). *Adult learning on the Internet: Engaging the eBay auction process.* Unpublished Doctoral Dissertation. Stillwater, OK: Oklahoma State University.

Gibbons, M., Limoges, C., Nowotny, H., Schwartzman, S., Scott, P., & Trow, M. (1994). *The new production of knowledge: The dynamics of science and research in contemporary societies.* London, UK: Sage.

Gibb, S. (2008). *Human resource development: Process, practices and perspectives* (2nd ed.). Hampshire, CT: Palgrave Macmillan.

Gibson, C. B., & Saxton, T. (2001). *Consultants in the cupboard: How third party involvement affects team strategic decision outcomes.* Working Paper. Los Angeles, CA: University of Southern California.

Gibson, C. (1996). Do you hear what I hear? A framework for reconciling intercultural communication difficulties arising from cognitive styles and cultural values. In Erez, M., & Early, P. C. (Eds.), *New Perspectives on International Industrial/Organizational Psychology.* San Francisco, CA: Jossey-Bass.

Gibson, C. B., & Cohen, S. G. (2003). *Virtual teams that work: Creating conditions for virtual team effectiveness.* San Francisco, CA: Jossey-Bass.

Gibson, C. B., & Gibbs, J. L. (2006). Unpacking the concept of virtuality: The effects of geographic dispersion, electronic dependence, dynamic structure, and national diversity on team innovation. *Administrative Science Quarterly, 51*(3), 451–495.

Gibson, C. B., & Zellmer-Bruhn, M. E. (2001). Metaphors and meaning: An intercultural analysis of the concept of teamwork. *Administrative Science Quarterly, 46*(2), 274–303. doi:10.2307/2667088

Gibson, C. B., Zellmer-Bruhn, M., & Schwab, D. P. (2003). Team effectiveness in multinational organizations: Evaluation across contexts. *Group & Organization Management, 28*(4), 444–474. doi:10.1177/1059601103251685

Giddens, A. (1984). *The constitution of society: Outline of the theory of structuration.* Berkeley, CA: University of California Press.

Gilbert, A. J., & Ivancevich, J. M. (2000). Valuing diversity: A tale of two organizations. *Academy of Management Executives, 14*(1), 93-105. Retrieved from http://web.ebscohost.com.ezproxy.library.unlv.edu/bsi/pdf?vid=19&hid=5&sid=1358b5cf-cbb2-4bcd-9062-b9e27e267f8a%40sessionmgr7.

Gilbert, D. U. (2005). Kontextsteuerung und systemvertrauen in strategischen unternehmensnetzwerken. *Die Unternehmung, 59*(5), 407–422.

Gilbert, J. A., Stead, B. A., & Ivancevich, J. M. (1999). Diversity management: A new organizational paradigm. *Journal of Business Ethics, 21*(1), 61–76. doi:10.1023/A:1005907602028

Gill, D. (2005, November). Dealing with diversity. *Inc Magazine,* 37-38.

Gill, S. (2010, February 8). What gets measured gets done...or not. *The Performance Improvement Blog.* Retrieved from http://stephenjgill.typepad.com/performance_improvement_b/2010/02/what-gets-measured-gets-doneor-not.html.

Gill, R. H., & Creighton-Zollar, A. (1998). Diverse self-directed work teams: Developing strategic initiatives for 21st century organizations. *Public Personnel Management, 27*(2), 187–200.

Ginsberg, M., & Wlodowski, R. (2009). *Diversity & motivation: Culturally responsive teaching in college.* San Francisco, CA: Jossey-Bass.

Giovannini, M. (2004). What gets measured gets done: Achieving results through diversity and inclusion. *Journal for Quality and Participation, 27,* 21–27.

Gitlin, T. (1987). *The sixties: Years of hope, days of rage.* New York, NY: Bantam Books.

Giulianelli, D., Cruzado, G., Rodriguez, R., Vera, P. M., Trigueros, A., & Moreno, E. (2011). Advances in new technologies, interactive interfaces, and communicability. *Lecture Notes in Computer Science, 6616*, 62–72. doi:10.1007/978-3-642-20810-2_7

Giuliani, R. W. (2002). *Leadership.* New York, NY: Miramax Books.

Giunipero, L. (1981). Developing effective minority purchasing programs. *Sloan Management Review, 22*(2), 33–42.

Gladwin, T. N., Kenelly, J. J., & Krause, T. (1995). Shifting paradigms for sustainable development: Implications for management theory and research. *Academy of Management Review, 20*(4), 874–907.

Glazier, J. A. (2003). Developing cultural fluency: Arab and Jewish students engaging in one another's company. *Harvard Educational Review, 73*(2), 141–163.

Glick, B. J., & Day, N. E. (2000). Teaching diversity: A study of organizational needs and diversity curriculum in higher education. *Journal of Management Education, 24*(3), 338–352. doi:10.1177/105256290002400305

Glomb, T. M., & Liao, H. (2003). Interpersonal aggression in work groups: Social influence, reciprocal, and individual effects. *Academy of Management Journal, 46*(4), 486–496. doi:10.2307/30040640

Goffman, E. (1961). *Encounters.* Indianapolis, IN: Bobbs-Merrill.

Goffman, E. (1963). *Stigma: Notes on the management of spoiled identity.* New York, NY: Simon & Schuster.

Goizueta Executive, M. B. A. (2011). *Emory University's online course catalog.* Retrieved from http://www.goizueta.emory.edu/cgi-bin/generate/microsite_info_req.pl?display=form&section=emba&tactic=140.

Golden, T. (2007). Co-workers who telework and the impact on those in the office: Understanding the implications of virtual work for co-worker satisfaction and turnover intentions. *Human Relations, 60*(11), 1641–1667. doi:10.1177/0018726707084303

Golden, T. D., Veiga, J. F., & Dino, R. N. (2008). The impact of professional isolation on teleworker job performance and turnover intentions: Does time spent teleworking, interacting face-to-face, or having access to communication-enhancing technology matter? *The Journal of Applied Psychology, 93*(6), 1412–1421. doi:10.1037/a0012722

Goldsmith, M., & Walt, K. (1999, December/January). New competencies for tomorrow's global leader. *CMA Management,* 20-24.

Goldstein, I. L., & Ford, J. K. (2002). *Training in organizations* (4th ed.). Belmont, CA: Wadsworth Group.

Goleman, D. (2004, January). What makes a Leader? *Harvard Business Review,* •••, 22–34.

Golembiewski, R. T. (1979). *Approaches to planned change: Part 2.* New York, NY: Marcel Dekker.

Golembiewski, R. T. (1995). *Managing diversity in organizations.* Birmingham, AL: University of Alabama Press.

Gómez-Mejía, L. R., & Balkin, D. B. (2002). *Administración.* Spain: McGraw-Hill.

Gong, Y. (2006). The impact of subsidiary top management team national diversity on subsidiary performance: Knowledge and legitimacy perspectives. *Management International Review, 46*(6), 771–789. doi:10.1007/s11575-006-0126-2

Gonsiorek, J. C., & Weinrich, J. D. (1991). The definition and scope of sexual orientation. In Gonsiorek, J. C., & Weinrich, J. D. (Eds.), *Homosexuality: Research Implications for Public Policy* (pp. 1–12). Newbury Park, CA: Sage.

Gonzalez, J. A. (2010). Diversity change in organizations: A systemic, multilevel, and nonlinear process. *The Journal of Applied Behavioral Science, 46*(2), 197–219. doi:10.1177/0021886310367943

Gonzalez, J., & Denisi, A. (2009). Cross-level effects of demography and diversity climate on organizational attachment and firm effectiveness. *Journal of Organizational Behavior, 30*, 21–40. doi:10.1002/job.498

Goodman, P. S. Ravlin, E. C., & Argote, L. (1986). Current thinking about groups: Setting the stage for new ideas. In P. S. Goodman (Ed.), *Designing Effective Work Groups.* San Francisco, CA: Jossey-Bass.

Gordon, G. G., DiTomaso, N., & Farris, G. F. (1991). Managing diversity in R&D groups. *Research Technology Management, 34*(1), 18–23.

Gordon, J. (1995, May). Different from what? Diversity as a performance issue. *Training (New York, N.Y.)*, 25–33.

Gostnell, G. M. (1996). *The leadership of African American women: Constructing realities, shifting paradigms.* Portland, OR: Portland State University.

Gowdy, H., Hildebrand, A., La Piana, D., & Mendes Campos, M. (2009). *How five trends will reshape the social sector.* Irvine, CA: The James Irvine Foundation.

Graetz, K. A., Boyle, E. B., Kimble, C. E., Thompson, P., & Garloch, J. L. (1998). Information sharing in face-to-face, teleconferencing, and electronic chat groups. *Small Group Research, 29*(6), 714–743. doi:10.1177/1046496498296003

Grant, J. (1988). Women as managers: What they can offer to organizations? *Organizational Dynamics, 16*(1), 56–63. doi:10.1016/0090-2616(88)90036-8

Graves, E. G. (1997). *How to succeed in business without being white.* Scranton, PA: HarperBusiness.

Gray, K., & Paryono, P. (2004). A conceptual model of workforce education and development systems. In Rojewski, J. W. (Ed.), *International Perspectives on Workforce Education and Development* (pp. 17–42). Greenwich, CT: Information Age.

Gray, M., Kurihara, T., Hommen, L., & Feldman, J. (2007). Networks of exclusion: Job segmentation and social networks in the knowledge economy. *Equal Opportunities International, 26*(2), 144–161. doi:10.1108/02610150710732212

Greenberg, J. (2011). *Behavior in organizations* (10th ed.). Upper Saddle River, NJ: Prentice Hall.

Greene, A. M., & Kirton, G. (2011). Diversity management meets downsizing: The case of a government department. *Employee Relations, 33*(1), 22–40. doi:10.1108/01425451111091636

Greenwald, A. G., & Banaji, M. R. (1995). Implicit social cognition: Attitudes, self-esteem, and stereotypes. *Psychological Review, 102*, 4–27. doi:10.1037/0033-295X.102.1.4

Greer, B., Matlbia, T., & Scott, C. (2006). Supplier diversity: A missing link in HRD. *Human Resource Development Quarterly, 17*(3), 325–341. doi:10.1002/hrdq.1177

Greer, L. L., Homan, A. C., De Hoogh, A. H. B., & Den Hartog, D. N. (2012). Tainted visions: The effect of visionary leader behaviors and leader categorization tendencies on the financial performance of ethnically diverse teams. *The Journal of Applied Psychology, 97*(1), 203–213. doi:10.1037/a0025583

Gregerson, H. B., Morrison, A. J., & Black, G. S. (1998, Fall). Developing leaders in the global frontier. *Sloan Management Review*, 21–32.

Gregory-Mina, H. (2010). The importance of teams and how to lead teams through change initiatives in 21st century organizations. *The Business Review, Cambridge, 16*(1), 60–66.

Greller, M. M., & Simpson, P. (1999). In search of late career: A review of contemporary social science research applicable to the understanding of late career. *Human Resource Management Review, 9*, 309–347. doi:10.1016/S1053-4822(99)00023-6

Griffith, K. H., & Hebl, M. R. (2002). The disclosure dilemma for gay men and lesbians: "Coming out" at work. *The Journal of Applied Psychology, 87*(6), 1191–1199. doi:10.1037/0021-9010.87.6.1191

Groschl, S. (2011). Diversity management strategies of global hotel groups: A corporate web site based exploration. *International Journal of Contemporary Hospitality Management, 23*(2), 224–241. doi:10.1108/09596111111119347

Grunin, S. (2011). *Becoming more competitive: How diversity and inclusion can transform your organization.* Paper presented at the Presentation on the Diversity & Inclusion White Paper Activity at the May 12, 2011 ACT-IAC Human Capital SIG Meeting. Retrieved June 17, 2011, from http://www.actgov.org/knowledgebank/ documentsandpresentations/Documents/Shared%20Interest%20Groups/Human%20Capital%20SIG/How%20 Diversity%20and%20Inclusion%20Can%20Transform%20Your%20Organization%20-%20Susan%20 Grunin-HC%20SIG%202005-11-11.pdf.

Gruszczynska, A. (2009). *Queer enough? Contested terrains of identity deployment in the context of gay and lesbian public activism in Poland*. Doctoral Dissertation. Birmingham, UK: Aston University.

Gudykunst, W. B., Guzley, R. M., & Hammer, M. R. (1996). Designing intercultural training. In Landis, D., & Bhagat, R. S. (Eds.), *Handbook of Intercultural Training*. Thousand Oaks, CA: Sage.

Gudykunst, W. B., & Hammer, M. R. (1984). Dimension of intercultural effectiveness: Culture specific or general. *International Journal of Intercultural Relations, 8*, 1–10. doi:10.1016/0147-1767(84)90003-8

Guerot, U. (2003). *On the future of Europe* (p. 5). Deutschland.

Guerrier, Y., & Wilson, C. (2011). Representing diversity on UK company websites. *Equality, Diversity and Inclusion, International Journal (Toronto, Ont.), 30*(3), 183–195.

Guidestar. (2010). *The nonprofit research collaborative: November 2010 fundraising survey*. Retrieved June 17, 2010 from http://www2.guidestar.org/ViewCmsFile.aspx?ContentID=3117.

Gumbrell-McCormick, R. (2011). European trade unions and 'atypical' workers. *Industrial Relations Journal, 42*(3), 293. doi:10.1111/j.1468-2338.2011.00628.x

Gumpert, D. E. (1979). Seeking minority-owned businesses as suppliers. *Harvard Business Review, 57*(1), 110–116.

Gunawardena, C. N., Nolla, A. C., Wilson, P. L., Lopez-Islas, J. R., Ramirez-Angel, N., & Megchun-Alpizar, R. M. (2001). A cross-cultural study of group process and development in online conferences. *Distance Education, 22*(1), 85–121. doi:10.1080/0158791010220106

Gupta, A. K. (1988). Contingency perspectives on strategic leadership: Current knowledge and future research direction. In Hambrick, D. C. (Ed.), *The Executive Effect: Concepts and Methods for Studying Top Managers*. Greenwich, CT: JAI Press.

Gurin, P., Dey, E. L., Hurtado, S., & Gurin, G. (2002). Diversity and higher education: Theory and impact on educational outcomes. *Harvard Educational Review, 72*(3), 330–336.

Guzzo, R. A., & Dickson, M. W. (1996). Teams in organizations: Recent research on performance and effectiveness. *Annual Review of Psychology, 47*, 307–338. doi:10.1146/annurev.psych.47.1.307

Haas, M. (2010). The double-edged swords of autonomy and external knowledge: Analyzing team effectiveness in a multinational organization. *Academy of Management Journal, 53*(5), 989–1008. doi:10.5465/AMJ.2010.54533180

Hackman, J. R. (2002). *Leading teams: Setting the stage for great performances*. Boston, MA: HBS Press.

Hailey, V. H., Farndale, E., & Truss, C. (2005). The HR department's role in organisational performance. *Human Resource Management Journal, 15*(3), 49–66. doi:10.1111/j.1748-8583.2005.tb00153.x

Halaby, C. N. (2003). Where job values come from: Family and schooling background, cognitive ability, and gender. *American Sociological Review, 68*, 251–278. doi:10.2307/1519768

Hales, C. (2005). Rooted in supervision, branching into management: Continuity and change in the role of first-line manager. *Journal of Management Studies, 42*(3), 471–506. doi:10.1111/j.1467-6486.2005.00506.x

Hall, D. T., & Richter, J. (1990). Career gridlock: Baby boomers hit the wall. *The Academy of Management Executive, 4*(3), 7–22.

Hall, E. T. (1987). *Hidden differences: Doing business with the Japanese*. Garden City, NY: Anchor Press/Doubleday.

Halpern, P. (2006). *Workforce issues in the nonprofit sector: Generational leadership change and diversity*. Kansas, MO: American Humanics.

Halter, M. (2000). *Shopping for identity: The marketing of ethnicity*. New York, NY: Schocken Books.

Hambrick, D. C., Cho, T. S., & Chen, M. (1996). The influence of top management team heterogeneity on firms' competitive moves. *Administrative Science Quarterly, 41*(4), 659–684. doi:10.2307/2393871

Hambrick, D. C., Davison, S. C., Snell, S. A., & Snow, C. (1998). When groups consist of multiple nationalities: Towards a new understanding of the implications. *Organization Studies, 19*(2), 181–205. doi:10.1177/017084069801900202

Hambrick, D. C., & Finkelstein, S. (1987). Managerial discretion: A bridge between polar views on organizations. In Staw, B. M., & Gummings, L. L. (Eds.), *Research in Organizational Behavior*. Greenwich, CT: JAI Press.

Hambrick, D. E., & Mason, P. A. (1984). Upper echelons: The organization as a reflection of its top managers. *Academy of Management Review*, *9*, 193–206.

Hammer, M. R., Gudykunst, W. B., & Wiseman, R. L. (1978). Dimensions of intercultural effectiveness: An exploratory study. *International Journal of Intercultural Relations*, *2*, 383–393. doi:10.1016/0147-1767(78)90036-6

Han, P. C. (1997). *An investigation of intercultural effectiveness of international university students with implications for human resource development*. Unpublished Doctoral dissertation. Fayetteville, AR: University of Arkansas.

Handfield, R. B., Krause, D. R., Scannell, T. V., & Monczka, R. M. (2000). Avoid the pitfalls in supplier development. *Sloan Management Review*, *41*(2), 37–49.

Hannigan, T. P. (1990). Traits, attitudes, and skills that are related to intercultural effectiveness and their implications for cross-cultural training: A review of the literature. *International Journal of Intercultural Relations*, *13*, 89–111. doi:10.1016/0147-1767(90)90049-3

Han, P. C. (2008). An investigation of intercultural effectiveness for foreign-born faculty in Taiwan. *The International Journal of Learning*, *15*(10), 165–174.

Han, P. C. (2011). Developing intercultural effectiveness competencies: The journey of transformative learning and cross-cultural learning for foreign-born faculty in American higher education. In Boden, C. J., & Kippers, S. M. (Eds.), *Pathway to Transformation: Learning in Relationship*. Charlotte, NC: Information Age Publishing.

Hansen, F. (2003). Diversity's business case doesn't add up. *Workforce*. Retrieved from http://findarticles.com/p/articles/mi_m0FXS/is_4_82/ai_99986376/?tag=content;col1.

Haq, R. (2004). International perspectives on workplace diversity. In Stockdale, M. S., & Crosby, F. J. (Eds.), *The Psychology and Management of Workplace Diversity* (pp. 277–298). Malden, MA: Blackwell.

Harbison, F. H. (1973). *Human Resources as the wealth of nations*. Oxford, UK: Oxford University Press.

Harder, R., Keeter, J. M., Woodcock, B. W., Ferguson, J. W., & Wills, F. W. (2005). Insights in implementing collaboration engineering. In *Proceedings of the 38th Hawaii International Conference on System Sciences*. Big Island, HI: System Sciences.

Hardiman, R., Jackson, B. W., & Griffin, P. (2010). Conceptual foundations. In Adams, M., Blumenfeld, W. J., Castañeda, C., Hackman, H. W., Peters, M. L., & Zuñiga, X. (Eds.), *Readings for Diversity and Social Justice* (2nd ed.). New York, NY: Routledge/Taylor & Francis Group.

Harrington, M. (2009). What is your diversity management recession strategy? *Profiles of Diversity Journal*. Retrieved from http://www.aimd.org/.

Harris, D., & Kleiner, B. (1993). Managing and valuing diversity in the workplace. *Equal Opportunities International*, *12*(4), 6–10. doi:10.1108/eb010604

Harris, L., Doughty, D., & Kirk, S. (2002). The devolution of HR responsibilities – Perspectives from the UK's public sector. *Journal of European Industrial Training*, *26*(5), 218–229. doi:10.1108/03090590210424894

Harris, L., & Foster, C. (2010). Aligning talent management with approaches to equality and diversity. *Equality, Diversity and Inclusion. International Journal (Toronto, Ont.)*, *29*(5), 422–435.

Harrison, D., Price, K. H., Gavin, J. H., & Florey, A. T. (2002). *Time, teams, and task performance: Changing effects of surface- and deep-level diversity on group functioning*. Retrieved May 29, 2011 from http://www.aom.pace.edu/amj/October2002/harrison.pdf.

Harrison, D. A., & Klein, K. J. (2007). What's the difference? Diversity constructs as separation, variety, or disparity in organizations. *Academy of Management Review*, *32*, 1199–1228. doi:10.5465/AMR.2007.26586096

Harrison, D. A., Kravitz, D. M., Mayer, L. M., & Leslie, D. L.-A. (2006). Understanding attitudes toward affirmative action programs in employment. *The Journal of Applied Psychology*, *91*(5), 1013–1036. doi:10.1037/0021-9010.91.5.1013

Harrison, D. A., Price, K. H., & Bell, M. P. (1998). Beyond relational demography: Time and the effects of surface- and deep-level diversity on work group cohesion. *Academy of Management Journal*, *41*(1), 96–107. doi:10.2307/256901

Harris, P. R., & Moran, R. T. (1987). *Managing cultural differences* (2nd ed.). Houston, TX: Gulf Publishing Company.

Hart, M. (1997). *Managing diversity for sustained competitiveness*. New York, NY: The Conference Board.

Hartenian, L., & Gudmundson, D. (2000). Cultural diversity in small business: Implications for firm performance. *Journal of Developmental Entrepreneurship*, *5*(3), 209–220.

Harvey, G. (2003). *Program on redefining diversity*. Paper presented at 4th Annual Summit on Leading Diversity. Retrieved March 10 from http://www.linkageinc.com.

Harvey, B. H. (1999). Technology, diversity and work culture: Key trends in the next millennium. *HRMagazine*, *44*(11), 58–60.

Harvey, C. P., & Allard, M. J. (2005). *Understanding and managing diversity: Readings, cases and exercises*. Upper Saddle River, NJ: Pearson Education.

Harvey, C. P., & Allard, M. J. (2008). *Understanding and managing diversity: Readings, cases, and exercises* (4th ed.). Upper Saddle River, NJ: Prentice-Hall.

Harvey, C., & Allard, J. (2009). *Understanding and managing diversity* (4th ed.). Upper Saddle River, NJ: Prentice Hall.

Harvey, M. G., & Buckley, M. R. (1997). Managing inpatriates: Building a global core competency. *Journal of World Business*, *32*, 35–53. doi:10.1016/S1090-9516(97)90024-9

Haslam, A. S., Reicher, S. D., & Platow, M. J. (2011). *The new psychology of leadership: Identity, influence and power*. Hove, UK: Psychology Press.

Hatch, E. K. (1995). Cross cultural team building and training. *Journal for Quality and Participation*, *18*(2), 44–48.

Havenga, A. J. (1993). Beyond affirmative action there is diversity. *PRO Technida*, *1*(10), 9–17.

Hawes, R., & Kealey, D. (1979). *Canadians in development: An empirical study of adaptations and effectiveness on overseas assignment*. Quebec, Canada: Canadian International Development Agency.

Hayes, S. N., Ofili, E. O., & Mitchell, J. E. (2010). *Racial/ethnic disparities: CVD in African American women*. Retrieved on February 26, 2010 from http://www.medscape.org/viewprogram/30681.

Hayes, E., & Flannery, D. D. (2000). *Women as learners: The significance of gender in adult learning*. San Francisco, CA: Jossey-Bass Publishers.

Hayes, K. H. (2000). *Managing career transitions: Your career as a work in progress* (2nd ed.). Upper Saddle River, NJ: Prentice Hall.

Hays-Thomas, R. (2004). Why now? The contemporary focus on managing diversity. In Stockdale, M. S., & Crosby, F. J. (Eds.), *The Psychology and Management of Workplace Diversity* (pp. 3–30). Malden, MA: Blackwell.

Hebl, M., Madera, J. M., & King, E. (2008). Exclusion, avoidance, and social distancing. In Thomas, D. M. (Ed.), *Diversity Resistance in Organizations* (pp. 127–150). New York, NY: Psychology Press.

Hegarty, W. H., & Dalton, D. R. (1995). Development and psychometric properties of the organizational diversity inventory (ODI). *Educational and Psychological Measurement*, *55*, 1047–1052. doi:10.1177/0013164495055006014

Heifetz, R., & Laurie, D. (1996). The work of leadership. *Harvard Business Review*. Retrieved on August 4, 2001, from http://mowgli.org.uk/wp-content/uploads/2011/02/laurie-jump-off-balcony-leadership.pdf.

Heil, G., Bennis, W., & Stephens, D. C. (2000). *Douglas McGregor, revisited: Managing the human side of enterprise*. New York, NY: John Wiley & Sons, Inc.

Heilman, M. E., Block, C. J., & Martell, R. F. (1995). Sex stereotypes: Do they influence perceptions of managers? *Journal of Social Behavior and Personality*, *10*, 237–252.

Helson, R., & Kwan, V. S. Y. (2000). Personality development in adulthood: The broad picture and processes in one longitudinal sample. In Hampson, S. E. (Ed.), *Advances in Personality Psychology* (*Vol. 1*, pp. 77–106). London, UK: Routledge.

Henslin, J. M. (2008). *Essentials of sociology: A down to earth approach* (8th ed.). Boston, MA: Allyn & Bacon.

Herek, G. M. (1990). The context of anti-gay violence. *Journal of Interpersonal Violence, 5*, 316–333. doi:10.1177/088626090005003006

Herek, G. M. (1996). Why tell if you're not asked? Self-disclosure, intergroup contact and heterosexuals' attitudes towards lesbians and gay men. In Herek, G. M., Jobe, J. B., & Carney, R. M. (Eds.), *Coming Out in Force: Sexual Orientation and the Military* (pp. 197–225). Chicago, IL: University of Chicago Press.

Herek, G. M., Jobe, I. B., & Carney, R. M. (Eds.). (1996). *Coming out in force: Sexual orientation and the military.* Chicago, IL: University of Chicago Press.

Heron, J. (1992). *Feeling and personhood: Psychology in another key.* Newbury Park, CA: Sage.

Heron, J. (1999). *The complete facilitator's handbook.* London, UK: Kogan Page.

Herriot, P., & Pemberton, C. (1995). *Competitive advantage through diversity: Organizational learning from difference.* London, UK: Sage Publications.

Hertel, G., Geister, S., & Konradt, U. (2005). Managing virtual teams: A review of current empirical research. *Human Resource Management Review, 15*(1), 69–95. doi:10.1016/j.hrmr.2005.01.002

Hewitt Associates. (2004). *Preparing the workforce of tomorrow.* Retrieved from http://www.hewitt.com.

Hewlett, S. A., Luce, C. B., & West, C. (2005). Leadership in your midst. *Harvard Business Review, 83*(11), 74.

Hewstone, M., Rubin, M., & Willis, H. (2002). Intergroup bias. *Annual Review of Psychology, 53*, 575–604. doi:10.1146/annurev.psych.53.100901.135109

Hicks-Clarke, D., & Illes, P. (2000). Climate for diversity and its effects on career and organizational perceptions. *Personnel Review, 29*, 324–347. doi:10.1108/00483480010324689

Higher Education Research Institute of University of Southern California. Los Angeles. (2008). *The American freshman forty-year trends: 1966–2006.* Retrieved May 22, 2011, from http://www.heri.ucla.edu/PDFs/pubs/briefs/40yrTrendsResearchBrief.pdf.

Highhouse, S., Stierwalt, S. L., Bachiochi, P., Elder, A. E., & Fisher, G. (1999). Effects of advertised human resource management practices on attraction of African American applicants. *Personnel Psychology, 52*, 424–442. doi:10.1111/j.1744-6570.1999.tb00167.x

Hinds, B. (2001). *Learning strategies in the African-American community of Enid, Oklahoma.* Unpublished Doctoral Dissertation. Stillwater, OK: Oklahoma State University.

Hinds, P. J., & Bailey, D. E. (2003). Out of sight, out of sync: Understanding conflict in distributed teams. *Organization Science, 14*(6), 615–632. doi:10.1287/orsc.14.6.615.24872

Hine, D. C. (1992). The black studies movement: Afrocentric-traditionalist-feminist paradigms for the next stage. *The Black Scholar, 22*, 11–18.

Hines, R. D. (1992). Accounting: Filling the negative space. *Accounting, Organizations and Society, 17*(3/4), 313–341. doi:10.1016/0361-3682(92)90027-P

Hite, L. M., & McDonald, K. S. (2006). Diversity training pitfalls and possibilities: An exploration of small and mid-size US organizations. *Human Resource Development International, 9*(3), 365–377. doi:10.1080/13678860600893565

Hitt, M. A., Miller, C. C., & Collela, A. (2006). *Organizational behavior: A strategic approach.* New York, NY: John Wiley & Sons.

Hodes, B. (2008). *Diversity best practices research for HCI summit: Full Report.* Bernard Hodes Group. Retrieved from http://emarketing.hodes.com/hci_may08/pdfs/HCI_ExecutiveSum_050208_FINAL.pdf.

Hoel, H., & Cooper, C. L. (2000). *Destructive conflict and bullying at work.* Retrieved from http://www.workplacebullying.org/res/umist.pdf.

Hoel, H., Faragher, B., & Cooper, C. L. (2004). Bullying is detrimental to health, but all bullying behaviors are not necessarily equally damaging. *British Journal of Guidance & Counselling, 32*(3), 367–387. doi:10.1080/03069880410001723594

Hoerr, J. (1989). The payoff from teamwork. *Business Week*, 56-62.

Hoerr, J. (1989, July 10). The payoff from teamwork. *Business Week*, 55-62.

Hofstede, G. (1980). *Cultures consequences: International differences in working-related values*. Beverly Hills, CA: Sage.

Hofstede, G. (1984). *Culture's consequences: International differences on work related values*. Beverly Hills, CA: Sage.

Hofstede, G. (1991). *Cultures and organizations: Software of the mind*. London, UK: McGraw-Hill International.

Hofstede, G. H. (2001). *Culture's consequences: Comparing values, behaviors, institutions and organizations across nations* (2nd ed.). Thousand Oaks, CA: Sage.

Hofstede, G., & Hofstede, G. J. (2005). *Cultures and organizations: Software of the mind*. New York, NY: McGraw-Hill.

Hogan, R., & Nicholson, R. A. (1988). The meaning of personality test scores. *The American Psychologist, 43*, 621–626. doi:10.1037/0003-066X.43.8.621

Hogg, M. A., & Terry, D. J. (2000). Social identity and self-categorization processes in organizational contexts. *Academy of Management Review, 25*, 121–140.

Hogg, M., & Abrams, D. (1988). *Social identification*. London, UK: Routledge.

Holladay, C. L. (2003). The influence of framing on attitudes toward diversity training. *Human Resource Development Quarterly, 14*(3), 245–263. doi:10.1002/hrdq.1065

Holladay, C. L., & Quinones, M. A. (2008). The influence of training focus and trainer characteristics on diversity training effectiveness. *Academy of Management Learning & Education, 7*(3), 343–354. doi:10.5465/AMLE.2008.34251672

Hollander, E. P. (2009). *Inclusive leadership: The essential leader-follower relationship*. New York, NY: Routledge/Taylor & Francis Group.

Holland, J. L. (1973). *Making vocational choices: A theory of careers*. Upper Saddle River, NJ: Prentice-Hall.

Hollingshead, A. B. (1996). Information suppression and status persistence in group decision making: The effects of communication media. *Human Communication Research, 23*, 193–219. doi:10.1111/j.1468-2958.1996.tb00392.x

Hollingshead, A. B. (1996). The rank order effect in group decision making. *Organizational Behavior and Human Decision Processes, 68*, 181–193. doi:10.1006/obhd.1996.0098

Holvino, E., & Kamp, A. (2009). Diversity management: Are we moving in the right direction? Reflections from both sides of the North Atlantic. *Scandinavian Journal of Management, 25*(4), 395–403. doi:10.1016/j.scaman.2009.09.005

Hom, P. (2007). *Women and minorities' high quit rates make corporate diversity difficult*. Retrieved March 10, 2011 from www.knowledge.wpcarey.asu.edu.

Homan, A. C., Greer, L. L., Jehn, K. A., & Koning, L. (2010). Believing shapes seeing: The impact of diversity beliefs on the construal of group composition. *Group Processes & Intergroup Relations, 13*, 477–493. doi:10.1177/1368430209350747

Homan, A. C., Hollenbeck, J. R., Humphrey, S. E., van Knippenberg, D., Ilgen, D. R., & van Kleef, G. A. (2008). Facing differences with an open mind: Openness to experience, salience of intra-group differences, and performance of diverse groups. *Academy of Management Journal, 58*, 1204–1222. doi:10.5465/AMJ.2008.35732995

Homan, A. C., van Knippenberg, D., van Kleef, G. A., & De Dreu, C. K. W. (2007). Bridging faultines by valuing diversity: The effects of diversity beliefs on information processing and performance in diverse work groups. *The Journal of Applied Psychology, 92*, 1189–1199. doi:10.1037/0021-9010.92.5.1189

Hong, L., & Page, S. E. (2004). Groups of diverse problem solvers can outperform groups of high-ability problem solvers. *Proceedings of the National Academy of Sciences of the United States of America, 202*(46), 16385–16389. doi:10.1073/pnas.0403723101

Hoobler, J., Basadur, T., & Lemmon, G. (2007). Management of a diverse workforce: Meanings and practices. *The Journal of Equipment Lease Financing, 25*(1), 1–8.

hooks, b. (1984). *Feminist theory: From the margin to center.* Boston, MA: South End Press.

Horn, J. L., & Cattell, R. B. (1967). Age differences in fluid and crystallized intelligence. *Acta Psychologica, 26*, 107–129. doi:10.1016/0001-6918(67)90011-X

Horwitz, S. K., & Horwitz, I. B. (2007). The effects of team diversity on team outcomes: A meta-analytic review of team demography. *Journal of Management, 33*(6), 987–1015. doi:10.1177/0149206307308587

Hostager, T. J., & De Meuse, K. P. (2002). Assessing the complexity of diversity perceptions: Breadth, depth, and balance. *Journal of Business and Psychology, 17*, 189–206. doi:10.1023/A:1019681314837

House, R. J. (1971). A path goal theory of leader effectiveness. *Administrative Science Quarterly, 16*, 321–339. doi:10.2307/2391905

House, R. J., Hanges, P. J., Javidan, M., Dorfman, P. W., & Gupta, V. (Eds.). (2004). *Culture, leadership and organizations: The GLOBE study of 62 societies.* Thousand Oaks, CA: Sage.

House, R. J., Spangler, W. D., & Woycke, J. (1991). Personality and charisma in the U. S. presidency: A psychological theory of leadership effectiveness. *Administrative Science Quarterly, 36*, 364–396. doi:10.2307/2393201

Howard-Hamilton, M. F. (2003). Theoretical frameworks for African American women. *New Directions for Student Services, 104*, 19–27. doi:10.1002/ss.104

HRC. (2008). *State of the workplace for gay, lesbian, bisexual and transgender Americans: 2006-07.* Retrieved January 27, 2011 from http://www.hrc.org/documents/State_of_the_Workplace.pdf.

HRC. (2011). *Statewide employment laws and policies.* Retrieved April 06, 2011 from http://www.hrc.org/documents/Employment_Laws_and_Policies.pdf.

Huang, W. W., Wei, K. K., Watson, R. T., & Tan, B. C. (2002). Supporting virtual team-building in GSS: An empirical investigation. *Decision Support Systems, 34*, 359–367. doi:10.1016/S0167-9236(02)00009-X

Hughes, R. L., & Howard-Hamilton, M. F. (2003). Insights: emphasizing issues that affect African American women. In M. F. Howard-Hamilton (Ed.), *Meeting the Needs of African American Women* (Vol. 104), (pp. 95-104). San Francisco, CA: Jossey-Bass.

Hughes, C. (2010). "People as technology" conceptual model: Towards a new value creation paradigm for strategic human resource development. *Human Resource Development Review, 9*(1), 48–71. doi:10.1177/1534484309353561

Human Capital. (2011). *Dictionary.* Retrieved on October 31, 2011 from http://dictionary.reference.com/browse/human+capital.

Human Rights Campaign. (2009). *State of the workplace.* Retrieved August 25, 2011 from http://www.hrc.org/documents/HRC_Foundation_State_of_the_Workplace_2007-2008.pdf.

Human Rights Campaign. (2011). *Timeline: The employment non-discrimination act.* Retrieved on 9/1/11 from http://www.hrc.org/issues/workplace/5636.htm.

Humphrey, S. E., Hollenbeck, J. R., Meyer, C. J., & Ilgen, D. R. (2007). Trait configurations in self-managed teams: A conceptual examination of the use of seeding for maximizing and minimizing trait variance in teams. *The Journal of Applied Psychology, 92*, 595–615. doi:10.1037/0021-9010.92.3.885

Hunter, W. D. (2004). *Knowledge, skills, attitudes, and experience necessary to become globally competent.* Doctorial Dissertation. Bethlehem, PA: Lehigh University.

Huselid, M. A., Becker, B. E., & Beatty, R. W. (2005). *The workforce scorecard: Managing human capital to execute strategy.* Boston, MA: Harvard Business School Press.

Hymowitz, C. (1999, April 6). Remote managers find ways to narrow the distance gap. *The Wall Street Journal*, p. B1.

i4CP. (2009). *Study of leadership competencies.* New York, NY: Institute for Corporate Productivity.

Idowu, W. (2004). Theorising conflict and violence: Contemporary Africa and the imperative of peaceful coexistence. *African Conflict Profile: Journal of the Centre for Ethnic and Conflict Studies, 1*(1), 1–17.

Iles, P., & Hayers, P. K. (1997). Managing diversity in transnational project teams: A tentative model and case study. *Journal of Managerial Psychology*, *12*(2), 95–117. doi:10.1108/02683949710164190

Ilgen, D. R., Hollenbeck, J. R., Johnson, M., & Jundt, D. (2005). Teams in organizations: From input-process-output models to IMOI models. *Annual Review of Psychology*, *56*, 517–543. doi:10.1146/annurev.psych.56.091103.070250

Inglis, T. (1997). Empowerment and emancipation. *Adult Education Quarterly*, *48*(1), 3–17. doi:10.1177/074171369704800102

Insight. (2008). *The 2007 telecommunications industry review: An anthology of market facts and forecasts.* Mountain Lakes, NJ: The Insight Research Corporation.

Irons, L. (2008). E-learning 2.0 and learning management systems (LMS). Retrieved December 7, 2008, from http://skilfulminds.com/2008/05/19/elearning-20-and-learning-management-systems-lms/.

Irving, J. (2009). Educating global leaders: Exploring intercultural competence in leadership education. *Journal of International Business and Cultural Studies.* Retrieved on July 2, 2011, from http://aabri.com/manuscripts/09392.pdf.

Isaacson, L. E., & Brown, D. (1997). *Career information, career counseling, and career development* (6th ed.). Boston, MA: Allyn & Bacon.

Islam, M. R., & Hewstone, M. (1993). Intergroup attitudes and affective consequences in majority and minority groups. *Journal of Personality and Social Psychology*, *64*, 936–950. doi:10.1037/0022-3514.64.6.936

Ivancevich, J. M., & Gilbert, J. A. (2000). Diversity management: Time for a new approach. *Public Personnel Management*, *9*(1), 75–92.

Jackson, C., Colquitt, J. A., Wesson, M. J., & Zapata-Phelan, C. P. (2006). Psychological collectivism: A measurement validation and linkage to group member performance. *The Journal of Applied Psychology*, *91*(4), 884–899. doi:10.1037/0021-9010.91.4.884

Jackson, S. (1992). Consequences of group composition for the interpersonal dynamics of strategic issue processing. *Advances in Strategic Management*, *8*, 345–382.

Jackson, S. (1996). The consequences of diversity in multidisciplinary work teams. In West, M. A. (Ed.), *Handbook of Work Group Psychology*. New York, NY: John Wiley&Sons.

Jackson, S. E., Brett, J. F., Sessa, V. I., Cooper, D. M., Julin, J. A., & Peyronnin, K. (1991). Some differences make a difference: Individual dissimilarity and group heterogeneity as correlates of recruitment, promotions, and turnover. *The Journal of Applied Psychology*, *76*, 675–689. doi:10.1037/0021-9010.76.5.675

Jackson, S. E., Joshi, A., & Erhardt, N. L. (2003). Recent research on team and organizational diversity: SWOT analysis and implications. *Journal of Management*, *29*(6), 801–830.

Jackson, S. E., May, K. E., & Whitney, K. (1995). Understanding the dynamics of diversity in decision-making teams. In Guzzo, R. A., & Salas, E. (Eds.), *Team Effectiveness and Decision Making in Organizations* (pp. 204–261). San Francisco, CA: Jossey-Bass.

Jacobs, D. (2004, September). In search of future leaders. *Human Resource Management*, •••, 22–27.

Jain, S. C., & Tucker, L. R. (1995). The influence of culture on strategic constructs in the process of globalization: An empirical study of North American and Japanese MNCs. *International Business Review*, *4*(1), 19–37. doi:10.1016/0969-5931(94)00029-L

James, K., Lovato, C., & Cropanzano, R. (1994). Correlational and known-group comparison validation of a workplace prejudice/discrimination inventory. *Journal of Applied Social Psychology*, *24*, 1573–1592. doi:10.1111/j.1559-1816.1994.tb01563.x

Jameson, D. A. (2007). Reconceptualizing cultural identity and its role in intercultural business communication. *Journal of Business Communication*, *44*(3), 199–235. doi:10.1177/0021943607301346

Jamison, C. (2007). Tapping the wisdom of the ages: Ageism and the need for multigenerational organizations. *OD Practitioner*, *39*(2), 14-17. Retrieved May 27, 2011 from http://www.kjcg.com/resources/articles/documents/KJ_TappingTheWisdom_AR_051507.pdf.

Janssens, M., & Brett, J. M. (1997). Meaningful participation in transnational teams. *European Journal of Work and Organizational Psychology, 6*(2), 153–168. doi:10.1080/135943297399141

Jap, S. D., & Ganesan, S. (2000). Control mechanisms and the relationship life cycle: Implications of safeguarding specific investments and developing commitment. *JMR, Journal of Marketing Research, 37*(2), 227–245. doi:10.1509/jmkr.37.2.227.18735

Jarvenpaa, S. L., & Leidner, D. E. (1998). Communication and trust in global virtual teams. *Organization Science, 10*(6), 791–815. doi:10.1287/orsc.10.6.791

Jaschik, S. (2011). The enduring gender gap in pay. *Inside Higher Education*. Retrieved from http://www.insidehighered.com/news/2011/04/052/the_enduring_gender_gap_in_faculty_pay.

Jaschik, S. (2011). The MIT again reviews status of women. *Inside Higher Education*. Retrieved from http://www.insidehighered.com/news/2011/03/21/mit_issues_new_report_on_status_of_women.

Jayne, M. E. A., & Dupboye, R. L. (2004). Leveraging diversity to improve business performance: Research findings and recommendations for organizations. *Human Resource Management, 43*(4), 409–424. doi:10.1002/hrm.20033

Jayne, M., & Dipboye, R. (2004). Leveraging diversity to improve business performance: Research findings and recommendations for organizations. *Human Resource Management, 43*, 409–424. doi:10.1002/hrm.20033

Jean-Marie, G., Williams, V., & Sherman, S. (2009). Black women's leadership experiences: Examining the intersectionality of race and gender. *Advances in Developing Human Resources, 11*(5). doi:10.1177/1523422309351836

Jehn, K. A. (1995). A multimethod examination of the benefits and detriments of intragroup conflict. *Administrative Science Quarterly, 40*(2), 256–282. doi:10.2307/2393638

Jehn, K. A. (1997). A qualitative analysis of conflict types and dimensions in organizational groups. *Administrative Science Quarterly, 42*, 530–557. doi:10.2307/2393737

Jehn, K. A., & Bendersky, C. (2003). Intragroup conflict in organizations: A contingency perspective on the conflict-outcome relationship. *Research in Organizational Behavior, 25*, 189–244. doi:10.1016/S0191-3085(03)25005-X

Jehn, K. A., & Mannix, E. A. (2001). The dynamic nature of conflict: A longitudinal study of intragroup conflict and group performance. *Academy of Management Journal, 44*(2), 238–251. doi:10.2307/3069453

Jehn, K. A., Northcraft, G. B., & Neale, M. A. (1999). Why differences make a difference: A field study of diversity, conflict and performance in work groups. *Administrative Science Quarterly, 44*, 741–763. doi:10.2307/2667054

Jenkins, C. J. (1983). Resource mobilization theory and the study of social movements. *Annual Review of Sociology, 9*(1), 527–553. doi:10.1146/annurev.so.09.080183.002523

Johnson, L., Levine, A., Smith, R., & Stone, S. (2010). *The 2010 horizon report*. Austin, TX: The New Media Consortium. Retrieved June 20, 2011, from http://wp.nmc.org/horizon2010/.

Johnson, A. G. (2006). *Privilege, power and difference* (2nd ed.). New York, NY: McGraw-Hill.

Johnson-Bailey, J., & Cervero, R. M. (2000). The invisible politics of race in adult education. In Wilson, A., & Hayes, E. (Eds.), *Handbook of Adult and Continuing Education*. San Francisco, CA: Jossey-Bass.

Johnson, J. P., Lenartowicz, T., & Apud, S. (2006). Cross-cultural competence in international business: Toward a definition and a model. *Journal of International Business Studies, 37*, 525–543. doi:10.1057/palgrave.jibs.8400205

Johnson, M., & Johnson, L. (2010). *Generations, inc: From boomers to linksters – Managing the frictions between generations at work*. New York, NY: American Management Association.

Johnston, D. A., McCutcheon, D. M., Stuart, F. I., & Kerwood, H. (2004). Effects of supplier trust on performance of cooperative supplier relationships. *Journal of Operations Management, 22*, 23–38. doi:10.1016/j.jom.2003.12.001

Johnston, W. B., & Packer, A. E. (1987). *Workforce 2000: Work and workers for the twenty-first century*. Indianapolis, IN: Hudson Institute.

Jokinen, T. (2005). Global leadership competencies: A review and discussion. *Journal of European Industrial Training*, *29*(3), 199–216. doi:10.1108/03090590510591085

Jones, D. (2004). Screwing diversity out of workers? Reading diversity. *Journal of Organizational Change Management*, *17*(3), 281–291. doi:10.1108/09534810410538333

Joplin, J. R. W., & Dauss, C. S. (1997). Challenges of leading a diverse workforce. *The Academy of Management Executive*, *11*(3), 32–47. doi:10.5465/AME.1997.9709231662

Judge, T. A., & Piccolo, R. (2004). Transformational and transactional leadership: A meta-analytic test of their relative validity. *The Journal of Applied Psychology*, *89*, 755–768. doi:10.1037/0021-9010.89.5.755

Judy, R. W., & D'Amico, C. (1997). *Workforce 2020: Work and workers in the 21st century*. Indianapolis, IN: Hudson Institute.

Kahnweiler, W. M. (2008). The work-life conundrum: Will HRD become more involved? *Human Resource Development Quarterly*, *19*(1), 75–83. doi:10.1002/hrdq.1226

Kamenou, N., & Fearfull, A. (2006). Ethnic minority women: A lost voice in HRM. *Human Resource Management*, *16*(2), 154–172. doi:10.1111/j.1748-8583.2006.00010.x

Kandola, R. (1995). Managing diversity: New broom or old hat? In Cooper, C. L., & Robertson, I. T. (Eds.), *International Review of Industrial and Organizational Psychology*. Chichester, UK: Wiley.

Kandola, R., & Fullerton, J. (1998). *Diversity in action: Managing the mosaic* (2nd ed.). London, UK: CIPD.

Kankanhalli, A., Tan, B. C. Y., & Wei, K. K. (2005). Contributing knowledge to electronic knowledge repositories: An empirical investigation. *Management Information Systems Quarterly*, *29*(1), 113–143.

Kanter, R. M. (1977). *Men and women of the corporation*. New York, NY: Basic Books.

Kanter, R. M. (1991, May/June). Transcending business boundaries: 12,000 world managers view change. *Harvard Business Review*, 151–164.

Kaplan, D. M., Wiley, J. W., & Maertz, C. P. (2011). The role of calculative attachment in the relationship between diversity climate and retention. *Human Resource Management*, *50*(2), 271–287. doi:10.1002/hrm.20413

Kark, R., & Shamir, B. (2002). The dual effect of transformational leadership: Priming relational and collective selves and further effects on followers. In Avolio, B. J., & Yammarino, F. J. (Eds.), *Transformational and Charismatic Leadership: The Road Ahead* (Vol. 2, pp. 67–91). Oxford, UK: Elsevier Science.

Karsten, M. F., & Igou, F. (2005). Career planning: A model for a diverse workforce. In *Proceedings of the North American Management Society track at the 2005 Midwest Business Administration Association Conference*. Chicago, IL: MBAA.

Kasl, E., & Yorks, L. (2002). An extended epistemology for transformative learning theory and its application through collaborative inquiry. *TCRecordOnline*. Retrieved on January 30, 2011 from http://www.tcrecord.org/Content.asp?ContentID=10878.

Kasper, G., Ramos, H. A. J., & Walker, C. J. (2004). Making the case for diversity in philanthropy. *Foundation News & Commentary*, *45*(6). Retrieved June 17, 2011, from http://www.foundationnews.org/CME/article.cfm?ID=3054.

Katila, S., & Merilainen, S. (1999). A serious researcher or just another nice girl? Doing gender in a male-dominated scientific community. *Gender, Work and Organization*, *6*(3), 163–173. doi:10.1111/1468-0432.00079

Kaye, B., & Cohen, J. (2008, April). Safeguarding the intellectual capital of baby boomers. *T&D*, 30-33. S

Kaye, B. (1997). *Up is not the only way*. Englewood Cliffs, NJ: Davies-Black.

Kealey, D. J. (1989). A study of cross-cultural effectiveness: Theoretical issues, practical applications. *International Journal of Intercultural Relations*, *13*, 387–428. doi:10.1016/0147-1767(89)90019-9

Kearney, E., & Gebert, D. (2009). Managing diversity and enhancing team outcomes: The promise of transformational leadership. *The Journal of Applied Psychology, 94*, 77–89. doi:10.1037/a0013077

Keating, L. (2002). Women mentoring women: The rewards of giving. *Women in Business, 54*(1), 28.

Keck, S. L., & Tushman, M. L. (1993). Environmental and organizational context and executive team structure. *Academy of Management Journal, 36*(6), 1314–1344. doi:10.2307/256813

Kegan, R. (1982). *The evolving self: Problems and process in human development.* Cambridge, MA: Harvard University Press.

Kegan, R. (1994). *In over our heads: The mental demands of modern life.* Cambridge, MA: Harvard University Press.

Kehoe, J. F., Dickter, D. N., Russell, D. P., & Sacco, J. M. (2005). e-Selection. In Gueutal & Stone (Eds.), *The Brave New World of e-HR,* (pp. 54-103). San Francisco, CA: Jossey-Bass.

Keller, J., & Loewenstein, J. (2011). The cultural category of cooperation: A cultural consensus model analysis for China and the United States. *Organization Science, 22*(2), 299–320. doi:10.1287/orsc.1100.0530

Kelley, C., & Meyers, J. (1995). *CCAI (cross-cultural adaptability inventory) manual.* Minneapolis, MN: National Computer Systems, Inc.

Kelley, T. (2005). *The ten faces of innovation.* New York, NY: Random House Currency Books.

Kellogg Executive, M. B. A. Program. (2011). *Northwestern University's online course catalog.* Retrieved from http://www.kellogg.northwestern.edu/Programs/EMBA.aspx.

Kelly, E., & Dobbin, F. (1998). How affirmative action became diversity management: Employer response to antidiscrimination laws, 1961 to 1996. *The American Behavioral Scientist, 41*, 960–984. doi:10.1177/0002764298041007008

Kenan-Flagler MBA for Executives. (2011). *University of North Carolina's online course catalog.* Retrieved from http://www.kenan-flagler.unc.edu/programs/emba/index.cfm.

Keogh, K. E. (2008). Workplace diversity and training – More than fine words. In Wilson, J. P. (Ed.), *Human Resource Development* (2nd ed.). London, UK: Kogan Page.

Kerno, S., & Kuznia, K. (2007). Modern career navigation: Preparing for success despite uncertainties. *Industrial Engineer, 39*(10), 31–33.

Kets de Vries, M. F. R., & Mead, C. (1992). The development of the global leader within the multinational corporation. In Pucik, V., Tichy, N. M., & Barnett, C. K. (Eds.), *Globalizing Management: Creating and Leading the Competitive Organization* (pp. 187–205). New York, NY: John Wiley.

Ketter, P. (2010). *Six trends that will change workplace learning forever.* Retrieved from http://www.astd.org/LC/2010/1210_ketter.htm.

Kickul, J., Lester, S. W., & Finkl, J. (2002). Promise breaking during radical organizational change: Do justice interventions make a difference? *Journal of Organizational Behavior, 23*, 469–488. doi:10.1002/job.151

Kidder, D. L. (2004). Backlash toward diversity initiatives: Examining the impact of diversity program justification, personal, and group outcomes. *The International Journal of Conflict Management, 15*, 77–102. doi:10.1108/eb022908

Kieseker, R., & Marchant, T. (1999). Workpalce bullying in Australia: A review of current conceptualizations and existing research. *Australian Journal of Management and Organisational Behaviour, 2*(5), 61–75.

Kiesler, S., & Cummings, J. N. (2002). What do we know about proximity and distance in work groups? A legacy of research. In Hinds, P., & Kiesler, S. (Eds.), *Distributed Work* (pp. 83–112). Cambridge, MA: MIT Press.

Kilduff, M., Angelmar, R., & Mehra, A. (2000). Top management-team diversity and firm performance: Examining the role of cognitions. *Organization Science, 11*(1), 21–34. doi:10.1287/orsc.11.1.21.12569

Kim, P. S. (1997). Globalization of human resource management in government: A cross-cultural perspective. In E. E. Holton, III (Ed.), *Academy of Human Resource Development Conference Proceedings,* (pp. 675-678). Atlanta, GA: Academy of Human Resource Development.

Kim, B., Burns, M. L., & Prescott, J. E. (2009). The strategic role of the board: The impact of board structure on top management team strategic action capability. *Corporate Governance: An International Review, 17*(6), 728–743. doi:10.1111/j.1467-8683.2009.00775.x

Kimmel, M. S., & Ferber, A. L. (Eds.). (2010). *Privilege: A reader* (2nd ed.). Boulder, CO: Westview Press.

Kim, S. S., & Gelfand, M. J. (2003). The influence of ethnic identity on perceptions of organizational recruitment. *Journal of Vocational Behavior, 63*, 396–416. doi:10.1016/S0001-8791(02)00043-X

Kim, Y. Y. (1991). Intercultural communication competence. In Ting-Toomey, S., & Korzenny, F. (Eds.), *Cross-Cultural Interpersonal Communication* (pp. 259–275). Newberry Park, CA: Sage.

Kim, Y. Y., & Ruben, B. D. (1988). Intercultural transformation. In Kim, Y. Y., & Gudy Kunst, W. B. (Eds.), *Theories in Intercultural Communication* (pp. 299–321). London, UK: Sage.

King, D. K. (1988). Multiple jeopardy, multiple consciousness: The context of a black feminist ideology. *Signs, 14*(1), 42–72. doi:10.1086/494491

King, E. B., & Cortina, J. M. (2011). Stated and unstated barriers and opportunities to creating LGBT-supportive organizations. *Industrial-Organizational Psychology: Perspectives of Science and Practice, 3*, 103–108. doi:10.1111/j.1754-9434.2009.01209.x

King, E. B., Gulick, L. M. V., & Avery, D. R. (2010). The divide between diversity training and diversity education: Integrating best practices. *Journal of Management Education, 34*(6), 891–906. doi:10.1177/1052562909348767

King, E. B., Reilly, C., & Hebl, M. (2008). The best of times, the worst of times: Exploring dual perspectives of "coming out" in the workplace. *Group & Organization Management, 33*(5), 566–601. doi:10.1177/1059601108321834

King, N., & Majchrzak, A. (2003). Technology alignment and adaptation for virtual teams involved in unstructured knowledge work. In Gibson, C., & Cohen, S. (Eds.), *Virtual Teams that Work: Creating Conditions for Virtual Team Effectiveness* (pp. 265–291). San Francisco, CA: Jossey-Bass.

Kirby, E. L., & Harter, L. M. (2003). Speaking the language of the bottom-line: The metaphor of "managing diversity". *Journal of Business Communication, 40*(1), 28–49. doi:10.1177/002194360304000103

Kirby, S. L., & Richard, O. C. (2000). Impact of marketing work-place diversity on employee job involvement and organizational commitment. *The Journal of Social Psychology, 140*, 367–377. doi:10.1080/00224540009600477

Kirk, G., & Okazawa-Rey, M. (2010). Identities and social locations: Who am I? Who are my people? In Adams, M., Blumenfeld, W. J., Castañeda, C., Hackman, H. W., Peters, M. L., & Zuñiga, X. (Eds.), *Readings for Diversity and Social Justice* (2nd ed.). New York, NY: Routledge/ Taylor & Francis Group.

Kirkman, B. L., & Shapiro, D. L. (2001). The impact of cultural values on job satisfaction and organizational commitment in self-managing work teams: The mediating role of employee resistance. *Academy of Management Journal, 44*, 557–568. doi:10.2307/3069370

Kirkman, B., & Mathieu, J. E. (2005). The dimensions and antecedents of team virtuality. *Journal of Management, 31*, 700–718. doi:10.1177/0149206305279113

Kirkpatrick, D. L., & Kirkpatrick, J. D. (2005). *Evaluating training programs: The four levels* (3rd ed.). Alexandria, VA: American Society for Training and Development.

Kirton, G., & Greene, A. M. (2005). *The dynamics of managing diversity: A critical approach* (2nd ed.). Oxford, UK: Elsevier Butterworth-Heinemann.

Kirton, G., Greene, A. M., & Dean, D. (2007). British diversity professionals as change agents – Radicals, tempered radicals or liberal reformers? *International Journal of Human Resource Management, 18*(11), 1979–1994. doi:10.1080/09585190701638226

Klein, K. J., & Harrison, D. A. (2007). On the diversity of diversity: Tidy logic, messier realities. *The Academy of Management Perspectives, 21*(4), 26–33. doi:10.5465/ AMP.2007.27895337

Klein, K. J., Knight, A. P., Ziegert, J. C., Lim, B. C., & Saltz, J. L. (2011). When team members' values differ: The moderating role of team leadership. *Organizational Behavior and Human Decision Making Processes, 114*, 25–36. doi:10.1016/j.obhdp.2010.08.004

Knight, D., Pearce, C. L., Smith, K. G., Olian, J. D., Sims, H. P., Smith, K. A., & Flood, P. (1999). Top management team diversity, group process and strategic consensus. *Strategic Management Journal, 20*, 445–465. doi:10.1002/(SICI)1097-0266(199905)20:5<445::AID-SMJ27>3.0.CO;2-V

Knoll, S. W., Hörning, M., & Horton, G. (2009). Applying a thinkLet- and thinXel-based group process modeling language: A prototype of a universal group support system. In *Proceedings of the 42nd International Conference on System Sciences*. Waikoloa, HI: System Sciences.

Knoop, R. (1995). Relationship among job involvement, job satisfaction, and organizational commitment for nurses. *The Journal of Psychology, 129*, 643–649. doi:10.1080/00223980.1995.9914935

Kochan, T., Bezrukova, K., Ely, R., Jackson, S., Joshi, A., & Jehn, K. … Thomas, D. (2002). *The effects of diversity on business performance: Report of the diversity research network*. Cambridge, MA: MIT Sloan School of Management.

Kolb, D. A., & Kolb, A. (2002). *Bibliography on experiential learning theory*. Retrieved from http://www.learningfromexperience.com/Research_Library.

Kolfschoten, G. L., & Santanen, E. L. (2007). Reconceptualizing generate thinkLets: The role of the modifier. In *Proceedings of the 40th International Conference on System Sciences*. Waikoloa, HI: System Sciences.

Kolfschoten, G. L., Appelman, J. H., Briggs, R. O., & de Vreede, G. J. (2004). Recurring patterns of facilitation interventions in GSS sessions. In *Proceedings of the 37th International Conference on System Sciences*. Big Island, HI: System Sciences.

Kolfschoten, G. L., & de Vreede, G. J. (2009). A design approach for collaboration processes: A multimethod design science study in collaboration engineering. *Journal of Management Information Systems, 26*(1), 225–256. doi:10.2753/MIS0742-1222260109

Köllen, T. (2007). Part of the whole? Homosexuality in companies' diversity policies and in business research: Focus on Germany. *The International Journal of Diversity in Organisations. Communities and Nations, 7*(5), 315–322.

Kolody, R. (1997). *Learning strategies of Alberta college students*. Unpublished Doctoral Dissertation. Bozeman, MT: Montana State University.

Konrad, A. (2003). Defining the domain of workplace diversity scholarship. *Group & Organization Management, 28*(1), 4–17. doi:10.1177/1059601102250013

Konrad, A. (2006). Leveraging workplace diversity in organizations. *Organization Management Journal, 3*(3), 194–189. doi:10.1057/omj.2006.18

Koper, G., Knippenberg, D., Bouhuijs, F., Vermunt, R., & Wilke, H. (1993). Procedural fairness and self esteem. *European Journal of Social Psychology, 23*, 313–325. doi:10.1002/ejsp.2420230307

Korac-Kakabadse, N., Kouzmin, A., Korac-Kakabadse, A., & Savery, L. (2001). Low- and high-context communication patterns: Towards mapping cross-cultural encounters. *Cross Cultural Management, 8*(2), 3–24. doi:10.1108/13527600110797218

Korinek, D. (1997). *An investigation of learning strategies utilized by Air Force officers*. Unpublished Doctoral Dissertation. Bozeman, MT: Montana State University.

Kormanik, M. (2009). Sexuality as a diversity factor. *Advances in Developing Human Resources, 11*(1), 24–36. doi:10.1177/1523422308329369

Korn Ferry Institute. (2008). *The cost of employee turnover due to failed diversity initiatives in the workplace: The corporate leavers survey 2007*. Retrieved February 1, 2011, from http://www.kornferryinstitute.com.

Korn Ferry International. (2004). *Diversity in the executive suites: Good news and bad news*. Retrieved February 8, 2011 from http://www.kornferry.com.

Koslowsky, M., Caspy, T., & Lazar, M. (1991). Cause and effect explanations of job satisfaction and commitment: The case of exchange commitment. *The Journal of Psychology, 125*(2), 153–162.

Kossek, E. E., & Lobel, S. A. (1996). *Managing diversity: Human resource strategies for transforming the workplace*. Retrieved May 29, 2011 from http://www.lavoisier.fr/livre/notice.asp?id=RAAWLSAXA6LOWB.

Kossek, E. E., Lobel, S. A., & Brown, J. (2005). *Human resource strategies to manage workforce diversity – Examining 'the business case'*. Retrieved May 29, 2011 from http://www.corwin.com/upm-data/7425_03_Konrad>02.pdf.

Kossek, E. E., Markel, K. S., & McHugh, P. P. (2003). Increasing diversity as an HRM change strategy. *Journal of Organizational Change Management, 16*, 328–352. doi:10.1108/09534810310475550

Kossek, E. E., & Zonia, S. C. (1993). Assessing diversity climate: A field study of reactions to employer efforts to promote diversity. *Journal of Organizational Behavior, 14*(1), 61–81. doi:10.1002/job.4030140107

Kossek, E., Lobel, S., & Brown, J. (2006). Human resource strategies to manage work force diversity: Examining "the business case". In Konrad, A. M., Prasad, P., & Pringle, J. K. (Eds.), *Handbook of Workplace Diversity* (pp. 53–74). Thousand Oaks, CA: Sage.

Kozlowski, S. W. J., Tone, U., Mullins, M. E., Weissbein, D. A., Brown, K. G., & Bell, B. S. (2001). Developing adaptability: A theory for the design of integrated-embedded training systems. In Salas, E. (Ed.), *Advances in Human Performance and Cognitive Engineering Research* (pp. 59–123). Amsterdam, The Netherlands: JAI/Elsevier Science. doi:10.1016/S1479-3601(01)01004-9

Kramer, R. (2005). *Developing global leaders*. New York, NY: The Conference Board.

Kramer, R. M. (2006). Social capital and cooperative behavior in the workplace: A social identity perspective. *Advances in Group Processes, 23*, 1–30. doi:10.1016/S0882-6145(06)23001-7

Kramer, R. M., & Messick, D. M. (1998). Getting by with a little help from our enemies: Collective paranoia and its role in intergroup relations. In Sedikides, C. (Ed.), *Intergroup Cognition and Intergroup Behavior* (pp. 233–255). Mahwah, NJ: Lawrence Erlbaum Associates.

Krause, D. R. (1999). The antecedents of buying firms' efforts to improve suppliers. *Journal of Operations Management, 17*, 205–224. doi:10.1016/S0272-6963(98)00038-2

Krause, D. R., Ragatz, G. L., & Hughley, S. (1999). Supplier development from the minority supplier's perspective. *The Journal of Supply Chain Management, 35*(4), 33–41. doi:10.1111/j.1745-493X.1999.tb00242.x

Kravitz, D. A. (2007). Can we take the guesswork out of diversity practice selection? *The Academy of Management Perspectives, 21*(2). doi:10.5465/AMP.2007.25356517

Kreitner, R., & Kinicki, A. (2004). La gestione delle diversità: Liberare il potenziale di ogni persona. In Kreitner, R., & Kinicki, A. (Eds.), *Comportamento Organizzativo* (pp. 39–68). Milano, Italy: Apogeo.

Kreitz, P. A. (2008). Best practices for managing organizational diversity. *Journal of Academic Librarianship, 34*(2), 101–120. doi:10.1016/j.acalib.2007.12.001

Krings, F., Sczesny, S., & Kluge, A. (2011). Stereotypical inferences as mediators of age discrimination: The role of competence and warmth. *British Journal of Management, 22*(2), 187. doi:10.1111/j.1467-8551.2010.00721.x

Krippendorf, K. (1980). *Content analysis: An introduction to its methodology*. Beverly Hills, CA: Sage.

Kristof, A. L. (1996). Person-organization fit: An integrative review of its conceptualizations, measurement, and implications. *Personnel Psychology, 49*, 1–49. doi:10.1111/j.1744-6570.1996.tb01790.x

Kruglanski, A. W., Thompson, E. P., Higgins, E. T., Atash, M. N., Pierro, A., Shah, J. Y., & Spiegel, S. (2000). To "do the right thing" or to "just do it": Locomotion and assessment as distinct self-regulatory imperatives. *Journal of Personality and Social Psychology, 79*, 793–815. doi:10.1037/0022-3514.79.5.793

Kuchinke, K. P. (2002). Institutional and curricular characteristics of leading graduate HRD programs in the United States. *Human Resource Development Quarterly, 13*(2), 127–143. doi:10.1002/hrdq.1019

Ladson-Billings, G. (1995). Toward a theory of culturally relevant pedagogy. *American Educational Research Journal, 32*(3), 465–491.

Ladson-Billings, G. (1998). Just what is critical race theory and what's it doing in a nice field like education. *Qualitative Studies in Education, 11*(1), 7–24. doi:10.1080/095183998236863

Ladson-Billings, G., & Tate, W. (1995). Toward a critical race theory of education. *Teachers College Record, 97*(1), 47–68.

Laiken, M. (2002). *Managing the action/reflection polarity through dialogue: A path to transformative learning.* NALL Working Paper #53. Retrieved on August 4, 2011, from http://www.nall.ca/res/53MarilynLaiken.pdf.

Lancaster, H. (1997, February 4). Black managers often must emphasize building relationships. *Wall Street Journal*, p. A-1.

Landy, F. J. (1986). Stamp collecting versus science: Validation as hypothesis testing. *The American Psychologist, 41*, 1183–1192. doi:10.1037/0003-066X.41.11.1183

Langbert, M., & Friedman, H. (2002). Continuous improvement in the history of human resource management. *Management Decision, 40*(7/8), 782–787. doi:10.1108/00251740210437734

Larkey, L. K. (1996). The development and validation of the workforce diversity questionnaire: An instrument to assess interactions in diverse workgroups. *Management Communication Quarterly, 9*, 296–337. doi:10.1177/08 93318996009003002

Larson, J. R. J., Foster-Fishman, P. G., & Franz, T. M. (1998). Leadership style and the discussion of shared and unshared information in decision-making groups. *Personality and Social Psychology Bulletin, 24*, 482–495. doi:10.1177/0146167298245004

Larzelere, R. E., & Huston, T. L. (1980). The dyadic trust scale: Toward understanding interpersonal trust in close relationships. *Journal of Marriage and the Family, 42*, 595–604. doi:10.2307/351903

LaSala, M. (2004). Lesbians, gay men and their parents: Family therapy for the coming-out crisis. *Family Process, 39*(1), 67–81. doi:10.1111/j.1545-5300.2000.39108.x

Lau, D. C., & Murnighan, J. K. (1998). Demographic diversity and faultlines: The compositional dynamics of organizational groups. *Academy of Management Review, 23*, 325–340.

Lau, D. C., & Murnighan, J. K. (2005). Interactions within groups and subgroups: The effects of demographic faultlines. *Academy of Management Journal, 48*(4), 645–659. doi:10.5465/AMJ.2005.17843943

Lavara, N. (2004). Los empresarios se implican en la conciliación de la vida familiar y laboral. *Entorno Social*. Retrieved from http://www.entornosocial.es.

Lave, J., & Wenger, E. (1991). *Situated learning: Legitimate peripheral participation*. Cambridge, UK: Cambridge University Press.

Lawler, E. E. III. (2003). *Treat people right! How organizations and individuals can propel each other into a virtuous spiral of success*. San Francisco, CA: Jossey-Bass.

Lawler, E. E. III, & Finegold, D. (2000). Individualizing the organization: Past, present and future. *Organizational Dynamics, 29*(1), 1–15. doi:10.1016/S0090-2616(00)00009-7

LBS. (2011). *About*. Retrieved from http://www.lbs.edu.ng/about-lbs/.

Lee, C. (1983). Cross-cultural training: Don't leave home without it. *Training (New York, N.Y.), 20*(7), 20–25.

Leibold, M., & Voelpel, S. C. (2009). *Managing the aging workforce: Challenges and solutions*. Hoboken, NJ: Wiley.

Leibowitz, Z. B., Farren, C., & Kaye, B. L. (1986). *Designing career development systems*. San Francisco, CA: Jossey-Bass.

Leinonen, P., & Bluemink, J. (2008). The distributed team members' explanations of knowledge they assume to be shared. *Journal of Workplace Learning, 20*(1), 38–53. doi:10.1108/13665620810843638

Leonard, J., & Levine, D. (2006, July). The effect of diversity on turnover: A large case study. *Industrial & Labor Relations Review*, 547–572.

Lepak, D. P., Liao, H., Yunhyun, C., & Harden, E. E. (2006). A conceptual review of human resource management systems in strategic human resource management research. *Research in Personnel and Human Resource Management, 25*, 217–271. doi:10.1016/S0742-7301(06)25006-0

Lewicki, R. J., McAllister, D. J., & Bies, R. J. (1998). Trust and distrust: New relationships and realities. *Academy of Management Journal, 23*(3), 438–458.

Lewis, P. (2006). The quest for invisibility: Female entrepreneurs and the masculine norm of entrepreneurship. *Gender, Work and Organization, 13*(5), 453–469. doi:10.1111/j.1468-0432.2006.00317.x

Lewis, S. E., & Orford, J. (2005). Women's experiences of adult workplace bullying: A process model of changes in social relationships. *Journal of Community & Applied Social Psychology, 15*, 29–47. doi:10.1002/casp.807

Leymann, H., & Gustafsson, A. (1996). Mobbing at work and the development of post-traumatic stress disorders. *European Journal of Work and Organizational Psychology, 5*(2), 251–275. doi:10.1080/13594329608414858

Liang, P. J., Rajan, M. V., & Ray, K. (2008). Optimal team size and monitoring in organizations. *Accounting Review, 83*(3), 789–822. doi:10.2308/accr.2008.83.3.789

Liff, S., & Dickens, L. (2000). Ethics and equality: Reconciling false dilemmas. In Winstanley, D., & Woodall, J. (Eds.), *Ethical Issues in Contemporary Human Resource Management* (pp. 85–101). New York, NY: Palgrave Macmillan.

Light, P. (2002). The content of their character: The state of the nonprofit workforce. *The Nonprofit Quarterly, 9*(3), 6–16.

Liker, J. K., & Choi, T. (2004). Building deep supplier relationships. *Harvard Business Review, 82*(12), 104–113.

Lincoln, Y. S., & Guba, E. G. (1985). *Naturalistic inquiry*. Beverly Hills, CA: Sage.

Linnehan, F., & Konrad, A. M. (1999). Diluting diversity: Implications for intergroup inequality in organizations. *Journal of Management Inquiry, 8*, 399–414. doi:10.1177/105649269984009

Litvin, D. (1997). The discourse of diversity: From biology to management. *Organizations, 4*(2), 187–209. doi:10.1177/135050849742003

Lively, S. (2001). *Learning, growing, and aging: Lifelong learners in the Academy of Senior Professionals in Bethany, Oklahoma*. Unpublished Doctoral Dissertation. Stillwater, OK: Oklahoma State University.

Livingston, R. (2009, July 7). The baby-faced Black CEO phenomenon. *Forbes*.

Li, W. (2009). Online knowledge sharing among Chinese and American employees: Explore the influence of national cultural differences. *International Journal of Knowledge Management, 5*(3), 54–72. doi:10.4018/jkm.2009070104

Lloyd-Jones, B. (2009). Implications of race and gender in higher education administration: An African American woman's perspective. *Advances in Developing Human Resources, 11*(5), 606–618. doi:10.1177/1523422309351820

Lockwood, N. R. (2005). *Workplace diversity: Leveraging the power of difference for competitive advantage*. Retrieved from http://www.shrm.org/Research/Articles/Articles/Documents/0605RQ.pdf.

Lockwood, N. R., Anderson, L., Gundling, E. O., Moore, K., Jr., Olivas-Lujan, M. R., Williams, S., & Wilson, J. R. (2009). *Creativity and innovation in human resource management: A sign of the times*. Retrieved from http://www.shrm.org.

Lockwood, S. (1997). *An investigation of learning strategies utilized by nursing students in Montana*. Unpublished Doctoral Dissertation. Bozeman, MT: Montana State University.

Loden, M., & Rosener, J. B. (1991). *Workforce America! Managing employee diversity as a vital resource*. Homewood, IL: Business One Irwin.

Loden, M. (1996). *Implementing diversity*. Chicago, IL: Irwin Professional Publishing.

Loden, M., & Rosener, J. B. (1991). *Workforce America! Managing employee diversity as a vital resource*. Homewood, IL: Business One Irwin.

Lopez, M., & Sánchez-Gardey, G. (2010). Managing the effects of diversity on social capital. *Equal Diversity and Inclusion: An International Journal, 29*(5), 491–516. doi:10.1108/02610151011052780

Lorange, P. (2003, September/October). Developing global leaders. *BizEd*, 24-27.

Lorbiecki, A., & Jack, G. (2000). Critical turns in the evolution of diversity management. *British Journal of Management, 11*, 17–31. doi:10.1111/1467-8551.11.s1.3

Lorde, A. (1984). *Sister outsider*. Freedom, CA: The Crossing Press.

Losey, M. R. (1993). Is sexual orientation an issue in the workplace? *HR News, 12*, 16–17.

Lubensky, M. E., Holland, S. L., Wiethoff, C., & Crosby, F. J. (2004). Diversity and sexual orientation: Including and valuing sexual minorities in the workplace. In Stockdale, M. S., & Crosby, F. J. (Eds.), *The Psychology and Management of Workplace Diversity* (pp. 206–223). Malden, MA: Blackwell.

Lublin, J. S. (2011, April 4). Coaching urged for women. *The Wall Street Journal*. Retrieved from http://online.wsj.com/article_email/ SB10001424052748704530204576237203974840800- lMyQjAxMTAxMDAwNDEwNDQyWj.html.

Luhmann, N. (2000). *Vertrauen ein mechanismus der reduction sozialer komplexitat* (4th ed.). Stuttgart, Germany: Lucius & Lucius.

Lukenbill, G. (1999). *Untold millions: Secret truths about marketing to gay and lesbian consumers*. Binghamton, NY: Haworth Press.

Luo, Y., & Peng, M. W. (1999). Learning to compete in a transition economy: Experience, environment, and performance. *Journal of International Business Studies, 30*(2), 269–296. doi:10.1057/palgrave.jibs.8490070

Lurey, J. S., & Raisinghani, M. S. (2001). An empirical study of best practices in virtual teams. *Information & Management, 38*, 523–544. doi:10.1016/S0378-7206(01)00074-X

Lynch, E. W., & Hanson, M. J. (1992). *Developing cross-cultural competence*. Baltimore, MD: Paul H. Brookes Publishing Co.

Lynham, S. A. (2000). Theory building in the human resource development professional. *Human Resource Development Quarterly, 11*(2), 159–178. doi:10.1002/1532-1096(200022)11:2<159::AID-HRDQ5>3.0.CO;2-E

Lynham, S. A. (2002). The general method of theory-building research in applied disciplines. *Advances in Developing Resources, 4*(3), 221–241.

Maass, A., Cadinu, M., Guarnieri, G., & Grasselli, A. (2003). Sexual harassment under social identity threat: The computer harassment paradigm. *Journal of Personality and Social Psychology, 85*(5), 853–870. doi:10.1037/0022-3514.85.5.853

MacDermid, S. M., & Witttenborn, A. K. (2007). Lessons from work-life research for developing human resources. *Advances in Developing Human Resources, 9*(4), 556–568. doi:10.1177/1523422307305493

MacGillivray, E. D., & Golden, D. (2007). Global diversity: Managing and leveraging diversity in a global workforce. *International Human Resource Journal*. Retrieved from http://www.orcnetworks.com/system/files/ global%20diversity%20int%20HR%20summer07.pdf.

Macgillivray, I. (2008). Religion, sexual orientation, and school policy: How the Christian right frames its arguments. *Educational Studies, 43*, 29–44.

Mackie, D. M., & Smith, E. R. (1998). Intergroup relations: Insights from a theoretically integrative approach. *Psychological Review, 105*, 499–529. doi:10.1037/0033-295X.105.3.499

Magazine, H. R. (2009). The multigenerational workforce: Opportunity for competitive success. *HRMagazine, 54*(3), 1–9.

Maier, M. (1999). On the gendered substructure of organization: Dimensions and dilemmas of corporate masculinity. In Powell, G. N. (Ed.), *Handbook of Gender and Work*. London, UK: Sage.

Mak, H., & Sang, J. (2008). Separating the "sinner" from the "sin": Religious orientation and prejudiced behavior toward sexual orientation and promiscuous sex. *Journal for the Scientific Study of Religion, 47*(3), 379–392. doi:10.1111/j.1468-5906.2008.00416.x

Maltbia, T. E. (2001). *The journey of becoming a diversity practitioner: The connection between experience, learning, and competence*. Ed.D. Dissertation. New York, NY: Columbia.

Maltbia, T. E., & Power, A. (2009). *A leader's guide to leveraging diversity: Strategic learning capabilities for breakthrough performance*. Oxford, UK: Elsevier.

Mancini, D. J. (2010). Building organizational trust in virtual teams. *Journal of Behavioral Studies in Business, 2*, 1–5.

Mannix, E. A., Griffith, T. L., & Neale, M. A. (2002). The phenomenology of conflict in distributed work teams. In Hinds, P., & Kiesler, S. (Eds.), *Distributed Work* (pp. 213–233). Cambrdige, MA: MIT Press.

Mannix, E., & Neale, M. (2005). What differences make a difference? The promise and reality of diverse teams in organizations. *Psychological Science in the Public Interest, 6*(2), 31–55. doi:10.1111/j.1529-1006.2005.00022.x

Mann, S., Varey, R., & Button, W. (2000). An exploration of the emotional impact of tele-working via computer-mediated communication. *Journal of Managerial Psychology, 15*(7), 668–690. doi:10.1108/02683940010378054

Markus, H. R., & Kitayama, S. (1991). Culture and the self: Implications for cognition, emotion, and motivation. *Psychological Review, 98*, 224–253. doi:10.1037/0033-295X.98.2.224

Marques, J. (2007). Diversity as a win-win strategy. *Management Services, 51*(1), 22–24.

Marshall Executive, M. B. A. (2011). *University of Southern California's online course catalog.* Retrieved from http://www.marshall.usc.edu/emba.

Marshall, J. (1993). Organizational communication from a feminist perspective. In Deetz, S. (Ed.), *Communication Yearbook* (*Vol. 16*). Newbury Park, CA: Sage.

Marsick, V. J., & Watkins, K. E. (1999). *Facilitating learning organizations: Making learning count.* Aldershot, UK: Gower.

Martin-Alcazar, F., Romero-Fernandez, P. M., & Sánchez-Gardey, G. (2011). Effects of diversity on group decision-making processes: The moderating role of human resource management. *Group Decis Negot.* Retrieved from http://wenku.baidu.com/view/5b7fb1f1f90f76c661371aa9.html.

Martin, P. Y. (2001). Mobilizing masculinities: Women's experiences of men at work. *Organization, 8*, 587–618. doi:10.1177/135050840184003

Martin, P. Y. (2003). Said and done versus saying and doing: Gendering practices, practicing gender at work. *Gender & Society, 17*(3), 342–366. doi:10.1177/08912 43203017003002

Martin, P. Y. (2006). Practising gender at work: Further thoughts on reflexivity. *Gender, Work and Organization, 13*(3), 254–276. doi:10.1111/j.1468-0432.2006.00307.x

Martins, L. L., Gilson, L. L., & Maynard, M. T. (2004). Virtual teams: What do we know and where do we go from here? *Journal of Management, 30*(6), 805–835. doi:10.1016/j.jm.2004.05.002

Maslow, A. (1970). *Motivation and personality.* New York, NY: Harper & Row.

Maslow, A. H. (1992). *Motivazione e personalità.* Roma, Italy: Armando Editore.

Masurel, E., Nijkamp, P., Tastan, M., & Vindigni, G. (2002). Motivations and performance conditions for ethnic entrepreneurship. *Growth and Change, 33*(2), 238–260. doi:10.1111/0017-4815.00189

Mathieu, J. E., & Hamel, K. (1989). A causal model of the antecedents of organizational commitment among professionals and nonprofessionals. *Journal of Vocational Behavior, 34*, 299–317. doi:10.1016/0001-8791(89)90022-5

Mathieu, J. E., & Zajac, D. (1990). A review and meta-analysis of the antecedents, correlates, and consequences of organizational commitment. *Psychological Bulletin, 108*, 171–194. doi:10.1037/0033-2909.108.2.171

Matveev, A. V., & Nelson, P. E. (2004). Cross cultural communication competence and multicultural team performance: Perceptions of American and Russian managers. *International Journal of Cross Cultural Management, 4*(2), 253–270. doi:10.1177/1470595804044752

Maxwell, G. A., Balir, S., & McDougall, M. (2001). Edging towards managing diversity in practice. *Employee Relations, 23*(5), 468–482. doi:10.1108/01425450110405161

Mayer, M. (1991). Social movement research and social movement practice: The U.S. pattern. In Rucht, D. (Ed.), *Research on Social Movements: The State of the Art in Western Europe and the USA* (pp. 47–120). Boulder, CO: Westview Press.

Mayo, M. (1999). Capitalizing on a diverse workforce. *Ivey Business Journal, 64*(1), 20–27.

Maznevski, M., & DiStefano, J. (2000). Global leaders are team players: Developing global leaders through membership on global teams. *Human Resource Management, 9*(2-3), 195–208. doi:10.1002/1099-050X(200022/23)39:2/3<195::AID-HRM9>3.0.CO;2-I

McAdam, D., McCarthy, J. D., & Zald, M. N. (1996). *Comparative perspectives on social movements: Political opportunities, mobilizing structures, and cultural framings.* Cambridge, UK: Cambridge University Press.

McCarthy, J., & Zald, M. N. (1977). Resource mobilization and social movements. *American Journal of Sociology*, *82*(6), 133–167. doi:10.1086/226464

McClenahen, J. S. (2005, January 1). Manufacturing & society: Creating values with values. *Industry Week.*

McConahay, J. B. (1986). Modern racism, ambivalence, and the modern racism scale. In Dovidio, J. F., & Gaertner, S. L. (Eds.), *Prejudice, Discrimination, and Racism* (pp. 91–125). Orlando, FL: Academic Press.

McCrae, R. R., & Costa, P. T. (1985). Updating Norman's 'adequate taxonomy': Intelligence and personality dimensions in natural language and in questionnaires. *Journal of Personality and Social Psychology*, *49*, 81–90. doi:10.1037/0022-3514.49.3.710

McCrae, R. R., & Costa, P. T. (1987). Validation of the five-factor model of personality across instruments and observers. *Journal of Personality and Social Psychology*, *52*(1), 81–90. doi:10.1037/0022-3514.52.1.81

McCrae, R. R., & Costa, P. T. (1990). *Personality in adulthood.* New York, NY: Guilford.

McCuiston, V., Wooldridge, B., & Pierce, C. (2004). Leading the diverse workforce: Profit, prospects and progress. *Leadership and Organization Development Journal*, *25*(73), 1–2.

McDonald, K., & Hite, L. (Eds.). (2010). Exploring diversity in the HRD curriculum. *Advances in Developing Human Resources*, *12*(3). doi:10.1177/1523422310375032

McDonald, P. (2008). The multigenerational workforce. *Internal Auditor*, *65*(5), 61–67.

McDonald, S., Lin, N., & Ao, D. (2009). Networks of opportunity: Gender, race and job leads. *Social Problems*, *56*(3), 385–402. doi:10.1525/sp.2009.56.3.385

McDonnell, A., & Collings, D. (2011). The identification and evaluation of talent in MNEs. In Scullion, H., & Collings, D. G. (Eds.), *Global Talent Management.* Oxford, UK: Routledge.

McGee, J. (1998). Commentary on corporate strategies and environmental regulations: An organizing framework by A. M. Rugman and A. Verbeke. *Strategic Management Journal*, *19*(4), 377–387. doi:10.1002/(SICI)1097-0266(199804)19:4<377::AID-SMJ988>3.0.CO;2-S

McGrath, J. E., Berdahl, J. L., & Arrow, H. (1996). Traits, expectations, culture, and clout: The dynamics of diversity in work groups. In Jackson, S. E., & Ruderman, M. N. (Eds.), *Diversity in Work Teams.* Washington, DC: APA Publishing. doi:10.1037/10189-001

McGregor, D. (2006). *The human side of enterprise.* New York, NY: McGraw-Hill.

McGrew, T. (1992). A global society? In McGrew, T., Hall, S., & Hel, D. (Eds.), *Modernity and Its Futures: Understanding Modern Society* (pp. 61–116). Cambridge, UK: Polity Press.

McGuire, D. (2011). Diversity training and HRD. In McGuire, D., & Jorgensen, K. M. (Eds.), *Human Resource Development: Theory and Practice.* London, UK: Sage.

McGuire, D., & Bagher, M. (2010). Diversity training in organizations: An introduction. *Journal of European Industrial Training*, *34*(6), 493–505. doi:10.1108/03090591011061185

McIntosh, P. (1988). *White privilege and male privilege: A personal account of coming to see correspondences through work in women's studies.* Working Paper 189. Boston, MA: Wellesley.

McIntosh, P. (1993). White privilege and male privilege: A personal account of coming to see correspondences through work in women's studies. In Minas, A. (Ed.), *Gender Basics: Feminist Perspectives on Women and Men* (pp. 30–38). Belmont, CA: Wadsworth.

McIntosh, P. (1998). White privilege and male privilege: A personal account of coming to see correspondences through work in women's studies. In Harvey, C., & Allard, J. (Eds.), *Understanding and Managing Diversity* (4th ed., pp. 35–47). Upper Saddle River, NJ: Prentice Hall.

McKay, P. F., & Avery, D. R. (2006). What has race got to do with it? Unravelling the role of racioethnicity in job seekers reactions to site visits. *Personnel Psychology*, *59*, 395–429.

McKay, P. F., Avery, D. R., & Morris, M. A. (2008). Mean-racial ethnic differences in employee sales performance: The moderating role of diversity climate. *Personnel Psychology, 61*, 349–374. doi:10.1111/j.1744-6570.2008.00116.x

McKay, P. F., Avery, D. R., Tonidandel, S., Morris, M. A., Hernandez, M., & Hebl, M. R. (2007). Racial differences in employee retention: Are diversity climate perceptions the key? *Personnel Psychology, 60*, 35–62. doi:10.1111/j.1744-6570.2007.00064.x

McKeachie, W. (1988). The need for study strategy training. In Weinstein, C., Goetz, E., & Alexander, P. (Eds.), *Learning and Study Strategies*. San Diego, CA: Academic Press.

McKnight, D. H., Choudhury, V., & Kacmar, C. (2002). Developing and validating trust measures for e-commerce: An integrative typology. *Information Systems Research, 13*(3), 334–359. doi:10.1287/isre.13.3.334,81

McLaren, A. (1985). *Ambitions and realizations: Women in adult education*. London, UK: Peter Own.

McLaughlin, H., Uggen, C., & Blacktone, A. (2009). *A longitudinal analysis of gender, power, and sexual harassment in young adulthood*. Paper presented at the American Sociological Association 104th Annual Meeting.

McLean, G. (2001). Human resource development as a factor in the inevitable move to globalization. In *Proceedings of the Academy of Human Resource Development 2001 Conference*, (pp. 731-738). Tulsa, OK: Academy of Human Resource Development.

McLean, G. N., Bartlett, K. R., & Chao, E. (2003). Human resource development as national policy: Republic of Korea and New Zealand. *Pacific-Asian Education, 15*(1), 41–59.

McLeod, P. L., Lobel, S. A., & Cox, T. H. (1996). Ethnic diversity and creativity in small groups. *Small Group Research, 27*, 248–264. doi:10.1177/1046496496272003

McMahan, G. C., Bell, M. P., & Virick, M. (1998). Strategic human resource management: Employee involvement, diversity and international issues. *Human Resource Management Review, 8*(3), 193–214. doi:10.1016/S1053-4822(98)90002-X

McMahon, M. A. (2006). *Responses to diversity: Approaches and initiatives*. Retrieved from http://www.shrm.org/.

McNamee, S., & Miller, R. (2009). *The meritocracy myth*. Lanham, MD: Rowman & Littlefield.

McNeil, R. (2011). The use of learning strategies in a learner-centered classroom. In *Proceedings of the 9th Hawaii International Conference on Education*, (pp. 4383-4393). Honolulu, HI: Hawaii International.

McNickels, J., & Baldino, C. (2009). Are African Americans still experiencing racism? In Harvey, C., & Allard, J. (Eds.), *Understanding and Managing Diversity*. Upper Saddle River, NJ: Prentice Hall.

McNulty, J. (2009). *Workplace learning in 10 years – My thoughts*. Retrieved from http://www.orbitalrpm.com/2009/workplace-learning-in-10-years-my-thoughts.

McPherson, J., Smith-Lovin, L., & Cook, J. (2001). Birds of a feather: Homophily in social networks. *Annual Review of Sociology, 27*, 415–444. doi:10.1146/annurev.soc.27.1.415

Meem, D., Gibson, M., & Alexander, J. (2010). *Finding out: An introduction to LGBT studies*. Thousand Oaks, CA: Sage.

Meldrum, M., & Atkinson, S. (1998). Meta-abilities and the implementation of strategy: Knowing what to do is simple not enough. *Journal of Management Development, 17*(8), 564–575. doi:10.1108/02621719810228425

Mello, J. A. (2007). Managing telework programs effectively. *Employee Responsibilities and Rights Journal, 19*, 247–261. doi:10.1007/s10672-007-9051-1

Mello, J. A. (2007). *Strategic human resource management*. Delhi, India: Thomson.

Mendenhall, M., & Oddou, G. (1986). Acculturation profiles of expatriate managers: Implications for cross-cultural training. *The Columbia Journal of World Business, 21*(4), 73–79.

Merriam, S. B. (2001). Andragogy and self-directed learning: Pillars of adult learning theory. In Merriam, S. B. (Ed.), *The New Update on Adult Learning Theory (Vol. 89*, pp. 3–13). San Francisco, CA: Jossey Bass. doi:10.1002/ace.3

Merriam, S. B. (2007). An introduction to non-western perspectives on learning and knowing. In Merriam, S. (Eds.), *Non-Western Perspectives on Learning and Knowing* (pp. 2–20). Malabar, FL: Krieger.

Merriam, S. B. (2010). Globalization and the role of adult and continuing education: Challenges and opportunities. In Kasworm, C., Rose, A., & Ross-Gordon, J. (Eds.), *Handbook of Adult and Continuing Education: 2010 Edition* (pp. 401–409). Thousand Oaks, CA: Sage.

Merriam, S. B., & Caffarella, R. S. (1999). *Learning in adulthood*. San Francisco, CA: Jossey-Bass.

Merriam, S., & Ntseane, G. (2008). Transformational learning in Botswana: How culture shapes the process. *Adult Education Quarterly*, *58*(183), 183–197. doi:10.1177/0741713608314087

Messerschmidt, J. W. (2009). Doing gender: The impact of a salient sociological concept. *Gender & Society*, *23*(1), 85–88. doi:10.1177/0891243208326253

Messick, D. M., & Mackie, D. M. (1989). Intergroup relations. *Annual Review of Psychology*, *40*, 51–81. doi:10.1146/annurev.ps.40.020189.000401

Metcalfe, B. D. (2008). A feminist poststructuralists analysis of HRD: Why bodies, power and reflexivity matter. *Human Resource Development International*, *11*(5), 447–463. doi:10.1080/13678860802417569

Meyer, J. P., & Allen, N. J. (1984). Testing the side-bet theory of organizational commitment: Some methodological considerations. *The Journal of Applied Psychology*, *69*(3), 372–378. doi:10.1037/0021-9010.69.3.372

Meyerson, D., Weick, K. E., & Kramer, R. M. (1996). Swift trust and temporary groups. In Kramer, R. M., & Tyler, T. R. (Eds.), *Trust in Organizations: Frontiers of Theory and Research* (pp. 166–195). Thousand Oaks, CA: Sage Publications.

Mezirow, J. (1990). How critical reflection triggers transformative learning. In Mezirow, (Eds.), *Fostering Critical Reflection in Adulthood*. San Francisco, CA: Jossey-Bass.

Mezirow, J. (1991). *Transformative dimensions of adult learning*. San Francisco, CA: Jossey-Bass.

Mezirow, J. (2000). *Learning as transformation*. San Francisco, CA: Jossey-Bass.

Mezirow, J. (2000). Learning to think like an adult: Core concepts of transformation theory. In Mezirow, J. (Eds.), *Learning as Transformation: Critical Perspectives on a Theory in Progress* (pp. 3–33). San Francisco, CA: Jossey-Bass.

Michael, R. T., Gagnon, J. H., Laumann, E. O., & Kolata, G. (1994). *Sex in America*. New York, NY: Little, Brown.

Michaels, E., Handfield-Jones, H., & Axelrod, B. (2001). *The war for talent*. Boston, MA: Harvard Business Press.

Michaelson, J. (2010). Ten reasons why gay rights is a religious issue. *Tikkun*, *25*(4), 34–70.

Miles, M. B., & Huberman, A. M. (1994). *Qualitative data analysis: An expanded sourcebook* (2nd ed.). Newbury Park, CA: Sage.

Miller, F. A., & Katz, J. H. (2002). *The inclusion breakthrough: Unleashing the real power of diversity*. San Francisco, CA: Berrett-Koehler.

Milliken, F. J., & Martins, L. L. (1996). Searching for common threads: Understanding the multiple effects of diversity in organizational groups. *Academy of Management Review*, *21*(2), 402–433.

Milliken, F., & Martins, L. (1996). Searching for common threads: Understanding the multiple effects of diversity in organizational groups. *Academy of Management Review*, *21*, 402–433.

Millman, J. (2007). *Hot new data: Selig center tells you which multicultural markets are exploding*. Retrieved February 2, 2011 from http://www.diversityinc.com.

Minton, H. (1997). Queer theory: Historical roots and implications for psychology. *Theory & Psychology*, *7*(3), 337–353. doi:10.1177/0959354397073003

Miville, M. L., Gelso, C. J., Pannu, R., Liu, W., Touradji, P., Holloway, P., & Fuertes, J. (1999). Appreciating similarities and valuing differences: The Miville-Guzman Universality-diversity scale. *Journal of Counseling Psychology*, *46*, 291–307. doi:10.1037/0022-0167.46.3.291

Moberg, C. R., & Speh, T. W. (2003). Evaluating the relationships between questionable business practices and strength of supply chain relationships. *Journal of Business Logistics*, *24*(2), 1–19. doi:10.1002/j.2158-1592.2003.tb00043.x

Mohammed, S., & Angell, L. C. (2003). Personality heterogeneity in teams: Which differences make a difference for team performance? *Small Group Research*, *34*, 651–677. doi:10.1177/1046496403257228

Mohammed, S., & Angell, L. C. (2004). Surface- and deep-level diversity in workgroups: Examining the moderating effects of team orientation and team process on relationship conflict. *Journal of Organizational Behavior*, *25*, 1015–1039. doi:10.1002/job.293

Molinsky, A. L. (2005). Language fluency and the evaluation of cultural faux pa: Russians interviewing for jobs in the United States. *Social Psychology Quarterly*, *68*(2), 103–120. doi:10.1177/019027250506800201

Monaghan, C. H. (2010). Working against the grain: White privilege in human resource development. *New Directions for Adult and Continuing Education*, *125*, 53–63. doi:10.1002/ace.362

Montebello, A. R. (1995). Inside teams: How 20 world-class organizations are winning through teamwork. *Personnel Psychology*, *48*(3), 686.

Montebello, A. R. (2003). Beyond teams: Building the collaborative organization. *Personnel Psychology*, *56*(4), 1070–1073.

Montei, M. S., Adams, G. A., & Eggers, L. M. (1996). Validity of scores on the attitudes toward diversity scale (ATDS). *Educational and Psychological Measurement*, *56*, 293–303. doi:10.1177/0013164496056002010

Mor Barak, M. E. (2005). *Managing diversity: Toward a globally inclusive workplace*. Thousand Oaks, CA: Sage.

Mor Barak, M. E. (2011). *Managing diversity: Toward a globally inclusive workplace* (2nd ed.). Thousand Oaks, CA: Sage Publishing.

Mor Barak, M. E., Cherin, D. A., & Berkman, S. (1998). Organizational and personal dimensions in diversity climate. *The Journal of Applied Behavioral Science*, *34*, 82–104. doi:10.1177/0021886398341006

Mor Barak, M. E., Findler, L., & Wind, L. (2003). Cross-cultural aspects of diversity and well-being in the workplace: An international perspective. *Journal of Social Work Research and Evaluation*, *4*(2), 49–73.

Mor Barak, M. E., & Levin, A. (2002). Outside the corporate mainstream and excluded from the work community: A study of diversity, job satisfaction and well-being. *Community Work & Family*, *5*(2), 133–157. doi:10.1080/13668800220146346

Moran, R. T., Harris, P. R., & Moran, S. V. (2007). *Managing cultural differences: Global leadership strategies for the 21st century*. London, UK: Butterworth-Heinemann.

Moran, R. T., & Riesenberger, J. R. (1994). *The global challenge: Building the new worldwide enterprise*. London, UK: McGraw-Hill Book Company.

Morgan, J. (2002). How well are supplier diversity programs doing? *Purchasing*, *131*(13), 29–33.

Morgan, R. M., & Hunt, S. D. (1994). The commitment-trust theory of relationship marketing. *Journal of Marketing*, *58*, 20–38. doi:10.2307/1252308

Morris, B. (2005). How corporate America is betraying women. *Fortune*, *151*(1), 64–71.

Morris, M. L., & Madsen, S. R. (2007). Advancing work-life integration in individuals, organizations, and communities. *Advances in Developing Human Resources*, *9*(4), 439–454. doi:10.1177/1523422307305486

Morrison, A. J. (2000). Developing a global leadership model. *Human Resource Management*, *39*(2-3), 117–131. doi:10.1002/1099-050X(200022/23)39:2/3<117::AID-HRM3>3.0.CO;2-1

Mortensen, M., & Hinds, P. (2001). Conflict and shared identity in geographically distributed teams. *The International Journal of Conflict Management*, *12*(3), 212–238. doi:10.1108/eb022856

Moss, P. I., & Tilly, C. (2003). *Stories employers tell: Race, skill, and hiring in America*. New York, NY: Russell Sage Foundation.

Mowday, R., Porter, L., & Steers, R. (1982). Employee-organization linkages. In Warr, P. (Ed.), *Organizational and Occupational Psychology* (pp. 219–229). New York, NY: Academic Press.

MPA. (2008). *Survey*. Retrieved March 1, 2011 from http://www.magazine.org.

MPCA. (2004). *Peace corps hotline*. Retrieved June 17, 2011, from http://multimedia.peacecorps.gov/multimedia/pdf/returned/hotline/hotline030104.pdf.

MPCA. (2011a). *Peace Corps' statement on diversity*. Retrieved June 17, 2011, from http://www.minoritypca.org/Peace.Corps.Diversity.pdf.

MPCA. (2011b). *MPCA*. Retrieved June 17, 2011, from http://www.minoritypca.org/index1001a.html.

Mroczek, D. K., & Spiro, R. A. (2003). Modeling intra-individual change in personality traits: Findings from the normative aging study. *Journal of Gerontology, 58*, 153–165. doi:10.1093/geronb/58.3.P153

Mueller, C., Finley, A., Iverson, R., & Price, J. (1999). The effects of group racial composition on job satisfaction, organizational commitment, and career commitment: The case of teachers. *Work and Occupations, 26*(2), 187–219. doi:10.1177/0730888499026002003

Mulholland, G., Özbilgin, M. F., & Worman, D. (2005). *Managing diversity linking the theory and practice to business performance. Change Agenda*. London, UK: CIPD.

Murray, A. I. (1989). Top management group heterogeneity and firm performance. *Strategic Management Journal, 10*, 125–142. doi:10.1002/smj.4250100710

Mushrush, W. (2004). Reducing employee turnover. *Creating Quality Newsletter*. Retrieved April 11, 2011 from http://www.MissouriBusiness.net.

Nabukenya, J., Van Bommel, P., Proper, H. A., & de Vreede, G. J. (2011). An evaluation instrument for collaborative processes: Application to organizational policy-making. *Group Decision and Negotiation, 20*(4), 465–488. doi:10.1007/s10726-009-9177-7

Nadler, L., & Nadler, Z. (1989). *Developing human resources* (3rd ed.). San Francisco, CA: Jossey-Bass.

Nancheria, A. (2009). Future leaders expected to wield soft power. *American Society of Training Directors*. Retrieved November 2, 2010 from http://www.astd.org.

Nancherla, A. (2006). The art of great training delivery: Strategies, tools, and tactics. *T + D, 60*(12), 87.

Nancherla, A. (2008, May). Nobody's perfect: Diversity training study finds common flaws. *T&D*, 20.

National Center for Public Policy and Higher Education. (2005). *FACT #1: The U.S. workforce is becoming more diverse*. Retrieved from http://www.highereducatin.org/reports/pa_decline/decline-f1.shtml.

National Center for Public Policy and Higher Education. (2005). *Policy alert*. Retrieved June 17, 2011 from http://www.highereducation.org/reports/pa_decline/pa_decline.pdf.

Navarrette, R. (2008). Commentary: What Olympic gold says about diversity in America. *CNN*. Retrieved from http://www.cnn.com/2008/politics/08/21/navarrette.demograhics/index.html.

Neal, A., & Griffin, M. A. (2006). A Study of the lagged relationships among safety climate, safety motivation, safety behavior, and accidents at the individual and group levels. *The Journal of Applied Psychology, 91*(4), 946–953. doi:10.1037/0021-9010.91.4.946

Neale, M. A., & Griffith, T. L. (2001). Information processing in traditional, hybrid, and virtual teams: From nascent knowledge to transactive memory. In Staw, B., & Sutton, R. (Eds.), *Research in Organizational Behavior* (pp. 379–421). Greenwich, CT: JAI Press.

Neal, R. A., Griffin, M. A., & Hart, P. M. (2000). The impact of organizational climate on safety climate and individual behavior. *Safety Science, 34*, 99–109. doi:10.1016/S0925-7535(00)00008-4

Nembhardt, I. M., & Edmondson, A. C. (2006). Making it safe: The effects of leader inclusiveness and professional status on psychological safety and improvement efforts in health care teams. *Journal of Organizational Behavior, 27*, 941–966. doi:10.1002/job.413

Nemeth, C. J. (1992). Minority dissent as a stimulus to group performance. In Worchel, S., Wood, S. W., & Simpson, J. A. (Eds.), *Group Process and Productivity* (pp. 95–111). Newbury Park, CA: Sage.

Nemeth, C. J., & Wachtler, J. (1983). Creative problem solving as a result of majority vs. minority influence. *European Journal of Social Psychology, 13*, 45–55. doi:10.1002/ejsp.2420130103

Nencel, L. (2010). Que viva la minifalda! Secretaries, miniskirts and daily practices of sexuality in the public sector in Lima. *Gender, Work and Organization, 17*(1), 69–90.

Neuliep, J. W. (2009). *Intercultural communication: A contextual approach.* Thousand Oaks, CA: Sage.

Neuman, G. A., Wagner, S. H., & Christiansen, N. D. (1999). The relationship between work-team personality composition and the job performance of teams. *Group & Organization Management, 24*, 28–45. doi:10.1177/1059601199241003

Neuman, J. H., & Baron, R. A. (1998). Workplace violence and workplace aggression: Evidence concerning specific forms, potential causes, and preferred targets. *Journal of Management, 24*(3), 391–419.

Ng, H., Pan, Y. J., & Wilson, T. D. (1998). Business use of the world wide web: A report on further investigations. *Information Research, 3*(4). Retrieved from http://informationr.net/ir/3-4/paper46.html.

Ng, E. S. W. (2008). Why organizations choose to manage diversity? Toward a leadership-based theoretical framework. *Human Resource Development Review, 7*(1), 58–78. doi:10.1177/1534484307311592

Ng, E. S., & Burke, R. J. (2005). Person-organization fit and the war for talent: Does diversity management make a difference? *International Journal of Human Resource Management, 16*(7), 1195–1210. doi:10.1080/09585190500144038

Nicolaides, A. (2008). *Learning their way through ambiguity: Explorations of how nine developmentally mature adults make sense of ambiguity.* Ed.D. Dissertation. New York, NY: Columbia.

Ninsin, K. A. (2009). West Africa's integration: The logic of history and culture. In Adejumobi, S., & Adebayo, O. (Eds.), *The African Union and New Strategies for Development in Africa.* Nairobi, Kenya: Codesria and DPMF Publications.

Nishii, L. H., & Özbilgin, M. F. (2007). Global diversity management: Towards a conceptual framework. *International Journal of Human Resource Management, 18*(11), 1883–1894. doi:10.1080/09585190701638077

NMSDC. (2008). *The new realities for minority business.* New York, NY: National Minority Supplier Development Council.

Noe, R. A. (2002). *Employee training and development.* New York, NY: McGraw-Hill.

Nonprofit Finance Fund. (2011). *2011 state of the sector survey.* Retrieved June 17, 2011 from http://nonprofitfinancefund.org/files/docs/2011/2011survey_brochure.pdf.

Norris, B. (2000). Managing cultural diversity within higher education: A South African perspective. *Intercultural Communication, 3.* Retrieved 4/06/2011 from http://www.immi.se/intercultural/.

Northwestern University. (2011). Kellogg school of management. *Kellogg Executive MBA.* Retrieved from http://www.kellogg.northwestern.edu.

Norton, J. R., & Fox, R. F. (1997). *The change equation: Capitalizing on diversity for effective change.* Washington, DC: American Psychological Association. doi:10.1037/10224-000

Nunamaker, J. F. (1997). Future research in group support systems: Needs, some questions and possible directions. *International Journal of Computer Studies, 47*, 357–385. doi:10.1006/ijhc.1997.0142

Nwoke, C. N. (2005). Nigeria and ECOWAS. In Ogwu, J. U. (Ed.), *New Horizons for Nigeria in World Affairs. Lagos.* Nigerian Institute of International Affairs.

O'Flynn, J., Sammartino, A., Lau, K., Riciotti, A., & Nicholas, S. (2001). *Attract, retain and motivate: A toolkit for diversity management.* Retrieved May 25, 2011, from http://www.mibru.unimelb.edu.au/template-assets/07/includes/diversity/Attract_retain_motivate_toolkit_diversity.pdf.

O'Leary, B. J., & Weathington, B. L. (2006). Beyond the business case for diversity in organizations. *Employee Responsibilities and Rights Journal, 18*(4), 283–292. doi:10.1007/s10672-006-9024-9

O'Leary, M., & Cummings, J. N. (2007). The spatial, temporal, and configurational characteristics of geographic dispersion in work teams. *Management Information Systems Quarterly, 31*(3), 433–452.

O'Neil, J. A., & Marsick, V. J. (2007). *Understanding action learning*. New York, NY: AMACOM.

O'Neill, M. (2002). *Nonprofit nation: A new look at the third America*. San Francisco, CA: Jossey-Bass.

O'Reilly, C. A., & Flatt, S. (1989). *Executive team demography, organizational innovation, and firm performance*. Working Paper. Berkeley, CA: University of California.

Oertig, M., & Buergi, T. (2006). The challenges of managing cross-cultural virtual project teams. *Team Performance Management, 12*(1), 23–30. doi:10.1108/13527590610652774

Oetzel, J. G. (1998). Culturally homogeneous and heterogeneous groups: Explaining communication processes through individualism-collectivism and self-construal. *International Journal of Intercultural Relations, 22*(2), 135–161. doi:10.1016/S0147-1767(98)00002-9

Oetzel, J. G., & Ting-Toomey, S. (2003). Face concerns in interpersonal conflict: A cross-cultural empirical test of the face negotiation theory. *Communication Research, 6*(3), 599–624. doi:10.1177/0093650203257841

Ogbonna, E., & Harris, L. C. (2002). Organizational culture. *Journal of Management Studies, 39*(5), 673–706. doi:10.1111/1467-6486.00004

Oikelome, F. (2011). Relevance of US and UK national histories in the understanding of racism and inequality in work and career. In Healy, G., Kirton, G., & Noon, M. (Eds.), *Equality, Inequalities and Diversity: Contemporary Challenges and Strategies*. London, UK: Palgrave Macmillan.

Olofsson, G. (1988). After the working-class movement? An essay on what's 'new' and what's 'social' in the new social movements. *Acta Sociologica, 31*(1), 15–34. doi:10.1177/000169938803100103

Olson, E. G. (2011, April 4). Wal-Mart's gender bias case: What's at stake?. *Fortune*.

Olson, C. L., & Kroeger, K. R. (2001). Global competency and intercultural sensitivity. *Journal of Studies in International Education, 5*(2), 116–137. doi:10.1177/102831530152003

Olusola-Oyewole, O., & Lamptey, A. S. (2008). *Developing links: EU-Africa cooperation in higher education through academic mobility*. Retrieved on 4/06/2011 from http://ec.europa.eu/education/external-relation-programmes/doc/confafrica/master3.pdf.

Orbitalrpm. (2009). *Website*. Retrieved from http://www.orbitalrpm.com/2009/workplace-learning-in-10-years-my-thoughts/.

Oreilly, T. (2007). What is web 2.0: Design patterns and business models for the next generation of software. *Communications & Strategies, 1*, 17. Retrieved from http://ssrn.com/abstract=1008839.

Ortiz, L., & Jani, J. (2010). Critical race theory: A transformational model for teaching diversity. *Journal of Social Work Education, 46*(2), 175–193. doi:10.5175/JSWE.2010.200900070

O'Ryan, L. W., & McFarland, W. P. (2010). A phenomenological exploration of the experiences of dual-career lesbian and gay couples. *Journal of Counseling and Development, 88*, 71–79. doi:10.1002/j.1556-6678.2010.tb00153.x

Osigweh, C. A. B. (1989). Concept fallibility in organizational science. *Academy of Management Review, 14*(4), 579–594. doi:10.2307/258560

Osman-Gani, A. M. (2000). Developing expatriates for the Asia Pacific region: A comparative analysis of multinational enterprise managers from five countries across three continents. *Human Resource Development Quarterly, 11*(3), 213–236. doi:10.1002/1532-1096(200023)11:3<213::AID-HRDQ2>3.0.CO;2-#

Ospina, S., El Hadidy, W., & Hofmann-Pinilla, A. (2008). Cooperative inquiry for learning and connectedness. *Action Learning Research and Practice, 5*(2), 131–147. doi:10.1080/14767330802185673

Ottley, A. H., Rosser-Mims, D., & Palmer, G. (2011). *The growing influence of spirituality in adult education: New opportunities to reach the adult learner*. PowerPoint Presentation. Retrieved on July 30, 2011, from http://www.indwes.edu/Search/?q=the%20growing%20influence%20of%20spirituality.

Overell, S. (2004). Painting over the cracks. *Personnel Today, 10*. Retrieved April 2, 2011 from http://www.personneltoday.com.

Oyler, J. D., & Pryor, M. G. (2009). Workplace diversity in the United States: The perspective of Peter Drucker. *Journal of Management History, 15*(4), 420–451. doi:10.1108/17511340910987338

Özbilgin, M. F. (2008). Global diversity management. In Smith, P., Peterson, M. F., & Thomas, D. C. (Eds.), *The Handbook of Cross-Cultural Management Research* (pp. 379–396). London, UK: Sage Press.

Özbilgin, M. F. (Ed.). (2009). *Equality, diversity and inclusion at work: A research companion*. Cheltenham, UK: Edward Elgar.

Özbilgin, M. F., & Tatli, A. (2008). *Global diversity management: An evidence based approach*. Basingstoke, UK: Palgrave.

Özbilgin, M. F., & Vassilopoulou, J. (2010). *Global talent management: The case of emerging economies*. London, UK: Chartered Institute of Personnel and Development.

Pace, A. (2011). OPM makes diversity a top priority. *T&D, 65*(6), 16-17.

Page, S. E. (2007). Making the difference: Applying the logic of diversity. *The Academy of Management Perspectives, 21*(4), 6–20. doi:10.5465/AMP.2007.27895335

Palanski, M. E., Kahai, S. S., & Yammarino, F. J. (2011). Team virtues and performance: An examination of transparency, behavioral integrity, and trust. *Journal of Business Ethics, 99*, 201–216. doi:10.1007/s10551-010-0650-7

Papadakis, V. M., & Barwise, P. (2002). How much do CEOs and top managers matter in strategic decision-making? *British Journal of Management, 13*(1), 83–95. doi:10.1111/1467-8551.00224

Parker, P. S. (2001). African American women executives within dominant culture organizations: (Re)conceptualizing notions of instrumentality and collaboration. *Management Communication Quarterly, 15*(1), 42–82. doi:10.1177/0893318901151002

Parker, P. S. (2005). *Race, gender, and leadership: Re-envisioning organizational leadership from the perspectives of African American women executives*. Mahwah, NJ: Lawrence Erlbaum Associates.

Parkhe, A., Wasserman, S., & Ralston, D. A. (2006). New frontiers in network theory development. *Academy of Management Review, 31*(3), 560–568. doi:10.5465/AMR.2006.21318917

Pascual, P. J. (2003). *E-government, e-asean task force, UNDP-APDIP*. Retrieved from http://www.apdip.net/publications/iespprimers/eprimer-egov.pdf.

Patton, M. Q. (2002). *Qualitative research and evaluation*. Thousand Oaks, CA: Sage Publications.

Paul, R., & Elder, L. (2009). *The miniature guide to critical thinking concepts and tools* (5th ed.). Dillon Beach, CA: Foundation for Critical Thinking Press.

Payne, R. (1990). The effectiveness of research teams: A review. In West, M. A., & Farr, J. L. (Eds.), *Innovation and Creativity at Work* (pp. 101–122). Chichester, UK: Wiley.

Peace Corps, G. L. O. B. E. (2009). *Lesbian, gay, bisexual & transgender US Peace Corps alumni*. Retrieved June 17, 2011, from http://www.lgbrpcv.org/articles/11_00globe.htm.

Peace Corps. (2011a). *Mission*. Retrieved June 17, 2011, from http://www.peacecorps.gov/index.cfm?shell=about.mission.

Peace Corps. (2011b). *Who volunteers?* Retrieved June 17, 2011, from http://www.peacecorps.gov/index.cfm?shell=learn.whovol.

Peace Corps. (2011c). *History*. Retrieved June 17, 2011, from http://www.peacecorps.gov/index.cfm?shell=about.history.

Peace Corps. (2011d). *Peace Corps today*. Retrieved June 17, 2011, from http://www.peacecorps.gov/index.cfm?shell=about.pctoday.

Peace Corps. (2011e). *Peace Corps fact sheet*. Retrieved June 17, 2011, from http://multimedia.peacecorps.gov/multimedia/pdf/about/pc_facts.pdf.

Peace Corps. (2011f). *Information session with diversity panel*. Retrieved June 17, 2011, from http://www.peacecorps.gov/index.cfm?shell=meet.regrec.event&eventid=97507.

Peace Corps. (2011g). *Press and multimedia: Press Corps director touts diversity*. Retrieved June 17, 2011, from http://www.peacecorps.gov/index.cfm?shell=resources.media.medstories.view&news_id=1104.

Peace Corps. (2011h). *Stories from the field*. Retrieved June 17, 2011, from http://www.peacecorps.gov/index.cfm?shell=resources.media.stories.

Peace Corps. (2011i). *Press and media: Diversity in the Peace Corps*. Retrieved June 17, 2011, from http://www.peacecorps.gov/index.cfm?shell=resources.media.medstories.view&news_id=1503.

Peace Corps. (2011j). *Agency jobs*. Retrieved June 17, 2011, from http://www.peacecorps.gov/index.cfm?shell=jobs.

Pearson, J. N., Fawcett, S., & Cooper, A. (1993). Challenges and approaches to purchasing from minority-owned firms: A longitudinal examination. *Entrepreneurship Theory and Practice*, *18*(2), 71–88.

Pekerti, A. A., & Thomas, D. C. (2003). Communication in intercultural interaction: An empirical investigation of indicentric and sociocentric communication styles. *Journal of Cross-Cultural Psychology*, *34*(2), 139–154. doi:10.1177/0022022102250724

Pelled, L. H. (1996). Demographic diversity, conflict, and work group outcomes: An intervening process theory. *Organization Science*, *7*, 615–631. doi:10.1287/orsc.7.6.615

Pelled, L. H. (1996). Relational demography and perceptions of group conflict and performance: A field investigation. *The International Journal of Conflict Management*, *7*, 230–246. doi:10.1108/eb022783

Pelled, L. H., Eisenhardt, K. M., & Xin, K. R. (1999). Exploring the black box: An analysis of work group diversity, conflict, and performance. *Administrative Science Quarterly*, *44*, 1–28. doi:10.2307/2667029

Pepsi. (2009). *Supplier diversity*. Retrieved on May 5, 2009 from http://www.pepsico.com/Purpose/Diversity-and-Inclusion/Supplier-Diversity.aspx.

Peters, P., & den Dulk, L. (2003). Cross-cultural differences in managers' support for home-based telework: A Theoretical elaboration. *International Journal of Cross Cultural Management*, *3*(3), 329–346. doi:10.1177/1470595803003003005

Peters, T., & Waterman, R. H. (1988). *In search of excellence*. New York, NY: Warner.

Petitt, B. (2009). Borrowed power. *Advances in Developing Human Resources*, *11*(5). doi:10.1177/1523422309352310

Pettigrew, T. F., & Martin, J. (1987). Shaping the organizational context for black American inclusion. *The Journal of Social Issues*, *43*, 41–78. doi:10.1111/j.1540-4560.1987.tb02330.x

Pew Hispanic Center. (2005). *Hispanics: A people in motion*. Retrieved April 1, 2011 from http://www.pewhispanic.org.

Pew Hispanic Center. (2011). *Hispanics account for more than half of nation's growth in past decade*. Retrieved March 25, 2011, from http://www.pewhispanic.org.

Pfeffer, J. (1972). Size and composition of corporate boards of directors: The organization and its environment. *Administrative Science Quarterly*, *17*(2), 218–228. doi:10.2307/2393956

Pfeffer, J. (1973). Size, composition, and function of hospital boards of directors: A study of organization-environment linkage. *Administrative Science Quarterly*, *18*(3), 349–364. doi:10.2307/2391668

Pfeffer, J. (1981). Management as symbolic action. In Staw, B., & Cummings, L. L. (Eds.), *Research in Organizational Behavior* (pp. 1–52). Greenwich, CT: JAI.

Pfeffer, J. (1994). *Competitive advantage through people: Unleashing the power of the workforce*. Boston, MA: Harvard Business School Press.

Pfeffer, J., & Fong, C. T. (2004). The business school 'business': Some lessons from the U.S. experience. *Journal of Management Studies*, *41*, 1501–1520. doi:10.1111/j.1467-6486.2004.00484.x

Phillips, K. W., Northcraft, G. B., & Neale, M. A. (2006). Surface-level diversity and decision-making in groups: When does deep-level similarity help? *Group Processes & Intergroup Relations, 9*(4), 467–482. Retrieved May 29, 2011 from http://peer.ccsd.cnrs.fr/docs/00/57/16/29/PDF/PEER_stage2_10.1177%252F1368430206067557.pdf.

Phillips, K. W. (2004). Diverse groups and information sharing: The effects of congruent ties. *Journal of Experimental Social Psychology, 40*(4), 497–510. doi:10.1016/j.jesp.2003.10.003

Phillips, K. W. (2009). To disclose or not to disclose? Status distance and self-disclosure in diverse environments. *Academy of Management Review, 34*(4), 710–732. doi:10.5465/AMR.2009.44886051

Pichardo, N. A. (1997). New social movements: A critical review. *Annual Review of Sociology, 23*(1), 411. doi:10.1146/annurev.soc.23.1.411

Pilcher, J., & Whelehan, I. (2004). *50 key concepts in gender studies*. London, UK: Sage.

Pitts, D. (2006). Modeling the impact of diversity management. *Review of Public Personnel Administration, 26*(3), 245–268. doi:10.1177/0734371X05278491

Pless, N. M., & Maak, T. (2004). Building an inclusive diversity culture: Principles, processes and practice. *Journal of Business Ethics, 54*, 129–147. doi:10.1007/s10551-004-9465-8

Plummer, D. L. (2003). Diagnosing diversity in organizations. In Plummer, D. L. (Ed.), *Handbook of Diversity Management: Beyond Awareness to Competency Based Learning* (pp. 1–49). Lanham, MD: University Press of America.

Plummer, D. L. (2003). *Handbook of diversity management: Beyond awareness to competency based learning*. Lanham, MD: University Press of America, Inc.

Polleta, F., & Jasper, J. M. (2001). Collective identity and social movements. *Annual Review of Sociology, 27*, 283–305. doi:10.1146/annurev.soc.27.1.283

Polzer, J. T., Milton, L. T., & Swann, W. B. Jr. (2002). Capitalizing on diversity: Interpersonal congruence in small work groups. *Administrative Science Quarterly, 47*, 296–324. doi:10.2307/3094807

Ponterotto, J. G., & Casas, J. M. (1991). *Handbook of racial/ethnic minority counseling research*. Springfield, IL: Charles C Thomas.

Ponterotto, J. G., & Pederson, P. B. (1993). *Preventing prejudice*. Thousand Oaks, CA: Sage.

Porter, J. (2010). The best executive M.B.A. programs. *The Wall Street Journal*. Retrieved from http://online.wsj.com.

Porter, M. (1995, May-June). The competitive advantage of the inner city. *Harvard Business Review, •••*, 55–71.

Portes, A., & Rumbaut, R. G. (1996). *Immigrant America: A portrait*. Berkeley, CA: University of California Press.

Powell, A. A., Branscombe, N. R., & Schmitt, M. T. (2005). Inequality as ingroup privilege or outgroup disadvantage: The impact of group focus on collective guilt and interracial attitudes. *Personality and Social Psychology Bulletin, 31*(4), 508–521. doi:10.1177/0146167204271713

Powers, B. (1996). The impact of gay, lesbian, and bisexual workplace issues on productivity. In Ellis, A. L., & Riggle, E. D. B. (Eds.), *Sexual Identity on the Job: Issues and Services* (pp. 79–90). New York, NY: Haworth Press. doi:10.1300/J041v04n04_05

PR Newswire Association. (2011). *Chrysler group named among nation's top supporters of engineering programs of historically black colleges and universities, 2011*. Retrieved from http://search.proquest.com/docview/863149112?accountid=14744.

Prahalad, C. K., & Hamel, G. (1990). The core competence of the corporation. *Harvard Business Review, 3*, 79–91.

Prahinski, C., & Benton, W. C. (2004). Supplier evaluations: Communication strategies to improve supplier performance. *Journal of Operations Management, 22*, 39–62. doi:10.1016/j.jom.2003.12.005

Pratto, F., Sidanius, J., Stallworth, L. M., & Malle, B. F. (1994). Social dominance orientation: A personality variable predicting social and political attitudes. *Journal of Personality and Social Psychology, 67*(4), 741–763. doi:10.1037/0022-3514.67.4.741

Preece, A. (2010). Embedding diversity: The obstacles faced by equality and diversity specialists. In Moss, G. (Ed.), *Profiting from Diversity: The Business Advantages and the Obstacles to Achieving Diversity* (pp. 137–148). New York, NY: Palgrave Macmillan.

Prensky, M. (2001). Digital natives, digital immigrants. *Horizon*, *9*(5), 1–6. doi:10.1108/10748120110424816

Prewitt, J., Weil, R., & McClure, A. (2011). Developing leadership in global and multi-cultural organizations. *International Journal of Business and Social Science*, *2*(13), 14–20.

Priem, R. L. (1990). Top management team group factors, consensus, and firm performance. *Strategic Management Journal*, *11*, 469–478. doi:10.1002/smj.4250110605

Pritchard, C., & Sanders, P. (2002). Weaving our stories as they weave us. In Yorks, L., & Kasl, E. (Eds.), *Collaborative Inquiry as a Strategy for Adult Learning: Creating Space for Generative Learning*. San Francisco, CA: Jossey-Bass. doi:10.1002/ace.60

Privitera, C., & Campbell, M. A. (2009). Cyberbulling: The new face of workplace bullying? *Cyberpsychology & Behavior*, *12*(4), 395–400. doi:10.1089/cpb.2009.0025

Pucik, V. (1984). The international management of human resources. In Fombrun, C. J., Tichy, N. M., & Devanna, M. A. (Eds.), *Strategic Human Resource Management* (pp. 403–419). New York, NY: Wiley.

Pugh, S. D., Dietz, J., Brief, A. P., & Wiley, J. W. (2008). Looking inside and out: The impact of employee and community demographic composition on organizational diversity climate. *The Journal of Applied Psychology*, *93*(6), 1422–1428. doi:10.1037/a0012696

Pullins, E. B., Reid, D. A., & Plank, R. E. (2004). Gender issues in buyer-seller relationships: Does gender matter in purchasing? *Journal of Supply Chain Management*, *40*(3), 40–48. doi:10.1111/j.1745-493X.2004.tb00173.x

Quinn, P. (2010). A multigenerational perspective on employee communications. *Risk Management*, *57*(1), 32–34.

Raeburn, N. (2004). *Changing corporate America from inside out: Lesbian and Gay workplace rights*. Minneapolis, MN: University of Minnesota Press.

Ragins, B. R. (2004). Sexual orientation in the workplace: The unique work and career experiences of gay, lesbian and bisexual workers. *Research in Personnel and Human Resources Management*, *23*, 37–122. doi:10.1016/S0742-7301(04)23002-X

Ragins, B. R. (2008). Disclosure disconnects: Antecedents and consequences of disclosing invisible stigma across life domains. *Academy of Management Review*, *33*(1), 194–215. doi:10.5465/AMR.2008.27752724

Ragins, B. R., Singh, R., & Cornwell, J. M. (2007). Making the invisible visible: Fear and disclosure of sexual orientation at work. *The Journal of Applied Psychology*, *92*, 1103–1118. doi:10.1037/0021-9010.92.4.1103

Ragins, B. R., & Wiethoff, C. (2005). Understanding heterosexism at work: The straight problem. In Dipboye, B., & Colella, A. (Eds.), *Discrimination at Work: Psychological and Organizational Base* (pp. 177–201). Mahwah, NJ: Lawrence Erlbaum Association.

Raisch, S., Birkinshaw, J., Probst, G., & Tushman, M. L. (2009). Organizational ambidexterity: Balancing exploitation and exploration for sustained performance. *Organization Science*, *20*(4), 685–695. doi:10.1287/orsc.1090.0428

Rajshekhar, R. G., Javalgi, A. C., Gross, W., Benoy, J., & Granot, E. (2011). Assessing competitive advantage of emerging markets in knowledge intensive business services. *Journal of Business and Industrial Marketing*, *26*(3), 171–180. doi:10.1108/08858621111115895

Ram, M., & Smallbone, D. (2003). Ethnic minority enterprise: Policy in practice. *Entrepreneurship & Regional Development*, *15*, 99–102. doi:10.1080/0898562032000075186

Rampak, S. Z. (2001, July 26). Matching workplace skills with technology renewal. *Business Times*, 7.

Rao, J., Wilson, J., & Watkinson, J. (2009). What is innovation? Part 2: A web view of how IBM approaches innovation. *Innovation at Work*. Retrieved May 7, 2011, from http://innovationatwork.wordpress.com.

Rao, S. V., Luk, W., & Warren, J. (2005). Issues in building multiuser interfaces. *International Journal of Human-Computer Interaction*, *19*(1), 55–74. doi:10.1207/s15327590ijhc1901_5

Ray, D. S., & Ray, E. J. (1998). Adaptive technologies for the visually impaired: The role of technical communicators. *Technical Communication, 45*(4), 573–579.

Reagans, R., & McEvily, B. (2003). Network structure and knowledge transfer: The effects of cohesion and range. *Administrative Science Quarterly, 48*, 240–267. doi:10.2307/3556658

Reagans, R., & Zuckerman, E. W. (2001). Networks, diversity, and productivity: The social capital of corporate R & D teams. *Organization Science, 12*, 502–517. doi:10.1287/orsc.12.4.502.10637

Reason, P. (2002). *Action research*. PowerPoint Presentation. Retrieved on May 19, 2011, from http://shsfaculty. swan.ac.uk/EmrysJenkins/Action%20Research/Powerpoint%20shows/Menu-web.htm.

Rees, C., Mamman, A., & Bin Braik, A. (2007). Emiratization as a strategic HRM change initiative: Case study evidence from a UAE petroleum company. *International Journal of Human Resource Management, 18*(1), 33–53. doi:10.1080/09585190601068268

Reichers, A. E. (1985). A review and reconceptualization of organizational commitment. *Academy of Management Review, 10*(3), 465–476.

Reich, R. B. (2010). *Aftershock: The next economy and America's future*. New York, NY: Alfred A. Knopf.

Renwick, D. (2003). Line manager involvement in HRM: An inside view. *Employee Relations, 25*(3), 262–280. doi:10.1108/01425450310475856

Reskin, B. F., McBrier, D. B., & Kmec, J. A. (1999). The determinants and consequences of workplace sex and race composition. *Annual Review of Sociology, 25*, 335–361. doi:10.1146/annurev.soc.25.1.335

Reynolds, L., Bush, E., & Geist, R. (2008). The gen y imperative. *Communication World.* Retrieved May 11, 2011 from http://www.emerginghealthleaders.ca/resources/Reynolds-GenY.pdf.

Rhinesmith, S. H. (1996). *A manager's guide to globalization: Six skills for success in a changing world*. New York, NY: McGraw-Hill.

Ricaud, J. S. (2006). Auditing cultural diversity. *The Internal Auditor, 63*(6), 57–61.

Riccò, R. (2009). *Shedding light on the Italian way to diversity management*. Paper presented at the 25th EGOS Colloquium Conference. Barcelona, Spain.

Riccò, R. (2011). *Guida operativa al diversity management*. Milano, Italy: OD&M Consulting. Retrieved May 25, 2011, from http://www.odmconsulting.com/survey/diversity-management/.

Riccò, R. (2008). Teoria e pratica della gestione delle diversità. In Neri, M. (Ed.), *Studi e Ricerche sul Tema Delle Relazioni di Lavoro* (pp. 188–225). Bologna, Italy: Pitagora Editrice.

Richard, O. C. (2000). Racial diversity, business strategy and firm performance: A resource-based view. *Academy of Management Journal, 43*(2), 164–177. doi:10.2307/1556374

Richard, O. C., & Johnson, N. B. (2001). Understanding the impact of human resource diversity practices on firm performance. *Journal of Managerial Issues, 13*(2), 177–195.

Richard, O. C., Kochan, T. A., & McMillan-Capehart, A. (2002). The impact of visible diversity on organizational effectiveness: Disclosing the contents in Pandora's black box. *Journal of Business and Management, 8*(3), 265–291.

Richards, H., & Freeman, S. (2002). *Bullying in the workplace: An occupational hazard*. Pymble, Australia: Harper Collins.

Ringer, A., Volkov, M., & Bridson, K. (2010). Cultural diversity in the modern tertiary environment: The role of assessment and learning approaches. In *Proceedings of the 2010 Australian and New Zealand Marketing Academy Conference, ANZMAC*. Christchurch, New Zealand: ANZMAC.

Rink, F., & Ellemers, N. (2007). Diversity as a basis for shared organizational identity: The norm congruity principle. *British Journal of Management, 18*, 17–27. doi:10.1111/j.1467-8551.2007.00523.x

Riordan, C., & Shore, L. (1997). Demographic diversity and employee attitudes: Examination of relational demography within work units. *The Journal of Applied Psychology, 82*, 342–358. doi:10.1037/0021-9010.82.3.342

Robbins, S. P. (2005). *Organizational behavior* (11th ed.). Upper Saddle River, NJ: Pearson Prentice Hall.

Roberson, Q. M. (2004). *Disentangling the meanings of diversity and inclusion.* Center for Advanced Human Resource Studies (CAHRS) Working Paper. Ithaca, NY: Cornell University.

Roberson, Q. R., & Colquitt, J. A. (2005). Shared and configural justice: A social network model of justice in teams. *Academy of Management Review, 30*(3), 595–607. doi:10.5465/AMR.2005.17293715

Robinson, G., & Dechant, K. (1997). Building a business case for diversity. *The Academy of Management Executive, 11*(3), 21–31. doi:10.5465/AME.1997.9709231661

Rocco, T. S., Gedro, J., & Kormanik, M. B. (Eds.). (2009). Sexual minority issues in HRD: Raising awareness. *Advances in Developing Human Resources, 11*(1).

Rocco, T., Landorf, H., & Delgado, A. (2009). Framing the issue/framing the question: A proposed framework for organizational perspectives on sexual minorities. *Advances in Developing Human Resources, 11*(1). doi:10.1177/1523422308328528

Rodriguez, S. (1997). Diversity and volunteerism: Deriving advantage from difference. *The Journal of Volunteer Administration, 15*(3), 18–20.

Roessler, R., & Nafukho, F. (Eds.). (2010). Disability, diversity, and discharge issues at the workplace: Implications for human resource development. *Advances in Developing Human Resources, 12*(4).

Rogerson, C., & Rogerson, J. (1997). The changing post-apartheid city: Emergent black-owned enterprises in Johannesburg. *Urban Studies (Edinburgh, Scotland), 34*(1), 85–103. doi:10.1080/0042098976285

Rogers, P., & Smith, J. P. (1994). *Nonprofit management and leadership: The status of people of color.* New York, NY: Nonprofit Academic Centers Council.

Roosevelt, T. R. (1990). From affirmative action to affirming diversity. *Harvard Business Review, 2*(90), 107–117.

Rosenbaum, J. E., Kariya, T., Settersen, R., & Maier, T. (1990). Market and network theories of the transition from high school to work: Their application to industrialized societies. *Annual Review of Sociology, 16*, 263–299. doi:10.1146/annurev.so.16.080190.001403

Rosen, R., & Digh, P. (2000). *Global literacies: Lessons on business leadership and national cultures.* New York, NY: Simon & Schuster.

Rosette, A. S., & Plunkett Tost, L. (2007). Denying white privilege in organizations: The perceptions of race-based advantages as socially normative. In *Proceedings of the Academy of Management Annual Meeting,* (pp. 1-6). Academy of Management.

Ross Executive, M. B. A. (2011). *University of Michigan's online course catalog.* Retrieved from http://www.bus.umich.edu/Admissions/EMBA/Whyross.htm.

Ross, R. (2011, July). Creating an inclusive environment. *Training Journal,* 28-30.

Rostosky, S. S., & Riggle, E. D. B. (2002). Out at work: The relation of actor and partner workplace policy and internalized homophobia to disclosure status. *Journal of Counseling Psychology, 49*, 411–419. doi:10.1037/0022-0167.49.4.411

Rothwell, W. J., & Sullivan, R. L. (2005). *Practicing organization development: A guide for consultants.* San Francisco, CA: Pfeiffer.

Rotundo, M., Nguyen, D. H., & Sackett, P. R. (2001). A Meta-analytic review of gender differences in perceptions of sexual harassment. *The Journal of Applied Psychology, 86*, 914–922. doi:10.1037/0021-9010.86.5.914

Rousseau, D. M. (1989). Psychological and implied contracts in organizations. *Employee Responsibilities and Rights Journal, 2*, 121–139. doi:10.1007/BF01384942

Rousseau, D. M. (1995). *Psychological contracts in organizations: Understanding written and unwritten agreements.* London, UK: Sage Publications.

Ruben, B. D. (1989). The study of cross-cultural competence: Traditional and contemporary issues. *International Journal of Intercultural Relations, 13*(3), 229–240. doi:10.1016/0147-1767(89)90011-4

Ruderman, M. N., & Hughes-James, M. W. (1998). Leadership development across race and gender. In McCauley, C. D., Moxley, R. S., & Van Velsor, E. (Eds.), *The Center for Creative Leadership Handbook of Leadership Development* (pp. 291–335). San Francisco, CA: Jossey-Bass.

Rupp, D. E., Bashshur, M., & Liao, H. (2007). Justice climate past, present, and future: Models of structure and emergence. In Dansereau, F., & Yammarino, F. J. (Eds.), *Research in Multilevel Issues (Vol. 6)*. Englewood Cliffs, NJ: Erlbaum. doi:10.1016/S1475-9144(07)06017-1

Russel, R., & Bohan, J. (2006). The case of internalized homophobia: Theory and/as practice. *Theory & Psychology, 16*(3), 343–366. doi:10.1177/0959354306064283

Ryan, J. (2007). Inclusive leadership. *University of Toronto*. Retrieved from http://fcis.oise.utoronto.ca/~jryan/pub_files/incleadership.pdf.

Rynes, S., & Rosen, B. (1995). A field survey of factors affecting the adoption and perceived success of diversity training. *Personnel Psychology, 48*, 247–270. doi:10.1111/j.1744-6570.1995.tb01756.x

Sagie, A. (1997). Leader direction and employee participation in decision making: Contradictory or compatible practices? *Applied Psychology: An International Review, 46*, 387–416.

Sagie, A., & Koslowsky, M. (2000). *Participation and empowerment in organizations*. Thousand Oaks, CA: Sage.

Sagie, A., Zaidman, N., Amichai-Hamburger, Y., Te'eni, D., & Schwartz, D. G. (2002). An empirical assessment of the loose-tight leadership model: Quantitative and qualitative analyses. *Journal of Organizational Behavior, 23*, 303–320. doi:10.1002/job.153

Salomon, M., & Schork, J. (2003). Turn diversity to your advantage. *Research Technology Management, 46*(4), 37–51.

Salopek, J. J. (2006). Leadership for a new age. *T+D, 60*(6), 22-23.

Sánchez-Apellániz, M., & Román, M. L. (2008). *Gestionar la diversidad: Políticas de recursos humanos para afrontar el entorno global*. Seville, Spain: Edición Digital@tres.

Sanchez-Huches, S., & Davis, D. (2010). Women and women of color in leadership. *The American Psychologist, 65*(3), 171–181. doi:10.1037/a0017459

Sanders, P. (2008). *The decision-making styles, ways of knowing, and learning strategy preferences of clients at a one-stop career center*. Unpublished Doctoral Dissertation. Stillwater, OK: Oklahoma State University.

Sandler, B. R., & Hall, R. (1986). The campus climate revisited: Chilly for women faculty, administrators, and graduate students. *Association of American Colleges and Universities*. Retrieved from http://dynamic.uoregon.edu/~jjf/chillyclimate.html.

Santas, A. (2000). Teaching anti-racism. *Studies in Philosophy and Education, 19*, 349–361. doi:10.1023/A:1005298916161

Santora, J. C., & Seaton, W. J. (2008). Age discrimination: Alive and well in the workplace? *The Academy of Management Perspectives, 22*(2), 103–104. doi:10.5465/AMP.2008.32739764

Santos-Paulino, A. U., & Wan, G. (2010). Introduction: Southern engines of global growth. In Santos-Paulino, A. U., & Wan, G. (Eds.), *Southern Engines of Global Growth* (pp. 1–7). New York, NY: Oxford University Press. doi:10.1093/acprof:oso/9780199580606.003.0001

Saposnick, K. (2003). *Managing diversity as a key organizational resource: An interview with David Thomas*. Retrieved from http://www.pegasuscom.com/levpoints/thomasint.html.

Sarra, J. (2002). Rose-colored glasses, opaque financial reporting and investor blues: Enron as con and the vulnerability of Canadian corporate law. *St. John's Law Review, 76*, 715–766.

Savicki, V., Lingenfelter, D., & Kelley, M. (1996). Gender language style and group composition in internet discussion groups. *Journal of Computer Mediated Communication, 2*(3). Retrieved May 14, 2011, from http://jcmc.indiana.edu/vol2/issue3/.

Schaie, K. W. (1996). *Intellectual development in adulthood: The Seattle longitudinal study*. Cambridge, UK: Cambridge University Press.

Schaie, K. W., Willis, S. L., & Pennak, S. (2005). A historical framework for cohort differences in intelligence. *Research in Human Development, 2*, 43–67.

Schaller, M. (1991). Social categorization and the formation of social stereotypes: Further evidence for biased information processing in the perception of group-behavior correlations. *European Journal of Social Psychology, 21*, 25–35. doi:10.1002/ejsp.2420210103

Schaubroeck, J., & Lam, S. K. (2002). How similarity to peers and supervisor influences organizational advancement in different cultures. *Academy of Management Journal, 45*(6), 1120–1136. doi:10.2307/3069428

Schein, E. H. (1975). How career anchors hold executives to their career paths. *Personnel, 52*, 11–24.

Schein, E. H. (1989). *Organizational culture and leadership*. San Francisco, CA: Jossey-Bass.

Schein, E. H. (1992). *Organizational culture and leadership*. San Francisco, CA: Jossey-Bass.

Schiele, J. H. (1996). Afrocentricity: An emerging paradigm in social work practice. *Social Work, 41*(3), 284–294.

Schneider, B. (1987). The people make the place. *Personnel Psychology, 40*(3), 437–456. doi:10.1111/j.1744-6570.1987.tb00609.x

Schneider, B. H. (1993). *Children's social competence in context: The contributions of family, school and culture*. London, UK: Routledge.

Schön, D. (1983). *The reflective practitioner: How professionals think in action*. New York, NY: Basic Books.

Schuler, R. S., Dowling, P. J., & DeCieri, H. (1993). An integrative framework of strategic international human resource management. *International Journal of Human Resource Management, 5*(3), 717–764. doi:10.1080/09585199300000056

Schwartz, R., Weinberg, J., Hagenbuch, D., & Scott, A. (2011). *The voice of nonprofit talent: Perceptions of diversity in the workplace*. Retrieved June 17, 2011, from http://www.cgcareers.org/diversityreport.pdf.

Scott, C. L. (2010). Preface. In Scott, C. L. (Ed.), *Leveraging Diversity: Multiple Settings, professions, Strategies and Theoretical Frameworks*. Geneva, Switzerland: Interscience Enterprises Ltd.

Scott, C. L. (2010). Preface. *International Journal of Human Resources Development and Management, 10*(3), 205–207.

Scott, J. C. (1999, January/February). Developing cultural fluency: The goal of international business communication instruction in the 21st century. *Journal of Education for Business,* ▪▪▪, 140–143. doi:10.1080/08832329909601676

Scullion, H., & Collings, D. G. (2011). *Global talent management*. London, UK: Routledge.

Segal, J. A. (1997). Diversity for dollars. *HRMagazine, 42*(4), 134–140.

Seidman, I. E. (1991). *Interviewing as qualitative research*. New York, NY: Columbia University.

Sen, S., & Bhattacharya, C. B. (2001). Does doing good always lead to doing better? Consumer reactions to corporate social responsibility. *JMR, Journal of Marketing Research, 38*(2), 225–243. doi:10.1509/jmkr.38.2.225.18838

Shah, M., & Ram, M. (2006). Supplier diversity and minority business enterprise: Case study experience of three US multinationals. *Supply Chain Management: An International Journal, 11*(1), 75–81. doi:10.1108/13598540610642493

Shamir, B., House, R. J., & Arthur, M. B. (1993). The motivational effects of charismatic leadership: A self-concept based theory. *Organization Science, 4*, 577–594. doi:10.1287/orsc.4.4.577

Shantz, A., Wright, K., & Latham, G. (2011). *Networking with boundary spanners: A quasi-case study on why women are less likely to be offered an engineering role*. Bradford, UK: Emerald Group Publishing.

Shapiro, D. L., Furst, S. A., Spreitzer, G. M., & Von Glinow, M. A. (2002). Transnational teams in the electronic age: Are team identity and high performance at risk? *Journal of Organizational Behavior, 23*, 455–467. doi:10.1002/job.149

Shaw, M. (2000). *Global society and international relations: Sociological concepts and political perspectives*. Cambridge, UK: Polity Press. Retrieved May 9, 2011, from http://www.sussex.ac.uk/Users/hafa3/global.htm.

Shen, J. (2005). International training and management development: Theory and reality. *Journal of Management Development, 24*(7/8), 656–666. doi:10.1108/02621710510608786

Shen, J., Chanda, A., D'Netto, B., & Monga, M. (2009). Managing diversity through human resource management: An international perspective and conceptual framework. *International Journal of Human Resource Management, 20*(2), 235–251. doi:10.1080/09585190802670516

Shen, J., Chanda, A., & D'Netto, B. (2009). Managing diversity through human resource management: An international perspective and conceptual framework. *International Journal of Human Resource Management, 20*, 235–252. doi:10.1080/09585190802670516

Shim, I. S., & Paprock, K. E. (2002). A study focusing on American expatriates' learning in host countries. *International Journal of Training and Development, 6*(1), 13–24. doi:10.1111/1468-2419.00146

Shin, S. J., & Zhou, J. (2007). When is educational specialization heterogeneity related to creativity in research and development teams? Transformational leadership as a moderator. *The Journal of Applied Psychology, 92*(6), 1709–1721. doi:10.1037/0021-9010.92.6.1709

Shore, L. M., Chung-Herrera, B. G., Dean, M. A., Ehrhart, K. H., Jung, D. I., Randel, A. E., & Singh, R. (2009). Diversity in organizations: Where are we now and where are we going? *Human Resource Management Review, 19*(2), 117–133. doi:10.1016/j.hrmr.2008.10.004

Shore, L. M., & Martin, H. J. (1989). Job satisfaction and organizational commitment in relation to work performance and turnover intentions. *Human Relations, 42*, 625–638. doi:10.1177/001872678904200705

SHRM. (2003). *Workplace forecast: A strategic outlook 2000–2003.* Alexandria, VA: Society for Human Resource Management.

SHRM. (2008). *2007 state of workplace diversity management: A survey report by the society for human resource management.* Alexandria, VA: SHRM.

SHRM. (2008). *Leadership summit on diversity and inclusion.* Alexandria, VA: SHRM. Retrieved from http://moss07.shrm.org/hrdisciplines/Diversity/Pages/inclusion.aspx.

Sidberry, T. B. (2002). Building diversity in organizations. *The Nonprofit Quarterly, 8*(2), 28–33.

Siegel, J., Dubrovsky, V., Kiesler, S., & McGuire, T. W. (1986). Group processes in computer-mediated communication. *Organizational Behavior and Human Decision Processes, 37*(2), 157–187. doi:10.1016/0749-5978(86)90050-6

Silverstein, M. J., Sayre, K., & Butman, J. (2009). *Women want more: How to capture your share of the world's largest, fastest-growing market.* Scranton, PA: HarperBusiness.

Simeon, R., Nicholson, J. D., & Wong, Y. Y. (2001). Comparisons of Asian and US workplace gender roles. *Cross Cultural Management, 8*(2), 47–59. doi:10.1108/13527600110797236

Simons, N. (2010). Leveraging generational work styles to meet business objectives. *Information & Management, 44*(1), 28–33.

Simpson, R., & Lewis, P. (2007). *Voice, visibility and the gendering of organization.* Basingstoke, UK: Palgrave Macmillan.

Sippola, A., & Smale, A. (2007). The global integration of diversity management: A longitudinal case study. *International Journal of Human Resource Management, 18*(11), 1895–1916. doi:10.1080/09585190701638101

Skeels, M. M., & Grudin, J. (2009). When social networks cross boundaries: A case study of workplace use of Facebook and LinkedIn. In *Proceedings of the ACM 2009 International Conference on Supporting Group Work (GROUP 2009)*, (pp. 95-104). New York, NY: ACM Press.

Slater, S. F., Weigand, R. A., & Zwirlein, T. J. (2008). The business case for commitment to diversity. *Business Horizons, 51*(3), 201–209. doi:10.1016/j.bushor.2008.01.003

Smith, L. L. (2002). Using the power of collaborative inquiry: Community women learn and lead themselves. In L. Yorks & E. Kasl (Eds.), *Collaborative Inquiry as a Strategy for Adult Learning: Creating Space for Generative Learning.* San Francisco, CA: Jossey-Bass. Rosenwasser, P. (2002). Exploring internalized oppression and healing strategies. In L. Yorks & E. Kasl (Eds.), *Collaborative Inquiry as a Strategy for Adult Learning: Creating Space for Generative Learning.* San Francisco, CA: Jossey-Bass.

Smither, R. D., Houston, J. M., & McIntire, S. D. (1996). *Organization development: Strategies for changing environments.* Scranton, PA: HarperCollins.

Smith, R. (1983). *Learning how to learn.* Milton Keynes, UK: Open University Press.

Smith, W. K., & Tushman, M. L. (2005). Managing strategic contradictions: A top management model for managing innovation streams. *Organization Science*, *16*(5), 522–536. doi:10.1287/orsc.1050.0134

Snow, C. C., Snell, S. A., Davison, S. C., & Hambrick, D. C. (1996). Use of transnational teams to globalize your company. *Organizational Dynamics*, *24*(4), 50–67. doi:10.1016/S0090-2616(96)90013-3

Society for Human Resource Management. (2009). *Creativity and innovation in human resource management: A sign of the times*. Retrieved from http://www.shrm.org/Research/Articles/Documents/09-0525_RQ_3_2009.pdf.

Solari, L. (2004). *La gestione delle risorse umane: Dalle teorie alle persone*. Roma, Italy: Carocci.

Somech, A. (2006). The effects of leadership style and team process on performance and innovation in functionally heterogeneous teams. *Journal of Management*, *32*(1), 132–157. doi:10.1177/0149206305277799

Sonfield, M. (2005, May 17). A new US definition of minority business: Lessons from the first four years. *Entrepreneurship & Regional Development*, 223-235.

Sorensen, J. B. (2000). The longitudinal effects of group tenure composition on turnover. *American Sociological Review*, *65*, 298–310. doi:10.2307/2657442

Speitzer, G. M., McCall, M. W., & Mahoney, J. D. (1997). Early identification of international executive potential. *The Journal of Applied Psychology*, *82*(1), 6–29. doi:10.1037/0021-9010.82.1.6

Spitzberg, B. H. (1989). Issues in the development of a theory of interpersonal competence in the intercultural context. *International Journal of Intercultural Relations*, *13*, 241–268. doi:10.1016/0147-1767(89)90012-6

Sproull, L., & Kiesler, S. (1986). Reducing social context cues: Electronic mail in organizational communication. *Management Science*, *32*(11), 1492–1512. doi:10.1287/mnsc.32.11.1492

Srinivas, K. M. (1995). Globalization of business and the third world: Challenge of expanding the mindsets. *Journal of Management Development*, *14*(3), 26–49. doi:10.1108/02621719510078957

Stalinski, S. (2004). Leveraging diversity: Moving from compliance to performance. *Journal for Quality and Participation*, *27*(4), 14.

Stanley, C. A., & Lincoln, Y. S. (2005). Cross race faculty mentoring. *Change*. Retrieved December 3, 2009 from http://www.findarticles.com/p/articles/mi_m1254/is_2_37/ai_n13794993.

Stanley, C. (2009). Giving voice from the perspectives of African American women leaders. *Advances in Developing Human Resources*, *11*(5), 551–561. doi:10.1177/1523422309351520

Stanley, L., & Wise, S. (1993). *Breaking out again: Feminist ontology and epistemology*. London, UK: Routledge.

Staoles, D. S., & Zhao, L. (2006). The effects of cultural diversity in virtual teams versus face-face teams. *Group Decision and Negotiation*, *15*(4), 389–406. doi:10.1007/s10726-006-9042-x

Staudinger, U. M., Marsiske, M., & Baltes, P. B. (1995). Resilience and reserve capacity in later adulthood: Potentials and limits of development across the life span. In Cicchetti, D., & Cohen, D. (Eds.), *Developmental Psychopathology: Risk, Disorder, and Adaptation* (*Vol. 2*, pp. 801–847). New York, NY: Wiley.

Stephan, W. (1985). Intergroup relations. In Lindzey, G., & Aronson, E. (Eds.), *Handbook of Social Psychology* (pp. 599–658). New York, NY: Random House.

Stephenson, C. (2004). Leveraging diversity to maximum advantage: The business case for appointing more women to boards. *Ivey Business Journal*. Retrieved from http://c0524352.cdn.cloudfiles.rackspacecloud.com/101220-leveraging_diversity.pdf.

Stern Executive, M. B. A. (2011). *New York University's online course catalog*. Retrieved from http://www.stern.nyu.edu/AcademicPrograms/EMBA/Curriculum/index.htm.

Sternberg, R., & Grigorenko, E. (1997). Are cognitive styles still in style? *The American Psychologist*, *52*, 700–712. doi:10.1037/0003-066X.52.7.700

Stevens, J. (2003). *The power of diversity in corporate America*. Retrieved February 15, 2011 from http://www.Linkage-Inc.com.

Stewart, M. M., Crary, M., & Humberd, B. K. (2008). Teaching value in diversity: On the folly of espousing inclusion, while practicing exclusion. *Academy of Management Learning & Education*, 7(3), 374–386. doi:10.5465/AMLE.2008.34251674

Stewart, M. M., Williamson, I. O., & King, J. E. (2008). Who wants to be a business PhD? Exploring minority entry into the faculty "pipeline". *Academy of Management Learning & Education*, 7(1), 42–55. doi:10.5465/AMLE.2008.31413861

Stockdale, M. S., & Cao, C. (2004). Looking back and heading forward: Major themes of the psychology and management of workplace diversity. In Stockdale, M. S., & Crosby, F. J. (Eds.), *The Psychology and Management of Workplace Diversity* (pp. 300–316). Malden, MA: Blackwell.

Stone, E. F., Stone, D. L., & Dipboye, R. L. (1992). Stigmas in organizations: Race, handicaps and physical unattractiveness. In Kelly, K. (Ed.), *Issues, theory, and research in industrial/organizational psychology* (pp. 385–457). Amsterdam, The Netherlands: Elsvier. doi:10.1016/S0166-4115(08)62608-4

Strommen, E. (1993). You're a what? Family member reactions to the disclosure of homosexuality. In Garnets, L., & Kimmel, G. (Eds.), *Perspectives on Lesbian and Gay Male Experiences*. New York, NY: Columbia University Press.

Stumpf, S. A., Watson, M. A., & Rustogi, H. (1994). Leadership in a global village: Creating practice fields to develop learning organizations. *Journal of Management Development*, 13, 16–25. doi:10.1108/02621719410071946

Subeliani, D., & Tsogas, G. (2005). Managing diversity in the Netherlands: A case study of Rabobank. *International Journal of Human Resource Management*, 16(5), 831–851. doi:10.1080/09585190500083392

Sullivan, S. E., & Mainiero, L. (2008). Using the kaleidoscope career model to understand the changing patterns of women's careers: Designing HRD programs that attract and retain women. *Advances in Developing Human Resources*, 10(1), 32–49. doi:10.1177/1523422307310110

Sung, W. C. (2011). Taking the fight back to title VII: A case for redefining "because of sex" to include gender stereotypes, sexual orientation and gender identity. *Southern California Law Review*, 84, 487–539.

Super, D. (2002). A life-span, life-space approach to career development. In Brown, D., & Brooks, L. (Eds.), *Career Choice and Development* (2nd ed.). San Francisco, CA: Jossey-Bass. doi:10.1016/0001-8791(80)90056-1

Sutton, R. (2002). *Weird ideas that work*. New York, NY: Free Press.

Suutari, V. (2002). Global leader development: An emerging research agenda. *Career Development International*, 7(4), 218–233. doi:10.1108/13620430210431307

Suyemoto, K., & Fox Tree, C. (2006). Building bridges across differences to meet social action goals: Being and creating allies among people of color. *American Journal of Community Psychology*, 37, 237–246. doi:10.1007/s10464-006-9048-1

Swaminathan, A. (2001). Resource partitioning and the evolution of specialist organizations: The role of location and identity in the U.S. wine industry. *Academy of Management Journal*, 44(6), 1169–1185. doi:10.2307/3069395

Swanson, R. A., & Holton, E. F. (2001). *Foundations of human resource development*. San Francisco, CA: Berrett Koehler. Rossi, J. (2007, November). What generation gap? *T&D*, 10-11.

Swanson, R. A. (2001). The discipline of human resource development. In Swanson, R. A., & Holton, E. F. (Eds.), *Foundations of Human Resource Development* (pp. 88–100). San Francisco, CA: Berrett-Koehler Publishers.

Swanson, R. A., & Holton, E. F. (2001). *Foundation of human resource development*. San Francisco, CA: Berrett-Koehler Publishers.

Syed, J., & Özbilgin, M. (2009). A relational framework for international transfer of diversity management practices. *International Journal of Human Resource Management*, 20(12), 2435–2453. doi:10.1080/09585190903363755

Szymanski, D., Kashubeck-West, & Meyer, J. (2008). Internalized heterosexism: A historical and theoretical overview. *The Counseling Psychologist*, 36(4), 510–524. doi:10.1177/0011000007309488

Taber, M. E., & Hendricks, W. (2003). The effects of workplace gender and race demographic composition on hiring through employee referrals. *Human Resource Development Quarterly, 14*(3), 303–319. doi:10.1002/hrdq.1068

Tajfel, H., & Turner, J. (1986). The social identity of intergroup behaviour. In S. Worchel &d W. Austin (Eds.), *Psychology and Intergroup Relations,* (pp. 7-24). Chicago, IL: Nelson-Hall.

Tajfel, H. (1978). *Differentiation between social groups: Studies in the social psychology of intergroup relations.* London, UK: Academic Press.

Tajfel, H. (1982). *Social identity and intergroup relations.* Cambridge, UK: Cambridge University Press.

Tajfel, H., & Turner, J. C. (1979). An integrative theory of intergroup conflict. In Austin, W. G., & Worchel, S. (Eds.), *The Social Psychology of Intergroup Relations* (pp. 33–47). Pacific Grove, CA: Brooks/Cole.

Tan, B. C., Wei, K., Watson, R. T., Clapper, D. L., & McLean, E. R. (1998). Computer-mediated communication and majority influence: Assessing the impact in an individualistic and a collectivistic culture. *Management Science, 44*(9), 1263–1278. doi:10.1287/mnsc.44.9.1263

Tan-Solano, M., & Kleiner, B. H. (2001). Effects of telecommuting on organizational behaviour. *Management Research News, 24*, 123–126. doi:10.1108/01409170110782720

Tapia, A. T. (2009). *The inclusion paradox: The Obama era and the transformation of global diversity.* Lincolnshire, IL: Hewitt Associates.

Tarrow, S. (1994). *Power in movement: Social movements, collective action, and politics.* Cambridge, UK: Cambridge University Press.

Tatli, A. (2006). Handbook of workplace diversity. *Equal Opportunities International, 25*(2), 160 – 162.

Tatli, A., & Özbilgin, M. (2009). Understanding diversity managers' role in organizational change: Towards a conceptual framework. *Canadian Journal of Administrative Sciences, 26*(3), 244–258. doi:10.1002/cjas.107

Tavris, C., & Aronson, E. (2007). *Mistakes were made (but not by me): Why we justify foolish beliefs, bad decisions, and hurtful acts.* Orlando, FL: Harcourt.

Taylor, A. S., & James, K. (2010). *Toward the well-being of all: Integrating diversity dynamics and organizational justice dimensions.* Paper presentation at the Academy of Management Meeting. Montreal, Canada.

Taylor, C. R. (2004). *An inquiry into the experiences of the African American women principal: Critical race theory and black feminist perspectives.* Augusta, GA: Georgia Southern University.

Taylor, D. M., & Moghaddam, F. M. (1994). *Theories of intergroup relations: International social psychological perspectives* (2nd ed.). New York, NY: Praeger.

Taylor, E. W. (1994). Intercultural competency: A transformative learning process. *Adult Education Quarterly, 44*(3), 154–174. doi:10.1177/074171369404400303

Taylor, F. W. (1911). *The principles of scientific management.* New York, NY: Harper & Brothers.

Taylor, V., & Raeburn, N. C. (1995). Identity politics as high-risk activism: Career consequences for lesbian, gay, and bisexual sociologists. *Social Problems, 42*(2), 252–273. doi:10.1525/sp.1995.42.2.03x0113i

Taylor, V., Van Dyke, N., Kimport, K., & Andersen, E. A. (2009). Culture and mobilization: Tactical repertoires, same-sex weddings, and the impact on gay activism. *American Sociological Review, 74*(6), 865–890. doi:10.1177/000312240907400602

Te'eni, D. (2001). Review: A cognitive-affective model of organizational communication for designing IT. *Management Information Systems Quarterly, 25*(2), 251–312. doi:10.2307/3250931

Teague, P., & Hannon, D. (2005). The changing face of supplier diversity. *Purchasing, 134*(13), 52–55.

Tejeda, M. J. (2006). Nondiscrimination policies and sexual identity disclosure: Do they make a difference in employee outcomes? *Employee Responsibilities and Rights Journal, 18*(1), 45–59. doi:10.1007/s10672-005-9004-5

Tempel, E. R., & Smith, L. (2007). *Nonprofits have a spotty record on diversity: Nonprofit times.* Retrieved June 17, 2011, from http://www.humanics.org/atf/cf/%7BE02C99B2-B9B8-4887-9A15-C9E973FD5616%7D/Smith-Tempel%20Article.pdf.

Terhune, C. P. (2008). Coping in isolation: The experiences of Black women in White communities. *Journal of Black Studies*, *38*(4), 547–564. doi:10.1177/0021934706288144

Terry, R. W. (1990). *For whites only.* Grand Rapids, MI: William B. Eerdmans Publishing Company.

Texas Executive, M. B. A. (2011). *University of Texas at Austin's online course catalog.* Retrieved from http://new.mccombs.utexas.edu/MBA/EMBA.

Texas Instruments. (2011). *2010 corporate citizen report.* Retrieved from http://www.ti.com/corp/docs/csr/index2.shtml.

The Executive MBA Program. (2011). *University of Texas at Dallas' online course catalog.* Retrieved from http://som.utdallas.edu/graduate/execed/execMba/.

The Nortre Dame Executive MBA. (2011). *University of Notre Dame's online course catalog.* Retrieved from http://business.nd.edu/executive_mba/.

Thomas, D. A., & Ely, R. J. (1996, September/October). Making differences matter: A new paradigm for managing diversity. *Harvard Business Review*.

Thomas, R., Jr. (2004). *Diversity management and affirmative action: Past present and future.* Paper presented at the Diversity Symposium: Equity, Affirmative Action and Diversity. Lansdowne, VA.

Thomas, D. A. (2001, April). The truth about mentoring minorities: Race matters. *Harvard Business Review*, 98–109.

Thomas, D. A., & Ely, R. J. (1996). Making differences matter: A new paradigm for managing diversity. *Harvard Business Review*, *90*(2), 107–117.

Thomas, D. A., & Robin, E. J. (1996). Making differences matter. *Harvard Business Review*, *74*(5), 79–90.

Thomas, K. (2005). *Diversity dynamics in the workplace.* Belmont, CA: Thomson Wadsworth.

Thomas, K. M. (2005). *Diversity dynamics in the workplace.* Belmont, CA: Thomson Wadsworth.

Thomas, K. M. (2008). *Diversity resistance in organizations.* New York, NY: Lawrence Erlbaum.

Thomas, K. M. (Ed.). (2008). *Diversity resistance in organizations.* Mahwah, NJ: Lawrence Erlbaum Associates.

Thomas, R. (1991). *Beyond race and gender: Unleashing the power of your total workforce by managing diversity.* New York, NY: American Management Association.

Thomas, R. R. Jr. (1990). From affirmative action to affirming diversity. *Harvard Business Review*, *90*, 107–117.

Thomas, R. R. Jr. (1991). *Beyond race and gender: Unleashing the power of your total work force by managing diversity.* New York, NY: American Management Association.

Thomas, R. R. Jr, & Woodruff, M. (1999). *Building a house for diversity: How a fable about a giraffe & an elephant offers new strategies for today's workforce.* New York, NY: AMACOM.

Thomas, R. Jr. (1995). A diversity framework. In Chemers, M. M., Oskamp, S., & Costanzo, M. A. (Eds.), *Diversity in Organizations: New Perspectives for Changing Workforce* (pp. 245–263). Newbury Park, CA: Sage Publications.

Thompson, J. L. (1983). Women and adult education. In Tight, M. (Ed.), *Opportunities for Adult Education.* London, UK: Croom-Helm.

Thompson, J. L. (1995). Feminism and women's education. In Mayo, M., & Thompson, J. (Eds.), *Adult Learning Critical Intelligence and Social Change.* Leicester, UK: NIACE.

Thompson, K., & Andrzejewski, J. (1988). *Why can't Sharon Kowalski come home?* San Francisco, CA: Spinsters/Aunt Lute.

Thompson, M., & Heron, P. (2005). The difference a manager can make: Organizational justice and knowledge worker commitment. *International Journal of Human Resource Management*, *16*(3), 383–404. doi:10.1080/0958519042000339561

Tihanyi, L., Ellstrand, A. E., Daily, C. M., & Dalton, D. R. (2000). Composition of the top management team and firm international diversification. *Journal of Management*, *26*(6), 1157–1177. doi:10.1177/014920630002600605

Time Inc. (2005). *Partnering for profit*. Retrieved on January 7, 2009 from http://www.timeinc.net/fortune/services/sections/fortune/corp/2005_04MinorityBiz.html.

Ting-Toomey, S. (1992). Intercultural communication. In Lederman, L. (Ed.), *Communication Pedagogy: Approaches to Teaching Undergraduate Courses in Communication* (pp. 157–171). Norwood, NJ: Ablex.

Tipper, J. (2004). How to increase diversity through your recruitment practices. *Industrial and Commercial Training*, *36*(4), 158–161. doi:10.1108/00197850410542392

Tisdell, E. J. (2003). *Exploring spirituality and culture in adult and higher education*. San Francisco, CA: Jossey Bass.

Tisdell, E. J., & Tolliver, D. E. (2003). Claiming a scared face: The role of spirituality and cultural identity in transformative adult higher education. *Journal of Transformative Education*, *1*(4), 368–392. doi:10.1177/1541344603257678

Tong, J., & Shaikh, S. A. (2010). Communications: Wireless in developing countries and networks of the future. *IFIP Advances in Information and Communication Technology*, *327*, 60–71. doi:10.1007/978-3-642-15476-8_7

Toosi, M. (2006). A new look at long-term labor force projections to 2050. *Monthly Labor Review*. Retrieved from http://www.bls.gov/opub/mlr/2006/11/art3full.pdf.

Torbert, B. (2004). *Action inquiry: The secret of timely and transforming leadership*. San Francisco, CA: Berrett-Koehler.

Tough, A. (1971). *The adult's learning project*. Toronto, Canada: The Ontario Institute for Studies in Education.

Townes, G. (2007). M/WBE suppliers find business opportunities with UPS. *New York Amsterdam News*, *98*(44), 6–34.

Townsend, A. M., DeMarie, S. M., & Hendrickson, A. R. (1998). Virtual teams: Technology and the workplace of the future. *The Academy of Management Executive*, *12*(3), 17–29. doi:10.5465/AME.1998.1109047

Townsend, P., & Cairns, L. (2003). Developing the global manager using a capability framework. *Management Learning*, *34*(3), 313–327. doi:10.1177/13505076030343002

Treleaven, L. (1994). Making a space: Collaborative inquiry as staff development. In P. Reason (Ed.), *Participation in Human Inquiry*, (pp. 138-162). London, UK: Sage. Retrieved from http://www.peterreason.eu/Participationinhumaninquiry/CHAP9.htm.

Trevino, L. K., Webster, J., & Stein, E. W. (2000). Making connections: Complementary influences on communication media choices, attitudes, and use. *Organization Science*, *11*(2), 163–182. doi:10.1287/orsc.11.2.163.12510

Triandis, H. C. (1995). The importance of contexts in studies of diversity. In Jackson, S. E., & Ruderman, M. N. (Eds.), *Diversity in Work Teams: Researching Paradigms for a Changing Workplace* (pp. 225–233). Washington, DC: American Psychological Association. doi:10.1037/10189-009

Triandis, H. C. (1996). The importance of contexts in studies of diversity. In Jackson, S. E., & Ruderman, M. N. (Eds.), *Diversity in Work Teams* (pp. 225–233). Washington, DC: APA Publishing. doi:10.1037/10189-009

Triandis, H. C. (2003). The future of workforce diversity in international organisations: A commentary. *Applied Psychology: An International Review*, *52*, 486–495. doi:10.1111/1464-0597.00146

Trompenaars, F., & Hampden-Turner, C. (1998). *Riding the waves of culture: Understanding diversity in global business* (2nd ed.). New York, NY: McGraw-Hill.

Truss, C., & Gratton, L. (1994). Strategic human resource management: A conceptual approach. *International Journal of Human Resource Management*, *5*(3), 663–686. doi:10.1080/09585199400000053

Tsui, A. S., Egan, T. D., & O'Reilly, C. A. (1992). Being different: Relational demography and organizational attachment. *Administrative Science Quarterly*, *37*, 547–579. doi:10.2307/2393472

Tudor, P. (2011). *Adding value with diversity: What leaders need to know*. Retrieved from http://www.tudorconsulting.net.

Tung, R. (1993). Managing cross-national and intra-national diversity. *Human Resource Management, 32*, 461–477. doi:10.1002/hrm.3930320404

Tung, R. L. (1981). Selection and training of personnel for overseas assignments. *The Columbia Journal of World Business, 16*(1), 68–78.

Turner, J. (1987). *Rediscovering the social group: A social categorisation theory*. Oxford, UK: Blackwell.

Turner, J. C. (1981). The experimental social psychology of inter-group behavior. In Turner, J. C., & Giles, H. (Eds.), *Intergroup Behavior* (pp. 66–101). Chicago, IL: University of Chicago Press.

Tushman, M. L., & O'Reilly, C. A. (1996). Ambidextrous organizations: Managing evolutionary and revolutionary change. *California Management Review, 38*, 8–30.

Tushman, M. L., & Rosenkopf, L. (1996). Executive succession, strategic reorientation and performance growth: A longitudinal study in the U.S. cement industry. *Management Science, 42*(7), 939–953. doi:10.1287/mnsc.42.7.939

Tyran, K. L., & Gibson, C. (2008). Is what you see, what you get? The relationship among surface –and deep- level heterogeneity characteristics, group efficacy, and team reputation. *Group & Organization Management, 33*(1), 46–76. doi:10.1177/1059601106287111

UE. (2003). *I costi e i benefici della diversità*. Retrieved May 25, 2011, from http://www.ec.europa.eu/social/Blo bServlet?docId=1440&langId=it.

Ulrich, D., & Brockbank, W. (2005). *The HR value proposition*. Boston, MA: Harvard Business School Press.

Ungricht, T. (1997). *Learning strategies of concurrent enrollment students at Utah Valley State College*. Unpublished Doctoral Dissertation. Bozeman, MT: Montana State University.

United States Small Business Administration. (2004). *Small business act (15 USC 637)*. Retrieved from http://www.sba.gov/regulations/sbaact/sbaact.html.

University of Iowa School of Social Work – National Resource Center for Family Centered Practice. (2009). *Supervision of intergenerational dynamics*. Retrieved February 13, 2011 from http://www.uiowa.edu/~nrcfcp/training/documents/Participant%20Packet%20Intergen%20Dynamics.pdf.

Urquhart, M. (1984). The employment shift from services: Where did it come from? *Monthly Labor Review, 107*(4), 15–22.

US Bureau of Labor Statistics. (2008). *Customized tables of data on gender of workers*. Retrieved from ftp://ftp.bls.gov/pub/special.requests/lf/aat2.txt.

US Bureau of Labor Statistics. (2008). *Customized tables of data on race of workers*. Retrieved from http://www.bls.gov/cps/cpsatabs.htm.

US Bureau of Labor Statistics. (2008). *Employed persons in agriculture and related and in nonagricultural industries by age, sex, and class of worker*. Retrieved from ftp://ftp.bls.gov/pub/special.requests/lf/aat15.txt.

US Census Bureau Economic Census. (2002). *Survey of business owners*. Washington, DC: US Census Bureau.

US Census Bureau. (2001). *Website*. Retrieved from http://www.census.gov.

US Census Bureau. (2002). *Website*. Retrieved from http://www.census.gov.

US Census Bureau. (2010). *Website*. Retrieved from http://www.census.gov.

US Congress. (2008). *Equality in job loss: Women are increasingly vulnerable to layoffs during recessions*. Washington, DC: Majority Staff of the Joint Economic Committee.

US Department of Commerce. (1999). *Best practices in achieving workforce diversity benchmarking study / U.S. Department of Commerce and Vice President Al Gore's national partnership for reinventing government*. Online doc. PRVP 42.2:R 27/2003012037. Retrieved June 17, 2011, from http://purl.access.gpo.gov/GPO/LPS30263.

US Department of Labor. (1965). *Executive order 11264, as amended*. Retrieved June 17, 2011, from http://www.dol.gov/ofccp/regs/statutes/eo11246.htm.

US Department of Labor. (2002). *Facts on executive order 11264 – Affirmative action*. Retrieved June 17, 2011, from http://www.dol.gov/ofccp/regs/compliance/aa.htm.

US DOL. (1978). *Uniform guidelines on employee selection procedures*. Retrieved from http://www.dol.gov/esa/regs/cfr/41cfr/toc_Chapt60/60_3_toc.htm.

US Glass Ceiling Commission. (1991). *A report on the glass ceiling initiative*. Washington, DC: US Department of Labor.

US Glass Ceiling Commission. (1995). *Good for business*. Washington, DC: US Department of Labor.

Van den Steen, E. J. (2009, August). Culture clash: The costs and benefits of homogeneity. *Harvard Business Review*.

Van der Vaart, T., & Van Donk, D. P. (2008). A critical review of survey-based research in supply chain integration. *International Journal of Production Economics*, *111*(1), 42–55. doi:10.1016/j.ijpe.2006.10.011

Van der Vegt, G. S. (2005). Location-level links between diversity and innovative climate depend on national power distance. *Academy of Management Journal*, *48*(8), 1171–1182. doi:10.5465/AMJ.2005.19573116

van Dick, R., van Knippenberg, D., Hägele, S., Guillaume, Y. R. F., & Brodbeck, F. C. (2008). Group diversity and group identifications: The moderating role of diversity beliefs. *Human Relations*, *61*, 1463–1492. doi:10.1177/0018726708095711

van Dijk, M. (2004). Career development within HRD: Foundations or fad? In T. M. Egan & M. L. Morris (Eds.), *2004 Academy of Human Resource Development Annual Research Conference Proceedings*, (pp. 771-778). Bowling Green, OH: Academy of Human Resource Development.

van Knippenberg, D., De Dreu, C. K. W., & Homan, A. C. (2004). Work group diversity and group performance: An integrative model and research agenda. *The Journal of Applied Psychology*, *89*(6), 1008–1022. doi:10.1037/0021-9010.89.6.1008

van Knippenberg, D., & Haslam, S. A. (2003). Realizing the diversity dividend: Exploring the subtle interplay between identity, ideology, and reality. In Haslam, S. A., van Knippenberg, D., Platow, M. J., & Ellemers, N. (Eds.), *Social Identity at Work: Developing Theory for Organizational Practice* (pp. 61–77). Hove, UK: Psychology Press.

van Knippenberg, D., & Schippers, M. C. (2007). Work group diversity. *Annual Review of Psychology*, *58*, 515–541. doi:10.1146/annurev.psych.58.110405.085546

Van Manen, M. (1997). *Researching lived experiences: Human science for an action sensitive pedagogy* (2nd ed.). London, UK: The Althouse Press.

Van Stralen, S. (2002). Making sense of one's experience in the workplace. In Yorks, L., & Kasl, E. (Eds.), *Collaborative Inquiry as a Strategy for Adult Learning: Creating Space for Generative Learning*. San Francisco, CA: Jossey-Bass. doi:10.1002/ace.55

Varadarajan, P. R., & Menon. (1988). Cause related marketing: A coalignment of marketing strategy and corporate philanthropy. *Journal of Marketing*, *52*(3), 58–74. doi:10.2307/1251450

Vardi, Y. (1980). Organizational career mobility: An integrative model. *Academy of Management Review*, *5*(3), 341–355.

Varmazis, M. (2007). Supplier diversity yields growth. *Purchasing*, 57-58.

Vecchio, R., & Bullis, R. (2001). Moderators of the influence of supervisor-subordinate similarity on subordinate outcomes. *The Journal of Applied Psychology*, *86*, 884–896. doi:10.1037/0021-9010.86.5.884

Verhaegen, P. (2003). Aging and vocabulary score: A meta-analysis. *Psychology and Aging*, *18*, 332–339. doi:10.1037/0882-7974.18.2.332

Vescio, T. K., Sechrist, G. B., & Paolucci, M. P. (2003). Perspective taking and prejudice reduction: The mediational role of empathy arousal and situational attributions. *European Journal of Social Psychology*, *33*, 455–472. doi:10.1002/ejsp.163

Vielba, C., & Edelshain, D. (1997). Are business schools meeting the challenge of International communication? *Journal of Management Development*, *16*(2), 80–92. doi:10.1108/02621719710164265

Virjee, Z. (2004). Cross-cultural learning in adult continuing education. *Education Canada*, *44*(2), 35–37.

Voelpel, S., Leibold, M., & Früchtenicht, J.-D. (2007). *Herausforderung 50 plus: Warum sie erfahrene arbeitnehmer optimal managen müssen und wie es funktioniert*. Erlangen, Germany: Publicis-Wiley.

Volkema, R. J. (2004). Demographic, cultural, and economic predictors of perceived ethicality of negotiation behavior: A nine-country analysis. *Journal of Business Research*, *57*, 69–78. doi:10.1016/S0148-2963(02)00286-2

Von Glinow, M. A., Shapiro, D. L., & Brett, J. M. (2004). Can we talk and should we? Managing emotional conflict in multicultural teams. *Academy of Management Review*, *29*(4), 578–592.

Vroom, V. H., & MacCrimmon, K. R. (1968). Toward a stochastic model of managerial careers. *Administrative Science Quarterly*, *13*(1), 26–46. doi:10.2307/2391260

Wagner, W., Pfeffer, J., & O'Reilly, C. (1984). Organizational demography and turnover in top management groups. *Administrative Science Quarterly*, *29*, 74–92. doi:10.2307/2393081

Walker, S. (2009). Reflections on leadership from the perspective of an African American woman of faith. *Advances in Developing Human Resources*, *11*(5). doi:10.1177/1523422309352439

Wang, P., & Schwarz, J. L. (2010). Stock price reactions to GLBT non discrimination policies. *Human Resource Management*, *49*(2), 195–216. doi:10.1002/hrm.20341

Wang, X., & McLean, G. N. (2007). The dilemma of defining international human resource development. *Human Resource Development Review*, *6*(1), 96–108. doi:10.1177/1534484306296305

Ware, J., Craft, R., & Kerschenbaum, S. (2007). Training tomorrow's workforce. *T+D*, *64*(4), 58-60.

Watkins, K. E., & Marsick, V. J. (1993). *Sculpting the learning organization*. San Francisco, CA: Jossey-Bass.

Watkins, K. E., & Marsick, V. J. (Eds.). (1996). *In action: Creating the learning organization*. Alexandria, VA: ASTD Press.

Watkins, K., & Cseh, M. (2009). Competence development in the USA: Limiting expectations or unleashing global capacities. In Illeris, K. (Ed.), *International Perspectives on Competence Development*. Oxford, UK: Routledge.

Watson, W. E., Kumar, K., & Michaelsen, L. K. (1993). Cultural diversity's impact on interaction process and performance: Comparing homogeneous and diverse task groups. *Academy of Management Journal*, *36*, 590–602. doi:10.2307/256593

Weaver, A. C., & Morrison, B. B. (2008). Social networking. *Compute*, *41*(2), 97–100. doi:10.1109/MC.2008.61

Wechsler, D. (1944). *The measurement of intelligence*. Baltimore, MD: Williams & Wilkins.

Weisband, S. P., & Reinig, B. A. (1995). Managing user perceptions of email privacy. *Communications of the ACM*, *38*(12), 40–47. doi:10.1145/219663.219678

Weisinger, J. (2005). *Understanding the meaning of diversity in a nonprofit organization*. White Paper. Retrieved June 17, 2011 from http://www.naccouncil.org/pdf/AR-NOVA%202005%20Paper%20Judy%20Weisinger.pdf.

Weisinger, J., & Salipante, P. (2005). A grounded theory for building ethnically bridging social capital in voluntary organizations. *Nonprofit and Voluntary Sector Quarterly*, *34*(1), 29–55. doi:10.1177/0899764004270069

Welton, M. R. (1993). The contribution of critical theory to our understanding of adult learning. In Merriam, S. B. (Ed.), *An Update on Adult Learning Theory* (*Vol. 57*, pp. 81–90). San Francisco, CA: Jossey Bass. doi:10.1002/ace.36719935710

Wennerds, C., & Wold, A. (1997). Nepotism and sexism in peer review. *Nature*, *307*, 341. doi:10.1038/387341a0

Wentling, R. M., & Palma-Rivas, N. (1998). Current status and future trends of diversity initiatives in the workplace: Diversity experts' perspective. *Human Resource Development Quarterly*, *9*, 235–253. doi:10.1002/hrdq.3920090304

Wentling, R. M., & Palma-Rivas, N. (2000). Current status of diversity, initiatives in selected multinational corporations. *Human Resource Development Quarterly*, *11*(1), 35–60. doi:10.1002/1532-1096(200021)11:1<35::AID-HRDQ4>3.0.CO;2-#

West, C., & Zimmerman, D. H. (1987). Doing gender. *Gender & Society*, *1*, 125–151. doi:10.1177/0891243287001002002

West, M. A., & Anderson, N. R. (1996). Innovation in top management teams. *The Journal of Applied Psychology*, *81*(6), 680–693. doi:10.1037/0021-9010.81.6.680

Wharton MBA for Executives. (2011). *University of Pennsylvania's online course catalog.* Retrieved from http://www.wharton.upenn.edu/mbaexecutive/academics/curriculum.cfm.

Wheeler, M. L. (1996, December 9). Diversity: Making the business case. *Business Week*.

White House. (2011). *American jobs act.* Retrieved on October 31, 2011 from http://www.whitehouse.gov/economy/jobsact/read-the-bill.

Whitehead, A. (2010). Sacred rites and civil rights: Religion's effect on attitudes toward same-sex unions and the perceived cause of homosexuality. *Social Science Quarterly*, *91*(1), 63–79. doi:10.1111/j.1540-6237.2010.00681.x

Whitfield, G., & Landeros, R. (2006). Supplier diversity effectiveness: Does organizational culture really matter? *The Journal of Supply Chain Management*, *42*(4), 16–28. doi:10.1111/j.1745-493X.2006.00019.x

Wiersema, M. F., & Bantel, K. A. (1992). Top management team demography and corporate strategic change. *Academy of Management Journal*, *35*(1), 91–121. doi:10.2307/256474

Wiersema, M. F., & Bird, A. (1993). Organizational demography in Japanese firms: Group heterogeneity, individual dissimilarity, and top management team turnover. *Academy of Management Journal*, *36*, 996–1025. doi:10.2307/256643

Wiesenfeld, B. M., Raghuram, S., & Garud, R. (1999). Communication patterns as determinants of organizational identification in a virtual organization. *Organization Science*, *10*(6), 777–790. doi:10.1287/orsc.10.6.777

Williams, R. H. (1995). Constructing the public good: Social movements and cultural resources. *Social Problems*, *42*(1), 124–144. doi:10.1525/sp.1995.42.1.03x0458p

Wilborn, L. R. (1999). *An investigation of the relationships between diversity management training involvement with the personal inputs and outputs of managers in the lodging industry.* Unpublished Doctoral Dissertation. Memphis, TN: The University of Memphis.

Wilder, D., & Simon, A. F. (2001). Affect as a cause of intergroup bias. In Brown, R., & Gaertner, S. (Eds.), *Blackwell Handbook of Social Psychology: Intergroup Processes* (pp. 153–172). Malden, MA: Blackwell. doi:10.1002/9780470693421.ch8

Wildman, S. M. (1996). Privilege in the workplace: The missing element in antidiscrimination law. In Wildman, S. M., Armstrong, M., Davis, A. D., & Grillo, T. (Eds.), *Privilege Revealed: How Invisible Preference Undermines AMERICA*. New York, NY: New York University Press.

Wildman, S. M., & Davis, A. D. (1996). Making systems of privilege work. In Wildman, S. M., Armstrong, M., Davis, A. D., & Grillo, T. (Eds.), *Privilege Revealed: How Invisible Preference Undermines America*. New York, NY: New York University Press.

Wilkening, B. (2005). *Political opportunities in the post-Soviet realm: A comparative case study of anti-regime mobilization and success in Azerbaijan and Georgia.* Paper presented at the Illinois State University Conference for Students of Political Science. Normal, IL.

Williams Institute. (2009). *Bias in the workplace: Consistent evidence of sexual orientation and gender identity discrimination.* Retrieved on August 25, 2011 from http://services.law.ucla.edu/williamsinstitute/publications/Bias%20in%20the%20Workplace.pdf.

Williams, C. (2011). Managing individuals and a diverse work force. In *Management* (pp. 452–487). Mason, OH: South-Western Cengage Learning.

Williams, K. Y., & O'Reilly, C. A. III. (1998). Demography and diversity in organizations: A review of 40 years of research. *Research in Organizational Behavior*, *20*, 77–140.

Williams, M. (2001). In whom we trust: Group membership as an affective context for trust development. *Academy of Management Review*, *26*(3), 377–396.

Willyard, P. (2000). *Learning strategies of first-generation community college students.* Unpublished Doctoral Dissertation. Stillwater, OK: Oklahoma State University.

Wilson, M. S., & Liu, J. H. (2003). Social dominance orientation and gender: The moderating role of gender identification. *The British Journal of Social Psychology*, *42*, 187–198. doi:10.1348/014466603322127175

Wingfield, A., & Byrnes, D. (1981). *The psychology of human memory*. New York, NY: Academic Press.

Wiseman, R. L., Hammer, M. R., & Nishida, H. (1989). Predictors of intercultural communication competence. *International Journal of Intercultural Relations, 13*, 349–369. doi:10.1016/0147-1767(89)90017-5

Witherspoon, R. (2006). Who's who in supplier diversity? *USBE & Information Technology, 19*(54), 28–31.

Woodruff-Pak, D. S. (1997). *The neuropsychology of aging*. Oxford, UK: Blackwell.

Woods, J. D. (1993). *The corporate closet: The professional lives of gay men in America*. New York, NY: Free Press.

Woods, S. E., & Harbeck, K. M. (1991). Living in two worlds: The identity management strategies used by lesbian physical educators. *Journal of Homosexuality, 22*, 141–166. doi:10.1300/J082v22n03_06

Workman, M. (2007). A proximal-virtual team continuum: A study of performance. *Journal of the American Society for Information Science and Technology, 58*(6), 794–801. doi:10.1002/asi.20545

Worman, D., Bland, A., & Chase, P. (2005). Managing diversity: People make the difference at work: But everyone is different. In *Change Agenda*. London, UK: CIPD.

Wrench, J. (2001). *Diversity management in the European context: A critical examination of organisational strategies for combating ethnic discrimination and exclusion*. Paper presented at the International Perspectives on Cross-Cultural Workforce Diversity: The Inclusive Workplace. Bellagio, Italy.

Wren, D. A., & Bedeian, A. G. (2009). *The evolution of management thought*. Hoboken, NJ: John Wiley & Sons.

Wright, P. M., Ferris, S. P., Hiller, J. S., & Kroll, M. (1995). Competitiveness through management of diversity: Effects on stock price valuation. *Academy of Management Journal, 38*(1), 272–287. doi:10.2307/256736

Wright, P. M., & McMahan, G. C. (1992). Theoretical perspectives for strategic human resource management. *Journal of Management, 18*(2), 295–320. doi:10.1177/014920639201800205

Wright, P. M., & Snell, S. A. (2005). Partner or guardian? HR's challenge in balancing value and values. *Human Resource Management, 44*(2), 177–182. doi:10.1002/hrm.20061

Wright, T. (2011). Exploring the intersections of gender, sexuality and class in the transport and construction industries. In Healy, G., Kirton, G., & Noon, M. (Eds.), *Equality, Inequality and Diversity: Contemporary Challenges and Strategies*. London, UK: Palgrave Macmillan.

Yakura, E. K. (1996). EEO, law and managing diversity. In Kossek, E. E., & Lobel, S. A. (Eds.), *Managing Diversity: Human Resources Strategies for Transforming the Workplace* (pp. 25–50). Oxford, UK: Blackwell Publishers.

Yammarino, F. J., Dionne, S. D., Chun, J. U., & Dansereau, F. (2005). Leadership and levels of analysis: A state-of-the-science review. *The Leadership Quarterly, 16*, 879–919. doi:10.1016/j.leaqua.2005.09.002

Yang, Y. (2005). Developing cultural diversity advantage: The impact of diversity management structures. In *Academy of Management Best Conference Paper 2005*, (pp. H1-H6). Academy of Management.

Yap, M., Holmes, M. R., Hannan, C., & Cukier, W. (2010). The relationship between diversity training, organizational commitment, and career satisfaction. *Journal of European Industrial Training, 34*(6), 519–538. doi:10.1108/03090591011061202

Yaw, A. D., McGovern, I., & Budhwar, P. (2000). Complementarities or competition: The development of human resources in a Southeast Asian growth triangle--Indonesia, Malaysia, and Singapore. *International Journal of Human Resource Management, 11*(2), 314–335. doi:10.1080/095851900339891

Yeo, S. (2006). *Measuring organizational climate for diversity: A construct validation approach*. Unpublished Doctoral Dissertation. Columbus, OH: Ohio State University.

Yin, R. K. (1999). Enhancing the quality of case studies in health services research. *Health Services Research, 34*(5), 1209–1224.

Yorks, L. (2005). Adult learning and the generation of new knowledge and meaning: Creating liberating spaces for fostering adult learning through practitioner based collaborative inquiry. *Teachers College Record, 12*, 9–25.

Yorks, L., & Kasl, E. (2002a). Toward a theory and practice for whole-person learning: Reconceptualizing experience and the role of affect. *Adult Education Quarterly, 52*(3), 176–192.

Yorks, L., & Kasl, E. (2002b). Collaborative inquiry as a strategy for adult learning. *New Directions for Adult and Continuing Education, 94*.

Yukl, G. A. (2010). *Leadership in organizations* (7th ed.). Upper Saddle River, NJ: Pearson.

Yuksel, M. (2011). Core competencies of managers in an emerging market. *Journal of American Academy of Business, 17*(1), 104–111.

Yussen, S. (1985). The role of metacognition in contemporary theories of cognitive development. In Forrext-Pressley, D. L., MacKinnon, G., & Waller, T. (Eds.), *Metacognition, Cognition, and Human Performance* (Vol. 1). Orlando, FL: Academic Press.

Zaccaro, S. J., & Bader, P. (2003). E-leadership and the challenges of leading e-teams: Minimizing the bad and maximizing the good. *Organizational Dynamics, 31*(4), 377–387. doi:10.1016/S0090-2616(02)00129-8

Zaccaro, S. J., Rittman, A. L., & Marks, M. A. (2001). Team leadership. *The Leadership Quarterly, 12*, 451–483. doi:10.1016/S1048-9843(01)00093-5

Zack, N. (2005). *Inclusive feminism: A third wave theory of women's commonality*. Lanham, MD: Rowman and Littlefield Publishers, Inc.

Zald, M. N., & McCarthy, J. (1988). *Social movements in an organizational society*. New Brunswick, NJ: Transaction.

Zanoni, P., & Janssens, M. (2004). Deconstructing difference: The rhetoric of human resource managers' diversity discourses. *Organization Studies, 25*(1), 55–74. doi:10.1177/0170840604038180

Zanoni, P., Janssens, M., Benschop, Y., & Nkomo, S. (2010). Guest editorial: Unpacking diversity, grasping inequality: Rethinking difference through critical perspectives. *Organization, 17*, 9–29. doi:10.1177/1350508409350344

Zelman, A. W. (1995). Answering the question: How is learning experienced through collaborative inquiry? A phenomenological/hermeneutic approach. *Dissertation Abstracts International, 7*(56), 2534.

Zenger, T. R., & Lawrence, B. S. (1989). Organizational demography: The differential effects of age and tenure distributions on technical communication. *Academy of Management Journal, 32*, 353–376. doi:10.2307/256366

Zenisek, T. J. (1979). Corporate social responsibility: A conceptualization based on organizational literature. *Academy of Management Review, 4*(3), 359–368.

Zhao, J. L., Nunamaker, J. F., & Briggs, R. O. (2002). Intelligent workflow techniques for distributed group facilitation. In *Proceedings of the 35th International Conference on System Sciences*. Big Island, HI: System Sciences.

Zin, R. M., & Talat, N. A. (2011). Can functional performances of HRM be improved with the adoption of IT? *The Cambridge Business Review, 18*(1), 48–53.

Zucker, L. G. (1986). Production of trust: Institutional sources of economic structure, 1840-1920. In B. M. Staw & L. L. Cummings (Eds.), *Research in Organizational Behavior, 8*, 53-111.

Zuckerman, A. J., & Simons, G. F. (1996). *Sexual orientation in the workplace*. Thousand Oaks, CA: Sage.

About the Contributors

Chaunda L. Scott is an Associate Professor and Graduate Coordinator of the Master of Training and Development Program in the Department of Human Resource Development (HRD) at Oakland University in Rochester, Michigan. Dr. Scott comes to Oakland University by way of The White House, The Harvard Graduate School of Education, and Teachers College Columbia University. At Oakland University, Dr. Scott teaches a variety of other HRD courses in the Undergraduate HRD Program, Masters of Training and Development Program, and the Honors College. Her scholarly research interests lie in the following areas: eradicating racism, workforce diversity education and training, human resource development, training and development, organizational culture, and organizational justice, and she has published her research in a number of respected journals. She has as well presented her research in such locations as South Africa, Oxford, UK, Beijing, China, Limerick, Ireland, Montreal, Canada, Washington D.C., and Minneapolis, Minnesota. In addition, Dr. Scott is the Founder and President of the Diverse Voices Initiative, created in 1999. Diverse Voices is a Michigan statewide higher education initiative that provides a supportive forum for Michigan higher education students, renowned scholars, business professionals, and community members to speak out in support of valuing all aspects of human diversity. She also serves as chair of the Academy of Human Resource Development's (AHRD) Cultural Diversity Special Interest Group, a member of the Academy of Management, and an appointed member of the Society of Human Resource Management Diversity and Inclusion Standards Task Force. Most notable in 2009, Dr. Scott received a Cutting Edge Research Award from the Academy of Human Resource Development.

Marilyn Y. Byrd is an Assistant Professor of Management and Marketing, University of Mary Hardin-Baylor, Belton, Texas. Dr. Byrd earned a BBA and MBA from Sam Houston State University in Huntsville, Texas, and a PhD in Human Resource Development from Texas A&M University, College Station, Texas. She teaches undergraduate and graduate courses in human resource management, organizational behavior, managerial communication, and business ethics. Dr. Byrd is a member of the Academy of Management and the Academy of Human Resource Development, where she serves as a steering committee member for the Cultural Diversity Special Interest Group. She was recently appointed to participate in the Society of Human Resource Management Diversity and Inclusion Standards Task Force that will be responsible for establishing standards for diversity professionals in the HR community. Dr. Byrd currently serves on the Editorial Board for *Advances in Developing Human Resources (ADHR)*. She co-edited the ADHR issue, "Giving Voice: The Socio-Cultural Realities of African American Women's Leadership Experiences," with Dr. Christine A. Stanley, Texas A&M University. This issue was the first ADHR issue devoted exclusively to African American women's experiences. Dr. Byrd is interested in contributing to research and literature in the area of leadership theorizing that reflects the multiple perspectives that shape the leadership experience. Her other scholarly interests include group dynamics in organizations, social systems in organizations, organizational social justice, and issues emerging from racial diversity in the workplace.

* * *

Phillip Acheampong is currently a graduate student pursuing Ph.D in a dual title degree in Workforce Education and Development and Comparative and International Education at Pennsylvania State University. His career emphasis is Postsecondary Technical and Community College Leadership. Mr. Acheampong came to Penn State University because he wanted to explore opportunities that will make him a change agent. His career goal is to assume a role as educational administrator, a practitioner, and a pioneer in career technical education setting. Mr. Acheampong sees education as a means to reduce poverty and improve quality of life with a focus on communities that are vulnerable. His research interests focus on educational policies that will provide technical skills that are responsive to economic opportunities among the youth. Mr. Acheampong believes career and technical education is the economic backbone of nations, yet it is the education sector that receives the smallest budget. Due to this inequality, Mr. Acheampong intends to explore opportunities that will influence policies that can impact career and technical education. Mr. Acheampong received his Undergraduate degree in Architecture and Masters degree in Vocational Industrial Education from Florida Agricultural and Mechanical University. In addition to the above, he attained his professional Master of Architecture degree from Savannah College of Art and design in Georgia, where he worked in the capacity of Architectural Coordinator for the local government doing historic preservation and restoration work. Phillip had the opportunity to work with graduate interns who were interested in developing their technical skills in building restoration and historic preservation projects.

Jeff M. Allen, Professor and Director for the Center for Knowledge Solutions, is a distinguished teacher and scholar in the area of learning and performance innovation. His research includes over fifty publications including articles, monographs, curriculum guides, and chapters. Dr. Allen has been a faculty member at the University of North Texas since 1994 and currently serves in the Department of Learning Technologies at the University of North Texas.

Güven Alpay is Management Professor in the Department of Management of the Faculty of Economics and Business Administration, at Boğaziçi University, Istanbul, Turkey. He received his PhD in Business Administration from University of Southern California, USA. His research interests include organization and management, strategic management, and global patterns of negotiation.

Tutaleni I. Asino is currently a Dual Title Ph.D. candidate in Instructional Systems and in Comparative International Education at Penn State University. He has over ten years of instructional design and training experience and consulting with organization ions on integrating new media into their communication strategy. Tutaleni's work experience includes: student affairs; web design; teaching in face-to-face and online classes in information technology and instructional design at both the graduate and undergraduate level. He has conducted cross-cultural research on the use mobile devices for learning and training.

His research interests include mobile learning, instructional design for mobile devices, contextually appropriate learning technologies, indigenous knowledge, and the role of culture in the development and evaluation of learning technologies. Tutaleni holds a B.A. in Political Science and Media Studies, a M.S. in Multimedia Technologies, a M.A. in Corporate Communication, and a M.S. in Instructional Systems.

Roxanne Beard is an Associate Professor of Organizational Behavior and Management at Ohio Dominican University in Columbus, Ohio, where she focuses on the application of leveraging mindfulness and personal spirituality as a means to transformative teaching and learning practices. Her research interests include leadership, the imposter phenomenon, the impact of mindfulness and spirituality on academic performance, and online learning pedagogy.

Robyn Berkley's research interests are in the areas of diversity, discrimination, and sexual harassment, along with ethics and corporate social responsibility. Her research has been published in scholarly journals such as the *Employee Rights and Responsibility Journal, National Womens Studies Association Journal, Journal of Small Business Management, Journal of Business Ethics*, and *Society and Business Review*. Her teaching focus is the area of Human Resources Management where she has taught classes in Staffing, Training and Development, and Compensation. At the Graduate level, she teaches HR Skills course for Non-HR Professionals and Managerial Decision-Making, including ethics and other decision-making challenges. Aside from being asked to serve as a speaker on human resource management issues both on and off campus, she also serves on the editorial board for the *Employee Rights and Responsibilities Journal*.

Pamela Bracey is currently an Adjunct Professor and a Research Affiliate of the Center for Knowledge Solutions in the Department of Learning Technologies at the University of North Texas. Pam also serves as a Curriculum Specialist for an Education Excellence grant which is funded by Texas Education Agency to develop professional development materials for Career and Technical Education teachers of the Information Technology Cluster. She holds a PhD in Applied Technology and Performance Improvement from the University of North Texas, M.S. in Higher Education Administration from Mississippi College, and B.S. in Business Technology Education from the University of Southern Mississippi. Her research interests include: career and technical education, gifted education, and professional soft skill development.

Jessica Briskin is the Content Developer for Affiliates Risk Management Services, Inc. (ARMS). She is responsible for collaborating with stakeholders, subject matter experts, and learners in the healthcare industry to design and develop eLearning courses. Jessica earned her Master's degree in Instructional Systems from Penn State University, and her Bachelor of Science in Communication, Management and Design from Ithaca College. She has comprehensive instructional design experience, including both corporate and K-12 arenas, as well as in higher education, working as an Adjunct Instructor. She is an active member of the International Society for Performance Improvement and has presented at their Annual Conference. She has also presented at Conference and the Association for Educational Communications and Technology and The Pennsylvania Educational Technology Expo. Jessica has been published in TechTrends and PerformanceXpress.

Claudia Buengeler is a Research Associate and Ph.D. fellow at Jacobs University Bremen, Germany. As an industrial and organizational psychologist, she has been working for various national and international organizations and consults companies in implementing leadership development programs. Her research interests comprise the manifold effects of leadership behaviors on teams that vary with regards to their levels of team diversity (especially age, personality, and attitudes diversity) as well as knowledge transfer in age-diverse teams. She presented her research at various international conferences such as the Annual Meeting of the Academy of Management or the International Workshop on Teamworking and has been a Visiting Research Fellow at the Roy E. Crummer Graduate School of Business, US.

Pınar Büyükbalcı is Research Assistant in the Department of Management of the Faculty of Economics and Business Administration, at Yıldız Technical University, Istanbul, Turkey. She received her PhD in Business Administration from Boğaziçi University, Turkey. Her research interests include International Strategic Management, Organization Theory, and Sustainability Related Value Management.

Norma Carr-Ruffino is Professor of Management at San Francisco State University, where she has been teaching since 1973. Currently she teaches courses in Managing Diversity and Creativity and Innovation. She developed the diversity and innovation courses, as well as a course she formerly taught, Leadership Skills for Women. She is the author of textbooks used in these courses at SF State and other universities: *Managing Diversity*, which is used in over 40 colleges and universities, *Leading Innovation*, and *Leadership Skills for Women*. Her other books include *The Innovative Woman, Diversity Success Strategies, Making Diversity Work, Business Students Guide*, and *The Promotable Woman*, which is available in Spanish and Cantonese as well as English and has sold nearly a half million copies worldwide.

Shani D. Carter is a Professor of Management and has been at Rhode Island College since the Fall 2001. She received a Ph.D. in Personnel/Human Resource Studies, Labor Economics, and Research Methods from Cornell University, a M.S. in Personnel/Human Resource Studies and Labor Economics from Cornell University, and a B.A. in Government from Cornell University. She teaches Human Resources, Compensation, Labor Relations, Foundations of Management, Organizational Theory, and Business, Government, and Society. She also has taught Human Resources Information Systems, Individual Behavior, Recruitment and Staffing, Professional Contribution, Human Resources Policies, Macro Human Resources, Training and Development, Statistics/Research Methods, and Business Communication. She has published more than 20 articles and conference proceedings on training methods, factors of cognitive ability, affect, skill certification, measurement, student learning outcomes assessment, coefficient alpha, skills shortages, diversity, gender, and government labor force projections.

Dominique T. Chlup is an Associate Professor of Adult Education and Human Resource Development in the Department of Educational Administration and Human Resource Development at Texas A&M University. Additionally, she is an Affiliate Faculty Member of the Women's and Gender Studies Program in the College of Liberal Arts. She is also the Associate Director of the College of Education and Human Development's Writing Initiative for Graduate Students entitled P.O.W.E.R. (Promoting Outstanding Writing and Excellence and Research). She received her Doctorate in Education from the Harvard University Graduate School of Education in 2004. She has over 85 publications in journals, books, technical reports, and refereed proceedings. She has delivered over 80 presentations for national and international audiences. She is a consulting editor for three major journals: *Adult Learning, Adult Education Quarterly,* and *TC Record.* Her research interests include the socio-historical dynamics of women's learning and issues emerging from the intesectionalities, diversity, and adult learning.

Ezeibe Chukwuebuka Christian is a First Class Honors degree holder in Political Science, University of Nigeria Nsukka. He currently lectures in the Department of Political Science University of Nigeria Nsukka, where he obtained his M.Sc. He has published in both local and international journals. His particular area of interest is African political economy. He has won numerous academic awards including the best faculty graduate in 2006. He awaits his dissertation.

Robert A. Eckhoff is a PhD candidate at Jacobs University Bremen, Germany. He holds a degree in Integrated Social Sciences (Jacobs), combining business administration, social psychology, and sociology. His papers have been published in *Human Relations* and the *Journal of Intellectual Capital.* He presented at leading international conferences such as the Annual Meeting of the Academy of Management, the American Psychological Association Annual Convention, the Annual European Group of Organizational Studies Colloquium, and others. He has been working as a human resource consultant for the EMPRISE Consulting Group and his research was supported by a PhD scholarship from the Foundation of German Business (Stiftung der Deutschen Wirtschaft). His current research interests include environmental conditions for fostering creativity, leadership, and entrepreneurship, as well as its relationships with diversity (specifically age diversity).

Kasia Ganko-Rodriguez is a Consultant **for The Kaleidoscope Group** L.L.C **with** extensive experience facilitating diversity and inclusion education sessions with leadership and individual contributors. Her expertise also includes instructional design, training solution strategy and planning, and organizational assessment consulting. Kasia conducts research and writes articles for The Kaleidoscope Group L.L.C. on various diversity and inclusion topics. Kasia holds a Master of Arts and a Bachelor of Arts from the University of Warsaw, the former in American Studies with a concentration in Cultural Studies and the latter in Teaching English as a Foreign Language. She has also completed four years of graduate study in Psychology of Intercultural Relations at the Warsaw School of Social Psychology.

Mariya Gavrilova, is a Doctoral Student in the Applied Technology and Performance Improvement program at the Department of Learning Technologies, University of North Texas. Mariya is a Research Affiliate of the Center for Knowledge Solutions and serves on an Education Excellence grant, which is funded by the Texas Education Agency to develop professional development materials for Career and Technical Education teachers. She holds an M.S. in Training and Development from UNT, BSBA in Marketing and Management, and BA in Spanish from Missouri Southern State University. Her research interests include organizational diversity, organizational creativity, strategic human resource management, and leadership development.

Julie Gedro is an Associate Professor of Business, Management, and Economics. She has a B.A. in Economics from the College of William and Mary; an M.B.A. in Information Systems from Kennesaw State University, and a Doctorate of Education (Ed.D.) in Adult Education and Human Resource Development from the University of Georgia. Dr. Gedro is certified as a Professional in Human Resources

(PHR) by the Society for Human Resource Management. Formerly a human resource management and development practitioner in finance, technology, and telecommunications, Dr. Gedro's work is informed by theory and practice. Her research focuses on leadership, ethics, equity, and productivity in organizations.

Apoorva Ghosh is a doctoral student with XLRI School of Business and Human Resources, Jamshedpur, India since June 2009. He is an active member and reviewer of the Gender and Diversity group of Academy of Management and has served on its committees, including the best student paper award committee. His research is published in management journals and presented in international conferences. He is also a 2012 Fulbright Scholar. His area of research interest is diversity at workplace. Within this area, he is working on identity deployment in the context of sexual orientation diversity and cultural competence. Apoorva has obtained a Bachelor degree in Mechanical Engineering from Gujarat University, India and Masters Degree in Quality Management from BITS Pilani, India. Before joining academia, he worked in manufacturing and consultancy industries for 6 years.

Bertie M. Greer is currently an Associate Professor in the Department of Management at Northern Kentucky University where she teaches both the core MBA and undergraduate course in Operations Management. She also teaches graduate and undergraduate elective courses in Project Management. Dr. Greer's primary research interests are in the areas of supply chain management, supplier diversity, project management, and change management. Dr. Greer has published scholarly articles in the *Journal of Operations Management, Journal of Business Logistics, Journal of Applied Behavioral Sciences, Interfaces, Human Resource Development Quarterly,* and other scholarly journals. She is a member of APICs (The Association for Operations Management), Decision Science Institute, Academy of Management and Institute of Supply Management. Dr. Greer has industry experience with Ford Motor Company, Chrysler, and Timken Roller Bearing.

Pi-Chi Han grew up in Taiwan. She received her Ed. D. from University of Arkansas, in Fayetteville, Arkansas. She has been influenced by both Chinese and American cultures. Her interdisciplinary academic background and cross-cultural learning experience have led her to adapt change flexibly. Professionally, Dr. Pi-Chi Han is an educator of global workforce development and a consultant of developing global talent and intercultural competence. She joined University of Missouri-St. Louis in the Fall of 2007. Her research interests have been focused on the study of investigating Intercultural Effectiveness (ICE) competencies for various demographic groups, and on the research of developing global talents and global leadership.

Doug Harris is the Chief Executive Officer with over 20 years of experience in the field of diversity consulting. As the leader of The Kaleidoscope Group L.L.C., Doug's knowledge and expertise guides organizations through the creation of customized strategies that address the specific diversity and inclusion needs of the business. Doug's extensive experience in managing cultural differences extends into the global arena. He has designed and delivered global strategic consulting solutions and cultural education workshops for multiple clients spanning across many public sector and private industries, including healthcare, financial, professional services, consumer goods, insurance, manufacturing, education, aerospace, government, and social services. His engaging style and unique ability to give diversity and inclusion meaning at all levels of the organization has made him a sought after and renowned diversity and inclusion thought leader, presenter, and facilitator.

James A. Hill serves on the faculty at The Ohio State University's Max M. Fisher College of Business in Operations Management, where he teaches graduate-level courses in supply chain management and operations planning and control. Hill is primarily interested in supply chain management with an emphasis on supply chain coordination. His current work examines behavioral contracts between buyers and suppliers exploring how psychological contracts affect supply chain performance. His articles have appeared in *Journal of Operations Management, Decision Sciences, Interfaces, Journal of Business Logistics,* and the *European Journal of Operational Research,* among others. Hill has extensive work experience in various management positions. His research and education in the area of supply chain management have included engagements with Pepsi Co., Scotts, Nestle, and Sherwin Williams, among others. Prior to arriving at Fisher Hill served on the faculty at the Owen Graduate School of Management at Vanderbilt University.

Astrid C. Homan is an Assistant Professor of Work and Organizational Psychology at the University of Amsterdam. She received her PhD from the Department of Work and Organizational Psychology of the University of Amsterdam in 2006. Astrid has been a Fulbright Scholar at the Management Department of Michigan State University and a Visiting Professor at Haas School of Business, University of California, Berkeley. Her main stream of research focuses on diversity, conflict, leadership, and team performance. Her work is published in outlets such as *Journal of Applied Psychology, Leadership Quarterly, Group Processes and Intergroup Relations,* and *Academy of Management Journal.* She is a regular reviewer for the *Journal of Personality and Social Psychology, British Journal of Management, Small Group Research, Organizational Behavior and Human Decision Processes,* and *Journal of Applied Psychology.*

Sujin K. Horwitz is an Assistant Professor of Management in the Cameron School of Business at the University of St. Thomas in Houston, TX. She received her Ph.D. in Human Resource Development and M.A. in Human Resources and Industrial Relations from the University of Minnesota. She worked as a cross-cultural trainer and consultant in human resources prior to joining the University of St. Thomas. Her research interests include diversity training and outcomes, cross-cultural HR issues, and leadership and teamwork in health care settings.

Claretha Hughes, Director of the College of Education and Health Professions Honors Program, Associate Professor, teaches Human Resource and Workforce Development in the Department of Rehabilitation, Human Resources and Communication Disorders, University of Arkansas, Fayetteville. She has extensive professional experience in business and industry and continues to serve as a consultant to international, national, and state organizations. Her research focuses on value creation through the use of human resource development and technology development. She is interested in the impact of values (1) on teaching and learning processes and motivation; (2) on organizational culture, change strategies, and leadership; and (3) on technology in the workplace environment and employee behavior. She is the 2009 University Council of Workforce and Human Resource Education Outstanding Assistant Professor. Dr. Hughes has a Ph.D. in Career and Technical Education from Virginia Tech, a MT degree from NC

State University, a BA in Chemistry from Clemson University, and an MBA from the Sam M. Walton College of Business at the University of Arkansas.

Sherita L. Jackson is a Training and Development Professional with a record of accomplishments in performance improvement and organizational development. Sherita holds a Bachelor of Science degree from Oakland University in Human Resource Development with a Specialization in Training and Development. She also earned a Master of Arts Degree in Training and Organizational Development from Oakland University. Sherita has over a decade's worth of experience developing training interventions for companies including EDS, Ford Motor Company, Deloitte, and AAA. She is currently an Instructional Designer at Thomson Reuters IP Management Services. Sherita is a board member of the Greater Detroit chapter of American Society for Training and Development. Her areas of research include performance improvement, diversity, and emotional intelligence. This is Sherita's first professional publication, and she looks forward to future research and writing.

Keith James received a Ph.D. in Social Psychology and Organizational Behavior from the University of Arizona. He is currently a Professor of Industrial/Organizational Psychology at Portland State University and does work on creativity and innovation in the workplace; organizational sustainability; organizations and disaster; occupational health psychology; and social-cultural influences on work outcomes. This chapter was completed while he was serving, with funding from the National Science Foundation (NSF), as a Grant Program Officer with the NSF's Education and Human Resource Development Directorate.

Katharina Janz is a Research Fellow in the WISE Research Group at Jacobs University Bremen, where she has been working on a project investigating the effects of the aging workforce on the innovation process using both experimental as well as survey designs. She has received a scholarship from the Volkswagen Foundation for her work on this project. Katharina's research interests include diversity, team processes and functioning, leadership, as well as aging workforce and demographic change management. She has a first degree in Psychology, and an MSc in Psychological Research Methods from the Universities of Winchester and Exeter (UK), and has been a visiting PhD fellow at VU University Amsterdam.

Ashwini Joshua-Gojer is a Doctoral Candidate at the University of North Texas. Her research interests include International HRD, cross-cultural research, and performance improvement. She holds two Masters degrees, one in Industrial Psychology and the other in Management. She has presented at many national and international conferences. Ms. Joshua-Gojer has taught at Wilson College, Mumbai, and other institutes in Western India. She is also a consultant in the corporate and non-profit sectors. She is presently pursuing her Doctoral degree in the Department of Learning Technologies at the University of North Texas.

David M. Kaplan is an Associate Professor of Management at Saint Louis University, where he is active in diversity issues on campus. He received his Ph.D. from the University of Illinois at Urbana-Champaign in Labor and Industrial Relations. In addition, he also holds degrees from the University of Wisconsin and Cornell University, and attended the University of New South Wales. His main streams of research focus on the individual and organizational implications of diversity and career management. This research informs his teaching in Talent Management and Negotiations. His publications can be found in journals such as *Human Resource Management, Human Relations,* and *Employee Responsibilities and Rights Journal.*

Esra Kaya has an MA in Human Resources Management and a BA in Psychology. She has been working at CEVA in Istanbul as the Human Resources Chief responsible for Turkey and Balkans since 2006. She is mainly responsible for Recruitment, Training, Performance Management Systems, Internal Communication, Customer Satisfaction Applications, and Regional Projects. In her recent role, she also acts as the SEMEA Regional Diversity and Inclusion Project Manager since 2009.

Yeonsoo Kim, Ph.D., SPHR, has been in HRM and training and development (currently known as Workplace Learning and Performance) field both professionally and academically for many years. Currently, she is an Assistant Professor of School of Environmental and Public Affairs in University of Nevada Las Vegas. In that capacity, she directs a graduate specialty in Human Resource Development and Human Resource Management, which is designed to prepare students for careers within HR fields in public and private sectors. Her research interests include strategic human resource planning, talent management, technical succession planning, and organization development.

David McGuire is a Lecturer in Human Resource Development (HRD) at Queen Margaret University, Edinburgh, Scotland. Dr. McGuire is highly recognized for his work in HRD and is widely published in this area. To date, he has published 2 books and over 25 research articles. Dr. McGuire's areas of interest include human resource development, perspectives on HRD, critical theory, competencies, and leadership and management development.

Rita C. McNeil is an Associate Professor in the Human Resource Training and Development department at Idaho State University. Dr. McNeil's major areas of interest are in workplace learning, adult learning methods, performance management systems, and corporate leadership training and development. As a practitioner and researcher, she has pursued a line of inquiry in adult workplace learning strategies and presents at regional, national, and international research conferences. Besides teaching undergraduate and graduate classes in adult learning methods, curriculum development, research methods, and instructional technologies for online learning, Rita guides student research projects focused on critical reflection in classroom practice. She serves as an organizational learning consultant in industry and as a co-editor for the *Journal of Adult Education.*

Ikeanyibe Okechukwu Marcellus, PhD, is a Senior Lecturer in the Department of Public Administration and Local Government, Faculty of the Social Sciences, University of Nigeria, Nsukka, Enugu State, Nigeria. He has published widely in both local and international journals. He has attended many conferences, workshops, and seminars. His major area of interest is public policy.

Naya Mondo, a native of Kenya, is a Doctoral Candidate at Columbia University – Teachers College in the department of Organizational Learning and Leadership. She is an Adult Learning and Leadership scholar/practitioner with over 21 years of experience in education, human resources, non-profit management, gender studies, and teacher training. Her research interest is women and leadership, collaborative inquiry, gender learning, individual and group learning, curriculum development, capacity building, diversity and inclusion, cultural competence, and leadership development.

Kemi Ogunyemi holds a degree in Law from the University of Ibadan, Nigeria, an LLM from the University of Strathclyde, UK, and an MBA from the Lagos Business School, Nigeria. She currently teaches Business Ethics and Anthropology at the Lagos Business School, while doing her PhD in Management at the School. Her consulting and research interests include personal ethos, work-life ethic, social responsibility, sustainability, and governance. After leaving the Nigerian Law School, Kemi worked as director, team lead, and mentor in various projects of the Women's Board (Educational Cooperation Society) before she joined Lagos Business School in 2006. She has also developed, directed, and taught in management and leadership programmes for Nigerians of all ages aspiring to impact their country and the world.

Adam T. Murry is a Doctoral Student in Industrial-Organizational Psychology at Portland State University and a Graduate Research Fellow with the National Science Foundation. His primary interests involve program evaluation, minority programs for Science, Technology, Engineering, and Math (STEM) education, Native American community development, scale development, and mixed methods research. Adam also sits as the Vice President of Native Hope International, a Los Angeles-based non-profit dedicated to serving urban Native communities and culture. Prior to matriculating to Portland State University, he worked as a Research Scholar in the National Institute of Mental Health's Career Opportunities in Research and the Sally-Casanova Predoctoral Fellowship. He is most thankful for his friends and family.

Hale Oner is an Assistant Professor of Business Management at Dogus University, Istanbul, was a Visiting Assistant Professor at Purdue University, Indiana, USA, in 2008-2009, and has been teaching Human Resources Mnagement at Groupe Sup de Co La Rochelle, France, as a Visiting Scholar since 2011. Dr. Zeynep Hale Oner holds a PhD. in Organizational Behavior specialized in leadership and an MBA from University of Stirling, Scotland. Previous to her academic life, she worked at Bayer Pharmaceuticals, Fiat Auto in Istanbul, North Yorkshire County Council, UK, and the United Nations Secretariat in New York. She has also taught English as a foreign language in England, Turkey, and the USA. Her recent book is *Intercultural Contextualization of Servant Leadership*.

Mustafa Özbilgin is a Professor of Organisational Behaviour at the Brunel Business School, London, and Co-Chair of Management and Diversity at the University of Paris-Dauphine, in France. He is an international research leader in the field of equality, diversity, and inclusion at work. He is the Editor-in-Chief of the *British Journal of Management* (Blackwell-Wiley). Professor Özbilgin holds a PhD from the University of Bristol, and a BA from Bosphorus University in Istanbul. His recent books include, *Global Diversity Management* (2007, Palgrave) and *Equality, Diversity, and Inclusion* (2009, Edward Elgar). His publications are available at: http://brunel.academia.edu/MustafaOzbilgin/About.

Laura A. Pasquini, Doctoral Student, Applied Technology and Performance Improvement, Department of Learning Technologies, University of North Texas. Laura is currently an Academic Counselor and Instructor with the Office for Exploring Majors, Undergraduate Studies at the University of North Texas. She holds an M.S. Ed in Elementary Teacher Education from Niagara University, NY, and an honors B.A. in History. Her research interests include the effects of emerging technology, collaborative learning environments, and personal learning networks for education and training.

Nicola Patterson is a Lecturer in Leadership and Management Development at Newcastle Business School, Northumbria University. Her teaching and research interests focus on gender, leadership, entrepreneurship, and small business. She has previously published a paper in the *International Small Business Journal* with Professor Sharon Mavin, exploring the post-hoc reflections of women entrepreneurs' career transition motivations for leaving their corporate careers to start up their own businesses.

Denise R. Philpot, an Applied Technology and Performance Improvement Doctoral Student in the Department of Learning Technologies at the University of North Texas, has more than 20 years of corporate experience in addition to being a certified Secondary Business teacher. She earned her undergraduate business degree from the University of LaVerne and her MBA in Organizational Behavior and Human Resource Management from UNT. Denise is excited about the prospects of helping organizations implement training strategies that improve productivity and reduce costs in addition to her first passion—teaching tomorrow's business leaders.

Rossella Riccò After a degree in Economics at the University of Modena and Reggio Emilia (Università di Modena e Reggio Emilia), in 2004, Rossella started a PhD in Labour Sciences at the University of Milan (Università degli Studi di Milano), focusing her researches on Human Resources. In September 2008, she took her PhD in Labour Sciences with a thesis titled "Diversity Management as Micro-Foundation of the Organisation and Person's Relation: Empirical Analysis on a Sample of Italian Based Companies" (Original title: La Gestione delle Diversità come micro-fondazione della relazione fra organizzazione e persona. Analisi empirica su un campione di imprese operanti in Italia). She is assistant in Organizational Studies and Human Resources at the Università degli Studi di Milano collaborating with Prof. Luca Solari. Her main research interests are diversity management, work-life balance, work flexibility, organisational justice, corporate social responsibility, organizational well-being.

Mercedes Sánchez-Apellániz is Associate Professor in the Department of Business Administration and Marketing at the University of Seville. She holds a Doctorate since 1995 in Business Administration and Management with the project titled "Women Managers and Organizational Culture: Towards a New Vision of Management." Responsible researcher of the research group "SEJ 488 Corporate Social Responsibility and Organizational Success" between 2010-2011. Her research interests include corporate social responsibility, gender in business, and cultural diversity management, with many international and national publications in these fields. Teacher in Master's degree in Gender Studies Master and in Strategic Management and International Business Master, both from the University of Seville. She belongs to the European Association of Business Management and the expert panel of the Press Association of Seville.

Cecilia Santillan received her Bachelor of Arts in International Studies, and a Master's in International Business from the University of St. Thomas in Houston, TX. She is currently researching virtual teams and their effects in global organizations, particularly in the area of diffusion of work values. She is interested in the practical application of theory in the workplace that incubates human capital and management activities that enable employees to develop their competencies. More of her research interests include cross-cultural management, managing technology, organizational change, corporate strategy, and team building in organizations.

Ramona T. Sharpe, PHR, CCP, is a seasoned Human Resources (HR) professional, adult educator, and human capital and strategy consultant. Ramona has more than thirteen years of experience in diversity and inclusion, workforce planning, training and development, project management, staffing, performance management, HR metrics, and talent management. Ramona has lead company-wide HR initiatives for fortune 500 companies as well as managed consulting projects for non-profit organizations and government. In addition, she has served as an Adjunct Professor teaching Professional Development at the university level. Ramona is currently a Doctoral Candidate at Teachers College, Columbia University, studying adult learning and leadership in the AEGIS Program. She has a MS in Human Organization Science (specializing in HR Development), a BS in Business Administration, and a BA in Psychology from Villanova University. Ramona is also a certified Human Resources Professional (PHR) and a Certified Compensation Professional (CCP).

DeVaughn G. Stephens is currently a Doctoral Student in the Human Resource and Workforce Development Education program in the Department of Rehabilitation, Human Resources, and Communication Disorders of the College of Education and Health Professions at the University of Arkansas – Fayetteville. His doctoral studies specialize in Human Resource Development with plans to receive his degree in 2013. DeVaughn has over 10 years of professional human resource management work experience in the U.S. government contracting/defense industry.

Olca Sürgevil, Ph.D., is a researcher in Management and Organization at the Department of Business Administration, Dokuz Eylül University (DEU) Faculty of Economics and Administrative Sciences. Her research interests include organizational psychology and diversity issues. She received her Bachelor's degree in Business Administration from DEU, and Master's degree in both Management and Organization from DEU and in Social Psychology from Ege University. She received her Ph.D. degree in Business Administration from DEU with her Dissertation on Workforce Diversity and Diversity Management. She has been employed at DEU as a Research Assistant since 2005.

Rafael Triguero-Sánchez is Researcher in the Department of Business Administration and Marketing at the University of Seville. He holds a Doctorate since 2010 in Business Administration and Management with the project titled "Managing Diversity in Organizations through Human Resource practices." He belongs to the research group "SEJ 488 Corporate Social Responsibility and Organizational Success" in 2011. His research interests include corporate social responsibility and diversity management, with many international and national publications in these fields. Professor in the department of Economics at the University of Pablo de Olavide of Seville. Teacher in Master's Degree in Hospitality and Tourism at the University of Seville during the 2011-2012 academic year.

Connie Watson has over twenty years of experience in higher education including the areas of student leadership, faculty, and staff development, and organizational learning. She is currently an Assistant Professor of Psychology at the Community College of Philadelphia, where she also coordinates the Community Leadership Program. Her research interest and areas of professional practice include transformational leadership, global/intercultural education, critical pedagogy, adult development, and positive psychology. Connie has an MS in Organizational Psychology and is currently a doctoral candidate at Columbia University – Teachers College in the department of Organizational Learning and Leadership.

Hsin-Ling Tsai, 3rd year dual title Ph.D. candidate in Workforce Education and Development and Comparative International Education with an emphasis on human resource development and organization development at Pennsylvania State University. Mrs. Tsai earned her BA in Accounting and English in Taiwan, and an M.S. in Elementary Education and TESOL in Connecticut. She was a Language Instructor and Career Counselor in NYC. In Penn State, she served as Diversity Specialist in Altoona campus and SPLED program with World Campus as Online Tech Support Assistant. In addition, she participated in several projects with Dr. William Rothwell and lead a Learning and Performance research team (graduate student team) to complete HR Encyclopedia Project. Her specialties are international talent recruiting, placement and retention, career counseling, cross cultural, and training and language teaching. Her current research interests are HRD/OD in international and multinational organizational setting, succession planning, recruiting and retention, social networking, career development, appreciative inquiry approach, and technology in learning and training.

Rosie Chen-Yong Williams is a Doctoral Candidate at Teachers College, Columbia University. Originally from Singapore, Rosie has worked in Asia, Australia, Africa, and the USA, in the areas of program planning, management, and leadership development. At Harvard Graduate School of Education's Office of School Partnerships, Rosie managed a Leadership Development Initiative designed for public school leaders. She has also been active in international development work, assisting in the building of leadership capacity of women in Madagascar. Presently, Rosie is the Executive Director of a leadership training company, Thinking Heads Global Pte. Ltd.

Maria Liu Wong is Dean of City Seminary of New York, and an EdD candidate in Adult Learning and Leadership (AEGIS) at Teachers College, Columbia University. She has graduate degrees in International Educational Development from Teachers College, and Urban Ministry from Westminster Theological Seminary. She has taught in New York City public and charter elementary schools, trained teachers in New York City and Ethiopia, and currently works in an intercultural urban learning community focused on theological formation. Her research interests are women and leadership, diversity, urban theological education, collaborative inquiry, interdisciplinary curriculum design, and faculty development. Originally from the United Kingdom, she lives in New York City with her husband and three children.

Aisha Taylor is currently pursuing a Ph.D in Industrial/Organizational Psychology at Portland State University in Oregon. Aisha works with Dr. Keith James researching leadership, innovation, organizational justice, and diversity in organizations. She is co-author on three book chapters regarding leadership, creativity, and diversity in the workplace. Prior to graduate school, Aisha lead the world's oldest and largest organization working for women's equality in the Catholic Church. As executive director of the Women's Ordination Conference (WOC), she was often called upon by major national and international media outlets to be an expert source on gender issues in church and society. Aisha has facilitated workshops and trainings on a range of topics for numerous educational institutions and non-profit organizations. Born and raised in California, Aisha earned a Bachelor's degree in Interdisciplinary Humanities and Chemistry from the University of San Diego.

Sven C. Voelpel is Professor of Business Administration at Jacobs University Bremen and Adjunct Professor at the EBS Business School, Germany. He has held numerous (Tenured, Visiting, and/or Honorary) Professorships at leading universities and business schools around the world, such as INSEAD, St. Gallen, Stellenbosch, IIMB, Tsinghua, and CEIBS, and Visiting Fellowships at Harvard University. His recent work is set against the background of demographic change and aging workforce management. At present, Sven C. Voelpel is working on leadership, innovation, and strategies for the survival and sustainability of businesses in times of demographic change, with particular attention to opportunities and risks with regard to innovation inherent in an aging workforce. Aside from his focus on organizational and team research, he also has a strong interest in methodological issues in team research. His work is published in outlets such as the *Academy of Management Journal* and *Leadership Quarterly.*

Aimee Tiu Wu is a Doctoral Student in the AEGIS program. She received her B.A. in psychology from De La Salle University Manila, Philippines. After her undergraduate work, she spent two years as a foreign language student at Beijing Normal University learning Mandarin and teaching ESL. With her passion for teaching adult learners, Aimee pursued a Master's degree in TESOL from New York University, while serving as a Learning Specialist. Aimee's higher education experience ranges from serving as Director of Academic and Disability Student Services to heading TRIO programs like Student Support Services. Her dissertation work involves inquiry into how doctoral mothers navigate graduate school, motherhood, and professional work. Her primary research interests include learning and motherhood, collaborative inquiry, educational equity for women and minority, diversity, and cross-cultural awareness.

Aileen G. Zaballero is a dual title Ph.D. candidate in Workforce Education and Development and Comparative International Education at Pennsylvania State University. Her research interest is to explore different leadership models that are impacting diverse settings and to understand the developmental perspectives as they apply to human learning. In addition, she is investigating collaborative approaches to develop effective leadership and cooperative work styles among diverse groups. Aileen's Master's thesis was an exploratory case study on the implementation of diversity initiatives that utilized OD concepts as an approach to a planned change process involving the entire organization. Aileen has presented and published on various subjects including: Global Trends in Workforce Education; Diversity Change Initiative; and Ethical Leadership. A member of ASTD, since 2008, she served on the board for the Las Vegas Chapter, is the recipient of the John Coné ASTD Membership Scholarship, and is CPLP certified since May 2009.

Index